WASHINGTON DESPATCHES
1941-1945

WASHINGTON DESPATCHES
1941-1945

Weekly Political Reports from
the British Embassy

Edited by
H.G. Nicholas

With an Introduction by Isaiah Berlin

Weidenfeld and Nicolson London

Contents

Introduction by Isaiah Berlin

This volume consists of a number of despatches, selected, edited and annotated by Professor Herbert Nicholas, which were sent by the British Ambassador in Washington to the Foreign Office in London during the war years 1941–5. The purpose of these Weekly Political Summaries, as they came to be called, was to provide the Foreign Secretary and members of his Department with information about changing attitudes and movements of opinion in the USA on issues considered to be of importance to Anglo-American relations. They were circulated more widely – to other ministers (including the Prime Minister) as well as to a considerable number of other British officials at home and abroad. My sole qualification for providing this prefatory note is that in the spring of 1942 I was seconded to the Embassy in Washington and charged with the task of preparing the first drafts of these weekly reports.

The reader may well ask himself why this particular job should have been entrusted to me. I doubt whether the explanation of this somewhat puzzling fact will satisfy those who believe that specialized tasks, particularly at critical times, should be performed by experts trained for the purpose ; it is certainly a vivid illustration of the way in which the appointments of temporary officials were made in Britain in wartime. My qualifications for this function were not obvious. Apart from such impressions as I gained in the course of friendly relations with American colleagues and pupils at Oxford, and an unbroken addiction, perhaps somewhat rare in England in those days, particularly in academic circles, to such American periodicals as the *New Yorker* and *Time* magazine – the latter since my first term at Oxford in 1928 – I had no particular knowledge of the United States. I had never been, or thought of going, there, at any time ; nor did I have any special knowledge or understanding of international affairs in general, or of Anglo-American relations in particular. In the summer of 1940, while still teaching philosophy at Oxford, I was asked by Mr (later Sir Harold) Nicolson, then Parliamentary Secretary of the Ministry of Information, whether I would consider going to Moscow as Press Attaché of the British Embassy : it was put to me, by Mr Gladwyn Jebb (later Lord Gladwyn) of the Foreign Office, who was concerned with such appointments, that, with my knowledge of Russian and interest in Russian culture, I could be of use at the Embassy in Moscow. I accepted, and was ordered to go to the capital of the USSR via the USA and Japan. By the time I arrived in Washington on what I supposed to be the first lap of my journey to Moscow, I was informed by the British Embassy that a message had been received in London from the British Ambassador to the Soviet Union,

Sir Stafford Cripps, that he had no need of my services, since whatever tasks a Press Attaché could perform at that time (it was the particularly dark period of the Soviet-Nazi Pact) were being attempted already, and that my presence would therefore be totally superfluous ; consequently the Foreign Office did not require me to proceed any further, and, upon being asked what it wished me to do, replied that my further plans were of no interest to it. My friends at the British Embassy in Washington put all this to me as tactfully as they could, and it was, I feel sure, largely due to their initiative that the Press Counsellor, Mr Stephen Childs, offered me a job in his under-manned Embassy office. I thanked him for his kindness and trust, but said that in the circumstances I preferred to return to the United Kingdom. He then asked me whether I would, at any rate, stay for six or seven weeks in order to analyse and write a report on the despatches of American correspondents of the Associated Press in Britain, which seemed to indicate, after the fall of France, a degree of depression and even defeatism in Britain which was not warranted by the facts, and some of which seemed to be having a deleterious effect on the public opinion of a country of whose goodwill and material aid we stood in desperate need. I agreed to do this provided I was allowed to go home after I had finished. In due course, having read a great many American newspapers in the New York office of the British Library of Information, I produced a report which to a considerable degree bore out the Embassy's initial impression. As a result, some representations in this connection were, so I was told, made to senior executives of the Associated Press : whether these had any effect I do not know.

I returned to Oxford at the beginning of the autumn term and resumed my work as a tutor at New College. In late November I received a letter from the Ministry of Information, informing me that I was overstaying my period of home leave and was required to be at my post in the Ministry's New York office. I said that I was not aware of holding any government post and that I was a don doing his job at the university. A correspondence followed, in the course of which I learnt that, on the strength of my AP report, and the recommendations of one or two highly placed Americans whom I had known in the past, I had been appointed to a post in the newly created office of the British Information Services (BIS) charged with the task of providing material about the British war effort to the American press and radio. The new office was headed by Alan Dudley of the Foreign Office, with John Wheeler-Bennett and Aubrey Morgan as its effective directors (an account of this is to be found in Sir John Wheeler-Bennett's published memoirs, *Special Relationship*). Everyone in the BIS and the American section of the Ministry of Information seemed to know of my appointment, I alone had not been informed. As this was the only wartime government post offered to me, I accepted it gladly, and worked in New York during the greater part of 1941 as an information officer. My task was to supply details of the British war effort to the press and other media connected with various social groups and religious minorities, such as labour unions, Jews, and some of the smaller Christian denominations. One of the most obvious functions of the BIS was to provide a survey of the press, radio and other media of communication over the entire spectrum of American opinion. This was regarded as being indispensable both by those in the Ministry of Information in London who prepared the data for dissemination especially in order to counter what was thought most damaging to Britain, and were needed no less by British officials in the USA engaged on tasks of this kind. In the course of my work I wrote reports on the attitudes to public issues in general, and to Britain in particular, of various groups whose views I studied (and some of whose representative figures I met and came to know), and to assess, so far as possible, the effect of these attitudes, both public and private, on American public opinion. In particular, I was concerned with the attitudes of the labour unions and their leaders, divided between the American Federation of Labor with its ties to the TUC, and its great rival, the Congress of Industrial Organizations, which for various reasons was at that time a good deal less friendly to Britain. It is, incidentally, this part of my activity that, so I was told, came to the notice of officials in the British Embassy in Washington, and, after Pearl Harbor, when I once more expressed a wish to return to England (since most of my 'clients' in America had by now become firm supporters of Britain and the war), moved them to ask for my transfer to Washington to take charge of political surveys.

The drafting of the Weekly Political Summaries had in earlier years been entrusted to relatively junior members of the British diplomatic mission in Washington, who performed it in such time as they could spare from their normal duties. Once, however, America had entered the war, the need to provide somewhat fuller information about the American scene was recognized, and this, in turn, was thought to require the services of at any rate one or two full-time employees, instructed to analyse and interpret congressional, administrative and public opinion and the influence upon it of individuals and groups in the USA in general and in Washington in particular.

The creation of a special Survey Section of the Embassy was a minute element in the great expansion of British activities in wartime Washington. New missions were established to represent the Treasury, the Ministries of Supply, Food, Aircraft Production, Political and Economic Warfare, Information, and other departments ; almost every Ministry in London had its representatives, in one form or another, in Washington or New York. Some of these British missions, in liaison with corresponding US departments, operated independently ; others, whose functions brought them into closer contact with the work of the Embassy, formed new sections of it, strictly understood to be temporary. The creation of these sections, as well as such other departures from tradition as the addition of, for example, a Labour Attaché (Professor R.H. Tawney was the first, and none too happy, holder of this office), were accepted by the Foreign Office with commendable stoicism, much as the classical public schools accepted the need for 'modern subjects', without undue efforts to resist the inevitable. There had been similar invasions during the First World War, although on a far smaller scale. The result was the creation in the American capital, at the beginning of the 'forties, of what was, in effect, a short-lived microcosm of Whitehall, the relationship of which with the relevant departments of the United States Administration turned out to depend to a high degree on the nature of the personal relations established between British and American officials. The new wartime auxiliaries, whom the various Ministries in London succeeded in persuading the Foreign Office to attach to the British Embassy, were relegated to a hastily constructed and ramshackle barrack which, for all its ungainliness, had its own quality : the atmosphere was one of agreeable informality, in contrast with the stiffer and more dignified atmosphere of the Chancery and the Ambassador's personal staff, and this may have had some influence on the more easy-going prose style of the Weekly Summaries and other reports of the Section to which I was attached.

The Survey Section, which prepared these reports, consisted of about three members. The material on which the Weekly Political Summary was based came in part from the surveys of the American press prepared in New York for the Ministry of Information in London. In addition, we made use of consular reports from various key posts in the country and those of BIS offices in New York and several other important cities, and, not least, exchanges with well-informed observers of the Washington scene – officials, politicians, journalists, diplomats – as well as such information as members of the British Embassy and other British Missions came by in the course of their regular work. All this was assessed in the light of our constantly growing knowledge of the character, connections, outlooks, allegiances, policies, interests, attitudes and personal feelings of individuals, government departments and political and social groups and movements in the USA. Our work was not secret : it resembled that of any foreign correspondent worth his salt, save that the reports, some of them in code went to a far smaller and more carefully selected group of readers. Some of these surveys were written in response to specific enquiries transmitted by the Foreign Office ; such enquiries were, as a rule, answered in special despatches which were not part of the Weekly Political Summary series, and are therefore not included here.

There was far less secrecy during the war on matters not connected with national security in Washington than, so it seemed to me, there was in London ; American society, even official, had a far looser texture and was more open than that of older, less socially mobile countries. This was, no doubt, partly due to the fact that a far higher proportion of amateurs – businessmen, lawyers, social workers, academics, and so forth – came to Washington to serve the Government, not only during the war or the immediately preceding period of 'preparedness' (as in Britain), but since 1933, with the New Deal.

The war transformed normal life in the United States far less than in the United Kingdom ; indeed, it was one of the main tasks of my Section to convey to the Government at home, where everything was centralized and totally subordinated to the war effort, that in the USA this was not so ; that political and economic life to a considerable degree continued as before, and that this fact, in particular some of the pressures and internecine feuds between individuals and power blocs, inherited from the New Deal and even earlier times, continued to characterize it, and themselves affected the war effort. In London this was not always sufficiently understood, especially when it manifested itself in the attitude of Congress, which in this respect was very different from that of Parliament.

The individuals to whom my colleagues and I talked about matters of public interest, for the most part knew quite clearly what we were doing, nor did we intend to conceal this from anyone. American officials who worked in the State Department or the White House with whom I discussed general issues did not tell me what they preferred the British Government not to know, nor did I expect them to do so ; unlike a journalist, I sought no scoops ; on the other hand, where they were not bound by the need for secrecy, they often discussed matters freely. This was, of course, even more true of journalists and others not bound by considerations of security ; such conversations led to free exchanges of view and friendships which long survived the war, and have been a source of lasting pleasure and abiding interest to me ; they certainly taught me more about America than newspapers or official documents or any other published material could possibly have done. My conversations, and indeed personal relations, with lawyers, bankers, academics who held wartime posts in the Washington hierarchy, as well as labour leaders, politicians, writers, journalists and public figures of all kinds, opened windows with far wider vistas than the political pages of newspapers or information contained in diplomatic cables or despatches, and supplied that (mistakenly so-called) 'background' knowledge which anyone who seeks to understand any country or society must have. A certain reciprocity obtained in these matters : American officials occasionally wished the British Government to be made aware of feelings and attitudes, and even specific policies, which they did not wish to formulate officially, in order not to provoke reactions or rejoinders that might complicate relationships in some sphere of delicate negotiation. The despatches of my Section could act as a channel for informal communications of this kind without committing anyone to anything, and thus occasionally proved useful in promoting understanding and clearing the air. It was as a result of these personal contacts that I soon learnt that politics in Washington were not only more open but far more personal and less institutional than they were in Whitehall. The State Department did have an institutional personality and continuity – its members spoke not so much of what this or that official thought, as of the attitude of 'the Department' ; this was to a lesser, but still significant, degree true also of the US Treasury. But it did not hold for a number of important agencies : if you asked a Washington government official what his job was, he was more likely to answer 'I work for Mr Ickes, (or Mr Forrestal, or Mr Nelson)' than 'I am in the Department of the Interior (or Navy, or the War Production Board)'. The relationships between the powerful satraps who governed provinces of the Administration, and between the groups of officials who 'worked for' them (and their relationships to individual journalists) seemed to me to be far more important than relations between established institutions, knowledge of which was indispensable to the understanding of the ways in which the British Civil Service and, to some degree, British Ministers too, thought and functioned. I sometimes wonder whether things have changed in this respect ; after more than thirty years during which I have had no connection with government or current policies anywhere, I cannot tell.

There were trends of American, and in particular Washington, opinion and public comment in which the Foreign Office and the Ministry of Information, naturally enough, took a special interest, and this accounts for the relative frequency with which they crop up in these despatches (as well as the regular quarterly and special reports for which my Section was initially responsible) : among them were such topics as Lend-Lease (and 'Reverse Lend-Lease') ; Isolationism and Pacific Firstism ; American expansionist ambitions ; British imperial policies, especially in India and the Far East, Hong-Kong and Singapore, in the Middle East and particularly Palestine, all of which were objects of traditional, sharp, well-organized criticism in the USA, as well as American policy on oil, civil aviation, foreign trade ; post-war plans, and the like. Occasionally we had to answer questions raised via the Foreign Office by some of our other clients – the Cabinet, the Colonial Office, the Service Departments, the BBC, and so on – to which it was important to convey certain differences which existed between the American Departments with which Britain had direct relations, and similar institutions in London ; in particular, to describe and account for the alliances of interest which were constantly forming and re-forming between various political and economic groups ; the tensions which arose between the old pre-war power blocs ; the ideological differences which divided the New Dealers, with their social aims and policies, on the one hand, from those, on the other, for whom the exigencies of mobilization of resources for the war took the first place ; and the corresponding changes of power centres, of relationships of leading personalities, and in the entire alignment of forces which was determined by all these processes.

The Foreign Office occasionally complained that it was being told more than it wished to know ; it was not lack of succinctness, but the sheer number of topics covered, and their ramifications, which led to mild protests, usually thinly disguised as a desire to ease the burden of its overworked cypher section. The Ministry of Information had a far greater appetite for the pabulum we provided, and if, in obedience to the Foreign Office, the supply grew thinner there were anguished cries from, e.g., Denis Brogan, the *doyen* of Americanists then at work as adviser to the North American Service of the British Broadcasting Corporation, who described the Weekly Political Summaries as his Ariadne's thread through the labyrinths of American politics, without which proper understanding of that complex field was in England totally unobtainable. Nevertheless, our master was the Foreign Office, and its wishes could not be disregarded. Consequently, we did report a good deal less than we believed or knew or regarded as worth knowing. Some of this residue spilt over into the private correspondence between Herbert Nicholas (of the American Division of the Ministry of Information) and myself, and may at times have been rather more interesting than the content of the official telegrams, though it did, perhaps, presuppose a somewhat more intimate knowledge of the American political scene than the majority of our readers could be expected to possess.

It should not, however, be inferred from this that the officials to whom these telegrams were circulated were for the most part unduly critical of their contents – on the contrary, we received much encouragement, and a good deal of informal praise ; in retrospect (which cannot fail to reveal avoidable errors of observation, judgment, emphasis, or sheer shallowness of assessment) much of it now seems to me a good deal more than our due.

To turn to the despatches themselves. The majority of those in this volume were drafted in the first instance by myself, but by no means all. I was away for relatively long periods in London ; I occasionally took leave for a week or two, and I was sometimes away from my office, either through illness or because I had been sent away on special missions to inspect British consulates or to attend conferences ; during those periods the despatches were drafted with great shrewdness and skill by Mr A.R.K. Mackenzie, Mr Alan Judson and occasionally by Mr Paul Scott-Rankine.* I was responsible only for the original drafts of the despatches. The despatches themselves were subject to various controls : I was naturally expected to exercise discretion – anything which I inadvertently disclosed that was considered at all likely to ruffle the sensibilities of important persons whose goodwill it was deemed politic to retain, had to be omitted or drastically modified ; thus the relative absence of character sketches of individuals, or accounts of their careers and origins, is mainly due to the fact that the Foreign Office showed no eagerness for such vignettes ; we were given to understand that they were best confined to highly confidential reports sent by couriers, and not included in the telegrams. Inevitably, leakages occurred ; although scarcely anything in these despatches was genuinely secret, the Embassy did not wish its comments on events, attitudes or persons to reach the American personalities concerned, and such leakages sometimes caused mild irritation. In addition to such self-censorship, my drafts, on occasion, went through a good deal of transformation : I delivered them, I think, on Thursday afternoons, to the Head of Chancery of the Diplomatic mission. He tended to show various portions of the draft to relevant officials in case they wished to urge some omission or

---

*To the best of my recollection I was away from Washington from June 1942, when I went to London, until late January 1943 ; between 26 September and 2 November 1943 ; between 18 March and 16 May ; between 15 July and 4 August 1944 and between 9 February and 4 April 1945. I was in San Francisco during the last fortnight of the conference in 1945. In July 1945 I left Washington to join the British Embassy in Moscow, and returned for a short while in 1946, some time after the despatches collected in this volume had come to an end.

alteration, or he might introduce these himself. The Minister, and in particular the Ambassador (who was the official source of all these messages), might from time to time add or subtract something. Such sentences as 'This story is supported by language used by Cordell Hull in conversation with myself . . .' or the like clearly do not come from my pen. The late Sir Michael Wright, as Head of Chancery, was particularly active in cutting out, altering and adding to the text. Nevertheless, I own to responsibility for the greater part of what is contained in these pages. After this length of years, I have little recollection of precisely what either I, or others in the Embassy, removed or altered ; the extant letters exchanged with Professor Nicholas occasionally remind me of it.

To re-read after many years documents in which one has had a hand is an exceedingly odd experience : one becomes aware, rather too often for comfort, how far one failed to realize the relative importance, or unimportance, seen in a longer perspective, of this or that view or development ; it is a very chastening experience. What it does bring back most vividly is how things seemed to one at the time. If this collection helps the interested reader to recreate the view of the political scene which, during years that now seem so remote, was common to some of the servants of the British Government during the war in Washington, it will have done something to help to reconstruct the past.

ISAIAH BERLIN

Foreword

As Sir Isaiah Berlin's Introduction makes clear, the interest of these despatches derives from the circumstances of their composition. The United States was engaged in its greatest struggle since the Civil War and chance brought to the British Embassy in Washington an observer of genius to describe it. Sir Isaiah has described the circumstances in which he came to be in Washington and in which the despatches were composed. His account makes clear that there were interruptions, excisions and additions to these compositions. His modesty about his own role should not, however, mislead the reader. The excisions and additions were trifling in relation to the whole. Even the interruptions due to his absences from his desk were less significant than might be imagined. His powerfully persuasive personality so impressed itself on his small team in the Reports Section of the Embassy that even skilled contemporary form-watchers could not always distinguish between what fell from the master's own hand and what should more properly be labelled 'School of Berlin'. Realization of this has reconciled me to the impossibility after all these years of establishing the precise authorship of every telegram, and indeed to the pointlessness of identifying other hands even in the rare instances where this could be done.

The main problem for an editor of these despatches is indeed quite an opposite one. It is to make from a total bulk of over 600,000 words a selection which will be balanced, manageable and coherent. In attempting this I have been guided by the conviction that the coherence of the despatches derives (apart from the distinctive angle of the author's vision) from the fact that they reflect the story not of the Second World War as a whole, but of America's part in it, and that even of that part they reflect not the whole national experience (if indeed that were ever capable of precise reflection) but of America's war as viewed from America's capital, Washington DC. To this one might add the third consideration that although the vision is in no way narrowed down to the day-to-day concerns of a British Embassy, it necessarily focusses on those events and circumstances which bear on the relations between Britain and the USA ; the war was, after all, a uniquely intimate moment in the long history of Anglo-American relations.

With these considerations in mind I have endeavoured in the first place to preserve the continuity of the story ; in the second to retain as much as possible of its vivid depiction of the politics of wartime Washington (while fully realizing, as the author did, that they are not the same as those of the nation as a whole) ; and finally to find room for all those elements in the narrative that have most relevance for the relations of the two allies. Even with such pointers to guide me the process of paring and selection was painful and, by its nature, imprecise and subjective. It was eased for me by Sir Isaiah's own advice and assistance, but I must make it clear that responsibility for the final selection is mine and mine alone. However, painful though it was to lose a full half of the original output, I found that there were certain compensations. Despatches written week by week and for an audience of diverse background necessarily require certain repetitions and reminders which are superfluous when the story is laid out in sequence. Similarly certain purely factual information for which space had to be found in the original (e.g. on economic conditions) can be more readily and comprehensively acquired elsewhere by a modern reader. Needless to say I have made clear in the text wherever any material has been excised or (this happens very rarely) where the wording has been modified in the interests of compression or clarification.

The despatches were written in midweek and telegraphed from the Embassy to the Foreign Office in London. Save that they were headed 'Weekly Political Summary' they did not outwardly differ from the hundreds of other messages which made part each week of the Embassy's regular telegraphic traffic. Thus in form they were, like all communications from overseas posts, despatches from the Ambassador to the Foreign Secretary, or, on occasions when either was absent from their post, from deputy to appropriate deputy. Thus the reader who encounters upon occasion the employment of the terms 'you' or 'yours' should read them as referring to Mr Anthony Eden, Foreign Secretary throughout almost all this period, though of course on occasions when the Foreign Secretary is visiting the United States he will be found referred to in the third person and the despatch will be formally addressed to the Minister of State. Similarly in Lord Halifax's absence from the Embassy despatches were sent as from the Minister, Sir Ronald Campbell (previously British Minister at Belgrade, 1931–41).

Initially the Weekly Political Summary took the form of a single midweek telegram sent in cypher. By degrees the length of the Summary increased to a point which overstrained both the capacity of the cypher staff and the digestion of the Foreign Office (though not to an equivalent degree of all the London readership). This led to the practice of splitting the Summary into two parts, the first (which contained the more urgent and, generally, though not always, the more important items) still sent by telegraphic cypher, the second sent by mail and *en clair,* and separately identified and numbered as 'Savingrams'. Thus if the reader encounters two despatches bearing the same date, what he usually has are the main telegram and the Savingram from the same Weekly Summary (though sometimes a day or two separated their composition and their dating). In addition to the Weekly Summaries the Reports Section also produced special reports, e.g. on election results. Since in composition (and usually in circulation) these did not differ from the Weekly Summaries, I have drawn upon them without any distinguishing label when it seemed appropriate.

The reader will observe that the weekly extracts tend to increase in scale as the war goes on. This reflects the fact that the Embassy's reporting itself became fuller, as indeed the volume of significant events itself expanded. In the interest of comprehensiveness I have included some material which antedates Sir Isaiah's assumption of his Embassy duties and continues after his absence in 1945. There is after all a unity about the period from Pearl Harbor to VJ Day which it seems to me important to preserve. And indeed by a pretty irony the same despatch which reports the celebrations of VJ Day describes the arrangements for the full-dress investigation of Pearl Harbor. The despatches in fact continued after the war was over. But the war's end robbed them of their distinctive quality. The Reports Section broke up, the London audience was scattered and indeed Washington itself lost its exclusive character as a listening post. Instead, therefore, of searching for a non-existent peroration, I have simply brought the curtain down on a date which had at least a profound symbolic significance for all Americans who lived to see it.

From Sir Isaiah's Introduction we have a graphic depiction of the processes of manufacture, so to speak, which produced the despatches in Washington. Perhaps as someone at one of their points of reception in London I may recall their function there. After American entry into the war American developments, American personalities, American assumptions and reactions assumed an importance for the day-to-day conduct of British policy, greater even than in the days when Britain was wooing the United States for 'aid short of war'. No department of government could afford to ignore the American dimension on even the most seemingly domestic of issues. Yet to convey this dimension to busy, preoccupied policy-makers was not easy. It could not be done by exhortation or the provision of mere information. Important ministers of state can be impervious to the one and too busy to absorb the other. The best chance of making an impact on these overburdened potentates lay in presenting them with a weekly serial of restricted circulation soon known for its highly influential clientele (was not the Prime Minister himself an *aficionado ?*), which provided penetrating insights into the ever-changing American scene, sympathetic yet sharply discriminating, written moreover in a style that surpassed the most brilliant reporting of the daily press. Thus it was that the weekly telegrams, quite apart from their service to the Embassy's immediate masters at the Foreign Office and related departments, developed their influence on a small but crucially important Whitehall public, and acquired a reputation unique among the official communications of the war. Thus, even if they did not still stand on their intrinsic merits as brilliant pieces of reporting, they would deserve the attention of any student of administration for their contribution to the shaping of British official thinking in wartime.

The material from which this selection has been drawn is now all in the Public Record Office under the class number FO 371. This is an enormous class and the years 1941–5 are covered by a huge array of pieces (i.e. individual files) ranging from FO 371/26146 to FO 371/44662. Unfortunately the filing system adopted takes no account of the Weekly Political Summaries as a separate sequence of despatches. They are mingled indiscriminately with a mass of other material and have to be ferretted out one by one. I have therefore not attempted to give source references for individual telegrams. For permission to draw on this material I am indebted to Her Majesty's Stationery Office, in whom the copyright reposes. For assistance in the reproduction and transcription my thanks are due to Mrs Colin Bundy and Mrs Meg Beresford. For editorial assistance at most stages of the project and particularly for research on the biographical appendix I am particularly indebted to Dr Kathleen Burk, uniquely qualified by her knowledge of both the American and British backgrounds. My thanks are also due to Mr Anthony Raven for his help in the preparation of the index and to Mr Michael Graham-Dixon, whose careful proofreading has greatly contributed to the accuracy of the text.

The expenses of acquiring and processing the material were met by a grant from the Commonwealth Fund of New York to whose generosity, as a sometime Commonwealth Fund Fellow, I feel doubly indebted. The grant was administered by, and the operation housed in, New College, Oxford, thus adding another debt to the many which I have incurred at the hand of the Warden and Fellows. And to an infinite number of scholars and librarians upon whose advice and services I have drawn I owe thanks which are none the less real for defying detailed acknowledgment.

OXFORD 1980
H.G.NICHOLAS

1941 and 1942

Although it was generally realized that a crisis had been reached in American–Japanese relations, the suddenness of the Japanese attack on American bases in the Pacific came as a great shock to the nation, the effect of which is likely to be all the more deeply felt as fuller information of losses in men and material becomes available. The immediate effect has been to make the country completely united in its determination to fight Japan to the end and indignant at this unprovoked and surreptitious attack. A significant feature of early press and radio comment is its tendency to view the Japanese attack not as an isolated move but as part of a concerted strategy agreed upon with Germany. Shortly after the first reports were received on afternoon of 7 December congressional leaders were summoned to a meeting at White House as result of which a joint session of both houses was summoned for 12.30 on 8 December to receive a message from the President in person. In this message, which was very warmly received, the President asked Congress to recognize that a state of war had existed between Japan and the United States of America since the attack on Hawaii. Congress, with only one dissentient vote, confirmed this on morning of 8 December.

The isolationist press has already come out in support of the President and in favour of war with Japan and Senator Wheeler [1] has expressed himself in favour of war. In a broadcast address Robert Patterson, [2] Under-Secretary for War, has appealed to the nation for a maximum effort to ensure sustained defence production on a twenty-four-hour basis. Meanwhile steps are being taken to round up all Japanese nationals and defence industries are being warned to guard against sabotage.

The war with Japan has naturally eclipsed all other issues, but the following is brief résumé of main developments during the week :

On 3 December the Administration suffered a further setback in Congress over the question of labour legislation when the House, by nearly a two-to-one majority, passed a drastic bill introduced by Representative Smith [3] instead of the milder Labor Committee measure favoured by Administration supporters. The Smith bill, which was rushed through by the same combination of Republicans and Southern anti-New Dealers who have opposed the Administration in other

---

1 Burton K.Wheeler, Democratic Senator from Montana since 1923 and leading isolationist.

2 Robert P.Patterson, lawyer and judge of Circuit Court of Appeals, appointed Assistant Secretary of War, July 1940, Under-Secretary, December 1940.

3 Howard Worth Smith, Democratic Congressman from Virginia since 1931 and leading conservative.

recent debates, prohibits the calling of strikes to secure a union shop[4] or for jurisdictional or organizational issues and freezes the *status quo* in regard to the open or closed shop. Strikes may only be called after a thirty-day 'cooling-off period' and after endorsement by a majority of the workers in a secret ballot conducted under government supervision. The bill provides machinery for mediation and conciliation and deprives unions striking unlawfully of their statutory labour rights. It also prohibits the importation of pickets into strike zones and the employment by unions of officials with criminal or subversive records.

In view of the outbreak of war, it is impossible to predict how this and other domestic issues will develop, but it seems reasonably certain that if and when an anti-strike bill is approved by Congress it will be much milder than the Smith bill.

A number of Senators are reported to favour an alternative measure introduced by Senator Ball[5] which merely establishes a procedure for the settlement of disputes and imposes no penalties.

It is quite possible that President may adopt the course urged by labour leaders, and supported by a number of industrialists, of calling a joint conference of labour, management and government representatives to establish a voluntary programme for uninterrupted defence production.

The Administration's defeat over the Smith bill, coming as it did after a number of similar reverses, was a further indication of the extent to which the President's control over the House has recently weakened. Revolt of the reactionary Southern Democrats has produced a serious split in the Democratic group with result that in all the recent debates the Republicans have again held the balance of power. New Deal influence in the House is at present practically negligible. Some commentators ascribe this development largely to the President's preoccupation with foreign affairs, which has resulted in a loss of contact between congressional leaders and the White House and in the weakening of presidential leadership. In the new situation which has now arisen however it is probable that the President's authority will be largely restored and that greater unity will be achieved in tackling vital domestic issues.

On 7 December the arbitration board recently appointed to settle the captive[6] coal mines dispute announced its decision awarding a union shop to the United Mine Workers ; although this verdict represents a further triumph for labour, it is unlikely to add much to the prestige of John L. Lewis,[7] who has recently been encountering opposition in his own union as a result of attempts to 'purge' union officials who support the President's foreign policy.

Some excitement was caused in latter part of week by announcement by a

---

4 Union shop : non-union workers may be hired, provided they subsequently join the union. Closed shop: only union members may be employed.

5 Joseph Hurst Ball, Republican Senator from Minnesota since 1940.

6 Mines owned by industrial firms for supplying their own fuel demands.

7 John L. Lewis, president of the United Mine Workers of America since 1920.

number of isolationist newspapers that they had evidence of a government plan for an American expeditionary force of five million men to launch an offensive against Germany in 1943. The existence of such a plan was not denied by the Administration but it was pointed out that it was the duty of the Government to make plans for all possible contingencies and, on 5 December, the Secretary for War[8] assailed the lack of loyalty and patriotism of those who published information of value to the country's enemies. The announcement of the plan occasioned little surprise and, as far as can be seen, has had no general effect on public opinion to date.

In a report issued 3 December, by a five-man congressional committee which recently returned from a tour of South America, the State Department were asked to investigate the competition of British with US firms in South America in the light of this country's programme for aid to Britain. The report stated that the committee had received indications that British firms were soliciting for delivery of goods which the United States of America, on account of priorities requirements, were not in a position to deliver.

17 December 1941

As was to be expected, the Japanese attack caused universal indignation and brought all sections of opinion together overnight. In view of the circumstances, it has not been unnatural that the first week of war has been one of considerable alarm, confusion, uncertainty and disillusionment. Concern regarding the seriousness of the losses suffered in Hawaii, fostered in the early part of the week by a host of alarmist rumours and absence of any authoritative statement as to the extent of the damage sustained, gave way to serious apprehension when news was received of the sinking of the *Prince of Wales* and *Repulse*.[1] The attack on Pearl Harbor was referred to by many as a 'major naval disaster' and the view was freely expressed in some quarters that the navy had been 'caught napping' owing to the negligence of high officers. Demands for an immediate enquiry and the punishment of those responsible were made in both Houses of Congress, but received little support and were rejected by Administration leaders, who pointed out that authorities themselves were not yet fully informed as to what took place, and called for confidence in the President, as Commander-in-Chief, to take whatever measures might be necessary as soon as the facts were known. At the same time it was announced that Secretary of the Navy,[2] who himself had not escaped criticism in Congress, had gone to Honolulu, and although the reason for his visit was not indicated, it was generally assumed to be for the purpose of making a personal investigation of the causes of the disaster. Meanwhile, confidence as regards the general military situation was somewhat restored towards the end of

8 Henry L.Stimson, Colonel in First World War, Secretary of State 1929–33.

1 British battleships sunk by Japanese air attack in Malayan waters, 10 December.

2 Frank Knox, publisher of *Chicago Daily News*, Republican, Colonel in First World War.

the week as a result of the announcement of the sinking and damaging of Japanese warships, and the news of the resistance being put up by the American garrisons in the Philippines and at Wake and Midway Islands, although there was little optimism regarding the ultimate fate of the last two of these outposts and considerable misgivings were felt about the first.

Other unsettling factors contributed to the general feeling of bewilderment during the first few days of the war. A series of air-raid warnings, which occurred on both the East and West Coasts on 9 and 10 December, caused great confusion and drew attention to the country's unpreparedness as regards civilian defence. Although the warnings in New York were later acknowledged to have been false alarms, the military authorities in the San Francisco area maintained that a force of about sixty hostile aircraft had been detected approaching the coast on the morning of 9 December and had later turned back to sea. Steps are being taken to reorganize and improve the system of civilian defence. In spite of the initial confusion which followed the entry of the United States of America into the war, however, there is little room for doubt as to the unanimity of feeling in the country, and the American people's determination to exert all their energies in prosecuting the war to a successful conclusion. From this point of view, the initial reverses in the Pacific have brought some compensating advantage, as also for their sobering effect on public opinion. All ideas of an easy victory over the Japs have vanished, and been replaced by a general realization that, as the President has warned the country, the war will be long and hard. Throughout the week declarations of solidarity and support have been forthcoming from all sections of the nation, including many erstwhile opponents of the President's policy, such as Wheeler, Lindbergh[3] and John L. Lewis. The America First Committee[4] has announced that it is dissolving itself. The view now commonly expressed by former dissident elements is that America is in the war for good or ill, and that all should unite their efforts to bring about the defeat of the totalitarian powers. It is also generally felt that Hitler is the ultimate enemy and Japan merely a satellite of Germany. The German and Italian declarations of war on 11 December had been fully expected and occasioned little surprise or alarm. On the other hand the feeling of American solidarity has been considerably strengthened by the action of those Latin-American countries who have entered the war at the side of the United States of America. There has been considerable speculation during the week regarding the position of Russia, and demands have been put forward in several quarters that the Soviet Union should declare war on Japan, or at least allow its bases in the Far East to be used by the United States of America and Britain. These gave way towards the end of the week, however, to a more sympathetic appreciation of Russia's position, and it was recognized that, having borne the brunt of the German attack, she might not feel able at the

3 Charles Augustus Lindbergh had made the first non-stop transatlantic flight in 1927 ; leading member of America First Committee.
4 Association of isolationists founded in July 1940.

moment to undertake a war on a second front. This was confirmed in a statement made to the press by M. Litvinov[5] on 14 December, which has so far provoked little adverse reaction.

The tendency of American public opinion during the last few days to adopt a more realistic attitude towards the war, was no doubt in large part the result of the sober advice given by the President in his first war-time broadcast to the nation on 9 December. In his address, the President admitted that United States of America had suffered a severe defeat at Hawaii, and he called on the nation to prepare for a long war which would require sacrifices and unceasing efforts from all. He emphasized that the Axis and Japan were conducting their operations in accordance with a joint plan, and warned the country that the coasts of the United States of America might be attacked by Axis forces. He urged the American people to beware of false rumours, and promised that adverse news would be made public as soon as the facts were established, and provided the information did not assist the enemy.

Roosevelt expressed his full confidence in ultimate victory, to assure which he announced a two-point programme of placing defence production on a seven-day-week basis and building new defence plants. Meanwhile, the Administration initiated a series of new measures with a view to organizing the country for war and co-ordinating the defence effort. On 11 December Congress approved a bill extending the duration of enlistments in the armed forces for the duration of the war, and removing Selective Service Act[6] restrictions on sending troops outside the Western Hemisphere. At the same time, legislation was introduced providing for the registration of all men between the ages of eighteen and sixty-four, those between nineteen and forty-four to be liable for military service. The bill, which would render possible an army of 7,500,000 men, is expected to be passed early next week on 12 December, while the Senate was passing a $10½ billion supplemental defence appropriation, including funds to strengthen the Army and Navy air arms. The Navy asked Congress to authorize an increase of 30 per cent in the fighting strength of the Fleet. The Supply Priorities and Allocations Board and the OPM[7] announced plans for intensified defence production and the expansion of existing plants. Meanwhile various security measures were taken, including prohibitions on the disclosure of military information and the detention of enemy aliens. By the middle of the week some 2,300 aliens had been arrested. It was announced that no arrests would be made on grounds of nationality alone, and that only those would be detained whom it was considered unsafe to leave at liberty.

On 11 December the President called a conference of Industry and Labour, which is to meet in Washington on 17 December to agree upon a policy for preventing the interruption of defence production by labour disputes during the period of the war. At the same time, it was announced that the Senate would

5 Maxim Litvinov, Soviet Ambassador to the USA, November 1941–August 1943.

6 Selective Service or Draft Act passed in June 1940.

7 Office of Production Management.

suspend consideration of anti-strike legislation pending the outcome of the conference. The President's action represents a last effort to achieve uninterrupted defence production by voluntary agreement and co-operation between labour and industry, instead of as a result of restrictive legislation. Although demands for an anti-strike law have continued during the week, they have been less insistent than before, and a number of industrialists are known to be in favour of a voluntary agreement between industry and labour. There thus appears to be a good chance that the conference may be successful. In the meantime, resolutions pledging whole-hearted support for the defence effort and calling for intensified production have been forthcoming from all sections of labour. A number of unions have already approached their employers with concrete plans for accelerating production by mutual agreement.

The sudden nature of the Jap attack and the losses suffered by the American forces brought a not unnatural first impulse to reserve war materials for American use and to regard the Pacific as the paramount area of operations. The President, however, and a considerable number of newspapers, at once took up the attitude, reassuring from our point of view, that the war must be regarded as a whole, that the supply of American material to other countries fighting the Axis must and would continue. The setback to American arms, and the circumstances in which it occurred, have served to suspend the tendency to criticize our conduct of the war, to allege inefficiency in use of American material, and to wish to remedy these inefficiencies by securing the employment of American experts and methods. Instead of this, and in spite of an extraordinary reluctance to start joint staff conversations in Washington, there is a new tendency on the part of Americans to seek our advice and the fruits of our experience in various fields such as civilian defence, owing perhaps to new-found doubts about their own efficiency. It is of real importance that we should be in a position to take this possibly transient opportunity, and that requests which we may send to London for information should be fully and promptly met. It would, of course, be unwise to assume that this comparatively humble state of mind will continue indefinitely or that there will not be differences of opinion and outlook in which the American side will be stated with cocksureness and the expectation that it should prevail. It would also be unwise to assume that we have only to draw a cheque on this country for it to be honoured. But that co-operation has been facilitated by America's entry into the war and the attendant circumstances can, I think, be assumed with some confidence, the more so since the reasons for self-reproach on account of failure to follow the hard path of duty, which existed amongst the clearsighted, have now disappeared.

.   .   .

23 December 1941

The general attitude to the war has remained substantially the same as last week, combining a realistic appreciation of this country's present difficulties with a sober confidence in the ultimate power of the United States to outproduce and outfight her enemies and a determination to get down to the task of winning the war with the utmost speed and energy. The situation in the Pacific and particularly the threat to Singapore are still causing very natural anxiety, although the country has been heartened by the successes of United States forces after their initial setback in Hawaii and individual tales of heroism are prominently featured in the press. Public opinion has also been considerably relieved by the report of the Secretary of the Navy on the circumstances of the attack on Pearl Harbor which was released on 15 December and from which it appeared that the losses sustained by the United States fleet were not as great as had at first been feared. This led some to ask who had been responsible for the alarmist reports of 'tremendous losses' which were current last week, but no satisfactory answer has so far been given although it appears probable that certain members of Congress were the chief culprits. While Mr Knox's report showed that the United States forces had fought with courage and skill once the action had started it admitted that they were not on the alert against the surprise attack and promised that responsibility for the error would be investigated immediately by a presidential commission. The report also revealed that the attackers had received great support from Fifth Columnists in Hawaii itself. The Board of Enquiry was appointed on 16 December with a Justice of the Supreme Court as Chairman. On the following day it was also announced that the Commander-in-Chief of the United States Pacific Fleet and the Generals commanding the Army and Air Force in Hawaii had been relieved of their commands. Admiral Kimmel, the former Commander-in-Chief of the Pacific Fleet, was also Commander-in-Chief of the United States Navy as a whole. He has been replaced in the former position by Admiral Nimitz[1] and in the latter by Admiral King,[2] hitherto Commander-in-Chief of the Atlantic Fleet.

. . .

. . . On 16 December it was announced that the President had placed Mr Byron Price, executive news editor of the Associated Press, in charge of a partly compulsory and partly voluntary censorship of press, radio and communications with the title of Director of Censorship. The establishment of a censorship has been received with remarkable calmness and absence of opposition by the press and general public. Its necessity is recognized as an indispensable wartime measure and the appointment of a newspaper man as head of the censorship has done much to reconcile the press. On 17 December Mr Leon Henderson[3] gave the country a foretaste of coming privations by announcing an 80 per cent cut in civilian consumption of rubber. Meanwhile Congress continued to rush through a series of defence measures. On 15 December it gave its approval to a ten billion dollar emergency appropriation for the armed forces and on the following

1 Admiral Chester William Nimitz, Head of the Bureau of Navigation (Personnel) since 1935.

2 Admiral Ernest J. King, since February Commander-in-Chief of the Atlantic Fleet.

3 Leon Henderson, administrator of the Office of Price Administration and Director of the Division of Civilian Supply of the War Production Board since 1941.

day passed a bill conferring on the President a number of emergency powers similar to those granted to President Wilson in 1917, including the power to redistribute the functions of government agencies, to establish a censorship, to control alien property and to award defence contracts without competitive bidding. On 19 December both Houses approved the new selective service bill which provides for the registration of all male residents of the United States between ages of eighteen and sixty-four, those between twenty and forty-four being liable for military service. Aliens in United States are specifically included in the new act. Army officials indicated that registration of new manpower under this measure might not begin for several months but that the action taken would depend on the war situation. . . .

.   .   .

30 December 1941

The principal event of the week was the arrival of the Prime Minister in Washington.[1] Though little was generally known of his discussions with the President, his public appearances at the President's press conference and before the Senate were such an unqualified success and made so strong and so favourable an impression on the public at large that they alone would have afforded sufficient justification for his visit. The only exception to the paean of praise for Mr Churchill's address to Congress was to be found in the comment of Senator Wheeler who was careful to dub the speech as 'clever'. . . . The President's announcement of the good progress of the discussions at the end of the week gave the public an indication that concrete results could be hoped for soon. The general impression created was one of complete Anglo-American harmony which, in the mind of the public at least, the unfortunate little incident at St Pierre et Miquelon[2] did nothing to mar.

.   .   .

On the home front the situation continues to be good and there has been no rift in the front of national unity. The President's Labor Conference which at the end of last week seemed to be on the point of collapse was brought to agreement on a three-point programme promulgated by the President, his points being that there should be no strikes or lockouts, that all disputes should be settled by peaceful means and that a War Labor Board should be set up to handle these disputes. The industrialists' desire to 'freeze' the situation in regard to the closed shop was ignored by the President's decision but they have announced their intention of accepting his finding. A 'wildcat' strike by welders in shipyards on the West Coast called against the wishes of the unions had little success and

1 Churchill arrived in Washington on 22 December, addressed Congress on 26 December, was in Ottawa from 29 to 31 December, and left the USA on 14 January.

2 On 24 December, while US–UK discussions over the future of these islands off the coast of Newfoundland were in progress, Admiral Muselier occupied them in the name of what Cordell Hull, the Secretary of State, described as the 'so-called' Free French.

movement for co-operation between the two branches of the labour movement is growing.

A Senatorial Committee has recommended drastic cuts in government expenditure for non-defence purposes. These cuts if accepted may result in considerable interference with civilian life but nothing could bring the war so thoroughly home to the average citizen of this country as the restriction, amounting to a ban, on tyres, resulting from the danger to the sources of America's supplies of rubber. This has been called America's automobile age and a lack of tyres would involve a profound readjustment in the way of life of every American family. It would also provide a particularly difficult task for the new Office of Defense Transportation which was set up by the President on 23 December 'to assure a maximum utilization of domestic transportation facilities of the nation for the successful prosecution of the war'.

5 January 1942

Though the Prime Minister has made no further speeches since his return from Ottawa, he has continued to be the centre of attraction and the outcome of his discussions with the President and of the meetings between Lord Beaverbrook[1] and the American Supply officials and between the British and United States service representatives are awaited with great interest. The signature on 1 January of the 'United Nations Declaration' was universally approved, and welcomed as a highly significant step, and the institution of a unified system of command in the South-West Pacific was equally well received. Although at one time, as was perhaps natural, the name of General MacArthur[2] had been canvassed as a candidate for the post of Commander-in-Chief, the appointment of General Wavell,[3] whose name commands widespread respect here, was greeted with much satisfaction. . . .

The Office of Production Management banned completely the retail sale of new cars and lorries on 1 January. A rationing system is to be introduced on 15 January. The production of passenger cars in the United States will stop for the duration on 31 January. . . . The CIO[4] has not failed to point out that it recommended months ago the conversion of the complete industry to war production, and there has been considerable criticism of the OPM and in particular of Mr Knudsen,[5] for failing to take steps to do this before. The CIO is also criticizing the labour policy of the OPM and has suggested that labour questions should be removed from its purview and centralized in the Department of Labor. The Brit-

1 British Minister of Supply, 1941–2.
2 Douglas MacArthur, Commander of US Armed Forces in the Far East, 1941.
3 Sir Archibald Wavell, Commander-in-Chief, India, 1941–3.
4 Congress of Industrial Organizations, a federation of industry-wide unions.
5 William S. Knudsen, Director-General, Office of Production Management.

ish system is quoted by Mr Murray[6] in support of this view in a letter to the President.

.   .   .

13 January 1942

The principal events of the week were the President's message to Congress on the State of the Union and his budget message. The immediate public reaction to the message on the State of the Union, with its enormous figures for armament production in 1942 and 1943, was that the programme, though staggering, was capable of being carried out. There is however a good deal of doubt and questioning about the supply machinery in the United States. It has been pointed out that it is useless for the President to attempt to perform efficiently and simultaneously the functions of Mr Churchill and Lord Beaverbrook, and various candidates for the post of the American Beaverbrook are being pressed upon the President. No one thinks that either of the present joint heads of the OPM, Mr Knudsen and Mr Hillman,[1] fills this bill. Some striking and dynamic figure is called for and Mr Walter Lippmann[2] and others have suggested that Mr Willkie[3] is the man for the job. Another suggestion is Justice Byrnes of the Supreme Court. Meanwhile the automobile industry, which will have to bear the heaviest burden in carrying out the President's programme, has been in consultation in Washington with the OPM and representatives of organized labour. The latter suggested a plan for a committee with equal representation of management and labour, which should be given directing control of the conversion of the industry to war production. The industrialists objected strongly to this, and the conference at one time was on the point of breaking down. Ultimately a seven-man committee with three management, three labour, and one government representative has been set up. It will however have a purely advisory role.

The budget which the President introduced to Congress on 7 January was described as the largest ever presented to any nation. It amounted to nearly $59 billion, $52 billion of which are for war purposes. Gross receipts from taxation for the year were estimated at under $18 billion. Meanwhile Congress continues to struggle with the Administration's price control bill, and the President received his first defeat in Congress since the outbreak of war, when the Farm Bloc[4] in the Senate, against his express wishes, pushed through an amendment giving the Secretary of Agriculture veto power over agricultural price ceilings

6 Philip Murray, President of the United Steel Workers of America since 1937 and President of the CIO since 1940.

1 Sidney Hillman, President of the Amalgamated Clothing Workers of America since 1915 and Associate Director-General (with Knudsen) of the Office of Production Management.

2 Walter Lippmann, author, editor, veteran of Paris Peace Conference and syndicated *New York Herald Tribune* columnist since 1931.

3 Wendell L. Willkie, Republican presidential candidate in 1940.

4 A bi-party group of Senators and Congressmen from agricultural constituencies formed in 1921 to secure legislation favourable to farmers.

imposed by the Price Administrator. The Senate has now agreed to a bill entirely different from that which passed the House, and the joint conference will have a difficult task in ironing out the differences and attempting to restrain the log-rolling[5] tendencies of members from agricultural constituencies. The Vice-President,[6] himself a successful ex-Secretary of Agriculture, considers that the Farm Bloc in the Senate have in reality rendered a disservice to the farmers. He has hopes however that the conference of the House and Senate will reach a satisfactory solution.

Criticisms of the Office of Civilian Defense (OCD) continue. La Guardia[7] told the press that he had no intention of resigning either the Directorship of that office or his post as Mayor of New York. The next day the House of Representatives voted against the wishes of the Administration to transfer the functions of the Office of Civilian Defense to the control of the War Department. This vote is of course not yet effective and meanwhile the President has appointed Mr Landis,[8] Dean of the Harvard Law School, as 'executive' of that office under La Guardia with undefined powers. It is typical of Mr Roosevelt's administrative methods, when one of his officials is criticized, not to displace him but to appoint somebody else to do the same job. The Landis appointment though welcomed in itself has by no means allayed the criticisms which have been levelled against the organization of civilian defence in this country.

The rapturous unity of the first weeks of the war is thus to some extent giving place to an atmosphere of criticism. Although the divisions are not following the same lines as those which split the country before Pearl Harbor, and although their main object is to increase the efficiency of the American war effort, they undoubtedly exist.

. . .

20 January 1942

. . . Average American is fully aware by now war will not be walkover for democracies and as he steels himself for sacrifices he has as yet barely felt, but which he has been told to expect to be considerable, there is natural tendency on his part to criticize war effort and authorities in charge of it. Public attention during past week has again been centered on shortcomings of situation at home. In this sphere main development has been appointment by President of Mr Donald Nelson[1] as head and organizer of whole of United States war production in capacity of head of new War Production Board (WPB). As indicated in last week's summary, establishment of a single authority to control and co-ordinate

5 'I'll help to roll your log if you'll help to roll mine.'

6 Henry Wallace (since 1940).

7 Fiorello ('the little flower') La Guardia, ebullient New Deal Mayor of New York, 1934–45.

8 James M.Landis, member of New Deal Securities Exchange Commission, 1934–7, Dean of Harvard Law School, 1937–46, Director of Office of Civilian Defense, 1942–3, Director of American Economic Operations and Minister to Middle East, 1942–5.

1 Donald M.Nelson, previously Head of Sears, Roebuck, the biggest mail-order company in the USA.

country's defence production has long been regarded as necessity in view of inadequacy of existing machinery, and therefore not surprisingly Nelson's appointment has received widespread approval. Mr Nelson has been given full control over all defence supply and production agencies, and even Board of which he is chairman has only authority to 'advise and assist him'. On face of it, presidential order setting up War Production Board confers very wide powers indeed on Mr Nelson. He has however not been made member of Cabinet, and to what extent he will in fact be able to establish his authority remains to be seen. Much will of course depend on extent to which he can count on continuing support of President. Mr Knudsen, hitherto Director-General of OPM, has been given post of Director of Production in War Department. There is some misgiving lest it may turn out that he clashes with Nelson in exercise of his functions.

Meanwhile criticisms of United States war effort in general and of supply machinery in particular have been continuing and have received support from report of special committee set up by Senate under chairmanship of Senator Truman[2] to investigate national defence programme. Report of this committee, which was appointed nearly year ago, contains severe criticism of national defence programme and reveals mismanagement on part of OPM and affiliated agencies. Report recommends, among other things, that all dollar-a-year men[3] should either give up their government jobs or sever their connexions with private industry. Nelson is reported already to be considering making certain changes in OPM under his new powers.

. . . Two important developments have taken place in sphere of labour. First is appointment by President on 12 January of National War Labor Board to assist in carrying out policy of 'no strikes no lockouts' recently agreed upon between labour and industry. Whether in fact both sides will be willing to submit disputes to Board, and accept decisions by this Board which has no statutory powers remains to be seen. In meantime, there is still considerable support for anti-strike legislation of moderate kind. Second development was surprise move on part John L. Lewis, proposing discussions with view to union between the two rival American labour organizations, the CIO and AF of L.[4] These overtures were immediately acknowledged and warmly welcomed by William Green,[5] President of AF of L, but Philip Murray, Lewis's successor as President of CIO, who was apparently not consulted beforehand, is much less enthusiastic. It is difficult to foretell at present what results may be. In general it may be said that 'climate' in labour circles favours unity and that everyone is competing for honour of being its author. But the genuine unity of ideas is still absent so that it cannot be taken for granted that unity discussions will be successful.

2 Harry S. Truman, Democratic Senator from Missouri since 1935.

3 Executives who work for the government at the minimum salary required by law.

4 The American Federation of Labor (AF of L), composed of craft unions, was founded in 1886. The Committee for Industrial Organization (CIO) was founded in 1935–6 by several dissident AF of L unions in order to extend industrial unionism to large-scale mass production industries.

5 William Green, President of AF of L since 1925.

On 14 January new Office of Censorship issued statement setting forth certain kinds of information not to be published, as being of assistance to the enemy. These regulations, which have been followed by similar ones for all radio services, have been received with general approval.

. . .

28 January 1942

The report of the committee of investigation into the disaster at Pearl Harbor was published 24 January and makes dismal reading. The Admiral and General concerned are roundly blamed for dereliction of duty and it is evident that the army and navy in Hawaii functioned in watertight compartments. Incredible as it may seem, up to the moment of the Japanese attack there had been no consultation between them in regard to the numerous warnings of impending hostilities which they had received from Washington. . . .

Senator Connally,[1] Chairman of the Foreign Relations Committee of the Senate, made an extraordinarily irresponsible statement on 21 January in the course of which he predicted the early fall of Singapore and attacked the Argentine Government for its attitude at the Rio de Janeiro Conference.[2] His remarks were at once disowned by the State Department and have since been much criticized.

Mr Nelson has been busy reorganizing the administration of war production. He has abolished the Office of Production Management, which was inaugurated a year ago under the dual headship of Mr Knudsen and Mr Hillman, and which has been freely criticized ever since. He has set up six divisions under the War Production Board to deal with purchases, production, materials, industry, operations, labour and civilian supply, the last two being headed by Hillman and Henderson respectively. A former director of the Ford Company has been given full powers to direct the conversion of the automobile industry to war production.

The conferences of the two Houses of Congress worked on the price control bill throughout the week, and finally produced a joint text which Henderson, the Price Controller, has described as 'practically worthless' as a weapon against inflation, although some of the more outrageous amendments introduced by the Farm Bloc have now been eliminated.

John L. Lewis's proposals for amalgamation of the two rival labour union organizations have come to nothing. They seem to have been generally regarded by everyone as an attempt by Lewis to gain for himself the control of a unified labour movement. Murray, his successor as President of the CIO, was furious at not being consulted beforehand, and the AF of L's original warm welcome soon turned to suspicion. At this point the President stepped in, summoned Murray and Green to the White House and rapidly worked out with them an alternative plan whereby each organization should nominate three members of a committee

1 Thomas Connally, Democratic Senator from Texas since 1929.
2 In particular Argentinian reluctance to accede to a forthright Western Hemisphere declaration for a rupture of relations with the Axis powers.

to consult with Mr Roosevelt on all questions relating to labour's participation in the war effort. This plan has been accepted by the AF of L and the CIO and no representative of Lewis's supporters in the latter organization has been nominated to the Board. One of the CIO representatives is generally believed to be a Communist. Lewis's reaction to this snub is not yet known, but there have been rumours that he may try to detach his organization, the United Mine Workers, from the CIO, of which it has hitherto been the main support. The Mine Workers have in the past been completely subservient to Lewis but it is far from certain that they would follow him in a manoeuvre of this kind. Meanwhile there has been some criticism of the President for his proposal to preside over the joint labour meetings himself, and it has been said that after giving up the attempt to be his own Beaverbrook he is now trying to be his own Bevin.[3]

4 February 1942

. . . The news of the landing of American troops in Northern Ireland . . . the publicity for which was skilfully handled, has been generally well received, and the public do not seem to have been much impressed by the criticisms of a few individual members of Congress who, moreover, were concerned not at the despatch of another American expeditionary force, but at the fact that this had gone to Europe rather than the Far East. The repeated attacks on American shipping by German U-boats off the Atlantic coast seem to have been received too complacently. Colonel Knox himself has been perhaps unduly optimistic on the subject, since some of his statements have given the impression that very few of the German submarines which have been in American waters have managed to make their way back to port. This renewed tendency towards complacency about the performance of the United States armed forces received encouragement from a speech by ex-President Hoover[1] who asserted that United States could not lose the war since they could neither be starved out nor invaded. American public opinion is notoriously mercurial, and the problem of morale has given rise to many conflicting theories of how to deal with it. The present mood is that America is doing all right. By playing up local American or Allied successes in the Pacific area the newspapers have contrived to give an impression of the situation which falsifies perspective. The American public is thus led to consider that the war news as a whole is good on any given day, when there is no ground for such conclusion. This risks two results. First that if the news of the day from the Pacific records local reverses the general war situation is regarded as bad to an undue degree. Secondly, this sort of treatment militates against the adoption towards the war of the healthy attitude that the United Nations will undoubtedly go through very bad times but that a successful outcome is not the less certain. Attention is too much concentrated on the present. This method of presenting the

3 Ernest Bevin, British Minister of Labour, 1940–5.
1 Herbert Hoover, Republican President, 1929–33.

news is deplored in many quarters, but little appears to be done from the side of the Administration to correct it.

But though the present mood is that America is doing quite well, it is felt that Great Britain's efforts are 'not so hot'. The rumours about the Australians and others doing all the fighting, etc., exemplified in a particularly unpleasant article by Mr Hearst[2] published on 28 or 29 January, though possibly Axis-inspired, find a ready market in that considerable section of the American public to whom criticizing the British is as natural an act as breathing. The matter has been reported to the Ministry of Information. But I would urge here as strongly as I can that remedial action should be taken as soon as possible. I myself saw several of the principal radio commentators two days ago in New York. I there tried to correct both this tendency to depreciate Great Britain by comparison, and also the two dangers referred to in preceding paragraph. Much could be done by producing facts and figures designed to put matters in their proper light. . . .

The Senate passed unanimously on 28 January the Second War Powers bill giving the Government additional authority over production, finance and raw materials. The bill now goes to the House of Representatives. The Senate was inclined to be critical of the so-called 'dollar-a-year men', the executives of important companies serving in the war production departments, but continuing to be paid by their own firms. Mr Nelson, however, has said that he cannot get on without them and the Senate, influenced by the present mood that Mr Nelson must be given everything he asks for, has told him that it will withdraw its objections. The announcement of the Combined[3] Anglo-American Raw Materials, Munitions and Shipping Boards was generally welcomed though apart from a large number of approving editorials it did not perhaps make as deep an impression as might have been hoped.

The Price Control bill, after being worked over for six months in Congress, at last reached the President for signature 30 January and received his somewhat tepid approval. The Farm Bloc in Congress, though some of their amendments were eliminated, thought that they had achieved a victory in the retention of the clause empowering the Secretary of Agriculture to impose a veto on the fixing of agricultural prices by the Price Control Administrator, and it was probably the idea that the Secretary of Agriculture was on their side that induced them to agree to the bill. Mr Wickard[4] has however made it plain that he is opposed to higher prices for farm products, and the Farm Bloc's victory is thus a pyrrhic one. They will no doubt try to take it out of Mr Wickard when he next wishes to put an agricultural measure through Congress. The full authority given to the Price Administrator to ration retail sales of all commodities should assist in checking price rises.

2 William Randolph Hearst, proprietor of coast-to-coast chain of newspapers.

3 In wartime usage 'combined' means Anglo-American and 'joint' usually means comprising US army, navy and air force.

4 Claude R. Wickard, Secretary of Agriculture since 1940.

The first serious strike since the United States came into the war is in progress among welders working in Pacific Coast shipyards. The reasons for the strike are jurisdictional and it has been denounced as 'intolerable' by the War Production Board. The CIO is delaying the introduction of the seven-day week in the automobile factories converted to war production by demanding double pay for Sunday work.

. . .

The overcrowded housing and the overburdened public services of Washington, due to the enormous increase in governmental agencies, have long given cause for worry, and the President at his press conference on 30 January expressed the view that 'parasites' should leave the capital immediately. He did not define 'parasites' but implied that all persons whose work did not contribute to national defence would be better out of Washington. These remarks caused a noticeable flutter in the Washington dovecots.

As far as public opinion is concerned one result of the present strategic anxieties is that the shares of Great Britain are going through one of their recurrent periods of slump. They will no doubt rise again as they have done before but the trend of the line on the graph has for some time now been a descending one and I am concerned by the indications that the innate inclination to think and hear ill of our country and of us so readily comes to the surface. I am confident that the heads of the Administration are wholeheartedly convinced that our two countries must work in the closest harmony during the war and after, and I firmly believe they will do all they can to this end. But the wish to collaborate closely and effectively is absent in many places and there are a number of quarters which should be more enlightened where it seems actively absent. Among some of the most senior officials of the State Department there is apparently a continuing anxiety to keep the hands of the United States Government free to deal with international problems, e.g. France and post-war Europe, as seems best to it, untrammelled by consideration of the views of other governments. This wish, which is not confined to State Department officials, is doubtless natural in ordinary times. But as a criterion for judging requests for collaboration in the day-to-day problems of wartime it is regrettable there is in the same circles a standing aversion from entering into closer relationships with Great Britain than with other friendly nations for reasons of old standing in the field both of internal and external politics. That entry of the United States into the war has made no visible change in this respect, has been rendered easier for the United States Government by the Declaration of the United Nations and the results of the Rio conference. We must in fact anticipate difficulties in the attainment both of wartime collaboration and still more of collaboration after the war. This is a situation which will require unremitting effort, patience and much wisdom to remedy. Something can perhaps be done by informed and imaginative publicity, an important part of which should be directed towards the promotion (e.g. by films, novels and anecdotes) of sympathy for our national character, individual way of

17

life and national ideals and towards the removal in this way of misunderstanding based on ignorance. We must clearly stand or fall by what we are, and a self-portrait falsified for the American taste would do more harm than good. But we can invite attention to our good qualities. We must moreover always base ourselves on the assumption that Americans are foreigners to us and we to them.

10 February 1942

The past week has been one of bickering. Congress has been attacked for voting itself pensions and has retaliated by attacking the Office of Civilian Defense and Mrs Roosevelt.[1] The President has been at odds with the Chairman of the Democratic Party,[2] and all Administration leaders, including members of the Cabinet, have been told to submit their speeches to the Office of Facts and Figures[3] instead of as hitherto to the President's secretary for clearance before delivery. The honeymoon of national unity is somewhat clouded.

The affair of the Office of Civilian Defense is working up for trouble. La Guardia has announced that he will resign, but has not fixed a date, and the attack is now mainly against Mrs Roosevelt and her protégés who have been given jobs in the organization, including a well-known film-star and a not at all well-known dancer who is drawing $4,600 a year for directing children's activities. Satirical attacks on the President's wife have been made in the House of Representatives, and the Administration are calling up all their forces in Congress to deal with a vote which will shortly be taken on the matter.

The Congressmen's indignation may be partly an attempt to divert attention from the public criticism of their recent action in voting themselves into the Civil Service pension scheme. This vote, taken at a time when Congress itself was leading a campaign for cuts in non-defence expenditure, has exposed the legislature to ridicule. The standing of the present members of Congress has never been particularly high in the eyes of the public and has hardly been raised by a series of complacent speeches in the Senate on 3 February, in which the majority of the speakers attempted to defend the Upper House against any share of responsibility for American weakness in the Pacific, the main charge against Congress being of course its continual refusal to agree to the fortification of Guam. The low opinion in which Congress is held may be reflected in the November elections, at which the whole House of Representatives and one third of the Senate come up for re-election. Mr Flynn, the Chairman of the Democratic Party, said in a speech that no misfortune except a major military defeat would be so bad for a country as the election of a Congress hostile to the President, and that vast confusion would result if there were a President of one party and a House of Representatives of another. This speech appears to repeat what is gen-

1 Eleanor Roosevelt, wife of President, appointed Assistant Director, OCD, 1941.
2 Edward J. Flynn, political boss of the Bronx, New York, Chairman of the Democratic Party since 1940.
3 Set up in October 1941 to assist in the 'dissemination of factual information' on the 'national defence effort'.

erally regarded as President Wilson's[4] fatal mistake of asking the country to return a Democratic Congress in 1918 and it was more or less repudiated by the President, who at his press conference on 6 February declared that the country needed Congressmen, regardless of party, whose record showed that they would back up the Government and the country's war effort. This statement has been generally applauded and has been publicly welcomed by Mr Willkie in particular.

The labour situation is healthier. The Pacific Coast welders' strike was strongly denounced by Nelson, Stimson, Knox and the Maritime Commission in a joint statement on 2 February, and has now more or less petered out. The question of double pay for Sunday work in automobile factories converted to defence work has been referred to the War Labor Board whose decision is expected to be accepted as final by both parties. . . .

The establishment of the Combined Chiefs of Staff in Washington was announced in the press on 7 February. This has given rise to some comments to the effect that Washington is replacing London as the centre of the war effort, and a New Dealer columnist reputedly close to the White House has written that 'When there are differences of opinion on strategy the appeal is to the President and not to the Prime Minister. In a real show-down the President undoubtedly can make his view prevail.' Although there is no reason to think that this view on the war is held by the President or the leading members of the Administration, it is undoubtedly widespread at lower levels. . . .

19 February 1942

The events of the past week have led to greatly increased criticism of Great Britain in this country. The friendly *Washington Post* wrote in an editorial on 15 February that 'It was perhaps inevitable that the dramatic escape of the German warships from Brest,[1] with all the implications that event may have for our own Atlantic Coast, should, coming on the heels of the Malayan fiasco and the collapse of the much advertised Libyan offensive, unleash a flood of indignation in this country.' This indignation gained fresh impetus from the unfortunately timed arrival in this country of American refugees from Penang who had some fierce comments to make on the circumstances attending the British evacuation of that port.[2] The saner people in this country are fully aware of the danger which this criticism of America's principal ally represents and have issued warnings against it. There is an undoubted danger that the former isolationists will take the opportunity of this phase of opinion to emerge as appeasers with policy of retiring

4 In October 1918 Woodrow Wilson announced that the 'return of a Republican majority to either House of Congress would . . . certainly be interpreted on the other side of the water as a repudiation of my leadership'. In November the Republicans won majorities in both Houses.

1 On 12 February : the *Scharnhorst,* the *Gneisenau* and the *Prinz Eugen.*

2 On 19 December 1941.

behind Hawaii and the Atlantic bases leaving the rest of the world to stew in its own juice. The Republican Party is evidently conscious of the danger that it might be exploited to this end and its responsible leaders, among them Willkie, Landon[3] and Martin,[4] have all warned against it and gone on record in favour of policy of fighting to the end. Willkie in a speech at Boston on Lincoln's birthday urged the party not to oppose for the sake of opposing but to do all it could to support the war effort and to get rid of inefficiencies. He suggested that General MacArthur be called back from the Philippines to become Commander-in-Chief of all the armed forces, a suggestion which is frequently being made from other quarters. Incidentally in this speech Willkie suggested that the legitimate functions of the State Department were being unduly infringed by some of the newly created governmental agencies. Martin, the National Chairman of the party, spoke at Kansas City on 15 February in same sense and Landon praised the Prime Minister's speech[5] in a press interview the same day.

While calling attention to the motes in British eyes Americans are becoming conscious of beams in their own. Though MacArthur's resistance in the Philippines continues to inspire legitimate pride it is realized if seldom actually stated that this is a sideshow and there is a certain feeling of frustration that apart from this small campaign American troops are not now actually fighting anywhere. The American public knows that there are United States forces in Northern Ireland and more recently in the Netherlands West Indies but those are zones normally remote from active operations and the American army as a whole is not at present actively engaged. The country is being told by many speakers, among others a prominent official in War Production Board and Admiral Standley, the newly appointed Ambassador to Moscow, that the United States of America can lose the war if they do not exert every effort.

The public is not sure that every effort is being exerted and is much disillusioned by signs of carelessness and inefficiency such as the fire which put the *Normandie* out of action.[6] Nelson issued a statement at beginning of week declaring that 1942 was the critical year in the existence of United States of America and that there was not a moment to lose in war production. In spite of this 10,000 mechanics employed by Ford were out of action for a whole day owing to a dispute about one worker and the welders' strike in the West Coast shipbuilding yards is still not entirely concluded. Admiral Land[7] admitted to a member of my staff the other day that he was far from satisfied as regards the labour situation in the shipbuilding world and feared that if this present state of affairs continued the rate of production of new ships would be affected. Relations between labour and government will not be assisted by refusal of House of Repre-

3 Alfred Landon, Republican presidential candidate in 1936.

4 Joseph Martin, Republican Congressman from Massachusetts since 1925, Republican leader in the House since 1939, and Republican National Chairman since 1940.

5 World broadcast, 15 February.

6 Burnt and sunk at her moorings in New York City on 9 February.

7 Emory Scott Land, Chairman of the US Maritime Commission since 1938.

sentatives to agree to a proposed appropriation for support of persons unemployed as result of conversion of industry for war purposes.

Congress so far has been still too busy trying to clear its own escutcheon from the blot of the Pensions vote to be very critical of other people, though I fear that attacks on British conduct of the war must be expected from some of the more irresponsible members. President asked Congress to suspend for duration of war section 7 of Neutrality Act[8] which forbids loans to belligerents (though this will not benefit United Kingdom since the Johnson Act[9] is still on Statute Book) and this was agreed to by Senate without much difficulty. Further Lease-Lend appropriation is also having an easy passage. Congress has been warned that Treasury will soon ask for an increase in National Debt limit.

The House is still restive about the Office of Civilian Defense (OCD) and has voted an amendment to an appropriation for that office in terms implying criticism of Mrs Roosevelt. Mayor La Guardia has now resigned as Head of the Office and Mrs Roosevelt has announced her intention of doing so. La Guardia in his final report has some implicit criticism to be made of Mrs Roosevelt. The latter has not retaliated but has been showing considerable impatience with her critics in the syndicated column which she publishes daily.

The public disillusionment referred to above is not confined to single instances of inefficiency or carelessness. There is now beginning a widespread feeling of concern (hitherto confined to comparatively narrow circles) over complexities of whole emergency government machinery, a suspicion that new boards are merely imposed upon existing ones to correct the inefficiencies of the latter, that these bodies largely overlap and hamper each other and that the efforts of the country are becoming 'bogged down' in a welter of clumsy machinery.

26 February 1942

. . .

There has been some anxiety that the Administration were not being sufficiently strict with enemy aliens or persons of enemy alien descent, particularly Japanese in the West Coast areas, and the campaign on this subject was led by Walter Lippmann, who is not generally regarded as an alarmist. On 20 February President issued an executive order authorizing Secretary of War to eject any citizens or aliens from military areas, and giving him power to define such areas, and a round-up of Japanese and of American citizens of Japanese descent is now taking place on West Coast. A Bill on the lines of the Official Secrets Act,[1] introduced in Congress on 16 February, seems likely to have a slow passage, being generally regarded as being too drastic in form. The objections raised to

8 Passed in 1937.

9 Passed in 1934, forbidding loans to countries in default to the USA on war debts.

1 British enactments of 1889, 1911 and 1920 designed to prevent espionage and unauthorized disclosures of state secrets.

this Bill in Congress and outside underline clearly one of the Administration's difficulties : the powers desired by the Bill are not in themselves considered objectionable, but it is feared or alleged to be feared that the New Deal elements in the Administration will use them to suppress criticism and not exclusively to preserve war secrets.

. . .

Mrs Roosevelt resigned from the Office of Civilian Defense on 20 February. In a subsequent broadcast she made it fairly clear that she had not done so voluntarily. Congress has again raised the issue of placing the Office of Civilian Defense under the control of the War Department.

The House of Representatives is still blocking the Administration's proposals for relief for persons unemployed as a result of the conversion of industry to war production. The major steel firms have come out with a pronouncement against a compromise on the closed shop proposed by the War Labor Board and a controversy bearing the seeds of trouble is feared. The Selective Service System has announced that leading members of trade unions may receive deferment from induction into military service.

The interest in the British rule in India and the Indian demands for a change of status, which is always prevalent here, has lately been showing signs of revived liveliness. . . . If the war situation adjacent to India continues to develop unfavourably, there is likely to be a good deal of comment upon the proportion of Indian fighting strength to India's total manpower, with which it will be desirable to deal in our publicity.

4 March 1942

There has been some increase of dissension and domestic bickering during the week. This tendency is probably in part the natural result of the fact that so far there has been little to report in the way of American military success beyond the defensive operation of General MacArthur. This continues to be splashed and the General's life is appearing in serial form in a Washington newspaper under title of 'MacArthur the Magnificent'. Colonel Stimson, however, made no secret to me a few days ago that MacArthur was of course under no serious Japanese pressure. There are also signs of a revival of party politics in preparation for the congressional elections in November. Public opinion is still very depressed over the situation in the Pacific and uneasy about the continued torpedoings on this country's Atlantic seaboard. News of Allied successes around Bali and Java and Colonel Knox's recent statement on the losses inflicted on the enemy by the United States Navy have provided some temporary encouragement, but have done nothing to stop dissatisfaction with the way the operations are being conducted from the centre. This has been increased by reports such as that broadcast by the NBC[1] representative at Sydney that American warships were using old

1 National Broadcasting Company.

and defective ammunition. There is a growing feeling, voiced by such responsible persons as Senator Austin[2], that the American forces ought to be getting to closer grips with the enemy. This sentiment has been publicly endorsed by General Marshall. . . .[3] It was in this atmosphere that it was announced on 28 February that General Short and Admiral Kimmel[4] would be tried by court martial at such time as 'the public interest and safety' permit on charges of dereliction of duty.

In his first 'fireside talk' to the nation since America entered the war, the President on 23 February made a point of replying to those of his critics who had been spreading the view that United States forces should be used exclusively for the defence of the American continent. He pointed out the disastrous results of such a policy, which would enable the enemy to cut allied supply routes and tackle the united nations one by one. He also denounced with unwonted asperity the rumourmongers who spread defeatist reports of American reverses. Otherwise the speech contained little of special interest apart from its emphasis on the fulfilment by the United States of 'our special task of production', an exhortation which was followed on 28 February by the announcement of new measures for an intensified war output. At the same time the situation on the production side is regarded as being more hopeful and there is much confidence in the ability of Donald Nelson to do a good job. In reply to a letter from the President urging increased production, Nelson on 28 February declared that as far as possible all war production plants would work on a twenty-four-hour-day basis, that 'outstanding industrial accomplishment both by management and labour' would be rewarded, and that plans were under way for establishing joint labour-management committees to consider suggestions for increasing production.

The attitude towards Great Britain remains critical (if rather less vocally so). Range and depth of this criticism is difficult to estimate, but all agree that it is substantial, but there are some signs that it is beginning to be tempered with an increasing willingness to give credit for past achievements, though we must expect its continuance until war prospects look better. There is a tendency to reserve judgment on the recent Cabinet changes until their practical results can be gauged and to call for a more enterprising and aggressive policy on the part of His Majesty's Government. This tendency derived some encouragement from the recent speech by M. Litvinov in which he maintained that Hitler could be beaten this year if the Allies launched resolute attacks on Germany from several different fronts. On the other hand the signature of the Lease–Lend agreement has been warmly welcomed as a token of future Anglo–American[5] collaboration.

In present circumstances an exuberant reception was hardly to be expected and in any case the fruits were likely to ripen slowly, but press comment has been

2 Warren R. Austin, Republican Senator from Vermont since 1931.
3 George Catlett Marshall, Chief of Staff, US Army, 1939–45.
4 Land and Sea Commanders at the time of Pearl Harbor.
5 The 'Master' Lend-Lease Agreement, setting out the terms of Lend-Lease and the conditions on which its final settlement should be based.

universally favourable and Mr Willkie hailed the agreement on 24 February as 'The most significant and beneficial understanding made between nations in the last many years.'

A recent report by the Princeton office of public opinion research is of interest. This report estimates that at the moment about one in every ten Americans would accept a peace offer from Hitler. If however the German Army were to overthrow Hitler and then make an offer of peace over a quarter of the American public would be prepared to accept it.

.   .   .

The President has been encountering further opposition to his policies in both Houses of Congress, which as the time of the elections draws nearer have been indulging in an unedifying exhibition of party politics. The main cause of the contention at the moment is the attempt of the Farm Bloc in both Houses to prohibit the Commodity Credit Corporation from selling government-held farm surplus at less than parity prices.[6] In spite of a last-minute appeal by the President on the grounds that such action would do irreparable harm to the war effort by creating inflation in food prices, the Senate passed a bill to that effect by a large majority on 25 February. The President made it clear that he would veto the measure if approved as a separate bill by Congress, and its passage through the House seems very doubtful. To get round the difficulty the sponsors of the bill talked of tacking it on as a rider to the $32 billion appropriation bill, which the President would naturally be reluctant to veto. That idea seems to have been abandoned but a fresh manoeuvre has been started in the House and the dispute between Congress and the Administration is still far from being resolved.

There has been further unrest on the labour front centering on the two main problems of the union shop and wage increases. Leon Henderson has expressed his opposition to the latter as leading to inflation and impeding the Administration's policy of stabilizing prices. Others, however, point out that price control is not yet a reality and that until it is labour should not be penalized by putting a ceiling on wages. Both questions will come up for review by the National War Labor Board at the hearings beginning this week in the dispute between the CIO and the 'Little Steel' companies,[7] which is regarded as a test case both for the Board itself and for the future relations between industry and labour during the war. There is considerable uncertainty at present over a number of war labour problems, including the question of the drafting of workers in defence industries, and several members of Congress have expressed their desire for the formulation of a clearly defined war labour policy, pointing out that the only statement of policy so far has been the President's declaration that there should be no inter-

6 Parity prices were designed to give farmers prices for their produce in balance with the prices farmers paid for what they had to buy. The prices farmers received between 1909 and 1914 were thought to represent such a balance.

7 'Big Steel' was the US Steel Corporation, which was responsible for nearly 40 per cent of American steel output. 'Little Steel' was a collective term for the other American steel-producing corporations.

ruption of defence production. In the meantime attempts to launch a new anti-labour drive have been made both in Congress and elsewhere, but so far have met with little success. On 27 February the House rather surprisingly rejected a proposal to suspend payment of extra overtimed workers for the duration of the war. The proposal was sponsored by Representative Smith, whose group of anti-labour Democrats had remained relatively quiescent since the shelving of his anti-strike bill in December. In the meantime the CIO and the AF of L have submitted a joint petition to the President asking him to renounce any plan for prohibiting wage increases and to create an independent agency within the Department of Labor to handle the problem of mobilizing industrial labour.

· · ·

12 March 1942

[Under an executive order of 2 March] . . . henceforward army will be divided into three branches of equal authority for ground, air and supply services operating under a relatively small general staff. Chief effect of this reorganization is to give air force a status corresponding to its importance in modern warfare. It is also expected to eliminate much overlapping and unnecessary administrative routine. This reorganization of United States Army was followed by announcement on 10 March that Admiral Stark, who has been Chief of Naval Operations since August 1939, was to be succeeded by Admiral King, Commander-in-Chief of United States fleet, who will in future combine duties of both posts. Admiral Stark is to take Admiral Ghormley's[1] place in London with title of 'Commander United States Naval Forces operating in European Waters'. It is too early yet to estimate effect of this change on Anglo–American naval relations. . . .

· · ·

Only important development during week in labour sphere has been action announced by Donald Nelson in course of a broadcast on 2 March calling for an all-out drive to raise production to new level to encourage establishment of joint management-labour committees in defence plants. This is undoubtedly a step forward for labour since it gives official sanction to a scheme which Philip Murray, President of CIO, has long been advocating. Committees are not however to handle specific management or labour problems but are intended to concentrate on organizing and improving production. In meantime President has indicated that he hopes shortly to reach a decision on government plans for mobilization of labour manpower.

On 3 March Secretary of Treasury[2] presented to Congress a tax bill of unprecedented dimensions providing for a minimum of $7.6 billion in new taxes. This, with addition of proposed social security taxes, is expected to raise Federal Government's revenue to about $27 billion in coming fiscal year. Proposals include drastic increases in income-tax rates, especially for middle-income groups.

1 Robert Lee Ghormley, appointed US Navy 'observer' in London in 1940.
2 Henry Morgenthau Jr, Secretary since 1934.

While necessity for a bill of this magnitude is generally accepted Treasury bill is not likely to be passed by Congress without considerable criticism. Among points already raised are advisability of widening scope of bill to cover lower-income groups not at present affected by increased taxes by reducing existing income-tax exemption schedules or by imposing a general sales tax. A bill to increase National Debt limit to $125 billion is at present before House. In meantime country has received further indications of some of privations which it will shortly have to bear. Leon Henderson has warned thirty million motorists that they must not expect any more tyres for three years and that even those they now have may be requisitioned. Secretary of Interior[3] has indicated that petrol rationing may begin shortly and WPB has given orders for manufacture of wireless sets and gramophones for civilian use to stop after 22 April.

Mr Hull,[4] who was far from well for several weeks in earlier part of year, is still in Florida recuperating and nothing is known about date of his probable return. Rumours are circulating that he may in fact resign either because of his health or because he feels that a younger man should be in charge of State Department at this moment. I have, however, heard nothing to tend to confirm accuracy of these rumours : on the contrary, only a few days ago one of Mr Hull's private secretaries assured a member of my staff that Secretary of State was well on way to recovery and that it would not be long before he was back in his office. Furthermore there are at moment quite a crop of rumours suggesting that other members of Cabinet are on point of resigning. Apart from Miss Perkins,[5] Secretary of Labor, whose resignation has been canvassed by newspapers for months past, there have recently been suggestions that Colonel Stimson is too old for his post and should retire, possibly to be succeeded by Mr James Wadsworth,[6] the well-known and highly respected Republican Congressman from New York State. President has discounted this talk of Cabinet changes and so far these stories have shown no signs of materializing, but it is perhaps significant that in a recent article by Walter Lippmann he pointed out that only one member of the Cabinet was under fifty and only three more under sixty.

20 March 1942

. . . Congress, which sometimes gives the impression of being unaware of what is going on in the outside world, continues to busy itself with log-rolling. The House of Representatives has now passed Department of Agriculture's Appropriation Bill with a number of economy cuts and with rider forbidding sale of government-held farm surpluses. Senate has still to consider this Bill. This action was taken in opposition to Administration wishes and in apparent defiance of a

3 Harold Ickes, Secretary since 1933.
4 Cordell Hull, Secretary of State, 1933–44.
5 Frances Perkins, Secretary since 1933.
6 James W. Wadsworth, Republican Senator from New York, 1915–27, Congressman since 1933.

warning on danger of inflation which President addressed to farmers on 9 March. What Administration will finally do about farm prices is still undecided but it was announced during week that President was considering dealing with the other most likely cause of inflation by imposing some kind of ceiling on wage rises.

.   .   .

Willkie, whom I saw a few days ago, is doing all he can to prevent the inevitable reaction against the Administration in forthcoming congressional elections from accruing to benefit of isolationist groups who are active underground. Much will of course depend upon how the war looks when election time comes. Meanwhile both members of Administration and others are a good deal perturbed by development of Negro problem under influence of colour propaganda by Japanese.

26 March 1942

General MacArthur's appointment to the Australian Command [1] aroused tremendous enthusiasm. A speaker in Congress described it as the best news of the war, Australian stocks rose on Wall Street and the General was seriously compared by a widely syndicated columnist with Alexander the Great and Napoleon. These panegyrics have aroused perhaps dangerous expectations of early and successful offensive action against Japan, and more sober reflection has produced warnings against expecting miracles and reminders that action depends on provision of material. The possibility of some offensive action to assist Russia continues to attract much attention, and the repetition by the Soviet Ambassador of a plea in this sense at a large dinner in New York was very warmly received. Meanwhile the Australian front dominates the headlines, and interest in that country has received strong support from the visit to Washington of the Australian Minister of External Affairs and from the dispute over Mr Casey's appointment. [2] Although comment on the latter incident has been restrained, the whole affair played into the hands of our enemies in this country who are glad of any excuse to criticize the stability and to cast doubts upon the unity of the Empire. Even in friendlier quarters the treatment of what appeared to be an intra-Imperial dispute showed traces of *Schadenfreude* and gave further evidence that the wave of anti-British feeling is running strongly. The existence of this feeling has been more evident in private conversation with Americans all over the country than in the press, which has on the whole shown a sense of responsibility in ignoring it, and there is no doubt that the Administration is much concerned about it. Mr Hop-

1 As Supreme Commander of all the Allied Forces in the South-West Pacific.

2 R.G.Casey, Australian Minister in Washington, was appointed on 19 March Minister of State, a member of the British War Cabinet, and representative of the War Cabinet in the Middle East. Mr Curtin, Australian Prime Minister, expressed regret at consequential loss of Mr Casey's services in Washington.

kins[3] spoke to me about it with some concern a night or two ago, and the President, in a letter read at a meeting in New York which was addressed by the Soviet and Chinese Ambassadors, the Netherlands Minister and myself, laid especial emphasis on the necessity for the United Nations to remain United. . . .

The creation of a war-time labour policy was the principal internal issue of the week, and the clamour in Congress for action on this question continues, reinforced by a record volume of mail addressed to Congressmen, which Green and Murray have declared is being organized by reactionary employers.

The main object of attack is the forty-hour week, but anti-strike legislation and prohibition of agitation for the closed shop are also being canvassed. The Administration, as so often in labour matters, speaks with two voices. Most government witnesses summoned by Congress during the week have advised caution, both the President and Nelson have defended the forty-hour week, and the latter has assured the CIO that labour's rights will not be infringed. On the other hand Arnold, the Assistant Attorney General,[4] told the Judiciary Committee of the House of Representatives that the unions were abusing their power, preventing the efficient use of men and machines and impeding distribution by undemocratic procedures. . . .

Lewis and the CIO are nearing an open breach and the former has been dunning the latter for some money owed by it to the United Mine Workers. There is still far from complete satisfaction at the rate of industrial production. Nelson for instance has said that production in New Jersey is only 49 per cent of its potential maximum and he has himself come in for private criticism from New Deal elements for being too kind to old friends in the War Production Board; the man in charge of the aircraft section for instance is said to be 'notoriously incompetent'. There is particular dissatisfaction with the shipbuilding programme, aggravated by the daily reports of shipping losses off the Atlantic coast and by the realization that the offensive action so dear to the hearts of the public depends on an acceleration of shipbuilding which is known to be seriously in arrears. . . .

It is announced that sugar rationing will be introduced at the beginning of May. The amount to be allowed per head has not been disclosed but it is expected to be half or three quarters of a pound per head per week. This restriction, slight though it is, will be the first real interference with the day-to-day existence of the American civilian. Though the sales of many consumer goods such as cars and refrigerators have been curtailed most people still have their old ones and in spite of the impending rubber shortage and warnings of petrol rationing on the East Coast there are no fewer cars on the roads than before Pearl Harbor. The shops are full as ever of all kinds of goods and the high standard of American living remains virtually unimpaired. To recent arrivals from England the absence of practically any outward evidence in America that there is a war on is something of a shock.

3 Harry L.Hopkins, head of Lend-Lease and confidant and 'expediter' to Roosevelt.
4 Thurman Arnold, Assistant Attorney General, 1938–43.

2 April 1942

In absence of any special development in the war, interest was concentrated on the home front where the principal battlefield was labour. On the whole the Administration has been for labour (the attack on labour by the Assistant Attorney General mentioned in last week's summary was repudiated by the Attorney General) [1] while Congress has been against labour. Even so faithful a supporter of the Administration as Connally, the Chairman of the Senate Foreign Relations Committee, is said to favour curbing labour's rights. Nelson again told a committee of the House of Representatives that he opposed suspension of the closed shop and the law requiring extra pay for work in excess of forty hours a week. He said he thought that double pay for Sunday and holiday overtime work ought to be dropped and this was accepted in principle by the CIO and the AF of L on 24 March. Both the latter organizations also announced that no strike for any cause will be called or tolerated for the duration of the war. If these two declarations are properly enforced much of the case for labour legislation may disappear, but the difficulties inherent in the differentiation in pay between industrial workers and the selectees called up for military service will still remain. . . .

Arnold, who last week was attacking labour, this week showed his impartiality by an onslaught on capitalist trusts. He accused Standard Oil of impeding the production of synthetic rubber in this country owing to its cartel agreement with IG Farben Industrie and of having disposed of a valuable American synthetic rubber invention to that concern. He also charged it with having attempted to arrange for resumption of business with Germany and Japan after the war and with having tried to break the British blockade. It has nevertheless been announced that prosecutions under the anti-trust legislation are to be avoided as far as possible during the war owing to the danger that they may interfere with production. The House of Representatives on 28 March attached to an appropriation bill a limit of 6 per cent on industrial profits earned in war production. If this provision passes the Senate and becomes law it will no doubt be used to reinforce the case for control of wages as a counterpart.

. . .

The controversy between Congress and the Administration is not confined to the labour issue. Republicans in the Senate and the House are supporting a bill to abolish the Civilian Conservation Corps and the National Youth Administration. These are two New Deal creations to rehabilitate or provide work for unemployed and a large section of Congress considers them to have outlived their usefulness. The Administration is anxious to keep them in being, influenced possibly not only by the services which they can still render to the unemployed but by the fact that their members provide strong voting support for the Democratic Party. The House of Representatives' Committee on Un-American Activ-

1 Francis Biddle, Attorney General since 1941.

ities (commonly known as the Dies Committee) [2] has claimed that a large num er of the high executives of the Board of Economic Warfare have Communist affiliations and the Vice-President, who is Chairman of the Board, has reacted strongly.

The President has sent a strong letter to the heads of the various government agencies urging them to eliminate the delay in deliveries of war material to Russia which apparently still persists in spite of Mr Roosevelt's previous announcement that it would be cured by 1 March.

. . .

8 April 1942

Though the agitation for labour legislation continues, it has now lost some of its force, partly owing to the strong opposition of Nelson and partly perhaps to the agreement of the unions to drop double pay for Sunday and holiday overtime. There were some exchanges in the Senate between Barkley,[1] the Administration leader, and Connally and it was finally agreed that the latter's labour bill should be brought up in the Senate on 20 April. Meanwhile the dispute within the CIO continues and there are rumours that Lewis will try to form a third labour movement, the nucleus of which would be the United Mine Workers which he dominates. Already the chief executives of the United Mine Workers in Illinois have been resigning from the CIO and the miners were conspicuously absent from the list of unions which signed a telegram sent by the CIO to General MacArthur and the Australian trade unions.

The need to organize American manpower for the war effort has for some time been apparent but there is considerable controversy as to who should have control of this question. Candidates are Hillman's manpower section in the WPB, General Hershey[2] of the Selective Service Administration, and McNutt[3] of the Federal Security Administration. The Department of Labor, otherwise the obvious candidate, is out of the running at least under its present Secretary. Hillman laid before the Senate Labor Committee on 2 April a plan for the mobilization of men and women to work in war industries but it does not follow from this that he has won the battle for control of manpower. Meanwhile the Department of Agriculture has tabled a plan for preventing the excess movement of farm workers into the armed forces and war industries.

. . .

Dies's attack on the Board of Economic Warfare has brought him much criticism and one member of his Committee has reported that the attack was made on Dies's own personal responsibility without reference to the Committee. The

2 After its notoriously xenophobic first Chairman, Martin Dies, Democratic Representative from Texas, 1939–45.

1 Alben W.Barkley, Democratic Senator from Kentucky since 1927 and Majority Leader of the Senate since 1937.

2 Major-General Lewis Blaine Hershey, Director of the Bureau of Selective Service since 1941.

3 Paul V.McNutt, Director of Federal Security Administration since 1939.

White House has pointed out that Dies's charges have been reproduced by the German radio and he has been accused once more of being more interested in smelling out alleged Communists than in exposing Nazi or Fascist activities. A few of the local brand of Fascists have been arrested recently. The latest is the notorious Pelley,[4] leader of the 'Silver Shirts', but the movements they represent have never been taken very seriously and the former isolationists who constitute the real Fascist material in this country are still uncurbed and very vocal in their advocacy of the new form of 'America First', which consists of concentrating on the defence of the American mainland and Hawaii to the exclusion of all else.

16 April 1942

The end of American resistance on Bataan was a severe blow, but it was generally felt that everything possible had been done and there was a certain tendency to contrast resistance here with that put up in British possessions in the Far East. The visit of Hopkins and Marshall to London turned attention to Europe and it was generally assumed that they had gone there to induce His Majesty's Government to take the offensive in Europe. The Soviet Ambassador, in a speech which paid a warm tribute to British resistance in the past, also called for more action now against Hitler. The breakdown in India is generally regretted,[1] but Sir Stafford Cripps's final statement was very well received and so far there has been no disposition to blame His Majesty's Government. There has been a certain tendency to regard the whole process of negotiation as a battle for American goodwill, and from this angle the issue has so far been favourable to Great Britain, and the prestige of the Congress Party leaders is now much lower than it was before Sir Stafford Cripps went to India, though they still have some defenders. The net result on public relations is likely to be satisfactory. Never again should glib generalizations about the simplicity of the Indian problem be accepted by the majority of people and never again should the Congress emissaries find it as easy to sow mistrust of Britain here. America has become better educated about India this past month.

Americans who are fond of criticizing the treatment of subject races by other people found similar troubles nearer home this week. The Navy authorized for the first time the enlistment of Negroes for general service, though not for commissioned rank, and this concession was criticized as both belated and inadequate by the Negro organizations. On 12 April the Administration found it necessary to warn ten industrial concerns holding big war contracts that they would incur severe penalties if they did not cease discriminating against Negro, Jewish and Catholic workers.

4 William Dudley Pelley, who founded in 1933 the Silver Legion of America, a fascist-type organization.

1 In February 1942 Sir Stafford Cripps, Labour politician and lately British Ambassador to Russia, was appointed Lord Privy Seal and Leader of the House of Commons in Churchill's coalition Cabinet. In March he undertook a mission to India to present British proposals for realizing Indian self-government. These were rejected by the Indian Congress Party and the Moslem League on 11 April.

The Secretary of Commerce[2] in his attempt to find a scapegoat for the rubber shortage is reported as having told the Senate Committee that the British and Dutch monopolies had prevented him from building up a stockpile while continuing to sell rubber to Japan up to the eve of Pearl Harbor. Steps to deal with these allegations are under consideration. Mr Jones seems to be taking criticism of his past record rather hardly. He came to blows with Mr Eugene Meyer,[3] the owner of the *Washington Post,* at a party last week, apparently on account of a leading article in the *Post* strongly criticizing the Secretary.

23 April 1942

In spite of the return to power of Laval,[1] which led to the recall of United States Ambassador for consultation and was taken very seriously by public opinion as implying a further step towards complete Franco–German co-operation, the week showed signs of certain rising spirits about the war. Hardly had the Secretary for War promised America that she would shortly be passing to the offensive, when the news of the air raid on Tokyo was published. Though there was no information from American sources about this raid, the news was received with jubilation by the public. The visit of Marshall and Hopkins to London was generally thought likely to lead to an offensive in Europe. Optimistic speeches about war production in the United States were made by Nelson who said that the combined production of the United States of America, Russia and England, now exceeded that of the Axis nations, and by the Under Secretary of War, Patterson, who claimed that the United States' tank output had already surpassed that of the Axis.

The controversy as to who should organize American manpower, . . . has now been decided in favour of McNutt, who on 18 April was made chairman of a newly established War Manpower Commission which will supervise the distribution of American men and women in industry, agriculture, and, within certain limits, the armed forces. The new Commission was authorized to propose legislation for the mobilization and utilization of manpower, which suggests that compulsory allocation for war tasks may be under consideration. The appointment of McNutt to this position is generally interpreted as a blow to Hillman, who was known to consider that manpower came within his sphere. He has been appointed special labour adviser to the President but many of the functions of his section in the War Production Board have been taken over by the new Commission and it is thought by some that this may mark the beginning of the end of his political career.

. . . The CIO has warned Congress that restrictive legislation on labour is

---

2 Jesse Jones, of Texas, millionaire, Secretary of Commerce, 1940–5.

3 Eugene Meyer, publisher of *Washington Post* since 1933. Previously Governor of the Federal Reserve System.

1 Pierre Laval, appointed Head of Vichy Government on 14 April, despite US warning that any such appointment would be unacceptable to them.

liable to imperil the no-strike agreement accepted by the trade union organizations for the duration of the war and has also in conjunction with the AF of L come out in strong opposition to the freezing of wages. Lewis has not yet had an open breach with the CIO, but he is carrying on without their support or concurrence a campaign to unionize dairy farmers, which is causing a certain amount of alarm in agricultural circles.

The first of party primaries for autumn elections was held in Illinois at beginning of last week. The most notable result was the re-nomination by large majority of Senator Brooks[2] as Republican candidate for his present seat. Brooks was one of leading members of the former isolationist group in the Senate and he voted consistently against Administration's foreign policy right up to Pearl Harbor. Although Brooks's Republican opponent was an avowed supporter of President's foreign policy, he was an unimpressive candidate, whereas Brooks himself has a large personal following in Illinois and the result of the election was largely due to considerations of local machine politics which are very powerful in Illinois, and not primarily to wider issues. Furthermore there was much apathy among the non-isolationist Republicans who did not go to the polls because they did not want to vote the Democratic ticket. This, I am told, was largely due to the impression these persons have gained that they are not being told the truth about the war, or, in other words, they would vote for Roosevelt since they approved his foreign policy if only they could feel that they were really being led. . . .

National Committee of Republican Party is now meeting in Chicago. It was presented with two resolutions on war and foreign policy. One, sponsored by Mr Willkie, pledged the party to complete support of Government in carrying on war, and committed it to post-war co-operation with other countries. The other, by Senator Taft,[3] agreed in supporting Government in the war but made no mention of post-war developments. A compromise resolution was finally adopted affirming obligations of United States to assist in world co-operation after war. This resolution was widely acclaimed by certain sections of Republican press as meaning abandonment of isolationism by the right wing.

Social Justice, Father Coughlin's[4] organ, has been banned from the mails, and Department of Justice are investigating a number of seditious anti-Administration and anti-British statements which it has been publishing recently. Though *Social Justice* finds few defenders, there has been some anxiety lest this move should be first step in restricting freedom of press, and a move to ban all foreign-language newspapers in this country has now been disowned by the White House.

General Electric is latest of great corporations in this country to have been

2 Charles Wayland ('Curley') Brooks, Republican Senator from Illinois, 1940–9.

3 Robert A. Taft, Republican Senator from Ohio since 1939.

4 Charles Edward Coughlin, a Detroit 'radio priest', whose National Union for Social Justice, founded in 1934, attracted a wide following for its blend of populist economics, anti-semitism and isolationism.

shown by Department of Justice to have had connexions with German firms detrimental to American war production, German opposite number in this case being Krupps. Two of largest steel corporations in this country have been accused by War Production Board of repeated and deliberate violations of priority regulations.

I myself spent ten days in Texas between 9 and 18 April and took the opportunity of visiting one of the flying schools for the RAF, a couple of shipyards at New Orleans and Houston, and a large new heavy bomber factory at Fort Worth. An encouraging spirit of determination everywhere and universal pro-British feeling. The RAF cadets were very popular. Though Texas of course is not the United States, it is worth remembering that there is a good deal right through the country to set against the anti-British feeling I have referred to earlier. . . .

There are however signs of return to the former critical attitude on matters relating to British Far Eastern and Indian policy. In a recent off-the-record conference with the press Mr Sumner Welles[5] is reported to have said that the offer to India should have been made sooner and endorsed the view that some dramatic statement should have been made to rally the Eastern peoples to the war against the Axis.

28 April 1942

. . . Industry is still under fire ; manufacturers of plastic glass used in military aircraft have been accused of having formed a cartel with German firms and Imperial Chemical Industries to restrict the supply of such glass, and it has been charged that owners of certain patents have been holding up construction of 'Flying Fortresses'.[1] President on 20 April ordered seizure of the four plants of Brewster Aircraft Corporation on grounds of inefficient management.

Among recent developments which have brought war more nearly home to American public are the declaration of whole Atlantic seaboard as a military area, suspension of retail sales of sugar which will shortly be followed by rationing, and announcement that rationing of gasoline is imminent in eastern states. To eliminate shortage in latter area the building of a pipeline from producing districts has again been proposed though lack of steel may make this impracticable. . . .

6 May 1942

The principal event of week was publication on 27 April of President's message to Congress containing his plan for combating what he does not like called 'in-

5 Sumner Welles, career diplomat, Under-Secretary of State since 1937.

1 Popular name for Boeing B17 monoplane bomber.

flation'. This plan contained seven points. Heavy taxation on personal and industrial profits (President said his objective was that no one should receive tax-free income in excess of $25,000 a year), price ceilings, wage stabilization, stabilization of agricultural prices, purchase of war bonds, rationing of essential commodities and restriction of credit. On the following day an order was issued by Office of Price Administration freezing prices of all major items of civilian supply. President in his speech on 28 April emphasized extent to which his programme would call for sacrifice from every section of community and made it plain that American standard of living would have to be reduced. As a result of this programme various draft bills for dealing with labour situation have been shelved, at least temporarily, and for present at any rate it is hoped that misinformed agitation about the forty-hour week will die down. Public reaction to programme was mixed. Objectives were generally approved but methods were criticized. Of President's seven points five can be put into effect without further legislation under his existing powers. Two require congressional action, namely increases in taxation and the stabilization of agricultural prices, and on both of these prospects are not good. Ways and Means Committee of Senate watered down Administration's tax proposals in a vote on 1 May wishing to leave a greater profit incentive in industrial production, and Farm Bloc, headed by Senator Bankhead,[1] have made it plain they think there is no chance of President's proposal on agricultural prices going through. Furthermore Murray, claiming to speak both for CIO and AF of L, announced on 3 May that both wings of labour movement are unalterably opposed to any system of wage freezing, though he did not definitely say that he opposed President's programme on this point. Retailers and manufacturers are complaining that price-fixing programme means ruin for them and Office of Price Administration has announced that it would rather pay subsidies to manufacturers than allow infringement of price control. Finally critics of President's plan complain that it fails to touch the real danger of inflation, namely the enormously increased purchasing power of persons with lower incomes, and it has been suggested that only sound method of dealing with this is British one of a sales tax, which, however, is strongly opposed by labour movement and has been turned down by President.

. . .

Mr Winant[2] returned to London last week. He has not received much publicity during the few weeks that he has been in the United States for some of which time he was ill and in the country, but he saw the President several times and I have no reason to doubt that he still carries as much weight with the Administration and is still as generally respected as hitherto. Rumour has it that he was offered the post of Secretary of Labor in place of Miss Perkins but that he de-

1 John Hollis Bankhead II, Democratic Senator from Alabama since 1931.

2 John G. Winant, US Ambassador to Great Britain, 1941–6, and Director of the International Labour Organization, 1938–41.

clined it, wisely no doubt from his own point of view, despite his popularity with labour dating from his ILO days.

13 May 1942

The news of the battle of the Coral Sea overshadowed all other developments of the week, even including Madagascar and the surrender of Corregidor. It is not the first naval action of the Pacific war to be hailed by the American press as the greatest since Jutland though its actual results are still unknown and no attempt is being made to suggest that the balance of sea power in the Pacific has been affected by it. . . .

The Secretary of the Treasury recommended to the Ways and Means Committee of Congress the lowering of income tax exemptions to $1,200 incomes for married persons and $600 incomes for single persons. This proposal is politically very unpalatable to Congress but the clamour for the taxation of the lower incomes (as a means of combating inflation) has been growing and it seems that this proposal is the only alternative to a sales tax which is even less popular. The President, although still strongly opposed to the abolition of the CCC[1] and the NYA,[2] has now recommended to Congress that their appropriation for 1943 be cut by 75 per cent as compared with that for the current year and they should be restricted to activities directly connected with training for war purposes.

A few more results in the primaries for the autumn elections have not shown any very marked trend of public opinion. . . . Rather surprisingly a recent Gallup poll suggested that if the elections were held today there would be a considerable Democratic gain throughout the country. Flynn,[3] National Chairman of the Democratic Party, has been acquitted by a grand jury of all complicity in the charges of misuse of municipal supplies, but the whitewashing is too thorough to be altogether convincing.

Rationing has at last got started. Sugar is now rationed and petrol in the eastern States will be as from this week. The first is not severe but the second will make a marked change in the way of life of the areas affected, temporarily at any rate. In addition to the restriction on sales of petrol the limiting of the sale of tickets for railways and long-distance buses is also said to be impending.

1 Civilian Conservation Corps.
2 National Youth Administration.
3 Charged 1941–2 with use of New York City paving blocks to pave private courtyard on his estate. Grand jury exonerated him, but suspicions remained.

14 May 1942

[In] the 1942 elections for Congress and State governorships . . . the Republicans expect a small addition to their strength.

. . .

The anti-Administration forces at the elections will be composed as follows:

(a) Virulent subversive bodies such as Father Coughlin's *Social Justice,* recently denied mailing privileges ; Mrs Dilling's [1] anti-semitic and anti-Roosevelt 'We the Mothers' ; and the very numerous small semi-Fascist groups. This criminal and lunatic fringe is quite potent and is made considerable use of by more respectable anti-Administration groups.

(b) The solid core of the disbanded 'America First' Committee, e.g. timid businessmen and all those who fear and distrust the central government.

(c) Americans of German and Italian blood and certain elements of Dutch and Scandinavian extraction, especially first- and second-generation immigrants, many of whom may be anti-Fascist but who are either connected by ties of sentiment with their European kinsmen or anxious not to be reminded of the Europe from which they have escaped.

(d) Anglophobes or Russophobes, e.g. the Irish and the Roman Catholics. The Roman Catholic Church, especially in the northern half of the United States, is on the whole anti-Roosevelt and anti-British, while the bulk of United States public opinion is still anti-Russian. The dangers possibly consequent on a Russian victory are much played upon by the isolationist press.

(e) Republicans who, while endorsing the President's foreign policy, think it important to maintain active political opposition in order to achieve a more effective prosecution of the war.

(f) Groups who have special grudges against the Administration, e.g. the labour leader John L. Lewis, some sections of the Negro population, and small businessmen hard hit by priorities and without defence contracts.

(g) Wall Street, fearing State Socialism.

The Office of Facts and Figures estimates that seventeen million Americans in one way or another oppose the prosecution of the war ; that 30 per cent of the population would be willing to discuss peace terms with the German Army if Hitler were disposed of ; that 10 per cent would make peace with Hitler on the *status quo,* and that 9 per cent would be quite willing to see the United Nations defeated.

Labour has recently been the subject of a strong campaign by the press and in Congress by Southern Senators and Representatives demanding severe wage and hour legislation and state control of unions. The President, by exceptionally skilful handling, has saved labour from this frontal attack. However, the President's formally stated policy against wage increases is liable to attack from organized

1 Mrs Elizabeth Dilling, Director of the Patriotic Research Bureau and head of one of the sections of the 'Mothers' Movement', part of Father Coughlin's Christian Crusade.

labour and in particular the CIO. Lewis and his friends both in the AF of L and the CIO are proposing to outbid moderate leadership in labour by opposing the Administration's efforts to control the rise of wages. The present policy of moderate labour leaders is to support the President and at the same time to demand a rise in wages. This attempt to stave off a crisis cannot last long but on the outcome will depend both the attitude of labour in the election and the extent to which the labour issue will determine its result.

The Communists, following the strict Party line, are for all-out war effort with no discussion of wages.

.   .   .

Anti-British feeling is still strong, stronger than it was before Pearl Harbor, though the Cripps mission to India has improved matters. This state of affairs is partly due to the fact that whereas it was difficult to criticize Britain while the United Kingdom was being bombed, such criticism no longer carries the stigma of isolationist or pro-Nazi sympathies. The attitude of Australian spokesmen has not made matters easier, and many criticisms come from the Chinese and Madame Chiang Kai-shek[2] in particular, and are now being broadcast through Clare Booth,[3] returned from the Far East choc-a-bloc with anti-British stories. In some official circles there is still rather keen suspicion of the general intentions of the British, who are thought to be too concerned to preserve their bargaining position after the war as well as their prestige as a first-class Power. This feeling is partly due to the efforts of our Allies on occasions to play Britain and the United States off against each other, partly to German and Austrian refugees who have deserted Britain in favour of the United States, and partly to the widespread ignorance of the extent of the output and effort of the United Kingdom in the industrial and military sphere.

In any post-war planning it is assumed that the white peoples have lost their Asiatic possessions forever. On the one hand the Board of Economic Warfare, under Vice-President Wallace and his *alter ego* Milo Perkins,[4] are dreaming of a kind of world New Deal. This group of self-confident, country-bred liberal reformers have prepared blueprints to reorganize the world in order to secure the best distribution of persons and things with a bold programme, which ignores racial and political differences, for spending the vast natural resources of the United States upon world reconstruction. These social reformers firmly believe that political and national organization is secondary to social arrangements.

The Willkie-Welles-Luce[5] group, on the other hand, see the world as a vast market for the American producer, industrialist and trader. They are believers in

2 Wife of General Chiang Kai-shek, Commander in Chief of the Chinese armed forces and President of Executive Yuan since 1939.

3 Clare Booth, author, journalist and playwright, wife of Henry Luce, publisher of *Time, Life, Fortune,* etc.

4 Milo R.Perkins. President of the Federal Surplus Commodities Corporation since 1939, Executive Director of the Economic Defense Board since 1941 and Executive Director of Board of Economic Warfare, 1941–3.

5 Henry R.Luce, periodicals publisher, with missionary zeal for shaping the post-war world in the image of what he called 'the American Century'.

the American Century, energetic technicians and businessmen filled with romantic, equally self-confident, economic imperialism, eager to convert the world to the American pattern.

Besides these two real power groups there is the Farm Bloc, powerful, but with no foreign policy except the belief that food will win the war, and the various movements advocating forms of neo-Wilsonian international organization. The latter are weak though widespread in academic and professional circles. They hold vague ideas about joint police power and free trade with the British Empire, but compared with the tough-minded visionaries of the two main groups they are of little political significance.

The clash between those who plan world social and economic arrangements and the dynamic militant technocrats is perhaps the most important political manifestation at the moment.

20 May 1942

. . . Sinkings of merchant ships off Atlantic and Gulf coasts continue at an alarmingly heavy rate and American public do not as yet seem to have grasped vital significance of matter from their own point of view. Interest over amount of petrol that Congressmen may be allowed has far exceeded that over sinking of a merchant ship a few miles from mouth of Mississippi. Incidentally I learn that apparent inability of United States Navy to protect their merchant ships, even within United States territorial waters, from destruction by enemy submarines thousands of miles from their home ports, is having a lamentable effect on American prestige in places such as Cuba.

. . . .

Browder,[1] Secretary-General of American Communist Party, who has been serving a prison term for a passport fraud charge, has been released by President. Mr Roosevelt gave two reasons for freeing him, firstly that sentence imposed was longer than normal one for such offences, and secondly that release would have a tendency to promote national unity and allay any feeling that unusually long sentence was due to Browder's political views. The majority of press comments have approved President's action and anticipate favourable repercussion on Russo–American relations, but there has been some criticism from conservative and religious quarters largely on grounds that whether or no Browder's imprisonment was due to political reasons his release undoubtedly was. Browder himself has announced his intention to give full support to the President in the prosecution of the war.

Rationing of petrol for private cars was instituted during week in eastern states amid considerable acrimony. There have been many complaints that 'X' cards entitling the holder to unlimited petrol have been issued under false pretences or

1 Earl Browder, Secretary-General of the American Communist Party since 1930.

as a result of political pressure. As a result, the holding of 'X' cards has become almost a badge of shame and dealers have refused to sell petrol on them. Holders' names were at first kept secret but have now been made available to the public. These cards have been issued to the whole diplomatic corps and to most British officials here and I have enjoined careful restraint in their use on my staff. Members of Congress were at first told that they would not receive 'X' cards unless they could justify them individually. There were immediate protests in Congress, and as a result 'X' cards were issued to anyone in the Senate and House of Representatives who asked for them. This claim to special privileges aroused a storm of criticism only slightly less than that which blew up when Congress, shortly after Pearl Harbor, voted pensions for its members, but Senate defeated by 66 votes to 2 a motion suggesting that its special privileges should be renounced. Debate on this motion was extremely heated and there were charges that the press was endeavouring to lower prestige of Congress. Press retaliated by saying that Congress had lowered its own prestige by its actions and in fact its reputation is now extremely low.

War Department on 14 May assumed control of civilian airlines in United States with a view to eliminating competitive services and taking over as many transports as possible. Civilian air travel will henceforward be severely curtailed.

. . .

Elements in President's anti-inflation programme which require legislation have not made much progress. Leaders of Farm Bloc after seeing President have reiterated their opposition to his views on lowering agricultural prices, and the Secretary of Treasury's proposals for lowering income-tax exemptions have been held up in Congress and subjected to criticism by the AF of L. The House of Representatives 12 May voted a more than 100 per cent increase in pay for soldiers and sailors. This has not yet been approved by Senate.

President has signed a bill creating a Women's Army Auxiliary Corps and recruiting will start shortly. One Roman Catholic Archbishop has counselled his flock against joining it.

. . .

27 May 1942

United States opinion has been passing through an optimistic phase. This optimism was stimulated by events such as the landing of American troops in Ireland and Doolittle's[1] account of the Tokyo raid and also received a certain amount of encouragement from official pronouncements. The President for example was surprisingly optimistic about shipping situation in a message published on National Maritime Day. On the other hand the Administration seem suddenly to have become alarmed towards the end of the week lest public opinion should have become too complacent and both the President, at one of his press conferences, and Mr Hull in a set statement, solemnly warned the country against over-

1 James H. Doolittle, General in the US Army Air Corps.

optimism. This tendency of the Administration to blow first hot then cold can hardly produce that steadiness of morale which it is presumably desired to achieve, and it lends force to the view that the Government would do better to interfere less and leave public opinion to form its own conclusions.

. . .

Mr McNutt in a speech in New York on 20 May dropped a hint that compulsory mobilization of labour for war industry might shortly become necessary. Open warfare between Murray and Lewis has not yet broken out but it can hardly be long delayed and Murray's supporters in the CIO have been attacking Lewis publicly. Murray has been elected President of the newly formed United Steel Workers of America, in which position he will receive a salary. Hitherto his only salary has been that drawn as Vice-President of the United Mine Workers. The latter union is holding a general meeting in Washington this week, at which Murray's position will no doubt come up for review, in which case he may try to challenge Lewis in the latter's own stronghold. Murray meanwhile has expressed disapproval of a message which the Executive Council of the AF of L had sent to the CIO proposing negotiations for amalgamation between the two bodies. Amid these internal controversies Sir Walter Citrine's[2] proposals for co-operation with the Soviet trade unions have not secured as much attention as they would have commanded in quieter times, and have encountered a good deal of difficulty with the American Federation of Labor, both in regard to the proposals themselves and in regard to position of CIO.

. . .

The President has issued an order making it plain that in regard to the conduct of foreign policy and negotiations with other countries the Board of Economic Warfare must recognize the supremacy of the State Department.

. . .

There has been an unusually large crop of political scandals recently. . . . There has been criticism of the President's appointment to a Federal Judgeship in New Jersey of a member of the corrupt Hague[3] machine in that State. Finally the *New York Post* has published charges involving the Chairman of the Naval Affairs Committee of the Senate in an extremely unsavoury trial in New York. Senator Walsh[4] who was a persistent critic of the Administration's pre-war foreign policy has been exonerated by the Department of Justice and the other ex-isolationists in the Senate have claimed that the charges were part of an attempt to 'smear' all members of Congress who before Pearl Harbor opposed involvement in war.

Mr Lewis Douglas[5] has been appointed Deputy Head of the War Shipping

2 Walter Citrine, General Secretary of the British Trades Union Congress since 1926 and President of the International Federation of Trade Unions since 1928.

3 Frank Hague, Mayor of Jersey City since 1917.

4 David I. Walsh, Democratic Senator from Massachusetts since 1919.

5 Lewis Douglas, Director of the Budget, 1933–4 ; President of the Mutual Life Insurance Company since 1940.

Administration entrusted with the supervision of the movements of shipping. I understand that Sir A. Salter[6] warmly welcomes this move.

4 June 1942

. . .

Mr Welles made an important speech on 30 May during the Memorial Day celebrations at the tomb of the Unknown Warrior. He reiterated his criticism of the United States of America for having failed to play their part in the reconstruction of the world after the last war and declared that there must be no repetition of this mistake. He urged the necessity for the organization of an international police power in the post-war world and expressed the belief that the United Nations would become the nucleus of a world organization of the future. He also denounced discrimination between peoples on the grounds of race, creed or colour and said that the age of imperialism was ended.

. . .

Congress is getting restive about the Government's administration of rationing and has been talking of withdrawing some of the war powers which it voted to the Administration in the early days of the war, though such talk is not likely to lead to effective action. A report on the rubber situation by the senatorial committee under Senator Truman was also very critical of the Government's handling of the situation. Congress, with an eye on the elections, is making a bid for popular support by increases in army pay, but as usual they have muddled things. The Senate voted to double the existing pay to make it $42 a month and the House went one better with a rise to $50. They have refused to accept each other's figures and meanwhile another payday has passed without a rise of any kind.

Both Congress and the President are being very cautious in their approach to the army's request for the conscription of men of eighteen and nineteen, which is thought to be an unpopular move.

Willkie told a member of my staff recently that he thought the extreme isolationists would be gradually eliminated from the Republican Party in the course of the primaries. A number of them, for instance Representatives Tinkham[1] and Schaefer,[2] have already decided not to seek re-election and this should start the process going. Fish[3] would probably not be nominated though there might be a hard fight for this. Nevertheless Willkie expects the Republicans to lose fifteen to twenty in the House when the elections take place.

From another source I learn that Willkie is still thinking of trying to get the Republican nomination for Governor of New York State. He is not anxious to

6 Sir (James) Arthur Salter, Head of the British Merchant Shipping Mission to Washington since 1941.
1 George H. Tinkham, Republican Congressman from Massachusetts since 1915.
2 Edwin M. Schaefer, Democratic Congressman from Illinois, 1933–43.
3 Hamilton Fish, Jr, Republican Congressman from New York since 1919.

stand for the sake of having the Governorship, despite its value as a jumping-off place, since there is not much for him to do in that position. The State has been efficiently administered recently and there are no great changes to be made. But he would rather stand himself than see Dewey[4] as Governor since this would seriously prejudice his own presidential chances in 1944. Lehman,[5] the present Democratic Governor, is not standing for re-election and the Democrats, having no outstanding candidate to succeed him, are pessimistic about the results of the election.

The battle between Lewis and Murray has now come into the open and the executive board of the United Mine Workers has removed the latter from his position as Vice-President of the Union. Murray proposes to take the case to a general meeting of the union. Whether the Mine Workers will leave the CIO or not remains uncertain.

The Attorney General has caused considerable consternation by ordering the immediate deportation of Bridges,[6] the Australian leader of CIO West Coast organization, on grounds of membership of Communist Party. Since outbreak of Russo–German war Bridges has been doing excellent work in keeping West Coast shipping and shipbuilding moving and order which would have been popular in many quarters a year ago has now been widely criticized. The Department of Justice, however, under Attorney General, is very hot against Communists both in feeling and in action, as shown by remarks which Mr Biddle has more than once made to a member of my staff. Mr Biddle has on these occasions talked strongly against Bridges and his activities. Bridges is appealing against the order which it has been suggested in well-informed quarters was issued without President's knowledge and it is hardly probable that it will be put into effect.

· · ·

11 June 1942

Welles' Memorial Day speech, reported last week, continues to arouse comment and is held by some to have been inspired by H.F.Armstrong,[1] editor of *Foreign Affairs,* and other members of State Department advisory committee on post-war reconstruction, over whose weekly meetings Welles presides. Discussions, and indeed the existence of this committee, are strictly secret. Welles and Wallace may be regarded as President's right and left hands on post-war matters. Principal points on which Administration is considered by certain informed persons to have made up its mind are:

(a) necessity for a long armistice, possibly lasting several years, before final settlement is made;

4 Thomas E.Dewey, lawyer, 'gang busting' District Attorney, 1937–40.

5 Herbert H.Lehman, Governor since 1932.

6 Alfred (Harry) Bridges, President of the International Longshoremen's and Warehousemen's Union since 1937.

1 Hamilton Fish Armstrong, editor since 1928.

(b) establishment of an international police force;

(c) abolition of colonial empires;

(d) equal access for all democracies to raw materials of world.

These are the sort of proposals which are being very widely discussed here and for the moment at any rate seem to receive wide, if not yet very profound, approbation. The approbation is likely to be more keen and wide with regard to (c) and (d) – ideas easy for Americans to subscribe to spontaneously – than for (a) and particularly (b) which are not kind of idea inevitably to pull a trigger. A guest present at a private dinner given to President by Welles and attended by the Litvinoffs and Brazilian Ambassador said that President talked along lines of Welles's speech and condemned the discussion of territorial arrangements before victory as likely to arouse resentment and suspicion in America, feelings with which he said he personally sympathized. Welles's speech is held by some to have been prompted by a cable sent to Washington by Winant reporting in full London *Times* article on Wallace's speech. Wallace is known to have received a letter from Henry Luce in which Luce congratulated Wallace on his speech and offered him unqualified co-operation despite Wallace's explicit rejection of Luce's 'American Century' outlook. How much this gesture means remains to be seen.

President, with consent of Congress, has signed declarations of war against Hungary, Roumania and Bulgaria. This action has been widely linked to pressure from Russia and to Russo–American conversations. The Russians are also reported to have pressed for a declaration of war against Finland. There is, however, still considerable pro-Finnish feeling here and M. Procopé[2] is actively disseminating view that Finland is involved in war against her will and looks to United States for protection of its rights after war.

The isolationists are definitely on march again and are boasting of their successes in recent congressional primaries. Their claims contain sufficient substance to justify their contention that Willkie's forces have so far made little progress against regular Republican Party machine which is on whole still inclined towards isolationism. The anti-Administration drive in Congress is being pressed. Question of pay of armed forces has been settled but other issues such as the muddle in rationing scheme, alleged failure of War Production Board to cope with rubber shortage and failure to implement plans for extracting a synthetic rubber out of great wheat surplus (for which British–Dutch cartel share the blame with American rubber companies and Secretary of Commerce) form favourite means of attack on Administration. It seems likely however that it will be decided to devote a large proportion of available wheat to production of synthetic rubber ingredients. If so, much satisfaction will be given to wheat farmers and Farm Bloc and isolationists will lose a powerful weapon. So far only concrete victory in Congress of anti-Administration forces has been abolition of

2 Hjalmar Procopé, Finnish Minister to the United States 1939–44.

Civilian Conservation Corps. National Youth Administration, which was similarly attacked, has survived unimpaired. Isolationism has received sudden support from Baptists whose northern convention refused to pass a resolution calling for 'defeat of the Axis, the restoration of sovereignty to enslaved people and triumph of freedom and democracy'. Presbyterian convention, after a strong pro-war resolution, modified this later with formula 'we have no alternative as a nation but to engage in this war'. This demonstrates the continuing existence of genuinely religious, as opposed to subversive, pacifism in United States and with isolationist attitude exemplified by *New York Daily News* must be taken into account as a limitation of measure of approval given to points (a) and (b) of policy attributed to Administration in opening paragraph above.

The general opinion in moderate congressional and administration circles is that from the point of view of national interest, Biddle has made a bad mistake in ordering the deportation of Bridges as a Communist. He has gained the embarrassing praises of isolationists and the disapproval of the left wingers, who see his action as inopportune. Biddle has explained that he was merely carrying out the will of Congress and no other.

The anti-Communist note has been sounded loudly by John L. Lewis, President of the Mine Workers' Union, whose rift with the CIO is now complete. The exchanges between him and Philip Murray, President of the CIO, have reached new heights of virulence. Murray has proposed that a joint committee of AF of L and CIO be established, not only for promoting general labour unity but for the purpose of adopting common political strategy in defence of the Administration's policy. The attitude of the American Federation of Labor to this remains sceptical. The powerful isolationist bloc of AF of L is not anxious to reach an understanding with Murray. The relations between AF of L and CIO are considerably more strained than at the beginning of the year. Fourteen of the forty-four CIO unions are reported to be under Communist domination, and it is primarily this which is frightening the AF of L off. There is little doubt that the occasion of the Lewis–Murray breach will be used to attach Lewis still more firmly to the general isolationist front now that open revolt has broken out inside the CIO. The efforts of the Administration are directed towards securing a workable alliance between Murray and Green as against the extremes of isolationism and communism. The management–labour committees now set up in factories by the War Production Board appear to be working smoothly according to a private poll conducted by industrialists.

Several minor 'Fascist' leaders have been tried and condemned but it does not appear that steps will be taken in the near future to prosecute Father Coughlin. This is interpreted in some circles as being due to the fact that the Administration is averse to a major campaign against Coughlin's numerous followers at this moment since it is nervous of the possible effects upon United States Catholic opinion. The hierarchy is said to be seriously divided on this issue.

20 June 1942

. . .

The most widespread reaction to the Anglo-Russian Treaty[1] and the US-Russian agreement[2] was deep satisfaction that the Russian claims have been satisfied, the security of Europe guaranteed by the twenty years' treaty, the Second Front in 1942 apparently promised and yet the Atlantic Charter preserved intact, and no concessions made to Russian territorial demands. Even the isolationist and Midwestern press pronounced itself satisfied.

But there was also an important minority view held by prominent columnists and influential political leaders of both parties. This takes the form of self-congratulation that the Atlantic Charter, after nearly being reluctantly abandoned by a Britain too weak to resist Russian demands, was rescued at the eleventh hour by the powerful intervention of the United States Government, in particular Mr Roosevelt and Mr Hull.

In this interpretation, advanced by Krock[3] and Clapper[4] and Lippmann, followed by a handful of minor columnists, His Majesty's Government, hard pressed and afraid of offending Russian susceptibilities, had very nearly, albeit with a heavy heart, arrived at an arrangement with Russia to parcel out various European territories, thus sowing the seeds of a new war; only the combination of American power and American moral resolution averted this disaster. While one could understand and sympathize with the British predicament, it was fortunate indeed that the United States was able to step in in time, etc. Senator Barkley, Henry Luce and several other politicians, journalists and New Dealers have spoken privately in this sense and taken the line that the United States alone now possesses the combination of material power, strength and devotion to principle without which the peace cannot be won.

. . .

Vice-President Wallace in his speech on the 8 June delivered himself of an apocalyptic version of America as 'the chosen of the Lord' in whom the culture of Palestine, Rome and Britain are to be brought to a final fruition. America has accepted a divine mission to save the world and Roosevelt is to be its instrument. 'English in language, we are not British in blood or customs', said the Vice-President. 'We have too many Irish, Germans, French, Jews, Italians, Greeks, Russians and Poles for that. South America is not Spanish or Portuguese and North America is not English.' A paean to Pan-Americanism follows. This speech is of importance because it is the most unbridled expression to date of the

---

1 Signed on 26 May 1942. It provided for full collaboration between the two countries during and after the war and was to run for twenty years.

2 Lend-Lease Master Agreement, signed 11 June 1942.

3 Arthur Krock, Washington correspondent for the *New York Times* since 1932 ; deeply conservative and noted for his 'exclusive' stories.

4 Raymond Clapper, political commentator for Scripps-Howard newspapers since 1936.

view of the New Deal as the New Islam, divinely inspired to save the world, a faith of which Wallace is the leading exponent. It was indirectly answered by speeches by Landon and Dewey and the President of Harvard,[5] in which they, in various ways, advocated caution with regard to post-war planning and warned America not to overlook its own national problems in the rosy haze of idealistic post-war speculation. The two recent speeches by Wallace and the declaration made by Sumner Welles have been followed by a renewed advocacy on 17 June by Welles of a cooling-off period before a final peace settlement and of the need to use instruments designed for war, such as Lend-Lease agreements, as the framework around which the peace will be constructed. These speeches are now beginning to provoke a definite resistance in isolationist circles; even comparatively restrained anti-Rooseveltites are heard to murmur that any attempt on the part of the United States Government to associate itself in any scheme of world reform will cause a split in American opinion comparable to and greater than that which occurred at the end of the last war. The Scripps-Howard newspapers whose isolationism has been muted for some time are slowly but surely reviving the issue again as a part of the anti-Roosevelt congressional campaign. This attack cannot be regarded as very formidable so far.

The appointment of Elmer Davis[6] as Director of Office of War Information (OWI) has been greeted enthusiastically almost everywhere.

. . .

The President's fifth report of his administration of Lend-Lease is an important document inasmuch as it stresses the fact that Lend-Lease is an instrument not only of war but of peace and is to play a dominant part in weaving the pattern of the post-war policies of the United Nations. This sentiment echoed by Sumner Welles (*vide supra*) is being widely discussed in Congressional circles which feel that if the President proposes to make Lend-Lease agreements political substitutes for formal treaties in order to avoid recourse to Senate ratification, Congress had better bestir itself and demand that such agreements be referred to it directly since they are becoming major instruments of foreign policy. It may be that Congress will try to pass legislation to enable it to take a direct part in ratifying such agreements. Other points made by the President are that American production is reaching the proportions of a flood, that the main problem now is that of distribution, and that 'Lend-Lease in reverse'[7] has made Lend-Lease machinery genuinely reciprocal.

. . .

Administration is seriously worried about feeling among the coloured population, which according to every survey is apathetic to the war which it considers a white man's conflict. Administration loses no opportunity of publicly insisting

5 James B. Conant, President of Harvard since 1933.

6 Elmer Davis, previously news analyst, Columbia Broadcasting System, since 1939.

7 Arrangement by which goods and services more readily procurable locally were made available to US forces on British soil on the same basis, *mutatis mutandis,* as the USA made Lend-Lease material available to its allies.

upon Negro rights, condemning labour unions for exclusion of Negroes and generally trying to create a strong pro-Negro attitude wherever this is possible. The influential Phelps-Stokes Committee[8] has been stimulated to prepare a report on future of Africa, which will shortly appear as part of campaign to arouse favourable interest in Negro problem among general public. Findings of this Committee are said to be critical of British administration in Africa.

After Lewis-Murray fight, labour scene is relatively quiescent. Sir Walter Citrine's visit has failed to result in establishment of an Anglo-Russian-American Committee, but has produced a proposal for a joint committee between TUC[9] and AF of L which if ratified by British TUC will keep British and American labour more closely in touch than has hitherto been case. Apart from that Sir Walter's visit has had few if any positive results. Although his public addresses have been well received in Washington and New York and in factories in West, AF of L does not feel any better disposed to the TUC because it has managed to frustrate Citrine's plan for a tripartite United States Anglo-Russian Trade Union Committee. CIO feel resentful at not being directly brought into the negotiations by Citrine. . . .

. . .

27 June 1942

The Tobruk disaster[1] overshadowed all other events this week. The slump in public feeling was particularly sharp after the boom stimulated by the publicity given to the Coral Sea[2] and Midway[3] successes and the unhappily optimistic news from Libya. The combination of the British defeat in Libya, the Russian position in the Crimea, and Kharkov,[4] and the Japanese operations off the West Coast has caused the kind of sudden collapse of morale to which the American public is peculiarly prone. Press editorials have been restrained and indeed in large measure sympathetic. The sharpest attacks on the British conduct of the Libyan campaign come in American press despatches from Cairo and London which have led to a wave of anti-British talk and feeling in congressional and other political circles unknown since Pearl Harbor. Editorial restraint is due in some degree to the sedative influence of the United States Government information services. (Mr Hull told me two days ago that he had issued instructions to State Department press people to do all they could to check tendency to criticize British.) . . . The solidarity of most Australian spokesmen and the recent speeches of Hopkins and Dewey have also helped. Both the latter denounced the tendency to blame the British for everything. The former delivered a rousing 'pep talk' in which he reiterated faith in the British, spoke of opening a Second,

---

8 Phelps-Stokes Fund of New York City, a leading philanthropic foundation.

9 (British) Trades Union Congress.

1 Libyan fortress which fell to Germans under Rommel, 21 June 1942.

2 Three-day naval engagement in Pacific, May 1942.

3 Battle of Midway Island, which saved Hawaii from possible Japanese invasion, June 1942.

4 On 1 July the Germans claimed the capture of Sevastopol. Kharkov had fallen in May.

Third and Fourth Front and reaffirmed the war aims of the New Deal originally stated by Mr Wallace and Mr Perkins.

The only Senator who gave violent public utterances to anti-British talk which has filled lobbies of Congress was Ellender[5] of Louisiana who bitterly protested that there was little point in supplying the British with war material since they invariably lost it all. There are, he said, four million inactive troops in Britain continually being reinforced by fresh American units, which deprives United States of badly needed warships, a sight to 'nauseate and disgust' both Americans and British who watch them waiting for an attack which may never come. Why was last Indian convoy not diverted to Egypt ? President Roosevelt must assume unified command and galvanize apathetic British. He was in this seconded by Senator Wheeler and others. . . . I understand from a moderately reliable source that Senators Pepper,[6] Connally and Smathers[7] are moving into closer line with Ellender. This is important since Pepper and Connally have often been spokesmen of left and right wings respectively of Administration. Ellender is a supporter of Administration and cry for unified military command is gathering momentum in many quarters. British prestige has for moment fallen lower than at any time since loss of Malaya, owing not so much to actual loss of Tobruk as to conviction that this was due to a hopeless and incurable incompetence, on part both of fighting soldiers and of High Command.

Anti-Administration forces are trying with some success to use mounting congressional jealousy of its own prerogatives as a stick with which to beat Administration. Numerous speakers in Congress have been publicly and privately exclaiming against usurpation of their legislative powers by growing power of bureaucracy. This represents in small part Jeffersonian sentiment, but is much more largely part of a concerted campaign by industrial and other interests which find that their lobbies are able to bring more pressure on members of Congress than on Administration. It is no accident that National Association of Manufacturers has started a nationwide publicity campaign to boost its own services to community and to agitate about danger of a post-war social order which may in some respect curb private enterprise. Backers of these campaigns have in private quite cynically admitted that charges with which they support them do not bear examination but that if they serve to incense Congress against vast executive machine on grounds that it is depriving Congress of power and patronage and is relentlessly driving country into some kind of collectivism, they will serve their purpose. They charge that New Deal is trying to do to States of Union precisely what Mr Sumner Welles is practising with regard to Latin America, binding them more and more closely to central government by systematic economic subventions for which they and their representatives in Congress pay price of political independence.

5 Allen J. Ellender, Democratic Senator from Louisiana since 1937.
6 Claude D. Pepper, Democratic Senator from Florida since 1936.
7 William H. Smathers, Democratic Senator from New Jersey since 1937.

Truman Committee has just published a report very severely criticizing incompetence of 'dollar a year' men in War Production Board. . . . In an obvious attempt to deflect an attack on Mr Nelson suspected of coming from New Deal, House Military Affairs Committee has published a report assailing New Deal agencies for squandering national resources on domestic projects instead of diverting them to accumulation of war supplies. Mr Jesse Jones is specifically excluded from this attack as having done his best in face of rubber monopoly (this is latest fling at Anglo-Dutch Cartel). Assistant Attorney General Thurman Arnold, celebrated trust-buster, has occasioned a certain amount of distress to his old New Deal associates by predicting that end of hostilities will usher in an era of unexampled expansion and prosperity for private enterprise in America which will emerge with unprecedented financial and economic strength, provided state confines itself to curbing monopolies (and in particular international cartels) and gives a free hand to private producer.

Mr Churchill's visit[8] naturally attracted immense attention, although it was a less sensational event than his previous visit which marked a high watermark of friendly Anglo-American relations. At first it was interpreted as meaning that a decision on Second Front was at last to be reached, then Libyan news provoked view prominent in both press and private conversation and stimulated by Associated Press despatches from London, that Mr Churchill had come to beg for American help in Middle East. Tense atmosphere which is always created by Mr Churchill's appearances in Western Hemisphere heightened sense of military crisis and has undoubtedly sharpened both favourable and adverse comment on British.

· · ·

Visit of Sir Walter Citrine and its negative political result has left American Federation of Labor content but suspicious, and CIO profoundly irritated. I am informed various CIO leaders, including Mr Murray himself, privately express some indignation at supineness with which TUC allows AF of L to prevent it from closer contact with important section of United States labour which is engaged in basic war industries, and possesses a younger and more dynamic outlook. . . .

· · ·

29 June 1942

Some prominence was given in the press and elsewhere to my remarks in reply to a question concerning the post-war programme enunciated by Governor Stassen[1] of Minnesota who last week presided over the Annual Conference of Governors at Asheville at which I was a guest. Stassen, who may be a Republican candidate for the Vice-Presidency in 1944, adumbrated the establishment of a post-war union of democratic states in which these states, while retaining their respective sovereignties, could concert united international policies. Stassen's not very precise but vigorously anti-isolationist plan is symptomatic of the limits

8 18–25 June, 'to reach a final decision on the operations for 1942–43' (Churchill, *The Hinge of Fate*, ch. 22).
1 Harold Edward Stassen, Republican Governor of Minnesota since 1938.

of the most advanced Republican thought. For practical purposes Mr Willkie and Mr Stassen are now the chief protagonists of views reflected in the Luce publications, notably in *Fortune,* which is at no great distance from the more cautious proposals of Mr Welles, and are totally at variance with those of Mr Wallace's school. There is a vague proposal afloat for an International Reconstruction Finance Corporation which would fit with Mr Welles's view.

3 July 1942

The depression caused by the British reverses in North Africa naturally continues and is reflected in much private anti-British talk. It is, however, not as profound as the events might be thought to warrant. The press, so far from indulging in anti-British criticism, has for the most part taken the precise opposite line of editorially denouncing any tendency to belittle the British war effort, if only because that would directly play into Axis hands. This is obviously inspired by the Administration but the success of the efforts to curb American propensities to rail against the blunders of their British allies indicates a genuine growth of a sense of responsibility on the part of American editors and news commentators in the face of considerable provocation offered by the news despatches from United States correspondents in Cairo and London. The glories of Britain in 1940/41 are recalled to restore a proper sense of proportion in estimating Britain's part in the war and this is perhaps the best antidote we can use. Mr Willkie (in a recent speech) and his friends are of course doing their best to support the pro-British administration line. Mr Elmer Davis's and Mr Byron Price's offices fully realize the dangers to America of anti-British taunts and have taken the lead in co-operating with my press officers in setting this sympathetic tone. There is no doubt that the prestige of the British army command has fallen low. There is some talk that no American soldiers would consent to serve in Europe under British command, that British strategy is fundamentally conservative, defensive and believes in the tactics of attrition, and that the war will not be won unless not only American production but also the offensive spirit and the new world *élan* of Americans is allowed to dominate in the strategy of the United Nations, and great hopes are consequently being placed on the ability of General Eisenhower [1] to communicate this new spirit to the tired allied command in the Eastern Hemisphere. Suggestions that the President should be Supreme Commander-in-Chief continue to appear. The view is that, if Russia holds, and it is widely assumed that it will, and if the great American striking force is launched in Europe in 1942 the Germans will be defeated. The British have done and will do their best but it is not on them, not even on the RAF and the British fleet, that victory will depend.

Much criticism continues to be expressed of both the censorship and the publicity policy of the Cairo authorities. Similar criticism is heard of the allegedly evident failure of British Middle Eastern intelligence.

1 Dwight D. Eisenhower, appointed Commander of US Forces in Europe in June 1942.

The joint statement of President Roosevelt and Mr Churchill[2] was received with general satisfaction, particularly the portion of it which dealt with the necessity of aiding China and Russia. . . . Direct criticism of the President as Commander-in-Chief has died down and criticism of Mr Churchill for the most part took the oblique form of speculation about the storm he would have to face in England on his return.

. . .

There is a good deal of criticism among liberals of the policy of the State Department towards Vichy which is regarded as being more supine and inept than at any period in the past. Its feeble conduct of negotiations with Admiral Robert[3] in Martinique[4] is held to be a striking demonstration of this. So long as this criticism is confined to New Deal circles it is unlikely to affect the Administration's policy nor are there any signs at present that it will spread in influence. For example Senator Connally, to whom a member of my staff recently spoke, defended the policies of the Department along traditional lines and said that in order to secure maximum support for the allied Second Front in France it was necessary for the United States to cultivate relations with Frenchmen in France, a task which the British were not in a position to do.

The New York State internal situation continues to be confused. Mr Farley,[5] who is backing the Democratic candidate, Bennett,[6] has definitely refused nomination for himself. Perhaps he does not consider the chance of a Democratic victory in New York State to be sufficient. A new 'Draft Willkie Committee' headed by a publisher named Rinehart[7] is pressing their candidate's claims with much local labour support and Mayor La Guardia's blessing against the two political machines. Mr Willkie has finally refused nomination in a speech in which he exhorted his followers to follow the principles of enlightened pro-Roosevelt Republicanism and disclaimed all ambition of glory for himself. Persons close to Mr Willkie are said to be quite certain that he would not reject the proffered crown if he thought that his followers were in a position to give it to him. He is much too shrewd a politician not to realize that his chances against both political machines are negligible unless a popular landslide, of which he perceives few symptoms, suddenly begins. Mr Dewey, for whom no one, not even his own supporters, pretend any enthusiasm, is still a favourite by a narrow margin. Mr Bennett, who is a complete obscurity, has deemed it wiser to say and do nothing.

2 A brief report on their conferences in Washington.

3 H.Robert, French (Vichy) High Commissioner, West Indies, since 1940.

4 In May, Roosevelt despatched Admiral Hoover, Commander of the Caribbean Sea Fleet, to Martinique, where, after protracted negotiations, he effected a local arrangement with Robert designed to prevent use of the French West Indies by the Axis.

5 James A.Farley, US Postmaster-General 1933–40 and Chairman of the Democratic National Committee 1932–40.

6 John J.Bennett Jr, Attorney General of New York 1931–42.

7 Stanley Marshall Rinehart Jr, President of Farrar & Rinehart since 1929.

The army supply bill of nearly $43 billion is hailed as the greatest single appropriation in United States history. But Congress and the public in general, who make a brave show of being eager to sacrifice their substance, are truculently opposed to the very rigorous price-control policies of Leon Henderson. Congress proposed to hamstring him by refusing an adequate appropriation for his office. Henderson and a large group of conservatives both in the press and outside are engaged in uttering desperate warnings of coming inflation unless some such plan as Henderson's is rigorously applied. This has thus far had little effect upon a Congress jealous of its own patronage (which Henderson continues to ignore) and anxious to avoid the unpopularity with constituents which drastic measures of this type must entail, particularly with the elections so near. Labour says that it cannot see why it alone should retrench when employers propose to ignore the President's programme so far as it affects them. Congress is in a rebellious mood and has completely stopped the normal appropriation for the Department of Agriculture owing to a deadlock between the House and Senate Committees. The Department of Agriculture is in a nervous condition, unwilling to retract its demand for power to sell wheat stocks at parity which it regards as essential, but frightened of Congress. Congress is in no mood to yield and will probably win. . . .

The Negroes continue to be a source of anxiety to the Administration. Paul McNutt, doubtless with one eye on the Presidential Election of 1944, has delivered an address out-doing Willkie in rhetorical appeal to a Harlem audience. A pro-Negro plank is evidently a *sine qua non* in the presidential platform and the Democrats are making every effort to prevent the Republicans from profiting by the attitude of the South. For the first time in recorded memory several important Southern papers have begun to defend Negro rights and to claim better treatment for them, plainly a result of Administration initiative. The situation is rising to a climax with the case of a Negro share-cropper named Waller who killed his white landlord. He was condemned to death, was temporarily reprieved by his State Governor and has now been executed. The attempt to create a new Sacco-Vanzetti case[8] out of this is growing. A special report on the Negro situation will reach you shortly.

. . .

11 July 1942

. . .

Trial of German saboteurs captured by FBI[1] and arrests and coming prosecutions of members of German-American Bund[2] and other subverters has captured

---

8 A *cause célèbre* in which two aliens were tried and convicted on a murder charge in April 1920. The conduct of the trial left much to be desired and although the Governor of Massachusetts approved a Commission of Inquiry which in 1927 reported the trial to have been fair, their consequential execution was widely deplored.

1 Eight saboteurs landed from submarines in Long Island and Florida and were captured in New York and Chicago by the Federal Bureau of Investigation.

2 Organization of German Americans who were Nazi sympathizers, formed in 1936.

attention of public. Story of capture has been told in melodramatic terms by Hoover,[3] Director of FBI. In every part of the United States newspaper editors and broadcasters are demanding the death penalty for the captured Germans. The story has aroused people to a heightened consciousness of the internal enemy, and has increased anti-German feeling without intensifying general war-mindedness. Hoover loses no opportunity of advertising himself and his organization but tactical considerations might have prevented publication on this occasion but for the support given Hoover by the Attorney General who views with anxiety the complacency and careless disregard of potential Fifth Column activities on the part of the average United States citizen.

The deadlock in Congress over the agricultural and the price administration issues continues to be serious. An appropriation has been passed this week enabling the Department of Agriculture to carry on for another month, but the stubborn refusal of the House Committee to accept even the compromise offered by the Senate Committee (whereby only a limited quantity of farm products would be sold below parity) in the face of stern words from the President about selfish and unpatriotic 'Pressure Groups' and of a barrage of hostile criticism from sections of even the most conservative press has created a genuine crisis. This attitude on the part of House members is doubtless due to the fact that with elections coming in the autumn the majority of Representatives particularly from the agricultural states cannot afford to risk a break with the powerful Farm Bureau[4] and its equally powerful big business allies over any major issue. Only one third of the Senate is due for re-election as against the entire House of Representatives, hence the more conciliatory attitude on the part of farm Senators towards the pressing demands of the Administration which is backed by the majority of public opinion. Indeed this is the only internal issue for a long time on which organized labour, the more conservative members of the Administration and the main body of the Republican press see eye to eye. A somewhat smaller but nevertheless very strong body of opinion both in the press and in the country at large supports the firm attitude taken by Leon Henderson who is still engaged in bitter conflict with Congress over the appropriation for his office. Something has been done to bring the dangers of inadequate price control and consequent inflation home to the public. The violent opposition both in the Senate and in the House (and it may be added throughout organized labour) to Henderson's plans, in particular that of covering the United States with a network of price supervisors, is yet another indication of the fear of the impending election which always tends to increase the irresponsibility of Congress and to start an open season for the pressure of the Washington lobbies. There is a good deal of general discontent both in the press and outside with the degree to which the President's anti-inflation programme has been ignored and 'politics as usual' have been allowed to

3 J.Edgar Hoover, Director of FBI since 1924.

4 Farm Bureau Federation, the most powerful of the farm organizations, mainly representative of more prosperous farmers of Midwest and South.

overshadow the urgent needs of the war and national interest generally. Attacks on Congress are multiplying fast. They have spread to the person of the President who was alleged to have exercised pressure to secure the appointment as a judge of a nominee of Mayor Hague of New Jersey, a notoriously corrupt political boss, in order to keep Hague in line for the coming Congressional elections.

Congressional and public opinion has finally forced Nelson into a reorganization of War Production Board which is not however regarded as radical enough by a majority of his critics. Sharp encounters with Senators Norris[5] and Gillette,[6] who accused him of undue favour towards oil companies, the rubber shortage, together with multiplying charges of various inventors that their suggestions have been ignored as a result of big business pressure, and the general feeling that he is not prepared to fight too strongly have resulted in a general diminution of Mr Nelson's prestige which is lower at the moment than at any date since his appointment. Scheduled mission of his assistant Reed[7] to England is held to represent a concession on Nelson's part to concerted attack on Reed who was alleged to be dedicated to a 'business as usual' policy.

Some diminution of stature is observed also in case of Elmer Davis who was sharply attacked by Stimson at a recent press conference and whose office it now seems is not after all to control publicity of service departments, State Department and White House. The inevitable friction between Office of War Information and service departments is growing sharp and has reached a climax in collision between OWI and War Department over Davis's demand for publication of an official account of saboteurs' trial. President arbitrated between Davis and Stimson and amid much excited newspaper comment an uneasy truce was declared. State and Justice Departments are likely to win similar autonomy for themselves. An attempt to canalize all government information in OWI thus cutting correspondents off from their familiars in other government departments provided a rebellion and an unofficial *démarche* of Washington correspondents and has been shelved. OWI's situation resembles the corresponding confusion in London in 1941 in almost every particular.

. . .

18 July 1942

. . .

After being upbraided by President, Senator Barkley, and entire national press, House agricultural bloc finally capitulated to Senate and passed amended Administration measure whereby certain agricultural products may be sold below parity. This is important because it indicates that Farm Bloc does not feel at moment sufficiently powerful to oppose combination of Administration, labour

---

5 George W.Norris, independently minded Republican Senator from Nebraska since 1913.

6 Guy M.Gillette, Democratic Senator from Iowa since 1936.

7 Philip D.Reed, Chairman of Board of GEC 1940–2, with Office of Production Management 1941, Chief of Bureau of Industries WPB 1942. In London July 1942 to January 1945.

and public opinion, even where its most intimate interests are affected. Its defeat represents a substantial victory for strong-minded Leon Henderson whose prestige is high at moment. Recent primaries in Oklahoma which were held this week and resulted in renomination of majority of previous incumbents who are mostly solid New Dealers led by erratic Josh Lee[1] and nomination of a Rooseveltite Governor strengthen this trend. Nation has been frightened by prospect of inflation, and, except in completely 'machine'-managed states, old-fashioned type of reactionary Farm Bloc candidate whose positive platform consists almost solely of a promise of higher prices for agricultural products is unlikely to succeed. Defeat of ex-Governor Murray, more commonly known as Alfalfa Bill,[2] in Oklahoma primaries, is an indication of this. On other hand, nominations of Burdick[3] and William Lemke[4] in North Dakota primaries are a move against Administration. Representative Burdick is a straight isolationist and represents Non-Partisan League,[5] a section of North Dakota Republicans. Lemke was 'Union', i.e. Farmer-Labor Townsendite[6] presidential candidate in 1936, when he was supported by Coughlin and polled 9,000,000 votes. It is clear that New Deal and Mr Wallace have not impressed more progressive aspects of their policy sufficiently on more backward states to destroy influence of these primitive agrarian bred-in-the-bone isolationists wedded to various crackpot schemes of which Townsend old-age pensions plan was only most celebrated. Ex-Representative Lemke is a simple reactionary Farm Bloc nominee, a typical 'friend of the people' who has consistently voted for labour. His almost certain election to Congress in November will not strengthen progressive wing of Republican Party. When it is remembered that arch-isolationist Nye[7] is one of North Dakota Senators, while other is Langer,[8] who narrowly escaped unseating for fraudulent practices, and that political machine is dominated by very conservative railroad unions, this result is hardly surprising.

New York State situation is only a little clearer than it was last week. Flynn, National Chairman of Democratic Party, and Representative Kennedy,[9] leader of Tammany Hall, have publicly withdrawn their support from Bennett and have offered it to Senator Mead.[10] Farley continues to back Bennett. President is clearly supporting Flynn who can count on support of both wings of American

1 Joshua B.Lee, Democratic Senator from Oklahoma since 1937.

2 William H.Murray, Governor of Oklahoma 1931–5.

3 Usher L.Burdick, Republican Congressman from North Dakota since 1935.

4 William Lemke, Republican Congressman from North Dakota 1933–41 and Union Party candidate for President, 1936.

5 A farmers' organization, centered in North Dakota, which in Minnesota became the Farmer-Labor Party, and favoured such socialist policies as state control and ownership of flour and packing plants.

6 Organization founded by Francis E.Townsend in 1934 and advocating old-age pensions on a lavish scale.

7 Gerald P.Nye, Republican Senator from North Dakota since 1925.

8 William Langer, Republican Senator from North Dakota since 1941.

9 M.J.Kennedy, Democratic Congressman from New York since 1930.

10 James M.Mead, incumbent Democratic Senator for New York since 1939.

Labor Party,[11] Senator Wagner[12] and all New Deal and liberal elements in New York State. Mr Dewey's backers are naturally delighted at so ugly a split in Democratic ranks. It is difficult to predict result of struggle, which may resolve itself into a duel between President and Farley for control of New York State. Upon its outcome now that issues have been drawn so sharply much depends with regard to future of Democratic Party and to presidential election in 1944. One of conclusions which may be drawn from dozen primaries so far held is that unless local machine is completely unbeatable labour support is required for Democratic nomination. . . .

Senator Cabot Lodge,[13] whose chances of re-election in Massachusetts had been somewhat jeopardized by his connexion with machine of discredited Senator Walsh, has recovered his position by serving as a military observer in Libya. Lodge has just returned to Senate and if he is re-elected his solidly isolationist record together with his newly won prestige may make him a formidable opponent to Administration. It is interesting that in private he has spoken in a friendly and favourable way of British forces in North Africa and attributed their difficulties and reverses to circumstance (outside their control) – that Great Britain, like United States, disarmed before war and neglected military training and provision of equipment. It was not therefore their fault that, as British officers had said to him, they were still amateurs versus professionals. Mr Lodge also said that visit to Libyan front and participation in actual fighting with our forces had given him quite a new outlook and that such experiences inevitably had this effect. It does not follow that Mr Lodge, whose constituency contains many Irish voters, will repeat these remarks publicly nor that his attitude towards United States foreign policy after war will be affected.

. . .

A difficult situation has developed with regard to labour. Mr Murray of CIO had some time ago asked for a one dollar a day raise for his steel workers. After a long period of public and private discussion, War Labor Board (WLB) awarded 44 cents per day. Labour members of board voted against this proposal and CIO is at present not disposed to accept it, on ground that steel manufacturers had virtually conceded that they could afford a dollar raise. I am informed that person who had greatest influence in preventing full amount was Leon Henderson, who had won President to his view that any concession involving a breach of anti-inflation programme would lead to a general breakdown of that programme. The urgency of Murray's demand is probably due not merely to needs of situation but even more to his fear that his rival Lewis will automatically win CIO to his side as only labour leader with an unbroken record of victories against employ-

11 Founded in New York City in 1936, as breakaway from Tammany's control of the Democratic Party, but frequently supporting Democratic candidates. Often known as 'ALP'.

12 Robert F. Wagner, Democratic Senator from New York since 1927.

13 Henry Cabot Lodge Jr, Republican Senator from Massachusetts since 1936.

ers. Persons close to Mr Murray are gloomily predicting steel strike or the holding of a referendum on decision among steel workers. Public opinion in press and outside strongly supports WLB decision and danger of a strike does not look serious at moment. But Roosevelt-Murray alliance is strained just now. Labour in general is complaining that President is too absorbed in conduct of war to attend to domestic issues with his customary solicitude. Labour in an election year holds a strong position as recent primaries have shown but Mr Murray's case is too weak to enable him to force through spectacular concessions at this moment. At same time no obvious method of compromise has been suggested from any direction.

.   .   .

25 July 1942

. . . Advocacy of a Second Front has increased largely as a result of the Russian reverses. An influential section of editorial opinion, by no means confined to isolationist and pro-Russian, has been insisting that the danger of such an operation now is more than outweighed by the greater danger likely to arise if it is delayed. . . . Much publicity, some of it engineered by circles close to the Soviet Embassy, was given to the visit paid by the Russian Ambassador to the President in the course of which he is reported to have made an urgent plea for immediate action. Russian officials have been more than usually gloomy and tend to complain that the publicity given by Captain Lyttleton[1] and British Information Service here to our shipments to Russia give a false picture of Russian resources. United States despatches from London have consistently played up Lord Beaverbrook's agitation in England. Joseph Curran,[2] the radical labour leader lately returned from England, is telling everyone he meets of the desire of the common people of Britain for immediate action, frustrated only by the, to them, incomprehensible dalliance of their Government.

.   .   .

Two mass meetings held this week in New York and Chicago called for a Second Front. That called on 22 July by CIO in New York was supported by a message from Willkie and called among other things for rupturing United States relations with Vichy and Spain. A similar resolution was passed on 19 July at a meeting held in Chicago under auspices of Slav Congress, a new and well organized institution with clear pro-Russian sympathies but not dominated by Communists. Together with this agitation goes the corollary demand for united command at any rate of American armed forces. Willkie has once more called for MacArthur as Commander-in-Chief. MacArthur is also persistently called for by Krock alone among the better known journalists. The recurrent Washington rumour that MacArthur is here and bound for England has revived once more. Possibly to take some of the wind out of the sails of this movement, the President

1 Oliver Lyttleton, British Minister of Production 1942–5.
2 Joseph Curran, President of the Maritime Union since 1937.

has appointed Admiral Leahy,[3] the lately returned American Ambassador to France, to be Chief of Staff to Commander-in-Chief, i.e. to himself. In spite of excited speculation which this appointment evoked, informed political and military observers are doubtful whether creation of this post will do much to alter the *status quo*. President has long needed an adviser to co-ordinate for him military and naval information and to perform liaison with departments and services connected with war, and it may be that this is the function which Admiral Leahy is to fulfil, but position is still uncertain. Admiral Leahy, who earned President's confidence in 1937 when he was Chief of Naval Operations, is now well known for admiration and affection for Marshal Pétain[4] to which he has this week again publicly testified and for his belief in wisdom of United States policy towards Vichy. On this subject he is known to see eye to eye with Mr Hull, who according to widespread Washington gossip continues to be more reserved in his attitude to Free French than any of his colleagues, largely because he is unable to forget the insulting terms used to describe him by sympathizers with de Gaulle in radio and press at time of St Pierre and Miquelon incident.

.   .   .

Donald Nelson and the War Production Board are going through one of the most difficult phases of their harassed career. In spite of the growing unpopularity of the various political pressure groups recently condemned both by the President and the national press, Nelson is beginning to lose ground under their concerted attack. His most formidable foe is the congressional Farm Bloc led by Senator Gillette which has long charged him with mismanaging the rubber situation by yielding to the pressure of the oil companies which are alleged to have succeeded in sabotaging various plans for the more economical production of synthetic rubber out of grain alcohol. Vice-President Wallace in an article in the *New York Times* of 12 July maintained that the desire to create a self-sufficient home-grown synthetic rubber industry represented a political move towards a 'New Isolationism'. The answer to it was given by the easy defeat which the Farm Bloc have this week inflicted upon the Government in the Senate over this issue, by passing a bill authorizing the establishment of an independent rubber production board with the clear implication that the War Production Board has proved unfit to take charge of this matter. Nelson and the Administration leaders protested vehemently but in vain. The House will probably accept this proposal and the President may then feel compelled to secure some delay by vetoing it. In an attempt to mend the situation he invited Chief Justice Stone[5] to investigate the entire rubber situation but Stone declined the invitation. The view is growing both in and out of Congress that government agencies have been led to their ruin by 'dollar a year' men who represent big business to the detriment of the country

3 William D. Leahy, Ambassador to France 1940–2, and Chief of Staff 1942–9.

4 Henri-Philippe Pétain, Commander-in-Chief of the French Army in First World War and Head of the French Government (Vichy) June 1940–4.

5 Harlan Fiske Stone, Associate Justice of the Supreme Court 1925–41 and Chief Justice since 1941.

at large. If Senator Gillette and his agrarian allies win their fight difficult days lie ahead for Nelson's organization, whose every step will be viewed with intense suspicion. To add to his difficulties the War Department is pressing Nelson hard for a larger share of control of production and allocation. Complaints are frequently heard in Washington political and business circles against the lack of encouragement given by the Government to technical enterprise. A Louisiana shipbuilder named Higgins[6] whose orders have been cancelled has stimulated a wide campaign in his favour, while the claims of a more celebrated figure, the shipbuilder Kaiser[7] of California, to be able to build 5,000 giant airships capable of carrying 500,000 equipped soldiers or 500,000 tons of material in a day to Europe [sic] – though they may be incapable of fulfilment – have attracted much popular attention. War Production Board has thus far refused the necessary steel allocation. Since Kaiser's shipbuilding achievement is the outstanding miracle of this war in the field of United States production his voice carries great authority, and much indignation – though probably largely uninformed – on his behalf is expressed in Washington political salons. They have found their clearest spokesman in Walter Lippmann who in his column maintains the United States is losing the war not through major errors of policy but because of the morass of confusion, indecisiveness and obstruction in which the audacious plans of the great industrialists who represent American genius at its most fertile are dissolved into nothing.

The threat of inflation is producing more and more nationwide support for Leon Henderson. Henderson's fearlessness and tenacity have made him the most genuinely respected member of the President's wartime administration. While Nelson is slowly but steadily moving downhill Henderson is still rising. Of the chief groups arrayed against him labour is not likely to cause his downfall, both because it is not strong enough and because Green and Murray are likely in the end to accept a solution leading to a *de facto* wage stabilization. A labour–management conference on wage levels called by the White House this week revealed both sides in a surprisingly accommodating mood. As for big business, the Chambers of Commerce and the Farm Bloc, they are for the moment in too much disrepute with the country at large to attempt a major offensive. Anxious cries of widening gaps in the price ceiling are being uttered from all quarters. I am informed that Henderson has very recently offered to resign, remove the price ceiling and let prices rocket to the skies. The President knows him to be a man of his word and remembers the effect of his previous resignations. Consequently I anticipate that the stringent measures recommended by Henderson will be implemented in some form in the near future, although doubtless clothed in a kind of ingenious disguise.

Public morale in general is not high at the moment. In spite of its condemnation of pressure groups, public opinion in general is still insufficiently war-

6 Andrew Jackson Higgins, successful designer and mass producer of landing craft.

7 Henry J. Kaiser, industrialist – builder of bridges, dams and ships and manufacturer of steel, aluminium, etc.

minded, according to surveys made by various journalists, a view on the whole confirmed by the experts of OWI. Midwestern Governors have protested that the sale of war bonds in their States has been a success but despite this the apathy which has kept voters away from recent primaries extends to other fields and this week has been filled with newspaper articles and conferences by officials concerned with the best methods of counteracting this. The appointment of Willkie's friend, the Midwestern editor Gardner Cowles,[8] an energetic and capable man, to take charge of home publicity has been well received by the press and radio. If MacLeish[9] ever returns to OWI he is not likely to pull as much weight as formerly. There are reports from the Detroit region concerning unrest among workers in the war industries who are unsettled by the lack of a stable wage policy and by stories of vast profiteering by the owners sedulously disseminated by agents of John L. Lewis, who continues to co-operate closely with the die-hard isolationists and even according to some with Henry Ford[10] (who has been campaigning against the Democratic and New Deal candidates in the Michigan primaries). The Negro situation is still unquiet in Detroit following the race riots of several months ago, and the Republican pro-Negro campaign still led by Willkie is gaining ground in the North. In the South following complaints of persecution by the Negro singer Hayes,[11] Governors Talmadge[12] of Georgia and Dixon[13] of Alabama made truculent anti-Negro statements which have stimulated racial feeling.

. . .

The trial of the German saboteurs has been superseded in public attention by the arraignment of native subversive groups. Under a blanket indictment which covered twenty-eight persons the Attorney General has included such celebrated figures as Mrs Dilling[14] of 'We the Mothers' of Chicago, who at one time spoke of killing the President, William Griffin, publisher of the *New York Enquirer*,[15] Gerald B. Winrod[16] whom the late Huey Long[17] once described as a better demagogue than himself, Pelley and Viereck,[18] both of whom are in prison already, and most of the other well known sedition-mongering native Fascists. While no

8 Gardner Cowles, publisher of *Des Moines Register*, President of Cowles Magazines Inc. (publishers of *Look*), President of the Iowa (later Cowles) Broadcasting Company.

9 Archibald MacLeish, poet, and Librarian of Congress since 1939; formerly Director of US Office of Facts and Figures (1941–2).

10 Henry Ford, motor manufacturer, individualist and right winger in politics.

11 Roland Hayes, tenor. For incident see G. Myrdal, *An American Dilemma*, pp. 1339–40.

12 Eugene Talmadge, Democratic Governor of Georgia 1933–7, 1940–3.

13 Frank M. Dixon, Democratic Governor of Alabama 1939–43.

14 See 14 May *supra*.

15 A newspaper circulating mainly in Yorkville, largely German district of New York.

16 The Rev. Gerald B. Winrod, a notorious anti-semite, publisher of *The Defender*.

17 Huey P. ('The Kingfish') Long, demagogic Governor of Louisiana 1928–32 and Democratic Senator from Louisiana 1932–4.

18 George Sylvester Viereck (1884–1962), poet, romantic, German by birth, emigrated to USA in his teens, closely associated with German propaganda outlets in USA, e.g. Flanders Hall publishing house. Imprisoned on charge of violating Foreign Agents Registration Act.

doubt this indicates a genuine move on the part of the Attorney General against disloyal groups its effect should not be overestimated since Father Coughlin's organization which is far more sinister and formidable than all the rest taken together continues as yet to operate underground unmolested ever since its organ, *Social Justice,* was officially suppressed. This will probably continue as long as the war remains a rather distant phenomenon to so many Americans. Among far too wide a section of the American people this is not even yet a really popular war. Until a great body of American troops begins to take part in actual fighting dissatisfaction with the Government's alleged mismanagement will continue in the case of many to occupy with private grievances the forefront of their thoughts to the detriment of the objects for which a better management is desired. Against this we must place the fact that the American war production effort continues to be remarkable.

1 August 1942

Mr Hull's speech of 23 July is an important political pronouncement. Hull is held both by country and by press in higher respect than any other Cabinet officer or member of Congress. He is to the average American the most distinguished living embodiment of traditional American virtues and his prestige and influence derive not merely from his office but from conviction which he inspires in a large section of United States electorate that it is his wise and moderating influence alone which acts as a brake upon impulsive extravagances of New Deal. His words are consequently listened to with a respect and attention almost as great as that accorded to President, and fact that President heralded Hull's speech as one of outstanding scope and importance increased sense of expectancy which preceded it. It had a varied reception. Even Secretary's warmest admirers conceded that it was compounded of generalities and seemed somewhat thin and remote from immediate issues of the war. Such points as seemed at all novel, e.g. advocacy of a world court and of an international force to secure world peace, were received with acclamation by entire press and public with exception of acute isolationists. Advocacy of conditions under which international trade would flow freely between independent states is in line with Hull's deepest convictions which have preoccupied his thoughts during entire latter portion of his life. Spokesman of State Department told press that his statement that only those who fought for it were entitled to freedom and independence after the war referred directly to Gandhi and possibly to Vichy, and that somewhat vague allusion to fact that each people would work out its own individual destiny referred to USSR. With no other directives to guide them press interpreted speech accordingly. But real importance of speech consisted not in what it said but in what it omitted to say. It had long been known that Hull had felt disquiet at what he considered utopian pronouncements on post-war policy by Messrs Wallace and Perkins, and indeed that he felt even less sympathy with their type of political revivalism than Welles, and had moreover been feeling strongly that, apart from the President, he, rather than the Vice-President, was entitled to make authoritative pronouncements on foreign policy of United States. It was rumoured that for months he had been preparing a thunderbolt to launch at the Pied Pipers of the New Deal. If that had been his original intention there was little direct evidence of it in speech itself. I learn that speech was largely drafted by Leo Pasvolsky[1] who is in charge of post-war planning in State Department. This very cautious official is thought to have persuaded Secretary to dwell on points of agreement rather than disagreement with previous official spokesmen on United States foreign policy which may have resulted in a great toning down of the original. . . . Speech makes it clear that latest ideas of New Deal have had little influence on thought and policy of Secretary of State and his immediate advisers, among whom Berle[2] now claims leading place.

I am informed that it is Berle who has induced Department to order a million copies of speech for distribution in localities in which Wallace's 'people's war' speech is still exercising a steady influence. Mr Wallace's followers may read more into Hull's words than they convey but this in itself serves to reveal how deep a gulf they believe to exist between their own and State Department's point of view.

. . . New York election is still occupying much attention. Governor Lehman has now publicly endorsed Senator Mead. Assistant Secretary of State Berle defended himself against Farley's charge of neglecting his proper duties by asserting that government of New York was a national issue and as such was vital both to war and coming peace. The two wings of American Labor Party have composed their differences to extent of offering united support to Mead while Farley continues to assure public that Democratic Party is solidly behind Bennett. At Willkie's own request the 'Willkie for Governor Committee' in New York was formally dissolved. President said testily at his press conference that he only spent two minutes with Mead. This was intended to counter the disfavour with which his palpable interest in this election has been regarded both in press and in general Washington talk. There is a certain tendency on part of Republican press to shed crocodile tears at alleged ingratitude which President has displayed towards his old henchman Farley. This is a repetition of similar talk in 1940. Mead is obtaining growing support in New York State and if he succeeds in defeating Bennett in primaries Democratic chances against Dewey look better than they ever have before. In conversation with me a few days ago Willkie expressed view that unless there was a serious cleavage in Democratic camp over questions of real principle Mead was fairly certain to be elected. Willkie emphasized the importance of Irish Catholic vote in New York State (no less than sixty-one out of sixty-two Democratic county chairmen are of Irish extraction) and

1 Leo Pasvolsky, economist, Special Assistant to the Secretary of State (for post-war planning) since 1939 and Chief of the Division of Special Research since 1941.
2 Adolph A. Berle Jr, New York lawyer and Assistant Secretary of State since 1938.

pointed out that that was largely why President had felt able to back Mead, who was an Irish Catholic with a good record with labour, against the candidature of Farley, the leader of Irish. As regards the quarrel between President and Farley, Willkie felt that if Farley were to win and Bennett be nominated this would mean in effect that it would be Farley and not the President who would nominate the Democratic candidate for President in 1944. This in turn would mean (1) the end of any fourth term aspiration on part of President, (2) a great decline in President's authority over Congress between now and 1944 (Congress would be turning to rising sun) ; (3) a growing tendency to regard the Democratic Party as led by its reactionary elements (for that is what Farley and his supporters are) and a consequent improvement in prospects of Republicans which, as another American present suggested, could then become party of liberalism.

In the meanwhile, in Texas Democratic primaries which are tantamount to election, Senator O'Daniel,[3] a rabid and irresponsible anti-Rooseveltite and anti-labourite, whose buffooneries are more appreciated in his native state than in Senate, failed to obtain a margin of more than 50 per cent over his rivals and therefore is due to stand once more against his chief opponent Judge Aldred,[4] a moderate New Dealer, on 22 August. He has however polled a surprisingly large number of votes for a man with perhaps lowest reputation in Senate. This, as well as similar developments in the fifteen primaries which have now been held strongly indicate that an isolationist pre-war record is no hindrance to re-election, and that campaign of Willkie supporters to eliminate persons with such records has thus far been a conspicuous failure. . . . Administration appears to be giving comparatively little beyond routine support to pro-Roosevelt candidates, and is said to be trusting to its achievements before November when elections are held.

These achievements are however being more and more vigorously criticized, both in Congress and outside it. Congress is in a state of exceptional sensitiveness to hostile talk about itself, having been subjected to a constant barrage of abuse on part of press for 'politics as usual', a conspicuous example of which was recent leader in *Washington Post* said to have been written personally by proprietor Eugene Meyer denouncing 'political profiteering' and quoting the disgust with behaviour of politicians and the pressure groups on part of a recently returned young United States military aviator. As a result Congress tends to vent its irritation upon Administration and press. Willkie in his conversation mentioned above confirmed that position of Congress was very low in the country, though he seemed to regard this as a chronic state of affairs and not one which was likely to be remedied under existing parliamentary system. Expert political observers prophesy a period of bigger and more numerous public 'scandals' of which rubber crisis (President has as good as promised to veto the bill setting up an independent authority for production of synthetic rubber) and shipping and transport plane issues are only the beginning. Situation is by some gloomily

3 Wilbert Lee O'Daniel, Democratic Senator from Texas since 1941.

4 James V. Aldred, US district judge since 1939.

compared to that of France in first year of war. The Truman Committee charges that present steel allocations which have resulted in a refusal of priorities to Kaiser, whose exploits and promises were referred to in last week's summary, and to the somewhat less convincing Mr Higgins of New Orleans, have been mismanaged by War Production Board 'dollar-a-year men' whose natural penchant inclines them towards old established firms and stifles efforts of new and imaginative enterprises. Nelson has won one of his skirmishes with Army and Navy Munitions Allocations Board, and has secured right of determining allocation of raw materials. Enough congressional and newspaper criticism has been directed at War Production Board to widen its authority considerably and to increase demands for drastic measures on part of President with regard to stabilization of prices and wages and reorganization of entire production front. Judge Rosenman,[5] who is often called in during such moments of crisis, has been conferring with Leon Henderson and other officials and one of the periodic reshuffles of functions and officials may therefore be expected soon.

The dramatic step taken by the Supreme Court in reassembling in midsummer to consider the validity of the habeas corpus plea made by the attorneys of the German saboteurs recently tried by a military tribunal was the object of much discussion. The Court has decided that the military tribunal was legally constituted and the defendants legally held in custody and in comment so far noticed this has been welcomed as establishing the power of the executive to deal with a decided danger to the country in a state of war. In the meanwhile the isolationist trio – the *Chicago Tribune,* the *New York Daily News* and the *Washington Times Herald* – went to the extraordinary length of attributing dubious motives to the Administration in indicting the native-born subverters whose trial was reported in last week's summary. The only nationally known rabble-rouser still at work is Gerald L.K.Smith,[6] Huey Long's supporter, who has embarked on a campaign of 'tires for all' actively supported by the isolationist press. His activities appear to be the last ember of an obsolescent sect of troublemakers who have been succeeded by forces no less sinister but outwardly more respectable deriving from 'America First' and, some people allege, operating quietly through big business rather than by direct violent agitation.

The precise position of Admiral Leahy, recently appointed Chief of Staff to the President, is still obscure to the general public. There is a good deal of fervent hope on the part of anti-New Deal elements that he will succeed in replacing Harry Hopkins in the President's favour now that Hopkins has been married and is therefore likely to leave the White House. This is mere wishful thinking at the moment however and rests upon an overestimation of Hopkins's influence with the President and a possible misunderstanding of the function

5 Samuel I.Rosenman, lawyer, counsel to Roosevelt when Governor of New York, 1929–32, special counsel (and speech-writer) to President 1943–6.

6 Gerald L.K.Smith, preacher of native American fascism, a leader in 'Share the Wealth' movement, said to have been supported by Harry Bennett of Ford Motor Company.

which the President expects Leahy to fulfil. According to one moderately reliable source, the President expects Leahy to confine himself to co-ordination and condensation of all current strategical and other military information. There is no reason for supposing the President as yet looks upon Leahy as a political adviser in any sense.

Labour is still in ferment. Dan Tobin[7], who is perhaps the most powerful of the AF of L leaders, has been conferring with various anti-Communist and semi-isolationist labour leaders for the purpose of creating a united front against the left-wing section of the CIO. The President is known to have summoned him and given him a stern talking to. Tobin, whose loyalties oscillate between the President and the Roman Catholic Church, has for the moment withdrawn his forces and abandoned his 'unity talks' with John L. Lewis and other labour isolationists. Meanwhile Mr Murray of the CIO, discontented with the War Labor Board's ruling in the case of the 'Little Steel'[8] demands which established the principle that wages should be raised in strict accordance with the rise in the cost of living, is privately appealing to British methods as having been far more successful in promoting labour–capital solidarity. . . .

8 August 1942

Henry Kaiser is the personality of the week on the production front. Kaiser's records in shipbuilding which have set the pace for all other shipbuilding yards constitute a typical American success story capturing public imagination. His confident go-getting businesslike pronouncements on his cargo plane project have been eagerly seized upon by a frustrated public as the way to victory. Kaiser has found support in many quarters. Senators Thomas[1] of Utah, McNary[2] of Oregon and Josh Lee of Oklahoma are making political capital by supporting the scheme in public and making it difficult for the Administration to turn down a scheme which has aroused such wide and exaggerated hopes. . . .

The War Production Board has now approved a plan for 500 air transport superplanes provided the work can be done without interfering with combat plane programme and the Navy Department is expected to instruct Kaiser to build one hundred 70-ton Mars Flying Boats, as a starter, with approval for 400 more if he succeeds. Kaiser is also to build on an experimental basis a 200-ton freight plane.

This is not the only problem which has placed Nelson and the War Production Board on the defensive. The turning down of Higgins's shipbuilding contract, Truman's charges against the Bureau of Ships of negligence or wilful misconduct

7 Daniel Tobin, President of the International Brotherhood of Teamsters since 1907.

8 In response to demands for higher wages War Labor Board evolved formula based upon the claims of workers in 'Little Steel' (see footnote 7, 4 March 1942) by which wages were held to 15 per cent above January 1941 level.

1 Elbert D. Thomas, Democratic Senator from Utah since 1933.

2 Charles L. McNary, Republican Senator from Oregon since 1917 and Minority Leader of the Senate since 1933 ; Republican candidate for Vice-President, 1940.

in connexion with the latter affair, the alleged existence of a black market in steel and allegations that the much suspected Bethlehem Steel exercises a sinister influence on the shipbuilding programme of the Maritime Commission, the rubber tangle, and charges that the War Production Board is over-easy on civilian industries have all tended to dissatisfaction with the War Production Board and the Maritime Commission.

The next big showdown for the War Production Board, it is said, will be the question of a balanced programme. There are numerous signs that the holding up of some parts of the programme for lack of raw materials is prejudicing the success of the whole production front. In order to meet this Nelson has reorganized the internal set-up of War Production Board and some of the criticism may be met by the appointment of Ernest Kanzler, the man who converted the automobile industry to war purposes, to be Deputy Chairman of the Board with the special assignment of looking after programme progress and balanced production. Kanzler is a brother-in-law of Edsel Ford and was formerly Vice-President of the Ford Motor Company in charge of production.

There is a widespread feeling of dissatisfaction with the President, Congress and war agencies for too much appeasement of pressure groups generally and it seems unlikely that the farm group in Congress will attempt to revive the synthetic rubber bill which was vetoed by the President on 6 August. In doing so the President reasserted the authority of the War Production Board as opposed to the interferences of Congress in this field but at the same time he sought to appease public dissatisfaction with the rubber tangle and War Production Board's handling of it by handing it over for investigation to a committee presided over by Bernard Baruch,[3] the Donald Nelson of the First World War. The other members are President Conant of Harvard and Dr Compton[4] of the Massachusetts Institute of Technology. The review to be undertaken by the committee will have a wider scope than rubber ; 'it will form a basis for future action with respect to such matters as nationwide gas rationing and motor transportation.'

SECOND FRONT

A large section of the public is becoming more and more bewildered by the war. There is no call for action, no outlet for enthusiasm, no glimmer of success. These people do not understand what is happening in the distant war theatres nor why the United States Forces are inactive. Hence a kind of puzzled boredom about the war in general. At the same time the war effort is constantly hampered by the party struggle which runs along in a subdued form on the stage of Congress and more merrily behind the scenes.

The opening of a Second Front in Europe is a major subject of both private and public discussion. Any public speaker who raises the subject is assured of press attention and as the autumnal conventions increase in number it may be

3 Bernard Baruch, financier and 'adviser to Presidents'.
4 Karl T.Compton, physicist, and President of MIT since 1930.

expected to be thrashed out before influential audiences in the weeks to come. The two opposing points of view have been expressed this week by, amongst others,

(1) Senator Pepper who pointed out that the instincts of peoples were better than the bound minds of discipline-nurtured men ;
(2) the more cautious CIO leader, Reuther,[5] who stated before the Resolutions Committee of the War Convention of the UAW–CIO, one of the largest unions in America, that the timing of the offensive cannot be based on emotion but must be determined by the military leaders of the various nations.

The division for and against does not follow party lines or the usual classifications of opinion although the arguments for and against are slanted by preconceived likes and dislikes. Former isolationists express their anti-British bias in criticizing the British for not opening such a front and for waiting for the Americans. There has been some suggestion in left-wing circles that influential Americans and Britons of the 'Cliveden' way of thought[6] are holding back the project of a Second Front simply because Russia is Russia, and Lady Astor's speech[7] has provided ammunition to this school of thought. So far as the press is concerned, the most militant demands for opening a Second Front come from the West and Middle West. The Southern and Eastern papers tend to be more cautious. Reports from the country districts and small towns in the Middle West show that there is greater enthusiasm for the war than in the larger towns or in the East.

The cognate subject of a generalissimo of the Allied forces in the European theatre and whether this should be a British, American or Canadian general has not yet become a subject of widespread discussion despite the stimulation given by London despatches on the subject. The demand that an American be appointed is by no means confined to former isolationist and anti-British circles and one of the arguments advanced is that American generals are more used than the British to handling the vast problems of supply involved in a Second Front.

NEW YORK STATE ELECTIONS

The New York State primaries take place next week and the tempo and bitterness of the exchanges between the Roosevelt-Lehman-Mead supporters and the Farley-Bennett supporters has been stepped up. Bennett is alleged to be an anti-semitic nonentity whose election would line up the Church and Irish against the Jews in breach of old traditional paternalism by which the Irish admitted the Jews to an inferior share of the Democratic political spoils. Farley suggests that

5 Walter P. Reuther, Director of the General Motors Department of the United Auto Workers Union since 1939.
6 Anti-Russian appeasement sentiment associated with group around the Astor family whose country seat was Cliveden in Buckinghamshire.
7 Nancy Astor was the American-born wife of Viscount Astor, proprietor of *The Times*. Her speech at Southport on 1 August, while expressing 'gratitude' to the Russians, emphasized that they had been 'allies of Germany' and had only now 'come into the fight'.

Mead is an ex-isolationist and anti-New Dealist. Farley's political future is at stake as if Mead is nominated he can hardly remain chairman of the State Democratic Committee running Mead's campaign for election.

.   .   .

PRIMARIES AND NOVEMBER ELECTION

Primaries have been suffering in public interest because of lack of any first rate issue to enable voters to base their choice on something more than personalities of candidates and local controversies. The success of anti-labour Howard Smith in Virginia primaries where he was opposed by an organized labour representative, and defeat in Kansas primaries of Reed[8] who said that anti-labour racketeering was first issue as far as he was concerned, suggests that attitudes towards organized labour cannot be made a first issue from whatever side it is approached and failure of the pre-Pearl Harbor policy to influence Republican choice almost suggests lack of public interest in that issue. Willkie asked that war aims be eliminated as an issue in November election through subscription by both major political parties to a three-point pledge to aim for complete victory, for non-appeasement and for a stable post-war world. The only issue left is that upon which Willkie thinks Republicans should base their programme, criticism of Administration's conduct of war.

.   .   .

LABOUR PEACE

Peace offer made by Murray of CIO to AF of L springs first from desire of CIO leaders to meet criticism of increasing jurisdictional disputes and secondly a genuine desire to assist in winning the war, further evidence of which has been recent decision of CIO leaders in some states to support candidates in primaries not on their labour record but on their record of support for Administration's foreign policy before and after Pearl Harbor. In view of collapse of a similar peace move some months ago it does not seem likely that Murray would have made this offer without some real hope of achieving more effective co-operation between AF of L and CIO. The attitude of AF of L to this proposal is still quite uncertain and it cannot yet be assumed that anything will come of it. But whilst any real merger in a grand Labour Council still seems unlikely to result at any rate for some months the move should result in a reduction of jurisdictional disputes, more peaceful relations between the two bodies and a correspondingly improved prestige for organized labour amongst general public. President Roosevelt is reported to have told AF of L and CIO leaders that he would welcome any peace move which was not dictated by John L. Lewis. The present prospect is that Lewis will refuse to merge with anybody except Lewis. If therefore Murray carried main body of CIO with him and if AF of L on its side reached an agreement with it, Lewis, who is already refusing to pay the dues of United Mine Workers to CIO and is attempting to increase his union following outside

8 Clyde M. Reed, Republican Senator from Kansas since 1939 and unsuccessful candidate in the Republican gubernatorial primary.

ranks of Mine Workers, would presumably break last thread which binds Mine Workers to CIO and stand out against identification with either of two master federations. This would leave a divided labour movement, but it would be Lewis versus the rest.

16 August 1942

India. In regard to India attitude of Administration is sympathetic and generally helpful while reaction of general public is satisfactory. Gandhi's policy up to his arrest [1] was extremely unpopular with press and public opinion generally. . . . If British policy in India proves successful, then American opinion seems disposed to approve it. A typical reaction in high official circles is that while Britain's previous record in India on industrialization and education was none too good, the British had no option but to arrest Gandhi – an eminently 'bad man' from point of view of war effort.

Widening interests. The presence of American troops in Solomon Islands brings home scattered allocation of American fighting services. There are American troops in over thirty different parts of world of which twenty-one are said to be potential fronts. Political problems caused by their presence, news stories and letters home, have had a general educative effect in making Americans realize the existence of world problems. It is natural that this new-found interest should frequently manifest itself in imperial daydreams and facile schemes to put world right. Though specific suggestions for a Pan-Arabic Confederation or for an African trusteeship may ignore long-standing difficulties, their value lies in acquainting America with world problems. *Fortune* [2] recommends creation of 'Indonesia' for East Indies, Siam and Malaya. In other quarters condominium for Korea is advocated. In addition local problems are forcibly brought home to American forces on the spot. American officers forced to land at Foynes in mufti get a new approach to concept of neutrality. More and more does one hear it stated that Americans will have to take their share of world control. Carr's *Conditions of Peace* [3] has been widely reviewed in this light. Though at the moment evidences of imperialist ambitions are fairly frequent it may be doubted if they will be lasting. They are rather first signs of beginnings of a grasp of world affairs. However, extension of dominion of United States through a series of widely flung bases may well remain a permanent feature of United States policy (Greenland and Iceland happen to be painted same green as Alaska and United States on map in Cabinet Room in White House). This again tends to involve

---

1 After the failure of the Cripps mission Gandhi and other leaders of the Congress Party launched a campaign of civil disobedience against the war and British rule in India. This led to their arrest in early August.

2 Influential business monthly, a Luce publication.

3 E.H.Carr's incisive analysis of inter-war diplomacy, *The Twenty Years' Crisis* (1939), guaranteed a wide hearing for his views in wartime Britain and the USA.

United States in problems which have hitherto been regarded as too remote for appreciation or consideration. Insistence on air power and air communications reinforces this lesson.

. . .

Production. There is a general reluctance on political grounds to impose total war, whether it be drafting of eighteen to twenty-year-olds advocated by Stimson and repudiated by Roosevelt, or regimentation of labour advocated by McNutt and opposed by organized labour. Diffidence in restriction of civilian consumption is embarrassing internally because of shortages of labour and materials and externally in South America where lack of vital United States exports is alleged to be due to excessive demand.

Primaries. Isolationists are glorying in fact that isolationist and ex-isolationist incumbents are obtaining renomination in Republican primaries in New York, Ohio, Nebraska and Idaho this week. It is difficult to imagine a stronger case on pre-Pearl Harbor isolationist issue than that built up against arch-isolationist Hamilton Fish in New York. He was however elected by substantial majority despite his alleged connexion with Nazi agents and an appeal by Willkie urging Republicans to defeat him. To date twenty-four of forty-eight states have held their nominating primaries and only three alleged isolationist incumbent Representatives (including the notorious Sweeney[4] from Ohio who made himself conspicuous by his anti-British remarks during royal visit in 1939) and no Senators (unless Bulow[5] can be ranked as an isolationist) have been defeated, while many times that number of isolationists have been nominated by large majorities. As always in American politics, machine candidate has won in primaries in most cases. As usual too the machine is behind the incumbent in office, because if he were to obtain nomination without political boss's support, machine's share of federal patronage would be lost. Local issues and machine pledges and loyalties are more important than pre-war isolationism, charge of which can be so easily turned away by resolve to get on with winning the war 'now we are in it'. Other reason that this accusation fails to stir primary voter (in any case largely a professional voter) is that, like jury in a criminal case, half have done same or worse and other half have never heard of such a thing. Between isolationists and noninterested, primaries do not produce sufficient electors with a moral fervour.

22 August 1942

. . .

A showdown seems widely anticipated between the WPB and the army and navy as to who has the final say in the production of a balanced flow of material to production centres. It is rumoured that Nelson obtained a slight advantage in

4 Martin L. Sweeney, Democratic Congressman from Ohio since 1931.
5 William J. Bulow (b. 1869), Democratic Senator from South Dakota since 1931.

the shape of a memorandum conceding him better control over army and navy procurement. Criticism is widely directed at the lack of unity between strategical objectives and production requirements and it is said that arrangements will have to be made for Nelson to be much closer to military decisions which must be translated into terms of supply.

Another subject hanging fire was the peace moves of the AF of L and the CIO but it is unlikely that any negotiations will take place until late September.

So far as Congress is concerned many problems packed with political dynamite may be expected to be postponed until after the elections, such as those relating to labour policy, manpower allocation, rationing of civilian goods. It is even thought that the tax bill which will affect more citizens than any ever passed by Congress in American history, on which the Treasury has been requesting speed since last January, has little or no chance of passage before November. If the bill were to include a sales tax which has been hotly debated by spokesmen of labour and management in recent weeks in and out of Congress it might be particularly unpopular with the electors.

Shortages. Meat shortage in certain parts of country caused confusion and uncertainty and there has even been consideration of possibility of a voluntary rationing scheme. An attempt was made to clarify situation by Mr Hendrickson,[1] Agricultural Marketing Administrator, who told retail meat dealers in Chicago that the reasons for the meat shortage are huge shipments to armed forces, to Russia and to Britain, the increased domestic consumer demand and the inequalities in the price ceilings as between areas. To meet this problem Hendrickson said that all purchases for the allies had been temporarily reduced to make meat available for domestic consumption and that prices being paid for meat for shipment abroad were being held below OPA[2] ceiling. A further contribution to solving this problem was made by Mr Wickard, Secretary of Agriculture, in a speech which is arousing nationwide attention. He stated that he was now prepared to approve a plan for imposing price ceilings on livestock prices. This anti-inflation move is an important concession to Leon Henderson's price control programme. The part of Mr Wickard's speech however which is attracting most attention is his willingness to abandon his earlier defence of a price control provision which forbids farm price ceilings lower than 110 per cent of parity. Wickard acknowledges the reversal of his previous position which was held by some to have been an important factor in enabling the Farm Bloc, last year, to read into the price control act a prohibition against ceilings on farm prices at less than 110 per cent of parity. It is not yet clear whether he will insist on ceilings no lower than parity but his speech is a step in direction of reaching price control before parity as the first consideration. There may be opposition to this from Farm Bloc and a sharp

1 Roy F. Hendrickson, Administrator since 1941.
2 Office of Price Administration.

battle in Congress, but Wickard should have considerable support from public opinion in general which has been critical of pressure activities of Farm Bloc.

. . .

Willkie. Willkie with blessing of President is about to visit Near East (including Turkey, Iraq and Persia). He will seek to correct the impression that is held to have spread over Europe and certain countries in Near East that American production is hampered by labour and management troubles. He has made it a condition that he should be back in this country before November elections. If he were to intervene in these after his return this would recall his intervention to save Lease-Lend bill after his dramatic return from England in Spring 1941.

. . .

Negroes. One aspect of situation which has received little attention to date is interest being taken in Indian situation by the Negroes. Negro opinion, as is shown by, amongst other incidents, continued acts of violence in Harlem, at present time is in a very sensitive and critical phase regarding questions of discrimination in industry and in general, the segregation of Negro blood by Red Cross, a recent lynching, etc. Negroes are now drawing parallels between their lot and that of Indians and their press is giving prominent display to news from India and to favourable comments on side of Gandhi and Congress Party. It is also important to remember in this connexion that certain papers which have very large circulations and which are traditionally unfriendly to Britain's cause anywhere are champions of Negro cause, and *New York Daily News,* the white paper with largest Negro circulation of any, has not been slow to exploit alleged inconsistency between our treatment of Congress Party demands and the Four Freedoms.

. . .

New York's Democratic Gubernatorial Nomination. New York State nominating convention brought to a conclusion a long and bitter party political struggle by nominating Attorney General John J. Bennett of Brooklyn for Governor over Senator James M. Mead of Buffalo by 623 to 393. The result was a great personal triumph for James A.Farley over President who had supported Senator Mead right up to last moment. The objectives of both sides were control of the powerful New York State delegation at 47th Democratic National Convention which will nominate Democratic candidate for Presidency in 1944. The result has therefore important indications in relation to possibility of President standing for a fourth term particularly in view of fact that Farley was one of strongest opposers to President standing for a third term. Regarding use to be made by Farley of his power, it is pointed out by some observers that Farley's working philosophy in Democratic Party approximates to that of Willkie in Republican Party, i.e. Farley is a supporter of President's foreign policies but as regards domestic policy he holds that greatest hope of continued social betterment lies in protection of individual initiative and free enterprise. It is even suggested that in some future administration Farley might have his eye on post of Secretary of State.

. . .

29 August 1942

. . .

Inter-Departmental Disagreement. President's recent order to officials not to air their disagreements in public has been endorsed generally in press despite fact that this will close some valuable sources of news to them. It is reported to have led some administrators to refuse to answer certain questions explaining the 'why' of the news. Confirmed critics of President declare that bickering of departments results from faulty organization of war agencies and tendency of President 'to appoint one man to do four jobs, four men to do one job, or both'. As foreshadowed in this summary a fortnight ago, Nelson of WPB is now fighting back fiercely against his critics and his new 'get tough' policy has been widely publicized. He has let it be known that because of shortage of critical materials, armed forces would receive top priorities for offensive weapons only. He has assumed complete control over flow of critical materials including those for the army. For some time army and navy have been trying to get top production of every kind of weapon needed to wage war in any part of world at any time. Nelson's move involves a check on these efforts and a curb on powers of Somervell,[1] Chief of Army Supply, who is a forceful, able and ruthless administrator, a stronger character than Nelson, pushing ahead while WPB hesitates. Nelson has also now issued orders revoking the blank-cheque powers which army and navy field agents hitherto held over priorities. Nelson also has asked representatives of trade unions to discuss with him their demands for greater participation in generalship of war production.

. . .

Manpower. Failure to draft nineteen- and twenty-year-olds is giving rise to widespread criticism, partly as it is thought that despite urgency of demands of army, drafting of younger men is only delayed for political reasons until after November elections. Decision has been highlighted this week by General Hershey's warning that married men, some with dependents, will have to be taken into army early this winter and Stimson's announcement that enlistment age for skilled men has been raised to fifty. Younger men are preferred by army authorities but unless age limit is lowered by Congress supply will soon be exhausted. Young men are also less likely to include skilled workers and key men urgently required in industry are often drafted owing to failure of present system to exclude them. One of the reasons given for unsatisfactory production is necessity of frequently replacing foremen who have been drafted. While army obviously requires great numbers of technicians it is pointed out that it is wasteful of in-

1 General Brehon B. Somervell, Assistant Chief of Staff (Supply) since 1941.

dustrial manpower to draft or exempt men not according to their place in war effort but with regard to whether they have dependents or not.

New York Gubernatorial Elections. New York Gubernatorial Convention nominated Thomas E. Dewey as Republican candidate by acclamation after a film version of Dewey's life had been presented in place of a nominating speech. Convention had in its background potentialities and preparations for 1944 presidential nomination which characterized Democratic convention reported last week. . . . GOP[2] leaders amongst whom Dewey has a powerful backing have selected with notable care party's candidate for Lieutenant-Governor in Wallace,[3] District Attorney of Schenectady, who is reported to be a non-Willkie man. Should present ticket be elected and Dewey become President in 1944, Wallace would of course succeed to Governor's chair with two years left to serve. Dewey is obviously doing his best to obtain support from Willkieites who are numerous in New York State by drafting of a party programme with a strong Willkie internationalist flavour, by his reaffirmation of his opposition to Hamilton Fish, recently bitterly condemned by Willkie, and by removing any seeming challenge by Dewey to Willkie's prospects of becoming Republican presidential nominee. Dewey will also obviously wish to do everything possible to cover up Willkie-GOP rift in order to take as much advantage as possible of Democratic split.

. . .

American Labor Party have now nominated their own candidate for Governorship, as they threatened to do if Mead was rejected. They thus threaten to take away from Democrats votes with which their supporters gave Governor Lehman a small majority over Dewey in 1938. Fact that Roosevelt did not call off American Labor Party which has its roots in New Deal movement is interpreted by some as meaning that New Dealers are out to prove their strength. Farley's victory from this point of view can be regarded as an attempt to break away from New Deal combination of Democratic Party. If Farley's candidate Bennett wins, Farley may become rallying point for anti-New Deal Democrats in nomination of a presidential candidate and put himself behind someone like Paul McNutt for President.

. . .

Poll Tax. Another section of 1942 New York State Republican platform which is likely to appeal to Willkie and his desire to recapture Negro vote, lost in recent years in great numbers to New Deal, is statement that 'existing race prejudices as exemplified in poll taxes, discrimination in war production and armed forces, makes our otherwise solemn pronouncement of democratic practices a hollow mockery'. Subject of poll tax, which virtually deprives Negroes of vote in certain states, has been injected into the Senate discussion of a bill permitting men and

2 'Grand Old Party', a sobriquet for the Republican Party.
3 Thomas W. Wallace. He was elected, but died the following year.

women in armed forces to vote by mail. Senator Curley Brooks of Illinois, *Chicago Tribune* protégé, notorious pre-Pearl Harbor isolationist and confirmed Roosevelt-phobe, proposed a Senate amendment exempting members of armed forces, which are said to include about four hundred thousand Negroes, from payment of poll taxes required by Tennessee, Georgia, Alabama, Mississippi, Texas, Virginia, South Carolina and Arkansas. Brooks presumably did this partly with object of creating popularity with large Negro population in his state, although these are not subjected to poll tax, partly out of a desire to embarrass the Democratic forces. House previously rejected a similar proviso, but the Senate has adopted amendment by a vote of thirty-three to twenty over opposition of Southerners who termed it 'an invasion of states' rights to determine qualification of their voters'. The Senate has now passed the bill itself by a vote of forty-seven to five but dilatory tactics by the opposition and unpopularity of poll tax clause amongst southern Congressmen may make the legislation virtually inoperative for this year's election.

. . .

5 September 1942

Home Front. A number of developments pointed to a tightening up of the American war effort on the home front. Nelson's 'getting tough' announcements have been very popular and other heads of war agencies are reported to be about to follow his example, including the President. Speculation about the President's Labor Day speech gave an impetus to the advocacy of firmer policies and the speech itself is anxiously awaited by the various groups, labour, farmers, consumers, taxpayers, who think they will be materially affected by it.

. . .

Consumers in general are affected by the recommendations of Wickard's Food Requirements Committee, that meat rationing be put into effect in about four months and that the present supplies of meat, the largest on record, be immediately regulated.

Recent reports that the production of civilian goods and services in the second quarter of 1942 was only 8 per cent less than during the same period in 1941 appears to show that many restrictions can be made without real hardship, but whether this can be done without widespread public criticism of the particular authorities responsible depends on how restrictions are presented and the ability of political leaders and pressure groups to exploit the situation in an inflammable pre-election atmosphere. There is no doubt of willingness of the American people to subject themselves to wartime restrictions. Outcries, however, take form of saying that restrictions are unnecessarily applied for sake of artificially building up 'war consciousness' and inequitably distributed. The vastness of the American continent gives rise to regional feeling since people in an area in which shortages do not exist do not subject themselves willingly to restrictions applied to nation as whole.

Poll Tax. Congressmen have been summoned back to the Capitol to act next Wednesday on legislation giving men and women in the armed forces a vote in November elections. As reported last week poll tax exemption is the chief controversial issue in connexion with this bill. . . . For the Southerners the issue is largely a racial one but there are constitutional questions involved, some arguing that to abolish the poll tax by an act of Congress would be plainly a step towards ending the right of states to control their elections. There is also a strong technical argument that it is unconstitutional to prescribe the qualification of voters for Federal office when the Constitution specifically provides that the qualifications for such voting shall be prescribed by each state. Such racial issues continue to be increasingly prominent and political observers have been surprised at the success of Eugene S. Blease [1] in South Carolina, who came within an ace of defeating the present United States Senator Maybank [2] for the Democratic senatorial race after a campaign which Blease had fought mainly on 'a white supremacy' basis. White supremacy is also providing the major plank in the platform of the notorious Eugene Talmadge whose campaign for the Governorship of Georgia is in the last bitter stages.

Elections. Clare Booth Luce, the wife of Henry R. Luce, has announced her candidature in the Republican nomination in Greenwich, Connecticut, reversing her previous decision not to stand. It has also been reported that she might become the keynote orator for the State Convention. . . . Considerable interest is being taken in the campaign for nomination as Republican candidate for Senator in Michigan of Gerald L. K. Smith, one of the most successful followers of Huey P. Long of Louisiana. He cannot be dismissed as a lunatic fringer. His whirlwind battle for the Republican nomination is thought by some to have a sporting chance of succeeding. Smith is unquestionably a dangerous character. He does not have the limited religious appeal of Father Coughlin, the dominant anti-semitic note of Pelley, or the one-sided outlook of most of the lunatic fringe, but seeks similar objectives and endeavours to make his appeal as universal as possible to attract as many disgruntled groups as possible.

China. The question of extraterritorial rights in China was raised some weeks ago by Senator Thomas of Utah in the Senate and now on the anniversary of the Nanking Treaty [3] one or two fairly important papers have asserted that United States and Britain should formally renounce these extraterritorial rights. Prime Minister's declaration on 18 July that we were ready to negotiate with the Chinese Government after the declaration of peace is quoted as inadequate by Anne O'Hare McCormick [4] in the *New York Times*. There is no doubt that there

1 Eugene S. Blease, brother of Senator Coleman Blease, and Chief Justice of South Carolina Supreme Court.

2 Burnet R. Maybank, Democratic Senator from South Carolina since 1941.

3 1842, between Britain and China, concluding the so-called 'Opium War', ceding Hong Kong to Britain and opening other Chinese ports to foreign trade.

4 Anne O'Hare McCormick, political columnist for *New York Times*.

is latent in this country a certain amount of emotional sentiment for such a re-nunciation and a news item might easily touch off widespread advocacy of it in the press.

Associated Press. The Government has ordered the Federal District Court to order the AP, the most important news-gathering organization in the United States, to open its membership rolls to any newspaper willing to pay its propor-tionate share of the cost of gathering news. This decision, which amounts to a Department of Justice anti-trust suit against the AP, rises directly from the news-paper war between the *Chicago Sun* and the *Chicago Tribune*. The *Chicago Sun*, which has been a consistent supporter of Administration policy, has been denied the AP services in Chicago as the *Chicago Tribune* and Hearst's *Chicago Herald-American* refuse to waive objections (the anti-Administration *Washington Times Herald* has also been denied the franchise of the AP). (It is worth noting in connexion with the often rather unfriendly tone of the AP that Colonel Mc-Cormick[5] is one of the Directors.) The most important newspapers in the country are involved in this dispute as their exclusive rights in certain areas to the AP service gives them advantage over new competitors. As might be expected they are almost unanimously supporting the point of view of the AP. The refusal of the Federal Grand Jury to return an indictment against the *Chicago Tribune* for the disclosure of military information has given rise to a considerable criticism of the Administration by the press on the grounds that it is attempting to use the law to punish its political enemies and reward its friends.

The Justice Department has also been in conflict with the Dies Committee this week. Almost a year ago the Committee sent complaints to the Department of Justice against 1,121 government officials and workers for investigation. The Federal Bureau of Investigation has now exonerated the workers, finding that there was enough evidence to force the resignation of only two of the employees listed. Representative Dies retorts by accusing the Attorney General of favouring employment by the Government of persons admittedly members of organizations which the Attorney General himself had branded as subversive. In official and business circles there is still a considerable fear of Communism, while in the country generally there is no enthusiasm for Russia comparable to that felt in the United Kingdom. Russian secretiveness is the subject of much criticism. The pessimism of Litvinoff and the Russian communiqués is discounted. However since the Prime Minister's visit there is much less talk of the possibility of Russia making a separate peace.

. . .

14 September 1942

President's message to Congress. On Labor Day, 7 September, President sent his anxiously awaited message to Congress on problem of inflation. He followed

5 Robert Rutherford McCormick, eccentric, powerful, reactionary and isolationist proprietor of the *Chicago Tribune*.

this up that evening with a speech broadcast to the nation justifying message and reporting on state of the war. In his message to Congress President asked for legislation by 1 October which would specifically authorize him to control cost of living. He coupled this with statements that if Congress failed to act adequately he would enact that legislation should hold farm prices at parity or recent levels whichever is higher, that individual incomes be kept below $25,000 a year and that unnecessary wartime profits be recaptured by taxation.

Constitutional issue. First issue raised in Congress was a constitutional one. Senators Taft and La Follette [1] protested hotly against assumption of dictatorial powers by President which, once precedent had been established, could be used in other fields, reducing Congress to mere shell of a legislative body. There was talk of another 'Supreme Court fight'. *Chicago Tribune* produced a steaming editorial entitled 'It is Revolution if He Tries It' and *New York Times,* less sympathetic than rest of press, asked if it was worth breaching Constitution to secure a difference of 10 per cent in farm prices which might in turn mean a difference of only a fraction of that amount in cost of living. This sort of opposition has however quickly died down for the present. Political observers agreed that past interpretations of constitution, particularly under wartime presidents, gave President immense undefined powers, e.g., Lincoln had exercised powers specifically entrusted to Congress by constitution but had justified this course on ground of necessity of war.

Public reactions. Public and press opinion has not so far responded to constitutional issue and has given overwhelming support for immediate action albeit criticizing both Congress and President for past delays. Although President spoke to a smaller radio audience than that of some of his historic foreign policy speeches of recent years, he spoke to people when many congressmen were in their constituencies mending their political fences for November elections, i.e. at a time when they were most sensitive and susceptible to direct pressure from home public opinion rather than from Washington lobbyists.

Congressional reactions. Congress were not therefore in a position to challenge President themselves on a constitutional issue but obliged to respond to his challenge to deal with inflation problem themselves or give him power to do it. If they refused to do either, constant criticism for selfishness and obstructionism, to which they have been subjected since ill-fated 'pensions grab' of last winter, would be disastrously confirmed and strengthened just prior to November elections. If they acceded to President's request they were placed in position of acknowledging that they had been wrong in contributing to inflation by writing 110 per cent of parity provision into law and wrong in refusing to take it out after President's message of 27 April. They were resentful at position in which

1 Robert M. La Follette Jr, Progressive Republican Senator from Wisconsin since 1925.

they were placed, do-it-or-I-will tone of speech and implication that they had fallen down on their job and that a slow-moving Congress required an ultimatum dateline to act on a vital war issue. Least unprofitable course for them to follow from point of view of political prestige was to produce an act in which they rather than President provided for stabilization of wages, farm prices and profits and to shift responsibility for inflation back to President's reluctance to use his powers to restrict inflationary wage increases. Administration spokesmen however made it clear that what they wanted was not an act creating specific inflation controls but an overall authorization giving President power to stabilize every-thing which goes into cost of living notwithstanding existing laws. On 14 September Senator Brown[2] of Michigan introduced a bill authorizing President to stabilize prices and wages, salaries and other factors affecting cost of living on general basis of levels existing on 15 August last.

Stabilization of wages. Key issue from this point of view became President's attitude to labour of which press, and to some extent public opinion, have long been distrustful. . . . Widespread feeling that Government and WLB has been too lenient towards wage increase was represented by a strong demand in Congress for either a presidential commitment on kind of wage action President would take or a wage-control blueprint by Congress itself. In days following presidential message to Congress this issue overshadowed need for farm price legislation which was taken for granted. Administration showed itself fully alive to strength of this feeling. An executive order was issued dramatically from White House prohibiting payment of double time for work on Saturdays, Sundays or holidays falling within regular forty-hour week. . . .

. . .

Farm reactions. Meanwhile power for obstruction of farm lobby, usually one of the most powerful lobbies, has so far been successfully immobilized. The two most powerful farmers' organizations are American Farm Bureau Federation, which represents the more prosperous farm owners and tenants, who are by reason of their employing more labour more sensitive to the need for wage restrictions, and the National Grange, the oldest and most conservative-minded farm organization in the country. These two organizations are both opposed to President's proposals regarding farm price parity. They argue that there is no real danger that a rise in farm prices will start a general inflationary movement. Prices of some commodities, e.g. wheat and maize, are still below parity. Where prices are substantially above parity (hogs, soya beans, beef, wool) the reason is that Government has set levels or acquiesced in them in order to induce the higher production that is required. The farmers' organizations have never asked for over parity prices. The motive of President according to farm lobbyists is not fear of inflation. He is merely out to make political capital by suggesting that Farm Bloc

2 Prentiss M. Brown, Democratic Senator from Michigan since 1936.

in Congress has placed the whole war effort in danger by refusing to pass measures necessary to prevent inflation. Finally President is asking power to control farm prices and has undertaken to exercise corresponding control over industrial wages, but there is no assurance that he will honestly carry out this undertaking and his past record suggests that he will not do so. Apart from question of equity as between farm prices and industrial wages, high wages in industry are attracting hired men off farms and thus creating a severe labour scarcity. The danger of present situation is not of inflation but of a serious drop in farm production. On the other hand, whilst Goss,[3] The Master of Grange, is of course predicting in public strong congressional opposition, in private he has made it clear that he does not expect much support from farm Senators for uncompromising opposition of the lobby. Moreover the attitude of farming press and reports from those who have recently returned from farm districts in the west make it clear that demands of farmers' organization go far beyond what the rank and file farmer wants. President of Farmers' Union, the most progressive of farm organizations, which represents the lower income tenant farmer and hired labour, has announced firm support for Roosevelt's demands. Wickard, the Secretary for Agriculture, asserts that his own recent conversion to price fixing for farm prices is typical of the great body of farm opinion.

Leon Henderson's position. Should President's proposals be adopted this will constitute a great personal triumph for Leon Henderson, the head of OPA. He is reported to have been largely responsible for inflation sections of President's broadcast which bears many similarities to a recent speech of Henderson's. His views appear to dominate Administration policy on this subject and an anti-inflation bill is said to have been drafted in OPA. He has been very unpopular with Congress for refusing to bow down to congressional patronage in making appointments and Congress recently endeavoured to check his organization by refusing it adequate funds for its administration. It should now be a source of some satisfaction to Henderson that he should be the one to inspire one of the strongest rebukes by a President to Congress in history of United States and that this rebuke should be so enthusiastically endorsed by the nation's press even to the point of suggestions in some important papers that whole organization of Congress and its committees is archaic and should be reformed.

Departmental reactions. On day following the President's broadcast Henderson came out with a fighting speech declaring that 'from here on we intend to fortify the President with a strengthened insistence' upon compliance with price regulations. Leaders of other agencies have followed suit in declaration of 'get tough' policies which are increasingly advertised and advocated as such. Paul McNutt,

3 Albert S.Goss, Farm Credit Administration 1933–40.

chairman of War Manpower Commission, declared twelve western states a critical labour area, preventing certain defence workers changing their jobs in that area without Federal permit. Office of Defense Transportation declared that it would assume control of commercial vehicles, about five million of them on 15 November, and ordered a third of New York cabs to surrender their licences. Baruch's rubber committee came out with a demand for nationwide gasoline rationing and a national speed limit of thirty-five miles per hour which was endorsed and passed to Congress by President who said that recommendations made by Committee would be put into effect as rapidly as arrangements can be made. The Senate Finance Committee voted in favour of a 5 per cent victory tax to be collected on 1943 earnings of perhaps as many as 43,000,000 individuals ; whilst approving rises in individual income taxes in lower middle range they imposed a heavy tax damper on public travel, specifically stated as not a revenue-producing tax by Chairman of Committee. Committee is now said to be trying to finish its work on bill by weekend.

. . .

19 September 1942

Inflation. Throughout the week Congress had two bills before it in response to President's demand for action to control cost of living. House bill introduced by Representative Steagall[1] was an obviously selfish attempt of Farm Bloc leaders to exploit situation and national emergency by a redefinition of parity by forcing up all farm prices and other measures. It has now been replaced by another House bill which is similar to bill introduced by Brown and Wagner in Senate reported in last week's summary. Both bills have now been completed and endorsed by congressional committees and will be discussed on the floor next week. Both bills delegate specific authority to President to put a ceiling on farm prices and to stabilize wages and salaries. Both in effect carry repeal of mandate made in January 1942 forbidding fixing of ceilings on farm products at less than 110 per cent of parity. Either of them would give President very broad power to handle situation through agencies designated by him. Main difference between measures is regarding wage stabilization. Senate bill gives President more or less unrestricted authority to effect stabilization in any manner whatsoever with suggestion only that in so far as practicable he try to keep both wages and salaries where they were on 15 September. New House bill however recommends use of so-called Little Steel formula developed by War Labor Board, which would limit wage increases to not more than 15 per cent above levels prevailing 1 January 1941. Senate Committee originally inclined to use Little Steel formula but some sections of organized labour are putting up opposition to it as smacking of rigid wage freezing which Murray says 'will destroy morale of American workers'.

. . .

1 Henry Bascom Steagall, Democratic Congressman from Alabama since 1915.

Primaries. The primaries are now completed except for conventions in Rhode Island and some run-offs [2] in Louisiana. The most outstanding characteristics of these primaries compared with other off-year primaries has been the apathy shown in both voting and the attendance at political meetings. Big national issues have been absent from the contests which have been decided largely on local problems and controversies, the personal popularity of the candidates, the power of political machines and hard work, organization and experience in the local field. Although observers some months ago had predicted that in view of the general unpopularity of Congress an unusual number of incumbents would be defeated, only four incumbent Senators – all Democrats – and nineteen House members, including thirteen Democrats and six Republicans, have been counted out. Considering the number of sitting members that ran again, this is a normal casualty list for off-year primaries (e.g., in 1938 the Democrat incumbents were reduced by four Senators and seventeen House members). All nine Republican Senators won the right to run again in November while Senator Norris, the lone Independent, has yet to announce whether he will run again. The attempt of the interventionists to make pre-Pearl Harbor isolationism an issue has had very little effect in the primaries (as between Republican and Republican, etc.) but might be somewhat more influential in the actual elections (as between Republican and Democrat) if related to the political philosophy of individual candidates as a whole. In only one of the senatorial defeats, that of Bulow of South Dakota, was isolationism a prominent issue, and voting against Bulow was also influenced by his opposition to the New Deal and his support of congressional pensions.

Liberals have taken considerable encouragement in the last two weeks from the defeat of Governor Talmadge of Georgia for the Governorship of that State and Gerald L.K.Smith who (see previous summaries) was standing for the Republican nomination for the Senatorship in Michigan. On the other hand liberal hopes not confined to his constituency had been placed in the candidature of Representative Eliot [3] for the Democratic nomination for the House for the eleventh congressional district in Massachusetts. He was beaten by former Governor Jim Curley, [4] who is trying to stage a political comeback after several defeats at the polls in the general elections. Eliot was regarded as a friend of the Administration and a young man with a great future. Regarding the actual chances for the elections in November, Republican sources are putting out confident claims that they are sure to enlarge their minority in the House of Representatives and have a reasonable chance of obtaining control of the House. It is not possible for the Republicans to obtain control of the Senate, only one-third of which comes up for re-election. The Democrats are similarly rallying their ranks with the warning

2 A second primary election between the two candidates who received the largest number of votes in the first primary.

3 Thomas H.Eliot, Democratic Congressman from Massachusetts since 1941.

4 James M.Curley, Irish Democratic boss, previously Mayor of Boston and Governor of Massachusetts, who fell out with New Deal in 1935.

that the loss of the House is a possibility and even an issue as they point to the dread example of President Wilson's loss of control of the House in 1918.

. . .

26 September 1942

ANTI-INFLATION

Congressional debate on proposals to control cost of living has now resulted in a clash between views of executive and legislature which Administration leaders declare might have eventually to be settled by Supreme Court. Second half of bill was amended by powerful Farm Bloc to include a redefinition of parity prices including all farm labour costs. This converts the anti-inflation bill into a pro-inflationary measure raising ceilings to 112 per cent of parity. President had already declared his unalterable opposition to principle of this amendment which he said would destroy possibility of achieving genuine price stabilization. OPA estimates that amendment would lift overall living costs by 5 per cent and would add from three to three and a half billion dollars to the nation's annual food bill.

But despite these facts and certainty of arousing a storm of indignation across the country, Farm Bloc leaders have succeeded in stampeding House into passage of bill with their amendment attached to it and re-urging farm Senators to reject any attempt at compromise in Senate. They contend that amendment is necessary to insure an adequate supply of farm labour and to protect country against a serious food shortage next year. A Republican move to provide a temporary freezing of all prices and wages to give Congress ninety days to draft another programme referred to in last week's summary was rejected. In passing this bill and in yielding to pressure of farm lobby, House has challenged President to exercise his veto and carry out his promise to act immediately to stabilize both farm prices and wages if Congress failed to do so by 1 October. Should Senate follow suit this would involve President in task of controlling these by decree under his general war powers as Commander-in-Chief or by virtue of very wide war powers granted to him by Congress after Pearl Harbor.

Farm Congress members appear to be choosing course of action of most immediate political advantage to them personally in Washington and in their constituencies. By voting for higher farm parity ceiling they will propitiate farm organizations who have had some 250 lobbyists at work in Congress. At the same time, provided that bill sent to White House is so inflationary that President will veto it and act himself, any unpopularity for anti-inflation action will be passed to the President and his opponents will charge that he is acting as a dictator against the will of the people as expressed in Congress. There would of course be very great feeling against Congress for having allegedly abdicated its legislative functions in face of a crisis but so far as November elections are concerned Congress may assume that if voting is light organized opposition of farm organizations is a greater menace than public indignation amongst those who do not bother to vote.

It should also be noted that by inviting a veto Congress is forfeiting present opportunity of writing wage control into statute books. Labour groups have announced new measure as a 'farmers' benefit and anti-labour bill'.

Vote in House was not along party lines. Democrats were almost equally divided and ninety-seven Republicans supported farm amendment with fifty-four against.

In completing their bill before Senate had completed theirs House has succeeded in strengthening hands of farm Senators and attempts to reach a compromise in Senate bill have so far failed. Majority leader Barkley is however now claiming that he has enough votes to get through Senate a compromise measure by which parity formula would remain unchanged but President would be directed to allow for farm labour costs in fixing price ceilings. Objection of farm organizations to this is that allowance for farm labour costs is left too much to President's discretion.

MANPOWER PROBLEMS

Whilst much of opposition to President's programme in Congress can be attributed to powerful pressure of farming organizations to exploit situation in order to obtain higher farm prices, farmers across country are genuinely and seriously disturbed at farm labour shortage. This provides a feeling of disgruntlement which farming organizations may be expected to exploit and which incidentally may provide a powerful protest vote for Republican Party in election. Supply of farm labour has been drawn off by demands of military service and by attraction of higher wages and shorter hours in war industries. Secretary of Agriculture Wickard has issued a warning that nation will face a food shortage next year unless it acts quickly to solve critical farm labour problem. Both Wickard and Hershey, Head of Selective Service, have suggested possibility of passing a law to keep people on the land.

Farm labour question is itself a part of manpower problem which is assuming critical proportions and is likely to receive nationwide attention in the same way that problems of WPB, of rubber, inflation, etc., have successively occupied forefront of attention in the past few months. Concern over manpower shortages has mounted steadily for last few weeks. Presidential order giving War Manpower Commission of McNutt authority to transfer any of 2,300,000 federal employees without their consent, and Commission's order freezing labour in certain western industries were received favourably by press. But on the broader question of finding enough workers for all essential farm and industrial needs criticism of governmental policy and of muddle has been considerable and supplies ammunition to Farm Bloc opposition in Congress. Manpower needs are developing on all fronts, military as well as industrial, in factory as on farm, e.g. a group of midwestern agricultural leaders recently declared that production of foods and fibres needed for war will be seriously affected unless Government moves within thirty days to allocate manpower to farms as well as industrial plants. There is however suspicion that Manpower Commission and Selective Service are not co-operating as they should and that they could work out a plan to solve most of problems if they wanted to. In testimony before Tolan Committee [1] both Hershey and McNutt have testified that no final authority exists to allocate manpower between armed services and industry. Contemplation of such contrasts as 500,000 jobless in New York City and jobs going begging on West Coast causes dissatisfaction. This has been highlighted this week by Kaiser's dramatic call for 20,000 New York workers for his West Coast works and still more dramatic crowds thronging employment agencies in New York in response to it. There is also criticism of conflicting official statements on general draft policy and dissatisfaction reported in previous summaries that only political considerations are postponing drafting of men under twenty until after elections.

REPUBLICAN PLATFORM

In an unusual caucus meeting Republican members of House of Representatives have drafted a wartime platform providing probably most coherent Republican programme so far released. This includes patriotic support of President, opposition to a negotiated peace and a responsible role for the United States in building a secure future peace, with important proviso that in so doing United States' independence, American way of life and system of government be not endangered. Last point follows lead of Republican National Committee which on the instance of Willkie passed a similar post-war resolution last spring. Platform was introduced by some Republicans who had in the past supported President's foreign policy, but references to post-war world and programme in general have been worded so vaguely that, like Willkie resolution as finally amended, it can be interpreted by both isolationists and interventionists according to their own lights. New programme may meet Democratic criticism that Republicans are somewhat less behind the war effort than themselves and save the party from some embarrassment in election through its association with isolationists.

DIPLOMATIC ASPECTS

Diplomatic aspects of America's role in the war have received more attention recently than in former weeks. British operations in Madagascar,[2] Herriot-Jean-neney letter to Pétain,[3] Vichy's protest against United States bombing of Northern France, measures against Jews, have evoked vigorous denunciations of Vichy Government in press and some firm statements by Administration. Reaction

1 Select Committee (of the House of Representatives) investigating National Defense Migration ; chaired by John H. Tolan, Democratic Congressman from California since 1935.

2 Because of suspicions that Vichy French authorities on the island were collaborating with the enemy, British forces landed and forced the French to surrender on 5 November.

3 On 5 September, Vichy Government ordered that by 1 October all Jews in Vichy France should be confined in prison camps and subsequently deported to Germany. This provoked protest from Edouard Herriot as President of the Chamber of Deputies, and Jules Jeanneney as President of the Senate.

to statement of Finnish Minister[4] that Finland will stop fighting as soon as security is guaranteed is dealt with in a separate telegram. Myron Taylor's[5] long audiences with the Pope are arousing widespread but uninformed speculation associated with persecution of Jews in France and occupied countries, post-war aims, etc. Possibility of a future peace offensive by Axis is increasingly discussed and prepared for. Statement of Mr Grew,[6] recently American Ambassador in Tokyo, that the Japanese would not automatically crack after defeat of Hitler has been widely noted.

5 October 1942

INFLATION

The President has acted with spectacular speed on the Act passed by Congress directing him to stabilize prices, wages and salaries approximately at the levels of 15 September, summary of which is contained in my immediately following telegram. He has directed the National War Labor Board to limit wages and salaries, the Office of Price Administration to put ceilings on rents and prices other than agricultural and the Department of Agriculture and the OPA to co-operate in holding down farm prices. He has set up the Office of Economic Stabilization with broad policy-making powers to control the cost of living. At the head of the OES he has put Associate Supreme Court Justice (formerly Senator) James F. Byrnes, who has been a fairly consistently pro-Roosevelt Southerner since the early days of the New Deal.

The President's prompt action within a matter of hours after the passage of the anti-inflation bill and some twenty-eight days before the 1 November deadline set for him by Congress, is in strong contrast to the weeks of furious debate and lobbying in Congress.

The new act represents a compromise between the Administration supporters and the Farm Bloc. It includes limitations on farm prices for which the President asked in his Labor Day broadcast. It does not contain the redefinition of parity to include farm labour costs for which the farm lobby originally asked. It is sufficiently close to the President's wishes to avoid the serious constitutional struggle between the Legislature and the Executive which at one time seemed imminent. It is in form at least a victory for the President's ultimatum to Congress and this appearance of victory is of real political value in an election year.

On the other hand the Farm Bloc leaders claim that theirs is the substance of the victory since farm labour costs have been the chief subject of dispute and the act directs the President to give adequate 'weighting' to such costs when fixing farm price ceilings. They claim with some justice that if the act is administered

4 Hjalmar Procopé.
5 US Representative to the Vatican.
6 Joseph C. Grew, Ambassador to Japan 1932–41 and Special Assistant to Secretary of State since 1942.

in strict accordance with the intent of Congress this 'weighting' should ensure them the prices they originally sought by a revision of the parity formula. Further increases in farm prices are not only authorized but partially guaranteed because the bill provides for a floor as well as a ceiling on farm prices. Should prices drop the Government is to maintain them at from 85 to 90 per cent of parity by loans to farmers not only now but for two years after the war. Finally, both the farmers and those who are opposed to the Administration's labour policy generally claim that in incorporating wage stabilization in the act they have succeeded in one of their most important objectives, namely to force the President to adopt a firmer policy towards wage increases by agreeing to parallel farm price increases at every step. It will now be their objective to exercise a similar pressure in Congress by increasing the anti-Administration and anti-labour representation at the November elections.

PRESIDENT'S TOUR

The President this week returned from a fortnight's coast-to-coast tour of the war factories and shipyards which the press and radio had hitherto been forbidden to mention. In a press conference remarkable for the hot-tempered tones in which it was conducted by both the President and his audience, the President took advantage of the publicity attached to the release of this news to administer a public rebuke.

(1) To Congress for its delay in passing the anti-inflation bill and for interfering in war matters upon which it could not have adequate information.

(2) To a minority of the press and radio for distorting the truth in accounts of the war effort and especially to certain unnamed columnists for their ignorant and sententious views, and

(3) To certain Administration officials for confusing the people by, for example, statements that the United States was losing the war. Congress have taken their rebuke comparatively quietly in the atmosphere of harmony in which they are endeavouring to dissipate the bitterness created by the anti-inflation debate. The Administration officials are of course silent. The press representatives however have not been so quiescent. At the conference referred to, the newspapermen cross-examined the President as to which columnists had been 'ignorant and sententious'. They aroused his anger when they pointed out that he had begun by praising the press for its self-discipline in not mentioning his tour and that he was now proceeding to castigate them for their treatment of the war. The fact that the press and the radio were forbidden for security reasons to refer to the President's presence at various places despite his being seen by large numbers of workers has caused widespread irritation amongst editors who claim that they have been placed in a ridiculous position in the eyes of their readers. A number of them have now sent a formal protest to the White House and the whole affair seems to have led to fairly widespread criticism of the President and his advisers.

ELECTIONS

Observers are predicting an exceptionally small vote in the November elections. Apart from general lack of interest in the local election struggles, the absence of soldiers from their districts and the wide migration of war workers into new localities are important factors in reducing the active electorate. Some estimate that fully twenty million fewer votes will be cast this year than in 1940. Leaders of both parties are endeavouring to dissipate this apathy but it is generally agreed that it is likely to keep more votes from the Administration supporters than from the Republicans.

One fact brought out by the anti-inflation debate is the lack of certainty in the President's control of his own party. The consequence of this may be that though the Republicans may fail to get control of the House of Representatives in November, the balance of power on certain big controversial issues such as inflation or labour legislation may be controlled not by the White House but by a combination of Republicans and anti-New Deal Southern Democrats.

This estimate presents a considerable contrast to that recorded in earlier telegrams to the effect that the Democrats might increase the number of their seats by about twenty. There are indications that Republican propaganda will increasingly be directed against the information and censorship policy of the Administration and be accompanied by claims that the Administration is not only failing to give an informative lead to the country but is covering up its blunders by excessive and burdensome censorship. . . .

WILLKIE

Willkie's dramatized tour,[1] particularly his activities in Russia, have obtained for him prominent publicity across the country. This publicity is probably increasing his popularity with the man in the street and middle-of-the-road opinion generally. Perhaps because they are conscious of this fact and fear his political influence on his return, his opponents both in Congress and in the press have become increasingly vocal in criticism of him. His optimistic statements regarding the Egyptian situation were quickly seized upon some weeks ago as encouraging the same sort of complacency which had such unfortunate consequence in the Middle East. His opponents have now seized on his statement about the public prodding of the military into a Second Front to endeavour to associate him with extreme left-wing organizations and to charge him with general irresponsibility. Senator Connally, the Chairman of the Senate Foreign Relations Committee, has also declared it 'most unfortunate that Mr Willkie has been so free with his comment and his newspaper headlines while he was in Russia'.

. . .

Manpower. A warning by Selective Service Director Hershey that even schoolboys of fourteen and upwards may have to put in a few hours a day at 'essential

1 During September and October Wendell Willkie made a 'goodwill tour' to Africa, the Middle East, the USSR and China which he later described in his book, *One World*.

work' kept manpower problem to fore. This problem continues to be regarded as one of the most pressing as well as most difficult at present facing the country. Complaints of serious shortages of manpower continued from farms, war contract plants, and essential civilian service organizations. Although a sweeping national service act is not regarded as possible at this moment, there are suggestions in responsible quarters that eventually scheme following general lines of British manpower mobilization will have to be adopted. . . .

. . .

Political warfare. During recent weeks there have been signs of a growing demand that psychological and political warfare should be reconsidered on bolder and more positive lines. Awareness of what propaganda may accomplish is reflected in Ernest K.Lindley's[2] plea that OWI overseas service 'should have all money it thinks it can use effectively'. OWI budget is at present in its final stages. In committee isolationists have shown themselves suspicious of possible postwar implications of political warfare work of OWI and Elmer Davis, the Director of OWI, has declared himself in favour of an organization of collective security based on United Nations after the war. Announcement of final appropriation for this work which will be very large may give rise to considerable discussion of subject. Colonel Donovan's[3] Office of Strategic Services, which is very jealous of powers and activities of OWI in this field, may hope to gain some ground if OWI is subjected to widespread criticism. Many writers over a period of time have argued that United Nations need a more definitive statement of war aims before this propaganda can be really successful. They complain that present broadcasts to Europe and Asia deal in generalities incapable of meeting Goebbels' propaganda material.

. . .

Shortages. Talk of a food shortage caused by lack of farm labour has already followed usual pattern of rubber shortage, man-power shortage, etc., where Administration leaders make inconsistent statements and thoroughly confuse the public. In any case 'shortage' is hardly the right word and is only being used masochistically. Petrol rationing has now been widened to include the whole country but according to OPA estimates it will not be effective for another six weeks.

12 October 1942

Stalin's letter.[1] Stalin's letter to the Moscow representative of the Associated Press has been widely interpreted as an appeal for a Second Front. It has given

2 Ernest K.Lindley, Washington political commentator for *Herald Tribune* syndicate who closely reflected White House opinion.

3 William J.('Wild Bill') Donovan, first Director of the OSS, which was charged with the collection and analysis of foreign information and with carrying out special operations under the control of the Joint Chief of Staff.

1 In a 'personal' letter of 3 October to Moscow correspondent of the Associated Press Stalin complained that the Allies were doing less than the USSR to defeat the Axis and ought to discharge their obligations fully and on time.

a more realistic tone to Second Front debate which had been increasing since Willkie's references to 'prodding the military authorities'.

The various spokesmen of public opinion have been comparatively quick to answer the increasing Russian pressure. The President had already made it clear in response to queries about Willkie's references that he had no intention of being stampeded into Second Front action by public pressure. Sumner Welles was quick to answer Stalin indirectly at his press conference the next morning, declaring it to be the intention of the United States to give every possible assistance to the Russian armies. Later in the week, before the National Foreign Trade Convention, he carried this a point further, declaring that whether that assistance be through the furnishing of arms, equipment and supplies or by forcing a diversion of the German armed forces upon Hitler through the creation of a new theatre of operations, the fullest measure of every means of help would be given. William Green, President of American Federation of Labor, rejected an impassioned plea of Jack Tanner,[2] the fraternal delegate of the Trades Union Congress, for a Second Front made at the Convention at Toronto, declaring that such matters should be left to the military authorities to decide. The nation's press has come down even more firmly after Stalin's letter on the side of leaving the decision to the military authorities, as a result of Stalin's statements. They had altready given a lukewarm reception to Willkie's prodding statement. A few newspapers go further, showing impatience with Russian pressure, and ask what Russia did to open a Second Front when the democracies were at bay in the West. Fervent anti-Communists of course denounce Second Front agitation as Communist-inspired. Official and press reactions have however not so far had any great influence on the public, which continues to show an uneasy interest and to enquire for failure to begin a Second Front. In some unofficial quarters there is a tendency to place responsibility for this on Britain as for alleged falling down on Russian supplies. On the other hand Stalin's letter has had the effect of causing a certain amount of stocktaking of actual aid sent to Russia. Two weeks ago left-wing newspaper *PM* [3] made sensational charges that anti-Russian feeling amongst certain officials was preventing despatch of American aid for building of a high-test gasoline plant, despite direct order from the President that this should be done. This week they charged that William M. Jeffers, new rubber czar, was delaying delivery to Soviet Union of a truck tyre plant promised Russia fifteen months ago. Such charges are symptomatic of the suspicion one meets from time to time that anti-Russian feeling is hampering the war effort. In fact there does appear to be a certain amount of disagreement amongst officials as to the possibility of increasing aid to Russia on a scale suggested by terms of Stalin's letter. Some point to shipping difficulties as making aid on such a scale impossible. Others point out that if intensity of effort of Russian resistance at Stalingrad can

2 Jack Tanner, General Secretary of the British Amalgamated Engineering Union 1939–54.
3 New York tabloid left-wing afternoon newspaper.

be duplicated here such problems would be solved. Some also point out that Britain has done more in the way of supplying Russia than United States. . . .

. . .

Inflation. The appointment of Byrnes as head of the Office of Economic Stabilization has been generally well received. Anti-New Dealers are relieved that the New Deal Supreme Court Justice Douglas[4] was not, as was anticipated at one time, appointed to the post and take comfort from the close association between Baruch and Byrnes. Byrnes is himself a quiet, middle-of-the-road, extremely tactful liberal. He has exceptional talents as a compromiser and conciliator and fresh experience of Congress which he only left last year. He is not committed to any extremes either for or against the views of any of the groups with whom he will have to deal, e.g. farm, labour, business. The worst that has ever been said of him is that he is a smooth politician, that he has no administrative experience and that he is exceptionally loyal to his party and his President. President Roosevelt has now appointed the Board to assist Byrnes, with two representatives each of Labour, Agriculture and Management. They are the Presidents of the CIO and the AF of L, James G. Patton,[5] the President of the Farmers' Union, who has been a consistent supporter of the President's farm price views, and Edward O'Neal, President of the American Farm Bureau Federation, who has consistently opposed them. Management is represented by Eric A. Johnston, President of the United States Chamber of Commerce, and Ralph E. Flanders, President of the Jones and Lamson Machine Company. The next step in controlling inflation is recognized to be the enactment of tax legislation. This week Secretary Morgenthau warned that he would ask for legislation to produce another six billions in addition to the yield required from the present tax bill. The present tax bill is still in process of debate and the Senate has approved the largest single levy ever made on American income, the so-called victory tax of 5 per cent on gross income after $12 a week, a tax which is expected to yield some $3½ billion annually. The present tax bill is being bitterly condemned by the CIO, AF of L and the Railway Brotherhoods as the hardest tax blow in history dealt the poor man, by the Senate Finance Committee as 'soak the poor and spare the rich' tax legislation. The vigour of labour's protests are likely to be increased by the rejection this week of La Follette's proposal to increase corporation taxes, the failure of Congress to consider with any seriousness the President's $25,000 limit as an integral part of their programme and the revival of support in the press and Congress for the sales tax proposal.

. . .

The withdrawal of the United Mine Workers with 500,000 members under John L. Lewis from the CIO is held by some as likely to weaken the CIO in its forthcoming peace negotiations with the AF of L.

4 William O. Douglas, Associate Justice of the Supreme Court 1939–80.

5 James George Patton, President of National Farmers' Co-operative Union and President of National Farmers' Union since 1940.

18 October 1942

Manpower. Steps for the solution of the manpower problem and concern over the muddle associated with it continue to follow the very familiar pattern which has preceded the 'solution' of the inflation problem, rubber problem, and others in recent months. Public opinion has been confused by conflicting official statements on the subject by the unco-ordinated agencies concerned. Many are critical of Administration's alleged lack of an 'overall programme' (a phrase which is becoming a Washington catchword). Few people have much confidence in Manpower Commission which is composed of representatives of the agencies competing for manpower. McNutt with his eye on presidential election has tried to please everybody and accomplished little. Proposed solutions contained in various bills before Congress all by-pass McNutt in favour variously of General Hershey, of Selective Service, of President, or of a new agency. Main issue is between (a) the compulsory drafting of labour accompanied by orders freezing men in their present jobs, and (b) mobilization and more economical distribution of present manpower without the exercise of any other powers than agencies at present possess. Attitude of labour is that full mobilization of present manpower and absorption of surplus labour without job freezing can meet the manpower problem and that until there is a proven need for compulsion all possibilities of voluntary arrangements should be tried. President at present stage appears to be willing to give a fair trial to voluntary solution advocated by labour, but he declared in his broadcast on 12 October that if voluntary methods did not suffice to solve problem new legislation would have to be adopted, and his speech has done much to prepare opinion for this course. So far as manpower problem of the army is concerned President has also prepared public opinion by his broadcast for drafting of eighteen- and nineteen-year-old youths. He explained that a youthful army was a better fighting army and that lowering of draft age would mean quicker victory and smaller casualties. Both Houses of Congress are now rushing through a bill to reduce draft age to eighteen years in response to President's request for legislation. In the course of this and other legislation Congressmen, with an eye on the elections, are now endeavouring to show there are times when they can act with kind of speed demanded by a country at war. If this bill is passed nearly half a million youths will be summoned in December and four hundred thousand in January, rest to be inducted in February. Calling of family men scheduled for November would be postponed until March. Pressure for action to solve manpower problem of the army has been increased and much confusion and criticism removed by Colonel Stimson's clear statement that an army of seven and half million men is the limit for army before end of 1945. Realization of size of army required and production required to supply it has given rise to consideration of new problems such as the conflicting demands of equipping the other United Nations and equipping the American army, and problem of a balanced war effort for the United Nations.

Willkie. Willkie's interview with the President on his return from his journey was used by Willkie to emphasize the agreement between the President and himself by publicizing President's denial that he had criticized Willkie while he was abroad. Willkie reiterated his plea for a Second Front and the suggestion he made last winter that General MacArthur be made single head of American military operations. Willkie's statement that he would make a report to the nation shortly corresponds to his usual tendency to speak of himself as the official leader of the opposition or even as a sort of unofficial Vice-President. Willkie personally is confident that he has done a good job in convincing the peoples of the countries he visited that America is powerful and bound to win and that those who are not with the United Nations are against them. Willkie's stock is at present very high across the country, perhaps higher than at any time since his return from England in 1941 or even since period immediately following his nomination [1] at Philadelphia. The imagination of the people has been caught by a tour from nation to nation in which he has succeeded in keeping himself constantly to the fore. His report to the nation which may take the form of two or three radio addresses is therefore being anxiously awaited by politicians who believe it will have considerable influence on the elections. The effect of Willkie's influence on the Republican vote would be a complex one but it may be taken for granted that the main weight would be directed against the pre-Pearl Harbor isolationists.

Poll Tax. The House of Representatives has passed by a majority of three to one a bill abolishing poll taxes in State elections for federal officials. Although nationwide opinion has not been aroused on the issue, liberals throughout the country and all who value the Negro vote in the northern states have been advocating the repeal of the poll taxes for some time on the grounds that they disenfranchised Negroes and poor whites in the southern states, that less than a fourth of the citizens of poll tax states vote in national elections as compared with two thirds in the other forty states, and that the tax is used to favour the incumbent regime unfairly.

· · ·

POST WAR

There has recently been a revival of public interest in post-war problems and it is likely that they will increase. Administration has for some time been deliberately arousing interest in post-war problems in general although they want to avoid conflicts on specific subjects which might excite Congress or otherwise become current political issues. . . .

There will be an ebb and flow in public interest but now that United States is in war a steady growth is probable. In periods when war effort is being brought home to them at home or abroad there is likely to be an ebb. It is therefore difficult to judge significance of any one burst or slackening of activity in press.

1 As Republican candidate for the Presidency on 27 June 1940.

Recently there seems to have been a renewal of activity but it is unlikely that post-war questions will be a vital issue in forthcoming elections. Administration do not want it and a revolt within Democratic machine is improbable on this issue.

Although individual Republican isolationists, particularly in Middle West, such as Senator Capper,[2] have shown signs of reviving isolationist propaganda in relation to post-war world, Republican Party as a whole could hardly make it an issue except by raising general question of isolationism versus intervention and that seems unlikely. If specific proposals had been adumbrated by Administration, opposition might be forthcoming and a vital issue arise but this is what Administration have been careful to avoid. They are deliberately going slow and testing public opinion by sending out high officials to talk to business and other groups. Two kinds of general economic framework have been outlined by Administration with respect to international post-war organization, one more clearly and persistently by the Hull group, other more vaguely and sporadically by Vice-President and Milo Perkins group. Statements on political side have been infrequent and do not show a cleavage of opinion of kind shown in economic matters. Cleavage on economic side is counterpart of well-known division between planners and their opponents in domestic affairs. Hull group believe that positive measures of government control or guidance internally do not necessarily involve planning on grandiose scale advocated by planners nor do they believe that grandiose planning at home or internationally is necessary to attain a large measure of international collaboration. A recent statement by Vice-President urging importance of restoring free enterprise in export industries after war has been interpreted as a step in direction of Mr Hull, while Berle, though not wholly renegade from extreme New Dealers, in his last speech proposed no more in way of positive measures to free world trade than would command Hull's assent.

This difference in outlook on planning will persist and will produce clashes on specific proposals in international sphere. Tariff issue, that bundle of vested interests combined with false economic doctrine, amongst planners and non-planners alike will also persist. Strength to movement for isolation will come from both these sources, from ranks of idealists and reactionaries, but hard core of isolationism will exist independently of either and it is this 'isolation on principle' that is chief threat to a steady American foreign policy and chief concern of Administration.

. . .

24 October 1942

MANPOWER

On the subject of manpower, still the nation's No. 1 unsolved problem, criticism and pressure for drastic measures showed a decline. This was due partly to the

2 Arthur Capper, Republican Senator from Kansas since 1919.

President's speech of 12 October, partly to the satisfaction at progress being made by Congress in drafting the nation's youth. . . .

One of the main problems continues to be weakness of McNutt's administration of his Commission and his personal position generally. The Tolan Committee which supports labour's point of view in opposing conscription of labour has now charged WMC[1] with inefficiency and declared bluntly that

> The agencies charged with responsibility for manpower mobilization are not yet ready to assume the further responsibility for administration of National Service Act. If such an act imposes universal service upon all the citizens of United States before these agencies are so reorganized to carry out manpower mobilization that will inspire confidence in the American people the effect upon our entire war effort is bound to be bad.

McNutt has also been openly attacked in the Senate for playing politics in making appointments to his field organization across the country. He is unpopular with organized labour as an advocate of compulsion ; with New Dealers as a 'non-New Dealer potential Democratic Presidential candidate' ; and with the Army because he wishes to absorb General Hershey's selective service organization. The lessening of demand from press and general public for compulsory measures is a further trend against McNutt's views.

The President has advised against attempts to deal with problem by rigid legislation, following his usual course of advocating legislation which hands over a problem to the Administration after the specification of an overall objective. Public opinion generally would welcome any clearcut programme, voluntary or otherwise, and although organized labour is bitterly opposed to freezing men in their jobs it might be prepared to accept a certain amount of regimentation if this were imposed by a pro-labour President rather than an anti-labour Congress, the position being somewhat similar to the attitude of organized labour to proposals to freeze wages when Congress in the inflation debate was threatening to do this by legislation.

Meanwhile further steps are being made to deal with the problem immediately by voluntary means. The most prominent this week has been the announcement by Under-Secretary of War Patterson that four thousand miners would be released from military service in an attempt to relieve the shortage of copper and other critical materials holding back war production. There are also rumours that the figure of seven and a half million required in 1943 by the Army might be reduced by as much as two million.

The Draft bill. The bill to draft the eighteen- and nineteen-year-olds has made comparatively rapid progress but obstacles to the passage of the bill continually arise from the desire of Congress to include provisions and safeguards for the nation's youth in order to answer the criticism of indignant mothers in an election

1 War Manpower Commission.

in which the feminine vote is of exceptional importance. These safeguards the Army and the Administration regard as impracticable but the latter are obliged to go through the spectacular motions of forcing the bill on a reluctant Congress in order to save the face of Congressmen in their constituencies. Thus the President himself has been obliged to take the blame for objecting to an amendment specifying that youths under twenty be given a year's training before assignment to combat duty. In a similar way the bill narrowly escaped a prohibition rider introduced by Senator Josh Lee of Oklahoma, itself a 'Dry' state, to establish 'Dry' zones in and adjacent to army camps. Lee has a great reputation as an orator before church groups and prohibition organizations and this bill was said to be backed by the powerful and wealthy prohibition church lobby. For a few days serious fears were revived of this being the thin edge of the wedge for some national prohibition amendment similar to that produced by the last war. The firm opposition of the Secretaries of the War and Navy finally gave sufficient courage to Senators to throw out the amendment by referring it to the Military Affairs Committee. Support for prohibition has recently been growing, although not in any way comparable to the developments of the last war. The General Federation of Women's Clubs has asked the Administration to stop the alleged increasing intoxication among the armed forces and a recent Gallup poll found that if the question of country-wide prohibition were put to a vote in a national referendum 38 per cent of the population would vote 'Dry'. This is 5 per cent greater than in 1936.

TAXATION

The new tax bill has at last been passed by Congress and signed by the President. The main features of interest are that the normal income tax rate is raised from 4 per cent to 6 per cent ; surtaxes now ranging from 6 per cent to 77 per cent are increased to range from 13 per cent to 82 per cent ; the maximum is reached at the 200,000 dollar level of income. Personal and dependants' exemptions are reduced. In addition a flat, so-called 'victory tax' of 5 per cent to be withheld at source is imposed on gross income above 624 dollars a year subject to certain credits. . . . The Corporation tax is raised generally from 31 per cent to 40 per cent and a flat 90 per cent excess profits tax substituted for the present scale rising from 35 per cent to 60 per cent. . . . Nearly all the excise taxes are increased and in particular the tax on personal transportation is raised from 5 per cent to 10 per cent and a new 3 per cent tax is to be levied on freight. On the other hand the social security taxes on employers and employees which were scheduled to rise to 2 per cent on 1 January are frozen at their present 1 per cent. . . . The Treasury has labelled the measure as inadequate and Mr Morgenthau has called for additional six billions of revenue. It is however not expected that a new tax bill to raise this additional revenue will be introduced until after 1 January next.

. . .

NY ELECTION

The New York State election continues to be the outstanding contest to be decided on 3 November. Various straw polls show Dewey and Bennett fairly close to each other, with Dewey in the lead, and Alfange,[2] the Labor Party candidate, drawing votes away from Bennett. Bennett has been endorsed by Roosevelt, Governor Lehman and Senator Mead, all of whom opposed his nomination. Alfange has been recently endorsed by Mayor La Guardia. The latter move is generally expected to work in Dewey's favour because it will take votes from Bennett in the New York City area where he needs them to make up for the inevitable upstate deficiency. Many New Dealers do not wish a Bennett victory because it will strengthen the control of Jim Farley over the Democratic Party and correspondingly weaken that of Roosevelt. Roosevelt himself has however emphatically and publicly declared that he does not believe in such 'protest' voting against Bennett and denied that his support of Bennett is lukewarm.

ANTI-NEW DEALISM

One of the most interesting trends in recent weeks has been the obvious effort of business circles to revive anti-New Deal feeling with the charge that the New Dealers are using the war to force a rigid planned economy on the nation and eliminate private enterprise from the national life. At the same time the anti-New Dealers point out that business enterprise is winning the war by its efforts, that the end of the war will provide unprecedented opportunities for business expansion, that private enterprise must take full advantage of this and that private enterprise is the only means of saving the country from a permanent bureaucratic totalitarianism. This leads them to attack governmental post-war planning as such. The similarity of the argument used by various business publications, including the organ of the United States Chamber of Commerce, and the coincidence with which these arguments are determined suggest an organized pro-business anti-New Deal campaign with a view to influencing the character of the Congress elected on 3 November and accumulating support for more sweeping changes in 1944 and after the war.

31 October 1942

WILLKIE

Mr Wendell Willkie's broadcast to the nation constituted major subject of political discussion throughout the week. Willkie renewed his demand for a second fighting front in Europe, expressed the hope that our forces in India would soon begin an all-out attack on Burma, denounced the stupidities of censorship, attacked the theory usually associated with the President that private citizens not

2 Dean Alfange, New York lawyer, supporter of New Deal. Had been unsuccessful Democratic candidate for Congress in 1941.

expert in military affairs should refrain from criticism of the conduct of the war, described United States aid to their allies as tragically small, criticized American Government's 'wishy-washy' attitude towards the 'problem of India', which he declared to be in a very real sense an American problem, and said that in Africa and the Middle East as well as China and the whole Far East freedom means the orderly but scheduled abolition of the colonial system. He also made a series of ill-informed remarks about the Near East and criticized United States representatives in that part of the world and in China. On balance the speech must be regarded as anti-British, although this was very probably not Willkie's intention, owing to the emphasis on Russia and China as allies, almost to the exclusion of Britain, and the indirect criticisms of British policy.

But too many subjects of controversy were raised by Mr Willkie's speech for it to provide a powerful impetus to any one current trend of opinion. It has not, for example, caused any nationwide revival of agitation for a Second Front or for American intervention in India. The aspect of the speech most discussed by our American friends in private conversation with us here has naturally been what is regarded as Willkie's criticisms of old-fashioned British imperialism, and although the speech pays a handsome tribute to the British Commonwealth of Nations, the tone of reference to India and Africa and the Far East is an echo of *Life*'s [1] recent 'Open letter to the British people', whose author, Russell Davenport,[2] assisted Willkie in the preparation of this broadcast. . . . Liberals have tended to give a slightly bewildered welcome to this new recruit to their ranks and do not see behind Willkie the more frankly American imperialist ambitions of Henry Luce, Pan-American Airways[3] and other advocates of American economic penetration of the world.

To some extent speech was an attempt to steal the President's thunder in advocacy of Atlantic Charter as a basis for world peace and the President himself was quick to assert that both Secretary of State and himself had pointed out on several occasions that the Atlantic Charter had always been intended to apply to all humanity. The Administration have however carefully refrained from being drawn into controversy over a speech which they regard as not being primarily directed against the Administration.

The Secretary of State has defended the State Department's policy in its relations between Great Britain and India, declaring that at the moment a critic has advantage over those who are charged with the responsibility of conducting foreign affairs, and he also replied to Willkie's remarks about United States representation abroad, but he does not appear to have made any reference to the ambassador whom Willkie alleged to have worked for more than twenty years amongst people whose language he had not bothered to learn. This is generally

1 Weekly pictorial magazine of Luce group. 'Open letter' was criticism of British Imperial policy.

2 Russell W.Davenport, Chairman of Board of editors of *Fortune*.

3 Reference to Juan T.Trippe, President of Pan-American Airways.

taken as a reference to Clarence E. Gauss,[4] the United States Ambassador to China, who had recently been the object of criticism from other quarters as well and who is expected shortly to be replaced. It is generally accepted that Willkie's criticisms of the Administration will attract votes to Republican Congressional candidates but not to any sensational extent. From a long-term point of view Willkie continues to be a source of confusion in the political scene. He may be endeavouring to mould a new party of Republican internationalism within the old party but at present the rebirth of the Republican Party is in a period of embryonic chaos.

· · ·

MANPOWER

The two most controversial issues brought up by the manpower problem have been postponed, the question of the drafting of the teenage groups until after the elections, and the legislation for compulsory service indefinitely.

The Senate, despite powerful opposition by the Administration and the War Department, persisted in requiring a year of training for eighteen- and nineteen-year-old conscripts before they assume combat duty outside continental United States. This is described by the War Department as a crippling amendment and Under-Secretary of War Patterson said this week that if the mandatory provisions for deferment of college students and a year's pre-training for youths are written in the bill it would be as well that it should not pass at all. In allowing this controversial question to be brought to a vote in the Senate so near to elections, the President is said to have acted against the advice of Democratic congressional leaders but in accordance with the demands of the army and in the hope that he could repeat his success in compelling an unwilling Congress to repeal the 110 per cent of parity restrictions on the control of farm prices.

The failure of Senators from the 'solid' South to support the President on this occasión, despite the fact that their election is assured, was notable. In view of the imminence of elections further discussion of the bill in Congress was postponed until after 2 November.

Administration congressional leaders are now using the threat of a presidential veto and they hope that after the election a fairly acceptable compromise regarding this amendment will be possible. It is anticipated that something which is alleged to approximate to the British system will result, i.e. the exemption of youths from overseas service until they have passed their nineteenth birthday.

Bitter opposition which labour has been expressing in recent weeks to compulsory controls over manpower was supplemented this week by the protests of management and farm groups, whilst labour and management officials in the War Manpower Commission itself were reported to be ready to resign if McNutt failed to transmit to the President without alteration their report showing concern at the pressure on McNutt for a compulsory industrial service law. McNutt has

4 Clarence E. Gauss, career foreign service officer, US consul in various China posts 1907–40, US Ambassador at Chunking since 1941.

described this group as an advisory one and has been endeavouring to 'get tough' in the same successful way that Nelson 'got tough' with the War Production Board. The result however has been that the McNutt universal labour draft plan has, it seems, been shelved by the President indefinitely since, after a conference at White House with the President, Green, AF of L President, and Murray, CIO President, declared that the President had told them he would postpone consideration of national service legislation.

. . .

FOOD SHORTAGE

Meanwhile the food crisis arising out of a shortage of farm labour is approaching. As usual there are demands that a national food administrator should be appointed and such an appointment is believed to be now under consideration by the President in consultation with Byrnes, the Director of Economic Stabilization. The major bottlenecks are

(1) Shortage of farm labour. This has been partly alleviated by a new policy of deferring farm workers and the fact that winter is slack period for arable work. The crisis will however come in the Spring.

(2) Lack of transportation and refrigeration apparatus for perishable foods for the long-distance trade.

(3) Shortage of metal for farm labour-saving machinery. Heavy cuts in the production of such machinery have just been announced.

(4) Government purchasing for the Army and Navy and the United Nations.

(5) Hoarding, which is produced partly by premature government announcements of rationing.

(6) Waste both in families and in food factories.

(7) Confusion in rationing.

(8) A struggle between the War Production Board and the Department of Agriculture as to which should have supreme power over administration of the problem. The War Production Board is backed by a large segment of the food processing industry and the Department of Agriculture by the CIO and AF of L. The President of the latter has now publicly endorsed Wickard, the Secretary of Agriculture, for the post of Food Administrator. Possible future changes in the daily life of the community were symbolized this week by the announcement that the coffee ration would only produce one cup a day. This has come as a shock and there has been widespread hoarding prior to the date in November when rationing will take effect.

THE WAR

Hanson Baldwin's [5] revelations regarding the circumstances of the loss of American cruisers off the Solomon Islands [6] have caused widespread concern and are taken as being confirmed to some extent by the replacement of Admiral Ghorm-

5 Hanson W. Baldwin, military and naval correspondent of *New York Times*, 1937–42.
6 In the Battle of Santa Cruz, 25–26 October.

ley by Admiral Halsey.[7] There are rumours of a shake-up in the Navy Department, some even suggesting that Knox, who is said not to be hard enough on his admirals, might have to go. There is a general feeling that the mess is due to lack of co-operation between the Army and Navy and between the two commands in the Pacific. The developments have increased the demand for a unified American command and this has been paralleled to some extent by a demand for a single United Nations command. General MacArthur's disavowal of political ambitions is being interpreted as an endeavour by him to remove what has been alleged to be a serious obstacle to his assumption of a unified American command suggested by Mr Willkie. Opinion regarding the Pacific is growing increasingly restive and should the Solomons be lost or it transpire that any major losses have been concealed, a public explosion may be expected. The wartime censorship and the silence on war losses have been criticized by at least two Democratic Senators and one Republican Senator in the course of the week as disastrous to national morale and as engendering general suspicion amongst the people that they are being deceived. There is an increasing lack of confidence in navy communiqués as a result of the cumulative record of late releases since Pearl Harbor. The criticism of wartime censorship is bitter and strong throughout newspaper circles and sections of Willkie's speech relating to this were amongst those most widely praised.

· · ·

STABILIZATION

Byrnes, the Director of Office of Economic Stabilization, has now issued salary regulations in accordance with the cost of living act. These regulations forbid the payment to any employee of an amount of salary which after deduction of the federal income taxes on the whole salary would exceed $25,000. The aim of this regulation, which was originally proposed by CIO, is to make it easier to win the co-operation of labour in sacrifices in hours, wages and living conditions. It will of course reduce the incomes of many big business executives, e.g. film executives, as the payment of such large salaries has for some time been a method of reducing taxable corporation income. The amount of purchasing power which it will remove from the market is not large and it is being criticized by the 'rich' as an attempt to introduce social reform as a drastic war measure. It is also pointed out that the proposal was specifically turned down by Congress and that Byrnes is straining to the limit the powers granted under the act in putting forward such a regulation. Compulsory bond buying and a spending tax appear to be the next proposals for raising revenue and draining off purchasing power.

1 November 1942

POLL TAX

Legislation dealing with the poll tax, referred to in previous summaries, has not yet reached a vote in the Senate. The Senate Judiciary Committee have now

---

7 William F. Halsey, previously in command of aircraft of the Pacific Fleet.

reported favourably on it. There is still talk of the possibility of a filibuster [1] and of other forms of obstructionism by the Southern Senators. Unless final passage is obtained for the bill by the end of the year it will have to start through the next Congress from the beginning.

Reports of contention between Negroes and whites continue to be received here from the consulates and a number of political issues have highlighted this subject, e.g. the struggle over the poll tax, firstly regarding the vote of the Negro soldiers and secondly regarding the anti-poll tax bill itself. Currently there have also been the Arnall [2]-Talmadge gubernatorial contest in Georgia in which the race issue played a prominent part, the friction between coloured and white soldiers in Great Britain, the arrest of eighty-one Negro members of the Ethiopia Peace Society in Chicago, the lynching of Negro children in Mississippi and other attempted lynchings. As concessions to pro-Negro sentiment there have been the invitation of the Daughters of the American Revolution [3] to Negro singer, Marion Anderson, to sing in their hall, the naming of the Negro-staffed Liberty ship *Booker Washington* [4] and the appointment of a Negro as the ship's captain. It is, too, not impossible that the Administration's interest in the Caribbean has as one of its motives a desire to show interest in Negro welfare while diverting attention to an area outside the Union but near enough to secure some credit from Negroes of the United States of America. Southerners, however, feel that their attitude to the Negroes and the defensive nature of their position is not sufficiently appreciated by the Northerners or by the Administration and continue to reiterate their intention to uphold white supremacy.

Neither the press nor the American Information Services appear to be giving sufficient publicity to the contribution of Negroes to the war effort, both in industry and in the Armed Services.

This question is not yet a nationwide one in the same way that manpower, food shortage, inflation, etc., have been nationwide problems, but it might become one and observers in the South say that only an incident is needed to bring about a flare-up there.

7 November 1942

. . . Almost all . . . political questions have of course been materially altered by the large Republican gains in Congress.

Labour. Congress is now showing a desire to re-examine past labour legislation and present war labour policy. Initiated by anti-New Deal Democrats, a move is in progress to suspend or repeal forty-hour-week laws in view of manpower

---

1 Speech deliberately prolonged to delay a vote. Made possible in US Senate by absence of enforceable provisions for closure of debate.

2 Ellis G. Arnall, Attorney General of Georgia since 1939.

3 Pompous association of ladies claiming descent from those who fought in the American War of Independence.

4 Booker T. Washington, the great conciliatory black leader in the post-Civil War period.

shortage. Moderate Republicans show signs of being alarmed at extremism of such measures which would probably be smothered by Administration in Senate or vetoed by President. But effort of Republicans to force Administration to adopt a less sympathetic policy towards labour corresponds with one of the objectives of their election campaign as outlined in previous weekly summaries and they will probably attempt to use their increased strength for this purpose. War Labor Board has already shown signs of attempting to head off this drive by announcement of a 'pretty damn tough' policy to be followed in dealing with its assigned part in economic stabilization. Wage rates prevailing on 15 September last have been described as 'proper' and only in cases which meet specific conditions will increases be approved. Board will not approve wage increases for purpose of influencing or directing flow of manpower. President has also quickly stepped in to defend past labour legislation, declaring that examples in England and Germany proved that a working week longer than forty-eight hours was not conducive to greater production. Nelson on other hand said at a press conference that extension of work week from present averages would bring greater productive efficiency.

Tariffs. President has now asked Congress for authority to suspend any law including tariffs which interferes with free movement of persons, property and information into and out of United States. This message to Congress issued on election day has so far attracted little attention but it seems likely that there will be opposition stiffened by Republican successes in the elections. Senate Minority Leader McNary has described message as a request to 'tear down tariff barriers'.

Draft bill. Administration leaders are predicting that House will back up Secretary Stimson's demand for defeat of Senate amendment to draft bill calling for a year's training in United States for teenage draftees. This will come up for consideration in House on 9 November. Administration opposition to this amendment should now be strengthened since Congressmen need no longer fear indignation of the electors.

Question of size of Army proposed by War Department has remained a subject of controversy in certain sections of press and in lobbies. At first there was general satisfaction that General Marshall was able to give a specific figure, coupled with relief at refutation of fantastic numbers which had been suggested. Argument is now increasingly heard that even figure of seven and a half million which includes two million Air Force is too large and that, beyond a certain point, the greater the armed forces the smaller must be the proportion of equipment for them and consequently for the other Allies.

Those who take this point of view include both the extreme opponents of Administration and those of a more liberal frame of mind. Former protest against indiscriminate snatching of men by Draft Boards while war production falls and agriculture feels the labour shortage. There are some reports that Administration also feels that seven and a half million figure is too large.

Our successes in Egypt [1] have been quoted as lending support to arguments for lowering Army's estimates of its manpower requirements in order that more weapons can be sent to the allies.

Though it seems unlikely that figure of seven and a half million will be substantially cut down, it is nevertheless probable that criticism will produce a more realistic point of view as to both composition and use of ground forces which are being created. This in turn should improve allocations of equipment and material.

.   .   .

8 November 1942

.   .   .

ELECTIONS TO CONGRESS: CONSEQUENCES

Following is a preliminary assessment of consequences of election. A further report will be sent as soon as a more detailed analysis of various contests is available.

(a) Democratic Party has had much heavier losses than anyone expected both in House and in Senate, heavier also than are usual in an off-year election. They hold nominal control of new House of Representatives by a margin of no more than eight votes and will face a tight squeeze when House has to elect its Speaker on 3 January. On many domestic and economic issues Southern Democrats in past have lined up with Republicans against Administration. If, as seems likely, Southern Democrats continue to follow this course Administration may well lose control of Congress on domestic and economic issues. On other hand a greater amount of party discipline among Democrats can be expected.

(b) Substantial changes in membership of major House Committees and new chairmanships in some minor committees will result from Democratic casualties in election. While Democrats will retain all chairmanships and nominal voting control of all the Committees, they may have to yield next January to Republican demands for larger representation on some of more important groups.

(c) Democrats now control only twenty-four governorships. (There is a strong possibility of their increasing this to twenty-five in one contest still in doubt.) Republicans control twenty-two, Progressives one. Republican gains in governorships are of particular importance in view of fact that they include some of most important states, such as New York and California. Republicans are now in a position in these areas to use distribution of patronage to build up support and strengthen their party machines for elections of 1944.

(d) Results have considerably weakened New Deal in Congress. Practically all those who have advocated restrictive labour legislation in last two years have been re-elected and others with similar views have been added. Many of those who fought against such legislation have been defeated. The new Congress can be expected to be even less amenable to Treasury tax proposals and restrictions

1 British Eighth Army victory at El Alamein, 23 October–4 November.

on farmers. Two men in Congress who fought particularly hard for the President's price control programme, Senator Prentiss Brown and Congressman Williams,[1] were defeated while many of the opponents of such legislation have come back. Democratic Party is now dependent for its majority on larger segments (e.g. conservative Southern Democrats) who have shown themselves opposed to many aspects of New Deal particularly labour legislation. Strong revived anti-New Deal drive which has been reported in recent weekly political summaries was getting into its stride prior to election. For a week or two a number of influential newspapers and magazines have been campaigning against forty-hour week. Immediately after election and without waiting for new Congress, opponents of recent labour legislation renewed their efforts to suspend wages and hours law for duration of war and demanded repeal of National Labor Relations Act. Also symptomatic of determination of certain sections of Congress to exploit election results for this purpose, but more subtle, is proposal of Senator Vandenberg[2] for a victory 'coalition', with politics and New Deal out for duration. Wing of Democratic Party which is opposed to New Deal is now declaring that country does not want New Dealism at present time. New Dealers have so far in public been comparatively silent on this issue but in private New Deal leaders such as Hopkins and Henderson are adopting a very firm attitude and declaring that they have no intention of compromising in or out of Congress with anti-New Deal forces, despite the elections.

(e) For first time since New Deal came into power Republicans are within striking distance of control in both House and Senate. It is even possible, although not probable, that special elections as a result of death might give Republicans control of House before another general election. Eight Republicans in place of Democrats would swing balance. For first time since 1932 line-up in Senate makes it possible for Republicans to obtain control at a subsequent general election. Hitherto it has been impossible for Republicans to look forward to getting control of Senate in a single election. Fourteen Democrat Senators outside solid South will have to face Republican opposition in 1944 and if Republicans gain eleven more seats (i.e. two more than they picked up this time) in addition to those they won this year they would control Senate. It is also to be remembered that certain types of legislation and Senate consent to treaties require a vote of two-thirds of Senate and this two-thirds is no longer controlled by Democratic Party.

CAUSES OF ELECTION CHANGES

Spokesmen of all sections of political opinion are of course interpreting results as mandate for whatever point of view they can faintly claim the nation to have endorsed. These are accompanied by (a) usual post-election affirmations of unity and (b) wartime affirmations that vote was in no sense a manifestation of any desire to slacken war effort.

1 Clyde Williams, Democratic Congressman from Missouri 1927–9, 1931–43.
2 Arthur H. Vandenberg, Republican Senator from Michigan since 1928.

Republicans claim that nation's vote was more than just usual swing in favour of the 'outs' in an off-year, that it constitutes re-establishment of a Republican trend that will continue in 1944 and is a public protest against Administration's conduct of war, against mishandling of news (of way in which bad news has been withheld), against New Deal, against forty-hour week, etc. Others say that it should be regarded especially as farmers' revolt against recent stabilization legislation and muddling of manpower situation and as a general protest against alleged pampering of labour during past decade.

Democrats point to lightness of vote, to fact that draft and industrial migration led to large numbers of young voters not using their ballot, and that such young voters contain a larger proportion of Democrats and New Dealers than Republicans. New Deal Vice-President Wallace has pointed out that in times like present an abnormally large proportion of voters are people who are well-to-do and hence are more likely to be Republican. The last point is not very convincing but it is likely that increasing prosperity decreases voters' dependence upon and their support of New Deal institutions. Wallace also declared that Democrats have established a modern record for keeping control of both branches of Congress for six straight elections.

Democrats also console themselves with thought that loss of an overwhelmingly large majority will restore a sense of party discipline and prevent party degenerating into mutually competitive and at times mutually antagonistic parts. This argument is however also somewhat unconvincing in view of likelihood that, as explained above, solid South will continue to be a competitive bloc against rest of Democratic Party on domestic issues and will probably hold balance of power in both Houses.

So far as can as yet be ascertained majority of contests were not decided on big vital and topical national issues which have provided Democrats with big majorities of last few years. In present year many of the contests therefore have swung back to old pattern of American elections in which local influences traditionally played an important part. States which had been traditionally Republican prior to New Deal reverted to Republicanism, e.g. Ohio, South Dakota, Iowa. Farmers who had traditionally been Republicans before New Deal and felt that New Deal Administration was not giving them a fair deal over farm prices reverted to this traditional Republicanism and there were consequently big losses of rural votes in Illinois, New Jersey, New York and Michigan. These rural votes were not offset by labour vote as had been expected by Democrats because industrial migration and draft had reduced weight of Democratic industrial vote.

. . .

Attempts to drive out confirmed pre-Pearl Harbor isolationists from Congress have been an almost complete failure. Outstanding amongst successes of such isolationists were election of Representative Hamilton Fish in New York State, Representative Day in Illinois,[3] Senator Brooks in Illinois, Representative Barry

---

3 Stephen A. Day, Republican Congressman from Illinois since 1941.

in New York.[4] These surprising results are explained in some quarters as meaning not an endorsement of isolationism but a refusal by the electorate to condemn those who had preached policies which they claim majority of electors endorsed before Pearl Harbor. Others however regard these returns as an ominous sign of public apathy to the war which in a wartime election was regarded as less important than local loyalties and issues. By others again fear is expressed that elections show beginning of a trend to post-war isolationism in Republican Party. This last view is for example held strongly by Milo Perkins, while other New Deal enthusiasts talk gloomily of election being a vote against 'idealism' in favour of a return to 'Hardingism'.[5]

Willkie's pre-election speeches no doubt swung many into Republican camp on grounds of dissatisfaction with war effort but it is important to note that Republican successes are not a triumph for Willkie type of Republicans but for right wing of Republican Party and machine politicians who are usually opposed to Willkie. Success of Republican isolationists illustrates this fact and overshadows comparatively minor Willkie successes such as those of Representative Clare Luce in Connecticut and the new Senator Moore[6] of Oklahoma, who was a Willkie Democrat drafted by Republicans to defeat Senator Josh Lee. It is a widely held view that Willkie will not now be able to obtain Republican nomination for President in 1944 if he wishes it. Here again however time alone can tell. It is to be hoped but it cannot be held to be certain that he will not be tempted to rally support in party by an anti-imperialism campaign which would very easily become anti-British.

15 November 1942

Developments in North Africa and France have given rise to an emotional response comparable, although in reverse, to the German *blitzkrieg* in Western Europe in the spring of 1940. The news of the landing of United States forces in Africa was like cool water to a parched throat. It was badly needed to counteract the feeling of frustration and meaninglessness which has been a depressing feature in recent months. As the days passed with the impetus provided by streamer headlines and special broadcasts and a welter of sensational and often conflicting rumours and speculation, public opinion took a turn towards over-optimism in the same way as after the fall of France it had turned to over-pessimism. On the Stock Exchange 'War' stocks fell and 'Peace' securities such as the bonds of occupied countries had a noticeable rise. Daily one hears talk of the war being over in six months. The Administration is making obvious endeavours to check these unhealthy tendencies. The President at his press conference recalled an earlier warning by himself against giving way to peaks of overconfidence and

4 William B. Barry, Democratic Congressman from New York since 1935.
5 Harding's presidency, 1921–3, was notable for its *laissez-faire* attitudes and easy-going public morality.
6 Edward H. Moore, Republican, lawyer and businessman.

valleys of depression. The situation in the Solomon Islands [1] is still giving rise to considerable public anxiety. The developments have naturally been a great triumph

(a) for the President – Mr Churchill's public handing of the honours to the President [2] contributed materially to this;
(b) for the State Department – Their policy is usually taken as having been vindicated, although some of their severest critics refuse to change their opinion and argue that the State Department is still leaving the Fighting French Movement [3] out of the picture and putting their hope in a 'Third France' which is neither de Gaullist nor collaborationist; and
(c) for the armed forces whose achievement of a unified command on this front is particularly praised.

The mobilization of an enthusiastic public opinion behind the war effort has been greatly assisted by the realization that the North African campaign is not limited to one single objective but appears to be a carefully devised plan of strategy which it is thought will prove to be the turning-point of the war.

The President has also come in for considerable praise, (a) because of his single-minded adherence to a plan despite the agitation of the critics;
(b) because he refrained from falling into the temptation to arrange for the campaign to begin before the elections.

These developments, happily preceded by the enthusiastic reception of the British victory in the Battle of Egypt [4] combined with the continued British success, have caused a notable improvement in sentiment towards us and it is likely that the general attitude of American opinion towards the British war effort will show continued improvement in the next few weeks, not only because we have demonstrated our ability to fight, but because Americans themselves are no longer in that mood of irritated frustration in which a scapegoat is eagerly sought.

It is still too early to attempt to define the programme of the opposition to the Administration in the present Congress. Some of the week's developments, however, give one a tentative indication, for example

(a) *Labour legislation.* . . . Plans are being developed to attempt to push through a strong anti-labour programme which might include the outlawing of strikes and jurisdictional disputes during the war, the prevention of unions from contributing to political campaign war chests, the application to unions of the federal Anti-Racketeering Act, [5] the elimination of time-and-a-half for work in excess of forty

---

1 Where fighting for Guadalcanal was still in progress.

2 Churchill in Mansion House speech of 11 November acknowledged significance for El Alamein of Roosevelt's prompt despatch of US aid after Tobruk.

3 *France Combattante:* the new title adopted by de Gaulle's Free French in July 1942.

4 British 8th Army victories at El Alamein and elsewhere in North Africa.

5 Act making it a criminal offence to interfere with foreign or interstate commerce by violence or intimidation.

hours. The drive against what is called the forty-hour week is the most powerful section of this attack and comparisons with Britain, where it is alleged a fifty-six-hour week is in operation, have frequently been made by opponents of organized labour, particularly after Mr Morrison's[6] speech on British per capita production.

A report of Senator Truman's Committee is now being quoted as proposing the lengthening of the work week to forty-eight hours. The main issue is of course whether overtime should be paid after the forty hours, since more hours can now be worked in a defence industry provided that the employer is willing to pay time-and-a-half overtime. The Truman Committee recommends that under certain circumstances overtime payments be in war bonds cashable only after the war. Labour for its part is demanding a greater part in the administration of the war effort and making counter charge of inefficiency against management.

(b) *Congressional organization.* The Republicans are settling down to the job of organizing their opposition procedure in Congress. Representative Joseph Martin of Massachusetts has decided to resign the Chairmanship of the Republican National Committee in order to devote his full time to leading the minority in the House. Amongst the proposals which he is supporting is one for a joint bipartisan committee to represent Congress in consultation with the White House on the conduct of the war. This recalls the unfortunate history of the similar Congress committee in the Civil War and is not too popular even in the Republican ranks because it seems inevitable that it would involve interference with the responsibility of the executive arms of the Government. Proposals which Representative Dirksen[7] of Illinois has been advocating for some time to modernize congressional procedure have now come in handy for exploitation by Republican opposition. . . .

(c) *Taxation.* The new Congress will assuredly use its strength to oppose any attempt to modify present system of taxation and there is likely to be a strong revival of agitation for a general retail sales tax; the latter has so far been opposed by Administration. Senator Vandenberg has already proposed a moratorium on new taxes for a year, at same time urging that immediate steps be taken to ensure sale of five times as many war bonds as are now being bought. His views appear to reflect views of rest of Senate Republican minority.

MANPOWER

President this week predicted that 9,700,000 would be serving in United States armed forces thirteen months hence, i.e. about one out of every five American males over fourteen years of age. The Brookings Institution[8] estimates with such

---

6 Herbert Morrison, British Home Secretary since 1940.

7 Everett McKinley Dirksen, Republican Congressman from Illinois since 1933.

8 Washington-based research foundation specializing in fields of government and public policy.

an army nation would require a total labour force of 62,262,000 persons in 1943 and 65,000,000 in 1944. Between these two goals lies struggle between industry and armed forces not only for overall numbers of men but for skilled men, the army declaring that it needs almost twice as many skilled technicians as it has been able to recruit to date. Criticism of War Manpower Commission continues. This week Truman Committee accused it of not evolving a basic policy in seven months' existence. The Truman report also proposed immediate abolition of voluntary enlistments and demanded one official to be responsible for military and production manpower requirements. The report added that in absence of any overall manpower policy it would be a mistake for Congress to consider passage of any drastic compulsory legislation. Baruch, whose power behind scene at present time through such friends as Byrnes of OES and Eberstadt[9] of WPB is an increasingly important factor in political-industrial scene, is again reported to be actively engaged in advising the President on this problem in consultation with McNutt. The President himself is reported to be considering a change in Administration set-up. Yet another 'Czar' might be appointed as a Director of National Service to have jurisdiction over manpower mobilization in all its aspects including authority over both Selective Service System and United States Employment Service. Both McNutt's and Hershey's systems would be preserved but it is unlikely that either would be chosen for this post. The teenage draft bill followed in previous summaries has now been passed and signed by the President, stripped of the training amendment which had been opposed by the Army and the Administration.

. . .

21 November 1942 [Special election survey]

The elections took place in an atmosphere unfavourable to Administration. The apathy of electorate had been demonstrated in primaries and continued to be most frequent subject of comment up to polling day. Political observers on both sides had rightly anticipated not only that vote would be an exceptionally light one but that this would count more against Democrats than against Republicans. The vote proved to be the smallest since 1930. Out of an electorate of 60,000,000 only 28,000,000 went to polls, that is about one half number of voters in last presidential year, 1940. For some time before elections news from chief battlefront in Pacific had been depressing and apparent absence of enterprise on European Front contributed further to a general sense of frustration. Such encouraging news as there was did not offset this because confidence in official bulletins had been undermined as a result of too many belated admissions by Administration that what had been reported as successes for American arms were in fact reverses. The people were dissatisfied with conduct of war both at home and abroad, displeased with their official representatives in Washington

9 Ferdinand Eberstadt, Vice-Chairman of the War Production Board.

and whole Washington 'Bureaucracy' and discontented at failure of local officials to cope with new problems created by restricted transportation, a shortage of housing, rationing, etc. Such feelings were increased by activities of almost all the press which had for nine months presented both Congress and Washington officials in an unfavourable and sometimes ridiculous light. This depression and discontent might have been crystallized by a great national issue into the sort of nationwide outburst of alarm or indignation which precipitates a crisis. But no such compelling issue was produced by either party. The consequence was a mood of political apathy in which the average citizen felt no urgent call to vote. Local issues and personalities held the stage and unwillingness of unprofessional voter to go to poll left political 'machine' as strongest single factor in many crucial contests.

In welter of local issues certain national trends are nevertheless discernible, all of them more or less unfavourable to Administration. The New Deal originally came into power with help of at least three great political forces in addition to traditionally Democratic solid South and Democratic urban political 'machines'. These forces were organized labour, the farmers and the 'forgotten man'. All three had been victims of great slump.

Of these three labour alone today continues to support Administration. Even this support is lukewarm and limited by recent developments. Alleged favour shown by President to CIO has cooled ardour of AF of L. Organized labour regards Leon Henderson's attempts to stabilize wages as a stab in back. High wages has somewhat dulled labour's gratitude and former dependence on New Deal is forgotten. Moreover conscription and migration further reduced total number of possible industrial voters. Natural though it was, this alliance with labour cost Administration dear. Anti-labour feeling had risen to a considerable height. Patriotic indignation at union racketeering and at strikes in war industries, contempt and irritation at the complexities of labour politics, comparisons between industrial worker's wages and those of soldier and farmer, all continually whipped up by predominantly Republican and anti-labour press, produced a powerful urge in many sections of the public to force Administration to put an end to its policy of 'pampering' labour. Farmers too were angered by Administration's labour policy because conscription and rise in industrial wages had produced a farm labour shortage at a time of peak harvest. Meanwhile manufacturers were loudly complaining against forty-hour week and cry had been taken up nationally by press. Outside Administration, labour had few friends. Even Mr Willkie, seeking support wherever available, cautiously abstained from taking up embarrassing cause of American labour.

If support of labour for New Deal was of less value in election than hitherto, that of farmers had been transformed into definite and often bitter opposition. The farmers' vote was not only a large one in total but vital in a number of marginal states which were swung this time into Republican fold. The farmers felt that they had been abandoned by Administration and New Deal and treated much more harshly than labour. Conscription had stripped them of their hired hands but seemed to leave industrial labour much less handicapped. Manpower Commission had failed to solve their problems, tyre rationing had penalized them more severely than urban dwellers and the Baruch report[1] had ended their dreams of an immense new synthetic rubber industry. Their reputation for patriotism had severely suffered in course of great inflation debate and they lost fight over control of farm prices. War Production Board appeared to discriminate against them in holding up their orders for labour-saving machinery. When Administration was not unfriendly to farmers it seemed preoccupied with problems other than theirs. Mr Wallace's eloquence was not a sufficiently consoling antidote to their wounds and they were not in need of old New Deal type of assistance. It was small wonder then that the farmer, traditionally a Republican before 1933, reverted to his former voting habits.

The third great source of New Deal votes had been the forgotten men, but today wartime prosperity has more or less absorbed the earlier victims of economic depression. New victims of wartime dislocation blame party in power for all their ills. Further strong support which New Deal might have expected from young groups of population was offset by their depletion by military mobilization and dislocation due to transfer of labour.

As for Democratic machines they did their best and to them and solid South Administration owes solid backing of Democratic Congressmen which enabled it just to retain its majority.

Mr Roosevelt's continuing popularity was not an issue in election. President's early interventions in Democratic primaries had been unsuccessful and with memory of Wilson's disastrous efforts in 1918, he remained aloof from election and thereby probably avoided losing face.

With no great national issues at stake, strenuous efforts of local Republican organization yielded a bumper harvest, particularly in marginal districts. Each party had a deep cleavage running through it but the Republicans managed temporarily to cover their differences far more effectively than Democrats, whose open splits in such crucial areas as New York, New Jersey, California and Pennsylvania played straight into Republicans' hands. Republicans also received further assistance from fact that there are more outstanding Republican than Democratic Governors. Democrats could not match personalities and promised patronage of Governors Stassen of Minnesota, Bricker[2] of Ohio and Saltonstall[3] of Massachusetts.

Isolationism was not an issue in election. The war as a necessary evil has been soberly accepted and is squarely faced. But it is not a crusade such as we saw in 1917 and average citizen is rarely swept on a wave of patriotic emotion. (That

1 Report prepared for President advocating sweeping changes in US system of rubber production and appointment of a 'rubber czar'.

2 John W. Bricker, Republican Governor of Ohio since 1939.

3 Leverett Saltonstall, Republican Governor of Massachusetts since 1939.

this is case is shown to some extent by repeated arguments of such men as Luce that provision of moral issue is essential and by their not unsuccessful efforts to mobilize as such the idealistic and vague anti-imperialist emotions that are always more or less ready to hand and that are now becoming articulate.) The average citizen rarely therefore bore resentment against pre-Pearl Harbor isolationists as such and all efforts to rouse him to anger against them failed. Pre-war isolationism was to most of voters no crime and in any case domestic policy loomed far larger in people's eyes than considerations of foreign policy, both in present and in post-war period. While a seam of isolationism is clearly visible in ranks of Republicans returned, no wave of isolationism, nor indeed any other kind of wave, is perceptible. On the other hand the successful candidates, while they are obviously not isolationists today, come from circles which have not shown any interest in foreign affairs and to that extent they are nearly all potential isolationists to-morrow. . . .

Despite appearances Willkie has failed to make any substantial inroads into Republican machine which remains essentially nationalistic. This does not augur too well for an enlightened post-war policy on part of Republican Party.

Elections have made clear nature of split inside both major parties. Democrats are split principally on internal policy – New Dealers versus conservative Democrats; Republicans are split on foreign policy – Willkie and Luce versus Joe Martin, the retiring chairman of Republican National Committee, and the majority of national organization. Despite all cross-currents this is the fundamental pattern. In election anti-Administration group won in each case. Balance of power in new Congress lies with old-fashioned Republicans on one side and combination of Southern Democrats and Mr Farley's anti-Rooseveltites of industrial North on the other. New Deal must therefore lean for its power not on Congress but on patronage and power of an Administration in office.

At moment Southern Democrats are in a peculiar position. Their adherence to Democratic Party has been largely dependent upon tacit understanding that they will remain masters in their own states. With increase of federal interference and gradual industrialization of the South, accelerated by war, this privilege is seriously threatened, and if in the course of current debates in Congress poll tax, which is foundation upon which absolute rule of Southern Democrats rests, is abrogated by Congress at instigation of Administration, bonds which tie South to Mr Roosevelt's cause may snap, and Southerners may find themselves in position of an 'Irish Party'.[4] They will then be tempted to exploit to the full their present position in Congress. Republicans are certainly aware of possibility of such an anti-Roosevelt alliance, particularly over internal issues. Once detached in this way from Democratic Party, Southern Democrats, at present solidly interventionist and pro-Roosevelt, may veer unpredictably even in their foreign policy.

4 The Irish Nationalist Party which operated throughout most of nineteenth century, after 1870 in loose alliance with British Liberal Party.

In view of above factors it is fairly probable that new Congress will attempt to reassert itself vigorously in following directions:

(a) by attempting to impose restrictions on labour ;
(b) by seeking reductions in domestic expenditure – expenditure for farmers, however, will not be attacked because Farm Bloc, always strongest bloc in Congress, has emerged from elections stronger than ever despite press campaigns against it ;
(c) by systematic committee investigation of conduct of war ;
(d) by an attempt to reorganize Congress in such a way as to increase Republican strength under cover of overdue 'parliamentary' reforms ; and finally
(e) by a determined effort to assert control of Congress over, or at least closer association of Congress with, the conduct both of war and coming peace and foreign policy in general.

While this last might not be wholly disadvantageous, this general atmosphere alarms the most capable and energetic of New Dealers such as Milo Perkins and Leon Henderson. They are thoroughly aware of combination of forces arrayed against them. A none-too-friendly Congress unlikely to be easily controlled by Administration has now been added to other great anti-New Deal factions, namely the press, nine-tenths of which have been consistently hostile to New Deal for last half-dozen years, the military authorities in Washington and big business administrators in supply agencies. Both of last two are alleged to be doing everything in their power both individually and in combination with each other to bypass New Deal administrators and agencies. Some New Dealers attempt to see in this combination of big business with army authorities, taken together with present campaign to reassert principles of free individualism and private enterprise, a sinister conspiracy to wrest power from their progressive hands and turn back clock to Republican idyll of Coolidge[5] and Harding with a pinch of fear of Fascism thrown in to taste. Despite congressional losses the leaders of New Deal are in no mood to compromise and will certainly advise President accordingly. President may be expected, as always, to compromise. In speaking of New Deal we should remember that country as a whole may be said to endorse its general objective (abolition of privilege and abusive exploitation of public, improvement of underdog's lot) and to have swallowed its broad achievements. Dislike for New Deal is, I think, now directed mainly against theoretical 'intellectual' planning and its exponents.

A conservative reaction against experimentation in domestic and foreign policy dates back to 1938. In 1940 it was checked by imminent approach of war. It is now beginning to show its head again. At moment a large part of American sentiment seems unwilling to be committed to endorsement for this country of

5 Calvin Coolidge (1872–1933), president from 1923 to 1928, associated with heyday of Republican individualism.

degree of social planning which is apparently winning some favour with British and European thought.

What light, if any, do elections throw upon presidential election of 1944 ? It would be futile to attempt any prediction on an event which is subject to so many unknown factors, unrelated to recent election. This much may however be hazarded. A fourth term for Roosevelt seems likely only if (1) he is swept into power on crest of a wave of victory ; (2) if a particularly ineffective candidate of Landon or Taft type wins Republican nomination ; (3) if Republican Party develops a frankly reactionary obstructionist policy in next two years.

Is it likely that tragedy of 1919 will repeat itself ? If victory occurs before 1944 we can assume that Mr Roosevelt will lead his forces with infinitely greater political skill, though less compelling moral force, than Mr Wilson. Moreover no isolationist figures comparable in national stature to Borah[6] and Lodge[7] are yet perceptible. The most influential isolationist Senators are aged Hiram Johnson[8] of California, Vandenberg of Michigan, and Taft of Ohio. Senator Wheeler, though he is at present under a cloud, is, with his personal popularity and parliamentary skill, still a force to be reckoned with. Certainly the isolationist tradition must be expected to reassert itself to a degree that cannot now be measured. As against it may be set perhaps a growing recognition that for United States to get into one war may have been bad luck but to have got into two looks like something wrong with system. Both isolation and the League of Nations appear to have failed. Will their failure be powerful enough to lead American opinion to a recognition of necessity of what appears the only other alternative ? It may.

The personnel of new Congress is somewhat less friendly to Britain than its predecessor. They may be expected to echo current criticism of our policy in India and be affected by anti-imperialist cry. While as regards post-war schemes much lip service is paid to international co-operation, there is considerable suspicion of achieving this by too close or rather, perhaps, too exclusive Anglo-American partnership. Hence volume of talk about importance of developing a United Nations outlook which is also reinforced by real necessity of not ignoring or appearing to ignore China and Russia. But there are few signs that any concrete machinery for realizing idea of United Nations is taking definite shape in public opinion. Many of those who advocate idea would hesitate to see a closer link with USSR, while beyond lip service to United Nations idea little attention is paid to claims of smaller nations. There is undoubtedly a wide expectation that effect of war will be greatly to increase United States influence in world and some dream of a vague federal world-wide scheme. Traditional resistance to

6 William E. Borah (1865–1940). Republican Senator from Nevada (1907–40) whose advocacy of isolationism stretched back to his role in 1919 as an 'Irreconcilable' opposing US entry to the League of Nations.

7 Henry Cabot Lodge (1850–1920), Republican Senator from Massachusetts (1893–1920), who led the Senate fight against ratification of the Treaty of Versailles.

8 Hiram Johnson, 1866–1945. Republican Senator from California since 1917.

European commitments is intensified in Congress by contention, frequently advanced in congressional circles, that President's attention is centred on Europe to detriment of Pacific, and in particular that he is too tender to interests of that feudal institution, the British Empire. New Congress is very far from being Russophile. In some circles fear is entertained that if Britain appears arm in arm with Russia at peace table, she may prove a formidable negotiator.

Despite undoubted presence and strength in present Congress of many obscurantist forces, isolationism, hatred or suspicion of Britain, of Russia, and above all of New Deal and Roosevelt, it cannot be emphasized too strongly that opinion is still fluid, that no crystallization has occurred within either of major parties. A repetition of disaster of 1919 cannot yet be called likely even if we must never dismiss from our minds possibility that extant forces with similar potentialities, though of rather different character and strength, may develop. A voice speaking with national authority, whether British or American, can still provide a focal point round which scattered forces of present will crystallize. The elections have demonstrated that there is no single great wave of national sentiment flowing in any direction. It is most important that by our dealings both with public opinion and with the Government we should continue to exert such influence as we may upon direction in which sentiment will flow.

I do not recommend or see any need for any revision of our present policy.

21 November 1942

Encouraged by results of the election, forces opposed to Administration both in and out of Congress are asserting themselves strongly in many fields.

(a) The House Ways and Means Committee have rejected a request by President for broad powers to suspend in time of war federal statutes affecting movement of war goods, information and persons into or out of the United States. The Committee will now draw up a substitute measure with more specific and restricted authority. This is first setback for Administration after election and may be expected not to be the last. The opponents of Administration claim that election showed will of people to be opposed to giving unlimited powers to President such as those envisaged by new War Powers bill. The setback is however thought by Department of Justice to be more apparent than real as Committee is preparing with assistance of Department of Justice their own bill to accomplish objects President had in view.

(b) The Farm Bloc shows signs of attempting to reopen their opposition to Administration policy of keeping down farm prices. National Grange[1] Convention this week asked Congress to order a thorough-going research to determine not merely a better parity formula but just what is farm population's fair share of national income.

1 Fraternal organization of farmers, especially strong in the North East, generally conservative in policies.

(c) Administration's extension of gasoline rationing to whole nation is now being opposed in Congress, and Oklahoma delegation in House claim support of more than a hundred Representatives for a resolution to postpone coast-to-coast rationing (now due on 1 December) for ninety days in hope that such a postponement would prove definitely that rationing is not necessary in West.

(d) Encouraged by strength of their position as controllers of a balance of power in new Congress, the Senators from solid South this week swung into a filibuster in opposition to the Administration-supported anti-poll tax bill. The stakes in the struggle are now quite different from the comparatively straightforward question as to whether a poll tax should be exacted from those wishing to vote in the Federal elections or the question of the constitutionality of Congress intervening in a matter which the Southern Senators regard as a State and not a Federal prerogative. The Administration has been endeavouring to force bill to a vote and has thus been brought into open conflict with Southern Senators at a time when their support is becoming most vital to it as a result of Democratic casualties in elections outside the South. Some suggest that feeling being aroused by filibuster makes even more likely a voting coalition between Republicans and Southern conservative Democrats. Republicans are sympathetic to principles of anti-poll tax bill and anxious to court Negroes in Illinois, New York and other states where their vote sometimes provides balance of power. They are however pleased at embarrassing situation in which Administration finds itself and anxious not to alienate Southern Senators whose votes they are likely to need in opposing Administration's domestic programme. The majority leader, Senator Barkley, has come under rather heavy fire as a result of his endeavours to break down filibuster. He is charged with being more subservient to White House than to majority which he leads. There is a move afoot to get members of Democratic majority in Senate to settle disputes over legislation in next Congress in party caucuses rather than through offices of Senator Barkley who now acts as White House go-between. It is also rumoured that Barkley may be chosen to fill Byrnes's vacancy on Supreme Court.

(e) An active movement against a Roosevelt fourth term is beginning to be discussed and Roosevelt has been urged openly to renounce a fourth term. New Dealers are of course reported to be advising President that if war is still going on in 1944 he must continue as chief director of United Nations war effort, and if war has ended his must be chief instrumentality in making a peace based upon the Four Freedoms. The anti-New Deal Democrats however claim that mid-term elections have effectively disposed of a fourth term and they can be relied on to attempt to block the President's candidacy in Democratic National Convention in 1944 in same way as they attempted to block a third term in 1940.

Discussion of party politics now centres round meeting of Republican National Committee in St Louis on 7 December. The main issue will be appointment of a Chairman to succeed Joseph W. Martin. Candidate most frequently mentioned has been Werner W. Schroeder, the National Committeeman in Illinois. He is an isolationist of extreme type, a friend of Colonel McCormick of *Chicago Tribune,* and is reported also to have the support of Herbert Hoover and Senator Taft. Schroeder's appointment is being bitterly opposed by sections of Republican Party opposed to isolationism, outstanding amongst whom are Governor Stassen of Minnesota and Willkieites. Willkie is reported to be prepared to go to St Louis if necessary to oppose Schroeder's appointment. . . .

. . . I had a long conversation with Mr Willkie on 17 November which may have done something to clear the air. He is certainly not anti-British and his latest speech to a British War Relief meeting in New York on 20 November was intended as an olive branch. Relations between Willkie and President are reported to be increasingly strained and even bitter partly because of Willkie's continual interference in matters of foreign policy, a field in which prior to Willkie's grand tour his agreement with the President had always been emphasized. Willkie's references to Vichy France situation in North Africa and to Darlan[2] in above-mentioned speech were toned down as a result of Colonel Stimson's direct intervention. In original draft he referred to American leaders as imposing on French people the very man who helped to enslave them and to the Government's long appeasement of Vichy as finding a logical conclusion in collaboration with Darlan, Hitler's tool. This was later eliminated and passage criticizing in retrospect the State Department's appeasement of Vichy was substituted. Willkie holds that censorship and holding up of his speech before transmission abroad until after President had issued his own statement on Darlan was a personal affront to himself as an individual and he is at present campaigning for freedom of criticism of American Government's policy and freedom of international discussion affecting after-the-war future. Most of all Willkie resents directive to foreign newspaper correspondents requiring that if they sent his speech it must be accompanied by an interpretation denying that it was intended to apply to North African situation. He is also very sensitive to criticism and went so far as to complain to Walter Lippmann that he, Lippmann, was a British propagandist.

The reactions to agreement with Darlan have been dealt with in my telegram No. 5621. Since that time the President's clarification of the situation appears to have satisfied majority of press but a minority still argue that it is never wise to sacrifice principle and that useful as arrangements may be from military standpoint, they nevertheless constitute a threat to Allied morale and political prestige. Some are pointing to rumpus created by appointment of Darlan as a sample of kind of problems that will have to be faced when nation after nation is in course of liberation from Nazi tyranny.

2 When US forces landed in North Africa Admiral Jean François Darlan, Commander-in-Chief of the French Forces, aligned himself with them and instructed all Frenchmen to co-operate with Eisenhower. In return he was recognized as French High Commissioner in North Africa. When this arrangement was criticized as signifying collaboration with Vichy, where Darlan had been Foreign Minister, Roosevelt on 17 November described it as a 'temporary expedient justified solely by the stress of battle'.

29 November 1942

. . .

United States censorship of messages going from United States, especially to Britain, is at present coming in for criticism from all sides. Present censorship policy goes far beyond field of military information. For example, news held back from Britain recently includes references to poll tax filibuster, strikes, industrial shortcomings, criticism of British policy in India, of the Administration and of State Department's policy.

The usual isolationist opponents of Administration attack censorship on grounds that foreign countries are not allowed to hear criticism of New Deal or of the Administration or of conduct of war on American home front.

Liberal circles object strongly to censorship of poll tax filibuster and are also incensed by operation of censorship preventing British people learning of criticism in United States of British policy in India. Their latter objection is not purely academic as both liberals and Willkie internationalists would obviously like to exercise strong pressure on British Government to revise their policy in India by alarming British people as to anti-British sentiment in United States. Some liberals make no secret of fact that they must act now on India for if war continues to move favourably for our side, American people will lose its present interest in India.

Middle-of-the-roaders, including some of our friends, express alarm at long-term evils which are likely to result from people of each country not knowing what is being said in other's about political aspects of war and argue that United States and Britain would have a greater opportunity of coming to an understanding if there were a free interchange of ideas.

8 December 1942

. . .

Congress shows signs of an increasing tendency to assert itself against the executive as though to indicate that even more opposition may be expected from the new Congress when it assembles in January. Thus for example the recent passage of an Administration measure involving concessions to the Republic of Panama [1] was hotly opposed by a group of Senators led by Hiram Johnson and Nye on ground that such a step required a formal treaty and consequently ratification by two-thirds of the Senate. The suspicion was openly expressed that the measure was a *ballon d'essai* floated by the Administration – that if it was allowed to pass the Roosevelt Government might, by the use of executive orders,

---

1 The Panama Resolution was an attempt to settle by a $10 million payment several longstanding issues between Panama and the USA and to express appreciation of Panama's making available some hundred military sites without charge.

120

end by arranging the terms of peace at end of war without submitting them to Congress for ratification. The Panama Resolution was voted with a majority of less than two-thirds of the Senate, which the anti-Rooseveltites claimed as a significant fact and a token of growing intention on part of Congress to insist on its due share in respect of foreign policy. The President's request to suspend tariff and immigration restrictions has been similarly attacked in Congress because it would increase President's powers, and that in respect of two matters about which there are strong feelings in certain sections of the legislature. The bill has been pushed through the House Ways and Means Committee but has some way to go before it is passed. If it is left to the next Congress to deal with, its chances like those of some other Administration measures are considerably lessened. Anti-New Deal opposition is growing inside and outside Congress. Thus the farm parity price bill successfully opposed by Administration last September has unexpectedly been revived by a Southern Democrat and quickly passed by the House. It includes farm labour costs in the parity formula, without which, it is claimed, farm wages cannot be brought into line with higher industrial wages and the drift of farm labour to towns checked. President may try to veto the bill in which case an attempt to override the veto will certainly be made in present mood of Congress which is likely to continue into the next session. New Dealers, fearing that a crisis in their affairs has arrived, are unhappy and predict a growing wave of isolationism. They point out that most of the candidates for the Chairmanship of the Republican National Committee not only did not feel it necessary to denounce isolationism but for the most part went to some trouble to clear themselves of charge of intervention before Pearl Harbor. They deplore the failure of Willkie's campaign inside the party and while benevolent to Willkie's liberal internationalism maintain that the great success of his recent pronouncements in the Middle West was due to the stimulus they gave, however unintentionally, to Anglophobe isolationism. The tougher New Dealers believe that attack pays better than defence ; thus Leon Henderson informed the 4,000 industrialists at the War Congress called together by the Anti-New Deal National Association of Manufacturers (NAM) that American people must be prepared for more control and restrictions, more bureaucracy and rationing, more regimentation, before victory can be achieved. This was naturally not too well received by his audience. Henderson's stock, which has been very high, is slowly declining largely because of the poor publicity of his Department. His words today have little more national appeal than Mr Nelson's speeches.

Henry Kaiser, West Coast shipbuilder, has tried to make political capital for himself by proposals about the automobile industry made at same NAM Congress. Though his ideas have been criticized, Kaiser enjoys a position which could not be left out of account if he gave proof of political ambitions. He is certainly the most spectacular spokesman of American business against the New Deal that has so far emerged.

. . .

Beveridge report[2] has received a friendly and at times an enthusiastic reception in national press and has been presented as a very big news story across country. Criticism of Britain has not recently taken the form of fear that it may be drifting too far to left. Willkie's speeches, Indian situation, transfer of Sir S. Cripps[3] and interpretations of Prime Minister's 'Hold on to our own'[4] speech have tended to revive picture of Britain as a stronghold of reactionary imperialism and Beveridge report has been widely greeted as at any rate a partial refutation of that. Liberal press as well as most London despatches somewhat diluted this impression by qualifying praise of report with acid predictions that Tory majority in Parliament will never allow so enlightened a piece of legislation to pass. It must be remembered that many middle-of-road Americans wish to see more liberalism in Britain which in general they imagine to be far more backward than in their own country. Hence general approval of Beveridge report which is regarded as a great blow struck for social progress against heavily entrenched *ancien régime*. At fringes, attitudes vary as might be expected. Stern individualists review scheme as yet another step by starry-eyed idealists to replace personal liberty with inefficient state despotism. New Dealers on other hand are apt to talk as if they were mildly jealous of having their limelight stolen by British of all people and their praise of report is somewhat tinged with surprise. Progress of report will be jealously watched from this side of ocean and any real or alleged steps to whittle it down will be chalked up against us by liberals and anti-British conservatives alike as typical British surrender to 'ruling class'. Fact that so much trouble had been taken by German propaganda to minimize report was played up prominently by press.

The Washington struggles for manpower and procurement control have been at any rate temporarily resolved by appointment of McNutt as sole authority over manpower (which transfers Selective Service from army to his office and increases his powers over industry considerably) and by a compromise between Nelson and General Somervell. Latter was reported by isolationist press, which supports Somervell, as a triumph for Nelson, by the pro-Administration press, which dislikes army control, as a triumph for Somervell, and by cautious *New York Times* as a typical Roosevelt compromise. Thus each section of press is preparing ground upon which it will blame its own particular scapegoat if arrangement, which looks precarious, fails to work. Meanwhile McNutt, who is regarded as a possible Democratic candidate for Presidency in 1944, has been given a task which may politically make or break him. Secretary of Interior Ickes, who is said to have turned down Labor Secretaryship, has had his powers over oil industry extended. His efficient management of this task has

2 Report of committee headed by Sir William Beveridge recommending sweeping extension of British system of social security.

3 From post of Leader of House of Commons to Minister of Aircraft Production.

4 Mansion House speech, 10 November : 'I have not become His Majesty's First Minister in order to preside over the liquidation of the British Empire.'

converted him from being a political liability into an asset to Administration.

Scope and frontiers of Lehman's new powers as Relief and Rehabilitation Administrator is not clear to anyone yet, certainly not to himself. He is known to be wondering, as are others, what his precise relation is likely to be to Paul Appleby,[5] Under-Secretary of Agriculture, and fervent Wallace-ite in his appointment to 'Office of Foreign Territories' in State Department. But Lehman spoke to me this afternoon in warm terms of Appleby. Selection of Lehman has been well received as he is a man of known moderation, integrity and competence. President in appointing him was heard to remark 'I want to see some of those Goddamned Fascists begging for their subsistence from a Jew'. Transfer of Appleby is probably a further stage in process by which Mr Welles has been securing for State Department the direction of all activities touching foreign policy and post-war problems which was at one time threatened by various New Deal agencies.

The entrenchment of Darlan, his public appearance with Eisenhower, Mr Stimson's letter to Austrian Pretender Otto[6] accepting his help in recruiting for an Austrian unit in United States Army and other alleged straws in wind, have increased despondency and alarm in liberal circles and Austrian issue has naturally stirred up strong feeling among anti-Habsburg Central European minority groups and among liberal Austrians. State Department privately disclaim all responsibility for this move which they attribute to White House and War Department. The War Department equally privately maintain that they acted with full knowledge and encouragement of State Department. Rumour that Felix Frankfurter[7] had interceded for Otto with President is indignantly disclaimed by Justice. He declares that he neither knew of nor took interest in arrangement and proposes to protest to Mr Hull formally against propagation of this rumour by a high official of latter's Department. Under-Secretary McCloy[8] of War Department told a member of my staff that Frankfurter is not involved and that initiative came from White House. So far as public opinion is concerned, while support of Darlan is generally approved by man in street and by majority of press as a necessary move with immediate dividends, Austrian issue has made little impression beyond attacks in liberal press. There is talk of Myron Taylor as having initiated it at instigation of Vatican and members of American Catholic hierarchy.

Republican politics. The struggle between Willkie forces and Old Guard within Republican Party referred to in previous summaries has resulted in election of a

---

5 Paul H. Appleby, Executive Assistant, Department of Agriculture, 1933–40 ; Under-Secretary since 1940.

6 Otto de Bourbon Habsburg (1912–54), son of Charles I. Refugee in USA after fall of France.

7 Felix Frankfurter, Supreme Court Justice, 1939–62, and friend of Franklin Roosevelt.

8 John Jay McCloy, New York lawyer who joined War Department in 1940 as special consultant to Stimson and became Assistant Secretary in April 1941.

compromise candidate as chairman. . . . Spangler[9] is sixty-two-years old, an Old Guard veteran party man of Hoover and Coolidge type. On matters of foreign policy he has not been an isolationist and is sometimes identified with moderate internationalists. He is a rabid anti-New Dealer and declared about New Deal on election, 'I have been after that animal since 1932 and I hope that in 1944 I can be there at the kill.'

13 December 1942

The 77th Congress may adjourn next week. Last week saw a continuation of the guerrilla warfare against the Administration which has been conducted in the Congress since the election and which foreshadows the major offensive which is likely to be conducted by the anti-New Deal and anti-Administration forces in the new Congress.

On balance the Administration came off second best in the week's struggles, e.g. suffering a major congressional defeat when the House Ways and Means Committee buried the Administration's bill to increase the President's power over tariffs, immigration, etc. In the Senate the Judiciary Committee gave some very rough handling to a bill adopted by the House to entitle the Office of Censorship to inspect communications between the United States and its territories and possessions, e.g. between Seattle and Alaska. Senator McCarran[1] of Nevada, a member of the Senatorial silver bloc, carried on a one-man filibuster against a measure covering the release of government stocks of silver to war industries. This is the third filibuster since the election and the fact that it provoked relatively little indignation anywhere is a symptom of the anti-Administration mood in Congress and of its renewed self-confidence, partly due to the fact that the isolationist press, satisfied with Republican victories, has abandoned its campaign to ridicule Congress. So paradoxically enough, an incidental result of the filibuster and general obstructionist mood of anti-Administration Congressmen has been the stalling of the bill sponsored by the Farm Bloc which Administration leaders were not certain that they could stop. This bill was designed to include the cost of farm labour in the maximum price fixed on farm products and thus would have revived the inflation battle of early autumn.

The Republican members of the Senate Banking Committee have launched an attack on the Board of Economic Warfare identified by conservatives with the New Deal. Behind this is the old struggle of Jesse Jones of the RFC,[2] a bellicose old dealer, and Henry Wallace and Milo Perkins of the BEW.[3] The RFC once exercised veto power over the BEW and was stripped of the authority by the President last spring because Jones was held to have failed to speed up the pur-

9 Harrison E. Spangler, from Iowa.
1 Patrick A. McCarran, Democratic Senator from Nevada since 1933.
2 Reconstruction Finance Corporation.
3 Board of Economic Warfare.

chases of critical materials on the scale required. Wallace and Perkins succeeded in persuading the Senate Committee in a secret conference that the BEW was doing 'what', in Chairman Danaher's[4] words, 'most of us want done'. This, although a defeat for Jesse Jones, may be counted as a round won by the New Deal.

With the addition to Jeffers and Byrnes of McNutt, Wickard and Ickes as 'Czars' of manpower, food and petroleum respectively the Administration is now approaching to the position of having a potential shadow cabinet to guide the war effort on the home front which only partly overlaps with the official cabinet.

As the 'Czars' require no senatorial confirmation and do not constitutionally function as a single body, they represent a development of the purely personal powers of the President who continues to be criticized in the press and political circles for failing to provide any regular machinery for settling their boundary disputes. No concessions have been made to the Republicans regarding representation in this group of administrators and anti-New Deal Democrats and Republicans point out bitterly that the membership is still largely confined to old New Dealers, in spite of the admission of Messrs Nelson, Byrnes, McNutt and Jeffers to this group.

Some of those who attended the Republican meeting which elected Harrison E. Spangler as its party Chairman in St Louis give some interesting forecasts of future Republican policy. As to these forecasts it would be a grave error to assume that because Schroeder was successfully eliminated by Willkie the party machine has ceased to be largely isolationist or that Willkie success has given an internationalist swing to the party. The Republican platform will most probably continue to be dominated by a desire to preserve party harmony by taking no precise or detailed stand on any major foreign issue. The campaign will be doubtless principally aimed against the New Deal, the President and the Administration and will then, the party managers hope, accumulate the required majority of votes without the need for formulating any positive policy on any issue in dispute among Republicans, the chief of which is foreign policy. This would not suit Willkie and even middle-of-the-road Republicans might revolt against it.

A similar split between old- and new-guard Democrats seems likely to occur in the election of a party Chairman to replace Ed Flynn, probably sometime in January. Mr Farley has not been idle among the local political machines and his strength is held to have grown despite his defeat in New York State.

. . .

20 December 1942

The next Congress due 6 January is expected to witness a serious struggle for power with the President over both foreign affairs and the many issues left un-

4 John A. Danaher, Republican Senator from Connecticut since 1939.

decided by the previous Congress, such as agricultural prices and the increase in the President's powers. It would seem that the Republicans will, in order to preserve internal harmony, confine themselves to whittling tactics avoiding major issues.

A major showdown might be labelled by the Administration as obstruction of the war effort and would widen the gap which divides Willkie and Stassen from the solid semi-isolationist centre. Spangler, the new Chairman of the Party Central Office, has promised co-operation in the war effort but opposition on purely internal issues such as a fourth term and government expenditure. Spangler is a colourless party organizer, a faithful henchman of Governor Bricker of Ohio (the present Republican favourite in the presidential race), and like the latter is ignorant of foreign affairs. He is supposed to have remarked that 'there wouldn't be many votes to be won in Russia or Tibet'. He was elected as a pure stopgap. The fight between Bricker and Willkie for control of the party is still to be fought out. As foreign policy is to be played down by the Republicans, their most notorious isolationist Congressman, Hamilton Fish, was induced to resign from the Foreign Affairs Committee of the House and transfer his activities to the very important Rules Committee, where he remains an obstructionist force in reserve to be used only as a necessary expedient in internal policies. Congressional foreign policy is moulded rather in the Senate than in the House and as a leader of diehard Anglophobe isolationists Senator Brooks of Illinois is a far more formidable and intelligent figure than Fish could ever be. Willkie is delighted by his negative victory in eliminating Schroeder, at any rate for the moment, since this gives him and his followers a new weight in Republican counsels after a period of relative decline. He continues to be closely advised by Joseph Barnes [1] of OWI, originally foreign editor of the *New York Herald Tribune,* who accompanied him on his recent journey and who has for some time held strong pro-Russian and anti-imperialist views. Barnes is at present the chief link between Wallace and Willkie, who do not meet directly but are closer to each other with regard to foreign policy than is generally imagined. Wallace, as would some other members of the Administration, uses language in private about India and colonial problems which is not far from Willkie and about which I myself had the opportunity of discussion with him last night. He however condemns Willkie's public treatment. . . .

The average American continues to accept the present North African regime and criticism is confined largely to liberals in the press and government and a handful of officials. A member of my staff was told by a reliable source that there is a tendency on the part of at any rate Mr Berle to preserve divided authority among the French until the day when the United States is prepared to mould France and its possessions into whatever pattern seems desirable at the time and that the present distribution of power between Darlan, de Gaulle, Rob-

1 Joseph Barnes, on staff of *New York Herald Tribune* 1935–41.

ert, etc., while not deliberately designed by the State Department, meets its desire to prevent crystallization of French round any one individual or party until the time is ripe, i.e. until the United States Government or the United Nations have formulated a definite policy. This is borne out by Mr Berle's remark to His Majesty's Minister that he thought the Darlan arrangement should be left undisturbed until the United Nations were ready to invade France. A vigorous defence of Eisenhower's arrangements with Darlan has been voiced by the isolationist Senator Vandenberg. Willkie replied with a warning that more American lives may be lost as a result of the weakening of the internal resistance in Nazi-occupied lands produced by the pact with Darlan. General Sikorski[2] has attempted to support moderate counsels by praising de Gaulle and defending the arrangement, while expressing the hope that all elements opposed to Axis may work together. The President made his views clearly known by personally publishing Darlan's promise to retire after France is reconquered, and Mr Hull conferred with the Fighting French and repeated that by the rules of the Atlantic Charter no attempt was being made to foist Darlan upon a France which will not have been consulted, and urged unity upon all anti-Axis groups. Most of the press defends Eisenhower's step as a military necessity. Willkie's opposition is echoed outside the liberal press only in the *New York Herald Tribune*. A few papers express resentment at British criticism of an American military move.

I am told that Leon Henderson has resigned from the OPA largely because he felt that his own unpopularity with Congress and the people jeopardized the future of his organization unless the President was prepared to fight his battle in the teeth of popular sentiment. The President was evidently not ready to do this and he will probably be succeeded by Prentiss Brown, ex-Senator from Michigan, whose fight against the Farm Bloc is said to have cost him his seat. Brown is more conciliatory and an altogether smaller figure than imperious and formidable Henderson of whom the last has probably not been heard. The defeat of this great champion of the New Deal is much deplored by his colleagues, notably Mr Byrnes, but the New Deal has scored this week in the victory which the Board of Economic Warfare claims over Jesse Jones's RFC and his friends in the Senate.

.   .   .

27 December 1942

.   .   .

Republicans are naturally pressing for greatly increased representation in congressional committees. They threaten to combine with considerable number of anti-New Deal Southern Democrats in support of

(a) Farm Bloc which having swept Henderson away feels in aggressive mood. In fact wealth and real income of farmers is far higher today than during

2 Wladyslaw Sikorski, Polish Prime Minister in exile and Commander-in-Chief, on a visit to the United States.

halcyon days of United States agriculture from 1910 to 1914, but this fact has received scarcely any publicity.

(b) Restrictive labour legislation in Congress outlawing strikes in war industries, abolition of forty-hour week and compulsion of unions to disclose their accounts to public authority, and reconstitution and toughening of War Labor Board. . . .

(c) A drastic curtailment of 'bureaucracy', which is opposition's name for Administration and their expenditures, and increase of . . . congressional as against New Deal patronage. By abolishing Works Progress Administration,[1] perhaps greatest symbol of New Deal, President has done something to placate his critics. Southern Democrats are in a fighting mood but if patronage is redistributed in their favour (negotiations are proceeding on this subject within Democratic Party) this feeling will be considerably abated. Postmaster General Walker[2] is rumoured to be about to accept chairmanship of Democratic National Committee. According to a New Deal informant, Joseph Kennedy's[3] offer of his services in that capacity was summarily rejected.

There is a very noticeable increase in discussion of post-war plans both in and out of press, certain definite trends having emerged this week. McNary, Republican leader in Senate, defined his party's aims as a vigorous protection of American economic position, defence of American standard of life and of American trade. He declared that time had arrived for discussing post-war plans and that while everything should be done to preserve international security and co-operation it was policy of his party to prevent squandering of American resources abroad. McNary, perhaps most popular Republican in Congress and an amiable and exceptionally shrewd and experienced politician, evidently feels this to be right moment to pour cold water upon internationalist eloquence of both Willkie and Wallace. . . . New Dealers feel none too optimistic about their own political future. Secretary of Interior Ickes is reported to have said that 'New Deal was beat', only two true New Dealers survived, himself and President, while forces of darkness were gaining so fast that he proposed to send his own children to be educated in more liberal atmosphere of England.

A further knock at New Deal was given when Igor Cassini, of bastard Russian and Italian origin and a venomous society columnist of isolationist *Times Herald*, printed a violent attack on a Lucullan party given by Baruch as a wedding present for the Harry Hopkinses. Dinner consisting of innumerable costly dishes with champagne, French perfume for ladies, was attended by many prominent New Dealers who at same time could be quoted as having urged public to tighten its belt. They have as a result been castigated as a privileged praetorian guard. As a counter-measure nationwide publicity was given to Baruch's million dollar

1 Or WPA. Set up in 1933 to provide employment through public works.
2 Frank C. Walker, Postmaster General since 1940.
3 Joseph P. Kennedy, US Ambassador to the United Kingdom 1937–41.

contribution to a number of charities including British, Russian and Chinese relief.

Other items of interest are (a) signing of a new commercial agreement with Mexico which has been well received by press ; (b) announcement by Elmer Davis of a British Division of OWI under Ferdinand Kuhn,[4] late *New York Times* correspondent in London, which indicates a growing appreciation of necessity of explaining America and combating anti-American sentiment in Britain, evidence of which is beginning to penetrate into this country.

4 Ferdinand Kuhn Jr, on *New York Times* since 1925, chief London correspondent 1939–40.

1943

Assassination of Darlan[1] has dominated discussion in public and private. News of his death was greeted in some Administration circles, though not by general public, with genuine gloom, based on belief that Eisenhower and Murphy[2] had come to look on Darlan as being both loyal and indispensable and had decided to back him against the intrigues of Noguès[3] and Boisson.[4] They privately expressed fears that the uncompromised but more passive Giraud[5] would fail to control the very difficult situation. Public criticism of State Department's policy led by Lippmann has abated somewhat, while columnists who act as mouthpieces of the Department stressed Darlan's loyalty to the United States and echoed the President's sharp condemnation of the assassination and Stimson's praise of the Admiral's wisdom and loyalty. . . . Report current at present that Giraud is prepared to offer de Gaulle a military but not a political appointment has therefore met with much approval in political circles. Chautemps's[6] call for unity has not cut much ice. There is a definite feeling in Administration circles that in some quarters in Great Britain there is a desire to see established in North Africa something more like a French Government, however provisional it might be termed, than these circles would favour. . . .

Wallace's speech of 28 December[7] has so far excited less comment and more general approval than his previous addresses. He amplified this speech in a radio debate where he advocated an international air force, an international authority for world projects and a maintenance of Hull's reciprocal trade programme (which individual Congressmen have announced will not be renewed when matter comes before Congress in June). In the speech he delivered on Wilson's birthday he vied with Welles in enthusiastic praise of Wilson whom the people of the United States had failed. In radio discussion he pointed lesson by warning of World War III which was at present being planned by German staff and which only economic justice and international co-operation could prevent. Wallace is plainly concerned to allay anxieties of those who regard him as a dangerous visionary and with this in view offered an alliance to progressive industrial and

1 In Algiers on 24 December.

2 Robert D. Murphy, career diplomat, Roosevelt's personal representative with rank of Minister to French North Africa.

3 Auguste P. Noguès, French Resident-General in Morocco.

4 Pierre Boisson, Governor of French West Africa.

5 General Henri Giraud, French High Commissioner, North Africa, in succession to Darlan.

6 Camille Chautemps, Vichy Vice-Premier in North Africa.

7 A broadcast on post-war policy of USA and United Nations.

business leaders (he did not mention Kaiser but was widely interpreted to mean him) whose aid Wallace's *alter ego,* Milo Perkins, has always regarded as indispensable to social and economic schemes with which his and Wallace's names are associated. Both sides – the New Deal and its opponents – are busily gathering forces and making alliances in preparation for the struggle, whose violence result of last election and its interpretation by Republican Party seems to have made inevitable. Mr Wallace has clearly made a tactical retreat, possibly to bid for support of progressive Republicans against nationalists and isolationists in both major parties. The gap between him and Willkie is fast growing narrower. New Dealers are divided in their opinion of the speech. The left wing condemns it as spiritless and 'appeasement minded'. The moderates find in it evidence of consummate tactical skill and point with satisfaction to the generally favourable reception which it has had at the hands of all but the most conservative elements in the country.

A major offensive is to be expected in Congress over next Lend-Lease appropriation bill and Stettinius[8] rightly anticipates troubles. Senator Butler[9] has formally given notice of his intention to call for an inquiry into the operations of Lend-Lease agency and is encouraged by Wheeler and Capper. Although the American public believes that principal purpose of Lease-Lend is to arm and equip its Allies, at back of its mind there is a suspicion, still sedulously fomented by isolationists and other Anglophobes, that the British abuse such funds by diverting them to promote their foreign trade and to other similar purposes. One line of attack is likely to be that the United States supplies us with food under Lease-Lend out of which the British Government make money by resale. President is not likely to retreat on this particular front even if it entails withdrawal by his forces elsewhere. If Congress proves contumacious he may well attack in his turn and fix responsibility for consequences of any defeats of Administration squarely upon Congress itself. The attempt, which McNary swiftly crushed, to oust Austin of Vermont, of the powerful Senate Foreign Relations Committee, from his position as Deputy Leader of Republican Party in Senate, on ground of excessive 'internationalism' should not be overlooked. Senator Austin is more Anglophile than internationalist, which is indeed a fault that many isolationists find it difficult to forgive. Another grave defect in their eyes is that he is prepared to consider a general lowering of United States tariffs for the sake of international peace.

. . .

Other points of interest are

(a) The bad press which Finns have been enjoying in contrast to e.g. the Swedes, whose courage is often praised. This reached a climax when State Department ordered discontinuance of Finnish propaganda in United States. The

8 Edward R.Stettinius, industrialist, appointed Lend-Lease administrator 1941.
9 Hugh A.Butler, Republican Senator from Nebraska since 1941.

small but active pro-Finnish lobby in Washington seems to be lying very low at present.

(b) A striking advertisement signed by 'Loyal Americans of German Birth', which included various well known names, appeared in several prominent Eastern papers. It called upon the Germans in the Reich to throw off the Nazi yoke, and upon Germans in the United States to say where they stand by joining committee. The declaration was drafted by Dorothy Thompson[10] and gesture has no ulterior significance so far as can be learned beyond causing a certain degree of embarrassment to German-Americans which was doubtless intended. Anne O'Hare McCormick in a recent article in *New York Times* made the traditional plea that the decent anti-Nazi majority of the German people be not forgotten. She told a member of my staff that she was encouraged to make this plea by Sumner Welles, of whose unofficial Political Advisory Committee she is a member.

9 January 1943

The optimism caused by the Russian news[1] is considerably tempered by the slow-down in Tunisia. Tunisian news has been meagre, and the press in the absence of feats of American arms has limited comment to a minimum. More press space is occupied by discussions of commodity shortages and the rationing muddle than by any other single subject. The wave of resentment against the responsible 'bureaucrats' who are represented as at once arbitrary and incompetent is mounting still and was echoed by Speaker Rayburn[2] who virtually in the names of both parties promised strong measures to put down these busybodies. In this atmosphere of righteous indignation and a novel consciousness of its own power the 78th Congress met to hear the President's report. Congressman Martin, the Republican leader, had pledged his party to winning the war, the restoration of the prerogatives of Congress and the preservation of the Constitution, of private enterprise and of a free press. He denounced 'the blanket powers and blank cheques' given to administrators and spoke of severer control of appropriations, curtailment of the number of government agencies and lighter taxation on business. He laid special stress on coming American supremacy in air transportation : 'America must rule the air.' Since a good many Southern Democrats sympathize with this traditional Republican platform and prepare to vote accordingly, the President appears to be facing an uphill task. His address on the state of the Union was conciliatory and omitted the detailed proposals for social security (which had been expected) on the advice of Democratic leaders who begged the President to play down New-Dealism. The speech gave general satisfaction. Republican circles echoed Wheeler's description of it as 'very clever.

10 Dorothy Thompson, syndicated liberal columnist from 1928 to 1942, wife of Sinclair Lewis.

1 Successful Russian offensives on Middle Don and Caucasus.

2 Samuel Taliaferro Rayburn, Speaker of the House of Representatives since 1940 and Democratic Congressman from Texas since 1913.

. . . It dealt entirely with generalities with which every right thinking person could agree.' Even Representative Fish agreed that it was a very fine speech. Clare Luce, however, who has privately intimated that she looks on herself as the voice of China in Congress, questioned the reference to the volume of aid to China. Silence greeted the President's reference to post-war social welfare, sparse applause his reference to Britain, louder applause the words on Russia and the mention of China brought thunderous applause.

Stettinius has been heavily briefed on reciprocal aid but no showing he makes is likely to prevent the use of the occasion of the new Lend-Lease appropriation for libels upon British use of Lend-Lease funds and of charges against officials administering them. The story of Beaverbrook's wedding present to Hopkins,[3] though denied by both parties, is still circulating and many old lies are bound to be dragged out once more. The Chinese have staged the recall of their Military Mission amid complaints about inadequate American assistance in a manner enabling isolationists and proponents of Pacific over Atlantic warfare to charge the Administration with favouritism towards the British over the Chinese, who are alleged to be at end of their tether and liable to capitulate unless assured of much more effective support. The champions of the Pacific front will no doubt quote a recent speech by Grew, who gave warning that a major offensive against Japan postponed until after Hitler's defeat would come too late. Admiral Halsey's surprising prophecy that Japan would be defeated this year was received with polite incredulity in the press and disavowed by Elmer Davis. The Navy Department appear to attach no importance to his remarks.

Hull, in whose economic faith reciprocal trade is the first article, has been kept in continuous public favour by a most successful campaign launched by his Department designed to represent him as having pursued a consistently wise and courageous policy against prevailing ignorance and political obstruction. The publicity on his French policy and the publication of the White Paper[4] (reprinted by the New York Times) dealing with the last decade of United States foreign policy, have both materially contributed to this. This canonization of the Secretary of State may be expected to have the merit of lessening the likelihood of a repetition of Lodge's success in undermining Wilson in 1919–20 since conservative Republican opinion has deep respect and faith in Hull who genuinely abhors isolationism as a species of sin, and looks on the war as having in effect begun in 1931. There is no doubt that recently the State Department has been gaining both in power and prestige and that its technical plans for securing executive control of post-war American policy and the making of the peace is likely to be seriously challenged by Congress alone. There are two resolutions in Congress for establishment of a mixed Senate-House Committee to decide issues of

3 The *Chicago Tribune* had alleged that Beaverbrook had given emeralds to the value of 500,000 dollars to the bride on the occasion of Harold Hopkins's wedding on 31 July 1942. Beaverbrook described the story as a 'fabrication from first to last'.

4 A collection of diplomatic documents published as *Peace and War: US Foreign Policy 1931–41*.

both peace and war. There is no doubt that Congress is determined to assert itself in this as in every other respect. Only when the Foreign Relations and Affairs Committees have been appointed will it be possible to estimate what the effect of this is likely to be.

. . .

Colonel Donovan does not disguise his satisfaction over his triumph over Sherwood[5] and Elmer Davis in securing control over psychological warfare for the Chiefs of Staff. The President at his press conference denied that Sherwood or Barnes had resigned. Elmer Davis is reported to be seeking a compromise solution, but as he is not interested in foreign operations Donovan's victory is probably complete for the present.

. . .

15 January 1943

Paul Appleby, Under-Secretary of Agriculture, has resigned from the newly-created Division of Occupied Territories. Appleby is moderate New Dealer whom Welles and Acheson[1] had with apparent success persuaded to enter the Department, and began by developing happy relations with his new colleagues, including the new Director of Foreign Relief and Rehabilitation, Herbert Lehman. He told a member of my staff that his regard for his colleagues, including Lehman, was unimpaired, but that Lehman's insistence on including rehabilitation, in its widest aspects, as well as relief, within his sphere of competence, appeared to him to render his own prospective functions largely otiose. Rather than indulge in the fashionable pastime of jurisdictional border warfare, whereby rival officials spend their time in appeals to the President to defend them against encroachment and for the recovery of lost powers, he preferred to leave the field of battle and make a dignified withdrawal to his own Department of Agriculture. This may, in fact, prove to be a shrewd move on his part, as the struggle for power in the field of reconstruction is likely to be very bitter, and the State Department in its present mood would do its best to prevent even a moderate New Dealer from capturing genuine control of this field. . . .

17 January 1943

The President's budget speech was well received with a noticeable feeling of pride in its very size and in the United States financial power which it presupposes.

Comment on President's opening speech in Congress, both in private and public, continues to exhibit relief over his abstention from indulging in utopian world planning of the type associated with Wallace. Congress and the press are in a high anti-utopian mood at the moment and Governor Lehman has taken care

---

5 Robert Emmet Sherwood, playwright, Director of Overseas Operations OWI since 1942.
1 Dean Gooderham Acheson, lawyer, Assistant Secretary of State since 1941.

to say publicly that his plans for relief and rehabilitation are thoroughly realistic and practical. In the meantime Governor Stassen of Minnesota has been expounding his plan for a world state governed by a world parliament which is far the most radical scheme yet advanced by a responsible person. It is instructive to note that his suggestions which would have attracted violent criticism had its author been a New Dealer were received tolerantly, if not enthusiastically, coming as they did from a respected anti-New Deal Republican.

Congress is known to be in a stern mood and nervous government departments are busily appeasing it. The word has gone round the economic agencies, particularly OPA, to which Prentiss Brown has been duly appointed, that they must show themselves accommodating to Congress and not choose this moment for standing on points of principle or show too much zeal in defending policies.

. . .

Congress plainly intends to assert itself during present session and a crop of enquiries are threatened. Nye proposes to investigate the food muddle to prove that Administration is incompetent and exporting beyond the margin of safety. La Follette wishes to forbid export of butter. The Tolan Committee has reported that war effort is the product of 'the unorganized might' of the nation and that manpower conscription and labour freezing is a false remedy for a situation only curable by a strong central authority for production and manpower. Rubber Controller Jeffers utters sombre warnings about the growingly grave rubber shortage which he considers due to reach a crisis in the autumn. Senator Gillette continues to denounce the Baruch report and the blindness of the Administration to the rubber situation. In this strongly charged atmosphere the appointment of Edward Flynn, Chairman of the Democratic Party and ex-boss of the Bronx, to succeed Nelson Johnson[1] as United States Minister to Australia with vague powers as presidential representative of ambassadorial rank in South West Pacific touched off a violent explosion in the press, radio and everywhere else. 'Boss Flynn' became a serious embarrassment to the Administration both on account of the particularly strong feeling against bosses in general shown by the results of the recent election and because Flynn was not a success either as boss or as Democratic organizer after he failed to hold Tammany together during the New York gubernatorial election. Moreover the municipal 'paving block' scandal[2] of which he was the central figure has never been satisfactorily cleared up despite his official exoneration. Administration may have expected some resistance to this appointment but it could hardly have foreseen the general shriek of indignation which the nationwide press emitted and has continued to keep up. Willkie declared that repetition of the idealistic slogans of Mr Wallace simultaneously with disreputable practices was typical of the Administration and declared that Flynn was being got off in order to appoint to the chairmanship of the party someone better capable of securing the 1944 term for Roosevelt. The only columnist who

1 Nelson T. Johnson, career diplomat, Minister to Australia 1941–46.

2 Allegation that Flynn had used some city labour and materials to refurbish a courtyard on his country estate.

feebly attempted to defend Flynn was sharply attacked for it by his own newspaper.

Senator Bridges[3] proposes to lead the anti-confirmation fight in the Senate and has tied Flynn's name to various scandals including the notorious Serge Rubinstein[4] whose lawyer Flynn is. The gibe is now going the rounds that the President has forgotten that Australia is no longer a penal settlement.

. . .

The labour situation is becoming disturbed once more. Both AF of L and CIO have played their political cards badly and have allowed the impression to grow among the public that jurisdictional disputes and 'politics as usual' continue in their ranks. The view that Republicans in Congress are unlikely to vote for severe restraints on labour in order not to lose labour support in 1944 is described as overoptimistic by gloomy labour leaders who cannot see how the Republicans can resist the temptation to support the Southern Democrats who have politically nothing to lose by attacking labour. The most immediate issue is the AF of L-CIO collision in the Kaiser shipyards which CIO has referred to the National Labor Relations Board. The dispute has seriously hampered work in the Kaiser shipyard and has led to explosions of bad feeling along the entire West Coast. 'Wildcat' strikes in the anthracite mines in West Virginia have brought further odium upon the heads of labour and its leaders are convinced that some restrictive legislation is inevitable and are very nervous. Despite this pessimism it seems unlikely that drastic anti-labour legislation will occur. The Administration and portions of Congress will certainly resist it and labour leaders have had considerable experience in last-minute compromises with the politicians whenever a major crisis seems otherwise unavoidable.

Appointment of Judge Rutledge[5] to Supreme Court in place of Byrnes has been received with considerable approval by press, Congress and American Bar. Satisfaction was caused by fact that President should at last have decided to choose a member of Federal Bench rather than a politician or personal friend. Rutledge, who is forty-eight, is a Kentucky Democrat who has spent most of his life in Missouri and Iowa and was Dean of two law schools in Middle West. He approved of President's plan to enlarge Supreme Court in 1937 and is counted an ally by New Dealers in Court, Douglas and Black,[6] and as somewhat naïve by Justices Frankfurter and Jackson.[7] His marked interest in social welfare and warm approval of New Deal demonstrates that President feels strong enough politically not to make concessions to those strong sections of public and legal opinion which prefer to see learning allied to greater conservatism in Supreme Court.

3 Henry Styles Bridges, Republican Senator from New Hampshire since 1937.

4 Serge Rubinstein, international financier, defendant in successive actions involving financial malpractices.

5 Wiley B.Rutledge, former Dean of the Washington University and University of Iowa Law schools, who served on the Court until 1949.

6 Hugo LaFayette Black, from Alabama, Justice of Supreme Court since 1937.

7 Robert Houghwout Jackson, Justice of the Supreme Court, 1941–5.

. . . James Dunn,[8] adviser on European affairs in State Department, has been appointed to be Department's representative on psychological warfare committee of Donovan's organization. Sherwood told a member of my staff that Dunn is regarded as most effective possible antidote to New Deal and anti-clerical attitude of Sherwood's Foreign Publicity Division of OWI. Sherwood is shortly to proceed to Africa as a presidential emissary. Attempt to substitute him for Murphy has failed.

24 January 1943

The least publicized and perhaps most significant political event of week was special congressional election in Sixth Missouri District. It was occasioned by death of Republican Representative Bennett[1] whose son Marion Bennett,[2] also Republican, was returned by a majority of nearly 14,000 votes, a majority of some 60,000 more than his father had received. Missouri is politically still a borderline state and large Republican swing indicates that anti-Administration wave is still rising and weakens Democratic claims that last election might have gone better for them but for lack of good war news. Vote was much heavier than expected and Bennett carried all electoral counties including those hitherto considered Democratic strongholds. Missouri has long oscillated between the two parties and this clear reaction is therefore most indicative.

I am told that Senator McNary is privately attacking internationalists of his own and the Democratic Party with great vehemence and talking of way in which Congress and people will yet show President how greatly out of touch he is with American sentiment on subject of foreign policy. Since McNary is adroitest of congressional politicians, and a reliable weathercock of Republican opinion, his tone is a fair indication of present temper and hopes of opposition. Certainly Wallace's views, particularly on post-war reconstruction, are widely held to be too vague and idealistic and to be inspired rather by general humanitarian sympathy than by regard for facts and for American needs. Attitude of general public and of Congress is better represented in article in *New York Times* of 17 January which advocates a 'go slow' policy and general caution. Berle in a recent private address said that State Department was well aware of its duty not to commit country beyond limits reached by United States public opinion. He professed to regret fact that rhythms of British and American political life were so systematically out of harmony with each other – that precise moment at which Britain moves left America invariably moves to right and *vice versa*. He regarded last election as a typical example of this.

Newspaper and general comment on North African situation is still divided and confused. Lippmann's article criticizing Murphy and policy of State Depart-

8 James C. Dunn, career diplomat.
1 Philip A. Bennett, elected to Congress 1941.
2 Marion Tinsley Bennett, lawyer, member of Congress 1943–9.

ment which is echoed by *Washington Post*, Clapper and a number of liberal papers led to angry words from Hull at two press conferences. Members of my staff have been told by United States officials half in earnest that Lippmann is evidently in our pay. Bullitt[3] on the other hand accuses him of drawing his inspiration from Communist sources. Mouthpieces of State Department in press are reported to have been primed on issue by Leahy who is said to be bitter at opposition to North African policy from both American and British sources. Peyrouton's appointment[4] has produced a new blast from the anti-Vichyites. State Department are telling journalists that they do not like it but that Giraud insisted.

There is a good deal of Washington talk of how all will be settled when President and Prime Minister reveal results of their reported deliberations with de Gaulle. Isolationists' reaction to this is that America has evidently made a mess of things in North Africa and that this should teach her in future to keep out of all foreign entanglements. Even moderates and liberals are sobered by the news. They are beginning to realize the kind of political difficulties which face any plan for a new world and are plainly taken aback.

Democratic Convention as expected appointed Postmaster General Walker Chairman of the Party in place of Flynn. Walker is an affable Roman Catholic politician whose relations with Farley continue unimpaired. His intention is reported to be to heal breaches within the Democratic Party and to reconstruct Southern Democrat-Irish Catholic-New Deal alliance of former days. That this will not be easy is shown by ferocious mood of Southern Democrats who retain congressional control of Democratic Party more strongly than ever in their hands, and have shown their temper by defeating nomination of Marcantonio,[5] near-Communist Representative from New York, to Judiciary Committee to which Speaker Rayburn tried to appoint him.

Attacks on Flynn continue but his confirmation as Minister to Australia is made more probable by unpopularity in Congress of his assailant, Senator Bridges of New Hampshire. Nevertheless episode will doubtless be used again by opposition. Willkie is using it widely and has stated in public that Flynn was ousted from Chairmanship of Democratic Party because President found it easier to run for a fourth term without his help. No fourth term hints emerged from Democratic National Convention, largely it must be surmised for fear of embarrassing President, since in Democratic circles its possibility and desirability is certainly being canvassed, although it is recognized that Mr Roosevelt's chances do not look too promising at moment. But Democratic Party is lacking in other candidates of even degree of popularity of Willkie or Bricker (dubbed 'an honest

3 William C. Bullitt, Special Assistant to the Secretary of the Navy June 1942–4, previously US Ambassador to USSR 1933–6, and to France 1936–41.

4 Marcel Peyrouton, Vichy Minister of Interior 1940–1. Appointed Governor General of Algeria, 1943.

5 Vito Marcantonio, Congressman (Republican) from New York 1935–7, and (American Labor Party) since 1939.

Harding'). I hear privately that White House circles regard Willkie at present as only dangerous candidate. He has probably weakened his position by recent speeches with more educated sections but has undoubtedly appealed to masses by his emotional presentation of large issues. Cabot Lodge of Massachusetts is said to be a promising dark horse for Republican primaries. Lodge is renewing his contemptuous references to British Army in his recent talks to army camps. Willkie on the other hand appears anxious to show his Anglophile feeling and to look on himself as a misunderstood friend of the British. He has gone out of his way to express his friendly sentiments to all his British acquaintances and was extremely affable to me in New York recently where he took pains to appear in public with me.

Strike in anthracite mines is virtually over as a result of President's threat to put army in control. Miners' leader Lewis has played his cards with his usual skill. Fundamentally miners' strike is against him and high union dues which he exacts, but as a strike is legal only against management a rise in wages is what is formally demanded. Lewis has in theory aligned himself with the Administration which he does not love while miners have been saying that they prefer control of army to that of Lewis. Lewis virtually said that he was waiting for April when coal contracts are up for renewal when he will demand a general wage rise. Administration will in that event face awkward situation as army can scarcely expect to run entire coal industry.

. . .

The Negro situation is not widely publicized as it is full of embarrassment to Administration. The Fair Employment Practices Committee suddenly suspended hearings of grievances submitted by Randolph,[6] head of coloured union of Pullman conductors (based on fact that Negroes are gradually being forced out of Railroad Brotherhoods where new type of machinery is leading to reduction of staff), for fear that resentment which a pro-Negro verdict would cause in railroad unions and in South generally might provoke bitter feeling and even race riots. Negro leaders are much more vocal and aggressive than they have ever been and are said to be bitterly disappointed at failure of war to change status of their people. Communists who were once their most ardent champions are now telling them to forget their grievances for duration of war, which has produced hostility to Communists among coloured population, together with a general anti-white sentiment which makes for fertile soil for Japanese propaganda. Administration is worried by this and relevant officials are apt to wring their hands and gloomily predict race riots after this war similar to those which occurred after last, so long as Northern labour union and solid South continue in their present obstinate mood. Feeling among whites in South is said to be very strained, and an illustration of this is that I have been earnestly warned by friends not to visit Tuskegee Negro University in a projected trip to Alabama unless I

6 Asa Philip Randolph, President of Brotherhood of Sleeping-Car Porters since 1925.

can go under cover of Governor for fear of impairing Anglo-American relations in the South.

. . .

In connexion with recent murder of Italian anarchist Carlo Tresca,[7] the Mazzini Society[8] and Italian labour leader Luigi Antonini[9] have publicly attacked Office of War Information for a misguided policy of trying to force loyal Italian organizations to accept Communists in an endeavour to accomplish unity. Cranston[10] of OWI who is person principally under fire told a member of my staff that he was convinced that Berle was behind it since Berle wants way cleared for his own negotiations with right wing and some Fascist minority groups. While I have no supporting evidence and Italian desk at State Department expresses little interest in Tresca affair, Cranston's suspicion is based on steady opposition by Berle and State Department to OWI's policy of trying to draw together all anti-Fascist American groups.

1 February 1943

Biggest story of week is naturally the 'unconditional surrender' conference at Casablanca.[1] While a great deal of enthusiasm was displayed throughout press and radio with virtually no carping even from isolationists, there is more than an undercurrent of disappointment at fact that main issues on which decision was expected, namely Allied council, unified command and settlement of North Africa, were not mentioned in communiqué and private comment in both journalistic and political circles complains of absence of any obvious concrete results and expresses wonder about absence of Russian and Chinese representatives. All this was loudly voiced by Willkie who said that results were disappointing, for which he was attacked by *New York Times*. The public is eagerly expecting important practical measures to be announced soon and press perceives intimations of this in a 'Wait and See' statement by President's Secretary, Stephen Early.[2] There will be a serious sense of 'Let-down' if announcement of such results is too long delayed. Lippmann with obvious relief after his campaign against State and War Departments welcomed communiqué warmly as putting an end to all talk of a negotiated peace and possible arrangements with Axis satellites and contrasted this with President Wilson's offer to negotiate on basis of the Fourteen Points. . . .[3]

. . .

7 Anti-Fascist refugee, assassinated in New York, 11 January.

8 Established by anti-Fascist exiles in 1940, dedicated to principles of *Risorgimento* and overthrow of Fascism.

9 General Secretary of NY Local 89 of International Ladies Garment Workers' Union, President of Italian-American Labor Council since 1941.

10 Alan Cranston, member of the Foreign Languages Division of OWI.

1 Churchill–Roosevelt conference, 14–23 January, held at Casablanca, Morocco, after which Roosevelt announced the decision to impose 'unconditional surrender' on the Axis powers.

2 Stephen T. Early, Roosevelt's press secretary since 1937, former newspaperman.

3 In October 1918.

The Lend-Lease report presented by Stettinius which from our point of view is very satisfactory has produced a fair amount of favourable publicity for Lend-Lease in general, although fact most prominently played up in press was that a third of United States tanks and aircraft had been sent to Britain while relatively little publicity was given to reciprocal aid. The last may be remedied by Stettinius's thus far excellent personal evidence and OWI in their own publications have put heavy stress upon it. There is some feeling in Republican circles against Lend-Lease power being concentrated in hands of President and suggestion has been made for some kind of commission to work it. In the main, the attack on Administration, if it develops, will spring from general dissatisfaction with its management of the internal economic situation and the knocks which we may get in course of this will be largely incidental. On the other side it should be noted that Winant delivered a very meaty speech at Baltimore to the Council of State Government on 25 January which contained one of the most informative, detailed and favourable accounts of the organization of British Home Front yet published here. It was from our point of view the best possible thing he could have done. It obtained literally no publicity and steps are being taken to ensure somewhat wider distribution for speech than is normally obtained by releases of State Department. At same meeting Jeffers, the Rubber Czar, delivered an unexpected and very fierce attack on 'expediters and loafers in Army and Navy Departments' who in his opinion seriously interfered with his rubber plans. He had a clash with Elmer Davis over this when latter complained that speech had not been cleared through his office. The struggle between demands for synthetic rubber, high octane gas and corvettes for U-boat warfare is at its height. Altogether it may be said that domestic issues and domestic irritations are more responsible for political moves both in Congress and outside it at this moment than foreign issues and attacks upon us here are more often than not the by-product of assaults on the Administration.

Casablanca Conference allayed storm over North African situation somewhat, but Hull is still highly sensitive on this subject, most passionately concerned to justify his Department's policies at press conferences and is said to have been restrained with some difficulty from attacking Lippmann directly. He said that 'vicious and violent vituperation' had been poured on State Department and by implication on Eisenhower and President at moment at which vital agreement between de Gaulle and Giraud was being effected by Allied leaders and that 'persons up on Mount Olympus' (i.e. Lippmann) were uttering criticisms without wishing to learn facts. He became particularly incensed by a question about Peyrouton, whose appointment shook even middle-of-road commentators. . . .

Flynn comes up for confirmation by Senate next week having received a favourable report from Foreign Relations Committee which voted for his confirmation by fifteen to ten. His opponents included seven Republican members of Committee and three Democrats, George,[4] Van Nuys[5] and Gillette. They may

4 Walter F.George, Democratic Senator from Georgia since 1922.
5 Frederick Van Nuys, Democratic Senator from Indiana since 1933.

not have forgotten that they were amongst Senators whom New Deal, assisted by Flynn who was then National Democratic Chairman, had attempted to purge unsuccessfully in 1938. La Follette, unexpectedly but with typical independence, voted for him. Connally will make principal speech in favour of Flynn, and Vandenberg tells me that Flynn's chances of confirmation are slender, since forty-six Senators are determined to vote against him and entire issue therefore hangs upon two or three votes. I asked how it was that the President whom even his fiercest opponents credit with consummate political skill came to provoke this situation. Vandenberg said that President was a very shrewd politician but was liable now and then to make appalling blunders and this was one of them. The loss of face on the part of the President if Flynn is not confirmed will be considerable. Willkie on other hand says that Flynn jumped gun by announcing his appointment first, thus forcing President's hand. Latest indications are that Flynn may probably himself withdraw and that if he does not Senate will decline to confirm.

Wallace's speech last week evidently meant to be conciliatory, in which he visualized a classless society composed entirely of a middle class, received some ironical comment in press, while his defence of competitive spirit and private enterprise was passed over in comparative silence. His speech is a symptom of general retreat of New Deal. Its opponents speak of a disorganized rout noticeable in a number of Departments. OWI is being pressed hard by an alliance of State Department and Donovan's Office. Department of Agriculture, long a New Deal stronghold, has dropped Parisius,[6] who was a champion of aid to small farmers of expansionist programmes, in favour of advocates of policies more favourable to Farm Bloc which represents mainly big agricultural interests. Board of Economic Warfare claims to have captured three agencies from RFC but has had to yield rubber control to Jesse Jones to whom Jeffers gave it. Anti-New Dealers feel that now is moment to strike and anti-Hopkins campaign was evidently timed to coincide with this general Republican anti-Roosevelt drive. On the other hand, attempt to set up a congressional committee to advise President on conduct of war which is being pushed by Vandenberg (Republican) and Maloney (Democrat)[7] in Senate so far has had little success with Military Affairs Committee. More importance is attached to a proposal of Senator Wagner to set up a mixed congressional-White House committee on post-war aims which has not yet been embodied in a bill since Wagner is thought to be in close touch with President on this.

Agitation for setting up a Special Aviation Committee in Congress to deal with wartime but more especially post-war commercial aviation is in full swing. There are eight bills on subject in Congress while Rules Committee whose Chair-

6 Herbert W.Parisius, Wisconsin Wallace-ite, Director of Food Production, Department of Agriculture, 1942–3. He left to join OFRRO (Office of Foreign Relief and Rehabilitation Operations) as economist field inspector.

7 Francis T.Maloney, Democratic Senator from Connecticut since 1935.

man, Hamilton Fish, is strongly in favour of such a committee is now considering. Principal opposition comes from Military and Naval Affairs and Inter-State Commerce Committees which have no wish to be deprived of control over this province. A strong letter by Rickenbacker[8] advocating Special Committee has been published and members of both parties in Congress have made glowing speeches on need for American post-war supremacy in air as a cardinal national peace aim. This has been supported by a recent speech by Governor Stassen who has long been an advocate of air expansion and topic is occasionally referred to by Wallace. Senator Brewster[9] has so far been only prominent person who has openly complained that Lend-Lease of aircraft to Britain might prove obstacle to American ambitions after war, but Representatives Magnuson[10] of Washington and Sumners[11] and Kleberg[12] of Texas are speaking of Britain as a dangerous post-war rival in this field and have talked of how they came across British Missions for whose enterprise they professed admiration already at work on this in South America.

.   .   .

Republican National Committee has appointed James Selvage[13] as its Chief Publicity Expert in place of Budington Kelland.[14] Selvage who was previously Publicity Director of NAM (National Association of Manufacturers) is credited with writing Hoover's speeches for some time and although never a member of was in intermittent contact with America First Committee. He is said to be a flexible person capable of swift self-adjustment to changing situations.

6 February 1943

. . . Guy Ramsey's[1] interview with Giraud,[2] quoted by President, strengthened general impression that North African situation was improving. This view is not shared by liberals. Thus President's assistant, Isador Lubin,[3] lately back from London and North Africa, does not in private conversation disguise his admiration of what he assumes to be British point of view and compares our occupation of Tripoli with situation in French North Africa greatly to advantage of former.

8 Edward V.Rickenbacker, President of Eastern Air Lines, First World War air ace.

9 Ralph O.Brewster, Republican Senator from Maine since 1941.

10 Warren G.Magnuson, Democratic Congressman from Washington 1937–45.

11 Hatton W.Sumners, Democratic Congressman from Texas 1913–47.

12 Richard M.Kleberg, Democratic Congressman from Texas since 1931.

13 James P.Selvage, in charge of publicity for National Association of Manufacturers 1933–8, member of public relations firm Selvage & Lee 1938–58.

14 Clarence Budington Kelland, popular *Saturday Evening Post* writer of detective and humorous fiction, put in charge of publicity for Republican National Committee in 1941.

1 Correspondent of London *Daily Mail*.

2 President expressed approval of stance taken by Giraud in the interview, namely that he would accept help from any source, including Vichy's *Service d'Ordre de la Légion*. The President added that this dovetailed with de Gaulle's views and 'there was no dispute there'.

3 Isador Lubin, New Deal economist, Commissioner of Labor Statistics in Department of Labor 1933–46 ; Special Assistant to President 1941–5.

Outside liberal press, columnist Drew Pearson[4] is most widely read among those who attack State Department in this connexion. Opponents of Department accuse it of a bad attack of 'Peyroutonitis'.

New Dealers seem somewhat depressed about degree to which, according to some of them, President has decided to back State Department's policy in North Africa. Edgar Mowrer,[5] in particular, who seemed on point of going to North Africa, told a member of my staff that he decided to abandon his efforts in view of rigid opposition of State and War Departments which he did not think he or Elmer Davis could overcome. He has now resigned from OWI. New Dealers in general seem greatly upset about turn of United States foreign policy over which they believe they can no longer exercise any noticeable influence.

. . .

In Congress anti-New Deal trend is clearly perceptible. Chief topics discussed in it this week included alleged muddles of manpower, food and related problems with view prevailing that Administration has bungled these badly. Pepper-Kilgore bill to set up an overall Office of War Mobilization to deal with home front even more comprehensively than at present dealt with by Byrnes's Office of Economic Stabilization is once again before Senate. . . .

. . .

Flynn's request of withdrawal of his nomination as minister to Australia is understood to have been extracted by majority leader, Senator Barkley, who assured Flynn that his non-confirmation by Senate was made certain by the opposition of Boss Crump[6] of Tennessee, a powerful Southern Democratic politician. There is much jubilation in senatorial circles at this conspicuous victory over Administration which is a clear sign of the times, although his triumphal return from Casablanca served to shield the President from any immediate exultation at his own expense on the subject.

. . .

Negro situation has been further aggravated by spectacular resignation of Hastie,[7] Stimson's coloured adviser on Negro issues. Hastie told press that he resigned because scant attention was paid to him in his own department, in particular by Army Air authorities, typical in his opinion of generally unfair treatment of Negroes which Administration evidently had no intention of curbing. President on 3 February announced that he had told McNutt to call a conference on discrimination in war employment with a view to strengthening powers of Committee on Fair Employment Practices.

A luncheon occurred this week in Washington of progressive conservatives,

---

4 Drew Pearson, syndicated columnist and radio commentator notable for his sensational 'investigations' into private lives and state secrets.

5 Edgar A.Mowrer, correspondent for *Chicago Daily News* in both world wars.

6 Edward H.Crump (1895–1954), absolute boss of Memphis and, by extension, of Tennessee, 1909–48.

7 William H.Hastie, previously Dean of Howard University Law School.

some of whom were members of old Fight for Freedom Committee.[8] Gathering, which Tom Lamont[9] was unable to attend, included Mrs Dwight Morrow,[10] Walter Lippmann, Raymond Clapper, and was addressed by Winant and Herbert Agar.[11] It was decided to form an informal group to press for an enlightened conception of peace and several persons who were present expressed view that group, which is very Anglophile, was likely to do serious work in this connection, particularly if, as was its present intention, it remained anonymous and private.

. . .

. . . Willkie has been saying in private that British correspondents in United States did not do justice to Republican Party which in view of its probable victory in 1944 was in his opinion short-sighted. He expressed privately view that either he or Bricker would be nominated (and elected) in 1944 and that he himself could get nomination easily if he would consent to make certain sacrifices of principle.

13 February 1943

This week has seen a great rise in controversy principally concerned with United States internal affairs. Administration is under fire from many quarters and is showing signs of trimming its sails before the winds of opposition which are blowing strong. Main line taken by opposition in its press, the congressional debates and in general Washington talk, is that Administration is still dominated by impractical idealists and pettifogging bureaucrats, poor guardians of national interests of United States both within and without. This attitude is not confined to Republicans but is found equally among anti-New Deal Southern Democrats. Truculent criticism of this kind has been prominent this week, and Administration, some of whose members appear fully alive to dangers of this campaign, is behaving as if it had decided to give impression that it is in sympathy with this realistic nationalism rather than trying to arrest it. Welles has recently stressed that interests of United States, and not sentimental altruism, are to be guides of American foreign policy. Henry Wallace, somewhat awkwardly and unconvincingly, has likewise tried to give impression that he too is not prepared to sacrifice national interests of the nation to purely idealistic considerations. Secretary Knox sounded this note most loudly in his recent evidence before the Appropriations Committee of House investigating Lend-Lease, when he said that he was in favour of planning at once to secure Pacific bases for defence of United States

8 Fight for Freedom, organization launched April 1941 as ginger group from Committee to Defend America by Aiding the Allies, to advocate a more outright American policy to defeat the Axis.

9 Thomas W.Lamont, Chairman of J. Pierpont Morgan, bankers.

10 Mrs Dwight Morrow, widow of Dwight Morrow, US diplomat, and mother-in-law of Charles Lindbergh.

11 Herbert S.Agar, London correspondent of *Louisville Courier-Journal* 1929–34 ; later editor 1940–2 ; prominent figure in Southern literary renaissance.

and had put this in secret session to the Naval Affairs Committee (which received it well and has since appointed a special sub-committee to consider this question). Knox explained in answer to a question that he was in favour of immediate action because he felt that best time for this kind of negotiation with foreign powers was at a moment when they were in need of assistance from the United States ; it was plain to those who heard him that he was seeking to give impression that he for one was no airy idealist, but a tough-minded Midwestern 'horse trader' who could be thoroughly relied upon to strike a hard bargain for United States. On 11 February Tydings and Reynolds, violently anti-Administration Democrats, demanded the West Indian bases [1] in perpetuity for United States as a natural return for the handsome United States Lend-Lease shipments to Britain which provided the United Kingdom, not merely with food, but with cash from sales to the public. McNary, who leads Republicans in Senate, agreed with them, while several Senators protested on grounds that this showed dissension among the Allies. Doubtless these outbursts are staged principally for benefit of Administration ; nor are Reynolds and Tydings popular spokesmen in any sense ; nevertheless mood which they are exploiting is a widespread consciousness of great and growing national strength and a significant pointer to attitude, not indeed of people at large, who are for most part uncertain and confused, but of many influential opinion-forming groups whose voice is likely to be heard more and more loudly as peace draws nearer. Walter Lippmann told a member of my staff that present mood differed from that during close of last war principally in that whereas twenty-five years ago the American people were powerfully affected by the band of internationalist crusaders and vast majority of thinking Americans were emotionally in favour of a single political world association, today there is an inclination towards a 'hardboiled' businesslike foreign policy and thinking is in terms of hard and fast agreements of a very specific nature, designed to increase security or prosperity of their country. This description applies perhaps more to the temper of Administration than to that of people or majority of Congress, who are more attracted to large than to limited arrangements, but it is the case that the American people, without perhaps abandoning its fundamental love of idealism, is today nervous of its vocabulary and applauds realistic language which seems a guarantee against once more being lured into uncertain paths by foreign sirens. This expresses itself in a variety of ways, some of them opposed to each other, in agitation to concentrate on strengthening the home front at cost of export of either men or materials, and on the other hand in expressions of the 'American Century' type which is at present most conspicuous in advertisements of aircraft interests calling upon the United States to dominate the air ; but in whatever form it is winning territory from supporters of New Deal and has forced Administration into a temporary tactical retreat.

1 The six sites in the Caribbean the lease of which Britain exchanged for fifty over-age destroyers in September 1940. Millard E. Tydings was Democratic Senator from Maryland 1927–51, and Robert R. Reynolds was Democratic Senator from North Carolina 1932–45.

Past week has been full of controversies typical of this anti-Administration drive. A stormy debate occurred in House over an indictment by Dies Committee of thirty-nine alleged radical 'crackpots' employed by Administration. An amendment to Appropriations bill whereby these persons were to be dismissed forthwith without appeal was indeed defeated but a specific rider dismissing a coloured Treasury official named Pickens accused of radical opinions was passed, although by a small majority, and was abrogated on next day amid great hubbub, after Northern Republican leaders had impressed upon their followers the unwisdom of alienating coloured vote by apparent discrimination against a Negro. Meanwhile Dies Committee itself was re-elected although against stronger opposition than in previous years. Faced with gathering opposition on part of both Congress and such powerful lobbies as American Legion[2] and farm organizations, the Administration made considerable concessions. White House caused the Department of Justice to appoint an interdepartmental committee with powers to investigate all government employees charged with politically disreputable views or activities. Not satisfied with this, the House appointed its own committee to perform precisely the same function, its membership representing a compromise between extreme and moderate pro-Diesites. It may be significant in this connexion that Maloney, Chief Prosecutor in case which is at present pending against a number of subversive political organizations with which various isolationist Congressmen have had dealings at various times, has been removed from the case. The Attorney General received a visit on this subject from Senator Wheeler whose name is mentioned in case and who has long been threatening to investigate Department of Justice if it did not cease to 'persecute good American patriots'. Similarly Thurman Arnold, the 'trust busting' Assistant Attorney General, has been 'promoted' to federal bench to the immense relief of big business which he has fought with fury and success for some years. Curbs have been put on broadcasts of columnists Winchell[3] and Drew Pearson. The radio, like the film industry, is a newer and far more timorous industry than the press and its millionaire owners are at once more anxious to play in with Administration, and to avert public criticism and political attack than press. OWI, for example, has succeeded in doing far more through the radio than through press, but on other hand the networks are more easily stampeded into retreat by opposition.

The criticism of food, manpower and general commodity shortages has if anything increased since last week. The isolationist and anti-Administration press have been asking how it is possible to provide food for the great United States Army apparently required by War Department and at same time for Lend-Lease and for Lehman's relief and rehabilitation schemes. While farmers are unable to get agricultural machinery or manpower, Army is increasing its draft bill, the higher wages of labour keep up drain of manpower into towns, and Administra-

2 Organization of ex-servicemen, formed after First World War.
3 Walter Winchell, syndicated gossip-peddler and broadcaster.

tion shows neither understanding of problems nor capacity to cope with them. This kind of criticism, which is normal staple of anti-Administration pressure, is now shared by wide sections of Congress and public and has been led with considerable success by Herbert Hoover who is making an effective comeback. In public speeches and in evidence before Congressional Manpower Committee Hoover has made sharp criticisms of Administration's incompetence and has as usual received much favourable comment from isolationist columnists and spokesmen and in particular from Senator Wheeler who described him as his candidate for Presidency in 1944. Hoover has been seeing something of Messrs Wheeler and Nye who have in turn been conferring with Lindbergh and other 'America Firsters' and is said to be busily discussing reorganization of their party. Hoover, who is plainly anxious to avoid weakening his position by acquiring a reputation for Anglophobia, has at one and same time paid tribute to British Empire and British heroism in war, and at same time collaborated in an article with Hugh Gibson [4] in *Collier's* magazine, harping on desirability of feeding occupied Europe. The article makes a number of unflattering references to British official attitude in this matter and praise is given to Turks for calling British bluff in matter of feeding Greece. A meeting in Carnegie Hall is shortly to occur to protest against blockade at which Hoover is principal speaker. Isolationist press is engaged in painting the new Hoover – a man full of vigour and imagination allied to mature wisdom and political shrewdness, who would make obvious candidate for Presidency. I am told that Hoover's fundamental views have not greatly changed and that his accession to any kind of power would certainly strengthen forces behind narrow American nationalism as opposed to that branch of Republican Party which favours international and in particular close Anglo-American collaboration as only basis of a sound post-war settlement. On the other hand, when I met him privately two or three weeks ago he spoke with utmost emphasis on necessity of United States and British Commonwealth joining to police the world after war and said more than once that American opinion would be willing to accept that idea.

Administration is endeavouring to put an end to manpower confusion and has authorized McNutt, the Manpower Administrator, to declare that in certain specified districts civilian mobilization will be put into effect, shifting and tying individuals to certain specified types of essential war work. This has aroused a protest from those who believe that resources of voluntary action have not been exhausted (McNutt continues to say that he believes in this too), of those who believe that measure does not go far enough, and finally from all those who disapprove of compulsion by executive regulations. The views of the latter are embodied in a resolution offered by Senator Austin and Representative Wadsworth whereby manpower mobilization would be enacted by Congress instead of War Manpower Board. Provisions of this bill do not so much differ from McNutt's order as lay down the principle that power to mobilize population of

4 Hugh Gibson, retired diplomat, Ambassador to Belgium 1927–33, 1937–8.

United States of America lies in Congress and not in Administration. In the meanwhile Byrnes has published an order enacting that a forty-eight-hour week be made compulsory in certain essential war industries, the workers to be paid time-and-a-half after the first forty hours. This extends actual week worked by several hours and offers a wage policy which is substantially the same as that already adopted. It has been received with modified rapture both by the labour organizations and by employers. Principal effect is likely to be greatly increased purchasing power on part of industrial workers, which according to most critics must inevitably lead to an inflation which no amount of control by Office of Price Administration can materially check. Byrnes admits that prices may rise somewhat but denies that they will rise to index figure of 180 obtaining during last war and cannot therefore lead to inflation in its worse sense. . . . Clare Luce's speech in Congress which described Wallace's 'global thinking' as 'glob-aloney' (a catchword already being ridden to death by isolationist press) together with exhortation to United States to emulate what she described as commendable British enterprise in securing a strong position in future air transport, may be taken as eloquent summary of view of the American Century group publicized by her husband's journals. The answers of Henry Wallace and Mrs Roosevelt pleading for greater internationalism and reproaching her for stirring up strife among Allies obtained little general response. It is clear that Mrs Luce expresses popular sentiment prevailing at this moment on subject more accurately than do her opponents.

. . .

Prime Minister's speech [5] received here unqualified welcome which all but his references to imperial issues invariably obtain. It is too early to assess reactions to President's Lincoln Day address of the 12th [February] but his unequivocal tribute to British Armies in North Africa and his evidence of close Anglo-American collaboration should do something to still unfriendly gossip in press on our differences. Its firm words on post-war aims – on determination to prevent unemployment at home and guarantee of free self-determination of reconquered countries abroad, together with deliberate linking of names of de Gaulle and Giraud and emphatic reiteration of pledge to fight until the unconditional surrender of Axis – should set at rest both honest doubting as well as ill-intentioned speculation about true purposes of Allies, which is a permanent ingredient of the very uneasy atmosphere of Washington but has lately increased beyond the normal. His repudiation of Fascism has an obvious bearing on situation in North Africa and other countries which may be liberated. Speech bears very obvious marks of Sherwood's authorship.

. . .

. . . OWI, little loved as it is by State Department and by OSS, and on whole unpopular with Congress, will be facing difficult times before Congress in a few weeks' time, when its budget comes up, since it is viewed by anti-Administra-

---

5 In House of Commons, 11 February.

tionists as a typical home of money-wasting New Deal intellectuals. Elmer Davis's integrity and courage should, however, prove equal to any odds that may be set against him, and retirement of MacLeish should help rather than hinder his defence.

. . .

21 February 1943

The struggle between military and civilian influence in the WPB which had been simmering for many months came to a head this week. I am told that army procurement authorities with a certain amount of big business backing have for some time wanted to put Baruch in Nelson's place and have been pressing the President to do so. Eberstadt, who is a protégé of Baruch's and a War Department man, would have become Baruch's deputy under this arrangement. One or two columnists began to back Baruch and Eberstadt and rumours began to circulate of Nelson's impending resignation. Nelson evidently decided to precipitate a showdown and with the President's consent dismissed Eberstadt and appointed C.E.Wilson [1] (who had earlier been given certain of Eberstadt's powers) as his deputy in charge of all programmes. This is an open slap in the face for the War and Navy Departments and the internecine struggle which had previously been fermenting under, if near, the surface has now virtually emerged into the open. The President's move was fairly well received in congressional circles which on the whole regard the growing power of the military in internal economy of the United States with increasing disfavour. President's decision to back Nelson is interpreted as a move to curb a growingly powerful interest – a combination of high army officers led by General Somervell and industrialists – against which there is much feeling at the moment particularly on the part of small business organizations which complain that they are being squeezed out of existence. In connexion with this the Patman Small Business Committee of the House [2] published a report violently attacking the 'almost traitorous' plan attributed to the Administration to destroy small business and thereby the American way of life, and to dismantle United States industry for Lend-Lease shipments abroad which could only have the effect of industrializing foreign countries and strengthening the future competitors of the United States. How long Nelson, who is not a born fighter or a born organizer, will be able to retain his newly-won position remains to be seen.

. . .

Remarks of Clare Luce on need for overwhelming American air power are credibly reported to have been partially written by one of the air experts of State Department who now complains that she left out the sense and used only the rhetoric in his text. She obtained background for her speech from Sam Pryor, [3] Vice-President of Pan American Airways and Republican political boss of Con-

1 Charles E.Wilson, President of General Electric Co.

2 Wright Patman, Democratic Congressman from Texas since 1929. The Small Business Committee which he chaired was set up in response to the fear that small business might suffer under pressure of war measures.

3 Sam F.Pryor Jr, Republican National Committeeman from Connecticut 1937–41.

necticut, who persuaded her to run for Congress, and from Sam Meek,[4] also prominent in politics, of her congressional district, who is a member of firm of J. Walter Thompson. He and Sam Pryor were responsible for advertisements of Pan American Airways emphasizing need for American supremacy in post-war civil aviation. In this connexion it is worth noting that Berle gave excellent evidence on this issue. His remarks on dangers of conflict of narrow nationalists and on necessity for a sensible civil aviation agreement between ourselves and America as well as his observations on the difficulties in the way of post-war American control of air installations built out of Lend-Lease funds were most useful. Mrs Luce is reported to have received over 2,000 approving letters on her speech but was clearly disconcerted at strong isolationist support which she obtained and which she hastened to disown. She has since been explaining to everyone that she was asking for control of American skies by America and not for American air control of the world. But Dorothy Thompson for one is accusing her of 'double talk'. Lippmann told me a few days ago that he did not think too much importance should be attached to Mrs Luce's speech, which she herself had imperfectly understood and that in the days that had passed *bon mot* in congressional circles was that there had been much clarification of loose thinking.

After-effects of her speech are however a lively reminder of the fact that political lines have been changing lately and that issue is not one between isolationists and anti-isolationists so much as between varying degrees of nationalism. Former is supported from different standpoints both by jingo ex-isolationists and by 'American Century' followers of Mr Luce as well as supporters of big army plans. These groups are to some extent embarrassed at finding themselves in the same camp but are equally opposed to liberal internationalists whether of Wallace or of Hull variety.

.   .   .

Newspaper editors and proprietors who held a conference in Washington were deeply impressed by General Marshall's talk to them. His plans for a large army may in consequence be more sympathetically treated in the press than hitherto. At dinner to press men which I attended Mr Byrnes told the press that if it was to play part of William Tell in criticizing internal policies of Administration, it must be careful in shooting at apple not to kill its own child. . . .

Anti-New Deal campaign is in full swing. James Farley has concluded a highly successful tour of the South, most of whose politicians are devoted personal friends of his, and is said to be busily building anti-New Deal bloc. Democratic Chairman, Postmaster General Walker, is determined to remain on good terms with him. I am told that Farley is unlikely to offer himself as presidential candidate unless he is certain of very solid support in his Party. Whether the South is willing to support a Roman Catholic for Presidency in return for guarantees on coloured issue seems very dubious at present.

4 Samuel W. Meek, advertising executive (Director of J. Walter Thompson Co. 1925–63), Director of *Time* 1922–70.

Refusal of appropriations for National Planning Resources Board by House has left that New Deal agency without current funds. President protested against this at a press conference saying that any funds given to Board now would save national resources at a later stage, continuing line of his speech to White House correspondents in which he indicated that while policies of Administration were aimed at creating a world in which private enterprise would provide jobs for all returned soldiers, ultimate responsibility for this rested squarely on the shoulders of Congress itself. In this connexion it is interesting to note that American Legion is actively recruiting incapacitated men back from fighting fronts and is said to be preparing to absorb into its ranks great army which will return after the war in order to play a more active part in national politics and prevent a recurrence of the situation in which ex-servicemen found themselves at the end of the last war. They look to Rickenbacker as a valuable champion. 'America Firsters' are said to be making overtures to Roane Waring,[5] Commander of the Legion, so far it is said without much success.

. . .

Arrival of *Richelieu*[6] is used as a peg by press allies of State Department on which to hang praise of North African policy which it is maintained turns out to have been far more profitable than ignorant persons had supposed. Hullites are led by Krock who emphasizes that Hull's policy was equally that of the President, an obvious attempt to discomfit liberals who still decline to admit that President was responsible for North African policy or else say that he was and is badly advised. Fact that large numbers of the *Richelieu*'s crew are deserting to Fighting French because they cannot stand pro-Axis policy of their officers has so far been kept out of the press.

. . .

Madame Chiang Kai-shek who addressed both Houses of Congress separately on 18 February was accorded an unprecedented ovation and her line, familiar enough among Chinese spokesmen, that Japan was a more formidable enemy than Germany and should be accorded priority of treatment, was greeted with loudest applause of any passage in her speech, the whole House standing. Her references to post-war international co-operation were more tepidly received. Senator Connally said privately that he was expressing the view of the majority of his followers in recording his opinion that she was the greatest woman in the world and that it would be a historical blunder not to pay the deepest attention to her views.

28 February 1943

Tunisian reverses[1] have not at any rate as yet made a profound impact upon political scene. Main political battles, that between Congress and Administration

5 Roane Waring, Memphis lawyer, Commander of Legion since 1942.

6 French 35,000 ton battleship, removed to Dakar in 1940, and, after Allied landings in North Africa, moved to the USA for refitting.

1 Battle of the Kasserine Pass, 19–22 February 1943.

and that between various 'blocs' and administrative 'czars' (carried on inside and outside Congress) are if anything more intense this week. McKellar[2] bill requiring Senate confirmation of federal employees with a salary of more than $4,500 (thus giving Senate wide patronage and control over civil service) has been approved by Committee and is now before Senate. Farm Bloc secured a senatorial majority of 78 to 2 for Bankhead bill which forbids any deduction from parity prices on account of subsidies. This is directly contrary to a recent presidential order and has raised wheat prices on Chicago exchange to unprecedented heights. . . . In the meanwhile food situation is clearly more difficult than public has been allowed to suppose, and although general new food rationing scheme has been quietly received, Wickard's attempts to convey that consumption of food may have to be drastically reduced is leading to a good deal of rumbling in a land used to considering itself as overflowing with the world's goods. While this may not precipitate a serious crisis, the fact that not a single important Administration measure has yet been allowed to pass by 78th Congress makes Administration's and particularly Mr Byrnes's task almost impossible at times. President's tactics at present seem to be to give Congress as much rope as it is asking for. While underlining in his public speeches and press conferences where he thinks blame for insufficient concentration on war and therefore ultimate responsibility lies he refrains from counterattacking on floor of Congress with a Democratic force which might prove insufficient. Some Republican leaders appear to have realized where their present impetus may take them, for Senator Taft, who is as uncompromising an anti-Rooseveltite as anyone, has publicly warned his colleagues not to thwart Administration too far lest they find themselves saddled with responsibilities which they are not organized to bear. The *Saturday Evening Post* and Scripps-Howard press also plead for more caution on part of Republicans. President appears to be manoeuvering in expectation that Congress will swing pendulum too far against Administration with inevitable popular reaction to follow. Liberals suggest that the more responsible members of the opposition will turn back before it is too late and save the war effort. There seem no signs of this at present. Willkie has been urging Republicans to 'go on affirmative: do something besides criticize'. General public is confused. Both Wickard and McNutt are under fire. Usual crop of rumours is circulating about their imminent dismissals with inevitable speculation about their successors. Justice Douglas, a tough and somewhat nationalistic New Dealer, is mentioned as a possible successor to McNutt with enlarged powers.

President made a very obvious reference to the congressional and in particular the Farm Bloc tactics in his Washington's Birthday speech which referred to conditions set on their allegiance by some American colonies, the perpetual desire on the part of many in Washington's army to return to their fields and farms, sneering attitudes adopted by some towards ideals of Revolution as cloudy and impractical, and compared this with similar attitudes in present-day America. A

2 Kenneth D.McKellar, Democratic Senator from Tennessee since 1917.

Democrat departing from the Washington dinner was heard to observe 'on Lincoln's birthday he thought he was Lincoln. Today he thought he was Washington. What will he say on Christmas Day?'

. . .

Hoover has now joined Dewey, Vandenberg and Taft in disclaiming all presidential ambitions. In meanwhile fourth term issue is gathering momentum. Governors Neely[3] of West Virginia and Maw[4] of Utah have publicly called upon Mr Roosevelt to stand for a fourth term, while aged Congressman Sabath[5] of Illinois told the press that he had discussed this with the President who was 'not at all keen' to serve a fourth term and had conveyed that he would prefer to be allowed to take a part in peace settlement outside White House. President cannot of course at this stage be expected to do anything but disclaim fourth term ambitions. Nevertheless his followers appear to be growing more and more convinced that the Democratic Party is unlikely to win the election without him, in this sharply differing from Jim Farley who appears to continue to gather support within the party in South as well as North against Roosevelt's renomination. Violent attacks of Patterson–McCormick press on prospect of a fourth term were echoed by Rickenbacker, who, in a speech at Albany, criticized 'labor oligarchy' as well as 'inner clique of bureaucracy which is thinking only of a fourth term', rousing violent labour protests and prompting Congressman Rankin[6] to suggest that Rickenbacker similarly address Congress. Rickenbacker's speeches are said to be written by anti-Administration columnist George Sokolsky,[7] while his publicity is said to be in hands of Republican Party experts subsidized by National Association of Manufacturers.

There is still a certain amount of talk on circumstances in WPB which led up to dismissal of Eberstadt and implied defeat of Baruch's ambitions by Nelson. Nelson announced that he could no more think of resigning than could a soldier in Guadalcanal. His new deputy, Wilson, appears to have full support of New Deal experts in WPB who look on Baruch as a reactionary influence. Baruch speaks of having no desire to hold public office and occasionally says that he hopes he is man enough to admit grave errors in his celebrated rubber report. Several government chemical experts are alleged to be saying that if plans for synthetic rubber out of wheat had been placed before them a year earlier, they might have been adopted and a far more satisfactory situation would have resulted. Senator Gillette may yet lead his cohorts in another battle for the conversion of midwestern wheat into rubber. At any rate Wallace has been encouraging Weizmann[8] to continue his researches and to ignore Jeffers, rubber czar, whom, according to Weizmann, he described as 'subhuman'.

3 Matthew M.Neely, Democratic Governor of West Virginia 1942–5.

4 Herbert B.Maw, Democratic Governor of Utah 1941–5.

5 A lolph J.Sabath, Democratic Congressman from Illinois sine 1907.

6 Jonn E.Rankin, Democratic Congressman from Mississippi since 1921.

7 George E.Sokolsky, China correspondent in interwar years, syndicated columnist, *New York Sun* and elsewhere, 1940–50.

8 Chaim Weizmann, President of the Jewish Agency for Palestine 1935–46 ; first President of Israel.

Lend-Lease Powers Act has now been voted unanimously by Foreign Affairs Committee for consideration of House without amendments regarding increased aid to China and post-war aviation which had been feared. While there is not much doubt that it will pass smoothly, hearings have revealed most clearly the lines at present trodden by American expansionists as expressed by Representatives Dewey[9] and Maas.[10] While these men at present stand for no more than a particularly up-and-coming section of the Republican Party, nevertheless they present a rising and not a diminishing trend. Maas is a straightforward Pacific naval imperialist. Dewey of Illinois, whose recent proposal for an international bank with 51 per cent American participation was subject of our telegram No. 809, assumed throughout that America would in fact be the dominant post-war power, and that its coming hegemony must be assumed in all future plans. Although Mrs Luce is still anxiously explaining that by air supremacy she meant no more than control of the air over the United States, nevertheless dreams of world domination are widespread, and while they may yield to Mr Hull's or the President's wiser counsels, their strength must not be discounted. Senate Finance Committee has now unanimously approved a resolution by their chairman, George, to establish a special Senate Committee to investigate and recommend post-war economic policies and planning.

. . .

. . . *Precise meaning of Stalin's last speech.*[11] The President denied that Stalin said that he meant to stop at his own frontiers in all circumstances but obscurity which surrounds Russian intentions leads to a good deal of worried speculation. Fear and suspicion of Russian post-war purposes is high throughout the United States, and Hanson Baldwin in *New York Times* spoke thoughts of many when he said that really convincing argument for a big United States army was need to prevent spread of Russia and Communism over Europe after the war. This view is to be found naturally most frequently among churches and in Republican Party, but post-war department of State Department is said to be deeply imbued with it and so are sections of Office of Strategic Services and it is widespread in military circles. Citrine's failure to get AF of L to enter into a joint committee with British and Russian unions shows how deep this feeling is also within ranks of American labour. Those sections whose aim seems to be to hurt Administration by sowing maximum of disunity are playing at same time on two inconsistent fears that Russians will sweep all before them in Europe and establish Communism everywhere and that Russians will stop at their own frontiers and make a peace with Germans disadvantageous to United States and Britain. Another facet of this is the line that Russian successes are causing grave concern in high quarters because they are inexplicable, that 110 best German divisions have not

9 Charles S. Dewey, Republican Congressman from Illinois since 1941 (Assistant Secretary of Treasury 1924–7).

10 Melvin J. Maas, Republican Congressman from Minnesota 1927–33, 1935–45.

11 An Order of the Day to the Red Army, 22 February, which averred that it was 'not created for the purpose of conquest of foreign countries, but to defend the frontiers of Soviet land'.

fired a shot for a year, that the Luftwaffe has gone intact into retirement and submarines, though as supreme as ever, have deliberately refrained from attacking Murmansk convoys. All this, it is concluded, bodes some deep German–Russian plot. . . .

. . .

OWI is exultant this week over its alleged victory over OSS since they now claim to have recaptured the entire field of foreign propaganda. OSS are still silent on the subject. There is a good deal of talk about this in the press and in Washington. It is too early to say how genuine or permanent this may be but it is unlikely that Sherwood who is leaving for London and North Africa would have left without securing his rear to some degree.

7 March 1943

During this week there has been a noticeable rise in discussion of post-war planning set off by Sumner Welles's Toronto speech in which he announced that inter-Allied discussions on this topic were due to begin. Statement was qualified by his explanation on return to Washington that discussions would be largely on a technical level. President has been induced to give a go-ahead signal to Welles who is the prime mover in this matter. President's recommendation at a recent press conference that widest discussion of post-war plans is desirable is in line with publicity now given to inter-Allied conversations and conference on refugees, post-war currency, etc., existence of plans for which have been received with thus far favourable comment. . . . There is a good deal of talk also on the fact that differences between the Allies, notably Poles and Russians, will continue to be aggravated so long as United States attitude remains obscure and all parties are allowed to rest large hopes on United States support for their particular point of view.

Presidential campaign of 1944 appears to have started in earnest with Willkie officially unfurling his flag in *Herald Tribune* which promptly attacked Governor Bricker (who is regarded as Willkie's most formidable Republican opponent at present) for absence of an enlightened foreign policy. Willkie's present strength seems largely to consist in his negative powers. There is an impression in Republican Party circles that no candidate has a chance to gain nomination without at any rate some support from Willkie's wing of party. Few indications have occurred so far as to foreign policy plank of anti-Willkie Republicans, whether of Dewey, Bricker or Hoover persuasions, and it seems unlikely at present moment. Meanwhile a deputation of Democratic politicians led by Democratic Chairman, Postmaster General Walker, was stated to have called on the President to plead for a fourth term to which the President has thus far not responded. There has been usual irony from anti-Roosevelt columnists and others over what are represented as disingenuous efforts on the part of the President to exhibit reluctance to stand. Talk in Democratic circles turns on proposition that while a

158

fourth term would plainly represent a graver departure from constitutional practice than even third term, no other Democratic candidate with vote-drawing powers is anywhere in sight. There is no evidence that President has begun to reach a decision on the subject. Meanwhile attacks in Congress continue on OWI's pictorial biography of the President which is charged with being a pure piece of fourth term propaganda. Elmer Davis has made a suitable reply.

There is no great change in manpower, food and labour disputes which continue to exercise Congress and nation. There are five anti-strike bills at present before the House. House Rules Committee has approved Hobbs's[1] anti-racket bill denounced by labour unions. Senate Military Affairs Committee has recommended deferment of farm workers for military service despite strong army opposition. Hoover continues to attack Administration's food policy. More publicity has been given to black markets which have developed in food and particularly meat trade. Strike at Boeing plant has provoked a great deal of angry anti-labour comment. John Lewis is preparing to resist decisions of War Labor Board over his demand for a two-dollar raise for bituminous coal workers and appears to be trying to regain his ascendency over organized labour by representing himself as the only major labour leader who has not 'sold out' to Administration. McKellar bill, widely attacked as a crude method of extending senatorial patronage, has emerged from committee in a form so unrecognizable that its own author now disowns it. News of execution in Russia of Polish Jewish labour leaders, Alter and Ehrlich,[2] has led to exceptionally bitter anti-Soviet feeling on the part of Jewish labour unions in New York and of American labour and liberal groups generally. It will be interesting to learn effect of this on Willkie who thought that he had successfully interceded on behalf of these men with Stalin at a time when it appears that they were dead and known to Stalin to be dead.

A good deal of anxiety about Russians' post-war intentions still prevails particularly in conservative circles and as a corollary of this there is much talk about necessity for more aggressive military and political action to ensure that American point of view is given adequate weight in post-war arrangements. Sympathy for Finland continues to be expressed despite Ryti's speech.[3] There is still a good deal of apparently unwarranted speculation about possible peace feelers extended through Archbishop Spellman[4] by Italians and Finns, and prominently publicized statement that United States is shipping more oil to Spain than is available to the eastern states of the United States has provoked some sharp criticisms from liberals and a lukewarm defence from their opponents. A similar reaction is noticeable in case of Supreme Court decision to quash Viereck verdict[5] with

1 Samuel F.Hobbs, Democratic Congressman from Alabama since 1935.

2 Henryk Ehrlich and Victor Alter, killed in February 1943.

3 Risto Ryti, President of Finland, who on 2 February claimed that the United Nations must recognize Finns' right to fight for life and freedom.

4 Francis Joseph Spellman, Roman Catholic Archbishop of New York since 1939.

5 Conviction set aside on grounds that he was not an agent but acted on his own initiative, also that prosecutor had incited prejudice in the jury.

the now usual dissent of Justices Black and Douglas which has caused such heartburning among young New Dealers and triumphant headlines in Mc-Cormick–Patterson press. Old-fashioned liberals applaud Chief Justice Stone's appeal against infusion of hysteria into judicial process and proudly hold up this judgment as evidence of strength of American justice in defence of constitutional liberties. Pacific First school is gaining support as a result of publicity accorded to Madame Chiang's movements and tumultuous reception at a mass meeting in New York which incidentally was an exclusively Republican affair. Dr Evatt's [6] anticipated arrival is expected to strengthen it further. Recent American air victories in the Pacific have restored MacArthur to headlines.

I am informed on reliable evidence that President has created a small 'secret' War Cabinet consisting of Byrnes, Hopkins, Leahy, Baruch and Rosenman. Apparently it is to meet at irregular intervals and have at any rate as yet no official standing or official existence of any kind. It is too early to say whether this body is likely to exercise more influence than is already wielded by its members as individuals. Only notable addition to President's 'unofficial family' is Baruch who is on excellent terms with his other colleagues and is said to be somewhat mollified by this after his disappointment in failing to supplant Nelson, but his relations with the President are said still to be marked by slight strain. Persons close to the President are said not to attach great importance to this committee at any rate at present.

Administration won its first victory in Congress this week in defeating Nichols [7] bill to set up a House aviation committee. There was heavy lobbying against it on the part of Military, Naval and Interstate Commerce Committees which argued that a separate committee even on purely civilian aviation would merely tend to create a new lobby competing with other transport interests. Defeat of this measure caused some distress among supporters of air supremacy school to which expression was given in House but it may indicate that Congress is not at present liable to be swept into indiscriminate legislation on this topic.

.   .   .

14 March 1943

Although situation in the fields of manpower, labour and price adjustment is still confused with apparent disagreements within the Cabinet, notably between Stimson and McNutt (the last is losing power and prestige steadily), the sheer productive effort of this continent is still gathering strength and speed and effects of this can be felt in the sense of its own power on the part of the American people which is steadily rising despite internal crises and military setbacks which may characterize any given week. It is this sense of rising power in the international field which gives a concrete basis to the post-war talks of which there has been much this week.

6 Herbert V.Evatt, Australian Minister for External Affairs since 1941.
7 John C.Nichols, Democratic Congressman from Oklahoma since 1935.

The most important item in this field is the rider attached by the Senate Foreign Relations Committee to its unanimous endorsement of the renewal for one year of the Lend-Lease Powers Act, which states 'the Committee believes there is no authority in the Lend-Lease Act to warrant any general post-war commitments of post-war policies in agreements made under the terms of Lend-Lease Act'. Senator Taft in an off-the-record talk laid heavy stress on the fact that Article 7 of the master agreement [1] was thus not formally binding upon the Government of the United States. No post-war commitments of any kind are or should be entered into now. These remarks were made in the course of a talk in which Taft repeated the old isolationist questions whether an international police force powerful enough to discipline say the United States, if ordered to do so by an international authority, were practicable or acceptable to the American people and again whether a plan to reconstruct the world would not necessarily entail a greater draining of United States resources for the benefit of peoples of lower standards of life than the American people would countenance. The chief butt of Taft's observations was Governor Stassen of Minnesota who has been campaigning in the East for his plan of world reorganization. His present programme, outlined before large meetings in Washington and New York, consists of seven points : (a) temporary administration of Axis territories ; (b) trusteeship of liberated peoples until they establish suitable governments of their own choice ; (c) United Nations airways and seaways supervision ; (d) a world police force ; (e) the improvement of standards of health, of literacy and of academic freedom ; (f) increase of world trade on basis of private enterprise ; (g) acceptance of a worldwide Bill of Human Rights which he has outlined. He laid greater stress on (g) and less emphasis than on previous occasions on an international world parliament, saying that more than one governmental method may be useful in achieving the desired end. Stassen is a rising force in America. His youth and his earnestness and his reputation as an outstandingly successful midwestern Governor with a level-headed and concrete approach to political problems and a strong anti-New Deal bias in internal affairs has given him a reputation for solidity and reliability which will stand him in good stead if and when he returns to politics after his service in the Navy. Partly on account of the flatness of its contents and exposition his world plan, radical as it may seem, has not acquired that flavour of utopianism which the public is now inclined to detect in everything that e.g. Mr Wallace may choose to say. Stassen is half Norwegian, half Czech and is viewed even by his opponents as a typical 'one hundred per cent' American, a symbol and an epitome of America's most characteristic virtues. Welles has also been speaking about the future and beyond declaring (in answer to a question about the acquisition of strategic bases in the Pacific) that Japan must be disarmed and security in the Pacific achieved, specially repudiated the

1 Article which provided that 'the final determination' of the Lend-Lease settlements shall be such as will 'promote mutually advantageous relations'. It committed signatories to 'the elimination of all forms of discriminatory treatment' and to 'the reduction of tariffs and other trade barriers'.

notion of the Pacific as a purely American lake. It is however fairly typical of present mood that various newspapers seized on the fact that when announcing that the United States had no desire to acquire permanent bases in Latin America, Welles said nothing explicit about refraining from acquisition of British, Dutch and French bases and tried to draw unspoken implications scarcely contained in Welles's words. In the meanwhile there have been continued stirrings on this topic in Congress and on 12 March the Senate set up a Committee on post-war policy under the Chairmanship of Senator George, a conservative Southern Democrat and former Chairman of the Senate Committee on Foreign Relations. . . .

Fourth-term agitation is continuing. Anti-Rooseveltites are using every weapon available for assailing what they believe to be the President's decision to stand for a fourth term. Congressman Lambertson's[2] attacks on the President's sons in the House, attacks on owi's alleged pro-Roosevelt propaganda, etc., are part of this campaign. Columnist Drew Pearson has provided accounts of a difficult interview between a truculent Democratic delegation and the President on this topic, which bears every sign of being largely mythical, while Mrs Roosevelt has tried to assuage the situation by making the sombre observation that the subject was not fit for discussion in wartime since in 1944 all concerned may be dead. In the meanwhile Jim Farley has not been idle. A member of my staff was told by one of Mr Farley's henchmen that Farley after his tour of the South had made two provisional decisions, to fight bitterly against a fourth term for Mr Roosevelt and to investigate whether Mr Byrnes could not, in spite of having left Roman Church, be made acceptable to Roman Catholic vote which Farley can probably control. If Byrnes were acceptable to Roman Catholics, and his Catholic past is outweighed by his Episcopalian present in the South, his reputation as an honest, level-headed and adroit 'middle-of-the-road' Democrat might make him a strong candidate with support in both parties, particularly if Republicans choose so uninspiring a figure as Bricker. It seems highly improbable however that Byrnes would ever consent to stand in opposition to the President at the Convention. Farley is said to be meeting Bricker next week to convince himself of his potentialities. According to one of his lieutenants Farley recently paid calls on everyone of consequence in Washington with the exception of the President who, knowing that Farley's behaviour was controlled not by personal likes or dislikes but by realities of political power, is said to have been slightly shaken by the fact that Farley should have so deliberately ignored him, and to have started a series of indirect negotiations with Farley for the purpose of coming to an arrangement. There is also an ill-substantiated rumour that the President would stand down if appointed principal American negotiator of the peace. Whole story is of course no more than gossip from Farley's headquarters and Mr Byrnes's closest friends say that he knows nothing of it. There is no doubt that the President attaches great importance to Catholic vote and his inter-

2 William P.Lambertson, Republican Congressman from Kansas since 1929.

view with Joe Kennedy this week may not be unconnected with this. Liberals interpret his foreign policy in Spain and North Africa as directly affected by his anxiety not to alienate the more than twenty million Catholic United States voters. Persons close to White House say that the President is fully resolved to stand again, and that unless he does no Democrat has a chance of being elected. A recent Gallup poll showed 58 per cent in favour of a fourth term if war was still on in 1944 and 44 per cent if it was over.

The Standley affair[3] naturally drew a great deal of speculation as to whether or not the Admiral had been put up to say what he did, and whether the speech by Wallace with its double warning, to Russia to abandon notion of world revolution, and to the United States and Britain not to encourage Russophobia in their own or other countries, and to abstain from 'double crossing' the USSR, was or was not a mere coincidence. There is no reason to think that it was anything else. Importance not unnaturally was attached to Wallace's disconcerting words on the 'grave probability' of a Russo–German combination but this is, according to Wallace's intimates, to be put down entirely to his desire to frighten Congress concerning possible consequences of their anti-Russian mood, and not to any secret information. It is also worth remarking that Wallace normally clears his text with the President and his friends are certainly under the impression that the President knew and approved speech. There is no reason to think that the President any more than State Department either knew in advance or approved of what Standley said. Correspondents who went to Welles's press conference got the impression that while he was deeply displeased at Standley's failure to consult Department on his remarks and had made this clear to Standley, he did not propose to push the matter any further and had decided to ignore the incident. Personally however I shall be surprised, from an observation that Welles made to me a day or two ago, if Standley is not recalled. I am told that there are two schools of thought in Department, the Russian experts who regard soft words as useless with the Russians and are privately delighted by Standley's remarks as being the only kind of talk which the Russians understand and respect, and group led by Welles which believes that gentler treatment and a certain degree of concession will succeed in breaking down Russian reserve and suspicion, a result which is indispensable for common successful prosecution both of the war and of the peace. Standley's statement that all he was referring to was the contribution of United States to Russian war relief and other charities has gone down quite well in spite of its apparent inconsistency with his earlier reported remarks about lack of Russian publicity for United States 'planes by the thousand' and the sensitiveness of Congress about lack of appreciation for its generosity, i.e. Lend-Lease aid. Press vastly exaggerated degree of bother about this in Congress and apart from allowing Wheeler and Fish to ventilate suspicion of Russia, in-

3 Admiral Standley, US Ambassador, said in Moscow on 8 March that news of American aid was being kept from the Russian people and the Russian authorities sought to give the impression that the war was being fought by Russia alone.

cident seems of relatively little internal consequence. Sumner Welles's anxiety to liquidate issue may be due to his realization of danger of stirring up fear and dislike of USSR which is a very strong and constant background factor here. Ex-Ambassador Bullitt, whose anti-Soviet views are well known, in a speech at Philadelphia said that United States policy to the USSR should be the method used with an obstinate donkey, a carrot, 'a real carrot', should be held before its nose and a club, 'a real club' (which this country possesses), behind its tail. Unless this is done 'Stalin would grab both'. Stassen who was present protested strongly against this remark. Willkie availed himself of the opportunity of simultaneously attacking Wallace and Standley for suggesting that such absurd possibilities as ulterior Russian motives, an American tendency to double-cross (these words of Wallace have scarcely made him more popular with the public) and mutual suspicion could ever infect relations between America and Russia. Willkie is doing his best to keep himself in the public eye but although his influence should not be underestimated and in fluid state of affairs so strong a personality is bound to play a powerful role, he does not look like becoming formal or actual leader of Republican opposition. Martin, minority leader in House, is said still to look upon him without enthusiasm. Recent Gallup poll on chances of Republican nomination for Presidency among registered Republican voters gave an easy lead to Dewey followed by Willkie, Stassen, Bricker and Saltonstall in that order.

Labour situation is not greatly changed. A decision to limit number of men in armed forces to 10,800,000 in 1943 has appeared in the press and appears to be accepted by both Nelson and McNutt, the latter claiming that this would not cut too deeply into civilian and production needs. AF of L and CIO after a brief and completely abortive effort to achieve unified political representation in Washington against fierce opposition to its claims in Congress and over entire country, are today more disunited than ever. Efforts are still being made to effect a tie-up between certain CIO unions and progressive Farmers' Union, a move which was opposed equally by the powerful Farm Bureau (which controls congressional Farm Bloc and exercises more influence than before over Department of Agriculture) and by the more reactionary unions within AF of L. John L. Lewis is busily promoting a crisis over his wage demands for bituminous miners and the situation within the ranks of labour is therefore somewhat chaotic. . . .

Lend-Lease Powers Act was passed by an unanimous vote of Senate and by a majority of 407 to 6 in the House. Of the six, three came from Ohio, three from Michigan, the last being gnarled anti-Administrationists. Connally and Vandenberg spoke with great eloquence and effect in favour of it in the Senate and it was passed without amendment. . . . OPA, under ex-Senators Prentiss Brown and Clyde Herring,[4] is suffering drastic changes which are costing several New Deal heads. Congressional critics are privately saying that the main division

4 Clyde L. Herring, Democratic Senator from Iowa 1937–43.

within Washington departments is that between disinterested servants of public interest and those zealous Rooseveltites who identify this interest with a fourth term for their leader, and predict combing out of the latter. Something of the kind does seem to be occurring but is unlikely to be pushed to lengths involving a serious political reorientation of New Deal agencies. Feeling between Congress and President is exceedingly sharp. . . .

20 March 1943

Mr Eden's arrival and the proposal of four Senators for immediate creation of a United Nations Organization to deal with problems of war and peace has led to a burst of speculation and discussion on post-war questions unparalleled in this war. Movement towards official consideration of post-war issues has been gathering momentum. Welles has been advocating publicly and privately the need for action in this field, and Congress also has bestirred itself. Senatorial opinion cuts across party lines. A dozen Senators of both parties genuinely sympathize with Welles and favour idea of immediate conferences on specific topics between representatives of relevant United Nations. Vast majority of Senate seems to feel that, whatever happens, Senate should at all costs assert itself whether to initiate or to dissent from any given scheme, but above all to curb independent action by the executive. This mood has effect at once of stimulating interest in post-war planning and of increasing suspicion of any specific suggestion made by Administration. The climax of this – the earliest phase of public discussion of post-war world – came with five-point resolution of four Senators, Ball of Minnesota (a nominee of Governor Stassen) and Burton[1] of Ohio, Republicans, and Hatch[2] of New Mexico and Lister Hill[3] of Alabama, Democrats. This resolution urged United States initiative in setting up an organization of United Nations representatives to prosecute the war, to establish provisional governments in freed territories, to organize rehabilitation, and to create machinery for settling international disputes and a 'World Police' to back its decisions. Senator Ball told a member of my staff that he alone is original author of resolution although he had apparently had help in drafting from others, notably Senator Truman of Missouri. According to an informed source Ball obtained support of Burton who is Senator Taft's chief rival in Ohio and a hot anti-Brickerite, and the two invited Hatch, the champion of 'pure politics'[4], and Lister Hill, the chief Democratic whip, to associate themselves with the resolution. Sumner Welles was consulted and, without subscribing to particular scheme or committing SD [State Department] in any way, gave it some encouragement in line with his policy of cultivating potential congressional supporters of any form of anti-isolationism. The

1 Harold H.Burton, Republican Senator from Ohio since 1941.
2 Carl A.Hatch, Democratic Senator from New Mexico since 1933.
3 Lister Hill, Democratic Senator from Alabama since 1938.
4 As author of the Hatch Act regulating campaign expenditure.

same source reported that Hull, after tart observations about not wishing to be told by Congress how to run foreign affairs, warned President that so specific and strong a proposal would lead to a bitter debate in Senate and in country, and was very premature. Senators Connally (Chairman of Foreign Relations Committee) Barkley (Majority Leader) and Wagner took the four Senators to visit President on 14 March. Byrnes and Hopkins were also present at meeting. They were promised no specific support, and President though benevolent apparently repeated Hull's warnings. Connally, who regards himself and his Committee as sole and proper source of senatorial action of this kind, was a trifle frosty to Ball and Burton, and complained of amateurishness of scheme and method of publicity adopted, and Ball is saying in private that Connally's *amour propre* is at stake and that scheme will only have a chance of adoption if it is radically altered and emerges as Connally Resolution. Barkley told press that he liked scheme in general. Some rumbling from isolationists began to be heard but in spite of it Ball, apparently following the tactic of asking more than he expects to obtain in order to leave room for a strategic retreat, introduced his resolution in Senate on Tuesday. Connally, who in meanwhile had had time to sound out senatorial sentiment, evidently confirmed Hull's fears that formidable and violent opposition was being planned by the isolationists. He consequently hedged on his earlier statement that Foreign Relations Committee would definitely consider resolution, talked gloomily of serious consequences likely to spring from an immediate debate upon this issue, said that neither SD nor White House had given him a lead in the matter, and finally suggested that he might designate a seven-man sub-committee of Foreign Relations Committee to consider the resolution. His private opinion appears to be that resolution is too specific to be safe object of debate in Senate and that a more general expression of American willingness to co-operate with other powers would be wiser. Senator James Davis[5] is so far the only member of Foreign Relations Committee to put his complete opposition to the resolution on record. Senator Thomas of Utah is only member to endorse it without qualification (Senator Guffey[6] is expected shortly to join him). The attitude of press is more favourable than that of political groups in Washington, and oscillates between full approval and more cautious line taken by such commentators as Krock and conservatives, who think that a more modest proposal would have a better chance of smooth passage, and would achieve effect of committing Congress to some kind of internationalism without causing a violent controversy which would be fatal to American and indeed United Nations solidarity. As for the President, at a press conference, he finally came out in favour of broad general principles of resolution after stressing that this was a matter strictly within province of senatorial prerogative, and added that it would not hurt the world to know where America stood in matter. As for general public it is, I believe, ready to welcome any suggestion represented to it as constructive

5 James J. Davis, Republican Senator from Pennsylvania since 1930.
6 Joseph F. Guffey, Democratic Senator from Pennsylvania since 1935.

especially if it entails American leadership but in general it has little sense of direction and is a trifle bewildered by latest plans and lack of guidance from Washington. Senator Ball, who has received enthusiastic endorsement from Willkie, is said to be ready to press on with his resolution come hell or high water, although there does not seem to be much prospect of his succeeding at present.

General impression which emerges from this welter of facts and expressions of opinion is that public opinion would support a formulation of peace aims, that Administration is inhibited from doing so principally by uncertain mood of Congress and nervousness concerning Russian intentions, that Congress, and in particular Senate, is in principle willing to consider subject but that in practice Democrats and Willkie Republicans are insufficiently sure of their strength to risk what would certainly develop into a battle with their opponents, and finally that tact and goodwill shown by the Secretary of State for Foreign Affairs[7] has helped to clear away much congressional suspicion of British intentions, and of secret methods which Britain is thought to employ for their fulfilment, a view still entertained widely in this country, particularly in Middle West and among its representatives in Congress. There is no doubt that in spite of unskilful and confused manner in which Ball resolution was brought forward, the four Senators have performed a valuable service in helping to publicize and crystallize the issue before Congress and public, and not least in providing Administration and congressional leaders with an opportunity of representing a set of more acceptable proposals of their own as a statesmanlike concession to opponents of Ball resolution. There is no evidence as yet for isolationist story that this is a deliberate Willkie-ite manoeuvre to force hand of Administration.

Mr Eden's arrival, coinciding as it did with reception given by press and radio to Ball resolution, was hailed as an added token of serious intentions on part of Allies to consider problems of peace . . . . Roscoe Drummond[8] (*Christian Science Monitor* correspondent) told a member of my staff that Sumner Welles had summarized obstacles blocking path of Russo–American understanding as being (a) the lack of any formal Russo-American agreement; (b) the danger that if no agreement on basic principles is reached before autumn it may be too late; (c) the stranglehold over foreign policy maintained by thirty men in Senate; (d) Stalin's lack of confidence both in Standley and in Litvinov which created a diplomatic barrier. Drummond reproduced this, without attribution, in *Monitor*. Suspicion of Russia's post-war intentions hovers like a ghost haunting American peace planners during their most expansive moments and has become an almost obsessive fear with certain members of SD, notably Mr Berle.

Eden's off-the-record luncheon with members of Foreign Relations and Foreign Affairs Committees was occasion for fresh speculation and comment. Most

7 Anthony Eden.
8 James Roscoe Drummond, with *Christian Science Monitor* since 1924, chief of Washington Bureau since 1940.

of those who attended declared themselves well satisfied, and described the occasion as 'delightful' and 'most encouraging'. Isolationists present were taciturn but offered no subsequent criticisms. They did however convey to isolationist press the impression that Secretary of State 'threw cold water on idealistic peace planning' and advised against 'detailed blueprints now for post-war conditions'. This last point was made more widely although an important section of press which had begun by being preoccupied with Russia has swung to an interpretation of Mr Eden's visit as being concerned with closer co-operation between all four major powers. The deepest impression on friends and critics alike was evidently made by Mr Eden's statement that Britain had no secret agreements or understandings with her Allies. His 'off-the-record' remarks, some of which leaked to press immediately, did a great deal to allay suspicion against which they were directed. Connally referred to 'very fine effect' of Mr Eden's visit and meeting with members of Congress and to 'the harmonious concord between Great Britain and the United States'.

· · ·

John L.Lewis, who is pressing on with his wage demands, is once more manoeuvering himself into the centre of the picture as the most dangerous demagogue in America. Brown, Chairman of OPA, has pointed out that if Lewis set the pace Green and Murray must follow, and if their demands are met, inflation is inevitable. Crisis in this situation cannot be far off now. The Administration does not appear to be doing much to avert it.

Mr J.P.Morgan's[9] death was an event of national significance. It symbolized the passing of an epoch and underlined the gradual decline of Wall Street as a centre of influence, and the transfer of its former power to great centres of production in Ohio, Michigan and West Coast.

At the Cleveland convention of Federal Council of Churches, after a prolonged debate, a resolution was passed asserting that the Protestant churches of America were not at war but in the war. The debate in general indicated strong pacifist sentiment, partly due to sense of guilt which is felt by many American Protestants at excessive martial zeal on the part of churches in last war. The Chairman of its commission for post-war studies has announced a six-point plan: (1) international political collaboration; (2) control of economic and financial acts which may disturb international peace; (3) organization to adapt the treaty structure to changing conditions; (4) autonomy for subject peoples; (5) international armaments control; and (6) religious and intellectual liberty.

· · ·

The Disney[10] bill repealing President's executive order establishing a $25,000 ceiling over incomes is a symptom of present acute tension between executive and legislature.

National income of United States in 1942 has reached the record figure of $119.8 billion (against $95.6 billion in 1941).

9 John Pierpont Morgan, banker, b. 1867.
10 Wesley E.Disney, Democratic Congressman from Oklahoma since 1931.

Gallup poll of Democratic voters' choice of presidential candidates (parallel to that of Republicans reported last week) puts Wallace first with 57 per cent, a rise of 7 per cent since last December, with McNutt, Byrnes and Justice Douglas some way behind. These figures were based on assumption that Roosevelt did not stand again. . . . Little importance attached to such polls particularly at this distance from election.

28 March 1943

Public support for formulation of an official United States post-war plan brought to a head by Ball-Burton-Hill-Hatch Resolution (referred to in our last summary) has, according to all available evidence, been mounting steadily in all parts of the country although not to the point of forcing Administration or Congress to take any immediate decision. Nevertheless President thought it necessary to deny allegation that he was cool towards Resolution. Hull, without giving explicit support to Ball Resolution, said that any declaration by Senate on American post-war collaboration would be 'helpful and encouraging' because it would give a lead to waverers.

Senate Foreign Relations Committee has appointed a sub-committee to consider and report on all pending resolutions dealing with post-war policy, i.e. those recommending specific post-war plans such as Ball, Gillette, Thomas and Pepper resolutions and those only setting up government machinery to promote such plans as suggested by Senators Kilgore[1] and Wiley.[2] Sub-committee consists of Senators Connally (Chairman), George, Barkley, Thomas and Gillette (Democrats), White[3] and Vandenberg (Republicans) and La Follette (Progressive). Of these Barkley and Thomas are wholehearted Rooseveltites, Connally and George are anti-isolationist Southern conservatives, White is a mild internationalist, Gillette a doubtful case, Vandenberg a respectable nationalist and La Follette an eccentric isolationist. There is thus an anti-isolationist majority of five without any dyed-in-the-wool isolationism in minority group.

Senators Guffey of Pennsylvania and Maybank of South Carolina pledged 'wholehearted support' to Ball Resolution, as did twenty-six of the fifty-five new Republican Representatives in Congress. It is noticeable that of the seventeen states represented in this last group there are few representatives from Middle West. A canvass of Senate's twelve new members is reported to show at least eight who are cool to Resolution, largely, it is said, under the influence of Minority Leader McNary who has both in public and in private spoken unfavourably of proposals for close political and economic international co-operation.

Taft said in a press interview that Senate ought to go on record as favouring the creation of machinery which the United Nations could employ for peace problems after the war but he persisted in his strong opposition, as reported last

1 Harley M.Kilgore, Democratic Senator from West Virginia since 1941.
2 Alexander Wiley, Republican Senator from Wisconsin since 1939.
3 Wallace H.White Jr, Republican Senator from Maine since 1931.

week, to United States entrance into commitments now on schemes for government relief and rehabilitation of reconquered areas, and more particularly to establishment of an international police force. Isolationist press is now openly hostile to scheme. Senator Willis[4] has attached routine isolationist amendment to Resolution giving notice that a two-thirds majority of the Senate is required for adoption of any such scheme by the United States. Messrs Hoover and Gibson, who are anxious to give evidence of constructive thought, have publicly spoken in favour of international police force. A half-forgotten figure, ex-Senator Reed of Missouri,[5] who was very prominent a quarter of a century ago in the fight against the League of Nations, suddenly spoke out loud and strong from the depth of Missouri against Resolution and tried unsuccessfully to revive the old cry of foreign entanglements. He was given little publicity outside Middle West and is probably no longer of account. Senator La Follette attacked Resolution on ground that its adoption would in any case commit the United States to nothing concrete and then attacked its specific proposals on usual isolationist grounds. It seems clear that a large and widespread volume of sentiment exists in favour of a congressional declaration in general terms of post-war intentions which is likely to bear fruit in the not-too-distant future. In order to avoid controversial debate and to secure its adoption by a satisfactory vote in Senate, whatever resolution emerges from Committee will certainly be one designed to provide common ground for divergent opinions, but may none the less serve both as a pointer and as a stage in the development of senatorial thought. Welles told Foreign Secretary and myself the other night that he was well satisfied with the way in which things were moving.

The first reaction to Mr Churchill's speech[6] was one of wide and warm approval. Dorothy Thompson said that it was the greatest speech of his career, and Lippmann thought that Mr Churchill had dispelled once and for all impression that he took little interest in post-war settlement. This favourable primary reaction is still fairly general but secondary effects are now discernible. A stream of sharp criticism was, as might be expected, directed by a number of radio commentators and in press against lack of reference to China among the powers on whose co-operation future settlement must rest. Point that Europe, after all, was subject of discussion, was made here and there but Sinophiles everywhere and one or two government-inspired columnists such as David Lawrence[7] and Constantine Brown[8] and, most important of all, House Majority Leader McCormack,[9] echoed by Sol Bloom,[10] Chairman of House Foreign Affairs Com-

4 Raymond E.Willis, Republican Senator from Indiana since 1941.

5 James A.Reed, Democratic Senator from Missouri 1911–29.

6 Broadcast 21 March endorsing Beveridge Plan and envisaging post-war planning between Allies.

7 David Lawrence, Washington syndicated columnist, founder and editor of *NY News and World Report*.

8 Constantine Brown, co-author with Drew Pearson of *The American Diplomatic Game* (1935); correspondent of *Washington Star*.

9 John W.McCormack, Democratic Congressman from Massachusetts since 1928.

10 Sol Bloom, Democratic Congressman from New York since 1923.

mittee, criticized the speech on these grounds. Chinese Embassy as well as MacArthur lobby gave every sign of acute unease and resentment and there is widespread talk in Washington of the deep concern alleged to be felt by interested parties about precise significance of Mr Churchill's references to partial demobilization should Germany be defeated before Japan. Madame Chiang made an unmistakable reference to this in her Chicago speech reported to have been inserted at last moment. Chinese lobby in United States, supported as it is by 'Pacific First' school, has shown its strength by this loudly discordant note which is unlikely to be stilled by references to Mr Churchill's words earlier in speech on his determination to crush Japan.

.   .   .

3 April 1943

Mr Eden's speech at Annapolis [1] attracted exceptionally favourable nationwide attention and discussion. The entire text was reprinted not only in leading New York newspapers but in a number of important journals in South and West. Even the *Chicago Tribune* found little to criticize.

The most widely and heavily stressed point was his vow to fight to the end against Japan. There is no doubt that the misunderstanding of Mr Churchill's words about partial demobilization and his apparent omission of China from list of great powers on whom reconstruction would rest produced a deep uneasiness throughout the country, the full extent of which was only revealed by the universal expressions of relief, simulated or real, which Mr Eden's words called forth. Although only a few lines of Mr Eden's speech were devoted to this topic, a casual reader glancing through the American press of this week would suppose that this was the main burden of his address. Headlines on the front pages of virtually every newspaper proclaimed it and editorials loudly welcomed the laying of this bogey. Madame Chiang, who (as reported last week) modified her speech to meet Mr Churchill's statement, went out of her way to praise Mr Eden's remarks and to express satisfaction at being allied to a country which produced such spokesmen. On the other hand a member of my staff was told by Pearl Buck [2] that Madame Chiang had assured her that Britain had no serious intention of fighting on against Japan. China is a national passion with the United States (despite rigid United States adherence to its Oriental Exclusion Act [3]) and any British act or word affecting China elicits an immediate and sharp response here.

The other principal points in Mr Eden's speech which were impressed upon the general public were (a) his denial that His Majesty's Government had entered into any secret agreements and (b) his general plea for collective security.

1 On 26 March. It ranked China with the USA, the USSR, and Britain in their war and post-war responsibilities.
2 Pearl S. Buck, novelist, Nobel Prize winner (1938), active Sinophile.
3 Passed in 1882, in the wake of a wave of Chinese immigration and high unemployment in California. The restriction was additional to those imposed by the ordinary US immigration laws.

Mr Eden's visit is universally described here as an outstanding success. The President, the heads of the State Department and the various influential Senators and Congressmen have privately been singing the praises of the Foreign Secretary's candour and realism. The President in his press conference spoke of 95 per cent agreement among the United Nations and took trouble to emphasize the non-exclusiveness of the Anglo-American conversations and the fact that they were but a prelude to many future conferences on specific topics such as food, refugees, oil, minerals, etc. In answer to a question whether he proposed to see Stalin soon he replied that hope springs eternal in the human breast. It may be of interest to note that Vice-President Wallace, now on a goodwill tour of Latin America, is engaged in learning Russian with, it is said, more enthusiasm than he ever put into his Spanish lessons.

The only aspect of Mr Eden's visit which attracted criticism was the suspicion voiced most prominently by Lindley (who continues to be an Administration mouthpiece) that the British Government entertained a desire to mediate between Russia and United States. This was interpreted in some quarters as an attempt by Britain to recover her traditional position as the manipulator of balance of power between Russia and United States as formerly between France and Germany. A senior member of the State Department remarked to a member of my staff that the United States did not wish to see that game started again and that although Stalin might well be the devil of the coming peace, United States thought it possessed a long enough spoon to sup with him without assistance of other powers. This attitude is fairly characteristic of circles least well disposed to Russian claims, such as European Division of State Department and the relevant sections of OSS. Meanwhile Bullitt repeated his warnings that if any one of the United Nations should violate the provisions of the Atlantic Charter, the people of the United States would turn again in disillusion to isolationism. This was interpreted by some as a reference to possible post-war encroachments by Russia on the integrity of its smaller European neighbours. Lippmann reproved Bullitt and said that to present to the American people the alternatives of either underwriting now specific solutions of complicated European disputes or withdrawing into isolation was the kind of intransigence on the part of Wilson which prevented American entrance into the League. Bullitt's remarks were addressed to a conference held by Coudenhove-Kalergi's[4] unimportant Pan-European Conference to which however both Hull and Welles sent carefully worded non-committal messages. Bullitt, who is perhaps the most rabidly anti-Soviet of all high United States officials, has of late been talking against Welles in what is even for him a wildly irresponsible fashion. This would be of little importance if it were not that Bullitt still has some access to the President.

The lines of the struggle within the Republican Party are becoming clearer. It is now plain that the Ball Resolution is to be the main weapon of offence directed

4 Count Coudenhove-Kalergi, founder and President of Pan-European Union in interwar years.

against Bricker and his group by the Willkie-Stassen wing of the party. . . . A member of my staff was told by one of the Cowles Bros,[5] who are Willkie's staunchest adjutants, that they were sanguine of defeating the old guard over issue of foreign policy since if they accepted challenge they would be routed, while if they did not such passivity at a critical moment would destroy them. On the other hand Cowles was not too optimistic about Willkie's own chances and opined that someone else, probably Dewey, might step into breach with a moderately internationalist programme made to suit whatever is the mood of the public.

The response to the Ball Resolution appears to have been more enthusiastic than the isolationists had calculated and it is perhaps as a result of this that Senator Taft delivered a speech of some importance in Cincinnati in which he advocated his own notion of a League of Nations with far more limited powers of controlling the acts of sovereign states than Ball Resolution which he condemned. Evidently the isolationists feel their position to be too weak at the moment to make a frontal assault upon their opponents and they are beginning to conduct flanking movements of the kind adopted by Lodge in 1919, i.e. of making counter-suggestions to any given scheme proposed by the Willkie-ites or the Administration designed to confuse the issue.

Some Willkie-ites maintain that President is deliberately damping down the agitation in favour of the Ball Resolution because its sponsors would be enabled thereby to steal too much Administration thunder. That there is nothing in this is shown by fact that, as I am informed from a most reliable quarter, the President has transmitted Hull's suggestions of a modified version of the Ball Resolution to Connally for consideration of Senate at earliest politically favourable moment. Meanwhile debate on issue has died down, with Guffey and other Administrationists warning about the horrors of a return to normality, while Wheeler and Reynolds dwell on disturbing obscurity of Russian intentions. Senate Foreign Relations sub-committee is now examining various post-war plans submitted to it. In line with our earlier reports the President and Farley are said to be entering on a tug-of-war for Catholic vote. The South is still simmering against New Deal but it is far too early to estimate what chances are of conservative anti-Roosevelt coalition of South and North which Farley is said to be promoting. Influential A F of L leader Tobin has warned Administration that labour will abandon Democrats unless a stronger pro-labour policy is adopted and various Southern governors have uttered similar warnings concerning racial and states' rights issues but these are probably no more than routine pre-election moves.

. . .

The passage of resolutions by the legislatures of Illinois, Indiana, Michigan and Iowa limiting presidential tenure to two terms and similar resolutions pending in Missouri, Nebraska, Wisconsin, while a relatively small snowball at pres-

5 John and Gardner Jr. For Gardner, see p. 61, n. 8. John was publisher of the *Minneapolis Tribune*.

ent, will if it spreads to the anti-New Deal South become a formidable movement even if it does not attain its objective, which is a constitutional amendment.

John L. Lewis this last week declared in evidence before the Truman Committee that in view of the imposition of the 'Little Steel' formula limiting wages irrespective of new increases in the cost of living, he now regarded his promise not to strike as not necessarily binding. Committee has now issued a report on labour situation condemning Lewis for backing down on this promise and deploring the split in organized labour which led to competitive appeals to the rank and file by different labour organizations. The report however unexpectedly conceded that 'Little Steel Formula', the Maginot Line of the War Labor Board, might conceivably require to be modified. Referring to the split in organized labour, Tobin of the AF of L told press that he saw no hope of any AF of L-CIO understanding in predictable future. This is an attitude shared by Dubinsky[6] (New York labour leader known to be advising Willkie on labour matters and Dewey on state politics).

Dubinsky is said to be contemplating a journey to Chungking. His contemplated journey to Russia is now definitely out of the question as a result of Ehrlich and Alter executions. These executions seem to have left a lasting scar on wide section of United States labour and liberal opinion. Green of AF of L and Carey[7] of CIO formally condemned them and latter is consequently under fire from left-wing CIO unions.

I learn that Bridges, the Australian West Coast labour leader, thinking to profit by controversy in CIO circles over recent visit of Citrine, recently delivered a violent diatribe against Britain before the CIO executive committee and proposed an anti-British resolution. Philip Murray condemned this attitude in very sharp and personal terms and caused a defeat of the resolution by a vote which, save for Bridges' vote, was unanimous.

10 April 1943

Discussion of your visit mostly stresses benefits gained by 'meeting of minds' and there is little suggestion that major decisions were adopted or adumbrated. . . . General press and Washington estimates of British foreign policy which had previously regarded Anglo-Russian accord as a subject for speculation now take it as a fact beyond dispute, whether they view it favourably or not. This is sometimes attributed to obscurity and unreliability of future American intentions and American indecision on this is often unfavourably compared to reported growing clarity of British and Russian intentions. . . .

6 David Dubinsky, President of International Ladies' Garment Workers' Union (ILGWU) since 1932.

7 James B. Carey, President of United Electrical, Radio and Machine Workers of America 1936–41 and 1950–65.

Luce publications have issued a fervently enthusiastic special Russian issue of *Life*. There is also a good deal of simple fervour in Willkie's published trave-logue [1] for which he is most warmly praised by Lippmann. In this connexion it may be noted that Berle went out of his way to condemn various views which have been not without cause commonly attributed to him. In a recent speech he stressed (a) that suspicions of Russia's expansionist ambitions were unjustified in view of vast task of internal reconstruction which will face her after the war ; (b) that notion of a *cordon sanitaire* of buffer states on Russia's western border was an outworn concept of bad old diplomacy and stultified by modern air power ; and (c) that suspicions that Britain was working to capture world trade were baseless since trading interests of the United States and Britain coincided and expansion of United States trade entailed corresponding expansion of British markets and *vice versa*. There follow some compliments to British Empire and hopes of a settlement based on an accord of Big Four Powers, etc. . . .

Bankhead Bill (see previous summary for 28 February) occupied centre of congressional stage. After passing both Senate and House by thumping majori-ties due in part to desire to show Administration how far it might go, it was vetoed by President with a mildly worded explanation of its inflationary dangers. Bankhead tried to rally a two-thirds majority needed to overrule veto, found to his surprise that this was unobtainable and executed a retreat by getting his bill recommitted to Agriculture Committee where it will hang as a permanent threat over head of Administration ready for use whenever Farm Bloc feel strong enough to pounce again. Administration proved just not strong enough to cut off Bankhead's retreat by defeating anti-veto resolution which would have killed the bill this session. What saved the President as much as anything was the terrifying spectre of John L.Lewis with his wage demands supported by Mine Workers' advertisements in press. Farm Bloc bill is ready for use by Senate if the President shows signs of giving in to labour demands. Anti-labour sentiment in Congress is at least as strong at the moment as loyalties to farm interests and meeting of two forces has produced an unstable equilibrium. Taxation plans are still utterly confused. President on 9 April dramatically forbade by executive order both wage and price increases beyond specified limits. As there is very deep and wide national anxiety about inflation this will be well received by the public.

. . .

Currency, Food and Refugee Conferences [2] are little discussed, last least of all. British and American currency proposals are now prominently before the public. President vetoed publication of latter to avoid awkward questions. Mor-genthau, after telling enquiring correspondents that no leakage would occur, gen-

---

1 *One World,* report and reflections on his trip to Middle East, USSR and China, a best-seller.

2 On 1 April Morgenthau announced that representatives of United Nations were about to confer in Washington on post-war currency stabilization (forerunner of Bretton Woods). Food and Agriculture Conference met at Hot Springs, Virginia, 8 May–3 June. Conference on Refugees met at Bermuda, 19–29 April.

erously exonerated Britain when it did and planted suspicion vaguely on one of the Allied Governments in London. . . .

. . .

Mayor Kelly[3] of Chicago has been re-elected by a majority of about 118,000. Alleged traditional tie-up between Kelly-Nash machine[4] and Colonel McCormick's forces is thought to have played its part. Despite drop of 70,000 from previous majorities this represents a definite Democratic victory in key state of Illinois. Michigan State elections went to Republicans. There is evidence of vigorous anti-isolationist agitation by Stassenites in Middle West.

A flurry was caused by Eisenhower-de Gaulle incident[5] with what is now routine comment from two well established camps in this controversy. Hull used occasion to repeat that military considerations alone weighed with him and protested that what he had been criticized for was failure to take political sides when he preferred to concentrate on winning the war. Anti-Gaullist sentiment is deeper than ever in official circles.

General Marshall's order under Stimson's instructions that no serving officer may run for political office is widely taken as directed against alleged (and denied) ambitions of MacArthur who in any case soon reaches retiring age. It has caused so far little beyond inevitable indignation of such anti-Rooseveltites as Vandenberg and Patterson press to whom it is routine grist for their political mills. Krock surprisingly exonerates President on this score. La Guardia's effort to become a general eventually frustrated by army and congressional opposition has caused some merriment.

Truman and Military Affairs Committees are publicly vying in their anxiety to visit fighting fronts. Marshall declared that he would obey orders and transport whole of Congress to fronts if so instructed.

Anti-New Deal campaigners started a new drive against 'professors' in OPA which is still being busily purged.

The status of Eire has led to some discussion. Two critical articles, one by Miss Hinkson,[6] the other by Professor Commager[7] (latter in *New York Times Journal*), finally provoked the Irish Minister into publishing an answering article in the same journal in which he claimed that the United Kingdom (a) benefitted by the neutrality of Eire, and (b) would not have surrendered the bases[8] if it thought their loss a danger in wartime, and then produced familiar stuff on partition and historical anti-British grievances.

3 Edward J.Kelly, Mayor and Democratic boss of Chicago since 1933.

4 Alliance between Mayor Kelly and Patrick Nash (National Committeeman) that ruled Cook County, Illinois (Chicago), during most of Roosevelt era.

5 Statement on 7 April by Eisenhower expressing 'surprise' at Fighting French assertion that de Gaulle had postponed visit to North Africa at Eisenhower's request.

6 Pamela Hinkson, Anglo-Irish novelist and journalist, who worked for the British Ministry of Information 1939–45.

7 Henry Steele Commager, historian and commentator on public affairs.

8 Under the 1921 Treaty which created the independent state of Ireland the United Kingdom retained three Irish ports as naval bases, but in 1938 they were handed back to Eire.

18 April 1943

British military prestige is at its highest at moment owing to vivid personalization of Montgomery and the Eighth Army in press and radio.[1] British exploits have been widely, at times almost fulsomely, played up, which has so far provoked only a mild counter reaction, e.g. an isolationist attack on military commentator Fielding Eliot[2] who has caused some irritation by drawing a comparison too unfavourable to Patton's[3] forces. The film *Desert Victory*[4] has created great enthusiasm in the East which will doubtless spread. There is no doubt, as Lewis Douglas of War Shipping Administration remarked to a member of my staff, that Anglo-American tension has declined and critical feeling, although potentially strong, has entered a passive phase. This steep rise in goodwill of a very mercurial public opinion was very noticeable during, and was considerably strengthened by, the good effects of your recent visit. Raymond Gram Swing[5] privately told a member of my staff that your words had made a favourable impression upon such anti-Administration leaders as Taft and McNary, and that our American friends were wondering how best to capitalize on this gratifying situation. In contrast to this, Mme Chiang (who is vaguely rumoured to be thinking of taking up the Indian problem in a big way) seems to have irritated Administration members and key politicians in Washington, principally by appealing over their heads to the general public. Popular devotion to China was probably heightened by her visit, but both White House and such friends of China as Senator Thomas of Utah and Senator Pepper and even Pearl Buck are said to be critical of Soong family[6] oligarchy and to wonder, on the basis of information by United States officials returned from China, what proportion of United States supplies are used against the Japanese and what proportion against local Communists. Mme Chiang spoke of 'an end to mandates under any one country' and regionalism. Her public complaint that Chinese were not even notified of diversion of arms from China to, say, North Africa, is not likely to improve her stock in official circles even if it excites sympathy among the public. The controversy between Knox and MacArthur[7] and their followers in Australia and Washington concerning degree of present menace to Australia has done something to split the 'Pacific

1 Apropos of second battle of Alamein, advance across Africa to Tunisia, and the breaking of the Mareth Line on 27 March.

2 Major George Fielding Eliot, military correspondent for *New York Herald Tribune* and Columbia Broadcasting System since 1939.

3 George S. Patton Jr, veteran of First World War and swashbuckling commander of the Western Task Force of 'Torch', the Northwest Africa operation.

4 British official film of the 1940–1 North African Campaign.

5 Raymond Gram Swing, commentator on foreign affairs for Mutual Broadcasting System since 1936, widely known in Britain for BBC broadcasts on US affairs.

6 Charles Jones Soong, a Shanghai merchant, had lived in America and become a Methodist before returning to China. Madame Chiang was his daughter. His son, T.V. Soong, banker, became Chiang's Foreign Minister.

7 MacArthur and Blamey (his Australian ground commander – see note 1, page 180) had alleged a large Japanese army and naval force were threatening Australia. Knox had denied that Japanese naval strike forces were so powerful and (April 16) emphasized that the USA had two fleets operating in the Pacific. However Stimson (15 April) promised increasing flow of planes to Australia.

Firsters'. They are still in full cry but some among them find it difficult to cry for despatch of same planes to China and MacArthur at same time.

Administration and opposition have both invoked Jefferson, whose bi-centennial is being celebrated, as the champion of their opposed doctrines. President praised him as a planner who looked to today and tomorrow, hated by those who looked to today and yesterday. Hull delivered a routine oration to the Pan-American Union and stressed that it was the most successful experiment to date of co-operation between sovereign states. Welles in letter to Professor Barton Perry,[8] . . . who had referred to criticisms commonly levelled at State Department as the home of 'embattled reactionary sentiments', quoting its alleged favour to Franco, Otto and Mihajlovic,[9] its antipathy to Free French, and its failure to cope with Indian problem, replied with a routine but very courteous defence of United States foreign policy, denying alleged favouritism and defining aims of United States foreign policy as the swiftest possible military victory with the least loss of American lives, followed by a fair and lasting peace, and complaining that 'surface developments had been taken as an indication of basic policy'. As for India, while United States was naturally much concerned, the problem was complicated. The Indians would be enabled to choose their form of government freely after the war, nor could he conceive how active United States intervention in Indian affairs could be viewed as a test of liberalism. Welles is undoubtedly concerned with good opinion of serious and influential liberal groups in this country and loses no opportunity of representing his views as being close to their own. He was duly hailed by Lippmann. Berle, speaking at dinner of the *New Leader,* a social-democratic anti-communist weekly, discoursed on 'the kindly revolution' which was America's way, reminded his audience of his own past connexions with American liberalism, denounced and discounted effects of disruptive foreign ideologies on American soil and in general represented himself as champion of American liberalism against totalitarian influences. I am told that the more hardboiled members of the audience and in particular the press table considered the speech a somewhat disingenuous effort to dispel general suspicion with which his political activities are regarded.

. . . I am told that Willkie thinks his chances would be greatly improved by a fourth term bid by President since his value to his party would be heightened inasmuch as he regards himself as sole candidate known to be capable of standing up to Roosevelt. Willkie's book *One World* continues to obtain wide praise. Stassen, who has reviewed it for *New York Times,* after conventional praise finds fault with overcriticism of British Colonial system and underemphasis of perils of Communism, as well as insufficient attention to religious issues.

.   .   .

Agitation concerning lack of facilities offered to press at forthcoming Food and Refugee Conferences has grown into a nationwide protest by journalists and

8 Ralph Barton Perry (1876–1957), Harvard Professor of Philosophy and disciple of William James.
9 Draza Mihajlovic, General in command of Chetniks, Serbian resistance forces.

broadcasters. Commentators and editorials maintain that this is an attempt on part of White House and State Department to conduct important discussions in camera, which may establish a precedent for coming peace negotiations, an attack on popular rights, a Star Chamber proceeding leading straight to abhorred secret diplomacy of European ill-fame. While Lippmann was ambiguous, Lindley . . . feebly defended Administration. Resolutions are before both House and Senate demanding press representation at these conferences. Elmer Davis has given impression that he sides with press on this issue but has been overridden. It is probable that if press has recourse to leakages uncorrected by official information the resultant embarrassments will be attributed by all sides to blundering on part of President. Senate House Joint Agricultural Committee, as well as minority leader Martin, now demand admission of congressional 'observers' to conference and various Congressmen utter dire warnings of Roosevelt's fate if, like Wilson, he forgets Congress.

President's anti-inflation order has met with widespread popular approval but controversy between John L. Lewis and coal operators continues with however much accession of popular sentiment to Government side. Hobbs Anti-Racketeering bill has passed House with a mild amendment safeguarding previous labour acts. Philip Murray at a press conference replied to charges of labour absenteeism by declaring that the country was threatened with overproduction at an early date and resultant dislocation and unemployment. Meanwhile War Department continues to press for Wadsworth-Austin manpower mobilization bill, McNutt is still stalling it, and press attacks on absenteeism continue. While no one denies shipping shortage, informed persons maintain that while a remarkable task has been achieved in sheer accumulation of war material, in particular of munitions, it could be argued that synchronization and co-ordination have not been so efficient, so that certain goods have been overproduced at expense of now more urgently needed commodities, since vast production machine is too unwieldy to be easily readjusted to new needs. Production agencies are well aware of these dangers (although public is not) and will doubtless bend every effort to avert prospect of unemployment and absenteeism at one end and shortages at other.

Comment on monetary plans is still thin, and suggestion that British plan favours Britain unduly and seeks to nullify the United States advantage as a gold possessing power, although occurring here and there particularly in financial press, has not yet developed into an even minor campaign, but there is no telling. Association of Lord Keynes's [10] name with British plan has excited anti-New Dealers' suspicions and flames may yet be fanned. Morgenthau said off the record that he contemplated no international monetary conference, only a series of *ad hoc* consultations between individual Governments concerned.

.　.　.

---

10 John Maynard Keynes, economist and adviser to H.M. Treasury since 1940.

Resignations from OWI continue. A round dozen of offficials have left domestic branch saying that they could not bear the substitution of ballyhoo for objective reporting by promotion agents and advertisers introduced by Gardner Cowles. Elmer Davis spoke of 'a clash of personalities', and Cowles described statement as 'the bunk'. Cowles himself is rumoured to be thinking of resigning in July to prepare Willkie's campaign. John S. Knight,[11] the anti-Rooseveltite newspaper owner, lately appointed Censorship Liaison Officer in London, is described to us by a Consul as vain, a climber and like his wife socially very ambitious and chosen by Byron Price in order to alter tone of American news despatches from London which are regarded as being too pro-British and critical of United States Government at present.

. . .

25 April 1943

Tunisian news and homage to Montgomery have yielded to headlines and divergent views over the Pacific war. The statements of MacArthur, Blamey,[1] Evatt and Quezon[2] and replies of Stimson and Knox were whipped up into an 'issue' by the press in which there is a tendency to sympathize with MacArthur. Senator Chandler[3] now leads the senatorial Pacific bloc. The gruesome news of executions by Japanese of several of Doolittle's men together with new details of the raid[4] and expressions of horror on part of the President, Hull and various Senators have poured oil on these flames and have sharply increased the stimulus of national anger and humiliation which makes of Pacific front permanently a more burning issue than European front is ever likely to be. It is known that some members of OWI had earlier been pressing for publication of the available atrocity stories as an antidote to complacency about the war and preoccupation with internal controversies, as an incentive to production and the bond drive, and as a safety valve for pent-up frustration concerning the Pacific front. Japanese anniversary broadcasts of the executions may have forced the timing somewhat. Morgenthau told me two nights ago that he was not satisfied with the temper of the country – not that it was not very determined but he wanted it to glow with whiter heat. He is broadcasting in Midwest on 25 April with this object. Oddly enough he said the West Coast was worst buyer of war bonds.

(a) The President's southern tour is said to have convinced him that while the South and especially the local Democratic machines were disgruntled, particularly over patronage by federal agencies which too often went to non-machine Democrats or even Republicans, the alarming picture painted by Farley's followers had been over-drawn. The Democratic Party would not secede. States' rights,

11 John S. Knight, proprietor of *Detroit Free Press* and other journals.

1 General Sir Thomas A. Blamey, Australian Commander-in-Chief Allied Land Forces, South-West Pacific, since 1942.

2 Manuel Quezon, first President of Philippines 1935–44.

3 Albert B. Chandler, Democratic Senator from Kentucky since 1939.

4 Raid on Tokyo, 18 April 1942, led by Colonel James H. Doolittle.

as Governor Arnall of Georgia pointed out, are not in the end a real issue in the South, which economically depends too much on federal help to afford such political autonomism as Midwestern, Mountain and Western States can indulge in. At most the South might give trouble at the Convention and then as usual vote the straight Democratic ticket. I was given same kind of picture in Alabama two weeks ago. Meanwhile ex-Governor Landon in New York delivered a Bricker-like talk on the 'ambitious and dreamy bureaucrats' of the Treasury with their world plans, demanded a United States War Council similar to that established by Wilson, and said it was time that America took over world leadership, not as an imperialist power but in the spirit of honesty, integrity, decency, etc. He said that every farmer west of the Alleghenies would vote against Roosevelt. 'The critter's (group undecipherable) is set.' Landon's main purpose in visiting New York seems to have been to sound out Dewey on the Presidency. Dewey is reported to have flatly declined and Landon thereupon set off for Ohio, i.e. to Bricker 'the man who will save the party from Willkie, the country from Roosevelt and the world from Wallace'. This may mean no more than that Dewey at present intends to wait for 1948 unless he is drafted in 1944 by such acclaim as reasonably ensures the Presidency. Willkie (who is said 'to aim at being Mr and Mrs Roosevelt in one') is in a sanguine mood since the sales of his book have broken all records.

(b) The President's speech in Monterrey[5] followed lines earlier set by Welles, including the thesis of Pan-Americanism as a model for the post-war world, a new doctrine towards which both Roosevelt and Welles have conspicuously been moving. Welles had stressed that non-intervention and reciprocal trade concessions were the foundations of Pan-American system and, without naming her, strongly attacked Argentina. After the usual Pan-American fanfare President duly denounced the exploitation of any country by groups in any other, and his visit and speech were probably intended mainly to foster the goodwill helpful to discussions of such United States-Mexican issues as oil, railways and labour and perhaps to underline importance of Mexico as against Argentina. . . .

The AP poll of Senators[6] on their attitude to a 'world police' has been criticized as misleading since it put a question about means not ends. Nor has the press taken it very seriously. Nevertheless the results cannot be waved aside. The fact that a third of the Senate put its opposition on record, however casually, has given pause to optimists within the Administration although I am told that Welles is not too depressed by the result as among the twenty-four who voted in favour he recognizes several of his own converts. He thinks that his missionary work continues to bear fruit. The group of thirty-two non-committal Senators, some of whom took refuge in the proposition that it was unwise so early in the

5 On 20 April, when he met President of Mexico at Monterrey. Speech advocated world free of exploitation and pledged fight to finish against Axis.

6 Question was : Do you favour committing the Senate and country now to a post-war course of preserving the peace through an international police force ?

war to examine, let alone adopt, so specific a commitment, contains more reputed interventionists than isolationists, including such key Southern Democrats
as Barkley, George, Byrd.[7] It also includes the arch-isolationists Brooks and
Reed and key Republicans McNary and Vandenberg. While there is of course
nothing conclusive about this poll, it indicates that the number of Senators at
present reluctant to assent to serious international commitments is well over the
third required for a Senate veto. The dominant motive of the straddlers, apart
from some honest doubt as to value or meaning of the notion of 'world police',
is the desire to wait until effect, if any, of the poll upon the electorate can be
ascertained. This is highly symptomatic of Senate's vacillating attitude to foreign
policy, where, apart from the twenty-four who may be taken to represent the
solid core of anti-isolationism, the internationalist leanings which Senators are
willing to express in conversation are often too weak to determine actual voting
unless bolstered by really telling considerations usually concerned with internal
and often highly local issues. Of the Senate Foreign Relations Committee seven
replied in favour, eight against, six were uncertain, two were absent. I am told
that Senate Minority Leader McNary, Hull and Connally are now engaged in
drafting a compromise resolution on post-war international co-operation to be
introduced by Connally and supported by McNary in the Senate in place of the
Ball Resolution at present stalled in Committee. It is to be very general and
innocuous. As McNary recently observed to a friend of his 'all we're for is an
early spring and a late fall and we're against the man-eating shark' which is said
to be Oregonian for a bromide. The Senator also told our informant that Russia
had in fact better be allowed to have the Balkans – as she possessed them for so
long – and then as an afterthought 'and we'd better throw in Serbia and Bulgaria
as well, and we'd better not say anything about territorial aggrandizement, Joe
Stalin might not like it'.

Congress has again rapped the knuckles of Administration by (a) depriving
President of his present power of currency devaluation (b) getting through its
first committee stage in the House a motion to forbid the Treasury to use its two
billion stabilization fund for any international financial scheme such as that currently discussed with the British ; c) ordering an investigation of the Farm Security Administration whose beneficiaries, the small farmers, are all that remains
of the Administration's agricultural allies, and by finally talking about congressional representation at all international conferences.

Protests about exclusion of the press from Food Conference continue to extrude the problems of the conference itself from public notice. Various associations of newspaper men in the country, including the Associated Press, met in
conference in New York this week and these protested so sharply that Marvin
Jones,[8] chairman of American delegation, was reduced to maintaining that the

7 Harry F. Byrd, Democratic Senator from Virginia since 1933.

8 John Marvin Jones, Democratic Congressman from Texas 1917–41 ; Judge of the US Court of Claims since
1940.

President was joking when he spoke of keeping away the press. He himself told me on 24th that this storm in the conference teacup would soon abate. The Bermuda Conference has had a thin press ; the despatches in United States press satisfactorily emphasize the main difficulties and play up Law[9] on the dangers of arousing false hopes in occupied countries and Dodds[10] on the part already played by Britain and United States in harbouring refugees. The liberal press and two scathing editorials in *New York Times* and *Washington Post* have attacked the conference as a hollow mockery and have given some prominence to demands of Jewish bodies. . . .

VARIA

(a) OWI, whose appropriation bill is up before Congress, is in for a difficult time and is unlikely to escape intact.

(b) House Committee hearings on reciprocal trade pacts are completed and debate is due. American Economic Association and, more surprisingly, the National Association of Manufacturers have pleaded for their renewal but minds of Committee are on tax bill which is stuck in a hopeless welter of compromises and counter-compromises. Hull tartly observed that an amendment to bill necessitating majorities in Senate or House for any given trade pact would destroy the act completely. Senator George, echoing this : 'if Russia and England conclude that we are not going to co-operate in restoration of post-war order they might say "we had better get together now". One could take Eastern Europe and one Western Europe and we would have same old balance of power again. It might have a serious effect on fighting of the war itself.' State Department's economic adviser Feis[11] told a Chicago audience that colonial raw materials should be pooled after the war for benefit of all United Nations.

(c) Poles, who are agitating vehemently against Russia over alleged Smolensk atrocities[12] and along lines of Polish Ambassador's letter to *Life* criticizing Joe Davies's article,[13] privately complain of British 'appeasement' of Godless Russia and are supported in this by various Roman Catholic groups including National Catholic Welfare Conference[14] (the Catholic Press Syndicate), which is

9 Richard K.Law, head of British delegation to Bermuda Conference, Parliamentary Under-Secretary for Foreign Affairs 1943–5.

10 Harold Willis Dodds, President of Princeton University 1933–57, head of US delegation to Refugee Conference.

11 Herbert Feis, Economic adviser to Department of State 1931–43, special consultant to Department 1944–6.

12 On 12 April the Germans announced the discovery of graves of 10,000 Polish officers 'murdered' by USSR at Katyn, near Smolensk. Russians denounced 'vile fabrication'. Poles confirmed 8,000 officers lost and never traced and asked for investigation by International Red Cross. On 25 April Soviet Government broke off relations with Polish Government. International Red Cross declined to investigate unless requested by Russians as well as Poles.

13 Joseph Edward Davies, lawyer and financier, US Ambassador to USSR 1937–8. His article said Poland's Eastern territories had originally been taken from Russia. Ambassador's letter denied this.

14 Voluntary and unofficial agency, established in 1919, to promote Roman Catholic thinking and action in the field of social reform. Its Washington HQ was highly organized and enjoyed easy access to Congress and the Executive.

playing up atrocity story, and by Polonophiles who charge OWI with broadcasting appeals to Poles to yield to Russian demands, also of course by *Chicago Tribune,* etc. . . .

(d) Colonel McCormick evidently intends to follow up his sensational interview with *PM* in which he urged incorporation in the United States of Australia, New Zealand, Canada, Scotland, Wales, etc. Entertainment value of this campaign should be considerable since we are assured that the Colonel is in deadly earnest.

2 May 1943

. . . The Russo-Polish imbroglio has produced less public interest outside Washington than might have been expected. The news was received generally more in sorrow than in anger by public opinion and most of the press. The pro-Polish Simms[1] of Scripps-Howard and the Russophobe Hearst papers speak of a 'diplomatic defeat for Britain and the United States who permitted matters to reach such a pass', and similar criticism is more mildly expressed elsewhere. The isolationists led by the Patterson press take line that the Russians are predatory and the Polish Government bitterly reactionary (and therefore popular with the conservative British Government). The situation is typical of the appalling conflicts which will continue to rend the old world and perhaps it is just as well that this sorry mess should have been disclosed now and not at the peace conference. Colonel McCormick, with an eye on the large Polish population of his area whose representatives have been supplying him with ammunition, has attacked the USSR for designing 'the rape of Poland', encouraged by British Government. It is worth noting that the Midwestern press follows the national trend. It is not in general noticeably pro-Polish and tends to deplore the comfort given the Nazis and to avoid irritating either side. Polish press here is divided into the anti-Sikorski papers of both Right and Left, to whom this is naturally climax of their anti-Russian campaign, and the more restrained organs which regret that the Russians should have made this Goebbels's triumph possible. Communist press takes the obvious line and advocates suspension of United States diplomatic relations with Poland. In meanwhile Litvinov, who is preparing to pay a short visit home, is said to be exceedingly morose and sullen on this and every subject, while the Russian experts of State Department in private say that a tougher attitude to Russians would be rewarding. They concede that Polish assumption that they can count on United States support has considerably affected the situation. They also anticipate some move by the handfuls of Polish Congressmen after present recess which will feed the flames although they are not politically important and not anxious to incur the charge of pursuing sectarian politics. Some congressional logrolling with other groups will doubtless be attempted.

1 William P. Simms, foreign editor of Scripps-Howard newspaper chain since 1922.

A far more menacing issue is the coal strike scheduled by John L. Lewis for 1 May. 17,000 miners are idle now. Lewis scarcely disguises his intention to break the War Labor Board as he broke its predecessor and to settle only after this has heen achieved and in any case to negotiate with no one short of the President himself. The press, the public and the Administration seem at the moment ready for a showdown with Lewis, who is branded by his opponents as the No. 1 enemy of the people. President is well aware that in resisting Lewis he will have great public support behind him and could once and for all scotch the constant charges that he is 'coddling' labour. On the other hand Lewis is clearly playing on the fact that President Roosevelt can ill afford to celebrate a victory over labour. Murray of the CIO has put on record and advertised in the press labour grievances about rising prices and frozen wages to show that the last reasonable advocate of minimum labour demands is Murray and not Lewis whose victory would be a defeat for moderates in labour and the Administration equally, and leave labour no alternative but to adopt Lewis's methods. Commentators and Washington officials are nervous about the coming conflict but on the whole wish to get the crisis over now, a view privately shared by some of the progressive leaders of the CIO. President has warned that the mines may be occupied by federal troops. Unless Lewis executes one of his last-minute *volte-faces* a major collision seems inevitable. Senator Connally's old anti-strike bill, shelved at the President's request about a year ago, has been resurrected and will be considered by the Senate shortly. Taft opposes on the ground that by abolishing the War Labor Board it gives Lewis what he most ardently desires. Taft however spoke to me two nights ago in very anti-labour tones and I should guess that unless the Administration wins out on this issue both decisively and quickly, there will be strong congressional pressure for some anti-strike legislation.

. . .

The House Ways and Means Committee has passed the Reciprocal Trade Agreements Bill without amendment, save that of Dewey of Illinois whose rider empowers the President to suspend reciprocal benefits on specific commodities to countries permitting the operations of cartels controlling those commodities in a way prejudicial to the United States national interest. This seems to add nothing to the Administration's existing powers and is a piece of political publicity – partly designed to meet the advertisements in which Standard Oil announced surrender of its Buna patents to the Government in an attempt to whitewash itself before the public. The genuineness of this move has been impugned by a journalist who maintains that these German patents in any case now belong to the Alien Property Custodian. The bill now awaits debate in the House and passage through the Senate. . . . The Panama Concessions bill which raised a congressional flurry some time ago as an alleged encroachment on the senatorial treaty-making prerogatives, was passed by thirty-seven to nineteen in the Senate, a triumph for the Administration.

. . .

185

The feud between rubber czar Jeffers and Under-Secretary of War Patterson over the allocation of priorities for rubber and aviation petrol has emerged into full and widely deplored limelight. Nelson has given somewhat ambiguous support to Jeffers, Forrestal [2] to Patterson. There is a general demand for the establishment of a single authority, say the popular Mr Byrnes, who would adjudicate in such disputes before they become public property. The disputes are to be considered by Truman Committee. The Administration now admits that the shipping losses last year exceeded construction and further revelations are expected from the Truman Committee. Forrestal declared that the escort vessel programme was retarded by the Joint Staff's decision to concentrate on 'destroyer escorts' which, according to the Committee, were demanded by the British and displaced the construction of tankers as well. The somewhat depressing effect of this on the public has only been slightly offset by the promise of Batt [3] of WPB of 1,000,000 planes by the end of this year. General Somervell has sharply denied the well authenticated story that a more than sufficient stockpile of arms to last for the duration has already been accumulated and said that the United States Army would not be fully equipped before the end of 1944. . . .

. . .

Joseph Martin, minority leader in the House, announces the formation of a committee of thirty-three Republican members of the House of Representatives to study post-war domestic problems, though doubtless it will cover international questions as well. The formation of the committee served notice on the Democratic Party that they, and in particular the New Deal, have no monopoly of post-war planning and may expect carefully prepared opposition. The committee is too big to be anything except representative and its members are in fact drawn from all parts of the country, from all congressional committees, both domestic and foreign, and represent all degrees of Republicanism, from Judd [4] and Powers [5] to George Dondero. [6]

8 May 1943

COAL STRIKE

A coal strike began on 1 May. President empowered Ickes as Fuel Co-ordinator to take over mines if necessary and hope was expressed among press and public that Lewis would find his match in this toughest of New Dealers. On 2 May Ickes-Lewis conference occurred. Lewis later maintained that Ickes offered to negotiate a new contract with operators. Ickes denied this. At 9.40 p.m. Lewis announced that he had ordered miners to return to work for fifteen days, allowing

2 James V. Forrestal, investment banker, Under-Secretary of Navy since 1940.

3 William L. Batt, President SKF Co. 1923–50 ; prominent figure throughout the war in US production and Allied allocation operations.

4 Walter H. Judd, Republican Congressman from Minnesota since 1943.

5 David L. Powers, Republican Congressman from New Jersey since 1933.

6 George A. Dondero, Republican Congressman from Michigan since 1933.

time for negotiation of a new contract (Lewis throughout does not speak of a strike but only of miners' refusal to work without a contract). At 10.00 p.m. President delivered a nationwide appeal to miners to return to pits. His speech turned on two theses :

(a) that he continued to be a friend of labour and was aware of menace of rising prices on which action would be taken,
(b) he was President and Commander-in-Chief and could not allow this stoppage by miners while their sons were fighting and dying abroad.

Although President was almost certainly aware of Lewis's move when he delivered his own speech, he had evidently decided not to allow his course of action to be demonstrably affected by Lewis's antics and possibly to let it be thought that Lewis had climbed down as result of some advance knowledge of President's text. His speech, a direct appeal to miners over Lewis's head, was widely acclaimed as a long overdue show of firmness but its effect was somewhat marred by fact that Lewis once more succeeded in stealing morning headlines. On 3 May Ickes, implementing suggestion of Miss Perkins, announced three-day week in now government-controlled mines which automatically increases miners' wages. President reaffirmed authority of War Labor Board, making plain that he would not have it by-passed. On 4 May most of miners were back at work although popular view is that President's words would not of themselves have sufficed to achieve this. Connally bill was debated in Senate and after amendments seeking to impose severe penalties on strikers in all war industries, or for disobedience of War Labor Board's decisions, and to abolish Wagner Act,[1] etc., had been duly defeated, and after Wheeler's effort to recommit bill as was demanded by CIO (Wheeler normally will play 'friend of the people' more especially if they are miners and if he can do so against Administration) had similarly failed, bill was passed by a large majority. It makes strikes or incitement thereto in war industries controlled by Government penal offence and increases powers of War Labor Board, previously a purely consultative adjunct of executive, enabling it both to enter labour disputes on its own initiative and to decide them. It cannot enforce penalties against failure to comply with its decisions but both sides obtain right to have immediate recourse to courts. Although not altogether to their taste, bill was not obstructed by Administration. It is now before House which may try to stiffen it. Effect of its passage may well be to restrict President's field of manoeuvre and provide Lewis with tension which suits his dramatic talents. Lewis truculently refuses to appear before WLB which has resumed hearings, accuses Ickes of going back on an alleged earlier deal between two as result of pressure from 'White House clique' and vaguely threatens a new strike when truce is over. Anti-Lewis feeling is high in country but tempered among Republicans by a scarcely concealed pleasure that this time a

1 National Labor Relations Act passed in 1935, establishing National Labor Relations Board.

really formidable and unscrupulous figure has blocked President's path, and there are those who sigh after Lewis as a Secretary of Labor in place of much abused Miss Perkins. Miners have won wide public sympathy by fact that their chief grievance is grievance of entire people – irregular rises in prices and faulty distribution, for which Administration is blamed (flattering comparisons are drawn with British and Canadian systems of price control and labour relations which are widely admired and praised). Consequently there is not that constantly rising anti-labour wave which would force Administration's hand although this may arise if strike breaks out afresh. If Connally bill is passed by House Lewis will be liable to arrest if he strikes. 'Let Senators try to dig coal with their legislations,' Mr Lewis is said to have cried. Many remedies are proposed, of which Dr Steelman's[2] guaranteed fifty-two weeks annual wages is most acceptable to Lewis. If something like this is tried as a basis of settlement President is certain to insist that it be done through WLB which he (and Congress) are as anxious to strengthen as Lewis to destroy. WLB is central instrument of co-operation between President and Murray, Green, etc., and its obliteration would destroy one of main supports of Administration's present political structure. Operators have tossed ball to WLB and have since preserved discreet silence but their spokesmen in press are expressing faint alarm that government control of private property may have come to stay, with bogey of gradual nationalization threatening. WLB is openly anxious to free itself from rigid 'Little Steel formula' which does not permit it to judge wage grievances on their merits. As Lewis appears more anxious to break WLB than to arrive at a settlement, a renewed strike and use of military to deal with it is predicted by competent government observers.

TUNISIAN VICTORY[3]

African war is regarded as won. Public is naturally jubilant and there is much emphasis among commentators on joint character of Allied victory. There is much happy anticipation of an early European invasion incensed by Elmer Davis's prediction that Europe might be invaded before capture of Bizerta, evidently an attempt at a personal war of nerves on his part.

RUSSO-POLISH IMBROGLIO

. . . Some ten Congressmen from Polish districts used occasion of Polish Constitution Day, 5 May, for delivering speeches which avoided all mention of atrocities but demanded restoration of frontiers of Polish State. Fieriest pro-Polish orators were Dingell[4] of Michigan and Dewey of Illinois. Sabath of Illinois observed that Poland might not have suffered her fate if Britain and France had not prevented her rearmament and (stranger still) forbidden her to pledge passage

2 John R. Steelman, Director of Conciliation, Department of Labor, since 1937.
3 With fall of Bizerta and Tunis, 7 May.
4 John D. Dingell, Democratic Congressman from Detroit, Michigan, since 1933.

to Russian troops during Anglo-Russian talks in 1939. While specific groups, e.g. Polish and Catholic, are mobilizing behind Polish Government's position, there is surprisingly little pro-Polish sentiment among general public. If Poles have made a serious effort to enlist general sympathy and promote a wide publicity campaign, their efforts have borne little fruit and absence of strong pro-Polish sentiment in United States outside Catholic Church has been made clear.

The Apostolic delegate,[5] a shrewd prelate, perhaps appropriately Titular Bishop of Laodicea, is understood to be in strongest sympathy with attitude of Polish Embassy and told a member of my staff that he had got well-known American Jesuit La Farge[6] to compile a pamphlet on 'The Pope and Poland'. He is also circulating present Pope's encyclicals on peace through Catholic Bishops. Chinese in this country also seem to be watching Anglo-American reactions to Russian move with tense interest and will doubtless draw a lesson from this to guide them in their own national policies.

Stalin's May Day speech and letter to *New York Times* correspondent[7] were most favourably interpreted save by confirmed sceptics and Russophobes. Line is everywhere taken that this was meant to placate rising anti-Russian sentiment. *New York Times*, in a typical leader, hailed both Stalin's and Sikorski's utterances as most constructive and gave much prominence to Joseph Davies's new mission to Moscow, declaring that he is to arrange for Roosevelt to meet Stalin alone but that conceivably Mr Churchill may also be invited to attend. Davies had been talking rapturously about his coming journey (need of which he has been assiduously impressing on President for some three weeks) and was immensely delighted by new film *Mission to Moscow*[8] which is politically popular with New York audience. It was vehemently attacked as a sham by Dorothy Thompson and Anne McCormick in *New York Times* and *New Republic* and defended by *Herald Tribune*.

. . .

Jews. Berle, who seems as anxious to clear himself of suspicion of anti-semitism as of Russophobia, sent a vigorous and flowery message to a semi-Zionist mass meeting in Boston saying that he would be less than candid if he concealed that invasion of Europe and total military defeat of Germany was the sole genuine means of saving the Jews of the Continent. Willkie in his message said 'We must not permit international power politics to close the door to a permanent Jewish homeland in Palestine'. This is in line with his new pro-Zionist orientation acquired since his return from the Middle East. Sales of his book are about to reach million mark and Twentieth Century Fox, of which Willkie is board chairman, are leading bidders for film rights.

. . .

5 Amleto Cicognani, Apostolic delegate to the USA 1933–58.
6 John La Farge, leading figure on influential Catholic Monthly, *America*, and editor 1944–8.
7 Emphasizing Soviet desire to see a strong and independent Poland.
8 Made from Davies's memoirs of same name.

Flurries. OWI front is disturbed by Milton Eisenhower's resignation[9] and there is a major flurry about 'red brick house on R Street',[10] a scandal investigated by House Military Affairs Committee. Various high officials of Government including Knox appear to have been lured to this establishment (by prospect of meeting various Senators, Archduke Otto, etc.) operated by a tout[11] for various business concerns in search of war contracts. Growing publicity will doubtless damage some politicians but no New Dealers are so far implicated. Three Senators involved are Republican interventionists. Press treats episode as a front-page story and reminisces about 'little green house in K Street' of Harding's days.

. . .

13 May 1943

Prime Minister's arrival. The unexpected arrival of the Prime Minister against a background of news of German collapse in North Africa and somewhat overoptimistic headlines on risings in Axis-occupied Europe has produced a mood of high good humour in Washington and throughout the nation. Military composition of the Prime Minister's party and in particular the appearance of Wavell and other officers from India has led to nationwide speculation about likelihood of an early combined attack in Pacific. The only voice protesting against division of the war into two rival fronts is that of Lippmann, whose article was reprinted as an advertisement by a commercial firm. The isolationist press has joined in general welcome of Mr Churchill along its usual line deploring that no such patriot was in power in America. Beaverbrook's appearance has excited little comment beyond a rumour reported by Daniell[1] from London that he had a pet scheme for reconciling the Russians and Poles that has caused some anxiety in Polish circles here. With this went the further rumour that a Cabinet post had been promised him if he could make it work. While 'Pacific Firstism' is less vociferous than for some time it is deeply ingrained and this has prevented general 'second front' agitation, which has in any case not been much in evidence in the Communist press. Elmer Davis has as good as promised the invasion of Europe for the summer.

Russo-Polish relations. Nothing fresh. Polish papers continue the anti-Russian campaign. Sharp criticism of the film *Mission to Moscow* continues, led by an elaborate 'exposure' in the *New York Times* of 9 May by John Dewey and Suzanne La Follette[2] who drew up a budget of historical distortions with which the

9 From post as an Associate Director, OWI, on appointment as President of Kansas State College.

10 Allusion to the 'little green house on K Street' utilized by Harry M.Daugherty, Attorney General in the heyday of Harding's corrupt administration as a clearing-house for doubtfully legal operations.

11 John P.Monroe (previously Kaplan).

1 Francis Raymond Daniell, *New York Times* chief London correspondent since 1939.

2 John Dewey, Professor of Philosophy at Columbia University; Suzanne La Follette, journalist and cousin of Senator; their letter, 2½ columns long, appeared on 9 May.

film teems. Several officials of the State Department express feelings of amused indignation. Litvinov departed gloomily, complaining that he had been out of touch with his Government for too long and that Moscow did not seem fully to appreciate the situation here. Meanwhile Mrs Roosevelt has been mending New Deal fences. Speaking to a youth conference she went out of her way to denounce Communist students for their typical double-dealing tactics. In this she follows other members of the Administration (to which for all purposes she belongs) in sincerely disavowing various unpopular sympathies (which are widely attributed to her).

Reciprocal Trade bill. Welles delivered an exceptionally vehement speech on past economic sins of tariff-raising nations and re-emphasized the crucial political importance of passing the Reciprocal Trade Agreements Bill. After a House Debate used by Republicans to criticize the depressing effect of Hull's policies on the American producer and to demand increased congressional power, the Act was passed by the House by 342 to 65 (195 Democrats, 145 Republicans, 2 others, against 52 Republicans, 11 Democrats, 2 others) for two instead of three years. All the other amendments were defeated by majorities of forty and fifty except the proposal to give Congress veto power over treaties within sixty days of conclusion which was defeated by the significantly narrow margin of twenty-one votes. But the result compares strikingly with the fact that in House votes in 1934 only two Republicans voted in favour, in 1937 three, in 1940 five (Senate, 1934, five Republicans in favour, in 1937 and 1940 none). The isolationist press openly deplored this result. A number of anti-isolationist Republicans make the point that Hull by making a major issue of the vote and speaking of it as a crucial test of future United States foreign policy (which in their opinion it is not) forced the opposition into treating it as a central party issue which according to their estimate lost Hull over forty votes. On the other hand, as the *New York Times* points out, this made Hull's victory more important. . . .

Coal Strike. The uneasy 'labour truce' continues. Public comment on it has waned. The President has granted wider wage adjustment powers to the War Labor Board, enabling it to correct 'gross inequities' but within the framework of the 'Little Steel Formula'. This is expected to prevent the threatened resignations from the Board of its labour members. The prophets are divided as to whether Lewis will or will not strike on 19 May if his demands are not granted, the majority inclining to the view that he will not. . . .

. . .

Bombing of Rome. The Gallup poll in answer to the question 'Do you think Allied Air Forces should bomb Rome ?' recorded 37 per cent yes, 51 per cent no, 12 per cent no opinion; of Catholics 67 per cent, Protestants 52 per cent, non-Church members 40 per cent gave the answer no.

24 May 1943

The 'Pacific First' issue blew up this week with a long and passionate speech on the 17th by Senator Chandler (Democrat, Kentucky) supported by Senators Bridges (Republican, New Hampshire), Shipstead (Republican, Minnesota),[1] Wheeler (Democrat, Montana), and Tydings (Democrat, Maryland). Chandler, who had been pursuing a pro-Chinese line for some time, made a considerable impression on his colleagues particularly in warning that unless Russia co-operated in war against Japan, she would, after defeat of Germany, be left to share Europe together with a Britain absorbed in task of watching Russia. America in the meanwhile would remain involved in an increasingly difficult, possibly hopeless, war against a much strengthened Japan. Shipstead, a routine isolationist, dwelt on Wilson's failure in 1918 which he attributed to England and France, and revived the hoary tale of British failure to support Stimson over Manchuria,[2] Wheeler took up Chandler's point that with an army of two millions in India facing sixty thousand Japanese in Burma, Wavell had obviously made no real attempt to invade Burma and thus to open only available door for aid to China. Chandler at intervals hinted that he would not have spoken as he did but for encouragement and information from high sources. There is much speculation as to what these are. Another explanation offered to account for Chandler's behaviour is that after his growing differences with his fellow-Kentuckian, Senator Barkley, majority leader, he chose popular Pacific issue as a 'surefire' method of asserting his independence of Administration (as opposed to party) control. Doubtless Chandler has not forgotten President's appearance against him in Kentucky primary in 1938.[3] This may not be the whole story but if it is even a part of it, it offers the most striking possible illustration of the influence of local politics on national affairs. The isolationist press (and Drew Pearson) strongly took up his argument that if British would only use the two million soldiers stationary upon their shores, the United States could devote itself to settling the Japanese. Chandler has been attacked with exceptional violence by *New York Herald Tribune, Washington Post* and *New York Post*. The Prime Minister's speech[4] could not therefore have been more opportune. It was acclaimed universally as a masterpiece and demand for reassurance about British intentions in the Pacific of which the Americans seem never to weary was once more proclaimed to have been finally satisfied. The Prime Minister received his usual ovation, shared on this occasion by the Duke and Duchess of Windsor[5] whose appearance in the gallery caused interest and pleasure. Even the unfriendly press conceded

1 Henrik Shipstead, Senator from Minnesota since 1923.

2 In relation to Japanese attack on Manchuria, 1931–2, when Stimson was Secretary of State.

3 Year in which Roosevelt (generally unsuccessfully) tried to prevent renomination of anti-Administration Democrats.

4 Churchill addressed Congress on 19 May, pledging British support for defeat of Japan, but insisting overthrow of Nazis must come first.

5 After the fall of France, the Duke (formerly King Edward VIII) was offered and accepted the governorship of the Bahamas, which he held until 1945.

that Mr Churchill 'triumphantly carried his audience with him', and various Senators including hardboiled isolationists spoke with appreciation both of his speech and of his subsequent remarks at a lucheon of Foreign Relations and Foreign Affairs Committees. Senator Chandler was heard to mutter about interpretation of Gettysburg[6] unwelcome to Southern ears, and told journalists that his fears had not been allayed but he and his supporters did not prevail against general enthusiasm. The Prime Minister also had opportunity of meeting about thirty Senators and Congressmen of both parties at Embassy and spoke briefly to them with great effect. Although such moods are evanescent and the fires of 'Pacific First' will continue to burn, Mr Churchill's visits and speeches create a volume of goodwill towards Britain which nothing else can parallel.

It is too early to estimate general implications of Food Conference. It got off to an uneventful start against continuous and still increasing barrage of protest by the press against its exclusion, about which virtually all major newspapers and radio networks have whipped themselves into a great rage. This, together with more interesting events, has caused little attention to be paid to the subject itself although Mr Law's statement at his Washington press conference (which was a success) has become a sort of official text for favourable press comment. Isolationists are divided between attacking prospect of America squandering its food to its own detriment upon a starving and shiftless world, and dire warnings that if this secrecy is a token for the future neither Congress nor the people will tolerate it and will tend to block Administration plans irrespective of their merit unless they are taken into its confidence. One or two columnists close to State Department have hinted that the Department regrets this secrecy enjoined by the President as much as anyone. I am informed that relations between press and British Delegation are happy enough. American Chairman, Marvin Jones, is conspicuously embarrassed by seething attitude of correspondents and somewhat nervous of congressional reaction. On the evening of the 19th Representative Bradley of Michigan,[7] a notorious scourge of the Administration, appeared unannounced at Hot Springs implying that he had come to investigate whether anything was being 'put across' the nation. Jones welcomed him warmly and invited him to return with any colleagues he wished to bring. Bradley left apparently mollified but vowing to return. He did so later with Representative Smith[8] who talked about need for congressional supervision. Practical consequences of this are not likely to amount to much but it indicates the general mood. After a minor flurry, English was agreed to as the sole official language of the Conference although M. Alphand,[9] the French delegate, extracted a somewhat hollow

6 'Gettysburg was the decisive battle of the Civil War . . . yet far more blood was shed after the Union victory at Gettysburg than in all the fighting which went before.' (WSC)

7 Frederick Van Ness Bradley, Republican Congressman from Michigan since 1939.

8 Joseph L. Smith, Democratic Congressman from West Virginia since 1929.

9 Hervé J.C.Alphand, French diplomat, director of economic affairs for the Comité Français de Liberation in London 1941–4. Ambassador in Washington 1956–65.

promise that this was not to be regarded as a precedent. Conference has now dispersed into sections, Mr Law to preside over Section 4 concerned with creation of permanent international machinery.

. . . The United States official attitude to Poles, which is correct but not too sympathetic, is a marked contrast to affability with which President Beneš[10] has been greeted by the President and Mr Hull. He professes to be entirely satisfied with his visit, to have found a genuinely strong desire to collaborate with Russia on the part of the President and Mr Hull, and told a member of my staff that while a Czechoslovak-Polish federation was essential in stability of Europe, he could not see how democratic Czech Government could collaborate unless Poles acquired a genuinely democratic government and unless further they adjusted their differences with USSR, which at present had little cause to suspect the Czechs but only too much to distrust the Poles. Poles seek comfort not only in Roman Catholic circles but among Republican politicians who, as Hoover told a member of my staff, see an opportunity of detaching Polish vote from Roosevelt at any rate in key Polish states of Michigan and Illinois.

Various neutrals are said to be reporting to their Governments on the fast rising American production and consequent invincibility of the United States and its Allies. Colonel Beigbeder[11] is said to be reporting in this sense to Madrid and Danish Minister told a member of my staff that Swedes are doing likewise. . . .

Vice-President Wallace has delivered two speeches, one acclaiming Latin-American common man, Indians, Bolivian miners, and Chilean democracy, a land where Roman Catholics and Communists have equal means of self-expression, and next day a second, more important speech to American Labor Party. He told his audience that if America was to avoid Communism it must promote full employment within a 'Capitalist Democracy'. By this frank avowal of faith in private enterprise he has placed himself on the side of the anti-Communist labour conservatives, of whom Dubinsky is most representative, disappointing only those who had long mistakenly seen in him some kind of socialist. Communism clearly presents itself to Wallace not so much as a menace but as the only possible efficient alternative to order which he and the majority of Americans infinitely prefer. American Labor Party has now decided to back his Vice-Presidency in 1944, and is crowing over the 'Radicals' who had once regarded Wallace as their own. While Wallace's political position is certainly weaker than it was six months ago he seems almost unconscious of this and almost indifferent and continues along his chosen path – a peculiar amalgamation of New Deal economics with his own brand of agrarian Christianity – unperturbed by the pessimism of his followers.

Coal strike. The coal truce continues uneasily, having been extended to 1 June, but Lewis has with his usual skill created a major diversion by applying for

10 Edvard Beneš, President of Czechoslovakia 1936–8, President of Provisional Government 1940–6.
11 Colonel Juan Beigbeder, Spanish Foreign Minister dismissed by Franco, October 1940.

membership of American Federation of Labor. This is a culmination of a long flirtation between him and the American Federation of Labor conservatives, Woll,[12] Hutcheson,[13] and Dubinsky, who think that if they recapture him they can hold him in leash and moreover celebrate a financial and political triumph over CIO. Lewis's position became uncomfortable after Ickes, with whom alone he seemed to wish to deal, clearly stated in a letter to Lewis that War Labor Board was sole proper agency for reopening negotiations with the operators. Lewis, who certainly (and not without reason) counts on dominating any organization with which he is associated, has scored again by serving the American Federation of Labor with the dilemma of either accepting him and the liabilities of his reputation or of rejecting one of most powerful single unions in the United States, which would inevitably be ill-received by some American Federation of Labor leaders and so cause an internal split in that organization. American Federation of Labor leaders (although not Green, who knows that his days are counted if Lewis enters) are apparently disposed to buy Lewis at almost any price and 'straighten things out' afterwards. . . .

Taxation. Still worse confusion prevails in sphere of taxation where Senate's Ruml like proposal[14] has been duly defeated by the House influenced by President's threat to veto a bill so conspicuously favouring the rich. All sides acknowledge a deadlock since everyone has now spoken and no one appears ready to compromise. This jeopardizes the essential withholding tax proposal scheduled for July. The solution seems to lie in reciprocal attrition and ultimate exhaustion of all sides. We appear to be in for a long and dreary stretch of positional warfare with the Treasury Department frustrated and for time being relatively powerless.

Witch-hunt. The congressional drive against radicals in Administration, seeking to oust two employees of the Federal Communications Commission and Lovett,[15] secretary of Virgin Islands, for subversive views, has resulted in a large House vote in favour of dismissal blocked by Senate Finance Committee after a plea by Ickes against such a bill of attainder. If the charges against Cox[16] (who is investigating Federal Communications Commission) of being paid for representing a commercial network before a federal agency (it is illegal for Congressmen to do so) is ever taken up by Justice Department the Federal Communications Committee issue may provoke great stir. Attorney General Biddle is said to be acutely nervous of taking issue with this aggressive and influential

12 Matthew Woll, President of International Photo-Engravers' Union 1906–29, Vice-President of AF of L.

13 William L.Hutcheson, President of United Brotherhood of Carpenters and Joiners 1915–53, first Vice-President of AF of L 1940–53.

14 Beardsley Ruml, Treasurer of Macy's department store, advocated a pay-as-you-go income tax plan that would begin by 'forgiving' all or part of 1942 taxes.

15 Robert Morse Lovett, Government secretary, Virgin Islands, 1939–43 ; notably liberal Professor of Literature at Chicago University 1893–1936.

16 Ed Eugene Cox, Democratic Congressman from Georgia since 1925.

Southern labour baiter. The Supreme Court has lately confirmed the control of commercial networks by Federal Communications Committee. ·′

. . .

29 May 1943

Mr Churchill. The Prime Minister's press conference[1] was enthusiastically received. References mainly taken up in subsequent talk were those concerning assurances on the Pacific, Italy and the hint to Russia on Japanese intentions. There is a vague assumption in sections of press and general talk that a Second Front at any rate in Western Europe is unlikely this year, that the Pacific War will be intensified and that main attack on Germany will be from the air. This is for the moment accepted without excessive murmuring. Mr Churchill's personal popularity is such that according to a current wisecrack if Colonel McCormick's plan to acquire the British Empire materialized Mr Churchill would find himself chosen by acclamation the first head of the Anglo-American Empire.

Russia. The dissolution of the Comintern[2] was duly welcomed by Hull, Willkie, etc. The vast majority of press, radio and public opinion generally regard it as a sensible liquidation of a useless instrument which had been a cause of constant Russo-American friction. All sides consider it as a deliberate step on the part of Stalin towards understanding with the West. The Russophile liberals acclaim it without reservation as confirming their brightest hopes. The radio commentators are far more enthusiastic than the press, which both of the right or left views it with certain suspicion but expresses pleasure and relief at a move which on the very lowest estimate must proceed from an obvious desire to please the democracies. Dorothy Thompson perceives in it a culmination of the Russian swing to nationalism. The isolationists, who on the whole accept this interpretation, either, like former Under-Secretary Castle,[3] discount it altogether, or warn that this manifests a very natural 'Russia First' attitude analogous to Churchill's 'Britain First', with the old Lindbergh moral that United States would be best advised to adopt an equally nationalist policy and stop dealing in flabby internationalism. Congressman Dies wistfully remarked that this may mean no further business for his Committee and was duly pressed to continue his fine work in a speech by a diehard colleague. Trotsky's daughter proudly announced that Fourth International[4] was now the sole bulwark of the proletariat. The dissolution together with Davies's spectacular second 'sub-mission'[5] coinciding with the current showing of film *Mission to Moscow* has produced at least a momentary ripple of benevolent feeling towards Russia amid the prevailing suspicion

1 On 25 May.

2 The Third Communist International or Comintern, founded by Lenin in 1919. Its dissolution was announced from Moscow on 22 May.

3 William R.Castle, career diplomat, Under-Secretary of State under Hoover 1931–3.

4 A somewhat shadowy organization set up by Trotsky's adherents in 1936.

5 Joseph Davies was received by Stalin on 20 May.

and antagonism. Mr Berle told a member of my staff that he valued this act chiefly as indicating that Stalin had decided to make clear to the Russian public that era of revolutionary adventures and international conspiracies was over. On the other hand he viewed Oumansky's[6] appointment to Mexico with suspicion – Oumansky was an intriguer and would probably try to play Latin-American nationalism against the United States. Cassidy's lately published book[7] contains a somewhat unfriendly account of Prime Minister's visit to Moscow.

Coal. The coal situation is improved as Lewis is negotiating with operators under the aegis of War Labor Board. Board rejected miners' $2 increase demand, miners have rejected the 80 cents offered them. Nevertheless Lewis has evidently decided to work for his ends by peaceful methods. . . .

Lend-Lease. Lend-Lease appropriations bill was passed by the House (309 *vs* 4) with an amendment forced by the Farm Bloc that none of funds provided are to be used for subsidies to growers of Lend-Lease agricultural products. During the debate Lend-Lease administration, in particular Stettinius, were again warmly praised by members of both parties as the one Roosevelt agency above reproach, and there was some mention of reverse Lend-Lease from Britain and Australia. On other hand sporadic demands were again made for a dollar and cent account of extent of such aid, and scarcity of help to China was once more emphasized. The President's last report gave impression that aid to Russia, being in some categories greater than that to Britain, was adequate.

Isolationism. Some publicity has been given by isolationist papers to a speech by Senator Taft of which no official text is available. . . . [He favoured] a modified League with general covenants and bilateral treaties directed against international aggression. Better access to raw materials and more rational economic relationships between states were needed than were made at Versailles but tariff policies could not be controlled by force of decree. America would assume a greater responsibility in Far East than in Europe where Mr Churchill's European Council would have primacy but armed force should not be used save against physical aggression or to enforce disarmament. An international police was absurd but there was no loss of sovereignty 'in a treaty binding us to send our armed forces abroad on the finding of an international body. Being soverign we could refuse to keep our promises. Being Americans we would not refuse', but added that this country was not fighting for the Four Freedoms and an American crusade was no more justifiable than Hitler's. Taft, who is the most honest and respected as well as the narrowest of isolationists, is said, despite his earlier retirement in favour of Bricker, to be still nursing presidential ambitions made stronger by Bricker's continued dimness. . . .

6 Constantine A. Oumansky, Soviet Ambassador to the USA 1938–41.

7 *Moscow Dateline*. Henry Cassidy was United Press correspondent in Moscow from 1940–4.

Food Conference. Food Conference is exciting less comment. The press relatively mollified. British delegation are widely praised for their exceptionally successful press arrangements which are held up as a model to the United States. . . .

Reciprocal Trade. The Reciprocal Trade Agreements bill is not out of the wood. Main question worrying Administration is the Danaher amendment empowering Congress to veto agreements six months after their conclusion . . . . Although issue thus depends on a small handful of votes Administration seem confident that amendment will be defeated. As Hull has declared this vote to be crucial test of future policy, the amendment quite clearly is intended as a political demonstration and not as a practical measure and is admitted to be such by both sides. Meanwhile Senator Ball is fuming about the supposed shelving of the Ball-Hatch resolution by Senate Foreign Relations Committee.

. . .

China. The Kennedy bill to abrogate the (anti-Chinese) Exclusion Act has been duly protested against by American Legion and the AF of L, and Committee is hearing witnesses. The Sinophiles are somewhat disturbed by effects of its possible defeat on China. Madame Chiang Kai-shek is said to be prepared to say something on this when it is over. Although still very popular with the mass of Americans, there is a good deal of critical and even libellous comment about her in Washington both in Government and outside it, concerned both with the Soong oligarchy in China and with the over-lavish and almost imperial display which attended her triumphal tour across the country.

War Mobilization Board. President's creation of a new Office of War Mobilization on 28 May headed by Byrnes followed an article on previous day by Krock (whose relations with Administration are said to be worse than ever, as a result of the exceptionally rabid part believed to have been played by him in egging Chandler on to his Pacific speech) confidently predicting Byrnes's impending fall. This new office, concerned with 'production, procurement, transportation, and distribution of military and civilian supplies, materials, and products', is regarded as being of the first importance in as much as it places Byrnes in genuine control of the entire wartime economy of the country, making him in fact what he has often been called but has never been, 'Assistant President of the United States'. He is to be guided by a committee of Stimson, Knox, Hopkins, Nelson and his own successor as head of Office of Economic Stabilization, Judge Vinson.[8] Vinson is an ex-Congressman from Kentucky, reportedly of liberal views. His powers over wages, prices, labour, etc., although in fact not as great as Byrnes's had been, are nevertheless expected to equal those of Nelson. Appointment meets the needs of the Kilgore bill[9] and may make the possibly

8 Frederick M. Vinson, Democratic Congressman from Kentucky 1925–9, 1931–8.
9 See despatch of 28 March 1943.

strongly supported Maloney bill (to set up a civilian supply administration) otiose. Baruch, who would have liked Vinson's post, is said to be very disgruntled. Attacks on the tottering OPA continue and there is talk of diverting Prentiss Brown's powers, at any rate over food rationing, to the homespun and more popular Food Administrator, Chester Davis.[10]

Polls. Fortune poll on the fourth term for Roosevelt indicates (a) if war is over 59.2 per cent are opposed to it ; (b) if war is in progress all occupational groups except those in highest income brackets would favour it (45 per cent of the executives in favour, a slightly larger percentage against, 77 per cent of industrial and farm workers in favour). 56.6 per cent favour an active part by United States in post-war international organization with a court [sic] and police force. 72.8 per cent favour sending money and materials to other countries for post-war rehabilitation. 80 per cent believe that United States should work with Russia although this may not be easy. 70.4 per cent believe that Mr Roosevelt has done a good job, 21.2 per cent thought his performance fair, 4.1 per cent regarded it as poor. 36.9 per cent want a United Nations Council to rule Germany for ten or more years, 20.7 per cent favour international government to rule Germany for a hundred years, 11.2 per cent wish to partition her among the victors, 3.7 per cent wish to kill a Nazi for every person killed by Germans in occupied countries. *Fortune* takes this to indicate a reasonable and unvindictive attitude towards the German settlement.

5 June 1943

Aftermath of Mr Churchill's visit. Aftermath of Prime Minister's enthusiastically received visit has taken form of what is now routine admiration for his personality and skill. Incorrigible 'Pacific Firsters' have taken refuge in the aside that irresistible Mr Churchill and his adroit British advisers have as so often bamboozled innocent Americans into forgetting their true Pacific interests and continuing with European plans. This is said indulgently, but not without some genuine bitterness about supposed gullibility of United States Administration. *Time* magazine has produced a map of Europe (which now embellishes some offices of War Department) captioned 'The not too soft underbelly of the Axis' showing Pyrenees, Alps, etc., in high relief as a row of jagged teeth. But fact that incorrigibles are incorrigible does not detract from immense effect of Mr Churchill's speech and visit.

Coal Strike. After a deceptive lull Lewis, who seemed determined about his demand of $1.50 per day, struck again while operators stuck at $1.00. War Labor Board conveyed that it would resign en bloc if its recommendations were

10 Chester C.Davis, President of the Federal Reserve Bank of St Louis 1941–51.

set aside by Administration. Ickes blamed operators' board, ordered discontinuance of miners-operators conferences while strike lasts. Leaders of AF of L and CIO, apart from conferring with President, sit by with folded hands evidently reluctant to risk any move. President ordered miners to return to work on 7 June with Ickes responsible for effecting this under terms originally recommended on 25 May by WLB. When miners start work conferences are to be resumed. After a grim four days during which virtually no coal was mined, President implied that he might induct strikers into army. House substituted labour-curbing Smith-Harness[1] bill for milder Connally bill which almost bans strikes in war industries, and a Southern senator demanded jailing of Lewis for treason. Lewis once again capitulated. Byrnes, who with Ickes was active in this situation, feels vindicated. President's prestige is bound to rise even in labour circles which feel that Lewis jeopardized their position. Bill will doubtless be toned down by Senate. View is freely expressed everywhere that, but for Lewis, Congress might well have delayed action. If really severe anti-labour legislation goes through, Lewis may yet emerge as obvious champion of a martyred group. Of this Administration is only too well aware. Lewis's ties with Republicans and isolationists, in particular with Hoover, are perceptible in Republican speeches in Congress and in isolationist editorials which exonerate miners and place blame on President to whose alleged bungling entire situation is ascribed. No other labour leader could have got away for so long with as much. Only all-out anti-Lewisites in Congress are Southern Democrats. Lewis's request for affiliation with AF of L (see last summary) seems to have struck a snag in resistance of those who anticipate difficulty in curbing Lewis once he has made his way into fold. Conflict is between anti- and pro-Rooseveltites in AF of L. Green and Murray have formally protested against what they maintain to be 160 per cent rise in food prices and blame OPA. That luckless agency, still convulsed by inner strife and left *in extremis* by most commentators, breathes still. CIO presses not for its abolition but for its strengthening. Likewise it adjures President to abate not a little of powers of WLB.

Office of War Mobilization (OWM). Effects of Byrnes's new office (see last summary) cannot be judged until it gets under way. It has temporarily at least satisfied great public clamour for a war cabinet and increasing tempo of United States production, impressive evidence of which was given in Byrnes's 'fireside talk', may serve to redound to his credit and strengthen his position. It is doubtful whether his new position will in fact effect greater co-ordination than his previous office had achieved since this depends on personal temperament more than official status and Byrnes's chief virtue has thus far been persuasiveness and tact, particularly with Senate. Nor is degree of real authority given him by President as against Hopkins, who is technically under him, at all determinable. There is

---

1 Forest A.Harness, Republican Congressman from Indiana since 1939.

talk that Stimson was (a) not consulted about committee of which he is a member, (b) required to attend in person which he finds a burden, (c) his department is trying to place an interpretation on order whereby OWM is merely an anti-inflation instrument and has no real jurisdiction over military supply. Nelson apparently was equally surprised, considered resignation, was put on OWM committee, reconsidered and stayed. Doubtless Byrnes's competence and seriousness of President's intentions will be tested by whether War Department will in fact get away with this. Judge Vinson's (see last political summary) political function is evidently to do for House what Byrnes is doing and will continue to do for Senate. There is talk in Republican circles that Byrnes's appointment clearly shows that he and not Wallace is being groomed for 'Vice-Presidential running mate' next year, since this would furnish much needed Southern Democrat, making Hull very much less indispensable. Some think that Protestant Byrnes's Catholic origins would prejudice his chances both in South and with Catholics, but most political observers on whole discount this. Others mention Speaker Rayburn as a likely Vice-President. Wallace's friends who are said to be busily instructing him in art of practical politics are obscurely hinting that he might possibly qualify as a Secretary of State. Nothing seems less likely at the moment. There is no reason for supposing that President has begun to make up his mind on any of this or that he will do so until last possible moment.

Reciprocal Trade Agreements. Reciprocal Trade Agreements bill was voted by Senate 59 in favour (41 Democrats, 18 Republicans) against 23 (14 Republicans, 8 Democrats and La Follette). This large majority has fully justified Administration's confidence which was widely doubted particularly in Congress itself. Crucial battle occurred over Danaher amendment (making agreements terminable six months after cessation of hostilities) which was defeated by 51 to 33 (i.e. fatal third of Senate voted against intention of bill – 7 Republicans and 7 Democrats crossed party lines). Other 'crippling' amendments were defeated by larger majorities. . . . Despite the fact that the bill is but a mild curb against protectionism and was extended for two instead of the customary three years, the voting must be regarded, as Hull sees it, as an important victory for the Administration. Hull and Welles repeated so often that passage was a 'crucial test' of future American policy that it was debated and voted as such. The value of this move against isolationism is not made smaller by the fact that it is mainly symbolic. The debate was instructive; it was far more concerned with the constitutionality of the process – delegation of power to the executive, agreements operating in place of treaties, etc. – than with the commercial issue itself. The deep congressional jealousies and fears of usurpation of its peacemaking powers by the executive by piecemeal encroachment emerged again and again.

Post-war. Welles continued his educational campaign with an article and a speech at Durham, NC, to the Southern Negro College. He was, as always, lucid, concrete and sane, speaking again of (a) the need for a provision of specific military forces by the nations to crush aggression and enforce disarmament, (b) a world court, (c) freer trade, (d) an end to racial and religious minorities in the new egalitarian order. His utterances continue more accurately than anyone else's to convey the general drift of thought of this Administration. Bullitt continues to try to 'smear' him, but so far his *chronique scandaleuse*[2] has proved too much even for the isolationist press.

. . .

Tax bill. Tax bill (see last summary) finally passed.

Food Conference. Food Conference is considered to have ended in a success after its shaky start. This is of some political importance here since it is an augury for future United Nations conferences. Many tributes have been paid to British delegation and Mr Law.

13 June 1943

. . .

French North Africa. News of united National Committee[1] was in general acclaimed chiefly by liberals, radio and in greater section of press, and was received with private misgivings by certain United States officials. Members of State Department are said to be somewhat disconcerted by turn of events and one or two are inclined to blame Monnet[2] for 'selling out' to the Gaullists. French experts of General Donovan's office are on other hand said to be pleased. For the moment official satisfaction is displayed, but should a new Giraud-de Gaulle break develop, the Department and its press mouthpieces would doubtless play it up and revert to their original sniping. Despite all evidence to the contrary it is still basically felt that composition of Committee represents a British victory over American influence. Local Fighting French and their supporters do not disguise their jubilation. Congress throughout appears to have no interest whatever in French affairs.

Labour. Public satisfaction with Lewis's apparent capitulation was swiftly shattered by his announcement that it was to be but a temporary truce – until 20 June – and his continued attacks on War Labor Board. After a deadlock between Lewis and operators during which each side ridiculed the other, and Lewis de-

2 The story which obtained wide but initially underground circulation was to the effect that Welles had made homosexual proposals to a Negro sleeping-car porter. The allegation was ultimately brought to the notice of Hull and Connally at the instigation of Bullitt. It was held to be the direct cause of Welles's resignation.

1 Committee of National Liberation formed in Algiers, alternately presided over by de Gaulle and Giraud.

2 Jean Monnet, Deputy Secretary-General of League of Nations, chaired Anglo-French Economic Co-ordination Committee 1939–40, served on British Supply Council in Washington 1940–3.

scribed operators' tactics as farcical, he broke operators' front by a dramatic separate peace with O'Neill[3] of Appalachian operators. O'Neill left conference leaving his colleagues in a state of bewildered indignation at his 'treachery'. There is much suspicion that his principal motive was identical with Lewis's – a desire to discredit Administration and its War Labor Board, for which not even alliance with Lewis was too expensive. The price may however turn out to be fatal to Lewis let alone the rest of labour – since Congress this time seems genuinely determined to put an end to strikes of this type and Senate and House committees considering Smith–Connally bill (see last two political summaries) have produced a stern compromise (which passed House) making incitement to strikes (but not strikes themselves) in war industries as well as payment of strike benefits a penal offence, imposing a thirty-day 'cooling-off period' before a strike may legally occur, and requiring a secret ballot of workers in plant concerned and forbidding use of union funds as political contributions (Senator Hatch proposes to offer a bill putting similar restraints on employers' associations). Amendments requiring registration of unions and publication of union funds were defeated. Byrnes is rumoured to be in favour of this compromise. Labour is naturally bitterly opposed, particularly to secret ballot clause which removes control over strikes from union chiefs and transfers it to men in local plants, a serious blow at power of trade union leaders (which indeed may be precise reasoning behind it – popular cry is that workers are patriotic enough and are forced into destructive courses by their irresponsible leaders). Large Republican vote against bill is due partly to anti-Administration feeling often used by Lewis, partly to fear of losing labour vote which Administration's stern measures may drive into their embrace. The compromise bill has passed the Senate by 55 to 22 (30 Republican, 25 Democrat, versus 18 Democrat, 3 Republican and La Follette), i.e. by a combination of Republicans and Southern Democrats. If, as seems likely, President signs it, a renewal of the strike (on 20th of this month) when new truce expires, would ultimately entail formal fine and arrest of Lewis and his colleagues. Danaher and Walsh, who lean heavily on a poor Irish vote, attacked bill, while Pepper delivered the most violent denunciation of Lewis to date. Ickes has caught spirit of the times in imposing a collective fine of nearly three million dollars on soft coal miners for four days' strike following contravention of contract, but left a conspicuously introduced loophole for its remission by local arrangement. Lewis has denounced this as illegal and as 'a brutal application of economic sanctions', and there is much violent outcry at the pits. There is a rising tide of anti-labour feeling among armed services. Soldiers form majority of assailants on Negroes and Mexicans particularly widespread in Los Angeles, publicized by press as attacks on 'zoot-suited hoodlums'.[4]

3 Charles O'Neill, President of United Eastern Coal Sales Corporation 1934–49.

4 The zoot-suit, an extravagant youth fashion, originated in Harlem and spread to the West Coast, where it was especially adopted by Mexican teenagers.

Republican tactics. Various candidates continue active. Willkie has been acclaimed by Negroes for his continued stand on their behalf (Negro votes may alter vote of at least three Northern states). There is a rumour that Willkie and Pearl Buck will head a new committee against racial discrimination. Appointment of Father Haas [5] to head the Fair Employment Practices Committee underlines close interest of Roman Church in Negro minority. Bricker delivered a routine blast at New Deal, the 'political parasites' swarming in Washington, and secrecy concerning recent food conference at Hot Springs. While Bricker's attack on conference was not surprising in itself it underlines peculiar fact that international conferences have been made to appear suspect as such by a part of press which represents them as at once futile and trifle sinister as occasions for secret diplomacy. On the other hand most Hot Springs correspondents and a fair proportion of editorials welcome accomplishments of conference as an excellent omen for international collaboration. Congress likewise appears to have got over its tantrums over being excluded. . . . Hoover continued his attacks against alleged mismanagement of food situation, said that owing to New Deal's scarcity system the country would find itself unable to feed its Allies if war came to an end this year. He recommended centralization under a competent Secretary of Agriculture, demanded more men on the land, and spoke with gloom about domestic food shortage. Latest figures of Department of Agriculture promising in 1943 a crop at most no greater than 1942 (partly as a result of recent floods and inclement weather) seem partially to bear this out.

· · ·

. . . There is a considerable flurry in New York over resignation of local OPA Director, Porter,[6] who resigned on grounds that he was unable to cope with pressure concerning OPA appointments exerted by politicians – principally Senator Mead and various Tammany bosses. Problem of patronage has always been acute and failure to observe its rules was one of causes of Leon Henderson's fall. Ex-Senator Prentiss Brown is alleged to have appointed ex-Senator Herring precisely to organize a more traditional distribution of spoils. New York Republicans naturally intend to make full use of this minor scandal. Meanwhile Senator McKellar's bill seeks to impose senatorial control over all federal appointments of policy-making officials. (Various financial and other criteria of what constitutes policy-makers are being discussed.) This attempted substitution of senatorial patronage for that of Administration is swiftly maturing again.

· · ·

China. The Anti-Exclusion bill having been rejected in one form has been reintroduced in another. This is still attracting attention. There is growing nervousness of effect on China if it is defeated. Several papers demand swift passage for

5 Francis J.Haas of Catholic University, prominent advocate of social reform, later Bishop of Grand Rapids.

6 Paul A.Porter, initially newspaper reporter and lawyer, special counsel Department of Agriculture 1932–7, Washington counsel to CBS 1937–42, deputy administrator in charge of rent division of OPA 1942–3, then transferred to War Food Administration.

it. (An attack on Ambassador Gauss and United States representation in China generally has appeared in *Christian Science Monitor*.)

. . .

19 June 1943

. . .

The Finns. The Finns, after missing two years, have paid their debt instalment and have been loudly acclaimed for it by the isolationist papers which said that the conspiracy of silence about the gallant people's conduct was scandalous. Despite all, the Finns are not unpopular and M. Procopé's social connexions with anti-Administration circles in Washington stand the Finns in good stead. Much delight was given to his enemies when his name with those of the Ministers of Eire and Argentina were taken by an OPA inspector for 'pleasure driving' to attend a dinner with the celebrated hostess, Mrs McLean.[1]

Labour. The Connally-Harness-Smith Labour bill is waiting the President's signature. The 'truce' expires on the 20th, the date for signature is the 20th. The President will not sign before the 20th and Lewis-Roosevelt war of nerves is thus in full blast. President is said to be impressed with fact that public opinion and Congress will be bitter if he does not sign, while labour will be no less bitter if he does. The whole of organized labour (in broadcasts and advertisements) and several government Departments are urging him strongly to veto the bill, but not with an intensity threatening a real explosion unless he does so. The betting in some White House and other government circles is that he will not veto the bill, but this is regarded as being far less probable than last week. There is no evidence that President has reached even a provisional decision on this as yet. There seems no doubt that he would have signed the original milder Connally bill without a qualm – and without much resistance from labour – and he may return the bill to Congress to amend, particularly if the miners refrain from renewing the strike. The provisions in the bill most objectionable to labour seem to be

(a) Prohibition of use of union funds for political campaigns,
(b) The secret ballot required for strikes in plants not managed by the Government, both of which destroy power of union leaders. . .

. . .

Post War. The House Foreign Affairs Committee has unanimously passed a resolution introduced by Fulbright,[2] an Anglophile ex-Rhodes Scholar and one of its most effective and enlightened members, pledging Congress in favour of the 'creation of appropriate international machinery with power adequate to establish and to maintain a just and lasting peace among the nations of the world, and as

1 Mrs Evalyn Walsh McLean, who entertained at her estate 'Friendship'.
2 J.William Fulbright, newly-elected Democratic Congressman from Arkansas.

favouring participation by the United States therein'. As a concurrent resolution this requires approval by the majority of the Senate. This attempt to prod the Senate Committee into some sort of action on the budget of post-war proposals pigeonholed in its archives, was described by the House majority leader, Mc-Cormack, as 'one of the historic documents of the day'. It was fairly well received in the House (which may debate it next week) save by one or two isolationists who bitterly chided their friends on the Committee for letting the resolution pass unanimously. Vorys[3] explained that the resolution committed nobody to anything but merely put on record general non-isolationist sentiment which was surely not untimely. The Senate received the matter with coolness and some irony. Connally (at whose committee it was aimed) said that it was 'mild and cryptic' and that his committee would produce its own resolution in its own good time. Messrs Ball and Burton (who had been consulted by Fulbright and his friends) welcomed the move. It is too early to estimate public and press reaction but the unanimity and impatience shown by committee indicate that general anti-isolationism is making even the Wheelers and Tafts moderate their language and pay lip service to international ideals, which in itself represents progress. Pressure for action on the topic has undoubtedly increased. Ball, who is genuinely indignant at delays of Foreign Relations Committee and wants more specific proposals passed by Congress, told a member of my staff that he thought it useless to wait further and proposed with Burton, Hatch and Hill to stump the country in support of their ideas. The tour of this quartet should be a novel event in the local political scene.

The appointment of Acheson as the Assistant Secretary responsible for co-ordinating the various agencies concerned in the administration of conquered Axis territories has not yet been made public. He is, according to the President's latest order, to preside over an interdepartmental committee including the Treasury, the War and Navy Departments, BEW, Lend-Lease, and OFRRO. The order drafted by Wayne Coy[4] in the Office of the Budget represents victory for the State Department whose general authority over all foreign civilian operations now seems established beyond doubt.

. . .

The Office of War Mobilization has acquired Baruch as an adviser (he had held this position less formally for some time) and lost a possible secretary in Oscar Cox (Assistant Solicitor General and Lend-Lease Counsel). Cox, who is a very capable and still rising young New Dealer, and a protégé of Hopkins, had originally accepted the post but apparently demanded that the appointment be formally made and announced by the President himself. When the President, out of deference to Byrnes, declined to do this, the arrangement was abandoned, according to Cox because Hopkins had advised him that he would prove of greater value in his present position, according to Byrnes because Cox had de-

---

3 John M. Vorys, Republican Congressman from Ohio since 1939.
4 Wayne Coy, Assistant Director, Bureau of the Budget, since 1942.

manded far too much and had shown over-ambitious inclinations. Benjamin Cohen,[5] described by Baruch as 'the elder statesman of the New Deal', thus still remains weightiest executive below cabinet rank within new office.

Congress. The Senate has defeated by a narrow margin the Bankhead Resolution raising agricultural prices, largely for fear of Lewis's and general labour wage demands which would prove harder to resist. The food and agricultural situation is subject of warm controversy in Congress and press. Landon has once more pitched in on the side of Hoover and the Farm Bloc. Chester Davis, Food Administrator, is said still to be opposing subsidies to grocers, probably because of the fear that the public will grow accustomed to low food prices which may ruin farmers if and when subsidies are withdrawn after the war. Republican critics maintain that subsidies divorced from an all-embracing scheme of inflation control increase the 'inflationary gap' at least as much as higher prices could and add to this the evil of a new crop of bureaucrats. . . .

Congress versus OWI. In a sudden explosion of temper the House, after approving of appropriations submitted for the majority of government agencies with certain cuts, directed its fury against OWI. By a vote of 218 versus 114 (160 Republican plus 55 Democrat plus 3 versus 108 Democrat plus 5 Republican plus 1) it abolished all funds for Domestic Division of OWI on motion of Starnes[6] who said that American people wanted no Goebbels or Gayda[7] but only freedom of the press. Elmer Davis implied at a press conference that he would have no choice but to resign if this went through, adding that he differed from Goebbels at any rate in that his distinguished colleague did not have to go to the Reichstag for his funds. . . . Meanwhile the Overseas Branch is left intact largely because of growing consciousness in America of its world problems and the need to propagate its views beyond its frontiers as a weapon both in war and in coming peace. Sherwood declared that the presidential candidates of both parties would get equal publicity in overseas propaganda and that the contest would be presented as an example of the democratic process at its best.

The 'zoot-suit' riots (see last political summary) are still causing concern and Negroes have been mobbed in Detroit, Alabama, Texas and Pennsylvania in a sudden fraying of national temper. The Mexican Ambassador has complained and Hull reports that no cases of violence to Mexican citizens occurred. The white-hot account in this week's *Time* is worth reading. The uneasy mood of the South emerged in the sudden refusal of South Carolina to contribute to the Dem-

5 Benjamin Cohen, New York lawyer, draftsman of much New Deal legislation, and Assistant to the Director, Office of Economic Stabilization, since 1942.

6 Joe Starnes, Democratic Congressman from Alabama since 1935.

7 Virginio Gayda, Italian journalist (1885–1944), who as editor of the *Giornale d'Italia* from 1926 to 1943 was a recognized spokesman for the Fascist régime.

ocratic Party funds so long at any rate as Negro political support was sought by the national party on an equal basis with the white vote.

26 June 1943

General mood. There has been a bewildering (if temporary) confusion of national feeling across the country.

(a) In Washington it showed itself in what Lippmann described as the hysteria of the House which pounced upon OWI and OPA and drastically cut their appropriations (see last political summary) and in congressional speeches which vied with one another in denouncing the incompetence of the Administration in managing the home front. Although one of the strongest statements was made by five Democrats (three of them faithful New Dealers, Senators Kilgore, Murray [1] and Thomas of Utah), there is reason for suspecting a concerted Republican drive to discredit the Administration by barracking and obstruction. This view is not the fault of mere Democratic propaganda since one or two key Republicans have in private admitted to some anxiety lest these tactics, rewarding though they be politically, may not go too far and harm the war effort. The man behind this campaign is Selvage, Publicity Director of Republican Party, originally of the NAM. He is probably the main force behind the drive against OWI and is said to have got *Reader's Digest* to order a leading article by Max Eastman,[2] the Trotskyite, attacking Russia and OWI in one.

(b) Last week's race riots in Los Angeles and elsewhere and the far more serious outbreak this week in Detroit have upset people everywhere. The activities of Fascist groups in Detroit, and the friction between the several hundreds of thousands of white labour imported from the South, and the Negro immigrants, as well as the lack of car petrol which keeps the population cooped up in the city during holidays, are not regarded as entirely sufficient to explain the mounting tension. The state of emergency is now over. But Negroes complain of lack of adequate protection from the police. Southerners in Congress as usual attribute this to bungling Northern interference with the stable social structure of the South.

(c) The political struggle and consequent uncertainty which surrounds the problem of farmers, subsidies and general price regulation has naturally affected farmers, retailers and their customers everywhere, and Republicans as well as dissident Democrats are using these issues as political weapons. Add to this the labour crisis and the military lull which has helped to move the troubled home front into the centre of attention, and the confusion of minds becomes intelligible. Such national fogs have occurred before, and this one will probably clear in time, but the Administration, faced with universal dissatisfaction, has an uncommonly steep task before it. Anti-Roosevelt columnists are playing it for all they are worth, and Lippmann, back from his tour across the country, has addressed

1 James E. Murray, Democratic Senator from Montana since 1934.

2 Author and editor, originally Marxist, subsequently anti-Stalinist.

severe words to the President on his lack of clear guidance to the nation and failure to bring facts home to the public.

Labour. President's customary skill in handling of critical issues has failed to prevent awkward developments. Coal 'truce' expired on Sunday and on Monday Lewis ordered men back to work implying that this was conditional upon continued control of plants by Administration, i.e. Ickes. WLB did not budge from its refusal to raise wages or allow portal to portal pay.[3]

Operators and their press supporters complained that even if Connally-Smith bill passed, anxiety to implement its provisions would dispose Administration to take over more and more plants for duration which was a form of socialist expropriation, an end for which Lewis was plainly working. Ickes worried them further by saying that he expected to run mines for a longer period than had been anticipated but he reassured operators somewhat by saying that he was a mere emergency custodian and no bar to agreements between unions and operators under auspices of WLB, only possible method of ultimate solution. Since then situation has deteriorated. (a) Miners, disappointed at Lewis's failure to raise their pay, are dribbling back to work very slowly and according to latest reports scarcely 50 per cent are back at work. (b) President, who according to faithful Lindley and all other sources had been inclined to sign Connally–Smith bill after listening to representations by Green and Murray, who justly claimed that their continued support of no strike pledge against Lewis was politically costly to them, appeared to haver until last moment. On 23rd he announced that he would offer Congress a resolution raising draft age for non-combat military service to sixty-five years (Selective Service Act limits this to forty-five) enabling a draft of striking miners to mines. Describing action of miners' leaders as 'intolerable, stirring up anger and disapproval of an overwhelming mass of American people', he instructed Ickes to operate mines under his executive order of 1 May and WLB directive of 8 June. This not only failed to stem great and rising anti-Lewis tide, but served notice to anti-labour forces that, with draft order an obvious alternative to bill, a veto of bill was probably in offing and thus presented them with two days in which to organize a counter-offensive. Senator Connally had earlier 'besought' President to sign bill and various Senators threatened to revolt if he failed to do so. Nevertheless an immediate vote was not expected and some presidential supporters are said to have left for a long weekend (there are lurid stories of their efforts to return in time to vote frustrated by lack of petrol). In an electric atmosphere President's veto of bill was read to Senate on afternoon of 25th and eleven minutes later was overridden by that body on Connally's motion (56 to 25, 6 over required two-thirds) amid cheering from galleries packed with men in uniform. An hour later House in tense silence voted with Senate (244 *v.* 108) and bill became law. President's veto message approved Connally portions of Connally-Smith bill and criticized provisions most odious to labour – secret

3 Payment calculated to cover whole period at place of work between arrival and departure.

ballot clause which, he pointed out, would increase instead of diminish strikes by encouraging independent action by workers in plants, and prohibition of political contributions which deserved mature consideration and was not relevant to bill. Message, prepared in Bureau of Budget, was regarded as insipid and further irritated Congress, precipitating first congressional annulment of presidential veto on a serious issue since veterans' bonus episode in 1936.[4] Such loss of face on part of President as is involved – and opinion would differ as to how great this will prove to be – may to some degree be compensated by fact that by this act he continues his hold on loyalty of organized labour which had been severely strained, since he can now plausibly attribute responsibility for all future complications to an irresponsible opposition in Congress. Moreover bill will satisfy at any rate some of angry anti-labour feeling in country and among United States troops abroad. This at least is explanation given to their indignant allies privately by Senators Pepper, Hatch and Hill (whose anti-veto votes turned issue in Senate) for their action, which they claim cannot do President any serious political damage. They stoutly deny that President has lost his grip and maintain that a happy solution has been reached. Senator Wagner, who is much distressed, is said to have referred to his colleagues as 'a Reconstruction Congress.[5] Very very bad.' Meanwhile several more Carnegie Illinois steel plants have ceased work and Eric Johnston, President of United States Chamber of Commerce, delivered a slashing attack on knock-kneed dilly-dallying of Administration on home front.

Food. . . . Chester Davis is rumoured to be meditating resignation because he finds that lack of direct access to the President (he must approach him through economic stabilizer Vinson) as well as lack of control over food rationing and food prices makes his position insupportable. Davis is supported by a group of anti-Administration columnists thirsting for the blood of OPA and is at present an obvious Trojan horse in the Administration fortress. Byrnes has spoken to various Congressmen on the undesirability of creating a food czar (see our last political summary) but despite this the House Agricultural Committee (18 *v.* 8) voted to vest Davis with plenary powers over rationing and prices. . . . The President described this agitation for a food czar as a red herring diverting attention from the central question of inflation. 'Suppose the Archangel Gabriel were made food czar, could he supply more food at the present cost?' he asked. Higher prices would benefit only the rich. . . .

French situation. The despatch in the *Philadelphia Inquirer* reporting that instructions had been received by British officials here to drop de Gaulle in favour of Giraud is only the sharpest example of the line taken by the greater part of the

4 In January 1936 Congress re-passed the Veterans' (ex-servicemen's) Bonus bill over Roosevelt's veto.

5 The Congress which, in the so-called 'Reconstruction' period after the Civil War, was continuously at odds with President Andrew Johnson and in 1867 attempted to impeach him.

press, and by the usual 'well-informed' American political wiseacres in Washington. Starting from the theory, which nothing has effectively shaken, that His Majesty's Government have throughout supported de Gaulle against Giraud who is backed by United States Government, commentators claim to see a palpable change in the attitude of His Majesty's Government which has finally decided to abandon the too importunate de Gaulle in favour of the steadier Giraudists. This, accepted as fact by both sides, leads Giraud's champions and State Department mouthpieces to congratulate us on our timely conversion, and naturally has aroused liberals and de Gaullists led by Lippmann to intensified defence of de Gaulle and condemnation of what is now taken to be common Anglo-American 'expediency' policy. The view that His Majesty's Government is merely anxious to support the National Committee and not this or that General obtains scarcely any credence, if only because despatches from United States correspondents in London convey that a change of heart towards de Gaulle has definitely occurred in 'British Government circles'. The eventual attitude to this of the State Department can be easily predicted, since it is likely to be deeply influenced by the report which Matthews,[6] who is bound to be regarded as an expert on all British attitudes, brings with him.

·   ·   ·

28 June 1943

·   ·   ·

Civil Liberties. There is much rejoicing in the liberal camp at (a) the reversal of the Gobitis (Jehovah's Witnesses) case[1] whose children, by a new judgment of the Supreme Court, may not be penalized for failing to salute the United States flag. Frankfurter, who delivered the original anti-Witnesses judgment, which had made a great stir at the time, is somewhat bitter and there is much crowing audible from his opponents of both the right and the left ; (b) the acquittal by the Supreme Court of Schneidermann,[2] an ex-member of the Communist Party, whom Willkie defended from the government denaturalization order. Communism is thus no longer automatically a ground for loss of citizenship.

·   ·   ·

Post-war. The week was crammed with post-war pronouncements. The Governors' Conference at Columbus, although technically non-political, was naturally the centre of much political manoeuvring and speculation. The Scripps-Howard press represents Dewey as having secured a great personal triumph, overshadowing Bricker (the host) and other presidential aspirants. Dewey delivered the now routine condemnations of the Administration's food policy, and of isolationism,

6 H. Freeman Matthews, Acting Chief Civil Affairs Officer, on Eisenhower's staff, London, Algiers, 1942–3.

1 Case involving followers of Jehovah's Witnesses sect who refused on grounds of conscience to salute the US flag.

2 William Schneidermann, Russian-born Californian Communist. US Government tried to revoke his naturalization order as having been fraudulently obtained, but Supreme Court contended that in 1927 (when he obtained it) the aims of the Communist Party were not unconstitutional.

and is evidently being played up by the Republican leaders as evidence that Willkie holds no monopoly of Republican collaborationist sentiment ; even Bricker stated that he favoured American participation in a world organization to preserve the peace if universal common consent could be gained ; though he was typically vague about details. Praise of the Fulbright Resolution (see last political summary) by the Scripps-Howard press is final proof of Republican desire to display its anti isolationist face, at any rate for the present. The Governors hotly demanded implementation of States' rights ; Governor Neely's call for a fourth term for the President was received by the Democrats with resignation rather than enthusiasm.

General Marshall told the Governors that even if bombing brings Germany to her knees only a land invasion can finally finish her off, that land blows at Japan may come sooner than is expected, and that the United States may still lose the war if its home front continues to be torn by strikes and race riots and weakened by complacency and the slackening of production. This reference to Assistant Secretary of War Patterson's comments on the 5½ per cent falling off of production (said to be resented by WPB) is widely carried by the press. Joe Davies delivered a routine encomium of the USSR.

Republican Chairman Spangler adduced some not very striking evidences of a continuing Republican swing, and wound up with a gibe at OWI, the Aunt Sally of anti-Rooseveltites.

Senator Taft after mocking the notion of a superstate has, significantly for him, called for force to preserve the peace and the covenants between nations. . . . But the most important speech of the week was undoubtedly that of Senator Lodge.

Lodge is a popular, politically astute and exceptionally capable representative of the harder-headed younger Republicans, and his remarks expressed what many of them think but do not often say. The gist of his statement was that since the other great powers conceived their vital interests clearly – Britain with her desire to preserve her Empire, Russia with her territorial aims in Eastern Europe – it was high time for the United States to do likewise, if they are not to be left without the strategic imports which at the present rate of expenditure they will have need of after the war. A statistical list of these followed. He poured a practical man's scorn on the notion of world or regional organization unsupported by a previous attempt to harmonize their national purposes by the major allies. The speech achieved relatively little publicity save in *Time* magazine, but is considered to have made a profound impression upon Lodge's fellow Senators and is an important expression of the attitude of a genuinely powerful cross-party group. . . .

3 July 1943

National mood. While war news, in particular American Pacific offensive and bombings, feeds public optimism and there is continued speculation about collapse of Italy, state of home front has scarcely been improved by resignation of Chester Davis, the sensational Wallace-Jones row, congressional blocking of Administration's anti-inflation bill counterblocked by President's veto, and disturbed aftermath of race riots. Opposition is publicly and privately jubilant. Willkie told a member of my staff that he is convinced that this is last nail in Administration's coffin and that their doom in 1944 is sealed : he fears that Republicans will romp home too easily, without an adequate opposition. What he may mean is that his party may be able to afford a machine candidate like Bricker and do without his own greater popular appeal. Krock in *New York Times* quoting *Manchester Guardian* and *Tribune* has expressed the common Republican annoyance at the unjustified understandable popularity of President in Great Britain and complains that the *Guardian* ignores reasons behind congressional opposition. He quaintly compares an analogous humiliation of Pitt by Parliament when Napoleon was in Boulogne.[1] All commentators but President's faithfuls are lecturing Administration on its incompetence, led by Lippmann who is calling for more young blood in an ossifying collection of office-holders. The public and perhaps sections of Congress are certainly at sea about such issues as food subsidies, inflation, etc., and failure on part of the President and his close lieutenants such as Byrnes and Vinson to explain these topics to the public, is attributed to advice of Hopkins, who is reported to be urging, as so often, that these storms will blow over quickest if no attention is paid to them. Speaker Rayburn told a member of my staff that he regards this as fatal advice but on other hand observed that chances of a fourth term depended far more on temporary mood of people during the four months before election than on anything occurring today. Deep general relief will be felt when Congress recesses, though the end is not yet in sight. . . .

Labour. Labour situation is slightly improved by gradual but steady return of miners to work. . . . Both Green and Murray have come out with loyal declarations of 'No Strike' support of the President. Lewis is silent and situation is in uneasy quiescence at moment. Nobody seems certain as to how and when coercive powers of bill will be implemented. Lewis is said to be debating whether or not to go to courts on issue of 'portal to portal' payments. Refusal to meet railroad union wage raise demands has increased tension in that quarter.

Food. Chester Davis's resignation was expected and President's curt refusal to allow him to continue with his programmes for awhile (which Davis had requested) is said to spring from White House irritation with Davis's alleged plots with Opposition. . . . Administration's plans have been rudely shaken by recent heavy vote of both Houses to forbid the use of subsidies (except to stimulate production) as a rider to bill extending for two years and increasing to $3,400,-000,000 the lending powers of Commodity Credit Corporation, upon which in-

---

1 In 1805 when Pitt was defeated by the Speaker's casting vote on the issue of Dundas's conduct as Treasurer of the Navy.

ternal loans, i.e. much of economic life of the country, depends. The President has vetoed it in a strong and lucid message, drafted in Byrnes's office, declaring that action of Congress opens the doors widely to inflation which would hit the unorganized millions and set farmer against the soldier, the worker and consumer. Although both Houses voted against subsidies by more than two-thirds, the House, unprepared to face consequences, has sustained the veto (154 versus 228 ; less than two-thirds) and an alternative measure is likely to emerge. CCC will be extended till 1 January by emergency legislation, while subsidies issue pends. Chester Davis's successor, Judge Marvin Jones, although a popular ex-Congressman of some twenty-three years' experience, is not precisely the stuff of which successful 'czars' are made. A man of unimpeachable integrity, goodwill and absolute devotion to Administration, he is not, unlike his predecessor, a firm or clear-minded man, as those who attended Hot Springs Food Conference best know – and earnestness and a kind heart seem scarcely sufficient to cope with a stubborn Farm Bloc and a seething Congress. His appointment, despite his elevation to Byrnes's War Mobilization Board (exclusion from which was one of Davis's main complaints), seems to indicate that President clearly wishes to leave decision in the hands of Byrnes and Vinson and has decisively rejected the notion of a plenipotentiary food administrator or appeasement of Farm Bloc. . . .

Flurries. The Vice-President, evidently irritated by political neglect of him by all parties (including White House), has evidently decided to reassert himself. No sooner were full appropriations for BEW accepted by Congress without a murmur (they await an automatic passage by Senate) after a striking exposition of its case by Milo Perkins, than Wallace published an attack on his old foe, Secretary Jesse Jones, worded in bitter and unbridled terms. Jones was charged with deliberate prevention of BEW (by withholding funds, general obstruction and presentation of false accounts of its activities inside and outside Congress) from building stockpiles of 'critical materials' and general exercise of wide functions which it acquired in April 1942. Jones replied that this was pure malice. Press loudly deplored this unedifying public exhibition (had the President not expressly forbidden public feuds between his subordinates ?) and then with greatest gusto provided the public with full details, and was duly reprimanded for it by President who observed that some publishers evidently forced their writers to demean themselves to such activities. This led to a fresh outburst in nettled opposition press of stories of a situation which by this time had acquired a strong flavour of *opéra bouffe*. Jones is said to have been seen carrying a gun in true Texan fashion and spoke of wishing to meet Wallace man to man. Byrnes, whose official duty it is to reconcile Administration feuds, summoned both men and uttered soothing remarks about inevitable clashes of men of strong views. He refused to be drawn on resolutions before House and Senate to investigate Wallace's charges. Congressman who said that all that had occurred was that 'a bureaucrat called a bureaucrat a bureaucrat' failed to do justice to depth of cleavage. Wallace and Jones called on Byrnes amid a large mob of onlookers barely held off by police. The meeting bore no fruit although Wallace formally declared that he did not wish to impugn Jones's patriotism or honour. Jones declined to be mollified, spoke of dastardly attacks and demanded full investigation. House Rules Committee and Senators Byrd and Bridges have promised that this will be done and issue is bound to crop up in Jones's appearance in Congress on other matters. Wallace conveyed that BEW would seek direct grants of funds from Congress. There is much general speculation on whether Jones can afford to continue in office after public loss of face on this scale and Farley's dissidents would doubtless welcome him into their ranks. As Jones owes his position largely to wide influence in the South particularly among small bankers and businessmen, episode is not calculated to narrow rift between Southern Democrats and Roosevelt's followers. Eugene Meyer, who was once physically assaulted by Jones, described him in his *Washington Post* as a menace to war effort. Lippmann aroused feeling in SD by his suggestion that all that remained was for some French official in Algiers to lecture an AP correspondent on the disgraceful lack of American unity. But the French had too much good taste for that. Opposition is naturally delighted by the row which illustrates that enmities among Democrats which are bitterly personal and born of too long association in office are profounder and more implacable than the merely political and ideological differences which divide Republicans. . . .

French. Giraud's announced coming arrival has stirred the SD's regulars to a routine exposition of de Gaulle's defects and political intrigues. . . . Now that His Majesty's Government are represented as having finally accepted American lead in this matter, criticism is directed mainly at de Gaulle with obliquer reference to Britain as originally responsible for building him to his present stature. The first of three articles by Demaree Bess[2] from Algiers in *Saturday Evening Post* on invasion of North Africa stresses Giraud's refusal to deal with anyone but Americans before and during the event. . . . Neither Hull nor Welles are anxious to see Giraud here at this moment and this visit, like the embarrassing appearance of Liberian President,[3] is ascribed to the lighthearted hospitality of President himself. Anne McCormick, who has talked with Hull, stresses in *New York Times* that Giraud is arriving in a purely military capacity and that 'it would be unfortunate if visit should strengthen impression that this Government is backing Giraud against de Gaulle. Nothing must be done to prejudice the ultimate choice of French people.' The sensitiveness of SD on this topic continues.

· · ·

11 July 1943

Congress, to general relief, adjourned on 8 July until 14 September. After a wild confusion of resolutions and counter-resolutions, the Administration by one sen-

2 Demaree C. Bess, correspondent for *Saturday Evening Post* 1938–50.
3 Edwin J. Barclay.

atorial vote won the right and the funds to pay food subsidies. Senator George, who almost defeated this single-handed, denounced rule by 'political commissars' attached to Byrnes, Vinson, etc. Anti-Administration press took up this cry, pointing (not without some justice) to e.g. Wayne Coy and Ben Cohen, etc., as real controllers of internal policy. President is said to be confident that contact with their constituents and diminution of the anti-Administration publicity afforded by congressional debates (as well as increase in government propaganda) will cause members of Congress to return more amenable to the Administration and that October will see inevitable reaction against Congress whose fury will have been spent, giving him a wider field for manoeuvring. Republicans say (and believe) the precise opposite. President's hope will not be realized if food and particularly prices policies provoke commodity shortages and price rises causing strikes, acute discontent, etc. There is a rumour that Coy is to succeed Prentiss Brown and no one prophesies a very long official life for Marvin Jones who has taken the place of Chester Davis on Food Production. Despite warnings by Somervell, Patterson, etc., about falling off production and danger of complacency, it should be noted that the vast industrial output continues to defeat all records.

FRENCH

Welcome to Giraud has been signal for unleashing of an anti-de Gaulle campaign of remarkable ferocity of which Callender's [1] despatch in *New York Times* of 7 July and the suddenly disseminated story of the Gaullist oath [2] (ascribed by UP [United Press] to State Department and spread in the background by General Odic) mark the climax. Drew Middleton's [3] despatch in the *New York Times* of the 8th was seized upon by liberals and most moderates as giving truer picture but Callender's version which, it is confidently asserted, was inspired by Hull personally, comes much closer to official attitude, according to which de Gaulle is a dangerous near-Fascist against whom drastic steps may have to be taken by United States Government and His Majesty's Government (belated change of heart by whom is noted with grim satisfaction). . . . Liberal press attacks publicly and others deplore privately 'British sacrifice of moral prestige' acquired during the Darlan deal for favour of the White House and State Department. President's remarks about continuance of non-recognition of the National Committee are likely to increase this. Meanwhile all French here, including Giraud,

---

1 Harold Callender, *New York Times* correspondent. In Washington 1942–3, Paris 1944–59.

2 General Giraud arrived in Washington from Algiers on 8 July and was greeted with a seventeen-gun salute. Harold Callender, writing from Washington, attributed to de Gaulle an 'unco-operative attitude', and described him as 'animated by dictatorial tendencies' and personifying 'fascistic impulses'. The UP despatch alleged that the US Government was in possession of a secret document 'in the form of an oath of allegiance' taken by 'Gaullist agents' by which they recognized him 'as the sole and legitimate leader of France'. Drew Middleton, writing from Algiers, warned that the Allies were alienating French goodwill by intervening on the side of Giraud.

3 Drew Middleton, AP correspondent with British and Allied forces 1939–42; in same capacity with *New York Times* 1942–6.

have been wounded and incensed by President's remarks at a press conference on 9 July that 'there isn't any France at the present time'.

The press no longer conceals that Giraud's visit is political as well as military. Welles is on a short vacation possibly for more than health reasons ; he is alleged to have hinted to his intimates that he wished to steer clear of this issue. This fits his general tendency to hold himself as available haven for liberals in distress. He told Zionist representatives that abrogation of Crémieux Law[4] and his own defence of it was a bad blunder and would be rectified. Same line taken by James[5] in *New York Times,* 4 July.

Senatorial committeemen Russell[6] (Democrat, Appropriations and Naval, chairman of group), Lodge (Republican, Appropriations and Military), Chandler (Democrat, Military), Mead (Democrat, Appropriations and Truman Committee) and Brewster (Republican, Naval and Truman Committee) who are to tour United States war fronts, propose to visit London shortly and have wide terms of reference to investigate most American activities abroad ('the matter of materials and the distribution of materials'), including post-war fate of American-built air bases and activities of OWI. Lodge and Brewster are real heavyweights, Mead and Russell pro-Roosevelt Democrats and Chandler an irresponsible. Their findings will doubtless form basis for congressional attitude on many issues.

FLURRIES

Wallace-Jones. The Wallace-Jones row continues. The President refuses to intervene. Commonest theory is that Wallace and Perkins, after successful congressional hearings and the acquisition of Baruch by Perkins as a powerful ally against Jones, feel BEW sufficiently strong to make attempt to drive Jones out of their field worth trying. Substance of Wallace's charges to some degree corroborated by weak defence put up by pro-Jones press. Democratic majorities in Committees defeated Jones's attempt to obtain congressional investigation, at any rate until next session, when issue may be too stale.

FCC. The investigation of the Federal Communications Commission by the congressional committee, whose Chairman is the fiery Southern reactionary, Eugene Cox of Georgia, has begun. The fact that a charge against Cox (initiated by FCC) of performing paid service for a government agency (illegal in case of sitting Congressmen), although filed with the Justice Department, seems too hot to the Attorney General to touch, has often been made public and left unanswered by Cox. Indignation that he, of all men, should have been appointed by Rayburn to inquire into FCC activities (Cox moved for investigation in obvious self-defence) has, after being voiced for weeks in the entire liberal press, been taken up by the *Saturday Evening Post,* which finds the proceeding wholly in-

4 The *Décret Crémieux* of 1870 enfranchised the Jews in Algeria.
5 Edwin L.James (1890–1951), managing editor of *New York Times* 1932–51.
6 Richard B.Russell, Democratic Senator from Georgia since 1933.

defensible. James Fly,[7] Chairman of the FCC, is a fairly tough customer, and has fought back with great spirit. The main charges are (1) that the Commission possesses powers of control both over the major radio networks and the numberless local stations, which strengthens 'New Deal despotism' over free speech and private enterprise (and incidentally hampers the exercise of local patronage and graft by State and Federal bosses and politicians), and (2) that its efficient radio monitoring service cuts across military and naval intelligence and endangers national security (the Army and Navy do not conceal their desire to acquire full monopoly of monitoring as of all foreign intelligence. Nor does Brigadier-General Donovan). Senator Taft (Republican, Ohio) duly denounced FCC as a menace to the liberty and property of American citizens, while Wheeler, who hates the FCC (which has produced too many instances of quotations from, and praise of, him by Dr Goebbels) turned his blast with equal fury against the 'plutocratic East Coast owners' of the major networks, whom he accused, as so often, of open pro-Roosevelt bias in allotment of time to political broadcasts (these 'plutocrats', who are the timidest of men, are particularly careful to avoid precisely that). After some rumbling in the opposition press about coming evidence by service representatives against the FCC, the President, after a private appeal by Fly, formally prohibited subpoena of Service and Budget Bureau witnesses or files in the case on security grounds. Cox demanded to know who was master, President or Congress? The issue is a far-reaching one in that the control of all commercial broadcasting is at stake ; the question of monitoring facilities, important as it is, is the lesser of the two. The enquiry represents an intersection of the Administration v. Congress, Army v. Civilians, and Vested Interest v. New Deal wars.

Elk Hills.[8] The enquiry into the Elk Hills oil contract between the Navy Department and Standard Oil, now disowned by Knox, is pushed remorselessly by the Justice Department investigator with Ickes's full blessing.

· · ·

18 July 1943

The excellent news from Sicily, Russia and the Pacific[1] has induced a mood of elation which, apart from chronic domestic anxieties, only the French imbroglio somewhat marred. The State Department's anti-Gaullist campaign is still conducted mainly through Lindley. . . . His reproduction on 12 July of an 'official confidential British directive' charging de Gaulle with Anglophobia, Fascist in-

7 James L. Fly, Chairman of FCC since 1939.

8 The Navy's contract excited the suspicions of the Justice Department, as a result of which the request for a $1.7 million appropriation 'for certain expenses' in connection with it was withdrawn in June. The proposal that Standard Oil should develop and operate the naval oil reserves in Elk Hills, Wyoming, was criticized as a 'give away'.

1 9 July : Allied landings in Sicily ; 15 July : Russian reports of heavy German losses at Belgorod, and reports from MacArthur of US successes in New Guinea.

clinations, etc., provoked strong reactions in Washington and New York press and political circles (if not beyond). The *Washington Post,* after recording editorially that British Embassy knew nothing of such a document, claimed that it was inconsistent with the Prime Minister's official statement[2] of 1 July and protested against the use of alleged secret documents by officially favoured correspondents as weapons in a 'war by innuendo' against de Gaulle. Lindley continued his serial with a piece describing Anglo-Gaullist friction in Syria in 1942 with details obviously supplied by American officials anxious to demonstrate that His Majesty's Government has reason to be as badly disposed to de Gaulle as the United States. The President's statement that the only symbol of France was France herself and that there is no France at present (with the implication that American recognition of the National Committee was most unlikely) is probably doing more to unite local Giraudists and de Gaullists here on a common nationalist anti-American and possibly anti-Anglo-Saxon basis than any other factor. The allegedly insufficiently deferential treatment of Giraud by United States authorities has further assisted this process which Hoppenot's[3] appointment to Martinique[4] and the official honours shown to Giraud have done little to check. The French expert of *Time* declares that the President wishes to eliminate all French influence from the peace settlement which is to be dictated by America, Britain and Russia alone. Elsewhere the State Department rather than the White House is criticized. Mr Hull remarked to a recent visitor how monstrous he thought Lippmann's criticism of him 'considering all I have done for the Jews'. President's toast to Giraud and 'the elimination' of Germany is variously interpreted ; the commonest view taken is that it indicated a general sentiment without specific implications about destruction of the German nation, etc. His latest statement implying United States neutrality as between the French factions and praising the unhurried tactics which secured Martinique and Guadeloupe adds nothing to the situation.

The Wallace-Jones controversy. The President has produced a drastic solution to the Wallace-Jones controversy. Both men have been sharply rebuked in letters subsequently published by White House. Jones has been shorn of all those agencies whereby he participated directly in the war effort. He remains Secretary of Commerce with only routine responsibilities. Attempt to train Wallace as an administrator and to bring him up as Assistant President seems finally to have been ruled off as a failure. Board of Economic Warfare over which he presided has been abolished. Its staff is to go with the agencies taken away from Jones (the RFC and its subsidiaries, USCC,[5] Export-Import Bank, Oil, Metal, Rubber

2 In the House of Commons, in which Churchill denied it was the Government's policy to take sides between Frenchmen.

3 Henri Hoppenot, of French purchasing mission.

4 To take over control of the French West Indies on behalf of the Committee of National Liberation.

5 United States Commercial Company.

Reserves, etc.) to form a new Office of Economic Warfare under Leo Crowley,[6] the Alien Property Custodian, who is to be responsible to Byrnes. The personalities involved are so picturesque and political cross-currents inside Democratic Party so numerous, that it is tempting to tell the story as though it were principally a palace revolution. Byrnes, who comes out of the struggle with greatly increased authority, appears to be President's chosen instrument for consolidating the South. Leo Crowley, a successful Wisconsin big business man, who has been outstandingly loyal to some of New Deal measures, is a pious and active Roman Catholic. His preferment may consolidate Catholic vote and middle Democratic business opinion. Only old Jacobins of New Deal who follow Wallace and Perkins feel betrayed and they must support President in any case. Behind all these principal actors is Baruch, who through his close connexion with Byrnes may in future enjoy influence in United States economic external affairs. In terms of political intrigue around the President, the *coup* has been well timed. The President allowed the Wallace-Jones controversy to run long enough for the public throughout the country to get really indignant. He then gave a demonstration of his authority and of his capacity to discipline, indeed to rebuke publicly, his one-time closest political friend, Henry Wallace, whose nomination as Vice-President he forced through a reluctant party convention in 1940. This was done precisely at the moment when Congressmen had got back to their constituencies blaming the President's incurable weakness in disciplining his subordinates for maladministration and scandalous internecine warfare in Washington. The other side of the story is less picturesque. It has been clear for over a year that the idea of a Board of Economic Warfare consisting of Cabinet members under chairmanship of Vice-President failed to do what was expected of it, to resolve inter-departmental disputes in external economic affairs without requiring perpetual reference to President. On many occasions when substantial issues of policy have arisen, a minority of Board, usually Service Departments, have insisted on referring matter to the President. Once Byrnes had been appointed as Economic Co-ordinator, the system of BEW, which ventilated disputes which it was powerless to resolve, was bound to come to an end at some time, as it had the effect of putting on the President's desk the very type of issue that Byrnes' appointment was meant to keep from him. Many of the more competent Washington agencies have felt that staff of BEW, under leadership of Milo Perkins, was maladroitly administered and was a principal source of both confusion and delay in many fields. Crowley made it a condition of taking on new Office of Economic Warfare that Perkins should go. If this means that there will be a gradual comb-out in personnel of BEW and a better control of their activities in future, the change can only be for the better. It is well known that Crowley himself works in effective collaboration with State Department as well as commanding confidence of the President. He is no crusader but an astute and resolute

6 Leo T. Crowley, US Alien Property Custodian 1942, previously chairman of Federal Deposit Insurance Corporation.

custodian of American interests at home and abroad. The President may well have strengthened his position with the country and, by giving satisfaction to the Catholics, taken some of wind out of Farley's sails. Hopkins, who has always been irked by Wallace, shows evident relief, though he sadly remarked to a member of my staff 'the Bankers would be pleased. The New Deal once again has been sacrificed to war effort.'

19 July 1943

FOOD, PRICES, AND LABOUR

(a) The appointment of Paul Appleby, Under-Secretary of Agriculture, to be the American representative on the interim International Food Commission, is probably due most of all to the fact that no other official of similar status could be found to fill this position. Appleby, who is a high-minded agrarian idealist of the school of Wallace, is looked on with some disfavour by certain members of the State Department on account of what they consider to be the naïveté of his ideas, his peculiar amalgam of economic idealism with undiluted Midwestern politics and a general amateurishness of approach. There is no doubt, however, about his very strong and sincere Anglophile feeling in spite of certain important differences of outlook. His relations with Mr Hull have not been good since his resignation under obscure circumstances during the Peyrouton flurry. His principal ally in the Department is still said to be Acheson.

(b) The food policy of Judge Marvin Jones seems to consist largely in pegging prices at their present level. His attitude is perhaps best illustrated by remarks which he made in the course of a conversation at which a member of my staff was present. He was asked whether the price of hogs, whose numbers have now reached 75,000,000 and are rising with record-breaking speed, would be lowered. 'No sir,' he said, 'this Government is morally obligated to support the price of $13.75 per 100 lbs as at present.' 'And the price of corn? Could not that be raised and provide feed for the Eastern dairy farmers?' 'This Government is morally obligated', said Judge Jones even more solemnly, 'to keep the price of corn at $1.07.' 'Won't we suffer a terrible corn shortage if you go through with your incompatible moral obligations?' 'We must take our punishment like men,' said Judge Jones firmly. 'It will be the hogs that take the punishment,' observed Mr Paul Porter of the War Food Administration. Not much progress is therefore to be expected there. Judge Jones possesses qualities of heart, a sterling character, and unswerving loyalty to the Administration, but he is thought to have few other qualifications for his crucial post.

(c) Meanwhile the prices of commodities are still rising, and Prentiss Brown is still being eyed askance by Messrs Vinson and Byrnes. Lou Maxon,[1] Deputy Administrator, a crude promotion expert brought in to placate businessmen and

1 Lou R.Maxon, founder of advertising agency, 1929.

anti-New Deal Congressmen, has left the OPA after a routine blast at the su. it of young lawyers and professors alleged to be bedevilling that organization. Meanwhile the continuing flabby management of the price system, in particular of basic foodstuffs, is probably the real cause of labour unrest, inasmuch as there is no intrinsic rift or cause for any between labour and management, or labour and government, appearances notwithstanding. It is the rise in prices, rather than the failure to raise wages, that is causing genuine concern to the most loyal of all the President's supporters, Philip Murray of the CIO, who privately wonders how long his men can be expected to endure this ever widening gap. The impression that there exists some basic disharmony between organized labour and the Administration is probably due to the overdramatization of the clash between Lewis and the President by the general, predominantly anti-labour, press, which prefers to play up colourful personalities and avoid the duller and more fundamental issue of wages *v.* prices. . . .

. . .

Germany. At the recent international conference of Christian leaders, held under the auspices of the Federal Council of Churches at Princeton, and attended by several members of my staff, there was much evidence of (a) warm feeling towards the German Protestant and particularly Confessional Churchmen on the part of corresponding American clergy ; (b) the view that the German Protestant Church was a possible foundation for the reconstruction not only of Germany but all Europe ; (c) the view that the relatively unravaged Germany would be a natural economic foundation for the reconstruction of Europe ; (d) that the problem of Germany was the problem of Europe, that Germany was, as it were, geographically and spiritually the natural leader on the European continent, since the conquered countries would be far too broken to be able to function effectively. This coincides with similar sentiment to be found not only among German Americans or refugees but in some naval circles, and among 'Pacific Firsters', some of whom are described as dedicated to the notion that a strong Germany is the sole means of preventing an ever stronger Russia from interesting herself too much in the Pacific and, it may be, Alaska. It is evident that the views of Germany's principal European victims concerning Germany have not sufficiently sunk in here, perhaps because of excessive if intelligible timidity on the part of the propaganda officers of the smaller nations. One of the causes of pro-German sentiment among Protestants is continuing remorse about the militant pro-war attitude adopted by the Protestant Churches during the last war.

Post-war. Senator Connally, in response to the rich proliferation of public, semi-public, and private post-war plans and resolutions, and in particular in response to the scheme whereby itinerant evangelists of the Fulbright Resolution, drawn from the House and Senate, are speaking against isolationism up and down the land, has announced that the Foreign Relations Committee of the Senate would produce a resolution of its own during the next session, clearer and more concrete than the Fulbright Resolution. Meanwhile the George Committee, which is charged with consideration of post-war economic policy of United States of America, has requested the Brookings Institution to become its principal research centre. Brookings, the most conservative of the economic research foundations, largely operates on funds provided by General Motors, the Chase National Bank and other financial and industrial enterprises. Advice to approach Brookings was almost certainly given to George by Jesse Jones, long connected with George politically and in matters of Southern patronage, and with Brookings through its financial sponsors. If Brookings accepts, the sober, conservative and 'business' character of the findings of the George Committee will follow inevitably. . . .

24 July 1943

Production, labour and prices. The continued good news from Sicily and Russia maintains public optimism at a level which is evidently regarded by the Administration as dangerously high. Hence a series of warnings by Hull, Knox and other officials on prevalence of exaggerated hopes of an early end to war. Knox spoke of 'steady loss of production in war plants now in its third month, and almost criminally careless belief that war has already been won'. This was echoed by Vice-Admiral Horne[1] who spoke of naval plans for a Pacific war lasting until 1949. Forrestal prophesied need for a sevenfold increase of the Navy. Hanson Baldwin denounced fallacy of supposing that peak production had been reached, founded, in his view, on growing public conviction, supported by polls, that European war is certain to end this year or next (Admiral Halsey's notorious prophecy that war would end this year is held by some to have caused largest single let-down in production). This was finally capped by WPB Vice-Chairman Wilson's statement that of 8,500 planes scheduled for July only 8,000 at most would be reached, that 300,000 tons of steel had been lost by coal strike, with corresponding discrepancies between schedules and probable achievement in construction of ships. . . . While the situation is far from critical, and general flow of war materials continues on a prodigious scale, this publicity is intended to regalvanize sagging war workers, possibly under impulsion from the Truman Committee, which continues to discover waste and faulty production, most recent case of the last being in one of Curtiss Wright Aircraft plants. Management blames unco-operativeness by labour leaders, labour bitterly complains about unregulated rise in prices, and Green and Murray have debated the dismissal of OPA Director Brown whom they (and privately some members of Vinson's and Byrnes's offices) blame for the situation. The President said that appropriations required for price regulation would have to be referred to Congress, i.e. wait till September. There has been no more talk of over-production of munitions and the like. The President still seems determined soon to return the mines to the own-

1 US Vice-Admiral Frederick J. Horne, Vice-Chief of Naval Operations 1942–6.

ers. Negotiations for Lewis's readmission into the AF of L fold seem to be proceeding successfully, if slowly. Lewis has negotiated a separate contract with Illlinois operators including portal-to-portal pay, etc., and effect of this test case referred to War Labor Board is being attentively watched.

Rome. Bombing of Rome has been greeted by press and public opinion generally as a routine and necessary measure, though there is much Washington speculation as to how American Catholic opinion is reacting. The Catholic hierarchy, led by Cardinal O'Connell[2] of Boston and Archbishop Mooney[3] of Detroit, head of National Catholic Welfare Conference, a key organization, have expressed sadness and regret that this course of action should have been required, even while they recognized Fascist responsibility in using Rome for military purposes. This note of open regret and carefully controlled resentment was voiced by several influential bishops including interventionist Hurley[4] from Florida and is not so far adopted by average Catholic periodical. Other somewhat less important and more liberal prelates approved bombing and were supported by one or two liberal Catholic organs. Principal Washington rumour is that hierarchy after Pope's message is working hard under cover to bring pressure on President to prevent repetition of bombing and are urging Murray of CIO, who is a pious Catholic, to speak to President. American Catholics are traditionally nervous of charge of double allegiance and may well try to avoid publicity and confine themselves to work behind the scenes. Catholic Senators Murray and O'Mahoney[5] publicly justified the bombings. President in his press conference justified action strongly as saving American lives and spoke at length of long and fruitless efforts on his part to get Fascists to declare Rome an open city. 'We pleaded and used every argument.' He then renewed his plea that this be done. A member of my staff obtained impression from conversation with an influential Jesuit that his colleagues thought that the ado would suffice to make a repetition of raid unlikely.

New Deal. New Dealers still seem somewhat stunned by blow to Wallace. A visitor reports that President in conversation with him said: 'Republic must retreat in order to advance.' Wallace is to deliver a speech on 'America's Future' on 25 July in Detroit calling for a progressive New Deal programme for American social and economic organization after the war. He is apparently to denounce 'scarcity' economics, give an apologia for his own actions, a declaration of loyalty to President and a warning against social strife. I am told by one of his friends that he submitted text to President who annotated and approved it and hinted that if Wallace took things quietly he would not after all be left to languish

2 William H.O'Connell, appointed Cardinal 1911, Archbishop of Boston 1907.

3 Edward Mooney, Archbishop of Detroit since 1937.

4 Joseph P.Hurley, Bishop of St Augustine 1940–9 ; Archbishop 1949–67.

5 Joseph C.O'Mahoney, Democratic Senator from Wyoming, 1935–53, 1955–60.

long. CIO is said to be making elaborate arrangements for his reception in Detroit (local headlines are said to have been set up : 'Wallace Hearse turns into Band Wagon'). Meanwhile Byrnes reaffirmed Hull's final authority over policies of Crowley's new Office of Economic Warfare. The State Department is still fast gaining political and administrative ground, and whatever fate of specific departments of BEW, its existence as a semi-autonomous political entity seems finally at an end. Crowley is thought to entertain no cravings for independent authority and is likely to listen to Hull, Jones and possibly his Catholic friends without attempting a strongly personal line. Ickes, whose stock is high both with labour and with business (he has been a singularly popular Petroleum Administrator), has emitted a typical blast at dollar-a-year men. He wished to say, speaking as one of the few surviving New Dealers, that it was Knudsen, Nelson, Stettinius, business leaders, not New Dealers, who were running this war with all its faults (this is an oblique hit at his *bête noire* Hopkins, who is said to have had much to do with appointment to responsible positions of up-and-coming businessmen with liberal inclinations). Ickes made a separate attack on Prentiss Brown's OPA petroleum rationing policy. Despite President's ukase during Wallace affair whereby officials must either refrain from public criticism of each other or resign, Ickes seems too strong for such treatment at present. He seems too shrewd to risk President's real displeasure unless he feels either strong enough to do so safely or doomed already. Last seems least likely at present. OWI admitted in somewhat confused fashion that they had passed speech. President said he knew nothing about it.

French affairs. Time's attack on United States policy towards de Gaulle . . . was echoed emphatically in an unsigned editorial in *Life* by Russell Davenport. Luce publications are plainly set to denounce on radical lines prevalent United States foreign policy while retaining a moderate Republican tone on domestic topics (Willkie's line). Leahy's mouthpiece, Constantine Brown, now takes line that Giraud, while an adequate military figure, is politically inept, indicating that attempt to build him up as a great Frenchman is to be abandoned. Giraud's remarks in Montreal about National Socialist achievement[6] went largely unnoticed except by *New York Times*. I am told that he publicly said in New York : 'They say that I am not intelligent. This is not true. I am very intelligent.' General flurry about French affairs seems to have died down somewhat and State Department gives signs of a calmer and slightly more favourable attitude to Committee.

27 July 1943

On 23 July the well known German-American propagandist, George Sylvester Viereck, was once again sentenced by a Federal Court in Washington for violat-

---

6 Giraud was reported by *New York Times* on 17 July as saying, 'Not all is bad in the National Socialist system. Some of its accomplishments have been magnificent.'

ing the Foreign Agents Registration Act.[1] A few days previously he had been found guilty by the jury on a number of counts which charged him with informing the German Government on matters of political interest in the United States, with disseminating information to individuals in the United States as the agent of a foreign principal, and of failing to give the State Department a comprehensive account of his activities. Amongst the publications which he had distributed in the United States were a number such as 'British Tyranny in India', 'The Hundred Families Which Rule the Empire', and 'Lord Lothian vs Lord Lothian' which were published by the notorious Flanders Hall, a publishing house which was financed and directed by Viereck himself. The evidence on which the prosecution relied to secure conviction on two of six counts was almost wholly supplied by His Majesty's Government in the shape of Viereck's correspondence, which was intercepted by the Imperial Censorship in Bermuda.

1 August 1943

Mr Wallace and the President. Wallace's much heralded speech at Detroit on 25 July was clearly intended to lay down latest liberal line, i.e. unconditional support through thick and thin of the President as being, despite all, in the last analysis a true liberal (Wallace is said to have received numerous messages from New Dealers enquiring whether further adherence to the President was justified : this was his answer), war on 'American Fascism' whether in the guise of isolationism, monopolistic big business or other forces hostile to the welfare of the people, support of labour, an economy of expanding production alone capable of giving employment to returning soldiers (with a threat of what might happen if jobs were lacking at the end of the war) and a routine exhortation to international co-operation. Wallace's delivery has much improved. He spoke with a bold conviction sometimes almost smacking of demagogy. It seems probable that he proposes to continue as principal champion of New Deal liberalism which in America is tied with Bryanite[1] tradition of anti-big-business 'populism', rescue of 'little man' from tentacles of monopolistic capitalism, rather than a direct tendency to collectivism and state ownership. Public reaction was not too favourable to the Vice-President. Liberal press as expected acclaimed his speech but middle opinion seems profoundly bored with Wallace and New Deal ideals even if the fiery eloquence of which Wallace seems incapable might conceivably still stir them. Conservatives counterattacked, charging Wallace with 'name calling' and wantonly dividing the nation by tying label of Fascism to some of its best elements in order to shift to them blame for growing government despotism. Although the President in his speech of 28 July made a gesture of support to-

1 Passed in 1938, to control the activities in the USA of Axis and related agents, engaged in subversion or propaganda. Its main effect was secured by obliging such persons to register with the US Government.

1 William Jennings Bryan, candidate for presidency, 1896, on a ticket which fused appeal of Democratic and Populist Parties.

wards Wallace by his reference to foes of an enlightened foreign policy, it seems probable that Wallace and his followers will on the whole have to stand alone while election issue is so uncertain and the President is making alliances. Nevertheless it would be a mistake to suppose that Wallace is out for good. If he can rally sufficient liberal support by next year his Vice-Presidential chances are quite fair. Senator Guffey's support of a second term for Wallace can scarcely have been made without some White House support. Hopkins is alleged to favour Byrnes.

President's own address[2] was undeniably a campaign speech against a background of triumph of allied arms ascribed in large measure to the Administration's successful plans. A vision of platform for 1944 dimly floated into view. There was something in it for everyone. Most concrete proposal outlined six steps whereby returning soldiers would be looked after, provided Congress understood its duty. Alternative – scenes of unemployed veterans selling apples under last Republican régime – was sharply evoked. Ship production was prodigious. There was no cause for anxiety about national economy provided that each citizen loyally co-operated with his government. Finally a *bonne bouche* : lifting of coffee rationing and a promise of an abundance of sugar. As for foreign policy Fascism would be crushed remorselessly, there would be no appeasement, no truck with Fascism anywhere. A handsome compliment to Mr Churchill (a name more and more to conjure with in addressing the American public) and generous praise of British arms, with more conventional references to Russia and China and a reminder that larger part of task is ahead, completed a somewhat monotonously delivered speech, incomparably less effective, even to American ears, than Mr Churchill's own recent words. President's obvious determination to tread cautiously in face of intense scrutiny by his enemies in both parties, of his every word and move, seems to have had a damping effect on Sherwood's muse (I am told that he is mainly responsible for this as for most other of the President's political speeches). Spangler immediately attacked President's postwar programme as shameless fourth-term campaigning and demanded that his own strictures be communicated to United States troops abroad together with the President's speech. Landon is to reply in a few days. All this is normal enough routine.

Italian situation ('the ship leaves the sinking rat'). Reactions to Italian situation are made confused by swift succession of events. Initial jubilation over Mussolini's fall[3] was accompanied by presentation of Badoglio as a simple and honourable soldier and veteran anti-Fascist. This was rapidly succeeded by scepticism and opinions split into various groupings which are continuously altering under impact of events. 'Unconditional surrender' is formally acclaimed by vir-

2 Broadcast, 28 July.

3 Resignation on 25 July. Pietro Badoglio, Marshal of the Italian Army and Chief of the Italian General Staff, assumed power 'by order of King'.

tually entire press and public opinion but there are noticeable differences from Darlan situation. While liberals are vehemently protesting against a deal with the King and Badoglio, conservatives are curiously divided, while e.g. Krock and Lawrence are strongly advocating negotiation with the King and Badoglio and in company with semi-official Lindley attacking OWI for discrediting 'authorized foreign policy of United States Government according to preferences of Communists, etc., in OWI'. *New York Times* editorially speaks of 'Shadowy authority of a puppet king' and 'martial law . . . to protect Fascist gangsters from popular recriminations' and while Simms (Scripps-Howard foreign editor), an old ally of State Department's French policy, follows a cautious line neither attacking nor urging such a deal, Scripps-Howard editorials for four days have delivered broadsides against 'craven king and "butcher of Ethiopia" who wishes to save as much totalitarian loot as possible'. It is not yet clear what line if any State Department is giving its mouthpieces. It seems most probable that while favouring negotiations between Eisenhower and the new Italian regime they, and in particular Berle and Dunn, are determined not to go through the nightmare of Darlan crisis again. They may prefer someone else, e.g. His Majesty's Government, to pull these particular chestnuts out of the fire while they themselves continue to protect themselves behind formula of unconditional surrender, in fact this time themselves play role *vis-à-vis* His Majesty's Government which they believe His Majesty's Government had played *vis-à-vis* themselves over the French. This may account for a certain number of hints in the press about British readiness to deal with Badoglio, side by side with praise of Churchill for his uncompromising speech.[4] Most obvious feature of the situation is evident lack of specific guidance to the press and consequent adoption by commentators of views of their particular friends among officials without an effort towards a concerted Administration line. *Time* is anti-Badoglio and anti-King. *Life* is anti-King but faintly pro-Badoglio, *Newsweek* favours both. *PM* has discovered a book by Badoglio dedicated to 'the Fascist Nation'.

Italo-Americans are sharply divided. One may distinguish (a) ex-Fascist press which now protests its Americanism, hopes for a strong US alliance with new Italy shamefully betrayed by Mussolini to the Germans, and cautiously refrains from specific reference to Badoglio and the King, (b) new 'American Committee for Italian Democracy' (alleged to have been inspired by Berle via his New York labour contacts) headed by Justice Pecora[5] (Democrat) and well known conservative labour leader Antonini, and containing Pope[6] (editor of ex-Fascist daily *Progresso*) and Forte[7] (head of once pro-Fascist order 'Sons of Italy'). This body, which probably represents largest number of American citizens of Italian

4 In Parliament on 27 July, insisting on unconditional surrender by Italy.

5 Ferdinand Pecora, Justice of New York Supreme Court since 1935.

6 Generoso Pope, millionaire head of New York construction business, publisher of popular Italian newspaper, Tammany Hall leader.

7 Felix Forte, Republican, Associate Justice Massachusetts Supreme Court.

origin, affirms loyalty to United States Government, demands unconditional surrender, asks for territorial integrity 'in spirit of Atlantic Charter', says nothing about Badoglio, but warns against possibility of Communist control in Italy and implies abhorrence of Italian revolution. (c) Other bodies of workers of Italian origin (e.g. members of Hillman's union) with more left-wing inclinations have denounced Antonini for associating with ex-Fascists (Antonini, like his master Dubinsky, is first and foremost an anti-Communist) and attack the King, the Pope, Badoglio, etc. (d) Now very weak Mazzini Society dominated by liberal Italian refugees attacked new Committee, called for a message assuring Italy of territorial integrity and its 'old Colonial outlets' and attacked new regime. Sforza,[8] its President, is expressing himself with almost comically exaggerated caution as one who may at any moment be called to higher spheres, but Salvemini[9] is true to form. Venerable Don Sturzo[10] said that fall of Mussolini did not necessarily entail that of Fascism and that 'powerful financial interests' were behind new cabinet which, but for Guariglia,[11] he condemned. Beyond that are numerically weak Communists who attack American anti-Communist Italian Committees, the King and the Pope. Pecora Committee is probably most important of these bodies and may be expected to follow State Department line with Mazzini Society sniping from a somewhat Gaullist position. Sherwood, after a public rebuke to his office by the President, was forced to apologize on their behalf for action of OWI which in its broadcast to Britain and not (according to OWI) to Europe or Italy quoted columnist Grafton[12] on 'Fascist Badoglio and moronic little King'. . . . A crisis in overseas section of OWI with resignations threatening is in progress. A notice instructing them to conform to and sustain State Department's line is said to have been circulated to all heads of government departments by the President.

4 August 1943

. . .

American-German ferment. The statement of the Free German Committee[1] in Russia is still exciting comment. It has been attacked by the majority of the German refugee and German American groups. Its only defenders are the Communists and, in addition, the 'American Friends of German Freedom', . . . who, with the *New York Herald Tribune,* echo the line adopted by Alexander Werth[2]

8 Count Carlo Sforza, born 1872, Italian Foreign Minister 1920–1, anti-Fascist, exile in USA since 1939.

9 Gaetano Salvemini, historian, anti-Fascist refugee appointed to professorship at Harvard in 1933.

10 Luigi Sturzo, Sicilian priest and Christian Democrat leader who fled to USA in 1940.

11 Raffaelo Guariglia, official in Foreign Ministry, became Foreign Minister under Badoglio 1943–4.

12 Samuel Grafton, associate editor of *New York Post* 1934–49, and author of daily column, 'I'd Rather Be Right', 1939–49.

1 National Committee for Free Germany organized in Moscow in July from anti-Nazi prisoners of war, notably Field-Marshal Paulus, who was German commander at Stalingrad.

2 Alexander Werth, Moscow correspondent of the *Sunday Times,* 1941–6.

in the *New York Times*. Broadcasters such as Swing, Strout,[3] and Howe[4] argue that this merely emphasizes the lack of clear policy on the part of Britain and the United States. Dorothy Thompson has interrupted her vacation to announce that the spell is broken, Fascism is dead and the Italians cannot continue the war, Badoglio or no Badoglio, but whereas Allied propaganda to Italians intelligently assumes that Italians do not love Fascism, our propaganda to Germany stupidly assumes the opposite – only the Russians have had the sense to realize this. . . . Bullitt, who is thought to have a good chance of becoming Mayor of Philadelphia (a step towards the Senate or other elective office), regularly stimulates such talk. His attitude is in part the product of acute frustration in his Washington posts. . . .

Labour. The salient facts of the week are :

(a) The continued pressure of Green and Murray for a 'roll back' in prices to the levels of 15 September 1942. In labour circles it is said that the President conveyed to Murray and Green that this was unlikely of achievement but that the Little Steel formula might be relaxed to allow wages to rise somewhat although not to the level demanded by the trade unions.

(b) Lewis's sudden application to the War Labor Board for a ratification of his new Illinois contract (which entails a $3.00 raise per day) is a typically shrewd manoeuvre since it heads off issuance of a subpoena by the War Labor Board compelling his presence. It faces the Board with sudden recognition on the part of a hitherto implacable foe with a request, rejection of which would equally provoke the Illinois operators and the miners, while acceptance of it breaks the 'hold the line' formula for wages which the War Labor Board has on the whole kept fairly taut.

(c) The acceptance of the miners' application for reaffiliation with the AF of L is regarded as virtually certain by most observers, but doubted by a minority. The anti-Communist forces in the AF of L, i.e. the great majority, are solidly in favour of this, since the miners are thought to provide an unbreakable bulwark against leftist penetration. It is rumoured, without, however, much discoverable foundation, that the White House has done its best to prevent this development and has failed.

(d) There is an elaborate struggle for control over the (New York) American Labor Party between Hillman and Dubinsky. Hillman is said to have contracted an alliance with the left wing of the Party (the Communists) led by Representative Marcantonio, Joe Curran of the Maritime Union, etc., while Dubinsky is an implacable right winger. The call for a compromise solution issued by Hillman was rejected by the right wing and the focal points of the struggle are likely to be at the ALP primaries, due 10 August, and in the by-election of the Lieutenant-

3 Richard L. Strout, Washington correspondent for the *Christian Science Monitor* since 1925, also wrote as 'TRB' in *The New Republic*.
4 Quincy Howe, news analyst for CBS News since 1942.

Governor of New York State in place of the deceased Republican Thomas Wallace.[5] Efforts are said to be in progress to induce Berle to accept nomination for this office ; it is doubtful whether he will stake his post in the State Department on so uncertain an issue. This is more important than it appears because the election of a Democrat to this office would make it more difficult for Dewey to accept nomination as presidential candidate since this would automatically entail the surrender of New York State to a Democratic Governor, a prospect which the Republican machine can hardly be expected to encourage. It may be imagined what elaborate convolutions are occurring on the part of the friends and enemies of Messrs Dewey and Berle in this complicated situation with Owen D. Young[6] as a permanent dark horse.

7 August 1943

State Department. Sanguine hopes of Italian surrender, controversy as to the right American 'line', and reaction to British criticisms of it, etc., have given way to disappointment at Badoglio's continued resistance. The general and Italian-American press continues along previous lines, i.e. from the Hearst (and ex-Fascist Italian) papers which urge an armistice with any available Italian Government, if only in order to check the possible spread of Communism, to left-wing denunciations of Anglo-American 'appeasement', with all intermediate shadings. . . . A foreign journalist tells us that Hull told him privately 'the only true friends America has in Europe are the Italians'. Asked why, he added 'at any rate they do not have a paper called *The Times*', apparently a reference to the 'appeasement' of Russia attributed here to *The Times* of London. Welles is back, and a reference to his well-known differences with Hull has finally occurred on the front page of the *New York Times,* which published a story dwelling on the sharp personal feuds and administrative chaos of the State Department, and alluded to a report which the President's administrative assistants had compiled, criticizing the alleged inefficiency of the Department. Apparently Wayne Coy, now Assistant Director of the Budget and principal author of the report (it exists, although its existence was promptly denied by Steve Early), had 'leaked' it some weeks ago to the *New York Times.* Hull at a press conference defended his Department against criticisms which have been growing in the press (e.g. the first article on the Department in *Fortune* written by a former member of it, and other similar press comment), in proportion as the Department has increased in strength and scope of authority. Krock characteristically followed up with an article on 6 August, confirming the existence of bitter feuds between Hull and Welles, Acheson and Berle, etc., and then as usual blamed the President for ignoring this, governing by personal appointments and failing to strengthen the

5 Dewey's running-mate in 1942.

6 Owen D. Young, lawyer and business executive, Chairman of General Electric 1922–39, 1942–4, famous for his Reparations Commission work, which produced the Young Plan (1929).

hand of Mr Hull who alone could, if properly treated, acquire a loyal staff and set everything right. Krock, who veers between the extremes of vindictive spite and sycophantic flattery, has for some months held up Mr Hull as a paragon of virtue gratuitously frustrated by the greatly inferior persons among whom it is his bad fortune to be compelled to function. . . .

Home Front. General Somervell continues his anti-complacency campaign by announcing that only two-fifths of the total programme of war production scheduled for 1943 had been completed in the first half of the year.

Landon's fierce attempt to turn tables on Wallace by denouncing New Dealers as the true Fascists of America, as well as Republican criticisms of campaign promises in the President's last speech, coming whence they do, are routine political moves too commonplace and disingenuous to convince even the converted. Wallace is being pressed (see political summary of 1 August) by his followers to allow them to speak their minds about the President's 'betrayal' of the liberal cause, and warning that the decimation of their ranks will otherwise lead to complete collapse before the election. Wallace continues to advise them to hold their horses, perhaps to avoid being pushed too far into the open as the leader of disgruntled radicals, but has spoken at Des Moines of 'the glorious fight' to be waged between the forces of the light – labour and farmers – and those (capitalists) who hate Roosevelt and not Hitler. The *New York Times* editorially reproved him sternly for such wartime politics. Landon's appeal to anti-New Deal Democrats is the first public effort of this kind (although Farley is still credited with private intrigues in this direction). So far there is no evidence of any response in official Democratic quarters. Anti-New Dealers are however triumphant about the results of the Mississippi gubernatorial primary which is going strong against the government candidates, and is likely to result in a contest between two equally anti-fourth-term politicians. Bricker has informed the world that he holds no views of his own on any topic and would accept any position formally adopted by his party. This should prove a useful gift to Willkie-Deneen Watson[1] camp. Leo Crowley has been charged with lack of guts by the liberals for demanding the resignation of an OEW economic analyst named Bovington[2] denounced by Dies. Photographs published in the anti-Administration press, revealing this official as a eurhythmic dancer in a peculiarly grotesque pose, rang his knell. The incident illustrates the acute nervousness of flustered Washington departments before the anti-New Deal witch-hunt.

The disagreeable spectre of the 1944 budget has appeared once more. The President repeated his earlier demand for a 'stiff programme of taxes or savings or both'. Morgenthau compared rates in Canada and the United Kingdom with the lower figures in the United States, which has not proved too popular a move.

1 Deneen Watson, Chicago lawyer, ardent Willkie-ite, who formed the Republican Post-war Policy Association in May 1943 to campaign for an internationalist plank at the Republican Convention.

2 John Bovington. He refused to resign and was dismissed on 4 August.

He wants to increase taxation revenue by 12–13 billions in 1944 as compared with 1933 but Senator George declared that 5–6 billions was the maximum possible increase. George could not see how the full sum demanded – a threat to the middle classes 'on which depend the strength and vitality of any civilization' – could be raised (and in an election year too). This clash is likely to grow and may become an increasingly dark cloud by the time Congress reconvenes in September. A nervous desire to defer grasping the nettle is only too evident everywhere. One of the obvious methods of closing the inflationary gap is compulsory savings but the Treasury is resolutely opposed to this and proposes to launch an intensified campaign for voluntary sacrifice by the public, with posters to illustrate the greater burdens borne by Canada and Great Britain.

14 August 1943

Absence of Russia from the forthcoming Anglo-American Conferences has revealed a fast increasing anxiety here about her general relation to the United States and Britain. Uneasy speculation takes various forms, discussion of reasons for Russian non-participation, of the possibility of a separate Russo-German peace whether or not along lines adumbrated by the 'Free German' Moscow manifesto, and finally demands for concerting of some sort of definite political plans in agreement with Britain, if only for short-term purposes, with which to meet the clear and set plans with which the Russians are credited. Persistent Russian failure (possibly somewhat allayed by realization of her position *vis-à-vis* Japan) [1] to take part in Anglo-American Conferences has generated no rise in anti-Russian sentiments (except possibly in service circles) but rather an unconcealed nervousness about purposes of that formidable power and their effect on war and the peace. The *New York Times,* in a carefully written leader of 9 August, tries to explain the American attitude to the three main possible points of difference, the Second Front, Germany and the Baltic States, and takes a new and unusually conciliatory line. Through it and most other press comment runs the slightly helpless feeling that at no time since Pearl Harbor have the Western Powers drifted so far apart from the USSR, and scepticism about the utility of further Roosevelt-Churchill conferences unattended by Russia. Talk in Washington always comes round to the recall of the Russian Ambassadors from London and Washington as positive evidence of this lack of unity. Allied diplomacy is blamed for this as much as Soviet chilliness. A Midwestern observer tells us that disenchantment over Italy, like all other military or diplomatic setbacks in Europe, offers material to those isolationists who harp on the theme that Americans are inevitably bound to sink in the European morass and had far better keep out of such difficult terrain altogether.

1 It was not until 8 August 1945 that the USSR declared war on Japan.

India League Meeting. The India League[2] celebrated the anniversary of Gandhi's arrest by a minor campaign, led off by Claire Luce, who spoke demanding immediate liberation of Nehru,[3] whom she described as a figure nobler than any possessed by the Anglo-American powers. Her speech was phrased in her sharpest, most barbed anti-imperialist style. . . .

. . . Mrs Luce did not attend [in person] and her speech was read by Roger Baldwin, Treasurer of the India League and of the Civil Liberties Union. The speech asked the audience to imagine animals in the zoo, each with a quart of milk a day and all the required vitamins, excellent plumbing, railways, electricity, etc. What made the animals want freedom? It is surely right to imprison them when they ask for freedom and protest they do not want milk. Offer them two quarts a day but be sure there is no nonsense about freedom, and when they are not animals, but human beings, it is all the more important to make sure that they show no signs of escape. The speech went on with ironical praise of Mr Churchill. The human animals imprisoned for wanting to get out of the zoo at any rate knew just where they stood with such frank talk as the Prime Minister's, but where did Roosevelt and Wallace stand? They were not the King's First Ministers ; they were just trailing in the King's First Minister's wake. Mr Roosevelt was behaving like Pontius Pilate. His conduct was less excusable than that of Mr Churchill. Mrs Luce's speech proceeded to demand the immediate liberation of Nehru and all other political prisoners. The general tone of the meeting was anti-British. The Chairman, Dr Carpenter,[4] quoted Sir Firoz Khan Noon[5] that 'not one Indian likes the British and wishes them well', but admitted that the British were liberal in what they allowed to be printed in Indian newspapers. The communal issue was a British fabrication.

15 August 1943

Labour. The negotiations concerning the readmission of Lewis and his union into the AF of L have struck a snag. The Executive Council has voted against a minority of pro-Lewisites to defer decision on this until the AF of L convention in October. The formal occasion was the protest of the AF of L's own 'Progressive Mine Workers' Union who claimed that the AF of L could give a charter to only one union of miners. But what appears to have swung the balance is the defection from the groups favourable to Lewis of the important figure of Daniel Tobin, who, it is said, had been spoken to by White House emissaries on the subject. . . .

2 US organization advocating independence for India.

3 See p. 70. Jawaharlal Nehru, Gandhi's colleague, was also arrested in August 1942.

4 J. Henry Carpenter, Chairman of American Committee in Aid of Chinese Industrial Co-operatives 1941–3.

5 Sir Firoz Khan Noon, Defence Member of Viceroy's Executive Council, India, 1942–5 (Prime Minister of Pakistan 1957–8).

The AF of L has again gone on record against abrogation of the Oriental Exclusion Act (i.e. against admission of Asiatic, in particular Chinese, labour).

Grievances about rising prices have not abated (although a small reduction in the cost of living is announced by the Labor Department) ; the manpower situation appears to be the weakest factor in the entire field of production, both on account of alleged absolute shortage (a most implausible claim) and the lack of control over the movement of labour from industry to industry still prevailing here. The Manpower Commission's announcement that fathers would be called up in October has met with very lively opposition on the part of Wheeler, who has long made this an issue, and May,[1] Chairman of the Military Affairs Committee of the House. General confusion prevails on this topic. The CIO has definitely decided to work for a fourth term. The AF of L, while apparently prepared to collaborate in electing or defeating specific candidates for Congress, has declined to consider a general political alliance with the CIO at any level, as compromising. The OWI estimates unionized labour strength as : AF of L 6,500,000 ; CIO 5,000,000 ; Railroad Brotherhoods 420,000 ; unaffiliated 1,100,000.

. . .

Jews. Drew Pearson's article purporting to describe the successful pressure exercised by the Zionists to prevent the publication of an Anglo-American statement deprecating Zionist propaganda in this country, although studded with his usual errors of fact, contains evidences of derivation (as usual) from high and fairly well-known United States Government sources in the State and War Departments. The statement has caused some agitation in Jewish circles and Baruch and Rosenman have made it known to their friends that they would view with some perturbation any statement likely to cause a more than usual stir in the Jewish cauldron. Military Intelligence, however, who are said to have been anxious to get an official condemnation of Zionist agitation, regarded as provocative by the Arabs in the Middle East, are said to be exceedingly irritated by the successful pressure of the Zionist lobby. The attitude of the State Department on this is not certain, but neither Hull nor Welles appear to be particularly well disposed towards a declaration of this type. Stimson and Morgenthau are said to be against it, and the President to be in two minds but on the whole favourable to it.

21 August 1943

Russia. Press and general conversation continues to be filled with anxious perplexity about Russia's intentions, her absence from Quebec,[1] etc., and the rumours of a new crop of German peace feelers made via neutral countries, alleged broadcasts from Berlin, etc., increase the suspicions of those who in any case

1 Andrew Jackson May, Democratic Congressman from Kentucky since 1931.
1 Quebec Conference, 11–24 August, involving Churchill, Roosevelt and Canadian leaders.

believe Russia capable of a separate peace. This has been offset somewhat by press rumours of a coming Anglo-American-Russian meeting in London. The Italian situation, Russian silences, press stories of the alleged desire to negotiate on the part of Pétain and/or Laval, of Vichy agents in Lisbon, and Hoare's meeting with Franco,[2] stimulated discussion of arguments for and against 'unconditional surrender'. This has been most vigorously taken up, not only by the near-subversive press led by Representative Clare Hoffman,[3] which after dormancy has raised its head to agitate for a negotiated peace to 'end the bloodshed', but also by *PM* and reputable commentators. . . . . Reluctant admiration for power and organization clearly affects the thought even of those conservatives who abhor Communism and fear the existence of so powerful a reservoir of it as Russia, but who suppose, on the principle of 'if you can't break 'em, join 'em', that business can and must be done with her. . . .

Food and Foreign Policy. Food is a politically explosive substance in the United States of America and the 'leak', apparently by one of Wickard's people (subsequently corroborated by Wickard who said that it strayed beyond its terms of reference), of the report of an interdepartmental sub-committee on United States food allocation policy expressing grave misgivings as to the amount of food likely to be left over from the internal needs of the United States for Lend-Lease, for Lehman's UNRRA[4], etc., together with news stories that the War Food Administration would be forced to cancel its original undertakings to these bodies, coupled with reports of astonishingly large food demands by the United States Army, has created a situation in which any news of large new appropriations of food for foreign purposes might be ill received by the public and Congress, unless it were demonstrated convincingly that the home economy would not suffer. . . .

. . .

There is no 'hard' news on the Hull-Welles front. The right-wing commentators continue to predict at any rate a change in Welles's status, while liberals deplore this possibility. Naturally Washington is alive with rumours of every possible kind : such as an alleged ultimatum by Hull to the President to which the President is, equally unplausibly, said to have replied that Hull could dismiss Welles if he wished but that he, the President, would never do so, etc. There is still no reason for supposing that any decision has been reached on the matter, although one or two of Mr Hull's recent visitors say that they received the impression from him that he was conscious of victory of some kind. *Life* magazine has published an unusually vehement attack on the Department and Hull

2 Sir Samuel Hoare, British Ambassador, held meeting with Franco, the Spanish dictator, on 20 August.

3 Clare E.Hoffman, Republican Congressman from Michigan since 1935.

4 United Nations Relief and Rehabilitation Administration designed to succeed OFRRO as an international agency (though heavily US-controlled) under Herbert Lehman, who was formally elected Director-General at first session of UNRRA's Executive Council, Atlantic City, November 1943.

(who is represented as a very jealous and formidable departmental 'feuder' from the hills of Tennessee) for having a 'no policy' policy (which results usually in emerging on the side of Fascism and not democracy). An appeal is made to Hull 'as a man who has taken more punishment for his Chief than any man in Washington' to ask Mr Roosevelt for determination at any rate of a minimum policy. This is significant, both because of *Life*'s wide circulation and because it represents a genuine public uneasiness at apparent absence of a consistent United States foreign policy.

. . .

Labour. The strengthening of the War Labor Board by the White House directive which empowers it to take over any plant the management or workers of which do not comply with a WLB decision (which puts the most effective sanctions possible into the Board's hands as an executive agency) is welcomed by conservatives and not deplored by liberals, because of the reputation of Davis[5] and his closest colleagues for fairmindedness and a liberal outlook.

No one pretends to know what is passing in the mind of John L. Lewis as a result of the conspicious rebuff . . . administered to him by the AF of L executive (after, it is said, a 'straight talk' between Tobin and Democratic White House agents) in deciding to forward his application for reaffiliation to the AF of L convention without recommendation, while returning the dues which the Mine Workers' Union evidently hoped would stampede the AF of L into immediate readmission of them. It should not be argued, however, that Lewis will not ultimately be readmitted if he is prepared – and this is a very large if – to waive the demand that his famous Union called 'Local 50' be admitted, in his own words, 'as is', i.e. with unimpaired powers of raiding other unions – the most dreadful of all bugbears to well-established trade unionists. ('Local 50' is designed to include workers in other industries connected even remotely with the mines.) A new tone towards Lewis is indicated by the fact that the War Labor Board has instructed that the 'check off' of union dues, which the Government automatically performs when it takes over a plant or mine from its owners, be discontinued until and unless Lewis complies with the decisions of the Board.

28 August 1943

RUSSIA

. . .

Despite attempts of reassurance by State Department officials concerning Litvinov, his replacement by the dimly competent and taciturn 'economist' Gromyko[1] was generally interpreted as a deliberate advertisement of its displeasure by the Soviet Government. State Department does not appear to have had definite knowledge of this move until a request for *agrément* for Gromyko arrived

5 William Hammatt Davis, New York patent lawyer, Board chairman, January 1942–5.
1 Andrei A. Gromyko, Counsellor at USSR Embassy, Washington, 1939–43.

about a fortnight ago. Privately some of its members agree that this, together with the publication in the official Soviet bulletin here of the criticisms of Anglo-American schemes for European Federation (quoted from Soviet *War and the Working People*), can mean only a deliberate stiffening of the Russian attitude. United States officials seem to have been telling journalists that Stalin was invited on at least five occasions to participate in Allied conferences, and that his caginess is not due to any negligence on the part of the United States. The liberal press has of course attributed the Russian attitude to broken promises of a second front, inadequate Lend-Lease aid to Russia, the obstacles to Bogomolov's [2] journey to North Africa, etc., and there is the usual undercurrent of suspicion, apparently communicated by at least two members of the State Department to journalists, that the British are pursuing their regular tactic of hinting that the United States attitude is the principal obstacle to a more liberal British policy towards France, Russia, etc. . . .

Welles's resignation is by some interpreted as a final touch in the failure to achieve a proper understanding with Russia and the symbol of the beginning of the new stiffer policy. There is no sign that such a development would be welcomed by public opinion whose Russophobia is more than balanced by a nervous longing to achieve agreement with a power that appears to it as formidable and frightening.

. . .

Such indications as His Majesty's Embassy have received from the State Department itself do not support the existence of a desire on the Department's part to cold-shoulder Russia.

Food. There is growing talk, particularly among Republicans who voiced it at a recent meeting of their Midwestern 'grass roots' leaders, that the food situation in United States is such that foreign demands cannot be met in the manner expected by OFRRO or Lend-Lease. Consequently these agencies will probably have to tread with particular wariness in making their requests and allocations, although no serious criticisms have so far been made of the level of shipments to the United Kingdom (as opposed to Europe). A favourite thesis, even among some of the enlightened, is that not direct relief, but supply of implements enabling Europe to recover its own productive capacity is the most rational contribution which the United States can make towards world recovery. Such talk, which probably emanates to some degree from the War Food Administration, comforts those who are persuaded that America is in no position to feed Europe on a large scale for any length of time after the war. Possibly to counteract this, the President's letter to Congress, accompanying the latest Lend-Lease report, published 26 August, explicitly promised relief and food to the liberated peoples

2 Alexander E. Bogomolov, Soviet Diplomat, Ambassador to London 1941–3. Appointed as envoy to Free French in Algiers. Soviet press alleged he had been obstructed by the Anglo-American authorities, who in turn attributed delay to Russian tardiness in recognizing French Committee of National Liberation.

of Europe as well as containing a very significant assertion that 'the United States wants no new war debts to jeopardize the coming peace. Victory and a secure peace are the only coin in which we can be repaid.' So far the only serious attention which has been paid to this comes from the isolationist newspaper trio[3] which triumphantly points out that as they had always suspected no return for Lend-Lease would be obtained by the American people, from *New York Times* which says that the term 'mutual aid' would, if this is the intention of Congress, be more appropriate, and from the *Wall Street Journal* which is unexpectedly sympathetic.

. . .

New York Politics. General Haskell,[4] with a good record in Hoover's European Relief organization of the last war and at present a member of Lehman's OFRRO, has been unanimously nominated by the Farley-led Democrats and the American Labor Party (often the makeweight in New York State elections) as a Democratic candidate for Lieutenant-Governor of the State. He is known to be backed by the White House, and unlike the muffed campaign for Senator Mead in the gubernatorial election in 1942, adequate steps seem to have been taken to ensure Democratic unanimity. His chances are regarded as moderately bright despite the present Republican preponderance in New York. If he is elected, Dewey may find it impossible to offer his candidacy as President since this would automatically abandon New York and its delegation to the Democrats. Hamilton Fish has publicly come out in support of MacArthur, who, if Dewey does not stand, might conceivably yet emerge as the chosen anti-Willkie Republican candidate. The choice of Haskell has silenced the gossip about Berle's chances in the same field.

Labour and Industry. The War Labor Board, provided with a set of 'teeth' (see Savingram of 21 August) has this week begun to use both rows (against labour and management) with a vengeance. It has firmly laid down decisions in a number of wage disputes which have been accepted. It rejected Lewis's claims by eight to four majority (labour members dissenting) and voided his contract with the Illinois operators (see Savingram of 5 August). A general Brewster Aeronautical strike was averted (although one of the plants is still on strike) as was a similar Allis Chalmers development.

. . .

Jews. Busy preparations are continuing for the American Jewish Conference due to begin this week and likely to be dominated by the Zionists. The official protest against the manner in which the Palestine gun-running trial[5] was conducted has apparently been deferred until the end of the trial. The Zionist members are now

---

3 *Chicago Tribune, Washington Times-Herald* and *New York Daily News.*

4 William N. Haskell, in charge of field operations in OFRRO 1943–4.

5 In mid August two British soldiers and two Jewish civilians, all of whom pleaded guilty, were convicted of smuggling arms into Palestine as part of a large operation linked with the Jewish Agency.

openly attacking Arthur Sulzberger[6] and the *New York Times* for leading the campaign against them. There seems no doubt that Sulzberger, so far as lies in his timorous nature, has generally decided to expose what he regards as a dangerously chauvinist movement. *PM* prominently displays articles on slaughter of Jews in Europe and the *New Republic* has issued a special fifteen-page supplement on 'The Jews in Europe – how to help them'. . . . The tone is relatively moderate with criticism of His Majesty's Government and the United States Government about evenly divided.

5 September 1943

. . .

Prime Minister's speech. The troubled American public looked forward to Prime Minister's Quebec speech [1] with exceptional eagerness and received it with clear satisfaction. Tension about Anglo-American relations with Russia has been rising sharply, and the speech, regarded as a bold grasping of the nettle by Mr Churchill, did something to relieve it. Apart from one or two left-wing New York commentators and *New York Herald Tribune,* which thought that mere words however apposite were not enough to solve the political crisis, the press and radio evinced delight at strength and frankness of passages on Russia and on France.

Distinction drawn in speech between leaders and people of Italy harmonized closely with opinion prevailing on this subject here, while representatives of exiled governments are for once reported as being amply satisfied by references to Yugoslavia and Greece. The news reports from London that a tripartite conference was being discussed by Messrs Eden and Maisky [2] generated the first small wave of optimism in what was hitherto a sea of uneasy perplexity. Confidence in Anglo-American, particularly American, diplomacy *vis-à-vis* Russia has been badly shaken in this country and the Russian issue is being presented to the public (even by those not friendly to USSR) as a crucial test of its quality now and in the future – good evidence of effectiveness of Russian psychological warfare here. Naturally the turmoil within State Department adds to disturbed feeling.

Welles. Despite fact that no official word on Welles's resignation has been heard and that there is reason to suppose that President has not finally accepted it yet, and may still be casting about for a means of continuing Welles in his service, the fact that a number of Latin American and other diplomats have received valedictory messages from Welles duly leaked out in the press and his resignation is being taken for granted as a public fact. Welles is still at Bar Harbor,[3]

6 Arthur H. Sulzberger, publisher of *New York Times* since 1935.
1 Broadcast on 31 August.
2 Ivan Maisky, Soviet Ambassador to the UK 1932–43.
3 Maine coastal resort, where Welles had a summer place.

plunged, according to his latest visitors, in deep melancholy which can have been relieved but little by surprisingly warm and widespread tributes which sections of the press and radio have offered (together with an unusual volume of indignation at alleged attitudes of President and Hull) to this cold and buttoned-up, and consequently hitherto scarcely popular, figure.

Foreign diplomats do not trouble to conceal from their friends their profound distress at eclipse of an official upon whose conspicuously good grasp of foreign affairs and effective collaboration they had been wont to look as their greatest single asset – Lippmann, Clapper, Swing are sorrowfully saying that with departure of Welles, whom they know, like and respect, their sole genuine point of contact with State Department has disappeared, and this field will henceforth be left to such tame official mouthpieces as Lindley, Kingsbury-Smith,[4] Callender, and the widely disliked Krock. Political tipsters are betting heavily in favour of Messersmith[5] as Welles's successor, and state that Armour's[6] and still more Long's[7] and Berle's shares are declining. Messersmith, a career member of State Department now Ambassador to Mexico, is a brusque and honest conservative who acquired as Consul General in Berlin and Minister in Vienna an irreproachably militant anti-Nazi reputation. He is said to have quarrelled with Welles when both were at the State Department in 1940, and is believed to be not too popular in Mexico, of whose political trends he is said to be critical.

The Pearson Flurry. Drew Pearson, who knows Welles intimately, in column after column attributed Welles's fall to the fact that he alone in the State Department had consistently pressed for a more understanding and intelligent Russian policy, against the alleged Russophobia of Hull and his advisers, Dunn and Pasvolsky. His broadcast allegation that Hull was among those who wished to see Russia 'bled white' in the war brought down on him fierce outburst by Hull, released by State Department, branding his words as a diabolical falsehood, followed by another official release asserting that nothing had been kept from Russians and that complete Russo-American harmony prevailed. Next day came personal condemnation of Pearson by President who called him a 'chronic liar' acting in bad faith towards his country – words, according to journalists present, said in a burst of spontaneous fury. Pearson has long been one of the most malicious and irresponsible political muckrakers in United States and this two-fold attack by President and Hull does him too much honour. It may have been due not merely to acute official sensitiveness on Russian and French issues, but to other recent gossip by Pearson including story about alleged refusal of Welles to support Hull's own presidential ambitions in 1940. Pearson's replies have been adroit and calculated to wound.

4 Joseph Kingsbury-Smith, correspondent for International News Service (INS) covering the State Department 1941–4.

5 George S. Messersmith, career diplomat, Minister to Austria 1934–7.

6 Norman Armour, career diplomat, Ambassador to Argentina 1939–44.

7 Breckinridge Long, Assistant Secretary of State 1917–20, 1940–4.

The ferocity of attack on Pearson has led some of his colleagues to suggest that President and Hull surely have graver issues to occupy them than a campaign against a tiresome critic – the *Washington Post* defines him as a fearless Socrates. As Pearson is a mischief-maker (thus his recent assertion that Mr Churchill at Casablanca insisted on a 70/30 ratio of American *v*. British invasion troops did us damage here) he has no reputation to save and nationwide notoriety which he has reaped will doubtless principally serve to stimulate his circulation. Episode has served to exaggerate Russian issue and provided a cue for left-wing press, in whose eyes Welles is now a Liberal martyr sacrificed to a 'reactionary clique' in the State Department. Although Pearson's picture of Welles as a casualty in the ruthless march of the anti-Russian Hull has not gained much general acceptance, it has added to nationwide feeling of discomfort and suspicion about the 'inside story' of Welles's removal, and has increased Washington speculation occasioned by scandalous campaign against him by Bullitt and others. Although the impression, which Welles's friends seek to convey, that he has resigned on grounds of conscience and political principle, has not got across, general dismay at his retirement cut far deeper than the indignation of liberals at the deprivation of Wallace.

. . .

One of the consequences of Welles's (still not confirmed) resignation is fact that Government of United States is at present dominated, apart from President (whose influence is still growing), by an ascendancy of right-wing Southerners – Hull, Byrnes, Vinson and Jesse Jones. Wallace is said to have remarked to a recent visitor 'if the President continues to appease Southern reactionaries he will lose his place in history'.

France. Recognition of the National Committee[8] was greeted with varying degrees of approval and disapproval along established lines. The Gaullist *Herald Tribune* and the liberal press complain sharply of the grudging tone of the American formula which is contrasted with the stronger Russian declaration. The right-wing press welcomes the reservations in the American declaration. Middle-of-the-roaders expressed general satisfaction. Scarcely any invidious comparisons between the American and British notes have been made. The Fighting French representative is officially satisfied and unofficially not too disappointed. There is scarcely any talk of any kind of possible Anglo-American differences on this or any other issue at Quebec.

. . .

Jews. The American Jewish Conference which met this week in New York and claims to represent at least two and a half million persons (a million and a half is probably nearer the mark) has, as predicted, by an overwhelming majority

8 On 26 August Roosevelt welcomed the establishment of the French Committee of National Liberation in Algiers, but only as 'administering those French overseas territories which acknowledged its authority' and not as a 'government of France or of the French Empire'.

passed a number of Zionist resolutions, chief of which are: demands for a Jewish commonwealth in Palestine, control of immigration by the Jewish Agency, the abrogation of the White Paper of 1939,[9] steps likely to result in the creation of a Jewish majority in Palestine, and all the other familiar Zionist claims. The American Jewish Committee, a financially and politically influential but self-co-opted body, publicly dissented from the Palestine resolution, and while endorsing the demands for mass immigration into Palestine and abrogation of the White Paper, declared through its spokesman Judge Proskauer[10] that in view of the troubled state of the world and the difficulty of predicting conditions after the war, it deeply regretted that a resolution likely to embarrass the Governments of the United Nations in the midst of a critical situation should have been insisted upon by the majority of the Conference. In temperate and dignified words it therefore dissociated itself from the demand for a Jewish commonwealth and spoke of 'the continuance of an international trusteeship to safeguard the Jewish settlement in Palestine and the fundamental rights of its inhabitants, to prepare the country to become in a reasonable period of years a self-governing country under a constitution and a bill of rights that would protect the basic rights of all'.

The American Council for Judaism, pledged specifically against Zionism and every other form of Jewish nationalism, and backed by the wealthy Rosenwald family[11] of Chicago, but otherwise containing few well-known names and representing a negligible minority, published a strong anti-Zionist statement while the Conference was sitting. It was very prominently displayed in the *New York Times,* doubtless because of the strongly anti-Zionist views of its publisher, Arthur Sulzberger. This bold act duly provoked its unanimous condemnation by the Conference and led to personal attacks on Sulzberger reproduced in *PM* and other newspapers. The existence of these three dissenting bodies makes it clear that American Jews are deeply, if very unequally, divided on the issue of Zionism (the vast majority of individuals and associations are pro-Zionist). The whole thing has thus far caused little general stir.

. . .

Office of Economic Warfare. Jones is said to be obstinately clinging to the financial agencies which the President's order . . . transferred to Crowley's new Office of Economic Warfare, reportedly in the hope that Congress will decline to assent in the transfer of the relevant appropriations. As a result of a shuffle, Messrs Rosenthal[12] and Oppenheimer,[13] who were regarded as New Dealers of the Milo Perkins school, have been dropped. On the other hand, the post of temporary Executive Officer has been taken by Lauchlin Currie,[14] one of the

9 British statement of policy, issued 17 May 1939, affirming that it was not a part of British policy that Palestine should become a Jewish State and fixing quotas for Jewish immigration.

10 Joseph M.Proskauer, Justice, Supreme Court of New York, 1923–30.

11 Proprietors of mail-order house of Sears, Roebuck.

12 Morris S.Rosenthal, Assistant Director in charge of imports, Board of Economic Warfare 1942–3.

13 Monroe Oppenheimer, General Counsel of the Board of Economic Warfare 1941–3.

14 Lauchlin Currie, Administrative Assistant, White House Office, since 1939.

President's six 'anonymous assistants' and a New Dealer *pur sang*. This is probably typical of the 'one step forward, two steps backwards' political policy at present pursued by the President. (It is rumoured that Justice Rosenman is to be permanently transferred to the White House.)

Currie. Currie, who is probably well known to your Department owing to his connexion with political and financial affairs in the Far East, is a Canadian educated at the London School of Economics; he is a somewhat pernickety and acid, if sincere, anti-imperialist of the *New Statesman* variety, and his sentiments towards Britain are deeply coloured by his passionate feeling for China on which, with Owen Lattimore,[15] he has been the President's principal recent expert. He is both tough-minded and capable, and his outlook on economic foreign policy which he is to administer may well be somewhat similar to what that of Mr Harold Laski[16] would be were he charged with this function. It would, therefore, be sanguine to expect frictionless co-operation on his part. With his friends Ben Cohen and Wayne Coy, he is virtually the only unregenerate New Dealer remaining in a position of real importance.

12 September 1943

MR CHURCHILL

Mr Churchill's presence here, his talk to press and Harvard speech,[1] together with flood of excellent war news, induced uncommon exhilaration in Washington which has done something to lift the gloom brought on by Welles' affair and gathering Russian cloud (see last political summary). The altogether exceptional position which Mr Churchill occupies in American national life and politics was underlined by the reaction to his Harvard speech. Core of it – need for and potentialities of Anglo-American partnership – was greeted with expected variations in warmth, ranging from enthusiasm on the part of the Anglophile section of East Coast broadcasters and press, to usual barrage of opposition by Patterson-McCormick-Hearst papers. . . .

. . .

General political atmosphere has admittedly been singularly favourable, during the jubilant mood induced by joint military successes widely attributed to President and Mr Churchill to the notion of continued close Anglo-American collaboration, and the call for an Anglo-American military alliance by impeccably conservative Dewey has helped.

Naturally the flowering of this seed depends both on events and on the behav-

15 Owen Lattimore, Professor of International Relations at Johns Hopkins University, and Deputy Director, Pacific Operations, OWI, 1942–4.

16 Harold J. Laski, Professor of Political Science at the London School of Economics and Labour Party intellectual.

1 6 September, on receipt of an honorary degree.

iour of political parties, but there has rarely been so much sentiment benevolent to Anglo-American association, and the psychological moment for the presentation of main views of future Anglo-American development could hardly have been better chosen.

At his 'off-the-record' talk at a Washington press luncheon on the 4th, Mr Churchill, who spoke with magnificent gusto and candour, captured the minds and hearts of his important and professionally sceptical audience to a degree which, according to some of them, was without parallel. Lippmann, whose column that morning paid homage to personality and achievements of Mr Churchill (enlarging upon the irresistible impact and life-giving properties of his visit in the stifling atmosphere of Washington intrigue and gossip), told a member of my staff that he and his colleagues of the Elite, Swing, Clapper and the rest, had been most deeply moved. Swing added that Mr Churchill's breadth of vision and generous attitude towards France and Russia, his freedom from petty resentments, and the thrilling effect of his all-embracing and infectious imagination were indeed marks of a very great man. References to it as a memorable occasion ('I would have travelled a thousand miles') were very frequent. So far as words can affect ingrained American attitudes towards their own and the world's future, Mr Churchill's electrifying utterances do so. . . .

REPUBLICAN CONFERENCE

The meeting at Mackinac Island[2] has, despite all efforts on the part of Republican columnists to represent it otherwise, yielded forth a mouse. It was, as expected, dominated by the old guard. Resolutions on domestic affairs followed the routine anti-New Deal line and apparently provoked little discussion. Vandenberg, who presided over the Foreign Affairs Committee, imparted to the final foreign policy resolution a peculiarly pompous and non-committal quality, similar to that which characterizes his attitudes and utterances in the Senate. Vandenberg has successfully substituted the neo-isolationist notion of an irreducible American 'sovereignty' as a barrier to internationalist planning, for the older bogey of 'entangling alliances', and a fight developed over this new or revived nationalist symbol between the old guard and some of the enlightened among the Governors, easily won by Vandenberg and the party machine. The 'sovereignty' point was, of course, much to the fore in the debates on the League of Nations in 1919 and weighed heavily with the Senate at that time. Vandenberg perhaps thinks it a useful substitute name for the policy now blown upon under its name of 'Isolationism'. Taft was, as usual, baldly isolationist–and although such 'internationalists' as Governor Baldwin and Senator Austin did their feeble best, and Dewey, who was very much the *jeune premier* of the occasion, caused a great flutter by unexpectedly and without a word to any other Republican delegate calling for a continued Anglo-American military alliance, the ultimate res-

2 Meeting of the Republican Advisory Council, 6–8 September, at a resort in Lake Michigan, designed to evolve a generally acceptable statement on post-war policy in advance of 1944 party convention.

olution muffled all this completely. Dewey was read out of the party by the *Chicago Tribune,* and signs of a possible Willkie–Dewey deal against the old guard began to be spoken of. Kelland's similar proposal seems to have been virtually ignored.

Dewey at this press conference apparently did as well as Bricker did badly. His success with the press and bold attempt to outbid Willkie on foreign policy seems to have stirred bitter resentment and jealousy among the Vandenberg-Bricker midwestern group. A comic flurry, almost a panic, is said to have been engineered by a journalist who paid a bellboy in the closely guarded conference hotel to page Mr Willkie (who had been most carefully excluded) for over an hour.

LEND-LEASE

The President's revocation on 7 September of the message in his covering letter transmitting the forthcoming quarterly Lend-Lease report to Congress which had declared that victory and peace were 'the only coin' in which the United States of America wished to be paid, is apparently due not to any sudden pressure put on him by any interest, but to his own fear of appearing quixotic to Congress and the American public in an election year. I am informed that when the *New York Times* leading article . . . calling attention to the significance of this step, was brought to his attention, he protested that he had never meant anything of the kind, and when faced with the official and approved text, decided to advertise his disapproval of the section dealing with repayment before the issue could blow up in Congress. OLLA,[3] which apparently got wind of this intention, made little or no effort to argue against it, although an OWI official told a member of my staff that OWI had made an effort to point out its unfortunate effects and had tried to persuade the Treasury to help them, but without success.

There are rumours, but not a shred of evidence, that Morgenthau had warned the President against 'unconditional surrender' of this type as weakening him far too much in any possible future negotiations with other nations, particularly Britain.

Be that as it may, there is no reason to suppose that the President acted otherwise than on his own untrammelled judgment, without consultation, and that his desire to seem a shrewd Yankee trader may tend to obstruct the efforts of those who wish to eliminate the threat of a resurgence of a war debts issue over Lend-Lease repayment. The President seems prepared to assist in educating the American public towards a truer appreciation of the nature of reciprocal aid, a task in which OLLA officials and Acheson sincerely believe, only if it involves no political cost to himself.

It should however be remembered that it is one of the President's tactics, springing from his love of dishing the Opposition, to issue a denial of an inten-

3 Office of Lend-Lease Administration.

tion to embark on some bold and necessary course of action shortly before in fact performing it (e.g. the destroyer deal in 1940,[4] the convoying of ships in 1941,[5] etc.) ; consequently this withdrawal should perhaps not be taken too tragically. But there is no reason to think that he will budge from his position at present. I gather that he has not spoken to the Prime Minister or any other British official on the subject.

.   .   .

STATE DEPARTMENT

Welles is still at Bar Harbor. His resignation has not officially been accepted and no successor has been announced.

The resignation of James LeCron,[6] an intimate 'bible belt' friend of Wallace and a brother-in-law of the Willkie-ite Cowles Brothers, giving as his reason the deliberate obstruction and incompetence of State Department officials, is part of the general anti-State Department campaign occurring at present.

.   .   .

So far as the press is concerned, the State Department is at present the target of all major commentators : Shirer,[7] Clapper and Mowrer are open assailants. With the departure of Welles, Swing has in his discreeter fashion also turned against it. It is forced to rely on such obedient mouthpieces as Callender, Krock and Kingsbury-Smith whose statements now tend to be discounted in advance and reach a far smaller public than the discordant voices of Drew Pearson, Clapper, etc. But a Scripps-Howard editorial defends the Department and Hull as effective opponents to the New Deal. The President appears to be increasingly filled with resentment against the press which he regards as perversely irresponsible. This does not make his press conferences easier or more popular and, consequently, facilities for popularizing official policy through the press are at a low level at the moment.

18 September 1943

The return of Congress, war news and realization of domestic tangles to be faced by returned Congress have had a sobering effect after a month of exaggerated optimism over war and of ferment of home issues.

Domestic issues. Two main domestic issues before Congress are 'Fathers Draft' against which Wheeler is crusading and Fulbright foreign policy resolution. There was a very considerable flutter over Canadian announcement about demobilization of two-and-a-half divisions. Hull refused to comment on Canadian

---

4 Exchange of fifty overage US destroyers for lease of bases in British West Indies.

5 'Shoot on sight' order, etc., September 1941.

6 James D.LeCron, Director, Food Supply and Nutrition Division, Office of Co-ordinator of Inter-American Affairs.

7 William L.Shirer, war correspondent for CBS News 1939–45.

internal politics but President manfully defended decision, stressing particularly relative proportions of military effort of Canada and United States of America. There is also much excitement about renegotiation of wartime government contracts in favour of business.

Pacific Firstism. Senator Chandler delivered a characteristic MacArthur speech and Patterson papers have attacked Mountbatten as 'a princeling' whose selection in preference to MacArthur [1] demonstrated powerful influence of reactionary British over American decisions.

Hull's speech. Hull's speech,[2] although attacked by liberals and such customary critics of the Department as Lippmann and *New York Herald Tribune* as empty and obsolete (*Herald Tribune* leader of 13 September is most trenchant criticism to date), and regarded as disappointing by more progressive among Washington officials, was well received on whole by press (less well on radio) and general public opinion. Reassuring repetition of ancient truths coupled with admission that force may have to be used to secure peace clearly has a comforting effect upon a public still deeply uncertain of the world it wants after war, and fact that an utterance consisting mainly of vague generalities should have had a favourable (if not specially enthusiastic) reception in so many quarters is perhaps best index of inchoateness of public thinking on this issue. Lindley as always and Raymond Moley,[3] more out of anti-New Deal sentiment than feeling for Hull (who ousted him very fiercely in 1934), rallied strongly to support of speech which in places was regarded as a faint reflection upon Mr Churchill's bolder pronouncement.

. . .

STATE DEPARTMENT

Rumours (some of which have appeared in the press) about the probable reorganization of the Department are circulating widely. A member of my staff was shown by a United States official the 'blueprint' of one such plan, apparently inspired by Leo Crowley, head of the Office of Economic Warfare, according to which Welles's post would be dissolved into three Under-Secretaryships charged with political, economic and cultural activities respectively. According to tipsters, the present favourite for the Under-Secretaryship in charge of political and diplomatic activities is still Messersmith (at present Ambassador to Mexico) ; Crowley apparently is plotting to get the economic overlordship for himself ; and cultural, i.e. propagandist, activities, may be placed under Breckinridge Long. There is no doubt that plans of this kind have been submitted, although none have, so far as is known, been accepted as yet either by Hull or the President.

1 Lord Louis Mountbatten, British Chief of Combined Operations 1942–3, appointed Supreme Allied Commander, South-East Asia, at Quebec Conference.

2 On 12 September.

3 Raymond Moley, columnist and contributing editor of *Newsweek*, renegade New Dealer.

Crowley's purposes seem evident enough: he occupies an exposed and uncomfortable position as Head of the Office of Economic Warfare ; he would prefer to integrate this Office into the structure of the State Department, which would secure for him (provided he becomes the Economic Under-Secretary) at once the protection of Hull's prestige and power, and greatly increased control over all foreign economic activities. Under a scheme of this kind Lend-Lease, OEW, OFRRO, etc., would become feudal appendages of the State Department, which would, through Crowley, exercise in practice that control over these (and possibly Nelson Rockefeller)[4] offices to which it is in theory entitled already. Crowley's elevation would please the Catholics ; the main losers would be Acheson and Finletter,[5] whose political influence is not a factor. Behind Crowley moves the great meddler Corcoran[6] to whom Crowley himself freely attributes his rise. Byrnes is said to be favourable to some such scheme as likely at once to conciliate the Catholics, and to do something, as any radical reorganization must, to still the clamour against the inefficiency of the State Department, if not in the liberal, at least in the general, press.

There is no doubt that the strength and wide extent of popular reaction over Welles's dismissal was a complete surprise both to the State Department and the White House. As part of the projected reform the State Department is said to be thinking of setting up an intelligence and survey department of its own, which will enable it to keep in touch with popular sentiment, and perhaps to influence it, which it is prevented from doing at present by the extreme isolation in which it works.

If a Cultural Affairs Division is set up its relations with the Overseas Branch of OWI and possibly with General Donovan's office may create problems ; whatever immediate solution is effected, such a division would be intended to become the residuary legatee after the war of all existing United States propaganda agencies, and may, at any rate in the Western Hemisphere, grow to be a powerful arm of the American Government.

WALLACE

The fact that Wallace regards his enforced freedom from executive office as an opportunity for intenser political activity emerges clearly in his recent speech in Chicago. . . . His continued attacks on 'cartels and monopolies' (in the best William Jennings Bryan tradition) with names named, e.g. that of Standard Oil, are plainly destined to be one of the main planks of the radical platform, whether or not Wallace, as its creator, himself stands for elective office during the coming year. The condemnation of 'Cartels' is, of course, also one of Eric Johnston's favourite battle cries ; this curious combination of right and left may, if it does

4 Nelson A.Rockefeller, Co-ordinator of Inter-American Affairs since 1940.
5 Thomas K.Finletter, Special Assistant to the Secretary of State since 1941.
6 Thomas ('Tommy the Cork') Corcoran, co-draughtsman with Benjamin Cohen of much New Deal legislation.

nothing else, create a new and formidable bogey capable of being used against British interests.

Wallace's suggestion that the President preside over the ultimate Peace Conference (presumably while still in office, i.e. during his fourth term) indicates that the present policy of the left wing of the New Deal is to continue to support the President with remorseless fidelity despite his deviations, while fiercely attacking interests which they conceive to be hostile to him, whether or not this suits the President's actual purposes. There is no evidence that the suggestion about the Peace Conference (when asked whether Mr Churchill could not equally well occupy this position, Mr Wallace smiled and replied 'I am an American') was conceived in collusion with the President or anyone else in the White House or in the Administration. Wallace's personal stock continues to be low since the bulk of organized (as opposed to individual) support for his ideas comes only from the CIO and the Farmer's Union, the latter the weakest, if the most progressive, of the farm organizations. His recent remarks and in particular his seven new 'freedoms', however serviceable as a New Deal programme, contain as the press was swift to note no more indication of the means of attainment of these ends than the more publicly popular abstractions of Mr Hull (which are the favourite target of the left wing). They have made far less impression here, than . . . they [appear to] have made in Britain.

Wallace seems at present a distinct political embarrassment to the President, who, nevertheless, as is his wont, still throws him an occasional sop, since the hour may come when left-wing support of this type may yet prove useful and even indispensable. There is as yet no evidence of any real growth of that renovated New Deal Party which disgruntled radicals, some leaders of the CIO and New York liberals yearn for. Wallace is still its most natural leader but his lack of political gifts is the gravest handicap to the success of such a movement. His influence and that of his friends is perhaps smaller at this moment than at any time since the mid-term elections of 1930.

ROSENMAN

The announcement that Judge Samuel Rosenman of the New York Court of Appeals is leaving the Bench to become the President's full-time legal adviser formalizes a long existing arrangement. Rosenman, who has for a long time been exceptionally close to the President, possesses little vanity or ambition, a limited, if exceptionally lucid, intelligence, and is wholly devoted to the President's interests, with neither taste nor desire for political intrigue. The President has used him in the past to draft the reorganization of collapsing government agencies, as a general draftsman of public messages and of economic legislation, as a collaborator with Sherwood on his public speeches, as editor of his speeches and as private legal adviser. Rosenman's gentle and conciliatory temperament, which has preserved him from normal Washington feuds and imbroglios, ensures that this move will cause minimum jealousy within the existing White House entourage.

. . .

25 September 1943

FULBRIGHT RESOLUTION

As had been generally expected, Fulbright Resolution, putting Congress on record as favouring United States participation in creation of appropriate international machinery with power adequate to establish and to maintain a just and lasting peace, was passed by House of Representatives by an overwhelming majority after a brief, meagrely attended and, apart from diatribes of extreme isolationists, unenthusiastic debate. Triumphant claims of original supporters of resolution that this represents a victory for post-war participation and a landmark in United States international relations require considerable modification. Inclusion of Republican amendment laying down that participation should be 'through constitutional processes' set further restrictions upon a participation already limited by brevity and vagueness of resolution itself. Passage of this resolution makes consideration of any more specific proposals improbable at this time. Some observers regard resolution as little more than a 'vote against sin' which commits United States to nothing, passed by a section of Congress which will not eventually be responsible for final decisions on foreign affairs. It is of some significance that one of the most influential speeches in support of the resolution was made by Representative Wadsworth (Republican, New York) who, as a Senator in 1919, while expressing similar generally participationist views, upheld fight of Senate against League of Nations in form presented by Wilson. Finally passage of Fulbright Resolution has not so far even succeeded in prodding Senate into action, since Senator Connally, Chairman of the Senate Foreign Relations Committee, has made it plain that Senate will not in the immediate future debate any of post-war resolutions in view of danger of producing 'irritations or vexations at a critical period' on subjects of 'vital interest to our Allies'.

Supporters of resolution however claim with some justice (a) that it has divided the ranks of the opposition and isolated in their extremism Ohio, Michigan, Illinois isolationist diehards ; (b) that it crystallizes and highlights participationist trend of public opinion to which returning Congressmen were obliged to yield ; and (c) that it marks the ebb of the isolationist tide and provides a basis for further advance.

Further evidence of participationist trend of opinion is given by this week's proceedings of annual convention of the American Legion which has each year since 1939 provided a reliable cross-section of American opinion on foreign affairs. This time the Legion has come out strongly in favour of American participation in an 'association of free and sovereign nations implemented with whatever force may be necessary to maintain world peace'. (Use of word 'sovereign' in this resolution should be noted however as an increasingly popular reinsurance formula.)

MARSHALL

Rumours of changes in status of General Marshall, at present Chief of Staff, and murmurs of alleged dissatisfaction from General MacArthur with the Roosevelt-Churchill strategy, have provided opponents of Administration with means of attacking conduct of war, a field in which reports from returning Congressmen and reactions to President's message to Congress have shown Administration to be least criticized by public opinion across country.

Extreme isolationist newspapers and former 'America Firsters' had for some time been propagating rumours of disagreements at Quebec between British and American High Commands and endeavours by British to oust General Marshall. *Army and Navy Journal* had published an editorial suggesting that Marshall 'had come into conflict with powerful interests which would like to eliminate him from Washington picture and place in his stead an officer more amenable to their will'. This provided isolationists with an opportunity to alarm both Congress and public with forecasts of demotion of one of most highly respected generals by alien-minded President at behest of selfish British. Marshall's global control of nation's strategy and his effectiveness as Chief of Staff in urging requirements of Pacific front would be lost. British, according to Representative Jessie Sumner[1] of Illinois, a shrewish Anglophobe disciple of *Chicago Tribune,* were also trying to oust Admiral Leahy and to keep MacArthur from highest military command for sake of Royal Lord Louis Mountbatten. Frankfurter, Hopkins, etc., were also allegedly in plot to elevate to post of Chief of Staff General Brehon Somervell, classified for sake of this story as a 'New Deal' General. Chairmen of both House and Senate Military Affairs Committees, Senator Reynolds and Representative May, both noted for their irresponsibility and former for his rabid isolationism, expressed themselves seriously and righteously alarmed at injection of politics into conduct of war.

A consistently loyal supporter of President and of close co-operation with British, General Marshall himself remained aloof, silent and impartial to these flurries. His stock in country is at present extremely high. His biennial report to nation on transformation of American armed forces has been widely acclaimed and in his recent evidence before a congressional committee he scored a notable victory over opposition to drafting of fathers. He has never been associated with those at present endeavouring to make him a martyr and recently denounced as despicable publication by Patterson papers of an article impugning morality of WAC.[2] When after a week's interval it was announced by Kirke Simpson[3], a correspondent very close to White House and a member of President's per-

1 Jessie Sumner, Republican Congresswoman from Illinois since 1939.
2 Women's Army Corps.
3 Kirke Simpson (1908–45), Washington correspondent for the Associated Press.

sonal 'Cufflinks Club'[4], that far from being demoted Marshall was 'Roosevelt–Churchill choice for a worldwide field command to lead all Anglo-American forces in smashing of Axis', spurious nature of campaign against both Administration and British was generally accepted and absurdity of British 'getting rid' of a general by having him put in charge of their own forces in most vital operation of war was frequently pointed out.

Isolationists however continue to suggest a plot, latest version being that presented by Representative Paul W. Shafer[5] (Republican, Michigan) who charges that Marshall is being removed in order to create a global WPA[6] programme through War Department for purposes of capturing a fourth term.

Article in *Army and Navy Journal* was uninspired and written in good faith by publisher, a close friend of Marshall's, who was concerned at continuance of rumours of Marshall's removal. Terms in which article was written seem to have been due partly to concern by professional army and navy circles that appointment of Marshall's successor might be a political one and partly to a genuine belief by some of Marshall's colleagues that he might be more useful in Washington. They are also said to be conscious of difficulty of refusing supplies to a European theatre in charge of Marshall and fearful of resultant fire to which they would be exposed from powerful 'Pacific Firsters'.

. . .

WILLKIE

Willkie . . . has now outlined a platform for 1944 in the current issue of *Look* magazine, the weekly organ of the Cowles family. This has been backed by full-page advertisements in the daily press, presenting Willkie as another Lincoln (the period chosen for the analogy is that of the Second Inaugural),[7] a man to bind up the nation's wounds and achieve a 'just and lasting peace among races and with all nations'. The article is Lincolnesque in its crusading terms and its faith in the people and reflects the mood of exalted crusading idealism in which recent visitors to Willkie declare him to be. . . . [T]he article makes a direct appeal (a) to minority groups, the protection of which is given the first place of honour on the platform ; (b) to disgruntled liberals in terms which some liberals have described as sounding more like Wallace than Landon ; (c) to the small businessman in its advocacy of freedom of opportunity both against the Government and against cartels ; (d) to critics of the OPA and unpopular home front agencies in its denunciation of bad administration ; (e) to the participationist trend of opinion in its advocacy of a new foreign policy ; (f) and to the former mass supporters of the New Deal in its proposal of 'absolute guarantees' against unemployment. . . .

4 Presidential intimates, such as his press secretary and personal physician, who wore gold cufflinks that Roosevelt gave them.

5 Paul W. Shafer, Republican Congressman from Michigan since 1937.

6 New Deal agency criticized (and praised) for the grand scale of its public works programmes, providing employment (and patronage).

7 Lincoln's speech on his inauguration for a second term as President, when end of Civil War was in sight.

Present discussion of Willkie's chances range from the North Carolina Governor's wisecrack that 'we are going to win the war whether the next President is Republican, Democrat or Mr Willkie', and Southern Representative Rankin's sarcastic questioning whether the world or the GOP are 'prepared for the Second Coming of Lincoln', to Mr Willkie's own personal declaration to his friends that he will get the nomination on the first ballot.

· · ·

3 October 1943

STETTINIUS AND CROWLEY

Appointment of Stettinius as Under-Secretary of State and creation of Office of Foreign Economic Affairs (OFEA) under Crowley means in brief that

(a) foreign economic policy will be formulated by President and by Hull in State Department and latter will now have benefit of Stettinius's practical experience in operational field,

(b) this policy will be executed outside State Department by Crowley who will be responsible to President and who has made it clear that whilst he will operate within framework laid down by Roosevelt and Hull he will brook no interference by State Department with operation of agencies incorporated in OFEA. Demarcation of frontiers is thus now clear except for some doubt as to position of Dean Acheson's Office of Foreign Economic Co-ordination, whose operational functions are expected to be transferred from State Department to Crowley. Dean Acheson will thus no longer be immersed in operations and will be able to devote more time to formulation of policy both economic and political. Whether peace will reign on both sides of these frontiers depends largely on personal relations of Crowley and Hull, which are and have long been cordial, and on their ability to settle amicably day-to-day problems of what is policy and what is operations.

· · ·

Berle in talking to a member of my staff lamented departure of Welles but praised appointment of Stettinius and added that he would himself do all he could to promote idea that Welles's great experience should be used, possibly in connexion with Latin American affairs. Another member of State Department remarked with some malice that changes at last established place of Governor Lehman. It is too early to forecast whether new executive order will result in far-reaching changes. There should be a clearer focussing of policy discussions in State Department although there may be a transitional period while Crowley is feeling his way in overhauling related functions and personnel of 'Federated Agencies'. Task of reporting on question of overlapping between four agencies has been entrusted to Stone of Budget Bureau.[1]

Political observers of all shades of opinion interpret appointments as a further move by President towards political forces of right and towards mollification of Congress.

1 Donald C. Stone, made a career in public administration, Assistant Director of Bureau of Budget 1939–48.

Stettinius in particular as Lend-Lease Administrator displayed his ability to get everything he wanted from Congress despite bitter controversies and campaigns which had surrounded subject of Lend-Lease. Crowley, a close friend of Hull's, has also been on excellent terms with Congress. Since he retains direction of Federal Deposit Insurance Corporation and of Alien Property Custodian's office in addition to all agencies now under OFEA he will be one of biggest spenders of Government in country and will need congressional support to a corresponding degree.

Appointment of Stettinius, son of a Morgan partner, ex-Chairman of United States Steel, and a brother-in-law of Trippe of Pan-American Airways, should also be acceptable to enlightened but conservative business groups and it is of some political significance that Stettinius started his career in Washington as a liaison officer between big business and New Deal in early days of NIRA.[2] A sound banker and utilities man, previously nominated to control Federal Deposit Insurance Corporation and Alien Property Office precisely because of his high public reputation for business integrity, Crowley represents middle-of-the-road section of Democratic Party which has not followed Farley in his fight against New Deal and fourth term but has supported Administration's foreign policy and advocated a conservative domestic policy without reaction. Since he is one of most influential laymen and No. 1 finance man of Roman Catholic Church, Crowley's appointment will also appeal to Catholic vote. On other hand neither Crowley nor Stettinius have proved themselves unacceptable to New Dealers and Hopkins himself is understood to have pressed Stettinius's claim to Under-Secretaryship. Liberals are at present too relieved that appointment was made from outside what they call 'Fascist' ranks of State Department to criticize move to right.

Add to above consideration President's previous support of Hull, representative of South, *vis-à-vis* Welles, and Crowley's influence with progressives in his home State of Wisconsin, and it will be seen that reorganization has something in it for almost all political groups upon which President's continuance in office may depend.

It is now generally accepted that Hull will go in person to tripartite conference wherever it may be held and both appointment of Stettinius and of Harriman[3] as Ambassador to Moscow are expected to appeal to Russians who are alleged to prefer dealing with hard-headed realistic typical American businessmen rather than liberals or career diplomats.

SENATORS' WORLD TOUR

Senators Mead, Russell, Lodge and Brewster this week returned from world battlefronts fortified with vivid evidence from their contact with fighting forces to support causes which they held most strongly when they left some months ago. Prestige and news value of Senators' pronouncements have of course been

2 National Industrial Recovery Administration, centrepiece of early New Deal programme.
3 W.Averell Harriman, Chairman of Union Pacific Railroad, Lend-Lease Co-ordinator in London 1941–3.

considerably enhanced by trip. Apart from a poor impression of war effort in India which they describe as 'infected with Singapore mentality', they have been very greatly impressed by evidences of British power, organization and ability. . . .

.   .   .

Post-war resolution. Decision of Senate Foreign Relations Committee . . . to postpone consideration of post-war resolutions despite passage of Fulbright Resolution gave rise to a sharp and unfavourable reaction not only in Washington but in press and on radio across country. 'Isolation', declared Raymond Clapper, 'has won opening battle in United States Senate.' Ball-Hatch group, whose post-war resolution has now been pigeonholed for some six months, delivered an ultimatum declaring that unless action took place within three weeks on a post-war resolution they would force a debate by moving to recall their resolution from Foreign Relations Committee to floor of Senate. Vandenberg group of Republican Senators also urged immediate debate in accordance with strategy decided upon at Mackinac of eliminating foreign policy as a political issue and concentrating Republican attack on Administration's domestic policy. Finally President indicated to congressional leaders at a White House meeting that he also wanted action now and he provided Foreign Relations Committee with a justification for a retreat in form of off-the-record reports of 'new developments on diplomatic and military fronts'. Committee have accordingly yielded and are now drafting a resolution of their own as a substitute for Fulbright Resolution.

.   .   .

Congress prospects. Congress has now settled down to reconsideration of some of 'hardy annuals' left unsettled when they recessed. Federal Communications Commission have secured a tactical victory in ousting of Representative Eugene Cox (Democrat, Georgia) Chairman of House Committee investigating FCC. Cox's resignation both as Chairman and as a member of this Committee was brought about by campaigning of Eugene Meyer in his *Washington Post* and tireless efforts of Clifford Durr,[4] one of FCC Commissioners who steadily bombarded Judiciary Committee and Speaker Rayburn with evidence of Cox's allegedly illegal acceptance of $2,500 cheque from a radio station involved in a case pending before FCC. It is not likely however that Committee itself will relax an investigation of FCC which has its roots in long struggle of radio companies against federal control. Another old issue between liberals and Southern 'diehards' will come up next month when Senate Judiciary Committee will hear witnesses, including Biddle, on bill to repeal poll tax which was passed by House in last session but killed by a filibuster. Fight to repeal Chinese Exclusion laws has now moved from House where repeal is blocked in Immigration Committee to Senate where Senator Andrews (Democrat, Florida)[5] has introduced a new bill for repeal. Finally both Administration and Farm Bloc are now mobilizing

4 Clifford J.Durr, lawyer and FCC Commissioner since 1941.

5 Charles O.Andrews, Democratic Senator from Florida since 1937.

their forces for a renewed battle along usual lines – higher farm prices and subsidies.

9 October 1943

In the course of the week the Senators who recently returned from the battlefronts unloaded enough criticisms of British worldwide activities and enough anti-British stories 'to supply', as one Senator put it, 'the *Chicago Tribune* for a year'. The statements made by the Senators to friends, pressmen and colleagues were almost universally accepted at their face value and obtained exceptionally wide circulation (1) because these were reports straight from the front by United States Senators who were all of them, with the exception of Chandler, highly respected by their colleagues (two are members of Truman Committee and will report to that body direct); (2) because Senators were, as they carefully pointed out themselves, none of them notoriously isolationist, Anglophobe or 'America Firstish', (3) because they avoided direct publication to the press of the most sensational charges and disseminated these to their colleagues in one of the few secret sessions of the Senate in American history and to newspaper men in off-the-record talks for publication without attribution; (4) because the accusations were not patently anti-British but directed primarily at exposing the utter failure of the Administration's agents overseas to stand up against British competition in global organization. In particular, the criticism of the Senators was directed at the inadequacy of State Department direction and personnel abroad, at Mr J.M. Landis, the former New Deal head of the OCD now in charge of American economic operations in the Middle East, and at the overseas branch of OWI. The fact that the stories of tough poker-playing British imperialists were used chiefly to highlight the ineptitude of the soft 'whist-playing' Administration appointees abroad did not, however, prevent the reports from providing valuable fuel to unfriendly critics of British policy and indeed increased the credibility of the stories in the eyes of the man in the street.

With much careful detail the Senators described how smart, hard-headed but patriotic British officials and businessmen (in Senator Brewster's words 'a bunch of cunning and scheming brutes') were daily outwitting, ousting and frustrating the naïve and inexperienced American officials. Steadily British diplomats and Board of Trade representatives were building up, often with the assistance of Lend-Lease materials, a world monopoly of civil aviation and a network of trade connexions across the globe. In Newfoundland, in accordance with the destroyers-bases deal, the Americans were allowed to build for their own use a modest military base on an unsuitable fog-bound site whilst the British poured millions of dollars worth of Lend-Lease material into the magnificent Goosebay airbase, complete with mahogany fittings and other luxuries, for the exclusive use of Anglo-Canadian airlines after the war. In North Africa, where the hated British had last November been obliged to wear American uniforms to avoid the wrath of Oran-mindful [1] Frenchmen, Murphy and his staff were now cooped up on the sixth floor of the British Residency without even a doorplate to their credit or a reliable elevator service. As the battlefronts moved forward in the Mediterranean area, an 'army' of retired British admirals and other high-ranking officers stepped into the posts and quarters evacuated by the advancing Americans, hopelessly out-ranking and out-witting the modest lieutenants commissioned by the American authorities for the occupied territories. In India the British kept inactive but under arms vast reserves of troops, whilst the people rotted in abject misery and the New Deal American representatives spent their time fomenting revolution by promising the moon to the dejected masses after the war. As an example of British methods abroad, one Senator told how the Egyptian King had refused to see the British Ambassador who was pressing the retention of a corrupt pro-British Prime Minister and how the 400 lb British Ambassador had then broken his way through the palace gates with the assistance of British tanks and a detachment of field artillery.

The Senators are also reported to have said that the British had substituted their own labels for American markings on Lend-Lease goods and transported them to Turkey and India to gain a more favourable post-war status with those countries. In addition, the British had accepted under Lend-Lease some supplies, such as petroleum, which they could supply themselves. In another instance, 30,000 trucks were allocated for civilian use in Australia at a time when only 15,000 were released to civilians in the United States.

The Senators competed with each other for attention. Despite his conscious intellectual superiority to the tactics employed by his colleagues, and despite the reproaches of his friends and even of his wife, Lodge showed himself determined to lose none of the political limelight so abundantly available and even stole a march on the others by reporting direct to the Senate in open session the day after his arrival. Chandler, the last to arrive back in Washington, who was rumoured to have dropped in on Hearst *en route* from the West Coast, aims at becoming the chief standard-bearer of the 'Pacific Firsters' in the Senate and directed his main attack on the Pacific and Asiatic conduct of the war, declaring that the British did not want a strong China because of Hongkong and were unenthusiastic even over the Burmese campaign. Russell, usually a mild-mannered and inconspicuous Southerner, went back to the destroyer-bases deal to lament the shortness of a ninety-nine years' lease, 'no time at all in the life of a nation.' Even Mead, the only Roosevelt man of the five, produced a batch of clippings in the Senate to show how the British and Australian press took all the credit for American victories.

The statements of Brewster, Chandler and Lodge were notable for their inter-

1 Oran, scene of British naval action against French, June 1940, to prevent French fleet falling into German hands.

nationalist-imperialist tone and terminology. Brewster, a pre-Pearl Harbor inter-ventionist, in an off-the-record talk to the press which he said would be substan-tially what he would say to the Senate, referred frankly to the requirements of American Manifest Destiny and *Pax Americana* and called for a strong American team overseas of businessmen and business-like officials to compete with the efficient, closely-integrated British team. Brewster has hitherto regarded Britain as a junior partner of the United States in this war and his present attitude reflects the shock which certain rather disillusioning discoveries have given him. The United States of America, according to Chandler, should adopt a policy of de-fence imperialism and hold on to strategic outposts in both the Pacific and the Atlantic including those formerly belonging to France, Denmark, etc.

From a party political point of view, both Brewster and Lodge may also be regarded as competing against the Middle Western isolationists for leadership in Republican politics. To do this they must show that they can make an attack on the Administration on internationalist grounds more effective than the *Chicago Tribune* type of tirade. The tour has provided them with an opportunity to do this but to attain their objective they must present a picture of the Administration as an inept and blundering sheep amongst the Allied wolves.

Apart from the plea of the professional Anglophobes, the first reaction to the Senators' reports has not primarily been critical of the British. They are, how-ever, producing a widespread feeling that those in charge of American affairs abroad must catch up with the British, copy and better their methods. The Administration earlier in the week started to deal *seriatim* with the earlier charges of the Senators regarding oil and aviation but are now presented with an almost impossible task of presenting in balanced form the true facts regarding past, present and future developments in every corner of the fighting fronts.

· · ·

We are now entering into the four-yearly rutting season in the reproduction cycle of the American Congress and Presidency. The behaviour of the five Sen-ators is a reminder, if this were needed, that the traditional ferocity of political manoeuvre and debate during this period is not (repeat not) likely to be abated because the nation is at war.

· · ·

Presidential candidates. In a sweep through West and Middle West, Mr Willkie is said to be completing his plans for a comprehensive pre-convention appeal over heads of GOP managers in at least a dozen states from Massachusetts to California. In San Francisco he confidently declared that Republican Party was 'drifting rapidly' towards his own viewpoint. In Chicago, where party man-agers are more bitterly opposed to him than in any other State, he gave interview-ers impression that he might make a dramatic stand in Illinois primaries. Nation-ally he succeeded in building up considerable interest and speculation regarding speech which he is to make on 15 October in St Louis. . . .

The Tax bill. The debate over Treasury's new tax programme asking for $10½ billion 'for the third successive year, the biggest tax bill in history', promises to be even longer and more bitter than that of 1942–3. Both Administration and Congress are extremely sensitive to effects of proposals on voters in 1944 election. First reaction from leaders of both parties has, therefore, been to endeavour to place responsibility squarely on Administration for imposts which they feel are bound to be extremely unpopular. The new burdens, they declare, go far beyond what average person is able to pay. Morgenthau's case is not only that money is needed for war effort but that there still remains an excess of purchasing power over available goods of many billions of dollars and that as much as possible of this 'dangerous' money must be siphoned off if inflation is to be avoided. As usual, however, Treasury seems to show no ability to get this case over to the public or to rank and file of Congress. . . .

18 October 1943

OPPOSITION STRATEGY

Behind week's major political developments looms determination of Opposition to put up an intense and bitter fight to discredit Administration before November 1944. Willkie's speech at St Louis attacking Administration on all fronts, an attempt to press for court-martial now instead of after war of Kimmel and Short for their responsibility for Pearl Harbor, way in which criticisms of travelling Senators have been built up in Republican press, clamour for 'investigations' in Congress and attempt by John L. Lewis to capture American Federation of Labour for Republican Party all testified to comprehensiveness of Opposition attack. It became clear that Anglo-American relations are likely from time to time to become a pawn in this game because, as one columnist put it, opposition are 'looking for an anti-English issue' in order to attack Administration. It is significant therefore that Senator Nye should stir an angry debate in Senate by reviving old story that has long circulated that Mr Churchill held that it would be a tragic catastrophe if American people failed to elect President Roosevelt for a fourth term and it would be even worse if he should be re-elected with a Republican Congress. (Nye attributes this story to Drew Pearson but it was originally traced to Roy Howard [1] after his return from England.)

'TRAVELLING SENATORS' ACCOUNT

It is now possible to attempt to assess our credits and debits amongst repercussions to reports of five travelling Senators.

Debit

(a) In Congress investigations are being called for. Senate Interstate Commerce Committee has voted to include in its investigation of international com-

1 Roy W. Howard, President of Scripps-Howard Newspapers since 1936.

munications by wire and radio 'Control of foreign governments over common carriers authorized by them . . . and character and extent of competition with foreign companies in communications to and from United States and nature and degree of competition with American companies'. An old pigeonholed resolution of Senator Butler (Republican, Nebraska) for an investigation of Lend-Lease was dusted off to be brought before Senate Appropriations Committee after Butler had described Lend-Lease as 'most colossal dole of all time'. Senator Ellender (Democrat, Louisiana) has demanded that Lend-Lease be placed under rigid controls requiring that United States Government receive bases, raw materials and other concessions in exchange for American supplies and has supported this with a fantastic computation of relative British and American national debts in which he brought British *per capita* figure down to $164 by dividing total public debt of British Empire (i.e. United Kingdom, dominions, India, crown colonies, protectorates and condominiums) by its vast total population. This feat of political arithmetic has however aroused general ridicule.

(b) Reports have unquestionably provided material for and strengthened confidence of those already inclined to isolationism, to economic nationalism and to Anglophobia.

(c) They have reawakened doubts of those near-isolationists who were beginning to show signs of 'coming around' to more enlightened views. They have provided opponents of Administration with a means of attacking hitherto relatively immune mechanism and execution of governmental policies with charge that their Administration agents are either subservient to British or incompetent to resist wiles of their British opposite numbers. Critics of British policy on congressional committees will now take every opportunity of cross-examining officials along these lines.

(d) Outside Congress we must add to debit side powerful stimulus which has been given to circulation of anti-British stories, emotional appeal of these to traditional American fear of cunning and slickness of foreigner, and encouragement of cynicism about all dealings with foreigners. Some of these stories may eventually be forgotten but subjects of Lend-Lease, of Anglo-American civilian co-operation overseas, and of American rights to bases overseas will now be sensitive national issues for many months. In particular it is going to be very difficult to remove impression that we are a bunch of card sharpers in matter of Lend-Lease.

Credit

(a) Our friends in Senate attempt to reassure us along lines that, in words of Senator Ball writing to a member of my staff, 'In the long run it is a healthy thing to get some of these complaints out in the open where we can get answers and discuss them', yet it is questionable whether this item on credit side can always be cashed in view of fact that answers are often too involved and too slow in coming to register with either Congressmen or man in the street.

(b) We can also write to our credit very considerable volume of critical press and radio comment charging Senators with irresponsible mischief-making. (Approval is virtually confined to McCormick-Patterson press.) Disapproval is widespread. Heated disagreement within group as to what was actually said to them by MacArthur and others has also made them a little ridiculous, whilst Mead deserted them on floor of Senate itself as soon as Roosevelt made clear his opposition.

(c) Personal unpopularity of Chandler with his colleagues, a hangover from quarrels *en route,* and of Lodge, an ex-newspaperman who once again outsmarted others by negotiating for sale of rights for an account of trip to a weekly magazine, are also factors on our side. Fact that Senator Lodge so blatantly ignored General Marshall's specific and personal request not to discuss bases or Marshall's views on them has not improved his prestige or popularity.

(d) Nor can any popular leaders today afford to ignore effect on public opinion of a rebuke by Mr Churchill even though this be promptly rebutted by diehards as an intolerable interference with American internal affairs.

(e) For what it is worth we can also claim as a credit Administration's defence of British position which could hardly fail to be forthcoming since attack is primarily one against Administration through British 'territory'. Eagerness of President to reply was shown by way in which he forced subject on one press conference which had begun to break up without any question on this subject at all and he was also disappointed when this session finally broke up before all pile of data on his desk had been revealed.

(f) In so far as the intense attention paid to the Senators' reports is a projection of American interest overseas, the debate confirms and encourages the participationist trend of opinion.

(g) We take some comfort from the return to our support of various previous pre-Pearl Harbor friends in response to this challenge. . . .

I have recorded the above at perhaps greater length than the importance of the five Senators in the overall picture warrants because the affair throws into relief a number of interesting tendencies. It is still too early to make a final judgment of the repercussions, especially as there may be an open debate in the House of Representatives. But I draw the following provisional conclusions :

(1) While the affair will make certain questions such as Lend-Lease more sensitive and difficult to deal with for some time to come, the present signs are that it is not (repeat not) likely to have any lasting adverse effect on the American attitude towards Great Britain. It may even prove in the long run to have a useful effect.

(2) Events seem to be confirming the wisdom of abstaining from any official British replies to the Senators' allegations.

(3) While the McCormick-Patterson press is running the story on isolationist lines, the general tendency up and down the country is to draw the contrary conclusion, that the United States must put her own house in order and become sufficiently lean and tough to play the part in world affairs which her interests require and which she is beginning to want to play.

(4) Between now and the elections next year, political attacks on the Administration involving Anglo-American relations are inevitably to be expected.

(5) The allegations that the British Commonwealth is a monopoly of communications in certain areas to the detriment of the United States is likely to need most careful consideration to see whether some remedial action or agreement is required.

. . .

22 October 1943

MOSCOW CONVERSATIONS

Speculation about Moscow conversations [1] is popular, ill-informed and sometimes wild. Many of officials who would normally 'guide' opinion through State Department pipelines to press are, of course, in Moscow itself. Despite warnings given by Lippmann and others against newspaper talk of 'settling fate of world for next hundred years', the conversations are receiving a considerable build-up and almost any published results from conference will be in danger of coming as an anti-climax. Expectation of momentous decisions is increased by fact that it is now accepted that any subjects which any of delegates wish to bring up will be discussed. The general mood is one of suspense and anxiety. Signs and auguries of success are eagerly sought after. Cordiality of Gromyko's speech on 'March of Time' Radio programme, the reorganization of United States military representation in Moscow, Russian participation in acceptance of Italy as a co-belligerent, the signature of new Lend-Lease agreement in London and progress of Senate's post-war resolution are pointed to as hopeful signs.

Main conflict is thought to be between American principles and Russian interests. The British by themselves are thought to have been unable to resist Russian demands. There is however little tendency amongst Americans to campaign for small nations upon whom Russia's demands may fall heavily. Those who look to Russian policy as a touchstone of realism and those on the left who normally criticize State Department's lack of high moral principles are both silenced by difficulty of predicting either what Russia will demand or accept. The complexity of ideological problems involved in early stages of any post-war settlement inhibits controversy. The struggle between Tito [2] and Mihajlovic for leadership in Yugoslavia, the feeling that there is a possibility of something approaching civil

1 Moscow Conference, 19–30 October, of British, USSR and US foreign ministers.

2 Tito, assumed name of Josef Broz, Yugoslav Communist whose Partisans were rivals to Mihajlovic's Chetniks in organizing resistance to Axis.

war in Poland and Greece when day of liberation comes, and obvious complications of Italian situation have prevented both conservatives and anti-Fascists from taking sides too confidently in disputes like that over Darlan.

Political repercussions of conference are likely to be considerable. Opposition are preparing ground for charges (a) that American representation abroad has once again been weak and inept ; (b) that the Four Freedoms of small nations have been sacrificed to Russian imperialism ; (c) that Hull, transported in 'strange' vehicles to 'strange' places far from Washington and Tennessee, has been outwitted by practised astuteness of Mr Eden or unscrupulous intransigence of Russians in same way that Wilson was outsmarted by Lloyd George and Clemenceau ; and (d) that United States has gained nothing by meddling with European frontier problems and should confine itself to consideration of general character of organization of the peace.

SENATE POST-WAR RESOLUTION

Determined to put up a stiff fight for a stronger and more specific post-war resolution, the supporters of the Ball-Hatch resolution in the Senate take great pride in the role of a 'little group of wilful men', this time on the anti-isolationist side. Despite the valiant efforts of Senator Pepper, the Senate Foreign Relations Committee refused to make any stronger the very general post-war resolution, which they have now approved and passed to Senate for debate next week. Whilst the interventionists are attacking the resolution for its 'studied ambiguity', the isolationists are preparing to demand a statement of the position of Russia and Britain before the United States commit themselves. The material provided by the travelling Senators will no doubt be revived in the course of the debate.

Meanwhile the interventionists at present in a vigorous fighting mood affirm their determination not to let the Senate wreck peace. Representative Fulbright revealed the strategy behind the current determination of the House to assert itself in foreign affairs, declaring 'it is time we all realized that the executive process of submitting a joint resolution to both Houses of Congress is just as constitutional a method of ratifying treaties or taking any other step in foreign relations as is the so-called treaty process requiring a two-thirds vote of the Senate' (a joint resolution requires only a majority vote of each House for passage). Supporters of the Fulbright Resolution are already beginning to campaign on this theme.

.   .   .

Sumner Welles. Freed from the duties and responsibilities of office, Mr Sumner Welles is now a valuable and active propagandist for the anti-isolationist forces. His first speech as a private citizen backed up the efforts in the Senate of the Ball-Hatch group with whom he worked closely when in office. He also made frontal attack on abstract theorizing about sovereignty and on the argument being advanced by the isolationists in the Senate that a foreign policy declaration cannot be made until other countries have advanced their views.

. . .

Willkie. After a careful inspection and mobilization of his political forces from coast to coast Willkie in his speech at St Louis launched a full-scale offensive to gain control of Republican Party and assure his nomination in 1944. His strategy is (1) to convince both Republican leaders and rank and file that a positive crusading programme based on somewhat more liberal foreign and domestic policy is in accordance with finest traditions of Republicanism, does not in effect differ greatly from their own platform and is more likely to win votes than a purely anti-New Deal, anti-Roosevelt negative strategy of carping and sniping at the OPA, Mrs Roosevelt, War Food Administration, etc. ; (2) to force the compliance of GOP local leaders with a truculent attitude of 'take me or lose election', best summed up in his remark to St Louis bosses 'I do not know whether you are going to support me or not and I do not give a damn. You are a bunch of political liabilities anyway' ; (3) to push Republicans into a 'Band Wagon' movement by a demonstration of his supreme self-confidence in his ability to muster a majority in convention in first ballots.

Aided and abetted by a sudden cold spell which reduced audience considerably, the political bosses in Missouri, led by bitterly anti-Willkie Edgar M. Queeny,[3] did their best to sabotage his address by inadequate publicity arrangements, half-hearted notices, noncommittal introductory speeches, etc. The local effect was also reduced by Willkie having to suppress applause in order to keep within the thirty minutes allotted to him over radio (he still had nine paragraphs to go when he was cut off to make way for a programme called 'People are Funny'). Nationally, however, speech has increased his political prestige considerably and by quickly following it up with conferences with Republican Congressmen in Washington, he has brought a number of waverers back into his camp. The timing of warning against British 'intervention in American politics' (a matter on which we know that he has long felt rather strongly) was no doubt calculated to fit in with his latest collaborationist speech.

. . .

The expected appointment of Chester Bowles,[4] the general manager of the OPA, to head that organization merely recognizes the position which he has held *de facto* for some time, since Prentiss Brown has for some months left most decisions to Chester Bowles and spent much of his time in Florida or Michigan. This appointment will place in a position of power yet another hardheaded businessman and is therefore in accordance with the move to the right. Prentiss Brown who is reported in the press to be under consideration for a place on the

3 Edgar Monsanto Queeny, Chairman of the Board of Monsanto Chemicals 1943–60, trustee of Herbert Hoover Foundation.

4 Chester Bowles, Connecticut state director of OPA 1942–3, general manager OPA July–October 1943.

Federal Reserve Board cannot be described as having been ousted by business pressure since criticism of the OPA has seldom been directed at him personally. (Chester Bowles is a member of the firm of Benton & Bowles, who organized the advertising and were one of the original supporters of the 'America First' movement. The Benton[5] of the same firm was one of Eric Johnston's companions on his recent trip to England.)

31 October 1943

FEA REORGANIZATION

When a month ago Leo Crowley took over Foreign Economic Administration he was faced with two possible courses of action, either (a) to co-ordinate federal agencies and leave their identities intact, or (b) to merge them into one administrative unit and reorganize entire structure to that end. His statements to his staff at that time appeared to indicate that he intended to follow course (a). In reorganization announced this week he has followed course (b). . . . Described without exaggeration by Crowley himself as 'most far-reaching consolidation of government agencies in the war', the reorganization is sweeping in its implications both regarding administrative structure, policy and personnel.

Significance of this is first in construction of a more workable, streamlined and centralized organization, at any rate on paper. Lend-Lease Administration, Office of Economic Warfare, Office of Foreign Relief and Rehabilitation, Foreign Procurement Division of Commodity Credit Corporation and part of Office of Foreign Economic Co-ordination now lose their identity in fact as well as in name. Work of FEA will now be conducted by two bureaux. A Bureau of Supplies will deal with all export and import controls and foreign requirements including Lend-Lease under direction of William H. Schubart,[1] Senior Vice-President of Bank of Manhattan and a friend of Jimmy Warburg's.[2] A Bureau of Areas will deal with operations in liberated, enemy and other areas under direction of James L. McCamy,[3] former Assistant Director of OEW.

Secondly, reorganization is yet another 'move to the right'. Knollenberg,[4] a New Dealer, is retained with title of Executive Adviser, duties which he himself regards as vague and uncertain. Others of like sympathies such as Van Buskirk[5] are placed in positions in which their powers are comparatively small and their tenure of office uncertain. This group may well be out of the organization before

5 William Benton, Vice-President of University of Chicago 1937–45, Chairman of Board of Encyclopaedia Britannica 1943–5.

1 William H. Schubart, Vice-President of Bank of Manhattan 1929–43. In United Kingdom in 1942 on mission for Departments of State and Agriculture.

2 James P. Warburg, banker, OWI official 1942–4.

3 James L. McCamy, previously Professor of Government, Bennington College, and Assistant to Secretary of Agriculture 1939–41.

4 Bernhard Knollenberg, librarian of Yale University 1938–41.

5 Arthur Van Buskirk, Deputy Administrator for Operations, OLLA, 1942–3.

Christmas. In place of above are brought in, either as part-time consultants or as administrators, friends and business associates of Crowley's from banking circles, Federal Deposit Insurance Corporation (FDIC), New York politics and United Fruit Company. These include

(a) Samuel Zemurray,[6] a one-time Bessarabian fruit pedlar who has risen by shrewd and hard-headed business ability to be president and largest shareholder of United Fruit Company ; (b) Executive Vice-President of that company, Arthur Pollan ; (c) Joseph D.McGoldrick,[7] comptroller of New York City and one of a number of Roman Catholics brought in by reorganization ; (d) Henry W. Riley,[8] a Southerner long associated with Crowley both in FDIC and Alien Property Custodian's Office.

Thirdly, reorganization presages a tougher attitude towards us on such subjects as Lend-Lease. Some of our closest friends in Office of Lend-Lease Administration have been set aside and have been replaced by hardheaded businessmen who are credited by our friends with a disposition to regard Office of Economic Administration as a spearhead for protection and promotion of American business in course of war and an aggressive American export policy after it. In a jocularly disgruntled spirit Knollenberg's friends warned a member of my staff who found them appropriately celebrating their 'liquidation', of the 'dire' consequences of the change and probable toughness and aggressiveness of their successors towards the British.

SENATE POST-WAR RESOLUTION

Senate debate over post-war resolution has refused to follow traditional pattern of isolationist minority attacks on interventionist trend of Administration foreign policy. Opposition to Connally Resolution has come from a bipartisan group of young and enthusiastic interventionist Senators who have seized and held initiative throughout in their endeavour to make resolution stronger and more specific. Senator Wheeler's opposition to passage of any resolution at all came late in debate and seemed anti-climactic and almost irrelevant.

. . .

Senator Connally's fight to keep resolution in most general terms has received support from widely different quarters. President has declared himself in favour of a resolution in 'general' terms. Connally's Resolution is said to have blessing of Hull and picture has been presented of Hull anxiously awaiting text to be cabled to Moscow. Extreme isolationists such as Senator Nye and at least two of four surviving Senators who fought League Covenant in 1919 support resolution although some of them contemptuously make it clear that they regard it as platitudinous and non-committal. Senator Taft supports it as 'doing nothing more than enunciate general principles of foreign policy' and he characteristically at-

6 Samuel Zemurray assisted in framing Agricultural Adjustment Administration (AAA) codes.
7 Joseph D.McGoldrick, comptroller of New York City 1938–45.
8 Henry Ware Riley (1902–59), banker.

tempts to confuse issues by going further to urge use of existing machinery of League of Nations and of World Court to simplify task of organizing nations for collaboration after war. Veterans such as Alf Landon and Herbert Hoover indirectly support resolution by warning of dangers of one alternative, namely an Anglo-American military alliance which Landon described as 'joint isolationism'. . . . . Faced with choice between a mild resolution passed by an overwhelming majority and a strong resolution approved 'by a narrow squeak' after a long struggle, middle-of-roaders in Senate have chosen former. Consequently Ball-Hatch group have made few converts and have been charged in cloakrooms with depreciating before world importance of resolution. . . .

. . .

STRIKES

Labour situation has again become troublesome. Nearly 50,000 miners are already on strike. A strike ballot is being taken among one and a half million railroad workers. The miners' 'no contract no work' truce from June last expires at midnight Sunday 31 October when a nationwide coal strike may take place. Rejection by United Mine Workers of War Labor Board's proposed 'model' wage agreement in Illinois case as well as four cents an hour increase to anthracite miners is expected at any moment.

An appeal by President Roosevelt followed by the taking over of the mines by Government is possible this weekend. If President returns mines to Government, any miner who struck work or remained on strike would become liable immediately to severe penalties under Smith-Connally Act. President is faced with problem of deciding to whom he should hand mines. In June he handed them to Ickes but Ickes did not see eye to eye with War Labor Board and seemed to favour John L. Lewis at expense of stabilization programme.

It is difficult to predict John L. Lewis's course of action. Wildcat strikes began as soon as mines were handed back to the owners. UMW[9] have not taken any drastic action such as expulsion of strike leaders to stop them from spreading. While Lewis has outwardly opposed strikers he has at same time given inflammatory accounts of miners' grievances. If mines come under government control he can urge miners to work for Government without loss of face and Smith-Connally Act will discipline his followers for him. It should be borne in mind also that Lewis is applying for acceptance of his application to return to A F of L which has a fairly strong non-strike policy.

. . .

Taxation. The House Ways and Means Committee continues to struggle desperately to find some method of taxation which will not be too disastrously unpopular in an election year. Commentators on both sides begin to deplore the 'shameful cowardice' of both Treasury and Congress. Sales tax was finally

9 United Mine Workers Union.

turned down by the Committee but the fight for it will of course be revived on the floor of the House.

7 November 1943

MOSCOW AGREEMENT

Moscow Agreement[1] was greeted with excited jubilation on all sides. It was interpreted as a practical assurance of Allied unity, both during and after the war, and a major political victory against Axis endeavours to divide Allies and manoeuvre for a separate peace. Despite after-effects of influenza the President was in an exceptionally cheerful mood on 29 October when he 'jumped the gun' by announcing a 'tremendous success' at his press conference. In private conversation over weekend he pointed to inclusion of China[2] and rebuttal of those who talked of disunity amongst Allies as alone making conference worth while.

The interventionists in press and Congress led by supporters of Ball-Hatch Resolution gave way to an, at times, almost lyrical enthusiasm over post-war implications of Declaration and potentialities of new commissions[3] in providing practical nucleus for a general security system. Senator Carter Glass (Democrat, Virginia),[4] the aged champion of American participation in League of Nations in 1919–20 and of American intervention in 1939–41, speaking to Senate from his sickbed, dramatically pleaded that tragic drift to war of 1919–41 period should not be repeated. This gave powerful stimulus to drive which quickly got under way and resulted in endorsement by an overwhelming majority in Senate of article 4[5] of seven-point Moscow Declaration as an addition to Connally Resolution. Senate vote of 85 to 5 in favour of Resolution . . . left only diehard core of Hiram Johnson, Shipstead, Langer, Wheeler and Reynolds still in open opposition. The unexpectedly prolonged debate of which both Senate and nation has grown weary was thus swept to a happy and harmonious close by a wave of optimism about American foreign policy which had few if any precedents since start of war. Isolationists did not feel strong enough to make any frontal attack on Moscow Declaration despite strong and in some cases exaggerated interventionist interpretations which were placed on it. Some attempted to raise bogey of secret commitments. Others, cynically disregarding their one-time criticisms of such documents as Atlantic Charter, borrowed weapons of liberals and idealists in an unsuccessful drive led by Senator Danaher (Republican, Connecticut) to write Atlantic Charter into Connally Resolution with broad implication that this should be a sort of guarantee of frontiers of Poland and Baltic States. Senator

1 Communiqué issued at end of conference emphasizing closer collaboration in all spheres.
2 China joined other three in signing 'Declaration on General Security'
3 European Advisory Commission and Advisory Council re Italy.
4 Carter Glass, aged eighty-five, Democratic Senator from Virginia 1920–46.
5 Recognizing necessity of an international organization for peace and security.

Wheeler (Democrat, Montana) referred to our guarantee to Poland in February 1939.[6] If Russia, Wheeler asked, now kept Polish territory would Britain now come to Poland's aid against Russia ? The outcome of Conference is regarded by all sections of opinion in Washington as a great personal triumph for Mr Hull who is assured of an enthusiastic welcome home. President is happy to encourage this growth in Hull's popularity since it involves no threat to his own prestige, Hull's views are not likely to conflict with his own and any increase in Hull's already powerful influence over Congress and people means increased support for ratification of Administration's ultimate settlement of peace. Stettinius also paid his tribute and Hull's friends in press triumphantly reminded his former critics of their talk of his feebleness, senility and Russophobia, traced principles of Moscow Agreement back to Hull's speeches of September 1943 and described how his frankness and directness had contributed to reaching agreement in Moscow. Hull's influence would moreover, they pointed out, ensure it a more friendly consideration in Congress than would have been given to an agreement brought back by any other representative, e.g. Welles. Many officials in State Department had been particularly indignant at *Time* magazine's description of personnel of delegation as Russophobe reactionaries and Stettinius recently sent for Luce and upbraided him, adding somewhat indignantly that he (Stettinius) did not like being described as looking like Charlie Chaplin himself. Luce based his case on freedom of press and on a demand that State Department should disprove surely irrefutable facts about Dunn, Bohlen,[7] etc.

. . .

COAL STRIKE

As soon as coalmine strike became nationwide, President took over mines and handed them to Ickes for operation. President's directive to miners to return to their jobs now under government operation was however generally ignored in major producing states. With authorization of President, Ickes promptly negotiated an agreement with, and satisfactory to, John L. Lewis whilst miners were still on strike. The decision gives Lewis some 75 per cent of $2.00 extra a day for which he had asked in the spring. It is blow to War Labor Board who had refused to approve such an increase only last week and had disapproved of negotiation with union while its members were on strike. Representatives of public on board are reported to be bitterly charging that President, in taking Ickes's side, has let them down. They are now faced with choice of either suffering a serious, if not fatal, blow to their prestige or rejecting the new contract thus again precipitating a country-wide strike. The Ickes-Lewis contract is however likely to be approved by a majority of Board since labour representatives will probably be supported by owners' representatives who know that cost of increase in wages will ultimately come out of public funds.

Meanwhile success of John L. Lewis forced leaders of other unions into more

6 Guarantee issued by Neville Chamberlain to defend Polish independence, 31 March 1939.

7 Charles E. Bohlen, career diplomat, First Secretary in Moscow, 1942–4.

aggressive labour action and United Steel workers were understood to be preparing to reopen their wage agreements. Many observers now expect a slow but steady rise in prices in approaching months.

SUBSIDIES

In longest message he has ever sent to Congress the President this week demanded that Congress pass food subsidies as only means of rolling back food prices and maintaining stabilization plan. He promised farmers reasonable prices by this means. To consumers he declared that an abandonment of present policy 'would increase cost of living, bring about demands for increased wages and start a serious and dangerous cycle of inflation'. Briefly President's case is that so far as relationship of national income to war effort is concerned the cake is now baked and a slice for one section of population can only be enlarged at expense of another section. He left no doubt that he will veto any bill seeking to prevent use of subsidies. First reply of Farm Bloc was to charge President rather unrealistically with playing politics on eve of this week's elections, with 'sowing a lot of words in order to reap a lot of votes'.

. . .

ELECTIONS

Republican gains in this week's scattered elections give further evidence of right-wing trend in the country. They increase probability of a strongly Republican House after next year's elections but they shed little light on outcome of presidential struggle itself. . . . With few exceptions Republican candidates attained outstanding successes, even greater successes in some contests than Republicans appeared to expect. In winning governorships of marginal states of Kentucky and of New Jersey Republicans now control administrations of a majority of states in union. In capturing Lt-Governorship of New York they have assured a Republican control of state should Dewey be drafted into Republican nomination for Presidency. William C. Bullitt (Democrat) lost Philadelphia mayoral election. Hartford (Connecticut) elected a Republican Mayor for first time since New Deal sweep of 1932. Apart from a minor success in Cleveland mayoral contest Democrats could not extract any comfort from any of results. On the other hand claims of Republican leaders that results constitute a forecast of sweeping victories in 1944 are somewhat exaggerated.

Elections demonstrated an accentuation of Republican trend but they were fought on local issues and should not necessarily be treated as representing a vote of no confidence in Administration. Vote in New York State can be interpreted as a demonstration that voters did not wish to confuse Dewey's successful Republican administration by electing a Democratic Lt-Governor. Voters in New Jersey and in Kentucky may have been protesting against corrupt machine politics in those states. However should election of 1944 be fought on local issues it now appears likely that even if Roosevelt is elected President in 1944 he will be confronted by a Republican majority in House of Representatives and a reduced Democratic majority if not an actual minority in Senate. Farley and conservative anti-fourth-term Democrats are naturally exploiting result to warn Democratic Party that Roosevelt cannot win election for them, that American people are tired of being kicked around, etc. President himself takes an increasingly aloof and non-partisan view of Democratic politics and in a private conversation with a member of my staff attributed failure of Democrats partly to fact that their organizations are stale and tired after a decade in power. In so far as results demonstrate successful working of Republican Party machines results should give more satisfaction to routine Republican leaders than to Willkie section of party. . . .

One feature of election results that has attracted considerable attention has been failure of organized labour to swing decisive blocs of votes or outbalance rural Republican votes despite strenuous and enthusiastic efforts of labour organized in contests in New York, New Jersey and Detroit.

14 November 1943

Moscow pact. General satisfaction with the results of the Moscow Conference has reached a climax with Hull's triumphant return, accompanied by only expected reservations by the isolationists and disgruntled European minority groups. Krock asserted that the Four-Power Declaration largely followed the lines of Hull's thought, had been conceived by the Secretary over a year-and-a-half ago, and steadily developed by the Political and Security Advisory Committees of the State Department (headed by Welles and Norman Davis[1] respectively) amid unseemly and ignorant abuse of Hull and the Department by the New Dealers. This interpretation of events is now largely accepted by more impartial opinion-forming groups and writers. The fact that approval of the Moscow Pact can be combined with opposition to the New Deal 'muddlers' gives it a permanent bedrock of conservative support. The President has caught the mood and deliberately went out of his way to pay homage to Hull by meeting him at the airport. According to White House sources the President is still obsessed by the nightmare of Wilson's fate in 1918 and perceives in Hull's role a strong guarantee of keeping conservative opinion in the Senate and in the Government on co-operationist lines in the making of the peace. So far as this calculation is justified, it is clearly equally in our own interest to support the belief of the dominant part played by American initiative in the matter. The inclusion of the Moscow formula in the Connally Resolution has to some degree placated the 'ginger group' of internationalists led by Senators Pepper and Ball, and although there is still some talk heard among liberal critics of unnecessary loop-holes left by the too general terms of the Resolution, the view that Connally averted disordered and acrimonious debate by manoeuvring the rejection of all the offered

1 Norman H. Davis, career diplomat, Under-Secretary of State under Woodrow Wilson, Chairman of American Red Cross.

amendments is held by several political observers, including Lippmann, who privately said that a long and bitter debate would almost certainly have led to a feebler compromise. For the moment public opinion has crystallized strongly around a solution which is regarded as both enlightened and realistic, and isolationism has been forced to content itself with ineffectual sniping around the edges. The influence of the crusade begun by the Protestant churches, inspired by John Foster Dulles[2] and Senator Ball, which has sent evangelists to preach internationalism in the churches, is not to be underestimated.

The disgruntled. Talk of betrayal of the border states to Russia, the dangers of four-power politics, and emphasis on the inclusion of safeguards of sovereignty which alone enabled arch-isolationists like Senators Nye or Brooks to vote for the Resolution, is not widespread, and to be found only in definitely isolationist circles. . . . As for minority groups, Polish officials, in a mood of despair, tell their friends that they regard Moscow as a betrayal by their United States and British allies which they cannot be expected not to resist. The relatively moderate release issued by the Polish Ambassador is, I am told, not to be taken as an index of the very bitter feeling aroused. As, however, the influential Catholic weekly *Commonweal* has suddenly begun to discourse on the shortcomings of the Polish state, it may be assumed that any effort by the Poles to mobilize general Catholic opinion on their side will not get very far unless other unexpected developments come to their support. The Yugoslav officials are naturally uttering loudly about the evidences of alleged British abandonment of Mihajlovic as stressed in newspaper despatches reporting General Wilson's recent statement. The Greek Embassy continues to be engrossed in internecine warfare, with the very vocal local opponents of King George apparently led by an official of Greek origin in the Office of Strategic Services. The Baltic representatives are suffering in silence. None of this amounts to much effective opposition either in public or private.

Labour. The unpopularity of John L. Lewis has reached the highest peak yet achieved even by him. The recent granting of his wage demands by Ickes is interpreted as a crushing blow to the Administration and the public by the majority of the press, a public humiliation of the War Labor Board and a general disaster. The public and business members of the War Labor Board do not disguise their nervousness of the results on the rest of labour. Ickes's allies say privately that but for this the New York-Washington service might have ceased functioning for lack of fuel a week ago. Whether or not this is special pleading to justify Ickes's 'appeasement' of labour, there is no doubt that Lewis has handsomely won his 1943 campaign, and the rest of labour – notably railroad workers dissatisfied by Vinson's refusal to grant their wage demands, as well as Murray's steel workers – have now no alternative but to press on with their own campaigns

2 John Foster Dulles, corporation lawyer and eminent Presbyterian layman, later (1953–9) Secretary of State.

with the full force of strike threats, etc. Philip Murray of the CIO is said to be in a distressed state, and the failure at the CIO Convention to pronounce for a Roosevelt fourth term is described by observers as directly due to dissatisfaction at the surrender to Lewis. Many think that the AF of L can now scarcely take long to readmit him into its ranks. Feeling against Ickes, who is accused of unscrupulous self-seeking, is hot in the Byrnes-Vinson entourage. Attacks on labour by farm leaders and spokesmen for industrialists have naturally increased in vigour, and the difficulties of the Administration in pushing its subsidies and tax policies through Congress (the House has so far agreed to two of the requested twelve billions taxation) have been materially increased by Lewis's coup, which has put a formidable weapon into the hands of the opposition. I am told that a good deal of anti-Roosevelt bargaining is going on between such industrial leaders as Eric Johnston and Roosevelt's many enemies in the AF of L.

Anti-British sentiment. The aftermath of five Senators still continues. Appointment of a Senate Sub-Committee containing Nye, Tydings and Brooks by Appropriations Committee to investigate Lend-Lease was conceived in no very friendly spirit and effects upon mood which prompted it of the publicity received by Mutual Aid White Paper remains to be seen. Initial reaction to it and President's covering message are favourable on the whole but it is far too early to judge. Nye complains that amount of information 'falls far short' of what is wanted and this is likely to be Anglophobe line. Actual anti-British sentiment may or may not have increased but various politicians have begun to report its increase to British and American friends and mere fact that this should have become a favourite topic of Washington after-dinner discussion – in a politely commiserating tone if British visitors are present – is in itself regrettable. If this indicates a genuine development it is mostly due to a shift of national attention from the war (which despite warnings by highest British and American authorities is on whole regarded as tending fast to inevitable victory) to post-war problems and first and foremost of these prospect of Anglo-American economic rivalry.

UNRRA. Conference got off to a good start[3] against background of relatively friendly press comment very different from hostile barrage which preceded Hot Springs Food Conference in the spring. . . . Observers in Atlantic City report mood as cordial and say that Acheson has things well in hand. He was apparently genuinely reluctant to accept chairmanship of Council which was in effect thrust upon him. Opening of conference coincided with Hoover's statements before a congressional committee defending his relief proposals and an attack on British brutality and part played by this Embassy in blocking Quaker Relief plans made by Howard Kershner,[4] the Quakers' European Director, in 1939–40.

3 Meeting of UNRRA Committee at Atlantic City of 10 November.
4 Howard E. Kershner, author, lecturer, director of relief in Europe for American Friends Committee 1939–42.

Refugees. Gillette's motion in Senate to set up a twelve-man special congressional committee to cope with problems of European refugees is not taken too seriously by anyone and is in nature of political demonstration rather than a concrete proposal. Willkie and Dewey have both supported demand of opening of Palestine for Jewish immigration, Willkie's statement being in strong terms.

. . .

Dewey. There is evidence that Dewey, popular as he is, is genuinely determined not to run for the Presidency since he calculates that even if this causes Willkie to get the nomination, the latter will either be defeated by Roosevelt and so be finally eliminated, or, if elected, will inherit the troubled post-war years which he will probably mismanage, allowing Dewey to be elected at a later period as a figure of unblemished repute and a great administrator. I saw Willkie recently and he is very confident, both about the general Republican prospects and his own, the more so now that Bricker has definitely declared his intention to stand. He says that it is nothing less than an insult to Governor Dewey and General MacArthur to suggest that they are not men of honour or not telling the truth in their disavowal of presidential ambitions. Willkie is said to be backed by the strongest financial interests in the East, including the Morgans and powerful press interest and insurance companies. The efforts of John D. Hamilton, ex-chairman of the Republican Party,[5] to mobilize feeling against him in the Middle West have so far borne no more conspicuous fruit than Farley's similar efforts on the anti-Roosevelt front, but he has not been long at work. The sudden suggestion by Senator Johnson[6] (Democrat) of Colorado to draft General Marshall as Democratic candidate drew a general blank, and Marshall himself has been a good deal disturbed and annoyed at the suggestion. MacArthur as a candidate of the Republican old guard, should Bricker finally prove useless, should not be overlooked.

Labour politics. Hillman has told various persons (picked up by *Time* magazine) that he had collected a pro-Roosevelt fund of $5 million. Those allegedly in the know say that Democratic Chairman Walker has only $1 million at his disposal, which would give labour a very considerable voice in Democratic councils. Wallace's followers are busy rallying liberal and labour opinion around him, with much success in the CIO. They declare that more than three million communications have arrived at the White House pressing for Wallace's renomination as Vice-President. This is in order to convince the President that he would lose more labour and liberal votes by dropping Wallace than he would gain by nominating a 'safer' man like Rayburn or Byrnes.

22 November 1943

Internal tensions. The lobbies are working overtime. A concerted attack is in full blast upon government agricultural subsidies. Representatives of the Farm Bloc,

5 John D. Hamilton, lawyer, Chairman of Republican National Committee 1936–40.
6 Edwin Carl Johnson, Democratic Governor of Colorado 1933–7, Senator since 1937.

bankers, manufacturers, are pouring into Washington from all corners of the United States, yearning for the restoration of the 'law of supply and demand', i.e. booming prices and profits restricted only by very limited taxation. This, coming together with the severe pressure exercised by the railroad unions to overturn Judge Vinson's refusal to break the 'Little Steel formula' in their favour, has at last made inflation an immediate menace. The railroad (and for that matter steel, leather and other workers) naturally cannot see why their wage demands are rejected when those of Lewis's miners have been granted so freely. The railroad unions have more wealth, prestige and political support than any other in the country. The mere fact that the Administration, and in particular Vinson, whose support of price regulation has angered the lobbies and pressure groups, are their chief opponents, has paradoxically assured the railroad workers of conservative congressional support against the Administration. The general mood of grab-as-grab-can, with prospects of huge wartime profits tantalizing industry and farmers and labour alike, has provoked some sincere indignation among the general public and its spokesmen such as Clapper. The Government's original tax bill seems definitely dead and buried by Senator George, who evidently supposes that one sixth of the sum originally demanded (twelve billions) will suffice to skim off the vastly increased purchasing power of the public. The OPA, under its third director, the 'sound' business executive Bowles, is nevertheless again under savage attack. Byrnes's stock has slumped as a result of alleged ineffectiveness, and he looks like becoming a second Donald Nelson. Meanwhile, the appointment of Baruch some weeks ago to organize post-war economic planning and in particular the peacetime reconversion of United States industry has pleased the conservatives. Nelson has apparently had to be reassured by the President who explained that Baruch's function was advisory and that the execution of post-war readjustment would belong to WPB. A member of my staff had a very gloomy picture of the post-war United States situation drawn for him by the disgruntled Leon Henderson, now in private practice, who sharply disagreed with optimistic official prognostications of a post-war boom, and held that lack of confidence and security will inhibit post-war investment and production. As for Baruch, a member of my staff was told by a close White House collaborator of his that despite his reputation for audacity and imagination, Baruch has become a complete safety-firster, unlikely to back any scheme unless it had first received virtually universal approbation, and so far from being a grey eminence, exercises little genuine influence on events. His value resides in the past prestige which his name enjoys with the general public and, in particular, with the press.

· · ·

Republican tactics. The Bricker-Landon-John D. Hamilton-Hoover tactic is entirely concerned with thwarting Willkie, and Bricker may be expected to make some initial gains. Hamilton and Landon are at present still engaged in persuading the various state delegations to nominate 'favourite sons' for the Republican

Convention. This is to prevent a coagulation in favour of Willkie by a majority of Republican electoral votes, and to create a kind of open stock exchange in which votes can be traded at the last moment by the old-line professionals who it must be assumed are against Willkie, and might come to agreement on some alternative candidate, whether Bricker or someone else. It is some tribute to Willkie's present lead that such guerrilla tactics have to be pursued by his opponents in an effort to scatter his strength, since a frontal assault seems impolitic. Willkie has publicly protested against these squalid stratagems, and professes great confidence in his ability to defeat them. I find in some well-informed quarters the feeling that the Republican handkerchief will finally come down on Dewey, but nothing clear is likely to emerge out of this pattern until at the earliest the spring of 1944. Senator Reynolds, chairman of the Military Affairs Committee, a pro-Fascist Democrat and regular hero of the 'lunatic', i.e. Fascist, fringe, has at last proved too much for even North Carolina; as no political organization seems prepared to support him, he has said he will not (to general relief) seek re-election. Senator Nye is talking about a third party to oppose the equally fatal internationalist platforms of the Democrats and the Republicans. As the latest champion of self-determination he asserted that the Germans are entitled to Fascism after the war if that is their will. None of this need be taken too seriously.

27 November 1943

.   .   .

Mosley. A disproportionate amount of attention has been given in press and radio here to the Mosley [1] agitation in England. There is relatively little comment, but wide interest in the demonstrations against his release, and although a handful of newspapers support His Majesty's Government's position, the general tone is one of support for the Labour protests which have been very copiously reported from London. The Communist press is naturally most voluble about this but interest in the case is very widespread, and a member of my staff, recently returned from Missouri, reports that academic groups he visited questioned him on this topic more pressingly than even on such hoary issues as India, Second Front, etc. Mr Morrison's speech has so far made little impression. It should occasion no surprise that the only newspapers which virtually omitted all mention of the Mosley affair are the two Patterson papers.

.   .   .

The Chinese Exclusion Act. The President is about to sign a bill which rectifies a 'historic mistake' by removing the Oriental Exclusion Laws from the statute book. While the actual effect of this will admit no more than 105 Chinese per

---

1 Sir Oswald Mosley, leader of the British Union of Fascists, was detained under the Government's emergency powers in May 1940 ; his release in November 1943 by Herbert Morrison as Home Secretary, owing to a serious deterioration in his health, provoked widespread protests.

annum into the United States, the moral effect of this gesture was emphasized by the President. Sinophile sentiment has received a strong fillip from the reports of the five Senators who took a very strongly pro-Chinese attitude on arrival and have privately criticized both British and American local policies in unoccupied China.

29 November 1943

Internal tensions: subsidies to growers and processors. War news was overshadowed by House debate on subsidies which ended in an amendment to outlaw them, voted by 173 to 102. Bill still has to come before Senate and may, if it passes, be vetoed by President. If vote is indication of real relative strength of parties, veto may stick as less than overriding two-thirds majority voted for amendment. Moreover certain members may have voted against subsidies to please their farm constituents while hoping that presidential veto would in fact protect them from economic consequences of their action. Nevertheless this defeat of Administration is important both because of possible effects on national economy if subsidies are killed off, removing effective control of profits, and because it underlines relative helplessness of Administration on domestic issues when it is opposed by entrenched interests and lobbies. Vote for amendment seemed mostly composed (it was a voice vote and not officially attributed) of Farm Bloc which stood solid, anti-New Deal Southern Democrats who to some degree overlap with Farm Bloc, and some anti-Administration Republicans. One of clearest divisions was that between urban and rural Congressmen. Urban (or consumer) bloc was poorly organized and last-minute appeal to housewives to consider effect which sudden leap in prices would have upon their lives fell completely flat. Principal strain which ran through debate was distrust of Administration's efficiency or fairness in carrying out any form of federal control. Fulbright (Democrat, Arkansas, who is in all ways enlightened enough) put this most clearly:

> in spite of theoretical soundness of subsidies . . . neither people nor this Congress believes that programme will be efficiently or properly administered. Reason for this . . . is found in a long series of relatively insignificant instances of unwise but more especially arbitrary actions of various administrators. . . . In short we have little confidence in wisdom and efficiency of those agencies that must administer programme.

This is refrain today most frequently heard in all connexions in all parts of United States.

Fathers draft. Conflict over drafting of pre-Pearl Harbor fathers which again may lead to a presidential veto of their reservation of deferment is but another instance of anti-Administration current which on all but foreign policy is powerfully obstructing Government's main policies. It does not indeed appear to be disturbing war production (Nelson's latest statistics on this are most encouraging) but it naturally gives a sense of constant insecurity to those members of Administration who are engaged on planning for national or international economic future and makes for search for safety in short-term programmes and avoidances of all long-term commitments.

Foreign v. Home Policy and Congress. It appears clear that while President's support of Hull has yielded rich returns in terms of national support of his foreign policy, his specialists in handling of Congress on internal policy, Messrs Byrnes and Vinson, have not despite their congressional connexions succeeded in achieving a dependable working relationship with their old colleagues. Perhaps even superior skill would not have availed in face of tough, old-established economic pressure groups. Any estimate of international economic collaboration by United States must take into primary consideration very specific intentions of these groups which so clearly know what they want. Their purposes and their tactics are, as Administration has learnt to its frequent cost, relatively little subject to fluctuations of public opinion and remain a constant, definite and more or less predictable factor where all else is so vague and liable to sudden mercurial changes of national mood. And so far as labour has a consistent political policy (as e.g. in case of AF of L) it now tends to look for a direct working arrangement with industrial groups if only as reinsurance against defeat of its anyhow none too reliable Administration allies.

UNRRA. Press has published inaccurate but friendly accounts of conference and irreducible opposition has not been disturbingly vocal. United Kingdom Delegation has covered itself with considerable glory and has thus far under capable management of Colonel Llewellin[1] achieved all its main objectives. It should be emphasized that this could scarcely have been possible without closest relations between United Kingdom and United States Delegation. Acheson kept unswervingly to general understanding arrived at when Mr Law was here and displayed a loyalty, wisdom and unexpected strength which made co-operation with American Delegation most fruitful factor in situation. Russians were also co-operative.

. . .

Most conspicuous result thus far is emergence of Combined Boards[2] with unimpaired and indeed increased importance. A new and more favourable attitude to Boards was shown by Americans. Latter admitted privately to official fear of excessive shift of balance to London occurring. Satisfactory settlement of Lehman's claims was reached whereby *paying* Allies continue applying for relief directly to Combined Boards (while non-payers go direct to UNRRA) but Boards do not allocate materials in short supply without consultation with Lehman re-

1 J.J.Llewellin, Minister Resident in Washington for Supply and Head of the UK Delegation to UNRRA Conference.
2 See n.3, 4 February 1942.

garding priority of allocation, etc. This gives Lehman more than purely advisory but less than veto function *vis-à-vis* Combined Boards. Old OFRRO officials are inclined to be plaintive about this and compare alleged domination of Big-Three at Atlantic City unfavourably to more 'democratic' procedures at Hot Springs but such disgruntlement on part of these woolly-minded individuals seems best proof of practical utility of actual decisions reached. General prospects for international conferences held in United States appear much improved by general efficiency of arrangements, particularly those for public relations, and strong popular prejudice here which initial handling of press by Administration at Food Conference had excited seems to be in process of dissipation.

Armed Forces vote. Lucas bill[3] to enable soldiers abroad to vote in presidential election (though it seems not in primaries) has stirred up powerful opposition among Southern Democrats who correctly perceive there is immediate danger to poll tax system since Southern coloured soldiers cannot well be prevented from voting with their white comrades, which would establish a powerful new precedent, and from Republican Old Guard which appears to believe from evidence before them that Roosevelt remains overwhelmingly popular with younger soldiers (i.e. vast majority) and that while Willkie may conceivably draw off some of these neither Dewey nor Bricker nor any other conservative has faintest real hold upon them. Hence artificial barrage of Republican criticism of voting methods suggested, talk of danger of government propaganda about to be unloosed on innocents abroad by OWI, and so forth. Administration has patiently answered most of these charges but as most of them are specious and politically inspired answers have made no real difference to opposition, leaders of which are Senators Taft for Republicans and Connally for Democrats. But opposition is in an embarrassing position since it cannot very well afford to be accused of wishing to deprive 'soldier boys' of an opportunity to vote in face of all efforts of the President and Administration to give them that right.

General Patton. Patton affair[4] has blossomed forth into national scandal and absorbs newspapers, radio and conversation to an absurd degree. Much abused Drew Pearson has been acclaimed by several newspapers as a fearless champion of popular rights and true benefactor of nation against a stupid and obscurantist military authority, and while extenuating circumstances are urged in favour of Patton his guilt is held almost universally to be sufficient to justify his removal from Field Command, and voices of those few in Congress and in press who wish to allow Eisenhower to act as he thinks best are for moment drowned by far vaster clamour of those who demand immediate disciplinary action. Senate Military Affairs Committee is to hold an enquiry and Stimson's declaration that he and Marshall have adopted a policy of giving full freedom of appointment to

3 Scott W. Lucas, Democratic Senator from Illinois since 1939.
4 Uproar occasioned when General Patton allegedly slapped an invalid soldier in hospital.

theatre commanders and have faith in Eisenhower has not allayed storm. While facts were known to a number of newspapers and individuals here for a month, method by which it was allowed to leak, then denied, then admitted by Army authorities is a model of incompetent handling. Incident itself will doubtless blow over soon but fact that such an episode can preoccupy national attention to overshadowing of all else carries its own moral. Left-wing press has tried to turn it into a political drive against conservative Army generals. Apart from managing to turn fresh limelight on General Somervell, who is now accused of engineering a doubtful army contract for Canadian oil, it has not succeeded.

5 December 1943

Cairo Conference. [1] Anglo-American-Chinese statement on Japan which naturally drove off other news from front pages (after considerable premature publicity) was received with mild acclamation. Determination to compress Japan ruthlessly fits American mood, and inclusion of the Chiang Kai-sheks at Cairo has aroused expected enthusiasm. Swing's suggestion that Cairo indicates a move in British policy away from a traditional interest in a strong Japan has been echoed in various quarters. A motley group including congressional isolationist core have also pointed to the silence over post-war status of Hong Kong, French Indo-China, Dutch East Indies and Sakhalin.

. . . The fact that Russia is held to have given tacit approval to the declaration on Japan is greeted with warm satisfaction by those who were genuinely nervous of the degree of Russian collaboration on Pacific matters even after the Moscow Conference, and there is renewed optimistic talk about acquiring Russian Pacific bases.

.   .   .

6 December 1943

.   .   .

REPUBLICAN POLITICS

(A) *Willkie in the South.* Willkie has been touring the solid South. While he cannot hope to sway it to a Republican banner, he evidently hopes to breed discontent with the present Administration and to capture the Republican convention delegates from the South, who traditionally vote with Ohio, i.e. Taft and Bricker. There is no evidence that his oratory has produced any unexpected results. A typical episode was reported from Houston (Texas) where a prominent local Republican millionaire had addressed a series of politically embarrassing questions to Willkie. Willkie at his meeting professed never to have heard his name, whereupon the man read out two letters in which Willkie had addressed him as 'My dear Roy', a *contretemps* which Willkie does not appear to have

1 Held 22–26 November and attended by Churchill, Roosevelt and Chiang Kai-shek.

carried off with his usual aplomb. The book written by Nelson Sparks, ex-mayor of Akron, Ohio, a notorious vigilante, and Frank Gannett's [1] campaign manager in 1940, entitled *One Man – Wendell Willkie,* purporting to describe the financial dealings preceding Willkie's nomination in 1940, including the alleged part played by Tom Lamont, Mrs Ogden Reid, [2] Lord Lothian, [3] etc., has not, outside the isolationist press, caused much of a stir. One or two of the isolationist Michigan gang in Congress are demanding investigation of the charges. It is not a skilful piece of work, and although issued in the same format as Willkie's own *One World* does not appear to be selling at all rapidly.

(B) A recent Kentucky by-election which led to the victory of a Republican by an unexpectedly large majority underlines, if it needs underlining, the unmistakable Republican swing now noticeable everywhere. Whatever the excuses adduced by the Democrats for other similar results, the Kentucky episode cannot be explained away by any special pleading, as the Republican majority is considerably higher in this generally Democratic district than its Democratic majority of the last election, and this has been gleefully emphasized by Krock and other anti-Administration spokesmen. In the meanwhile, John D.M. Hamilton, who has been touring the Middle and West with funds allegedly supplied by Joseph Pew, [4] the Pennsylvania Sun Oil magnate, who is a ferociously anti-Willkie-ite, has taken the trouble to deny that he is engaged on a 'stop Willkie' or indeed 'stop anybody' campaign. This denial, echoed by Landon, has deceived no one. Stassen's supporters are said to be collecting strength for their man, starting with the Nebraska primaries and those of his own Minnesota, whose Republican committees have decided to offer him as presidential candidate. According to *Time* magazine they are carefully refraining from invasion of states which propose to offer 'favourite sons' [5] to the conventions, hoping thereby to avoid fights now and to secure allegiance at a later stage, when a deadlock between, say, Dewey and Willkie may make room for the blameless and high-minded Stassen, with his unimpeachably conservative record on domestic legislation. The latest definite candidate for the Presidency is Representative Everett M. Dirksen of Illinois, a well-known Republican economy zealot and terror of New Deal agencies, a capable and energetic reactionary who insists that he is standing not as a political manoeuvre or for bargaining purposes but in the genuine hope of being elected President. . . .

. . .

Overseas United States Soldiers' Vote. The Administration bill to give voting powers to some eleven million men and women in the United States armed forces abroad was killed in the Senate by 42 to 37 (24 Democratic and 18 Republican

1 Frank Gannett, publisher of a chain of newspapers circulating in upper New York State.

2 Helen R. Reid, wife of the publisher of the *New York Herald Tribune.*

3 Philip Kerr, Lord Lothian, British Ambassador to Washington 1939–40.

4 Joseph N. Pew devoted his fortune since 1933 to defeating Roosevelt and promoting the most conservative Republican candidates possible.

5 Favourite son – a candidate whose own state delegation is committed to voting for him on the first ballot.

v. 25 Democratic and 12 Republican). The defeat of the bill was engineered principally by the Southern opposition, thirteen of whom came from poll tax states. The desire to prevent a breach in the poll tax political structure was the paramount Southern consideration. . . . As for the Republicans, their motive was different from that of Southerners, since they fear the reported pro-Roosevelt sentiment among the troops abroad. . . .

The proposal which has been substituted by the Senate retains to the states control of voting qualifications, which guarantees segregation of coloured troops on the part of states which demand it, and thus provides infinitely wider opportunity for local manipulation. Senator Lucas, therefore, described the substitute adopted by the Senate (42 *v*. 37) as 'worse than nothing' ; the bill now goes to the House, whose Privileges and Elections Committee has already voted in its favour (9 *v*. 4). The Bill merely 'recommends' that each state make available to its overseas citizens facilities for voting, leaving it to their discretion to do what they please. . . .

11 December 1943

Pro- and Anti-Russianism. Presence of Stalin at Tehran [1] and immensely wide publicity given to meeting and to interchange of courtesies between Prime Minister, the President and Stalin has served to maintain enthusiasm originally aroused by Moscow Conference. According to Consular reports the nationwide current of feeling more favourable to Russia and of internationalist sentiment is rising still. Anti-Russian front is now equally clearly discernible and consists principally of Catholic hierarchy, national minorities' press (especially German and Polish) and that strong section of Republican Party which is closest to more isolationist circles in services, in big business and among Midwestern politicians. Ex-Governor Landon, for example, uttered sharp public criticism of Pact and his friends, plainly worried by this tactical blunder, quickly sent Hoover to set him right. A day later Hoover duly announced that ex-Governor Landon had quite clearly not meant what he had so clearly said and that he was like everyone else fundamentally in favour of Moscow Pact, etc.

Publicity. Criticism both official and in American press of the publicity for Conferences had risen to flood proportions. No one had a kind word for British and resentment against original Reuters 'scoop'[2] despite Tass's and subsequent scoops is still genuine and raw. Minister of Information's defence has been inadequately quoted and summarily dismissed in press. Elmer Davis is viewed as a feeble and pathetic figure more in need of help himself than capable of doing

---

1 Tehran Conference, 28 November–1 December, attended by Churchill, Roosevelt and Stalin.

2 Reuters reported the Cairo Conference (held, for security reasons, in great secrecy) twenty-four hours before the official release time. This turned out to be due to accident of a Reuters' man passing through Cairo *en route* to London from Chungking, who gave the story to the Reuters' representative at Lisbon when his plane stopped there.

anything for others, while Byron Price, the Chief Censor, has found it necessary to issue a statement begging press to take no notice of any further attempt to restrain them from publishing information unless it comes from only body authorized to act in matter, i.e. civilian censorship authorities. This doubtless refers to Patton incident but is meant no less as a general underlining of solidarity of United States Censorship with press against bullying from within and 'unethical' competition by foreign press services and is probably intended to allay storm of criticism of alleged Administration incompetence in protecting American international interests. . . .

General Smuts's speech.[3] There has been surprisingly little press and radio reaction to Smuts's speech (such as there is was mostly critical) but a great deal of private talk in Washington. It is probable that people here have so far only read versions sent by American correspondents which did not include passages about Commonwealth and Empire. Speech is regarded as somewhat puzzling and only genuine veneration in which Smuts is held by almost everyone here prevents a more critical attitude from being adopted. There is a good deal of questioning whether this founder and champion of the League can have come to advocate a 'naked' balance of power view which makes it imperative for Britain to surround herself with European satellites solely for purpose of propping herself up against Russia on one hand and United States on other. On other hand Smuts's flat statement that an Anglo-American condominium was not feasible or desirable echoes much sentiment prevalent here and is a very useful corrective to view too often taken that we come as a suppliant seeking an American alliance because without it we should be unable to hold our own in a post-war world dominated by Russia. Mixture of imperial sentiment and confession of economic weakness in speech are ingredients calculated to secure least sympathy in this country. The omission of reference to China was, of course, remarked, and French here are very offended about role or absence of it to which they are relegated, but it is doubtless salutary to have existence of our strong pro-European sentiment conveyed and it could have come from no one so well as Smuts whose prestige amongst opinion-forming persons and groups here is perhaps second only to that of the Prime Minister, since his upbringing, personality and general outlook are almost too perfect an embodiment of American national ideal combination of benign practical wisdom with vision, strength and enterprise of rugged pioneer.

Mr Rayburn and Mr Knox's speeches. So sharp have discordant xenophobe voices evidently become, that Speaker Rayburn, long embodiment of sanity and good sense, who speaks from floor only on solemn occasions, delivered a much applauded address to House warning against insidious effect domestically of discussion of Russia's or Britain's post-war ambitions and their possible detrimental

3 On 25 November to Empire Parliamentary Association in London. It advocated, *inter alia*, regional groupings in Commonwealth centred around principal Dominions and United Kingdom.

effects on America's future. An eloquent and intensely pro-British speech was delivered by Secretary Knox stressing community of interests between Britain and United States since foundation of American Republic, citing many instances in which British power alone, particularly on oceans, rescued the growing Republic, and inveighing against deep-rooted delusion that British inevitably competed with and outwitted the innocent Yankees. He ended with declaration that world could and would be made secure only by inevitable co-operation of British and American Navies in policing the sea lanes of world. Knox had shown me his speech in advance and had it approved by Mr Hull. It is all too rarely that we get such warmth in public statements about us and this very friendly attitude on Knox's part should be remembered when there may be disposition to criticize him for taking up an occasionally 'tough' attitude about Pacific bases, etc.

13 December 1943

Republican politics. The anti-Willkie forces are on the march on several fronts. Congresswoman Clare Booth told a member of my staff that in her opinion Willkie was done for, that it all happened with great suddenness, but that suddenly and simultaneously various Republican leaders had come to the unanimous conviction that he was not merely an undesirable but an easily avoidable candidate. Henry Luce, however, according to all available information, shows no disposition as yet to start selling his shares in Willkie, nor do the Morgan interests. Willkie's addresses to Senate and House Republicans appear not to have turned out well for him. He is reported to have taken the same overbearing tone before both bodies, saying in effect, that he was a man of destiny whom the Republican Party, and indeed the nation, needed, whether they knew it or not ; that nothing could stop his rise to power, and that he did not, therefore, care whether he obtained their support, since, when the hour came, they would find that they had no alternative. The mystical assurance of a dedicated man, which he had adopted some months ago before the disgruntled Republicans of Indiana, apparently failed to stir the seasoned congressional politicians, and lowered Willkie's stock in his own party, although perhaps not fatally as yet. Willkie stock is the most speculative article in the political market and follows a more zigzag course than any other commodity.

The appointment of Charles Halleck[1] to succeed Ditter[2] as chairman of the Congressional Republican Committee, although he represents Indiana and moved Willkie's candidature at the Republican Convention in 1940, does not augur well for Willkie. Halleck's voting record has since then been isolationist and his popularity with the majority of Republican Congressmen is social and not political. This choice is the clearest single indication yet that despite alleged change of heart what still counts most among Republicans is the machine and not an enlightened attitude to world affairs.

1 Charles A.Halleck, Republican Congressman from Indiana since 1935.
2 John William Ditter, Republican Congressman from Pennsylvania 1933–43.

Thus ex-Governor Landon, the most energetic of the anti-Willkie-ites, is immensely busy at present, and has emerged as a prominent standard-bearer of the old guard. His recently declared disapproval of the Moscow Pact obviously represents the considered stand of his wing of the party on international relations (Willkie said that if this was the party's stand they should seek a leader other than himself) and his Washington press allies (one of whom tried to sound out a member of my staff) are talking fairly openly about the necessity for an alliance with Britain – under President Dewey or President MacArthur – to protect the Western World against Russian influence. Landon has publicly proclaimed Dewey as the best hope of the party in 1944, which Dewey for once did not trouble to deny, allowing himself to be photographed with Landon at a New York press conference. Dewey's unexpected failure to decline the proffered crown has, of course, stirred speculation about the renewed possibility of his candidature, especially as Landon, according to the gossips, gave Dewey tangible proofs based on Hamilton's trip to the recent rapid growth of his popularity in the Middle West.

Republican plans at present appear to contemplate the entrance of a number of candidates – Bricker, Dewey, Willkie, MacArthur, Stassen, Dirksen – for the presidential primaries, each backed by a respectable number of nominations, to be followed by the usual elimination of those with least support, and the emergence of Dewey in the final heat. At present, however, all is still speculation and darkness.

·   ·   ·

Subsidies. Justice Byrnes delivered a very forthright radio address, warning the country that if the present tactics of pressure groups succeed in breaking through the anti-inflationary 'line' held by the Administration, the decent and prosperous post-war life hoped for by the American people could not be built. Byrnes, who understands Congress well, must have been aware that such an appeal over the heads of the Farm Bloc and conservative Democrats would add to their irritation and must have judged the situation to be serious enough to warrant this step. The Farm Bloc immediately riposted with a statement issued at a Farm Bureau meeting in Chicago and Chester Davis, the ex-War Food Administrator, while conceding that farm prices were at present fair enough, promptly denounced subsidies as a direct stimulus to inflation.

·   ·   ·

AF of L. The three main wings of labour are pursuing their respective paths. The AF of L is inert as usual. Its President, Green, has spoken to denounce the rumoured Russian plan to press Germans after the victory into armies of labourers for the rebuilding of the Russian economy destroyed by the Germans, as the creation of 'slave labour' ruinous to the interests of world labour in general and contrary to the ends for which this war is being fought. This is the line with the consistently anti-Soviet line of the AF of L leadership, and betrays the influence of local German social democrats to whom AF of L leaders lend a willing ear provided that their anti-Communist record is guaranteed beyond question.

CIO. Support of President Roosevelt continues steadily, and Sidney Hillman, organizer of its political campaign, claims that his war chest of over $5 million is the one solid factor in the situation. The campaign to secure sufficient support for Wallace to assure him of a place on the Democratic ticket continues sporadically.

John L.Lewis. Negotiations with the mine owners are pursuing a tortuous course and are still uncompleted. The *United Mine Workers Journal* is, with some justice, accused by the liberal press of having become a kind of labour version of the *Chicago Tribune,* inasmuch as it attacks the Administration, the prosecution of the war as too long and costly, the Russians, the British (Laski is singled out as a British agent of the White House 'clique' with the function of selling British labour to British capitalists) and so forth. The ties between John L.Lewis and the reactionary Republicans seems as strong as ever.

. . .

Wages. The virtually unanimous vote of the Senate to accede to the demands of the Railroad Brotherhoods for a wage raise denied them by Messrs Byrnes and Vinson is partly the result of pressure by the railroad lobby (which is prepared to come to terms with the exceptionally powerful and well-organized railroad unions), partly a desire to spite the Administration, partly genuine belief that Vinson is being mulish over a trivial issue. But this intrusion into executive action by Congress shakes the foundation of Vinson's authority, and although he does not appear to be contemplating resignation as yet, a new effort will, it seems, be made to convince key Democrats of Congress privately that their present behaviour is ruinous alike to their party and to the economic welfare of the United States. If this fails, Vinson says he will resign.

20 December 1943

Aftermath of Cairo and Tehran. . . . There is a striking contrast between the virtually universal enthusiasm with which the Moscow agreement and Hull's part in it were greeted, and the somewhat tepid approval of the President's activities. This is doubtless largely due to the fact that the Moscow declaration relieved anxieties and was relatively concrete in content. But there is also a very noticeable contrast between the confidence reposed in Hull and the mixture of admiration for the President's skill in negotiation, with fear of 'cleverness', and suspicion of an insufficiency of principle and 'Americanism' on his part, a powerful ingredient in the formation of public opinion here. A journalist told a member of my staff that a high State Department official told him that he feared that the

President had given away much of what Hull had secured from the Russians, and this, however apocryphal, is a fair index of talk among some officials, particularly those from whom, as happens here so often, the full details of the transactions within their own special province have been withheld.

Gossip on European policy. There is naturally a good deal of general talk and gossip of varying degree of reliability. The Greek Ambassador is reliably reported to have said that at his last interview with the President the latter had told him that no fuss would be made by the United States Government about the incorporation of the Baltic States by Soviet Russia, and that after much trouble an appropriate formula to cover this had at last been found. The Greek Ambassador then inquired about Poland. According to our informant, the President made gestures of mock despair and said that he was thoroughly tired of the Polish problem, and had told the Polish Ambassador so in clear language, and warned him personally about the effects of continued Polish agitation. The Polish officials are naturally deeply disgruntled about the whole situation and are not particularly well disposed towards us at the moment. This holds also of the Yugoslavs, who draw some crumbs of comfort from the fact that the text of Hull's statement on military aid to the Partisans was somewhat more general and guarded than Mr Law's statement to the House of Commons. The anti-Tito press detects disturbing signs of left-wing leanings in the new British attitude to Tito but this is offset to some degree by the general expectation in the press of an Allied attack through the Balkans which is held to justify placation of the left and this demonstrates to Scripps-Howard editorialist that the much criticized 'appeasement' of Darlan and Badoglio is not confined to right-wing groups. Brigadier Maclean's [1] report is reported to have made a considerable impression upon the relevant officials in the State Department, since those who know him regard him as unlikely to be swayed by pro-Partisan bias. London despatches have begun to paint the Brigadier in picturesque terms to the American public.

Hamilton Fish Armstrong told a member of my staff that there was considerable feeling in the Department about what was thought to be a somewhat too cynical and brutal abandonment of Mihajlovic in favour of his rival, and some indignation among both officials and the press about alleged British refusal to let American correspondents interview the Chetnik [2] chiefs. Armstrong himself, who is, of course, particularly versed in Balkan affairs, and a friend of Fotich, [3] takes a somewhat gloomy view of our behaviour. He is busily trying to find middle ground for himself and his Council on Foreign Relations to occupy, and has therefore rediscovered the existence of the Croat peasant party and of Subasich [4] who is equally opposed to Communists and present Yugoslav Government

1 Fitzroy Maclean, British liaison officer with Tito and Partisans.
2 Mihajlovic's guerrilla forces.
3 Constantin Fotich, Yugoslav Ambassador in Washington.
4 Ivan Subasich, *Ban* (governor) of Croatia at time of German invasion.

and therefore seems worthiest of American support. On being asked whether he agreed with the view recently advanced publicly by Lippmann, and privately by others, that neither the Baltic nor the Middle East form genuine spheres of American interest, and that pressure of minority groups on these issues would therefore merely irritate the American people and Administration without achieving anything, Armstrong disagreed sharply and said that this was true only if a reactionary Republican government came in (which he admitted was perfectly possible), but that so long as anything like the present foreign policy continued the United States would take an active interest in these regions as well as the Balkans, and would listen to the views of minorities, some of whose leaders, e.g. Louis Adamic,[5] were, in his view, professional charlatans, in contrast to others, e.g. Sforza, a man who, in his opinion, the Foreign Office had treated with insufficient courtesy. Armstrong continues to be on excellent terms with Hull and Welles simultaneously, and told a member of my staff that Hull was immensely pleased with Litvinov's support of his, Hull's, main contention at Moscow that only provided that the Russians made concessions could he undertake to swing American opinion into line of general world co-operation.

Hull in Moscow. The general confidential account of officials here is that Hull told the Russians that unless such concessions are made, whether or not they conflicted with Russia's immediate interests, both his country and theirs would lapse into isolationism, a danger which in his opinion could still be averted, but only if the Russians played. Litvinov, according to these accounts, behaved with exceptional courage in expressing vigorous agreement with Hull, and this, according to Hull, probably tipped the scales.

President in Tehran. Not much has yet been heard about the President's interview with Stalin save that President is supposed to have started a conversation about the border states, and asked Stalin if he did not think that self-determination would be a proper principle to apply to the smaller nations on her frontiers. Stalin wished to know what precisely the term 'self-determination' meant. The President, evidently unwilling to mention specific countries by name, said something about the determination of government by the majority vote of specific nationalities. Stalin quickly said 'Agreed. Next point', and throughout took advantage of the President's constitutional reluctance to make his language sharp and specific. Hence it is now thought here that plebiscites are contemplated by Russia at least in Poland, Bessarabia, etc., the reality of which no one here is liable to overestimate.

UNRRA. The congressional hearings of Messrs Acheson, Crowley and Lehman have gone off favourably for UNRRA. Crowley was informed by the Foreign

5 Louis Adamic (1899–1951), immigrant from Yugoslavia, author, and (beginning in 1940) editor of *Common Ground*.

Affairs Committee that it was a pleasure to them to know that matters were in such solid and capable hands, and Crowley happily assured the Committee that they were indeed secure with him. Lehman does not seem to have liked this inasmuch as it appeared to give the impression that sovereignty lay with FEA and telephoned Acheson to complain. Acheson tried to take the line that Lehman was now a great international official, placed high above any servant of the United States Government and would perhaps do best to ignore the Committee's summons as in his new capacity he was not bound to appear. Lehman was neither mollified by the elevation ascribed to him, nor did he take kindly to the advice to ignore Congress, duly appeared, and came off well. . . .

The Prime Minister. At this moment newspaper offices in Washington are being flooded with enquiries about Mr Churchill's condition.[6] Even the isolationist *Times Herald* led off editorially with a prayer for his recovery, perhaps the most striking evidence of the universal respect and affection in which he is held by the American nation.

Oil. A good deal of public attention has been paid to the politics of oil recently, notably to the views of Secretary Ickes, who, as Petroleum Co-ordinator, is insistently repeating two points with ever increasing emphasis : (1) that present sources of United States oil are insufficient to tide the country over a period of more than 10–15 years ; (2) that the sooner America imitated British oil policy, in particular the governmental control of Anglo-Iranian, the better for the United States. According to the *New York Times* his panel of experts has produced a report whose main recommendation is that private enterprise should alone be encouraged to run the industry and that the chief duty of the United States Government is to give more vigorous diplomatic and other support to its nationals, wherever they may be at work, on the analogy of similar support offered to their nationals by other Governments. Mead delivered a temperate speech on this in the Senate, quoting liberally from Ickes, describing existing Anglo-American arrangements with approval and pleading for a clear United States policy. In this he was supported by Lodge. No anti-British nuances occurred. Although the controversy between those who favour government partnership or control and the champions of private industry may complicate the issue, the general drive for more oil for the United States is under way publicly and privately, and the Republican opposition is trying to use it as a stick to beat the Administration.

Home Front. The subsidies issue continues to simmer strongly, but the Administration now has solid hopes of getting the vote postponed until February. I am told that several New Deal Congressmen have turned their offices into campaign rooms and have been flooding the mails with literature and suggestions for put-

6 Prostrated on 12 December with an attack of pneumonia 'among the ruins of Carthage'.

ting pressure on their colleagues. The unexpectedly strong representations made by various consumers' groups, particularly women's organizations, are thought to have pushed the farm lobby forces back and made a compromise solution more probable. What happens then is difficult to foretell. The 'Southern revolt' over the soldier vote, led by the Farm Bloc leader Senator 'Cotton Ed' Smith [7] and Bailey [8] of North Carolina, led to a display of Victorian eloquence which obtained an appreciative press, and served a new notice to the Administration that the South must be appeased to the full limit if a Democratic victory, even with Roosevelt as a candidate, is to be thought of at all. The unexpected protest of the bedridden veteran Carter Glass against the Southern stand was naturally hailed by the liberal press which made him its hero for the day, but his solitary voice seems unlikely to stem the Southern tide running high at present. This tide is exemplified by suggestions for various Southern presidential candidates – Byrd, Arnall, etc. – which at present are simply expressions of discontent and means of organizing resistance.

.   .   .

REPUBLICAN POLITICS

'The trend is in the bag' – Landon.

'The GOP could win with a Chinaman' – Anon.

The only development since last week is a routine anti-New Deal speech by Bricker and a vehement attack upon him by House majority leader McCormack, who has made the obvious comparison between Bricker and Harding again and again. Clapper gloomily wonders (as do many others) whether a situation similar to 1920 may not arise and Bricker find himself elected as a result of a deadlock between the equally matched Willkie and Dewey. Senator Langer's demand for an investigation of Nelson Sparks's charges that Willkie's nomination was bought by the 'East Coast (Anglophile) plutocrats' is to be examined by a five-man sub-committee early next year, which will technically only consider whether the facts justify a formal investigation. Gardner Cowles, himself 'smeared' by Sparks, published indignant rebuttal, citing Willkie's various refusals in 1940 to 'trade' with other Republican groups. Some anti-Willkie Republicans are said to be wondering whether this 'smear' campaign, pleasing enough in itself, might not boomerang, in that it may discredit all Republicans in the eyes of the public by suggesting that what Willkie was alleged to have done once, will be done even more naturally by Bricker's or Dewey's millionaire supporters. A member of my staff, who has been talking to Mrs Ogden Reid, obtained the impression that while proposing to continue her present investment in Willkie, whose stock is still high, she was well aware of the possibility of having to switch to someone else in time, and would endeavour to do so as gracefully as possible, after some formal *casus belli,* which no one could have much difficulty in picking with Willkie. Landon's efforts to be a President-maker

---

7 Ellison DuRant Smith, Democratic Senator from South Carolina 1905–44.

8 Josiah W. Bailey, Democratic Senator from North Carolina since 1931.

are now said to be viewed in shrewd Republican circles as something of a liability, since the clumsy rescue of him by Hoover last week (see summary of last week) put him in a ludicrous light and cannot well be repeated often. His remarks, favourable to Governor Green of Illinois[9], are therefore regarded as of no significance. Green (regarded by some as the *Chicago Tribune's* chief hope) is now at daggers drawn with the latest official presidential aspirant, Representative Dirksen (see political summary of 6 December). Colonel McCormick's Detroit speech is said to be regarded as a deranged performance by some of his own followers (not unlike Northcliffe's Cologne Speech in 1920).[10]

Vandenberg has extracted out of the Secretaries of War and Navy an assurance that serving officers are permitted to offer their candidatures for the Presidency, which clears the path for both MacArthur and Stassen. Apart from the fact that the Administration could not well have refused, a split in the Republican convention vote is not likely to be displeasing to it. As for Dewey, those who know him say that he is now genuinely worried about the possibility that the Republicans may win the election in any event, which he had not thought probable before, and that his own chances for the future would be gravely prejudiced by the victory of, say, Willkie in 1944 ; he is, therefore, genuinely perplexed about what do do. Current polls indicate a slight rise in MacArthur's stock.

.   .   .

27 December 1943

Domestic front. Congress has recessed after three months of support of Administration's foreign and military policies and grim obstruction of its domestic plans. Issues in suspense due to be resumed in January include taxes, subsidies, excess profits, soldiers' vote, mustering-out pay, poll tax, etc. Failure of Congress to pass Administration's price-regulating and taxation bills has provoked warnings of dangers of inflation by Administration spokesmen and press but country at large cannot be said to be inflation-conscious. This is partly accounted for by fact that it has proved able to meet its military commitments with one hand, while with the other pouring out a quantity of consumer goods to satisfy, except for certain restricted categories such as automobiles and refrigerators, vastly increased demand due to higher wages and general boom atmosphere. Volume of sales (almost 60 per cent above 1923–9 levels) of consumer goods to vast mobs of eager purchasers this Christmas has broken all records. It is expected that by end of year sales of consumer goods will have totalled ninety billions of dollars higher than peak year 1929. Fact that more concern is felt in industrial circles about technique of peacetime readjustment and shutting down in line with this of several minor plants (which in one case led to a strike of laid-off workers) coupled with remarks by various industrialists, notably Kaiser, that

9 Dwight H. Green, Republican Governor of Illinois 1941–5.
10 Presumably reference to Northcliffe's articles in *Daily Mail* and *Times* after his visit to Cologne, 'Incognito in Germany', the first public manifestation of his insanity.

peak of production has been passed, has naturally made people more conscious of their post-war needs and ambitions than of present economic perils. It is not surprising if in this atmosphere Administration's warning voices are relatively little heeded, either by special interests or people at large and Congress, while disposed to collaborate in foreign policy, does not feel sufficient popular pressure in favour of Administration's attempts to check profits, curb prices and hold wages. Any domestic anti-administration line (even if it is pro-labour) is *ipso facto* welcomed by major lobbies at moment.

Death and interment of New Deal. President in answer to a journalist's enquiry said that in his opinion 'New Deal' is an obsolete description of Government's policies. It was needed in 1932 and now it is 1943. Thus New Deal has been formally relegated to history. Republicans naturally replied that this very understandable attempt on part of President to jettison memories of twelve years of maladministration will deceive no one ; as for his substitute for it of 'win the war' as a slogan, that was direct pilfering from Republican armoury. Fact that New Deal as a movement had been virtually dead for some time has long been taken for granted. This looks like its formal epitaph.

Tax bill. Senate Finance Committee's substitute for Administration's bill reducing it to a sixth and postponing increase in social security taxes has provoked an angry outburst from Morgenthau who pointed out (a) that successful senatorial pressure to prevent renegotiation of wartime contracts would lead to 'truly extortionate profits', and (b) that as matters stood, Treasury would virtually be better off with no tax bill at all as proceeds of renegotiation, together with scheduled increase in social security taxes (both of which Senate's bill reduces), would scarcely yield less than Senate bill itself. This together with publication of Administration's projected budget (for some $96 billion) is likely to cause some rough passages in January when fact that there existed unexpended balances of appropriations (e.g. thirteen billions for Army and four billions for Navy) will be liberally quoted by Opposition. Senator George, Chairman of Finance Committee and reported foe of profit-curtailing renegotiation, has been accused by Drew Pearson of suspicious collusion with a lobbyist of United States Chamber of Commerce. Pearson's expected testimony on this before investigating congressional committee has thus far failed to materialize because George was prevented from attending by indisposition until day when Pearson in his turn could not appear. There is some private gossip about this, New Dealers maintaining that they have facts to support Pearson, and Southern conservatives duly indignant.

Judge Vinson's problems. Subsidies issue has been deferred until February with both sides fully armed and polishing their weapons. Vinson is said to be working hard to keep House Committee firm in its opposition to Senate's action and is meantime in deep trouble with railroad unions which still threaten to strike on 30 December. It is almost inconceivable to vast mass of American public that so solid and trustworthy a body as railroad employees could perpetrate a nationwide strike. Unions bank on this and are well aware of their bargaining position (railroad unions have won all their previous battles) anticipating that Administration is likely to yield rather than face strike. Consequently Vinson's gallant attempt to hold wage line may be broken by weight of popular and political pressure. But President appears to have returned in a tough mood and bluntly told railwaymen that he had completed arrangements to turn over railroads in event of a deadlock. Railroad workers indicated that in that event they would call off strike. Finally President declared that he would personally arbitrate the issue. Two of unions involved accepted this. President is said to have talked with unusual bluntness about his intention to resist pressures of special interests at all costs. His popularity among all Democratic groups is still, according to Gallup, immensely higher than anyone else's (85 per cent ; Wallace who comes next 6 per cent ; rest nowhere). His prestige is high at the moment.

European relief. Combination of pressures has forced a resolution through Foreign Relations Committee of Senate, calling upon State Department to work out in co-operation with Britain, Sweden and Switzerland a system of moving food supplies to peoples of Nazi-occupied Europe (e.g. from Argentine). Behind this is Hoover who is intensely jealous of Lehman. He has been bullying Lehman through those Hooverite members of Lehman staff whom Lehman took on in a vain effort to placate ex-President. With him stand arrayed not only pacifist, Quaker and 'soft peace' groups but Roman Catholic hierarchy which is said to see immediate relief as an important means of securing prophylactic influence over Europeans against dangers of Communist undergrounds and Russian penetration. There is a liability in both executive and congressional circles to look upon relief as a method of winning European goodwill, a commodity in which United States and Britain are both interested and which therefore is a natural object of political competition. This may explain Senator Gillette's obscure observation (quoted in press) to Foreign Relations Committee that he had been informed by high Administration authority that sole obstacle to provision of relief to European children came from Britain and that by passing this resolution Committee would usefully strengthen President's hand against British opposition. There is evidence for supposing that American officials, while keeping to their general agreement with us on blockade policy, have in one or two cases expressed dissatisfaction with it 'off the record', to such figures as Kershner (see political summary of 14 November) who is tied to a specific pacifist group connected with Wheeler, sympathetic to French and Germans, but directed against Poles and even more Russians. In absence of serious opposition to motion and possibly for fear of political persecution at home if they chose to oppose it, Senate Foreign Relations Committee has unanimously recommended motion for senatorial consideration and in one fell swoop also passed a resolution to recommend to President establishment of a committee composed of political, military and economic experts to assist rescue of Jewish victims of Nazi persecution, a motion previously blocked in Foreign Affairs Committee of House (after a fortnight of hearings) by evidence of Assistant Secretary of State Breckinridge Long. Both resolutions are due to be debated in Senate in its next session. An official of State Department told member of my staff that in his considered opinion nothing would come of Jewish resolution.

Labour. The American Labor Party (a New York and New Jersey New Deal organization) recently visited the White House to say that unless the Soviet Embassy did something to prevent the penetration and demoralization of its ranks by the New York Communists, it would be compelled to dissolve altogether. As it often holds the balance of power in the New York State elections, the threat to the Democrats is a real one, and the President's labour advisers are likely to do everything in their power to prevent this attempted suicide. The appointment of Lee Pressman,[1] General Counsel of the CIO, long known for his Communist sympathies, as one of Hillman's chief officials in the joint labour pro-Roosevelt campaign has further irritated Dubinsky and his anti-Communist right wingers and Pressman's appearance on behalf of the steel workers who, encouraged by the railroad unions, are in their turn threatening a strike (one wildcat strike has already occurred) is a grave nuisance to those Roosevelt tacticians who realize that without a fairly solid labour vote the President's chances of re-election are slim.

. . .

Cairo and Tehran. Rumours are flying around the town and have, of course, been published by Drew Pearson to the effect that there was considerable friction between the President and the Prime Minister, particularly over Pacific questions, the role of the Chinese in the reconquest of Burma, etc. The commonest rumour is that the President got on exceptionally well with Stalin and less so with Mr Churchill. The Czechs say that they have heard this, with the variant that Stalin for his part remained unimpressed by the President. The majority of these rumours appear to have trickled down from the members of the United States military staff present in Cairo and Tehran. It is possible but not probable that the President, while of course not giving countenance to such rumours, has done nothing to check them because it is in his interest to dispel public impression that he and the United States Administration are under the spell of the Prime Minister. The President would doubtless find it difficult to denounce Pearson again, particularly after the latter's accurate revelation of the Patton affair, and his fairly well-known contacts with the high officers in the War Department.

. . .

1 Lee Pressman, New York lawyer, early New Dealer in AAA and WPA, general counsel for CIO and United Steel Workers 1936–48.

1944

War news. Despite satisfactory war news from Russia and Italy, sinking of *Scharnhorst*[1] and good reception of President's Christmas talk, there is a pre-invasion tension pervading both press and general talk. Senator Johnson (Democrat, Colorado) charged that it had been decided to compose a European invasion force of 73 per cent Americans *v.* 27 per cent British. This was angrily echoed by Wheeler, Nye and Chandler . . . who spoke of coming invasion as 'little short of mass murder'. This although most handsomely rebutted by United States Chiefs of Staff, who said that nobody doubted that both Britain and America would throw all they had into assault, has nevertheless planted seeds of uneasiness in mind of public. Eisenhower's appointment[2] stirred relatively little interest as appointment of an American invasion chief (e.g. Marshall) had in any case long been taken for granted and British appointments have been received with routine approval. What is really worrying commentators and public (although there has been a natural reluctance on part of well-disposed to ventilate it) is anticipation of vast American losses and effect of this on public, an anxiety set off by no corresponding exhilaration or excitement at prospect of coming to grips with Germans on a mass scale. Wheeler talks ominously about public reaction in event of failure of invasion. He has of course been attacked for this in responsible press but not perhaps with that violence which genuine indignation provokes. Prevailing mood is somewhat grim, outwardly calm, inwardly a trifle tremulous. The statement widely attributed to Justice Byrnes, that 400,000 casualties were to be expected, has further increased this. Elmer Davis is said to be much insulted at this new bypassing of OWI by, of all people, the referee of interdepartmental disputes himself, and a redefinition of functions of his unhappy agency will doubtless once more be attempted. The outgoing chief of OWI's domestic branch has also spoken of need for greater 'realism' in presentation of war news. While all this does not indicate any kind of weakening of fibre and will have no effect on operational decisions or execution, it is worth remarking that atmosphere is one of nervous expectancy rather than enthusiastic anticipation. . . .

Poles. The Poles are fermenting as usual, and Dewey is alleged to be surrounding himself with Polish politicians in search of the Polish vote. *New York Times*

1 German pocket battleship sunk on 26 December 1943 by units of the British Home Fleet off North Cape, Norway.

2 As Supreme Commander of Allied Expeditionary Force in Western Europe.

on 30 December in a leader, which seems of some importance, discusses the Russo-Polish problem, urging Stalin to make a 'bold declaration' on the lines of the Atlantic Charter, saying that he had no wish to incorporate in Russia 'peoples who do not choose to go there willingly after a free plebiscite' to be held by the major allies. It gloomily reviews the alternatives :

(a) A possible alliance between the Republican vote-seekers and the Polish-Americans which would split the country on an irrelevant issue and do Poles no good and possible harm, and

(b) Cynical annexation of Polish territory by Russia (which United States would clearly not try to prevent by force) which would produce disillusionment in America with a drift to isolationism, etc. Author holds no brief for sanctity of any given Russo-Polish frontier and reminds his readers that original old Polish frontier was acquired by force at a moment of Russian weakness and that Russian strategic frontier demands are not unreasonable. Article is significant if only because it seems to express what appears to me to be opinion of average enlightened official and unofficial persons and institutions here concerned with foreign affairs at present. Yugoslav Embassy is scarcely pleased with continuing stream of pro-Partisan despatches from Cairo and elsewhere, but despite sympathy felt for its point of view in certain sections of State Department it is hardly likely to be effective at moment.

Japan. There has been a renewed discussion of future of Japan. Perhaps as a reflection of voices raised against 'enslavement' of Germany after war among which is that of President himself in his Christmas talk, there has been talk in State Department circles about need for co-operation with Mikado and possibility with skilful treatment of canalizing Shintoism in a pro-Allied direction. Hornbeck[3] alone appears to think that theory of usefulness of Mikado in this connexion is a delusion. This translation of allied Italian policy into Japanese terms is attributed by Kuh[4] from London to British official inspiration. Ambassador Grew (still Special Assistant to Hull) has focussed discussion by declaring that Japan must be given adequate economic outlets after her defeat if seeds of a new Pacific War are not to be planted. Thus far this attitude has not been denounced despite universal 'exterminationist' anti-Japanese feeling here of man in street. . . .

Domestic politics. . . . Railroad strike has collapsed in face of firm action by President who put railroads under army control (an action which was received with unruffled satisfaction by public). Railroad situation will clearly be useful for enemy propaganda but is not likely to have direct material effect here on transportation. Steel workers likewise returned to work and despite sporadic

3 Stanley Kuhl Hornbeck, career diplomat, Chief of Division of Far Eastern Affairs, State Department, 1928–37, Adviser on Political Relations since 1937.

4 Frederick R.Kuh, London correspondent of *Chicago Sun-Times* 1942–51, noted for his scoops.

strikes by shipbuilding workers, etc., labour situation is in a state of precarious quiet although pressure continues. Tipsters are predicting some sort of compromise of soldier vote issue.

Presidential prospects. (a) President at his press conferences, evidently feeling that his announcement of the death of the New Deal last week was somewhat too brusque, this week delivered a handsome obituary notice enumerating the many achievements of the defunct order. As this sounded like electioneering, he was asked about his fourth term intentions by a favourite correspondent and snapped back that the question was 'picayune', which had the effect of reminding those present of the manner in which he used to award 'dunce caps' to correspondents who asked him similar questions in 1940. Hence a new wave of prophecies that he does intend to stand again. He spoke of supersession of 'Dr New Deal', needed by the patient in 1932, by 'Dr win the war', needed now. Wallace, asked to comment, said that he 'wouldn't attempt to improve the jewel'. . . .

(b) Colonel McCormick's official refusal to offer himself to the Illinois primaries robs Willkie of a useful foil. The MacArthurites are preparing to step into this breach. The General's candidature is beginning to look real. His committee say that MacArthur has not himself been consulted. The Republican situation appears very confused, with a desire by the bosses for a Bricker or a Taft or any other Harding, coupled with uneasy realization that only a Willkie or a Dewey whose 'East Coast outlook' is suspect to the Midwest could produce the necessary avalanche of votes. Everyone is waiting for everyone else to act and the political war is still in the stage of confused crisscross skirmishing between and within the major parties. Daniel Tobin, perhaps the most influential AF of L labour leader, has in print expressed his opinion that Willkie is likely to emerge as the Republican candidate, but has so far himself cautiously repeated his support for Roosevelt. This, if it means anything, means that AF of L has offered Willkie, who has been flirting with labour lately, a place second to Roosevelt on its list of candidates. I am reminded of Ickes's old epigram about Willkie as 'the rich man's Roosevelt'. American labour unions, particularly in the conservative AF of L, are staunch supporters of the moneyed interest.

. . .

The resignation of Burke,[5] the Head of Communications Division of the State Department, is the culmination of a long series of disagreements with other officials of the Department on post-war air policy, principally Berle. Burke has long been known as a protagonist of the 'chosen instrument' doctrine[6] and has helped Clare Luce with more than one of her speeches on this topic. He is said to be joining Juan Trippe's Pan-American in some capacity, which both personally and ideologically will suit him better than the constant bickering with the

5 Thomas Burke, Chief of the Division of International Communications, State Department.

6 Principle that the Government should give exclusive backing to the organization or corporation best able to promote the interests of the USA, e.g. Pan American Airways in South America.

majority of his committee colleagues whose continued opposition to the 'chosen instrument' policy may be inferred from Burke's resignation.

9 January 1944

The Marshall flurry. The explosion touched off by General Marshall's off-the-record press conference [1] was evidently far more violent than he or Stimson had anticipated, whether or not because of United States Army Intelligence reports indicating the actual and probable effect of threatened strikes in United States steel and railroad industries on the wavering Axis satellites. Marshall at this conference (conferences of this sort are quite normal and given by many high officials including the President) struck the table and said with genuine anger that the behaviour of the labour leaders in question might easily prolong the war at a vast cost in American blood and treasure. Marshall is perhaps more universally admired in the United States than any other individual, and is regarded as a figure of such unimpeachable impartiality, integrity, efficiency and ancient American virtue as to be almost beyond criticism. A statement from him, therefore (his identity was disclosed by a Florida newspaper, and the War Department, twice shy after the Patton case, did not attempt to deny it), was a bolt from the blue and caused an immense sensation. The labour leaders Green and Murray reacted instantly and sharply, and defended their position, Green naïvely going so far as to say that despite the railroaders' threat no strike was ever actually in question. A handful of Senators of both parties, mindful of votes but unprepared to attack the still sacrosanct Marshall, took the line that not the workers but the bungling of the Administration was to blame for what was a truly appalling state of affairs so accurately revealed by Marshall. This line was eagerly seized upon by the dyed-in-the-wool Republican railroad unions themselves, which repeated their old line that Byrnes and Vinson gave fatal advice to the President and the Administration was alone to blame for the railroad crisis.

It is very notable that there was not that volume of support for Marshall and wave against labour which might have been expected – the anonymity which shrouded his statement, the sweeping nature of the charge, the supposed lack of evidence about the use which the enemy was making of these stories, etc., were taken as occasions for criticism of Marshall's act, sharp in the case of the liberal press, milder in the case of the rest. There is no doubt that were the spokesman anyone other than Marshall, indignation against so bitter an onslaught by a public official against a particular section of the population (while saying nothing of the scarcely more edifying behaviour of other special interests) would have been more pronounced even despite the present unpopularity of labour. As it is, it is widely assumed that Marshall meant precisely what he said – that the psychological effect upon the tottering Axis satellites of such an exhibition of American

1 On 31 December an 'anonymous spokesman' sharply criticized labour and asserted that strikes had given Hitler a propaganda weapon which might delay uprisings in Europe and so prolong the war.

impotence together with the diversion of his soldiers to the administration of United States railroads might, in fact, lead to dangerous consequences, and that there was no political bias or purpose concealed in his remarks. . . .

. . . There is no evidence that the President (as well as Stimson and Patterson) was consulted by Marshall, although Early indicated that his thought moved along the same lines as Marshall's. The actual incident may die down, but as a move likely to increase anti-labour sentiment and demoralize labour support for the President, it is of real importance. The reaction of the moderates is one of embarrassment at so violent a pronouncement by so respected a figure however well substantiated. Respected and admired though Marshall will doubtless continue to be, his unique position, as a figure lifted above the political battle, has been, at any rate temporarily, shaken.

. . .

Russia and Poland. The spectacular Russian advances, while of course welcomed, have pushed into fresh prominence the Russo-Polish question which is discussed, if anything, with more heat in private than in the press or radio. There exists as yet nothing describable as widespread national American sentiment on this subject, and Hull has repeatedly tried to curb anti-Russian propaganda by Poles in frank talk to the Polish Ambassador[2] on this topic. The Polish Ambassador declares himself worried by an alleged statement to him of Mayor Kelly of Chicago that 90 per cent of Illinois Poles who had previously voted solidly for Roosevelt were now ready to vote for almost any other candidate. While the sincerity of Ciechanowski's anxiety may be doubted, it is becoming clear that the Polish vote, which may be crucial in such borderline states as Illinois, Pennsylvania, Michigan, Connecticut, etc., has been profoundly affected by both events and by propaganda principally from the New York Knapp (the anti-Government Nationalist Pilsudski-ites).[3] Willkie's article in the *New York Times* ('don't stir distrust of Russia') on 2 January, warning the minorities against undue agitation but advocating the need for an equitable arrangement, to be found in consultation with Russia, to adjust the status of the border states, was probably meant as a crumb of comfort for the disgruntled minorities. On the 4th Willkie was still praised by the *Daily Worker* as a 'good' Republican and a true friend to the USSR. On the 5th the *Pravda* article suddenly pitched into him as a political gambler, meddler and opportunist of the first water. As there are few persons in this country familiar with the sardonic pleasure which the USSR is liable to take in tripping up its over-zealous bourgeois suitors when these are guilty of tactless behaviour, there is very general surprise. The semi-official Lindley gloomily predicts that this worsens Russo-American relations. Sullivan[4] speaks of inter-

---

2 Jan Ciechanowski, Polish Ambassador 1941–5.

3 'Komitet Narodowy Amerikanow Polskiego Pochodzenia' (National Committee of Americans of Polish Descent).

4 Mark Sullivan, long-established journalist, syndicated columnist, *New York Evening Post*, 1919–23, and subsequently *New York Herald Tribune*.

ference in United States internal affairs. As for Willkie he is said to be completely dazed by this stab and has so far only stated that he adheres to his views. The anti-Willkie-ite right wing led by Hoover is naturally said to be crowing with delight. The White House is said to be surprised but not wholly displeased. Hull is reported to be displaying considerable gaiety on the subject. Interpretation varies between those who take the article as prompted by the Russian desire to teach a lesson once and for all to anyone daring to raise unmentionable topics, e.g. about the Baltic States, and those who suppose that the Russians have decided that they need the re-election of Roosevelt, and look on Willkie as merely causing a diversion which may land them with a Republican President, who, even if he is Willkie, will find himself in the grip of forces on the whole antipathetic to the USSR. Be that as it may, Mr Willkie's next reaction is being waited for with considerable, and in places malicious, interest. The Poles are naturally pleased, and some among them are trying to pin their hopes on Churchill inasmuch as they do not expect any further genuine aid from the President. The more serious-minded Poles are quite aware of the fact that the politicians at present exploiting Polish anti-Russian sentiment in a Republican direction will do little enough for them in the event of being returned to power with the help of Polish votes. (See *New York Times* leading article on Russian–Polish relations referred to in last week's political summary).

10 January 1944

. . .

Cartels. The drive against cartels is continuing, and the Justice Department's prosecutor Wendell Berge[1] has now formally brought civil suit against not only the Duponts[2] but also Imperial Chemicals[3] (under the Sherman Anti-Trust Act)[4] which thus is brought into the limelight after a long period of obscurity. The inclusion of ICI in the suit provides that flavour of sinister international monopoly which is one of the traditional bogeys of the American man in the street, and clears such attacks of any suspicion of a New Deal campaign against private enterprise. . . .

. . .

Jews. The campaign against the White Paper conducted now by extreme Zionists, moderate Zionists and non-Zionists, each in accordance with their own preferred technique, is rising to a climax and is proving embarrassing to the Administration. The American Palestine Committee[5] (which roughly corresponds to the Old British House of Commons pro-Palestine Committee), headed by Sena-

1 Wendell Berge, Assistant Attorney General, Department of Justice, since 1941 and Head of the Anti-Trust Division since 1943.
2 Du Pont de Nemours & Co., US chemicals combine.
3 Imperial Chemical Industries (ICI), UK chemicals combine.
4 Introduced in 1890 by Senator John Sherman to combat business tendencies towards monopoly.
5 Constituted in 1941 to secure removal of immigration restrictions in Palestine.

tors Wagner and McNary, has now enlisted the services of Senator Vandenberg, who has evidently concluded that there is no Arab vote in the State of Michigan. A full page advertisement by this body, more moderate in tone, but not in substance, than the usual advertisements, has appeared and was swiftly followed by a far more unbridled revisionist advertisement calling on America to avert civil war in Palestine by doing justice to the Jews and foiling the plans of the Colonial Office. It is now an open secret among Zionists that after consulting Postmaster General Walker (who is the chief Democratic tactician) on Jewish sentiment Hull is contemplating some sort of friendly bromide to placate the Zionists, which of course merely serves to increase Jewish pressure. . . .

Crowley's chickens have come home to roost in unprecedented quantities this week when the very real inefficiencies and ineptitudes of the collection of economic agencies grouped under FEA have been exposed to intensive criticism. A pincer movement seems to be converging on it from liberal and conservative quarters – the pro-New Dealers Drew Pearson and the editorialists of the Scripps-Howard press and the *Washington Post* vied with each other in telling stories of its lack of method and control, of scores of officials rendered idle and demoralized by lack of direction, and of resignations (Knollenberg has gone from Lend-Lease, the banker Schubart has joined Lazard Frères, New York, Lauchlin Currie is said to be moving out, etc.). All this has so far been left unanswered by Crowley who appears to have lost most of his friends in the press. I am told that the press campaign was stimulated simultaneously from two sides – from the State Department, which forms the natural opposition to FEA, and from the old followers of Wallace and Perkins who lay low until they had convinced themselves that Crowley had in fact failed and was an easy target on which to vent the accumulation of their bitter feeling.

Labour. The Marshall episode . . . has served to move the position of labour back into the limelight. Elaborate computations have appeared in the newspapers estimating man-hours lost through strikes compared with 1941 and 1942 with results not too discreditable to labour, since the general argument is that although more strikes have occurred in 1943 than in 1941 or 1942 fewer hours were lost with many more men in employment and a vaster general production than any previous period. The railroad strike is to be settled by a new tribunal set up by the President ; the steel workers hope for a revision of the 'Little Steel' formula ; the rest are in a state of deceptive quiescence. In general labour is in a nervous state, since, despite the high levels of its present wages, it is faced with the spectacle of unparalleled profits being garnered by industry, a prospect of substantial decrease in employment in 1944 (the beginnings of which are already in sight) and the danger of violent unpopularity through the combination of the growing power of the anti-New Deal forces in the country, and the indignation (of which Marshall is known to be painfully aware) of the armed forces abroad with the 'soft' lives of industrial workers at home. Rickenbacker's American

Legion anti-labour blasts[6] were a clear symptom of the kind of mood into which returning soldiers may only too easily slide, and which reactionary groups will be only too well prepared to exploit. The nightmarish memories of anti-labour pressure which occurred after the last war haunt both the AF of L and the CIO, and it is instructive to note the prophylactics on which various sections of labour place their hopes, each in accordance with its own temperament. The bulk of the CIO still pin their faith to a liberal Administration, i.e. Wallace, but since they do not seriously believe in the Vice-President's power to save them, they look ultimately to the President, despite his at times very ambiguous attitude towards them. Hillman, who leads this group, is campaigning busily and reports political progress. The AF of L and the Railroad Brotherhoods with their conservative cast of mind and deep distrust of state control in any form are looking towards some sort of compromise with the more progressive industrialists as a possible path of salvation, and conversations between such labour politicians as Robert Watt[7] and such industrial opportunists as Eric Johnston are typical of this kind of rein-surance. Although the bulk of the AF of L may, despite Johnston's and Willkie's blandishments, nevertheless vote for Roosevelt in the end, it will do so without enthusiasm as a *pis aller*. The main preoccupation of this section of labour led by Woll, Green and Meany[8] is to conserve its gains, and refrain from foreign adventures and compromising political entanglements. The acutest form of this is the continued refusal to have any dealings with the Soviet trade unions, and the persistent rejection of all of Citrine's efforts in this direction. Fear of Communism is plainly stronger in this group than desire for international labour solidarity, and for that reason Citrine's invitation to the AF of L to attend his international trade union conference in London in the summer is likely to be turned down (Fenton,[9] a prominent AF of L leader, told a member of my staff that the presence of the Russian and of the very reactionary Catholic French-Canadian union representatives ruled attendance out as far as his people were concerned). . . . Meanwhile, there is no one in the Administration who seems capable of handling labour authoritatively for the President, perhaps because the latter tends to do so more and more himself, thus to some extent undermining the authority of the officials he has charged with this task – Byrnes, Vinson, Chairman Davis of the War Labor Board, Secretary Perkins, Paul McNutt, etc. All these, bar Miss Perkins who remains passive, are very unpopular with labour at the moment. This unpopularity is played upon by those anti-Roosevelt political industrialists who believe that they can create a common anti-Roosevelt labour-capital front before the next election. They count on using the political disgruntlements of the minority groups in labour – Poles, Slovaks, Irish, Jews and others – as so

6 Eg. at Boston on 4 January.

7 Robert J. Watt, AF of L international representative since 1936, previously Vice-President of the Massachusetts State Federation of Labor.

8 George Meany, plumber, President of the New York State Federation of Labor 1934–9, Secretary-Treasurer of the AF of L since 1940.

9 Francis P. Fenton, Director of Organization for AF of L, labour representative on OPA, WPB, etc.

much additional cement. From all this, it will be seen that the labour situation is confused and tense at the moment. . . .

The two present eyesores in labour's field of vision are the Farm Bloc's pressure for higher prices, and resistance by industry and its senatorial supporters (e.g. Senator George) to renegotiation of contracts on which profiteering is thought to be occurring or likely to occur. The Administration is, however, trying to take serious measures on this. . . . Meanwhile the Service Departments' threat to expose excessive corporation profits is said to be putting the business pressure groups into a more reasonable frame of mind with regard to renegotiation of exorbitant contracts.

17 January 1944

President's message. President's message to Congress,[1] a part of which he broadcast, was received with moderate favour. It was his first purely political speech for some time, in as much as it did not confine itself to painting dangers of failing to implement Administration's anti-inflationary measures but specifically appealed to certain designated sections of population – in this case fixed salary groups such as clergymen, teachers, etc., who were warned that they would be hardest hit by present inflationary trends unless he were empowered to check them. While it was not a typical campaign speech it was taken by most observers as clear evidence of intention to stand for re-election. Others less plausibly maintained opposite on ground that proposal for a national service law, in effect conscripting labour, could not but alienate workers in a way in which no sane presidential candidate would dream of deliberately doing. Labour draft was section of speech regarded as its core and main purpose, although President has made clear that his proposals stand or fall together. Opposition to such an action is at present powerful, not merely within AF of L and CIO (whose leaders have formally denounced it), but in Congress and among pressure groups which rightly perceive a threat to their freedom of operations from such a move. Despite therefore routine support which it obtained from loyal Democrats and Republicans who have always favoured such a measure (e.g. Messrs Austin and Wadsworth on whose abortive bill proposal is modelled) and very real support of Stimson and service departments, general view is that it is unlikely to pass Congress. President asserted that for three years he had refrained from such a proposal and that war could indeed be won without it but at far greater cost. He thus very deftly pinned responsibility for, and possible consequences of, its defeat equally on to labour and managements as well as Congress. This has left opposition somewhat uneasy about blame which may fall on it if nothing is done, a position against which they have little ammunition save vague cries about 'Fascism' of national service legislation and either inadequacy or difference of con-

1 State of the Union message, 11 January, calling for conscription for civilian service, a ban on strikes, realistic taxation, subsidies for essential foodstuffs, limitation of profits and wider social insurance.

ditions of similar legislation in Britain. President's own references to 'Fascism' as goal of 'right-wing' reactionaries (recent denunciation of whom by C.E. Wilson he quoted with approval) demonstrates how meaningless a slogan this term has become. His budget proposals reiterated some of substance of address to Congress. Explicit assumption that war may last until autumn of 1945 is in line with serious concern felt e.g. by Stimson about over-optimism in this respect. Undertones of Marshall's reproof to labour which was given with Stimson's knowledge and approval (Byrnes seems to have known nothing of it) is an additional factor in making not unlikely passage of some sort of further anti-strike legislation. There is no doubt that President appreciates that he is thought to have allowed Home Front to slide and has taken first steps to demonstrate that there is henceforth to be a firm hand at the helm. How far this will go beyond level of stern exhortation remains to be seen. Baruch has always opposed a national service act in this country on ground that no one in present Administration is competent to administer it ('Who will he get to run it ? McNutt') and that such a law would make confusion worse confounded under present conditions. Few persons here seem prepared to assert opposite. I was interested to hear Adolph Berle at a private party last night making no secret of his own disagreement with national service proposal on same ground as Baruch's.

Polish question.[2] . . . There is said to be much uneasy speculation in the White House as to whether political and patronage sops offered to Roman hierarchy by Democratic bosses will prove sufficient to restrain Church from active advocacy of Polish cause before and during elections. There is talk of impending resignation of Democratic Chairman Walker as being due to his failure to accommodate the Church in this respect. One of the most significant facts is that volume of explicit pro-Polish sentiment is not greater than it is. American respect for power and success seems to be strongest single factor in situation. There is no great love for Russia but there is great respect and admiration, and general sentiment, discernible in the press and in conversation of young 'tough-minded' Washington and other executives whose temper is likely to shape American policy in future years, is that Russia is doing only sensible thing for a rising great continental power, that America's resources enable her to act likewise, that on a hard and unsentimental basis the two countries will be able to agree after some hard pokerplay without intermediary of Britain or any other 'old' power whose day is passing. They do not deny that Atlantic Charter is being infringed and Wilsonian ideals are going by the board but since Russians wish it so, this is perhaps way world is inevitably going and it would be a foolish luxury to continue to wag a warning finger at Russia in name of ideals which United States knows it does not propose to implement by force. This mood, more influential at moment (although this may change) than attitude of academic or church circles, in effect means that

2 The Russians had offered Poles the Curzon Line as a future frontier. The Poles asked the USA and the UK to mediate between them and the Russians, who affected to treat this proposal as a rejection of their offer.

cause of Poland is regarded as a serious enough embarrassment in view of large Polish vote in key states but not as an issue sufficient to divide nation, at any rate as yet. This attitude is noticeable even in State Department where cue has been given by Mr Hull's allegedly continuing pro-Moscow enthusiasm. The chances of direct understanding with Russia and consequently diminished need for a close alliance with England is said to be an attitude widespread at present in Administration circles. Poles are on the whole getting more warnings not to divide nation than sympathy from most of important persons they consult. This naturally adds to their exasperation and Mikolajczyk[3] is likely to find atmosphere here far from easy.

18 January 1944

Republican politics. The meeting of Republican chiefs and party bosses in Chicago went as expected. Governor Wills[1] of Vermont, where, as in all New England, Willkie sentiment is strongest, denounced the old party liners whom he openly accused of manoeuvring to force some new Harding upon the public with all the horrors of a new 'normalcy'. The bitterness of the attack was officially deprecated by most Republican leaders in Chicago. It represented the spearhead of the nationwide drive into which Willkie has been putting all his energies lately and which have so far certainly not yielded him all he expected ; the straw vote in Chicago made him even with Dewey (21 each) while Bricker, MacArthur and Stassen, etc., trailed behind. In view of the far more intensive activity by Willkie's agents than by Dewey, this has somewhat depressed the Willkie-ites. Some among them are vaguely hoping for increased popularity on the part of their candidate as a result of the attack on him in *Pravda*. This attack (although it is generally realized that it was aimed beyond Willkie at American policy makers generally) will probably do Russia a certain amount of damage here as Willkie is unlikely to forget or forgive, and can stir up considerable sentiment against the USSR. He is alleged to have argued that since the Russians have now put international issues on a basis of naked power politics, the President, tied as he is to the Atlantic Charter, cannot successfully campaign in such an atmosphere. This elaborate casuistry is curiously unlike Willkie's normal somewhat crude processes of thought. At least two members of my staff who have seen him fairly recently report that he is very disgruntled and, in that mood, liable to be unbalanced, inclined to anti-British utterances, and to genuine or self-induced suspicion that British 'pull' will lose him the election. Meanwhile, Spangler's tactless observations about arranging a private poll with the help of Army officers to sound out political opinions among United States troops abroad, have further diminished the stock of that dreary party hack. There is some demand that he be replaced by a more presentable personality. The press on the whole gives the impression of a greater strength for Dewey at Chicago than for

3 Stanislaw Mikolajczyk, Polish Prime Minister 1943–4 (Minister of the Interior 1941–3).
1 Henry William Wills, Republican Governor of Vermont since 1941.

any other candidate, and the Governor has for once declined to reaffirm his reluctance to stand, which has led to excited speculation about a positive decision to stand on his part. He is known to have been seeing a good deal of Hoover lately, who has been trying to provide him with conclusive evidence of his (Dewey's) mounting popularity. Meanwhile, Bricker's speech in Detroit at the beginning of the month was apparently, as usual, a dull, dismal failure. Senator Taft told me a few days ago that he had been disappointed in Bricker's progress and that it now looked more like Dewey. Such votes as Bricker is able to muster are, therefore, to be taken more as a gauge of anti-Willkie sentiment than a tribute to his own negative qualities. California's decision to put up Governor Warren[2] as a 'favourite son' is a blow to the hopes of the Willkie-ites, who had hoped to capture that state (with its twenty-five votes and possible gravitational influence on other West Coast states) for their candidate in the first instance without the need for elaborate bargaining at the convention itself. The Polish question is still regarded by Republicans as a possible weapon against the Administration. Governor Landon is said to have telephoned to Mr Hull recently to enquire why no guarantees for Poland were obtained at the Moscow Conference. Hull is said to have suggested that he go to Moscow himself and plead the Poles' cause with Marshal Stalin in the name of the great Middle West ; Landon asked whether Hull really thought this might save the Poles. Hull begged him on no account to forget to take a specific commitment from the Republican Party to go to immediate war for the integrity of Poland, should the Russians prove obdurate, and a clear promise from the United States Army and Navy to lend them assistance in that event. Landon, who began by taking Hull's words seriously, is said to be much wounded by this irony and to be sulking in Kansas. This story is supported by language used by Hull in conversation with myself, but without mention of names.

. . .

United States Communist antics. Browder's declaration that the United States Communist Party is to be disbanded, only to be reconstituted as an 'association', is not taken too seriously by anyone, and has provoked much ironical comment. More significant are his remarks about the continuation of 'Communist education' within the framework of the two-party system appropriate to the waging and winning of the war against Fascism. Dorothy Thompson perceives in this the new Stalin line directed not to the promotion of revolutionary regimes but to the preservation of world security for which the continuation of stable capitalist governments is indispensable, and comments on the fact that a little body of true Marxists walked out of the hall when Browder began to enlarge upon the beauties of the United States two-party system.

The President's budget message. The President's Budget Message and his message to Congress on the State of the Nation two days previously might well have

2 Earl Warren, Republican Governor of California since 1943.

been expected to arouse the American public to a state of apocalyptic fervour, but both messages seem to have been received coolly. The astronomic figures which are to be the measure of the nation's sacrifice in the coming year are subject to banal comment, and have been received on the part of the legislators with anything but enthusiasm.

.   .   .

23 January 1944

Pravda outburst. Russian thunderbolt on subject of alleged British secret parleys with Ribbentrop [1] was sensationally headlined and our and your prompt denial of it stopped what might otherwise have developed into widespread speculation of truth of *Pravda* canard (as opposed to its political implications) especially as State Department's *démenti* although equally prompt was couched in somewhat frigid tones. General reaction was one of complete bewilderment and wild speculation and liberal press lamented that fruits of Tehran should so soon have showed signs of turning sour. . . .

.   .   .

Majority of press interpreted Russian move as a rebuke to Britain for alleged support of Polish Government-in-exile and there was much speculation on Russian dissatisfaction with attitude to Polish question alleged to be entertained in London with liberal undertone implying that there was some ground for such dissatisfaction.

. . . View that Russians may be building up towards their own separate peace has been negligibly sparse nor has there been any evidence of belief in *Pravda* allegation. There is talk in Washington about

(i) Possibility that Russian move is meant to divide Britain and America by displaying distrust of former, thus opening road wider for more direct collaboration with latter without British intermediacy or even continuous consultation. This represents wishful thinking on part of certain circles particularly in Navy and to a smaller degree State Department who feel after Tehran that the future of the world depends on a tough-minded United States-Russian relationship with no third powers interfering and that if the Russians prefer a game of diplomatic poker to more enlightened techniques only the United States is powerful enough to do so successfully.

(ii) That if this represents a 'hands off' warning by Russia not merely with regard to Poland but with regard to South Eastern Europe generally (hence allusions to 'reliable Greek and Yugoslav sources') there is little that can be done to prevent it.

(iii) That this represents merely another sharp prod for an immediate Second Front disapproved by Mr Churchill. This has naturally revived rumours of dis-

1 On 17 January *Pravda* alleged that two British representatives had met and discussed with the German Foreign Minister plans for a separate peace. The Foreign Office issued a flat denial on 18 January.

agreement between the Prime Minister on one hand and Roosevelt and Stalin on the other on this and other topics at Tehran. . . .

     .   .   .

Republican politics. . . . Dewey's stock is high. In a recent off-the-record press conference at Albany, Dewey is reported to have repeated his Mackinac foreign policy proposals, saying, however, that when he commented at that time about a post-war military alliance with Great Britain he thought that there had already been an agreement to that end with Roosevelt and Churchill, but later discovered it to be a mere newspaper rumour. However, he still favoured such an alliance – with Russia and China and other nations to be drawn in as soon as possible. It might not be expedient to plan a post-war military alliance with Russia at this time because when the war with Germany ends, the war with Japan still may be on. That would lead to some difficulty if Russia merely sat on the sidelines and did not help go after the Japanese. The general impression of our informant on this is that Dewey does not intend to go beyond generalities. . . . The view is gaining ground that if Dewey receives the nomination he will not decline it. When asked 'Are you willing or ready to use General Sherman's formula "If nominated, I will not run and if elected I will not serve"?',[2] Dewey replied 'The answer to that is that I am wholly and exclusively occupied with administrating the affairs of the State of New York, period, close quote.' The *New Yorker* comments 'Close quote, open campaign.' *Verb. sap.*

     .   .   .

30 January 1944

Russian relations. Excitement over *Pravda*'s allegations about British negotiations with Ribbentrop has subsided considerably and State Department have certainly advised press and radio to let issues die down. . . .

In Russian section of State Department, possibly in consequence of new 'pro Russian' trend, view prevails that diplomatic peace should be preserved at all costs and that your statement of 26 January was a trifle stiff.[1] Russian reaction to it is awaited with greatest interest. If reception is strongly adverse, that will be taken at any rate by Department's East European experts to mean that Russia has decided to settle frontiers unilaterally in defiance of general spirit of Moscow and Tehran. . . .

     .   .   .

Soldiers' vote. Congress has tied itself into knots over this very ticklish issue . . . and is consequently arousing the resentment of the general public and the personnel of the armed Services, who have more than once had to be rebuked for cheering or booing in the Senate gallery. The Southern Democrats, concerned

2 Approximate terms in which William Tecumseh Sherman, Civil War hero second only to General Grant, wired the Chairman of the Republican National Convention in 1884.

1 Eden stated in the House of Commons that the UK Government did not recognize any territorial changes made in Poland since the outbreak of war.

lest their poll tax system be undermined, by letting negro soldiers vote, and the Republicans, who despite Spangler's indiscreet claims to the contrary are deeply concerned lest the soldiers' vote goes to their Commander-in-Chief, have both been holding out for a state ballot arrangement whereby each state would arrange for the voting of its own soldiers. . . . The President has now made a bold entry into the field. He has blasted the state ballot proposal as a 'fraud' and has denounced those men whom he accuses of wishing to rob the eleven million fighting men 'who have no lobby to fight for them on the Hill'. This has naturally produced an explosion of rage from Senator Taft and the Republicans generally who see in this an electioneering move (which indeed it is) likely to win valuable support. The prospects for the Administration's federal ballot proposal are consequently somewhat brighter.

ELECTION POLITICS

A. *Democrats*. The Democratic National Committee meeting in Washington resulted as expected in an enthusiastic launching of a fourth term for the President, even while he himself maintains his favourite sphinx-like pose. The talked of rebellion by discontented elements, led by Quigley[2] of Nebraska and a Midwest group, came to nothing, and there are signs that a good many disgruntled Democratic office-holders, faced with the rising Republican sentiment in the country, will be glad when the time comes to shelter behind the President and his immense prestige. The Committee's somewhat ingenuous assertion that 'Our Allies are praying with us for the continuance of his [the President's] services' has not yet produced the eruption that might have been expected, though it has been attacked by the Scripps-Howard press. The speech by Speaker Rayburn, who filled the President's place, was notable mainly for its ill-concealed attack on Willkie as 'an imitation liberal' and Wallace's speech for its lyrical defence of the New Deal. An AP poll on the vice-presidential nomination resulted in 18 votes for Rayburn, 14 for Wallace, 7 for Farley, with a majority of the Committee still undecided. . . . Frank Walker gratefully climbed down from the key post of National Chairman in which he has never been happy, and was replaced by Robert Hannegan,[3] a Missourian protégé of Senator Truman. A Roman Catholic, like Farley and Walker, he is young (forty), vigorous and has made a decent record as Commissioner of Internal Revenue but is almost an unknown to the party hierarchy. He has been duly hailed by Democrats as a second Farley, but it remains to be seen whether he will display that great master's astounding gift for personalizing every local 'ward heeler' in the Democratic ranks from New York to California. Farley remains an enigma. The weight of his influence, especially in New York State, is considerable but no one can apparently tell which way he is going to throw it.

2 James C. Quigley, Democratic National Committee member from Nebraska 1936–52.
3 Robert E. Hannegan, initially Chairman of the St Louis Democratic Committee 1934–42.

B. *Republicans.* Willkie has announced that he will not after all enter the California primary in which Governor Warren has entered his own name, but that he expects to enter the primaries in Wisconsin, Nebraska, Pennsylvania, Oregon, and New Hampshire. The retreat from California (with its twenty-five votes), although hedged about with a face-saving statement that he saw no need to do so after obtaining Warren's assurance that he was not committed to 'stop Willkie-ism' or anything else, probably represents genuine fear of losing to Warren. As for Wisconsin (one of the first large states to hold primaries), the latest Gallup poll shows Dewey well in the lead ; (Dewey 40 per cent, Willkie 20 per cent, and MacArthur 15 per cent). . . .

Elmer Davis. Elmer Davis has let it be known publicly that he has offered his resignation to the President unless he is given clear authority over all branches of owi. The immediate occasion for this arises from a projected reorganization in the Overseas Division and Robert Sherwood's unwillingness to sack three of his Overseas Division chiefs at Davis's request – Warburg, Barnes and Johnson[4], whom Davis, apparently on the basis of an elaborate dossier prepared by one of his people, regards as insubordinate. However, the Davis-Sherwood tension is of long standing and in a way repeats the Hull-Wallace feud, for Davis has long felt keenly the direct access which Sherwood has had to the White House. Not much interest is taken in it in the press at the moment, but if Davis resigns (the President seems less likely to let Sherwood go) he may become a martyr, and 'revelations' in the press about the Overseas Branch activities are almost certain to be poured out and cause a flurry.

5 February 1944

Japanese atrocities. Publication of Japanese atrocities[1] stirred public opinion most deeply as might have been expected . . . but fact that it has not increased 'Pacific Firstism' appreciably is a welcome indication of better perspective in which war is now viewed by average American. Why, it is asked, can this information which must have been available for some time so suddenly be released? Following has been confidently advanced in press and elsewhere :

(a) it was done to boost sales of war bonds ;

(b) it has nothing to do with bonds but was done to demonstrate need for a national service act, an unanswerable reply to labour grousers ;

(c) Big Four have finally decided that Pacific has too long been neglected and is a clear indication of a shift in strategy ;

(d) negotiations are in progress for a new *Gripsholm*[2] to exchange prisoners

---

4 Edd Johnson, Chief of Overseas Division, owi, 1942–4.

1 Disclosed by Anthony Eden to House of Commons on 28 January. Referred particularly to maltreatment of prisoners of war.

2 The *Gripsholm*, a Swedish ship, brought home US diplomats and others in June 1942.

and publication is meant to 'soften up' Japanese into acceding to proposed arrangements ;

(e) negotiations for such an exchange have finally broken down and publication previously withheld is therefore no longer dangerous ;

(f) true explanation (half suggested by Lindley) that *Chicago Tribune* would have published these facts if Administration had not forestalled it.

This welter of hypotheses shows how ill informed 'well-informed sources' here can be when Administration combines to choose not to tell them and indicates that when genuine leaks occur they are scarcely ever accidental.

. . .

Soldiers' vote. 'Soldiers' vote' after boiling hotly in Congress has precipitated a first-class crisis. After some reluctance to have their names recorded by roll call, House opponents of Administration's plan, stung by President's charge of 'fraud', voted against Administration's Worley bill[3] 224 votes to 168 and then passed original Senate Bill sponsored by Republican and Southern Democrats by 328 votes to 69. In this great majority were included many original sponsors of Administration's Worley bill (including author himself) who, conceding defeat to champions of States' rights, seem to have decided to jump on the Southern bandwagon for fear of displeasing Southern or other anti-Roosevelt electors by backing a cause which looked lost already. Final House vote occurred late at night amid scenes of chaos and passionate excitement and opposition press is exulting loudly over this thumping defeat of Administration on a really crucial issue. . . .

Jews. Jewish pressure is rising still and has succeeded in gaining for resolution now before Congress (demanding that United States Government use its good offices to promote abrogation of White Paper and creation of a Jewish Commonwealth in Palestine) support of Majority and Minority Leaders in both House and Senate. From this it may be assumed that it will probably go through with virtual unanimity. This is viewed with some concern by non-Zionist Jews but they appear to prefer an anti-White Paper declaration saddled as it is with a for them unwelcome rider about Jewish State to nothing at all. While such a joint resolution would not commit United States Government to any action its significance should not be minimized as its passage imposes inevitable curbs on pro-Arab tendencies of Near Eastern Office of State Department on Palestine issue. Isolationist columnist O'Donnell[4] as a result of a Zionist press conference reports that Prime Minister told Weizmann that support of United States Congress is precisely what he needs to strengthen his hand against White Paper supporters in his own Government. Certainly all Jewish leaders seem convinced of this.

OWI. The President has now publicly admitted the existence of a disagreement between Sherwood and Elmer Davis and the betting at present is slightly in

3 Francis E.Worley, Democratic Congressman from Texas since 1941.
4 John P.O'Donnell, *New York Daily News* correspondent and columnist.

favour of Sherwood. According to one well-informed source the President sent for Davis and Sherwood, expressed his regard for them both, and upbraided them for starting a public brawl at such a moment. They replied that the matter had now gone too far in public for a negotiated peace on the basis of the *status quo*. The President persisted and said he declined to hear of resignations. The deadlock continues unaltered. Byron Price is said to be strongly disinclined to take over any part of so rickety an edifice.

Internal Shifts. Wayne Coy, one of the toughest and most efficient of the younger New Dealers, has resigned as Assistant Director of the Budget to become assistant to Eugene Meyer on the *Washington Post,* and ultimately, I am told, to inherit that newspaper which might otherwise end by falling too completely under the spell of the ebullient Mrs Meyer. His successor is Paul Appleby, previously Under-Secretary of Agriculture. This is variously interpreted. Mr Byrnes told a member of my staff that it was due to a desire on the part of Harold Smith,[5] Director of the Budget, egged on by Wayne Coy, to take Appleby 'off the shelf' on which he had been reposing for some two years, and give him a post of genuine responsibility. The Bureau of the Budget performs some of the functions of the British Treasury in scrutinizing and controlling the appointments and functioning of government departments, and Harold Smith, an honest, efficient and self-effacing Midwesterner, much trusted and used by the President, has acquired a considerable degree of influence over the machinery and consequently over the policies of the Administration. Most recent efforts to 'house clean', e.g. the Foreign Economic Administration, State Department, etc., have originated in critical reports by the Bureau, and Appleby, who is still an unrepentant liberal, will doubtless make most of his new opportunities. Those who regard his approach to commodity policy, in particular international food problems on which he had been working, as excessively confused, express relief at his transfer. Others, particularly in Byrnes's office, predict that he will prove a strong and beneficently liberal force in his new post. It seems clear at any rate that Appleby's strong Anglophile sentiments remain unimpaired, nor does anyone doubt his personal integrity. He expresses genuine delight with new functions.

.   .   .

Congressman Sheppard[6] (Democrat, California) suddenly delivered a violent and carefully prepared blast at Trippe and Pan American, alleging undercover activities in a mysterious Washington house with mysterious funds. He also took the time-honoured line of revealing the octopus in its full horror with tentacles spreading to many other financial and utility companies, and mentioned the interest of Leo Crowley, Admiral Standley and Norman Davis as well as a fact little known in public, that Trippe is Stettinius's brother-in-law.

5 Harold D. Smith, Director of the Budget, State of Michigan, 1937–9, and Director of the US Bureau of the Budget 1939–46.
6 Harry R. Sheppard, Democratic Congressman from California since 1937.

The United States has this week lost two of its most prominent publicists. The veneration for William Allen White,[7] 'the sage of Emporia', an almost ideally pure embodiment of American character and ideals, was universal, and his small-town Kansas paper acquired a nationwide reputation for the vigour and independence of its editorial page. White's contribution to our cause, as organizer in 1940 of the Committee to Defend America by Aiding the Allies, was an unforgettable service. Raymond Clapper, who died in an air accident in the South Pacific, was not only one of the most widely syndicated press columnists (180 daily papers) but was an exceptionally level-headed, candid, diligent and well-informed correspondent, whose voice articulated the reactions of the average decent small-town Americans, i.e. of the majority of the American population, more faithfully than any other man. We shall feel his loss the more if, as one rumour goes, he is to be replaced in the Scripps-Howard papers by Henry J.Taylor,[8] a nationalistically inclined sensation-monger, with views close to Roy Howard's own aggressive outlook.

12 February 1944

. . .

OWI dismissals. Dismissal of Warburg, Barnes and Johnson from OWI constitutes a personal victory for Elmer Davis, a shattering and possibly fatal defeat for Sherwood and further proof of disintegration of OWI. . . . One reason why President backed up Davis is said to be that nobody was prepared to work with overseas branch if Warburg and others remained. Sherwood after offering his resignation is carrying on out of loyalty to President. Presumably with very little authority he goes to London, in his own words 'To save what he can from the wreck', and in those of his critics 'To avoid facing the music'. His stock is very low both within his own office and in official circles generally.

Jews. Current high Zionist pressure was again evidenced when hearings were held before House Foreign Affairs Committee on two identical resolutions, HR 418 and 419, urging United States to use its good offices towards freer Jewish immigration into Palestine and towards creation there of a Jewish Commonwealth. Zionist witnesses spoke of many conferences and meetings, with hundreds of delegates from all over United States which all adopted with virtual unanimity resolutions similar to if not identical with the resolutions appearing before Committee. Hearings however did not centre around problems existing in Palestine but rather round question of where majority of Jewish sentiment in United States lay on issue. Zionists managed to persuade Committee that non-Zionist Jewish opposition in this country, though eloquent and persuasive, represented only a very small fraction of American and Jewish opinion. Republican

---

7 William Allen White, editor and publisher of the *Emporia Gazette* 1895–1944.
8 Henry J.Taylor, correspondent for Scripps-Howard chain.

minority however was evidently disturbed lest the passage of resolutions should convey any hint that United States is prepared to stand behind establishment of such Jewish National State with armed force if necessary and is worried too lest an expression of congressional opinion in case of Palestine might complicate matters in wider field of reconstituted governments in reconquered territories and encourage other minority nationals in United States to press for acceptance of their own particular claims. Though no further hearings are at present scheduled it seems likely at this moment that some modifications will have to be made in wording of resolutions before they are reported out of Committee. Representative Baldwin[1] (Republican, New York) told a member of my staff that resolutions would not pass and might not even be reported out of Committee. It is said that War Department are writing a letter to Committee saying that resolutions are untimely from a military point of view. Alleged views of Mr Churchill were quoted freely by both sides in support of their cases.

. . .

13 February 1944

Soldiers' vote. Debate in the Senate on the soldier vote bills became hotter and more confused than ever, the climax being reached when the Chair ruled that a bill did not necessarily have to make sense before it could pass. The passage of two contradictory bills in one, a federal vote bill tacked on as an amendment to a state ballot bill already passed last December, capped a week of legislative manoeuvring and counter-manoeuvring that left not only seasoned observers but Senators themselves completely bewildered. . . . The odds, however, are in favour of the state ballot, since the Senate passed the federal ballot bill only by a narrow margin and the House, having passed a state ballot bill by an overwhelming majority, has now pigeonholed the Senate's federal ballot bill in its Elections Committee. Further, since it is the Administration which is trying to alter the *status quo* by substituting Federal for State voting machinery, they will be the losers if the present deadlock should result in no legislation at all being passed.

. . .

Taxes. A Senate–House conference committee reported out the expected compromise version of the Administration's tax bill which in its original form had made provision for raising $10½ billion but which in its final form this week provided for only $2⅓ billion. The compromise has been accepted by both Houses with easy majorities, and the bill is now on the President's desk. It is considered probable that he will allow it to become law without his signature though labour leaders are currently pressing him to veto it. A veto appears improbable[2] since the main objection to the bill has been largely removed. The objection was a rider attached which virtually abolished the renegotiation of contracts by the War and Navy Departments ; a compromise on renegotiation has been reached which is reported to satisfy those two departments.

1 Joseph Clark Baldwin, Republican Congressman from Manhattan 1941–7.
2 President did, however, veto tax bill on 22 February.

Subsidies. The Senate also this week voted down any efforts at compromise on the Administration's food subsidies programme. The Farm Bloc's Bankhead bill, which would ban most of the existing food subsidy programme after 30 June of this year, is expected to pass without any amendments or modifications. Since the House has already approved a similar bill, only a presidential veto can now save the Administration's price-rollback programme. Such a veto is widely anticipated and it is thought unlikely that Congress will override the veto. This situation parallels that of last summer when the President vetoed a similar measure attached as an amendment to a bill extending the life of the Commodity Credit Corporation. If, as is expected, the pattern is repeated, a separate bill extending the life of the Commodity Credit Corporation will be introduced and passed immediately following the presidential veto. The press has been strongly critical in recent months of the selfishness of the opposition to subsidies by pressure groups, and it is likely that the President will gain prestige in this matter again at the expense of Congress.

.   .   .

19 February 1944

An exceptionally quiet week. The Russo-Polish issue was conspicuously played down in press, plainly under inspiration of State Department which seems to have continued line laid down by Hull at press conference given before he went to recuperate in Florida, in which he spoke of difficulty of reconciling just Polish and Russian claims and conveyed that less partisan talk on this subject the better. He added that it was after all a British responsibility since United States was uncommitted. Stettinius, who is now in charge, in a 'frank' talk to a small group of newspaper correspondents at a private luncheon appears to have led off with a peculiar story that word had arrived from Moscow implying that Stalin was contemplating a personal message to Willkie dissociating himself and his Government from the now famous attack on Willkie in *Pravda*. One American newspaperman is saying that he had gathered that Joe Davies had written to Litvinov explaining that damage to USSR had been done in United States by *Pravda* attack and that Stalin's rumoured move was result. Stettinius also said (echoing Hull) that a larger reform of State Department was contemplated than had so far occurred, involving injection of genuine new blood (possibly Nelson Rockefeller) and that a really 'tough' Department would duly emerge if he had his way. . . . There can be no doubt of Stettinius's genuine ambition to recast Department on lines which he considered more adequate for present-day needs, particularly for dealing with international commercial and economic policy on more vigorous lines. . . .

.   .   .

Oil. This issue continues to be widely discussed and is especially highlighted by publication of Truman Committee's report on this question which gives a detailed description of situation and takes a line more or less analogous to five Senators, i.e. emphasizes depletion of United States resources and necessity for a more aggressive oil-acquiring United States policy, particularly in Middle East. Report was obviously drafted principally for home political consumption and cannot of course be taken as authoritative in any way or as representing views of any executive agency of Government. On whole it is objective and is mainly critical of defects of United States governmental machinery which is invidiously compared with British. Truman Committee will now pass out of the picture and be replaced by new committee of nine with delegates from the Lands, Commerce, Interstate Commerce and Foreign Relations Committees of Senate and a chairman nominated by President. Ickes's announcement on contemplated pipeline[1] has been criticized both from left and from right – from left as dollar diplomacy and evidence of sinister power of oil interests, from the right as a new 'entering wedge' into private enterprise on part of Government. If Ickes intended to precipitate issue in a form in which it can no longer be ignored (and it is said that he did) he has succeeded and, as in matter of civil aviation, issue has become one on which the Administration knows that it must act in full glare of public attention.

20 February 1944

PRESIDENTIAL POLITICS

(a) *Republicans*. The Lincoln Day speeches of Dewey and Willkie have been in line with their previous utterances, and Governor Bricker has made his much heralded Washington debut. His reputation, which had sunk to zero, rose somewhat : he is now definitely known to exist – and his supporters seem to believe that if this knowledge does not evaporate too quickly, he may yet prove the rallying point for conservatives. The press has, on the whole, described him with tolerant amiability, and has congratulated him on the frankness of his replies to unfriendly questions, even when they admitted their somewhat humdrum content. . . .

.   .   .

(b) *Democrats*. Wallace's attack on Wall Street fell flat, even more so his denunciation of the growing influence of American fascists ; when, under pressure, he finally identified these as Colonel McCormick, the anti-climax reached its nadir. Nor has his prediction that the President will be re-elected caused a sensation. Such passionate desire to secure renomination for the Vice-Presidency is unique in United States history : this odd spectacle is observed with pain or enjoyment according to the sympathies of the onlooker.

.   .   .

27 February 1944

The greatest sensation of week is of course Senator Barkley's resignation as Senate Majority Leader. I have no information leading me to suppose that it was

1 On 6 February Ickes announced an agreement between the Petroleum Reserves Corporation, which represented the US Government in foreign oil matters, and Standard Oil of California and Texas. Under this the USA would construct and maintain a pipeline from S. Arabia and Kuwait to the Mediterranean.

other than a spontaneous explosion on Barkley's part, preceded though it undoubtedly was by accumulating resentment on part both of Senate as a whole and of conservative Democrats, for both of which Barkley feels that he speaks. President's recent strategy can be consistently interpreted only as based on a decision to take offensive against Congress whenever he feels that his case seems to him sufficiently strong. The underlying reasons are probably :

(a) A recognition of necessity to reassert his leadership in internal matters after some neglect in favour of attention to matters concerned with conduct of the war.

(b) A modicum of election tactics. Only a realization that conciliatory tactics did not succeed in bringing a conservative Congress to his side and would not do so in future, can have decided President to issue so blunt and uncompromising a series of messages to Congress as those over soldiers' vote, subsidies and taxes. This naturally did not fail to breed corresponding bitterness particularly among Southerners who have continually been forced to choose between unity and strength of the Democratic Party on the one hand and permanent political interests and lifelong convictions on other. Such rumblings as have been heard usually ended inconsequentially in efforts to build up Senator Byrd as a rival Democratic presidential candidate, a tendency naturally encouraged by Farley and his disgruntled friends. Barkley, who has served President with faithful devotion for many years and owes his position as Majority Leader to him, has, it is known, been assailed by a combination of practical personal considerations and conscientious political qualms about his position as principal organizer of policies in which he did not believe. His position in Kentucky has for some time been somewhat shaky and his re-election, which comes up this year, has been regarded as far from certain. His reputation as a blindly devoted agent of White House has not helped him in that border State and doubtless advice of his local political friends together with growing persecution of him by main body of Southern Democrats, led by such intransigents as George and McKellar, have proved too much for him personally. Conflict between Rooseveltite and Southern conservative trends in the party has made life intolerable for his predecessors, particularly late Senator Robinson[1] who nearly seceded over Supreme Court fight.[2] A member of my staff who has spoken to several of Senator's friends reports them as saying that although Barkley's act was sudden and committed virtually without consultation, it has, in rallying South round him, undoubtedly saved his political life. It seems unlikely that President anticipated this move and his letter as much as says so. It is difficult to see how even if he did foresee it, he could have modified his policy (though he might have modified his veto message which was couched in highly provocative terms), since he is reported by his closest advisers to feel that appeasement of Congress would prove fatal to his

1 Joseph Taylor Robinson, Democratic Senator from Arkansas 1913–37 and Majority Leader 1933–7.

2 Roosevelt's unsuccessful attempt to secure legislation enabling him to increase the numbers of Supreme Court justices, 1937.

chances of re-election. It is too early to determine effect of this crisis but it already seems clear that painful negotiations with South will have to be conducted by White House, whose contacts with it have been growing thinner and thinner, if Democratic unity is to be restored. President, like everyone else, understands that without Southern conservatives his re-election is virtually impossible. On the other hand rebellious Democratic elements are not unaware that their own political fortunes may be jeopardized if the party swings too far away from President whose vote-getting powers are unchallenged within the party. . . . Barkley's prompt re-election by an enthusiastic majority was immediately interpreted as meaning that he would now be spokesman for Senate in White House rather than vice versa. However President's letter to Barkley and warmth of regard for President still evident in Barkley's reply is leading some observers (e.g. Scripps-Howard press) to question this assumption. It would be rash to assume that President's powers of persuasion are exhausted and that a satisfactory compromise cannot be patched up, though there is no doubt that breach has been a dangerous one. . . . Some well-informed observers declare that tax bill itself is a sorry compromise containing many of worst parts of both Treasury's and Congress's measures and say blame is equally divided between Administration and Congress. However overriding of President's veto was not based on tax bill so much as on a Congress versus executive basis. House voted overwhelmingly to override (299 to 95) while Senate next day overrode veto by an even larger margin 72 to 14.

. . .

Truk.[3] Admiral Nimitz is the new hero of the day and his exploits in Pacific have drawn much attention from other fronts. This is first relief after relative stagnation of Italian Front to American reader and press has made most of it. European realities have been recalled to him however by speech of Mr Churchill but Pacific news still dominates attention.

Mr Churchill's speech.[4] This was as always hailed with immense enthusiasm particularly by radio commentators although one or two newspapers were evidently made restive by very meatiness of the speech. Early reactions of minorities principally affected are such as might be expected – the Poles are gloomy and depressed, some officials of Yugoslav Government in Washington are speaking of resigning, while Greeks complain that reference to depressing confusion of their country at a time when they were under the impression that some sort of agreement was being patched up between warring factions, came as a very nasty surprise to them. Possibly they feel a trifle compensated by hostile reference to Bulgaria which must also please the Yugoslavs. . . .

3 Devastating attack on Japanese naval and air units on Truk Island, 16 and 17 February.

4 In the House of Commons, 22 February, reviewing progress of the war and policy with regard to Italy, Yugoslavia and Poland.

Baruch Report.[5] . . . The recommendations of the report were not wholly unexpected in view of its conservative authorship. Its presupposition that the
Administration should relinquish control of the industrial life of the country as
rapidly as possible once the emergency is over and should create facilities for its
recanalization into the old channels of private enterprise, has been exceedingly
well received by the entire conservative and middle-of-the-road press, with only
the expected amount of criticism by the liberals. Points to be noted are that its
reception might have been less cordial if the Service Departments had not
reached a far better understanding with the War Production Board and the other
economic agencies concerned than had been the case a year ago. The clear statement in the report that the war was far from won, and that to begin transformation to civilian economy would be highly premature and prejudicial to the war
effort, has done much to relieve those who looked with anxiety on the tendency
in public opinion, and even more strongly in the business world, to look on
victory as so foregone a conclusion that it was only natural for producers and
distributors to plan their activities in terms of probable peacetime conditions
rather than the immediate requirements of the war. The report was written by
Messrs Hancock,[6] Herbert Swope[7] and Sam Lubell[8] (the last collaborated also
in the Baruch Rubber Report and is a facile journalist originally connected with
the *Saturday Evening Post*). If the Administration adopts this report as a plank
in its economic platform, it could probably amass a great deal of conservative
support, particularly in the South : it is unlikely to wean Mid-western or Western
anti-Rooseveltites, whose natural reaction is to praise the report but to add that
it will come to nothing if the Roosevelt Administration is charged with its implementation. The only discordant reaction came from the Senate where Senator
George, who does not in general disagree with the conservative attitude of the
report, is evidently jealous of the prerogatives of his own Committee which,
with the help of Brookings Institute, issued a strangely neglected report, if anything more orthodox than Baruch's, more than a fortnight ago. Apart from this
jealousy which takes the form of demanding that Congress, in particular the
Senate, set up the Committee to conduct post-war reconversion, and not an
agency responsible to the White House (this despite the clear provision in the
Baruch report that Congress must authorize various recommended policies before any action can follow) there is a sharp disagreement on demobilization. The
Baruch report specifically rejects a separate Bureau of Demobilization on the
ground that such an office may develop a vested interest in demobilizing as many
persons as possible in the shortest time, irrespective of the national interest, and
prefers to entrust this duty to those original offices – chief among them the Office

5 Baruch Report on War and Post-war Adjustment Policies, issued on 18 February.

6 John M. Hancock, industrial banker, partner in Lehman Bros, close associate of Baruch.

7 Herbert Bayard Swope, editor of the *New York World* 1920–9, publicist, adviser to the Secretary of War.

8 Sam Lubell, reporter on the *Washington Post* 1936–7, *Washington Herald* 1937–8, freelance 1938–41, general secretary of the Baruch Rubber Survey 1942.

of War Mobilization, headed by Baruch's friend Byrnes – which were charged with mobilizing the national effort and are, therefore, best qualified to unwind the strands with due regard to the various interests and issues involved. Under this scheme it is suggested that Will Clayton[9] of Texas, Jesse Jones's assistant on RFC and the world's greatest cotton operative, take charge of industrial reconversion, while General Hines,[10] long experienced in the Veterans' Bureau, should take charge of demobilization. Clayton's efficiency, lucid mind and capacity for getting on with people, has made him many friends in circles less traditionally orthodox than he is himself, the reasons for which will be appreciated by those members of British delegations, particularly to the Food Conference, who have come in contact with him. So high is his stock at the moment that Hull is said to want him as one of his new Assistant Secretaries in the State Department, while Byrnes is demanding him to undertake reconversion.

There is also a rumour that Hamilton Fish Armstrong, long a confidential consultant to State Department committees, was sounded out on the possibility of entering the State Department as an Assistant Secretary, a move which would please many liberals in view of Armstrong's well-known integrity and liberal outlook, but that he declined on the ground, probably justified, that he had more scope for influence in his present unofficial position. Tom Finletter's resignation in the State Department has finally been made public. He is merely one of a series of frustrated liberals, preceded by Feis, to whom the Administration, and in particular the State Department, appears to offer inadequate elbow-room.

Dewey has asked that his name be withdrawn from the Wisconsin primary, where Willkie, Stassen and MacArthur are also entered and Gallup polls suggest Dewey is in lead ; but I have found no well-informed observer who believes that he is any the less likely to accept the Republican presidential nomination if it is offered to him.

The 'soldier vote' remains in a hopelessly deadlocked position after seven meetings between the Senate and House conferees.

5 March 1944

The Barkley affair. It is now becoming possible to see what is valid and what is not, in all the deduction and speculation arising from the Barkley incident. No (repeat no) permanent split has been created in Democratic Party by episode which of itself is unlikely to affect President's chances of a fourth term. Barkley's stock has risen dramatically which will assist him materially in his own campaign for re-election in Kentucky. But it seems far-fetched to talk of him as a potential presidential candidate pushed through by anti-Roosevelt Democrats and far from certain that he is from now on the champion of Senate versus White House. He may perhaps show more independence *vis-à-vis* President but on his

9 William L.Clayton, Assistant Secretary of Commerce 1942–4.
10 Frank T.Hines, Administrator of Veterans' Affairs 1930–44.

past voting record it is difficult to see him becoming spokesman of conservative George-Byrd bloc any more than of New Dealers, and it is doubtful how far Barkley will be able to live up to greatness which some people would like to thrust upon him. Unfortunate consequences of affair from White House point of view seem to be twofold. (1) An open rebuke was successfully administered both in Barkley's resignation and in heavy overriding by both houses of veto of tax bill. This was as much a rebuke to White House political tactics as to White House tax policies. It expressed growing resentment felt in Congress against President's tendency to 'put it on the spot'. The tax veto was however a particularly suitable issue for a congressional stand because taxation has always been jealous preserve of Congress. Various commentators have suggested that President has been badly advised especially by Treasury, over tax issue, and Lippmann declared flatly that a new Secretary of Treasury is needed. Opposition press have tried to pin blame for explosive veto message on to Rosenman but apparently some of its more provocative passages may have come from Vinson, Byrnes and President himself. (2) It meant that President's tactics by which many observers believe he was beginning to build up his record *vis-à-vis* Congress as part of a fourth-term campaign, have been exposed and discussed throughout the nation and may have been correspondingly weakened. President has still much support for himself in country over this matter (e.g. amongst labour and armed forces), and even papers which condemned his tactics on tax bill have warned Congress that it must still demonstrate that it can do more than obstruct. For meantime the resentment of Congress seems more likely to be taken out on domestic than on war or foreign policy issues. Willkie tried to score off both parties at once by condemning President's veto message as 'violent and ill tempered' and declaring that 'dramatic resignations and over-sentimental reconciliations' (i.e. Barkley's) provided no answer to administration's economic mismanagement. But his failure to include Congress in his condemnations since they were passing a 2½ billion tax bill in place of 16 billion one he had so recently advocated has led his potential left-wing supporters (e.g. *New York Post*) to criticize his apparent inconsistency.

. . .

State Department. White House has requested Congress to authorize expansion to a worldwide basis of cultural relations activities which State Department now conducts in Latin America, China and a few other countries. Proposal provides for greatly expanded use of movies, radio, educational exchanges, overseas libraries, etc., to interpret America abroad and suggests that reciprocal arrangements might be worked out for spreading of information about other countries in United States. Cultural enthusiasts in State Department who have felt somewhat lost since their original patron Sumner Welles was removed seem to have found new champions in Stettinius and Howland Shaw [1] and may now be able to get on

1 G.Howland Shaw, career diplomat, Assistant Secretary of State 1941–4.

with some of their oft-postponed plans. They still face many difficulties from Congress (which has already suggested a cut in State Department budget), from commercial film and radio interests and from other governmental agencies already active in this field, but it does seem increasingly likely that State Department will be dominant agency in operating America's post-war overseas publicity. Old rumour is again circulating that co-ordination for inter-American affairs will eventually be absorbed in State Department and that Nelson Rockefeller will be appointed as one of two new Assistant Secretaries of State whose creation Mr Hull recently announced and authorization for whom application has now been made to Congress. OWI have evinced little surprise at State Department proposals but they accept them as one further indication of their own demise as soon as shooting stops.

'The Times' on Germany. The Times editorial[2] arguing against a partition of Germany has been prominently reported in *New York Times* and *Herald Tribune* and is causing some eyebrow raising in Washington. . . . Mr Walter Lippmann told a member of my staff that *The Times* leader coupled with Smuts's speech was being taken to indicate a strong body of opinion in London in favour of building up Germany against Russia.

.   .   .

6 March 1944

Soldiers' vote. The fortnight-long deadlock over the soldiers' vote was finally broken when a compromise measure was announced by which the Federal ballot would be used as a supplementary measure, available to members of the armed forces for whom no provision for voting had been made by individual States. Immediately following this announced compromise, the House conferees insisted that the measure apply only to service men abroad and, rather surprisingly, the Senate conferees gave way. It will be the responsibility of the State Governors and Legislatures either to amend their State constitutions if no absentee voting provisions exist or to supply ballots to men overseas, if requested, by 1 October. If neither of these things is done, overseas soldiers may use the Federal ballot, provided it is declared acceptable under the laws of the States from which they come.

.   .   .

Jews. Further hearings on the Jewish Commonwealth Resolution are quite likely, but the pendulum now seems to be swinging away from the Zionists. The opposition of the War Department is becoming known and Constantine Brown, frequently a State Department mouthpiece, condemned the Jewish pressure as ill-timed and militarily embarrassing to the Allies, especially the British. Supporters of the Resolution in the Foreign Affairs Committee feel that Chairman Sol

2 Of 29 February.

Bloom by delaying tactics has destroyed the Resolution's chances and that he, in fact, never intended to do more than make a show for the benefit of his Jewish constituents. The intervention of the Egyptian Premier and the Iraqi and Syrian statements [1] against the Resolution have provoked an outburst from Representative Celler [2] who charged that the machinations of the British Colonial Office were patently responsible for the protests. The State Department feels that Arab outbursts will only tend to arouse irritation in the United States and so keep the issue alive, but in view of the desire to secure oil resources in the Middle East they may be expected to have some effect.

Senator McNary. With the death of Senator McNary, Senate Minority Leader, the Republicans have lost their ablest parliamentarian and one of the strongest influences in the party. He was a leader of the Farm Bloc in the Senate, and on foreign affairs, though he was Willkie's running mate in 1940, he occupied a straddling position between the isolationist and internationalist wings of the Republican Party. Senators White, Vandenberg and Taft are most often mentioned as possible successors and considerable jostling is said to be going on. It is still possible, however, that rather than risk an intra-party squabble, the Republicans may decide to retain, till the next Congress convenes, the recent arrangement (made on account of McNary's illness), whereby White acts as Acting Floor Leader and Vandenberg as Acting Chairman of the Senate Republican Conference. The Republican freshmen are known to be pressing for a clear-cut reorganization.

. . .

Political realignments. Some curious realigning of political supporters seems to be under way. Communist publications are solemnly wagging a finger at Mr Wallace for his sweeping condemnations of cartels and Wall Street. There are good cartels and bad cartels, they now announce, and good and bad on Wall Street, and there is no justification for indiscriminate attacks by wild-eyed liberals. The Communists' new zeal for national unity is assuredly carrying them into strange places. At the same time the Hearst papers and Lewis's *Mine-Workers' Journal* are swapping articles – on a basis of mutual aid against Roosevelt.

11 March 1944

American foreign policy. The week has been marked by a sharp upsurge of uneasiness about the vagueness of American foreign policy in particular and Allied war aims in general. This has been brought to a head by various factors – the continued evidence of Russian diplomatic aggressiveness *vis-à-vis* Poland

---

1 On 28 and 29 February Egyptian and Iraqi Governments protested to the United States on the statements made to the Senate Committee about the creation of a Jewish State in Palestine. The Syrian and Lebanese Governments followed suit.

2 Emanuel Celler, Democratic Congressman from New York since 1923.

and Finland, the aftermath of Prime Minister's speech,[1] the President's casual revelation of proposed Italian ship transfer, etc. Resulting mood is reminiscent of the uneasiness of last summer when many commentators, led by liberal critics of State Department, were deploring America's lack of any clear policy. Now, however, the dissatisfaction is evident amongst groups of almost all shades of political opinion. . . .

The impression is gaining ground that Atlantic Charter has been abandoned, certainly by Russia and Britain, that even the Moscow Declaration is outdated and that the future is being shaped more in accordance with 'unknown deals' made at Tehran where Stalin emerged as dominant figure in a new game of politics.

Attitudes to British policy vary. Our friends feel that we are doing our best in a very difficult situation, with little positive help from Washington. They say that the Prime Minister's speech shows that we are making our choices, even if they are unpleasant and regrettable ones, whereas Washington is simply procrastinating. But the bulk of opinion, including the liberals and Wilsonian idealists, seem to feel that we are abandoning all high principles and resorting to the old discredited policies of expediency, national interest and balance of power. *The Times* editorial of 29 February on Germany's role in Europe is cited as evidence of this, and so are the Prime Minister's remarks on the Badoglio regime,[2] which drew an impassioned protest in *Herald Tribune* from six prominent Italian liberals (Salvemini, La Piana, Borgese, Toscanini, Pacciardi, Venturi).[3] Blame for the unsatisfactory situation in Italy is generally placed on our shoulders and Anglophobes like the *Chicago Tribune* as well as sentimental lovers of Italian culture suggest the strategy of attacking the soft underbelly of the Axis has been a blunder.

Meanwhile, Sumner Welles has delivered an attack on the haphazard way in which the European Advisory Council ('a poor makeshift' consisting 'merely of the United States and Soviet Ambassadors and a minor official of the Foreign Office') is tackling the problems of Germany and Europe in the absence of an adequate United Nations Council.

It is against this background that announcement of Stettinius's impending visit to London has come. It has been uniformly welcomed as, at least, a ray of sunshine. Stettinius's stock is high at the moment and he is personally looking forward to his London trip. Disclosure that he will take with him Matthews,

1 *Vide supra,* 27 February.

2 'I am not yet convinced that any other Government can be formed at the present time which would command the same obedience from the Italian armed forces.'

3 George La Piana, church historian, emigrated to USA 1913, taught at Harvard 1926–47.

Giuseppe A. Borgese, in USA since 1931, Professor of History, University of Chicago, 1936–52.

Arturo Toscanini, world-famous conductor. Left Italy in 1928 as protest against Fascism. Was conductor of New York Philharmonic Orchestra 1926–36, NBC Symphony Orchestra 1937–53.

Randolfo Pacciardi, journalist and Italian Republican Party politician, exile in the USA 1940–4.

Franco Venturi, historian of the Enlightenment.

Wallace Murray,[4] Isaiah Bowman[5] and a Lend-Lease official is producing the usual speculation about the purposes of his trip. There is a strong undercurrent of feeling in Washington however that while the trip may clear many technical points, the real clarification of American policy can come only from the White House itself.

Italian shipping. Circumstances in which President revealed proposal to give Russia one third of Italian fleet, or the equivalent thereof, have aroused much surprise and have increased the irritation with President's failure to take the country into his confidence, especially since Tehran, as, it is frequently said, the Prime Minister does with the British people. At an earlier press conference President had been asked about a call he received from Soviet Ambassador. He replied that Mr Gromyko had brought a question from Stalin which he, the President, was now trying to find an answer for. On 3 March he was asked if he had yet found the answer to Stalin's question. He at first professed not to recall the incident and then, upon further prompting, remarked 'Oh, that' and went on to say that it concerned the disposition of the Italian fleet. This casualness in revealing what was taken to be a matter of high policy has aroused more comment and hostility than actual question of disposition of Italian shipping. On latter point press opinion has been almost evenly divided between those who say Russia is justified in claiming a fair share of the 'spoils', and those who see further evidence of British-American appeasement of Russian demands.

.   .   .

France. There is increased pressure on State Department and White House to clarify America's attitude to French National Committee. . . . It is known that a statement on America's attitude to the Committee, prepared by War and State Departments, has been lying on President's desk for some time, and the rumour has been that, while State Department has overcome its earlier squeamishness, President's personal feelings towards de Gaulle were still proving a bottleneck. Reports from moderately reliable newspapermen suggest that statement when it comes will be a disappointment to Gaullists and liberals.

.   .   .

Oil. Subject of petroleum continued to be much in evidence in press and particularly Mr Ickes's unloved brainchild, the Arabian oil pipeline scheme of the Petroleum Reserves Corporation.[6] Having been attacked as a potential source of international conflict and betrayal of the Atlantic Charter, a waste of public funds, a victory for two large oil companies over their rivals at government expense, a step to involve United States Government in the petroleum industry

4 Wallace S.Murray, career diplomat, Director, Office of Near Eastern and African Affairs, State Department, 1944–5.

5 Isaiah Bowman, geographer, President, Johns Hopkins University, since 1935, veteran geopolitical Washington sage, Vice-Chairman of Advisory Council of State Department on post-war foreign policy 1943–5.

6 Corporation set up by US Government in July 1943 to acquire and develop oilfields outside the United States.

against the will of the people in the industry itself, and a furtherance of foreign oil cartel arrangements, it is now being attacked by the Petroleum Industry War Council as a typically fascist approach to the whole problem. In the meantime forthcoming conversations between ourselves and United States Government on general subject of petroleum have been announced to an eagerly awaiting press whose impatience for some definite statement had been causing Mr Stettinius considerable anxiety. Simultaneously with announcement that preliminary discussions were to be held on a technical level, the composition of the American committee to conduct the ministerial-level talks which are expected to follow was made public. It consists of the Secretary of State as Chairman, Secretary Ickes, Vice-Chairman, with Patterson, Forrestal, Charles Rayner,[7] Petroleum adviser of the State Department, and Charles Wilson, Vice-Chairman of WPB. This committee is a culmination of struggle between Department of State and Ickes for control of American foreign oil policy, victory seemingly going to State Department. In this connexion Mr Stettinius remarked to a member of my staff 'we saved you from Ickes'.

Ickes however has never yet played a willing second fiddle and is still determined to dominate the conference, but his position with the oil industry has been severely shaken through his advocacy of pipeline scheme, which it is reported is now only backed seriously by President and Secretary Knox. Current gossip is that both Ickes and President seriously misjudged political effect of pipeline scheme. They had expected attack from major oil companies which they would have welcomed as political capital. However the most vocal opposition has come from small independents, an important and influential voting factor, with strong influence in Congress.

Jews. American Palestine Committee on 9 March held an all-day conference in Washington which had been planned some time back as a trump-card in their campaign to force their Zionist resolution through Congress. The speakers and supporters included Vice-President Wallace and Paul McNutt (who were extremely cautious and non-committal) and Wendell Willkie, Senators Taft and Wagner (who fully endorsed the Zionist demands), together with many labour and church organizations. Actually however the peak of Zionist influence was passed over a week ago and things have been going against them since the opposition of General Marshall, Mr Stimson and the State Department, as well as the Arab protests, became publicly known. A few hours before the Washington meeting convened, Drs Wise and Silver[8] went to White House and came out with a statement from President which seems at once to mark his concession to Zionist pressure (and five million Jewish voters in the background) and to seal

7 Charles B. Rayner, Chief of Petroleum Division of the Office of Economic Affairs, State Department.

8 Co-Chairmen of the American Zionist Emergency Council. Stephen S. Wise, New York rabbi, founder of the Zionist Organization of America. Abba H. Hillel Silver, Cleveland rabbi, President of Zionist Organization of America.

the doom of congressional resolution for time being. White House statement said that United States Government had never approved the White Paper, that President was happy that doors of Palestine are open today to Jewish refugees, and 'that when future decisions are reached full justice will be done to those who seek a Jewish national home'. There was finally a reference to 'hundreds of thousands of homeless Jewish refugees'. Zionists who had been in a mood of disappointment over what seemed to be the imminent failure of their efforts and of sharp resentment against the War Department, Arab, and alleged British interference, will probably accept this statement as the best they can achieve meantime. They are openly attributing the War Department's attitude to concern for American oil interests in Middle East.

· · ·

The Administration and Congress. An indication of the extent of resentment of Congress against recent White House tactics has been seen in the letter of Senator Truman (normally a 100 per cent Roosevelt man) to the *St Louis Star Times* sharply rebuking the press for ridiculing Congress and declaring bluntly that the President 'got just exactly what was coming to him' for his attack on Congress in the tax veto. Apart from this, there have been no further repercussions to the Barkley incident though the press has noted that Barkley did not return to Washington for the conference of Democratic congressional leaders at the White House a few days ago. The belief at the moment is that the White House feels that congressional ire must be allowed to die down. Hence the decision to give way to the demand of a Senate committee to question Jonathan Daniels, one of the President's administrative assistants, regarding appointments in the Rural Electrification Administration, a demand which Daniels had at first resisted to the delight of anti-Administration forces who saw a chance of building up the incident into another *cause célèbre*. Hence, too, the decision of Vinson and Bowles to have informal conferences with Senate and House leaders prior to the impending debates on the renewal of the Price Control Act. Representative Wolcott[9] (Republican, Michigan) has already warned that he intends to reopen the fight over consumer food subsidies by introducing into the Price Control Extension Bill an amendment to outlaw them.

· · ·

Baruch Report. The Baruch report has had a very good reception as an outline of America's industrial reconversion programme. Even Philip Murray in a letter to Donald Nelson has declared himself 'completely sympathetic' to its 'basic assumptions'. It seems that the real fight will centre round the techniques and personnel by which the report is implemented. Senator Styles Bridges, while defending the report itself, has warned in the Senate against trying to carry it out without the consent and co-operation of Congress. The WPB is also determined to have a finger in the pie, and Murray's letter to Nelson contained a strong

9 Jessie P. Wolcott, Republican Congressman from Michigan since 1931.

demand for labour representation. The National Farmers' Union (the only farm organization which has recently been loyal to the Administration) stands out alone in its sweeping criticism of the report itself and has protested violently against the appointment of Clayton as administrator, because of his business connexions as the biggest cotton broker in the world.

18 March 1944

Italy and Soviet-British-American relations. Soviet recognition of Badoglio came as a complete surprise and State Department found it difficult to conceal their astonishment from press. Such a development is of course a gift to Russophobes and isolationists who are quick to point out that Russia is going her own way and that Moscow declaration like Atlantic Charter was never more than window-dressing behind which Soviet leaders are working out their own schemes. Alarm about implications of high-handed, independent and unpredictable line of Russians is increasing amongst genuine internationalists. Freedom House[1] (composed of earnest internationalists, Wilsonian idealists, etc.,) has issued an anxious appeal to Soviet protesting against her tactics towards Poles. It is signed by such people as William Agar,[2] Raymond Leslie Buell,[3] George Fielding Elliot, Justice Pecora, Robert Watt of AF of L, etc. In general however criticism of Soviet action in Italy has not been as violent and widespread as might have been expected and this seems due to deep discontent with Washington's own apparent lack of any policy on almost all outstanding problems (see last week's telegram). . . .

What many commentators agree is that Soviet is scoring off Britain and America not only in Eastern but in Western Europe by the indebtedness it derives from its advance recognition first of de Gaullist and now of Badoglio régimes. 'Wheel of fortune is turning fast,' Mrs McCormick said in *New York Times,* 'and all that remains is for Stalin to join the Pope in a plea to spare Rome.'

One byproduct of affair is to increase demand noted last week for more information about what is going on behind diplomatic curtains. This is true of much of rank and file of both parties in Congress though especially of Republicans who are out to make what political capital they can out of Administration's silence. It is also true of entire press and radio who grew used to almost unlimited access to information in peacetime and who now feel frustrated and impotent. Dilemma of Administration especially in an election year when almost anything can be used to make political controversy is easy to understand.

. . .

1 Freedom House, founded October 1941, as symbolic antithesis to Nazi Braunhaus, at 32 East 51st St, New York, to serve as information centre to anti-Nazi groups, became residuary legatee of Fight for Freedom Committee after Pearl Harbor.

2 William M.Agar, brother of Herbert Agar *(vide supra,* 6 February 1943), geologist, author, Chairman of Board of Freedom House.

3 Raymond Leslie Buell, lecturer at Fletcher School of Law and Diplomacy 1938–46, and adviser on foreign affairs to *Time.*

Anglo-American friction. There has been an unpleasant rash of gossip stories in Washington recently about irritations and disagreements arising between American policy-makers and ourselves. We are portrayed as being irritated about Ickes's pipeline invasion into our 'sphere of influence' in Middle East. Before Soviet action American authorities were pictured as being irritated with Prime Minister's leanings towards Badoglio-Victor Emmanuel régime. There have also been rumours of disagreement over certain aspects of Lend-Lease. But most serious has been growth of rumours that we were again stalling on invasion of Europe and that Stilwell[4] could get no active co-operation from Wavell or Mountbatten in Burma. Some of this criticism of our military strategy has undoubtedly reached press from United States Army and Naval officials possibly of the middle èchelons. Two days ago however General Marshall summoned one of his selective off-record conferences and warned press sharply of follies of irresponsible criticism of Britain, stories which he said could only have a bad effect on morale of American soldiers fighting with their British allies. Marshall is proving a valuable friend these days for he has used his unrivalled reputation with Congress and press on several occasions in our interest, notably in turning scales against Zionist Resolution, in Eire crisis and in situation described above. General Pat Hurley,[5] who also opposed Zionist pressure perhaps because of his interest in oil of Middle East but who had been reported as source of some of criticisms of our Burma tactics, also talked off record with press this week. He suggested that reports of the five senators about America being outwitted in the Middle East and elsewhere were greatly exaggerated and that whatever day-to-day frictions might arise it was stupid to blink fact that maintenance of a strong British Empire was essential to America's own interest. There is little doubt that American military authorities are realizing, not without prompting on our part, that anti-British gossip mongers may seriously damage Allied cause at this critical juncture but tendency to play up points of Anglo-American friction is distinctly more perceptible than it was some months ago.

Eire. There has been almost 100 per cent support for combined American and British pressure on Eire to expel Axis representatives. Almost only exceptions are two New York Irish American papers (*Irish World* and *Gaelic American*) which now as always are fanatically anti-British and a certain softness towards De Valera[6] evident in Boston papers. Hull at his press conference used his old argument that lives of American boys were being endangered and this never seems to fail with press. General Marshall also spoke out strongly at a private conference declaring that situation in Eire was as serious as Spain and that War

4 General Joseph W.Stilwell, Chief-of-Staff to Chiang Kai-shek and Commander of 5th and 6th Chinese Armies in Burma, and of US forces in China, Burma and India.

5 Patrick J.Hurley, lawyer, Secretary of War 1929–33, negotiated with Mexico for five expropriated US oil companies, 1940, personal representative of President on numerous occasions in Second World War, especially in Middle East and China.

6 Eamonn De Valera, Prime Minister of Ireland 1932–48.

Department had definite information of Axis's spying and sabotage via Dublin. Press and radio seem ready for whatever further moves interests of security may demand. In general we have been coming in for considerable praise (e.g. from a conservative like Mark Sullivan) for our tactful handling of Eire during war. It seems that America's traditional sympathy for Irish is quite outweighed today by fact that safety of American boys is involved and it is also true that Irish American population is much more absorbed in American scene than it was in 1918.

. . .

Jewish Resolution. Jewish press has been enthusiastic over President's statement on Palestine, and Arab press, while still vitriolic against Zionists, has tried to make best of it insisting that important thing is that Palestine's future be settled at peace table and not by political pressure. Jewish press is now complaining of alleged censorship of President's statement by our censors in Palestine and I have already received a telegram from Drs Silver and Wise protesting this. A member of my staff who has talked with Dr Silver found him much encouraged by his recent interview with President whom (he says) he found very favourably disposed to Jewish cause though impressed with Marshall's testimony[7] and intending to take up matter further with Britain at an early opportunity. Zionists are bitterly resentful against what they call double-crossing of State Department who they allege first approved and then opposed congressional resolution and are already girding themselves for next round of struggle.

20 March 1944

Soldiers' vote. Both the Senate and the House have now passed the compromise Soldiers' Vote bill – the former by a vote of 47 to 31, the latter by 273 to 111, votes which suggest that Administration forces, though too weak in the House, would be strong enough in the Senate to sustain any veto that may come. Congress is so wearied of the entire affair that there is a general disposition to accept the compromise as the best that could be expected in the circumstances. Immediately following the House passage of the bill, the President telegraphed the Governors of all States asking them to advise him (1) whether the use of the supplementary federal ballot provided for by the bill was, in their judgment, authorized by the laws of their State, and (2) whether they will take steps to enable the ballots to be certified acceptable prior to 15 July, if not acceptable under existing laws. It is too early to report the result of this survey, but by this move the President has skilfully put much of the responsibility for any subsequent veto on to the Governors who have lately been vociferously defending States' rights and their capacity to assume full responsibility under them. In the event of subsequent difficulties in providing ballots for the soldiers, the President will, of course, now be provided with a campaign issue with great appeal to the soldiers' families – a prospect which causes considerable apprehension in Republican quarters. At the moment many commentators feel that, whatever hap-

7 At his press conference, *supra*.

pens, the actual percentage of soldiers who will vote in November is now destined to be small.

GOP Steering Committee. The Republican Old Guard won out over the younger group when the Republican Conference in Congress decided against appointing a new Minority Leader to succeed McNary (see Political Summary Savingram of 6 March), and elected instead a new temporary steering committee containing several well-known conservative nationalists with Taft as Chairman. Vandenberg is named acting Chairman of the Republican Conference and White, a cautious middle-of-the-roader, is retained as acting Floor Leader. Liberal Republicans, who have been pressing for the party to take a definite stand and who deplore the attempt to drift into power on an anti-New Deal wave, point to the omission of the internationally-minded Austin, who until recently was assistant Republican Leader, and say that Styles Bridges is the only member of the new Committee who is a wholehearted internationalist. This manoeuvre emphasizes the rift between congressional Republicans and Willkie who has always condemned the 'Win by default' tactics of the Old Guard.

New Hampshire primary. As was expected, Wendell Willkie scored a success in the New Hampshire primary this week when six of the States' eleven delegates pledged to him were successful. Two of the other winners were pledged to Dewey, and the other three were unpledged. There is some difference of opinion as to whether the three unpledged delegates are pro- or anti-Willkie. New Hampshire has always been regarded as a Willkie stronghold, both Governor Wills[1] and Senator Bridges being outspoken Willkie-ites. Too much is not, therefore, being read into this result, and political observers are withholding judgment until after the Wisconsin primary on 4 April which is expected to be a more revealing test of strength.

Labour. Several developments in the labour world are worth noting:

(a) The President recently urged the AF of L to accept the CIO (which is not formally affiliated with the ILO) as a co-representative of American labour at the forthcoming ILO Conference at Philadelphia. William Green has now rejected this proposal as impossible and has threatened to withdraw the AF of L if the CIO is included.

(b) The War Labor Board has rejected a petition from the AF of L to 'modify realistically' the Little Steel Formula which is the basis of wage stabilization, offering the reason that the Senate Banking Committee is proposing in the immediate future to hold hearings on the entire stabilization programme.

.   .   .

Parliament's invitation to Congress. Parliament's invitation to Congress to send a delegation to London has aroused considerable interest on Capitol Hill but not

1 Sic. Wills was Governor of Vermont. Doubtless Robert O. Blood is meant.

much attention elsewhere. Privately members show some keenness to be selected but the demands of the forthcoming election campaigns, plus the fears of being involved in what might become labelled a 'junket' make them cautious. Representative Jessie Sumner spoke for the diehards when she said she did not expect to be invited, having been 'exposed' to England already. 'It didn't take', she explained.

25 March 1944

AMERICAN FOREIGN POLICY

Pressure on administration to clarify American foreign policy which in press and Congress has reached greater proportions than at any time during the war had its effect this week in a series of moves by Hull. First was issuing of a seventeen-point statement on principles of United States foreign policy culled mainly from Hull's own speeches in 1942–3, second was a two-hour executive session with Senate Foreign Relations Committee in which Hull later said he covered whole field of foreign affairs, third was announcement of a forthcoming broadcast in which he has promised to give more detail on seventeen-point statement, and fourth was a private conference with twenty-four internationally-minded Republican Congressmen who had addressed a public letter to him demanding more information on mysteries surrounding Administration's foreign policy.

Seventeen-point declaration prepared by Messrs Pasvolsky and Carlton Savage[1] has certainly not quieted widespread uneasiness. So far Hull's strongest supporter, doubtless to Secretary's embarrassment, seems to be the *Daily Worker* which glowingly defended statement as an adequate definition of United States policy against attacks of 'Rightist reactionaries and irresponsible liberals' and especially Willkie, who according to the *Worker* now exemplifies worst in both these camps. (This alignment is not quite so freakish as might appear. Hull still frowns on criticism of Moscow Conference, his personal triumph, and in this he is joined by Communists who defend Moscow and more especially Tehran as high points of Allied unity and oppose all questioning of accomplishments of these conferences, apparently sensing that such questioning is largely motivated by suspicion of Russia.) . . . General feeling is that it is too late in the day to be satisfied with abstract principles and that all important issues on which a clarification of American attitude has been demanded are still shrouded in mystery. State Department officials privately do not place too much importance on statement admitting that it contains nothing new but incline to believe without knowing much about Secretary's exact intentions that he will go further in his promised broadcast.

It is known that there was at least one point removed from statement at last minute (Hull had earlier told pressmen that there would be eighteen to twenty

1 Carlton Savage, general consultant to Secretary of State since 1943.

points) and we are reliably informed that this was a declaration on postponing settlement of all territorial questions until after the war. In his session with Foreign Relations Committee, Hull is said to have taken line that nothing must be allowed to interfere with successful prosecution of the war and to have rebuked those who want to precipitate other issues such as boundaries, Lend-Lease, settlements, etc.

Future of Atlantic Charter has been brought into full focus by Hull's statement, coming as it did almost simultaneously with Prime Minister's remarks on the Charter in Commons.[2] Any suggestion of betrayal or 'revision' of Charter provides of course ammunition for isolationists and Administration's opponents and is liable to have a depressing effect on idealistic groups who have used Charter as a weapon in their battle to get America to accept international obligations after the war. There have also been increasing charges recently that Prime Minister following Stalin's example has 'buried' Charter. Yet there is considerable feeling voiced by *New York Times* and other liberal papers that something or other must be done to clarify Charter's implications in the light of realities of world situation as of today. This results in considerable publicity being given to rumours of a forthcoming conference between Prime Minister and President and perhaps Stalin. Despite dissatisfaction with aftermath of Moscow, Cairo and Tehran there seems to be considerable faith that another conference might help to improve and clarify relations between the Allies, or at least it is popularly felt that nothing much worse could happen than present rumours of apparent disagreements and unilateral actions.

Soviet recognition of Badoglio. Soviet recognition of Badoglio threw American press into a state of confusion from which it has not yet emerged. It reopened all bitter feuds between Communists and other left wingers. *Daily Worker* waxed furious against such 'irresponsible liberals' as the *New York Post* and *PM*, while *PM* took its hat off to its old enemy, Hull, for his firm assurance that America would not follow Soviet example. Meantime much of conservative press is more interested in enjoying discomfiture of American liberals than in voicing sentiments about Italy. One of most significant effects of Soviet policy coupled with many other signs of unrest and division in Europe has been to increase anti-European trend. Lippmann maintains that it is futile for America to say that she will only take part in European affairs on her own high terms but this is precisely line that isolationists (e.g. Senator Wheeler who is busy advocating a federation of Europe) are adopting and it is one with considerable appeal in this country.

France. President's statement at his press conference on 17 March that he had reached a decision on question of role of French Committee of National Liberation in liberated France and that his formula had been communicated to London

2 'As the changing phases of the war succeed one another, some further clarification will be required of the position under the document . . . and it must be a subject for renewed consultation between the principal Allies.'

revived widespread discussion of French situation. There has been much speculation, some of it reasonably well-informed, about contents of formula. It has
been generally accepted that it gives great latitude to General Eisenhower and
that in particular he is given discretion to deal with French authorities other than
Committee. This gave rise to suggestions mostly emanating from Algiers that
United States Government were not averse if need be from doing a deal with
Vichy. Callender's reports from Algiers to *New York Times* about French anxieties on subject evoked a heated statement from State Department to the effect
that it was ridiculous to suggest that United States Government could contemplate co-operation with Vichy. Department also revealed that French Committee
had been officially informed by United States Chargé d'Affaires in January that
United States Government had no intention of having any further dealings with
Vichy. In suggesting that French Committee were acting disloyally in expressing
anxiety about United States intentions, State Department chose to overlook fact
that there was plenty of material in the United States press about American intentions which was calculated to cause the French serious anxiety.

There is a considerable undercurrent of anxiety lest the President may have
allowed himself to be governed by his supposed personal antipathy for de Gaulle
and while in the absence of detailed knowledge of contents of his formula, discussion is necessarily somewhat speculative, there is an obvious lack of confidence in the Government's French policy particularly in those circles which have
always criticized American reluctance to deal first with the Free French and then
with the Algiers Committee. There is also discernible some regret that latest
developments do not seem to offer much prospect of an early improvement in
Franco-American relations. There is some speculation as to whether His Majesty's Government will be prepared to endorse the President's line.

Eire. There have been virtually no defections from solid support for United
States pressure on Eire. Underlying sympathies of some of the Catholic papers
and some St Patrick's Day speeches are unmistakable but very few seem disposed openly to question American policy especially in view of Hull's insistence
that the lives of American boys are at stake. Administration is of course keeping
one eye on Irish vote and while there is little evidence of lobbying so far some
people in Washington are wondering whether election fears are causing Administration to hesitate to exert further pressure on Eire. Critics of Administration's
foreign policy suggest that America has now been snubbed by Argentina, Finland and Eire in turn and that in none of these cases does Administration seem
willing or able to press its policies to a successful conclusion.

. . .

Oil. Knox speaking for Navy Department continues to be a warm advocate of
controversial pipeline scheme. He maintains that it is sound from an economic
standpoint that it is a form of national insurance that United States should have
adequate oil reserves and that it marks birth of a foreign policy on oil. He has

invited public support by ascribing opposition to machinations of selfish oil companies. At same time he is trying to reassure opponents of governmental intervention in private business by picturing board of directors of Petroleum Reserves Corporation as being entirely composed of men whose views would normally be against such a development. . . .

26 March 1944

Soldiers' Vote. The compromise Soldiers' Vote measure still lies unsigned on the President's desk. Replies from forty-seven Governors to the President's wire . . . gave an inconclusive picture of the situation. It appears that some twenty-one States could or might use the federal ballot and that twenty-two will probably not use it, the rest being uncertain. The President has until 31 March to decide what action he will take, but there are increasing doubts that he will consider it worth risking another veto fight.

. . .

Lend-Lease. The Lend-Lease Renewal bill has finally been unanimously approved by the Foreign Affairs Committee after an unexpected series of executive sessions. I am informed that these sessions were largely due to demands by Republicans that adjustments be made because of the improvement in the British dollar balances in the United States. These moves came to nothing and the only amendment attached to the bill was one by Representative Wadsworth (Republican, New York) designed to prevent the President from assuming economic or military obligations through the Lend-Lease programme without congressional approval. It seems that Wadsworth offered his very generally worded amendment to forestall more crippling moves by House members who are apprehensive that the Executive's powers over Lend-Lease might be used to change the tariff structure.

UNRRA. The conference report on UNRRA was accepted by both Houses this week by satisfactory majorities and without the proposed amendments forbidding UNRRA to indulge in religious, educational or political activities in liberated areas. . . .

Willkie in Wisconsin. The Republican primary in Wisconsin (4 April) is attracting nationwide attention. The situation is an unusual one. Three of the candidates (MacArthur, Stassen and Dewey) are not even known to be seeking the presidential nomination and are not in Wisconsin. The fourth, Willkie, is very much in Wisconsin and is campaigning through the State, accompanied by a large retinue of newspapermen, as if the presidential election itself rather than a State primary were at stake. Willkie clearly feels that he must win the Wisconsin primary handsomely if he is ever to convince the Republican Party that he could be a successful presidential candidate. It is too early to say what success he is having, but it is clear that the divorce between him and the Spanglerites is becoming steadily wider and in Wisconsin he has also become entangled with Stassen's supporters. Stassen, who is serving with the Navy in the South Pacific, has announced in a public letter to Secretary Knox that he will not actively seek the Republican nomination but would feel obliged to accept it if offered to him. Willkie is clearly disappointed at this stand since he had been hoping to gain support from Stassen's followers if Stassen removed himself from the 1944 campaign. In Wisconsin Willkie is also hoping to capture votes from Progressives and Democrats who, under Wisconsin laws, are allowed to vote in the Republican primary.

.   .   .

31 March 1944

Internal front (manpower, food, coal, etc.). A number of clouds still hang menacingly over the home front – the Manpower bill, with its great powers for Mr Byrnes, which has finally squeezed through the House but may get emasculated again in the Senate ; the soft coal strike which John L. Lewis has, in what is now a routine manoeuvre, suspended over the head of the nation largely in order to obtain government control of the mines, causing a dislocation which he now knows he can exploit more skilfully than the other parties to the dispute ; and most publicized of all, the food muddle, with its foreign implications. The press is behaving fairly responsibly about this, i.e. although they inevitably publicized Elmer Davis's extraordinary statement from London about the superiority of the British meat ration over that of America. There is due stress given to the disastrous consequences, particularly in liberated Europe, if, for domestic reasons, insufficient shipments of food and other materials are made from America.

.   .   .

Aubrey Williams. [1] The defeat of Aubrey Williams, the President's candidate as Rural Electrification Administrator, by a large senatorial majority, which came as a kind of revenge for the pressure exercised to secure Wallace's nomination as Secretary of Commerce, does not seem likely to be the last chapter of this sad story. The attack on Aubrey Williams, which was based on his New Deal and Negrophile sentiments, as well as his alleged godlessness, provoked violent resentment among both Negroes and the CIO. The testimonial dinner to him, at which Mrs Roosevelt and Wallace spoke, was intended to be an opening shot in the PAC[2] campaign to use this case in their general fight against the conservatives and it would be surprising, indeed, if, with so good a case, the liberals prove unable to capitalize on it heavily in the 1946 [sic] elections. The Southern Democrats are not likely to feel the main effects of this, since they are usually entrenched beyond the reach of the liberal opposition, but the Northern Republi-

1 Aubrey Willis Williams, archetypal early New Deal radical, National Youth Administrator 1935–43.
2 Political Action Committee, an organization set up by the CIO in 1943, with Sidney Hillman as Chairman, to promote the political interests of trades unions.

cans, who voted against Williams, are seriously threatened with a mass defection of the coloured vote in their States as a result of propaganda revolving around this case alone. Aubrey Williams is described as a man with a blameless private and public record. (He was a competent administrator of the defunct National Youth Administration.) The unbridled speeches made against him in the Senate are likely to be used again and again in 'borderline States' during the next two years, where the Negro and CIO vote are of crucial weight. The conservatives are naturally exultant and read in all this a hopeful sign of the times.

Mr Lloyd George's death.[3] Long and handsome tributes were paid to Mr Lloyd George in a great many American newspapers. The years have apparently effaced earlier memories of his conflicts with Wilson or his alleged responsibility for an unsatisfactory peace, and the eulogies treated him as a great historical personage secure in his immortality.

International communications. Secretary of the Navy Forrestal's advocacy of a single government-sponsored communication system has met with a good deal of opposition in the press, which reflects the views of those who automatically shy away from government control, however advantageous in the short run, as meaning the thin end of the totalitarian wedge. It should be remembered that this subject, which may not occupy the attention of the British general public, in view of its technical look, is here highly charged with political significance and is second only to aviation and oil as a subject of passionate and publicly expressed feeling.

1 April 1944

American foreign policy. Widespread disquiet about Administration's foreign policy continues. Neither Hull's seventeen points nor his sessions with Senate Foreign Relations Committee and twenty-four Republicans have materially improved situation. Foreign Relations Committee are reported to have been relatively unimpressed by Hull's exposition of his policies and deputation of internationalist Republicans remained openly critical after their session, Secretary complaining with some feeling that their statements to press were 'garbled and inaccurate'. According to these press reports Hull's main points at private conference were :

(a) he took to Moscow a definite plan for dealing with Germany which was shelved by British and Russian delegates ;

(b) Britain and Russia are not on speaking terms about Polish border and State Department is trying to act as peacemaker ;

(c) State Department believes Finland should accept Russian peace offer ;

3 On 26 March 1944.

(d) there is no call for undue concern about Russia's recognition of Badoglio which was partly provoked by British-American failure to keep Soviet fully informed of Italian developments ;

(e) American policy in Balkans is to liberate occupied countries and let people choose their own governments.

Hull is still a mighty influence and a revered leader to mass of ordinary Americans. But bloom of his Moscow triumph is wearing off and certainly in Congress and amongst Washington press corps his stocks are not rising at the moment. Rumour persists that Mrs Hull is demanding that he shall retire as soon as November elections are over.

.   .   .

Meantime virtually every Republican leader seems to have decided that Administration's foreign policy is after all as vulnerable as its domestic policy. Hoover has charged betrayal of Finland. Dewey has criticized secrecy surrounding Tehran. Senator Vandenberg (Republican, Michigan) has declared that whether Administration likes it or not foreign policy is now going to be a prime election issue. Willkie has announced that Administration's policy has 'lost direction', that Atlantic Charter has been abandoned and Poles deserted. Fourteen Midwest Republican Congressmen have challenged Hull to tell public 'What are we fighting for' and 'What are conditions German nation must expect to secure a cessation of hostilities', and Spangler has rounded off criticisms by predicting that Administration's policy towards Eire, Italy and Poland will swing Irish, Italian and Polish votes solidly to Republicans. Administration spokesmen, Senators Connally (Democrat, Texas) and Tunnell[1] (Democrat, Maryland [sic]), have begun to hit back, declaring that critics are sowing disunity amongst Allies and pointing to isolationist record of some of Administration's loudest opponents but they have made little headway so far. Administration's best-received counter-move to date has been Connally's announcement that Hull has requested formation of subcommittees of Senate and House foreign affairs committees to hear and advise him on State Department's plan for an international peace organization. . . . These subcommittees will be set up immediately after Easter recess.

.   .   .

2 April 1944

.   .   .

Manpower situation. The armed services' need for 1,160,000 men by 1 July to provide a total of 11,300,000 is causing numerous headaches in both the War Department and Selective Service Headquarters. The conflict centres round the desire of the Army to obtain younger men, many of whom are now employed as expert technicians in vital war production plants. A move to nullify the occupa-

1 James Miller Tunnell, Democratic Senator from Delaware since 1941.

tional deferments of men between eighteen and twenty-six sent Donald Nelson hurrying to the White House to obtain a modification of this plan which in his opinion would seriously cripple war production. The solution put forward this week by Selective Service headquarters, which has always been reluctant to draw heavily on the father class, was to induct sufficient numbers from the large pool of physical rejects for use as 'labour battalions' and in the many non-combatant army activities. This solution is being bitterly contested by the army authorities, who refuse to lower their physical standards and who have countered with a suggestion that the Selective Service should draft into war industry from the 4F [1] class a sufficient number to replace those younger men now deferred as essential workers.

Several members of Congress, who have all along favoured national service legislation, have privately pointed to this muddle as an excellent example of the confusion and delay caused by lack of total mobilization legislation.

. . .

American Labor Party – New York primary. Interest in the New York primaries this week centred in the battle for control between the right and left wings of the American Labor Party. This party functions virtually only in New York State (and is, therefore, a misnomer) but is of national significance in that it controls 400,000 votes which can constitute the balance of power between Democrats and Republicans in the most powerful State in the union, and a borderline State this year. Only this week Colonel McCormick offered this fact as 'proof' that a small group of communists, by holding the balance of power in the key State, actually rules the entire United States. A bitter inter-tribal war has been progressing between the right wing of the ALP, headed by David Dubinsky, and the left wingers, headed by Sidney Hillman, Chairman of the CIO Committee for Political Action, backed vociferously by the New York communists. The bitterness has been intensified by the personal antagonism of Dubinsky and Hillman as presidents of the rival Ladies Garment Workers' (AF of L) and Amalgamated Clothing Workers' (CIO) Unions respectively. In this week's primary the left wing of the ALP emerged victorious. The full significance of this is not yet clear, but the following can be said :

(1) The President stood, and still stands, to get almost the full support of both factions. The right wing, because of their animosity towards the Soviets, might be more conditional supporters, though virtually only the *New York Post* shows signs of a serious flirtation with Willkie. The Hillman left wing victory puts the President's more zealous and unconditional supporters in control ; but at the same time it gives the opposition (cf. Colonel McCormick above) the chance to raise the old bogey of communist control. The Dies Committee has just released a 215-page report 'exposing' the personnel and techniques by which communists allegedly control the key posts in Hillman's organization ;

1 Lowest category ; physically, mentally or morally unfit.

(2) The American Labor Party as at present constituted has suffered another setback for the right wing (including Dubinsky's powerful union) has now announced its determination to break away. What Hillman will make of his victory in the circumstances remains to be seen. There have been many charges from embittered right wingers that his real hope is to use his position as head of the CIO Political Committee eventually to manoeuvre himself into the leadership of a new national political labour organization ;

(3) Mayor La Guardia, a member of the ALP, by his fence-sitting attitude has probably lost ground politically and has certainly incurred the resentment of the right wing, who declare themselves betrayed.

Little interest was taken in the Democratic and Republican voting, for in both cases the party organization's picked candidates, uniformly loyal to Roosevelt and Dewey respectively, were accepted virtually unopposed.

.   .   .

The President, as seemed increasingly likely, did not attempt to veto the compromise Soldiers' Vote bill, allowing it to become law without his signature.

.   .   .

8 April 1944

Wisconsin primary. Outstanding event of the week has been overwhelming defeat suffered by Wendell Willkie in Wisconsin primary. Extent of his defeat was wholly unexpected and surprised even his bitterest opponents. During his 'barnstorming' of the State, Willkie had stated that he would be satisfied with a majority of convention delegates but that if he received less than half he would concede that his chances of gaining nomination would be virtually finished. Willkie gained not a single delegate. Dewey received fifteen delegates pledged outrightly with two claimed for him. Stassen received four delegates and MacArthur three. Immediately following results Willkie, who had moved on to continue his campaign in Nebraska, announced that he was abandoning his campaign for Republican presidential nomination but would continue the fight to get Republican Party to accept his principles.

Some close observers point out that Willkie's failure was due almost entirely to his inability to sway over 'maverick'[1] voters – the independent and more progressive elements in both parties towards whom Willkie's campaign was chiefly aimed. Vote was even lighter than it was four years ago when independents and progressives stood solidly behind Roosevelt. Therefore these observers conclude present light vote was made up almost entirely of old line Republicans whom Willkie uncompromisingly denounced during his campaign. . . . These observers also argue that result is a sign that independent vote, which it is generally agreed will be decisive in November, refused to desert the President or cross over even into ranks of enlightened Republicans. Democratic reckoning is

1 Texan for cattle bearing no brand ; hence one who will not attach himself to a regular political party.

based however on at least a normal size vote in November but Gallup organization has just worked out a prediction (for whatever it may be worth) that total vote will probably be only two-thirds of what it was in 1940. Despite Willkie's efforts to put fight on basis of what principles Republican Party would stand for issue was decided largely on basis of personalities. Evidence of this is fact that views of neither Dewey nor MacArthur on major political issues have yet been made known. Unexpectedly good showing by both Stassen and MacArthur will undoubtedly put new life into their supporters though neither of them are likely seriously to challenge Dewey. Bricker has now declared that he will intensify his own campaign for nomination and hopes to pick up much of Willkie vote while Vandenberg has renewed MacArthur's claim to serious consideration. It is Stassen however who is most likely to benefit from the withdrawal of Willkie. MacArthur's success is believed to be due mainly to fact that he is a native son of Wisconsin while Stassen's strength is for most part an overflow from neighbouring Minnesota. Dewey's triumph is a triumph for the Republican machine. Anti-Willkie-ites, isolationist nationalists and Roosevelt-haters emboldened by Willkie's overwhelming defeat are joyously and emphatically asserting that result is a complete repudiation of the internationalism which Willkie preached and a clear indication that country wants neither Roosevelt nor a carbon copy of him. More progressive Republican papers, while regretting Willkie's defeat, hail the principles for which he fought and call upon Dewey as the now almost certain standardbearer of the Republican Party to come forth in the not too distant future and proclaim his position on vital issues. Whether Dewey will do so seems extremely problematical for his present sphinx-like pose seems to be producing good dividends.

There is of course considerable speculation as to Willkie's future course of action. It is even being half seriously suggested that Willkie may go so far as to come out in favour of a fourth term for Roosevelt if the Republican Party refuses to incorporate in its platform some of his more enlightened principles especially regarding foreign policy. Professional liberals such as *PM* and New Dealers are now proclaiming that the die has been cast and that all liberal and progressive people have little choice but to rally solidly behind Roosevelt for re-election.

. . .

Supreme Court. Supreme Court has handed down by an 8 to 1 majority a ruling that Negroes cannot legally be barred from voting in Texas Democratic primaries. This decision reversed one made in 1935 which held that court could not interfere with voting qualifications and restrictions determined upon by a political party. Current decision written by Justice Reed[2] is based upon determination of intent and Texas Democrats have made no efforts to hide their intent to bar Negroes from polls in their elections. Observers do not believe that this decision will have any significant influence on outcome of this year's elections but South

2 Stanley Forman Reed, Associate Justice of the Supreme Court since 1938.

has obviously been stirred by this 'threat to white supremacy'. Even usually cautious and self-contained Senator George insisted after decision that rules governing party primaries in individual states should not be interfered with by Federal Government. Typical reaction by Southern politicians came from Representative Nat Patton[3] of Texas – incidentally one of staunchest admirers and supporters of Britain and the British Empire – who declared that Texas would find some way to 'work out a Democratic primary for white folks'. This Supreme Court ruling is but one more move in long struggle over colour question and though its long-range effects may be considerable nothing of immediate importance is expected to arise from it.

Churchill's vote of confidence.[4] Considerable disquiet is being evidenced over general political situation in England. This has centered mainly round Churchill's demand for a vote of confidence, though continuing coal and shipyard strikes, alleged evidences of failure of party truce and reports of your own impending resignation from Foreign Office are also being taken as indications that all is by no means well in England. Press reports give impression that there is deep dissatisfaction over domestic policy and that British public no less than American is apprehensive over apparent lack of Allied unity and uncertainty as to foreign policy. . . .

. . .

16 April 1944

Hull's broadcast.[1] Hull has once again demonstrated his ability to retrieve his hold on confidence of country when it has seemed to be slipping. His broadcast had a very favourable reception and seems to have turned tide of criticism of Administration's foreign policy. . . . Unqualified opposition is confined very largely to the diehard isolationists who are weeping crocodile tears over betrayal of Poland and small Baltic countries and the torpedoing of Atlantic Charter. The strange *bouleversement* by which Hull has become to the McCormick-Patterson papers 'Platitudinous' and 'Senile' and to *Daily Worker* a 'revered' national leader is again noticeable.

France. Hull's statements on France have been generally accepted as adequate, although those perennial champions of de Gaulle, the *Washington Post* and *New York Herald Tribune,* remain critical and Lippmann has pointed up apparent inconsistency between President's press conference remarks on 7 April, when he said no one could tell who would be acceptable as the Government of France, and Hull's statement that 'the President and I' are disposed to deal through

3 Nat Patton, Democratic Congressman from Texas since 1935.

4 On a minor issue, an amendment to grant equal pay to women teachers, which was carried against the Government by one vote. Two days later the Government won a confidence vote by 425 to 23.

1 On 9 April.

French National Committee. According to Lippmann it was President's misleading emphasis on Eisenhower's overall control that precipitated the ouster of Giraud,[2] since de Gaulle realized that Eisenhower, as Allied military commander, would deal with Giraud, as French Commander-in-Chief who would be liable to recommend to Eisenhower administrators of stamp of Pucheu[3] and Peyrouton. Generally Giraud's ouster has brought little change in established anti-Gaullist and pro-Gaullist blocs of opinion. There is a certain weariness evident in press's reactions to whole protracted French problem.

Atlantic Charter. Hull's statement that Atlantic Charter is not a code of law but a general guide has been well received by moderates and liberals, but isolationists have fastened on it as evidence that Washington is now busy appeasing Russia and Britain.

. . .

Neutrals. [Hull's] announcement of a toughening attitude towards neutrals has been roundly approved without arousing very extensive comment. *PM* has reopened its campaign against State Department's 'appeasement' of Franco. Liberals are also protesting against sending an official American exhibit to forthcoming Barcelona Trade Fair. Meantime Acheson and others are telling us that Secretary's speech and public approval of it makes it necessary to hold a very firm line in negotiations at Madrid.

Consultations with Congress. Hull's plans for bipartisan discussions with Congress (see political summary of 1 April) have been warmly received in Congress and press. Both Wiley and Kefauver resolutions[4] have of course long ago set before Congress proposals for regular consultations on foreign policy between different branches of government. Hull has been cool towards proposals from legislative side which savoured of infringement on State Department preserves. But he is keenly aware of importance of carrying Congress with him in shaping foreign policy and his latest plans while not going as far as Wiley or Kefauver resolutions and while maintaining initiative firmly in State Department's grasp, should be helpful in overcoming legislative suspicion of 'secret diplomacy' and in preventing kind of impasse Wilson faced in 1919.

. . .

Breckinridge Long, Assistant Secretary of State now in charge of relations with Congress, also presented in a New York speech an elaborate picture of State Department's manifold researches and consultative procedures for avoiding 'mistakes of unhappy past'. He revealed what seems to be outline of peace plan

2 He was induced to resign as C.-in-C. of French Army on 9 April.

3 P.Pucheu, Vichy Minister of Interior 1941–2.

4 In September 1942 Alexander Wiley, Republican Senator from Wisconsin, submitted a resolution calling for a Foreign Relations Advisory Council. In November 1943 Estes Kefauver, Democratic Congressman from Tennessee 1939–49, submitted a resolution to have cabinet members and agency heads report to House of Representatives.

which Hull had said was now ready for congressional examination, basic points being

(i) an international security organization ;

(ii) agreement by major nations not to use force without approval of this organization ;

(iii) 'major nations and any other nations to be agreed on' should accept responsibility of maintaining adequate military forces to keep peace.

. . .

Meaning of Wisconsin. Willkie's sensational defeat has naturally produced a nationwide flood of comment on political temper of country. Isolationists have come right into the open triumphantly claiming Wisconsin vote as a repudiation of internationalism. . . . Senator Wheeler, whom it is difficult to remember as a Democrat, has advised Republicans that if they have courage to stand uncompromisingly for nationalism in November, they will win, but if they attempt a 'weasel-worded' internationalist platform their chances will decline. At other extreme crusading liberals also rather gloomily see Wisconsin as a victory for a renascent isolationism though it does make them close ranks behind the President. Truth seems to be that Wisconsin was in the first instance neither an isolationist nor an internationalist victory, but a victory for GOP County Chairmen, as Willkie himself admitted in New York. Wild speculation on Willkie running as a Democratic vice-presidential candidate or forming a third party has rapidly subsided. His own associates believe that he will now devote his attention to 'smoking out' Dewey. As regards Willkie's supporters it seems that internationalist Republicans will go in the first instance to Stassen, potential liberal and labour supporters will return to the President, and orthodox Republicans will go to Dewey, as Willkie's principal New York State supporter Rolland Marvin[5] of Syracuse and *New York Herald Tribune* have already done. At the same time there have been many tributes to Willkie's courage and honesty which clearly outran his judgment in selection of Wisconsin as a battle ground. His eclipse as a candidate leaves him respected as a personality.

Nebraska–Illinois primaries. In Nebraska primary Stassen came out on top, though probably more significant was the fact that over twenty thousand voters took the trouble to write in Dewey's name though he was not on ballot. Stassen's supporters have taken new heart both because of their candidate's favourable showing in Wisconsin and Nebraska and because of Willkie's withdrawal but neither they nor anyone else believe that Stassen is a serious threat to Dewey in 1944. Their redoubled efforts are directed more to manoeuvring themselves into strongest possible position before bargaining with Dewey camp. In Illinois General MacArthur was victorious – but against negligible opposition. His supporters have chosen this moment to publish a series of letters which the General has

5 Rolland B.Marvin, Mayor of Syracuse 1930–42.

exchanged with Congressman Miller[6] (Republican, Nebraska) since last October. To Miller's alarming description of New Deal menace MacArthur replied that it was 'sobering' and a challenge to every patriot. To Miller's suggestion that he could carry every State the General replied that this was a 'flattering' thought. MacArthur gave no direct admissions of political ambitions but his interest is now unmistakable, likewise his hurt feelings at being 'subordinated' in Pacific strategy. Prevailing opinion is that these coy admissions have come too late to make him a serious contender. They may in fact further damage his chances in the general situation as they will certainly prejudice him with many responsible Republicans. According to columnist Thomas Stokes,[7] Senator Vandenberg's only reply when asked if he had received any letters from MacArthur was 'ha, ha, good afternoon'.

. . .

. . . In a recent conversation with His Majesty's Consul General in New York Dewey reavowed his desire for collaboration with Britain and expressed concern over what he thought was a fresh wave of anti-British sentiment in America. He suggested that these waves seem to coincide with Russian victories which were so exaggerated as to make British effort seem negligible. He expressed deep suspicion of Russian secretiveness and sympathy for Mr Churchill who, he felt, was being blackmailed into a European invasion which would be bloody though doubtless inevitable. He declared that Stalin told General Pat Hurley (only American who had got close to him and that by arguing fiercely) that he had to be secretive about Russia's military position because if he told Britain they told Americans and in no time the German Intelligence had the whole story. Dewey has been seeing a great deal of John Foster Dulles whom he calls his most intimate friend and there is no doubt that his own views are being modified by Dulles's brand of rather academic and anti-colonial internationalism. A highly successful New York lawyer, Dulles is grandson of a former Secretary of State under President Harrison[8] and has been professionally active in international affairs ever since he attended Hague Conference in 1907. He is said to have collaborated with Clarence Streit on *Union Now*.[9] Most recently he has been chairman of 'Commission to Study Basis of a Just and Durable Peace', set up by Federal Council of the Churches of Christ in America. This commission has been proclaiming 'six pillars of peace' – an international political framework, international economic agreements, provisions for adapting peace treaties to changing conditions, international plans for achieving 'the goal of autonomy for subject peoples', international control of military establishments and protection of religious and intellectual liberty. Dewey's interest in such high-minded goals is of course sure to be strongly conditioned by his own innate caution and by

6 Arthur L.Miller, Republican Congressman from Nebraska since 1943.

7 Thomas L.Stokes Jr, columnist and Washington correspondent for Scripps-Howard chain, 1936–44.

8. John W.Foster, Secretary of State, June 1892–February 1893. (His uncle, Robert Lansing, had also been Secretary of State, under Wilson, 1915–20.)

9 Clarence K.Streit, *New York Times* League of Nations correspondent 1929–39. *Union Now* (pub. March 1939) advocated a federal union of democracies as the only alternative to world war.

powerful political and economic pressures in Republican Party. While there are strong grounds for believing that he has tentatively promised Secretaryship of State to Dulles, we are also informed by a reliable newspaperman that Dewey assured him that, if elected, he felt it would still be essential to make use of international prestige of President Roosevelt and of Hull in war and peace negotiations. Two or three months ago when I saw Dewey myself, he said that he could not imagine any Republican President not seeking to make use of Roosevelt's special gifts and knowledge.

. . .

Wallace's visit to China. The surprise announcement of Wallace's impending visit to China is causing some heartburning. Apparently the idea of a trip abroad was worked out personally between Wallace and Mr Roosevelt. The intention was for the White House to announce it in suitable terms at a later date. Unfortunately the President mentioned the plan at a recent Cabinet meeting and from there it leaked to other 'well-informed quarters'. . . .There is much difference of opinion as to whether the trip is a 'build-up' or a 'brush-off' politically, but those nearest the President and Wallace say that, while no decision about the Vice-Presidency in the coming election has been taken, the President still shows warm affection for 'Henry'.

24 April 1944

. . .

Dewey. In a conversation with Sir Ronald Campbell, Walter Lippmann said that he believed that Dewey (whom he had recently seen in New York), and his adviser, John Foster Dulles, were genuinely favourable to American participation in world affairs and, which was even better in Lippmann's eyes, to an Anglo-American alliance. In Lippmann's view no Republican candidate can afford to ignore dominant desire for American collaboration now shared by rank and file of both parties. When Sir Ronald raised question whether Dewey's value to common cause would not depend on degree to which he might be beholden and therefore subservient to 'old guard' Republican machine, Lippmann agreed but argued that since Wisconsin primary and Willkie's discomfiture, Dewey had become largely master of machine. It was no longer a question of Dewey going to the machine, the machine would now have to come to Dewey. There is much to confirm Lippmann's theses. Thus on collaboration issue, Dewey is unquestionably trying to disentangle himself and party from old isolationist label. For political reasons he seems unwilling to take action that might alienate large groups of conservative Midwest supporters and there is no doubt that many ex-isolationists are rallying to his cause but he has publicly disowned Gerald K. Smith who has been trying to hitch his disreputable 'America First' wagon to Dewey's star and he has declared privately that he believes that McCormick-Patterson press would support him as against Roosevelt but would part company with him two months after he took office. Again on his relations with party, there are many rumours of nervousness at GOP headquarters and amongst su ᛫h potentates as Joseph Pew and Ernest Weir,[1] the Pennsylvania millionaires who have been looking for a 'manageable' candidate of the Bricker stamp. It now seems that from their point of view the 'stop Willkie' campaign drive accomplished rather too much too soon and has left Dewey in an almost unchallengeable position without his having made commitments to anyone. Because of anomalous position, Dewey being an overwhelming favourite without being an admitted candidate, prospects are that Republican convention will become an 'open' convention, with large numbers of candidates arriving officially uninstructed but known to be sympathetic to a 'draft Dewey' movement. An open convention is of course the nightmare of machine politicians whose influence depends on being able to trade support as between candidate and candidate. There are accordingly rumours of 'stop Dewey' movement being organized but it does not look as if it would have much chance of success, for time is short, Dewey is in an immensely strong position and supply of alternative candidates has begun to run short. Bricker, the machine's original hope, has failed to catch public eye. MacArthur's chances have been damaged by indiscreet disclosure of his letters to Congressman Miller and Stassen support is not at present of a kind susceptible to machine manipulation.

Republican National Committee this week selected Governor Warren of California to give keynote address at convention. This selection was made after long discussions in which names of Clare Luce, Senator Vandenberg, Governor Griswold[2] of Nebraska, Eric Johnston and others were pushed. Warren was a safe if not a compromise choice for he is so middle-of-the-road that he is acceptable to most sections of party. Geography played a part in selection since permanent chairmanship of convention went again to Joe Martin from Massachusetts and West Coast *amour propre* had to be considered. There is a tradition against keynote speaker finding a place on party ticket and there are rumours that Warren is more interested in being Attorney General than Vice-President but choice does not seem to rule out obvious possibility of a Dewey-Warren ticket. In fact if Warren made a good impression at opening of convention his chances of vice-presidential nomination would doubtless boom. (Stassen first made his national reputation as keynote speaker at Philadelphia in 1940.) Choice also puts Hoover in a strong position for he remains a dominant influence in California and is favourable to Warren. Rumours persist that he still has hopes of squeezing the Secretaryship of State out of Dewey or Warren.

. . .

Oil. The Anglo-American oil talks[3] have opened with relatively little publicity considering explosive controversy which has surrounded Ickes's pipeline pro-

1 Ernest T. Weir, founder and Chairman of National Steel Corporation.

2 Dwight Palmer Griswold, Governor of Nebraska 1940–6.

3 When the pipeline proposal met mounting resistance, support grew for negotiating an agreement with the British as the major producers in the area. Initially the talks took place on a technical level (see Herbert Feis, *Three International Episodes*, 1946).

posal. There have been usual suggestions in press that British technical representatives being more experienced and more closely tied to government may overpower or outsmart Americans. However atmosphere in talks themselves has so far been of the most cordial and frank nature. James Moffett[4] has widened his fulminations against Petroleum Reserve Corporation to include Anglo-American talks and is charging that they are simply a smokescreen for formation of a gigantic cartel under British control. It is difficult however for American officials or oil industry itself to take anything he says seriously. Suspicions have also been voiced in and out of Congress of sinister financial tie-ups and secret deals involving appeasement of Arabs. Meantime Secretary Knox continues his defence of pipeline and declared before a congressional committee, as you already know, that American companies want USA aid because of their fear of British interference. It is questionable how far Secretary seriously believed this ; he may have produced argument as a means of gaining favour for much criticized pipeline by playing on congressional suspicions. I have since taxed him with spreading mischievous rumours. He expressed relief at my reassurances and is now earnestly hopeful that forthcoming talks will clear away all misunderstandings. Herbert Feis, until recently Economic Adviser in State Department, is latest to blast Ickes's scheme suggesting that proposed arrangements do not give United States Government adequate control over oil firms and at same time are calculated to irritate other governments. Congressional opinion seems to be that pipeline project may be put on a hook at least in its present form until special Senate Oil Investigating Committee has completed its study of America's overall oil needs and interests.

Aviation. Controversy on civil aviation questions has died down since Berle's talks in London. He himself is well satisfied with his trip and is said to have made a favourable report before an executive session of Senate Foreign Relations Committee.

26 April 1944

Lend-Lease Renewal bill. The Lend-Lease Renewal bill passed the House by 334 to 21, the only amendment being the Wadsworth Amendment (see Political Summary Savingram of 25 March) prohibiting the President from incurring obligations, via Lend-Lease, with respect to post-war economic, military or political policy 'except in accordance with established Constitutional procedures'.

. . .

The Leased bases. A three-man sub-committee (Hébert,[1] Democrat, Louisiana ; Sterling Cole,[2] Republican, New York ; Hess,[3] Republican, Ohio) of the House

---

4 James A.Moffett, chairman of the board of California and Texas Oil Company 1936–53.
1 Felix E.Hébert, Democratic Congressman from Louisiana since 1941.
2 William S.Cole, Republican Congressman from New York since 1935.
3 William E.Hess, Republican Congressman from Ohio 1929–37, 1939–49.

Naval Affairs Committee, back from a tour of South Atlantic naval bases, has recommended that immediate steps be taken to gain perpetual title to the bases leased by Great Britain in return for the fifty over-age destroyers. The sub-committee cited the $130 million which the United States Navy alone has spent on these bases and declared that it would be a mistake for the United States ever to abandon them. There is little doubt that such a report will be received with considerable favour by many members of Congress.

Robeson and an African Charter. The Council of African Affairs, of which Paul Robeson[4] is founder and chairman, have used the famous singer's birthday as an occasion to launch a drive for an African Charter. Declaring that 'America should listen to Roosevelt's interpretation of African affairs rather than Churchill's', Robeson urged increased commercial relations between America and Africa, American support for raising of social and economic conditions in Africa, and a guarantee of self-government for Africans within definite time limits. Dr Max Yergan,[5] Director of the Council, has recently been seeking guarantees along these lines from Villard[6] and others of the African Division of the State Department, and a proposal for an international agency, patterned on UNRRA, to supervise Africa's post-war development has been sent by the Council to the President and Mr Hull. Robeson has, of course, the full support of the Communists (who also play a prominent role in the Council of African Affairs), but the campaign, which may grow, is very small fry compared with the recent Zionist pressure, and the eight to nine thousand people, mostly Negroes, who turned out to the Robeson birthday rally in New York seemed to have been as much attracted by the galaxy of entertainment stars on the platform as by the political programme.

Food for Europe. Representative Hamilton Fish's resolution 'respectfully urging' the United States Government to work out with other governments a system of relief for starving peoples in Europe was passed by a voice vote in the House. Fish made a subdued, reasoned speech suggesting that the British people, like the Americans, were now ready to accept a relaxation of the blockade since its principal purpose had been served. Clare Luce has also made an impassioned, religious plea in the *Herald Tribune* for immediately shipping food to 'the innocent children of our Allies'. The future of the resolution is not predictable. No official statement has been made by the Administration and the net effect in the public mind is to leave us still bearing the major responsibility for the blockade.

. . .

30 April 1944

Bases. Question of America's post-war need of extra bases for defence purposes is coming to the fore. Pressure is increasing for America to stake her claims

4 Paul Robeson, Negro singer and actor.
5 Dr Max Yergan, elected President of National Negro Congress in place of A.Philip Randolph, 1940.
6 Henry S.Villard, Chief, Division of African Affairs, State Department, 1944–6.

without delay. This is especially true of the Pacific, where spokesmen as varied as Walter Lippmann, Governor Bricker, Knox's *Chicago Daily News* and McCormick's *Chicago Tribune* all openly urged acquisition of Japanese-mandated islands and other not clearly specified bases. However Curtin's[1] press conference suggestion that questions about Pacific bases should be left for the Peace Conference seems to have been accepted without controversy. Question of our leased bases in Western Atlantic has also come into the news and two members of Naval Affairs Sub-Committee, which last week urged the permanent annexation of the bases, have protested against the Prime Minister's remarks in the Commons on this subject.[2] However Hull told newspapermen that this was a question for their great-grandchildren to take up seventy-five years from now and Representative Bloom, Chairman of Foreign Affairs Committee, probably as usual at prompting of State Department, also decried the agitation, and so it does not look as if Administration is interested in working up pressure on this subject.

. . .

American foreign policy. Bricker and Dewey have both delivered themselves of major declarations on foreign policy in the past week. Outstanding feature of both was abandonment of isolationist principles and acceptance of American collaboration in an international organization, sponsored by Britain, America, Russia and China. Statements were of course very general but neither could give any comfort to *Chicago Tribune* or isolationist diehards in Congress. They were both acknowledgments of the continuing trend of American opinion over past year, and at the same time silent testimonies to Willkie's efforts to rouse Republican Party from its stagnation on foreign policy.

. . .

Meantime Senator Connally has come out against any revision of two-thirds majority rule on treaty ratification, and it seems still more likely than last week that latest efforts of Representative Bloom and others are doomed to failure. . . . Eight-man Senate sub-committee appointed by Connally to consult with State Department . . . has been well received by the press for its representative character – four Democrats (Connally, George, Barkley, Gillette), three Republicans (Vandenberg, White, Austin) one Progressive (La Follette) – personnel being almost identical with those who drafted original Connally resolution. It has a more conservative complexion than supporters of Ball resolution would like but it is a powerful group and whatever it approves should stand a very favourable chance of gaining necessary two-thirds acceptance by Senate as a whole. The committee have had their first meeting with Hull and weekly sessions are now planned. Connally made a strong speech at a law dinner on Saturday night stressing all implications of Senate resolution that bears his name.

. . .

1 John Curtin, Australian Labour Prime Minister 1941–5.

2 When asked if he was aware that the House of Representatives had recommended the permanent acquisition of the Western Hemisphere bases leased to the USA by Great Britain, Churchill replied that there was no question of 'any cession of British territory'.

1 May 1944

Election prospects. Dewey and Roosevelt are more firmly ensconced than ever as the presidential favourites as a result of the primaries in Pennsylvania and Massachusetts this week. Pennsylvania's coveted bloc of seventy delegates to the Republican convention, traditionally unpledged and usually perched invitingly on the shoulders of a favourite son (e.g. the Governor) for a few opening ballots in order to be available for the best bargain, was strongly pulled to Dewey's side, over 130,000 voters 'writing in' his name, with less than 10,000 for each of the other candidates, including Governor Martin[1] of Pennsylvania. This, of course, puts Dewey in a powerful position as against the Pennsylvania machine. . . .

In Massachusetts the President won a convincing victory over ex-Governor Joseph Ely,[2] who was protesting a fourth term. The anti-fourth term efforts of Senator Byrd, James Farley and others have been making little headway, and the President is now almost universally taken to be the Democratic nominee.

Jews. Zionist pressure continues. Congressmen say they continue to get heavy mail, and Senator Styles Bridges, Representative Clare Luce and Sidney Hillman have all berated the White Paper at Zionist rallies in the past week. Meantime press announcement has been made of the research project to be undertaken by Robert Nathan,[3] former WPB executive, to estimate the absorptive capacities of Palestine. Considerable publicity is also being given by the liberal press, and, of course, by the *Daily Worker,* to the allegations of anti-Semitism in the Polish Army in Britain, and Representative Dickstein[4] (Democrat, New York) raised the matter on the floor of the House.

Knox's death. The sudden death of Secretary Frank Knox removes from the Navy Department a vigorous advocate of Anglo-American co-operation and of full participation by a strongly armed United States in world affairs, and a very good friend of the British Commonwealth. His paper was also a bulwark in the Middle West of the more international outlook over the long period when Colonel McCormick's *Chicago Tribune* and Knox's *Chicago Daily News* were the only major dailies in the Chicago area. First reports are that the Under-Secretary of the Navy James Forrestal will become Acting Secretary and that no permanent appointment will be made until after the election.

. . .

The Senate Foreign Relations Committee unanimously approved the Lend-Lease Renewal bill in one of the shortest hearings on record : half an hour.

---

1 Edward Martin, lawyer, Republican Governor of Pennsylvania since 1943.
2 Joseph B.Ely, lawyer, Democratic Governor of Massachusetts 1930–5.
3 Robert R.Nathan, New Deal economist, Chairman of planning committee of WPB 1942–3.
4 Samuel Dickstein, New York Democratic Congressman 1923–47.

6 May 1944

Russo-Polish-American relations. News that an American Catholic priest, Father Orlemanski,[1] was visiting Stalin aroused quite a flutter of excitement. Anti-Administration press immediately went to work and have been playing up alleged irregularities surrounding his passport and travel arrangements and especially fact that he failed to get permission of his Bishop for trip. State Department have taken little trouble to hide their lack of enthusiasm regarding this as one more instance where White House went over their heads. Hull has tried to make the best of it by telling press that Orlemanski and his companion Professor Lange[2] of Chicago University are travelling merely as private citizens. But whatever Orlemanski's exact status, it is impossible to keep Catholic angle out and Catholic spokesmen have already condemned trip as 'phoney Russian propaganda'. Meantime intimate connexions between Catholic Church and Polish cause have again been underlined by stinging denunciations of Orlemanski as a Judas Iscariot, etc., which have come from Polish-American elements in Congress, notably Representative Lesinski[3] (Republican, Michigan). A delegation claiming to represent six million Polish-Americans have demanded from Hull an explanation how Orlemanski came to receive travel facilities. Lesinski who sponsored delegation has boasted that he will write and wire and if need be camp on Secretary's doorstep till an answer is received. Orlemanski is an American-born priest whose parents came from Eastern Poland. He has lived and worked in Springfield, Mass., for twenty-eight years. He has been known to resent strongly intensive propaganda of Polish Government representatives in America, believing that Polish-Americans should react as American citizens rather than as a foreign-controlled pressure group. This antipathy inevitably brought him into contact with minority groups of Polish liberal intellectuals like Lange and labour leaders like Krzycki,[4] Vice-President of CIO Clothing Workers' Union and organizer of Polish-American Trade Union Councils. Orlemanski himself in 1943 founded Kosciuszko League, organized principally to collect aid for Kosciuszko Division in Russia, and toured Canada (where his activities incurred Catholic displeasure) and Middle West setting up branches. When State Department showed themselves to be cool to the project Stalin, it is widely believed, intervened personally and asked President to facilitate trip. Msgr Ready[5] of Catholic Welfare Conference has declared with unconcealed satisfaction that 'very clever men of Moscow in their latest innings in propaganda game have made no hits, no runs and one more error'. Meantime anniversary of Polish constitution has been seized on by pro-Polish groups and representatives from Polish communities as well as anti-

1 Rev. Stanislaus Orlemanski, parish priest from Springfield, Mass.

2 Oscar Lange, Polish-born Professor of Economics who became US citizen, publicly advocated Russo-Polish *rapprochement*.

3 John Lesinski, Republican Congressman from Michigan since 1933.

4 Leo Krzycki, Vice-President of CIO Clothing Workers' Union, national chairman of American Slav Congress.

5 Michael J. Ready, general secretary of Catholic Welfare Conference 1936–44.

Administration spokesmen like Senator Wheeler and Representative Clare Luce have been sounding off against Administration's threatened betrayal of Poles.

Council for a Democratic Germany. Announcement has been made of a new organization, Council for a Democratic Germany, sponsored by prominent German refugees from political, educational and artistic fields and including all shades of Catholic centre, Social-Democratic and left-wing opinion. Backing for programme has also come from such Americans as Reinhold Niebuhr,[6] Dorothy Thompson, William Agar, William Allan Neilson,[7] Justice Pecora, etc. Council urges application of Atlantic Charter to Germany, suggests inclusion of a disarmed Germany in a general European system and warns against dismemberment or destruction of Germany's productive resources. Author Rex Stout[8] who with Emil Ludwig[9] represents only Vansittartite groups in United States has protested loudly against unrepentant tone of Council's programme. . . .

Anglo-American oil talks on technical level have ended. More headway was made in less time than either side had dared to hope. State Department have released a generalized statement on findings looking towards orderly long-term development of world's oil resources by means of an international advisory oil commission. This announcement has been received calmly enough by press. Oil remains a highly inflammable subject in this country but talks seem for time being to have taken heat out of controversy by strengthening feeling that something was at least being done. Arabian pipeline played little part in talks and generally seems to be receding from prominence at least as a major issue. Americans have now submitted their report to Special Senate Investigating Committee and to Hull's political committee and attention is turning more hopefully to next move which is expected to be Anglo-American discussions at a ministerial level.

Stettinius. Stettinius gave Washington correspondents a highly enthusiastic account of his London trip. He said he had told Hull he was now convinced that State Department had waited too long before sending a working group to 'cover the waterfront' with Foreign Office and that many troublesome points had dissolved rapidly when frankly discussed. He paid warm tribute to Prime Minister, yourself and Sir Alexander Cadogan[10] and reiterated his faith that Britain and America must and will stick closely together after war.

Primary elections. Senators Hill of Alabama and Pepper of Florida whose seats were being contested by anti-Roosevelt Democrats both won their primaries this

---

6 Rev. Reinhold Niebuhr, philosopher and theologian, Professor at Union Theological Seminary since 1928.
7 William Allan Neilson, Scottish-born educator and English scholar, President of Smith College 1917–39.
8 Rex T.Stout (1886–1975), best-selling thriller writer, active in Fight for Freedom Committee.
9 Emil Ludwig, popular biographer and historian, born in Germany, came to USA in 1940.
10 Sir Alexander Cadogan, Permanent Under-Secretary, Foreign Office, since 1938.

week and seem certain of re-election. Since both Hill and Pepper campaigned on their record as Roosevelt supporters fight was widely taken as a test case of Democratic unity. Opposition stooped to lowest form of racial appeal but result seems to show that though Administration may have to trim its sails rumours of a serious Southern rebellion can be dismissed.

Only Democratic office holder to be defeated this week was Representative Starnes of Alabama and this upset is being duly claimed as a victory by CIO Political Action Committee who had campaigned against him because of his Dies Committee activities.

Whole Indiana Delegation to Congress (nine Republicans and two Democrats) was renominated without serious opposition, which coming after a similar result in Illinois may be regarded as a sign that little change is to be expected in fairly solid Republican Middle West.

. . .

8 May 1944

State Department changes. Joseph Grew has replaced Stanley Hornbeck as Director of the State Department's Office of Far Eastern Affairs. Like so many other recent State Department shifts, this one is the result of a conflict of personalities more than of policies. Hornbeck's assistants have long found him a difficult work-mate and recently declared a virtual strike. Grew's appointment seems sure to be approved except by the liberal elements, e.g. Representative Will Rogers[1] (Democrat, California) and the Marshall Field papers, who have been attempting to drum up suspicion of his pro-Emperor sentiments. Grew's public standing is at present very high. Indeed there are attempts to make him appear almost as omniscient as Joseph E. Davies, a picture which hardly squares with the facts of his Tokyo record and applies still less to Dooman,[2] who then, as now, was his chief adviser. It is generally assumed that Grew will now be relieved of his stopgap role as the State Department's representative in international civil aviation negotiations, a step which will be welcomed by the aviation interests who have been critical of his inexperience. Hornbeck seems to have been 'kicked upstairs' and is to devote himself to post-war problems in the Far East. Grew's appointment will, of course, tend to even up the excessive Chinese sentiment which some State Department people felt characterized the old Far Eastern Division.

13 May 1944

. . .

President's return. President's return from his secret recuperating centre, now revealed as Bernard Baruch's estate in South Carolina, has been news of the

1 Will Rogers Jr, Democratic Congressman from California 1943–4.
2 Eugene H. Dooman, career diplomat, Counsellor of Embassy, Tokyo, 1937–41.

week. First effect has been to quell rumours that he is too ill to run again. Pressmen came away from his first press conference agreeing that he looked bronzed and fit. He even scolded them vigorously for giving the country a biased presentation of news of Montgomery Ward case,[1] a sure sign to many that he is in battling political mood. Simultaneously Robert Hannegan, Democratic National Chairman, and Senators Truman and Barkley emerged at Jefferson Day dinners as the frontline champions of a fourth-term drive. Hannegan and Barkley did Dewey the honour of selecting him as the butt of their most withering sarcasm, delving into his 1940 speeches for anti-Russian passages and hopelessly inaccurate estimates of America's productive capacity. The lines of strategy of opposing camps are beginning to clarify. Republicans are going to try to make capital out of 'The Tired Old Leaders' in Washington, alleged to be patently incapable of undertaking task of peace-building. Democrats are going to stress that experience of the present war leaders cannot possibly be thrust aside in favour of novices like Dewey and his associates. Nomination of James Forrestal, Under-Secretary of Navy, to fill Knox's place in Cabinet, ending the wild rumours that Willkie or Stassen were to be given the post, was in some measure unquestionably influenced by both these factors. For Forrestal's relative youthfulness (fifty-two) – average age of Cabinet being over sixty-four – and his experience in war councils are both assets. In this sense nomination is good politics though not as sensational as the appointment of a prominent Republican would have been. Forrestal is a Wall Street Democrat, roughly of the Stettinius-Harriman stamp, who has made a very creditable record since 1940 supervising the Navy's vast expansion programme. His nomination has been well received by both parties, and by War and Navy Departments, and seems certain to be confirmed. He has recently come out as an opponent of plan to merge the armed services under a single command, at least until much further study has been made of the situation.

Russo-Polish-American relations. Father Orlemanski's visit to Russia is having varied repercussions. On the one hand it has given Russophobes, Catholics and Poles something to howl over. Even *New York Times* has belaboured Orlemanski as a rather shallow cleric fishing in very deep waters. Virtually no one has risked saying anything good about the trip so far, though his statements have been given full and fair publicity and Episcopal Bishop of Massachusetts has called on his critics to be silent till he has explained his position. Orlemanski arrived back in Seattle on the 10th, had an unpleasant brush with inquisitive pressmen at the airport and left without saying anything. In Chicago he revealed Stalin's devotion to freedom of conscience and worship and his opposition to persecution of the Catholic Church. He added 'I have wonderful news on Poland, but this will

---

1 Throughout the spring of 1944 Montgomery Ward, the mail-order house headed by Sewell Avery, had been defying a War Labor Board order to negotiate with a CIO union. The President consequently ordered the seizure of the plant. Avery was photographed being carried out in the arms of two burly soldiers. There was much uproar about Government's alleged seizure of private property.

come at a later date'. Meantime the *Springfield News* (Massachusetts) has produced a banner headline 'local priest wins Polish freedom'. President – perhaps unchivalrously but certainly adroitly – has referred all questions about the trip to Mrs Ruth Shipley,[2] Head of State Department's Passport Division. Mrs Shipley has reputation as a veritable ogre of formality and rectitude, who is not only above reproach but beyond intimidation. . . .

.   .   .

Lend-Lease Renewal bill. Senate has renewed Lend-Lease Act for one year by a vote of 63 to 1 reflecting overwhelming support for Lend-Lease as a war measure. Wadsworth amendment was strengthened by Vandenberg so that President is now prohibited from incurring post-war obligations not only with regard to final settlement but as regards any aspect of Lend-Lease. . . .

14 May 1944

Primaries. Presidential and congressional primaries in Ohio and West Virginia have served mainly to confirm prevailing trends. As was expected, all of Ohio's Republican delegates went to Governor Bricker, while all the Democratic endorsed a fourth term. Similarly, West Virginia's delegates went solidly to Dewey and Roosevelt respectively. It is now calculated that both Roosevelt and Dewey have already sufficient support to be nominated on the first ballot of the conventions.

22 May 1944

Presidential election prospects. Political picture has brightened distinctly for Administration. Washington gossip is now not only tipping off President as a probable winner in November but suggesting that he may not after all have to contend with a hostile Congress, a prospect which seemed almost inevitable two months ago. This belief that Administration has passed through trough of its misfortunes springs from various circumstances, President's renewed health and vigour, collapse of much talked-of Southern revolt seen in primary elections, victories of such unqualified Administration stalwarts as Senators Pepper and Lister Hill and emergence of CIO Political Action Committee as an election factor of considerable potentiality. Members of turbulent Dies Committee investigating 'un-American activities', long a thorn in the side of CIO, were marked down 'for special treatment' by Political Action Committee. Now within last two weeks Dies himself has withdrawn from November elections (claiming ill-health) and two of his henchmen, Representatives Starnes of Alabama and Costello[1] of California, have both been defeated in primaries. Political Action Com-

2 Ruth B.Shipley, inexpugnable, uncircumnavigable Chief of Passport Division since 1928.
1 John Martin Costello, Democratic Congressman from California since 1935.

mittee are jubilantly claiming major credit for these upsets. Degree of their influence is debatable but that they were a factor in each case cannot be denied. Districts of Dies, Starnes and Costello have each seen a substantial influx of war workers to new war plants. Political Action Committee has gone to work energetically to get these 'migrant' workers to register and turn out at polls. Results seem to show that they are having some success. Committee was organized some months ago, not primarily to campaign for any one candidate, though it has this week publicly endorsed a fourth term for the President, but to combat traditional political apathy of ordinary American labour union member. Originally it was hoped that it would operate amongst CIO and AF of L alike but sectarianism prevailed and William Green ordered his officials not to collaborate with what he called a CIO-dominated and even Communist-dominated concern. For a time there was talk that since extreme left wingers had manoeuvered their way into certain key positions, Committee might prove a political liability to the President who was believed to be burying New Deal in view of rightward swing in country. This thesis seems much less plausible today. John L. Lewis's failure to regain admission to AF of L means that he is left without a national vehicle for his anti-Roosevelt policies and that little serious disaffection from Democrats is to be expected in AF of L ranks. Meantime Political Action Committee is grimly mobilizing five million CIO voters. This combined labour backing will prove influential and perhaps decisive in many key industrial areas. Willkie might have wooed some labour support (and northern Negro support) away from the President. There does not seem any likelihood that Dewey will.

. . .

The Republicans still lack a clarion call like third term or interventionist issues on which they campaigned in 1940 and both national conventions, with serious competition removed, promise much less excitement than usual. Dewey's managers badly want Governor Warren of California as vice-presidential candidate in a desperate effort to win California and they may prevail but Warren personally is known to be cool to vice-presidential suggestion. If he held out, Bricker would become most obvious candidate. Democratic vice-presidential candidates have narrowed down to Wallace, Truman and Barkley, with some talk of Rayburn. We are informed that Quentin Reynolds,[2] the war correspondent, is being seriously considered as Democratic keynote speaker, doubtless to add colour to an otherwise dull convention.

. . .

Russo-Polish-American relations. People find it a little difficult to take the Orlemanski affair seriously but 'surprise' tactics in Soviet diplomacy have become so familiar that it is still considered possible that Orlemanski may be part of some great design of Stalin's either to sell America on Russia's Polish policy or to secure a *rapprochement* with Roman Church. Events followed thick and fast

2 Quentin Reynolds, associate editor, *Collier's* Magazine, 1933–45, war correspondent, London, etc., 1940 and after.

after priest got back to Springfield, Massachusetts. Four hours after his arrival his Bishop suspended him and bade him retire to a monastery. Orlemanski protested publicly that he was being 'crucified', adding, according to press reports, 'if Stalin hears things like this, he will be very displeased', and announced that he was taking his case to the Apostolic Delegate[3] in Washington. However at that moment he disappeared and next report from Catholic sources was that he was in a state of physical and mental collapse. This was followed by release of his full apology, including promise to 'cease and separate himself from all activities not in accord with rule and mind of Church', by rescinding of suspension order and the report that he may after all be back at his post in a few days. No one seems quite sure what will happen next. Meantime Polish Embassy are publicly challenging him, if he really has a solution from Stalin for Russo-Polish difficulties, to make it known without delay.

.   .   .

26 May 1944

President's position. President's position continues strong. Although Democrats of Texas and South Carolina demonstrated restiveness by refusing to pledge themselves to him, this looks at present no more than a storm in two smallish teacups and not necessarily an omen. Gallup estimated that Roosevelt and Dewey are running neck to neck with Dewey leading in New York but he may not be a wholly unbiassed witness on this subject. Dewey is still gathering support and Bricker's chances are still declining. Dewey himself is said to be contemplating prospect of nomination without much joy since he is caught in dilemma of either risking defeat in this year or if he declines to stand an uncertain prospect in 1948 made more dubious by annoying party bosses if he resists their pressure this year as well as possible emergence of a more compelling figure – Stassen, Eric Johnston or an unknown by 1948. Republican bosses seem to be in two minds. Some still believe that Dewey will win : some are above all anxious to avoid a Landon landslide which Bricker might cause and reasonably count on Dewey at any rate to pile up votes. *Life* in an editorial maintains that a Midwestern Republican President alone could guarantee that adhesion of entire country to his foreign policies – since otherwise Midwest would feel unrepresented and consequently dissident. Views differ as to policies Dewey would pursue if elected. A member of my staff was recently told by one of Dewey's followers that Governor upon being asked whether he favoured tariff revision said that he was himself favourably inclined but that Republicans in Congress would not accept it indicating that he proposed to do nothing to antagonize them. This seems key to Dewey's general reluctance to take initiative on any policy likely to displease an influential section of his party. Nor does it seem so certain as some time ago that House will inevitably turn isolationist or even Republican.

3 Mgr Amleto G. Cicognani.

Nomination of Progressive Wayne L.Morse[1] as Republican senatorial candidate from Oregon in place of rabidly isolationist Holman[2] is a prominent feather in Progressives' cap. Unexpected efficiency of CIO Political Action Committee in mustering labour votes for President and in defeating reactionary candidates in South and elsewhere is now anxiously conceded by conservatives who no longer underestimate significance of defeats of Starnes, Dies, Costello, Holman, etc., and view with gloom lessened likelihood of a political investigation of Hillman's CIO Committee for allegedly infringing Smith-Connally Act forbidding labour unions to use their funds for political campaigns.

British foreign policy. I shall report further next week on reception of Mr Churchill's[3] and of your own speeches which were on the whole favourably received. Perhaps most significant point is that formation of world organization with American participation is taken almost for granted and that debate centres on other aspects of matter (see below). Press criticism is mainly confined to routine complaint that Americans must wait for political guidance from Churchill rather than Roosevelt and that Atlantic Charter is being torn up (Scripps-Howard). There is usual alignment on de Gaulle and some attacks upon defence of Franco. Publication of Forrest Davis's articles[4] (on Tehran) expounding President's 'grand design', the pivot of which is reported to be desire to bring Russia into concert of Great Powers at all costs, combined with Mr Churchill's words about executive council of Great Powers,[5] looks like having effect of altering direction of criticism on part of what might be termed the Atlantic Charterites. Whereas previously they represented issue as one between Mr Churchill who desired naked power politics versus American Government which inclined towards Atlantic Charter the issue is now viewed as much more one between Mr Roosevelt (and indeed Mr Hull) backed by Mr Churchill in desire to placate Stalin versus proponents of a world organization with power more equally distributed among smaller nations or blocs of them, whose chief spokesmen in this country are now Sumner Welles and Senator Ball, the Minnesota Stassenite.

Zionists. Zionist agitation has relatively abated as a result of the defeat of the proposed congressional resolution on Palestine by General Marshall's intervention, as well as of private messages from Weizmann which, I am told, sharply criticized his followers for their disastrous strategy and cautioned them against any further brouhaha pending delicate negotiations in which he was likely to be concerned in London. . . .

.   .   .

1 Wayne L.Morse, progressive Republican Senator from Oregon since 1945. Dean and Professor of Law, University of Oregon, 1931–44.

2 Rufus C.Holman, Republican Senator from Oregon since 1939.

3 Churchill spoke in House of Commons on 24 May, Eden on 25 May.

4 In *Saturday Evening Post.*

5 Churchill on 24th : there would have to be a World Controlling Council, composed of the greatest states.

Poles. The Orlemanski affair seems to have died down and there is reason for supposing that the lifting of the suspension order by Bishop O'Leary[6] was due to an intervention by the Apostolic Delegate, who pointed out that his act unnecessarily prejudiced the possibility of such negotiations as the Vatican may wish to conduct with the Kremlin, and, moreover, gave Orlemanski the dignified status of a martyr.

.   .   .

30 May 1944

Prime Minister's speech. While earliest reactions welcomed Prime Minister's frankness and completely restored vigour with only usual complaints from liberals, later press and radio reactions are unusually critical. Passages on Spain[1] seem to have overshadowed rest of speech and stimulated widespread disapproval particularly marked in general talk in New York and Washington.

This is especially true of New York syndicated radio commentators. These broadcasters always tend to be more sharply leftist than press and ever since Spanish Civil War Franco has been one of their *bêtes noires.* They now profess to be deeply shocked by Prime Minister's kindly references to Spanish Government and in particular by his remark that war is growing less ideological, and several of them protested informally to me while I was in New York. . . .

.   .   .

. . . A member of my staff was told by a prominent member of Democratic National Committee that his colleagues regarded reference to 'less ideological' character of war[2] as likely to damage President's position in elections since it was in direct contradiction to Democratic Party line in favour of a fourth term.

4 June 1944

MR CHURCHILL'S SPEECH

Spain. News and radio comment continues to be very critical of Mr Churchill's statement about Franco. Letters of protest are being received daily at Embassy and are increasing. President casually remarked at his press conference that Spain's curtailment of supplies to Germany seemed to him insufficient. Mrs Roosevelt observed at her press conference that Mr Churchill had doubtless held views he recently expressed on Spain for sixty years although if told that he was trampling Atlantic Charter into dust[1] he would probably be deeply shocked. This week's *Life* editorial contrasts Mr Churchill's alleged cynicism with conscience of America as yet dormant though awake in Midwest, particularly in La Fol-

---

6 Thomas M.O'Leary, Bishop of Springfield, Massachusetts, since 1921.

1 Churchill 'appreciated Spain's refusal to listen to German blandishments' and described himself as 'speaking friendly words about Spain'.

2 Churchill : 'As the war has progressed it has become less ideological in its character.'

1 Churchill : 'The Atlantic Charter remains a guiding signpost. . . . It in no way binds us about the future of Germany.'

lette's Progressive Party. All this has kept alive both Washington speculation on Prime Minister's words on Spain and on precise degree of disagreement between Prime Minister and President on this as well as on other issues. Acheson who is known to hold strong views on Spanish policy told a member of my staff that he was profoundly upset by this statement and other members of State Department have shown similar disapproval. A frequent comment made by Americans who pride themselves on their political realism is that while they understand that a pat on the back to Spain may have been required they are puzzled by extraordinary warmth and compliments ('an orchid perhaps but why a bouquet ?'). Isolationists are said to be tantalized by desire to proclaim that speech provides final evidence for what they have believed all along – that this war was not being fought for an idea nor for anything else for that matter – but evidently (unlike editors of *Life*) do not feel that they have quite sufficient material for this thesis as yet. This is perhaps first speech by Prime Minister which so far from being received with enthusiasm with which his words are normally received here, has evoked widespread concern almost entirely due to references to Spain and to lessened influence of ideology in war. . . .

France. Prime Minister's remarks about France evoked relatively little comment, largely no doubt because those who would normally have been critical of speech as being insufficiently forthcoming to French Committee attribute this to need for His Majesty's Government to keep in step with President.[2] Failure as yet to reach any agreement with French Committee is now generally attributed to President's well-known personal antipathy to de Gaulle which has been subject of critical articles by Krock, Marquis Childs[3] and others. It is noteworthy that State Department is no longer blamed even by those who were formerly most critical of Hull's French policy. . . .

Future World Organization. President's and Hull's recent statements on progress achieved with regard to formulation of United States draft of a plan for a World Organization have been received with approval by public opinion. Hull has genuine reason for congratulating himself on fruits of his Fabian tactics. Senate Foreign Relations Committee is in a favourable frame of mind and press indications of what draft is likely to contain have gone down, so far as we can judge at present, satisfactorily. President's and Hull's statements are generally considered to have been stimulated in part by necessity for capping Prime Minister's and your statements on subject in Commons and there is noticeable emphasis in Hull's statement on American origin of draft, extent to which American work on

2 Churchill explained failure to recognize the Committee of National Liberation as the Government of France by saying he was not sure that 'it represents the French nation in the same way as the Governments of Britain and the United States represent the whole body of their people.'
3 Marquis W.Childs, liberal columnist with United Features Syndicate 1944–54.

problem outdistances that of other nations and direct connexion of this with Moscow Declaration (omitting Cairo and Tehran). It is plainly greatly in our interest to encourage so personal a presentation of topic by Hull, as it not merely serves to spur him to further effort but is undoubtedly useful with Congress which is far more likely to accept a proposal if it is apparently American (and particularly Hull's) in inspiration and is not necessarily in complete accord with counter-proposals of other nations. Hull's statement that Senate Liaison Committee of eight was fundamentally in accord on principle of settlement and disagreed only on timing of ultimate decisions, is probably technically accurate. . . . . Connally, an astute parliamentarian unlikely to commit himself to any losing cause and guided by shrewd calculation of expediences, said in a private conversation to a journalist that he thought that Committee of Eight had gone further under his own and Hull's tuition than he had himself expected a few months ago and that slowness of progress was therefore thoroughly justified. I am told that Hull's statement at his press conference on 1 June on equality to all nations was exceptionally tart in tone, and despite State Department's desire not to allow it to be so presented, was taken by those present as a slap at Van Kleffens's[4] words on fears of small nations as well as an indirect reference to imperialism everywhere. It has been welcomed as such by India League and there is a tendency in a section of press to interpret it as a reply to Prime Minister's remarks about ideology. A member of State Department tells us that Hull's words were also in part inspired by a feeling in the Department that the Big Three motif had been slightly overplayed and that something was needed as a sop to that section of public which is loyal to Administration but dislikes prospects of power politics and might be induced to restrain its qualms until election, provided that reassurances about democratic international intentions of United States Government are given it from time to time. Hence Hull's sermon on traditional role of America in encouraging free governments among all nations. A reliable journalist who has recently had a long interview with President tells us that latter reiterated theses expounded in Forrest Davis's recent articles in *Saturday Evening Post* on Tehran Conference, stressing particularly paramount necessity of bringing Russia in and winning her trust by displaying full confidence in her representatives in Moscow and abroad. He also told him that his remark at press conference about compatibility of United States draft for a World Organization with retention of full American sovereignty and integrity was intended for those 'tiresome persons who continually brought these words up and otherwise had no special significance'. President remarked that M. Monnet had an interesting plan for economic reconstruction of Europe entailing internationalization of 'metallurgical heart of Europe', i.e. portions of Rhineland, Alsace-Lorraine, Luxembourg, Belgium, etc., which Monnet proposed to discuss with Harry Hopkins when he returned. I have previously reported Monnet's view on these general lines.

4 E.N. Van Kleffens, Dutch Minister for Foreign Affairs 1939–46.

6 June 1944

Internal politics. The Governors' Conference did not yield any unexpected results. After the usual tub-thumping about the importance of States' rights versus federal authority, Bricker declared himself in effect an out-and-out isolationist, against military alliances, against a world police force, etc., and for nothing in particular. He was evidently not merely irritated by Dewey's progress but did not trouble to conceal his loss of temper when he challenged prospective presidential candidates to stop hiding and to declare their platform as he had done. When one of the correspondents, probably with malice aforethought, addressed him as Governor Dewey, he barked back 'Don't call me Dewey'. Dewey was duly addressed as Governor Bricker by another correspondent and was asked if he minded as strongly as Bricker appeared to resent the converse. 'I have been called by many worse names than that,' he replied. Dewey's speech was in his customary semi-committal vein with an approving, though glancing, reference to the necessity for international co-operation. The whispering campaign that the President's health is none too good, and that the Vice-Presidency is therefore a crucial issue this year, since the President might well, even if re-elected, be forced to abandon his office by ill-health, is once more on foot, culminating usually in the question 'Do you want Wallace as your President ?' . . .

Southern politics. South Carolina (with eight electoral votes) proposes to hold a second Democratic convention after the Chicago national convention to decide only then whether or not to support the party's chosen candidate. The Texas Democratic convention has quite clearly indicated its hostility to Roosevelt, and has threatened to dispute the claims of the delegates of a rival 'rump' Democratic convention which has duly plumped for Roosevelt. The Southern Democrats now claim that Virginia and Mississippi are in an equally disaffected mood. The machinery which these dissident Democrats threaten to use is the exercise of the right technically vested in a State's official electors to vote freely whichever way they choose. Normally such voting is a foregone conclusion since the State's electors are expected to vote for the chosen party candidate. But if they do not do so, it is just possible that neither Roosevelt nor his Republican rival will secure an absolute majority of the vote of the electoral college, in which case the election is 'thrown into' the newly elected House of Representatives, which would perhaps give the Republicans a better chance than the ordinary direct vote. It still does not look at all probable that this eventuality will materialize and the entire manoeuvre may be no more than an ordinary piece of bargaining by the South, with which to bully the convention in Chicago on such burning Southern issues as the coloured vote (the recent Supreme Court decision that a 'white primary' is unconstitutional is reported to have wounded Texas deeply) and alleged economic discrimination in favour of the North. The bark of the Southern Democrats may, as so often, turn out to be far worse than their bite. At any rate, this is what most experienced Washington observers with no axe to grind are saying.

Labour. The sputtering of legal and wildcat strikes recently, together with the much publicized issue of the grievances of the workers likely to be left unemployed by the reconversion of the Brewster Aeronautical plant under Kaiser's new reorganization, has drawn much attention to the problems of re-employment of 'laid off' workers and to labour unrest generally. The issues are perhaps not serious in themselves, but are symptoms of the kind of difficulty likely to occur when real reconversion begins, and have drawn attention to the need for more practical and immediate attention to the problems of re-employment than the very general discussion of this in the Baruch report and other Washington media. . . . The State Department has added Watt of the A F of L, a conservative figure known to the ILO, J.R.Walsh,[1] a regular of the CIO, and Professor Sumner Slichter,[2] of Harvard, an orthodox economist, as advisers of the Department's Labor Relations Division under Otis E.Mulliken.[3] Meanwhile the CIO Political Committee has been formally denounced by the Republican Party, whose chairman Spangler accused Attorney General Biddle of deliberately failing to prosecute them under the Corrupt Practices Act, and inquired whether the farmers' group were similarly entitled to wage political warfare. This is additional evidence of the fact that the CIO Committee has made itself politically sufficiently formidable to provoke a full-dress Republican counter-offensive. Hillman is said to be very cock-a-hoop about it all, with the result that he placidly ignores his rival Dubinsky's attacks upon him and his organization as 'a Communist-dominated outfit'.

11 June 1944

Invasion. After excitement of first impact[1] there was a subsidence into tranquil confidence. False alarm three days previously which on the whole caused more amusement than annoyance (and incidentally delighted Roy Howard and UP hitherto subject to endless gibes from its rival AP for announcing a false armistice on 7 November 1918) did something to reduce force of impact. Description by *New York Times* of British mood as one of 'sober fatalism' fits this scene also though good if meagre news and relief at absence of immediate large casualties makes for high confidence. Considering almost automatic tendency of United States press and public to attribute all good things to American authorship there has been relatively little explicit emphasis on primacy of American troops, most headlines speak of 'Allied' invasion and 'Allied' advances and while this may

1 J.Raymond Walsh, Professor of Economics, Williams College, 1940–2 ; Director of Research and Education, CIO-PAC, 1942–4.

2 Professor Sumner H.Slichter, Professor of Economics, Harvard, 1940–59.

3 Otis E.Mulliken, Chief, Division of Labor Relations, Office of Economics Affairs, State Department, 1943–6.

1 D-Day, 6 June.

do scant justice to our part in enterprise (since 'Allied' probably means principally United States and Canadian to most readers) it denotes what for this country represents something approaching sober restraint, almost hesitation, before launching into irresistible flood of pure self-praise which if things go well we must expect at a later stage. With no headlines to advertise it our part will remain relatively unknown to public and much underlining of extent of it will be needed to counteract prevailing tendency natural enough in persons reared for years on a straight diet of Americanism and exhibited by present tone of Washington gossip to jump to conclusion that American troops, ships and material predominate. But even this must be set off against quite fair coverage in bodies of news despatches given to British action. Nor have radio commentators been demonstrably unfair in this respect, they have paid a due tribute to Montgomery[2] and British forces but are otherwise insufferably tedious even to local audiences since having very little positive information and obliged to keep up a flow of talk they have been driven to endless reiteration and regurgitation of the same exiguous collection of facts provided by communiqués. Forced back upon their own imaginations which have proved singularly sterile they have taken to monotonous recapitulation which was bound to produce a somewhat numbing effect even on unborable American audience. President's radio talk on Italy on 5th was placidly received, his prayer on 6th was well received, responding well to serious mood of the moment. General tone of opinion is sensible and not over-optimistic, large casualties are expected and there is no observable change in normal life of country.

Future World Organization. Although invasion has pushed it into background interest excited by President's announcement[3] that time is ripe for discussion of American draft by major Allies continues in political circles. There is reason for thinking that texts of draft have been shown to a few privileged journalists and members of Senate Liaison Committee seem to have been talking pretty freely. Marquis Childs, who is much in the know, in his column enumerates main heads of draft and speculates on whether Welles had seen it when he attacked tendency to 'power politics' of Allied conversations, having apparently been privately assured that Welles had in fact been shown it by President. Krock on 8 June published an account of reported divergences between Prime Minister's tendency to regionalism and objection to this on part of what Krock calls 'entire Foreign Office to a man'. A friend of ours tells us that he probably obtained this information partly from someone in State Department and came to conclusion which he printed that American view accords more nearly with Prime Minister's than with that of Foreign Office. . . .

Southern revolt. The Democratic 'revolt' in Texas, South Carolina and Maryland has, as expected, spread to Mississippi, whose Democratic convention declined

2 Bernard Law Montgomery, Commander in Chief, British Group of Armies, Northern France, and of Allied invasion forces until Eisenhower established his headquarters in France, 1944.

3 At an impromptu press conference on Memorial Day (30 May).

to 'instruct' its delegates to vote for any particular candidate. This cannot prevent the renomination of the President for which there are enough pledged delegations already, but it could lead to a fight about the Vice-Presidency and to a crisis in the actual election. As to the second of these points, Democratic wiseacres are saying that the States of South Carolina, Texas and Mississippi do not themselves possess enough electoral votes to affect the issue unless New York fails Mr Roosevelt ; if this happens, they suppose that other Northern States will follow suit, since an anti-Roosevelt trend is unlikely to be confined to New York alone. If this occurs, the South alone cannot save Roosevelt, while the Middle West and Rocky Mountains are anti-Roosevelt anyway. However, the Democratic leaders genuinely do not seem to anticipate any such contingency despite the election this week of a Republican Congressman for a Democratic New York district, and therefore discount the Southern rebellion altogether. All this elaborate talk amounts to no more than their belief, which is probably justified, that not enough Southern voters are likely, in any event, to vote for a Republican or a rival Democrat to make any real difference, whatever the Southern conventions may do.

Vice-Presidency. As for the Vice-Presidency, the most formidable rival to Wallace seems at present to be Justice William O.Douglas of the Supreme Court, although he himself has strenuously denied such ambitions. It will be remembered that Douglas was an original favourite for the Vice-Presidency in 1940 and was then discarded mainly because of the absence of sufficiently definite political affiliations. He is an exceptionally vigorous young New Dealer with a sharp tongue and the air and convictions of a hard-hitting frontier radical (he was born in Oregon), the fiercest opponent of tradition in the Supreme Court, and is described to us as a kind of left-wing American nationalist in outlook and a great favourite with Mrs Roosevelt. He is, by Washington gossip, commonly grouped with Ickes in the dissident anti-Hopkins New Deal *fronde.* His friends tell us that he has the backing of many disgruntled Democrats – principally the discarded ex-favourite Tommy Corcoran, now a corporation lawyer, and through him, of influential Catholics such as Joe Kennedy, Leo Crowley and Bishop Shiel.[4] One of his best friends is Eliot Janeway,[5] a malicious and effective writer in *Fortune,* who is wooing Luce, who is at present without a presidential candidate, in favour of Douglas. The very nature of the present support for Douglas may prove distasteful to the President, who shows no signs of wishing to drop Wallace.

· · ·

Socialists. The Socialists have duly renominated Norman Thomas[6] on the usual anti-imperialist platform. This party has not the smallest political weight, nor has its demand for a negotiated peace, worded, curiously enough, in language

4 Bernard J.Shiel, Auxiliary Bishop of Chicago since 1928.

5 Eliot Janeway, economist, author, also director of specialist business research publications.

6 Norman M.Thomas, clergyman 1911–31, Socialist Party candidate for Presidency of the United States 1928–48.

369

closely resembling the Pope's recent pronouncement to the same effect, made any noticeable impression.

. . .

18 June 1944

Invasion. Comment and talk continues to be surprisingly sober without that display of mercurial flights to extremes to which the American public temperament is often prone. Nor have we now anything truly serious to complain of concerning the public presentation of the British effort. Naturally American exploits greatly overshadow ours, but despite Pearson's malicious disinterment of the old rumour about 30–70 Anglo-American proportion of troops involved (which accords with widespread belief that many more United States than British troops are taking part) it is my definite impression that we have after a slow start obtained a degree of publicity which is as good as we could expect in view of all the powerful traditional influences and national predilections which weight the scale against us. The Prime Minister's visit to the front was given great prominence and Stimson's statement about the excellence of Allied collaboration and the fact that we bore the brunt of the German onslaught has helped to illuminate the true position, at any rate in Washington. A constant flow of news and vivid appraisals of it from European sources will however be needed, if the right balance is to be maintained.

De Gaulle. The steady rise of public sentiment in favour of full recognition of de Gaulle, to which there were increasingly fewer dissentient voices in the press latterly, appears to have been checked by the stories of de Gaulle's last-minute cancellation of orders to the French liaison officers to proceed to France.[1] The mixture of exasperation and a somewhat triumphant 'I told you so' attitude among officials in the White House and State Department may be easily imagined – and Lindley, the unswerving exponent of the official view, characterized de Gaulle's latest move as coming 'very close to being a stab in the back'. This act is likely to be most heavily capitalized by the anti-Gaullists, since de Gaulle's appointment of the Commissioners for Normandy and the protests about the invasion francs, while they have profoundly annoyed officials here, are likely to be judged along familiar lines by the pro- and anti-Gaullists. The cancellation of the liaison officers is different in kind, since it can be represented not as flowing logically from normal Gaullist claims, but as a deliberate act of irresponsible pique almost amounting to sabotage of the Allies at a critical moment. The most is therefore being made of it, both in the press and in the Washington official and unofficial world. . . .

Hull was plainly disgruntled, but when questioned at his press conference did

1 All but about twenty out of hundreds of liaison officers were withdrawn by de Gaulle in protest against the non-recognition of his Committee before the invasion. The 'invasion francs' bore the imprint of no government or bank ; they were intended for the use of invasion troops.

not explicitly charge de Gaulle with unco-operativeness but contented himself with a strong implication to that effect. When asked whether French policy was in the hands of his department or the White House, he tartly left the answer to the questioner's imagination. Recognition of de Gaulle by the four European Governments has not aroused much public comment. It is clear that these developments have occasioned more than routine irritation and the French situation is, in responsible circles, viewed with genuine gloom and perplexity as creating an acute and immediate problem to which, in present circumstances, there is no obvious or easy solution. Recognition seems more remote than ever at the moment and de Gaulle's latest moves seem to provide the Administration with precisely the ammunition it has so long desired for future use against the champions of the General's claims.

Poles. Mikolajczyk[2] has, according to all accounts, made a good impression upon officials and members of Congress (he spoke to the Senate Foreign Relations and House Foreign Affairs Committees). While he may have done a service to his people by conveying impression that reasonable Poles exist, and so added to the sadly depleted stock of goodwill for them in Washington, he does not, so far as we can learn, seem to have obtained anything tangible from the President or anyone else. This would seem to be confirmed by Polish recognition of de Gaulle, which would scarcely have been granted if they had anything serious to lose from diverging from official American policy at this moment. Oscar Lange is now here having presented long memoranda to the President and Stettinius. He also held a press conference at which he distributed an official statement to the press, gist of which was :

(a) that Soviet Government and Union of Polish Patriots[3] and leaders of Polish Army in Russia were equally anxious to arrive at a democratic solution ;

(b) that if an internal crisis in Polish Government abroad was made necessary by such a 'reorientation' of policy, it should not be evaded ;

(c) this requires 'an immediate stoppage of anti-Soviet propaganda by Polish Government agencies and organizations dependent on the Polish Government' ;

(d) a civil administration would have to be established in Poland once Polish forces in the USSR enter Polish territory irrespective of whether an agreement with Polish Government-in-exile is reached or not. This might have result of excluding 'an important and valuable part of the Polish political groupings' from final solution, unfortunate for both Poland and America.

In addition he seems to have said, in answer to questions,

(a) that most members of Polish Government were not respected by Polish soldiers in Russia ;

(b) that Russian military administration would not (repeat not) be set up in Poland after defeat of Germans ;

2 Mikolajczyk's visit to Washington began on 5 June and lasted nine days.
3 Russian-organized body of Poles mainly living in Western Ukraine and Western White Russia.

(c) that Polish soldiers to whom he spoke desired a democratic Poland with the bigger estates divided but not nationalized, big industries nationalized, small businesses left intact, and monopolies abolished ;

(d) a western frontier pushed as far as 'we can get away with it', e.g. East Prussia, Silesia, Pomerania. On eastern frontier, on which as might be imagined he was severely pressed by his audience, he was obstinately vague and said that boundary questions were 'unimportant at this time'. He throughout implied but refused to assert explicitly that he had Russian authority for his statements. He impressed his audience as being a serious and well-intentioned person.

. . .

Nothing very concrete is expected to follow from Mikolajczyk's conversation with Lange, the measure of Polish despair (or realism) is perhaps best conveyed by a reported private remark to a journalist of a high Polish official here that 'henceforth, Poland can rest its hopes only on its great French Ally'. Some observers think that they detect a certain cooling in local Franco–Soviet relations.

Post-war. The President's full-dress declaration[4] of the substance of the American plan for post-war organization, the formal and carefully planned character of which was emphasized by the presence at his press conference of Messrs. Hull, Bowman, Norman Davis, Pasvolsky, etc., is symptomatic of the far more definite and at times almost aggressive attitude towards foreign affairs which has for some time characterized the Administration. Ever since the President decided to capitalize to the fullest – as indeed he well might, in view of the confused and hollow statements of the opposition – on his foreign policy as an election asset the Administration has tried to impress the country with the new and more vigorous spirit which inspires its policies. The new decision to take a strong line in foreign affairs emerged most prominently in the tough attitude towards the neutrals which has done more to improve the position of the State Department with the press and public opinion at large than any other recent move. The explosions which the Prime Minister's reference to Spain touched off far and wide indicates the strength of this recent trend. Well aware that he has excited widespread suspicion of following too closely Mr Churchill's alleged tendency towards power politics, the President, by sonorously announcing the plan for a world council, has strengthened his own position by a public display of initiative in seeking to rescue the world from the opposed and equally fatal pitfalls of a naked power alliance on the one hand and of a weak and impractical internationalism on the other. The substance of the 'American plan' is conservative enough to suit all but the diehards of both camps – Senators Connally and White gave it faint praise ; Senator Ball criticized it as merely a feebler version of the League ; Senator Vandenberg conveyed that he is favourable to it so far as it squares with the Mackinac declaration (with which it does not indeed disagree) and anyhow regarded it as a basis for discussion. . . .

4 On 15 June.

Reconversion. There has been a good deal of talk about the necessity for implementing the Baruch report, and the Senate George Committee has issued a long list of principles for post-war economic internal policy. There is talk in White House circles that the President, after his stay with the author, has come to the conclusion that the Baruch report, so much cried up by the conservative press, was a hollow performance, too empty to provide even general answers to the critical economic questions with which this country is likely to be faced, and that in looking around for someone else to perform this task, his eye has come to rest on Chester Bowles, head of OPA, the only government official who thus far has managed a deeply unpopular task with competence and public satisfaction. Be this as it may, Baruch has now formally disbanded his office and returned to private life from which, according to his critics, he should never have been permitted to emerge. Nevertheless his report (with nothing better in sight) continues to be the mainspring of loud demands from both private and congressional committees for legislative action along lines recommended in it. Baruch's personal prestige has indeed declined somewhat and his name is no longer the infallible guarantee of public approval.

Extension of Price Control bill. The week-long debate in both Houses on the extension of Price Control and Stabilization Acts ended with the measures' passage with several major amendments. The bills now go to a Conference Committee for the ironing out of differing amendments attached by House and Senate. There is considerable speculating as to whether the Conference Committee can work out a bill that will be able to avoid a presidential veto.

· · ·

By-elections. For the first time in thirteen years the Democrats have now lost their technical majority in the House. Two recent by-elections in Illinois and New York – the latter being formerly a Democratic seat – were won by Republicans, which have reduced the number of Democrats in the House to 216, or 2 below the technical majority of 218. Joseph Martin, House Leader of the Republicans who now have 212 members, declared, however, that there was no intention of trying at this time to reorganize the House. It is obviously to the opposition's advantage to have nominal responsibility for the House's actions remain with the Administration during the election.

· · ·

24 June 1944

The invasion. The mood is sober still, with suppressed excitement communicated by incomplete but good news of Pacific naval battle. American advance on Cherbourg has been most spectacular piece of news from France with natural result that our share of headlines on Normandy has sunk steadily since last week. Of five major events we naturally have no share in Pacific or Finnish fronts, our part in capture of Perugia and calm and efficiency with which the 'Robot'[1] invasion

1 Flying bombs, launched from Pas de Calais.

of our shores was met, have been adequately acknowledged. Burma front is a poor last to all these though clearing of Imphal road has been acknowledged as a British achievement. My impression however is that the exclusion of British news is not generally due to any deliberate policy of giving us less than our due on part of press but to evaluation of news in terms of its worth as publicity by headline writers and sub-editors. . . .

The Lyttelton flurry.[2] The results of Minister of Production's impromptu comment on America's provocation of Japan into war may easily be imagined since these ran dead counter to official version of events as published by State Department and contradicted Hull's deepest and sincerest beliefs. Nor did later amended version seem to satisfy Secretary who like the President had been concerned to hammer home the point that United States at all stages acted as it did, not out of sympathy with other powers but out of pure national self-interest however enlightened. This after all has been Administration's official reply to charge that President failed to live up to his 1940 election promise never to lead America into foreign wars (and this incidentally is surely view of America's policy which it is in our interest to encourage if we are to avoid expectation of repayments for Lend-Lease and of United Kingdom deference to United States policies based on a purely 'generous' American 'Aid to Britain'). The grist to anti-Administration mill of a statement giving impression that even members of British War Cabinet do not trouble to conceal a view on their part of American Administration's true role in 1941 opposed to that part which it represents itself, for political motives, as having played, has been eagerly welcomed by opposition. Inveterate isolationists like Senator Shipstead, Representative Jessie Sumner and McCormick-Patterson press have all taken Mr Lyttelton's side, professing astonishment that anyone should try to make an international incident of remarks which are so obviously true. The flurry about this in Congress despite 'demand' by Senator Lucas (friendly enough to us) for Lyttelton's resignation and Bloom's exasperation has not been as great as it might have been, at any rate as yet. It has been far more played up in press which has (in case of anti-Administration organs) connected it with Tyler Kent case,[3] ventilated by Senators Shipstead and Wheeler, and in combination with this has generated a sizeable issue. If any facts about Kent-Ramsay case could be made public without prejudice to security, it would do much to clear the air. Otherwise there is considerable dan-

2 Oliver Lyttelton, British Minister of Production, addressing the American Chamber of Commerce in London on 20 June, said that the United States had provoked Japan to such an extent that 'the Japanese were forced to attack the Americans at Pearl Harbor'.

3 In June 1940 Tyler Kent, a code clerk at the United States Embassy in London, was detected by British intelligence in the act of passing large quantities of secret documents from the Embassy to the Germans. With the ambassador's agreement he was charged under the Official Secrets Act, convicted in October and sentenced to seven years' imprisonment. His mother unsuccessfully filed suit with the US Supreme Court for his release. Kent was released in December 1945 and deported to the USA.

Captain Ramsay, a British subject detained in August 1940 under Defence Regulation 18B as a Nazi sympathizer (cf. Oswald Mosley), was not in any way connected with Kent.

ger that issue, i.e. alleged collusion between President and Mr Churchill behind
backs of United States Congress and people to make American entrance into war
inescapable, will be injected into election issue to our detriment and continue to
cloud pages of journalists and historians long after. Hull's prompt rebuttal of
Lyttelton's statement (if not long-winded recapitulation of story of Japanese
aggression) is an example to us all of an effective case of 'answering back' a
charge before it had time to sink in deeply, though Lyttelton's expression of
regret in House was prominently reported and on the whole well received. Attitude of most people is not one of indignation but rather of astonishment, amused
or pained, according to sympathies of the individual, that so huge a brick could
have been dropped at this particular moment, coupled with a certain suspicion
that what was said may well have been true. It is this last that renders so natural
Hull's flare-up. Hull himself is of course most anxious that incident should be
buried and forgotten as soon as possible and he told me on 22 June that he
thought flurry was mainly over.

Foreign policy : de Gaulle. The attitude to de Gaulle has not altered much since
last week. President on the 23rd reiterated his belief that more of France should
be liberated before questions of civil administration are taken up. The initial
tempest about refusal to send liaison officers to France has calmed down somewhat at any rate as far as press and public are concerned, but total effect has
been to stop pro-de Gaulle drift. . . .

Finns. The expulsion of Procopé has stirred expected protests of Procopé's anti-
Administration friends – Senators Vandenberg and Wheeler, Representative
Knutson[4] and Patterson press. What apparently happened was that Procopé's
well-known and systematic anti-Russian and anti-Roosevelt propaganda carried
on in the most obvious market for such wares, the anti-Administration salons of
Washington in which he was a great lion, finally exasperated President himself.
Press carries stories of warnings unofficially administered to Minister by officials
of State Department concerning this, and of his despatches to Helsinki contrasting official American advice to come to terms with Russia with reports of powerful pro-Finnish and anti-Russian sentiment pervading potent sections of United
States political and general opinion. Doubtless he was doing just this. The official policy of friendship with Russia is now in full swing and expedient of eliminating Procopé without breaking off relations with Finns seems a typical State
Department device intended to satisfy Russians without incurring too much public odium for persecuting a country whose regular payment of a small debt has
won them an unreasoning affection in sentimental heart of American public.

The political conventions. We have now entered into breathless interval before
actual match where weights and sizes of rival champions are widely hawked to

4 Harold Knutson, Republican Congressman from Minnesota since 1917.

the fanciers. Despite alleged eleventh-hour premonitions about Dewey's suspected over-independence of character, said to be felt by Republican bosses, and despite Bricker's brave words (and Taft's) about himself, it still looks as if Dewey is easily favourite, with someone like Warren as vice-presidential nominee. Willkie's widely distributed articles have caused a considerable flutter but not nearly large enough to make any immediate difference to his own position. His proposals for social security, the status of Negroes, labour and foreign policy have been most boldly liberal not to say New Dealish in tone ; there is no doubt that if he were candidate many liberal votes would stray in his direction. As it is he was smothered in liberal bouquets. The CIO Political Action Committee pledged to a fourth term for Roosevelt is said to be meditating distribution as a pamphlet of Willkie's very strongly pro-union article on organized labour (he recommends among other things a fixed minimum wage), omitting naturally his complimentary references to AF of L leader Dubinsky. Mrs Roosevelt has treated this with characteristic skill by praising Willkie's enlightened sympathy with New Deal ideals (which discredits him with Republicans) while suggesting that past Republican record has not been such as to make that party the most obviously effective instrument for carrying such radical policies as he advocates (thus suggesting that anyone agreeing with Willkie should vote for Democrats). Indeed so far as one can see the real effect of Willkie's utterances is to strengthen anti-reactionary groups, whether Democratic or Republican, which on the whole strengthens President. (It is said to have done this in Indiana.) The open snub administered to Willkie by Republican National Committee in refusing to ask him to speak at Chicago or to put him on any of convention committees is regarded as somewhat crude by some even of the old guard. Vindictive feeling against him in Taft–Bricker entourage is said to be very violent. Dewey's candidature was in effect announced by his agents, Sprague[5] and Jaeckle,[6] and he may well be 'drafted' on the first ballot if his agents can pull it off.

As for the Democrats, Wallace's pamphlet on Pacific is only significant political utterance of moment. General tone of it, cautiously and not unfairly though it is phrased in general, is Wallace's by now familiar brand of liberal anti-imperialism. Dutch Ambassador,[7] much troubled by Wallace's demand that the date of 'Liberation' of colonial possessions should be specifically announced, called on Hull to discuss this. Hull had pamphlet on his desk and before Dr Loudon embarked on this subject, asked him whether he had read that 'Bunk' or it might have been 'Junk'. Dr Loudon was evidently much relieved by this. . . .

.   .   .

2 July 1944

Invasion news. Invasion news shared the headlines with Republican convention. Our part is now far more prominently, in fact most generously, reported as a

5 John Russel Sprague, lawyer, Republican boss, Nassau County, New York, 1930–52.
6 Edwin F. Jaeckle, lawyer, Chairman of New York State Republican Committee 1940–4.
7 Dr Alexander Loudon, 1942–7.

result of the drive on Caen. Indeed it has received greater recognition than even that of the Russians, and successfully competed with Convention headlines. A good effect was also produced by an off-the-record press conference given by General Marshall at which he went out of his way to stress the prowess and exploits of English and Canadian invasion forces, the remarkable smoothness and effectiveness of Anglo-American collaboration, as well as Montgomery's quality as a leader. This is said to have made a considerable impression on correspondents. Marshall also spoke of 10,000 casualties in England as a result of Robot raids, with high praise for the stoutness of the British population. This demonstrates once again that Marshall is a staunch ally and that he helps wherever he can. Apart from this, Marshall once more evinced his indignation with Congress and labour, and general distaste for politicians and civilian 'meddlers' in military affairs. Dewey, who like everyone else is well aware of this, in his acceptance speech promised Marshall and King freedom from civilian control. The Administration may yet capitalize on this by pointing out (a) that it was, after all, Roosevelt who picked the United States Supreme Command, (b) that clamour against civilian control strikes at the very foundations of American republic.

The conventions. All reports agree that Republican convention in Chicago was a tame and tedious affair. The main task was obviously done behind closed doors, and the public results have had an air of excessive smoothness. Everyone admits that Dewey's managers, Brownell,[1] Jaeckle and Sprague, have done a remarkably slick job for their client. Once it was evident that Dewey was the leading candidate (and this may well have been largely affected by the polls of Dewey's admirer Gallup, which, whether accurate or not, seem to have played an exceptionally large part in convincing the Old Guard politicians that popular sentiment in fact much preferred Dewey to the other Republicans), they arranged that unanimous 'draft' of him which bore an air of such artificiality at the convention. In its heart of hearts a large body of American voters, particularly in the West and Far West, today probably longs for peace and quiet and a minimum of government, in short, for the cosy, dull and solid Bricker, but they also feel that this is to put comfort above duty, a piece of dubious self-indulgence which it must try to control. Bricker was clearly far more personally popular than Dewey, and is the true *amant de coeur* of the GOP. I am told that once the powerful largely Midwestern isolationist pro-Bricker 'Old Guard' reluctantly became convinced that popular support for Dewey would easily beat their candidate, they reconciled themselves to the inevitable, and decided to swallow Dewey, although they did not hide that he looked to them a disturbingly cold, tight-lipped, uncommitted and, from their point of view, tricky personality, who might easily not prove wholly amenable to the bosses and was, above all, very much not (repeat not) one of themselves. Having done this they then determined to protect their own

1 Herbert Brownell, New York lawyer, Thomas Dewey's campaign manager, 1948.

interests by assuring Bricker, who is flesh of their flesh, of, at any rate, the second place whence he could, if elected, control the party machine, keep Dewey in order as the faithful instrument of the wire-pullers of the Old Guard within his administration, and more particularly in the Senate (over which he would preside), much as Garner[2] was intended to be during the 1932–40 period. Warren was either induced to retire from the vice-presidential race – for he seemed certain to win if he so wished – or else voluntarily abandoned it, realizing that the Vice-presidency was an empty post under so young and power-loving a man as Dewey, whereas the Governorship of California might still prove a stepping-stone to national office at some future date. He may, moreover, have been influenced by the thought that if he resisted the party bosses and Dewey were defeated, his own political career would probably come to a close, not merely nationally but in California too. Bricker had no such considerations before him, since after being thrice Governor of Ohio, mere continuance in office cannot tempt him much. The atmosphere of the convention was, I am told, acutely anti-Willkie and anti-liberal. Bricker felt immensely at home, Dewey, described by *PM* as 'the candidate whom nobody wants very much', stirred no hearts. Thus if the nomination of Dewey was a reluctant surrender by the Midwest isolationists, the Hearst Californians, etc., to the business interests of the East, the nomination of Bricker was a concession to these same elements by the relatively moderate Republicans and international bankers and business groups. For there can be no doubt that Bricker's outlook is almost totally isolationist although he is not directly connected with any specific political group of undesirable aims or tenets.

The platform. Dewey himself has already told the world that the platform is a child of compromise and this is exceedingly obvious. It includes the stock attacks on, and promises to remedy the growth of, bureaucracy, of infringement of States' rights, etc., which closely copies Landon's platform in 1936 and Willkie's in 1940. There is in it not a scintilla of that progressive spirit for which Willkie has recently thundered and of whose need even more conservative elements are uncomfortably aware. The domestic programme is compounded of ancient platitudes, the lowest common denominator of anti-New Dealism ; even the labour plank, meant to catch, at any rate, the conservative A F of L, is evidently supported only by 'Big Bill' Hutcheson, the voice of John L. Lewis and the extreme conservatives of the movement. The careful avoidance of kind words for the Wagner Act and the obvious half-hearted acceptance of existing labour legislation eked out by the traditional and all-too-plausible attack on the chaos in labour administration, together with the promise to appoint a union official as Secretary of Labor (which probably means Hutcheson) has left the A F of L cold and CIO indignant. It is quite clear that here as elsewhere the Republicans have

2 John Nance Garner, Democratic Congressman from Texas 1903–33, Speaker 1930–2, Vice-President 1933–41.

written off the liberal vote and have decided to direct their appeal openly and unblushingly to business and the big farm organizations. The economic planks are said to be viewed by the specialists in the State Department and outside with considerable and very intelligible gloom. The plea for bilateralism is said to have represented a hard-won victory by the not too liberal Landon over the completely diehard protectionism of the notorious Grundy [3] of Pennsylvania, from which the general degree of enlightenment of the Republican leaders may be gauged. As for foreign policy, the result is a watered-down version of the Mackinac resolution, itself a model of tremulous caution. Indeed the fact that the *Chicago Tribune* which detected heresy in the Mackinac 'Charter' expressed contentment with the plank, indicates the interpretation placed upon it. Dewey is said to be well aware of its shortcomings, and, doubtless under pressure from Dulles, may try to give it more teeth. Willkie, humiliated and ignored by the convention, attacked the plank with passion and so did Governors Edge [4] of New Jersey and Sewall [5] of Maine. Although this did not produce a notable effect at the convention it has increased the profound uneasiness felt in liberal Republican circles, and such publishers as Luce, Mrs Ogden Reid, Eugene Meyer and the anti-Roosevelt Sulzberger find themselves in a quandary as to what line they should follow. Mrs Reid hopes that Dewey will, by his own exertions, extricate the Republican machine from the morass and set it upon the high road of international collaboration. Luce, who does not like Dewey, quite obviously does not know what to do – more particularly as neither he nor the staff which he has gathered around him seem temperamentally capable of turning from the strong internationalist meat with which he has fed his public for so long to the vegetarian diet now officially prescribed for the Republican Party. Luce has irrevocably committed himself to a crusade on foreign policy from which there can be no convenient turning. On the other hand, with no alternative, he may make a frantic effort to build up Dewey as a vigorous young Midwesterner unlikely to be got down by the dead weight of his party. Willkie's telegram of congratulations to Dewey was a formal gesture and can contain little behind it, unless Dewey, as now seems improbable, wishes to enter into that alliance with the liberal forces which Dulles and Lippmann would like to see and which his own powerful right wing will bitterly resist. As for minorities, the anti-poll tax and fair employment statement will doubtless catch some Negro votes, although the relegation of the poll tax issue to a constitutional amendment seems a deliberate shelving of it to the Greek Kalends. The Palestine plank, which is an attempt to capture the Jewish vote from the Democrats, is said to represent a conviction on the part of the Republican bosses that Zionism is today the only political creed which can rival devotion to Roosevelt in its hold on the mass of American Jews. Dewey's own

---

3 Joseph R.Grundy, Head of the Pennsylvania Manufacturers' Association and pre-war Republican boss of the State.

4 Walter E.Edge, Republican Senator 1919–29, Governor of New Jersey 1917–19, 1944–7.

5 Sumner Sewall, Governor of Maine 1941–5.

Jewish advisers, his old master Medalie[6] and the industrialist Roger Strauss[7], are not indeed Zionists, but probably are, like all American Jewish leaders, united in opposition to the White Paper. What is more remarkable is that nothing was said to the Poles or other discontented national minorities. Hoover mentioned Poland in his speech, but this was a personal statement, and the reason for the omission of this issue was said to be due to the belief that no one national minority could be mentioned without the alternatives of including the others or earning their resentment ; that such a course would lead to real divisionism of which the Democrats could make great play; to the conviction on the part of Dewey's manager Jaeckle that Poles and Catholics were not popular in the United States at the moment (hence his refusal to back a certain Congressman named Mruk[8] on these explicit grounds, which has led to a minor flurry in Polish and Catholic circles); and finally to the restraining influence of Dulles, who agreed the Jews had a special position in this regard and, like the Irish, did not count as a politically explosive national minority and so could be safely backed. The other planks, such as the promise of statehood to Hawaii, Alaska, Puerto Rico and the two-term limit for the Presidency, are too obvious to deserve comment. Dewey's acceptance speech with its stress on youth and concession of the good work of the New Deal's early days, feeble echo of Willkie as it was, was well received by the press with which indeed Dewey seems to stand exceedingly well. So were Warren's words on the fact that the United States was tired of eleven years in midstream and hankered for dry land. Hoover's speech seemed to make no impression, and Mrs Luce is held even by some of her admirers to have sunk to a level of sentimental gush which most of her hearers found it difficult to endure.

All in all, it was a singularly dreary performance and while it should be remembered that too much importance should not be attached to party platforms here, which are traditionally a patchwork quilt meant to cover the widest field of voters, yet the fact that Republican managers think, as they plainly must, that no more than this is required to collect a sufficient number of votes for Republican victory – that something more progressive might lose more votes than it would gain – leads to melancholy reflections upon the true state of mind of those solid blocs of American voters in industry and among the Western farmers upon whom Republicans traditionally lean.

Democrats, possibly with some justice, think that platform, despite Dewey's brave words, will on the whole increase President's chances which in any case seem high enough. There is a rumour that they propose to astonish public with

6 George Z. Medalie, New York lawyer, President of the Federation of Jewish Philanthropic Societies of New York 1941–5.

7 Roger W. Strauss, President of the American Smelting and Refining Company, Co-Chairman of National Conference of Christians and Jews.

8 Joseph Mruk, Republican Congressman from New York 1943–5.

a singularly short programme reciting past performance and stressing war, and to depend for rest on an all-too-easy pillory of Republican performance. An experienced political observer told us that real issue may still turn upon retention of Wallace. Whispering campaign about President's health continues and horrid prospect of Wallace as a more disastrous Andrew Johnson [9] is dangled before eyes of Southerners and conservatives – Wallace's own utterances have as yet had little effect here: his Siberian speeches were scarcely reported, Chungking statement only a little more so. On other side, many believed that Hoover has made his final bow and that inclusion of relief for Europe plank in platform is the sum of his influence. Dewey's man Brownell has succeeded Spangler as Party Chairman and the notorious Werner Schroeder, an Illinois isolationist, fought off by the Willkie-ites last year when he was put up for Spangler's post, is one of the four Vice-Chairmen. Unless Dewey displays qualities of imagination and eloquence as great as his tact with political bosses, Republican chance of victory seems somewhat lower than for some time. This however is not a view shared by Republicans themselves – e.g. as expressed in the Scripps-Howard papers – who appear to feel genuine optimism.

Reports from sources close to President portray him as confident of re-election. Meanwhile he continues to press for progress in post-war negotiations with us all along the line before the election. Public opinion appears to be with him on this. We have everything to gain and nothing to lose by seizing this opportunity while Administration and public opinion are at one. If President is re-elected we shall have advanced that much further – if he were defeated we should at least have made progress which it will be difficult to undo. Only serious danger lies in our hanging back now.

French affairs. The tension is somewhat relieved and Lippmann, who has been talking to McCloy and Acheson, has applauded improved atmosphere. Commentators continue to be divided along lines which I reported to you last week, but subject is engaging less general attention, and de Gaulle's conciliatory statement and President's hint of expected arrival has had a good effect on public as well as official opinion. What high officials seem chiefly nervous of is that some understanding will be reached between de Gaulle and ourselves, with Eisenhower as a party, which will then be presented more or less as a *fait accompli* to the Administration. High officials in State and War Departments seem more anxious about possible effect and rejection of this by President than of actual substances of such an agreement. M. Léger [10] is talking as bitterly as ever about de Gaulle. He recently refused to meet an important underground leader just out from France, and continues to be unconstructive and sulky.

9 President who imposed on the South after the Civil War the punitive régime known as Reconstruction.

10 Alexis St Léger, Secretary-General at French Foreign Ministry 1933–40, then escaped to USA where he did publicity work for Free French.

Latin America. Situation *vis-à-vis* Argentina continues to be exceedingly tense. Press is aware that something is exceptionally amiss, and naturally speculates on immediate causes of Armour's recall. . . .

. . .

Welles's forthcoming book on Foreign Policy is said to be even sharper than his articles and Republicans are waiting to pounce. Hull is in a fierce and determined mood about all this and is determined to do his best to give Argentinians the whipping he thinks they deserve and caused his spokesman to condemn Perón's[11] speech of 11 June[12] as guiding her towards a disastrous fate like that of Italy. Situation is full of dynamite and we have to tread with extreme caution here if we are to prevent a detonation in our own faces.

9 July 1944

. . .

The Presidency. The Republican platform continues to depress even the party's staunch supporters, and the East Coast dailies are outspokenly critical. You will have seen that Sumner Welles has added his voice to that of the other critics, and while allowing due meed of praise to his hobby-horse, the good neighbour policy, to which the Republicans paid some tribute, is severely critical of the rest. The points most widely criticized by him and others are :

(a) the injunction that trade agreements should be bilateral, each to be ratified by Congress, a course which would kill Hull's reciprocal trade agreements or any other effective substitute therefore;

(b) that all 'agreements' with foreign states – presumably not treaties only – be subject to the two-thirds rule in the Senate, which in its turn reduces effective foreign policy to a minimum.

(c) The ambiguous term 'peace forces', substituted, after a sharp internal debate, for 'adequate forces' to preserve the peace, a formula too clearly designed to be infinitely elastic.

On the domestic side the incompatibility of the demand for a simultaneous reduction of taxation as well as of the national debt provided a very glaring target for attack. The Democrats seem more and more inclined to confine their platform to the shortest possible statement, use the Connally resolution as their foreign policy plank, and for the rest point to the wordy farrago of the Republicans as evidence of their rivals' true state of mind.

. . .

. . . Most Washington correspondents back from Chicago on the whole tend to agree that the Republicans do not really hope for victory with anything like the ardent optimism of 1940 or 1936, and that the steadiest convention refrain was to 'bring the boys home'. I am told that Vandenberg remarked 'in 1936 they

11 Col. Juan Domingo Perón, dictator of Argentina since his military coup in 1943.

12 In which he asserted that there was no essential difference between Axis and Allied victory.

chased after me for the Vice-Presidency, in 1940 I chased after them for the Presidency, this time I guess I will just sit it out and make myself comfortable'. This seems to be the mood of many members of the Old Guard, delighted to have routed Willkie, suspicious of Dewey, and not too anxious to be embroiled in the troubled year 1945. Some say that Dewey himself is none too confident of the election, and has acquiesced in the inclusion in his committee of such out-and-out isolationists as Schroeder and in the support of the *Chicago Tribune,* in order to keep the machine intact and loyal to himself until 1948, above all anxious to avoid the errors of Willkie in 1940, who, with his Willkie clubs, alienated the conservatives and has paid dearly for it ever since. Dewey is said to be of the opinion that the liberal vote will be lost to him in any case, and that it would be stupid therefore to drive away the reactionaries in order to put Mrs Ogden Reid's mind at rest.

Willkie's attitude continues to be an enigma shrouded in a mystery. There are unsubstantiated rumours, denied by Willkie, that Clare Luce is acting as go-between between him and Dewey. Although Willkie is still sulking in his tent, some of his people tell us that a little encouragement would bring him to the President's side, and there are some who are still working to create an 'unbeatable' Roosevelt-Willkie ticket. If this does not go through and Willkie comes out for Dewey that may well, as in Landon's case, spell end of Willkie's career as presidential possibility. His six recent articles (see our political summary of 24 June), which doubtless were intended to be his nomination platform, are still causing a profound impression among liberals.

. . .

France. There is naturally eager speculation in press about outcome of de Gaulle's visit which has been very widely advertised. The anti-Gaullists have for the moment muffled their horns and there is much speculation about the results. There is a good deal of optimism based upon view, plausible enough, that President would not have encouraged visit or heralded it with so loud a fanfare if he did not expect to extract some immediate political profit from it, e.g. a degree of agreement likely to be welcomed by the public. The exceptional cordiality of both President's and Hull's reception of de Gaulle, and Leahy's conspicuous presence, played up by press, serve to confirm this hypothesis. If the General does not prove too insistent upon formal recognition, any adequate substitute for this, which would be popular here, would finally round out anti-Fascist front into which State Department has latterly been most anxious to shape its policies. (Its attitudes to Franco, Bonomi,[1] Argentina, Finland and European neutrals and above all Russia have had a favourable press here broken only by Welles's attacks on Latin-American policy of the Department.) If this carefully staged performance comes off and the French imbroglio is resolved or even reduced, President would be able to go to the polls with a shining diplomatic record from

1 Ivanoe Bonomi, leader of Rome's Committee of National Liberation who formed a cabinet of anti-Fascists when Rome was freed.

which earlier stains of appeasement and opportunism would largely have been washed. Invidious comparisons with various of our real or alleged attitudes and policies are in that event bound to be drawn if only to set off the purer quality of the 'new' and enlightened foreign policy now pursued by an America which has finally rediscovered its democratic soul. Whether this trend is encouraged mainly by President's acute sense of his own political advantage or by more disinterested motives, it is strong, has basis in popular support, and we would ignore it at our peril. Meanwhile visit is proving an unbroken success so far. The warmth of the greeting is said greatly to have melted the icy General ('My, I am glad to see you', said President – 'Why, it's good to have you with us', said Hull). De Gaulle so far broke down during his interview with the aged Pershing (despite the latter's insistent questions about Pétain's health – 'in 1940', said de Gaulle, 'he was really very well considering his age' – and only then remembered Pershing's[2] eighty-three years) as to leave his kepi behind. He declined at the last moment to address the Washington press club. His entourage explain this by fact that official conversations are progressing so well that the General wished to take no risks arising from embarrassing questions from journalists. Léger looks very black these days, Lippmann correspondingly contented.

Argentina. Recall of United States ambassador from Argentina, after figuring somewhat prominently in press and being accompanied by vague rumours of 'economic sanctions', of the implication of which public is unaware, has ceased for time being to be subject to much comment. But it would be a mistake to underestimate strength of Hull's feelings, supported as they apparently are by White House and by the public, against allowing an Argentine régime, credited with authoritarian principles and German connexions, from entrenching itself. The uneasy perplexity which surrounds Argentine problem is also responsible for undisguised warmth with which arrival of Padilla,[3] the Mexican Foreign Minister, has been received here. It is obviously hoped that he will help to unravel the knot. Armour has been offered post of Political Adviser on Latin American affairs which, he has indicated to his friends, he is most reluctant to accept.

The Zionists. The story now reaches us that the Zionist plank in the Republican platform was indeed drafted by Taft and Silver, but was originally rejected by the Republican Drafting Committee which felt somewhat uneasy. Thereupon Silver warned them that this would tie Zionists forever to the Democrats to whom indeed they were too close already. This did the trick. In due course Wise, who is the President's principal New York Jewish political manager, denounced the plank as unfair to the President (though presumably not to His Majesty's Government) and called on Bloom who duly testified that the President had often spoken to him of his desire to see the Balfour Declaration fulfilled. In the mean-

2 John J. Pershing, Commander-in-Chief of American Expeditionary Force in First World War.
3 Esequiel Padilla, Mexican Foreign Minister 1940–6.

while Stettinius has apparently again told several Zionist leaders that a Jewish State in Palestine was duly in store for them, and that in mid August he would take them to see the President who would confirm that an Anglo-American arrangement to create such a state was to be set in train. . . .

Bretton Woods Conference.[4] This has not excited any sizeable comment as yet. The conference itself appears to be going smoothly enough. . . . Criticism is so far confined to fears that the United States is being called upon to subsidize a pauperized world and more particularly to finance a British New Deal, and finally that the British delegation is infinitely more expert, i.e. astute, than the American. The climax of the opposition thus far was a letter opposing the monetary scheme in the *New York Times,* signed by twenty-one Republican Congressmen some of whom carry weight in Congress. But very little can be deduced from these symptoms about the real strength of the opposition once the scheme is tentatively adopted by United States Government representatives. What seems quite clear is that the public at large, and particularly opinion-forming individuals and groups, feel far more strongly about the necessity for measures for permanent political and military collaboration between the nations than about the economic equivalents. On the other side of the picture should be set the fact that Dewey, evidently estimating that the Republican platform was too obscurantist even for the GOP, has expressed himself as being in general agreement with Hull's trade policies.

15 July 1944

. . .

The Presidency. President, who never repeats his tactics, did not this year wait to be 'drafted' by Democratic convention but on 11 July informed his press conference, after locking the doors ('Out of humanity, to prevent accidents in the scramble'), that he had decided to accept nomination, if offered it. His reply to Democratic Chairman Hannegan's letter (informing President that majority of delegates were pledged to him) was drafted by Rosenman, and trotted out ancient phrases protesting that President was reluctant to stand, for his heart was in Hyde Park on banks of the Hudson, but that like a good soldier he must needs do his duty when the people command. With exception of one or two politicians like Senator Nye who seem to have been genuinely taken in by whispered rumour that Mr Roosevelt might not stand, statement was greeted along expected lines by friend and foe. Willkie laughingly said 'Is that news ?' and refused to comment. One or two Republican Senators allowed themselves some ribaldry but in general tension was relieved and Democratic leaders together with entire press and radio swooped down on real problem of convention – the nomination of the

4 United Nations Monetary and Financial Conference, 1–22 July.

Vice-President. At the moment total turmoil seems to reign in this field. There is no denying President's skill in turning the jealousies, the ambitions and interests of politicians and the curiosity of the press and public away from his own candidature and the party platform towards fundamentally less important question – Wallace or no Wallace ? (as Senator Tunnell observed 'campaigns aren't fought over the Vice-Presidency. They don't make or lose votes. How many votes did Mr Roosevelt gain in 1920 ?' – a view which however would not be universally endorsed). There seems to be no doubt that so far as Mr Roosevelt personally is concerned, he would genuinely prefer to have Wallace retained and this is known to his entourage. On other hand he must give some latitude within which Democratic leaders can exercise at least a semblance of freedom of choice, particularly as his opponents' view of him as an autocrat makes it necessary not to control convention too obviously or too strictly. A 'free' Democratic convention in which a genuine fight occurred on some second-rate issue, and was decided by a genuine majority of votes, would moreover contrast favourably with the unnaturally frictionless and mechanical unanimity of Republican convention. I am told that Wallace assured President that he would readily stand down if it was decided that his candidature was a serious danger to President's own chances. In return President is said to have assured Wallace of his personal loyalty. Newspapers have been tipped off that President will endorse Wallace warmly, without however that insistence on his nomination which he displayed in 1940 – if this leads to an open fight in convention it will in no way be directed against President himself. Wallace's friends are fighting hard to prove to Democratic managers that a sufficiently large number of delegates are already pledged to Wallace to make it dangerous to drop him if liberal and Negro votes are to be retained. Professionals working for Wallace are headed by Senators Guffey (the Pennsylvania delegation is therefore his) and Pepper (Florida) and possibly Governor Arnall (Georgia). Negro vote seems really vital since, as a writer in *New York Times* on 9 July put it, President might have won in 1940 even if he had lost entire electoral vote of solid South, but could not have won even with the South if he had lost Negro votes of crucial Midwestern and Eastern states with their large electoral votes, since Negro vote tipped the balance precisely there. Negro vote is still greatest factor militating against candidacy of such Southerners as Byrnes and Rayburn. Wallace has with him the CIO and liberal press. Justice Douglas has a good deal of inner New Deal support as well as such allies as Tom Corcoran, Joe Kennedy, Krock and possibly Luce, who see in him a tough-minded nationalistic young radical, a red-blooded American first and a liberal reformer second. Byrnes has support of middle-of-the-roaders and Southerners (his native state of South Carolina has pledged its delegation to nominate him for Vice-Presidency). Barkley, Truman and Winant are mentioned and name of Judge Sherman Minton [1] of Indiana, a New Deal ex-Senator and a

1 Sherman S.Minton, Democratic Senator from Indiana 1935–41, Judge of Appeals Court 1941.

favourite of President, has finally leaked into the press, but without much comment. Harry Hopkins is back, and would have liked Willkie as a candidate (Willkie's would-be platform, a vigorously liberal document, has just been published) but admits that it is too late for that now and is on the whole said to be inclined towards Wallace. He has long been at daggers drawn with Justice Douglas, who led Ickes's anti-Hopkins faction of New Deal, and his relations with Byrnes are said to be pretty cool. The Wallace-ites are fighting hard and even desperately. They claim to have enlisted the support of President's daughter, Anna Boettiger,[2] who lives at White House, and they have mobilized Drew Pearson whose recent statements charging Hopkins and Mr Churchill with plotting against the anti-imperialistic Wallace (as well as his analysis of China as torn between corrupt and over-Western Soongs and corrupt and feudal war lords, with no chance for the common man) are said to derive from Wallace's entourage. Newspapers are keeping a kind of log of number of Wallace's visits to White House and follow his progress with breathless and almost disinterested excitement. It looks at present as if a real fight might boil up during convention unless President personally decides to plump and force his decision on his party. Wallace's chances are good only so long as his opponents are divided between so many rival claimants.

De Gaulle. This has been very much General's week. His public pronouncements were very well received and impression which he personally made on American officials and others whom he met was considerably better than had been expected here. A steady crowd stood silently outside Blair House before which he occasionally appeared, an event not very common here. Dr Padilla, Mexican Foreign Minister, who stayed next door, was relatively ignored and ultimately called on de Gaulle to pay his respects. Anxiety to please was considerable on both United States and French sides and Hull is said to have expressed his satisfaction with de Gaulle's sentiments and impeccable behaviour. Receptions in New York seem to have gone off with immense *éclat* and undeniable dignity and unexpected ease of manner of the General made as deep an impression there as in Washington. He seems to have devoted much time to talk with Archbishop Spellman. Only New York newspaper owners honoured with invitations to dinner were Mrs Ogden Reid and Mrs Thackrey[3] (of unswervingly Gaullist *Herald Tribune* and *Post* respectively). Only important person who seems to have remained completely frigid was Admiral Leahy, who was conspicuously absent at airport, is said to have declined invitation issued by Hoppenot[4] and was conspicuously omitted from de Gaulle's valedictory speech in which he thanked Messrs Marshall, King and Arnold.[5] Official announcement

2 Anna Roosevelt Boettiger, wife of publisher of *Seattle Post-Intelligencer*.
3 Mrs Dorothy Schiff Thackrey, publisher of *New York Post* since 1942.
4. Henri Hoppenot (see 18 July 1943) was delegate of the Free French in Washington 1943–4.
5 General Henry H. Arnold, Chief of US Air Staff since 1942.

that National Committee is to have official status in civil arrangements in reoccupied France has done much to clear public air and newspapers indicate that Anglo-French agreements will be accepted by Americans after modifications insisted on by President. Public therefore is now clearly under impression that French–American relations have finally been straightened out and United States European policy has reached highest peak of popular support to date. Gaullist headquarters here seem reasonably satisfied with excellent impression conveyed by visitor although some of them scarcely conceal their continuing doubts about ultimate intentions of United States Government towards them which they feel were not fully revealed to General and which they still suspect of entailing desire to relegate France to a minor place in settlement of Europe (and still more in Far East). Hoppenot himself is said to be feeling strengthened by visit and probably proposes to continue to pursue firm, not to say truculent, tactics with which he recently achieved a small triumph over Attorney General Biddle. (Biddle apparently attempted to apply notorious Foreign Agents Registration Act to publications issued directly by Hoppenot's office on ground that it did not enjoy diplomatic immunity. Hoppenot refused and dared Biddle to do his worst. Nothing happened. This replica of de Gaulle-Roosevelt relations at a lower level is a fair indication of French attitude.)

.   .   .

16 July 1944

Bretton Woods. The Bretton Woods Conference pursues its peaceful course. The newspapers have published the fact, evidently leaked by the Americans, that pressure is being exercised on the Russian delegation to obtain their Government's answer on the subject of the extent of the Russian quota in the Stabilization Fund, which is now said to be the main factor holding up the decision on the subject. Senator Taft once again predicted the failure of Congress to ratify a scheme on the present lines, and Lippmann in his column, after pillorying Taft as a poor political prophet in the past, expounds the case of the debtor nations and how, bad as such a course may be, they might find themselves forced into barter and bilateralism if the great creditor nation, the United States, proves too obstinately unwilling to meet their demands. I am told that Taft's outburst, made before he had any concrete evidence of what in fact the Conference agreed to, has annoyed his own Republican colleagues at Bretton Woods so that even the obstinate Charles Dewey (Republican, Illinois), a confirmed opponent of the plan, who arrived as an observer at Bretton Woods, is now much nearer conversion than before. This also goes for Messrs Tobey [1] and Wolcott previously regarded as irreconcilables. . . .

.   .   .

The primaries. The general impression derived from the returns in the primaries to date is that they are following somewhat a routine outline, that is to say that

1 Charles William Tobey, Republican Senator from New Hampshire since 1939.

existent incumbents are as a rule renominated by their parties without much regard to their views on domestic or foreign policies. Only thus, for example, can one explain the renomination of a collection of representatives from Oklahoma holding very divergent views on both domestic and foreign policies from districts the sentiment of which on these topics is not known to vary at all widely. The main factors seem, therefore, to be as always local, and more particularly connected with the backing of particular business or farm groups, local patronage and jobs, etc. The only serious exception to this is the effective activity of the CIO Political Action Committee (reconstituted as National Citizens Political Action Committee) which, although it has had some failures, seems to have managed to eliminate a number of anti-labour reactionaries who otherwise might have romped home. The cases of Dies, Costello and Starnes are by now notorious. The latest addition is Congressman Vincent[2] of Kentucky whom the PAC successfully defeated. This has sufficiently troubled the Republicans to cause Gallup, who is an ill-concealed Deweyite, to ask the question 'If the CIO unions supported a candidate, would you be more likely to vote for that candidate, or against him' ? which naturally yielded a majority against such candidates (Republicans 68 per cent ; Democrats 43 per cent ; Independents 46 per cent). This may have its effect as propaganda but it does not seem to reflect the actual state of affairs, which it purports to describe and may succeed in altering.

. . .

USSR Henry Wallace and Eric Johnston arrived back this week from their trips to the Far East and Russia, and have been adding more colours to the already extremely bright picture being painted of America's post-war commercial markets in Russia and China. Wallace, who seems to have been more impressed with what he was shown in Siberia than with troubled China (though he underlined America's vital interest in peace between the Soviet and China), might almost have been speaking on behalf of the Chamber of Commerce itself in his glowing picture of what he called 'the manifest destiny of the west of America and the east of the Pacific' and the vast economic developments possible in that area. Eric Johnston talked along similar lines at a press conference about the 'limitless' two-way trade possible between Russia and America. In his enthusiasm he could see not one necessary point of conflict between the two countries and pictured a prosperous communist Russia and a prosperous capitalist America, fired with mutual admiration, as the major props of world peace.

. . .

23 July 1944

Reports of the attack on Hitler's life and of revolts inside Germany and resignation of Japanese Cabinet have been proclaimed in press with evident relish. Public excitement has been tinged with incredulity and there have already been warn-

2 Beverly Mills Vincent, Democratic Congressman from Kentucky since 1937.

ings from Hull, Patterson and Grew that Japanese Cabinet changes do not mean that Japan is about to sue for peace but spreading belief that the war both in Europe and Pacific is moving swiftly to a climax has naturally been greatly strengthened. Apart from these sensational items the nation's attention has been riveted all week on Chicago where Democratic convention has aroused vastly more excitement than Republican one three weeks ago. Everything else seemed in abeyance while nation concentrated on its political Donnybrook, to accompaniment of many self-satisfied reminders that America was only nation in world that could continue full and free elections while waging a total war.

Democratic convention. Convention has been an instructive, if not wholly edifying, reminder of curious nature of Administration with which we have been dealing for past twelve years. Democratic Party today is an unstable amalgamation of interests (conservative Southerners, northern Negroes, labour unions, left-wing radicals, Catholics, foreign-born groups and large city machines) brought together by fortuitous, historical and geographic circumstances and held together more by a common interest in retaining political power than by any single political or economic philosophy. (Happily for us the various groups are not (repeat not) generally divided over President's foreign policy.) Party convention provides a quadrennial testing ground of relative strength of these forces. It also provides a safety-valve by letting them blow off steam. At Chicago, since all groups had finally acquiesced in fact that Mr Roosevelt was their only possible leader for coming election, the battle for control became centred on vice-presidential candidacy, a post that is customarily filled as an after-thought. On the eve of convention the Southerners, Catholics and many of party bosses, including Hannegan, the National Chairman, and Rosenman, Byrnes and Hopkins of President's own entourage were opposed to Henry Wallace either as being a symbol of New Deal or as a political liability ; the labour unions, Negroes and New Deal liberals were supporting him ; while big city bosses (Flynn of New York, Kelly of Chicago and Hague of Jersey City) were playing a waiting game – though they have never been very warm to Wallace at any time.

The President, faced with a choice of dictating his own wishes and incurring sharp resentment in process, or letting different factions fight it out (within limits), chose the latter. In so doing he deftly transferred bad feeling which was inevitable in selection of a Vice-President whatever happened, from his own shoulders to those of party bosses. The convention was not an 'unbossed' one (perhaps there never is such a thing in American politics) but bossing this time was done in 'smoke-filled hotel rooms' in Chicago and not from White House. President thus comes out relatively unscathed (though Barkley and others who found they were not on his shortlist of favourites are not exactly in a happy mood), whereas most of factional chiefs, victorious and defeated, are licking some wounds. Mr Roosevelt first put regular Party Chairman, Hannegan, in charge of his interests and not a personal representative like Hopkins, as he had in 1940. He then wrote a letter to Senator Jackson,[1] the convention Chairman, which made clear that, while Wallace was his own first choice as Vice-President, it was up to convention to decide. This was signal for party factions to begin a wild hunt for suitable alternatives. A dozen candidatures sprouted overnight but it gradually became apparent that Senator Harry S. Truman of Missouri would be Wallace's most formidable opponent. This trend increased when Hannegan let it be known that Truman was one of those specially approved by President as acceptable alternatives if Wallace was not to be renominated. On first ballot Wallace received 429½ votes, Truman 319½, with fourteen other candidates receiving scattered votes – a successful manoeuvre by bosses to prevent a Wallace victory by first ballot. It was expected that several ballots would be necessary to reach a decision but early in the second it became apparent that both South and big city machines, who had up till then been much more against Wallace than for Truman, were prepared to accept the Senator and traditional 'band-waggon' started to roll, with Truman finally winning nomination by 1100 votes to Wallace's 66.

This result sheds considerable light on strengths of party factions. Southerners (with collaboration from party bosses) were strong enough to oust Wallace but not to elect a Southerner. The liberals, for whom Sidney Hillman of CIO Political Action Committee was spokesman and strategist, were not strong enough to get Wallace elected but were able to defeat Byrnes, the Southern favourite, and other candidates with anti-labour records. (Byrnes's candidacy collapsed as soon as Hillman let it be known that CIO disapproved.) The old line party regulars led by big city bosses held balance of power. By Friday Wallace's supporters were directing their fires at them, rather than at Southern conservatives, as their real enemies and much heat and bitterness was engendered on both sides. Hillman's forces were accused of trying to stampede convention with 'imported' supporters, as Willkie's followers were said to have done in Philadelphia in 1940, and big bosses were accused of unscrupulously manipulating and trading in secret conclaves. The outcome was a victory for the regular politicians, who are more interested in the reins of power and control of patronage than in any particular ideology, rather than a victory for either conservative or liberal wings as such, though liberals will certainly feel that President's tactics played into hands of unprincipled old-line politicians and are a further indication of his own move away from a crusading liberalism. Truman's victory was a personal triumph for Hannegan, the National Chairman, himself a Truman protégé from Missouri who had favoured Truman against Wallace all along.

Truman. Truman himself occupies a unique place in the party. He is something of a lightweight, 'just a country boy' (*ipse dixit*), who ran a haberdashery after coming back from war and was ruined through being too generous to his credi-

1 Samuel Dillon Jackson, Democratic Senator from Indiana, January–November 1944.

tors. He is liked by almost everyone for his impeccable honesty, affability and modesty. He has been a prominent supporter of Moral Rearmament movement.[2] Paradoxically he originally entered Senate as a nominee of corrupt and now defunct Pendergast machine of Kansas City – and Republicans will unquestionably bring this up during the campaign, but it is generally agreed that he has long since shaken himself free from such dubious associations. He is nevertheless much more of a 'practical politician' than Henry Wallace ('a Statesman', he is fond of saying, 'is just a dead Politician'). Even after entering Senate he remained a nobody until in 1941 he was appointed Chairman of the special Senate Committee to investigate the war effort. This bipartisan committee which now goes by his name has been one of the remarkable successes in war organization. It has an unstained reputation for fearlessly investigating every suspected waste, scandal or inefficiency in war effort and has won for Truman nationwide fame as the 'billion dollar watchdog'. But he has never taken much initiative in developing policies and ideologically holds a middle ground, being a faithful follower of party line (he has never been a member of Southern bloc) without being identified as a New Dealer. Hillman has declared that his labour record is perfectly acceptable. He was one of the earliest public advocates of a fourth term but he has never been one of the closest intimates of White House. In fact it is said that Hannegan met with considerable coolness in his early attempts to convince the President that he would make an ideal running mate. He has consistently supported President's foreign policy including post-war collaboration of the big four and until recently was still advocating an international police force. His capacity to fill presidential chair in an emergency raises obvious questions but as far as forthcoming election is concerned he strengthens the ticket, certainly making party harmony more possible, and respect in which he is held by his fellow Senators might prove a valuable asset to the President in securing Senate ratification of his foreign policies (the Vice-President presides over the Senate).

The platform. Platform is not a very distinguished document. It does not look as if Democrats themselves lay much store by it ('we do not here detail a score of planks. We cite action'). Apparently things got out of hand in Resolutions Committee, disagreements multiplied and draft which had been prepared in White House by Cohen and Byrnes (after earlier Rosenman attempts proved unsatisfactory) went by the board. Cohen was thereupon summoned to Chicago and Committee set to work, virtually recasting the whole platform. Foreign policy plank finally agreed on bears much more of the stamp of a Connally Resolution than a White House product. It is at least a little more forthright than Republican platform in advocating 'an international organization based on principle of sovereign equality of all peace-loving states' and the employment of 'armed forces' (as distinct from Republicans' vague 'peace forces') to prevent aggression but there is nothing very new in it and when a Texas delegate proposed an amendment

2 Offspring of Frank Buchman's 'Oxford Group'.

providing for an international air force, Senator Connally pounced on him and proposal was hastily squashed. References to colonialism and international trusteeship, which had appeared in earlier drafts, have all disappeared, nor are there any references to Poland or other European issues. The omissions are in fact as significant as declarations. There is no mention of 'white supremacy', a sign that Southerners lost to other forces in the party. On other hand the Negro issue is mentioned only in an extremely general statement favouring racial and religious equality. Wallace in seconding Mr Roosevelt's nomination declared that 'the poll tax must go', but there is nothing so concrete in platform and it is obvious that Democrats are looking to their past record as Negroes' friend to counter Republican bid for coloured vote. Jewish pressure again had its effect and there is a statement, approved by Hull, favouring 'the opening of Palestine to unrestricted Jewish immigration' and an eventual Free Jewish Commonwealth there which, while it does not go into details about the mandate as the Republicans did, should prove satisfactory to Zionists especially in view of their belief that things are now generally going their way. Both platforms this year stress free dissemination of news and Democratic reference to 'uniform communication rates', freed from Government's or private monopoly and protected by treaty, reflects personal pressure of Kent Cooper of Associated Press. This cry (directed of course at our allegedly monopolistic control of international communications) is getting growing support over here and only last week State Department revealed that it was hoped to begin discussions on international communications in Washington in the autumn.

President's acceptance speech. President's acceptance speech, which seemed much more skilfully drafted than his letter of acceptance, and which was extremely well received by convention, was a much clearer indication than platform of kind of campaign the Democrats will wage. Its setting – a naval base where President as Commander-in-Chief was surrounded by military and naval not political aides – and its emphasis on world affairs were both significant. The warning against handing over matters of such great moment to 'inexperienced and immature hands' was an obvious but adroit reply to the Republicans' emphasis on Dewey's youth and vigour. As we have anticipated when pressed in recent months for speeding up of international conferences it became quite clear in this speech that President hopes to present a series of completed agreements and going international concerns to electorate in November as evidence of effectiveness of his policies and needlessness of the fears that international collaboration will involve any drastic changes in American way of life.

29 July 1944

German revolts. First reaction to reports of revolt spreading inside Germany has been one of conspicuous almost affected caution though people are obviously now having difficulty in restraining high hopes which they unquestionably feel about an early conclusion of the European war. Press is apparently following an official lead from Washington and papers of all shades of opinion are stressing that much hard fighting lies ahead. That is the official line in Administration speeches as well, and in his broadcast report on his European trip Secretary Stimson emphasized that he had discovered no feeling amongst men on fighting fronts that Nazis were about to collapse. This emphasis doubtless reflects Administration's fears that any increase in already widespread optimism might dangerously accelerate scramble from temporary government posts and war industries back into civilian channels. Pointing up these fears has been the calling of a Republican caucus in August by Senator Vandenberg to press for more rapid consideration of demobilization plans. Generally mood being induced by press and Administration is all to the good. Reported conflicts between Nazi hierarchy and German Generals, suspiciously viewed as they have been, resulted in a good deal of comment which points out that both groups are equally guilty and which warns against fake peace feelers and any soft settlement with Germany.

The Poles. Russia's recognition of Polish Committee of National Liberation [1] has been accepted resignedly by press and public, who, while they may disapprove, feel that moral indignation alone can achieve little especially *vis-à-vis* Russians. Administration are not likely to raise much of a fuss in view of priority now being given to good relations with the Soviet Union. . . .

. . .

Election politics. Democratic convention has produced usual post-mortem discussions on how long such a loose conglomeration of interests could hold together without Mr Roosevelt's leadership. Lippmann philosophically explains convention as an example of the American political system at work ensuring that no party which represented only one class or section could ever win an election. *Life,* on the other hand, declares that Democratic Party is suspended by a thread, the life of a single man, and more surprisingly Lindley, who is often a White House mouthpiece, writing on stormy sessions at Chicago, declares pessimistically 'In words of chairman of one delegation ''we wired this contraption together for a single straight flight. Now we are being asked to turn loops and barrel rolls. The passengers are falling out all over the place and we may all crash at any moment.'' The ultimate disaster was averted but possibly only for four years.' This is sheerest speculation. No one can say with any assurance what will happen to the Democratic Party in next four years, though, depending on post-war conditions, extensive realignments seen quite on the cards. In the long view the role of Hillman's CIO Political Action Committee may prove to have been the most important development at the convention, marking advent of

1 Said to be intended to serve as the executive authority of the Polish National Council, a body of uncertain origin formed recently in Poland, in fundamental agreement with the Union of Polish Patriots, previously set up in Moscow.

American labour as a well-organized political pressure group, competing with politicians on their own ground for control of one of the major parties. The Democratic Party has long been a loose collection of forces, but while Southerners and city bosses were old familiar faces, the PAC was something new and the fact that it failed to put Wallace across successfully may be less significant than its future potentialities, for it took a combination of other forces to defeat it. PAC supporter has been quoted as saying 'The Democratic Party is fifty-two years old, PAC is one. Just give us a chance.' PAC which has been re-christened The National Citizens Political Action Committee with a base widened to include non-CIO liberals and thus avoid financial restrictions on campaign contributions imposed on labour unions by Hatch and Smith–Connally Acts, is a militant and well-led left-wing group. . . .

. . .

What does seem clear from Chicago is that Truman's nomination improves the chances of party unity during this campaign. *The Daily Worker*[2] and Southern conservatives are both explaining that he is perfectly acceptable to them. The American Federation of Labor are claiming that he was their candidate all along and that they and not Hillman's much publicized group proved to be 'kingmakers' at Chicago while the PAC are intensifying their efforts to bring out a maximum Democratic vote in November. Wallace has acclaimed the Roosevelt-Truman ticket as a victory for liberalism, party bosses are naturally happy over their eventual success and even Farley has announced that he will vote straight in November. There is thus an impressive semblance of general unity despite the fires which everyone knows to be still burning under the surface. Truman who is meanwhile well aware of his limitations (he is in truth almost a symbol of the virtuous 'little man' in high places), is said to be feeling extremely uncomfortable about greatness which has been thrust upon him. He certainly did not seek and almost certainly did not want the Vice-Presidency but he maintains manfully that 'Barkis is willin' '. It is now clear that Wallace, while he would doubtless have been a very easy target for Republicans in the campaign, had a great deal of popular sympathy on his side. This is becoming more apparent since people who are not quite sure that he would be politically advisable, feel free to express their sympathy with him now that they know they are not to be saddled politically with him or his much more suspect leftist followers. A great many people undoubtedly see in him and in his going a symbol of their own frustrated idealism and perhaps rather naïve hopes about a bright new world. Wallace came out of the Chicago imbroglio with his own integrity unbesmirched and his own stocks unquestionably higher than before the convention. He is now planning to make a series of campaign addresses on the President's behalf.

Republicans of course are turning their fires on 'communist-dominated' PAC

2 US Communist daily.

and city bosses as the two disreputable forces which control Democratic Party. Bricker has been claiming that hostility to Hillman's tactics will swing a large segment of labour vote to Republicans. This seems like wishful thinking. Lewis's *Mine-Workers Journal* has indeed come out for Republicans but it is doubtful if miners will follow Lewis's political lead as unitedly as they follow his industrial leadership. (He failed conspicuously to deliver CIO vote to Willkie in 1940.) And while American Federation of Labor makes no attempt to hide its hostility to Hillman's organization, William Green himself said at Republican convention that 80 per cent of labour vote would go to Roosevelt and that there was nothing that Republicans could do about it. The conservative Railroad Brotherhoods are of course also much happier with a Roosevelt-Truman than with a Roosevelt-Wallace ticket.

.　.　.

Under prompting Dewey has repudiated isolationist Representative Hamilton Fish (whom he had once before denounced in 1942) as he earlier rejected the support of Gerald K. Smith, making a bid at same time for the Jewish vote by charging Fish with anti-Semitism, but this effort to dissociate himself from discreditable isolationist elements may be cancelled out by Bricker's bland assurance at a press conference, which he held with Dewey at Albany, that he finds that he will have to change none of his pre-convention views to fit Dewey's campaign. He also indicated in reply to questions that he at any rate will be quite glad to accept votes from Colonel McCormick, Gerald K. Smith or from anybody.

.　.　.

Congressional primaries. Primaries in one or two Southern States have resulted in victories for several pro-Roosevelt nominees. The most notable was the victory of the pro-Roosevelt Governor Olin Johnston[3] of South Carolina over the colourful but obstructionist diehard 'Cotton Ed' Smith, a Democratic Senator for thirty-six years, leader of the 'white supremacy' school and one of the most outspoken critics of the President. Another Roosevelt victory was the success of Representative Fulbright in Arkansas in displacing the cautious and conservative Hattie Caraway,[4] only woman Senator, though Fulbright himself faces a final run-off against other Democratic rivals. Two further Administration gains were the defeats in Texas of Representative Richard Kleberg, a bitter anti-Administration Democrat, who was a moving spirit in the recent 'Texas revolt', and Nat Patton, likewise an arch-reactionary. Local and personal factors played too large a part in these changes to permit broad generalizations about a liberal trend. Yet it is an encouraging fact that where vigorous and adequate opposition has been forthcoming some of the worst of the dead wood in Congress is being removed. In addition to the above changes, the new Congress will be without Representa-

3 Olin Dewitt Talmadge Johnston, Governor of South Carolina 1935–9, 1943–5.
4 Hattie Wyatt Caraway, Democratic Senator from Arkansas 1931–45.

tives Dies, Costello and Starnes, of the witch-hunting Dies Committee, as well as the isolationist Senators Worth Clark[5] of Idaho and Rufus Holman of Oregon. Senator Nye squeaked through very narrowly in the North Dakota primary and it is said that he will again face a stiff fight in November. These Roosevelt victories may well have a sobering effect upon the 'Southern Revolt'.

6 August 1944

Reconversion. . . . . almost every prominent Administration spokesman has been brought forward in past week armed with facts and figures to show that complacency on home front can still play havoc with military plans and that war is far from won. General Somervell in particular read the Riot Act to a special press conference, declaring that production on EWP [sic] essential items was lagging and that there had been a 5.9 per cent drop in plane production last month. Nelson, Wilson, McNutt, Forrestal, Bard,[1] King, Connally and many others have added warnings of their own. 'Evaporation' of labour from war boom areas on West Coast is a cause of special concern. As a result we have unusual situation, as many Americans are noting, of the Prime Minister whose text has so long been 'Sweat and Tears' now radiating confidence while United States Government has taken up his earlier sombre tones. This doubtless reflects different conditions in two countries. People in Britain may need and certainly deserve encouragement as they end their fifth year of war, whereas in the United States war seems far removed and people have to be warned against slacking off and against a scramble back into civilian employment 'before it is too late'. (Complicating things for Administration is the fact that many Americans trust Prime Minister's judgment about course of war more than they do almost any American spokesman.) As regards demobilization and industrial reconversion plans, on which so little progress has been made despite the many reports and committees dealing with subject, Administration is thus caught in something of a dilemma. It is clear that pace of events demands action. Yet Administration (and particularly Service departments) has apparently been loath to turn spotlight on reconversion lest it increase feeling that war is almost over and start a scramble from war jobs. Now however Dewey and Republican Governors have taken up cry against Administration's unpreparedness and so Administration leaders especially Byrnes have taken bull by horns and are making efforts to speed up legislation. Warnings about production shortages, etc., are an obvious attempt to keep workers on the job till effective reconversion legislation has been passed. . . .

.   .   .

Post-war organization. Announcement of strong American team of diplomatic, military, naval and economic experts has brought some attention to forthcoming

5 David Worth Clark, Democratic Congressman from Idaho 1935–9, Senator 1939–45.
1 Ralph A. Bard, Assistant Secretary of Navy since 1941.

Four-Power talks at Dumbarton Oaks[2] on a post-war international organization but it is perhaps an encouraging sidelight on development of American opinion on international collaboration that such discussions could be planned and held in Washington and on eve of an election campaign with such little excitement and without immediately becoming a political football (it is of course also a measure of the overwhelming interest of current war news).

Election politics. Dewey has been making his first campaign tour and in process some of features of Republican strategy have become clarified. In contrast to bedlam which surrounded Willkie's campaign in 1940 with presidential candidate waging a one-man crusade and virtually ignoring party organization this year's campaign is going to be as cool, methodical and calculating as Governor Dewey himself. This also reflects mentality of those around him, for it has to be remembered that while Messrs Brownell, Sprague and Jaeckle did not produce any enthusiasm for Dewey at Chicago they did calculate and plan their campaign to put him across with no mean skill as result showed – 1056 to 1 for Dewey on first ballot. With Republicans, enthusiasm and inspiration are at a discount this year and organization and calculation (both as to voting probabilities and as to fluctuations in public feeling revealed in public opinion polls) are at a premium.

In accordance with this strategy Dewey's first campaign move was to go to a half-way meeting house in St Louis in borderline State of Missouri and confer with the other twenty-five Republican Governors. Existence of a Republican Administration in any State cannot by any means assure a Republican victory there in a presidential election. If it did, Dewey's chances would be decidedly bright for the twenty-six Republican Governors now represent States with 339 electoral votes and only 266 are needed to win. But a Governor does have control of choicest patronage in his State as Herbert Brownell, Dewey's new Republican National Chairman, well realizes and patronage shrewdly dispensed can spell added votes in elections. This aspect of trip seems considerably more important than elaborate discussion of Federal-State relations which were nominal theme of St Louis Conference. More than that, Dewey in this trip has made his first bow in direction of Governors' group rather than to Old Guard in Washington. Governors ever since their mild revolt against Old Guard dictation at Mackinac Conference (which they threatened to repeat at Chicago convention) have come to be regarded as a new, if loosely knit, bloc in Republican Party hierarchy – more youthful and in most cases more progressive than Old Guard of Messrs Taft, Vandenberg, Martin, Pew, etc. (They even contain one or two Willkie followers in their ranks.) Dewey was not of course originally an Old Guard candidate, though Bricker was, but neither was he one of most popular members of Governors' group. His coolness and aloofness tended to keep him apart. It

2 A mansion in Rock Creek Park, Washington, the property of Harvard University.

may be that this turning towards Governors should be counted to him for grace – at least it is a further hint that Old Guard no longer wields unquestioned power in party.

Republicans' counter-attack to Mr Roosevelt's 'Commander-in-Chief' argument also began to become clear. Dewey's line is now to concede that war is going well and insist that next President will be not primarily a Commander-in-Chief, but a peacetime President called upon to handle vast domestic problems that will follow military victory. From there he goes on to attack Administration on its most vunerable flank, its domestic policies, though whether he will be able to convince voters that there is anything in Republicans' record to suggest that they would have done better is much less certain.

Only one cloud seems to have arisen during trip : the brash announcement by Gerald K. Smith's disreputable and politically insignificant America First Party (to be distinguished from America First *tout court*) that they had elected Bricker as their vice-presidential candidate to run with Smith. Both Bricker and Dewey very hastily repudiated Smith and all his works, but as if to rub salt into wound the America First Party thereupon replaced Bricker with a close associate of discredited Father Coughlin. All this looked like Bricker's chickens coming home to roost, after his all-to-generous assurance to pressmen last week that he would welcome support from Smith or anyone else (and some of more enlightened members of Dewey's entourage must be praying 'Lord save us from our friends'). Internationalist commentators have noticed that Dewey has based his repudiations of both Representative Hamilton Fish and Gerald K. Smith on their alleged anti-Semitism and not on their isolationist record, a tactic doubtless dictated by hopes of his managers of winning over some Jewish support (especially in New York), and at same time of avoiding loss of any of those Midwesterners who are not yet so certain that isolationism was such a bad thing.

6 August 1944 (Savingram)

Congressional primaries. Congressional primaries in New York, Missouri and Kansas produced a number of interesting results, though the overall trend remains one of little change with most incumbents easily winning renomination. The exceptions were, firstly, the defeat of the anti-Roosevelt isolationist Senator Bennett Champ Clark [1] by the State Attorney General, Roy McKittrick, [2] in Missouri. McKittrick, who had full support of the CIO–PAC, campaigned on a straight pro-Roosevelt platform. He now faces a stiff fight in November against his Republican opponent, Forrest Donnell, [3] the present Governor ; of the two McKittrick is regarded as personally the stronger candidate. Another isolationist

1 Bennett Champ Clark, Democratic Senator from Missouri since 1933.
2 Roy McKittrick, lawyer, Missouri Attorney General since 1933.
3 Forrest C. Donnell, Republican Governor of Missouri since 1941.

to go down was the rabid Roosevelt-hater Representative William Lambertson of Kansas. His defeat was probably due as much to dislike of his despicable personal attacks on the President and his family as to his views on national and international policies. Isolationist Clyde Reed, however, had little difficulty in beating his CIO-backed opponent for the Kansas senatorial renomination.

The most newsworthy renomination, however, was that of the isolationist Republican Congressman Hamilton Fish in New York, despite the denunciations of both Dewey and Willkie and most of the press, opposition which he proved able to exploit in his district as 'outside interference'. However, his opponent, Augustus Bennett,[4] who ran him quite close, had already won the Democratic and American Labor Party nominations for the district, and running as an independent in November, stands a good chance of defeating Fish then.

The CIO–PAC is also hailing the victories in New York of Vito Marcantonio, Clayton Powell[5] and Donald O'Toole.[6] Marcantonio not only managed to defeat the Tammany Hall candidate Martin Kennedy (though Kennedy is now alleging that Tammany stabbed him secretly in the back), but won the Democratic, Republican and American Labor Party nominations and is, therefore, virtually certain of re-election in November. This is no mean feat for one who was strongly isolationist till Russia's entry into the war and is generally regarded as a loyal 'Party-liner', if not an openly declared Communist. His election literature reveals a bewildering set of claims : champion of the Negroes, of Irish freedom, of full Allied recognition for Italy, of Puerto Rican independence, and to cap it all, a loyal son of the Roman Catholic Church – all of this reflecting the heterogeneous racial groups which make up his district in New York City. In another newly created New York district which takes in Harlem, the Rev. Adam Clayton Powell, a six-foot Negro demagogue also with communist leanings, won all three primaries and also seems certain of election in November. If Representative Dawson,[7] Democrat, of Chicago, is re-elected, that will make two Negroes in Congress.

Philadelphia strike. The entire transportation system of Philadelphia has been dislocated this week by a strike, condemned by the CIO Transport Workers' Union leaders, which seems to have been started by the decision to appoint eight Negroes as car drivers rather than as road workers. The rank and file of the 5,000 white car-men thereupon explained that they had fallen sick, though some of their unofficial spokesmen told the press more frankly that the Negroes should be put back where they belong – 'on the road'. The War Manpower Commission and Fair Employment Practices Committee have both upheld the right of the

---

4 Augustus W.Bennett, lawyer, US referee in bankruptcy, 1923–44.

5 Adam Clayton Powell Jr, minister of Abyssinian Baptist Church, Harlem, 1937–60, Democratic Congressman 1945–67.

6 Donald L.O'Toole, Democratic Congressman from New York since 1937.

7 William Levi Dawson, Democratic Congressman from Illinois since 1943.

Negroes to promotion where qualified and the Army has now seized the transportation system. . . .

Because of the Negro vote, the strike has wide political implications. It may yet be that the Administration, by fighting the Negro battle in a strike which seems to be very widely condemned, at least in the North, may improve their chances of holding the Negroes in November. They will certainly have to make some gestures for Negro support because the Negro organizations have been condemning the token declaration on racial and religious equality, agreed on at Chicago, as 'not a plank, just a splinter'.

12 August 1944

President's trip. The President's trip to Pearl Harbor has been the other big news of the week. Whatever its connexions with forthcoming developments in the Pacific war, everyone here has viewed it first in relation to the election campaign, and even rank-and-file Republicans express grudging admiration at this latest display of the President's skill as a political opportunist. The absence of Marshall and King leaves doubts as to whether major strategic plans were really discussed, but Mr Roosevelt's identification of himself as Commander-in-Chief in a theatre where war is sure to be continuing in November is accepted generally as an adroit political manoeuvre. It should also help to meet the allegation, especially common in the West Coast States, that the Administration has tended to neglect the Pacific. The Republican bosses, of course, are fuming. The pictures of Mr Roosevelt talking happily with General MacArthur . . . seem likely to have the same effect as the display of bonhomie towards de Gaulle, in dispelling rumours that the President ever allows personal feelings to influence national policies. Mr Roosevelt, in taking up MacArthur's own cry of 'back to the Philippines', was also careful to underscore his anti-imperialist guarantees of independence for the Filipinos.

There are also well authenticated rumours that the President has been making overtures to Willkie to come and discuss foreign policies with him. It is said that his invitation stated explicitly that politics would not be mentioned, but the implications are obvious. . . . There are various indications that Dewey's managers are having little success so far in their wooing of Willkie. The *Herald Tribune*, Willkie's original champion, now supporting Dewey, boldly suggested this week that he should be offered Republican nomination for the New York senatorial race against Wagner, but the idea seems to have made little headway in Albany and a stock Republican politician with no known breadth of vision, Thomas Curran,[1] was adopted.

. . . . .

. . . At the moment the principle of continuing Lend-Lease after German war and until Japanese war ends seems to stand a fairly good chance of being upheld

1 Thomas J.Curran, lawyer, President of New York County Republican Committee since 1940, Secretary of State for New York since 1943.

(Stettinius himself upheld it unequivocally in a talk with the press), though special congressional enquiries into the matter could only tend to add extra restrictions as to what might be leased or lent, etc. Prospects of Lend-Lease programme being extended after Japanese war seem far dimmer. This is point seized on by the critical conservative-nationalist press which rebels at the idea of an American taxpayer supporting Britain's domestic economy. Stettinius himself said that he has never conceived Lend-Lease as 'a post-war instrument' and recalled that the Act (as we ourselves have insisted) is explicitly 'an Act to defend the United States'. If it should be our policy to request Lend-Lease (repeat Lend-Lease) aid for reconstruction purposes, it would be unrealistic to underrate formidable political opposition in this country under any Administration. . . .

Oil. The Anglo-American Oil Agreement[2] has been well received and with much less excitement than might have been expected, considering the storms that raged over the Arabian Pipeline project. The harmony achieved at the earlier technical talks thus paid good dividends. The United States representatives let virtually nothing leak out during the negotiations on this occasion and so public controversy was kept to a minimum. In the outcome Ickes is happy, the press is happy, the oil industry is said to be acquiescing silently, and a good many people are relieved that the nightmare of the pipeline scheme apparently did not recur. It is generally assumed that it was American principles that triumphed and Senator Connally, Chairman of the Foreign Relations Committee, spoke for many when he said that agreement meant that Britain 'would let our concessions alone'. He has given his Committee a week before holding the hearings which will go far to determine whether the Agreement will be treated simply as an executive agreement or as a treaty demanding formal Senate ratification. . . .

Fulbright. J. William Fulbright (Democrat) won his run-off against Governor Homer Adkins[3] in Arkansas and is now virtually assured of election to the Senate in November. Replacing the cautious and uncreative Mrs Hattie Caraway, Fulbright (a Rhodes scholar, and author of the Fulbright Resolution advocating American collaboration in international affairs) declared that he regarded his nomination as 'a mandate from the people to abolish war through close co-operation of all nations'. He should be a very useful addition to the Upper House.

20 August 1944

The War. High optimism about progress of European war naturally continues despite President's warning against expectation of a German collapse before ef-

2 Signed on 8 August by Stettinius and Beaverbrook, providing for an Anglo-American International Petroleum Commission with advisory powers. (The agreement, however, was rejected by the Senate in December on account of the hostility of Senator Connally and oil interests.)

3 Homer M. Adkins, Governor of Arkansas 1940–4.

fective invasion of German soil. Maitland Wilson's message [1] in connexion with Riviera landings has provided a needed reminder of degree of British participation. President's statement that German habit of throwing up the sponge to avoid occupation of German soil will not work again and that nothing Germany and Japan could do will prevent Allied occupation is widely and approvingly reported. If this is not done, he continued, the next generation (of Germans) will be told Germany 'won the war'. As for Japan, she 'must be sealed off from peace-loving world until she proves herself willing and able to live with peaceful countries'. Job of 'sealing her off' is principally a responsibility of the United States because, with exception of Burma theatre, the American forces in Pacific are stronger than those of her Allies.

Dumbarton Oaks. Dumbarton Oaks Conference has finally leapt into prominence as a result of many factors. Cadogan's statement at my press conference that we in general approved American proposals was prominently and favourably reported and has created general impression that whatever the attitude of the USSR our view was unlikely to deviate much from that of Americans although there might be differences of emphasis. . . . Hull and his officials generally are proving most co-operative and understanding. Hull was finally forced to break his reticence by a statement issued by Governor Dewey on the 16th. Dewey, possibly advised by Foster Dulles, and less probably by Welles, took the obvious line of supporting need of an international organization with force to back it but of expressing uneasiness at reports of 'cynical big-power politics', and predicted failure of any system which imposed military domination by the Big Four and did not give adequate representation to smaller nations. This is in some ways promising ground for Dewey since it implies not merely a traditionally American liberal outlook but gives pleasure to hyphenated groups within the United States and is likely to find response in anti-imperialist sentiment which in America stretches from distant right to remote left. Hull, who is particularly and no doubt sincerely incensed by any suggestion that he has abandoned internationalism, replied that charge was utterly baseless. For 150 years United States has been champion of small nations 'especially those striving to be free' (he has said this often before). He had consulted many American groups and foreign countries before these talks which in any case were not intended to be conclusive. He personally hoped that a full and final conference of the United Nations would occur this autumn but when pressed on this by correspondents emphasized that this was merely his personal hope and not an agreed plan. The last thing the United States wanted was a kind of military alliance of the Big Four to coerce the world which Dewey ascribed to it. Words of Moscow resolution were sufficient rebuttal. Senator Connally let fly at Dewey in characteristically sharp language and charged him with crude partisan politics. So did other Democratic

1 Henry Maitland Wilson, Supreme Allied Commander Mediterranean Theatre, 1944, issued communiqué emphasizing joint role of the British, American and French troops in the landings between Nice and Marseilles.

Senators. Vandenberg duly came to Dewey's defence and pontificated about wickedness of any settlement which ignored rights of smaller powers. Hull, answering a question, said that he would gladly discuss topic with Dewey if domestic politics were kept out of it. Dewey said that he would send Foster Dulles to represent him in conversations with State Department. The press tends to emphasize the fact that the very differences between Dewey and Hull serve to bring out underlying harmony of their views on general necessity of international arrangements. Certainly there is something quaint about Dewey as champion of pure Wilsonian doctrine against the 'cynicism' of Hull.

. . .

There is naturally much curiosity about our proposals, concerning which nothing has been hinted to any journalist if only in deference to Hull's wishes, but far more curiosity and anxiety in press and beyond attaches to intentions of the Russians. Relatively low-grade delegation of USSR has led to ill-concealed disappointment in official circles and to unconcealed complaint in one or two periodicals. Nevertheless atmosphere in which talks will occur is very much more friendly and favourable than exigencies of Republican politics would seem to suggest. Hull's sadly reiterated plea that domestic politics be kept out of so desperately important an issue is unlikely to achieve its full purpose although it may well shame some potential critics into silence and what is more important serve to keep broad mass of middle American opinion where it is now – fairly solid behind Roosevelt-Hull policy. . . .

Since above was written Dewey has accepted an offer by Hull of consultation and has delegated John Foster Dulles, who is generally believed to be his choice for Secretary of State if he is elected, to come to Washington for the purpose. Dewey added 'I am happy to extend my fullest co-operation to the end that result should be wholly bipartisan and should have united support of the American people'.

Bases. President's Bremerton speech [2] of 12 August was received with unanimous favour. Everyone agreed that Pacific war needed emphasis by contrast with sensational European developments and while professional Republicans denounced the President for undertaking a journey for allegedly blatant political purposes, moderate Republicans as well as all Democrats asserted that he was, after all, in fact Commander-in-Chief and that if some political advantage accrued to him from that position that was due to the nature of the position and not to some vaguely dishonourable use of it by its holder. President's remarks about Pacific bases were also received without any dissent. It is interpreted widely in press as meaning that no Pacific bases would ever again be exclusively controlled by any one of their present possessors – not only would Japanese islands revert to the United States but British, Dutch, French, etc., outposts would in future be held in some sort of joint trusteeship with the United States. This well-known

2 At Bremerton Navy Yard, Washington State, delivered from deck of a destroyer.

view of the President's is obviously greatly to the taste of nation at large and although there is no sign of a rising campaign on this topic (nor much talk of bases in exchange for Lend-Lease), it is clear that American imperialists and anti-imperialists alike take it more or less for granted that the President's wishes will in fact be realized. The McKellar bill now before the Senate, adding to specific bases Caribbean and West Indian (as well as Galapagos) Islands, is by now a very large and familiar straw in the wind. Control if not acquisition of at any rate Pacific bases has clearly achieved the status of an objective of United States national policy irrespective of the colour of the administration.

. . .

FOREIGN POLICY

(a)*China*. The most arresting [development] is the growing lack of enthusiasm for China, a fact which is striking indeed if compared with the prestige that country enjoyed, say, six months ago, not to speak of earlier periods. The continuous stream of stories about the financial corruption, the political dictatorship, the despotic suppression of opinion, etc., by the Soong oligarchy has finally seeped through widely. I am told that Wallace, on return, remarked after praise of Russia that in the case of China 'the higher one went to the more disgusted one became'. This reflects fairly accurately the disappointment of liberal opinion, which was the mainstay of pro-Chinese feeling here, not unaffected perhaps by quiet anti-Chiang Communist propaganda in this country which seems to have done something to undermine the Chinese myth. It would be too much to say that a realistic view of China obtains ; but in the press and everywhere else an ironical attitude to the claims of China to be a first-class power is only too observable. Surprisingly little mention, for instance, has been made of China in connexion with the talks at Dumbarton Oaks. The slump in general Chinese stock is an accomplished fact and appears to be increasing.

(b) *Italy*. The opposite has occurred in the case of Italy, towards which very soft sentiment is entertained. Not only Mayor La Guardia but many other organs of opinion either explicitly or by omission are letting it be understood that the Allies are perhaps being somewhat too harsh to the Italians, and that gentler treatment of a democratic government duly purged of Fascist and royalist elements should be adopted. There never was great antipathy to Italy here but now it would not be too much to say that it is viewed with considerably friendlier feeling than certain allies of the United States.

(c) *Zionists*. The Zionists, elated by the pro-Zionist resolutions of both the major parties, are said to be engaged on a plan to renew the abortive Palestine resolution killed in the spring by General Marshall. This time they say that they are certain of success. The politicians principally concerned are Senator Wagner and Representative Celler. They maintain that the army authorities will not again oppose objections, and that the full original resolution will pass both Houses.

One cannot tell what turn events may take, but there is reason for thinking that Stettinius and to some degree Hull are mildly favourable to such a move, or at least not sufficiently adverse to do much to hinder it. The Zionists hope to push their scheme through before the elections, when the Jewish vote in New York State is at its most crucial, and argue that this will successfully tie the hands of their most implacable opponents in the Eastern Division of the State Department. If there is anything in this, the State Department may take the line that they cannot do anything against Congress of which they are undoubtedly in considerable fear.

Presidential campaign. . . . Republicans place much hope on the deep resentment which the CIO-PAC Political Committee has excited. There seems no doubt that Hillman has somewhat overplayed his hand and has conveyed the impression of a more powerful and sinister force allied to Communists than in fact he is able to control. The Democrats are executing routine manoeuvres and are very satisfied with Truman as a future spokesman, inasmuch as they maintain, with much justice, that he and his wife are ideal versions of plain Mr and Mrs America and that this is what gets the voters. . . .

Reconversion. The War Production Board-Army feud looks like stabilizing into regular trench warfare. The political alignment appears to be : on one side Big Business within and without the War Department (together with their allies among the professional soldiers) who are anxious not to allow a switch to civilian production before, at any rate, they themselves are ready to participate in it. These are naturally not alone in taking this line, which is urged also by some perfectly honest Army officers who regard Nelson's estimates of war needs as unduly optimistic and prefer to err on the side of overproduction rather than be caught short by an unexpectedly long war. On the other side is arranged a motley collection of interests. These include some government economists and other specialists who maintain that the facts of production support Nelson's stand, and Small Business, which is naturally anxious to return to normal functioning before it is squeezed out by the returning onrush of Big Business. (The average small businessmen are very confused and muddled about their proper interests, and their lobbies in Congress voted against the Murray-Kilgore, and in favour of the George, bill [3] more out of conservative, small-town anti-labour sentiment and general aversion to the New Deal and government control, than from a rational calculation of their own economic interest which might dictate support of the Murray bill.) To these must be added such foes of all large combinations – cartels, unions, government centralization, etc. – as Senator O'Mahoney and Thurman Arnold ; and finally left-wing and liberal opinion in general. As a preliminary sketch of the post-war political topography of the economic forces, the

3 Murray–Kilgore (CIO sponsored) bill dealt with post-war reconversion, and would establish a Works Administration to promote employment and unionization. For George bill, see p. 411.

situation is peculiarly instructive. Both sides appear equally cavalier with the facts with which their statisticians busily ply them, and both tend to camouflage their true desires beneath a cloak of patriotic needs.

. . .

26 August 1944

. . .

Dumbarton Oaks. Everyone now has had their say and result has on the whole been encouraging – Dulles has seen Hull twice and both have spoken amiable bromides indicating that there was no very serious disagreement between them. Vandenberg claims unanimity with Dulles, and Willkie has made a cautious statement along lines of his ignored message to Republican convention, emphasizing need for agreement to employ force by definite commitment of states concerned to preserve security, and demanding wider publicity for issues raised if only in order to educate American public opinion sufficiently. President, having somewhat too impulsively denied to press that he had recently invited Willkie to discuss foreign policy, has now, press reports, been persuaded by his advisers to placate the wounded Willkie by writing to him again to denounce press for alleged inaccuracy, and to invite him once again. Earlier Willkie said that he would prefer to wait till after election, but could come. Even Taft observed that he saw no obvious points of disagreement between Republicans and Hull. Such harmony though it may seem almost too good to be true is hopeful as far as it goes, supported as it is by the very real progress being made at conference itself.

Dulles did however observe that he saw no reason why world organization should not remain a subject for 'bipartisan' debate in presidential campaign, that Hull and he had not reached complete agreement on this, and reiterated that more publicity might be given to discussions, courteously adding that such things must be left to Hull as the responsible official. This can only mean that Dewey does not propose to be deprived of a potentially strong election weapon by Hull's genuine desire to lift matter above party politics, which in its turn makes position of Dulles ambiguous, since he seems free to publish and make political use of anything communicated to him by the Secretary, and equally free to complain of secrecy, and to counterattack if, for precisely these reasons, information is withheld. . . .

. . .

It is reasonably certain that Hull will continue to keep relevant Senators informed of progress of talks (Vandenberg appears to have shown American plan to Dulles yesterday) which may prevent discussion from going too wide of the mark, at any rate in responsible political circles. Even irresponsible circles do not seem wholly beyond the Secretary's ken – notorious Fascist demagogue Gerald L.K.Smith, who has duly appeared in Washington and made a scene outside gates of Dumbarton Oaks, upon requesting a 'conference' was formally turned over by the Secretary to Assistant Secretary Breckinridge Long, who is to 'keep in touch' with this disreputable figure. Long is not very pleased by this and is trying hard to confine exchanges to writing. American negotiators are said to be filled with a kind of nervous confidence. Thus far the auguries for success seem favourable enough despite press imbroglio. Stettinius has taken delegates off for a weekend in New York.

The Oil Agreement. Notorious Pew, Pennsylvania Republican boss and chairman of Sun Oil Company, has fired a shot against Oil Agreement on ground that it means creation of a cartel, with usual American objections to that menace to free enterprise. Pew is not a lonely thinker, and this may mean some sort of campaign though not necessarily too formidable a one. Marquis Childs reminds his readers that it is difficult to tell when Pew is talking oil and when he is talking Republican politics. President has dished prophets by declining to define Oil Agreement as an executive agreement – a thing he has not done for a considerable time – and submitted it to Senate Foreign Relations Committee as a formal treaty. This he did apparently on advice from Connally and his colleagues and agreement thus becomes subject to the two-thirds Senate majority rule applying to treaties. The move seems *prima facie* characteristically shrewd and bold since it places responsibility for deciding upon first serious international commodity agreement of its kind upon Senate – if Senate votes it down it incurs much obvious odium over an issue which, though important enough, is not most crucially immediate : if it ratifies it as a treaty, it creates precedent of very great value. In either case this step protects the executive from increasing charges of usurpation of senatorial prerogative by means of executive agreements, which could clearly prove most dangerous at this moment, particularly if opposition decided to exploit them with real gusto, dragging in alleged trampling on rights of small nations and other irrelevant nonsense amid much popular acclaim. It also protects the executive from charges of sole responsibility for endorsing a cartel for favouring 'Big Business' and oil business at that. President has taken a risk but if he wins it will clearly have been more than worth while.

27 August 1944

Reconversion. The Nelson-Wilson duel has ended in the resignation of Wilson and Nelson's coming journey to China in the company of General Hurley. The deputy remaining in charge is Krug,[1] a young executive originally in Tennessee Valley Authority. The general atmosphere is well conveyed by the fact that the President has had to deny that the clumsy White House statement promising that Nelson would be away for several months was 'a kick in the teeth' to Mr Nelson. Both the President and Nelson have now formally placed on record their conviction that Mr Nelson had not in fact been 'kicked in the teeth'. It appears that Mr

1 Julius A. Krug, chief power engineer, TVA, 1938–40 ; Director, Office of War Utilities, 1943–4.

Nelson received two letters from the White House on the same day : the first declared that he would proceed to China for 2–3 weeks ; the second that he would be away for several months. The second letter, which was apparently based on one of the President's more light-hearted statements to Wilson in an effort to make him stay at his post, is said to have driven Nelson to considerable frenzy. He demanded a final showdown and won. Wilson's resignation was accepted by the White House apparently under pressure, not merely from Nelson only but from all those who pointed out to the President that concessions to Big Business were in themselves genuinely damaging to the country's welfare, and, moreover, inexpedient from the point of view of, and incompatible with, the President's general political position. Truman is said to have been particularly insistent on this point. Wilson accused Nelson's friends of systematic vilification of himself, and Nelson of lack of authority in his own house, and left openly disgruntled. The liberals do not conceal their delight at this apparent defeat of what they had long viewed as a sinister combination of Big Business and high Army officials. In his last press conference the President threw some doubt on the retention by Nelson of his post after his return from China. General rumour is that having allowed Wilson to go as a sop to Small Business and liberals, the President sees no reason for keeping Nelson whose amiable inefficiency is a byword. But in view of the President's habit of day-to-day decisions Nelson's doom cannot be regarded as by any means settled. The Chinese are said to be displeased by the role played by China as a distant repository for temporarily unwanted officials, often the first stage to total eclipse. Nelson's reported observations about China as a possible market for post-war surplus Army supplies fails to assuage local Chinese feelings.

3 September 1944

The War. War news is too good to encourage much contention in other fields. Our part in French campaign has obtained a slightly wider mention than last week, and tributes in Eisenhower's report of 31 August[1] have helped, but it still remains only dimly perceptible through clouds of glory trailed, naturally enough perhaps, by reported exploits of Generals Patton, Bradley[2] and Patch.[3] Capture of Amiens may improve this. Montgomery's elevation, generally warmly approved, has stimulated Chamber [sic] to talk of British outranking of Americans in military and diplomatic fields. Although the old warning voices are not mute and sternly warn de Gaulle that his civilian arrangements will be sharply watched, general consensus is today perhaps more pro-Gaullist than ever before, possibly because nothing succeeds like success, here especially.

.   .   .

1 Referred to Montgomery as 'one of the great soldiers of this or any other war' who had directed the operations of both American and British armies during the great victories of July and early August. At Caen the British had been up against 'the strongest defenses on the French front'.

2 Omar Nelson Bradley, Commander of US 12th Army Group in France 1944–5.

3 Alexander McC. Patch, Commander of US 7th Army in Southern France 1944–5.

Post-war planning : Dumbarton Oaks. Reston[4] duly published Chinese plan in his series of political scoops for *New York Times,* and much discussion is therefore in progress concerning main lines of what public believes to be the four plans.

. . .

Truman in his acceptance speech delivered a direct onslaught on isolationists, which he and Paul Porter, Democratic publicity director, who I am told wrote speech, know to be a sure fire target at moment. Isolationists know it too and are unlikely to expose themselves to a pitched battle. Administration is said to hope not only that talks will conclude in broad general agreement but that Senate will, with gentle treatment, be induced to swallow them whole. I see no reason at present to question this optimism.

. . .

No one knows quite how much to make of the Hull-Dulles discussions. Dulles spoke optimistically to press about having done 'something that is perhaps unique in American politics' but refused to agree with portions of his joint statement with Hull into which Secretary wished to insert words about removing issue from party politics and thus committing Dewey to some sort of alliance or silence on topic. Press correspondents tried to pry out of Hull more information about how he had handled Dulles but could get only cryptic reply 'Oh I treated him just like a Senator'. Dewey who has announced a plan for eight speeches on way to and along Pacific Coast plainly does not intend to preserve such silence. He is manoeuvring for a position which allows him to condemn President's alleged 'power political' ambitions while not reawakening now painful memories of Lodge and 'Death Battalion' of 1918–19.[5] Willkie, who is behaving coyly, appears similarly unwilling to throw into either scale an influence which may in event of a close election prove a makeweight until last possible moment. Dulles-Willkie-Hull triangle thus displays a remarkable combination of genuine pious effort to arrive at a bipartisan position with typically tough and vigorous political 'dickering' in approximately proportions in which these attributes are compounded in character of Foster Dulles. Drew Pearson has exhumed certain somewhat Lindberghian remarks made by Dulles in spring of 1939 in which he congratulated Germany on dynamism and capacity for taking her destiny into her own hands, etc., and much other explosive is doubtless being accumulated by Democrats with which to blow up Dulles at right psychological moment. Dulles himself is said to feel that mantle of Elihu Root[6] has fallen upon him. A Wilsonian bitterly remarked that this is only too true and only shows how greatly this mantle – too narrow to embrace other nations at the best of times – has shrunk of late.

4 James B. ('Scotty') Reston, *New York Times* correspondent, London, 1938–41 ; Washington, 1941 onwards.

5 The fourteen 'irreconcilable' Senators, including Borah and Hiram Johnson, dedicated to rejecting Wilson's Versailles Treaty.

6 Elihu Root, Republican jurist, Secretary of War 1899–1903, Secretary of State 1905–9, Senator from New York 1905–15.

Meanwhile Mr Hull has been having some trouble in squaring Mr Roosevelt's somewhat light-hearted remarks on Dumbarton Oaks talks with the official line. President appears to have observed at his press conference (a) that a new and better League would spring from these talks, (b) that it would be an improvement on old League in taking cognizance of such world questions as food, labour, etc., and (c) that it would have more efficient machinery for prevention of aggression by force. Naturally Mr Hull's audience wanted to know why, if so, talks were described as dealing exclusively with security, what was to happen to ILO or any of bodies set up or about to be set up as a result of recent conferences on economic issues. The *Baltimore Sun* pointed out that President first criticized old League for dabbling too much in non-security, e.g. economic issues, and then praised new body for including precisely such activities. All this Mr Hull found naturally somewhat difficult to reconcile with official line. He stuck to his guns about security as the sole proper topic of talks but observed that other relevant issues might naturally be discussed. He said nothing specific about relationship between economic organizations flowing from Hot Springs, Atlantic City and Bretton Woods Conferences save that they were separate from any organization discussed at Dumbarton Oaks, and generally stalled on issues on which journalists present finally decided, in view of obvious embarrassment caused him by the President's words, to spare him. . . .

Economic front. On the economic front, I am now told that Nelson was saved from extinction principally by Hopkins, who has always propped him up, but that the President is tired of Nelson's lack of character and will need some persuading if he is to reinstall him in any real capacity. Meanwhile the George Demobilization bill, a very conservative alternative to Murray–Kilgore Bill in that it leaves nearly everything to Director of Demobilization Office, leaves relief to States and does not provide for retraining, was itself so emasculated in the House (which strips even Director of his power) that something new may have to be attempted. If an excessively conservative Senate-House measure emerges, President could either veto it or – as some think likely – let it pass, condemn it and promise redress if he is re-elected, meanwhile letting it be used as a campaign weapon. Issue is one on which Administration must show liberalism if only from a purely electoral point of view. This political need may also be responsible for sudden anti-trust action [7] against two large railroads and Logan and Kuhn Loeb Banks instigated by Department of Justice (Attorney General said as much in private conversation). As season advances more symptoms of 'populism' may be expected from an Administration which needs support of hereditary enemies of Big Business if it is to be re-elected. To this extent Senator Truman's influence is clearly discernible. Wallace has been touring South West in a pro-Roosevelt campaign. His stock, as a dignified and defeated idealist, is

7 Launched in May 1944.

411

higher than it has been since 1942. He is said to desire Secretaryship of State in 1945 and Presidency in 1948.

The Phillips flurry.[8] Drew Pearson, who privately claims to have collected a considerable dossier of facts on India, publication of which would be unwelcome to His Majesty's Government, has caused a genuine flurry with his stories about circumstances surrounding Phillips's resignation. Senator Chandler, much the most irresponsible of the Five Senators, repeated Pearson's allegations that Phillips had been declared *persona non grata* in London and demanded an investigation by Foreign Relations Committee of the case which he thought in all respects discreditable to us. Later an obscure Congressman, despite denials by State Department and this Embassy that Phillips had been asked to leave, revived charge and tabled a resolution that Indian Agent General and Sir Ronald Campbell be similarly treated. This absurdity may have merit of reducing situation to farce, but Pearson has assured his friends that he intends to print more and more Indian material likely to do us damage. . . .

4 September 1944

Hard and soft peace. Diettmar's[1] reported appeal to the Allies for 'reasonable' terms stirred Hull to a stern reiteration of the 'no surrender' formula. This robust attitude which clearly represents that of the Administration was met with fairly general approval by the press, which is on the whole not 'soft peace' minded. . . . The strongest manifestation of a campaign for soft peace naturally comes from the German language press which displays a unanimity on this issue – a need for a strong Germany as a wall against Russia – which stretches from the extreme semi-Fascist right to the most left-wing Social Democrats and embraces all faiths and credos, save some Communists and the Jewish refugees. The Lutheran and Catholic newspapers take a somewhat analogous line both in the German-language and English-speaking press. Anti-Russian feeling characterizes the majority of the rest of the foreign-language press (the Czech and Communist papers being the most obvious exceptions).

Since a greater ratio of Americans in 1940 than in 1920 stated, according to a census, that a non-English language was their basic tongue, it may be imagined that this is influential particularly in the Middle West, and despite some views to the contrary and despite a general slight move towards a 'harder' view, there is little reason for supposing that there has been any dramatic mass change of heart. The robot bombings have undoubtedly had their salutary effect here too : mili-

8 William Phillips, career diplomat, visited India in 1943 as Roosevelt's personal representative. He wrote an account of the Indian situation for the President on 19 April in terms critical of British policy. This letter was published in Drew Pearson's column on 25 July 1944. After his return from India Phillips had been appointed to Eisenhower's staff in London. It was his resignation from this post on 19 July 1944 which occasioned controversy over whether he had been 'asked to leave'.

1 Lt-General Kurt Diettmar, leading German military commentator and broadcaster.

tary occupation of Germany and her disarmament are universally taken for granted and the White House is said to be as severe as ever ; but the groups more or less favourable to some sort of negotiated peace – the Roman Catholics, the Nonconformist churches, as well as many Episcopalians, humanitarians and liberals, a section of Big Business (particularly Midwest industrialists) as well as anti-Russians everywhere – compose a formidable body whose strength should on no account be underestimated.

.   .   .

11 September 1944

The inevitable consequence here of the victorious progress in Europe is that thoughts, acts and official pronouncements on readjustment to conditions of peace have come with a rush, and are preoccupying whatever attention is left over from the comfortable assurance of an early end to the European war. The War Department has published some of its plans for gradual demobilization of the army. Marshall's plan for a small permanent army reinforced by national military short-term service is universally approved in the press. The Secretary of the Navy has proclaimed that the navy, so far from demobilizing, would grow until it reaches a strength of over three and a half millions and implied that it would so continue. Krug, the new acting Chief of the War Production Board, has promised reconversion to peace economy of at least 40 per cent of the existing war economy, and this may not be regarded as sufficient in some quarters. The blessings of brand new motorcars and refrigerators are promised within a few months, Byrnes has relaxed the rationing of certain processed foods and promised wider relaxation in the near future. Faced with a flow of so much new fruit from the horn of plenty, the public is naturally not in a mood for long-continued self-discipline. Despite a certain underlying awareness of strains likely to be exacted by the continuation of the Pacific war, the thoughts of the average man, already long intent upon his personal post-war destiny, have now been virtually invited to proceed in that direction by the Government itself. Naturally this finds a strong echo in the press and in Congress. The pressure on the Administration to relax every possible war restriction is of course all the stronger because of their need to make the best possible appeal to the country in the pending election.

Dumbarton Oaks. An unexpected debate on American participation in the world organization was suddenly touched off in the Senate by a routine demand for American bases by the chauvinist Senator Brooks. A day later it was denoted by Krock and Reston as the formal prelude to a now inevitable 'grand debate' on the whole subject. The ball was set rolling by Senator Bushfield,[1] an unregenerate isolationist dinosaur of the 1918–19 type, who, basing himself on Reston's summaries of the plans in the *New York Times,* demanded to know whether

1 Harlan J.Bushfield, Republican Senator from South Dakota since 1943.

under the scheme discussed at Dumbarton Oaks the President would be entitled to plunge the United States into war without the consent of Congress and conveying unqualified opposition thereto. Senator Millikin[2] asked if the Senate could 'run out on the representative of the United States if it did not acquiesce in his views' on military intervention. Connally, who was caught somewhat off his guard, made a moderately artful but at times confused and evasive series of replies in the course of which he stated :

(a) That the plan under discussion precluded the possibility of armed intervention by the World Council without unanimous consent by the four major powers. This entailed the right of veto on the part of the United States which eliminated objections made a quarter of a century ago to article x of the League Covenant whereby, it was alleged, other powers were entitled to cause the United States to go to war without the consent of the American people or Congress.

(b) In answer to other questions, he and Republican minority leader White made clear that there were two turnstiles at least at which the Senate could control proceedings. Firstly, in ratifying the basic instrument – a formal treaty committing the United States to adherence to the new world organization. Secondly, in ratifying these series of special agreements – again in effect treaties – whereby the United States would pledge to other powers (presumably at least the permanent members of the Council were meant) the provision of specified armed assistance in specified circumstances for the preservation of security as part of the general plan. Thereby the constitutional prerogative of the Senate to regulate United States foreign policy would be amply preserved. Unless this was done, sudden aggression could never be checked. If Bushfield's desires were fulfilled the Senate might be talking and talking while Hitler was gobbling up Poland. Without speed, no real security. As for senatorial prerogatives, history provided plenty of instances of Presidents – McKinley[3] and other eminent Republicans – who took military action without consulting Congress. Here Connally reeled off an immense catalogue of such cases, doubtless providently supplied by the State Department. He ended with a grand patriotic peroration.

Thereupon Vandenberg expounded what looks like becoming basic text of the serious opposition. He asserted

(a) That neither Dumbarton Oaks talks, nor any other international conference, could frame terms of reference of United States delegate to Security Organization. This would have to be finally determined by Senate when ratification comes up of the basic instrument setting up the Organization. It could of course pledge itself to go to war whenever the United States delegate so committed it. But he, Vandenberg, could not agree to this nor would the American people.

(b) Yet he wished to leave executive some freedom of military action without control of Senate – within the region of security protected under Monroe Doctrine. Within that region Presidents have acted and Presidents should act to pre-

2 Eugene D. Millikin, Republican Senator from Colorado since 1941.
3 William McKinley, President 1897–1901, who took the USA into the Spanish-American War.

serve security on their own authority. Once they stray beyond this – once it is a question of using force 'outside of our normal zone at a level which is tantamount to a declaration of war' – joint action by both Houses of Congress alone can authorize it. This seems to amount to a strong demand for a hemispheric sphere of exclusive influence, with the rider that American representative in, say, a world council, should not be empowered to pledge United States of America to joint military action outside United States sphere without assent of Congress. Vandenberg then characteristically began to muffle the blow. There had been far too much talk about force. Much preliminary machinery to settle disputes by means short of war would have to be gone through first. By time that was done, if trouble still continued, the American Congress and people would surely have no doubt about who was to blame and would vote and act accordingly. And if Germany and Japan were now crushed who could the future aggressor be ? One of present Allies ? Was this thinkable ?

With all this Connally dealt well. He congratulated the able Senator from Michigan on his optimism but wondered whether his 'beautiful homilies' to Hitler and Hirohito would have sufficed to check them : a policeman was powerless without a visible stick even if he didn't use it. There matter rests.

Vandenberg's cat is now out of the bag. His moderately worded but basically isolationist thesis may become central text of the opposition on Foreign Relations Committee and in Senate. Emphatic distinction between indispensable hemispheric and more remote world security, and even more the disingenuous mixture of constitutional objections with argument that with advance of reason and of peaceful mediation the need for international machinery for the rapid use of preventive force will become increasingly remote, reminds one of similar subtleties of late Senator Lodge. Nor are Wheeler or Shipstead, Bushfield or Taft the tactical equals of Borah and his friends. Vandenberg is no desperate champion of losing causes, he is too much of an artful dodger and if public opinion moves against him strongly enough he will rapidly adapt himself to new situation by way of one of the many loopholes with which he invariably provides himself.

. . . United Press started a canard about an invitation issued to French Committee to join Dumbarton Oaks talks ; Connally, apropos of virtually nothing, delivered an attack on French incompetence in 1940 (though he thought well of their conduct of the Hundred Years War) and said that they must serve an 'apprenticeship' before being admitted to an equality with Big Four. French will doubtless infer that here as elsewhere he is Administration's mouthpiece. He probably expresses its sentiment if not its considered policy. French quarters have put in to other Senators routine of strongly worded requests that they should dissociate themselves from Connally.

Hull has exchanged courteous notes with Dewey apropos of his conversations with Dulles. Both sides agree to treat peace like war itself – as a non-partisan issue, the internationalist end is identical but expression of disagreement about means is allowed. Hull is clearly still labouring to avoid a 'grand debate' in

Senate and is said to dismiss the recent debate as so much summer lightning. Dewey, on being asked at a press conference whether United States member of the World Council should commit the United States to use force against aggression without instructions from Congress in each case, replied that 'such questions would have to be worked out by discussion and consultation'. For what it is worth, Dulles made no concealment to me a few days ago of his desire to avoid placing shackles on executive by requiring action of United States representative on the World Council to be subject to congressional approval. . . .

Meanwhile fresh evidence of growing sensitiveness to public criticism of State Department is provided by :

(a) the publication of official statement on Tyler Kent case.[4] This did not fail to note Kent's delinquencies but tended to convey that he was handed over to us as a favour at a time when our critical state made such favours impossible to refuse. Only Joe Kennedy's story to press made his treason to the United States amply clear. The isolationists (and Kent's mother) continue to complain that Senator Shipstead's charge – that Kent knew that Mr Churchill was inveigling President into alliance behind Mr Chamberlain's back – had not been refuted. But publication of facts has usefully cleared the air.

(b) A formal defence of Messrs Robert Murphy and Samuel Reber[5], attacked with exceptional violence by the *Washington Post* as well as *PM, Christian Science Monitor,* etc., as a couple of Vichyssois [*sic*] incompetents likely to bungle Eisenhower's policies in occupied Germany. Mr Hull recited Murphy's record, asserted accurately enough that he had confidence of White House and declared that Reber was far above petty prejudice and as able an officer as any in the Department. This latter, if not former, is, as you doubtless know, a fair enough attribution inasmuch as members of my staff who have dealt with him regard Reber as an exceptionally well informed, capable and unruffleable official, not too literally bound to his instructions, too astute and adaptable to be an over faithful slave of principle or conviction. The *Washington Post* replied with a second equally fierce denunciation. Murphy, who is here, wears a persecuted look and is said to be wondering how soon his half-German Milwaukee origin would be used against him.

. . .

'Hell hath no fury . . .'

Bullitt's article in *Life* on 4 September in which, after somewhat mystical praise of the Vatican, he represents the Italians whom he has met as mainly perturbed about exchanging the tyranny of Berlin for that of Moscow from which only London can save them, has naturally caused considerable stir. Bullitt's violent ideas on this subject are not new, and he appears to have put in the mouths of unnamed Romans fears and suspicions of Russia which seem to be identical with

4 On 2 September. *Vide supra*, 24 June, n.2.

5 Samuel Reber, career diplomat, Assistant to President's special representative in North Africa, 1943.

his own. The Communist press, following the lead of *Pravda,* has harshly attacked Bullitt as a 'bankrupt spy' and leader of the 'soft peace' party in the United States of America (and Britain). The article, written in Bullitt's most irresponsible and unbridled style, has also upset many moderate supporters of the Moscow Declaration. Some see in it a vindictive desire to damage the President, whose preoccupation with good relations with the USSR is well known and who, after the Welles affair, seems finally to have cast Bullitt off. The key to Bullitt's behaviour seems to lie in his frustration as a victim of unrequited love for the USSR, for France, and for President Roosevelt by all of whom in turn he was scorned and against whom he has systematically turned. So far, apart from the Communists and one or two liberal commentators, only Lerner[6] in *PM* has really trounced Bullitt for inciting to war against Russia (the article does indeed come near this), while much private indignation was shown by Lippmann who deplored Bullitt as a reckless mischief-maker and told a member of my staff that Bullitt joined the French forces only after Stimson refused him a commission in the United States Army, saying 'Why apply now, when you are fat and fifty, and not in 1917 when you were slim and young and twenty ?' Be that as it may, the sentiments expressed – hatred of the Soviet régime, fears of the bolshevization of Europe, desire to see Britain as a buffer – are certainly not confined to the author, least of all in Washington, though he has given the most brutally direct expression to this brand of isolationism. It is too early to assess reactions, particularly from the Catholic and 'hyphenated' press : but the relative scarcity of protest makes one wonder whether an equally provocative article in *Life* in the opposite sense – say one extravagantly praising the Russians and demanding the total occupation of Germany by them – would have met with a similar equanimity. There appears to exist greater uncertainty and indifference in the United States about the future of Europe – as opposed to specific dread of Russia – than Washington officials seem to believe, or at any rate reveal to us.

PAC *and* NAM. Hillman took some wind out of his enemies' sails by his testimony last week on the funds expended by his Political Action Committee, which revealed that far smaller sums had been expended than e.g. by the National Association of Manufacturers, whose representative tried to argue that the NAM spent its money in a non-partisan way ; that the millions of dollars spent by e.g. Duponts in the Landon campaign in 1936 was a private act on the part of Duponts, not a 'political' contribution by the NAM. The PAC is still a considerable bogey to respectable citizens, and is being used as such with skill by the Republicans, but it probably has prevented some of the defections from Roosevelt which his dropping of Wallace might otherwise have occasioned, and is, therefore, on the balance considered by some Democratic politicians to be more a gain than a loss. Hillman's effective challenge to the Senatorial Investigating

6 Max Lerner, teacher and columnist, 'neo-Marxist liberal'.

Committee to probe the funds of his big business opponents, seems to have had the added effect of checking what might otherwise have developed into a successful attack upon his own organization. But Hillman himself has now become one of the anti-Rooseveltites' favourite scarecrows, together with the Communist Browder. The AF of L, hostile to Hillman though they are, seem still to be gravitating, under the influence of Tobin and the rank and file union leaders, in the direction of the Democratic Party, despite the alliance between Dewey and Messrs John Lewis and Bill Hutcheson, who are not likely to split off more than a small segment of the labour vote in the Republican direction. Dewey's people are saying, possibly with some justice, that there is a certain reluctance on the part of migrant labour to register as voters because of the draft, since they vaguely feel that the less registered they stay the less likely the draft is to discover them.

18 September 1944

The War. Early victory in European campaign continues to be taken for granted and, apart from a still fairly faint undercurrent of worry about Russia's intentions, this allows attention to wander freely over future of Pacific war to which Quebec Conference has given a sharper point. There is a general sense in the press and in Washington talk that we are not doing as much as we ought on Asiatic mainland ; Drew Pearson's libels of our conduct in Burma, the reverberation of Phillips incident, etc., have reinforced the thought long embedded in the background of American consciousness that while our intention to fight in the Pacific may be genuine, the fruits of it will not be considerable and primary purpose of it is reconquest of our Far Eastern Empire, to which our title is in any case dubious. While this is a general trend it is not yet in forefront of public attention. Optimism about end of European war has naturally increased as result of a highly confidential and unreported small press conference held by General Marshall in which I am told that he predicted end of European war early in October. Meanwhile Admiral King at a similar press conference, doubtless with a view to damping expected decline of war-mindedness, seems to have talked soberly about difficulties and sacrifices still looming in Far East, and refused to predict date of Japanese defeat. There is some reported talk in Navy Department about possibility that when we do offer full naval aid in Pacific there may not be sufficient Pacific bases available to accommodate our full fleet, in which case we may be requested to limit our aid, which might well prove embarrassing. The feeling that Pacific is a sphere of exclusive American activity conflicts with a suspicion that we will not expend upon it as much of our resources as we could – yet both these contradictory trends may yet operate against us unless Administration takes timely steps to clarify position. There is growing speculation about what steps if any Russia will take against Japan – Lippmann told someone that he intended to tell her where her duty lay : such lectures are regarded as inexpedient by Administration officials who raise no eyebrow about criticism of our-selves in this connexion.

Post-war planning. There is a détente in talk about Dumbarton Oaks conversa-tions, partly owing to shift of limelight to Quebec. Main topic of interest is Republican position. If Vandenberg occupies middle position once held by late Senator Lodge, Senator La Follette is the Borah of the party, if a very much less gifted and formidable one. In his Wisconsin paper, *The Progressive,* he com-plains that far too much haste is occurring with regard to world organization – until nature of peace settlement has been publicly expounded and discussed and the nation knows what the new organization is to impose upon the world, how can American people authorize creation of a machine which will impose the will of strong nations upon the rest, perhaps unjustly ?

Far more important development is Dewey's Louisville speech of 8 September in which he repeated points of his acceptance speech, namely that it is more important to prevent a Third World War than to participate in it after it breaks out – that this must be done by non-partisan effort, hence the Hull–Dulles con-versations – that there must be no 'hush, hush, pussyfoot basis' to discussion. Moreover the two subjects of 'the immediate problems of victory' and 'long-term problems of organized peace' must be kept distinct. Germany and Japan must be utterly defeated and disarmed. Germany will probably have to be con-trolled by a disarmament commission which must eliminate or 'place under close supervision' industries convertible to war production. Germany must be forbid-den an aviation industry. Ruhr would be internationalized and made to work for economic rehabilitation of whole of Europe (there is reason for thinking that this idea comes to Dewey from Foster Dulles who in his turn was led to it by Jean Monnet). Japan, despite special Chinese interest, is a common responsibility. As for second task – world organization of all nations as sovereign equals – it extends beyond disarmament of Germany and Japan who are not the only possi-ble aggressors. Creation of it must be work of some sixty nations. Both parties have agreed that there should be a General Assembly of 'all peace-loving nations of world'. There should also be a Council 'small enough for almost continuous meeting and prompt action' consisting of major nations and representative of small nations. It should mobilize not merely force but moral pressure and eco-nomic sanctions. There should also be a World Court. But this is not enough. Mere force breeds revolt. Only justice to smaller nations will prevent it. 'The people of Poland, of France, of Low Countries, of Norway' have a stake as great as ours. 'We Americans and a few strong friends must not assume right to rule the world.' Nor should goodwill of the world be bought out of 'goods and labour of the American people' as the 'Washington wasters' desire. Goodwill will only flow to the 'self-reliant and independent'. After this Dewey continued his blasts against senile philosophy of New Deal. Present Administration was 'conceived in defeatism', is 'tired, exhausted, quarrelling and bickering', and has bungled for eight years. It even thinks that it is 'cheaper to keep men in the army than let them come home'. Only the sense of youthful strength, desire for full expansion of resources, and his (Dewey's) own vigorous efficiency – conviction that 'we have not even begun to build our industrial plant' – will save America; under new impact there will be jobs for all, etc. Last thing that is wanted is a world WPA.

All these, apart from relatively progressive stand on foreign policy, are anti-New Deal platitudes repeated by every Republican campaigner since 1934. It has not, so far as I can tell, produced a noticeable impact on public opinion and reference to wish to keep United States soldiers mobilized for fear of creating unemployment, founded as it was on a casual dictum of Selective Service Director General Hershey, a Republican, proved too much even for Republican press, some of which condemned it as false and unworthy. War Department's demobilization plans and Byrnes's general reconversion plan have since been published ; Dewey declared that they came far too late, but this comeback was clearly not very effective. But there are at least two strong factors working for the Republicans, apart from steady and familiar ones reported to you in recent telegrams and despatches – the principal among which is still the anticipated light vote, as e.g. in recent Republican victory in Maine. Republicans and Democrats both agree that the lighter the vote the better the Republicans will do. These are

(a) a real, if not wholly justified fear of Hillman's Political Action Committee on which Bricker has been concentrating his fire, representing it as a sinister un-American group managed by alien Hillman ('a pantsmaker from Russia', said John L. Lewis) in alliance with Communists. The Democratic manager, Hannegan, and columnist Marquis Childs complained of injection of 'racial prejudice', but it remains true that Jewish labour leaders from Lithuania scarcely inspire automatic confidence in rural and small-town America, and

(b) fact which Clare Luce and Joe Martin have made known pretty widely, that with majority of states now in hands of Republican state officials presiding over political activities, and especially over polling booths, a Republican majority, at any rate in the House, should duly materialize. Influence of local politicians in key places is naturally great, but against it must be placed the wave which inevitably accompanies a victorious presidential candidate. So long as Roosevelt is leading, as he still appears to be, a Republican House, with gloomy prospect of a President and the House in perpetual deadlock, is certainly no foregone conclusion. Indeed the belief that the House will be Republican whoever is President is not quite as prevalent among political observers as once it seemed to be.

.   .   .

19 September 1944

Cartels. The President's letter to Hull on the desirability of curbing and controlling cartels may be credited to the inspiration of the anti-trust Division of the

Department of Justice, still a home of fierce New Dealers, but was clearly good Roosevelt politics, inasmuch as there exists widespread popular feeling against cartels ; both because they are thought of as a wicked foreign invention, to which the British are particularly prone, and into which a few unprincipled American big businesses are at times inveigled ; and because of the perpetual fear which haunts small businesses of being swallowed up by cartelized Big Business. The present Administration is naturally sympathetic to such fears and entertains the further suspicion that unless something is done to prevent it, Big Business will acquire possession of big plants at present controlled by the Government so as to be able to limit or stop production after the war in its own monopolistic interest. Whatever opposition may be offered by special interests, there is no doubt that popular as well as departmental feeling is set strongly against the pre-war practices of such firms as Standard Oil or Duponts, and even more against foreign enterprises such as ICI behind which loom such sinister spectres as IG Farben. Biddle's recent remarks offer every indication of plans for a large-scale crusade by his department. ICI has been under fire for some time, Borax has just been severely and publicly accused by a Federal Grand Jury. Our position on such topics, however virtuous or sensible, is therefore liable to grave misunderstanding in the present climate of opinion. Hull's reply to the President promised an early international conference on world commercial policy in which the question of cartels is to be scrutinized with special care.

On saving the United Kingdom. There are signs that the Administration, banking and business circles alike are becoming aware that excessive suspicion of our economic intentions, with the unreflecting opposition to them which this stimulates, has gone too far, and may indeed end by being deleterious to America's own interest ; there is perhaps the idea that only by saving the United Kingdom from serious economic embarrassment after the war, can she be dissuaded from jumping over the precipice of economic autarky and resorting to bilateral pacts and cartel agreements as the Only Way Out. Apart from some recent and friendly remarks by Crowley and Charles Taft,[1] the more liberal brother of the Senator, in which, speaking as a State Department official, he attempted to explain the necessity for American support of British economy, which apart from its intrinsic merits, would alone make Britain capable of paying for imports from America, public pronouncements by bankers and their academic allies to this effect have also unfortunately been coupled with vigorous attacks on the Bretton Woods monetary agreements. The line taken is that the financial rehabilitation of the United Kingdom is the major requirement for world reconstruction and that a stabilized dollar-sterling rate will form an adequate foundation upon which world trade can be built up once more. This is what is generally referred to here as the 'key country' approach. It is the line endorsed by the American Bankers'

1 Charles P. Taft, lawyer, in Federal Security Agency 1941–3, Director Wartime Economic Affairs, State Department, 1944.

Association (which body has finally decided to go all-out in fighting the Bretton Woods agreements) and was endorsed in a speech last week by Winthrop Aldrich,[2] president of the Chase National Bank, whose speech may be considered the opening move in an organized drive by bankers against the Bretton Woods proposals, and is also believed to have been a trial balloon for Mr Dewey. Aldrich's speech (copies of which have been sent to you by bag) proposed a 'grant-in-aid' to the United Kingdom and warned that the sum involved might be a large one. He went on to indicate, however, that he thought that the rehabilitation of Britain was the major problem, in his mind, and that Americans 'must show courage in its solution'. Aldrich is, of course, a man of great influence in East Coast Republican circles in which Dewey moves. It is noteworthy that he dwelt at some length on the early need for eliminating trade barriers and controls of every type, and to this extent explicitly endorsed the Atlantic Charter and the Seventh Article of the Lend-Lease Agreement.

Telecommunications. Under the pressure of Kent Cooper, chairman of the AP (who has long been engaged on this) and his friends of the press, a campaign to obtain an international agreement on 'freedom of the press' seems to be on foot. The State Department seems to have conveyed to newspapermen that it had for some time been at work on a plan for this, and Hull said that he had always been in favour of full freedom of information on an international scale and would welcome steps towards it. The most concrete purpose of the campaign is the promotion of uniform international cable, etc., rates established under international authority. Congressman Fulbright has introduced a relevant resolution into the House and Senator Taft (and later Senator Connally) into the Senate. It is clear that the campaign derives its popular appeal from its opposition to censorship, secrecy, monopolies of information, etc., and that these are the motives which inspire Fulbright and his friends ; but reduction of rates for Americans is the principal goal of the more tough-minded proponents. At any rate support for the proposals seems wellnigh universal. So far, surprisingly little has appeared in the press specifically directed against alleged British monopoly in the field of communications.

. . .

Murphy. The correspondence on Robert Murphy's fitness to advise Eisenhower on German problems continues in the *Washington Post,* with fairly strong attacks by Edgar Mowrer by letter, and Representative Celler in Congress, mainly stressing Murphy's alleged connexion with the reactionaries in North Africa. Murphy himself called on Eugene Meyer, the proprietor of the *Washington Post,* and asked whether he had anything against him personally. Meyer told a member of my staff that he replied that as he did not have the pleasure of knowing Mr Murphy this did not arise but that he took full responsibility for the leading articles in question of which he completely approved, and proposed to continue in the same spirit. Thereupon Murphy asked the editor whether 'any foreign

2 Winthrop W. Aldrich, Head of Chase National Bank since 1930. Ambassador to Great Britain, 1953–7.

power' had influenced his articles, meaning apparently the Gaullists. The editor replied that this was a poor approach for a professional diplomat and he and Meyer both later asserted that they were much taken back by the crude manner in which Murphy took this up with them ; that they could not conceive how he could discharge his duties efficiently ; they would from time to time take care to say so loudly. Meanwhile, Mr Hull took the trouble to deny a spreading rumour that Brüning,[3] Treviranus[4] and others had been constituted into a secret advisory committee on German affairs at the instigation of Berle to advise Murphy. Despite this denial which was completely unambiguous, and so far as Hull himself is concerned, quite clearly sincere, it is not impossible that Brüning, etc., may on occasions in fact be consulted informally via the German refugees in OSS or other channels by the relevant officials of the State Department. Brüning is alleged to have remarked when invited to collaborate that 'he would do so only on condition that he was not expected to preside over the liquidation of the German Reich', but the whole story may well be apocryphal.

25 September 1944

. . .

The Peace Settlement. Morgenthau's reported views[1] about turning Germany into a 'pastoral' country form the subject of high-level departmental gossip. Hopkins is thought to support this and Harry White[2] to have drawn up plans. 'Elimination of the Ruhr industry will boost that of Britain and so make the Beveridge plan realizable' is the alleged trend of the Treasury argument. Krock, in one of his 'Well Poisoning' series, declares that Morgenthau has now replaced Hull as President's chief adviser on Germany. An Associated Press article states that Morgenthau's thesis is opposed by Hull and violently opposed by Stimson.

Pearson has published a story about indignation on the part of the President and Morgenthau at the allegedly excessive 'softness' of the combined Anglo-American handbook for invading Allied troops. Pearson also says that Murphy was appointed without the President's knowledge, which is a War Department canard and patently absurd. Others more plausibly see in this a concession to the Roman Church since Murphy is at once a faithful and pious son of it, and a faithful executor of White House policy, and therefore has the merit of at once placating nervous Russophobe Catholic opinion in the United States (as well as in Europe), without definitely veering from his official instructions. . . .

The same pre-election mood may have dictated the appointment of Lane[3] as Ambassador to the Polish Government. Even Stalin's recent visitor, Professor

---

3 Heinrich Brüning, Catholic politician. Became Reichskanzler March 1930 ; emigrated to USA 1934.

4 Gottfried Treviranus, Conservative, Minister under Brüning 1930–4, when emigrated first to UK, then to USA.

1 Presented to a cabinet committee on Germany. The plan proposed the division of Germany into three separate zones and the destruction of all Ruhr industry, mines, etc.

2 Harry Dexter White, economist, US Treasury official since 1940.

3 Arthur Bliss Lane, career diplomat, Ambassador to Colombia 1942–4.

Lange, does not deny that the latest Russo-Polish imbroglio has exasperated the American Poles, particularly those in touch with the equally authentic indignation said to exist in underground Poland. The President's latest move is therefore interpreted as an attempt at once to please the Poles and to give an impulse to the hoped-for reconstruction of the Polish Government on broader and more Russophile lines.

The Pacific. As for the Pacific, Chinese stock has never been lower in official circles and Chinese reverses are now irritably attributed to benighted political despotism in China. The reaction against the recent ecstatic enthusiasm about China could not be sharper. China is getting the treatment which we were accorded after Tobruk, and Chinese here appear to be in an unhappy state. As for our part of the Pacific, although we do not obtain the full credit we deserve there are signs that the fact that it was we who demanded a greater share in the Far Eastern campaign and the Americans who sought to limit it, has proved a shock to our sincere but misinformed critics.

. . .

Dumbarton Oaks. The press is not quite clear as to what has caused the check, but the best informed have no doubt that Russia's attitude towards the problem of voting in the Council by a state accused of aggression is the real reason. So far, this has produced direct criticism of the reported Russian attitude only from Max Lerner in *PM* which has surprised only those who underestimate his anxiety not to be considered as a Soviet mouthpiece. Complaints about secrecy have decreased since the substance of current discussions had not in fact been successfully concealed from the press, but the principal snag which the conversations have struck is still not a subject of serious public debate. If the positive achievements of the talks – more particularly the agreement to set up the various international institutions for the preservation of security – are made known, there is so far no particular reason to anticipate too great a let down in public feeling, particularly if the probable next step in peace is made clear. Naturally Dewey and Dulles could generate a storm on this if they wished. . . . Willkie is somewhat less likely to do so, partly because of reported lack of sympathy with the Dewey-Bricker ticket, partly because he seems to have suffered a breakdown in health and is semi-incommunicado. He may of course issue a press statement. The Hearst and McCormick presses continue to blast against the menace of Russia, but this by now has become a routine exhibition, though not without influence. The President spoke of 90 per cent agreement at Dumbarton Oaks, which he considered 'a darned good batting average', in an evident attempt to soft pedal the condition of the discussions until the election.

. . .

Dewey's speeches. Dewey has been touring the North West and West Coast. In Oregon he repeated that the Administration was quarrelsome, quoted specific rows, said that there were no indispensable men, and spoke of his 'unprecedented step' of non-partisan approval of the Dumbarton Oaks talks and their purposes. In Seattle he spoke on labour and demanded a 'real labour department' to replace the present chaotic welter of conflicting agencies, and promised to give the post to a labour leader. He defended the National Labor Relations (Wagner) Act as a guarantee of collective bargaining and denounced the Smith-Connally (strike controlling) Act which, after all, he said, had been drafted by two Democrats. This mild support of labour was not unexpected and fits with the conservative Lewis-Hutcheson anti-New Deal line. Lewis has duly denounced Roosevelt without explicitly mentioning Dewey, nor has Dewey allowed himself to be drawn on a possible alliance with the somewhat compromising Lewis. In San Francisco Dewey announced support of state intervention in supporting farm prices, employing labour not absorbed by private enterprise, and keeping interest rates on public debt stable, after which he inveighed against the muddles and petty tyrannies of the New Deal and its un-Americanism. Even this mild economic programme was found too New Dealish by the *New York Times*. While the speeches themselves, although delivered with streamlined competence, have not had a perceptibly strong effect, Democrats, who are worried by the low labour registration, are said to be pressing the President to deliver his most telling strokes not before the election, so much as before the end of registration, i.e., before mid-October when it ends in most states. With migrant labour estimated at some 12-13 millions of whom at least a third are voters, there is a serious danger that Roosevelt will lose the 5 million votes by which he conquered Willkie in 1940. Dewey is credited by some people with deliberate Machiavellianism in pitching his utterances in as low a key as possible to avoid stirring up new issues and so stimulate too high a turnout of voters, since he counts on apathy to work against Roosevelt. Although the odds quoted on Wall Street are still 8 to 5 on Roosevelt, and Gallup concedes growth of Roosevelt sentiment in seventeen States as against decline in ten, Democrats are said to be very nervous particularly about the effect of the 'clear everything with Sidney' anti-Hillman slogan.[4] The Republicans are said to be spending large funds to spread this in the hope that it will have the effect of 'Rum, Romanism and Rebellion' which killed the presidential chances of James J. Blaine.[5]

30 September 1944

The War. The Arnhem setback[1] has naturally had a sobering effect on the perhaps too complacent optimism about a very early end of the European war (this

4 According to Arthur Krock (*New York Times*, 25 July) Roosevelt, in connection with enquiries about the choice at the Democratic convention of a vice-presidential nominee, is supposed to have said 'Clear it with Sidney' – i.e. Sidney Hillman, head of the Political Action Committee (PAC) of the CIO.

5 A statement that the Democrats were the party of Rum, Romanism and Rebellion (i.e. drunks, Irish and Southerners) was reported to have been made at a New York public meeting in 1884 at which Blaine, the Democratic candidate for President, was present. His failure to deny the allegation was said to have cost him the election.

1 Arnhem, just north of the Waal mouth of the Rhine, where British Airborne Division was nearly wiped out in attempt to secure bridgeheads.

week's Gallup poll quoted 67 per cent convinced that it would end before Christmas), and it has evoked a generous flow of sympathy and admiration for the superb gallantry displayed by the British troops involved. The British share in European fighting is getting better play, and the Prime Minister's statement on the ratios of British and United States forces should buttress this. The Service Departments have impressed upon the public the probable length (one and a half to two years) of Pacific war by emphasizing the formidable resources wielded by the Japanese. This too will be strengthened by Mr Churchill's words. A more realistic public mood has therefore begun to prevail.

. . .

The Morgenthau-Hull-Stimson flurry. The leakage of Mr Morgenthau's reported views on post-war treatment of Germany via the *Wall Street Journal* and AP has pushed the Dumbarton Oaks talks into the background for the moment. It is not certain where the AP obtained its material, but there is some evidence for thinking it emanated from sources in the State Department irritated by this intrusion from the Treasury, and was intended to discredit Mr Morgenthau's views, which in the State and War Departments seem to be regarded as fantastically harsh, and, if given circulation, likely to stiffen German resistance to a new peak of fanaticism. Mr Hull at his press conference did not admit, but did not deny, that disagreements on this point existed in the United States Cabinet, and allowed it to be supposed that differences between the major allies might be present too. The President denied that disagreements existed ; press reports were 'essentially untrue in the basic facts'. In his speech to the Teamsters [2] he tilted at Republican jibes about 'quarrelsome, tired old men'. So far, with very few exceptions, the press and radio are uniformly hostile to the so-called Morgenthau-White plan to destroy German industry, dismember Germany, convert her into an agricultural or, as Admiral Land insists, into a pastoral country ('that would do the Germans and Japs a hell of a lot of good'). . . .

If the attack on Morgenthau serves to make the views of Mr Stimson and Mr Hull – who are very far from entertaining any 'soft' tendencies – seem attractively moderate by comparison, it may actually do some good. . . .

The State Department has let it seep through the press that Mr Morgenthau's escapade is now over and it has the situation once more well in hand. Mr Morgenthau and Mr Stimson have cancelled their press conferences, and the former is said to be readier to listen to the counsel of the latter, which, I am told, was not at all the case previously. The German-language press, needless to say, now demands the preservation of Germany more openly and boldly than ever.

Out of this brief storm has come at least a lightning flash which has illuminated the public landscape, revealing a state of wide ignorance and perplexity. If the Administration genuinely desires, as there seems no doubt that it does, to support a stiff post-war settlement, it still has time, and now also the opportunity, to educate its people accordingly. If this is not done, the gulf between the two may widen.

2 See below, p. 427.

Meanwhile the whispering campaign, according to which Mr Churchill is somewhat less anti-German than Messrs Roosevelt or Stalin (with the specific rider that sinister British financial and business interests are pressing him hard and successfully to spare Germany economically, not only as a bulwark against Russia but as an economic political desideratum of Britain's coming role as the leader of the new Europe), is being sedulously spread, and may sooner or later burst into print. It appears to come mostly from Americans returning from Britain and from semi-official American sources abroad, and one or two officials in the State Department are lending a worried ear to these rumours. . . .

Dumbarton Oaks. All this has obscured Dumbarton Oaks somewhat, but it now seems fairly clear that despite the sniping of the isolationists, any official announcement reciting the achievements of the talks (as Mr Churchill has done) will probably be taken to indicate that genuine progress has been made, and that a slower unfolding is now to be expected, accompanied by patient labour and further conferences, from which a more durable result is likely to emerge than if the original hopes for a swift climax and a final peace conference by January were realized. American officials do not wholly agree with this view, fearing that unless swift results are achieved before European victory, the public will cool off on this issue, and that speed is therefore of the essence. An AP despatch predicted at least another year of discussion before the final result. But Stettinius, questioned by the press, said he saw no reason for pessimism about providing the Senate with a full-fledged treaty to ratify by January; American pressmen do not take this seriously. . . .

The election. The President's speech to the Teamsters on 23 September was awaited with great impatience and justified it. It was, as you will have seen from newspaper texts, a return to the best and most ruthless of his old fighting days. It was compounded of the familiar amalgam . . . indignant gibes at his opponents' knavish tricks . . . sustained flights of sarcasm at their expense, by turns fierce and gay . . . and a general appeal to the common people against the rich and strong, with grim reminders of the Hoovervilles of 1931–2.[3] The press, being as in 1936 and 1940 heavily anti-Roosevelt, divided accordingly, and on the whole voted the speech a masterpiece of effective vituperation. The Republicans declare it inexcusably unfair (particularly the analogy between Republican propaganda and that of Goebbels), and shamefully flippant and undignified. Some Rooseveltites privately and publicly agreed with this, thought it a blunder for the President to stoop to a level at which his opponent could comfortably operate, instead of remaining on peaks too lofty for Mr Dewey to scale. The majority of pressmen on Dewey's train agree with this. Dewey hit back with something, though nothing approaching the full intensity of the incandescent rhetoric of his opponent, and made his first really violent counter-attack. The

3 Shanty towns occupied by unemployed victims of the Depression.

Republican press duly acclaimed him and expressed gratification that his latent fighting powers had finally found themselves. Despite the press the President's speech appears to have given widespread pleasure to the electorate. Its very pugnacity brought back to their memory the days of the great campaigns, and they are preparing with unconcealed delight to cheer gladiators to new excesses, in a fight grown violent at last after what had seemed too like a 'phoney war'. The President may have been moved by the thought that apathy worked in favour of his rival, that his principal need was to rouse the electors to register and vote (hence Wallace's encouragement in his last speech that men register if only to vote for Dewey, but above all vote), and that in order to produce this he must deliberately stir up the mud, knowing well that in an old-fashioned rough and tumble he would probably prove more than a match for his inexperienced opponent. Those, therefore, who criticize the speech on the ground that it laid the President open to direct attack by Dewey (who quoted Truman and Barkley and other Roosevelt supporters against him and taunted him with his unscrupulous reference to Goebbels) may well be beside the mark. The press wondered whether Paul Porter as well as the lately returned Sherwood, who has resigned from OWI, and Rosenman had, as usual, written the speech, but it bears every mark of the President's own hand.

Krock's sermon on the President's unworthy stooping to the demagogue's cheap tricks in so grave an hour is some index of the shock occasioned to his opponents. Some capital is being made by isolationists out of the fact that the President was wheeled in and did not stand to deliver this speech – a feeble cripple unfit to govern. This argument may be used further as the campaign advances, but the President's deliberate exhibition of robust exuberance makes this a somewhat unplausible thesis.

Hannegan has attempted to check the anti-Hillman campaign by charging Dewey's adviser Jaeckle with anti-Jewish and anti-Catholic bias. From this it is clear that the campaign will not be fought by the Queensberry rules. The audience no longer feels that it will be cheated of a show, and the President may well profit by the resultant atmosphere but there is no doubt that the Democratic organizers have become anxious, and their emissaries have suddenly sprung to feverish life in the constituencies.

1 October 1944

. . .

Campaign eddies. The 'Texas Revolt' against the President (see Political Summary of 6 June, p. 366) has duly fizzled out and, apart from the attempt by the ousted Senator from South Carolina, Ellison ('Cotton Ed') Smith, to organize a rural anti-Roosevelt group, supported by the powerful Farm Bureau, the Southern Democratic vote seems solidly pro-Roosevelt. Senator Ball (Republican, Minnesota) is warmly urging the defeat of isolationists at the polls. Ball is an undeviating Republican on domestic issues and his call to arms is not therefore likely to prove comparable to the boomerang which Wilson's similar plea in 1918 turned out to be, although it may well remain equally ineffective. Wheeler is talking, with some skill, about the conspiracy to involve the American people in 'secret arrangements' plotted at Dumbarton Oaks, and is making specious appeals for a European federation. But his brand of desperate isolationism has little influence. Ickes has begun to breathe fire, and in a typically tart and entertaining letter to Dewey, who has sworn to purge him, announced that this would not be necessary as he could not conceive of continuing in the unbelievable event of Dewey's election, and then denounced him as both a liar and an unimaginative nonentity, in the familiar Ickes fashion. He has so far coined nothing so apt as his unforgettable 'Barefoot boy from Wall Street', which probably cost Willkie dear in 1940. Willkie and the socialist Norman Thomas have pitched into both parties, as was to be expected; Willkie over the inadequacy of both platforms on the Negro issue, and Thomas first in the usual anti-Roosevelt tirade and then in a warning against Dewey as a 'sophisticated Harding'. On the other hand, Bricker declared that he was in favour of the use of force in suppressing minor conflicts between nations of a kind likely to lead to major wars. How this squares with Vandenberg's position is not clear.

. . .

7 October 1944

Foreign affairs. While the Chinese phase of Dumbarton Oaks has fallen into the background, the general issue of foreign policy was given a sharp fillip by Senator Ball's statement that this issue was of such vital importance that he could not bring himself to campaign for his party leader Dewey, because he was not satisfied that his position on foreign policy was unambiguously favourable to real international collaboration. Although Ball himself is a prominent if not a politically powerful Senator, this courageous statement by a man of known integrity, together with Willkie's eloquent silence (he is still in hospital), may make a greater difference than Republicans at present concede to the crucial 20 per cent 'independent' section of the electorate which appears still to be in some doubt about the candidates. The latest *New York Times* poll to examine how much support there is for an amendment substituting the majority of Congress for the present two-thirds majority of Senate as the number sufficient to ratify foreign treaties, has yielded the interesting result that out of nineteen aspirants to Senate, seventeen Democrats and only two Republicans favour this. The two Republicans have duly been congratulated by Willkie. Most replies were evasive and asked for time for reflection, but the general impression arising from this poll is that conservatism among the Republicans has not diminished appreciably. But it is almost impossible to estimate what the attitude of the party is likely to be on, say, recommendations arising out of the Dumbarton Oaks talks. Vandenberg is said to think that he has support of majority of his Republican colleagues in the Senate. Ball disputes this, and regards him as over-confident. . . .

The elections. As for election speeches, Dewey's routine promise to reduce taxes, and Bricker's equally familiar blast against 'deficit budgeting', are commonplaces regarded by even Republicans as such. The President, as a result, I am told, of his private reports on the reactions to his last speech, has judged the country to be in a better mood. If his last speech (generally conceded to have been a 'wow') succeeded in stirring up dormant political passions and exhilarating the audience with a spectacle of a leader who, whatever may have been thought of his levity, was clearly anything but a tired old man of failing powers, it will have gone as far as was safe in that direction, and something more weighty and solemn was now called for. Consequently, in a speech of unbroken earnestness he urged the voters to register and to vote, said that he would be sorry to win with a light vote and would almost prefer to lose with a heavy one, quoted the George Act to set minds at rest about early demobilization, and spoke of guarantees of equally early removal of industrial controls, deplored the obstacles to soldier vote, and above all disavowed all connexion with Communist (as well as Fascist or any other 'lunatic fringe') groups seeking to subvert the American way of life, and by implication defended Hillman and his Political Action Committee. As a defensive operation this may strengthen his supporters and contained antidotes to the 'Red Scare' propaganda which he charged the Republicans with spreading and looks like a series of reassurances recommended by his political managers. The real offensive is still to come, as both sides are aware. Gallup now estimates the probable Roosevelt-Dewey vote as 51 per cent – 49 per cent of a vote of 37½ millions to which he estimates the total vote will sink. . . . Sceptical Democrats observe that the Republican leaders have predicted 'the closest election since 1916', and an unquestionably Republican House on each occasion, since at least 1928 – a myth which has survived unscathed in the face of perpetual refutation. Indeed Senator Burton (Republican, Ohio) has just repeated it. The Negro vote seems still fairly solidly pro-Roosevelt (latest estimate is 78 per cent pro-Roosevelt, 22 per cent pro-Dewey). The 'Businessmen for Roosevelt' Committee, despite a sprinkling of prominent shipbuilders who are prospering at present, is not a formidable array. A speech by Ickes scheduled for 8 October is expected to be up to traditional standard of that celebrated purveyor of asperities, and is therefore awaited eagerly.

8 October 1944

Poles. The collapse of resistance at Warsaw has produced a considerable volume of pro-Polish comment with varying degrees of anti-Soviet emphasis. The Russophobes are naturally having a field-day, but even more moderate and thoughtful commentators are profoundly troubled about the Russian attitude, and the desire to let their consciences speak is obviously in conflict with their equally laudable fear of pouring oil into the flames and undermining faith in good Russo-American relations in the possibility of which they clearly strongly wish to believe. Open justification of Russia is, apart from the Communist press, scarcely anywhere to be found. There is no doubt that the Polish issue will, in one way or another, continue to exercise real influence, although the American Poles themselves appear to be lying relatively low possibly in order not to be accused of letting their European loyalties influence the presidential election (the Polish Ambassador's statement that the Russians deliberately prevented Anglo-American aid to Warsaw was published [so far] without much comment); the President's carefully non-committal words on the issue are said to have prevented the Polish vote from seriously slipping from him. . . . Russian treatment of Poland, together with her alleged obstinacy at Dumbarton Oaks, balanced by the strongly felt need and hope of her ultimate aid against Japan, etc., have transformed what had at one time been a largely pro-Russian wave into an attitude compounded of somewhat uneasy suspense and guilty conscience, tempered by a faintly pathetic hope that all will end well somehow. The line of the Administration – fullest possible understanding with the USSR – does not seem to have changed one whit.

14 October 1944

Dumbarton Oaks. Published text has obtained very widespread national approbation. Dewey's approval set official keynote for Republicans so that Democratic and Republican comment expressed equal favour of proposals which were regarded as conspicuously superior to constitution of League of Nations. Criticism there is, particularly on radio, which stressed (a) that uninspired official prose of document was hardly calculated to stir greatly needed enthusiasm of public opinion, and that somewhere and in some way document should have been made more moving, (b) that the Assembly was to be a mere impotent talking shop of too little consequence, (c) that unsettled '10 per cent' contained too many crucial issues, (d) isolationist press advised its readers to take a very careful look before approving – as if to say that public opinion made it inadvisable to attack document at present but that occasion might well arise when this would become tactically more practicable. . . .

Senators Connally (Democratic) and Austin (Republican) have published statements supporting resolutions of Dumbarton Conference. There is a certain amount of moderate optimism about outcome, supported by Stettinius in his last press conference although he would not commit himself to more than the hope (shared by Krock) that with Hull's expert steering the scheme would safely surmount all congressional hurdles. At same time, distrust of Russia is if anything still rising among public and Dumbarton Oaks has done nothing to reduce this nervous condition. . . .

As for the party front, Dulles informed a private correspondent who published his letter that re-election of President Roosevelt would make it less probable that Republican Senators on Foreign Relations Committee would support any international agreement sponsored by his Administration in view of the bad relations between President and Congress, and Senator Pepper duly denounced him for breaking bipartisan pact on foreign policy thereby. Senator Ball (see last week's political summary of 7 October) as well as some prominent Liberals are advocating defeat of eight Senators with isolationist leanings in coming elections, but it is doubtful whether these efforts will be effective since whether isolationist or not, these Senators are at present professing unexceptionably non-isolationist sentiment. Dewey's 'offer' to Hull to be his adviser on foreign affairs in event of his election, has provoked a cautiously worded statement in which the Secretary said that his loyalty was primarily to 'official head of Administration', President Roosevelt, and that he took the whole thing as a compliment to Administration's efforts in foreign policy. Hull's name is still greatest symbol of sound foreign policy in either party and both sides naturally wish to buttress themselves with his prestige.

Election politics. Texts of Dewey's speeches deserve little comment and much same factors prevail as last week. His attempt to point to Berle as sinister grey eminence responsible for New Deal's secret plan to Bolshevize United States economy (by quoting a sentence in a Berle memorandum wholly out of context) has occasioned more amusement than indignation among those acquainted with the Assistant Secretary's strongly held views on Communism. Lindley duly cleared Berle of the charge.

Democrats seem genuinely worried by lack of enthusiasm for Roosevelt on part of electorate. They correctly estimate that most electors will vote against either Roosevelt or against Dewey but not positively for either and that this means an apathetic and therefore a light vote favouring Republicans. On the other hand, registration in crucial Pennsylvania is said to have been, at any rate round Philadelphia, heavier than in 1940. New York is said (despite some confusion denounced as deliberate obstruction by Democrats and defended as accidental by Republicans) to have registered fairly well and if President has not obviously gained ground neither has Dewey. Wallace is off to stump the bitterest of anti-Roosevelt Middle West – Illinois, Ohio, Michigan, Kansas. Democrats are whispering that Michigan is by no means as Republican as some persons suppose since the CIO has done exceptionally well there. Leon Henderson is actively campaigning for Mr Roosevelt and is rumoured to have been offered a post as Eisenhower's economic adviser. *New York Times* evidently cannot bring itself to swallow Dewey and is said to be thinking of announcing open support of Roosevelt. *Washington Post* is pro-Dewey in all but name. President seems to have a solid hold over Italian vote particularly with American-Italians returning with comparisons of British and American behaviour in Italy unfavourable to the former. Pro-Italian sentiment is probably if anything higher here than pro-French and President has been consistently friendly to Italians culminating in his affable words to them on Columbus Day. He has similarly spoken to Poles on Pulaski

Day[1] after Dewey demanded 'clarification' of unsatisfactory Russo-Polish situation. He reiterated previous pledges about reconstitution of Poland as a great nation but stressed heavily that she must be 'representative and peace-loving too' and professed much ignorance of what had happened in Warsaw. Polish leaders have been told from some 'high source' that President's letter to Stalin of over ten days ago on this topic was very strongly worded. President is reported to be about to placate Jews too by sending a favourable statement to Zionist convention according to Stephen Wise whom President, as is his custom before elections, summoned for purpose of bargaining about Jewish vote in New York. There is a rumour that news of seizure by United States forces of one of the Philippines is to be held up until psychological moment before election and that USSR will according to preconceived arrangement declare war on Japan before 7 November. This last item appears to emanate from Admiral Leahy. Returning Americans teem with reports of strong pro-Roosevelt campaign now under way in Britain – they assert that nothing has been left undone to unite British public behind President and that dismay if Dewey is elected will be universal however well concealed. Democrats are (not very plausibly) complaining of lack of money. The desertion to them of advertising millionaire Albert D. Lasker,[2] who was Harding's campaign manager, should assist in this respect. Lasker is reported to have said that a choice between Roosevelt and Dewey was one between holding his nose and closing his eyes respectively and that he had never walked over a precipice with his eyes closed yet.

15 October 1944

Willkie's death. The death of Wendell Willkie came as a sharp and genuine shock to the public which did not suspect that he was in serious danger. Tributes to him are both sincere and universal. His impeccably liberal record, particularly on issues of foreign policy and latterly on issues of domestic policy as well, gave him a unique position, and Lippmann's eulogy of him as 'The conscience of the Republican Party', the disappearance of which makes a vote for Dewey a vote for Dewey and for nothing else whatever, seems universally felt. There is a general sense, too, that in him the most American of notable living Americans has passed away – most American because personally he seemed compounded of large-scale vision, a prodigious curiosity, equalitarian ideals, boundless energy, courage and gaiety, and a passionate desire to 'tell the world' – characteristic of the rough and uninhibited frontiersman, and at the same time of mixed immigrant parentage, all strong traits in the American picture, a picture which this very self-conscious nation is perpetually scanning and displaying to itself and to the world. There is no doubt too that from our point of view Willkie is a

---

1 Pulaski Day, 11 October, to celebrate death in 1779 of Polish and US Revolutionary War hero, fatally wounded at siege of Savannah.

2 Albert Davis Lasker, advertising executive, Chairman and owner, Lord & Thomas, 1908–42.

considerable loss since, despite a critical and occasionally ill-informed attitude towards our imperial, in particular Indian, problems, he genuinely admired the people and institutions of Britain, was a deeply convinced internationalist, and preserved a powerful hold over the imagination and loyalty of an articulate minority of the American public whose votes may well determine crucial political and economic issues. Naturally both parties are now fighting for his political legacy. His antipathy to Dewey was well known, and close friends of his say that he so deeply abhorred the isolationist trend of the Republican Old Guard that he would have abstained from voting altogether, believing that after Mr Roosevelt's death or retirement the liberals of both parties would be able to find no leader but himself. Be that as it may, the Republican leaders, particularly Luce, are busily protesting that had he lived he would have voted for Dewey – adducing his brother's testimony to that effect as evidence – while Drew Pearson, with whom he was certainly in frequent touch, maintains that he had assured him that he would vote for Mr Roosevelt. The most plausible report states that he proposed to wait until the last week before the election and might not have made up his mind even then. His death does not materially alter the balance of power, but if anything may throw those voters who, like Lippmann, cannot stomach an unadulterated Dewey, to Mr Roosevelt or cause them not to vote. The isolationists are trying to moralize about the mortality of man – when even a man who seemed so abounding in health as Willkie is suddenly cut off, how much more this might hold of the far from robust Mr Roosevelt – the 'President in the bath chair' theme is likely to be made more of as the election approaches. Tributes to Willkie ranged from the President's own generous and sincerely worded statement to Senator Nye's 'It is always a pity when a live wire goes'. The President is said to be genuinely distressed since, despite difficult moments with Willkie, relations between the two were unbroken since 1941, and the thought of collaborating with Willkie in some way had always been present at the back of the President's mind. British tributes to Willkie, including the Prime Minister's, your own and Mr Bracken's,[1] were given adequate publicity.

· · ·

Jews. The American Zionist convention is at present being held at Atlantic City and has received the usual congratulatory messages from Messrs Ickes and Majority House Leader McCormack, as well as Sumner Welles and Governor Dewey. Dewey, who had been nobbled by Rabbi Silver, an influential Cleveland Republican, declared himself unequivocally in favour of 'the reconstitution of Palestine as a free and democratic Jewish Commonwealth in accordance with the Balfour Declaration of 1917 and the resolution of the Republican Congress in 1922'. He also favours the 'opening of Palestine to unlimited, "Jewish" immigration and land ownership', and promises to assist in this, when President, in co-operation with Great Britain. The President is thought to be sending a

1 Brendan Bracken, Minister of Information 1940–5.

message too, although it is difficult to see how it could outbid Dewey's (maximalist) pledge.

.   .   .

The *Saturday Review of Literature* is about to publish results of a poll on the influence of newspapers and columnists which states that in the opinion of 160 members of the Capitol press gallery (a) the Washington correspondent who exerts the greatest influence in Washington is Arthur Krock (51 votes), Drew Pearson (32 votes), Walter Lippmann (19), no answer (18) ; (b) the Washington correspondent who exerts the greatest influence in the nation is Drew Pearson (56), Walter Lippmann (28), no answer (23), Arthur Krock (13) ; (c) the person of greatest reliability, fairness and ability to analyse the news is Thomas L. Stokes of Scripps-Howard (25) with Marquis Childs next. The newspaper 'most flagrant in angling or weighing news to suit its own editorial opinions' is the *Chicago Tribune* (65), *Washington Times Herald* (34), *PM* (29), *Washington Post* (2), *Daily Worker*, *New York Times*, Hearst papers, *Chicago Sun*, *Washington Star* (1 each).

22 October 1944

The not unexpected invasion of the Philippines by General MacArthur has naturally eclipsed all other war news. This event marks a great emotional climax ; the scar left on America by the loss of the islands was deep and the hope of triumphant return – heightened by MacArthur's dramatic pledge [1] to avenge the surrender of Bataan and Corregidor – has released a stream of pent-up feeling over the press and radio. Previously there was much sober comment on the Western European fighting with somewhat increased appreciation of the part played by British forces.

The presidential election. The tempo is noticeably increasing. Dewey is clearly developing a carefully conceived plan of action. Having established his positive platform, he has now passed into an open offensive against his rival on all fronts, personal, domestic, foreign. His technique is also clearly revealed as consisting of hammering away at the few places in the Administration's armour where it is believed to be most vulnerable. Thus in St Louis on the 16th and again in New York (at Mrs Reed's *Herald Tribune* Forum) on the 18th, he dwelt on the bitter quarrels which have torn the Administration and cited as notorious instances Wallace-Jones, Ickes-Davis, Ickes-Hopkins. He triumphantly quoted the admittedly startling executive order which, at any rate *prima facie,* appears to vest one another's powers in the War Food Administrator and the Secretary for Agriculture to prove that 'they' deliberately 'planned' such conflicts. How could an Administration so hopelessly divided at home carry authority abroad, when its

1 'I will return.'

agencies (say FEA and the State Department) quarrelled so furiously in front of the foreigners (e.g. in the case of Brazil) ? Dewey accused the President of 'personal secret diplomacy' which he shrewdly distinguished from the good work of Hull and his department. He appealed to the Italian, Polish, German and even Balkan votes (and the pro-French liberals) by declaring roundly that conditions in Italy are disastrous (he quoted the report of a returned United States labour leader), Poland has been confused and betrayed (cf. the battle of Warsaw), Roumania has concluded an armistice with the United States through the signature of a Russian General without Hull's even knowing the terms (this was duly denied by the State Department in a public statement). Non-recognition by the United States of de Gaulle was an obvious blunder (*'de facto* recognition' of de Gaulle by the President was followed by a UP story that His Majesty's Government was about to recognize a 'provisional' French Government with unofficial State Department intimation that it could not bring itself to believe that something so embarrassing to the United States Government could possibly be contemplated in London). Finally Dewey declared that America was 'paying in blood' for the failure to have prepared adequate armistice terms for the Germans, and has, through the publication of the proposals of Morgenthau, who anyhow had no business to make them, exasperated the Germans into fiendish resistance – 'the frenzy of despair'. All this was ably concocted, and added to repeated charges about the Administration's reluctance to demobilize soldiers with no jobs awaiting them (into which the President's aged uncle, Frederick Delano,[2] has now been dragged), and other time-honoured anti-New Deal charges, has put the Administration somewhat on the defensive. The long and elaborate statements issued by the White House refuting Dewey's points one by one, and evidently composed by the uninspired hand of Rosenman, bore the public. Unless the President seizes the initiative in his foreign policy speech on the 21st, Republican inroads will make themselves felt even in foreign policy – a field normally regarded as the Administration's favourite battleground. Dewey flattered Hull and praised Dumbarton Oaks as a 'grand beginning' and declared himself against 'reservations that would nullify the power of that organization to maintain peace'. This is triumphantly quoted by the Republican press as conclusive evidence of Dewey's true internationalism. (But a voice familiar to the old and middle-aged – that of ex-Governor Cox of Ohio,[3] Democratic presidential candidate in 1920 – declared that Harding too had offered lipservice to the League, that precisely those who supported Harding against himself and Franklin Roosevelt are now supporting Dewey and that Willkie was broken by them. Not Willkie but Hoover had been the voice chosen to speak at their convention.) Dewey thus sought to allay the respectable internationalists of his party, went on to repeat the Foster Dulles theses about disarmament and the internationalization of the Ruhr and, in fact, reduced his attack to the drawing and redrawing of the

2 Frederick A. Delano, Chairman of the National Resources Planning Board since 1934.
3 James M. Cox, newspaper owner, Governor of Ohio 1913–15, 1917–21.

portrait of the President as tired, listless, secretive, unscrupulous, despotic, inefficient and, above all, in a state of imminent collapse.

Registration, etc. On the other hand, registration has proved much higher than Democrats had hoped or Republicans had feared. Taken together with the absentee registrations, record totals were announced from several big cities including New York, Chicago, Detroit and Cleveland. It is reported that the total registration figures are about forty-five million as against Gallup's prediction of thirty-nine-and-a-half million. These evidences of the ability of Democratic field-workers to mobilize voters have caused some observers to reassess the situation in borderline States including even Michigan and Illinois which were previously considered 'reasonably safe' Republican. Roosevelt is now given 'a fighting chance' in these two States while his prospects in Pennsylvania and New York have also improved.

Press and other reports, official and unofficial, continue to uphold conviction that soldier vote will be heavier than has previously been expected and here again Roosevelt is generally accorded at least a 60/40 percentage. Gallup with his pro-Dewey leanings is wriggling somewhat obviously about all this and some expect him to predict Dewey's victory at the eleventh hour to tip the scales with wavering 'band-waggon jumpers' much as he did with his 'Roosevelt-Willkie 50/50' in November 1940.

The White House announcement that President Roosevelt would make a major campaign speech in Philadelphia on 27 October and reports that he will also speak in New York and possibly Boston may be evidences that Democratic managers realize that Roosevelt must make a fighting finish, that he must in fact campaign in 'the usual sense' whatever he may have wanted earlier. If brilliant home stretch spurts are particularly President's forte, and Dewey fails to offer more than he has and so to arouse enthusiasm save in the converted, this will offer President precisely the kind of political situation of which he is the greatest living master.

Meanwhile there is the solemn conversion of *New York Times* to Roosevelt, announced in a long and tormented editorial of 16 October which gave as its reason paramount importance of foreign policy today and greater fitness of Roosevelt in this field. The three columns, to judge from the soul-searching, hesitant style in which they were composed, were probably written (and there is other evidence for this) by Sulzberger himself, who is known to have struggled long and painfully between alternatives of domestic confusion for which he holds Roosevelt responsible, and more than a trace of Harding touch in foreign affairs which Dewey's entourage unmistakably conveys. Sulzberger's long delayed conversion is bound to have a considerable effect throughout the country, as *New York Times* still occupies a position of unique authority. This fact (enhanced by a kind of vote of confidence conferred on *New York Times* by a recent poll of newspapermen) has been universally recognized by friend and foe. Lippmann has also come out for Roosevelt on ground that Dewey cannot be trusted now with responsibility in foreign affairs.

Churchill-Stalin talks. Interest in Churchill-Stalin talks is subsiding and comment is now in a state of suspended animation, awaiting final announcement of Moscow results. Suggestion voiced last week that President's absence from the talks was due to his ill-health has been dropped and private speculation is divided between the theory that talks cover solely European problems, which are primarily affair of Russia and Britain and only secondarily of the United States, and suspicion that Anglo-Soviet relations need mending owing to clash of interests in Balkans and that Prime Minister has hurried to Moscow principally to effect a reconciliation of interests which will assure British domination of Mediterranean. As for the Poles there is nervous hope that a satisfactory compromise will be worked out – the latest news is interpreted to reinforce this. Conservative papers have continued to convey that Russian strategy is being dictated more by political than by military factors – a criticism made to a lesser degree about British campaign in Greece – accompanied by widespread expressions of regret over Russia's partiality for unilateral action. The ground-swell of Russophobia continues noticeably. . . .

World Security Council. An interesting development this week was the off-the-record seminar of questions and answers on the Dumbarton Oaks proposals given by Under-Secretary of State Stettinius for representatives of ninety-six organizations joined together under the title 'Americans United for World Organization'. The late Wendell Willkie was the prime mover in the formation of this group which includes organizations as diverse as the CIO and the National Association of Manufacturers, the American Bar Association and the Farm Bureau Federation, the AF of L and the Brookings Institution, the Bankers' Association and the Carnegie Endowment. The seminar was stated to be the opening move in a campaign by the State Department to promote public discussion of the whole problem of post-war security. The most significant item to emerge from this first meeting was a claim by 'Americans United' that the American public is strongly opposed to any voting procedure in the new World Security Council which would allow one of the major powers to vote on an issue involving itself. It is difficult to tell how much substance there is to this claim in view of the probable ignorance on the part of the American public of the pros and cons of, or indeed existence of, this as a crucial issue. And it may be that what does not hold of the 'public' holds still less of a nationalistic United States Congress. There are indications that the press has been enlisted in a campaign to interest the general public in the problems of post-war security. But the main issue still seems to be crystallizing around the extent of authority to commit the armed forces of the United States which should be granted to the American delegate on the World Council and whether that authority shall be subject to congressional ratification in each case. Senator Ball's question on this is still unanswered by either candidate. Dewey has ignored it ; Roosevelt dismissed it as trivial – 'I shall next be asked what the delegates ate at breakfast' he said, and was duly reproved by the press for ill-timed petulance.

. . .

Jews. Zionists are naturally jubilant about the President's unequivocal pledge to them[4] and Rabbi Silver, after acclaiming both Roosevelt and his own leader Dewey, said that he was sure that Mr Churchill – whose views on this were sound – would not look on such pledges with any disapproval.

28 October 1944

Presidential election. Democrats are notably more confident about President's chances than at beginning of month. Even though Hopkins's private predictions to his friends of favourable votes in more than thirty states may be over-sanguine, Democratic leaders have some genuine cause for optimism based on following :

(a) There has been a much larger registration than had at one time been expected particularly in big cities and particularly of labour vote which with some reluctance Democratic leaders concede to activity of Hillman's Political Action Committee. Registration has however not so far exceeded that of 1940 save in some cities (Chicago, Los Angeles, Baltimore, St Paul, San Francisco) against a lower registration in Pittsburgh and New York (this leaves some cases of ballots sent to soldiers abroad out of account), and with 2½–3 million soldier vote forecast by Gallup the total vote is expected to be slightly under total of 1940. A great fight is occurring both for New York and Chicago. In New York City, which is still predominantly pro-Roosevelt, the shakiest votes are said to be those of Brooklyn Poles and of Italians, although Democrats are hopeful of having made much progress with latter. Chicago is exceptionally unpredictable. In Ohio Democrats point to large labour registration of such cities as Youngstown, Akron, Toledo, Canton to show that state of Bricker and Taft may not be so safe a Republican stronghold after all. Be that as it may, the increased registration does demonstrate that Republican attacks on Hillman are not merely good election tactics but turn out to be directed against a genuinely effective foe. Columnists Childs and Stokes, who are trustworthy on this, both concede that Hillman's campaign was largest single factor in whipping up registration, Republican as well as Democratic, and to that extent rendered a service to American democracy. 'Clear everything with Sidney' (now played on record over a number of radio stations 'on the hour every hour') still seems to be working powerfully, despite fact that Krock, who originally gave it circulation, has protested in his column that he had made it clear that it concerned only Democratic vice-presi-

4 On 15 October supporting the opening of Palestine to unrestricted Jewish immigration.

439

dential nominations and not, as now used by Republicans, general field of Democratic Party and election strategy.

(b) Democrats draw comfort from combined effect upon 'opinion forming' individuals and groups of conversions of *New York Times,* of Walter Lippmann, of Senator Ball, of such of Willkie's supporters as Russell Davenport, Dorothy Thompson and Bartley Crum [1] (influential in California) as well as of President's foreign policy speech and of relatively ineffective reply to latter by Dewey.

(c) The knowledge of these facts has had an effect upon Democratic workers whose zeal has naturally become more intense with hopes of better political weather. . . . Dewey and Republicans generally also harp on dangers of a President permanently deadlocked with a Republican House and hostile Senate. Democrats reply that this argument is circular and prejudges the vote speciously – Rayburn now goes so far as to pooh-pooh the idea of a Republican House. Objection to fourth term is still powerful but Democratic optimism is clearly plausible if overdone.

Election speeches. President's foreign policy speech [2] was fairly widely acknowledged as being an authoritative, courageous and masterly performance for which the public had been waiting. The unequivocal stand on American delegate's powers in world council, while it might have provoked a bitter debate in the Senate had it been in session (and may do so still), does not seem to be having this effect on the elctorate, to which it probably does no more than convey the degree to which President has decided to commit himself and his party to full international collaboration. The warning that the President's 'old friends', Hiram Johnson and Joe Martin, as well as Messrs Nye and Fish, would head key committees in Congress (if Republicans won) seemed to sink in. Republicans are privately complaining that President knows, just as they themselves know, that whatever happens to President the Senate is most unlikely to contain a Republican majority and Johnson and Nye are not therefore likely in any case to acquire posts in question. However, as they obviously cannot say so publicly themselves, the President gets away with this particular stroke. Some observers think that his pro-Russian policy may alienate Catholic votes but it is clear the President has decided, perhaps rightly, that an absolutely unequivocal and open stand on foreign policy will profit him more than evasions to allay suspicions of this or that havering minority. Only obvious concession of this type in the speech was passage dealing with 'good Germans' in America which some among the 'hard peace' adherents, who interpreted it like everyone else as an appeal to New York and Midwestern German voters, deplored on ground that, however proper in substance, utterance of such sentiments at this moment might lead to too senti-

1 Bartley C.Crum, California lawyer, progressive and interventionist, founder member of Fight for Freedom Committee.

2 Waldorf-Astoria speech, 21 October : 'Our representatives must be endowed in advance . . . with authority to act.'

mental an attitude on part of United States troops in German territory. Reference to China was appreciated by representatives of that country. Poles are said to be gloomy about inadequate notice of them. One or two persons commented on absence of all reference to British, which may have been either accidental or perhaps due to a desire not to give any material to those who would wish to ascribe undue influence to the Prime Minister.

Republicans have attacked the speech on general grounds, but one or two of their leaders have in private conceded that while they thought speech to Teamsters of 23 September a deplorably cheap performance, they regarded this speech, whatever might be thought of its substance, as a noble declaration worthy of the President of the United States. President's sudden decision to ride through New York in an open car under drenching rain and his extraordinarily buoyant high spirits after it have done much to still rumours of his decrepitude. An entertaining poll by *PM* disclosed that the majority of the reporters who covered this event developed colds and chills apparently leading in one case to pneumonia. Mayor La Guardia, who only did half the trip, had to go to bed after it.

Dewey's reply, made at Minneapolis on 24 October, was not among his more effective. . . . The propositions that the President will not do because he (a) wilfully led America into war although (b) he appeased Japan and allowed scrap to be sent to her in 1940-1, but (c) is also a crypto-isolationist – as witness his scuttling of World Economic Conference of 1933, his signature of the Neutrality Act, his refusal to join the League of Nations – and finally (d) is guilty of doing nothing to prepare this country for war, is a case unlikely to carry conviction even in most bitterly anti-Roosevelt circles. Reiterated charges of 'cynical disregard of claims of small nations' probably cut a little more ice at any rate among minorities. Bricker's steady hammering on 'sinister' combination of Hillman and Browder, together with his simple, unceasingly repeated appeal to the average American's desire to return to the old traditional, decent, American way of life, back to the familiar and solid world which existed before the Great Depression, is of its kind a more effective anti-Roosevelt strategy and strikes deeper chords in heart of mass of voters at any rate in Middle and Far West and to some extent even in South, than the philippics hurled by Dewey as prosecuting attorney. Dewey's support of Dumbarton Oaks proposals with pointed emphasis on the rights of Congress (in course of his remarks about power to be given to American delegate to world council) has given *New York Times* and Lippmann an opportunity for repeating distrust of Dewey's attitude to foreign policy. His production of messages from such Republican leaders as Senators Vandenberg, Austin, Taft, White and Representative Martin praising his non-isolationist stand has provoked from Truman a demand that he formally disown his party's isolationist candidates for the Senate as well as McCormick and Hearst and so prove that he is no Harding and does not 'carry water on both his shoulders'.

Meanwhile Truman is getting his own share of mud with not much apparent capacity for responding in kind. In addition to association with Boss Pendergast's[3] machine, he is now charged with having been a member of Ku Klux Klan (which he indignantly repudiates) while Millikin, an otherwise obscure Colorado silver Senator called isolationist by Truman, suddenly snapped that 'to trade epithets with Senator Truman is like wrastling with a cipher', and Hannegan too is said privately to complain of lack of red blood in his nominee. Democrats do however find it worth while to crack up the generally respected Truman Committee as an advertisement for its chairman.

Senator Ball. Senator Ball's dramatic conversion to the cause of President Roosevelt on ground that Dewey's utterances on that subject were too ambiguous and could be interpreted to give equal comfort to both sides has naturally caused a stir. Isolationist mouthpiece John O'Donnell – the Drew Pearson of the right – is busily 'revealing' that this was result of intrigues by Hopkins who convinced Ball that if Dewey were elected there was no hope for Stassen or himself, whereas in opposite case they might well come into power in 1948. Ball did indeed spend an hour with Roosevelt and Hopkins and seems to have had few dealings with Dewey, but those who know him well maintain that he was guided by more sincere and honourable considerations – in fact by the reasons which he gave, since his faith in international co-operation is the passion of a crusader. Thought that Dewey's victory might put off his day and that of Stassen – if only by initiating a new Harding era – may indeed have influenced him since he naturally has some political ambition. Dewey's foreign policy declaration in Ball's own city of Minneapolis was obviously meant to underline fact that this was an unwise and premature move on a Republican Senator's part and some effort has been made to show that Willkie disliked Ball more even than he disliked Dewey. Some ground is lent to Republicans' thesis that Stassenites are displeased by Ball's 'bolt', by Mrs Stassen's affability to Dewey during his visits (though Ball's friends say she doesn't know what it's all about) and formal dissociation from Ball by Stassen's nominee, Governor Thye[4] of Minnesota. Senator Burton (of B2H2[5]) campaigning in Ohio said that Ball 'takes himself too seriously', but Ball told a member of my staff that his mail brought predominantly favourable comment from Minnesota, and mostly unfavourable remarks from the rest of the country. He has now denounced the Republicans' domestic obscurantism – e.g. on labour – and seems to be bidding for Willkie's mantle (or hairshirt) in earnest. His transparent sincerity is conceded by the more detached among Republicans who, probably rightly, see in him the beginnings of Norris or elder La Follette – with an outlook in field of foreign policy as generous and

---

3 Thomas J.Pendergast, Democratic Boss of Kansas City, under whose auspices Truman entered politics in 1922.

4 Edward J.Thye, Republican Governor of Minnesota since 1943.

5 B2H2. See p. 165. Resolution presented to Senate on 16 March 1943 by Senators Ball, Burton, Hatch and Hill advocating a 'collective world security system'.

independent as that with which these great isolationist champions of the common man viewed the domestic scene.

30 October 1944

Resumption of diplomatic relations with France and Italy. The recognition of de Gaulle's administration as the provisional government of France was received with universal satisfaction, with comment dividing itself along customary lines into those who took their cue from the State Department's text and hailed this as a logical step in the correct line throughout taken by the United States Administration, and those who said 'Better late than never' and treated the Department's line as a threadbare and disingenous face-saving device best overlooked in the welcome atmosphere of good sense and generosity. Some cynics remark that this was done only just in time since diplomatic recognition of Italy preceding that of France would have produced a peculiar impression. I am told that some Democratic politicians hope that the recognition of Italy will have a decisive effect on the Italian vote here.

.   .   .

World Organization. Stettinius is still obscure on whether and when the next step – an international conference of some kind – is to occur. Hull, who is still in hospital (I am told with a streptococcal infection) has published a full-length encomium of the President as fitted by achievement and character to cope with one of the most crucial issues in the history of the nation, and enumerated the recent achievements of American policy one by one. He is said to claim to be unable to remember Dulles's name – a sure sign of strong disfavour doubtless caused by Dulles's now notorious letter in which he suggested that Republican Senators might not work well with a Democratic Administration in the peace settlement. The President has duly altered this 'elect me or I won't play' attitude.

.   .   .

5 November 1944

Presidential election. War news is beginning to yield in public interest to rising tempo of election campaigns. There is no real change from last week. Polls and estimates of relative strengths of candidates succeed each other with increasing rapidity and total impression conveyed is that race is still neck to neck with odds slightly favouring the President. Democrats seem privately more confident than this, Republicans (although this does not show in press) more gloomy. . . . There is a whispering in Republican circles that Gallup while privately conceding 52 per cent to Roosevelt will, as a political move, come out on Dewey's side on the eve. Elaborate tightrope performance by 'Pollsters' is beginning to look a little ridiculous. Politicians and gamblers are therefore thrown back on their own less scientific resources, and reported large volume of recent Wall Street bets giving Roosevelt odds of as much as 17 to 5 must be based on evidence other than that provided by 'experts'. A very great deal of money is reported to be ready to change hands in this fashion. Some of it may represent efforts by wealthy persons to compensate themselves financially for a possible Roosevelt victory.

Neither candidate has notably added to his stature by last week's speeches. Dewey, speaking (28 October) in Syracuse to farmers, repeated much of Republican platform, held up ex-Food Administrator Chester Davis as a martyr of New Deal incompetence and made his usual promises. In Buffalo on 31 October he enunciated an eight-point programme promising social security, a floor under farm prices, lowering of taxation, better relations with Congress, etc., the only new points being pledges to simplify machinery of tax returns particularly for farmers (their present load of book-keeping appears to madden most of them) and a 'really' effective campaign against cartels. In accordance with his technique of harping on identical themes and altering only variations, he repeated charges against the President of selling privilege for $1,000 per purchase, of a desire to 'purge' Congress, of alliance with Communism, etc., and spoke of 'a just and lasting peace through an international organization with sufficient strength to prevent war'. Communist motif is said to be most repaying thus far. In Boston on 1 November Dewey took a line evidently designed to allay increasing charges against Republicans of stirring up 'racial and religious hostility' (Hannegan, a Roman Catholic, has, stressing his own faith repeatedly, thrown this in Dewey's teeth, referring particularly to use made of Hillman's 'non-American' origins by Bricker, Clare Luce, etc.) by saying that Communism was a menace even when home grown – thus Browder was born in America (he is in fact said to stem from an ancient Colonial family). As for Hillman – here audience booed and hissed particularly loudly – had he not been described by New York labour leader David Dubinsky (here audience, uncertain as to how this outlandish name should be greeted, seemed poised for booing) as a front for Communists (audience cheered) ? Dewey's expedient of quoting Dubinsky against Hillman to so largely mixed an audience as that in Boston, was plainly designed to clear himself of whispered charges of anti-Semitism. Yet there was a conspicuous difference between whole-hearted pandemonium which any mention of Communism or Hillman or of New Deal bungling aroused, and subdued and somewhat artificial applause which Dewey's references to ultimately immigrant origins of all Americans produced.

Meanwhile President in his speeches at Philadelphia and Chicago (where Mayor Kelly fulfilled his promise of 'Biggest goddam rally this city has ever turned out') dwelt on Administration's military and civilian record and obstruction of this by Republicans, praised work of Truman Committee, warned against racial divisionism and in general spoke with conspicuous assurance and force but without bold new strokes which characterized his foreign association speech on 21 October. He added a few words of appreciation of smaller nations in his broadcast on 2 November.

Both candidates seem now to have reached the stage where they appear intent upon holding their earlier converts rather than recruiting new adherents. Dewey is still ramming home such points as chaos of New Deal, the Communist menace, sale of privilege by the President, his ill-concealed hatred of private enterprise and his entrance into war as a desperate cure for unemployment. His strongest backers are Luce Publications. *Christian Science Monitor* also has come out for Dewey (it supported Willkie in 1940), while *New York Times* in its new role as the President's ally is doing quite an effective job of analysing and refuting Dewey's speeches one by one. In particular it insistently inquired what value there would be in Dewey's promised 'harmonious relations' with Congress, particularly a House dominated by men like Knutson, Martin and Hamilton Fish, since the better he got on with such men the more disturbing the prospect to foreign policy.

Reston reports from Midwest a combination of bitter-end isolationists of school of Colonel McCormick with disgruntled liberals of school of younger La Follette, somewhat resembling analogous pattern of 1918-19 in common opposition to Administration's internationalism (in this case Dumbarton Oaks Agreement). He does not however point out that unlike 1918 this is a largely Midwestern phenomenon only and thus far not observable on a nationwide scale. Senator Mead (Democrat, New York) has caused a mild flurry by alleging that he had evidence to show that Hoover and Dewey were conspiring to 'remove that corn Willkie from the Republican toe', a statement hotly denied of course by Republicans. Jesse Jones has made a speech of unqualified praise of the President's preparation for war and Ambassadors Winant and Harriman now here have made speeches for him. Stettinius has also made a brief statement. Lippmann (who has since left on a visit to England) has once more summed up against Dewey whom he regards as having conspicuously failed to grow to presidential proportions while Krock is elaborately arguing that Dewey would have less trouble with an almost certain Democratic majority in Senate than Roosevelt with not improbable Republican majority in the House. If Krock's (and other experts') estimates are right, a divided Congress seems certain whatever result, and the alternatives are the present Republican plus conservative Democratic coalition against Roosevelt as against the Democrat plus liberal Republicans against Dewey. But despite united verdict of most commentators and newspapers, a Republican majority in the House does not seem to me inevitable in the event of a victory by the President (Speaker Rayburn says that 20 to 45 Democrats will be added to present party strength in the House but this may well be overoptimistic), while defeat in senatorial primaries of some of Roosevelt's most rabid isolationist opponents makes his task in that field easier. Massachusetts Republicans are counting heavily on result of Truman's somewhat over-candid admission that Democratic Senator Walsh (who endorsed him) was actually as extreme an isolationist as anyone ('but we have two years in which to reform him'). Walsh has naturally taken much umbrage at this and as he is 'greatest vote-getter' in history of State, which itself appears to be teetering on a razor edge, Republicans are confidently predicting that this will tip balance in their favour. Every step has been taken to placate Walsh (somewhat discredited Chairman of Senate Naval Affairs Committee), and his acceptance of an invitation to accompany the President on his Massachusetts tour caused almost audible relief among Democrats. The offended Senator says that he will not however open his mouth – his friends say that he will continue to support ticket 'regardless'. Ickes continues to refer to Dewey as the 'chocolate soldier'.

Meanwhile Hillman, who has plainly overplayed his hand (even though his organization is now widely acknowledged to have played a dominant part in stimulating registration – total vote now looks like being not much below that of 1940), has done something towards seizing the bull by horns by seeking to clear himself of charges of pro-Communism in a series of public conferences. His appearance before Washington Press Club seems to have been something of a personal success for him according to both Lindley, who described scene and praised Hillman for his forthright and stumbling but honest eloquence, and by a member of my staff who confirms that he made a good impression on his critical audience. It is possible that intemperate attacks by Republicans may boomerang somewhat by provoking labour. Clare Booth seems justifiably nervous about her seat in Connecticut ('may she carry her pretty head for many many years,' said Hillman 'preferably outside of Congress').

There is no doubt that trend reported last week which has made industrial states like Michigan, Ohio and Rhode Island seem more dubious from Republican point of view than that party had originally assumed, is still continuing. PAC has whipped up labour vote in Michigan and Bricker's entourage is said to be troubled by inroads in Ohio. This does not of course affect solid anti-Roosevelt vote of Dakotas or rest of Corn Belt (Iowa, Nebraska, Kansas stretching to Colorado in West). Indiana, Wisconsin and Vermont seem only other solid Republican states – even Maine shows slight signs of thaw. There is no evidence that speeches of anyone other than principal candidates have made any appreciable impression. Latest Gallup poll indicates that only 57 per cent of Roosevelt supporters polled know that Truman is his 'running mate' – a higher percentage of Republicans have heard of Bricker. There is much speculation about last date on which the soldier vote, which in a close race may swing issue, will come in, and of effect of such intense suspense on conduct of public affairs.

Stilwell. Other outstanding piece of news has of course been recall of Stilwell[1] and accompanying flood of anti-Chinese stories in newspapers. Most violent and eloquent of these has been despatch by Brooks Atkinson[2] the veteran dramatic

1 Recall ordered by Roosevelt on 18 October, in response to Chiang Kai-shek's refusal to place Stilwell in unrestricted command of all Chinese forces.

2 J.Brooks Atkinson, drama critic of *New York Times* 1925–60, war correspondent in China and Russia 1942–6.

critic of *New York Times,* who has served as its correspondent in Chungking lately. It dwells on familiar theses – Chiang's corrupt autocracy, reluctance to fight Japanese, suppression of freedom of speech and liberal trend generally, etc. – with new gusto. This has been widely supplemented by AP and other agency despatches and has presented American people with spectacle of Stilwell as a martyr in the cause of prosecution of the war – the victim of his own ultimatum to Chiang to fight or lose American help. Issue has been obscured but only slightly by peripheral stories of alleged intrigues between Dr Kung[3] and Hopkins to support Chiang against combination of Nelson, Hurley and Stilwell, or rivalries between Stilwell, Chennault[4] and Ambassador Gauss, whose own resignation is attributed to indignation with behaviour of Chungking Government, but general picture of a wicked and deceitful Chinese régime unsuccessfully prodded by United States into resisting the common enemy rather than its own Communists is now firmly drawn. President at his press conference made a somewhat faint-hearted defence of Chiang, saying that flurry was due to a clash of personalities and nothing more – Chiang was after all within his rights : if he, Roosevelt, disapproved of a 'Britisher in Washington' he would naturally tell Mr Churchill about it – that 'honestly there was no politics in it', but this has not persuaded anyone. Thus far no allegation of British complicity in Stilwell's removal has been made, nor now that whole issue has blown so wide open, does it seem likely that any will, although there is a sprinkling of talk about possible effect on British commanders in Far East. Sinophiles are naturally much depressed by sudden transformation of a particularly well-loved ally (even though it has been losing favour rapidly lately) into a knock-kneed, shifty and somewhat Fascist-minded malingerer and Dr Judd,[5] the ex-missionary Representative from Minnesota, has struck the first blow in defence of Chinese by declaring that Chiang was intolerably provoked by Stilwell's ultimatum – a demand to be made Supreme Commander over all Chinese forces including the Generalissimo himself – which he had transmitted on behalf of President Roosevelt, himself a typical practitioner of 'personal' policy, but this will now scarcely help. The extraordinary spell which Chinese have managed to bind on Americans for so long seems broken for a long while. The pendulum seems now to have swung as excessively against the Chinese as a year or two ago it had swung in their favour. Shrewd observers did indeed predict at that time that this was only possible result of unreal heights of mystical adoration which were then being lavished upon China in this country. Rise and fall of this extraordinary political romance offers most strikingly instructive exhibition to date of astonishing instability of American popular emotion. Doubtless something nearer proper equilibrium will sooner or later be attained but upset has been considerable and it will take time for a sober view of facts to be achieved.

3 H.H.Kung, financier, Chinese Finance Minister and Vice-President 1933–44.

4 Claire Lee Chennault, originally in command of American Volunteer Group of pilots in China, then in 1943 General of Air Force.

5 An ardent Sinophile.

A somewhat similar disillusion may stem from latest Russian moves although Russophobia is one of more permanent deep currents in this country and fewer delusions have been harboured than on subject of China. Contrast between this and enthusiasm for both China and Russia at this season twelve months ago is indeed arresting. Our own position is enhanced by contrast. The sudden Russian refusal to take part in civil aviation conference in Chicago as well as its latest moves over Persian oil[6] coming on top of the Polish imbroglio cannot but have a damping effect. We get the impression that State Department, in particular Berle, were much disconcerted by Russian note on subject of Spain, Portugal and Switzerland[7] but dare not show it for fear of 'rocking the boat' during critical election week. I am told that Berle was at first inclined to take a somewhat stiffer line but in the end agreed to mild official line which regrets Russian decision, understands objection to Spain but scarcely to Portugal or unoffending Switzerland, and still hopes that USSR will allow its representatives to act as observers and feels sure that no real difference will be made by this sudden stiffening of attitude.

. . .

Henry J.Kaiser. An observant traveller lately back from the North West tells us that while there is naturally much excitement about, and admiration for, the immense activities of Mr Henry Kaiser on the West Coast, persons close to him as well as outside observers feel somewhat apprehensive that this organizer of genius but reckless gambler, who is buying up plants, and building on a prodigious scale, may be seriously overextending himself, and that, with the hostility to him of his powerful rivals, particularly in the established steel and aircraft industries, he may precipitate another Kreuger crash.[8] They allow that, on the other hand, his vast speculation may come off, in which case it will have been the most spectacular success of imaginative big business enterprise in the present generation.

8 November 1944

Returns to date indicate that Roosevelt majority is handsomely exceeding general predictions. This nationwide sweep, embracing at present over thirty States (with electoral total of over 400), added to every sign of a heavy vote, indicates a degree of popular support which naturally delights Administration. Hopkins is jubilant and describes the President as in the highest spirits.

Dewey 'conceded' election in generous and dignified terms at 3.15 a.m. on

6 In September the Russians had begun to press Iran for oil concessions. Iran resisted and in November Britain and the USA made supporting representations in Moscow.

7 The Russians contended that they could not attend the conference because 'among the nations taking part are Switzerland, Spain and Portugal, countries which for a number of years have carried on a hostile policy towards the Soviet Union.'

8 Ivar Kreuger, Swedish match manufacturer and financial tycoon whose operations led to a sensational crash in 1933.

radio. The President and Truman immediately telegraphed their thanks to Dewey.

10 November 1944

ELECTION RESULTS

On the basis of latest returns, the following facts are clear.

The new Senate. This will consist of fifty-six Democrats, thirty-seven Republicans and one Progressive (La Follette), with two seats (Pennsylvania and Missouri) still undecided. Eight and probably nine Senators of less or more isolationist tendencies will not return. . . . James ('Puddler Jim') Davis (Republican, Pennsylvania) will probably, when the soldier votes are counted, be succeeded by the highly respectable Myers.[1] . . . Moreover, Governor Saltonstall of Massachusetts (Republican) is likely to make a more progressive, if not so able, a Senator as Lodge (Republican, now in the Army). Fulbright (Democrat, Arkansas) is clearly an improvement on Hattie Caraway, and may well be appointed to the Foreign Relations Committee.

Of the new Senators, only Capehart[2] of Indiana is a probable obstructionist. If Missouri goes Republican and Pennsylvania Democratic, as expected, the Senate will once more consist of fifty-seven Democrats, thirty-eight Republicans and one Progressive. This would represent no change in proportions but a clear change of character: thirty-three Senators are men of clearly internationalist opinions, sixteen are Southern Democrats strongly inclined to vote with the internationalists, seven are moderate Republicans inclined to internationalist but liable to nationalist influences, and, therefore, somewhat uncertain, seven are Democrats of similar type, seven are straddlers of no fixed tendency, and twenty-five are more or less isolationist. Thus on the wholly pessimistic assumption that Davis of Pennsylvania is re-elected and that all the straddlers will vote with the isolationists, we might obtain an opposition figure of thirty-three, i.e. the fatal one-third minority. Against this may be set the facts that (a) if Davis is, as is probable, turned out, this is reduced to thirty-two, i.e. one below the fatal third. (b) The defeat of such notorious isolationists as Senators Nye, Holman, Danaher, and probably Davis, as well as of Representatives Fish (Republican, New York), Day (Republican, Illinois), Busbey[3] (Republican, Illinois), and Calvin Johnson[4] (Republican, Illinois) with some twenty others of the same general type, mainly on the issue of foreign policy, clearly indicates a strong popular trend, universally recognized as such, and unlikely, therefore, to be ignored by the more politically cautious or precariously placed among isolationist incumbents.

The general complexion (as distinct from strict party alignment) of the House

1 Francis John Myers, Democratic Congressman from Pennsylvania since 1939.
2 Homer Earl Capehart, Republican Senator from Indiana 1945–63.
3 Fred Ernst Busbey, broker, Republican Congressman from Illinois since 1943.
4 Calvin D. Johnson, building contractor, Republican Congressman from Illinois since 1943.

of Representatives has not of course been as much affected as that of the Senate. With its 435 members, the House looks at present as if it will not differ greatly from its predecessor, although the Democratic majority of over fifty gives the Administration a solid enough edge.

The House will doubtless be liable to control by the now familiar coalition of Republicans and Southern Democrats on domestic issues and of Democrats with progressive Republicans on foreign issues. It is worth remarking that the crucial Senate Foreign Relations Committee has lost the isolationists Champ Clark, Nye, Reynolds, and probably Davis, as well as the isolationist-inclined Gillette. While the Republican caucus is free to fill its two vacancies as it wishes, the Democrats, who are now rid of the only four isolationist members of that body, are unlikely to appoint isolationists to succeed Messrs Clark, Reynolds, Gillette and Van Nuys. Thus the situation here looks distinctly brighter. Carter Glass (Democrat, Virginia) and Hiram Johnson (Republican, California) attend this Committee more and more fitfully on account of old age and failing health; their rarely cast votes cancel each other. Johnson's successor can hardly be as intransigent. The less important House Foreign Affairs Committee, which in any case had a clear internationalist majority, has lost four Democrats and two Republicans (all internationalists) and as their successors are likely to hold similar views, they could not upset the majority in any event.

There seems little doubt that the result of the elections is interpreted by friend and foe alike as a strong expression of popular opposition to isolationism, at any rate in its acute form, and appears to indicate a general readiness on the part of this country to take full part in the affairs of the world, some say in a nationalist spirit, but to take part fully and vigorously nevertheless. This is conceded by the isolationist Patterson papers which try to find cause for satisfaction in the fact that a clearcut national decision has at any rate been reached. Coming from such a quarter this verdict can only be regarded as highly encouraging.

11 November 1944

Democratic victory. Hopkins turns out to have been a true prophet, and press (with exception of *PM*), as so often where political issues are involved, a false one on this topic. After the mass of predictions that victory by either candidate would be closest imaginable, that whole situation was uncertain to a degree scarcely to be conveyed, President duly accumulated a popular majority, which, according to latest figures, exceeds three million, and this has given him thirty-six States with an electoral vote of 432 (against Dewey's twelve States – two more than Willkie – with ninety-nine votes) plus an unchanged Senate and a Democratic majority in the House approaching fifty. Roosevelt's popular majority is smaller than during his three previous elections, and to this extent prophecy that this would be 'the closest-run election since 1916' is literally accurate (it would thus be incorrect to speak of a landslide). But the cardinal fact is that sentiments of American people have been expressed with unassailable clarity, and *New York Daily News* editorial which comforts its readers by saying that at any rate the issue (and it means that of isolationism) has at least been settled firmly, shows that result is accepted as clearest possible endorsement of Administration's foreign policy. Almost as significant as President's own re-election was defeat both in primaries and in elections themselves of leading isolationists in Senate and also the House (see below). The writing on the wall is clear for all to read. For the first time since Woodrow Wilson it is not wholly certain whether the isolationists can on paper muster fatal one-third of Senators required to block a treaty. At the same time some eight isolationist Senators were returned, and Administration will still have to play its cards carefully enough. Nevertheless elections have clearly set the seal of electorate on trend towards participation in world affairs which, as I have reported for past year, has been steadily growing throughout the country.

The campaign. The campaign grew in intensity as climax approached, and while Dewey did not in his final speeches say anything striking, Mr Roosevelt's Boston speech was perhaps the freest, most infectious and sparkling performance of entire campaign – he felt that he had his audience with him from first moment and was inspired by this to flights of virtuosity reminiscent of his greatest days. Whether or not as a result of this, Massachusetts gave him firm majority. Republican campaign was characterized by a calm efficiency and precision of calculated effects, the very opposite of the barnstorming tumult of Willkie's progress in 1940, but lacking in spontaneous enthusiasms of that remarkable procession. Its main emotional stimulus was desire for a rest – genuine inability to bear the thought of four more years of Mr Roosevelt. Democrats appeared fired by greater enthusiasm for their candidate than Republicans for theirs, and at least an equal distaste for his rival – they exploited such modern resources as radio with incomparably greater skill than Republicans, and last hour before the final election addresses of the two candidates was filled by Democrats with political songs and sketches which, while they might have seemed distasteful to the more fastidious, evidently 'went over big' with audience – particularly a ballad with the refrain 'That old red scare ain't what she used to be, ain't what she used to be, twenty long years ago', sung by Groucho Marx with infinite gusto. A song which reported Mr Dewey as having grumbled, fumbled, mumbled, stumbled, bumbled, etc., also went exceptionally well. This was, with astonishing inconsequence, interspersed by moments of sudden solemnity during which a man whose head had been patted by Abraham Lincoln quavered his appreciation of the New Deal, a Georgia voter aged eighteen echoed him together with a New Guinea veteran, and finally President read a Prayer. Republicans took refuge in unbroken austerity which they contrasted with unseemly high jinks of their irresponsible opponents. Dewey refused to admit defeat until early hours of morning and made his final admission a little after 3 a.m. in a genuinely dignified and handsome little radio address in which he wished success to his rival. President acknowledged this immediately but somewhat drily, by cable, and a similar exchange of courtesies occurred between Bricker and Truman. President told me however today that he had not yet received customary personal message of polite congratulation from Dewey.

Voting and election might seem to have been uncommonly decorous, particularly in New York where little of usual clowning occurred, and crowd in Times Square waiting for result was quiet and earnest. 'You see, America has at last come of age,' remarked an eminent American politician to a member of my staff, as they walked home from Broadway. On other hand Henry Wallace is said to have caused some perplexity to his police escort by suddenly leaping out of his car in middle of New York and setting off through Broadway at a steady trot and so into Central Park. The detectives puffed away behind him, slightly stunned by such behaviour, but without venturing openly to speculate about his motives or to question its propriety. Presently the Vice-President stopped and re-entered his motorcar which had followed him. He explained that he had merely felt the need for exercise. President is said to be very pleased with Wallace's aid to him during the campaign, and to be contemplating an important post for him – but he is said to be unlikely to offer him Secretaryship of State (which Wallace is said to want). In this connexion Mr Hull's recent breakdown in health has naturally sent speculation about his successor ablaze again, and names of Winant and Byrnes are mentioned, with Wallace considered improbable. Byrnes is reported to have told his friends that he might be forced to return to private legal practice as he is a poor man and cannot afford life in Washington on a public scale. Stettinius is naturally also mentioned within Department of State itself. President gave me impression when I saw him that Hull would be staying on anyhow for the present.

Cause of Roosevelt's victory. What are main factors in Mr Roosevelt's re-election ? First and foremost probably is the still magnetic power of his remarkable personality, and his matchless and acknowledged skill as a campaigner. There appeared to be no reason why, in principle, a Republican capable of exciting the nation and attracting the 'Independent' New Deal vote – say Willkie – should not have won this year. But no such person was chosen by the grand old party. Republicans scarcely attempted to maintain that their candidate was of a stature equal to the President's, and some even of the President's bitterest opponents could not but concede his unique quality. Nor should element of pride in leadership of a man whose greatness is acknowledged so widely abroad be discounted in the case of this most self-conscious of nations, increasingly certain of itself and keenly aware of the new figure which it cuts in the world. This was closely connected with widespread feeling that only Roosevelt possessed talents and outlook large enough to transact business with Mr Churchill and Marshal Stalin on their own scale, and this conviction was influenced by and itself influenced the continually growing interest in foreign affairs prevalent in this country, unquestionably the largest single issue in this election. Domestic issues may well have loomed largest regionally, but a general sense of America's inescapable role in world affairs seems to have permeated the consciousness of this nation. Dewey professed proper sentiments on this topic but in a none-too-certain tone. There was a feeling that he and the Republicans would fail to measure up to Russia. To Roosevelt's Gladstone there was no discernible potential Disraeli.

PAC. Among other factors was the undoubted influence exerted by the (CIO) Political Action Committee. Its influence can easily be exaggerated, but it did an extraordinary job in increasing registration and 'getting out the vote' in dubious areas, acting in this respect as the shock troops of the Democratic Party. The swing of Michigan to Roosevelt, no less than that of New York, Massachusetts, New Jersey and Pennsylvania was due in no small measure to the fervour of the CIO, whom the attacks of Dewey and Bricker on Hillman and the Communists did not intimidate. Their main regrets are

(a) (and this is shared astonishingly widely) the victory of Clare Luce in Connecticut, which the PAC leaders do not think they could have prevented, and

(b) the narrow victory of Senator Taft in Ohio, if confirmed by the final figures, which they now feel could have been prevented if a nonentity had not been pitted against him. Conservative Democrats are uneasily wondering whether they are not travelling in the company of a Frankenstein's monster – whether the PAC will not in effect prove to be the long discussed nucleus of a political labour party, or at the very least a cuckoo in the Democratic nest, likely to pitch out the Southern Democrats when the hour comes, and so cause the much dreaded and discussed split in the party with the inevitable political realignments. And indeed it is possible, but too early to tell, that political clashes between the New Deal, with the PAC as its vanguard on the one hand, and the combination of Republicans and Southern Democrats on the other, within the framework of the existing parties, will one day burst through this framework and radically transform the present party system to allow for the new political and economic realities. But this seems unlikely to happen during Mr Roosevelt's régime, although it may well begin in the vacuum which its passing will leave. The formal future of the PAC will be decided at the CIO convention which meets this month in Chicago. It seems likely to continue as a cardinal pressure group, whatever is resolved.

Two celebrated political old stagers have finally shown their weakness in this election. John L. Lewis once again failed to 'deliver' the miners' vote in Pennsylvania, West Virginia and Illinois. Jim Farley, alleged to have been helping Hamilton Fish under cover, seems completely finished. Political bosses as a class are clearly threatened by such mass organizations as the PAC.

Not to be neglected also is the exhibition of stamina – however it was contrived – which the President exhibited during his rain-soaked drive in New York, New Jersey and Philadelphia ; to turn bad weather to such brilliant political advantage was a manoeuvre which displayed Roosevelt's peculiar talent to its fullest extent.

It is unlikely that many believers of either side were converted in the course of the campaign, but Dr Gallup's 20 per cent of independents may have been swayed by political speeches, of which the best was perhaps Dorothy Thompson's eve-of-poll talk in which she seized on every hostile point made by the opposition against the President, ostensibly accepted it, and turned it to political credit. (Yes, he is a tired old man, at least as tired and old as Mr Churchill and Marshal Stalin ; Mr Dewey is not tired, why should he be, Mr Dewey has not worked, etc.) The newspaper articles which probably had the greatest effect were those of the *New York Times* in support of Roosevelt, of Walter Lippmann, and the striking editorials in the *Louisville Courier-Journal* (Barry Bingham[1] and William Agar) which although preaching to the converted, may have influenced the fact that Kentucky gave more votes to Roosevelt than Virginia. The brilliant anti-Dewey campaign of the *New Yorker* is a permanent memorial of American irony at its most unforgettable.

The defeats of Messrs Nye, Danaher, Holman, Champ Clark, Worth Clark, and probably Davis in the Senate; of Fish, Day, Maas, Busbey, Charles Dewey (Republican, Illinois), one of our sterner financial critics, and other isolationists in the House and their replacements by men and women of liberal outlook, cannot but make a profound difference to the attitude of Congress to international affairs. The more astute old isolationists may next turn their sails to this new wind.

11 November 1944 (Savingram)

Polls. The professional polling organizations were perhaps the most timorous of all the prophets. Dr Gallup finished with 51.5 per cent of the civilian vote. The final figures will not be clear until the soldiers' vote is counted, but on the basis of existing returns it is clear that more than 53 per cent voted for Roosevelt, which, although undeniably within Gallup's admitted margin of error (of 3–4 per cent), does not serve to strengthen the faith of the unconverted in the complete dependability of his polls. Perhaps his alleged Republican sympathies led him to underestimate the size of the total vote on which the percentages were based. . . .

His and other pollsters' errors, which are not in terms of percentages outrageous, are indeed within the realm of unavoidable human fallibility, which the experts themselves explicitly emphasize in every published prophecy. But the divergence between the predictions and the facts may be salutary to those inclined to lean too heavily upon these techniques. The full count will not be

1 Barry Bingham, publisher of *Louisville Courier-Journal* 1930–45.

completed until the last soldier vote is counted on 5 December, when it will be possible to compare this result with that of the professional prophets. . .

Field-Marshal Dill. The untimely death of Field-Marshal Sir John Dill[1] has called forth unanimous expressions of profound and genuine regret and appreciation. The *New York Times* and *Washington Post* in leading articles paid worthy and eloquent tributes to his character and unique position in Washington. The intimate understanding which he had achieved with his friend General Marshall, and to an almost equal extent with General Arnold and Admiral King, was a relationship unique among the military directors of any association of Allies, and was an asset of the highest order to Anglo-American relations, the loss of which will inevitably be felt as deeply by the Americans as by ourselves. His military funeral at the Arlington National Cemetery was a profoundly moving ceremony unlikely to be forgotten by those who attended. By special request of General Marshall the flags in the District of Columbia were flown at half mast on the day of the funeral – a unique tribute. The affection and honour in which he was held by his American colleagues was such that future historians will scarcely be apt to underestimate the part which his presence played, particularly before his health began to fail, in creating the remarkable effect which the institution of the Combined Chiefs of Staff has had upon Anglo-American relations, and the conduct of the war.

China. Anti-Chinese publicity continues, though the volume has naturally fallen off somewhat. The Chinese in Washington are very unhappy to see the result of so much careful emotional investment melt away so suddenly. Criticism of us in this connexion has been surprisingly sparse, although talk of our alleged apathy in Burma has recropped up here and there. Indeed, the absence of anti-British comment during the presidential election generally and over this issue in particular, has been gratifyingly noticeable. If it be asked why the Administration allowed the anti-Chiang campaign to rise as high as it did, the answer may well be (a) that it was not a deliberate move on its part but was caused by the Chinese crisis and the ultimate inability of any democratic government to prevent the indignation, whether real or drummed up, of a sufficient number of its officials and journalists from finding vent, (b) but on the other hand it may well be that Mr Roosevelt realized that the pro-Chinese lobby had been largely captured by his political opponents. While the nucleus of it is doubtless formed by the non-political groups of missionaries and disinterested Sinophiles (the basis of United States pro-Chinese sentiment is in the Sunday Schools) – together with serious United States students of China among officials who sincerely feel the political and economic future of the United States to be bound up with China – yet the political exploitation of this sentiment has largely been the work of such anti-

---

1 Field-Marshal Sir John Dill, Chairman of Joint Chiefs of Staff Mission 1941–4.

Rooseveltites as the Luces, Willkie, Pacific-Firsters, isolationists who see in it a useful foil to preoccupation with European issues, Anglophobes and other anti-imperialists, a combination opposed both to involvement in Europe, and to the foreign and to some extent domestic policies of the Administration. A counter-wave reducing the Chinese to something below their just proportions may therefore be not wholly unwelcome to the Administration, since a number of the warmest Sinophiles in it probably have left-wing sympathies and feel strongly about both the Chiangs. By a parity of reasoning the Luce papers, which fear Communism, defend Chiang and blame America for the imbroglio (cf. article in *Life*, 13 November, and the analogous trend in *Time*) but this is a deliberate political line, based on dread of American aid to a Chinese Tito and does not reflect general opinion.

18 November 1944

Aftermath of the election. While war news received the normal amount of attention, intensive discussion of the results of the election still predominates. Certain facts now seem clear :

(a) Roosevelt obtained over six-and-a-half-million votes in thirteen cities with a population of more than 500,000 against some four and a quarter million for Governor Dewey. Of these thirteen, the soldier vote is yet uncounted in St Louis, Philadelphia, Pittsburgh and Baltimore. Except for Ohio and Wisconsin, Roosevelt carried all the States containing these cities. Of the nationwide majority of over three million so far counted, over two and a quarter million was contributed by these cities. This powerfully supports the claim made by the PAC to have played a determining part in the election. Doubtless if Roosevelt had lost, the aggressive publicity of that organization would have been the first to be blamed. As it is, its role in the Democratic Party, and the American political scene generally, is likely to be very noticeable, if not in the immediate future, at any rate as the 1948 elections approach.

(b) The South, both deep and 'upper', shows definite signs of disaffection which might have been greater still and influenced events if the Southerners had had anywhere else to go. Roosevelt's majority there was considerably reduced since 1940 and, although the Democratic votes exceeded the Republican by something like three to one, Roosevelt carried Virginia, the Carolinas, Kentucky and Tennessee by sharply reduced majorities compared to 1940, and Dewey received the heaviest Republican vote in Louisiana recorded since 1876. At least three-quarters of a million of normally Democratic voters in the South failed to vote for Mr Roosevelt. While this did not begin to affect the ultimate alignment of the States (so that the result in the Electoral College would not have been affected even if Roosevelt had retained his earlier popularity) it does indicate that a New Deal candidate not endowed with the singular attributes of a Roosevelt can, in a foreseeable, if not near, future lose these States. The artificiality of the alliance between the New Deal (buttressed by the Northern Democratic political machines) and the South has been vividly demonstrated, and an anti-New Deal alliance is less unthinkable than it would have been even as lately, say, as 1942. Certain disaffected Southerners now maintain that the Republicans did not in fact contract such an alliance only because they laboured under the illusion that they could win single-handed (you will recollect Republican optimism throughout 1943) and that they will know better next time. But everything will clearly depend upon the record of the Democratic Administration in the next four years and no crisis is probable during Roosevelt's reign. But the mid-term elections of 1946 will not necessarily be more indicative than were those of 1942, with their clear Republican trend, which have caused so much of the overconfidence of the Republicans.

(c) Although the full vote has not been counted, it seems clear that besides obtaining the votes upon which the Democrats concentrated – labour, Negro, 'hyphenated groups' – not as many farmers seem to have voted for the Republicans as had been expected, e.g. in such States as Wisconsin, Minnesota, Illinois and New York. This was apparently due to nervousness about post-war agriculture, and a certain reluctant awareness on the part at any rate of the poorer farmers that in a crisis Roosevelt's administration would do more for them than Dewey with his Wall Street supporters. In the North-Western States, the issue of public power is the liveliest, and this apparently caused the adhesion to Roosevelt of Washington and Oregon. As for the Middle West the isolationists continue to concede that issues of foreign policy did largely affect the result and while the Patterson papers say that their day will come, the temporary victory of interventionism is openly admitted. The sweeping victory of Senator Lucas in Illinois, and the heavy defeat of Nye and the large pro-Roosevelt minority vote in North Dakota are arresting phenomena.

(d) For all the talk flowing around the two propositions that President's victory was due to reluctance on people's part to swap horses in mid-war, and that world has witnessed an inspiring exhibition of untrammelled democracy at work with the victor suitably warned by smallest majority of his career, the 'young Turks' will clearly try to revamp the organization of the party. Composed on the one hand of Willkie liberals like Ball, Saltonstall, and Russell Davenport as well as Stassen, on the other of ambitious persons of tougher views like Lodge, Sam Pryor, Juan Trippe and the Luces, this group may argue that, necessary as the solid financial contributors of the Pew-Gannett-Rockefeller type may be, the party will never win under guidance so uninspired, and that a bolder, more positive line must be developed. This may lead to a real struggle for the party machine, the outcome of which will depend on the general political situation in 1946 when the mid-term elections will bring this to an issue and Stassen may loom large. Until then nothing decisive is likely to emerge.

(e) Ickes has attacked the press for once again showing its remoteness from popular opinion and indeed the trade paper *Editor and Publisher* showed that

68.5 per cent of the press opposed Roosevelt and only 17.7 per cent supported him. There is no doubt that, as in 1932, 1936 and 1940, the press has shown its relative impotence to sway the election, a fact to be borne in mind in estimating the influence of the American press on major political issues. The radio supported Roosevelt by a much larger ratio.

(f) The continuing hold of President's international policy over the minds and hearts of American people seems thrown into clear relief by the large measure of general contentment with which his re-election has been received. The press, even anti-Roosevelt sections of it, report the defeat of isolationists and the 'clear mandate on foreign policy' now given to the President without bitter or uneasy undertones. The ultra-isolationist minority continues with its old refrain but it is quite clearly a minority and acknowledges this. The omens thus seem hopeful enough and seem to be so interpreted by the White House.

Cabinet shifts. Speculation on this topic naturally continues to bubble. I have no reason for supposing that Hull will go very soon but in view of state of his health, about which I hear reports that are by no means encouraging, I do not think he will remain very long. He himself will almost certainly wish to continue until he is satisfied that international organization with which he has so deeply identified himself, and upon which he has staked his reputation, has been provided with solid foundations. Provided his health permits, it is unlikely that he will be relieved of his post until he chooses to abandon it himself, although if his absences from his department grow more frequent, the President may feel obliged to supersede him. Press comment still speculates busily about this and I am told by some fairly well-informed persons that Byrnes, who has agreed to remain in his present office until end of the German war, only did so under impression that he is in line ultimately to replace Hull. Names of Stimson, Winant, Stettinius, Harriman, Grew are still bandied about. . . . Secretaryship of Labor is much discussed and name of its lately resigned labour conciliator Steelman, said to be backed privately by Miss Perkins (who seems genuinely anxious to leave a position gradually grown less and less tenable since 1932), and publicly by various newspapers, is much spoken of. I am told that Wallace could probably have this difficult post, beset as it is by rival and conflicting agencies, if he wished it but that he is for these very reasons not very likely to covet it and that he could probably also return to his old post of Agriculture. He is said by some to prefer Secretaryship of Commerce if only because of moral satisfaction which stepping into the shoes of his *bête noire,* Jesse Jones, would give him. According to most reliable sources the President has not made up his mind on any of these questions yet and may as so often act suddenly and probably on impulse and give everyone a surprise. It seems most unlikely at present that Ickes, Biddle, Stimson or Forrestal will disappear. There is some talk of traditional appointment of Hannegan, as head of Democratic machine, to Postmaster General in place of Walker since this office is source of much patronage. This is neither certain nor important. Tough-minded and scarred veteran of many Washington battles with private interests, James Fly of FCC has resigned and Democratic publicity chief Paul Porter, once a CBS Vice-President, has been appointed to succeed him. Porter is a spirited and very capable young New Dealer. Otherwise there is no conspicuous change. Public members of War Labor Board have agreed to remain in answer to the President's entreaty.

Churchill, Stalin, Roosevelt talks. There is naturally much speculation in press and radio about date and nature of forthcoming conference between Prime Minister, President and Marshal Stalin which is assumed to be likely to occur before end of the year. There has apparently been no inspired 'line' on this from the White House or State Department. I am told that Stettinius and Pasvolsky recently called at the White House and since Stettinius is plainly anxious to push on with discussions if only to keep them prominently in the public eye, one may assume that he favours an early meeting. But a columnist normally close to Leahy reports that the President is at present not too eager for this and a member of my staff was told by an official who should know facts that Stalin's reluctance to leave Moscow is at present the main obstacle. The President at his press conference confirmed that he had made no progress with plans for such a meeting. Public opinion is however favourable to an early resumption of talks and press regards President's hand as so much strengthened by result of elections that it voices expectation of meeting almost universally. President reasserted desire of all three principals to see each other as soon as possible, and suggested that he would not accept General de Gaulle's invitation to visit Paris until that had materialized. There are of course various rumours attributing President's alleged reluctance to meet with Stalin and Churchill to a variety of causes – a reluctance to discuss Polish issue, to take sides on reported Anglo–Russian differences, etc. – but this gossip appears to me to contain no substance. Stalin's speech was widely discussed and on the whole excellently received.[1] Russian absence from Civil Aviation Conference is no longer discussed.

The Press and the election. Ickes has publicly invited ('in friendly fashion') American newspaper publishers ('to give the country an explanation of facts which seem to me to indicate a progressively unhealthy and dangerous decline in the reader confidence . . . this nation has again questioned in ringing tones the right of the press to represent readers' opinion by selecting a President supported by only 17.7 per cent of the press and actively opposed by 16.5 per cent, with only 13.8 per cent representing themselves as neutral'. The facts are that Governor Dewey was supported by 796 newspapers (60.1 per cent of those surveyed with a circulation of 26,654,996 – 68.5 per cent of the total circulation under survey) ; Roosevelt was supported by 291 newspapers (32 per cent, circu-

1 Delivered on 6 November to Supreme Soviet, playing down differences, and emphasizing the need to establish an organization to prevent another world war and an alliance based on 'vital and lasting interests'.

lation of 6,902,243, i.e. 17.7 per cent of total circulation involved) ; Independents numbered 237 (17.9 per cent of those surveyed with a circulation of 5,356,807, i.e. 13.8 per cent of total circulation). The editor of *The Editor and Publisher*, which published these figures, replied that in New York, New Jersey, Pennsylvania and Illinois where Dewey had more press support than Roosevelt, Dewey captured 'a majority of the voting units' since Roosevelt's strength lay in the 'populous areas', and animadverted on the fortunate fact that, in the United States, newspapers indicated one point of view, electors voted for another and democracy flourished freely. This, however, cannot disguise the fact (and indeed is hardly intended to do so) that the press in the United States, to a conspicuously greater extent than in Britain, represents the political sympathies of its owners, and to that extent of affluent and normally Republican pressure groups of this country, and is not an accurate mirror of public opinion or of the relative strengths of the political parties; and their influence is, therefore, apt to tell most over issues which are not subject to major internal political controversy, or else relatively unaffected by them, for example opinions entertained of the policies and character of foreign countries, progress on the war fronts, etc. Those, therefore, who listened too much to the newspaper chorus which gave Dewey too high a chance of victory and dogmatically asserted that a Republican House was in any case inevitable (and they include, it seems, a good many of the diplomatic missions in Washington and other interested observers) found themselves very wide of the mark. . . .

· · ·

Business Conference at Rye. So far, no political or press repercussions appear to have resulted, and the routine views of certain members of the conference have been reported (e.g. Winthrop Aldrich, supported by the *Washington Post*, on the necessity of post-war loans to prop up British economy as against continuance of Lend-Lease). . . . Anti-cartel remarks by Eric Johnston, and others, and liberal anti-tariff sentiments were much in evidence. The Conference formally approved the British resolution on the Bretton Woods proposals about the International Reconstruction Bank. A *mot* which is circulating reads 'Bankers of the world unite, you have nothing to lose but your Keynes'.

The *New York Times* reports a virtual unanimity of opinion for repeal of the Johnson Act (forbidding loans to countries which failed to settle their war debt to the United States) in Congress and outside. Charles P. Taft (of the State Department) has spoken against the Act and Eric Johnston supported this attitude. Meanwhile the proponents of extension of the activities of the Export-Import Bank in making loans abroad point out the perfect compatibility of this with the Bretton Woods Reconstruction Bank.

· · ·

There is a rumour that Leo Crowley may go as United States Ambassador to the Vatican (as opposed to Kennedy, whose offer to contribute to the Democratic funds is reported to have been declined by the Democratic Party Chairman Hannegan).

25 November 1944

A kind of political détente seems to have followed the election and its immediate aftermath. Nothing has occurred on the war fronts to arouse more than normal comment. The 'lame duck' Congress is naturally enough not in a mood to embark on controversial legislation which its successor is almost bound to upset. Even the Democrats do not refer to the election as a landslide, and appear soberly conscious of the difficulties facing the Administration, particularly on domestic legislation. Both sides continue to recognize that on foreign policy the popular endorsement is unambiguous. As for Congress, what pleases the Administration most is not the retention of its majority in the Senate (which was expected) nor even the increase in its majority in the House (which many professional wiseacres had doubted so strongly as to be somewhat discredited by the result), but the composition of this new majority. Few even among the most sanguine New Dealers hoped to secure so valuable a group of allies, who if they succeed in banding together could perhaps offer more formidable support to the Administration on domestic as well as foreign issues than the conservatives have had to face since 1938. The soldier vote will not be fully counted until December but present indications show that the majority is, as was expected, about 67 per cent pro-Roosevelt. Breakdowns of the way in which specific social groups voted are not available yet, but again there are strong signs that voting was 'selective', i.e. that mass voting for a given party as such is decreasing, and that records of candidates played a part independently of their formal party affiliations. The decisive Roosevelt majority came from the industrial North. As in all his previous elections, the President could have afforded to lose the entire 'solid Southern' vote and still have been elected (and indeed the South proved itself somewhat disaffected: 145,000 votes for Dewey in Virginia against 235,000 for Roosevelt tells its own tale). Labour (according to hints by the 'pollster' Elmo Roper who came nearest to predicting the actual result) hints that a third of the labour vote did not go to Roosevelt, while a third of the normally conservative 'professional' and 'executive' group voted for the President. The Republicans, who can no longer convincingly blame their defeat (as often before) on the 'abnormal' situation (some among them now tend to concede that Willkie, for example, might have been elected), will inevitably be forced into some recasting of their platform and organization, and will be faced with the painful issue of inventing new positive political aims of their own. How drastic a reform the party will undergo the next eighteen months will show. There is some ground for supposing that the Old Guard is and feels feebler than it looks. Colonel McCormick told a Canadian journal that Dewey was a weak candidate and that

461

the Republican Party must become openly nationalistic and more Western or die.

The PAC very naturally feels cockahoop about its performance, since its new power derives as much from the general impression of the decisiveness of its role, as from its actual achievement which perhaps falls somewhat short of this. The CIO convention has decided to continue this organization for the purpose of general 'educational', i.e. specific, political work in local and national elections in 1945 and 1946. The convention tumultuously hailed Wallace who said nothing new but said it well, and hailed him as its presidential candidate for 1948. . . .

The AF of L reaffirmed its refusal to sit at the same table with the other guests whom the TUC invited to its London International Conference in February – the CIO, the Canadian Catholic unions, the USSR delegates, representatives of the 'wrong' Latin American groups, etc. – and then settled down to similar condemnations of the War Labor Board, and otherwise restated old positions showing no signs of change of its traditional outlook and time-honoured tactics. The vision of Hillman's coming visit to London to be received in triumph as the new Napoleon of American labour depresses the AF of L leaders very deeply. The CIO feel self-consciously young and vigorous by comparison and Hillman is riding high.

25 November 1944 (Savingram)

. . .

Conscription. An issue which is likely to become fairly sharp in the course of next year is that of compulsory national service on military lines, the need for which the President has reiterated several times recently. There is general agreement that training of this type will be necessary, but the President has not made it clear whether what he contemplates is direct military conscription and the training of a vast reserve army on the European model, or something more nearly approaching the CCC youth programmes which Congress abolished against his protest. In the present state of uncertainty the Quakers pointedly, and other church groups, Catholic and Protestant, more guardedly, have entered reservations concerning what to some of them may seem a programme of New Deal indoctrination ; the National Guard, perceiving danger of its own extinction in the wider scheme, also protested, and much skill will evidently be needed in piloting any bill designed to create the new organization ; but there seems little doubt that such a scheme, comprehensive, and with a radical influence on America's sense of its place in the world, will sooner or later go through, supported as it is by the War Department and veterans' organizations, probably sometime next year.

Blasphemy. The flurry caused by publication in *Time* magazine of the President's alleged exclamation from within his polling booth that 'This Goddamned thing won't work', leading to a solemn prayer to him to recant on the part of a Cali-

fornia Clergymen's association, followed by denials on the part of precinct officials that any such words had been overheard by persons near the booth in question, has now been happily allayed by Mr Roosevelt's partial admission that
while he might have used the word 'damned' he had not invoked the name of
the Lord in vain. The clergymen have now apologized for putting their faith in
Time magazine, and all is peace again. The fact that the President should have
found it necessary to make so explicit a statement on the situation is a sharp
reminder of how powerful the sentiments of the 'Bible belt' can still show themselves to be.

Varia. In the reorganization of congressional committees consequent upon the
new election, Senator White (Maine) temporarily succeeds to Nye's key position
as head of the 'Interim Republican Committee on Committees', which recommends appointments to the other committees, and is joined on this by the enlightened Austin (Vermont), but also by Brooks (Illinois and the voice of the *Chicago
Tribune*), as well as Willis (Indiana), an ex-isolationist, and the somewhat colourless Robertson[1] (Wyoming). These, together with Taft (Ohio) and Butler
(Nebraska), preserve the old reactionary balance. Meanwhile Senator Styles
Bridges (Republican, New Hampshire), a vociferous defender of the rights of
small European nations, is regarded as almost certain to be nominated to the
Foreign Relations Committee, while Messrs Gurney,[2] Reed, Taft, Tobey and
Wiley – non-too-encouraging a group – are due to have the second Republican
vacancy filled from their number. Meanwhile Senator Thomas[3] (Democrat,
Oklahoma) succeeds to their chairmanship of the Senate Agricultural Commit-
tee, which Wheeler rejected in favour of continuing as chairman of the Interstate
Commerce Committee, Senator Pepper (Democrat, Florida), an ardent New
Dealer, presides over the Patents Committee, while Senator O'Mahoney (Democrat, Wyoming) will have to be satisfied with presiding over Indian Affairs.
The Dies Committee, bereft of its leading members, has been pronounced dead
with much public acclamation. The appointment of Donald Nelson as the President's personal representative in China, with Cabinet rank, settles for some time
the fate of that harried, bewildered, but persistently loyal official. It has been the
subject of some criticism of the President's methods, which Krock told me a few
days ago had been summed up by the well-known Ed Flynn's saying that FDR
could always be relied on either to put four men to do one job, or one man to do
four jobs. As for the Cabinet, talk of new faces, particularly in the State and
Labor Departments, continues on lines reported in our last summary. It is worth
remarking that whatever their other failings, no better friends of Britain than the
present United States Cabinet (e.g. Messrs Hull, Morgenthau, Stimson, Biddle,

---

1 Edward V.Robertson, rancher and Republican Senator from Wyoming 1943–9.
2 John C.Gurney, Republican Senator from South Dakota since 1939.
3 Elbert Duncan Thomas, Democratic Senator from Utah since 1933.

Ickes, Jones, Miss Perkins, and for that matter Wickard and Forrestal) can well be imagined. It is at the level of Assistant Secretaries and below (Berle, Laughlin Currie, etc.) that difficulties begin. Meanwhile a firm friend has been lost us in Paul Appleby, who has left the Bureau of the Budget apparently (like Milo Perkins) to recoup his dwindling fortunes in private business.

Obituary. The most noteworthy deaths are those of Senator Ellison ('Cotton Ed') Smith, for thirty-five years Senator from South Carolina, a moderately picturesque and blindly diehard champion of the cotton lobby, defeated in the last primaries of his State, and of Boake Carter,[4] a renegade radio commentator, son of a British Consul in Baku, who developed eccentric Anglophobe views and before his death became converted to peculiar neo-hebraic religion apparently of his own devising. His broadcasts, which were nationwide, were listened to with considerable attention. In this connexion it is gratifying to note that one of our chief scourges, Upton Close,[5] an intensely isolationist commentator, has lost his network, perhaps defeated by the new spirit that is abroad.

27 November 1944

Appointment of Stettinius as Secretary of State is virtually certain to be confirmed by Senate. It indicates, in terms of current politics, a victory for Harry Hopkins over Byrnes who is a relatively independent personality. After the news of acceptance of Mr Hull's resignation (which is apparently due solely to reasons of ill-health) had been made known, Senators Connally and George, after expressing their regrets about Mr Hull's abandonment of his post, expressed their preference for Byrnes, a fellow Southerner and an intimate friend, as his successor. Two hours later, the President announced the appointment of Stettinius and it was implied that he had cleared this with Connally and George. It would seem that uncertainty about the post continued until the end. Stettinius told a member of State Department that he was Mr Hull's own choice as his successor.

Main immediate effect is a closer integration of State Department with the White House, which is doubtless all to the good. Stettinius is an original Hopkins protégé and has never forgotten it. The internal balance of influence within State Department, which might have altered under almost any other Secretary of State, will most probably remain almost entirely unaffected, and key roles of Dunn and Pasvolsky are . . . likely to continue. The Department itself seems vastly relieved (and delighted) at the continued *status quo*. The effect on Berle's position is not so clear. Some actually speak of him as a possible Under-Secretary, but all this is very vague at present. The President's intention to conduct his own foreign policy has now been, if anything, still more palpably demonstrated ;

4 Boake Carter (1898–1944), news commentator on Mutual Broadcasting System.

5 Upton Close, extremely right-wing radio commentator and correspondent, particularly on Pacific and Far East affairs, for NBC, 1941–4.

Hopkins's old (New Deal) prejudice against officialdom of State Department has in any case been melting of late, and he has been conducting business with individual heads of the Departments more widely than before. This habit will doubtless increase with the appointment of Stettinius. Stettinius is a specialist in 'public relations' with Congress and the public ; young, jovial, energetic, the exemplar of glad-handing, back-slapping, vigorous American executive, he provides the politically much needed contrast with both the 'tired old men' and 'Europeanized' diplomats so abhorrent to American people. With Forrestal, Harriman and now Stettinius strategically placed, the White House, and in particular Hopkins, are acquiring more integrated control than ever before. The long rumoured 'house-cleaning' of State Department is now most unlikely to occur, although Stettinius has undoubtedly introduced much improvement of the machinery. A good deal may depend on who is appointed Under-Secretary, concerning which there is too little evidence at the moment.

From our point of view this appointment, which Congress and public opinion will receive quite well, is likely to change very little. The Department will doubtless be run as before mainly by Dunn, while important decisions will even more systematically be referred to the White House, where Hopkins and, at some considerable distance after him, Leahy appear to possess the most considerable influence.

Mr Hull is expected to continue as an elder statesman and adviser to the President on world organization.

2 December 1944

The resignation of Secretary of State Hull was made public on 27 November, when a letter to the President was given to the press expressing Hull's bitter disappointment at having to relinquish his labours in the international field owing to ill-health. Since the rumours of Hull's failing health have, as I reported, been circulating persistently for some months, this news did not altogether surprise the general public for it was generally supposed (and quite correctly) that Hull's prestige was such that nothing but his own free choice could cause him to retire, and indeed, as it turned out, ill-health alone appears to have been the determining cause of the resignation. Speculation about his successor pointed to Byrnes, the War Mobilization Director, as a favourite by long odds, and indeed there is reason for supposing that Hull himself favoured him as the successor. Byrnes's influence with Southern Senators, back to his days as Congressman and Senator, is perhaps second only to that of Hull himself and equal to that of Senator George. He is trusted and moderately popular in conservative circles and the country at large. Moreover, it was felt that the President owed him some recompense for causing his candidature for the Vice-Presidency to be withdrawn earlier in the year, despite which Byrnes campaigned sturdily for the President. Senators Connally and George duly conveyed to the press on the morning of 27 November that they favoured Byrnes as the successor. Several hours later the press announced the appointment of Under-Secretary Edward N. Stettinius to the vacant post and published his own very warmly worded reply to Hull in which he paid due tribute to Hull's work and unique reputation, called him the father of the United Nations, and urged him to continue with his advice to the Administration in an individual capacity. Hull subsequently replied to this in a letter to Stettinius in which he praised his successor's loyalty and abilities and promised him his help whenever needed.

. . .

The appointment of Stettinius was received with well-moderated praise by the press and public opinion. The editorials and, to a lesser extent, the broadcasters dwelt upon the tragic loss which Hull's resignation constituted and vied with each other in eulogizing Hull's qualities of character and judgment which had made him for so long the symbol of traditional American virtue, the possessor of attributes of which many Americans instinctively think with pride as the national character at its best and finest. There is no doubt about the unanimity and sincerity of this nationwide outpouring of homage and personal regret at the retirement of this widely admired and indeed much beloved figure, whose very tartness and obstinacy have contributed to the image of him as a Grand Old Man, the father of the new American foreign policy, in whom almost infinite trust was reposed by the average unsophisticated American citizen. Both Houses of Congress echoed these for once profoundly felt sentiments. After expending their principal verbal resources on encomia to Hull, the press welcomed Stettinius too, in words indicating that they were prepared to give the young man a chance to prove himself.

. . .

White Papers. On this we had a very good week. Our (Reverse Lend-Lease) statement [1] on this subject, although to some degree swamped by the President's own latest report on this topic, [2] did in conjunction with the President's most eloquent testimony to the British contribution, create a receptivity among the public to the White Paper on United Kingdom war effort, [3] which thereupon received exceptionally widespread coverage and a volume of favourable comment with which our information experts are justifiably contented. The press, but more particularly the radio (whose voice is the louder) dwelt with virtual unanimity on the astonishing wartime achievements of United Kingdom while stress is still laid (both in conjunction with the President's Lend-Lease statement and the Morgenthau-Crowley-Stettinius statement on the subjects of Lord Keynes's recent conversations) [4] on the welcome diminution in the size of the

1 British Government's statement on Reverse Lend-Lease.

2 President's 17th Report to Congress on Lend-Lease Operation covering Reverse Lend-Lease period up to 30 June 1944, transmitted 24 November.

3 *Statistics Relating to the War Effort of the United Kingdom*, Cmd 6564, presented to Parliament in November.

4 Talks, began 5 October and ended 23 November, designed to execute Quebec Agreement that US aid to Britain should be adjusted to permit the British economy to begin conversion from war to peace.

'sacrifices' which America will have to make to her British ally, and there is some fairly routine but mild sniping from Anglophobes, yet not merely the volume but the appreciative quality of the comment – filled with admiration that so much could be done – on the statistical White Paper is greater than any similar British announcement has yet achieved. The moral which follows from this is that, when the story which we have to tell both is and rings true, the reaction here is strong, immediate and generous. [British Information Service] surveys provide full details of this. The White Paper may justly be described as the most effective blow yet struck in defence of our general economic position, and is likely to leave a lasting impression even on the kaleidoscopic American memory. The reports of our alleged request for United States Lend-Lease material intended for re-exports are correspondingly dying down, and the National Planning Association's clearly formulated demand for expansion of American imports was much better received than might have been expected. For the moment, atmosphere e.g. in Congress is favourable to reasonable arguments : how long this will last is another question.

The reports of press conferences by Mr Bracken in London and Mr Harold Butler[5] in Washington have received full and favourable publicity. Mr Bracken's words about our freely offered sacrifices of our accumulated Victorian inheritance appear to have caught the broadcasters' particular fancy.

Italy. The UP despatch from Rome reporting that Count Sforza had been stopped from becoming Italian Foreign Minister by direct British pressure, followed by reported official admissions in London that it had been indicated in Rome that such an appointment would in fact be very badly received by us, has been greeted with wholly adverse comment here, even by such confirmed friends as Swing and the vastly popular Heatter.[6] The general adverse attitude here towards our policies in Italy, entertained both in public and in official circles, will by now be familiar to you, and the blocking of Sforza allegedly because of his opposition to the House of Savoy which is most unpopular here will merely strengthen our bad name in this respect. It will probably also increase talk about our undisguised desire to fashion a Western European bloc of British satellites in Europe. Sforza, who is well known and well liked in Washington and New York, and indeed symbolizes Italian democracy to the American public, which has heard of scarcely any other anti-Fascist Italian, may well attain the status of a political martyr of the British, and I am told that his Italian opponents here may in that event rally to his side at any rate for a while. Your statement in Parliament was given some prominence but there has been no time for comment to develop. At the moment, moderate Liberals of the *Herald Tribune-Washington Post* type, who are probably not averse to giving us general support, are in a mood to chide

5 Harold Butler, British Minister in charge of Information at Washington 1942–6.
6 Gabriel N.Heatter, radio commentator with Mutual Broadcasting System since 1932.

467

us more in sorrow than in anger. Others talk more sharply. No support of our position is discernible anywhere.

. . .

2 December 1944 (Stettinius Special)

Stettinius's vast affability, sincere desire to be a friend of all the world and shining sincerity are qualities which cannot fail to endear him to the public, and offset the disadvantage (in some circles) of a Morgan and United States Steel past. There is probably far more real disappointment among serious-minded persons in Washington than either in the country at large or in the press at what e.g. Chief Justice Stone, in conversation with a member of my staff, referred to as 'a piece of incredible levity on the part of Mr Roosevelt.' The press is kindly disposed to Stettinius. His good work in Lend-Lease was duly recollected, and much advice on foreign policy, but more particularly concerning shortcomings of his Department, was pressed upon him, varying according to the shade of opinion of the writer or broadcaster. He can hardly be called either the people's or the Congress's or even Washington's own choice for his present office, but if there is no enthusiasm (save for the *New York Times* and Sol Bloom who virtually threw their hats in the air), neither is there any publicly expressed resentment or opposition except for a very few disparaging remarks in liberal quarters. The applause is moderate but benevolent, and there is virtually no booing. Senator Langer delivered a long speech in the Senate to block the appointment after the unanimous recommendation of the Foreign Relations Committee, and talked of Stettinius's failure in 1940-1 in connexion with the steel and aluminium industries, but Langer is a disreputable old radical and his long speech merely evoked loud praise of Stettinius from other Senators (of both parties). His confirmation was, of course, not in doubt.

Members of the State Department appear to be jubilant and, above all, relieved, about this choice. They wanted Wallace and Welles least of all (neither of these appointments ever seemed probable) and appear delighted to have this exuberant optimist, who bustles and backslaps but at the same time displays earnestness and genuine humility, defers to the judgment of experts, and has during his Under-Secretaryship warmed the hearts of officials inhibited and alienated by the cold, Curzonian manner of Welles. These officials believe that Stettinius has improved and will continue to improve the technical organization of the Department, and appear to feel confident that, while some changes in personnel (and other where) may come, the fundamental organization and the relative status and influence of individual members of the department will not alter greatly ; but they concede that much will depend on who is appointed Under-Secretary. The names of Berle, Lew Douglas and Dunn have all been mentioned. But Grew and Armour are the favourites with the odds slightly on Grew.

. . .

468

Most important of all, there is general conviction that Stettinius's appointment was due most largely to the President's determination to conduct his own foreign policy in a completely clear field, without having to reckon with another strong personality, either so formidable and independent a figure as Hull had been or such a one as Byrnes might to a lesser degree, owing to his congressional backing, have proved to be. Stettinius has, throughout his public career, risen as the protégé of Hopkins and it may therefore be expected that the State Department will tend to become a technical adjunct of the White House to a far greater extent than it could ever do under a head with a strongly marked character of his own. For, while it is true that on matters of policy few disagreements arose between Hull and the President, yet the latter had to walk with conspicuous wariness at times for fear of offending the old gentleman's easily inflamed susceptibilities. The President, it is thought, faced with an opportunity of a completely free hand, had seized it ; and to the extent to which the new arrangement ensures the integration of American foreign policy, and averts the nightmare of two foreign offices (such as had caused havoc when the staffs of Lansing and Colonel House [1] competed so sharply under Wilson) it is clearly an excellent thing. Whether the somewhat informal arrangements under which business is at present conducted at the White House will extend into the State Department and what its relations are likely to become with other departments in the absence of the authority wielded by Mr Hull, may depend to some degree on the strength displayed by the Under-Secretary upon whom a great new burden will come to rest. There is no doubt, of course, of the new Secretary's undeviating friendliness to Britain nor of his purity of motive and lack of any tendency to become the instrument of any sectional interests, nor for that matter of his devotion to, and determination to accept, complete guidance on all things from the President and Hopkins.

Some among the Southern Senators are said to be labouring under a sense of having been insufficiently consulted by the President on the appointment, and point to their *bête noire* Hopkins (who has never, so it is said, seen eye to eye with Byrnes or his friends) as the author of Stettinius's fortunes. But they feel no animus against Stettinius himself ; their resentment is probably directed, as traditionally it must be, against the President. Meanwhile, Stettinius does not disguise his elation at the turn of events, and is said to be meditating a conference of the United Nations in Miami in the Spring, an occasion and a venue which would display his social talents at their most exuberant and irresistible.

3 December 1944

A member of my staff was told by Senator George of Georgia, whom he met on the night of Stettinius' appointment, that he, George, and his friend Connally,

---

1 Edward M. House (1858–1938) as Wilson's personal confidant repeatedly acted for him in foreign affairs and often clashed with Robert Lansing, Secretary of State 1915–20.

Chairman of the Foreign Relations Committee, were in a rare rage about the whole thing. According to George, the preference of the Foreign Relations Committee for Byrnes had been made unmistakeably clear to the President but had met with opposition from Hopkins. Hull had in fact resigned on 22 November and Stettinius had promptly applied for the job, and had then been left in suspense for some five days, in the course of which he had gone about making nervous inquiries but without receiving a reply. George used this time in order to make inquiry of Hull (whom the President had visited in his sick bed on the 22nd) as to whom he, Hull, would prefer as a successor. George had not seen Hull, but received a message from him indicating that Byrnes was his choice and mentioning no other name. Any story that Hull had himself asked for Stettinius was, therefore, a falsehood. He, George, had known Hull intimately for many years and was sure that Hull would not say one thing to him and another to the President. It was with this in mind that George and Connally had spoken to the press of their preference for Byrnes. The President summoned the two Senators to visit him at 2.00 p.m. on 27 November, but at 1.55 p.m. he had despatched his note to the Foreign Relations Committee tendering Stettinius's name. George asserted that he and Connally felt angry about this but, knowing the President as they did, and labouring under no excessive affection for him (the President had attempted to purge George in 1938), they realized that this was a typical Roosevelt manoeuvre and that there was nothing to be done. They had nothing against Stettinius who, George said, was 'a nice enough lad if not too bright', but the Southern Senators would never forgive the President for this gratuitous and irresponsible whim and he would pay for it sooner or later. He (George) had been to see Byrnes to condole with him and Byrnes had remarked to him : 'When a man kicks you downstairs once, you blame him ; when you let him do it to you a second time, you blame yourself.' Byrnes was in a gloomy mood, sorry he had agreed to stay at his post till the end of the German war, but unwilling to resign immediately, since that would look much too obvious. George went on to denounce the President and his act, and said that the country had lost a great Secretary of State in Byrnes, but that, at any rate, he and his friends had saved it from Wallace and the 'crackpots'. As for Hopkins, they would get even with him yet. All this is, of course, no more than a case of typical, if particularly acute, senatorial disgruntlement, but George is perhaps the most powerful member of the Senate, and the fact that Jesse Jones is now the only Southerner in the Cabinet, and not a typical one, may land the Administration in some difficulties. On the other hand, the fact that the President should have chosen to disregard Southern sentiment may perhaps be an index of his own sense of his new power accruing as a result of the recent election. In any case, the story is characteristic of present relations between Roosevelt and the conservative members of his own party ; also of the way in which things are done and freely ventilated in Washington.

3 December 1944 (Savingram)

. . .

The so-called 'streamlining of Congress' (O'Mahoney- Monroney Resolution). [1]
This would provide for a number of needed overhauls, including the provision
of better technical, legal staffs for House and Senate committees, and the integration of overlapping committees in the House and Senate, the existence of which
necessitates the giving of identical testimony by busy government officials twice
or several times over to different committees at the cost of too much time and
labour. This reform appears to have a genuine chance of being adopted, as it is,
doubtless correctly, being represented to Congress as a measure designed to enable that body to draft its own legislation by employing staffs of experts rather
than leave the drafting of bills to officials in executive departments, who, as
often as not, are the real authors of much congressional legislation. As Congress
is at all times anxious to preserve and, indeed, extend its constitutional powers
against the dreaded encroachment of the Executive, it may well modernize itself
to resume the struggle with more up-to-date equipment at its disposal. The executive departments, particularly those of Justice and Interior, while they view
the 'rationalization' aspects with approval, scarcely conceal their doubts about
the effect of a Congress rampantly eager to initiate legislation without, and in
some cases contrary to, the advice of the relevant executive departments. Such
a development may occur, nevertheless.

Freedom of the Press. The newspaper lobby is conducting a two-prong campaign
of great vigour to secure the adoption of an official American policy against
censorship and for full freedom of the press and, less obviously, for uniform
cable rates. Kent Cooper of the Associated Press delivered himself with great
fire and eloquence on this in New York, while John S. Knight, chairman of the
Association of Newspaper Editors and Publishers, is to go to Europe to investigate the international situation. Senator Brewster and others have spoken in support of the United States position, while those who inquire whether it is thought
possible to establish complete freedom of the press (to look no further afield than
Latin America) by passing pious resolutions, are given little play in the newspapers. While there are no specific attacks on the British position, it is obscurely
felt that (a) there is one, and (b) it favours restriction and must be cleared away
if the new world is not to remain in chains.

. . .

1 Resulted in the establishment in 1945 of the La Follette–Monroney Committee which recommended the exten-
sive modifications in congressional structure and methods (particularly the committee system) embodied in the
Legislative Reorganization Act of 1946.
   A.S.Mike Monroney, editor of the *Oklahoma Daily,* Democratic Congressman from Oklahoma 1939–50,
Senator 1951–68.

Canada. Reactions to the Canadian conscription crisis [2] have been singularly restrained and, although two or three newspapers openly criticized the French Canadians, and there has been some scattered criticism of Mackenzie King's [3] tactics of an almost technical nature, the relative absence of outspoken comment on the crisis itself is a striking symptom of the prevalent fear of irritating the susceptibilities of the only completely dependable good neighbour possessed by this country. Belief in Canadian virtue is widespread, and there is much respect for the greater political efficiency of Canadian institutions. Hence the degree of American surprise at the fact that such a tempest should have blown up in that apparently quiet pool of good government, coupled with deep reluctance to let fly on the subject.

Conscription. The Federal Council of Churches has asked Congress to delay action on peacetime military conscription until after the war and said that the Council 'is not pronouncing judgment for or against conscription'. The American Federation of Labor expressed similar reservations on the subject and the measure will clearly require the most delicate and skilful possible piloting.

10 December 1944

THE ANGLO-AMERICAN EXCHANGES ABOUT ITALY AND GREECE

What began as the Sforza imbroglio turned into a wider controversy over policy in Europe. Coming on top of a rising wave of criticism of His Majesty's Government for interference, when unwarranted or of the wrong kind, in Italy and Greece, the first statement made by State Department provided a clear lead to press and radio upon which they seized with some avidity. In general public opinion is critical and suspects us of wishing to impose a specific – more or less reactionary – pattern upon Europe. . . .

. . . The overwhelming bulk of radio comment and Washington talk (now that Greek situation has supervened) varies between the uneasy and the deeply critical. While press generally represents this as being the sharpest divergence to date of British and American policies, some indeed, on the ill-wind theory, profess to see in this a healthy form of freedom to differ. Although it is doubtless the case that with replacement of military by more purely political factors, real conflicts of opinion are inevitably bound to crop up between Britain and the United States, and that most of these should perhaps not be taken too tragically, the present difference is more than that and springs from profound and permanent

2 Under the National Resources Mobilization Act (NRMA) the Canadian Government of Mackenzie King was empowered to impose conscription for home defence only. When in the autumn of 1944 the need developed for larger overseas forces than volunteers could supply, a political crisis developed. By an order in council of doubtful constitutionality a quota of 16,000 NRMA men was ordered abroad, provoking some disorder, arson, etc., in Quebec province.

3 William Lyon Mackenzie King, Liberal Prime Minister of Canada, 1935–48, and Secretary of State for External Affairs, 1935–46.

causes. In the first place increasing consciousness of its vastly expanding material power makes this country acutely aware of the absence of a correspondingly effective diplomatic technique. Hence the welcome given to the renovation of State Department, and with it, a desire for a brand new 100 per cent American foreign policy, not tied to Britain's apron strings. Any assertion of an independent, emphatically American line, is therefore exceptionally well received here. There is furthermore no doubt that in this country, which whatever its practices, thinks of itself as deeply libertarian, antipathy to our support of what are regarded as right-wing forces in Europe against the left is widespread although inhibited to some degree by fear of Communism. Hostile comment divides itself into outright condemnation of what is viewed as our repressive policies in Italy, Greece and to a lesser extent Belgium, and the more isolationist view that since the United States itself is evidently not prepared to assume large military responsibility in for instance Greece, it is scarcely in a position to abuse the British too much. However unfortunate British policies may in fact look and be, there is some recognition throughout all this of the inadequacy of a pure 'hands off' policy which smacks of isolationist escapism. In view of unanimous condemnation of British policy by all American correspondents from Mediterranean, it would be surprising indeed if the general press here adopted a more sympathetic tone. The atmosphere resembles nothing so much as the outburst which greeted the Prime Minister's so-called 'friendly words to Spain'[1] in May, recollection of which indeed affects thinking now, and it is quite clear that attention of public is concentrated not so much on e.g. Greek affairs as such, as on the attitude of Britain towards Greece, since it is reflections on political intentions of the British which mainly perturb and irritate American minds. This applies to a certain degree even to the case of Italy, although with the large Italian minority, Italian affairs loom large enough here in their own right. We are naturally blamed more heavily for support of right wing than of left, because that already is suspected to be our traditional political trend, and critics of Britain find a readier response to this view of us than to any other charge they may attempt to bring. It is probable for example that if we had been represented as supporting the liberal against the reactionary cause in Europe, volume of criticism would have been considerably smaller, if only because liberals are so much more articulate, and we should find bulk of press and radio on our side and should be attacked mainly by Russophobes (as in fact occurred in the case of Tito), who hate us and the Administration equally. It is only too easy for American public to think of British foreign policy as being inspired by principles of Metternich, and the verdict of many American diplomats and journalists here and in Europe on recent events lends credence to the view.

As for State Department, it is torn by a variety of influences. It still suffers from nightmare through which it passed during Darlan period, when it was

1 See summary of 4 June.

scapegoat of the nation. If therefore it can support anti-Fascist and liberal causes in public without detriment to America's immediate interests, it does so with an eagerness which shows that this is the part in which it best loves to see itself. It must be remembered that despite peculiar vagaries of their own foreign policy, Americans think of themselves as inflexibly dedicated to principles of liberty and equality everywhere, and Stettinius's first statement to that extent was drafted by persons in a state of genuine indignation and obviously sincere in their belief that this was proper attitude for a democratic and freedom-loving nation to adopt in its day of rising power. The reception of the Stettinius statement[2] by press and public showed that it did indeed strike a responsive chord in most American hearts. At same time there is a genuine fear in State Department lest storms arise to upset smooth passage of negotiations begun at Dumbarton Oaks, and from this springs a conflict between fear of upsetting the smaller nations and desire to keep relations with Britain and Russia on an even keel. When Stettinius and his subordinates perceived amount of dust which statement had raised, they attempted to back water, at least to extent indicated in Stettinius's second statement (on 7 December), in which he voiced agreement with Prime Minister's words on the Greeks' freedom of choice of their Government. Beyond this Stettinius felt he could not go, if only because of force of public (and congressional) sentiment with which in principle feeling of Department is in agreement. All this emerged in general backing given to matter (in spite of some criticism of manner) of his statement by almost entire press as well as such figures as Senators Connally, Ellender, etc. The most that our usual friends such as Swing and Heatter can say in public is that they well understand feeling of resentful protest which Stettinius's disavowal of British policy has caused in even liberal British press. In private they say that if the British can reach the point of shooting down men who had fought Nazis for three years, on whatever ground, how can there be any room for criticizing Stalin for similar behaviour? . . .

. . . While this immediate flurry may, if Greek situation dies down, duly evaporate, deeper currents which it has set in motion will continue to flow. Suspicion of British despotism in Europe is now thoroughly awakened, and such statements as Frederick Kuh's direct attack on complicity of British Ambassador in Athens are likely to be received with far more credence than before, and in general it may be expected that out of these events the isolationist elements will draw fuel. . . .

10 December 1944 (Savingram)

The State Department changes do not indicate any basic alteration in the policy or general characteristics of the Department but are designed to increase its effectiveness in working along existing lines by much the same methods as in the

2 Issued on 5 December, expecting 'the Italians to work out their problems of government along democratic lines without influence from outside'. . . . 'This would apply even more to governments in liberated territories.'

past, and is attacked so strongly by the left-wing press precisely for that reason ('The State Department is now a millionaires' club'). . . . The departures of Messrs Berle, Long and Howland Shaw seem to have gone singularly unlamented, both within and without the Department ; the two latter pulled little weight in any case, and Shaw, the most amiable of the three, is now to devote his increased leisure to full-time attention to the problems of juvenile delinquency which have long absorbed his interest. The position of Acheson (charged with international conferences and relations with Congress) becomes somewhat ambiguous *vis-à-vis* his more specialist colleagues, but particularly to Clayton, if Acheson is in any sense to continue to manage economic issues ; he himself appears somewhat uncertain as to what his exact new functions are to be. . . . The now far more needed close liaison with the White House is to be improved by the appointment of a special official to do this, so that the control which the President (and Hopkins) evidently intend to exercise over details of foreign policy can become systematized. Indeed, one of the reasons for the choice of the reliable Grew seems to have been the fact that ever since they were class-mates at Harvard personal relations between him and the President have always remained direct and warm. Informed sources maintain that Hayes [1] is definitely to leave Spain and Armour is to replace him ; if this occurs, and Crowley loses FEA, this, with the resignation of Shaw from the State Department, would sensibly diminish the number of Roman Catholics in positions of importance : Berle's departure (he is a Congregationalist who flirts with the Church of Rome) and McDermott's [2] widely expected (though not necessarily early) replacement would seem to increase this trend. Wilder Foote, [3] now in FEA, who ghosted Stettinius's book on Lend-Lease, is to be appointed as an aide to the latter, mainly to draft his speeches and statements.

11 December 1944

Biddle-Littell row. The dismissal of Assistant Attorney General Littell [1] by the President for insubordination, although in itself not an important event, has been interpreted by the liberal press as a defeat for the forces of light and a victory for Big Business of which Littell was a loud-voiced and implacable (and somewhat self-advertising) foe, and for cartels, and caused by Biddle's allegedly continued flirtation with the discredited Tommy Corcoran, now a lawyer lobbyist for business concerns. The emergence of Senators Kilgore, Murray, etc., as defenders of Littell is a symptom of the gathering conflict over the general issue, which is loosely connected with 'international cartels' and which is likely to arise at every

1 Carlton J.H.Hayes, historian, professor at Columbia University, Ambassador to Spain 1942–5.

2 Michael J.McDermott, career diplomat, Chief of the Division of Current Information, State Department, 1927–53.

3 Wilder Foote, assistant to Secretary of State. Vermont newspaper editor and publisher 1931–41, information officer in OEM (Office of Emergency Management) and OWI in charge of Lend-Lease information 1941–4.

1 Norman M.Littell, Assistant Attorney General, Lands Division, 1939–44.

level, administrative and legislative alike. Littell's attempt to demonstrate, at the expected congressional investigation, that Biddle is a dishonest intriguer is unlikely to succeed in the face of Biddle's obvious integrity.

17 December 1944

OPEN SEASON AGAINST BRITISH FOREIGN POLICY

Public feeling on this topic still runs high and is suspicious and disturbed. The Sforza episode has naturally receded before grimmer situation in Greece.[1] It is being asked whether there is an underlying divergence of political views and methods in treatment of post-war Europe between British and American Governments. Anglophobes in Congress, Fish, Day, Gavin,[2] Senators Brooks and Gillette have judged this the right moment for airing their views on British *Machtpolitik* against embarrassed but feeble protests of their more responsible colleagues. In official circles (as opposed to general public) there is growing as part of genuine uneasiness about Greek situation (together with some apprehension about whether and when Soviet Union may choose to intervene) an anxiety to compose our differences and to find some formula which would indicate continuation of a united Anglo-American political front without entailing loss of face or anything which might be interpreted as a retraction on part of State Department. Published British and United States statements on Italian Cabinet are fruit of this concern. Prime Minister's displeasure at apparent lack of solidarity coming as it does after his own unswerving support of position of United States Government in face of public clamour during Darlan and other crises, is appreciated by State Department but nowhere else. And even among responsible persons in the Department, this concern mingles with a feeling that these particular political difficulties of United States Government over Italian and Greek questions are not adequately appreciated on our side.

Our strongest press allies have been Hearst papers which acclaim Mr Churchill as long-wanted champion of humanity against the advance of the Red menace. There is also some support of our position as such (e.g. in *New York Times*) and our friends plead our glorious record of past achievement and Mr Churchill's part in them in extenuation. Too often defence of us takes form merely of questions as to why USSR, which has been guilty of harsher intervention in affairs of other nations, should escape such criticisms while Britain is treated to so full a measure of rebuke by United States Government and press and as a corollary whether American people wish to see Soviet or Communist domination of great

1 Conflict in Greece between rival resistance groups developed throughout 1944, with the USSR backing EAM, Communist-led National Liberation Front, and Britain backing the royalist government-in-exile in London and its local supporters. British troops arrived in Greece in October and George Papandreou, the royalist Prime Minister, was installed in Athens. But on 2 December EAM, through its military wing, ELAS, launched an uprising which threatened a Communist take-over. To prevent this, British forces were strengthened and were able to secure the regions around Athens and Salonika.

2 Leon H. Gavin, Republican Congressman from Pennsylvania since 1943.

parts of Europe. But what probably inhibits fuller support of even those who are worried by such considerations is a very general conviction that British Government (and more particularly the Prime Minister) is firmly resolved to effect restoration of King George of Greece as well as of other southern European monarchs which is repugnant to traditional sentiment of all shades of American opinion from most conservative to most radical. Resentment at idea of restoration of an allegedly unpopular monarch is a far stronger factor here than sympathies with EAM which are confined to liberal circles. Sforza's stories about Prime Minister's alleged insistence in conversation with him upon House of Savoy have therefore fallen upon fertile soil, as have steady stream of newspaper stories from London and from Mediterranean tending to paint a picture of reactionary clique of persons who had supported Fascist dictatorship of Metaxas[3] being foisted with violence upon necks of bitterly struggling Greeks by ruthless orders from Whitehall.

The belief that United States Administration deplores British action in Greece has naturally been heightened by publication by Drew Pearson in his column of what is probably an official paraphrase of Kirk's[4] telegram containing version of Prime Minister's message[5] to General Scobie[6] together with his comment that this document had been seen by a very few high United States officials who were disagreeably affected by its tone. Moreover reports of Labour Party's debate on this topic and of tone of British press have given impression that British opinion is divided and embarrassed (much as American opinion had been over Darlan) and this makes intelligible a general atmosphere in which, with so much opposition to us from so many quarters, such questions as those asked by Senators Kilgore and Murray (normally friendly enough to us) as to whether Lend-Lease was intended to supply one Ally with weapons to be used against another, have further fanned flames of moral indignation.

The close connexion established between events in Greece and propriety of continuing Lend-Lease to Britain (when her 'power play' is so generally viewed as directed against spirit of Dumbarton Oaks Agreement at least as much as attitude of Russians) has been increased by e.g. advertisement calling for investigation of Lend-Lease published by the largest fraternal Greek-American Association as well as by general suspicions cast upon result of Keynes conversations by such columnists as Krock, Pearson and spokesmen of NAM. Early liquidation of fighting in Greece would of course greatly ease situation and Senate, which at present seems thoroughly stirred up, may be in a better temper when Lend-Lease comes up next Spring. Moreover conversations between three Great Powers may do much to heal breach and American public opinion is notoriously mercurial.

. . .

---

3 General Ioannis Metaxas, dictator ('Prime Minister') of Greece 1936–41.
4 Alexander C. Kirk, Foreign Service officer since 1915, US Ambassador to Greece, June–November 1943.
5 'Do not . . . hesitate to act as if you were in a conquered city where a local rebellion is in progress. . . .'
6 General Sir Ronald Scobie, GOC British forces in Greece 1944–6.

SENATE AND STATE DEPARTMENT

Sforza's remark that although he had signed letter to Berle he had not written it,[7] did not please the State Department who thinks that this is meant to indicate that letter was written under their pressure (which may indeed be the case), nor are they too happy about leakage of Prime Minister's instructions to General Scobie quoted by Pearson in his column (see above) which he can only have obtained from sole sources in or close to four departments which had seen it. A witchhunt is on (a procedure which has proved singularly fruitless in the past) : Swing, fair as ever, while deploring our policy, said that the breach of confidence which made this leakage possible is considerably greater than any committed by His Majesty's Government in failing to consult United States authorities concerning Sforza and that it made diplomatic negotiations impossibly difficult. Such criticism of one broadcaster by another is rare indeed. In the meanwhile Stettinius duly shepherded his new assistant secretaries before Foreign Relations Committee where expected 'Field Day' was sharply cut short by Connally (who seems to have felt personally insulted by Senate's action in throwing back nominations which his Committee had approved). Main target of attack was, as reported to you, Clayton, and it seems clear that against him such charges as excessive trading with Germans and Japanese after moral embargo and other anti-capitalist charges such as have been bruited for some time by *PM* and Pearson will duly be advanced both in Committee and in the Senate itself. As for the rest, Brigadier-General Julius Holmes[8] was whisked off on a waiting airplane back to European Military Headquarters where he was said to be urgently required after a brief interrogation in course of which he was asked what connexion he had had with Darlan agreement. He said 'I drafted it and signed it with Robert Murphy' and told reporters outside that he was sorry that he was not questioned more extensively about a performance of which he felt proud. Rockefeller got off almost unquestioned. As expected Mr Grew was challenged on his views on Hirohito. His prepared statement seems to have satisfied all save *PM* and Pearson. MacLeish had a facetious autobiography quoted at him by Champ Clark, did well against him and spoke of his brother's death in last war with a solemnity which seemed to shame Senators into embarrassed silence. Dunn was asked by Johnson of California 'Where is the Atlantic Charter?', and indicated that it was right there and being adhered to. Senators Guffey and Murray tried to obtain his views about 'Mr Churchill's behaviour in Greece', but Connally ruled this as out of order and asked whether United States Senate would care to have questions about Stettinius asked before a British Parliamentary Committee. Stettinius himself delivered a short address in course of which he declared that a new and liberal policy was to be pursued by his Department. This should on no account

---

7 Letter was dated 23 September 1943. It pledged support for Badoglio, as 'the only way to destroy the last criminal remnants of fascism' was to 'adjourn internal Italian politics for the period after the struggle. . . . I pledge my honour to do this myself.'

8 Julius C. Holmes, President of General Mills Co., Brigadier-General 1943.

be treated as a mere pious platitude, since there is other evidence to show that the White House (and State Department) fully realize the unpopularity of some of the 1941–3 foreign policies and propose to give the world an example of democracy on the march, powerful and above all independent, backed by American initiative and business efficiency in the field of international relations. It is to be 'liberal and forward looking . . . vigorous and progressive'. Dunn denied hotly that United States diplomacy necessarily followed that of Britain. All concerned mentioned Hull's name with veneration whenever in doubt as to what their own policy was supposed to be. Chandler who apparently had come armed with a variety of questions was muzzled by Connally and is said to have made a considerable fuss about this in the 'secret' executive session. Committee finally endorsed Grew 15 to 4, Clayton 11 to 7, Rockefeller 12 to 7, Dunn 13 to 5, Holmes 15 to 4, MacLeish 11 to 10. . . .

. . .

Franco-Russian Pact.[9] Press and radio are naturally very busy with this, and after conceding that it clearly increases prestige of France and more particularly of de Gaulle himself, and saying something of the need for taking maximum security measures against Germany, they sound gloomier note. A sprinkling of papers allows that new pact should be easily fitted into general Dumbarton Oaks framework, but bulk of press comment is more suspicious and uneasy.

. . .

18 December 1944

Palestine Resolution. The Wagner-Taft Palestine resolution[1] was blocked before the Senate Foreign Relations Committee by Stettinius who appeared in person to explain why it was impolitic to pass it at present, and was deferred until the next session by a vote of 12 to 8. The State Department have issued a statement saying that in view of the 'delicate international situation' involved, it would not be wise to pass this resolution now. I learn that this appears to follow on a letter received (and kept confidential) by Senator Wagner from the President whom he had consulted on the matter, in which Mr Roosevelt said that he had been told that rash action now might precipitate a massacre of Jews in Palestine. This very considerable setback has naturally much upset the Zionists who are trying to play upon the feelings of those Senators who dislike such executive interference. There is some newspaper talk of introducing the resolution into Congress without the approval of the Foreign Relations Committee. Connally, who dislikes the resolution anyhow, will certainly do his best to prevent this : he has privately conveyed that he will try to kill it altogether, but that it may be forced through in the next session against his will. The Zionists have no choice but to bow before this latest obstacle, and the more far-sighted heads among them are severely

9 Signed 17 December 1944.

1 Introduced in the Senate early in the year, advocating opening Palestine for 'free entry of Jews' so that they may ultimately reconstitute it 'as a free and democratic Jewish Commonwealth'.

critical of the political ineptitude of the hamfisted Dr Silver which stimulated precipitate action in Congress without previous clearance with the White House. It may, therefore, be expected that all the local powers of Zionist persuasion will now be turned from the Senate at the White House itself, particularly as there is an impression in Zionist circles here that the Prime Minister, despite the situation created by Lord Moyne's assassination,[2] would take action favourable to the Jews if urged to do so by the President.

Work or Fight Order. The drift of labour from the factories will doubtless be checked by Byrnes's latest order to Hershey to conscript men between the ages of twenty-six and thirty-seven, not engaged on other essential war work. This will doubtless create natural reluctance on the part of workers meditating abandonment of war plants for other occupations. General Somervell is similarly delivering vigorous speeches on the need for manpower and increased production. All this has contributed its meed to the general swing of opinion from expectation of an end of at any rate the European war this year, to the assumption that the war might well last for much longer than was anticipated (earlier optimistic prophecies are sardonically quoted). Hence the big boom in war securities (largest since 1940) on the stock exchange, and e.g. sniping in Congress at the British Empire failing to conscript 'colonial troops' in sufficient proportions.

Spain. The recall of Carlton Hayes and the appointment of Norman Armour as United States Ambassador to that country is connected in the press and in general Washington talk with the new aggressive 'liberal and forward-looking' foreign policy which Stettinius promised to inaugurate. The simultaneous withdrawal of Hayes and Lord Templewood[3], which is generally taken for granted here, is held to presage the imminent fall of Franco, who cannot be expected to last long without that Allied support which is now expected to be denied him. The British are expected to favour a constitutional monarchy, the Americans to continue with their 'traditional hands-off policy'. The unofficial mouthpiece of United States foreign policy, Lindley, in his syndicated column defends the record of Hayes (and less warmly of Templewood) against charges of 'appeasement' or excessive pro-Franco sentiment. In an article in the current issue of *Harper's* magazine, Lindley and a fellow journalist named Edward Weintal[4] have printed an account of Hayes's mission, which they described as based on official documents and conversations with responsible officials, which seeks to demonstrate that he had performed a difficult job with great adroitness, honesty and success, and quote letters by him to the late Count Jordana[5] giving his reasons for looking

2 Lord Moyne (Walter E. Guinness), British Resident Minister in the Middle East since January, was assassinated outside his home in Cairo on 6 November 1944 by two Palestine Jews, members of the Stern Gang.

3 Previously Sir Samuel Hoare, British Ambassador to Spain since 1940.

4 Who produced during war years, in collaboration with Sir Wilmot Lewis of *The Times* of London, a weekly Washington review, *Foreign Correspondence*.

5 Francisco G. Jordana, Spanish Foreign Minister 1938–39, 1942–4.

on the Spanish régime as Fascist in character, and otherwise demonstrating his innocence of the charges brought against him by the United States liberal press. If and when Franco falls, United States opinion may be expected to watch for divergencies between British and American policy under the impression that we are likely to plump for a more conservative régime than is likely to be desired by the American Government and public.

24 December 1944

THE WAR

Reaction to setback on Western Front[1] has not yet had time to develop. The first response is that of reproach of those leaders of opinion who had underestimated cost of war in the West and feeling that although European war may last very much longer than had been expected, victory is not in doubt, although it will entail far heavier losses than had been anticipated. On the other side is Stimson's statement that if Germans lose this gamble, results would much shorten the war. There is as yet no great volume of recrimination either internecine or inter-Allied, although here and there (*Washington Post*) view is heard that diversion of troops on any 'non-essential' front – e.g. in Greece – is inexcusable, and there is some muttering about Russian 'inactivity' on Polish front. Byrnes told a member of my staff that some answer ought to be provided to complaints here about the 'disproportion' of British and United States forces in France, and Montgomery's alleged 'passivity' of which there had been, he heard, talk among United States generals on Western Front.

Depression about European politics has, if anything, deepened this week. Indignation with Britain has given way to a kind of disgruntled and disenchanted cynicism which says that it was foolish ever to have supposed that the European, and particularly Russian and British, leopards, could really have been expected to change their spots as the result of a few idealistic words from America – that 'power politics', spheres of influence, etc., were evidently a constant element in the European scene, and that the sooner America realizes this, the better for all concerned. This naturally feeds the isolationist tendencies of the waverers and depresses our friends. Indeed the most melancholy aspect of situation is that this time the main burden of blame comes not from our traditional enemies but from our disillusioned friends. A senior member of my staff, who has recently come back from a tour of the Middle and Far West, reports that today our sharpest critics are those normally disposed to support us. Our opponents take up a somewhat sanctimonious 'I told you so' attitude confident that this time our friends will have no ready answer to give. Thus Senator Ball sadly observed that for the first time he felt inclined to agree with Wheeler. The Italian issue has receded from the foreground, the Greek situation is still most prominent, and the Polish factor has now erupted, making the confusion of the public mind very much worse confounded. We have, as a result of the Prime Minister's statement on

1 i.e. successful German offensive in Ardennes.

Poland, lost a degree of support (over Greece) from such Russophobes as Hearst, who own to a certain disappointment with the early promise which we had shown over Greece. Our principal supporters now consist of that small group of opinion, reflected in such 'centre' newspapers as the *New York Times, Baltimore Sun, New York Herald Tribune,* etc., which looks on Russian intentions with suspicion (though without alarm), still feels much natural sympathy with the general outlook of the British Government and proceeds on the assumption that although there may be much to criticize in our Mediterranean policies, we are too old and valued an ally and understanding with us is too important *vis-à-vis* the USSR to be damned so harshly over a situation so confused. But beyond this small group of soft-voiced moderates and supported by those friendly but troubled Washington officials who regret the public pandemonium in which Anglo-American relations, complicated as they must in the best of cases be, are being carried on, we seem to have little visible support in any camp. Opinion continues to be divided between those vociferous isolationists and liberals who blame us outright, those more responsible circles who qualify their blame by citing extenuating circumstances, and that appreciable and well meaning group which, while feeling that there is little to be said for our policies, salve their consciences by equally harsh words about the beam in their own eye, and condemn unhelpful criticism or supine attitude of United States Government, and demand that United States either develop a positive foreign policy of its own (which they obviously prefer) or admit its helplessness. This group tends to point to Stettinius's statements as so many pusillanimous platitudes. This attitude is best summarized in the *Louisville Courier Journal* leading article 'The British are Wrong – What are We ?''. This, although a line less specifically critical of us than the former two, in the long run breeds lack of confidence in our foreign policy no less effectively. Senator Ball's view as expressed to a member of my staff was that his twenty-five isolationist colleagues now have far more grist to their mill than they could ever have dreamt of getting.

Although your speeches and Prime Minister's during past fortnight have been reported in the press, the public is not in a mood to absorb their substance, since it is preoccupied, not with specific rights and wrongs of the Greeks (although prevailing assumption is that those who side with Balkan kings are self-condemned) as much as with allegedly cold and calculating realism with which Britain and Russia are pursuing their national policies in Europe. This is viewed as showing a general temper so deeply out of sympathy with the American attitude, which looks fervently to Atlantic Charter and Dumbarton Oaks, as the only proper basis for building the future – and as proving therefore so great a spiritual distance between Europe and America – that that intimate collaboration between the Great Powers in building a new heaven and a new earth, which some here perhaps unconsciously and unrealistically have been expecting, is now seen receding beyond the clouds. Veering as many persons in this country do between extremes of sentimental idealism and 'dynamic' materialism, they have been awakened from former of these states so harshly, that they are divided between a wistful hope that this may be but a temporary lapse on the part of the British Government which the British people themselves will presently bring to an end, and a relevant admission that it is they who had overestimated goodwill of Europeans, and that the world is a far colder, bleaker, harsher place than they had led themselves to believe and that a mental readjustment must be made accordingly.

Polish issue. Prime Minister's speech on Poland[2] produced mixed reactions : it threw the two groups, the Russophiles and the Russophobes, into a kind of schizophrenia – the Russophobes who were pleased by our line in Greece could not stomach the 'betrayal' of Poland, while those liberals who look on London Polish Government as a reactionary clique little better than Fascists, could not forget events in Athens. Hence much confused talk in the press, conceding the necessity for a solution of a critical problem, stating reasons for and against the specific plan advocated by the Prime Minister, wondering whether or not the United States had any obligation to interfere or at least to speak out and generally unable to make up its mind what to think or say. As majority of United States press is conservative, general effect is not friendly to us, especially as the only group which remains profoundly upset is that wide front of liberal groups, the 'Dumbarton Oaks public', to which Messrs Dulles and Shotwell[3] address themselves, the clergymen and schoolmasters and country editors and members of women's clubs, to whom events in Greece and British stand on Polish question seem equally to violate their most cherished liberal convictions. Reports of a similar confusion in the House of Commons with the parties largely divided into pro-Polish Conservatives and pro-EAM Labourites have further increased impression that policy of His Majesty's Government is not basically supported by the British people or parliament, although the Prime Minister can obtain a vote of confidence by threatening to resign. Total picture is somewhat sombre therefore with reluctant admission but little understanding of our difficulties – less understanding of our purposes – and pronounced lack of sympathy with them even when they are more or less clearly comprehended. Sanest voice is still that of Lippmann, who urges his countrymen to understand that liberated Europe cannot be expected to put all its problems into cold storage and wait patiently for the overall final solution which will emerge from a series of international discussions – that such problems as those of e.g. security against Germany, or organization of formerly Nazi-occupied territories, are urgent and cry for, at any rate, an immediate beginning to the solutions ; that Europe is bound to arrive at a series

2 To the House of Commons on 15 December. Laying out the 'grim, bare bones' of the Polish question, Churchill reported British acquiescence in the Russian proposals for post-war frontiers – Russia to advance to the Curzon Line (so-called because drawn by the Western Allies after the First World War when Lord Curzon was British Foreign Secretary) and Poland to be compensated by the cession of about half of Eastern Prussia.

3 James T. Shotwell, Columbia Professor of History 1908–42, early advocate of League of Nations, Director of Carnegie Endowment for International Peace 1924–65.

of regional understandings to solve its own political and security problems which can later be fitted into a more universal structure – and that attacks upon such natural and healthy tendencies are to be eschewed. But his is a voice crying in a wide political wilderness. It should be added that Mr Stettinius's statement on Poland,[4] acclaimed by Polish Ambassador, has failed to give satisfaction to the press or public which sees it as cautious to the point of caricature. Lindley, as ever the voice of Administration, interprets it as advice to Polish Government to be reasonable and seek an arrangement with the USSR since nobody can help it if it doesn't – he defends frontier of Curzon Line ; if the Poles are wise, they will see that it is this that is in the minds of the United States Government despite their evasive formulation. Simms is unable to make up his mind whether betrayal of Poland – and of little nations generally – is or is not a worse thing than outbreaks of Communism in liberated countries.

. . .

Summing up. I have thought it right to give you a full account of the unfavourable reactions in what has been a difficult week. But in this country where criticism is usually shouted at the top of the voice it is often hard to tell when the surface is disturbed whether the waters are deeply moved. It does not follow from what is said above that the American people are about to swing sharply into isolationism or to sustained opposition to British policy. We have had the Polish question, which was likely to be the most difficult one, brought to a head while the debate over Greece and Italy was still going on. As the United States move out into world affairs we may expect many ups and downs of this kind and severe bouts of growing pains. It is noteworthy that following Prime Minister's speech on Poland, attention has to some extent shifted from discussion of British policy to heart-searching about American policy or the lack of it. I do not (repeat not) personally take as depressed a view as some observers of the latest trends here. The German counterattack is already having a sobering and healthy effect, and if American opinion has to adjust itself this does not necessary mean that the main currents of politics will change. Senator Connally a few nights ago spoke to me very confidently of his expectation to be able to get two-thirds of the Senate to support the Dumbarton Oaks plan, when it came before it, and that without imposing on the United States representative the necessity of reference back to Congress before voting for action.

The Senate and the Administration. The so-called 'filibuster' of three New Deal Senators with La Follette and Chandler to block the presidential nominations to Assistant Secretaryships of State finally collapsed after the President had made it clear that he would not alter his nominations and would make interim appointments for as long as was necessary until the Senate confirmed his nominees. In

4 On 18 December. Affirmed United States unequivocal support for Polish independence but refused to give territorial guarantees. The statement appeared to oppose the imposition of any settlement, but equally to withhold from Poland any hope of active support for its stand in the boundary controversy.

the final count, Grew was confirmed (66:7), Rockefeller (62:10), Clayton (52:19), Dunn (62:10), Holmes (61:9), MacLeish (43:23) (opposition in his case being entirely Republican). Despite a great deal of impatience in the press with this 'childish' exhibition, it has had a certain effect. The liberal Senators, particularly those associated with Wallace and the PAC, were clearly anxious to demonstrate that they regarded the President's appointments as over-weighted with conservative and 'Wall Street' influences, and as the party which had so notably swung the scale in the elections, they were determined to put the President on notice that such 'appeasement' of the 'right wing' – which they interpreted as an effort on his part to demonstrate his independence of Hillman and the radicals – would not be suffered by them in silence, and that they still possess considerable public power behind them. Pepper and his friends are said to be talking of continuing as a political group, a kind of liberal 'watch committee' authorized to meet and advise the President and Stettinius of the view taken by the liberals of the foreign and domestic policies of the Administration. The President is said to have tactfully agreed to this. He is reported as having assured Pepper (who appears to have acted disinterestedly inasmuch as neither the electors of Florida nor White House can have been pleased by this exhibition) that he would promptly get rid of any official in the Department who failed to execute his, the President's, wishes in the spirit and not merely in the letter. The total effect of this demonstration (which seems to have reduced Connally to a white heat of fury) is that a certain circumspection is likely to be exercised by the new Assistant Secretaries in the discharge of their duties, since they are painfully aware that they are being watched with narrowed eyes by the suspicious Senators. In the course of cross-examination, Grew denied particular sympathies for Hirohito, Dunn denied predilections for General Franco's régime. Holmes, after a moment of hesitation, said that his sentiments towards Russia were friendly. Clayton once more denounced cartels. MacLeish reasserted his strong sympathies for the Spanish loyalists, and Rockefeller in effect said nothing. But beyond the question of confirmations which were used as a peg for it, the Senate debate served to ventilate a great deal of angry feeling about the international scene. Vandenberg characteristically wondered how much of international agreement there could be in view of the European turmoil. Chandler said that he had realized what sinister use the British would make of Lend-Lease goods when on his famous world tour. Shipstead and Brooks made bitterly isolationist onslaughts on us, the aged and feeble Johnson (of California), propped up by his colleagues, made an almost inaudible speech saying that the Greeks should not be 'shot down like dogs' for wanting governments of their own choosing (and in this was obliquely supported in milder terms by Senator George speaking in his native Georgian). Finally the defeated Nye, addressing the Senate for perhaps the last time, predicted the third war (against the USSR) in fifteen or twenty years' time and solemnly entreated the Senate to resist British propaganda and keep America out of this disaster now so clearly made inevitable by the march of events in

Europe. Nothing was said to spoil this isolationist holiday, which brought back the spirit of 1939 so vividly. And many words were spoken regretting the passing of the Atlantic Charter, unhonoured and unsung, nor did the President's press conference, in the course of which he appears to have asserted that the Atlantic Charter does not exist as a formal document but on the other hand had been signed and might turn up (the State Department Bulletin of August 1941 printed it as a signed document – the press seems unaware of this) one day, improve the situation. His light touch, so often a method of getting out of a tight corner, sometimes seems to put too great a strain upon the earnestness of his own followers. Mr Roosevelt, who is said to be looking singularly well after his stay in Georgia, broadly hinted that lack of arrangements for a meeting with Messrs Churchill and Stalin lay outside his control. He was asked whether Mr Bevin had spoken truly when he said British policy in Greece had been approved at Quebec. He said that this had surely already been denied by the State Department, although the form of the denial had been polite, but the question was 'contentious', a new term which, he said, he had but recently picked up but proposed to use often. The *Washington Star*, he was told, headlined 'United States backs Poland on frontiers', whereas the *Washington Times Herald* printed 'FDR backs British Reds on Polish plan'. Which was true ? The President ducked this by saying that the *Star* was at least a newspaper which 'the other' – 'he could not call it newspaper' – was not – it was all very speculative. Was he moving to the right or to the left ? He was still 'a little left of centre'. That question had surely been answered eleven-and-a-half-years ago for good and all. Were the six State Department appointments to be regarded 'a little left of centre' ? All opinions were represented in the Administration, said the President, extreme right and extreme left. 'Do you find them all for you ?' 'It is surprising how many are.' Not a serious word was spoken during the entire press conference.

31 December 1944

The military-political situation. The reverses on Western Front have had a profoundly sobering effect on American public opinion. It had more and more tended to think that while the United States was engaged in fighting Germans and Japanese, its major Allies seized the occasion for somewhat disreputable political skirmishing on the side, leaving it to the simple and unsuspecting Americans to win the war (which they had indeed already as good as done). Coming when it did, Rundstedt's [1] breakthrough did much to dam or divert the flood of gloomy talk about the intolerable political mess in Greece and other parts of Europe, and had a steadying effect in forcing the average American to hesitate, if only for a moment, about the invincible might of his country, to reflect upon

1 Field-Marshal Karl R.G.von Rundstedt (1875–1953), German Supreme Commander in Western Europe 1943–4.

the still formidable dangers threatening him from east and west, and consequently upon the necessity for firmer understanding with, at any rate, his major Allies. Prime Minister's and your own flight to Athens was, generally, well received as striking evidence of 'gallantry', political imagination and a 'flexibility' which did a good deal to dissipate impression of Prime Minister – a compound of Lords Chatham and North – as a crusted and unbending eighteenth-century Tory which had undoubtedly been gaining ground during recent weeks. Journey itself is inevitably interpreted in a good many quarters as an admission that a mistake had been made in Greece, that the strength and popular support of ELAS had been underestimated by British political intelligence and that the wrong horse had consequently been backed by us. This view is one frequently heard in Washington and in liberal circles. But those who take it give the Prime Minister and yourself credit for a courageous willingness to adapt or modify policy.

As for conservatives they have raised a great lament, loudest in formerly isolationist circles, about the untimely demise of the Atlantic Charter, so cynically interred by Messrs Churchill and Stalin with scarcely a tear from Roosevelt or Stettinius. President's reference to it as embodying general ideals rather than specific precepts, and in this respect resembling the Ten Commandments (or Mr Wilson's Fourteen Points) has naturally not (repeat not) been too well received by his fundamentally earnest fellow citizens. But this has had its own favourable effects. For while what is regarded as the official British attitude to European settlement is still critically treated, several welcome signs are at hand of broadening of America's attitude to criticism of the Allies of the United States to one of including herself in the criticism. Thus the State Department's utterances on Italian and Greek situations, to which all enquirers are still being referred as the last word of American foreign policy, are assailed for their negativeness, unrealism and unnecessarily 'holier than thou' tone, and criticisms in the British press of America's unhelpful and irritating tendency to preach virtue to Europe, while engaged in dubious practices of her own, in, say, Latin America, have not passed unnoticed here, being received without apparently any noticeably disagreeable reactions. All of this, indeed, may have done good.

Criticisms of United States foreign policy. Sumner Welles continues his (now practically non-stop) attack on State Department's policies by chiding it for uttering basically sound sentiments concerning Greek crisis at a moment when such language could only do maximum possible harm, and says that if his expedient of a continuing United Nations Council for settling such disputes had originally been adopted, this debacle might have been averted. Lippmann, on the next day, agreed that State Department's attitude would not do, but pointed out that postponing political problems, an attitude so fatally adopted by United States Administration, is precisely what is responsible for the mess, since political arrangements in liberated countries cannot be expected to wait *in vacuo,* and to put them into cold storage is merely to invite unwelcome developments in the more immediate future. Lippmann, and also Swing, Harsch,[2] and a group of other influential commentators, attribute the military setback not so much to bad military intelligence on part of United States Command, as to faulty interpretation of it by its strategists, and Swing and others speak of a sad lack of imagination on part of high United States military authority. The fact that British generals can scarcely be blamed for latest developments (very few, including Pearson, imply that fault is partly ours), has inhibited what might otherwise have caused streams of vituperation in the irresponsible press. There has so far been no great cry for heads to roll. Stimson was provoked by some very tart remarks of the eighty-year-old Peyton March,[3] Pershing's Chief-of-Staff, into a warning about too much premature mud-slinging, and relief of Bastogne[4] has done much to diminish suspense of the public. Nevertheless, as a sharp blow to the rosy complacency and nebulous idealism which followed the presidential election, the military setback has undoubtedly proved a salutary if rough incursion of reality.

Public anxiety. There appears to be almost universal agreement that a meeting of the heads of the three major Allies is urgently called for. Your own and the Prime Minister's eagerness to do this is well known, and newspapers speculate about possibility of a meeting in February at a place within easy range of communication with Moscow, followed by a conference of United Nations' Foreign Ministers in March on American soil. Both Stettinius and President have evaded all queries of the press on this. So far as public opinion is concerned, its state is not unlike that before and during the first Quebec Conference in 1943, when absence of Russia led to considerable nervousness and demands for clarification of political situation. Now too there is a powerful and instinctive demand for something – evidence of real co-operation and agreement between the Great Powers – to satisfy the public that there is a plan, both rational and just, behind the seeming injustice and play of naked force which the liberals perceive in Greece, the conservatives and Catholics in Poland, and the 'Dumbarton Oaks' public in both. If the Greek crisis is settled reasonably soon (and announcement of the Regency and further assurances by the King that he will not seek to return unless on a clear popular demand can be counted on to do much good with the United States whose jaundiced eye had been fixed upon the highly unpopular symbol constituted by the King of the Hellenes) and a meeting of the big three is promised soon, much of the odium under which we still labour at present may lift in the relief which this would afford. In many quarters, official and other, the hope is expressed that the forthcoming meeting may formally approve your suggestion of regular meetings of foreign secretaries.

2 Joseph C.Harsch, *Christian Science Monitor* correspondent 1929–43, and CBS news commentator since 1943.

3 Peyton Conway March, US Army Chief-of-Staff in 1918, when Pershing was Commander-in-Chief.

4 Important road centre in the Ardennes region of Belgium, scene of an epic stand in the Battle of the Bulge by the 101st US Airborne Division, December 1944.

Supplies for Europe. The economic aspects of European unrest, which are not at all well understood here (together with the problem of shipping allocation and closely related ancient Pacific *v*. Atlantic issue) have so far been given clear, and from our point of view, satisfactory, public expression only by columnist Marquis Childs (writing apropos of visit of Minister of State).[5] Childs, who is to go to England and France shortly, has done his best to illuminate supply issues involved and the indissolubility of political from military aspects of effects of supplies or lack of them in Europe. Lindley gives a vague outline of what must be official reservations about our case, but in general the issue is not to the fore publicly. Yet American military losses have created a mood, although it may of course only be momentary, in which United States public opinion as well as officials may actually be ready to learn something of these disturbing facts if fed with adequate information. Here too, Lippmann, who feels very disgruntled about United States political policies, particularly *vis-à-vis* France, and has a grasp of European realities, may help. I am told that he is particularly pleased about his talks in London with the Minister of Information, whom he singled out for praise upon his return, in contrast with other eminent persons, who, he implied, had not been equally accessible to him.

Summing up. In general therefore it may be said that temporary concentration of criticism on our foreign policies is largely giving way to meditation on other troubles, and in particular on American foreign policy and on the military situation. It is increasingly evident that the criticism arose from a linking together of a series of happenings over a considerable period, among them Field Marshal Smuts's speech last year, the Prime Minister's statements some time ago about Franco, and suspicion that we were trying to reimpose the King on a reluctant Greece, support the House of Savoy in a reluctant Italy, and back reactionaries in Belgium. To such special factors is always to be added the instinctive feeling of the average American that he is unfamiliar with European problems, and that for some reason which he cannot precisely analyse, but with which he is vaguely annoyed and for which he is always ready to find a whipping-boy, his own large words and principles do not seem on all occasions to fit, but now that criticism of us has partly turned into self-criticism and the situation is once more fluid, anything we may do or say will have a maximum effect. Public opinion is in a mood of disappointment and uneasy questioning, but is also looking for reassurance and a clear voice to guide them.

5 Richard Law.

1945

Congress v. Executive. In Congress two movements appear to be on foot : (a) by Senator Pepper and his friends (as reported last week) to create a kind of left-wing 'ginger group' to keep the President up to the mark in both foreign and domestic policy. This appears to be gaining genuine ground among the liberals (who under chairman Thomas of Utah and Murray of Montana are to control the Military Affairs and Labor and Education Committees), although Mr Wallace's relation to it and indeed his general future remain obscure. After his last interview with the President, he emerged smiling and inscrutable, and said that they had much talk about reafforestation in Persia. Evidently the ousting of Jesse Jones from the Department of Commerce and his replacement by Mr Wallace is not proving easy. (b) The move started by Senators Hatch and Ball to rally support for the continuation of the Dumbarton Oaks policy, a move which they seem to feel has been made necessary by the low morale at present prevailing among the internationalists. There is much speculation about who will succeed to the five vacant posts in the Foreign Relations Committee, all abandoned by ex-isolationists. The Republicans seem bound to put in Styles Bridges (New Hampshire), once a supporter, now a critic, of the Administration's foreign policy, and possibly Chan Gurney (South Dakota), an amiable government supporter. Curiously enough Taft, who could be in the running, does not appear anxious to enter this committee, unlike Wheeler, who is making desperate efforts to do so. Fulbright seems pessimistic about his claims in view of his very junior status. Hatch is more hopeful.

. . .

Rapprochement with the USSR. A series of four long articles in the *New York Herald Tribune* expounding the need for closer commercial and cultural as well as political relations with Soviet Russia, of which three have appeared, are a straw in the wind of United States-Soviet relations. Stimulated by the pro-Soviet Foreign Editor of that journal, Joseph Barnes, the intimate of Wallace and of the late Wendell Willkie whom he accompanied to Russia, the first article by Barnes himself mainly complains that too little is known here about the Soviet Union and advocates a semi-official United States central institution for the spreading of relevant knowledge.

The War. The none-too-detailed news from the Western Front has induced a pensive mood in which the most noticeable strain is that this is no time for inter-

Allied squabbles and that there is far too much preventable misunderstanding occurring which an Anglo-American meeting at the highest level could surely do much to clear up. There is no doubt that while a misinterpretation of and opposition to our policy continues in many quarters, there is great and increasing anxiety for something which will clear the air and re-establish broken harmony. Most of the more responsible journalists are saying this privately, and number either say it in their articles or at the very least refrain from their previous public criticisms. Among these are Marquis Childs (who is shortly to visit Britain, France and Italy), Joe Harsch of the *Christian Science Monitor,* Swing, and the editorial writers of the *New York Times, Herald Tribune, Des Moines Register* and *Baltimore Sun.* . . . Lippmann points out most forcibly and clearly that the 'self-determination' article of the Atlantic Charter of which so much unfair play has been made was not, and cannot be, meant to apply to the interim governments of liberated countries whose duty it is to create conditions for free elections, and blames the American policy of procrastination for allowing situations to develop in which, in the absence of an agreed policy, political chaos inevitably develops. This is echoed by the *Washington Post* and liberal commentators. He ends it with a characteristic recommendation that the great specialist whose advice on this should be sought is de Gaulle. The demand for a more positive United States foreign policy is very persistent and intense. General adhesion to Dumbarton Oaks is felt to be insufficient.

British foreign policy. Although it cannot be said that either public or official opinion fully understands the reasons for, or whole-heartedly approves, British policy in the Mediterranean, the Prime Minister's and your journey[1] has had a beneficial effect. The continuation of fighting by ELAS, despite the appointment of Damaskinos[2] by the King of Greece (almost universally welcomed here), has given a jolt to the views of those who automatically identified ELAS with the light and Messrs Leeper[3] and Scobie with the forces of darkness. There is gradual realization that the situation is much more complex than had been imagined. Even the greatest of all the trouble-breeders, Drew Pearson, in his Sunday column begged readers to distinguish between the good democratic British people and the 'outgrown imperialism' of the Prime Minister, and went on to recite the sacrifices made by the British people in the course of the war, demonstrated by the British White Paper[4] : this, as compared with the easier life of the American people. The mood here is not exactly one of contrition, but certainly one in which any convincing explanation of our general position, political, military and economic, *vis-à-vis* both Europe and the United States, would probably be given a more receptive hearing than during any period since the publication of the White Paper. The State Department and the White House have scrupulously

1 To Athens, 24–28 December, to strengthen anti-ELAS forces and arrange a cease-fire.
2 Damaskinos, Archbishop of Athens, resistance leader, appointed Greek Regent December 1944.
3 Reginald W.A.Leeper, British Ambassador to Greece 1943–64.
4 See above, pp. 466–7.

refrained from pouring oil into the flames, and indeed have done their positive best to allay the storm. In these quarters, the visit of the Minister of State [R.K.Law] has undoubtedly contributed much to the decrease of ill-feeling. The President's message to Congress just delivered may be expected to do much to steady opinion.

The 'Economist' article. [5] Excerpts from the *Economist* article and the relevant comments of *The Times, Yorkshire Post*, etc., have of course been widely reproduced here. The effect has been strong and extensive. The great outburst of British criticism has obviously caught Americans unaware, and the reaction is filled with surprise. Views are divided between those who look on the *Economist* as a liberal, serious, fairminded and, on the whole, pro-American publication (as if the *New York Times* or the *Christian Science Monitor* suddenly burst out with a catalogue of British misdemeanours) and therefore express genuine astonishment at such violence of feeling from so respectable a quarter, and those who (like Simms and others) take it, in conjunction with *The Times*, as the voice of His Majesty's Government and particularly stress the connexion with the *Economist* of the Minister of Information or that of yourself with the *Yorkshire Post*. [6] Whichever interpretation is adopted the general reaction is that although the British attack was not unprovoked and the British cannot have been expected to take the flood of criticism poured by the United States press and radio lying down, yet the British are surely much too touchy and the tone of their retort is much too harsh. Some say (and the majority probably feel) that this is mainly due to the frayed nerves of the British and the fact that they feel for the first time politically and economically weak and inferior to the United States, a bitter pill which the British still cannot bring themselves to swallow. A country which feels itself as strong and secure as Britain did in the past would surely not be displaying such bitter irritation at United States criticism, however ill-founded and intolerable. On the other hand the combination of vague adherence and general virtue, of moralizing and nagging, with absence of American readiness to offer concrete political assistance in Europe, is conceded to be a sorry attitude for a great nation to display. Added to this, there is a general confused bewilderment of the uninformed who feel genuinely surprised by the fierce tone of the onslaught upon them coming from a people whom they quite naturally, even if

5 The *Economist* editorial appeared on 30 December 1944, in response to what it called 'one of the most violent and sustained' outbursts of criticism of the war years, with 'ammunition' provided by 'the American Government itself – or at least some part of it'. Complaining of 'lofty moral generalities', 'noble negatives' and 'hypocrisy', it asked whether the price paid for collaboration with the USA was not 'too high for what we are likely to get'. It concluded that 'a genuine American collaboration' should still be sought but that an end should 'be put to the policy of appeasement . . . with all the humiliations and abasements it has brought in its train'. 'They have twisted the lion's tail just once too often.'

6 Brendan Bracken had been a Director of Economist Newspapers Ltd but ceased to sit on the board on becoming Minister of Information in 1941. The *Economist* on 6 January 1945 went out of its way to deny any connection between Bracken and the views expressed in its editorial. The *Yorkshire Post*, also under an independently-minded editor, W.Linton Andrews, was owned by the Beckett family, to which Sir Anthony Eden's wife belonged.

not altogether justifiably, feel to be recipients of so many benefits, military and economic, at their hands. . . .

The President, asked about the *Economist* article, gently pointed out that some things are better not stated, that differences are inevitable and not in themselves unhealthy, and the Secretary of State has similarly refrained from comment and refused to be drawn by the somewhat provocative questions of the reporters. There is no doubt that Stettinius is personally most anxious to restore good Anglo-American relations in which he sincerely believes, and that his attitude has been thoroughly impressed upon the members of his Department, particularly his new 'General Staff' which he has organized with enthusiasm and effectiveness.

Wheeler. Meanwhile, Senator Wheeler has caused a mild sensation by introduction of a resolution in the Senate, details of which I have reported separately. His demands for a European Federation, a United Nations Council for Europe, plebiscites of peoples, etc., coupled with an invitation to Senate to speak its mind in view of President's evident 'reluctance' to do so, should have surprised no one. The isolationist line has for a long time been the 'we believe in the Atlantic Charter, but do you ?' argument that the real reason for isolationism is not its intrinsic desirability, but fact that European nationalisms are incurable, and that her own idealism should not betray America into undertaking international obligations in the end only likely to be sabotaged by the selfish squabbles of 'power hungry' States elsewhere. This is by far the most plausible, as it is the most dishonest, line used by the more unscrupulous opponents of international co-operation. Wheeler, who was thought to be anxiously pressing his claim to one of the vacancies in the Foreign Relations Committee, but has since given up hope and withdrawn, clearly perceived a heaven-sent opportunity for demonstrating that he is no 'bitter-ender' but after his own fashion a sincere internationalist while, at the same time, causing embarrassment to the British and American Governments as well as to the genuine internationalists of the B2H2 type. I am told that Wheeler is closely connected with a small but still unimportant [sic] group of Russophobes in and out of Congress, whose normal organ is the Patterson–McCormick Press which weeps over the slaughter of American manpower on the fields of France and Flanders, on the grounds that it can only weaken America before its inevitable struggle with the USSR. In a short talk that I happened to have myself with Wheeler the other night at a private party, it was clear that his thought is mainly shaped by his Russian fears.

Pearson complains of a 'leakage'. Drew Pearson, who has had the honour of a full-scale article describing his career and methods in the *Saturday Evening Post*, has followed his 'leak' of the Prime Minister's message to Scobie with yet another scoop – a British memorandum on the subject of supplies to Italy. This time I had wind of what was coming and the State Department was therefore enabled to issue a rapid counter statement which leaves nothing to be desired, in that it declares that no basic difference of policy between Britain and the United States exists on this issue and denounces the damage which unauthorized publication of such passages torn from their context must inevitably produce. As a result of this, Pearson himself is now quaintly complaining of a shocking 'leak' from his confidential files. The State Department appears genuinely upset at rate of increase in important leakages of information, and a frantic investigation is being made. There is a mild panic in Washington Departments about this and oss, for example, are complaining that circulation of telegrams is being withheld from them on the mere suspicion of insecurity. Whether these efforts will lead to a genuine tightening up of security here remains to be seen.

. . .

Domestic legislation. Byrnes's latest orders on the subject of the conscription of the 4-F class, as well as introduction of stricter rationing, has had the effect of a cold douche after the 'spending spree' which has exceeded all records this Christmas. Meanwhile Krock is strongly implying that Byrnes, whose theoretical powers, he reminds his readers, over the domestic life of the United States are second only to the President's, is felt to be their acknowledged leader by the Southern Democrats and all good anti-New Dealers ; and, indeed, Byrnes's friends have been saying that his influence in the White House is perceptibly growing. But all such political stock-market quotations vary from week to week and are profoundly unreliable. The only solid guidepost to White House politics is still the President's permanent tendency not to allow any one of his advisers overweening power, and as a corollary a tendency to placate whichever wing of his party, he has reason to believe, has been neglected too long. In this case, it may well be that he is inclining towards Byrnes in an effort to avoid provoking his more conservative supporters in Congress after his alleged promise to consult Pepper and his pro-PAC group following the tantrum about the State Department appointments. So the seesaw continues.

Dies Redivivus. Meanwhile the new House has given the President his first acrid taste of its new quality by voting, on a motion of the very reactionary Representative Rankin of Mississippi, to set up a committee to continue the work of the now dead Dies Committee to 'Investigate Un-American Activities'. Normally such motions must obtain the approval of the Rules Committee, although there is no statute to that effect, and are then set up as *ad hoc* committees for specific purposes, and unlike the permanent committees of Congress, can report facts but not recommend legislation. Knowing well that the new chairman of the Rules Committee will almost certainly block the measure so unwelcome to the Administration, the anti-PAC front by a snap vote passed a motion to appoint a permanent committee of the House to perform this function. This gives the new committee powers to recommend and initiate legislation and thus creates a more formidable body than its predecessor. The Administration, which appeared genuinely surprised by this 'revolt', mustered all its strength against it and was defeated 207 *v*. 186. The chief (and precarious) hope of the Administration now lies in blocking the measure in the Appropriations Committee, which will attempt to refuse funds. The combination is a familiar one of Southern Democrats and Republican conservatives, which looks like giving as much trouble to the Administration on domestic policy as heretofore. The chief purpose of the new committee is doubtless to prevent a repetition of the PAC triumph in 1946 while there is still time to discredit it.

Wallace and others. Meanwhile, speculation about Mr Wallace's possible appointment to the Secretaryship of Commerce continues, with a despatch in the *New York Times* asserting that he has definitely applied for this post in a letter written by him to the President.

. . .

Meanwhile liberals – as represented by *PM* – are said to be broken-hearted about the alleged White House veto on the appointment of Benjamin V.Cohen as counsellor of the State Department, a long disused advisory office of the level of the Under-Secretary, to which Stettinius is said to have recommended him. Cohen had resigned from his present position under Byrnes, then, pressed to reconsider this by Byrnes and the President, stayed. His future is still uncertain. I am told that Berle is definitely expected to go as Ambassador to Brazil.

14 January 1945

Despite setbacks on the Western Front there is no clamour here for any heads to roll among Eisenhower's staff. Montgomery's new post[1] was moderately well received, and Prime Minister's and Montgomery's warm references to United States soldiers are very widely appreciated. This absence of self-blame is doubtless partly due to recouping of their fortunes by Allied troops reported during last few days, partly to natural resurgence of automatic nationalist feelings of self-defence aroused by sharp criticisms of United States strategy and tactics in e.g. the British press. Attacks of *Economist* and other British organs have now had their full, and to some degree salutary, effect here but further efforts in this direction may well boomerang. There is intense desire on virtually all sides to call an end to this trans-Atlantic slanging match and resume co-operation. Latest editorial in *Life* attributes British criticism to 'political failure' in United States of America and gives an exceptionally sympathetic and friendly analysis of reasons for British anger. A worried attitude about Europe continues of course, especially over Russian recognition of Lublin Government,[2] but undertones of anti-Allied bitterness are vanishing and there is much genuine anxiety to help.

1 At end of 1944, during Battle of the Bulge, Field-Marshal Montgomery was given temporary command of all Allied forces north of the German salient.

2 The Polish Committee of National Liberation, with temporary headquarters in Lublin, on 31 December was reconstituted as the provisional Government of Poland and given unilateral recognition by Stalin.

President's message. President's annual message to Congress 'on state of nation' has had a favourable reception. There is general acknowledgment that within limits of generality which such messages must necessarily have, he has answered many of questions which have confused public opinion with a sufficient concreteness and firmness to give a genuine lead to bewildered public opinion and stimulate talk of a 'new era' in foreign policy. His domestic proposals – unequivocal approval of a national service act, qualified though provisions may be – have been received as inevitable by all save organized labour, with Murray of CIO still speaking of it as a 'quack remedy', similar words by AF of L and contentions by both that local labour bottlenecks do not need so drastic a national solution when voluntary system is so much part and parcel of American tradition. The same general support and sectional opposition is likely to greet President's demand for a draft of women as nurses for Army and Navy and for permanent compulsory military training for American youth. As for foreign policy the widening sense that there is many a beam in eye of United States public opinion which so sharply detects the motes in eye of other nations was most usefully reinforced by President's warning against perfectionism as an international policy no less fatal than isolationism, by his call for expansionist economies and by his words of solidarity in particular with British policy which were clearly intended to have, and to some extent had, the effect of pouring long needed oil upon troubled Anglo-American waters. . . . I am told that address was drafted mainly by Messrs MacLeish (who supplied historical analogies), Sherwood, Benjamin Cohen (who supplied reasoned words about Poland and Greece), and Rosenman who, as so often, provided general cement. . . .

Vandenberg's speech. Meanwhile Senator Vandenberg has made a spectacular move. Gist of it resides in his proposition that fear of inadequate means to enforce German (and Japanese) disarmament is main factor promoting distrust among Allies, therefore it would surely be a most constructive act to conclude an immediate security pact between major Allies at any rate for purpose of curbing possible rise of Germany and Japan at any future date after victory. He saw no incompatibility between that and general purposes of Dumbarton Oaks discussions, indeed he supposed that his pact might function as a cornerstone of an edifice ultimately to be constructed in accordance with present plans of Allied Governments. Senator Austin (Republican Vermont, Foreign Relations Committee) appeared to agree with this, having extracted from Vandenberg admission that the bilateral Russo-Czech, Anglo-Russian, Franco-Russian, etc., pacts were not inconsistent with such a purpose. Senators from both sides of the floor – Pepper and Ball, Fulbright and Wiley – have congratulated Vandenberg on his performance. Although there is no reason for supposing that Vandenberg is moved by other than mixture of genuine benevolence and intense desire to perpetuate his own name as one of main architects of future peace – (in substance proposal is the same as the one he propounded during Dumbarton Oaks debate held during conference itself in early autumn of 1944) – yet Connally and certain members of Administration perhaps with reason feel that adoption of this treaty, limited to security against Axis, might relieve consciences of many troubled Americans and so act as a partly unconscious deterrent to further steps towards a real international organization which must obviously embrace a much wider scope than this crucial but limited objective. On other hand spectacle of an ex-isolationist Senator calling for what in effect is a most entangling alliance is surely one to cause wonder and gratification. Questioned further about Dumbarton Oaks, Vandenberg said that his pact could be concluded immediately whereas general negotiations for a world organization would probably drag on for a good long time. Also that he was not prepared as yet to subscribe to any international instrument which would perpetuate a peace which might be unjust without providing machinery for its possible revision whereas his own suggestion would at least empower President to use armed forces of United States of America in all cases where security against ex-Axis powers demanded it without perpetual recourse for authority to Congress. Connally has promised to study proposal further and Vandenberg privately has told journalists that one of his intentions was to strengthen President's hand for his coming meeting with heads of other states by removing at any rate some of suspicion that whatever United States Government may propose the Senate would fail to dispose and as Vandenberg probably controls makeweight of two-third's majority of that body, this is clearly most important. Relevant State Department officials appear to oscillate between a feeling that Vandenberg might prove an embarrassing ally if placated too far, and fear of letting him go altogether with deleterious consequences to senatorial support for Dumbarton Oaks. Elaborate negotiations are therefore proceeding.

Foreign Relations Committee. Meanwhile reconstituted Foreign Relations Committee of Senate with the accession of ex-isolationist Wiley (Republican, Wisconsin) and the uncompromisingly internationalist Hatch (Democrat, New Mexico), Hill (Democrat, Alabama) and Lucas (Democrat, Illinois) now contains fourteen unswerving supporters of Administration's policies against nine Republicans of whom Austin is thoroughly enlightened. White and Styles Bridges are uncertain but have comparatively good records. Vandenberg and Wiley with isolationist voting records look on themselves as reasonable men in international affairs, and only Johnson, Capper, La Follette and Shipstead are diehard isolationists. There was apparently some move to attach 'strings' to Hatch's election but he rightly felt strong enough to refuse to bind himself to any conditions.

Senator Wheeler has once more shown his true colours by denouncing 'unconditional surrender' in a radio address as 'asinine' and likely to lead to much unnecessary bloodshed. Stettinius severely rebuked him for using words likely to encourage Germans to think that by persisting sufficiently they will gain better terms, and Vandenberg indirectly made his own position clear by saying that such a military pact as he suggested would bring about unconditional surrender sooner by making Allied intentions clear 'beyond peradventure of a doubt' to enemy. Some pro-Administration Senators are saying that Stettinius should not have troubled to scold Wheeler since that only gave him unnecessary publicity. Nevertheless in present fluid state of opinion, any firm announcement by Administration that its purposes have not altered, and giving answers to doubts and queries, undoubtedly does a great deal of good.

State Department on the march. Meanwhile State Department is on the march too and has asked in current budget of United States Government (of $83 million, less than 1944) for slightly over $75 million for itself – i.e. some $28½ million more than last year. Marquis Childs has written an article obviously inspired, describing intolerable physical conditions under which high officials of the Department are at present forced to work, and this appropriation if granted will enable Stettinius to modernize and expand his Department in order to perform those wider and more intensive labours which Administration and in particular President obviously regards as made necessary by far greater and more energetic part which United States of America is to play in international affairs. The 'new era' is confidently expected to dawn on all hands.

.   .   .

Landis. On his return from Cairo Landis, in an interview with the press, gave a characteristic account of his stewardship, saying that his principal tasks had been to liquidate Lend-Lease in the Middle East as far as possible in order to reopen and widen the normal avenues of commerce upon which in large measure the prosperity of that part of the world depended in his view. The main obstacle to this was paucity of dollar exchange in the hands of potential Middle Eastern customers as against sterling for which they did not find nearly as much use. This merely re-emphasizes Landis's by now familiar attitude, which he will doubtless carry with him to the grave (certainly to the Harvard Law School to which he returns).

21 January 1945

The general mood is mending fast. As a result of several factors – the victorious Russian drive,[1] MacArthur's Luzon operations,[2] Vandenberg's proposals[3] and, following from this, a renewed sense of bipartisan co-operation in the making of the peace, and the general and inevitable reaction to the orgy of recrimination between the American and British presses – there has been a marked rise in general confidence, particularly with regard to international affairs.

.   .   .

1 Red Army took Warsaw 17 January.
2 On 19 January four US divisions went ashore on Luzon.
3 See last week's summary.

National Service. The issue of national mobilization is still much to the forefront, with the publication of the letters to the President by General Marshall and Admiral King calling for 900,000 more recruits for the Army and Navy draft, and of the President's letter to the chairman of the House Military Affairs Committee supporting this. How much effective legislation will emerge against the combined opposition of organized labour and the National Association of Manufacturers remains to be seen. But sufficient pressure from the Service Departments should effect some action in this field. The President is asking for no more at the moment than a more thorough combing of the eighteen-forty-five age-groups already liable under selective service. It is interesting to note that the relative burdens of the United Kingdom, first made crystal clear to this country by the recent statistical White Paper on the subject, and then swamped by the uproar on the Italian and Greek affairs, is once more filtering through, and a number of appreciative and understanding references are once more beginning to occur to the British plight past and present.

. . .

The Moyne murder trial. This has obtained fairly wide publicity here, with the political angle heavily stressed and a little rumbling about censorship of the defendants' speeches in the Jewish and liberal press. *PM* is particularly rabid on all this, followed closely by the *New York Post*. There has been scarcely any other comment (beyond one unimportant senatorial outburst) but if there is not much pro-Zionist reaction there is scarcely any overt condemnation of the act either, since the general impression made by the United States newspapers' dispatches is that it is a typical political assassination committed by misguided but disinterested fanatics and as such is vaguely analogous to incidents in Anglo-Irish history.

Un-American Activities. The resurrected ex-Dies Committee is to be headed by Representative Hart[4] (Democrat) of New Jersey, one of Boss Hague's men, and, so long as the Hague machine co-operates with the CIO political committees as it did during the election, unlikely to encourage anti-labour investigations. Consequently, commentators are predicting that despite the inclusion of the very reactionary Representative Rankin (Democrat, Mississippi) in the committee, it is unlikely to emulate the witch-hunts of its notorious predecessor. But anything may happen.

. . .

China. The new view of China as being a land torn by internal conflicts and the greater part of it ruled by a very imperfect central government, which had not been in the forefront of attention lately, was once more strongly reinforced by the speech in Congress by Representative Mansfield[5] (Democrat, Montana) who returned from a tour of China on which he had been sent by the President. Mans-

4 Edward J. Hart, Democratic Congressman from New Jersey since 1935.
5 Michael J. Mansfield, Professor, Democratic Congressman from Montana 1943–5, Senator 1945–77.

field served as a marine in the Philippines in the last war and taught Far Eastern History in Montana. His account stated that both the Communists and the Kuomintang were more intent upon their own partisan purposes than upon defeating the Japanese, but after that went on to say that the Chinese Communists are not so much Communist as agrarian reformers, that they received no Russian aid, that they controlled some ninety million Chinese (a higher figure than given by anyone else so far) and controlled some 600,000 'good' troops, and that more democracy was to be found in the provinces under their control than elsewhere in China. As for the Kuomintang, he repeated the now familiar story of inefficiency and misgovernment, said that they were losing steadily to their Communist rivals, but wound up by saying that despite all this Chiang Kai-shek was still the only man capable of uniting the Chinese, the only national leader of sufficient stature 'to make China's independence and unity a reality'. 'As of this date,' said Mansfield, 'the Chinese house has a leaky roof and a shaky foundation. Whether or not that house can be put in order is a question mark.' Hurley, Nelson and Wedemeyer[6] are doing their best to promote much needed unity, but it is an uphill task. All this must by now be fairly familiar to the American Congress and public, and causes considerable distress in the Chinese Embassy. Mansfield made a friendly reference to British military activity in Burma.

22 January 1945

As stated in my telegram of 1 January, Wallace did apply for Commerce post and Jones did prove most difficult to oust. He is said to have offered to go gracefully if permitted to retain the obviously more important control of Reconstruction Finance Corporation and connexion with the network of agencies which control a good many of the war plants at home and operations abroad, besides many related economic mechanisms. This Wallace is said to have refused to accept. Meanwhile considerable pressure was steadily being put on the President by liberal Senators, representatives of the Political Action Committee and New Dealers in his own immediate entourage to fulfil Wallace's request. The President has always personally liked and approved of Wallace, and in this case not only gratitude for his devoted performance during the election campaign, but reasons of political expediency i.e. a desire to show that he was still 'left of centre' no doubt inspired him to make up his mind. Jones, after a personal talk with the President four days ago, is said to have refused to budge, and therefore had to be formally dismissed. Steve Early told the press that the White House did not anticipate that Jones would publish the exchange of letters, the gist of which is that Wallace deserved a reward for his past achievement and his work

6 General Albert C. Wedemeyer, Commander US Forces in China and Chief of Staff to Chiang Kai-shek 1944–6.

during the election (when Jones was suspected of slight disaffection) and was a really fit occupant of the office. Jones openly took issue with both points, and indicated that Wallace's appointment would not be well received by important interests. The whole issue is exacerbated by the fact that Wallace had been somewhat unceremoniously deprived of his job as head of Board of Economic Warfare (predecessor of the Foreign Economic Administration) colliding with Jones and Clayton (the latter was at that time in the Commerce Department) and this therefore represents ultimate victory for Wallace. Senators Connally and Bailey (Chairman of the Senate Commerce Committee) called on the President to advise against this move, but the President probably discounted this in advance, as Southern conservative sentiment against Wallace, demonstrated during the last Democratic convention, is notorious.

A Senate fight on the confirmation is therefore to be expected, with every effort by the Democratic whips to push the nomination through, and the opposition consisting largely of Republicans, bitterly anti-New Deal Southern Democrats and milder pro-Administration Southerners, who may abstain. Support for Wallace will come, besides party regulars and New Dealers, from Senators under pressure from labour and liberal elements in their States as well as anti-cartelists who see a champion in Wallace. Thus the exceedingly influential Senator George (Democrat, Georgia, Chairman of the Senate Personnel Committee) has already introduced a bill to remove all lending agencies in the Department of Commerce and put them under the control of an independent administrator, presumably of Cabinet rank. Whether or not this bill now before the Commerce Department goes through, it is a very obvious slap at Wallace. If he succeeds it would crucially weaken the Commerce Department and give Wallace no greater powers than e.g. Hopkins enjoyed as Secretary of Commerce during the President's second term before his rise to real influence. Jones's state, Texas, in the persons of Senators Connally and O'Daniel and several of the Texas House Delegation, has already spoken against the confirmation. Several Republicans have added their voices to this, while liberals – Senators Murray, Pepper, Guffey, etc. – are preparing for an all-out fight.

If Wallace is confirmed he is expected to devote himself to the support of small businesses and creation of conditions providing the '60,000,000 post-war jobs' promised by the President and the party ; on foreign economic policy, i.e. connected with his lending agencies, there is no evidence that his views have changed since his Board of Economic Warfare, Milo Perkins days. One press story says that among diplomatic appointments offered to Jones in the President's letter (a suggestion which he has rejected) was the London Embassy with Winant to succeed Perkins,[1] who seems genuinely anxious to go but is said to be staying indefinitely so long as the President's present inability to find a successor continues.

1 Frances Perkins, Secretary of Labor.

28 January 1945

The President. President's inauguration passed off without incident, his speech on this occasion was well received, and as it contained no controversial matter, aroused little comment. There is little doubt that despite all sectional opposition to him on specific matters, the President today carries the country with him to a far greater extent than e.g. Wilson did in 1918, and the criticisms of him on this or that sector of the anti-Roosevelt front should not today, whatever the future may hold, be taken as indicating the existence of an opposition sufficiently serious to upset his basic plans in their main outline.

Public opinion. Effect of the great Russian offensive upon public opinion has not been simple. First, and incomparably the greatest, consequence has of course been to lift drooping spirits and engender general buoyancy. But connected with it is a natural increase in anxious speculation about Russian political intentions in Europe, and, fed by the increase in discussion of British ends (with the Prime Minister's speech as the main text) and various rumours as to United States policies formulated for and by the President in anticipation of the forthcoming Big Three conference, there has been a very large amount of discussion of foreign affairs in the press and far beyond it. The President is credited with 'very tough' intentions with regard to Germany, something not very far off the 'Morgenthau plan' involving drastic disarmament, de-industrialization and the lopping of frontiers with an attempt at trichotomy as well. The establishment of an inter-allied body (possibly in Paris) to administer interim governments in all liberated territories, a far more powerful version of EAC, [1] to which such interim governments would be solely responsible is also said to be much in his mind. This of course is what Sumner Welles pursued so long and so vainly. In general the national attitude, with appropriate variations to the right and left varying in accordance with general political outlook, comes to something of this kind. . . . America must and shall collaborate in the affairs of the world, including even Eastern Europe. The Dumbarton Oaks proposals are a very acceptable basis upon which to found an international organization to which America must adhere. (This has been emphasized by the acceptance of it by sixteen 'Freshmen' Senators, also by John Foster Dulles's flock.) There is every hope that agreement both with Britain and Russia can be reached on fundamental questions, without sacrificing the principles held up to democratic peoples by their leaders. To do this America must boldly make concrete and positive proposals of her own, which she is prepared to back by her moral and material resources, and does not merely trail behind and offer criticism of the two other powers. In most cases, the name of France, and less frequently China, is added to the list of the major

1 The European Advisory Commission, set up in November 1943, was to advise the UK, US and USSR Governments on matters to do with the termination of hostilities with Germany.

powers concerned. Suspicion that British are pursuing a traditional 'balance of power' policy, principally intended to safeguard their own interests, has not been dispelled by any recent utterances of British spokesmen. . . .

. . .

Prime Minister's last comprehensive political general survey[2] has met with a mixed reception. The general core of the 'right centre' and 'left centre' press has praised it both as a masterpiece of exposition and as a powerful argument for recent British action. But, both on the right and left, there has been increasing criticism of this or that portion of his speech, and in direct proportion as Americans appear to become more ready to accept their own responsibility for participation in political solutions abroad, there is a tendency to scrutinize even the Prime Minister's golden eloquence with a sharp eye to the merits or demerits of specific concrete proposals, and an almost discernible effort to resist being swept away by the sheer power of his hypnotic style. Consequently passages on Greece and Italy, and to some extent on Poland, do not appear to have altered the existent tendencies of minds already moving in this or that direction, and opinion is on the whole somewhat puzzled or critical rather than acquiescent. But an immense amount is hoped from forthcoming conference, which is expected to set more definitely the pattern of future political developments than any previous events.

Movement of anti-isolationist opinion is marked by two significant declarations: (a) of a programme outlined by sixteen 'freshmen' Senators, who, led by the Democrat Fulbright (Arkansas) and the Republican Smith[3] (New Jersey), explicitly favour Dumbarton Oaks, full American participation in an international security organization backed by force, a treaty to keep Germany and Japan fully disarmed (à la Vandenberg) and finally full American participation in the organization of interim régimes in liberated and ex-enemy territories. As these 'Freshmen' contain persons (e.g. like Capehart of Indiana) normally suspected of insufficient enthusiasm for such courses, this is an important development, showing not merely a desire to assert themselves on the part of junior Senators, who doubtless rightly believe that as a bloc they will have more weight than they would dispersed in unimportant positions among many senatorial committees, but also a recognition of which way the wind is blowing, i.e. the unwisdom of opposing inevitable United States participation in world affairs. (b) The debate and ultimate decisions of Dulles's influential conference of various churchmen's and Wilsonian organizations, which led to defeat of the extreme anti-imperialist and near-isolationist positions of the 'Christian Century' group, and the unqualified adoption of Dumbarton Oaks with various reservations about rights of small nations, hard peace, colonies, etc.

All this is in general to be regarded as an encouraging trend, although it is wise to remember, particularly at such moments, that economic thought lags a

2 Delivered to House of Commons on 18 January.
3 Howard Alexander Smith, lawyer, Republican Senator from New Jersey 1944–53.

long way behind this political enlightenment, and seems much the tougher problem of the two for both British and United Statesmen.

Wallace-Jones. I have reported the text and details of the dismissal of Jones from his post as Secretary of Commerce and the appointment thereto of Wallace in previous telegrams. I am told that the President personally drafted his letter to Jones. Its extraordinary stress on the fact that his reason for acting as he did was his conviction that Wallace was, in virtue of his political services, entitled to the reward for which he had asked, has naturally stirred up the hornets' nest which no observant person could have failed to anticipate. The immediate reactions are very much such as might have been expected. The liberals and a section of more conservative-minded persons, who pride themselves on moving with the times, look on Wallace as both willing and capable of promoting schemes of full employment and the propping up of small businesses against the Big Business octopus, which is his avowed creed. The conservatives and business and financial interests generally are vociferously up in arms and flooding the capital with telegrams, messages and pressures of every kind. The staggering expanse of Jones's vast financial empire, deriving not from the Commerce Department but from the lending agencies, under, and connected with, the Reconstruction Finance Corporation (created by Hoover), has been once again impressed upon an astonished country and upon Congress. The result is an anti-Wallace campaign by the conservatives (and Scripps-Howard Press) who cannot forget Wallace's remark last year about seizing business by 'the scruff of the neck', and depict him as undeniably a man of probity and principle, but a notoriously scatter-brained dreamer who will surely squander the nation's resources with breakneck speed, a major menace to be averted at all costs. There is similarly a stream of criticism of the President for so blatantly exposing the raw realities of the spoils system by openly declaring that Wallace was appointed for solely political, i.e. partisan reasons. Pearson declares that the President had long ago determined to oust Jesse Jones in any case. And this may well be true since Jones's general outlook must have conflicted with that of the President at many points, and the major reason for retaining him had always been the exceptional support upon which he could count not only in the Senate, in which his influence had been second perhaps only to that of Hull, but throughout the business and financial community which his lending agencies had welded together into a very powerful political economic bloc. The President's uncompromising rejection of his services, therefore, is at the very least evidence of how strong politically he feels himself to be. Jones has not troubled to hide his anger, and in his reply to the President, referred sourly to the shock which the new appointment would give to the commercial community, and has left his office far from gracefully (Wayne Chatfield Taylor is the Acting Secretary).[4] Meanwhile his friend Senator George

4 Previously Under-Secretary of Commerce 1940–5.

(Democrat, Georgia) has introduced a measure to separate the financial powers of RFC from the Commerce Department on the grounds that so vast a strength should not reside in the hands of any one man. . . . He successfully introduced this measure before the question of Wallace's confirmation could come up, and has called Jones and Wallace as witnesses, ostensibly on the abstract question of whether the two powers should be separated. . . .

. . . There is no doubt that conservatives and businessmen are genuinely disturbed, that Jones's clients do not know where they stand, and that the bill advocating the separation of the two authorities (Commerce and RFC) may well pass, leaving Wallace largely stripped of effective machinery for action, and in a mainly advisory and research capacity (e.g. like the Secretary of Labor) for which latter alone Lippmann suggested that he was properly equipped. There is a tendency, even in the anti-Wallace press, to hold that a President is entitled to whatever Cabinet he appoints, since the ultimate responsibility is his and his alone, and Cabinet members are not responsible to Congress under the constitution. Nevertheless the Commerce Committee in a sudden vote declined to confirm Wallace 14–5 and adopted 15–4 George's scheme for the separation of powers of RFC from the Commerce Department. Although theoretically the matter is one for the entire Senate to decide, Wallace's chances cannot be said to look rosy after this and he appears destined to become a martyr in the cause of unrepentant liberalism once again. There may be an attempt at a counterattack by the pro-Wallace forces in the form of nationwide advertisements 'Vote for Wallace and 60 million jobs' by the old pro-Roosevelt businessmen's committee. But it is not a powerful body. Pepper naturally took up a cudgel in debate for the ex Vice-President, while the most extreme expression of opposition came from a Southern Congressman who observed 'any office which Wallace is qualified to fill ought to be abolished'.

What occurred in the President's mind is obscure. He cannot have forgotten Jones's more than ambiguous attitude towards his own fourth term as reported to him by his agents in Texas. For although Jones finally supported him in a brief radio speech, Jones's friends in Texas were scarcely supporters of Mr Roosevelt. As for Wallace, there is no reason for thinking that Mr Roosevelt does not still genuinely like and respect him. Certainly Wallace's behaviour during the election was impeccable in the face of vast provocation, and raised his reputation greatly throughout the country even among his opponents. The President is under considerable pressure from the liberals to offset appointments, particularly in the State Department, which New Dealers regard with open disapproval, and, in addition to Wallace, has appointed one or two other noted radicals to government posts of fair importance (e.g. Aubrey Williams to the Rural Electrification Administration). Yet the President trailed his coat so openly before the conservatives by his letter to Jones, that the more cynical observers are inclined to suspect that if Wallace is not confirmed, the President will not repine too much. In other words, that while he is genuinely prepared to accept Wallace as one of the major architects of the home front and by this means to placate the indignant New Deal faithfuls (in particular PAC and labour) who have done a very great deal to re-elect him, yet if Wallace is defeated, or deprived of power by Congress, that will be one political embarrassment the less, and the President will quite honestly be able to say that he had done all that was in his power, but that the Senate is a genuinely independent body very much not under his ultimate control. All that is clear is that he has with open eyes precipitated a crisis which will determine matters one way or the other and at least leave no doubt as to what the Senate and public opinion favour as well as put on clear record his own undeviating liberalism of purpose. Perhaps he thought that since the crisis between the economic views of the 'right' and 'left' was bound to burst out in any case it might as well boil itself out during his absence on a political expedition which was warily welcomed and supported by the majority of Americans irrespective of economic beliefs.

28 January 1945 (Savingram)

. . .

The Churches on the Peace. Protestant 'perfectionists', after a fighting speech by John Foster Dulles, suffered a slight but still noteworthy defeat in the Cleveland meetings of a conference called by the Federal Council of Churches of Christ. Many of the attending clergy rumbled on about power politics and the like, but Dulles insisted that the United States should take action instead of 'pleasurably immersing itself in the intellectual pastime' of 'devising ingenious formulae to deal with voting on an hypothetical security council'. A resolution endorsing Dumbarton Oaks was carried, although an eight-point programme for recommended 'improvement' was attached. Among the improvements suggested were (1) rejection of the right of any nation 'to vote when its case is being judged', (2) the development of a code of international law, (3) the creation of a Colonial Commission, (4) provision for 'eventual universal membership'. Dulles's chief opponent was C.C.Morrison,[1] editor of the influential and antiimperialist *Christian Century*. So far as the treatment of Axis nations is concerned, the conference followed a familiar line in asking for 'reconciliation of victors and vanquished', in opposing a partititon of Germany, in assuming that the German churches will play a large role in establishing German democracy and in demanding the end of 'the imperialism of the white man' and autonomy as 'the goal for all dependent peoples' in the Far East. Nevertheless, the principal difference between this most influential of all Protestant bodies and its Roman Catholic equivalent is that . . . the former finally approved Dumbarton Oaks without qualification, whatever their private misgivings, in order to avoid a return to 1918, whereas the Catholics qualified their support so heavily as almost to nullify the value of their support.

1 Charles C. Morrison, clergyman, editor of *Christian Century* 1908–47.

Canada. It is once again worth noting that the news of the Canadian 'mutiny' of troops unwilling to go on service abroad,[2] while baldly reported on the UP tickers, was sparsely reported and aroused scarcely any comment. This astonishing self-restraint, which is not practised with regard to any other country, is a tribute to the nervous respect in which Canada is held here.

A still further sobering influence was the only slightly subsequent publication of the report that some 12–13,000 United States soldiers are 'absent without leave' in Europe, mostly engaged it is said in some form of black-marketing.

5 February 1945

. . .

Mr Wallace. . . . . Wallace's supporters in Senate (see last political summary), realizing that there is at present no chance of endowing their men with Jones's full powers, concentrated on getting George bill (which divorced federal lending agencies from Department of Commerce) to the vote first, since they realized that unless it was stripped of its vast financial powers the Secretaryship of Commerce would be overwhelmingly refused to Wallace. This after much jockeying they succeeded in doing, and a very large majority passed George bill. It has still to come before the House. The President has indicated that he will not veto it which is part and parcel of pro-Wallace strategy. Next move is confirmation of Wallace himself to a Commerce Department reduced to its pristine and somewhat limited powers. Even this proved none too easy. A tie of 42 to 42 nearly defeated Administration's motion to defer confirmation until 1 March when tempers, it was hoped, would be cooler. But for a tactical slip by Senator Taft the Administration might have lost and Wallace have been defeated outright. In end the motion to defer was won by one vote, and at moment it seems fairly probable that Wallace will be duly confirmed in March in his reduced post. Most political observers seem to think that having made a demonstration of its independence and having rescued the $40 billion lending fund from possible control by Wallace, the majority of Senate will not in the end obstruct his admission into Cabinet. Senator Brewster gave as one of his reasons for supporting deferment his view that it 'might be smartest thing to do' to confirm Wallace inasmuch as he would be relatively powerless as Secretary of Commerce, whereas if debarred from all federal posts, he might easily become a political martyr of first order with considerable chances of emerging as a popular hero. Some carry this further and predict that it is in Wallace's interest to allow himself to be 'massacred', since this would prove the making of him as presidential candidate in 1948. And indeed this is far from absurd. Liberals, outmanoeuvred as some among them feel themselves to be by Mr Roosevelt, who has managed to pursue a skilful zigzag policy between them and his right-wing supporters, are in acute need of

2 In British Columbia the discrimination of the quota system (*vide supra*, 3 December, n. 2) provoked a near mutiny as troops on embarkation leave absconded.

a leader and with Willkie dead and Ickes too old and too rough and too independent, and Justice Douglas still too unknown, Wallace is their best natural champion. This emerged very clearly at a testimonial dinner given him by liberals in New York at which Mrs Roosevelt, perhaps his staunchest ally, paid a warm tribute to him and read a message from President which declared that country needed Wallace more than ever. Wallace at this banquet delivered an unusually clear and ably constructed profession of faith and contradicted his earlier statement to Senate Committee that he would accept Commerce post without lending agencies, saying that he would prefer not to do so if Jones's successor as federal leader were a man who was 'too little and too late'. He has now cautiously declared that he will say nothing till 1 March. Wallace's recent utterances have been distinguished by unusual forcefulness and economic good sense which give his followers a reason for hoping that the evangelical mysticism and liability to go off on disturbingly naïve tangents is offset by a more hard-headed conception of what is practicable on both foreign and domestic fronts. Wallace's performance during election campaign, and subsequently, has undoubtedly raised his prestige to a point higher than any since 1942. The opposition to him is of course the most formidable in country, coming as it does from entire anti-New Deal front, united on this as on no other issue. Opposition to Wallace in Senate consists either of bitter-end party-line Republicans, or Southern Democrats to whom Wallace's name is anathema. At same time there are those who might not strenuously object to his becoming Secretary of Commerce since they respect his integrity and good intentions – e.g. Lippmann in his articles – but who fear that President may, by executive order, transfer to him other offices, at present under control of FEA or other agencies, which again would give him those executive powers which they believe him not to be competent to discharge. Result therefore still hangs in balance. It has become most spectacular contest between liberals and their opponents since election itself. Roosevelt's own feelings are said to be curiously mixed – but that is a subject of psychological speculation on which no views can claim much factual support.

4 February 1945 (Savingram)

Labour. The most interesting developments in this field are (a) the imminent admission of John L. Lewis into the American Federation of Labor, which is said to be due to be consummated in February after a period of negotiation which has lasted for over two years. There is no doubt that if this happens, Lewis will attempt, and may succeed, in dominating that at present somewhat inert and old-fashioned institution and may make an instrument of great aggressive power out of it, since it possesses much wealth and latent strength, which its leaders have so far proved too unimaginative to use boldly. A renewal of a bitter period of fighting with the CIO may in that event be anticipated. In the meanwhile imprisonment technically threatens Lewis, if in the perennial squabble over the renewal of the bituminous miners' contract, he declares a strike similar to that of 1943. This would precipitate a major crisis. (b) Hillman's PAC is experiencing considerable internal convulsions on account of the disagreement of its right (or liberal) wing with the more aggressive Communist element. Hillman appears to be in favour of decentralizing it, which undoubtedly would deprive it of some of the power which it has accumulated during and as a result of the election. All this is being fought out now. Meanwhile both AF of L and CIO and all other labour organizations have united for the moment in unsuccessful opposition to the National Service bill and have produced various striking instances of the misuse of existing labour power designed to show that a more efficient management would eliminate the need for a more exhaustive draft. This is still largely supported by the representatives of the National Association of Manufacturers, a paradoxical alliance which only the peculiarities of wartime could have produced. On this issue the left wing of the CIO – the so called 'Communist' section of it – broke away from the united labour front, in support of the unadulterated bill.

.   .   .

Montgomery Ward.[1] The decision of Judge Sullivan[2] that the Administration acted unconstitutionally in enforcing the War Labor Board's decision upon that firm (after the spectacular physical ejection of Sewell Avery, its head, some time ago by orders of the Attorney General, had furnished infinite food for argument, and more particularly political cartoonists, all over the country) has put new heart into anti-New Dealers. The fact that Sullivan was originally appointed by President Roosevelt, while it may serve to clear the President of the recurrent charges of political appointments to the judiciary, seems to give particular satisfaction to his opponents. The decision rested upon a finding that the bill providing the relevant powers to the Administration covered only production and manufacture and not distribution. The Administration are appealing to the Supreme Court. A cartoon of Mr Avery triumphantly ejecting Mr Biddle duly appeared. The tug of war between business and labour continues unabated.

11 February 1945

MacArthur's 'I have returned',[1] his new cry of 'on to Tokyo',[2] the release of American military and civilian prisoners from Japanese prison camps and the satisfying reversal of Japanese and American roles in the Philippines in 1942 and 1945 have touched off in the press one of the greater emotional outpourings of the Japanese war. Unstinted praise is being lavished upon MacArthur as a 'mas-

1 *Vide supra* 13 May 1944.
2 Philip Leo Sullivan, US District Judge, Northern Illinois District, 1933–59.
　1 'People of the Philippines, I have returned' – message delivered by MacArthur to a microphone set up on the beach-head established on Leyte island, on 20 October, in the first stage of the reconquest of the Philippines ; it echoed his 'I shall return' pledge given on leaving Bataan in 1942.
　2 'On to Tokyo', MacArthur's exhortation to his troops after the capture of Manila.

ter strategist' and his champions, especially the Hearst-Patterson-McCormick press, have already renewed their campaign for MacArthur as supreme commander of all Allied forces in the Far East.

Big Three parley. The mood at the opening of the Black Sea parley[3] is one of passive expectation in which hope mixed with some anxiety rather than optimism is the keynote. Despite the great satisfaction felt that the Big Three are at last meeting again to iron out political differences and plan the final stages of the war against Germany, and possibly Japan, there is an underlying feeling that these occasional meetings by Mr Churchill, President Roosevelt and Marshal Stalin are not of themselves enough and must very shortly be supplemented by more continuous methods of liaison. Your own suggestion of regular meetings between the Foreign Ministers of the Great Powers is still widely favoured. The belief is widespread that the President has gone to the parley with a hand far stronger than was foreseen a month or so back. The almost universally acclaimed Vandenberg proposal to ensure against any rebirth of German and Japanese aggression, the *New York Times* poll on this in the Senate showing an encouraging measure of support, the declaration of the sixteen 'Freshmen' Senators coupled with unparalleled popular confidence in the President on foreign policy – all these are seen as strong cards in the President's hand at the conference : in particular the conviction that in President Roosevelt alone lies the last chance of ensuring a just peace settlement within the framework of the Atlantic Charter. British and Russian need for American economic assistance in the post-war period is cited as the main hope for a compliant attitude towards American moral demands. Writers and commentators are in fact peculiarly insistent that the President use the strong cards which he has been given to bring about solutions acceptable to the American Senate and people. Beyond such vague terms as the Atlantic Charter and 'democratic principles', it is doubtful if there is any appreciable understanding of what sort of settlement is desirable. The Hopkins mission to London, Paris and Rome[4] has produced the belief that Hull's recent policy of 'benevolent abstention' has now given way to a willingness to accept responsibility for peace in Europe always provided that the United States does not thereby become involved in a power politics system doomed to end in a Third World War, nor have to sanction bilateral decisions by any of the major powers.

. . .

There is speculation of the possibility of Russian participation in the war against Japan after the defeat of Germany. Hope, though no expectation, is widespread that she will thus materially shorten the war in the Pacific and though more enlightened circles declare that continued Russian neutrality would be understandable, it is certain that Russian refusal to fight against Japan would impose a severe strain on Russo-American relations. British participation in the

3 Yalta Conference, 4–12 February.
4 21–30 January.

Pacific is no longer discussed or brought into question. Except in *Chicago Tribune* and such quarters it is taken for granted that we will participate as fully as circumstances allow, but it is popularly anticipated that our role will be very secondary.

That our war effort in the Pacific is likely to be regarded as purely nominal if known at all to the great majority of Americans is brought out once more by the sparse news coverage given this week to British task forces' attack on oil refineries in the Dutch East Indies. This example once more underlines the lesson that, whatever the extent of our actual participation in the Pacific war may be, the general emotional attitude in the United States towards Britain after Germany's downfall will greatly affect the amount of credit we get for our effort.

· · ·

Little concern has so far been shown save on the part of the liberals over the exclusion of France from the Black Sea meeting. De Gaulle's announcement that any decisions made there would not be binding upon France until she had had an opportunity to discuss them on a basis of equality and his demand for French predominance from one end of the Rhine to the other, are regarded in certain quarters as tiresome and unreasonable and have served to some extent to lessen traditional sympathy for France's position.

The Vandenberg proposal. Senator Vandenberg in a speech at Detroit reiterated his conviction that a hard and fast treaty signed by major Allies for permanent demilitarization of the Axis is an indispensable forerunner of, and not a substitute for, Dumbarton Oaks as some had feared. Nevertheless it is interesting that Vandenberg's proposal has temporarily eclipsed discussion of Dumbarton Oaks, although latter is naturally somewhat in abeyance pending outcome of Black Sea parley.

· · ·

. . . While Vandenberg proposal continues to be widely acclaimed by press and radio, the measure of support for it in Senate was indicated over weekend by a poll of eighty-one Senators conducted by *New York Times*. This found sixty-three in favour and only nine outrightly opposed. Of the Senators unavailable for reply, nine are normally regarded as supporters of Administration's foreign policy. Only three made their support conditional upon treaty not interfering with formation of an international security organization, but thirteen of the sixty-three made their support conditional on Administration approval. This evidence of willingness on part of Senate to see United States of America enter into a permanent alliance against Axis makes an encouraging contrast with the fear prevailing a year ago of any outright commitments.

· · ·

Italy. An attack by a member of Congress on British policy in Italy, along with conflict at World Trade Union Conference over inclusion of delegates from Italy, this week brought out once more the fundamental divergence of British and

American attitudes towards Italian question. To the vast majority of American people, Italy never has been a real enemy and innumerable signs both among general public and in official circles point to fact that she is coming to be considered virtually as an ally. Representative Vito Marcantonio, of socialist American Labor Party of New York, attacked armistice terms for Italy as too harsh – 'they could have been no stronger had they been for Germany'. He asserted that Italy was to be called upon to give up all her colonies, turn over island of Pantelleria to Great Britain and even cede Trieste to Yugoslavia. The implication behind his statement was that this was all at British insistence. A few hours later Acting Secretary Grew issued a statement denying that the Italian armistice terms contain 'any provisions with respect to future settlements'. Nevertheless nothing will shake average American's conviction that Great Britain is determined to reduce Italy to virtual status of a British dependency and that only hope of 'democratic' Italy resides in support that United States of America may be able to afford her. Italo-American group with its many influential leaders in party, church and labour organizations has played its cards skilfully and consistently. As a result a psychological background has been built up against which Italy is coming to be regarded as a prodigal son to be welcomed back to Allied family with much killing of fatted calves, and if British (no one seems to think of French, Greek and Yugoslav claims) insist on regarding prodigal as a borstal boy, that attitude is both selfish and unjust. Whole campaign has brilliantly illustrated Italian (and Italo-American) political argument and one can only compare results achieved with what the large Polish-born element in this country might have succeeded in doing for their mother country had they possessed anything approaching Italian flair.

Bretton Woods. The American Bankers' Association in its long awaited report on post-war monetary policy has come out against the 'Fund' proposals endorsed at Bretton Woods, but has declared its approval of the proposed $10 billion International Bank for Reconstruction and has proposed to add to the Bank some of functions of the Fund. The bankers asserted that the Fund 'was contrary to accepted credit principles and went far beyond the standards heretofore accepted by the United States in recognizing and improving changes in currency values and the maintenance of exchange controls'. The bankers' report also calls for extended powers for the Export-Import Bank, and, as a corollary, the repeal of the Johnson Act (forbidding loans to countries in default on their obligations to the United States). Opinion is divided over the interpretation to be put on the bankers' strategy. The United States Treasury will strongly resist the bankers' proposed compromise. At his press conference this week Secretary of the Treasury Morgenthau rebuked the bankers for their counter-proposals and said he would regard endorsement only of the Bank proposal as the kiss of death to the overall Bretton Woods Plan. It is possible that many New York bankers do indeed view their own proposals in that light, but it is also true that many of them have seen in the Bretton Woods Bank an invaluable channel for virtually risk-free overseas capital lending. The enabling bill for implementing the Bretton Woods proposals is expected to be presented to the House in the near future. The leader of the opposition in the House told a member of my staff that any previous disposition among Republicans to go along with the President on post-war economic policy had been dealt a severe blow by the President's nomination of Henry Wallace to the Secretaryship of Commerce.

17 February 1945

THE YALTA CONFERENCE

Yalta communiqué has had an extremely favourable first reception. Great deal was of course expected from the conference and the opposition were prepared to raise hue and cry against secret diplomacy as they did after Tehran. In the outcome, the communiqué was meaty enough to satisfy almost everybody (even though not everybody agreed with it) and in saying that it was 'by far the best communiqué issued from any major conference' so far, Vandenberg voiced popular reaction. There is no doubt that White House and State Department are determined this time to avoid the charges that Americans have to get all their news about such conferences from Prime Minister's speeches. James Byrnes seems to have raced back to Washington to make sure that the first commentary on Yalta would come from American lips and his press conference in White House on 13 February has been very widely publicized. It is also said that the President plans to report to Congress and nation when he returns. Vice-President Truman is known to favour a direct appearance before Senate. This new solicitude towards press and congressional sensibilities should help to roll some clouds away and secure more support for Administration policies.

Main charges against Yalta (as against Tehran) in this country are likely to be that Stalin dictated terms of agreement and Byrnes was at pains to depict President Roosevelt in the influential role of a tactful chairman and as the author of the agreements on the Dumbarton Oaks voting issue, the liberated areas and the reaffirmation of the Atlantic Charter. This stress of course also meets the recent calls for the President to take a more firm stand for American principles. But there is a strong tendency to evaluate the conference in terms of Roosevelt's influence versus Stalin's with the British playing a subordinate role. The critics . . . are charging that Stalin scooped the pool : internationalists are claiming that he made concessions like everybody else especially over Poland and Germany ; and Administration supporters, as after Moscow, are trying to sell the agreement as being largely of American origin. Practically no one seems to have noted that in the agreement for joint American-British-Russian handling of liberated areas as well as in plans for quarterly meetings of Foreign Ministers, we achieved a good deal ourselves. But to have the American public believe that Yalta was an American success would be a cheap price to pay for acceptance of American participation in settlement of European problems.

It frequently takes the opposition some time to decide on lines of their attack in such cases as this and so full extent of criticism and sniping to come is unknown, but it is significant that Yalta agreement has already won words of approval not only from regular Administration supporters and internationalists of radio and press but from Herbert Hoover, Senator White, minority leader in the Senate, John Foster Dulles (who said that it showed that the United Nations could and would stick together after all), Senator Wiley, ex-isolationist Republican from Wisconsin, the turbulent Democratic Senators Chandler and Tydings and Luce's *Time* magazine. Senator Ball (Republican, Minnesota), spokesman of extreme internationalists, said that his apprehensions about Polish settlement were outweighed by his approval of the document as a whole. There is no doubt that after all the recent forebodings about inter-Allied clashes, people's hopes have been raised by this evidence that the Big Three could find so many points of agreement even though many cautiously add that the real test will come in translating paper agreements into action.

. . .

. . . It is already clear that Polish settlement will be main centre of controversy. Congressmen from Polish areas of Illinois and Michigan have been quick to condemn Yalta as another Munich, the Polish-American Congress are likewise infuriated and isolationist Senators like Walsh and Wheeler profess themselves shocked. On the other hand Leo Krzycki of the Polish Labor Council (representing some 600,000 American unionists) has approved the settlement and most radio commentators and a substantial number of papers across the country accept it as being as much as could be hoped for and as representing at least some concessions by Stalin. These papers not only include liberals and regular internationalists but such conservatives as the *Denver Post, Boston Globe, Detroit News* and the *Tulsa Tribune* (Oklahoma). . . .

While there is sure to be much discussion of Polish settlement, and even Byrnes confessed that it is not the kind of thing one could enthuse over, it does not seem that recent tendency to sympathize with the Poles but accept the inevitable (in a problem with which many Americans are growing weary) will be reversed. And as for Polish-Americans themselves (who, I am privately informed, are gathering in Chicago next Thursday to decide policy), while most of them feel obliged to be more Royalist than the King in public, not all of them are so totally hostile while talking in private. There has been little new comment on Italy's relations with United Nations, and the overture to French from Yalta seemed to have been quite well received. But French here and most of their friends are still touchy and declare that recognition of France as a great power in the security organization conference at San Francisco is no substitute for full French participation in decisions for reordering of Europe which were made in Yalta.

Vandenberg remains the great enigma and is manifestly enjoying the spotlight which is now always upon him. He expressed particular pleasure about the announcement on the demilitarization of Germany but added in an impromptu talk with pressmen that the Polish settlement might mean 'quite a lot or almost nothing. If this wiggling round the Curzon Line means Lwow and Vilna will be in the new Poland, that is one thing: if they are not, that is another.' In a later written statement to the press, however, he made no allusion to the Polish settlement. The question of whether Vandenberg will accept the President's invitation to join the American delegation to the San Francisco conference is arousing much interest and if he refused, e.g. out of deference to his large Polish constituency, he would become the rallying point not only of the diehard isolationists but of all those professing loyalty to internationalism but whose consciences forbade taking part in the building of an international order based on injustice. On the other hand if he accepted it would be much more difficult for dissidents to split the country. Vandenberg meantime is playing a coy game, saying that he has not yet received an invitation to San Francisco and that his acceptance is, therefore, 'what the President calls an iffy question'. He told me two or three days ago that he had written to the President seeking clarification on four points but did not disclose what these were. The prevailing feeling in Congress is that both vanity and political expediency will dictate acceptance, although he might possibly contrive some qualified acceptance declaring that he would feel free to criticize any decisions reached at San Francisco if he felt that they should be rejected in the Senate. Of course Vandenberg, who is no novice at politics himself, must be well aware that the President has adroitly put him in a spot where he has to demonstrate the sincerity of his recent internationalist professions.

. . .

San Francisco conference. The choice of the place and time for the United Nations conference has aroused the inevitable speculation. The San Francisco Consulate reports that the Pacific Coast is already giddy with excitement about the honour which has unexpectedly fallen to it – the holding of the conference in the United States is welcomed as another Roosevelt diplomatic victory – and virtually the only discordant note comes from Los Angeles which is finding it difficult to conceal its envy of its rival to the north.

. . .

The eight-man American delegation to San Francisco is widely accredited as another example of political wizardry on the part of the President. Orthodox Republicans are disconsolate in the face of such encircling tactics but there is no doubt that the country as a whole looks on the composition of the delegation with pleasure. It is not only irrefutably bipartisan (two carefully chosen internationally-minded Republicans, Representative Eaton[1] of New Jersey and ex-Governor Stassen of Minnesota, now in the United States Navy), but it does honour to the venerable Cordell Hull (though he is still in hospital and will probably act, if at all, in no more than an honorary capacity). It brings a woman to the peace table as has been so widely demanded (Dean Gildersleeve[2] is a

1 Charles A. Eaton, Republican Congressman from New Jersey since 1925.
2 Virginia C. Gildersleeve, Dean of Barnard College 1911–47.

respected women's college president, internationalist and Anglophile in outlook ; she has praised the Yalta Agreement as an Anglo-Saxon success). It includes a representative of the fighting services (Stassen) and three key members of Congress (Connally, Chairman of the Senate Foreign Relations Committee ; Vandenberg, chief Republican foreign policy spokesman in the Senate ; and Sol Bloom, chairman of the House Foreign Affairs Committee). The delegation in fact looks almost as carefully balanced though possibly not so well together as a rowing eight. The only striking omission is the name of John Foster Dulles ; the bitterness engendered during the election battle is evidently still too fresh to permit that.

. . .

Lewis and the AF of L. The general expectation that the application of John L. Lewis and his powerful United Mine Workers for re-entry into the American Federation of Labor would be accepted, has been upset at the last moment by a further demand for concessions by Lewis, and the AF of L Executive Council meeting in Miami adjourned without taking any formal action. Lewis's demand was for representation on the Executive Council, places on which, however, are only allotted by election as and when vacancies occur and no vacancies in this fifteen-member body at present exist. It is thought that this last remaining obstacle may be settled before many weeks. The Lewis move is aimed mainly at assuring him a voice on the Council which includes representatives of several unions with which he is engaged in jurisdictional disputes.

The future of OSS. The question of the post-war status of the Office of Strategic Services has produced a flutter on the Washington scene. General Donovan was commissioned some time ago by the President to draft proposals for co-ordinating overseas intelligence work after the war, OSS having at present status merely as a war agency. One of the few copies of Donovan's proposals, circulated to influential Administration figures, leaked mysteriously to Trohan[3] of the McCormick–Patterson papers who promptly dressed up the proposals in lurid colours in a front-page story as a super-spy and Gestapo system. Gossip has it that the information leaked deliberately, if not maliciously, from Military Intelligence which has long been jealous of OSS's interloping. The ensuing publicity has caused a good deal of heartburning in the Administration which fears that Congress might take fright. The proposals seem designed to provide primarily for carrying on OSS's work after the war and for co-ordinating the sundry political intelligence activities now carried on more or less independently by the War and Navy Departments, Commerce Department, State Department, etc. The separate intelligence sections would remain but they would be called on to make available the fruits of their labours to the new central unit which would be responsible directly to the White House rather than to the Joint Chiefs of Staff as OSS is at

3 Walter Trohan, Washington correspondent of *Chicago Tribune*, 1934–69.

present. This would, of course, give the United States a more extensive political intelligence service than it has had hitherto, but the principal reason for drafting the proposals now seems to have been that Donovan, who has no intention of seeing his creation die with the war, is keen to hold on to his best recruits who are threatening to drift away to more permanent jobs. It may indeed be that the *Times-Herald* leakage will queer the pitch but schemes for the more adequate protection of American interests against the wily British and unscrupulous Russians would normally find a not unfriendly reception in Congress these days.

Wallace nomination. The George bill, divorcing the lending agencies' powers from the Secretaryship of Commerce, has passed the House after much parliamentary manoeuvring by the opposition. The test came over a motion to send the bill back into Committee which would have delayed action until after the 1 March deadline when the Senate is due to act on Wallace's nomination. The Administration won with a margin of only 8 votes (204 to 196). All the amendments to stiffen the bill in the hopes of forcing a presidential veto were ruled 'out of order as not germane'. The George bill itself was thereafter passed overwhelmingly by 399 to 2. Since the President has agreed privately not to veto the George bill, it is thought that there will be little difficulty now in obtaining Senate confirmation of Wallace's appointment. One of the interesting aspects of the fight has been the growing fear among Wallace's opponents, particularly some of the Southern Democrats, that the very violence of the opposition might end by strengthening rather than weakening Wallace's prestige and might put him in a powerful position with the rank and file of the Democratic Party for the 1948 presidential nomination. In fact, one of the arguments used by the Speaker and the Democratic Party Whips during three days of intensive behind-the-scenes pressure was the rejoinder of Andrew Jackson when confronted by the Senate's rejection of Van Buren as Minister to Great Britain : 'You have broken a Minister and elected a President of the United States.'[4]

24 February 1945

Post-Yalta mood. There is now no doubt that Yalta has had a genuinely beneficial effect on American opinion. The first shouting may, as *Life* claims, have been a shout of relief that the Big Three partnership had not fallen apart, but while the initial enthusiasm has given way to more qualified and sober evaluations of the conference's achievements, with more references to the gaps in the report and with open hostility from the Catholic press, the Russophobes and other familiar special-interest groups, the predominantly favourable estimate is maintained. . . .

·   ·   ·

4 In January 1832.

This may not last ; it may be whittled away by what Lodge in 1919 called 'the indirect method of reservations' ; but it is a welcome contrast to the tone of the discussion over Greece two months ago. The doctrine of American responsibility for European order implicit in the Yalta communiqué, and the evidence of active American interest in Middle Eastern affairs seen in the graphic account (reportedly written by the President himself) of the President's meetings with the Middle East leaders in the Mediterranean, have been accepted without any notable outcry either in Congress or in the press. In fact there is evidence of many conservatives adjusting themselves to the inevitability of American participation in foreign affairs, and even to the economic implications of this.

. . .

Though the general mood is more favourable for the time being, it is necessary for us to keep a watchful eye on the continued tendency to measure Yalta and the future in exclusive American-Russian terms. While there is a good deal of suppressed suspicion of Stalin's long-term ambitions, this is overridden at present by the desire for American-Russian collaboration and indeed Russia has come in for a fair amount of credit since Yalta for her concessions over Poland.

. . .

Mexico City conference. As a result of last-minute pressure by the United States Government all twenty American Republics represented at the Mexico City conference [1] are at war with the Axis. The large United States delegation includes Congressmen of both parties, and an army of official advisers on all the principal subjects for discussion – collaboration in the prosecution of the war, economic co-operation, Dumbarton Oaks and the Argentine problem. It is the second item on this agenda that gives the Latin American representatives the chance to demand further assistance from Uncle Sam in bolstering up the sagging markets for their strategic materials. Satisfaction of these demands may be their price for their acquiescence in other spheres.

. . .

The United States delegation apparently goes to Mexico without any concerted plan for dealing with the Argentine. Sumner Welles has reiterated his demand for her readmission to the family, but other columnists have called, in more strident tones, for the continuation of the Hull policy, supporting their demand with highly coloured rehashes of old rumours of Nazi activity in South America. Stettinius is quoted as saying that there will be no appeasement and he is believed to have taken with him the State Department's long prepared indictment of the Argentine Government's shortcomings. Another of his principal advisers has compared the activities of Col. Perón's clique with those of Mussolini before the attack on Abyssinia. Nelson Rockefeller, the recently appointed head of the Latin American Division in the State Department, is a profound believer in the good neighbour policy and is inspired with hopes, natural to one who has taken

1 Inter-American Conference on Problems of War and Peace held at Chapultepec, near Mexico City, 20 February–14 March.

over a difficult problem, of a solution turning up, but even he has said that there can be no recognition of the Colonel's Government.

. . .

The home front. The encouraging news from the war fronts in Europe . . . makes it the more difficult for the public to accept the necessity of such unpopular eleventh-hour restrictions as Byrnes's midnight curfew on all entertainment places (though the possibility of a nationwide coal strike when Lewis's contract with the coal owners expires in a few weeks makes the fuel situation a legitimate cause for worry).

. . . Meantime a Gallup poll on the question 'Have you had to make any real sacrifices for the War ?' found 64 per cent with refreshing honesty replying 'No' as against 36 per cent who replied 'Yes'.

3 March 1945

THE PRESIDENT'S RETURN

President's gesture in going voluntarily to report to Congress immediately on his return from Yalta – his first appearance in Congress in two years – has made a good impression. His speech, of course, contained little that was new and this was quickly noted by some of his opponents (Congressman Halleck, Republican of Indiana, was most cutting – 'a pretty good report of reports already reported'). The familiar complaint is consequently again being heard that Americans are dependent on Prime Minister's speeches for knowledge of what goes on at Allied conferences. Report that President revealed to the three newspapermen who accompanied him on his return voyage that 'secret understandings' had been reached at Yalta which were not in the communiqué may mean extra criticism on this count. Senator Brewster has already fastened on to this point. However these factors seem to be definitely outweighed by goodwill which President has accumulated by going to Congress, when inevitably still fatigued, by his earnestness and by his unusually subdued and at times even hesitant but always conciliatory mode of delivery. Washington has been such a sea of gossip about his poor health – partly as a result of unflattering newsreel pictures of Yalta Conference – that President felt compelled to take notice of and scotch these rumours in his opening remarks. He also made one of his rare public references to his physical disability in asking Congress's courtesy to deliver his speech seated and his mention of his 10 lb steel brace seems to be arousing as much public discussion and sympathy as any of the more weighty parts of speech. It is significant that such habitually acid voices as John O'Donnell, Fulton Lewis[1] and Arthur Krock all concede that President has made a genuinely co-operative gesture.

It was noticeable that it was almost exclusively the remarks on Allied military

1 Fulton Lewis Jr, radio commentator, Mutual Broadcasting System, 1937–66.

accomplishments which drew applause while comments on political affairs were received without visible reaction, though President's reiteration of unconditional surrender as applied both to Germany and Japan provoked applause. His remarks on increasing military cohesion between the three Great Powers are being received with pleasure and General Marshall, whose stock remains as high as ever, has made another strong plea for continued Allied unity and avoidance of bickering at an off-the-record dinner with journalists in New York. President's exposition of political agreements reached at Yalta underlined in clear terms principle of American responsibility for what goes on in liberated Europe (where he admitted problems arise which have implications that are difficult for Americans at first to realize) as being only alternative to 'queer ideas' about spheres of influence which unilateral actions produce. He admitted that 'Big Three' had been too long separated and drew favourable attention to agreement to put into effect your own original idea of quarterly meetings between Foreign Secretaries. Speech was notable too for its conversational interpolations, and some of President's aides, who had deleted from early drafts certain references to de Gaulle, were surprised to hear an unexpected allusion to 'international prima donnas' creep back into text as delivered. Exposition of 'reparations in kind', which President admitted in his press conference on 2 March included possible use of German ex-soldiers to repair damage in Soviet Union, has been calmly received so far though Clare Luce (Republican, Connecticut) expressed fears of creation of a vast slave labour state in heart of Europe and announced that she favours 'cold cash on the barrelhead' since America could get no reparations in kind that would be of any value to her. (American Federation of Labor has also in the past been hostile to suggestions of forced labour.) The President also expanded his explanation of Polish settlement as an admitted compromise but one which gives best hope for a new strong and independent Poland.

Spokesman for Polish American Congress and diehards have of course pounced on this as an abject surrender but there is little sign of country as a whole rebelling. . . . (It has been said that many Americans have come to feel that no Government has right to be so small, so intransigent and so unsuccessful as London Poles.) Meantime State Department spokesmen have been explaining and defending agreement over radio and Lippmann is arguing that Yalta gives Polish people their first hope of a genuine democracy to replace totalitarian feudalistic régime which dominated them until 1939.

Yalta proposals therefore still hold the field. Idealistic Americans certainly have misgivings and chronic reactionaries continue to object to any and every suggestion of American involvement in unpleasant affairs. . . . Despite these protests and silence of many key figures like Vandenberg the mood of moment seems to be acceptance of trend of events as outlined at Yalta, with many a warm sigh of relief that at least the three Great Powers look as if they may stick together.

International Security Organization. The high priority given by Administration to Senate ratification of American participation in security organization to be set up at San Francisco was again apparent in President's speech and in his open bid for congressional support necessary to avoid Wilson's misfortunes of 1919. He stated explicitly that success of Yalta was in Senate's hands and in stressing how he laboured at Yalta to explain American Constitution to 'two other countries' he was obviously attempting to silence rumours that he would try to circumvent Senate by means of executive agreements. With Senate and American people he said there lay responsibility for world collaboration or the responsibility for another world conflict. There is a growing feeling that Senate will eventually approve American participation in security organization (William Clayton, Assistant Secretary of State at Mexico City conference, even declared that Administration 'confidently expected' that Bretton Woods proposals would be approved by Congress which seems even more controversial) and some people say that area of serious debate will be a much narrower one, i.e. that major effort will be not to block American participation and perhaps not even to block use of an American quota force without recourse to Congress but to make certain that American delegate cannot put full (repeat full) weight of United States of America behind Security Council without recourse to Congress. . . . Senator Vandenberg told me this evening that he was accepting President's invitation to attend at San Francisco.

. . .

The Pacific War. Reactions to Prime Minister's latest reiteration of our intention to make our full contribution against Japanese, as revealed in President's report of his Mediterranean talks, show that our policy on this matter has been having its effect. A number of papers not only commend declaration but for first time add, in the words of *New Orleans Times-Picayune* : 'It is welcome but unnecessary. One British pledge is enough and realities speak for themselves.' *San Francisco Chronicle* even calls assurances 'a trifle wearisome to hear repeated'. But it is repetition which seems to have paid dividends. At same time, there is no mistaking prevailing conception that Pacific war is in a special sense America's business and that our role will be decidedly a subsidiary one.

. . .

Coal situation. John L. Lewis has opened negotiations with coal operators for a new contract by 1 April ; but, even before negotiations had started, he had duly served notice under War Labor Disputes (Smith–Connally) Act of possibility of a bituminous coal strike in thirty days. In his opening speech at negotiations on 1 March Lewis declaimed at length against governmental interference in industrial bargaining and outlined a new eighteen-point list of mine workers' demands, including a 10 cent royalty on every ton of coal mined to be used by Union for Miners' Welfare (an ingenious circumvention of wage restrictions imposed by Little Steel formula), and full pay for all time, including lunchtime, spent underground. General press is solidly against Lewis's Napoleonic domineering and Administration is admittedly nervous, especially in view of meagre coal reserves, about possibility of strike which would involve 400,000 miners, but it is too early to predict likely outcome of negotiations.

· · ·

Wallace's cabinet appointment. Henry Wallace's appointment to the Cabinet as Secretary of Commerce was finally confirmed in the Senate by 56 to 32 votes. The last round of the long battle had little excitement in it, for the fact that the President *en route* home had signed the George bill separating the Secretaryship of Commerce from the control of the government-spending agencies which Wallace's predecessor, Jesse Jones, had also controlled, mollified the opposition sufficiently to get Wallace through. However, the bitterness and name-calling in the debates on the appointment of another well-known liberal, Aubrey Williams, as head of the Rural Electrification Administration, shows the depth of feeling which exists amongst the Southern conservatives and the majority of the Republicans against anything savouring of radical New Dealism. Williams's appointment has now received an unfavourable vote from the Senate Agricultural Committee (8 to 12), which means that it will be submitted to the Senate next week with an adverse report, and Williams's head may be the price which the conservatives exact for giving way over Wallace. The President on 2 March also cleared up the mystery as to whether Jesse Jones had in fact resigned from the control of the spending agencies by announcing that he expected to appoint a new Government Loan Administrator soon. Fred Vinson, Director of Economic Stabilization, is one obvious candidate and Marriner S. Eccles[2] is mentioned as another possibility.

11 March 1945

The dramatic news of capture of Cologne and crossing of Rhine, the continued good news from Pacific and Burma theatres, the hopes that general public have entertained of improvement in Allied relations since Yalta all contribute to brighter mood which prevails at moment. This, if it lasts, offers a good omen for San Francisco and crucial debates on post-war policies. Nationalistic, even imperialistic, instincts are still strong when economic issues come up but no one denies that White House is making an impressive effort to avoid the impasse which Wilson faced in 1919. The latest sign of the President's new solicitude towards Congress is his naming of Vice-President as his special link with the Senate on post-war policies. Truman may be intellectually lightweight but he has considerable gifts of bonhomie and tact and is as popular with the Senate (over which he presides) as Wallace was unpopular. I was told that he was one of most effective backstage organizers of support for Wallace's new Cabinet appointment

2 Marriner S. Eccles, business executive, Chairman of Federal Reserve Board since 1936.

and his room, like Garner's in early days of the Administration, is always open for consultation – or refreshment – where either Democrats or Republicans are concerned. With Truman smoothing relations between Congress and White House, Bohlen linking White House and State Department and Acheson linking State Department and Congress the improved liaison system seems to be in working order.

INTERNATIONAL SECURITY ORGANIZATION

The voting formula. The Yalta formula for voting in Security Council looks like reducing still further both scope and heat of debate over American participation in World Security Organization. The all-out internationalists are frank to express some disappointment and, despite the President's claim that formula was his own idea, the press has very frequently presented solution as a straight victory for Stalin ; yet all but purists seem prepared so far to support it as a realistic compromise. (It is surprising that American idealism has not been more vocal but a fiery warning against 'forsaking ideals' in *Life* magazine by G. A. Borgese, formerly of Milan, now teaching in Chicago, suggests that there may be more to come.) On the other hand nationalist-isolationist forces, from whom trouble on such matters can normally be expected, find it difficult to make an issue on a compromise which, while conceding something to Russia, also gives America a veto right on any action against her. This is just the kind of reservation the nationalists might have cried for. Senator Ball has indeed approved proposal which he says falls short of what might have been hoped for (an effective international security system) precisely because it 'cuts the ground from under the isolationists'. It therefore now seems that question of powers to be allowed to American delegate is not such a life and death matter, since he will not be called on to commit American forces except when all great powers are agreed. President is therefore being credited in some quarters with a stroke which at once met Russian demands and mollified Senate. Senator Ferguson [1] told a member of my staff that he thought the Senate debate might now be reduced to a matter of weeks rather than months.

Of course some people are declaring that in process the new Security Organization has been seriously weakened at the outset and references to great power domination are occasionally heard. Senator Bushfield (Republican, South Dakota) has deplored appeasement of Stalin and 'three-man domination of the world', as have Scripps-Howard papers. Senator Brewster (Republican, Maine) has talked pessimistically about another futile Holy Alliance. But for the moment such voices are greatly in the minority and prevailing tendency is to accept formula as a basis for action and that if disturbances occur in which great powers are involved, no voting procedure would save peace anyhow. Besides Ball, his companions of the famous B2H2 resolution (Senators Burton, Hill and Hatch)

1 Homer Ferguson, Republican Senator from Michigan 1943–55.

have also announced their support and Vandenberg is said to have told a private session of Republicans that while formula was 'morally wrong' it was 'practically of no moment'. Senator White (Republican leader in Senate) has also commented favourably. Perhaps most interesting endorsement has come from John Foster Dulles in a letter to *New York Times* which attempted to give theoretical as well as practical justification for what he called 'a statesmanlike solution of a knotty problem'. Dulles argued that much-used maxim that no nation should be a judge in its own case is not applicable to many of issues which may come before the Security Council, since it applies only where there is a pre-existing body of relevant law and provision has been made for referring justiciable cases to international court. He also pointedly claimed that formula closely followed recent Cleveland Church Conference declaration which was largely his own creation. Some of the other religious organizations who came out against the veto right after Dumbarton Oaks have still to be heard from.

Chapultepec Security Act. The other major development in this field has been the Chapultepec Security Act whereby all twenty American Republics at Mexico City pledged themselves to use force to repel any threat to one of them during remainder of present war and recommended continuance of these obligations post-war by adoption of appropriate treaties. The prevailing feeling in Washington is that this act – an expression of Latin American countries' anxiety for collective security against possible Argentine aggression – went considerably further than the United States Delegation had originally bargained for. . . .

. . . Act is frequently said to replace Monroe Doctrine by a historic new principle in which the United States acts not as hemispheric policeman but as a partner in genuine good-neighbour style.

. . .

Vandenberg's position. Vandenberg, in announcing his acceptance of invitation to San Francisco, referred to a 'cordial and satisfactory' interchange of letters with President which had guaranteed him 'freedom of action'.

. . .

In Senate on 7 March Vandenberg made his first public comment on Polish settlement at Yalta. He started by reading a press report of our own warning in the House to Lublin Government, went on to express his 'complete approval' and called on United States Government to be 'equally frank'. The acid test of new Government he declared will be whether Generals Anders [1] and Bor [2] are permitted to return freely to Poland. 'It is my dearest desire', he continued, 'that all these decisions made under pressure of war shall be temporary in fact as well as in name ; that they shall pass in full review at final peace table ; and that if

1 General Wladyslaw Anders, prisoner of war in USSR 1939–41. On release organized Polish Corps in Middle East.

2 General Tadeusz Bor-Komorowski, commander of underground army in Poland, 1943, and of the Warsaw uprising in 1944.

injustices still remain they shall fall squarely within asserted jurisdiction of new peace league for full, free, fair study and for recommended correction.'

.   .   .

Administration changes. Wallace has now taken over as Secretary of Commerce and his opening move was the appointment of an orthodox committee of businessmen to study the problems of Small Business. The impression is growing that he will start by making a careful effort to win over support, e.g. of Small Business *vis-à-vis* Wall Street.

.   .   .

The appointments of Vinson to be Federal Loan Administrator, William H. Davis, Chairman of the War Labor Board to succeed him, and George Taylor,[3] Davis's assistant, to the War Labor Board, indicate the White House's present desire to avoid unnecessary friction with Congress while the great issues of post-war policy are in the offing.

17 March 1945

.   .   .

Reorientation towards the Pacific. The tone of the Prime Minister's speech to the Conservative Party[1] has confirmed the prevailing belief here that the war in Europe is finally in its last stages. While there is an almost self-conscious avoidance of over-optimism in view of the disappointments of last December, the Military and Naval authorities are initiating extensive efforts to prevent any let down on VE day and to reorient people's thinking towards the Pacific. (The startling newsreel pictures of the bitter fighting at Iwo-Jima have already been assisting this process. They have been making a profound impression on the public and one symbolic byproduct is the new willingness to discuss the possible use of gas against the Japanese, an idea originally mooted by the *Chicago Tribune*.) General Marshall has had another of his secret sessions with his favourite group of journalists and broadcasters, and Admirals Halsey and Nimitz while in Washington have also had private conferences with the press. The effects of these talks are already discernible in the columns of the journalists and three themes are noticeable :

(a) The public must not expect large-scale demobilizations after VE day. Most of the United States forces in Europe will have to move to the Pacific and some may not even get a furlough in the United States before transfer.

(b) The Pacific theatre is changing so profoundly that any forthcoming reorganizations in the top command should not occasion surprise.

.   .   .

(c) The broad outlines of Pacific strategy now provide for American forces to tackle Japan direct while other Allied forces will be used for such specialized

3 George W. Taylor, Professor of Economics, University of Pennsylvania.

1 Delivered on 15 March, envisaging a general election in the summer and referring to the 'nearly continuous and ever more rapid progress of the war.'

tasks as removing the Japanese from their conquered overseas territories. The rationale for this division of responsibilities was offered in a succession of plainly inspired broadcasts by Gram Swing in which he declared

we are not going to spend American lives and treasure in freeing imperial possessions from the Japanese and then turn them back to their pre-war owners. It is for the British to clear the Japanese out of Malaya and for the Dutch to clear them out of the Netherlands Indies. If the Dutch do not have the strength to do it they must ask the British to help them. We are not going to do it. . . . We see it as our assignment to bear the responsibility of defeating Japan and that we are prepared to do by ourselves.

Such sentiments are being echoed elsewhere and all serve, along with Stettinius's off-the-record declaration to journalists that the trusteeship principle will be on the agenda at San Francisco, to bring questions about the future of dependent territories back into prominence.

Trusteeship.[2] This discussion has changed considerably from the fulminations against imperialism as such which were common two or three years ago. Though Stettinius hinted last week that he favoured the application of trusteeship not only to captured territories and existing mandates but to areas incapable of self-government, the discussion now commonly centres almost exclusively on the Pacific, and criticism of African colonies comes only from such Negro organizations as Paul Robeson's leftist Council on African Affairs. It is clear that Stettinius, the Office of War Information, and the War and Navy Departments are keen to ward off possible criticism by presenting America's fight in the Pacific as a battle for progress. The danger for us in such publicity is that while America is identified with the fight to free the world from the Japanese menace, we may become identified with a selfish fight to restore the *status quo* by recapturing our lost imperial possessions. Writers of as different backgrounds as the conservative William Philip Simms and the liberal Owen Lattimore (who accompanied Wallace to China and Siberia) talk of Russian prestige alone rising in the Pacific, and Lattimore in his new book *Solution in Asia* draws the conclusion that only more progressive policies by the Western Powers can prevent the Eastern peoples from turning towards the Soviet. Generally America's handling of the Philippines is presented as a goal to be aimed at. The Dutch are accorded second place because of their declarations of future policy in the Dutch Indies. We tend to come off a rather poor third and the French attitude is viewed as the most recalcitrant and least defensible of the European imperial powers. Apart from occasional suggestions by anti-Communists that China is liable to become another Poland with the Yenan Communists replacing Lublin and Chiang Kai-shek replacing Mikolajczyk, there is at present surprisingly little discussion of China's post-war role.

. . . .

2 In place of mandates system of League of Nations a scheme for placing 'backward territories' in the 'trusteeship' of the United Nations organization was put forward.

San Francisco conference. Interest in San Francisco conference rises steadily and one group after another have announced their determination to be represented – the Zionists, National Negro Council, National Association of Manufacturers, the CIO (the *New Yorker* comments 'to get hotel space in San Francisco now you have to declare war against Germany'). CIO staged a gigantic rally of 18,000 people in Madison Square Garden tying together Yalta, World Trade Union Conference and San Francisco, with Gromyko and returning CIO delegates to London conference as star speakers. Enthusiasm manifest was further evidence of new political orientation of CIO, spurred on by Hillman, and of the ascendancy of pro-Russian wing of American labour movement. AF of L, who had refused to participate in London, seemed to have been out-manoeuvred and are left uttering plaintive warnings to Administration about dangers of America's foreign policy being dictated by any international trade union gathering.

26 March 1945

Inter-Allied relations. With State Department continuing to discourage all speculation on such issues as Poland and Roumania, week has been unusually uneventful as regards diplomatic developments, and public's attention has swung back to domestic concerns, especially the food tangle and Byrnes's midnight curfew on entertainment places and restaurants. Enthusiasm over Yalta has inevitably somewhat melted but disposition to put a priority on harmony between the Big Three, and especially USA and USSR, continues. Consequently State Department has succeeded so far in preventing any great public issue building up over Roumania, Poland or Finland. Following Stettinius's statement on 15 March [1] there was increased talk of Roumania being a test of Yalta, and some internationalists showed signs of nervousness lest unilateral Russian action might undo Yalta's achievements, but in absence of hard news this has died away and issue is again out of public eye. White House and State Department experts are privately depressed about continuous eruption of snags e.g. the Polish, French, Arab, etc., crises. Polish negotiations have indeed progressed without usual glare of publicity. Question of who represents Poland at San Francisco is recognized to be an increasingly embarrassing one. Professor Lange of Polido Socialists (who visited Russia with Father Orlemanski last year) has suggested in *New York Times* that Poland might be represented by Osubka-Morawski, [2] Foreign Minister of Lublin Poles, Romer, [3] Foreign Minister in Government-in-Exile during Mikolajczyk's premiership, and a third person to be chosen by these two. Meantime American-Polish Congress have been telegraphing White House insisting that one of their number should be attached to United States delegation as

---

1 That the situation in Roumania was such as to require consultations between the Big Three.
2 Edward B. Osubka-Morawski, President of Lublin Committee 1944–5, Prime Minister of Provisional Government 1945–7.
3 Tadeusz Romer, Foreign Minister in London Polish Government 1943–4.

an observer. A *Herald Tribune* reporter has quoted a State Department official as suggesting that, if Moscow talks do not progress faster, San Francisco might have to start without the Poles, who would join conference later.

· · ·

United States delegation have now had two sessions with President and further 'team meetings' are planned. President has also visited Mr Hull who is still in hospital and whose appearance at San Francisco looks increasingly unlikely. State Department are meantime in process of assembling assorted list of advisers who will accompany American delegation. Vandenberg has released a letter from John Foster Dulles in which latter rejected idea of attaching himself to delegation or to Vandenberg personally as an adviser, but suggested that he might appear independently as Chairman of Federal Council of Churches Commission on a Just and Durable Peace. This does not I think mean that Dulles and Dewey intend to oppose San Francisco. In fact I am told that Dulles has two speeches on Dumbarton Oaks, one voicing unqualified approval which he makes to audiences in Middle West who still need convincing, and other proposing various amendments which he keeps for more internationally-minded East Coast. Nor does it mean any split between Vandenberg and Dulles (I am told that when invited recently to speak in Michigan, Vandenberg's home state, Dulles replied that he would first 'have to clear it with Arthur'). It looks more like a mixture of *amour propre* and hardboiled politics on part of Dewey and his advisers who, while giving approval to Dumbarton Oaks, are not prepared to surrender their independence by playing second fiddle in a Roosevelt-appointed delegation.

· · ·

Food Tangle. Full details of the furore over food supplies are reported to you separately, but it is worth noting that the subject has claimed more front-page space and editorial attention than at any time during the war. The crisis has again uncovered the deep-rooted American suspicion of being fleeced by the rest of the world and demands that America's own needs be considered first are widespread, but the Administration has come in for most of the direct criticism on this occasion. The Prime Minister's statement in the Commons[4] seems to have provided an effective check on criticisms of our own stockpiles. The President, who had promised to give the press a statement on the situation on 23 March, cancelled his press conference on that date.

· · ·

Palestine. According to confidential talk in Zionist quarters the President told Rabbi Stephen Wise that it had been agreed at Yalta that Palestine should be constituted as a Jewish State. This was to be finally settled by the Council of the world organization to be established at San Francisco. The President is supposed

4 On 21 March, rebutting exaggerated impression in certain American circles of Britain's food stocks and asserting that they amounted to 'rather less than 6 million tons' and would probably fall in November to 4.75 million tons.

to have added that Ibn Saud[5] was adamantly opposed to this despite the entreaties of Messrs Roosevelt and Churchill, but that this would have to be largely overcome or ignored. This, though nothing more than a rumour at present, has caused a rise in the spirits of Zionist leaders here which had been left drooping by the recent public remarks on Palestine made by the President and the Prime Minister.

31 March 1945

The headlines celebrating the phenomenal American advance east of the Rhine [1] – with occasional mention of British advance towards Munster – as well as Russian march to Austrian border have naturally made for intense expectation of early German surrender. The misinterpretation of a White House circular requesting the heads of missions, Government Departments, etc., to remain at their posts in Washington during San Francisco conference finally raised the temperature to boiling-point and Eisenhower's statement that Germans were done for precipitated on 27 March a nationwide rumour, disseminated by radio commentators, that end of European war was expected hourly. This was later scotched by press but general excitement continued to bubble for some time. There are no signs of any 'soft peace' undertones. Public opinion in general would welcome severe terms and reports of the stern attitude towards reparations on the part of principal Allied Governments is received with approval. So far neither churches nor trade unions have ventured to express their usual reservations.

In contrast with satisfaction caused by war news there is now much natural anxiety, more widespread at present in official Washington circles than in press and among public, about international diplomatic situation. Administration is plainly engaged in toning down exaggerated expectations concerning San Francisco conference.

. . .

Officials most directly concerned do not hide either from themselves or from their closer press contacts their worry about obstacles to understanding with USSR, particularly over Poland and Roumania, and latterly over Russia's intentions towards Turkey. Persia is seldom mentioned. There is no general chorus of anxiety as yet. The various disturbing possibilities are rather like apparitions raising their ugly heads from time to time, one diverting attention from another. Many events have contributed to this. Russia has now officially declared her intention to send no higher official than Mr Gromyko. The obvious implications of this, and the allegation of the columnists Drew Pearson and Constantine Brown that the decision was not well received by British and American Governments, have had their effect. At first in form of press leakages, later confirmed

---

5 Abdul Aziz Ibn Saud, King of Saudi Arabia 1932–53.
1 After crossings at Oppenheim and Worms on 26 March.

under pressure by White House while State Department sat by in embarrassed silence, the fact emerged that Russia intends to bring 'independent' Ukrainian and White Russian delegations with them to San Francisco. Concurrent statement that United States also claims three voices provoked obvious criticisms from Senator Vandenberg and Representative Bloom. Fulbright protested against such secret deals of this kind. There is indeed a wave of indignant or cynical comment in press which speculates on effects of so obvious a split inside the United States delegation, and enquires about the prospects of that equality of all nations large and small which Hull had preached so fervently ; which America, alone among the powers, was supposed to hold dear ; and of which the original democratic constitution of the Assembly was to be the sacred aim. But the fiercest fire is directed against secrecy – the admission by White House that a secret agreement was in fact reached at Yalta has conjured up one of the worst bugbears of American public opinion – the traditional horror of secret diplomacy calculated to concert sinister arrangements which will not bear the scrutiny of a free people. In this respect American journalists cease to be professionals and experience the strong emotions of the average American citizen. To all this is added the actual state of affairs in Poland and Roumania, the former naturally bruited about by the Polish Ambassador, who is an eloquent speaker and has at last a really effective case ; the old uneasiness now naturally much magnified about voting procedure in the Council ; the obscure behaviour of de Gaulle ; alleged British and French reluctance to discuss colonies and mandates and their fears of American intentions in that regard. There is some continuing uncertainty as to behaviour of Latin American countries, despite the accord reached at Chapultepec, in particular speculation about Russian attitude to possible admission of Argentina and anxieties of purists opposed to well-defined regional plans which may cut across a world organization. From all this it will be seen only too clearly why these and other occasions of conflict lower the spirits and confuse the outlook both of the public and of those most intimately concerned with conference itself. I am told there are some in State Department who would willingly postpone the whole affair if it were at all feasible to do so at this late date. Nevertheless, when the hour strikes an attempt will doubtless be made by Administration and its supporters to hold public opinion solid on crucial issues and to prevent disagreements from obtaining too much play.

. . .

Comment on San Francisco. Meanwhile, various American statesmen are making their views known to the public, with some indication of what line will be followed by those who share their views at the conference. Ex-President Hoover has written a series of widely syndicated articles in line with his previous well-known views. He makes seven main points : the need for a charter of human rights, i.e. of individual liberties ; arrangements for the possibility of the revision of all treaties every ten years ; the need for tight regional, political and economic organization ; the total disarmament of the enemy ; relative disarmament of the Allies ; the right to commit the United States to the use of force against aggression to be given not to the delegate at the council but to the President, subject to approval by the majority of the Senate and House Committees concerned with Foreign Affairs ; the need for implementing all decisions slowly and not in one fell swoop. This is probably in general harmony with the views of such Republicans as Dulles, who is going to San Francisco in a 'private capacity', and of other Republican leaders, particularly Vandenberg, who is a delegate. Stassen has similarly spoken in favour of the charter of human rights and warned against the debacle bound to be caused by excessive defence of national sovereignties against prevailing world trends. Fulbright in his maiden speech in the Senate echoed this warning concerning sovereign rights and he aimed principally at nationalists of both parties – the Vandenberg-Tydings school. He called for the burial of such persistent myths as the view that the United States was Anglophobe or Russophobe or anti-Semitic, and like Stassen made a strongly internationalist speech permeated with a certain degree of scepticism concerning San Francisco. Now that the Russians have shown their hand the air is likely to be fuller of similar pronouncements, and their tone sharper.

If the question of the number of votes to be controlled by the Big Three and general Russian intransigence is the biggest bogey visible at the present, that of the trusteeship of dependent areas is likely to rival it unless steps are taken to conjure it. If there is one subject upon which the bulk of United States opinion is united, it is the undesirability of colonial possessions as such. When Americans think of colonies they think of British colonies first. It is difficult to see how the most enlightened American officials can resist the impulse to reform or urge the reform of the institution of colonies and mandates, since it is one of their few points of genuine solidarity with those groups and individuals who oppose them in other fields, and moreover responds to their own most cherished convictions. At best they may try to avoid raising the issue altogether or sidetrack it in some way, but this is unlikely to pass unnoticed by newspapers and political groups and may form the subject of much adverse comment, some of it sincere enough but with anti-British implications. The colonial question is indeed apt to be the first to be raised in any group of representative and serious-minded Americans. Their interest is indeed only equalled by an almost complete lack of factual information and a general lack of ability to distinguish between the 'colonial' and the Indian question. The bodies most opposed to the raising of this subject at present are the United States service departments, openly anxious as they are to obtain outright possession of strategic bases, which would amount to colonial annexation. On this tack an unexpected ally, Robert Sherwood, lately back from the Pacific, observed that he did not see how islands, over whose conquest so much American blood had been spilt, could ever be given up by this country. The protagonists of this view are therefore among those most likely, if not to defend – for few do that – at least to refrain from attacking the British colonial and mandatory system. Since the visit of the Colonial Secretary,[2] Washington officials, particularly Mr Stettinius and members of his Department, seem convinced that His Majesty's Government looks with some disfavour upon mandates, an institution viewed here as one of the few genuine, if indifferently realized, achievements of the League of Nations, and really wishes to convert them into virtual colonies. Sooner or later this subject may form a topic of public controversy, the acuteness of which will depend to some extent on the degree of previous understanding reached between Americans and ourselves on basic principles.

Economic isolationism. As for isolationism, it has, as might have been expected, shifted from the political front, where it is at present too discredited to risk a serious trial of strength, and moved to economic fields where it can operate in a much more disguised, if even more destructive, fashion. The debate in Congress on the renewal of the Reciprocal Trade Agreements, with the new 50 per cent increase in flexibility requested by the President, is likely to be as serious a conflict as it always has been, for it leads to an opposition of representatives of special economic interests with economic reactionaries and isolationists *pur sang* ; the opposition at Bretton Woods has similarly been loudmouthed, with Leon Fraser,[3] ex-President of the Bank of International Settlements, going considerably beyond the regular bankers front : he spoke of the fund as a disguised grant-in-aid to Britain which Britain did not need or deserve, etc. – words apparently merely intended to curry favour with the more reactionary Senators. The fight over this is expected to be severe and the outcome uncertain. Mr Boothby's[4] letters to the *New York Times*[5] reported to you in a recent telegram are being used as ammunition by the financial and political opponents to Bretton Woods who make capital out of the fact that they have so far gone completely unanswered by Dr Harry White. Mr Boothby himself is said to be giving a good deal of aid and comfort to the more implacable anti-Administration members of Congress, who privately maintain that his intervention has tipped the scale and enabled them to guarantee, if not the defeat, at any rate the deferment of the Administration's proposals for a considerable time. Although there is a view in the State Department that Mr Boothby's intervention must sooner or later boomerang against him and his allies as a dark British intrigue doubtless undertaken on behalf of reactionary or sinister interests in Britain, this may be no more than so much wishful thinking on the part of these indignant officials. In the meanwhile, the *Reader's Digest,* which in effect is the voice of Big Business, has

2 Oliver Stanley, Secretary of State for the Colonies 1942–5.
3 Leon Fraser, President of First National Bank of New York 1937–45.
4 Robert J.G.Boothby, Conservative MP for E.Aberdeenshire 1924–58.
5 On 4 and 14 March, questioning the workability of the Bretton Woods proposals and wanting them shelved until after San Francisco.

printed a digest of Professor Hayek's notorious work, *The Road to Serfdom* (any number of off-prints of this at reduced prices would be supplied by the Book of the Month Club to purchasers). Wall Street looks on Hayek[6] as the richest goldmine yet discovered and are peddling his views everywhere. The Scripps-Howard papers have syndicated a digest of this digest, and the imminent arrival of the Professor himself is eagerly anticipated by the anti-Bretton Woods party, who expect him to act as the heavy artillery with formidable academic ammunition, a commodity at present insufficiently supplied by the somewhat thin writings of their university allies, faced as these are by the almost complete consensus of all the reputable economists in the country. Professor Hayek should not be surprised if he is invited to address the Daughters of the American Revolution to provide them with the latest weapons against such sinister social incendiaries as Lord Keynes and the British Treasury.

8 April 1945

San Francisco Conference. Anxieties and dissensions reported last week led to an immense depression during weekend. It soon became clear that things were being handled in a somewhat haphazard fashion apparently by President himself who is on holiday, with scarcely any systematic co-ordination with, or indeed information to, the State Department. If President ever supposed that his demand for three United States votes would act as a sop to those who would otherwise protest against the similar Russian demand, this calculation was plainly upset by results. The sharp change of key from the tone of sustained international idealism, which Stettinius has kept up with some consistency, to an atmosphere of concealed bargaining behind the scenes on a basis of sheer national expediency, was clearly too much for United States public opinion and proposals received a very bad press and genuinely shook United States delegation. When belatedly, after an acutely embarrassed silence, Stettinius gave out in the course of his reply to journalists that United States had decided to withdraw its original claim and to confine itself to one vote, the universal sigh of moral relief was almost audible. In this case even the crudest antennae would have sufficed to detect shock administered by this combination of the abhorred secret diplomacy together with a display of apparent disregard for principles accepted earlier, with no steps to prepare public for anything of the kind. MacLeish, as might have been expected, gave tongue to particularly melancholy reflections and went about enquiring how he was to defend his lately announced policy of 'candour to the people', when secret clauses were likely to pop up right and left, and President took steps with which he did not trouble to acquaint even highest officials responsible for foreign policy. President has since seen him and soothed him down considerably. Stettinius's general statement to the press did indeed do a good deal to allay perplex-

6 Frederick August von Hayek, Professor of Economic Science and Statistics at University of London 1931–50. His *Road to Serfdom*, a polemic against welfare socialism, was published in 1944.

ity and resentment which were mounting at an alarming rate ; while no one can be said to be precisely happy about prospects of San Francisco particularly with respect to the Polish issue, and the powers of the Assembly and its connexion with the rights and the reactions of the smaller nations, the steady support of the San Francisco shares by State Department, and confidence radiated by Stettinius have undoubtedly, with some help from this Embassy, propped up a jittery market and checked the onslaught of the bears effectively.

Attitude to Russia. It is worth noting that such is the respect for triumph and power that apart from the regular Russophobes there is no violent criticism of Russia's behaviour, demands and intentions, so much as disappointment, nervous perplexity, a search for motives, an attempt to put fairest interpretation upon her behaviour such as a genuine desire to introduce a greater federal flexibility into her system of republics, talk of her need for good European neighbours, etc. Poles are getting a correspondingly feeble press except from their steady friends whose influence is clearly declining with that of isolationism in general. On the other hand rejection of demand that Lublin Government be represented is well received as minimum concession to principle bound to be paid by the democracies. One of byproducts of this situation is that inevitably less is expected of San Francisco conference than say a week ago, which is doubtless all to the good, but that public enthusiasm which Yalta had originally induced has, equally naturally, melted away completely. Timing of Soviet denunciation of the pact with Japan has naturally done something to increase optimism regarding Russia's role. One or two State Department officials tend to look on this with mild scepticism as a smart Russian move to offset the distrust engendered by other Russian acts.

The attitude of United States delegates. There are improvements in other directions ; Krock reports, probably reliably enough, that American delegation have finally reached unanimity about granting of Russia's request for three votes if she persists in it, because they feel bound to support President's commitment, however unwelcome. If this means that Vandenberg, who previously announced opposition to this, has yielded ground, this represents a notable triumph for moderates. Hamilton Armstrong who is one of American advisers has apparently played some part in persuading Dulles (who has changed his mind and accepted post of Adviser) and through him the Republicans, that a split in delegation at this stage would create greater havoc than this particular concession. Dulles himself told me that he did not think votes were as important as many appeared to think. But while steps to steady public opinion have thus proved gratifyingly effective, talk within Administration itself naturally continues to be somewhat depressed, since it is realized that such solidarity of American opinion can scarcely be expected to survive the kind of disagreements which the Russian attitude seems at present to make inevitable at the conference itself. Nevertheless, a meed of praise is due to Stettinius, who, despite inevitable embarrassment, did not lose his head either in the face of contradictory instructions from the White House or of the rebellious press, but continued to peg away at the essential reasons for the conference without any display of personal uncertainty or resentment. His speech at Chicago, probably written by Clayton, firmly asserting that the economic issues – Bretton Woods and commodity policy, on which a conference is now officially to be held next year – were part and parcel of the general foreign policy of the United States and that the hopes of the American people for a stable world in which they shall be involved to a far greater degree than before will founder just as much upon a failure to support the Administration's economic as its political policy, was a brave, as well as timely, utterance in view of the considerable opposition to this from Wall Street etc., and is evidence that the Administration is genuinely prepared to go full steam ahead on the probably accurate supposition that it is now or never, that their duty is clear, that they have judged their moment and that their power is never likely to be higher. His robust optimism shows up well at such moments of public confusion and depression, and he has earned reluctant compliments from his harshest press critics. Senator McCarran, who spoke of the meetings of his group, i.e. the Silver Senators, with Administration and bankers' advocates as well as Mr Boothby, 'the leader of the opposition to Bretton Woods in England', declares them prepared to back Bretton Woods provided that silver is assured of an adequate role.

Vandenberg's eight amendments which chiefly stress the necessity of a charter of human rights, of ensuring machinery for the revision of any peace settlement and the necessity for greater power for the Assembly, have undoubtedly had considerable influence on his fellow delegates and are likely to be acquiesced in to some degree by the Administration. Whatever the Administration may therefore choose to tell us on the matter, Vandenberg's proposals clearly deserve your most earnest consideration. . . .

.   .   .

The resignation of Mr Byrnes [1] occurred in the same sudden, unpredicted and inconsequent fashion as most of the other strangely disconnected political developments of this peculiar fortnight. It was long known that Mr Byrnes wished to retire. Ever since his disappointments, firstly, in failing to secure the President's support for the vice-presidential nomination (when he had apparently been led to believe it was coming), then for the Secretaryship of State, which, it seems, he deeply desired, Mr Byrnes had been talking seriously of resignation. He has devoted himself too long and too honestly to public affairs to have acquired more than a very modest competence, and his friends report that he feels too poor to continue in office as well as too tired and insufficiently supported by the White House. Latterly disagreements with Mr Baruch, dissensions within his office

1 As Mobilization Director.

with Major-General Clay,[2] a strongly authoritarian character now sent to supervise civil affairs in Germany, and finally the imminent failure of the manpower bill (now defeated in the Senate) upon which his future policies rested, finally decided him to go now. He talked of this to American officials during the return from Yalta, but did not himself appear certain of the date. His resignation appears to have been as much a surprise to the White House as to the public, but the President evidently felt that he could not indefinitely prevail upon him to remain. He left at one of the most critical moments in his particular province with the food situation in a palpable mess and the manpower situation not much better. The President swiftly replaced him with Judge Vinson, the nearest equivalent to Byrnes in public life. Vinson is a Southern liberal, gifted with considerable common sense, slow but firm judgment and a range of sympathies and acquaintance which stretches from Southern conservatives in Congress to such out-and-out New Dealers as Justice Black. He is not too popular with labour at the moment on account of his unyielding firmness in holding wages during his period as Economic Stabilizer ; on the other hand he is very well viewed in Congress (in which he sat for almost fifteen years) and his confirmation to the most powerful internal post in the Administration went through with that lightning rapidity with which only the most popular public servants are allowed to pass that tricky turnstile. His attitude towards us is said to leave nothing to be desired, and perhaps the main disadvantage of his appointment is that being none too rapid a thinker he will probably take some time to acquire the knowledge of the situation which his office requires. While he may lack Mr Byrnes's uncanny sensitiveness to the gusts of public opinion and his famous Irish charm which so often won over potential opponents, he is, if anything, a solider and more disinterested man, less likely to yield to political and economic pressures and more likely to stick to whatever guns he may choose to select. His judgment of persons is said to be good and he is reported to overestimate the abilities neither of Crowley nor of Marvin Jones. Meanwhile the post of Federal Loan Administrator, vacated by Jesse Jones and torn from the grasp of Mr Wallace, into which Mr Vinson had been shunted, is once more unfilled. There is the usual talk of Joe Kennedy (who has been mentioned for almost every available post) who indeed is said to be backed by conservatives and Catholics. Crowley too is said to have his eye on it, as has Harold Smith, the inconspicuous but most efficient director of the Bureau of the Budget. Marriner Eccles and Justice William Douglas are occasionally spoken of. There is no reason for supposing that the President has made up his mind, or that when he has, this fact will be communicated to his advisers before it actually takes effect. Official Washington is prepared for anything. The President is away and a sudden fiat is expected at any moment.

Mr Justice Black and the Negroes. The New Deal is still very much on the defensive, and from time to time, therefore, requires manifestations of faith in principles and leaders, if only to determine the loyalties and opinions of its ad-

2 Lucius du B. Clay, career soldier, Deputy Military Governor of U S zone of Germany, 1945.

herents. The recent dinner to Mr Justice Black, who has pursued an undeviatingly radical path on the Bench to the occasional consternation of his more conservative brethren, was such an event. Black is a typical Southern radical by birth and upbringing, a 'poor white', who has frequently been mentioned for a number of political posts as one of the few still stout and undefeated fighting leaders of aggressive liberalism in the United States. The dinner was addressed by Senator Pepper, who made a fiery New Deal speech ; by Senator Barkley, who delivered a milder homily ; by Judge Vinson, whose presence symbolized his solidarity with even the extremest liberal principles ; and by the Attorney to the Department of Interior,[3] who gibed at what liberals regard as Justice Frankfurter's now undiscriminating conservatism. The meeting was notable for the presence of some two hundred Negroes, not often guests at Washington banquets. Coupled with recent political repercussions which occurred round the Aubrey Williams case it is now fairly clear that a really determined bid for the entire coloured vote in the North and South is likely to be made by the Administration. The only factor likely to moderate this is the Administration's need for Southern votes in the Senate in support of foreign policy (on domestic policy it knows it cannot expect them). There is similarly equally little doubt that unless the Republican Party makes a serious and successful effort to steal this thunder, it will lose the Negro vote for good. Since there are over twelve million Negroes in the United States, and the poll tax, gradually whittled at, seems bound sooner or later to be abolished in State after State, Negroes are likely to play an increasingly important part in virtue of the sheer weight of their vote, unless indeed those sanguinary racial conflicts, which some pessimists declare to be inevitable after the war, make of this a really violent issue, incapable of being settled by peaceful means.

· · ·

New spirit abroad. I was amused and gratified to observe that the harsh words used of my recent attendance at a State wolf hunt in Oklahoma by a Republican novice in Congress have for once evoked a stout and eloquent defence by no fewer than three of his colleagues from the South West, who denounced the offender as indulging in highly irresponsible mischief-making based on wide-ranging ignorance of the facts. These handsome bouquets represented, if nothing else, a changed temper of Congress in this regard – a far cry from the difficult days of 1941.[4]

14 April 1945

Mr Roosevelt's death.[1] The sudden death of President Roosevelt stunned the nation and Washington equally and first reaction is nervous helplessness and a

---

3 Fowler V.Harper, Professor of Law, University of Indiana, 1929–46, Solicitor to Department of the Interior 1943–5.

4 In March 1941 Halifax's acceptance of an invitation to take part in a fox hunt at Wilmington, Virginia, provoked a tempest of criticism for indulging in 'effete pleasures' in wartime.

1 On 12 April 1945.

strong instinct to unite and stand together during so grave a crisis. As a result of this President Truman is likely at any rate in the beginning to obtain all support he may require to discharge the immense new task by which he is all but overwhelmed. Critical voices are for moment stilled, grief is profound and universal and greatness of Franklin Roosevelt is passionately attested on all sides. His openest enemies have united to pay homage to his memory. Meanwhile confused speculation is naturally flowing everywhere about personality and future policies of new President and of impact of event upon the United States and world. Truman's modesty, geniality and honesty have won him golden opinions in Washington ; in country at large he is not so well known. I have met him and entertained him on more than one occasion and my feeling is that he is a man of principle and courage, of pertinacity and sound judgment and of goodwill particularly towards us. On all topics which matter most – post-war settlement and in particular international security, the future of Germany, Lend-Lease, Bretton Woods, etc. – his views are probably identical with those of his predecessor. He may not hold them in same wealth of personal knowledge of issues involved, or imaginative sweep, but as a number of shrewd Americans have been saying, e.g. Dean Acheson, Byrnes, Vinson, Frankfurter, Rayburn and others, his earnestness and open-mindedness are such that he is capable of being educated by his experts about all that really matters. He is singularly free from prejudice or self-willed obstinacy and is naturally inclined to seek an association with us (and more remotely the USSR) and if we establish a sound relationship with him from the beginning, things should go well if general Washington political structure remains reasonably stable. The most probable immediate development is likely to be an increase in powers of Senate and possibly of State Department which is bound to happen during periods of relative uncertainty, while it is still problematic to what degree White House will be able to assert its authority. One of Truman's strongest suits is his popularity in, and naturally liking for, the Senate and it may well be that legislation, particularly on foreign policy, once it is adopted elsewhere, in government Departments or at San Francisco, will be passed more easily by Senate from hands of President Truman than from those of his more imperious predecessor. How important this is needs no stressing. Truman is essentially a man of the people, a son of a Missouri farmer with a homely touch and a good deal of rustic shrewdness combined with political courage which made his well-known Senate Committee a genuine scourge of speculators and wasters in field of national defence. Although one of his intimates is Bob Hannegan, the Missouri political boss who is Chairman of Democratic Party, Truman is unlikely to dispense favours to political cronies or indeed in any other way remind public of Harding era. His firm adhesion to the enlightened international policies which his predecessor had so firmly set in train, his capacity for impressing those he meets with practical nature of his desire to improve the lot of the 'little man' both in his country and beyond and his genuine anxiety to listen to advice and to equip himself thoroughly for his immense task – all these promise well for continuance of the close Anglo-American association provided that new ties are forged to replace those which death of Mr Roosevelt so tragically snapped. Certainly there is every evidence of willingness on Truman's part for such a consummation. If new President is to assert himself process will inevitably take some time and during that interim centrifugal forces within Administration may make themselves felt all too prominently. It is important that this should not be viewed by us as a sinister symptom of a chaos to come or of a probable weakening of relations between us and United States. We shall doubtless go through a somewhat confused interval but from what I personally know of new President there is no reason for supposing that this will last unduly long or that inevitable lowering of level will turn out to be fatal. Truman's firmness in declining to defer San Francisco conference, his immediate consultation with Byrnes, his good relations with labour and with Southern Democrats (which earned him Vice-Presidency) and his passionate sincerity, are excellent auguries for the future. The Cabinet have in meanwhile been asked to remain at their posts and Secretaries of State, War and Navy will certainly do so for the present ; nor are any other immediate resignations expected although there are plausible rumours that Messrs Morgenthau, Biddle, Ickes and Miss Perkins will duly leave, with Fulton,[2] an energetic lawyer of New Deal tendencies who was counsel for Senate Truman Committee, as Biddle's possible successor. Hopkins's fate naturally causes widest speculation : Truman has already made a gesture towards him and Stettinius will almost certainly beg Truman to keep him as an invaluable repository if nothing else of late President's intentions and a link with foreign governments. It is too early to tell but it does not seem too probable that Hopkins, whose life was so completely wrapped up in that of his late master, will long be able to function in a new atmosphere. However that may be, Truman is likely to do nothing rash or desperate. He will listen to advice of his friends, Senators Barkley and Hatch, Speaker Rayburn and perhaps Byrnes, which will certainly be on side of light and reason. The two strongest members of his entourage would seem today to be Messrs Vinson and Clayton and, if a period of confusion ensues, theirs may be the strongest hands at the helm. Again we have nothing to fear and much to expect but the next two weeks will make prospects very much clearer.

San Francisco. The succession of daily headlines reporting rapid progress in conquest of Germany is now taken so much for granted, that interest was liable to centre on less certain fortunes of San Francisco conference. There are no startling developments on this front but the deep gloom of earlier weeks has been succeeded by mild pessimism penetrated by occasional rays of hope and a growing feeling that perhaps it would after all go off well on the night. There is still a certain amount of growling particularly in Scripps-Howard Press about Russian

2 Hugh Fulton, chief counsel of Truman Senate Committee 1941–4, lawyer in private practice since 1944.

demand for three votes ; the Polish issue has turned into a permanent cloud, the blackness of which is no longer disputed, with dwindling hope of a last-minute miraculous breeze, in form of creation of a new Polish Government, agreed by the powers, to blow it away. Widespread discontent has been at any rate temporarily averted by State Department's invitation to no less than forty-two political, social and economic organizations to appear as 'consultants' to United States delegation ranging from such eminently respectable bodies as Council on Foreign Relations and Foreign Policy Association through the two main Roman Catholic bodies and mutually opposed (Zionist) American Jewish Conference and (Non-Zionist) American Jewish Committee, the trade union organizations, the chief Negro association and ending with Rotarians, Kiwanis, Lions and Federation of Womens' Clubs. These bodies are at present too preoccupied by choice of delegates and planning of tactics to give tongue to their views and complaints which will doubtless obtain a magnificent airing at San Francisco itself. As for American delegation it has been decided that each of its members is to preserve full liberty not only of opinion and of action but of access to publicity of his or her views, with the quaint addition that they are nevertheless resolved to remain one and undivided and to preserve a solid front, whatever that may turn out to mean. The two most powerful individual members of it are still Connally and Vandenberg upon whose capacity to co-operate the effectiveness of delegation will doubtless ultimately depend. Vandenberg's success in getting his formula about justice as basis for settlement, vague as that may seem, has apparently put him into a complaisant temper and although he is said still to feel most strongly on question of votes, prospects of genuine solidarity between Republicans and Democrats backed by good work done behind the scenes by staunch Senator Austin, seem considerably higher than before. Vandenberg's chief brain trustee is still Dulles, with possibly ex-ambassador Hugh Wilson[3] (the last United States Ambassador to Germany), who had just been appointed political adviser of Republican Party. Hugh Wilson is a sensible and level-headed diplomat of the old school who is likely to act as moderating influence throughout. A wistful note is supplied by Secretary of Commerce, Henry Wallace, who after conferring with Stettinius said that he himself was not going to San Francisco, adding 'Ed Stettinius is a lucky guy'.

. . .

Colonial trusteeship. Subject of colonial trusteeship has now emerged into public notice although it is still not a subject of sharp public controversy. Press has revealed that serious disagreements exist between service departments on one hand and State Department on the other as reported to you in my last week's summary [see p. 533]. I am told by well-informed journalists that although experts at State Department would perhaps be prepared to follow Yalta Agreement and leave specific questions of classification of specific territories to ultimate

3 Hugh R. Wilson (1885–1946), retired career diplomat.

discussion and decision by a body to be set up at San Francisco, confining themselves at present to most general possible statements of principle, they are said
to feel nervous about possible behaviour of other powers at San Francisco ; in
particular of alleged desire on part at any rate of one of Arab representatives to
raise problem of Mandated British and French territories in Middle East at San
Francisco ; if this should happen they are reported to feel that they can scarcely
expect to get away with a mere generality and are consequently torn between on
the one hand desire to relegate this very ticklish political issue and on the other
the need for an American statement of policy on this topic which will at least
prevent an unfavourable press here and abroad. Although there is every reason
to think that they will keep such a declaration of intentions as a step to be taken
only in the last resort and that they will communicate it to us in advance should
they decide upon it, it is not impossible that, faced with a political crisis, they
will suddenly improvise something unilaterally ; hence need on our part not to
be caught empty-handed ourselves in such a contingency with nothing better than
a statement that these problems are outside scope of San Francisco discussions
seems to be all the greater. State Department at any rate seem genuinely anxious
to be as co-operative as possible and to help us keep this particular pot from
boiling over, but behaviour of other delegates and possible repercussions in a
San Francisco filled with aggressive pressure groups and through them in rest of
the United States may force their hand. The clearer therefore our own attitude in
the matter is meanwhile made to the public, the smaller opportunity for its mis-
representation, particularly by honest ignorance. There are however certain later
developments which I shall report separately by cable.

15 April 1945

Lend-Lease. The Lend-Lease bill, like all economic issues at present, aroused a
real opposition to the Administration. The House opposition had already succeeded in inserting into the Act extending Lend-Lease for a year an amendment
forbidding use of Lend-Lease funds for post-war relief, rehabilitation and reconstruction. Vandenberg harked back to his old thesis that the Administration must
not be permitted to use Lend-Lease as an instrument of post-war policy. Taft
recommended an explicit prohibition of export of any Lend-Lease materials of
value for reconstruction in the post-war period, particularly if it took the place of
straight loans or aid for rehabilitation (e.g. to the French) which ought to be
transacted by other and more traditional means. This amendment produced a tie,
39 *v.* 39 votes, broken by Truman's casting vote against the amendment. The
votes followed a straight party alignment with Republicans largely against, with
the notable exception of Austin and also, more surprisingly, of the ex-isolationist
Wiley of Wisconsin, whose vote in this sense may be said to have saved the day
for international collaboration. Such liberals as Saltonstall and Ball voted for the
amendment, which, following their similarly anti-Administration vote in the case

of Aubrey Williams, probably indicates that Ball at any rate, having been scolded, as I am told, by Stassen, for letting down the party by his support of Mr Roosevelt's candidacy, is now determined to 'stay on the reservation', i.e. prove his steady Republican loyalty.

Gallup poll. The following confidential unpublished Gallup poll reveals interesting facts :

In answer to question whether the United States and England should make a permanent military alliance after the war, 'that is, agree to come to each other's defence immediately if the other is attacked', 52 per cent replied affirmatively, 38 per cent negatively ; 30 per cent think that the United States has 'nothing' or 'not much' to gain from England after the war ; 15 per cent think that trade is the most important item of possible United States gain ; 9 per cent speak of co-operation as being the most important ; 8 per cent of 'goodwill, friendship, gratitude'. 'Payment of debt' is indicated by 4 per cent and 'bases of defence, air bases' by another 4 per cent. 'Peace', 'security', 'balance of world power', 'ideas', 'culture' get between 3 per cent and 1 per cent. 18 per cent think that British imperialism, 'jealousy of United States power', 'domination of Europe', 'take and don't give' is what the United States has most to fear from England after the war. 13 per cent are worried most by British designs on 'trade or airways competition' ; 11 per cent say that British 'won't pay debts, will have to lend them money'. 4 per cent say 'war, Britain might fight us' ; and 4 per cent suspect Russia and England of ganging up against the United States. 3 per cent complain of lack of goodwill ; 2 per cent fear Mr Churchill, but 26 per cent, i.e. the majority, declare that they have nothing (repeat nothing) to fear from Britain in any of these respects. Gallup further reports (this time publicly) that between 81 per cent and 85 per cent strongly favour world co-operation today as against between 21 per cent and 31 per cent in 1937 favouring adhesion to the League. There are no great differences in this vote either regionally or politically. 81 per cent think that the United States should join an organization with police power to stop war, rising from 26 per cent in 1937. There is no doubt that this does in fact correctly represent American sentiment at the present moment.

21 April 1945

National mourning. The nation is slowly coming to, but a consciousness that it has lost its greatest President has muted and slowed all activity. There is scarcely anywhere now a word of public criticism against the man who, if the press is any indication, was one of the most bitterly hated figures in America. The opposition press has printed scrupulously fair estimates of his personality and his achievement, and incidents of persons who have spoken disrespectfully of Mr Roosevelt, and were fiercely dealt with by angry individuals or institutions, are conspicuous only for their scarcity. There is everywhere a recognition that his abiding place in history is secure if only because he brought into existence a full-fledged new policy in domestic and in foreign affairs alike – indeed, in the latter sphere, he was virtually building in a vacuum so securely that with his death there is now no doubt of the survival of the form and lines of the policy associated with his name. Moreover, he has altered, perhaps in perpetuity, the concept of the duties and functions of the United States Government in general and of the Presidency in particular. It is so far a cry from the days when President Coolidge could say 'The business of the Government of the United States is business' that most Americans scarcely realize that the tradition of positive action towards social welfare with which they automatically identify the duties of any United States President (Willkie's and Dewey's programmes are handsome evidence of this), and which now seems so permanent, was established so recently and by the efforts of relatively so few men and women. Naturally there is much talk of the end of the great 'Roosevelt era' and the beginning of quieter times under 'a Democratic Coolidge'. But that, if natural, is superficial. If there is strong, and probably justified, expectation of the relaxation of centralized Washington control and of profoundly personal government, there is equally strong if less articulate assumption that the main federal reforms of the New Deal, and still more the world-embracing foreign policy for which the late President stood, will and should be carried on in the manner for which he had, in the end, secured the positive approval of the vast majority of the nation. It is against this background that Truman performed his first acts and spoke his first public words, and the fact that he was felt to pledge himself with genuine conviction and sincerity to the continuation of the basic policies of his predecessor – war until the enemies' unconditional surrender, full punishment of war criminals, and the continuance of present military direction, the renewal of Lend-Lease, support for reciprocal trade pacts and for Bretton Woods, the extension of social security – was realized with relief and approval by the vast majority of listeners in Congress and in the country. The absence from his speech of all fustian, and indeed of any false note, if anything increased the impression of whole-hearted dedication for which the country was eager. The isolationist McCormick-Patterson papers have handsomely offered not to attack Mr Truman for three, perhaps even six, months. The great waves of speculation and gossip, largely founded on hopes and fears rather than fact, reported in my last summary, naturally continue to fill the sudden void created by the catastrophe. But there is a new and growing conviction that no radical changes in central policy are desirable or to be expected – that the President will refuse to be stampeded into any dramatic reversals of policy or of dismissal of key individuals – that he is determined to act without precipitancy. Hence an atmosphere in which officials can carry on their work with sufficient confidence that their efforts would not be suddenly frustrated or deflected into some perilous unknown. Naturally reactions differ from group to group, from department to department. The stock-market rise is the highest since 1937. Conservative opinion is certainly convinced that a swing to the right – even if not very sweeping – is inevitable.

Foreign policy. The domestic agencies carry on much as usual – with Vinson secure in his new province as a trusted friend of President Truman, with Ickes still firmly entrenched and not likely to be driven out although he may choose to go of his own accord ('they would not dare turn old Ickes loose on the United States, they just would not dare,' Speaker Rayburn was overheard to observe). Ickes himself, with reference to possible supersession by Ed Pauley,[1] the Democratic Party's treasurer, is alleged to be muttering fiercely that he would 'get the hell out when the plunderbund boys muscle in. Hannegan is sniffing carrion like a South American condor', while Miss Perkins is still *en poste* but perhaps more likely to go (but she has been going for so long now that this is scarcely news) ; only Attorney General Biddle's resignation is still the object of really lively speculation. The agencies most shaken are those conducting foreign policy – the delicate structure deliberately created between the State Department and the White House, whereby the true directors of United States foreign policy were the President and Harry Hopkins, connected by a number of administrative links with the Department of State and with Stettinius. Lippmann in an unusually sharp article pointed out that Stettinius is now the constitutional heir apparent should anything happen to Truman and that, since he is not a popularly elected official, this is anomalous and unsatisfactory and that he must go, preferably before San Francisco, to avoid division of counsel. This is said to echo the opinions of several influential Senators who have nothing personal against the Secretary of State. There is naturally furious and widespread speculation about the position of Byrnes, so nearly Vice-President, so nearly appointed to the Secretaryship of State, and so dramatically back from his Sabine farm in South Carolina to advise his intimate friend, the new President. Byrnes has told one or two of his intimates that he abhors the thought of occupying so indeterminate a position as Hopkins, that he would have no objection to succeeding Stettinius, but that unified direction was imperative and that so long as Stettinius remains in office he, Byrnes, proposes to continue in his rural retreat. He claims also to have advised the new President not to allow a multiplicity of counsel, and to have recommended that on domestic matters the President should place paramount reliance on Fred Vinson, in foreign relations on Admiral Leahy. This last may mean no more than that his advice is against the retention of either Hopkins or Stettinius in key positions, and is a matter of avoiding direct reference to himself as the obvious candidate for such post. That Leahy is to be kept was made clear in the President's first speech ; the French are said to be somewhat downcast, quite naturally, at this. The situation is still obscure but Stettinius

1 Edwin W. Pauley, Chairman of Pauley Petroleum Inc., Treasurer of Democratic Party 1944–5.

seems most likely to go to San Francisco and, if he makes a great success of that, perhaps to continue permanently in office although no one seems to think that particularly likely. Truman himself sharply scotched the suggestion that he was on the point of replacing Stettinius with Byrnes ; nevertheless the rumours that a definite understanding with Byrnes exists persist very strongly. Possibly Stettinius's performance at San Francisco may affect this issue. But the new President is evidently determined not to rush matters, not to upset existing routine by wholesale house cleaning, and he is therefore likely to take his time over whatever new arrangements he may have in mind, and alter his personnel gradually and with a minimum of friction. This came out most conspicuously in the arrangements he has announced for the White House : he has appointed Matthew Connelly,[2] his unknown amanuensis in the Senate, as his personal secretary (Connelly is a moderate Roman Catholic from Massachusetts of apparently neutral flavour) and the equally unknown Reinsch[3] from his own Missouri as his radio and possibly press specialist. He has chosen an old 'War Buddy', Harry Vaughan,[4] as his military aide. At the same time he has requested the existing White House staff – Early, Hassett,[5] Daniels and Rosenman – to remain at their posts to train the new men. On 15 May Reinsch is to give way to Charlie Ross,[6] a seasoned old radical of the St Louis Post-Despatch, a schoolmate of Truman, and a shrewd and honest rural New Dealer, as Press Secretary. Similarly Fulton, the Counsel for the Senate Truman Committee who seems universally admitted to be 'a little right of the centre', is obviously designed for a key post whether or not he succeeds Biddle in the Department of Justice. The new President's act so few hours after his oath of office in driving to the Senate to take luncheon with the leading Senators of both parties is everywhere greeted as a symptom of the new 'era of good feeling' between the President and Congress and indeed between the two parties. Much of the prevalent talk about the new spirit of harmony between the Executive and Legislature is of course no more than exultation by conservatives at what they think is the knell of the New Deal, since Congress has been latterly conspicuously more conservative than the Administration. Some of these chickens may be being counted before they are hatched ; for, while it is true that new President feels happier in company of seasoned Senators than in that of energetic young reformers, his record as one of the solidest of all supporters of New Deal measures in Congress and Vinson's New Deal entourage argues that the switch to the right may not be as pronounced as conservatives hope ; and in this the left-wing press and labour take some comfort. Some of

2 Matthew J. Connelly, member of staff of Truman Senate Committee, Vice-Presidential Secretary, subsequently (1960) imprisoned for fraud and perjury.

3 James L. Reinsch, radio and television executive from Atlanta, adviser to White House 1945–52.

4 Harry H. Vaughan, in Truman's Artillery battery in First World War, his Secretary in Senate 1941–5.

5 William D. Hassett, suceeded Marvin McIntyre in February 1944 as a presidential secretary, draughtsman and confidant.

6 Charles Ross, chief Washington correspondent of St Louis Post-Dispatch 1918–34, on editorial staff 1934–45.

these confidently predict that the very liberal Senator Kilgore may succeed Madame Perkins in the Labor Department. Organized labour is not (repeat not) backing this unanimously. Morgenthau, who tendered his resignation last Saturday but withdrew it after the promise from Truman that he would lend him the same strong support as his predecessor, told a member of my staff that he thought that 'Truman was a genuine liberal. He means to stand by the people' and although his judgment sometimes errs on the side of naïveté there is a certain amount of other evidence for this. All that is known of the new President's economic views is his distrust, characteristic of his background, for big business and big finance, whether of the Wall Street or of the Detroit, or indeed of the Texas, type.

Who are to be the new President's close personal advisers? What are the main influences likely to sway him? To this there is as yet no clear answer. The Wallace-ites have already begun a whispering campaign against possible rivals of their leader in 1948, and have ascribed presidential ambitions to Vinson for which there is as yet no real evidence. Wallace himself appears to have no hand in starting such rumours and is on good terms both with Vinson and Truman, reasonably secure of his own position inasmuch as the new President is unlikely to oust a man who behaved with such gallant loyalty in the presidential campaign towards himself after being defeated by him for the Vice-Presidency. He has appointed a respectable Missouri banker, Snyder,[7] to be Federal Loan Administrator, and doubtless a certain number of appointments of party stalwarts and personal friends – all of whom tend to be middle-of-the-road Democrats of the somewhat humdrum type – are to be expected. Provided he continues to lean on Senators Barkley and Hatch and Representatives Rayburn and Wadsworth, on Messrs Byrnes and Vinson, as seems likely, a steady course will prevail and public life will be kept as free of notorious public scandals as, despite all its shortcomings, the New Deal has managed to keep it for many long years. The period of the 'Palace Guard' is certainly over. The fear of its supersession by naked boss rule seems altogether unfounded. Meanwhile the new President's attitude towards the San Francisco conference and towards Britain in particular seems entirely satisfactory. Mr Eden tells me that he obtained an excellent personal impression of Truman's sincerity and goodwill. Mr Eden is also much encouraged by the friendly and co-operative temper of the Senate Foreign Relations Committee with whom he had luncheon, contrasting notably with the more difficult mood during his visit of 1943. Senator Vandenberg told a journalist that the United States delegation felt the new President would be a tower of strength to them at the forthcoming conference, and that there were no destructive influences effectively at work. Senator Connally publicly congratulated Mr Truman on his swift grasp of foreign affairs and his support of the United States delegation. The sense of national unity is very strong and likely to remain so for some time. The power of Mr Roosevelt's ideals is today incomparably greater than if his broken health had led to a Wilsonian aftermath.

7 John W. Snyder, banker, manager St Louis Loan Agency, Reconstruction Finance Corporation 1937–43.

The Prime Minister's tribute to the late President was very well received and the Foreign Secretary's attendance at the funeral service could not have been more timely. The McCormick-Patterson papers complained that the Prime Minister had not seen fit to put in an appearance, but this was an isolated note from a discredited quarter. At the same time there is no doubt that a visit by the Prime Minister would be regarded as a natural and welcome event here and might do much to increase the prestige of the new President.

The Russo-Polish Deadlock. There is deep uneasiness, of course, over this issue which still hangs over the coming conference. However, the shock of the President's death and announcement of the arrival of M.Molotov,[8] which has throughout been reported as representing a feather in Mr Truman's cap, has served to dissipate what would otherwise have been the gloomiest of all political headlines. There is press speculation on what precisely Mr Truman meant to convey when he replied with emphasis at his first press conference (and was applauded for it) that the Russian Foreign Commissar would undoubtedly pay his respects to the President of the United States *en route* to San Francisco 'as he should', but there is no reason for thinking that any particular nuance is to be detected in this form of words. There is much praise on all sides for Truman's conduct of this, his first press conference, for his 'trigger-quick' replies and his obvious candour. Some of this springs from desperate desire to build him up to adequate stature, but much of it seems spontaneous and genuine. The Roman church has come out with a blistering denunciation of Marxism and a solemn warning of the fate in store for all settlements which ignore the rights of the smaller nations in favour of the big, as the trend of events from Dumbarton Oaks, through Yalta, and towards San Francisco seems to indicate to the ten bishops and archbishops who signed this document. It is perhaps an indication of the earnest and sober beginnings of realism and general hope concentrated upon the findings of San Francisco that this blast, which would normally have been taken up, and reverberated from the pages of the entire anti-Roosevelt press, seems largely confined to the intransigent Russophobe minority and Roman Catholic and Polish presses, without making much impression in the country as a whole. Everyone is aware that the test of President Truman and United States diplomacy is yet to come, and in the earnest mood now so intensely widespread there is no disposition to make the usual political hay, however favourable the opportunity. How long this will last is another matter and, if a genuine conflict breaks out between the USSR and other powers and remains unresolved for any length of time, the letdown in feeling, particularly doubts as to the new President's competence in imposing his personality upon events, will doubtless be correspondingly great. Meanwhile there is certainly no perceptible rise in pro-Polish feeling.

8 Vyacheslav Molotov, Soviet Minister for Foreign Affairs since 1939.

28 April 1945

Political détente. This has been at once a gloomier (because of Russian behaviour) and a calmer week than the preceding one. Calmer because new President has on the whole lived up to expectations of his well-wishers : instead of an immediate outbreak of intrigue around the throne and sweeping changes in high posts and a fierce struggle for power on part of old and new personalities, President Truman's clear intention of keeping his ship on an even keel is obviously being implemented at any rate for moment with conspicuous firmness. Thus we are treated to the unusual spectacle during this era of good feeling of such conservative lions as Mr Pegler [1] and Mr Krock (who describe the President as 'moderate and serious' and 'firm, vigorous and quick' respectively) lying down with such liberal lambs as Lerner ('his leadership is honest, straight-forward, liberal and crisp'). Meanwhile, Byrnes is sitting quietly in South Carolina, Stettinius was accorded warm public backing by the President in his speech to San Francisco, a firm line was pursued with regard to Polish problem and Administration is clearly solidly behind Mr Hull's trade policies, Bretton Woods, etc. All this has had a tranquillizing effect on public opinion which, after the first spasm of acute uncertainty, has avoided all signs of political panic and now, if anything, tends to overestimate the solidity of new establishment. That the President, a firm believer in party loyalty, is not wholly averse to regular patronage is attested by (not yet published) appointment of Ed Pauley, Democratic Party's treasurer and California oil magnate with a vigorous business sense, to position of American representative on Reparations Commission. . . . President also placated the South by according McKellar, Presiding Officer of Senate and arch-conservative from Tennessee, a seat in Cabinet. Result is that several old anti-Roosevelt Democratic Senators have dropped in at White House to offer their good wishes.

Victories in Europe. Naturally catastrophic collapse of German resistance over wide front to some degree cushions off political melancholy, although even here there is anxiety about how collaboration with Russians can be expected to proceed smoothly while they continue in their present unyielding mood. This is to some extent exploited by anti-Russian 'hyphenated' groups but it is important to realize that, with passing of the President, the tendency on the part of Roosevelt-haters to exploit grievances of groups with which they are not themselves directly connected and for whose real interests they may care little, shows signs of rapid subsidence. Thus, on Russo-Polish issue, real opposition stands in much clearer relief than before – it includes a section of Poles and Representatives of Polish districts in Congress, Roman Catholic Church and liberals impatient of naked play of power politics – but strength of this group, such as it is, is considerably smaller now that it is losing power of conjuring up, during moments of crisis,

1 J.Westbrook Pegler, sports writer who turned political columnist with New York *World Telegram*, Chicago *Daily News*, 1933–44 ; subsequently joined King Features (Hearst) syndicate.

the entire old anti-Roosevelt front ; Administration therefore, in its efforts to put forward whatever policy it may decide upon, gains greatly from disappearance of those obstructive forces whose power of blackmail used to inhibit its freedom of action so greatly before. Whether State Department uses its new freedom remains to be seen. This naturally applies to many other spheres of activity – economic as well as political – and is most considerable benefit conferred by an otherwise very ill wind.

The Russo-Polish issue. While confidence in Mr Truman is high the deadlock over Poland spreads very darkly over entire political heaven. From time to time stories appear in press indicating that some 'high personality in touch with Polish situation' or 'important foreign diplomat' has told a news agency that a solution has in fact been reached and a Polish government delegate is about to be seated. But in general, press is better informed than that and knows what everyone in Washington knows, that Eden-Molotov-Stettinius talks have proved inconclusive and that what slender hopes there are depend upon next reaction from Moscow itself. . . . In general existence of a united Anglo-American front on this problem is universally taken to be the case. Molotov appeared very cheerful on arrival, cracking jokes about no longer posing as 'Mr Brown' (his alias when last here) and contrasted strongly with obvious gloom of Harriman and Messrs Dunn and Bohlen, who displayed every characteristic of men butting their heads against a virtually stone wall. Molotov's press conference seems to have gone off quite well. When he asked whether he had made himself clear, the reporters unanimously chorused 'no' according to press accounts. Possibly you will obtain a further version of this from San Francisco.

The whole scene has shifted to San Francisco upon which all eyes are directed, but we have as yet no information as to the experiences of our delegation there. President Truman's speech was well received and his decision to remain in Washington was wise, if only because it gives the impression of something stable in an unstable scene, a competent Administration carrying on solidly while the welter of the Conference goes on. The opening speeches were duly acclaimed.

. . .

Buchenwald. The horror stories of treatment of prisoners in German prison camps, accompanied by a large number of grisly photographs in the press of the victims, have made the profoundest possible impression and are so far the greatest factor contributing to a hardening of sentiment. The returning congressional and press delegations are likely to intensify, if that is conceivable, the violent revulsion and anger which the flood of evidence, pouring out day by day from all the newspapers and radio stations in the country, have produced. The public so far does not appear to distinguish clearly which of these ghastly facts apply to American prisoners and which to Nazi victims generally, nor is there any undue insistence upon this. The plea of Elmer Davis (an obscure figure now) for a differentiation between Nazis and Germans, echoed in the *New Republic*, represents at present a small (and denounced) minority of opinion ; and the outcry against the 'pampering' of German war prisoners in the United States, bolstered by similar accounts from Britain, at present holds the field. The War and State Departments said that they proposed to adhere firmly to the Geneva Convention and denied 'coddling'. Whatever the realities of any tendencies to a 'soft peace', the public expression of them from any responsible quarter would be most bitterly unwelcome here at this moment. This does not affect of course such questions as the possible admission of Eastern and Central European immigrants into the United States, concerning which the old negative attitude exists in all its strength. Indeed the veterans' organizations are if anything likely to make it even more adamant. The question of war criminals has had a new and vigorous airing with the statement by Herbert Pell[2] that it is the lawyers in the State Department who are most directly responsible for unnecessary death and torture on the part of many Nazi victims by failing to issue real warnings, when it was still possible to do so, i.e. before the latest massacre, which might have had a restraining effect. This has naturally been taken up by the liberal press, who take Pell's word for it that he was himself dropped purely because of his unseasonable representations to this effect made from London to the State Department. The State Department has so far issued no *démenti*.

29 April 1945

Food. The situation is considerably darker with respect to food for Europe. The general public is not yet aware of the full gravity of it, and, although an organization called 'Food for Freedom' has circularized its members with a really enlightened statement calling for a self-sacrificing policy on the part of the United States for Europe's benefit, signed by many prominent liberal names (as well as the four leaders of the farm organizations), the power of General Somervell and his friends does not appear to have diminished. The latest Gallup poll shows 65 per cent in favour of rationing of butter, sugar, meat, etc., for one year after the end of the European war for the benefit of Europeans. But the controversy is unfortunately not for the public to decide.

Pressure groups at San Francisco. The pressure groups have, as might be expected, intensified their propaganda, particularly the Poles and the Zionists. The former proceed along usual lines. As for the Zionists, the extremists have worked up a fever – pamphlets, speeches, mass meetings, etc., etc. – while the more moderate Jewish Agency representatives trust to work in the purlieus and antechambers of San Francisco of their representatives invited by the State Department, and have kept relatively quiet in New York and Washington which now constitutes the rear. They do not, I am told, propose to raise officially the Pal-

2 Herbert Claiborne Pell, ex-Congressman (1919–21), American member of United Nations Commission for Investigation of War Crimes 1943–5.

estine question themselves unless the Arabs do so. At any rate, that is what they are saying to members of my staff, thinking perhaps that they had better save their fire for the institutions to be set up at San Francisco rather than the conference itself. But the tinder is there and a spark would set it ablaze in the now, alas, all too familiar fashion. This Embassy continues to receive letters about 'British atrocities' against illegal immigrants, in particular concerning the treatment of Eri Jabotinsky,[1] but this is by now routine. The forty-two United States 'consultant' organizations are by the press said to be chafing somewhat at the lack of official attention paid them ; MacLeish is attempting to assuage them. Doubtless their efforts will be reported to you direct from San Francisco.

6 May 1945

The war news.[1] Reactions to this were as might have been expected ; grisly details of the death of Mussolini and speculation about Hitler's last days and hours[2] flooded the headlines ; the end of the European war was prematurely announced by several newspapers and, originating apparently in remarks by Senator Connally in San Francisco, touched off popular demonstrations, more sustained than on the occasion of the previous false (radio) peace rumour until finally killed by President Truman's announcement that the report had no substance. Perhaps as a result of this such headlines as 'Hitler and Goebbels commit suicide', 'Berlin captured by Russians' – words so passionately longed for for so many months – came as a kind of anticlimax. Everyone knows that VE day may come at any hour, but the edge has to some degree been taken off that overanticipated thrill. Meanwhile, accounts of German concentration camps continue to pour in, and the violence of anti-German feeling generated by this shows no sign of abating. The return of Congressmen, and pressmen, and then of the soldiers themselves, with eye-witness accounts, seems likely to kill any chance that this feeling will soon evaporate. At the moment, the sense of horror and indignation is at least as intense as that previously excited only by the Japanese, which penetrated very deep : it looks as if this too will leave a scar just as unhealing.

. . .

San Francisco.[3] This has of course preoccupied everyone. From the very beginning a tendency developed to look upon the whole thing as a tug-of-war between the United States of America and the USSR, the elephant and the whale, with Britain in a somewhat less important role. Molotov's toughness has riveted general attention, and the mood, as reflected in the press and in conversation, varies

1 Eri Jabotinski, Zionist, who worked from Ankara on a scheme to smuggle 2,500 refugee Jews a week into Palestine. The British secured his deportation from Turkey and interned him.

1 On 2 May the Red Army completed the capture of Berlin, and German forces surrendered in Italy.

2 Mussolini died on 29 April, Hitler on 30 April.

3 Conference opened 25 April.

between anxious speculation as to whether a genuine alliance can ever be securely forged with so difficult a great power, and straight press blow-by-blow reportage in which Molotov is, e.g., reported to have scored one (admission of the two Soviet Republics) and lost two (on the Polish and Argentine issues). Despite the warnings in the press and elsewhere that nothing could be worse than the attempt to represent the United States and Soviet Russia as pitted one against the other so that every move is represented either as an American victory and consequently a Soviet defeat, or vice versa, this is precisely how the majority of the press has in fact treated it. On the admission of the two Soviet Republics there was little excitement. On the Polish issue public opinion in general supports the Anglo-American stand and Mr Eden is singled out for praise, both for the eloquence and for the substance of his opening speech, which was interpreted widely to have sounded the true keynote of what it was hoped the Conference might still become. On Argentina,[4] there was a very great deal of severe criticism of Stettinius's insistence on rushing the motion through, particularly from Lippmann and the liberal press. Senators Ball and Hatch protested against it but withdrew their protest after a conference with Truman, who apparently convinced them that the bargain with Latin America was essential, and, at Nelson Rockefeller's instance, commended Stettinius's tactics. Nevertheless, and despite the tendency particularly among the smaller newspapers to stress that inter-American solidarity is worth a very high price, there is a definite sense of guilt about a piece of such blatant appeasement by a country which had taken so much moral pride in its earlier anti-Argentine stand. This frequently took the form of complaint that Molotov had been presented with an altogether too good moral platform from which to point a finger of scorn at this high-principled and embarrassed country. Indeed, Argentina seems to have produced the only really passionate moments thus far : I am told that Vandenberg had to stop a Nelson Rockefeller press conference before the questioners became too offensive and the situation got altogether out of hand. Rockefeller is said to have persuaded Stettinius of the wisdom of this Argentinian move against Dunn's advice. Stettinius, who is very sensitive to press criticism, accosted Eugene Meyer, according to an account in Meyer's own *Washington Post,* in a San Francisco hotel lobby, demanding to know whether his journal, which had spoken of Stettinius as a bush-league Machiavelli, wished to undermine the American delegation ? Meyer evaded the issue but promises to continue to thunder. Among those most embarrassed are said to be the Czechs : Masaryk[5] knows he has no option but to vote with the Russians but, in view of the large Czechoslovak population in the United States and his own and his colleagues' friendly relations with the United States Government and Congress, this is proving intolerably difficult. There is a clear feeling, even among those who approved Stettinius's tactics as a disagreeable but inevitable choice of the lesser evil, that Molotov has scored a consider-

4 The motion to seat Argentina, motion proposed by Mexico but pressed by USA.
5 Jan G. Masaryk, Foreign Minister of Czech Government-in-Exile 1940–5.

able moral victory, a weapon in the hands of the Russians for general use and particularly handy if and when they choose to raise the question of Spain.

. . .

. . . The general attitude towards the Russian delegation is as towards so many strange visitors from Mars, concerning whom so little is known and whose behaviour is so inscrutable that any information, however trivial, is so scarce as to be immensely interesting and valuable as such. Thus the papers abound in stories of every gesture and remark issued from M. Molotov's delegation. Stories appear quoting with relief the remarks by a member of one of the other delegations that, despite his defeat on the Polish and Argentine questions, 'M. Molotov still appeared quite affable and genial' at a committee meeting. This atmosphere of goggle-eyed wonder and nervous anxiety about how things will ultimately turn out has made M. Molotov easily the central figure of the conference, with much admiration, but less limelight for either Mr Eden or the man whom the Republicans still steadily continue to describe as the most important man at the conference, i.e. Vandenberg – and with some sympathy for Stettinius's alleged flounderings. Nevertheless, there is still confidence that the present situation of Molotov versus the rest will give way to a more constructive common endeavour to produce concrete results and this is enhanced by the news that the Polish situation is showing signs of thaw at last. On specific points, the protest first by American trade unionists, then Citrine, about insufficient recognition given to organized labour at the conference has been noted without much comment ; the AF of L is openly pleased at this rebuff of the CIO and its Russian and British Allies. The question of trusteeships has not yet flared up, although the American plan is now fairly widely known and reported and the British insistence on mandates with a closed economic door as opposed to colonies with an open door, which the Americans would prefer, is reported in more serious newspapers so far without strong reaction. . . .

. . . As for the pressure groups, the Indians are engaged in routine exercises, the Jews (still smarting under the effect of the Duke of Devonshire's speech [6] in the House of Lords some weeks ago) are to some extent engaged in defeating their own ends by having split into four political groups, both Zionists and non-Zionists with incompatible demands.

Rumours. The town is naturally full of rumours about Truman's next batch of appointments. Hannegan's appointment as Postmaster-General may encounter some routine opposition in Congress, led by Missouri Republicans who have many personal grudges against him, but is likely to be confirmed as is that of David Lilienthal, reappointed to head the celebrated Tennessee Valley Authority, perhaps the New Deal's proudest domestic achievement. Francis Biddle is still Attorney General and Morgenthau is at the Treasury, but the days of both,

6 In the House of Lords, 29 March, the Duke being Under-Secretary of State for the Colonies. The speech was a refusal to grant extra certificates to admit additional Jewish refugees into Palestine.

particularly the former, are still considered counted by the most reliable political tipsters and by liberals who are displeased with Pauley's appointment to the Reparations Commission and are said to be consoling themselves with the thought that at any rate the Treasury is still as free from the breath of political scandal as during Mr Roosevelt's regime. Truman has summoned his old friend ex-Senator (now Federal Judge) Schwellenbach[7] from the State of Washington. This typically rural New Dealer, from a state in which public control of the sources of hydroelectric power is still the largest issue, is rumoured to be likely to succeed Miss Perkins in the Department of Labor. Schwellenbach is personally distrusted by some of his senatorial colleagues but his record on both foreign and domestic policy is impeccably liberal and he represents the type of anti-Big Business western Radical with whom Truman feels in natural sympathy. He is an astute politician and, if appointed, may do something to alleviate chronic distempers in the labour field. Various other appointments are rumoured, particularly for various Missourians. The President has been seeing considerable numbers of his old friends, apparently for purely hand-shaking purposes. A number of them is said to have secured free passes to the White House swimming pool ; beyond this the President is reported to have shown no tendency to fall in with their suggestions either about policy or about patronage. The entire Roosevelt White House staff is now under notice with the exception of McReynolds,[8] who says he sees no reason for going. It is not impossible that Mr Roosevelt's most intimate friends will ultimately drift towards forming a group around Mrs Roosevelt who declares that she proposes to devote the next six months to setting her private affairs in order. The irrepressible Senator Guffey of Pennsylvania has announced, much to Mr Truman's embarrassment, that he proposes to support him for a second term in 1948. Whilst Guffey no doubt has an eye on his re-election prospects in 1946 the main significance of this move is that it seems finally to kill Mr Wallace's chances for succession, since Guffey led the pro-Wallace wing of the regular Democratic Party and can scarcely expect to win with the support of the labour, liberal and coloured vote alone. Wallace is once more trying to convince the country that he is not a star-gazer by means of an article in the *Reader's Digest*, pleading for better opportunities for Small Business and denouncing an over-centralized economy controlled by the state in language worthy of Professor Hayek.

Irish 'neutrality'. Some prominence was given in the press to reports of Mr De Valera's visit to the German Ministry in Dublin to express condolence on Hitler's death, and to Salazar's[9] similar action, and the *New York Times* and *Herald Tribune* (also the *Washington Post*) have already delivered scathing editorials

---

7 Lewis B. Schwellenbach, Democratic Senator from State of Washington 1935–41, Federal Judge in State of Washington 1940–5, appointed Secretary of Labor, (*vide infra*) 1945.

8 William McReynolds, an administrative assistant.

9 Antonio de O. Salazar, virtual dictator of Portugal 1932–68.

pillorying Mr De Valera and conveying incredulity that such an act was possible, protocol or no protocol. It is clear that this latest evidence of partiality has made a truly disagreeable impression and it will be interesting to see if the Irish minister here reacts to it in any way.

. . .

Bretton Woods. The chances for the passage of both the Bank and the Fund seem vastly improved. Possibly, the most powerful influence in favour has been that of the very respectable Committee for Economic Development supported as it is by middle-of-the-roaders in finance and business. Much good work was done by the Boston banker, Ralph Flanders, and curiously enough Professor Hayek, at a meeting of influential New York bankers attended by both Winthrop Aldrich and various Morgan partners as well as by Mr Herbert Hoover and others, argued passionately in favour of Bretton Woods on the ground that its defeat would encourage British bilateralism and economic nationalism to a fatal degree. Whether or not this kind of argument proved a makeweight, the opposition of the American Bankers' Association appears to be melting and the Administration pilots of the deal are once more looking cheerful and predicting that it will get through with only minor amendments. . . .

Food. The Rosenman report[10] has now appeared in an abbreviated form, but it is still doubtful whether the implications of it for the American economy – i.e. the need for voluntary contributions in order to make the minimum available to starving European countries – has really sunk in. Marquis Childs, who has recently spent long enough in Europe to have observed its horrors ('What is Belgrade like ? Like North Dakota bombed', he observed at a dinner party), is pleading strongly for a realistic approach along Rosenman's lines. But very much more education – as much perhaps as Dumbarton Oaks and Bretton Woods required – may be needed if United States civilian supplies are to be rationed more drastically. The President is said to be showing signs of willingness to press the military authorities on this but, despite everything, the problem has still not been presented either to the public or to Congress with the desperate urgency which it deserves.

Crowley's report[11] was reported widely but superficially, and excited relatively little reaction. What the public minds principally is its own meat shortage.

. . .

Zionists. Apart from the general turmoil in the Jewish field over San Francisco, principally consisting of fear that the Arabs will secure seats on Commissions dealing with the Palestine issue, the most notable recent event in that field was

10 On civilian supplies for liberated countries of north-west Europe. It insisted that the USA should supply a 'substantial share' of civilian needs even if this meant a reduction in the US rations.

11 Based on conclusions reached by the British-American combined conference on world food supply and distribution. It called for an increase in food production, an acceleration of exports, and a reduction in US civilian consumption after VE day, below the level of the previous year.

a monster meeting in the Lewisohn Stadium in New York (alleged to have been attended by 60,000 persons) at which Senator Wagner formally denounced the British Government for its Palestine policy in terms now too familiar to need stating. The Zionists are counting heavily on Mr Truman's sympathy for their cause to which they add the conviction that, unlike the late President, he will not seek to play politics with them. This last represents pure wishful thinking rather than any basis of concrete evidence. The mass meeting was also attended and addressed by Mayor La Guardia whose stock is reported as steadily falling in view of Truman's well-known predilection for regular party workers. Without New Deal support, it is held that La Guardia cannot be re-elected and, if a regular Democrat is backed by the President (La Guardia is technically a Republican), the present Mayor's goose is believed to be cooked.

13 May 1945

End of European war. The premature leakage of surrender at Rheims by Associated Press caused the formal announcement of peace in Europe to peter out into something of an anti-climax. If the 8th of May was VE day, the 7th is now known in some circles as AP day. But of course it was an immense event. It spelt in a large sense the end of the war, notwithstanding all talk here during last three years of war against Japan as the real war, and despite all deliberate emphasis laid here for many months and especially now upon toll of lives and treasure which Eastern war was still likely to exact particularly from the nation. All the speakers dwelt on this but particularly Admiral King and Acting Secretary of State Grew, while President Truman, whose speech was written in Vinson's office, spoke of 'work, work, work' largely at request of Chiefs of Staff. The Japanese war is of course much more than a mere colonial war, however vast and bloody. For a long time Americans had been hoping and praying that they would quickly get their hands untied in Europe in order to throw themselves with all their strength upon the hated Japanese savages, and in that sense this is more of America's own war than the great world conflict with its climax on German soil. But the very fact that conclusion of Japanese war is so absolutely foregone, that it is merely a matter of time and that the Japanese, despite all vivid horror which they conjure up in American minds, have not dramatic identities and historical associations of the Nazi or even Fascist leaders, does to some degree relegate the Japanese war to category of a bitter and heavy duty to be fulfilled as rapidly as possible, but of limited scope rather than an operation of cosmic proportions. It is as if all available emotion had been expended upon the great individual monsters like Hitler, Goebbels, Goering, Mussolini, with little feeling left, at any rate at the moment, for the nameless mass of vermin as the Japanese are conceived to be. No doubt this will alter with time and further Pacific casualties, but great and memorable act remains the first. Remainder of tragedy is too obvious to excite passions to original pitch which they had attained. There is much sour comment in press on excessive courtesies shown to such characters as Goering, Schacht, Thyssen, Krupp, etc., and the softness this implies.

Japan. As for terms for Japan there are notes, though few and muffled at present, not merely in ex-isolationist press but e.g. the *Washington Post,* of the possibility of some modification of unconditional surrender in her case and optimistic speculation of likelihood of her early surrender when she perceives the hopelessness of her case, and woven into popular desire for Russian participation in the Pacific war there runs as a thin but just perceptible thread the thought that an American settlement of that area would be made if USSR were kept out of it. And there is an unsupported story by Freddie Kuh that a Japanese peace offer was recently rejected here. In connexion with this there is as yet little specific speculation as to exact part which Britain will play in Far Eastern war. Problem of British participation has of course been discussed intensively on and off since Pearl Harbor and despite reiterated statements to the contrary of Prime Minister and all other responsible British statesmen and newspapers, it is still generally assumed that we may not carry too much of burden. We must naturally be prepared for criticism from some quarters whatever we do : if we prosecute Eastern War with might and main, we shall be told by some people that we are really fighting for our colonial possessions the better to exploit them and that American blood is being shed to better purpose than to help ourselves and Dutch and French to perpetuate our unregenerate colonial Empires ; while if we are judged not to have gone all out, that is because we are letting America fight her own war with little aid after having let her pull our chestnuts out of European fire. There are probably elements throughout Navy Department likely to be prey to both these lines of simultaneous thought, torn as they are by desires to make Pacific victory as purely an American victory as possible and not to let us off too great a share of heat and burden of the day. These fears may turn out to be exaggerated and great part we are likely to play in second phase of war may obtain its due meed of recognition, but it will need unrelaxing emphasis by us on our role to see to it that it does. Despite flood of bigger news acknowledgment of British achievement in Burma appeared very widely.

Other Reactions. New York duly celebrated during the two VE days ; the crowds in Times Square behaved with all their traditional abandon ; an avalanche of ticker tape poured down, and at least one church announced VE day services 'every hour on the hour'. But the (German-American) Yorkville is said to have stayed quiet as the grave. Chicago displayed some ebullience, and the headline 'Halifax (i.e. in Nova Scotia) Has Hangover after VE day' led to some ribaldry, but in Washington and San Francisco all was relatively restrained and business-like. The broadcasts conveying the excitement in London were warmly received and are said to have moved listeners to tears. On all sides the right of the British people at last to enjoy themselves was acknowledged, and the radio, which has been consistently friendlier to us than the press, was filled with glowing recitals of our long story of endurance and resistance. The mood here is one of sober triumph : even this mercurial nation is for the moment at least made grave by the thought of the Pacific ordeals still to come, of the difficulties in the path of international reconstruction, and of the devastation of Europe grimly emphasized by the continuing testimony of German bestiality brought home by journalists and politicians beginning with the group of editors and publishers who recently visited Germany. The American-German press is still either silent or desperately softpedalling such stories of the concentration camps as they acknowledge, and cries for a hard peace are otherwise virtually universal. How long this may last it is difficult to tell, for American (like other) opinion cannot long bear the contemplation of the very disagreeable and of its grimmer implications. But at the moment, the public temper is strikingly different from that of a few months ago when the so-called Morgenthau Plan led to such widespread opposition. The victorious Governments need today fear no unfavourable public reaction to the harshest terms imposed upon the vanquished. While this fierce mood may not last, there is no doubt that the hard-peace school will never find a better time in which to strike.

San Francisco. As for the conference, it is not easy to tell precisely what the atmosphere is at San Francisco. From Washington the salient points seem to be these :

The Soviet Union still occupies the centre of the stage. The general impression of those friendly, hostile and uncertain in their feeling to it, is that the central tension is still between the USSR and the United States with other powers somewhat further in the middle of background. Molotov is still the limelight figure, and has emerged as a mixture of hard bargaining power and 'uncompromising realism' and a compound of intriguing irony and affability by which the press professes itself to be unexpectedly fascinated. For better or worse he has built up for himself a public personality which now shares the stage with Stalin himself, and the journalists, delighted by the discovery of a new major actor in the play, will doubtless continue to supply sufficient 'colour' to make him at least the equal of Litvinov in his impact upon the public mind. Mr Eden continues easily as the outstanding figure of the British delegation and has won golden opinions from all observers – even Drew Pearson, not to speak of Krock – as the wisest mediator and the clearest voice at the conference. By comparison Stettinius, despite Krock's affable words, does not seem to have grown in the estimation of the public. No one doubts his good intentions. Vandenberg and Stassen are still the biggest members of the United States delegation.

The most notable aspect of the entire situation is the remarkable and widespread restraint with which the press and radio treat the entire subject of relations with the USSR . . . So far from picking on the Polish issue, as they might well have done only a few months ago, in order to express that indignation with the arrest of the sixteen Poles, etc.,[1] which many of them probably feel in private, they strain every nerve to play down differences. They represent Russia within her limitations, and with her strange un-American scale of values, as continuing to be 'reasonable', and warn the public against forming up against her because of this or that specific disagreement with her policy. Partly this is due no doubt to sheer admiration (and apprehension) of victorious strength ; partly because the death of President Roosevelt has robbed the Polish issue of its uses as an anti-Roosevelt weapon ; partly because so many people are tired of what may seem petty European obstacles to the realization of a great global settlement ; but to a large degree, this is due to a genuine desire to arrive at a durable arrangement. . . . The fear of the failure of San Francisco is evidently still far greater than the fear of broken eggs provided that an omelette is, in principle, capable of being made. To this extent the pessimists who predicted chaos and disunity from the first are confounded.

. . .

The trusteeship question. Here there is vast confusion in the press and far beyond. On the one hand (a) the British plan (its disclosure before that of the Americans is regarded as a neat coup of British publicity) is viewed as a reactionary proposal to reduce mandates to a status of greater dependency than they had had under the League. The British desire to make the Assembly chargeable with the welfare of native populations of security as well as non-security areas (as against the American relegation of the first to the Security Council) is, in parts of the press, described as a British trick to give an air of greater liberality to an arrangement which, *in toto,* is far more imperialistic and coercive than the proposals of the Americans. On the other hand, there is (b) acute anxiety to retain full control of strategic bases, particularly in the Pacific, under untrammelled United States control. Persons who argue along the lines of (a) are often identical with those who passionately hold the latter proposition. These persons desire (1) that the new World Organization should prevent colonial powers from exclusive control of their possessions, and desire to accelerate the liberation of the dependencies by international action ; but (2) they desire also the greatest accumulation of power in the hands of the trustworthy democracies, i.e. principally their own. On the one hand, why should Americans shed their blood merely to return Hong Kong to the undesirable rule of the British ; on the other hand, a delegation of Senators appeared at San Francisco to see to it that nothing was done to give away a jot or tittle of what the United States Admirals demand in the way of control of the sacred fields of Saipan, Okinawa, Iwo Jima, etc., which might, unless something was done to stop it, find themselves back in the British Empire or even under non-American international control. Lindley is trumpeting away about America's fair share of Asiatic spoils, and Marquis Childs, otherwise a good enough friend to us, is gloomy about reactionary British intentions con-

1 Deputation from Polish Government in London, invited by Russia to visit Poland for talks, were arrested on charges of 'diversionary activities against the Red Army'.

cerning colonies. Senator McCarran, an old Nevada diehard, proclaims we have had one taste of the mandate way and it did not turn out very well. 'I'm a hell-tootin' American from out West, and I'm for keepin' the mandates under the Stars and Stripes.' Small wonder that there is appalling confusion on editorial columns with general motives of the need to break down British intransigence about one hundred per cent colonialism, need for United States control of bases, need for the freeing of subject peoples, need for economic arrangements beneficial to the prosperity of the United States of America : finally, as a kind of loose blanket flung over all, there are optimistic statements that the British, French and Dutch viewpoints, on the one hand, and those of the United States and probably the USSR on the other are not after all so very wide apart and that an acceptable, common scheme is now not far distant, with the guiding genius of Stassen, to whom at this point all American eyes look up, to give his moral *imprimatur* to this ultimate solution. All these strains enter into most of what is poured out on this subject with varying amounts of self-contradiction and perpetually shifting emphasis. But that the issue is now well to the forefront and that there is little if any support for the original British position as such, there appears no doubt. However, all this may look quite different from San Francisco.

. . .

AP leakage. About this there has been of course a veritable storm. Roy Howard, who was guilty of having personally reported the false armistice at the end of the last war, at first quixotically came to the defence of AP, saying that any good journalist would have done the same ; but as the facts gradually reveal themselves, more and more condemnation has begun to appear (ultimately from Howard's United Press as loudly as from anyone) and it is all that Kent Cooper's men here can do to stem the flood of criticism by putting out their own somewhat coloured accounts of their representative's action. Since Kent Cooper is the foremost champion of the 'freedom of the press' campaign, he finds himself in a somewhat awkward position because of this internecine press war. There is no doubt that, despite automatic adulation which goes to anyone who gets away with a scoop by whatever means, the whole episode has left a disagreeable taste here and may reduce the clamour against 'illicit censorship' for a time at least. The AP has now come forward with an official apology which nothing but a very black case could have extorted.

19 May 1945

. . .

. . . Lippmann on the 15th maintained that death of Roosevelt had robbed the United States of the man who knew how to maintain an independent position as between Russia and Britain, thus enabling him to mediate between them and act as a 'unifying power'. It was essential for the USA not to take sides strongly in

European disputes. This golden rule he argued had been broken by Messrs Stettinius and Rockefeller in their partisan support of Latin American position. Now that a European situation had arisen which was fundamentally an Anglo-Russian dispute, the United States, whilst it required to take up a position of its own, should not 'be drawn into this issue as a partisan' as it has been at San Francisco. In the general international interest the United States should exercise 'a wise reserve' particularly during the election period in Britain ; 'a more independent method of diplomacy on part of the United States will, as things stand now after Roosevelt's death, produce more international co-operation'. All this is of course in sharp contrast with Lippmann's earlier robustness, e.g. in January when he said 'that the United States could either keep out of European problems altogether' or 'accept responsibility jointly with the British . . . and the French . . . the one thing we cannot do is to sit on sidelines and proclaim high . . . principles'. Swing has similarly given vent to doleful utterances and has been admonishing the United States not to 'line up' with the British against Russia but to 'mediate'.

. . . Bert Andrews[1] in an article . . . in the *Herald Tribune* of the 17th gave a long account of alleged disagreements between the late President Roosevelt and Mr Churchill on the interpretation of Yalta formula on Poland. He quoted Lippmann as support for the thesis that President 'mediated' between Messrs Churchill and Stalin, thus tending to create impression that, if correspondence between Messrs Churchill, Roosevelt and Stalin were made public, it would reveal Britain as diplomatic aggressor in this case. . . . Stettinius to his great credit immediately issued a denial which does not seem to have been published and State Department officials have been at pains to refute the story. . . .

At a time when United States public opinion shows signs of being greatly exercised at the deterioration of Anglo-American relations with the Soviet Union this kind of thing tends to foster growing public misgivings as to whether present Administration is not allowing itself to be drawn along in wake of Great Britain towards a breach with the Soviets. More balanced leader writers are however stressing the need for Anglo-American unity of purpose in face of Russia's arbitrary interpretation of her security requirements. Indeed although Andrews included in his article a good deal of apparently correct detail about secret discussions of Moscow Commission on Poland (evidently gleaned at San Francisco) which gives an air of truth to his general thesis, it must not be assumed that our case has gone by default. The extent of Soviet backsliding upon its Yalta engagements seems by now fairly clear to general public. Criticism of our position thus springs from fear of trouble in Europe and Americans' part therein rather than from disapproval of our attitude as such. To this extent the picture has shifted from that of earlier weeks – when the United States and USSR were the

1 Bert Andrews, chief Washington correspondent of *New York Herald Tribune* 1941–53.

great protagonists in arena with Britain in background. Now emphasis is on Anglo-Soviet tension, with differing attitudes as to wisdom of United States backing of what is conceived to be a British position.

The attitude of press just described does not seem a true index of sentiment in either Administration, Service or congressional circles. Members of State Department have privately told members of my staff that they could easily provoke a storm by publishing even half the story of broken Russian pledges since Yalta and that statement on Venezia Giulia[2] represented the minimum of what could be said if this tempest was to be averted. US Navy officers, including Admiral King, are said to be talking about the unhappy possibility of a clash with Soviet Russia if she persists in her present courses and all talk about need for Pacific bases is permeated with this feeling. According to the Jingos the time to talk tough is now while United States strength is at its peak and not a decade hence when Russia has succeeded in building up her aggressive power in the Pacific. War Department is somewhat less affected by this mood and Mr Stimson, I am informed, has told President that Yalta formula about Polish Government is sufficiently ambiguous, if not to justify Russian interpretation, at any rate not to afford sufficient ground for talk of a breach of faith.

There is said to be a good deal of angry talk in Senate contingent upon publication of suspension of Lend-Lease to Europe which, although at first headlined by some newspapers as the total stoppage of supplies to Russia, was later modified by Grew and Stettinius as not meaning the cessation of all Lend-Lease supplies although possibly entailing a drastic reduction of European programmes. The relevant Senate Committee is said to have cross-examined State and FEA officials with some ferocity, the prevailing note being 'why should we help Russia when it is breaking all its Yalta pledges ?'. While United States policy on the whole issue has not yet crystallized, the President's friends are saying that he is merely biding his time for firm action, possibly until after meeting of Big Three. Our own position and in particular Mr Eden's public and private statements have met with a great deal of genuine sympathy in upper strata of Administration.

Meanwhile President Truman, whose genuine readiness to collaborate most fully in European settlement seems unquestionable, is said to be pulled one way by State Department, which still places Europe before Pacific or Latin America (despite Nelson Rockefeller), and another way by Service Departments which desire to begin transfer of troops to Pacific area as early as possible. Matters must clearly come to a head and in the showdown, the advice of such centrally placed officials as Vinson and even the quasi-retired Byrnes may play a decisive role, particularly as new President does not seem to place too much faith in present State Department (a reshuffle of posts and new appointments in it seem inevitable). Harriman says that he finds President very understanding and reason-

2 When Yugoslavs with Russian backing resisted British and American pressure to extrude their forces from Venezia Giulia or Istria, State Department in a press release on 12 May insisted that disposition of the territory 'must await a definite peace settlement'.

able on Soviet-Polish problem and that Hopkins is agreeably surprised by degree of grasp which he has shown of it. Baruch is also trying to put in his oar but so far I am told without success. He is very pleased with his visit to London and is telling everyone about the stern lecture which he read to British Cabinet on Bretton Woods and on the undesirability of reducing American tariff which he maintains shocked some members of it.

21 May 1945

Politics in New York. It now seems clear that Mayor La Guardia's statement that he will not offer himself for re-election as Mayor is only too genuine, since he knows that his chances of re-election would not be high. This is said to be largely due to the accumulation of grievances against his somewhat disconcerting political manners on the part both of the Republicans and the New Dealers, who originally combined to form the 'fusion' ticket[1] which defeated Tammany. A recent appeal for support sent out by his original patron, Judge Seabury,[2] failed to elicit an adequate response. The candidate of the straight Democratic Party ticket, whoever he may be (and it seems likely that it may be Brigadier-General O'Dwyer,[3] a New York district attorney, late of Italy, and now head of the War Refugee Board), thus has an excellent chance of being elected, particularly since President Truman is known to be a loyal party man and will almost certainly back the regular party candidate. In the meanwhile, a somewhat sinister alliance appears to have been concluded between Tammany proper and the left wing – more or less Communist – elements, led by Representative Marcantonio. This alliance may be said to combine some of the dirtiest and most effective politicians in New York City. The friction between both Hillman's left-wingers and Dubinsky's right-wingers on the one hand and La Guardia on the other is said to be mainly responsible for the melting away of La Guardia's original New Deal support. The door has thus been opened to this unholy Tammany-Communist alliance, and the alternatives now seem to lie between a nominee supported by at any rate some sections of the underworld, and a straight Republican probably at least as conservative as Dewey. New Dealers seem to have realized too late what they had let themselves in for, and are divided between self-reproach and complaints that La Guardia's high-handed methods are chiefly responsible for this unhappy situation. Since New York City is an exceedingly important factor in national, e.g. presidential, elections, the chances of a straight New Deal victory in 1948, say under Mr Wallace, are thereby yet further diminished. Failing the appearance of some new figure of impeccable political purity, e.g. Mrs Roo-

1 A temporary coalition of Republicans and labour elements in New York City which elected La Guardia Mayor in 1933, 1937 and 1941.

2 Samuel Seabury, anti-Tammany Democrat, famous for his 1930–1 investigation of the misgovernment of New York City.

3 William O'Dwyer, New York City magistrate, Roosevelt's personal representative on Allied Control Commission in Italy, 1944. Elected Mayor of New York 1945.

sevelt, or some of the persons mentioned by La Guardia himself as desirable successors to himself (e.g. Lew Douglas or Adolph Berle, or some other figure of national prominence) the prospect of the continuation of honest government in New York seems in jeopardy.

. . .

Office of Strategic Services and Office of War Information. I am told that the newspaper stories reporting that General MacArthur has warned the Office of Strategic Services off his theatre of command are substantially correct. His opponents say that General Donovan's position has been somewhat weakened by the death of Mr Roosevelt. Whereas Donovan's Irish qualities and passionate interest in the international political underworld, as well as his Republican affiliation and influence, were assets with the late President Roosevelt, who liked to attract influential Republicans to his side, President Truman is a stricter party man and somewhat shy of international ramifications. General Donovan himself, however, tells his friends that his relations with the new President are very satisfactory. The General, as already reported, has agreed to go to Europe to assist Justice Jackson in the work of the War Crimes Commission, which should suit his talents and expert knowledge of hues and shades of German parties and personalities. There is some nervousness within the Office of Strategic Services as to the future of that vast and omnivorous organization under the new regime.

. . .

TVA. Senators McKellar and Stewart,[4] the chief opponents of the renomination of David Lilienthal, have now announced that, as they are reluctant to oppose President Truman, 'whom they like', they would not press their case against renomination. This they accompany with a good deal of personal abuse of Lilienthal himself. It is clear, however, that the reason for cancelling their projected onslaught lies in the fact that President Truman has made it quite clear that he shares the general view of the beneficial work and efficient management of this remarkable agency, and that even McKellar prefers to avoid heavy defeat to the empty satisfaction of ventilating his sentiments on the floor of the Senate. Liberals (e.g. Marquis Childs) are naturally much elated.

Taxation. President Truman has once more shown his firmness and earned liberal applause by opposing Senator George's proposal to reduce taxation on the ground that this was not to be hoped for until the end of the Japanese war. George is perhaps the most influential of all Senate conservatives and does not disguise that he favours reduced taxation in order to preserve the 'middle-class ascendancy' upon which he believes the American way of life to be based. Truman's direct opposition to this influential personage, so different to the more skilful but more evasive methods which the late Mr Roosevelt sometimes employed under like circumstances, seems to have made weighty impression even

---

4 Arthur Thomas Stewart, lawyer, Democratic Senator from Tennessee since 1939.

in conservative circles. . . . In general, the impression seems to be that President Truman is grasping the reins of office very firmly indeed.

26 May 1945

The War. The hard fighting on Okinawa [1] has dispelled excessive optimism about a quick end to the Japanese war. The press takes the line that rejoicing about the end of the war is premature whilst so many American boys are dying in desperate Pacific warfare. Interest in this front nevertheless is somewhat forced since the turmoil in Europe obviously offers more real and exciting food both for speculation and anxiety. Russia in Europe, and the right way to treat Germany, are the real preoccupations that obsess the minds both of officials and the public.

. . .

A member of the Embassy staff found this week that in some of the more advanced New York political salons the Soviet Union seems to be exercising its old hypnotic effect : the victims either desire to struggle against the influence, or to succumb gracefully to so much supposed superior wisdom and power. . . . Meanwhile Mr Wallace in a recent speech denounced those who regarded Soviet and United States aims as irreconcilable. He described the United States and the USSR as the strongest powers emerging out of the 'thirty years' war', both bent upon improving the lot of the common man by the application of technology and 'scienomics' (a word of his own queer invention) and only liable to encroach on the sovereignty of their smaller neighbours for security reasons. His theme falls into the now all prevalent Big Two rather than Big Three pattern. . . .

The Hopkins mission. This growth of public anxiety doubtless decided the President to send Messrs Hopkins and Bohlen to Moscow and Joe Davies to London.[2] The first of these moves was probably prompted by the advice consistently given to Mr Truman by the principal European experts in the State Department (and outside), who feared an excessive deterioration of relations in Europe if nothing were done until the meeting of the Big Three which was itself likely to be delayed until after the British elections. Thinking also as they certainly were of the mounting tide of British indignation at the Soviets, of which they are said to be getting many reports from London, these experts showed every sign of anxiety to prevent the pot from boiling over. At the same time they may well have sought to impress upon the President what some of them have been telling us in private – namely that it was important to demonstrate to Russia and the world that Mr Roosevelt's foreign policy – 'The Grand Design' – was being continued in full strength by the new President. This was certainly understood to be the view of e.g. Messrs Leahy, Stettinius and Harriman. Indeed Leahy, Marshall and Stettinius are thought to have played a decisive part in convincing the

1 From 1 April to 21 June.
2 All on the same day, 23 May.

President that the ideal choice as emissary to Moscow was Harry Hopkins, if only because he is universally known to have been more closely associated with Mr Roosevelt's foreign policies than any other living man (and moreover enjoys a unique measure of confidence in Moscow, London and among the Chiefs of Staff of his own country). His task is evidently to try to relieve the tension, to convey to the Kremlin the dangerous effect of present Soviet policies upon American public opinion and the United States Government and to collect sufficient information about the present Soviet position to enable the American Government to determine its course of action whilst reassuring public opinion that it has an 'independent policy' of its own. Above all the Hopkins Mission seems to have sprung from a desire to keep matters moving during the most perilous period yet of inter-Allied relations, when the integrating force of the fight against the common foe in Europe has suddenly been withdrawn, and a passive policy could lead to disastrous misunderstandings and a series of progressively graver conflicts between the Big Three.

As for Joe Davies's London mission it seems to have been due both to his own well-known desire to continue to take part in affairs, and to President Truman's desire to employ party regulars as much as possible. The relatively non-party Hopkins is thus counterbalanced by Davies who is at once the symbol of pro-Soviet policy and married to a very substantial contributor to Democratic Party funds.[3] The decision to send both appears to have been abruptly taken. I am told that Hopkins did not really feel well enough to undertake this arduous journey but decided that the gravity of the situation demanded that he should go. Meanwhile Truman's press secretary Ross has announced that an early meeting of the Big Three is 'definitely in the works' and that the Hopkins-Davies journeys are but a prelude to and not a substitute for it. This meeting is urgently demanded by the press.

1 June 1945

.   .   .

British General Election. There is naturally a good deal of interest in this event. . . . In general a Conservative victory is expected. It is entertaining to note that the same phenomenon as could be observed in Britain during the United States presidential elections in 1944 now appears to be occurring in reverse in this country. The average American, whatever his opinions, looks on Mr Churchill as much the greatest visible symbol of the British role in world affairs, and would, therefore, be as surprised and shocked by his defeat as the British might have been had this occurred to Mr Roosevelt. Such members of the British Labour or Liberal parties as may happen to be in the United States will doubtless experience emotions very similar to those which affected American Republicans

3 Joseph Davies's second wife (m. 1935) was the wealthy heiress Marjorie Post Hutton.

in Britain during 1944, when they found to their consternation that the re-election of Mr Roosevelt was assumed to be both inevitable and intensely desirable by most British persons of whatever party to whom they spoke. It should be added that the liberal and left-wing press in the United States is likely to echo British anti-Churchill newspapers more closely than any British organs reflected the opinions of, say, the *Chicago Tribune*. There is a further possibility that, unless the tension with Russia is soon eased, Mr Churchill, who is widely reputed to be the protagonist of a tough line with Stalin, will be adopted as their stoutest champion by all United States critics of Soviet policy, and by the same token attacked by those who deem this attitude mistaken or dangerous. Intense interest is certain to continue in British political developments, and it is not probable that either the United States press or the United States radio will begin to practise that detached 'neutrality in thought and word and deed', once enjoined by President Wilson,[1] which they seemed to expect (and in a large measure, obtained) from us in 1940 and 1944.

. . .

United States Communists to take 'inventory' of their position. Recently the press from right to left printed virtually identical accounts of a 'crisis' in the United States Communist Party, now quaintly known as the Communist Political Association of the United States, a 'non-party organization'. A year ago, when the American Communist Party as such was formally disbanded, Mr Browder encouraged this organization to 'co-operate with' either of the two existing great political parties. The present crisis was precipitated by an article in the April issue of *Cahiers de Communisme*, an organ of the Communist Party of France, written by Jacques Duclos,[2] and believed to be inspired by Maurice Thorez[3] who is thought to have recently discussed the matter in Moscow. Duclos's general thesis is that Mr Browder's leadership was guilty of 'sowing dangerous opportunist illusions' in advocating the possibility of class peace in the United States, and thus deflecting the revolutionary movement of the working masses from its proper end, i.e. the seizure of power. He charged Mr Browder with having 'ended in practice in the liquidation of the independent political party of the working classes'. He accused him of leading a 'notorious revision of Marxism-Leninism. Nothing justified the dissolution of the Communist Party of the United States. . . . The constitution of the Communist Political Association could only result in anxiety and cloud the vision of the working masses', etc., etc. Browder has printed the article in the American *Daily Worker* and performed a routine grovel with great humility. He confesses that M. Duclos's words doubtless reflected the 'general trend of opinion of European Marxists in relation to

1 At the outbreak of war in Europe in 1914.

2 Jacques Duclos, deputy leader of French Communist Party under Thorez for many years, having joined it at its inception in 1920. Acting Secretary in Thorez's absence.

3 Maurice Thorez, Secretary-General of French Communist Party 1933–64. Fled to USSR in October 1939 and returned to France in October 1944, under amnesty from de Gaulle.

America' and 'thus demand our respectful consideration'. The press has in general seized on these servile words with much natural glee, pointing out at the same time that the incident foreshadows an imminent sharp change of line that will entail the elimination, or at any rate demotion, of Browder. They predict that William Z. Foster,[4] Browder's chief rival in the United States party, is likely to succeed him and that enthusiastic support of Messrs Roosevelt and Churchill, which was the 'line' ever since Tehran, is about to be abruptly reversed under direct orders from Moscow, back again to traditional opposition to 'national governments' with Mr Churchill as the special target. Whether or not this is so, it is clear that a major upheaval has occurred in the ranks of United States Communists, and that feverish party conferences are about to take place ; 'an inventory must be taken' to adjust the party line to greater conformity with the possibly more aggressive tactics now being pursued by European Communist parties. In this process Browder may well be discarded,[5] and much genuine ammunition provided to the anti-Soviet forces in the United States whose strength is potentially very considerable.

. . .

2 June 1945

United States relations with the USSR. Whilst Hopkins's mission, and reports of Stalin's affability to him, have had a tranquillizing effect, the accumulation of anti-Russian talk was obviously thought by the Administration to have reached a peak which made it imperative to take immediate steps to assuage it. Hence a series of inspired utterances intended to calm the atmosphere. The most important of these pronouncements was the speech of Stettinius, a masterpiece of cautious and tactful drafting. . . .

On the other side of the picture, the Roman Catholic order of the Knights of Columbus, taking their cue from an earlier pronouncement by the United States Roman hierarchy reported at the time, delivered a violent diatribe on the danger to Europe and the Christian tradition from the Eastern barbarians. This anti-Bolshevik tirade was echoed in a broadcast delivered by Congresswoman Clare Booth Luce, recently returned from her European travels, who alleged that mass desertions by Russian officers and men to the Germans had occurred in order to escape the intolerable Soviet tyranny. She had also been putting all this about in private, quoting, so it is rumoured, a high British personality in London to support her Russophobe views, and referring to China as the 'Poland of Asia' inasmuch as it displayed the same pattern of Soviet support of anti-Western Communists.

. . .

4 William Z.Foster led AF of L strike against Steel Trust in 1919 and secured largest vote of inter-war years (over 100,000) as Communist candidate for Presidency in 1932. In that year illness obliged him to yield leadership to Earl Browder.

5 He was. In July Foster was chosen as new national chairman of the party and in February 1946 Browder was expelled as a 'social imperialist'.

Mrs Luce's line on China is strongly supported in an article in the *Readers Digest* by Messrs Max Eastman and J.B.Powell [1] (a United States editor in China back from Japanese prison and torture) passionately denouncing the Chinese Communists and accusing United States Communists of spreading false information about the Chungking Government. Mr Soong's appointment as Premier of that Government was very favourably received here since he is regarded as the best type of level-headed liberal and as the most pro-Western member of his family.

. . .

As might be expected those sections of the press and radio normally critical of British policy, both from the left and right, are most vocal in accusing Britain of trying to drive a wedge between the USSR and the United States, in pursuit of her traditional balance of power strategy, which alone, it is alleged, could preserve her role of world arbiter. While this view is not (repeat not) traceable either to the White House or to the upper layers of the State Department, even they must be at pains in the prevailing state of public opinion to stress that United States foreign policy is free from undue British influence. Hence their public solidarity with us on the Levant question [2] is all the more highly to be commended as evidence that they are not allowing themselves to be stampeded into making unwise but popular gestures of a 'hands off' type as in the Greek imbroglio last year.

Stettinius speech. Awareness of this confusion in popular thought and the search for an official United States 'line' must have entered deeply into the composition of Stettinius's radio address of 28 May on the achievements to date of the San Francisco conference. It was an unexpectedly meaty speech, drafted indeed at San Francisco, but, I am told, most carefully checked with the White House; it gained widespread approval in the press, and did something to prop up Stettinius's declining prestige. The promise of a strong international security charter answers to the still fervent desires of virtually all sections of the United States public, and Stettinius's praise of the exemplary behaviour of the United States delegation was designed to please, and had the effect of pleasing, all parties. The relatively strong words on Argentina are the best proof of the degree of public uneasiness aroused by this issue, and may represent the convictions of those who, like Dunn and Pasvolsky, and possibly the President himself, have been none too happy about that aspect of the conference. The words on Poland were exquisitely balanced and impartial, and gave no handle to the anti-Soviet faction; while the extended praise of Molotov's co-operative behaviour rang comfortingly in the distraught atmosphere surrounding the crucial Russian issue. Stettinius also did his best with the troubled veto question, and altogether man-

1 John B.Powell, managing editor of *China Weekly Review*, Shanghai, 1917–41, made Japanese prisoner of war in 1941, exchanged and repatriated on *Gripsholm*, 1942.
2 Anti-French disturbances in Syria and Lebanon.

aged to avoid giving offence to anyone with considerable adroitness. The list of the objectives of United States foreign policy – total victory over Japan; a world settlement founded on justice and right; a better social and economic order; the limitation of national sovereignties made inevitable by international needs, which spelt the end of isolationism; and finally (perhaps the most significant point of all), the American determination to maintain its own policies to the full and to 'mediate' wherever necessary – were all received with acclaim by the press and public.

The myth of Mr Roosevelt as a great and wise mediator between the powerful figures of Mr Churchill and Marshal Stalin, whose policies might otherwise have come into open collision, seems to be deeply embedded in the popular consciousness of the American people. Indeed this popular myth, which spokesmen of the late Administration appear themselves to have fostered both after the Tehran Conference and at an even earlier time, is now so strong that it suits the book of United States officials, who are aware of the true facts, to earn automatic credit for American policies both present and future, by representing them as directed towards this virtuous end. No one, including high American officials themselves, who in private assure us that no particular significance attaches to the term employed in their chief's speech, seems at all clear as to what is entailed by the concept of the United States as a 'Powerful Mediator'. . . .

. . . Some commentators like Hanson Baldwin, who is close to the Service Departments, think of mediation as an uncommitted but positive role, opposed equally to an anti-Soviet 'line-up' with Britain and to 'appeasement' of the USSR. Others seem to understand by it a more negative and isolationist notion of the United States as intervening in world affairs only when Anglo-Soviet relations reach an inevitable crisis and a major collision threatens. Be this as it may, the blessed word 'mediation' seems to have gained popularity from alleged American subservience to Britain at San Francisco and it has undoubtedly made a profound impression.

The speech of Stettinius has led to a slight rise in stock of the State Department and of Stettinius, although most political wiseacres still firmly believe that Stettinius will soon have to go, which may well be true. Senator Willis has openly said so, and Lippmann has repeated in a very clear and emphatic fashion that what may have suited Roosevelt, who with Hopkins conducted his own foreign policy, will not do for Truman, who needs a State Department capable of formulating high policy, instead of, as he implies, drifting rudderless as at present. He declares that a wise and experienced political figure is required to guide foreign policy, not necessarily someone already deeply versed in foreign affairs (for such cannot be found) nor the kind of *salon* diplomatist who talks about 'Dear old Charlie in Bucharest'. His attitude seems accurately to represent the present state of popular, and probably White House, feeling about diplomatists in general and the United States foreign service in particular.

3 June 1945

The 'Era of good feeling'. In his relations with the public and the political parties, President Truman continues to bask in an Indian summer and his interview with Hoover and invitations to Landon and Dewey were enthusiastically applauded in large sections of the press as continuing the splendid 'era of good feeling' so different from e.g. the troubled period after Lincoln's death. The *Daily Worker* has stigmatized this affability to Hoover as a very sinister symptom of *rapprochement* with so notorious a 'Fascist beast', and *PM* is also censorious. The Cabinet changes are still favourably viewed by all concerned. The part in causing Biddle's dismissal played by Hannegan, who, I am told, is one of the new Attorney General Clark's [1] best friends, has not leaked out even to Drew Pearson. I am told that Truman's old antipathy to Biddle was the strongest factor in his unseating, and that one of the reasons for the nomination of the comparatively colourless Clark was the need to placate Speaker Rayburn (who advocated Biddle's retention) with the appointment of a friend and fellow Texan. Left and right seem equally enthusiastic in their praise of both Anderson [2] and Schwellenbach, whose appointments have been ratified by the Senate. Ickes is now the only unregenerate New Dealer left in the Administration. His retention is said to be due to the degree of political support which he still enjoys, and to his formidable personal qualities which make it imprudent to expel this fierce old fighter, with whom Truman is said to feel none too comfortable. Ickes would certainly hit back if any move against him were made, and this is all too well known to everyone concerned. One commentator has made the entertaining observation that Truman has in fact kept nearly all of Dewey's election pledges – a tendency to choose younger Cabinet members, to clear the Administration 'jungle' of overlapping and inefficient agencies, to establish better relations with Congress, to seek for talent west of the Mississippi. Truman's own position thus continues to be remarkably strong at the moment.

British General Election. Whilst the liberal and left-wing press (e.g. the Marshall Field papers in New York and Chicago, the Communist papers, etc.) hope for a Conservative defeat, the bulk of such newspapers as have expressed opinions either expect, or both expect and hope, that Mr Churchill will be returned to power. There is talk in the conservative press that a Labour victory would mean really dangerous socialism in Britain, and there is a general sense, very similar to that experienced *vis-à-vis* Roosevelt in Britain in 1944, that with Mr Churchill America knows where she is and is indeed most contented with her relationship, whereas a new administration is a leap into the unknown. This goes on side by side with complaints that Mr Churchill is needlessly antagonizing the

---

1 Thomas C. Clark, Texan lawyer, in Department of Justice since 1937, ending up as Assistant Attorney General.
2 Clinton P. Anderson, made Secretary of Agriculture, previously Democratic Congressman from New Mexico 1940–5.

Soviet Union, and dragging a reluctant America in his powerful wake into a dangerous anti-Russian alliance, with the implication that Mr Davies was sent to London to warn Mr Churchill that he is not to expect American support for so foolhardy a position. The conservative press and broadcasters continue to stress that only Mr Churchill provides a real guarantee of the full prosecution by Britain of the war against Japan, although relatively few newspapers actually avow their suspicion that Labour might be diverted by domestic interests away from full-scale Pacific warfare. It is encouraging in this connexion to note that Admiral Nimitz used the opportunity of visiting a British battleship to denounce mischievous rumours that the United States of America did not want the British fleet to participate in Pacific fighting. He professed not to know whence such evil rumours sprang, but whether or no this was disingenuous it is a significant and welcome fact that the Admiral should have gone out of his way to praise the British naval achievement in his area and to spike officially the ceaseless whispering campaign on this topic, of which no political observer in Washington can be unaware. Some persons, particularly among the broadcasters, wonder how, in the event of a Conservative victory in Britain, United States policy, which is 'left of centre', can be fitted in with a 'return to Toryism' across the Atlantic. Others apply this only to foreign policy in Europe and the Far East. A considerable number of newspapers, too varied to be classified, do, however, take the line that British foreign and military policy is too strongly set, particularly with regard to the Pacific war, to be altered by a change of administration. They hold that the elections, however inconvenient at such a moment of international strain and stress, are well worthwhile as an expression of the vitality of democratic institutions and cannot alter the firm bonds which unite Britain and the United States of America. Comments on the elections, however obvious the predilections of the editorialists, are moderate in tone but display no false inhibitions about 'interference in British domestic affairs'. The general tone continues to be most amicable.

9 June 1945

. . .

. . . The general atmosphere until a day or two ago was not one of hostility or of passion towards the USSR, but of steeply declining confidence in the international political stock-market. Owing however to the widespread desire for reassurance provided in an uncertain world, any turn for the better such as is now provided by the solution of the veto issue and the agreement with Tito about Trieste, must lead to a rapid improvement of public confidence until the next inevitable slump occurs.

As it is, even the left (non-communist) papers, radio commentators, etc., joined the general chorus of complaint against the Soviet attitude over the veto issue at San Francisco,[1] and news of Hopkins's general progress has not yet been

1 The Russians wanted the veto in the Security Council modified so as to safeguard any action they might take under various bilateral mutual aid pacts which they had negotiated in Europe.

given sufficient publicity to offset the mood of melancholy. The doldrums, which prevailed until the end of the week, were not unlike those before Yalta. The public and uninformed officials tended to wring their hands, whilst officials in the know went about with a slightly mysterious air of better things to come when it will become apparent that President Truman is pursuing a constructive American policy designed to remedy existing difficulties. The theme that United States mediation is needed continues to be sedulously propagated, with Lippmann and others assuring us that they mean no more than that America must continue to develop that policy of full responsibility in European affairs which was decided upon by President Roosevelt during the troubled days before Yalta. These pundits add that 'mediation' is merely a useful label with which to sell this policy to the immature public. Provided therefore that the results of the Hopkins Mission and of any subsequent formulation of United States policy can be represented as a mainly American achievement, it is distinctly possible that the present perplexities will once more as has so often happened in the past be succeeded by a period of faith and hope in which the United States will be represented as having at the eleventh hour again rescued the world from falling a prey to the fatal collisions of the other major allies.

It is significant that recent searchings of heart have not led to any serious relapse into isolationism. Even ex-Governor Landon declares that America must 'seize the balance of power'. The effect of shaken confidence in Soviet intentions – and, as a result of the Levant situation, in those of Britain and France as well – should thus lead to an even more fervent faith that President Truman, whose mind and heart seem so obviously in tune with those of the American people, will presently follow up his much acclaimed review of the Japanese war situation with an equally convincing statement of future United States policy, and with corresponding diplomatic action, which Americans of all parties can wholeheartedly support.

To sum up: the present mood resembles the dark moment before the dawn. When therefore the fruit of the Hopkins Mission is revealed to the public, together with any supporting evidence of a general improvement of inter-Allied relations, there is a risk that unless strongly played down by the highest quarters public jubilation may prove to be unrestrained. In the meantime a number of commentators have been drawing attention to the economic chaos in Europe and to the immense problems which confront the Allied Control Commission in Germany where it is pointed out that the prospects of effective inter-Allied collaboration are about to be put to the crucial test.

Possible changes in the State Department and the position of Mr Truman. As reported in earlier summaries, it seems certain that both Stettinius and Grew will be relieved of their posts in the fairly near future, the former no doubt after receiving warm praise for his work. The position of Mr Truman appears to be quite exceptionally strong, probably stronger than Mr Roosevelt's ever was. In a recent poll 80 per cent of Democrats and 70 per cent of Republicans declared that they wished for no change in the Presidency.

11 June 1945

British elections. Less was said on this topic in the press and radio than last week, and the old alignments continue. Mrs Patterson's [1] *Times-Herald* says that it proposes, as an unofficial member of the British Empire, to vote for Mr Churchill, insisting that a dukedom must be conferred upon him. At the same time it represents Mr Churchill in a singularly disagreeable cartoon as inviting a frightened and reluctant Uncle Sam to enter the Third World War. The *Daily Worker* has spoken against the Prime Minister, and so have the Field papers and the radical press generally. As the British election campaign gets into its stride, we may expect a corresponding rise in excitement amongst the local partisans, with the old anti-Roosevelt majority of the press plumping for Mr Churchill, and vice versa.

Bretton Woods and reciprocal trade. Contrary to earlier fears concerning ratification of the Bretton Woods agreement, the House passed the enabling legislation by an overwhelming vote of 345–18. Although an easy passage of the bill had been forecast after the adoption of the Wolcott amendments, the almost negligible opposition, nearly all of which came from the diehard or 'lunatic' fringe, is regarded as an encouraging indication of the Congress's real willingness to co-operate in international economic problems. No great difficulty is anticipated in the Senate on Bretton Woods especially in view of Governor Dewey's strong personal endorsement in a New York speech, though opposition over extension of Reciprocal Trade powers is reported still strong. . . .

It is amusing to note that Professor Friedrich von Hayek, upon whom the economic tories in this country placed so much hope, founded upon the Professor's indubitably anti-New Deal views, has proved a most embarrassing ally to them since his passion for free trade makes him no less hostile to tariffs and monopolies. His sincere refusal to be identified with the economic pressure groups which acclaimed his book as a major weapon to fight against planning of any nature have led to a succession of embarrassing incidents highly awkward for both sides.

FEPC and Congress. The President has shown considerable political courage in backing as strongly as he has the Bill to establish a permanent Fair Employment Practices Committee which is particularly anathema to all Southern members of Congress, since it is principally a measure to safeguard the rights of Negroes. This is perhaps the largest single issue on which the President has found himself in opposition to powerful sections of Congress. The others are his desire to be

1 Eleanor (Cissie) Patterson, cousin of Colonel McCormick and publisher of Washington *Times-Herald*.

given powers to reorganize federal machinery, which might deprive the Senate of considerable patronage, and the politically embarrassing issue of raising the salaries of members of the House. But despite all this, his relations with Congress continue to be exceptionally serene.

. . .

One World. The once-isolationist Representative Everett Dirksen of Illinois, a leader among Republicans and one of the most influential speakers in the House, hitherto regarded as something of a diehard, has delivered a speech on his trip abroad. Although containing little of specific note, its general tone was remarkably like the speeches made by the late Wendell Willkie after his world trip. The irony of this fact lies in the fact that Dirksen's trip was financed in large measure by surplus monies raised on his behalf last year for an anti-Willkie campaign.

16 June 1945

The USSR and the European situation. The news of what the Hopkins Mission to Moscow had achieved was greeted with relief but not with that unrestrained jubilation, the possibility and perils of which were mentioned in last week's summary. The feeling prevails that a new and fresher day has begun to dawn, but that the sun has still to rise. The mood, for once, is one of profound but sober satisfaction, and the danger of a subsequent revulsion of feeling has therefore greatly diminished.

The personal stock of Hopkins with the public and indeed Congress is higher than it has ever been. Even some of his most inveterate foes amongst conservative columnists and commentators seem to have discovered for the first time that he is a devoted patriot and the most skilful of American negotiators; a certain amount of vicarious credit is also assigned to Joe Davies, whose precise part remains, however, unknown. President Truman, and to some extent Stettinius, naturally enough benefit from the general satisfaction at the latest achievements of United States foreign policy. It is indeed perhaps as much due to the President himself as to anyone that the good news has not been allowed to lead to extravagant transports of feeling.

. . .

The general tone however both of press and radio comment and of talk amongst officials reveals a determined desire to think that everything has turned out to be very much better than might have been expected. . . .

. . .

The President himself gave the lead to the public at his last press conference where he spoke of 'pleasant concessions' by the Russians and appealed to journalists not to upset the apple-cart by intemperate remarks. The journey of the London Polish leaders to Moscow is being hailed as the best of omens (although this is somewhat offset by the Soviet announcement of the trial of the sixteen Poles); the forthcoming meeting of the Big Three is warmly welcomed but without that desperate note of urgency which used to be heard on past occasions; the press announcement of the American refusal to move out of Western Czechoslovakia has not stimulated worried speculation; although strong views to the contrary had been expressed by two of the newly returned Senators, it is generally taken for granted that the American forces in Germany should make an early withdrawal into the occupational zones. The widest possible publicity has been given to General Eisenhower's remark in Paris that he had encountered nothing in his experience of Soviet military and diplomatic leaders that impeded co-operation with the Russians.

There is now much hope that the Senate may ratify the San Francisco agreement before or during the meeting of the Big Three, i.e. while the present optimistic view prevails; and that the meeting itself will establish the lines of the coming Peace Conference in a manner acceptable to American and world sentiment. As matters stand, it is generally held that grave disservice is being done by those who cast doubts either upon Soviet Russia's intentions in Europe or upon the possibility of creating a stable world settlement. The Administration will no doubt do its best to see that such an outlook is maintained. Against the prevailing background there is a certain danger that sharp criticism of Soviet practices or intentions by other powers, and notably by Britain, would be condemned by the American public as ill-timed and as a petulant prodding of the Russian bear at a moment when, in response to tactful American treatment, he has shown himself quite prepared to engage in co-operative pursuits with other peace-loving creatures.

. . .

The President versus Congress. Although Arthur Krock already claims to detect rifts in the lute in the prevailing 'era of good feeling' between the President and Congress, his analysis seems premature. Points of disagreement have occurred until now over (a) the Fair Employment Practices (pro-Negro) bill, (b) congressional salaries, (c) expansion of the President's powers to reform the federal executive, (d) Reciprocal Trade Agreements, (e) appropriations for the Office of War Information. Whilst on all these issues Congress may not have done the President's liberal bidding, it looks at present as though he would finally succeed in carrying the day without the bad blood which accompanied Mr Roosevelt's disputes with Congress. Considering that occasional differences of opinion and indeed executive-legislative conflicts are an inevitable feature of the American political system, the wonder is that the clouds which have so far appeared on the horizon have been so few and far between: nor are there at present any signs of heavy weather. The 'honeymoon' continues. Senatorial attempts to uncover scandals – e.g. concerning alleged graft in the construction of the Pan American Highway, and concerning an alleged unpaid debt of General Elliott Roosevelt [1]

---

1 Elliott Roosevelt, second son of President, served in Army Air Corps, becoming Brigadier General in February 1945.

reputedly backed by his father, the late President – are routine muckraking activities, and not directed against the White House.

17 June 1945

Administration changes. The most recent change is that in the Navy ; Forrestal duly handed in his resignation which was rejected. Under-Secretary Bard, a Republican, has left and Artemus Gates,[1] previously responsible for the Naval Air Force, has succeeded him. Our people have enjoyed good relations, and in some cases warm personal friendship, with Gates too long to make this appointment need special comment here. Gates has been succeeded by John Lawrence Sullivan,[2] a Democrat once with the Treasury, described as a competent and well-disposed official. But the fact remains that the Navy Department is run by the Admirals to a larger extent than the War Department by the Generals, and that it is the very formidable Admiral King who sets the tone. As for the State Department the President systematically kills the recurrent suggestion that Stettinius is about to go and has started a new crop of speculation by announcing that Stettinius, Byrnes, Hopkins and Joe Davies (the latter two if their health permits) are all to accompany him to the meeting of the Big Three. With regard to the State Department itself, he told the journalists 'to keep on asking' about his coming reform. Hence increased expectation that a shake-up is imminent. Grew, Rockefeller and Holmes still continue at the top of the list of the proscribed. Various new jobs (e.g. that of Under-Secretary) are rumoured for Acheson. The stock of Byrnes has once again risen high, and it is strongly rumoured that the President is only waiting for the Big Three meeting, at which he can completely satisfy himself of Byrnes's quality, to make the final decision to substitute him for Stettinius. Meanwhile, McKim[3], the President's 'battery mate', has been removed from the White House and placed under Snyder in the Loan Administration. The gossip is that McKim was found working against Vinson – fell out with Hannegan – and so had to go.

Foreign propaganda. Relatively little stir has been caused by the publication by the Department of Justice of a massive report describing the activities of foreign publicity agencies in the United States. Even the McCormick-Patterson papers could not do much with the fact that the British have been the heaviest spenders with a little over two million dollars – a far cry from the fantastic sums hinted at by the Anglophobe press. (But in its editorial the *Chicago Tribune* did use of foreign propagandists generally the phrase 'the sack of America is the objec-

1 Artemus L.Gates, Assistant Secretary of Navy since 1941.

2 John Lawrence Sullivan, lawyer, Assistant Secretary of the Treasury 1940–4.

3 Edward D.McKim had been sergeant in Truman's artillery battery in the First World War. An insurance executive in Kansas City, Mo., he was brought to Washington by Truman when he became President, and was made his Chief Administrative Assistant.

tive'.) The Poles came next, with something under a million, then the Dutch, the Czechs and the French. As for the Russians, the report and subsequent comment by Attorney General Biddle (who is leaving at the end of the month) made it clear that the Soviet Union was thought to operate in other than public ways, and that the report was not concerned with possible infringement of an Act under which the Russians officially made no publicity. Although the immediate effects of this publication have so far not been adverse (indeed the usually critical commentator Quincy Howe wished long life to the BIS), it is impossible to tell when or how it may be used in the near or distant future by persons seeking to estimate the effect of British or other foreign propaganda on United States policies.

. . .

New York politics. The mayoral position is still in an incredibly confused condition. The following picture has so far emerged from an immense amount of jockeying to and fro between and by various bosses and controllers of political power in the State of New York. The strongest candidate in the Democratic primaries appears to be O'Dwyer, who successfully overcame the opposition of the bosses Kelly[4] and Flynn and, indeed, displayed sufficient political strength (a) to eliminate two fellow candidates for lesser State offices who were attached to his ticket by Messrs Kelly and Flynn, and (b) restore the candidacy of Hogan,[5] Dewey's successor as District Attorney and the most energetic gang-buster of the State, who has been strenuously attacked by those elements in Tammany connected with the underworld. The elimination of Hogan, the scourge of criminals, would have given immense capital to the opposition.

As it is, O'Dwyer emerges as a fairly strong candidate with a personal reputation somewhat better than that of his backers. He has been accepted not merely by Tammany but by the Labor Party as well, which means a combination of Hillman's CIO-PAC as well as the straight followers of the Communist Party line. Although a very personable and affable figure, O'Dwyer's handling of civil affairs as a Brigadier in Italy, and of his present functions as head of the War Refugee Board, have scarcely been distinguished. He has incidentally criticized British policy in Italy on what seems an insufficient basis of knowledge and probably for political reasons. Although his friends in Washington maintain that he is honest and liberal, the impression in New York seems to be that, whilst free from any taint of underworld connection, he is not a strong man, and would be largely run by the machine politicians.

Meanwhile the Republicans, the anti-Communist Liberal Party (AF of L and in particular Dubinsky's Garment Workers and their political allies) and the old Fusion party which originally supported La Guardia, have combined to choose as their candidate Judge Jonah J.Goldstein,[6] by origin a Jewish politico in Tam-

---

4 Frank V.Kelly, insurance executive and Democratic boss of Brooklyn since 1934.

5 Frank S.Hogan, lawyer, District Attorney, New York, since 1942.

6 Jonah J.Goldstein, New York philanthropist and lawyer with Democratic credentials going back to his days as Al Smith's secretary, Judge of Court of General Sessions 1939–56.

many, but long since separated from his original sponsors. The New York Consulate General reports that he is a sound and sensible friend of Britain and a decent man, and that his chances of victory partly depend on how much support he can win in the Democratic camp as a result of the internecine warfare in the ranks of his opponents. No straight Republican can hope to win in New York without some Democratic support – and Goldstein may be hoping to receive aid *sub rosa* from the two disgruntled Democratic bosses, whose backing of O'Dwyer may be something less than whole-hearted. I understand that Goldstein offers better promise of progressive government than O'Dwyer. He will doubtless be branded – unjustly as it now seems – as a Tammany man, although he has just refused the support which certain Democratic elements appeared ready to give him, doubtless in return for a suitable deal.

. . .

If O'Dwyer is elected the somewhat sombre picture recorded in telegram of 21 May still holds good. Whatever his personal virtue he is unlikely long to resist the political pressures which will be brought to bear on him. The outlook is, however, very much less depressing than anticipated if the Republican candidate (supported by Dewey) is elected. As for O'Dwyer, he certainly seems to be doing his best by repeated snubs to those concerned to kill the rumour that he is supported by Communists and underworld elements.

. . .

23 June 1945

. . .

The USSR. Relations with the Soviet Union are again on the upward grade. Soviet compromises at San Francisco, the Polish détente and the reported withdrawal of Russian troops from Czechoslovakia have contributed to a feeling that the Soviets are willing on occasion to give as well as to take in the solution of pending international problems. This has quickened anew the urgent American desire to find a durable *modus vivendi* with the Russians. Although the undercurrent of misgiving naturally continues and is certain to re-emerge at the next crisis, the favourable omens are encouraging a general sense of optimism.

This optimistic mood has been greatly stimulated by the simple but universally acclaimed statement of General Eisenhower that the individual Russian soldier is as friendly and easy to get on with as the American. His ability to inspire trust in the Russians and the high honour bestowed upon him by Marshal Zhukov [1] are pleasing evidence to Americans that, as he himself told them, 'it can be done'.

. . .

The triumphant return of Eisenhower and the proof he has given that an American is capable of winning the highest esteem abroad and of harmonizing Allied

1 Georgi Zhukov, Commander in Chief of Soviet armies on Eastern front in Europe.

differences have thus gone far to reassure his countrymen, who are perpetually haunted by the uncomfortable belief that they lack the necessary experience and guile to deal with the complex problems of the Old World.

. . .

24 June 1945

General 'Ike'. General 'Ike's' triumphant return was the most notable item of domestic news during the week. His modest bearing and friendly, informal ways stirred popular emotion. Enthusiastic crowds are reported to have outdone those which greeted Lindbergh's return and even that of Pershing after the last war. 'What Ike says makes sense' typified the attitude of the man in the street whose affection for the General was cemented by the conviction that he symbolizes something essentially American. Press headlines, editorials and radio comment all burst forth into paeans of welcome and praise, unstintingly asserting that nothing was too good for the General. Typical of this have been suggestions that Eisenhower's obvious ability to get on with the Russians would make him an excellent Ambassador to Moscow and it has even been proposed that he should be appointed to the Secretaryship of State. More sober opinion, however, feels that he will have a difficult enough diplomatic job in Europe and that his admitted talents will find plenty of scope on the Allied Control Commission. The General, who has himself roundly disclaimed any political ambitions, is also mentioned as an obvious candidate for Chief-of-Staff when General Marshall should wish to resign. His speech before Congress contained unusually warm tributes both to the Prime Minister and the British people, and his emphasis on the hopes of the American soldiers that the United Nations will remain united in peace as in war found a ready response in all quarters.

. . .

Associated Press monopoly suit. Considerable prominence has naturally been given in the press to the ruling handed down this week by the Supreme Court on the suit brought by the Department of Justice against the Associated Press under the Sherman Anti-Trust Act. In a 5 to 3 decision, the Supreme Court upheld a lower court ruling that the bylaws of the Associated Press violate the Anti-Trust Act and ruled that, in passing on applications for membership, the Associated Press must not take into account the effect of possible competition with existing members. The appeal of the Department of Justice that the lower court's ruling should be broadened was rejected. The press itself has so far been slow to react, in any decisive manner, though much is made by both sides of the danger to 'freedom of the press'. This lack of comment may be due to some extent to a belief that the ruling is not likely to have much effect in actual practice.

1 July 1945

The United Nations Organization. The limelight this week was focussed on the historic signing of the San Francisco Charter. The newspapers were filled with photographs of the delegates of the Great Powers signing the final document and the speeches by the various heads of the delegations were prominently reported. Commentators were good enough to draw favourable attention to my remark that an instrument had been forged which 'if men are serious in wanting peace and are ready to make sacrifices for it, they may find means to win it'.

. . .

Hope has been expressed in some quarters that ratification may be achieved before 19 July in order to strengthen the President's hand at the forthcoming meeting of the Big Three. Few observers believe however that this can be done quite so soon. As it is, President Truman will present the Charter to the Senate in person on 2 July and Chairman Connally has announced that Committee hearings will begin the following week. It is generally expected that the hearings will last approximately two weeks, whilst at least a further two weeks will be needed to enable the majority of Senators to air their views on the floor of the House. Ratification, which Ernest Lindley called 'as nearly certain as anything can be in the world of politics', may then be expected by the end of July. More than the necessary two-thirds of the Senators have already voiced their intention of voting in favour and it is not expected that more than a handful will ultimately oppose. Even such one-time opponents of internationalism as Wisconsin's La Follette and the *Chicago Tribune*'s 'Curley' Brooks have declared that they will vote for ratification. The isolationist Senator Burton K. Wheeler has made it known that he expects 'no organized fight' against the Charter and will not himself 'spearhead' any opposition.

As for public support, first returns from a nationwide Gallup poll show that 90 per cent of the people ready to express their opinion want the Senate to ratify the Charter and only 10 per cent are opposed. Whilst the omens all point to speedy ratification, they are based on the assumption that nothing will occur during the next few weeks to upset the applecart. In this connexion William Philip Simms, foreign editor of the Scripps-Howard newspapers, has warned that something may occur at the Big Three meeting which will play into the hands of the opposition. Intransigent isolationists are presumably awaiting just such a development. It will also be a matter of surprise if the debate in Congress does not ventilate the question of the powers of the American delegation to the World Organization, which figured so prominently in congressional discussion on Dumbarton Oaks. Indeed Senator Taft has already stated that he anticipates offering a reservation to the Charter to limit the powers of the United States delegate. Although the Executive already has authority to confer certain powers on the delegate this issue will have to be decided by both Houses of Congress. The real fight may thus occur over the American delegate's powers rather than over ratification of the Charter itself.

The Polish issue. Following immediately after the comparatively mild verdict on the Polish underground leaders [1] the announcement that success had attended the

1 Three were acquitted, one received a ten-year sentence, one eight, and ten others lesser sentences.

talks in Moscow for the formation of a provisional Government for Poland produced a sense of relief that another difficult barrier to an understanding with Soviet Russia had been overcome. The fact that three of the Poles named at Moscow for membership in the new Government will not in fact occupy posts in it, has so far received little notice but will almost certainly serve to provide ammunition for inveterate Russophobes. In further comment on the sentences passed on the underground leaders even the right wing press has done no more than to say that the Soviet charges were 'not wholly incredible' ; whilst liberals declared that the trials had vindicated the USSR in world opinion. Formation of the new Polish Government is generally regarded as the first step to unity within Poland itself, of which it is recognized that the ultimate test will be the holding of free elections. It is expected that Britain and the United States will shortly proceed to recognize the new Government and that this step will be of good augury for unity at the Big Three meeting.

The USSR. Comment on relations with Soviet Russia is almost uniformly characterized by a tendency to give her the benefit of every doubt and even to soften the contours of hard problems which call for international action. Indeed the American public is evidently anxious to persuade itself that solutions for all current difficulties with the Soviet Union can readily be found through the exercise of common sense and goodwill. This tendency has been most marked in the initial comment on the Russian demands on Turkey which have been fully reported in the press. The *Washington Post,* for example, stated that the Soviets had a strong case for the revision of the Montreux Convention[2] and it is generally thought that the whole question will be peacefully settled at the coming Big Three meeting.

. . . .

Resignation of Stettinius. The long-expected resignation of Stettinius from the post of Secretary of State has already been commented upon in my telegram No. 4500. It was announced today that he has been succeeded by Byrnes. There is naturally much private speculation about the effects of this new appointment on other members of the State Department. It is widely expected that Grew and probably also Nelson Rockefeller, Joseph Grew and MacLeish, and more remotely James Dunn and Holmes will be replaced and/or transferred ; that Clayton is likely to stay, that Ben Cohen will be given an appointment and so forth. Phillips, who acted as an Assistant Secretary of State during Dunn's absence in San Francisco, has now resigned. The State Department regulars are distinctly nervous about Byrnes, whom they suspect of viewing the Department and its traditions with a somewhat critical eye. There is some private speculation about a possible increase in the influence of Joe Davies and Baruch. Byrnes's friendship with Judge Vinson (his own nominee) is likely to promote greater harmony

2 The Montreux Convention (1936) allowed Turkey to refortify the Dardanelles, but banned warships of belligerent nations in any war in which Turkey was neutral.

than has hitherto existed between the economic and political aspects of United States foreign policy.

Although I am reporting fully on the subject by despatch it may be of value to submit the following comments on Byrnes, whose appointment as Secretary of State was confirmed today by the Senate. He is a product of the poor Irish immigrant ; good humoured, sensitive and quick-witted but of provincial outlook and somewhat unsure of himself. He is not in any sense a self-seeker and has amassed no fortune in the course of a highly successful career. His political and economic views are those of a moderate Southern Senator, i.e. conservative in social questions and particularly in regard to the Negro and labour problems, an ardent free-trader and a devoted personal follower of Mr Hull.

Having when a Senator built up his reputation as a singularly gifted promoter of the late Administration's policies, he sees himself, and is regarded by others, as a remarkably skilful composer of differences. Senators look upon him as one of themselves and his natural charm and tact have made him widely popular in Congress and Administrative circles. He is an intimate associate of the President who proposed him for Vice-President in 1944.

Being sensitive to opinion himself, he responds to courteous treatment and like many Americans he prefers simple candour to a more sophisticated approach. As one who faithfully reflects the prevailing mood of the Administration and the public, he is likely at the Big Three meeting to give the Soviet Union the benefit of many doubts and to seek to avoid major crises. It would be his object to return home with a reputation for having found a lasting *via media* for such divergent trends as may there seem likely to divide Great Britain and the Soviet Union. He tells excellent Southern stories.

2 July 1945

Labour. Strikes, which were largely to be expected at this time in view of the lay-offs and general uncertainty, have been played up in the press and have created a strong impression of growing labour unrest. War-plant strikes were reported in St Louis, Detroit, Akron (Ohio) and in Chicago, where the Army was finally forced to take over : the Labor Department's Conciliation Service reports that the daily average of strikes and walkouts has risen from twenty before VE day to approximately forty. The chief cause behind this unrest is undoubtedly labour's fear not only of post-war unemployment, but that with the end of the war and the reduction in overtime, the workers' take-home pay will be cut. The whole position of labour is further marred by the inability of the AF of L and CIO to reconcile their differences at this critical time ; this is exemplified by the spreading strikes in the Detroit automobile plants, where, in the process of partial reconversion both CIO and AF of L unions are refusing to carry the work forward unless the other union is excluded. Some 30,000 workers are affected. The Ball-Burton-Hatch Labor bill continues to be attacked savagely by labour leaders, including John L.Lewis and the left-wing press, as anti-labour and even as 'un-American'. Its general reception, however, has been favourable. It is praised in the press generally as an honest attempt to 'meet one of the most challenging post-war issues'. The need for revision of the Wagner Act and for the placing of responsibility on the labour unions as well as on management has equally been emphasized in more conservative newspapers. There has been a noticeable absence of speculation on the President's attitude towards the new labour bill. It is against this background that Madame Perkins this week bowed out to make way for Judge Schwellenbach, whose appointment as Secretary dates from 1 July.

.   .   .

Fairness to Negroes. The often threatened but seldom realized spectacle of a filibuster in the Senate was started by Senator Bilbo [1] (Democrat of Mississippi) in an attempt to block an appropriation for the President's Fair Employment Practices Committee. This appropriation, which is part of a bill containing appropriations for a number of important war agencies, has already been passed by the House, and authorization of the agencies' current funds is due to expire at the end of June. With the President scheduled to present the United Nations Charter to the Senate Monday and important legislation pending, an attempt is being made to end this filibuster by a 'cloture', which would limit each member to a one-hour speech. The enforcement of 'cloture', however, requires a two-thirds vote of the Senate which may not be forthcoming, as the Southern Democrats are opposing this Executive attempt to enforce equality for the Negroes in all questions relating to employment in industry.

8 July 1945

APPOINTMENT OF MR BYRNES AS SECRETARY OF STATE AND CHANGES IN THE UNITED STATES FOREIGN SERVICE

The appointment has been warmly acclaimed by almost all newspapers and radio commentators. Byrnes is generally regarded as the right man in the right place and is confidently expected by various groups to promote their pet schemes – whether by substituting more businesslike and 'forward-looking' men for old-fashioned or exclusively conservative officials ; or by increasing allowances to Foreign Service officers to enable them to represent the United States adequately without the use of private means ; or by integrating in the State Department the various overlapping foreign policy agencies, particularly in the economic field. Lippmann has given Byrnes his accolade and declares that together with Vinson, he should powerfully reinforce the new cabinet team.

The only sharp criticism of the appointment of Byrnes has come from the Citizens' Political Action Committee, representing labour and liberal groups,

1 Theodore G.Bilbo, Democratic Senator from Mississippi since 1935.

which accuses him of reactionary views on social questions, and from the Negroes, who offer similar complaints. These voices are largely drowned in the general chorus of approval. Max Lerner in *PM* predicts that Byrnes will be as strongly entrenched among his congressional allies as was Hull. This contention, which Lerner does not like, may well have been one of the strongest reasons in the mind of President Truman himself, a favourite of Congress, for appointing Byrnes. It is at any rate clear that the new Secretary of State has entered the game with some very powerful cards in his hand.

Benjamin V. Cohen, Byrnes's friend and assistant in recent months, has been appointed to the State Department, for the moment as a personal assistant to the Secretary. It is said that he will ultimately become Counsellor (a semi-obsolete office of equal rank with the Under-Secretary) or act as Byrnes's personal representative in Europe. He, as well as Dunn, are to accompany Byrnes to the Big Three meeting. Stettinius is said to have expressed a desire to have either Dunn or Pasvolsky, or both, follow him into the United Nations Organization, but neither seems likely to accept unless their position in the Department is rendered untenable, which does not seem probable.

The announcement by Hopkins of his resignation was made the occasion for a handsome tribute to his services by the President. Hopkins is stated to be planning to withdraw to New York to compile his memoirs and it is reported that he has accepted the post of impartial referee in the labour disputes of the Dubinsky Ladies Garment Workers' Union. With Hopkins and Stettinius out of the way, the fate of Harriman is naturally the subject of interested speculation. There are also growing rumours that Caffery [1] may be transferred from Paris, and there is some talk of the transfer of Kirk from Rome. I have heard no mention of a move for Winant. Obiously, however, all important foreign posts are about to be scrutinized and Hannegan, on behalf of the Democratic Party, is bound to demand an adequate share of the spoils.

Byrnes himself, whose appointment was unanimously confirmed by the Senate without the customary committee hearing, has declared that he will make no changes in the Department until the Bureau of the Budget has reported its views on the existing establishment. Hence nothing is certain, but all sources seem to agree that Rockefeller is doomed, and that some stiffening in United States policy towards Latin America and in particular Argentina may, therefore, be anticipated. Messersmith, United States Ambassador to Mexico, is said to be anxious to step into Rockefeller's shoes, but I know of no evidence that this is likely to occur. Julius Holmes is said to be personally unpopular with Byrnes and likely to go for that reason if for no other. Grew, whose departure has been confidently predicted by his critics for many days, may be kept on for a while if there is no immediate agreement about his successor, or if the successor requires to be groomed for a while before being appointed (this might apply e.g. to Pauley,

1 Jefferson Caffery, career diplomat, US Ambassador in Paris 1944–9.

whom Hannegan is said to be pushing). MacLeish may be dropped by the wayside, although no one seems to care greatly about his fate, since his influence in any case has not been very noticeable. Of the remaining Assistant Secretaries, Clayton seems likely to stay, since he has earned golden opinions for his intelligence, efficiency and drive even from New Dealers, and is in sympathy with Byrnes's general outlook. Acheson is, as usual, talking of going, and seems genuinely anxious to resume his private legal practice. There is still talk of his succeeding Crowley as Foreign Economic Administrator, of his promotion to the Under-Secretaryship of the State Department, and of his staying in his present position. If he goes, it will be of his own volition, since no one seems to be driving him. Dunn, at whom the liberal press has been growling, seems likely to remain ; his stand at San Francisco against Argentina is said to have earned him approval at the White House. He, moreover, continues to enjoy the confidence of Mr Hull, now back at his Washington home. Mr Hull in his turn is said to exercise a very considerable influence over Byrnes, for so long his most loyal collaborator in the Senate.

· · ·

8 July 1945

The general public mood is exceptionally benevolent and hopeful; indeed, wherever the average American looks he perceives favourable omens: President Truman's popularity is immense; the latest Gallup poll estimates that 87 per cent of the entire population approve of him, with Republicans scarcely less enthusiastic than Democrats. Indeed, a member of my staff was told by a typical Republican that, after twelve years of happy indignation 'against that man in the White House, it was no fun being a Republican today'.

With only Ickes, Wallace, Stimson and Forrestal remaining of the former Administration, the new Cabinet equally appears to satisfy everyone. The Charter is universally approved. In the foreign field the usual undercurrent of ultimate distrust of the Soviet Union has been muffled. Other problems seem on the way to solution. *Time* magazine even wonders what the Big Three will find to discuss. Shortages of civilian goods and labour strikes are so many flies in the ointment (Ickes delivered a severe public warning on 5 July about the critical coal situation). They are not however felt to be as acute as they might have been and, to the general public, the restoration of peacetime economy seems almost round the corner. The problem of feeding Europe this winter is fully appreciated by the Administration, but is not sufficiently realized elsewhere to disturb the prevailing buoyantly optimistic mood. The only serious exception is the casualty list of the Pacific war – hence an increase of sentiment in favour of modifying, or at any rate clarifying, the concept of unconditional surrender of Japan.

· · ·

The passage of the Charter may be regarded as virtually assured. The debate may however last a fortnight largely to enable Senators to make speeches for home consumption – what Connally has contemptuously termed 'honey-swog-gling'. Gromyko has said that it would be impressive if the United States of America and the USSR ratified the Charter at about the same time. British rati-fication is taken for granted. All this does not mean that we are necessarily altogether out of the wood since, however unlikely on present showing, the real debate may yet be staged on the question of the degree of military assistance due from this country to the organization, and on the powers of the United States delegate, with particular reference to his authority to use American armed forces without a specific vote by the Senate. The motion to confer such powers (in this case on Stettinius) will be debated in both Houses as it is likely to be made the object of a Senate-House resolution, i.e. subject to a simple majority vote of the entire Congress. In any case, these questions are unlikely to come up before the autumn.

.   .   .

Cabinet Changes. According to a completely reliable source, Morgenthau's resignation from the Treasury was primarily due to his feeling of personal incom-patibility with Byrnes. He is said to have demanded a showdown on his authority from the President, who thought it easier to let him go. His resignation was nowhere welcomed so much as in the State Department, which had for long resented his incursions into what it deemed its exclusive province. Indeed the news was said to have been greeted with dancing in the corridors, particularly outside Mr Riddleberger's[1] German Division. The press has given him a cour-teous but not enthusiastic series of obituaries. Morgenthau's departure may pos-sibly mean the retirement or diminution in influence of Dr Harry White, the principal American architect of the Bretton Woods scheme, which is itself suf-ficiently far advanced not to suffer excessively from whatever is in store for that none-too-easy official. The White House announced today that on his return from the Big Three meeting the President will nominate as Morgenthau's suc-cessor Judge Vinson. . . .

As might be expected there is now much talk of other Cabinet changes. Of the original New Deal Cabinet only Wallace and Ickes remain, and the fate of the latter is thought to be very precarious, although it may depend in some degree on his success in the oil negotiations, to conduct which he is about to proceed to London. It is rumoured that Ickes may be succeeded by Pauley or by Krug of the War Production Board. The general trend in Cabinet changes has been to reward loyal party members, particularly congressional leaders, and not to cast about too much for outside talent. The eyes of the public are incidentally now fixed on Truman to see whether he appoints a liberal or a conservative to succeed the Republican Justice Roberts[2] (the investigator of Teapot Dome and Pearl Har-bor incidents), who at the age of seventy is retiring from the Supreme Court.

1 James W.Riddleberger, Chief of Division of Central European Affairs since 1944.
2 Owen J.Roberts, appointed to the Court by Hoover in 1930, was a successful corporation lawyer when asked by Coolidge in 1923 to investigate the scandalous leases of Navy oil reserves in the Teapot Dome area of Wyoming.

Foreign Affairs – general. The prevailing outlook can be summarized somewhat as follows. In Big Three relations American influence will be exerted to prevent collisions between Great Britain and the Soviet Union, i.e. the notion of the United States as mediator ; in bilateral dealings with Britain a tough, businesslike and hundred per cent American line will be kept to the fore. Energy will be displayed in dealings with other Great Powers and a sharp eye kept on the supposed efforts of the wily foreigner to outmanoeuvre the United States. The acceptance speech of Byrnes with its stress on the need to live in peace with nations of a widely dissimilar outlook (written I am told by Ben Cohen) sets the general tone of a policy designed to promote toleration and to avoid major crises.

In a written reply to Congressmen who had questioned the State Department on 31 May about American foreign policy, Mr Grew has declared that 'it can be stated unequivocally that the United States Government has no tacit understanding or day-to-day working arrangement through which it has become *de facto* or otherwise part of an Anglo-American or any other front against the Soviet Union'. He added that 'conversely there is no truth in the assertions made by some that we are playing into the hands of the Soviet Union to the detriment of the British Empire or any other nation'. This communication also referred to the former foreign policy of President Roosevelt 'whereby the United States participated as an active force in all foreign questions involving American interests or policy'. Mr Grew assured the Congressmen that President Truman is continuing the policy of the late President who 'used his influence and that of the United States as mediator in those questions which, although not directly affecting our interests, might disturb international harmony if allowed to remain unsolved'.

. . . .

Interest of the USSR in European problems. No particular suspicion has greeted Soviet interest in the Straits and Tangier, and singularly little attention has been paid to the transfer of Ruthenia[3] and the dispute over Teschen.[4] There is a general tendency, to some extent encouraged by the highest quarters, to believe that whatever they portend in the long run, Russian claims to be heard on problems of the Western Mediterranean are to be welcomed at the present time if only because they appear to justify an analogous United States interest in Eastern European questions. . . . The liberal Chicago publisher Marshall Field recently told a British official that he had been horrified to discover that his normally Anglophile East Coast friends were bitterly complaining that Britain intended to manoeuvre the United States of America into war with the Soviet Union and that they would die rather than permit this to happen. Although somewhat gullible, Marshall Field probably accurately voices the views of others like himself.

. . . .

3 The easternmost portion of Czechoslovakia, transferred to the USSR by agreement between the two governments. It gave the Soviets a common frontier with Hungary.

4 A district traditionally in dispute between Poland and Czechoslovakia, occupied by Czech troops on 6 July.

15 July 1945

. . .

Ratification of the Charter. The Senate Foreign Relations Committee has completed hearings in the big Caucus Room and on 13 July recommended the Charter to the Senate for ratification by a vote of 20 to 3. Three members of the Committee have still to cast their vote. I am informed by Senator Connally that the debate on the floor will begin on 23 July and is expected not to last for more than a week or ten days. I understand he is working hard for unanimity.

Contrary to common expectation a few months ago, there has been no drama or excitement. Despite big attendance by an inquisitive public, it is felt that the issue has already been decided and that the Senate is merely going through the motions. 'The drama here is that there is no drama,' one commentator remarked. The hearings themselves have proceeded much more quickly than had been expected. They were opened by ex-Secretary Stettinius who, after explaining the main provisions of the Charter, justified the veto provisions on the ground that the Big Five must agree and act together if peace is to be maintained and that, if any one of the five were to embark upon a course of aggression, a major war would result, Charter or no Charter. He concluded by expressing his belief that 'no country has a greater stake than ours' in the Charter. The major burden of dealing with detailed committee questioning fell upon Pasvolsky, who gave assurances that the United States could withdraw whenever it wished provided its reasons for doing so did not constitute a threat to world peace, and that the security of the United States would in no way be impaired by the trusteeship provisions covering islands captured from the Japanese in the Pacific. Excepting in isolated instances, there has so far been no criticism from liberal quarters that the Charter places more stress on national sovereignty than upon internationalism, a point which has been made occasionally in press reports of the hearings.

In so far as it exists, serious opposition until now – comic relief was afforded by the appearance of various 'crackpots', one-man organizations and table-pounding female fanatics – has centred round steady questioning by Senator Millikin, whose main argument is that Congress must first sanction any use of United States armed forces by the Security Council. This received a forthright answer from Senator Vandenberg, who claimed that any attempt by Congress to retain complete control over the use of the nation's armed forces would violate not only the spirit of the Charter but also the Constitution of the United States. He asserted that in the last resort the Executive had used the armed forces of the country to restore or maintain order in various parts of the world no less than seventy-two times. This answer did not however appear to satisfy Millikin, and Senator Bushfield has indicated his intention of putting forward a reservation covering this question, even though he will vote for the Charter. Senator Hatch has suggested that Congress should define the powers of the United States delegate as equal to those conferred by the Constitution on the President, but Walter Lippmann and others have flatly declared that such is already the case with no room or need for argument. Millikin has been roundly condemned by the press for suggesting reservations, and, should any reservation be put forward, there seems little doubt that the Administration will easily dispose of it. . . .

Some observers are pointing out that the pattern of bipartisan co-operation between the Congress and Executive, which has resulted in this virtual unanimity, is no less significant for the future formulation of a continuing and constructive American foreign policy than for the early ratification of the Charter itself. The happy contrast between the situation today and in 1919–20 is being widely remarked upon, and is further heightened by the President's absence from Washington at this time. Even the Patterson–McCormick press grudgingly admits that any Senator who votes against the Charter will be a 'political fathead', adding contemptuously that the Charter anyhow 'is no more or less important than a resolution in which the Senate of the United States solemnly proclaims that it takes a vigorous and militant stand against sin, the man-eating shark, in-growing toenails and the heat of a Washington July'.

. . .

Big Three meeting and Germany. The question of food this winter for Germany and the liberated countries has been receiving more attention. It is pointed out that, whilst the liberated countries must have first consideration, the food situation in Germany itself must not be allowed to degenerate to the point where riots and chaos will result. Warning voices have again been raised in Congress that the United States cannot and should not try to feed and clothe the world; this was echoed by Clinton Anderson, the Secretary of Agriculture, although he added that the United States must do whatever it could to help. . . .

The foregoing and other critical issues that confront the Big Three are cited as the first great test for President Truman whose popularity continues unabated. Some satisfaction is derived from a feeling that, although Truman will be the junior member at the meeting, this drawback will largely be offset by the fact that united behind him stands the most powerful country in the world. The President's decision not to see either Marshal Stalin or Mr Churchill before the meeting has been noted in some quarters as further evidence that the true role of the United States must be one of impartial arbiter, and that Truman intends 'to shape a three-cornered policy'. In commenting on the visit of Davies to England before the Big Three meeting, Swing has stated that he 'will not be suspected by the Russians of tying American policy too closely to the British'.

. . .

Far East. With both the Okinawa and Philippine campaigns now successfully concluded, with reports of Chinese advances in South China and descriptions in the press supported by dramatic pictures of devastating huge-scale air raids on Japanese cities, there has come a feeling that Japan is rapidly being softened up for a knockout blow which will admittedly be costly enough when it comes. The belief that Japan herself is anxious to capitulate on terms less than unconditional surrender has been further nourished by stories of unrest and dissatisfaction inside Japan; reports over the Tokyo radio that the dean of Japanese journalists had openly criticized his government for 'dismissing the loss of strategic islands with superficial optimism'; the plea for cessation of hostilities on reasonable terms seen behind numerous threats of even heavier American losses than on Iwo Jima and Okinawa; the Japanese Government's declaration of a state of emergency for the railroads and warnings of imminent invasion.

Rumours concerning peace feelers were once again emphatically denied by Under-Secretary Grew who stated that no 'approach had been made to the United 'States Government, directly or indirectly'. He reiterated that the policy of the United States Government 'has been, is and will continue to be unconditional surrender'. . . .

. . .

British elections. Interest in the result of the British elections quickly subsided. Though there is evidence of some anxiety as to the outcome, the general assumption is that the Conservatives will get in with, however, a considerably reduced majority and that the Liberal Party may have made something of a comeback. Americans privately express amazement at British ability to wait three weeks for the results, a strain which they admit would be unthinkable in this country. As one commentator put it, the British must not only have 'hearts of oak but nerves of stainless steel'.

22 July 1945

Potsdam conference. The news blackout has left commentators foundering with speculative stories as to what is being discussed. Whilst the British press seems to be protesting violently, some American journalists at any rate have unexpectedly tempered their evident indignation with a tendency to rationalize and explain the necessity for a strict censorship. . . .

Interest in the actual proceedings is heightened here because the conference is universally felt to be a crucial test for the new President. He has the sympathetic backing of almost all sections of the country – far more than President Roosevelt could have commanded were he now in Potsdam. There is widespread hope that coming from Missouri (the 'show me', hard to convince, State) Truman will prove himself to be a negotiator at least the equal of his two more experienced partners.

Poland. An unusual assortment of right- and left-wing Russophobes have joined in a memorial to the White House deploring the appeasement of Soviet Russia in Poland and urging the release of the twelve Polish underground leaders, free elections and free speech, the withdrawal of Russian troops from Poland or joint occupation and the right of American journalists, Red Cross, etc., to enter Poland. The signatories included Herbert Hoover, Alf Landon, Father Gannon,[1] the prominent Catholic; William Green of the AF of L, Elliot Bell,[2] Dewey's adviser; Raymond Leslie Buell of the Foreign Policy Association; Justice Pecora; Benjamin Stolberg[3] and Isaac Don Levine,[4] renegade leftist authors. Buell apologized to a British official for a passing criticism of our Greek policy which the memorial contains and declared that it had to be inserted to satisfy the conscientious liberals. Meantime Vandenberg, doubtless with his large Polish constituency and his re-election fight next year in mind, had addressed a letter to Grew, in which he describes the Polish settlement as 'inadequate and unconvincing'. In a published reply to questions in the letter Grew promised that the State Department would use its full influence to gain access for American correspondents to Poland and to ensure – possibly by Allied supervision – that the forthcoming elections are free in fact as well as in name.

San Francisco Charter. . . . The Foreign Relations Committee's report on the hearings came out strongly against any attempt to compel the United States delegate to refer to Congress before committing the United States quota forces to action, declaring that this would clearly violate the spirit of the Charter. Provided the right of Congress to declare war is recognized, it seems reasonably certain that the Administration will be able to carry their thesis that the United States delegate is the representative of the President and therefore entitled to use the latter's well-established right to commit United States forces without special approval from Congress in every instance.

. . .

Bretton Woods. Meantime the Senate this week debated and passed the Bretton Woods proposals by 61 to 16. This victory on what has always been recognized as a more controversial issue than the World Security Charter ('political co-operation is all right but business is business' expresses much conservative sentiment) is being welcomed in enlightened quarters, and is believed to be especially timely in strengthening the President's hand at Potsdam. Taft led the opposition's rearguard action with considerable guile and received unexpected support in some of his manoeuvres from Senator Ball of Minnesota, normally a reliable internationalist Republican. The closest vote in the debate was produced by Ball's last-minute amendment proposing that member nations should abolish discriminatory currency practices within three years or be banned from the use of the fund (it was defeated 46 to 29). It was encouraging to see Vandenberg part company with Taft and other reactionaries on various points although he did support the Ball amendment. The House of Representatives duly confirmed ap-

---

1 Robert I. Gannon, President of Fordham University.

2 Elliot V. Bell, publishing executive and financial writer, Superintendent of Banks, New York, 1943–9.

3 Benjamin Stolberg, Marxist critic of New Deal, journalist and author, columnist for *New York Post* 1932–3, historian of ILGWU.

4 Isaac Don Levine, journalist and author, born in Russia, anti-Communist.

proval of the plan as passed by the Senate and it now only needs the President's signature.

28 July 1945

Far East. The twelve-point ultimatum to Japan[1] has had a very favourable first reception from the Senate and the press, although some liberals complain that it has 'weaseled on what they regard as the crucial question of the fate of the Emperor'. The ultimatum has clarified if it has not brought to an end the prolonged and confused controversy which has been going on over surrender terms for Japan. Both press and radio have been showing concern about the trend of American thinking on the subject and there was much discussion of a broadcast to Japan last week by a Captain Zacharias[2] of the United States Navy. The broadcast, already reported, seemed to suggest that the Atlantic Charter might apply to the Japanese if they surrendered without delay and warned them to surrender before the Russians entered the war. As this broadcast came from a Navy spokesman, it was interpreted in some quarters as evidence of the Navy's desire to finish off the war before Soviet Russia could stake out a claim to a share in the victory. Yet at the same time Senator Wiley had issued a statement summoning the Russians to declare war on Japan. Generally speaking it is believed that the Pacific war is rushing towards an early climax. The part played by British naval forces in the continuing bombardment of Japan receives fair notice in the press and Mountbatten's presence at Potsdam has also served to underline our growing interest and participation in the Pacific war.

British General Election. The news of Mr Churchill's sweeping defeat[3] was received with a shock of astonishment that was almost reminiscent of the reactions to the Pearl Harbor bombing. Newspapers headlined it as 'one of the most portentous events of our times' and the radio commentators naturally squeezed the maximum pathos and drama out of the news. Americans have unquestionably felt more directly involved in this event than in any other British or foreign election for many years.

The first reactions of the man in the street seemed to be that the vote revealed a strange ingratitude on the part of the British electorate. This first impression is wearing off, however, and the press have been very helpful in making clear that the election did not reflect on Mr Churchill's record as a war leader. Many newspapers have also reassured the public, as Mr Attlee himself pointed out immediately after the results were known, that Britain's new Government will continue the fight against Japan to the end. . . .

1 So-called Potsdam Declaration of 26 July, issued by Truman, Churchill and Chiang Kai-shek.

2 Captain Ellis M.Zacharias, OWI broadcaster to Japan, had spoken of unconditional surrender with its attendant benefits, as laid down by the Atlantic Charter.

3 Division of seats in the new House of Commons : Labour 393, Liberals 12, Conservatives and supporters 213.

As regards Foreign Affairs it is taken for granted that there will be no sensational departures in our policy but there is also a general expectation that there may be changes in our attitude towards Greece and Italy, towards the Franco régime, Palestine, the Colonies and India. Press opinion, shared by junior members of the State Department, is that the changes should actually make joint Anglo-American policies in some of these issues easier to achieve. It is also generally agreed that the result will put new vitality into the various left-wing parties on the Continent. The Zionists were quick to announce their pleasure at the turn of events and expressed confidence in the new Government.

Three probable consequences of the result are worth noting:

(1) There will be the liveliest interest in every move in British foreign policy in the coming weeks and this in itself will have the salutary effect of arresting the recent trend to ignore our role and concentrate on the purposes of the Big Two, i.e. United States and USSR.

(2) The result will cause some realigning of our supporters in the United States. Liberals and left-wingers, who were sympathetic to us during the darkest days of the war but became our most constant critics since the Greek Revolution of last December, will once again tend to rally to our side. Already we have had telephone messages from our left-wing friends welcoming us back into the progressive fold. Whatever steps we may feel compelled to take to safeguard our interests in Europe and in the Empire it seems certain that – at least for the next six months – liberals will be much less inclined to voice criticism of a Labour Government than they would of a Conservative régime following approximately the same course.

(3) Everyone here is well aware that the result has implications for the United States as well. Rugged individualists at the moment feel very much alone on a choppy collectivist sea. Labour politicians on the other hand are patently encouraged and the pressures on the Truman Administration from 'left of centre' seem likely to increase.

. . .

4 August 1945

Speculation arising from the unexpected Labour victory at home dwarfed everything else in public interest for most of this week, even the Senate's ratification of United States participation in the world security organization. The Potsdam communiqué has of course now captured the headlines and, despite disappointment at the silence on Russia's role in the Pacific, first reactions are favourable. The Senate has recessed until October amidst protests from the press, after admitting to itself and the country that many urgent domestic matters have been left unsettled. There is much anxiety both inside the Administration and elsewhere about the dislocations that may ensue if the Japanese war were to end this year.

. . .

Mr Churchill's very large American following, amongst whom are to be found many of the staunchest interventionists drawn from middle-class America, are still shocked by their hero's defeat. Although the press explains that Mr Churchill's war leadership was not in question, the sense of loss remains and we are frequently asked to explain the strange ingratitude which seems to have overtaken the English people. The extent to which Mr Churchill had gripped the American imagination is reflected in the nationwide cartoons and editorial tributes to what one paper called 'This great gladiator who bestrode the continents like a Colossus'.

The press, which did so little beforehand to enlighten its readers on the issues and trends of the election, has undertaken the most elaborate *post-mortem* examinations and explanations of the result. These include the leftward march of world events, the British people's war weariness and the desire for change, resentment against the 'autocratic' rule of Mr Churchill and his closest associates and (flattering unction) the democratizing impact of the American GI on the British social system. Generally speaking these analyses, even in conservative newspapers, have concluded in not unfriendly tones that no radical break with the past is involved in this 'middle-class revolution' and that the British tradition of orderly progress and moderation will prevail. Mr Attlee's personality, 'as British as Oxford, warm beer or cold toast,' remarked one commentator, is frequently referred to in support of this view ; he is already widely spoken of as the British Truman. Both *Time* and *Newsweek* magazines salute him this week with full-page portraits on their covers. Sir Stafford Cripps's broadcast to the United States on 30 July[1] has also been quoted as evidence of the firm democratic foundations of the British way of life.

. . .

Potsdam. The preliminary reactions to the communiqué are on the whole distinctly favourable. Initial radio and editorial comments hail it as a steady advance beyond Tehran and Yalta and praise the forthright language. The Council of Foreign Ministers[2] is taken as a special cause for hope and as providing the political machinery necessary for the transition period. The general terms of the settlement for Germany, while they have still to receive detailed analysis, are received with approval as hard but not intolerable. David Lawrence is so far the only commentator to say that the reparations provisions put impossible conditions upon Germany.

. . .

Charter ratification. The Senate ratified American participation in the World Security Organization on 28 July by the overwhelming majority of 89 to 2 (Shipstead and Langer). Stalin was pictured next day by a cartoonist as asking Truman 'How do you account for all this opposition ?', and Langer has in fact boasted

1 In which he emphasized that nationalization would rest on 'fair compensation' and that Labour's programme was 'limited'.
2 Created to prepare drafts of peace treaties with ex-enemy states.

he is really thousand per cent for the Organization. What might have seemed likely at one time to be an occasion for historic rejoicing, in view of America's guilty memories of 1919, has actually been received with calm approval and with many salutary reminders from the press that only continuing wholehearted American support can turn the paper Charter into an effective reality.

. . .

11 August 1945

It has been a tumultuous week of earth-shattering events. The press had hardly settled down to examine the long-awaited Potsdam communiqué when the atomic bomb burst upon them and buried every other issue deep on the back pages. The smoke of Hiroshima had scarcely subsided when the Soviet declaration of war on Japan supervened. This was followed in rapid succession by a second atomic bomb, the President's radio address, the Japanese surrender offer and the imminent end of World War II.

The psychological impact of these events upon the public, especially of the atomic bomb, was greater than anything America had experienced in the war, even Pearl Harbor, and profound changes in the currents of thought seem inevitable. The march of events has been so swift that the country on the eve of victory is more breathless than jubilant. The immediate effect has been to quicken the fears in responsible circles that with vj day upon her America will be shown to be dangerously unprepared for the economic and social problems of reconversion to peace.

The bomb. The stories of the atomic bomb appealed to everything most typical in the American nature. The lurid fantasies of the comic strips seemed suddenly to have come true. Headlines sagged under the weight of the drama and the superlatives they had to carry. One front page said simply 'seven pages on the greatest story of the age : Atomic Bomb opens new era : it will end all war – or all men : it will revolutionize human life'. The same newspaper announced on an inside page with more questionable taste that the Washington Press Club had produced a new Atomic Cocktail, price 60 cents, with 'only one to a customer'. The press generally has overflowed with diagrams, interviews with scientists, stories of the test in New Mexico, estimates of what an atomic bomb would do to Brooklyn, etc. The mood of the moment was caught by a cartoonist who pictured Truman presiding over an angelic cabinet with each member sprouting wings, a bowl of split atoms in the centre of the table and the caption 'the Cabinet meets to discuss sending an Ambassador to Mars.'.

However, along with a thrill of power and the instinctive pleasure at the thought of Japan cringing in abject surrender, America's deep-rooted humanitarianism has begun to assert itself and this secondary revulsion has been very marked in private conversation although it has not yet appeared in the press. Both the War Department and Office of War Information became genuinely concerned with the deluge of anxious telephone calls, arising especially from a widely published story by a scientist named Jacobson [1] that the devastated area would be polluted for seventy years by the bomb's radioactivity and also by the Japanese estimates of 150,000 casualties. Although Jacobson's story was subsequently refuted and he himself collapsed when threatened with ten years' imprisonment, there is a good deal of heart-searching about the morality of using such a weapon, especially against an enemy already known to be on his last legs. Virtually all comment agrees that the bomb has demonstrated our modern dilemma – a generation that has grown up intellectually must mature morally or perish. The Scripps-Howard papers turned to 'Locksley Hall' to give vent to their feelings, and the *Washington Post* resorted to W.H.Auden – 'We must love one another or die'. Meantime churchmen generally endorsed the President's appeal for divine guidance on how to use and control this revolutionary discovery. John Foster Dulles and one or two other religious leaders have urged the temporary suspension of its use on moral grounds.

Everyone read into the bomb story a vindication of his own favourite theory. Senator Johnson of Colorado said that it proved the stupidity of universal military training. Mrs Roosevelt said it proved the importance of such visits of goodwill as the Soviet trade unionists are now making in this country. The head of the National Association of Manufacturers saw it as a reason for accelerating industrial reconversion plans, and the press, patting themselves as always heartily on the back, took pride in having kept a secret. As oil shares dropped, oil and coal industry representatives came forward with vigorous reassurances that the new discovery would have little effect on existing fuels in the foreseeable future.

Politically it is clear that the bomb is doing more than Pearl Harbor or the war to obliterate the last vestiges of the isolationist dream, and in this sense it is a new weapon in the hands of the internationalists. At the same time nationalists are insisting that if America can only keep the secret she will be powerfully placed to make other nations, not least the Soviet Union, behave. The Patterson papers waved a warning finger towards the North and said that since Canada is a major source of uranium she 'ought to make herself America's out and out and exclusive ally' or patriotic Americans should bring her to her senses.

Generally speaking, the fact that the bomb is a British-American-Canadian invention has been recognized. Mr Churchill's statement and the comments of British scientists have been well publicized. In consequence the whole of Anglo-American teamwork has received a fillip. One American scientist was quoted as saying : 'There is no need to talk of an Anglo-American federation – it is here.' The President's radio assurances that Britain and America mean to hold on to their secret have been greeted with satisfaction as a powerful bargaining counter in the play of power politics and the organization of world peace. The Russo-phobes would like to gloat over this advantage which science has given the de-

1 L.O.Jacobson, one of a group of twenty-two scientists at Chicago University who called for a public statement on the destructive potential of the bomb and its likely effect on international relations.

mocracies but are restrained by the gnawing suspicion that Soviet scientists may be well on the way to the production of their own atomic bombs. A campaign is already under way, led by the left wing, to ensure that in the United States the patent rights and means of production are publicly controlled through Congress and are not placed in the hands of large oil or ammunitions combines.

Pacific war. Coming after the impact of the atomic bomb, the Soviet declaration of war, however welcome, was something of an anticlimax. All the appropriate tributes are being made to the cause of inter-Allied solidarity, but even State Department officials have privately expressed their belief that 'this time Moscow was caught off schedule'. Attention is now being forced on the question of what Russia's claims in the Pacific spoils will be. There is no disposition to deny that she is now a great Pacific power and will doubtless seek to recover her 1895 position in Manchuria and Korea. This, it is recognized, will precipitate many problems, but it is in the fate of China proper that the United States is most concerned. Again, in the overriding interests of Soviet-American harmony, it is being fervently hoped that Soong's talks in Moscow will produce a solution to outstanding Sino-Russian problems. Left-wing radio commentators meantime re-opened the campaign against Ambassador Hurley and his predispostion for the Kuomintang.

The official Japanese surrender offer has been greeted with delight and, from the inevitable ticker tape storms in New York City, it is clear that emotionally at any rate the war is already over in the public's estimation. At the moment however opinion is in wide disarray regarding the fate of the Emperor and an unofficial press canvass has revealed the Senate too is sharply divided on this issue. The public is too flushed with victory to consider the matter in the light of the actual administrative problem of Japan and there is much belligerent talk of treating Hirohito as just like any other war criminal. On the other hand it seems very doubtful whether the public – or indeed the fighting forces – would tolerate any considerable prolongation of the war over this issue.

Potsdam. Much of the analysis of the Potsdam communiqué has clearly been short-circuited by the other sensational events of the week but will doubtless mature later. The majority reaction is still soberly favourable if unenthusiastic and every comment serves to underline the growing preoccupation with Soviet-American relations. . . .

The terms for Germany are widely accepted as hard but not intolerable. But while they are viewed as morally justifiable there is an undercurrent of questioning . . . as to whether they will be economically practicable.

. . .

The Polish settlement which is said to contain the most diplomatic double-talk tends to be reluctantly accepted as the best obtainable given the overriding necessity of Soviet–American harmony. It is generally conceded however that the new Poland will be inevitably under Soviet domination. The workability of the proposed German-Polish boundary with the large migrations involved is viewed with some scepticism, although Professor Lange, now sometimes referred to as an unofficial Ambassador of the Warsaw Government in the United States, has vigorously defended it as clearing the traditional breeding ground of the Prussian Junker class. Senator Vandenberg, doubtless with his Polish constituents in mind, has protested against the indefiniteness of the communiqué's guarantee of a free press and free elections in Poland.

The proposal for the Council of Foreign Ministers is viewed as one of the most solid achievements of the conference.

.   .   .

12 August 1945

.   .   .

Hiram Johnson. The week saw the death at the age of seventy-eight of the last of the great immovable isolationists in the Senate, Hiram Johnson, Democrat of California. He was one of the main instruments of the Senate's rejection of the League of Nations in 1920. He opposed in turn United States membership in the World Court, reciprocal trade, Cash-and-Carry, Lend-Lease and even the bill passed four days after Pearl Harbor authorizing the President to send United States troops overseas. Consistent to the end, he voted against the San Francisco Charter in committee and, being too ill to appear, paired his vote against ratification in the final vote. The news of the atomic bomb, which coincided with the day of Johnson's death, seemed like a cosmic reminder that the era of America's former isolationism had closed. With his demise Senator Capper of Kansas, who at the age of eighty has recently been showing the first cracks in his own long record of isolationism, becomes Ranking Minority Member of the important Foreign Relations Committee. The *New York Times* is boosting Herbert Hoover as Johnson's successor, but so far Governor Warren has made no appointment.

.   .   .

18 August 1945

The week has seen the breathless waiting for Japan's surrender, followed by the nationwide celebration of the end of the war which totally eclipsed the rejoicing on VE day. All headlines have proclaimed the sweeping removal of wartime controls and, on the surface at any rate, a delighted America has seemed to be returning full tilt to a 'do as you please' mentality. True, those who stopped to think were sobered by problems of reconversion and future unemployment, by the shadow of the Soviet Union slanting halfway across the world, and by the portent of the atomic bomb which seemed at once to render the United States of America more powerful and more vulnerable. But for the moment most people were drinking the heady wine of victory, of a peculiarly American-made victory.

End of the war. Nervous tension mounted to a high pitch as a result of the Japanese delay in accepting Allied terms and the spate of false rumours, especially the peace flash on the United Press on Sunday evening. When I saw the President at midday on Tuesday morning he was a very worried man, pinned down in his office at the White House by a mob of news-hungry journalists parked on a twenty-four-hour vigil in the anteroom. He had just received a report that the messages from Japan did not contain the expected reply and he sorrowfully remarked that another atomic bomb now seemed the only way to hasten the end. However, later in the afternoon, the Japanese acceptance arrived, the historic announcement was made at 7 p.m. EWT,[1] and the whole country gave itself over to delirious rejoicing. Mr Attlee's broadcast, coming whilst people were still glued to their radios, made a very favourable impression as his first Prime Ministerial utterance.

In contrast to Armistice Day, 1918, it was delightful summer weather, and the crowds that had waited all day outside the White House were soon reinforced by tens of thousands more until the centre of the city became a seething mass of humanity. The crowds were rowdy, happy, occasionally destructive and universally disposed to let the problems of tomorrow look after themselves. Sunday 19 August has been designated a day of thanksgiving, and many people agreed with the President's dry comment that, after its orgy of celebration, 'the nation could do with some prayer'.

The more sober expressions of victory have been characterized by one central theme – America is now the most powerful nation in the world. Every newspaper has echoed this thought, but Admiral Leahy gave it official sanction in a broadcast in which he said :

Today we have the biggest and most powerful navy in the world, more powerful than any other two navies in existence. We have the best equipped and most completely mechanized ground force in the world. The Army and Navy together have the world's largest and most efficient Air Force. We possess, with our British Allies, the secret of the world's most fearsome weapon.

It is also true that Leahy paid tribute to those Allies 'who held the ramparts through long months of solitary trial and sacrifice', and that the President himself, in his reply to the greetings of the Diplomatic Corps, underlined in generous terms that 'we owe our victory as much to our Allies as to ourselves'. Yet in spite of these laudable efforts to preserve perspective, pride in America's unequalled might is the dominant mood of the moment and Mr Churchill's remarks on this subject in his Commons speech have been widely taken up.[2]

To the nationalists the consciousness of America's superior power becomes an excuse for a new brand of aggressive 'America-Firstism', with the United

---

1 EWT – Eastern War Time.

2 'The United States stand at this moment at the summit of the world. I rejoice that this should be so. Let them act up to the level of their power and their responsibility, not for themselves but for others, for all men in all lands, and then a brighter day may dawn upon human history.' (16 August)

States seizing whatever bases, etc., it may need to wave the big stick. To the internationalists and to the President and his advisers it implies the responsibility of United States leadership in the various instruments for world collaboration. The first group ignore us altogether, or regard us as a hindrance to America's interests. The second accept us as a valuable junior partner in an Anglo-American concern. This emerged quite clearly in the negotiations attendant on the Japanese surrender. The Administration seemed genuinely disposed to keep us informed of developments, whilst allowing us little enough opportunity to shape policy. This is doubtless less than we would like, but we may perhaps take comfort from the thought that more consideration was shown to us than to the Russians or Chinese.

Japanese surrender. The days of negotiation with a prostrate and despised enemy strained public patience. Although the responsible press united in support of the reply to the Japanese surrender offer, and Byrnes came in for many compliments, the general public were and still are much less tolerant of discredited deities. Some cried scornfully 'They can keep their Son of Heaven': others dismissed the treatment of the Emperor as yet another strange expedient which the State Department somehow appeared to find necessary. The man in the street seemed keener to hear about Admiral Halsey riding on Hirohito's white horse, as he had boasted he would, than to listen to explanations about the problems of administering Japan. This public impatience has certainly not been allayed by the unrepentant tone of Tokyo's pronouncements since the surrender and by the apparent Japanese stalling tactics. MacArthur's curt order of the 17th to send emissaries to Manila without further delay has been warmly welcomed.

Soviet Union and the Far East. It becomes daily more evident that the United States of America sees Soviet Russia as its only rival for world supremacy and at the same time has no desire to become unnecessarily embroiled with her. Thus whilst it has been taken for granted that MacArthur is the appropriate commander to receive the Japanese surrender, Ed Murrow's[3] broadcast from London, stating that Molotov had tried to convince Harriman that the surrender should be to a Russian, has been allowed to pass, although it provoked some indignant surprise at Washington. A small hint of rivalry to come was seen however in an incident on vj day, now made public by the *New York Herald Tribune.* The Mexican Ambassador, as doyen of the corps, had requested his United Nations colleagues to accompany him to the White House to express congratulations to the President. The Russian Chargé d'Affaires however demanded to know what he proposed to say and expressed dissatisfaction at his having omitted to make explicit mention of the Soviet Union's contribution to the victory over Japan. As a result all other United Nations Missions excepting the Soviet paid their respects to the President.

The speed of the Russian advance in Manchuria and Sakhalin – so reminiscent

3 Edward R. Murrow (1908–65), cbs correspondent, noted for his wartime broadcasts from London.

of Hitler's 1940 blitzes, said the *New York Times* – has been noted with mixed admiration and misgiving, but it is generally conceded that the USSR is entitled to regain Russia's 1904 position[3] in the Far East – although it is probably not realized what exactly this involved – and it is hoped that this will be possible without disturbing Soviet relations with China. For this reason the news of the new Sino-Russian agreement has been greeted with relief by the press and the announcement of the terms is eagerly awaited. At the same time there is an undercurrent of uneasiness at Chiang Kai-shek's latest difficulties with the Chinese Communists which newspapers have fully reported. There is certainly no enthusiasm for the Communists, apart from left-wing writers, who have been publicizing them as they did Tito a year ago. But enthusiasm for Chiang Kai-shek has also dwindled. America's main hope at present is that someone or something will rid her of this troublesome issue which seems to present in the Far East the same elements as the Polish problem; just as the situation in Siam may perhaps develop on a minor scale the same intractable Anglo-American difficulties as have occurred in Italy.

. . .

Meantime in clear response to the public mood, war agencies have been competing with one another in slashing of controls, and an impression is given that the gigantic and complex American war machine is being dismantled overnight. The War Department boasts that it has cancelled twenty-five billion dollars worth of contracts, and the Navy six billion. The Army has promised to release up to seven million men within eighteen months and the Navy up to two million. The cautious Mr Stimson reflected the prevailing mentality when he said that the War Department would 'try desperately' to free five million men in a year. At the same time the draft rate has been drastically reduced, and all civilian manpower controls abolished. Byron Price claimed the end of censorship and Elmer Davis indicated that he would soon preside at the burial of his war-weary Office of War Information. But to the general public the lifting of petrol rationing, together with the prospect of the progressive removal of rationing on most foods, seemed the most pleasant signal that the day of America's reluctant submission to irksome and badly-functioning controls was at an end. . . .

. . .

20 August 1945

Reconversion to peace. The prospect of widespread unemployment is not yet causing undue concern. But official and unofficial spokesmen are coming out daily with estimates of five to twelve million 'temporary' unemployed by next spring, and thoughtful people are wondering how the public will react to such predictions when the victory spell wears off. Meantime Big Business is coming forward with its own antidote to the gloom spread by government officials and

---

3 i.e. before Russia's defeat in Russo–Japanese War.

labour leaders (e.g. Hillman predicted ten million unemployed) by assuring the public that, if given a chance to operate freely, it can absorb most displaced industrial workers. The President of the National Association of Manufacturers has predicted fewer than 1½ million unemployed.

The Administration's own master plan for reconversion, completed under great pressure and issued as a 6,000 word report 'From War to Peace : A Challenge' by John Snyder, the reconversion director, has had a fair enough reception, although liberals condemn it as wholly inadequate. Snyder's overall rules for the transitional period, during which he admits the possibility of unemployment rising to eight million, are : (a) speedy cancellation of war contracts and release of materials and plants for civilian production; (b) rapid demobilization from the forces; (c) removal of many controls to speed reconversion and the retention of others for the same reason; (d) holding the price and rent lines to prevent inflation; and (e) 'holding wages in line wherever their increase would cause inflationary prices'.

Krug, Chairman of the War Production Board, . . . has decided to follow his own known view that the best plan is to get out of industry's way. He has therefore announced the cancellation of 600 of the 650 WPB controls. Simultaneously, the President himself has announced the imminent end of the War Labor Board, the overrule agency for investigating industrial disputes and wage demands, and has pointed towards a new wage policy which will permit wage increases as long as they do not affect price ceilings.

Thus, in spite of generalized talk by Snyder, Krug and others of the need to provide for orderly readjustment, it appears that we are entering a period in which the Government does not believe that extensive controls are either practicable or advisable.

.   .   .

Acheson's appointment. That the day of surprise last-minute appointments did not pass with the late President became apparent when, two days after he had announced his retirement from the State Department, Dean Acheson was reappointed and promoted to the post of Under-Secretary of State. Grew's desire to go had long been known and was undoubtedly hastened by the fact that he had been repeatedly bypassed by the President and Byrnes during the hectic Japanese surrender negotiations. It is said that he may yet accept the post of political adviser to MacArthur, but since he and Acheson have been leaders of the opposing State Department factions on soft or hard peace for Japan, the latter's promotion would not seem to foreshadow the kind of policies which Grew would look on with favour.

Acheson's appointment is a victory for the new Byrnes-Cohen-Truman team over that of the Stettinius-Grew-Dunn and the old school generally; for although a member of the Department since 1941, Acheson has never been especially intimate with its ruling caste. He owes his appointment at least in part to the good opinion he has won as State Department liaison officer with Congress, where he has impressed many of the President's old friends. Acheson's general outlook is that of a liberal conservative, and he has stood consistently against reactionary or narrowly nationalistic tendencies, especially on economic affairs. He is, in addition, warmly disposed towards us. Yet his talent – like that of Byrnes – is that of the smooth, sometimes excessively smooth, negotiator rather than of the administrator or overall planner. Since he and Byrnes are so similar in this respect, the question remains as to whence will come the much discussed need for a clarification of America's policy objectives.

Other State Department changes. The expected resignations of Archibald MacLeish and General Julius Holmes, two of Stettinius's Assistant Secretaries of State, have also been announced. No successors have yet been named.

25 August 1945

Japanese procrastinations. Although some commentators have explained the technical difficulties involved in making the Jap surrender effective, the general public has grown increasingly impatient with every sign of Jap procrastination. The impenitent tone of the Emperor's rescripts has undoubtedly hardened sentiment, and some of the current scepticism is reflected in a Washington witticism 'Do you think Japan's surrender will shorten the war?' Confidence in MacArthur is unabated, and he is being freely advised to 'rub the Japs' noses in the dirt'. Liberals are voicing loud misgivings about the outcome of this latest experiment in expediency and relate it to the earlier suspect manoeuvres with Darlan and Badoglio.

Far East and American-Soviet relations. The emergence of the United States as the strongest power in the world and 'the appearance of the Bear on the shores of the Pacific', as the *New York Times* put it, are felt to be the two most salient facts about the Far East. The interests of European imperial powers are regarded as decidedly secondary, especially as it is seen that some of these powers – France, Holland, Portugal – do not possess the strength to defend their overseas possessions.

The primacy of America's interests in the Pacific – 'an American lake' – has been underlined in all the newspaper and newsreel reviews of the end of the war. Admiral King spoke for the great bulk of opinion when he declared that, however altruistic she might become, America 'must always retain control of the sea and all areas vital to her defences'. At the same time a congressional sub-committee, after a 21,000-mile tour and extensive conferences with naval and military authorities, has issued an official report on America's strategic needs in the Pacific. This report, details of which have been telegraphed separately, roundly declares : 'We will have restored peace to the Pacific almost single-handedly, and if we are to be charged with the responsibility of maintaining that peace, we must be given the authority and the means by which to maintain the peace – one of the principal means being authority over strategic islands in the Pacific.' Liberals seem more or less to have abandoned their fight against United States imperialist tendencies, and the *Cleveland Plain Dealer* is a lone voice when it enquires how America can hold Russia to the Cairo Declaration or demand Britain to relinquish Hong Kong if she herself retains the Pacific Islands by unilateral action.

At the same time the emergence of the Soviet Union as a major Pacific power and its occupation of Manchuria and certain of the Kuriles Islands, are being watched with the closest interest. So far there is little talk of a Soviet domination of Asia, to parallel the gloomy prognostications of a Communist-dominated Europe. There is even a feeling that the terms of the Sino-Russian agreement show that the USSR has demanded rather less than might have been expected. There have, of course, been protests from the small American-Korean lobby, but there so far seems little disposition on the part of the public or the Administration to force any showdown in the Pacific on the basis of the present Soviet demands. Indeed, it has been put about that at Potsdam President Truman took a very firm line and succeeded in persuading Stalin to acknowledge the supremacy of America's interests in the Pacific.

The hope therefore prevails that it may not prove too difficult to heal the internal dissensions in China which are generally recognized to be the most likely cause of serious Soviet-American friction. In spite of reports from China of active clashes between the Communist and Chungking forces, this hope has been strengthened by the general belief that the Soviet Union does not, after all, propose to adopt Yenan as a Far Eastern Lublin. There is considerable support for the idea that the Great Powers, especially the United States and USSR, should use their good offices to hasten a compromise settlement between Chungking and Yenan, on a Chungking base. The *New York Times*, however, violently opposed such suggestions as unjustifiable interference and as bestowing on the Chinese Communists an undesirable prestige.

Hong Kong. The future of Hong Kong has sprung dramatically into the headlines and there has been much loose talk of the Chinese and ourselves racing to get there first. Whilst opinion is divided, the firm statements by the Prime Minister and yourself have undoubtedly given friendly papers a lead, and several of them have taken the trouble to explain and defend the legality of our position (*Washington Post, San Francisco Chronicle, Springfield Republican*). At the same time the President has refused to be drawn on the subject and has referred questioners to the State Department who have been indicating that the United States Government in no wise questions our sovereignty and feels that the future of Hong Kong is a matter for the Chinese and ourselves to settle. It looks as though the present Administration feels less strongly about changing the status of Hong Kong and other imperial possessions than President Roosevelt is alleged to have done. America's acquisitive mood towards the Pacific has in any case undercut much of the earlier criticism.

It would seem mistaken however to count on uniform sympathy for an unqualified and permanent return to the *status quo*. As a result of the American-Chinese honeymoon period and of President Roosevelt's reported pleas to Mr Churchill on behalf of Chiang Kai-shek, Hong Kong has become a symbol to Americans of an outdated era in the Pacific. . . . Generally speaking, opinion appears to favour not so much the relinquishment of our sovereignty, as a fresh consideration of Hong Kong's future, either on British initiative with the Chinese directly, or through the agency of the Council of Foreign Ministers as Byrnes seemed to suggest in his press conference this week, or through the United Nations security organization as various liberals are urging.

Europe. Byrnes has delivered himself this week of two separate strongly worded statements of disapproval of the Communist-dominated régimes in Bulgaria and Roumania. This forthrightness towards European problems is in marked contrast to the much more timid onlooker which characterized the State Department last winter and spring. In Roumania the United States Government is now even standing forth as the defender of a monarchy. To some extent these and other recent votes seem to have come about in response to the persistent public demand for a stronger and more independent American foreign policy. That this new forthrightness has its limits was indicated in Byrnes's explanation, after *Izvestia* had condemned supervision of elections as interference in domestic affairs, that America did not really believe in supervising elections but merely in freedom to observe and report. This remark suggested that the new line was also influenced by persistent demands in the press that the Administration should fight for the removal of censorship in Eastern Europe.

The more positive trend undoubtedly reflects the Administration's own conviction that with the war over and United States power at its zenith and secure in the possession of the atomic bomb, it is time for America to assert herself. Her role as they see it is not only to collaborate in international affairs but to assume a leadership which befits her pre-eminent position.

Your own warning in the Commons [1] of the dangers of a new totalitarianism in the Balkans, like Mr Churchill's earlier speech, has been very welcome to the State Department and conservative and middle-of-the road opinion supports a policy of frank dealing with the Russians. . . .

British policy. American fears about the implications of a Labour victory have certainly receded over the past week. . . . Your own speech of 20 August as already reported (in my telegram 5773) impressed the American public with the continuity and stability of British foreign policy. Many newspapers noting its

1 In the Debate on the Address, 20 August.

vigour declared that it was clear that you no more than Mr Churchill would preside over the liquidation of the Empire. Whilst conservative and middle-of-the-road opinion thus commended the speech, there is no denying that it disappointed liberals and the left-wing commentators. Some of them admit that in the flush of victory over 'Tory Imperialism' they had no doubt expected – and predicted – too much. Their complaint now is that they have got nothing at all. In their disappointment they draw attention not only to your attitude towards Russian activities in the Balkans, our warnings against intervention in Spain and your remarks on Hong Kong, but to the omission of references to India and Palestine in regard to which they had vaguely hoped for a liberalization of British policy.

End of Lend-Lease. However logical in view of the Act's original stated purpose, the abrupt end of Lend-Lease came as a surprise even in this country. The decision appears to have been made by the President himself, largely on advice from Leo Crowley, Head of the Foreign Economic Administration, and against the advice of other strong elements in the FEA and the Treasury. It seems that the President's well-known tendency to make speedy decisions, which is at once his strength and weakness, led him to take this position largely with the thought of forestalling the criticism which would indeed have inevitably come from Congress if Lend-Lease had been continued beyond VJ day. It is more doubtful whether he had at that stage given due consideration to the wider implications of the action as it affected other countries.

The speed with which the decision was made and announced has to some extent backfired, for newspapers have directed public attention to the abruptness of the decision even more than to the actual ending of the Lend-Lease programme. Our difficulties have in consequence come in for a fair share of notice and in some quarters it has even been suggested that the administration might be 'jerking the rug' from under our new Labour Government by presenting it with unsurmountable economic difficulties. While my own information does not confirm this in any way the suggestion has had the effect of winning to our side the liberals (e.g. Harsch, Swing, *PM*, etc.) who at the same time have been condemning our foreign policy. Whatever the outcome, this development . . . has at any rate resulted in bringing home our economic difficulties to the American public with more poignancy than ever before.

. . .

France. De Gaulle made a good start to his visit here with a shower of tributes to the United States delivered in tolerable English. At the White House dinner in his honour he referred to America and France as *'les deux piliers de la civilization'*. The press gave him a good reception and talk of bygones being bygones. Although the President indicated to me before de Gaulle's arrival that he proposed to indulge in some straight Missouri talking I gather from talks with

609

M. Bidault[2] and State Department officials, which I am reporting separately, that the conversations have proceeded in a generally friendly atmosphere. At the same time the President soon after seeing de Gaulle astonished his own aides at his press conference by lecturing twelve visiting French journalists on the need to present the United States in a fairer light in the French press. De Gaulle did not let this pass at his own press conference next day and admonished the American press in reciprocal terms. He seems to have carried the American journalists with him by his willingness to answer all the questions thrown at him, restating vigorously his views on the international control of the Ruhr, the permanent occupation of the Rhineland, France's economic difficulties and her unconditional sovereignty over Indo-China. A Foreign Office spokesman has been quoted in despatches from London as expressing doubts about France's capacity to take control of Indo-China. The State Department for their part are letting it be known that they fully approve of the continuance of French sovereignty there.

27 August 1945

Administration changes. Harold Ickes, whose status in the Cabinet was once as insecure as Morgenthau's, has played his cards much more adroitly, and with the help of some of his political friends (e.g. Senators Hatch and O'Mahoney) has been assured by the President this week that he can stay as long as he likes. The President also announced that Ickes will, after all, go to London to try to negotiate a new oil pact.

It is again being rumoured that Stimson will retire as Secretary of War on vj day. According to the press Judge Sherman Minton of Indiana, a former Senator and an influential Democratic Party official, will get the post, but I hear privately that Louis Johnson,[1] the Assistant Secretary of War in Roosevelt's Cabinet from 1937 to 1940, is a strong candidate.

. . .

Zionists. The President indicated this week that he had proposed to us at Potsdam that a policy should be worked out permitting as many Jews as possible to enter Palestine, but that no decisions had been reached. This revelation has, of course, put new fight into the assorted Zionist battalions, who seem to see more hope in Truman's more simple and direct approach to their problem than in his predecessor's delicate manoeuvrings. Senators Taft and Wagner, who have been associated before on such ventures, have canvassed their congressional colleagues about the possibility of producing an American equivalent of the Balfour Declaration. While Zionist pressure habitually creates its own counteraction, it has to be remembered that the argument of military expediency by which General Mar-

2 Georges Bidault, leader of French Catholic Left, became head of National Council of the Resistance in 1943, and was de Gaulle's Foreign Minister 1944–8.

1 Louis A. Johnson, West Virginia lawyer and politician, sent to New Delhi (March–December 1942) as Roosevelt's personal representative during Cripps Mission.

shall last year forestalled congressional action will no longer avail ; nor can we count on Roosevelt's capacity for finessing when the pressure is hottest.

. . .

Pearl Harbor. The press has been demanding the full facts on Pearl Harbor now that the war is over, and the President has indicated that he has requested the Secretaries of War and Navy to prepare a full report on which he will decide whether immediate trials should be held.

Drew Pearson's standing. An interesting sidelight on the influence and prestige of the columnist Drew Pearson is to be seen in the fact that the following national figures have been prepared to take over his column for one day each during Pearson's vacation – Fred Vinson, Henry Kaiser, Leon Henderson, Herbert Brownell and Philip Murray.

Sir Ronald Lindsay's [2] death. The press has paid more than usual attention to the news of Sir Ronald Lindsay's death, and there have been many moving tributes to his work as Ambassador here in the inter-war years.

1 September 1945

. . .

Sino-Russian treaty. All shades of public opinion have hailed the Sino-Russian treaty [1] with immense relief. The possibility of America becoming involved in a Far Eastern dispute on China's side against the Soviet Union has hung like a cloud over all those who hold that peace primarily depends on the cultivation of harmonious relations between the two great world powers, the United States and the USSR. Now unexpectedly the air in the Far East had cleared and the prospects of peace seem to have correspondingly enhanced. Even such a rabid Russophobe as Clare Luce has publicly confessed that her earlier trepidation was unjustified and has declared 'that the treaty exceeded even her most enthusiastic hopes'. In the mood of rejoicing congratulations are being handed out on all sides. T. V. Soong [2] is credited with a major diplomatic triumph : the Soviet Union is congratulated, even by Mrs Luce, on its exemplary moderation ; and the treaty is felt to be at once a vindication of and a victory for American policy in the Far East. The *Daily Worker* and its fellow travellers are red with confusion, but they try to make the best of things by insisting that, since Moscow is not going to recognize the Yenan Communists, Washington must stop buttressing the Kuomintang reactionaries. The more level-headed commentators point

2 Sir Ronald Charles Lindsay, in foreign services since 1899, British Ambassador at Washington 1930–9.

1 Sino-Soviet Treaty of Friendship and Alliance, signed 14 August ; in related notes the Russians recognized Chinese sovereignty in Manchuria and promised to give aid and support only to the Nationalist Government of China, i.e. repudiating the Communists. The Chinese agreed to recognize the independence of Outer Mongolia if a plebiscite endorsed it. The Manchurian railway was to be operated jointly and Dairen to be under joint control.

2 T. V. Soong, Prime Minister of China since July 1930.

out that it now depends upon Chiang Kai-shek to show moderation to the Communists and remind their readers that the treaty must be judged by the way it is carried out in practice.

· · ·

Lend-Lease. The abrupt termination of Lend-Lease[3] and the plain speaking by the Prime Minister and Mr Churchill have given rise to much lively discussion about our economic position. Sensational accounts of the statements in the Commons produced the inevitable reflex action, and many commentators immediately rallied to Truman's defence. It was repeatedly said, even by our friends in the Administration, that the British Government ought to have known and that the President's action was only logical. Senator Wagner, for example, said that he 'just couldn't understand the British attitude', and the anti-British Congressman Celler called on us to 'play cricket' and to open up the sterling area markets to American exports in return for economic aid. Outright chauvinists were openly jubilant at what they took to be evidence that the President had no intention of continuing to squander American resources overseas, especially for the purpose of salvaging a poverty-stricken and ungrateful British Empire. They seem likely to be much less pleased with the President's letter of 30 August accompanying the latest Lend-Lease report which states more frankly than President Roosevelt ever did that America should regard Lend-Lease as having been repaid in victory and declares that the wisest course might now be to write off most of the dollar balances involved.

· · ·

Oscar Cox, Deputy Director of the Foreign Economic Administration and one of our strongest Allies there, has been allowed to resign with scarcely a farewell from his chief, Leo Crowley. It seems clear that whether because of his Irish-Catholic background or for some other reason Crowley is going to prove something of a stumbling-block in our path. There are rumours however that he may not remain for long, and his economic views and those of Dean Acheson, the new Under-Secretary of State, are hardly consistent. Meantime Clayton has got back from London[4] and has been playing possum with all enquirers. America's economic policies hinge on these three men as much as anyone under the President.

The latest indications are that our friends in the Administration have been pulling themselves together. . . . It is expected that some new agreements will be reached during the Keynes mission,[5] although there is a great vagueness as to

---

3 On 21 August the President directed the Foreign Economic Administration to take steps immediately to discontinue Lend-Lease operations. In the House of Commons Mr Churchill described the manner of its discontinuance as 'rough and harsh' and Mr Attlee said that it put the United Kingdom 'into a very serious financial position'.

4 Where, at the British invitation, he had gone after Potsdam to discuss the British shortage of dollars and supplies.

5 Despatched to negotiate the settlement of the British Lend-Lease account and the line of credit designed to assist Britain in the transition from a war to a peace economy. It resulted in the Anglo-American Financial and Trade Agreement, ratified in Britain in December 1945 and in the USA in July 1946.

what form they should or will take. People tend to talk feebly in terms of loans or credits, and no one so far seems to have hit on any new concept or inspired phrase to succeed Lend-Lease which would bring out that more than commercial considerations are involved in aid to Britain at this time.

. . .

De Gaulle's visit. De Gaulle has now completed what must have been a most exhausting whirlwind series of visits to Washington, New York and Chicago. Throughout his stay he was never deflected from an obvious and almost painful desire to please. He not only kissed babies, as every zealous politician must, but Mayor La Guardia, Newbold Morris [6] and the American Chiefs-of-Staff as well. As a goodwill venture, the visit has been a success. It has certainly established de Gaulle firmly in the American consciousness as the undisputed leader of France and it has helped to bring before the public France's economic plight and her decided views on post-war affairs. It seems more doubtful whether it has offset the loss of prestige from which France has been suffering as a result of the depressing revelations of the Pétain trial and the tales of continuing cynicism and defeatism spread by returning soldiers.

. . .

Reconversion. The country continues to revert to peacetime conditions in a somewhat recklessly carefree mood. Unemployment has not yet reached serious proportions and there is a great deal of money about. Public interest is centred on how soon new cars, radio sets and refrigerators will be available, and the promise of 'nylons by Christmas' has raised feminine morale. The reappearance of traffic jams reminds people of headaches to come. As Mayor La Guardia put it : 'We are in for a spree – and then the damnedest hangover we've ever had.'

. . .

Pearl Harbor report. A sensation has been provided by the publication of the Army-Navy reports on Pearl Harbor, with their sharp criticisms not only of Kimmel and Short, the Field Commanders, but also of General Marshall, Cordell Hull and Admiral Stark. Although the Administration had apparently decided that it would eventually have to publish the reports, we are told in confidence that the whole 130,000-word document had to be rushed out at a few hours' notice because the *Chicago Tribune* had obtained copies and were about to publish it. None the less with the country still mellowed by victory this is perhaps as opportune a moment as any for the Administration to release the facts. The report contained no recommendations for court-martial or further punitive action and the Administration would clearly like to see the matter closed.

. . .

End of OWI. The President issued an order on 21 August abolishing the Office of War Information and directing Byrnes to take over the responsibility of disseminating American news overseas. The foreign information functions of the

6 Newbold Morris, Republican, President of the New York City Council since 1938.

Office of Inter-American Affairs were simultaneously placed under the State Department. This move had been freely predicted but came with unexpected suddenness. The State Department – itself in the throes of reorganization, and still lacking an Assistant Secretary in charge of information to succeed MacLeish – is not a little flustered by the hundreds of owi employees who have landed on its doorstep.

Dulles. Byrnes's announcement this week that John Foster Dulles would accompany him as adviser to the Council of Foreign Ministers in September is a hopeful augury for the continuance of a bipartisan United States foreign policy, for Dulles remains the confidant of both Vandenberg and Dewey. Dunn, as predicted, will be Byrnes's deputy on the Council, and Ben Cohen is also to accompany him.

. . .

Draft proposals. President Truman this week advocated the continuance of the military draft for men from eighteen to twenty-five, arguing that unsettled world conditions and 'equality of sacrifice' made this necessary. The proposal is being widely supported in the press, but there will undoubtedly be much batting to and fro in Congress before it is approved.

. . .

8 September 1945

. . .

Victory mood. vj day speeches on 1 September followed by the Labor Day orations on the 3rd, gave an interesting index of the victory mood in the country. It was a mood of nationalistic, even imperialistic, pride in what the President called 'the strongest nation on earth'. Yet it had an idealistic side too, for nothing was more noticeable than the note of rededication and the urge towards what Mac-Arthur called 'a spiritual recrudescence' that would save the world from the horrors contained in the atomic bomb. It was indeed precisely on account of the idealistic urge to 'make the world over' that this revived spirit of manifest destiny had such vitality.

This was not just a Big Business mentality. It was the mood of the Middle West and of the average American of whom President Truman is the embodiment. It is because the present Administration represents neither Big Business on the one hand, nor, unlike its predecessor, the Eastern New Deal intellectuals on the other, that this middle-of-the-road American mentality is so popular. . . .

Whilst optimism is now general, American business in particular has recovered from its midsummer gloom following the British election results. Victory had brought a fresh burst of pride in the production miracles of American capitalism : industry had been given the green light in the Government's reconversion programme : British socialism, far from being a threat, now seems destined to labour through heavy seas. Hence while Ickes and various labour leaders on Labor Day still maintained that the British election constituted the writing on the wall for reactionary American capitalism, business spokesmen like the *Saturday Evening Post* had recovered their balance and were proclaiming that there was no reason for America to go left because Britain had done so. Indeed it was argued in this quarter that the British people voted as they did in order to try to secure for themselves some of the fruits which American capitalism was about to provide in abundance for American citizens.

Labour leaders and liberals were naturally not so enthusiastic about this version of the American Century. They may however again take heart from the tone of the President's message to Congress, which prompted Republicans to ask whether the New Deal was dead after all. But there is no mistaking the exuberant, power-conscious mood of the moment.

Attitude towards Japan. There is mounting uneasiness about developments in Japan. The situation there is thought to resemble that of 1918 Germany or the brief Doenitz[1] régime, and there is a feeling that in the enthusiasm to spare American lives, the Pacific war was allowed to end before clear policies had been elaborated for the treatment of the Japanese ruling caste, the handling of war criminals, the extent of occupation, and so forth. The exclusion by Japanese guards of American newspapermen and officials from the opening of the Diet has offended national pride and the impenitent tone of Japanese official pronouncements raises serious questions about how Byrnes's proposed 'spiritual disarmament' of the Japanese people can be effected.

The Administration is not however unduly criticized at the moment, apparently because it is felt that MacArthur has so far shown firmness and initiative and may soon get the situation under proper control. It is also taken as a promising sign that the two leaders of the soft-peace school (Grew and his adviser, Dooman) have retired from the State Department, leaving Dean Acheson, a hard-peace advocate, in control. . . . Liberals also hope that a tougher policy is presaged by the State Department's release of the full story of Japanese brutalities towards war prisoners.

Far East. The optimistic glow shed by the Sino-Russian pact continues. *Life* magazine excitedly declares that Stalin and Soong 'have done as much to assure peace as all our flying Fortresses'. Chiang Kai-shek's speech[2] with its pledge of constitutional democracy has been taken as a hopeful sign ; and it is frequently said that it now devolves on him to reach a settlement with the Chinese Communists in a spirit of compromise and thus remove the main threat to international harmony in the Far East. The Russians have come out of the Sino-Russian

1 Admiral Doenitz, Commander-in-Chief of German Navy, took over direction of German state on Hitler's disappearance in May 1945 and encouraged acceptance of Allied surrender demands.

2 In VJ message Chiang on 4 September pledged himself to democracy, ruled out political armies and said military forces must be nationalized to recover national unity.

pact extremely well. . . . In the prevailing mood, the Soviet occupation of the Kuriles Islands and the inadvertent revelation by Byrnes that this question had been settled as far back as Yalta have been allowed to pass without much attention.

. . .

Lend-Lease. The President's suggestion on the cancellation of most of the dollar balances in Lend-Lease had a very favourable reception from the press (including even the *Wall Street Journal*), who agreed either that this was desirable, or at least that it was inevitable. However, the Republican opposition in the person of Senator Taft, seconded in milder terms by Vandenberg, instantly protested that in making such an announcement the President had thrown away America's principal bargaining weapon for securing her objectives in post-war negotiations. These congressional storm signals were at least partly responsible for Byrnes's statement of 1 September explaining that, notwithstanding the President's statement on dollar balances, there were still Lend-Lease settlements to be made. To some extent this statement played into the hands of nationalist-conservative opinion, for the very newspapers which had approved the President's statement now bethought themselves and decided that, after all, Lend-Lease was far from a closed book. The result was a new emphasis on bargaining in the discussions of economic aid to Britain. If, it was argued, Britain were to get further help on special terms there should surely be some *quid pro quo*. Britain should relax the Imperial Preference system or the sterling bloc restrictions (both of which have been said to contravene Article VII), and should certainly accept Bretton Woods without further delay. It was occasionally suggested in other quarters that Lend-Lease should not be closed until America had secured adequate post-war rights with respect to American-built landing fields and naval bases.

There is no doubt that the Truman Administration did the popular thing in unequivocally terminating Lend-Lease. Although regrets have been widely expressed over the abrupt handling of the affair, there has also been, especially in the Middle West, fiery indignation at what is viewed as our ingratitude in criticizing this move. The idea that America is used as a Santa Claus by an ungrateful and largely undeserving world still flourishes luxuriantly here and the present Administration, which puts such a premium on the harmony with Congress and on carrying public opinion with it, is very sensitive to this accusation. Hence the appearance of inspired stories suggesting that the Administration will play a tough bargaining role in the forthcoming negotiations and demand concessions on commercial policy in return for economic assistance. Friends close to the Administration try to reassure us that such stories are put about with an eye to public opinion and that the United States Government will, in fact, talk much tougher than it will act. There was some evidence for this in the tone of the background press conference which Clayton gave this week. Speaking off the record, he gave a very fair picture of our difficulties, underlined America's desire to help, and suggested that some middle way must be found between giving

Britain outright grants (which the American public would not support) and driving through a hard banker's loan (which Britain could not accept).

    .   .   .

Pearl Harbor. The Administration has given way, with obvious regrets, to the popular clamour for a full investigation of Pearl Harbor. Here and there it is occasionally remarked that the British are perhaps wiser in letting bygones be bygones over such disasters as Singapore and Tobruk. But there is too much political capital involved in the Pearl Harbor affair to make that possible in the United States. Barkley, the Administration leader in the Senate, forestalled the Republicans by introducing a resolution of his own to set up a ten-man Senate House Committee to conduct an investigation and report by 3 January 1946. In the subsequent debate, the scope of the enquiry had to be widened in response to Republican demands until Barkley agreed that 'it could go back to the time Japan invaded Manchuria'. Thus the affair has now gone far beyond Pearl Harbor and, for good or ill, we may witness a grand debate on United States foreign policy over the past twelve years, with dead cats flying in all directions. The fact that the Republicans intend to press for a twelve-man committee allowing equal Republican-Democratic representation, instead of for Barkley's proposal for six Democrats and four Republicans, reveals the political dynamite involved and the unsettling effect which this investigation may have on the recent progress towards a bipartisan foreign policy.

617

Biographical Notes

ACHESON, Dean Goodenham (1893–1971) : Lawyer with Washington firm of Covington, Burling. Secretary to Louis Brandeis, 1919–21 ; Under-Secretary of the Treasury, May–November 1933, resigning in disagreement over gold-buying policy ; Assistant Secretary of State, 1941–5 ; Under-Secretary of State, 1945–7 ; Secretary of State, 1949–53.

AGAR, Herbert Sebastian (1897–1980) : London correspondent for the *Louisville Courier-Journal* and the *Louisville Times,* 1929–34 ; literary editor of *The English Review* (London), 1930–4 ; editor of the *Courier-Journal,* 1940–2. Special Assistant to the US Ambassador to Great Britain, and director, British Division, Office of War Information, London, 1943–6. Prominent figure in the Southern Agrarian literary movement.

AGAR, William MacDonough (1894–1972) : Geologist and author. Brother of Herbert Agar. Chairman of the Board of Freedom House. With the Department of Public Information, UN, 1946–56.

AIKEN, George David (1892–1980) : Farmer and author of *Pioneering with Wildflowers* (1933) and other books. Republican Governor of Vermont, 1937–41 ; US Senator, 1941–75. Intractable isolationist before Pearl Harbor, but on domestic issues very liberal.

AITKEN, William Maxwell, 1st Baron Beaverbrook (1879–1964) : Canadian-born owner of Express Newspapers ; a close friend of Churchill's. Minister of Aircraft Production, 1940–1 ; Minister of State, 1941 ; Minister of Supply, 1941–2 ; Minister of Production, 1942–3 ; Lord Privy Seal, 1943–5.

ALDRICH, Winthrop William (1885–1974) : Son of Nelson Wilmarth Aldrich (1841–1915), 'boss of the Senate' at turn of the century. President of Chase National Bank, 1930–4, and Chairman, 1934–53. US Ambassador to Great Britain, 1953–7.

ALFANGE, Dean (b. 1897) : Lawyer and author. A radical liberal, he was the American Labor Party's nominee for Governor of New York in 1942.

ALLEN, Jay Cooke, Jr (b. 1900) : Liberal journalist. Foreign correspondent for the *Chicago Tribune* press service, 1925–34, 1937–8 ; foreign correspondent in North Africa, 1941–2 ; in government service in North Africa, 1942–3.

ALPHAND, Hervé Jean Charles (b. 1907) : Diplomat. Director, Comité des affaires economiques, London, 1941. French Ambassador to the USA, 1956–65 ; Secretary-General, Ministry of Foreign Affairs, 1965.

ANDERSON, Clinton Presba (1895–1975) : Involved in journalism, insurance and dairy farming. New Deal relief administrator in New Mexico, 1935–8. Democratic Congressman from New Mexico, 1940–5 ; Secretary of Agriculture, 1945–8 ; Senator, 1949–73 ; Chairman of Joint Committee (of Congress) on Atomic Energy.

BIOGRAPHICAL NOTES

ANDREWS, Charles Oscar (1877–1946) : Assistant Attorney General of Florida, 1912–19 ; circuit court judge, 1919–25 ; Justice of the Florida Supreme Court, 1929–32. Democratic Senator from Florida, 1937–46. A wholly unnotable Senator.

ANTONINI, Luigi (1883–1968) : General Secretary of New York Local 89 of the International Ladies' Garment Workers' Union since 1919. Chairman of the American Labor Party, 1936–42. President of the Italian-American Labor Council since 1941.

APPLEBY, Paul Henson (1891–1963) : Editor and publisher of the *Des Moines* (Iowa) *Register*. Executive assistant in the Department of Agriculture under Henry Wallace, 1933–40 ; Under-Secretary of Agriculture, 1940–4 ; Assistant Director of the Bureau of the Budget, 1944–7. Subsequently Dean of Maxwell School, Syracuse University.

ARMOUR, Norman (1887–1978) : Career diplomat. US Minister to Haiti, 1932–5 ; Minister to Canada, 1935–8 ; Ambassador to Chile, 1938–9 ; Ambassador to Argentina, 1939–44 ; Ambassador to Spain, 1944–5 ; Assistant Secretary of State, 1947–8 ; Ambassador to Venezuela, 1950.

ARMSTRONG, Hamilton Fish (1893–1973) : Editor of *Foreign Affairs*, 1928–72 ; Director, Council on Foreign Relations. Author of books on foreign relations, with a special interest in the Balkans. Unofficial White House adviser on foreign affairs, 1944–5.

ARNALL, Ellis Gibbs (b. 1907) : Lawyer. Attorney General of Georgia, 1939–43 ; Democratic Governor of Georgia, 1943–7. President of Columbus National Life Insurance Co., 1946–60 ; President of the Society of Independent Motion Picture Producers, 1948–60.

ARNOLD, General Henry H. (1886–1950) : Staff officer in First World War. Chief of the Army Air Corps, 1938–42 ; named Commanding General of the Army Air Force, 1942.

ARNOLD, Thurman Wesley (1891–1969) : Crusading demythologizer of capitalism. Mayor of Laramie, Wyoming. Professor, Yale Law School, 1931–8. Joined New Deal in 1933 as special counsel for the Agricultural Adjustment Administration, in charge of Anti-Trust Division ; Assistant Attorney General of the US, 1938–43 ; Associate Justice, US Court of Appeals, District of Columbia, 1943–5. Subsequently partner in the Washington law firm of Arnold, Fortas and Porter from 1945. 'A cross between Voltaire and the cowboy, with the cowboy predominating' – Robert Jackson.

ASTOR, Nancy Langhorne, Viscountess (1879–1964) : American-born wife of Viscount Astor, proprietor of *The Times*. First woman Member of the House of Commons, 1919–45. A conservative iconoclast. The Astor home, Cliveden, gave its name to the appeasement-minded politicians of the 1930s.

ATTLEE, Major Clement Richard, 1st Earl (1883–1967) : Leader of the Labour Party in Opposition, 1935–40, 1951–5 ; Lord Privy Seal, 1940–2 ; Secretary of State for Dominion Affairs, 1942–3 ; Lord President of the Council, 1943–5 ; Deputy Prime Minister, 1942–5 ; Prime Minister, 1945–51.

AUSTIN, Warren Robinson (1877–1962) : Lawyer. Republican Senator from Vermont, 1931–46. Very liberal on foreign policy, pretty conservative on domestic policy, with a special interest in China and Cuba. US representative to the UN, 1946–53.

AVERY, Sewell Lee (1873–1960) : President and Chairman of Montgomery Ward Co. of Chicago ; President of US Gypsum Co., 1905–37, and Chairman, 1937–51.

BIOGRAPHICAL NOTES

BADOGLIO, Pietro (1871–1956) : Marshall of the Italian Army and Chief of the Italian General Staff ; Prime Minister, 1943–4.

BAILEY, Josiah William (1873–1946) : Editor of the *Biblical Recorder,* 1893–1907 ; subsequently lawyer. US Collector of Internal Revenue for North Carolina, 1913–21. Democratic Senator from North Carolina, 1931–46 ; Chairman of the Senate Commerce Committee, 1938–46.

BALDWIN, Hanson Weightman (b. 1903) : Journalist with the *New York Times* since 1929 ; military and naval correspondent, 1937–42 ; military editor since 1942. Pulitzer Prize, 1942.

BALDWIN, Raymond Earl (b. 1893) : Republican Governor of Connecticut, 1939–41, 1943–6 : Senator, 1946–9. Associate Justice, Connecticut Supreme Court of Errors, 1949–59 ; Chief Justice, 1959–63.

BALDWIN, Roger Nash (b. 1884) : Noted civil libertarian, who began life as a sociology instructor and probation officer. Director, New York branch, American Civil Liberties Union, 1917–50 ; National Chairman, 1950–5. Treasurer of the India League.

BALL, Joseph Hurst (b. 1905) : Journalist on the St Paul, Minnesota, *Pioneer Press and Dispatch.* Republican Senator from Minnesota, 1940–9 ; Stassen protégé, appointed to fill the vacancy on the death of Senator Lundeen ; strong internationalist ; very active member of the Truman Committee ; defeated for re-election in 1948. Supported Roosevelt for re-election in 1944.

BANKHEAD, John Hollis II (1872–1946) : Lawyer, President of the Bankhead Coal Co., 1911–25. Democratic Senator from Alabama, 1931–46. Moderate conservative. Member of the Bankhead clan – son of John H. Bankhead, Senator 1907–20, and brother of William H. Bankhead, Speaker of the House 1936–40. Active supporter of New Deal agricultural policies ; was the link between Washington and the Alabama Farm Bureau Federation.

BARBOUR, William Warren (1888–1943) : Republican Senator from New Jersey, 1931–7, 1938–43. Engaged in thread-manufacturing business and other industrial enterprises.

BARD, Ralph A. (1884–1975) : Stockbroker. Assistant Secretary of the Navy, 1941–4 ; Under-Secretary of the Navy, 1944–5.

BARKLEY, Alben William (1877–1956) : Democratic Congressman from Kentucky, 1913–27 ; Senator, 1927–48, 1954–6 ; Majority Leader of the Senate, 1937–47, elected by Roosevelt's personal intervention ; Vice-President of the USA, 1948–52.

BARNES, Joseph Fels (1907–70) : Correspondent with the *New York Herald Tribune,* 1935–41 ; foreign news editor, 1939–41. Deputy Director (Atlantic Operations), Overseas Operations Branch, Office of War Information, 1941–4. Foreign editor of the *Herald Tribune,* 1944–8.

BARRY, William Bernard (1902–46) : Irish-born lawyer. Special US Attorney for the Department of Justice, 1933–5. Democratic Congressman from Queens County, New York, 1935–46.

BARUCH, Bernard Manners (1870–1965) : Financier and 'adviser to Presidents'. Head of the War Industries Board, 1918 ; adviser to the War Mobilization Board, 1943–5.

BEAVERBROOK, *see* AITKEN

BIOGRAPHICAL NOTES

BENĚS, Edvard (1884–1948) : Foreign Minister of Czechoslovakia, 1918–35 ; President, 1935–8, 1946–8.

BENNETT, Augustus Witschief (b. 1897) : Lawyer. US referee in bankruptcy, 1923–44. Republican Congressman from New York, 1945–7.

BENNETT, John James, Jr (1894–1967) : Assistant to E.R.Stettinius of J.P.Morgan & Co., 1915–25. Professor, Brooklyn Law School, 1928–31. Attorney General of New York, 1931–42 ; Deputy Mayor of New York City, 1947–9 ; Chief Justice, New York Court of Special Sessions, 1950. Chairman, New York City Planning Commission, 1951–5.

BENNETT, Marion Tinsley (b. 1914) : Lawyer. Republican Congressman from Missouri, 1943–9.

BENTON, William (1900–73) : Advertising man, founder of Benton & Bowles ; retired, 1936. Vice-President, University of Chicago, 1937–45 ; Chairman, Encyclopedia Britannica Inc., 1943–73. Assistant Secretary of State for Public and Cultural Relations, 1945–7. Democratic Senator from Connecticut, 1949–53.

BERLE, Adolf Augustus, Jr (1895–1971) : New York lawyer. Practised law, 1916–24 ; lecturer on finance, Harvard Business School, 1925–8 ; Professor of Corporation Law, Columbia Law School, 1927–71 ; co-author of Berle and Means, *The Modern Corporation and Private Property* (1932). Member of original Roosevelt 'Brains Trust'. Assistant Secretary of State, 1938–44 ; Ambassador to Brazil, 1945–6.

BEVIN, Ernest (1881–1951) : General Secretary, British Transport and General Workers' Union, 1921–40. MP (Lab.), 1940–51. Minister of Labour, 1940–5 ; Secretary of State for Foreign Affairs, 1945–51.

BIDDLE, Francis (1886–1968) : Lawyer. Chairman, National Labor Relations Board, 1934–35 ; judge, US Circuit Court of Appeals, 1939–40 ; US Solicitor General, 1940 ; Attorney General of the US, 1941–5 ; US member, International Military Tribunal (Nuremberg trials), 1945–6.

BILBO, Theodore Gilmore (1877–1947) : Governor of Mississippi, 1916–20, 1928–32 (only Governor of Mississippi to serve two terms). Democratic Senator from Mississippi, 1935–47 ; personification of the 'poor white', a master of personal invective and a rabid racist.

BLACK, Hugo LaFayette (1886–1971) : Democratic Senator from Alabama, 1926–37 ; sat in Senate as populist-progressive and, for most part, staunch supporter of the New Deal (despite early membership of the Ku Klux Klan) ; gained considerable attention with a vigorous investigation of the public utilities in Washington. Associate Justice of the Supreme Court, 1937–71.

BLAMEY, General Sir Thomas Albert (1884–1951) : Australian Commander-in-Chief, Allied Land Forces, South-West Pacific, 1942–5.

BLOOM, Sol (1870–1949) : In newspaper, theatrical and music publishing business. Democratic Congressman from New York, 1923–49 ; became Chairman, House Committee on Foreign Affairs, 1938. US delegate to the UNRRA and UN conferences, and signed the UN Charter.

BOETTIGER, Anna Roosevelt (1884–1962) : Roosevelt's eldest child and support of his declining months. Her second husband was John Boettiger (1900–50), whom she married in 1935, newspaper correspondent and then publisher of the *Seattle Post-Intelligencer*, 1936–45 ; editor and publisher, *Arizona Times*, 1947–8.

BIOGRAPHICAL NOTES

BOHLEN, Charles Eustis (1904–74) : Career diplomat. Assistant to the Secretary of State for White House Liaison, 1944–5 ; US Ambassador to the USSR, 1953–7 ; Ambassador to the Philippines, 1957–9 ; Ambassador to France, 1962–8 ; Deputy Under-Secretary of State for Political Affairs, 1968–9.

BORAH, William Edgar (1865–1940) : Progressive Republican Senator from Idaho, 1907–40. Crusader against League of Nations and leading isolationist in the 1930s.

BOWLES, Chester (b. 1901) : Advertising man ; Chairman of Benton & Bowles, 1936–41. Administrator, Office of Price Administration, 1943–6. Democratic Governor of Connecticut, 1949–51. US Ambassador to India and Nepal, 1951–3.

BOWMAN, Isaiah (1878–1950) : President of Johns Hopkins University, 1935–50 ; Vice-President, National Academy of Sciences, 1941–5. Chairman, Territorial Committee, Department of State, 1942–3 ; Special Adviser to the Secretary of State, 1943–5.

BRACKEN, Brendan Rendall, 1st Viscount (1901–58) : A close follower and friend of Churchill. Chairman of the *Financial Times*. MP (Cons.), 1929–52 ; Parliamentary Private Secretary to Churchill, 1940–1 ; Minister of Information, 1941–5 ; First Lord of the Admiralty, 1945.

BRADEN, Spruille (1894–1978) : Began as a miner ; involved in mining construction and other businesses. US Ambassador to Colombia, 1939–42 ; Ambassador to Cuba, 1942–5 ; Ambassador to Argentina, 1945. Assistant Secretary of State for American Republic Affairs, 1945–7. President of the Americas Foundation, 1960–6.

BRADLEY, Frederick Van Ness (1898–1947) : Salesman and business executive. Republican Congressman from Michigan, 1939–47.

BRADLEY, General Omar Nelson (b. 1893) : US Commanding general, 2nd Corps, North Tunisian campaign, 1943 ; Sicilian campaign, 1943 ; 1st US Army, Normandy campaign, 1944 ; 12th Army Group, 1944–5. Administrator, Veterans' Affairs, 1945–7 ; Chief of Staff, 1948–9 ; Chairman, Joint Chiefs of Staff, 1949–53 ; General of the Army, 1950. Chairman, Bulova Watch Company, 1958–73.

BREWSTER, Ralph Owen (1888–1961) : Republican Governor of Maine, 1925–9 ; Congressman from Maine, 1935–41 ; Senator, 1941–53 ; member of the Senate Committee on Foreign Relations and of the Interstate and Foreign Commerce Committee ; Chairman of the Republican Senatorial Campaign Committee for 1950, and subsequently charged with fraud involving campaign funds.

BRICKER, John William (b. 1893) : Republican Governor of Ohio, 1939–45. The favourite of his party's conservative wing, he was the Republican vice-presidential nominee, 1944. Senator from Ohio, 1947–59.

BRIDGES, Alfred Bryant Renton (Harry) (b. 1901) : Australian-born communist dockers' leader ; President of the International Longshoremen's and Warehousemen's Union since 1937.

BRIDGES, Henry Styles (1898–1961) : Republican Governor of New Hampshire, 1934–6 ; Senator, 1937–61 ; Minority Leader of the Senate, 1952–3 ; President *pro tem.* of the Senate, 1953–5.

BROOKS, Charles Wayland ('Curley') (1897–1957) : Illinois lawyer, and Assistant State's Attorney for seven years. Served with distinction in the US Marine Corps in First World War ; protégé of the *Chicago Tribune*. Republican Senator from Illinois, 1941–9.

623

BIOGRAPHICAL NOTES

BROWDER, Earl Russell (1891–1973) : Secretary-General, American Communist Party, 1930–45 ; expelled in 1946 for being a 'revisionist'.

BROWN, Cecil (b. 1907) : Radio reporter and broadcaster, CBS, 1940–58 ; news commentator, Mutual Broadcasting System, 1944–57 ; news commentator, ABC, 1957–8.

BROWN, Constantine (1890–1966) : Journalist with the *Washington Star,* specializing in international affairs, since 1931 ; co-author, with Drew Pearson, of *The American Diplomatic Game* (1935).

BROWN, Prentiss Marsh (1889–1973) : Lawyer. Democratic Congressman from Michigan, 1933–6 ; Senator, 1936–43. Administrator, Office of Price Administration, January-October 1943. Chairman of Detroit Edison Co. since 1944.

BROWNELL, Herbert (b. 1904) : New York lawyer and Republican behind-the-scences man. Member, New York legislature, 1933–7. Thomas Dewey's campaign manager, 1948. Attorney General of the US, 1953–7.

BULLITT, William Christian (1891–1967) : US Ambassador to the USSR, 1933–6 ; Ambassador to France, 1936–41 ; Ambassador at large, November 1941-April 1942 ; Special Assistant to the Secretary of the Navy, June 1942-June 1944.

BULOW, William John (1869–1960) : Lawyer. Democratic Governor of South Dakota, 1927–31 ; Senator, 1931–43.

BURDICK, Usher Lloyd (1879–1960) : Republican Congressman from North Dakota, 1935–45, 1949–57. Candidate of the Non-Partisan League ; pro-labour. Claimed eighth-generation descendance from Rhode Island followers of founder Roger Williams.

BURTON, Harold Hitz (1888–1964) : Mayor of Cleveland, Ohio, 1935–41, who established record of urban reform. Republican Senator from Ohio, 1941–5. Associate Justice of the Supreme Court, 1945–58.

BUSBEY, Fred Ernst (1895–1966) : Republican Congressman from Illinois, 1943–5, 1947–9, 1951–5.

BUSHFIELD, Harlan John (1882–1948) : Lawyer. Governor of South Dakota, 1939–42 ; Republican Senator, 1943–8. Established virtually one hundred per cent anti-liberal voting record.

BUTLER, Sir Harold Beresford (1883–1951) : British civil servant who became Director of the International Labour Office, 1932–8. Appointed first Warden of Nuffield College, Oxford, in 1939, but when war came acted as southern regional commander for civil defence. Head of British Information Service, Washington, with rank of Minister, 1942–6.

BUTLER, Hugh Alfred (1878–1954) : Grain miller. Republican Senator from Nebraska, 1941–54. Fierce isolationist and extreme diehard.

BYRNES, James Francis (1879–1972) : Democratic Congressman from South Carolina, 1911–25 ; Senator, 1931–41. Associate Justice of the Supreme Court, 1941–2. Director of Economic Stabilization, and subsequently Director, Office of War Mobilization, 1942–5 ; became known as the 'assistant President'. Secretary of State, 1945–7. Governor of South Carolina, 1950–5.

BYRD, Harry Flood (1887–1966) : Publisher and apple grower. Member of the Virginia State Senate, 1915–25 ; Democratic Governor of Virginia, 1926–30 ; Senator, 1933–66. Chairman of the

Senate Rules Committee (1944) and later of the Finance Committee. The Byrd machine in Virginia was legendary for its success in manipulating a restricted electorate and in its close ties with business.

CADOGAN, The Hon. Sir Alexander George Montagu (1884–1968) : British diplomat. Minister to China 1933–5, Ambassador 1935–6 ; Deputy Under-Secretary of State for Foreign Affairs, 1936–7, Permanent Under-Secretary, 1938–46 ; Permanent Representative of the United Kingdom to the UN, 1946–50.

CALLENDER, Harold (1892–1959) : New York Times newspaperman. European correspondent, 1926–40 ; South American correspondent, 1941 ; Washington correspondent, 1942–3 ; Paris correspondent, 1944–59.

CAMPBELL, Sir Ronald Ian (b. 1890) : Career diplomat. British Minister at Belgrade, 1939–41 ; Minister to the USA, 1941–5 ; Assistant Under-Secretary of State, Foreign Office, 1945–6 ; Ambassador to Egypt, 1946–50.

CAPEHART, Homer Earl (1897–1979) : Republican Senator from Indiana, 1945–63. Engaged in the radio, phonograph and television manufacturing business, hence known as the 'Jukebox Senator'.

CAPPER, Arthur (1865–1951) : Publisher and owner of the Topeka Daily Capital, 1892–1951, as well as of a large chain of rural papers and magazines ; owner of two Kansas radio stations. Republican Governor of Kansas, 1915–19 ; Senator, 1919–49. Member of the Senate Committee on Foreign Relations.

CARAWAY, Hattie Wyatt (1878–1950) : Democratic Senator from Arkansas, 1931–45 ; appointed on the death of her husband, Senator Thaddeus Horatius Caraway.

CAREY, James Barron (1911–73) : Organized the United Electrical, Radio and Machine Workers of America in 1936 (President 1936–41) and affiliated it to the CIO, of which he served as National Secretary, 1938–73. Appointed a member of the Production Planning Board, Office of Production Management, 1941. General President, United Electrical, Radio and Machine Workers of America, 1950–65.

CASSINI, Count Igor Loiewski (b. 1915) : Society columnist, pen name 'Cholly Knickerbocker'. Columnist, Washington Times-Herald, 1938–43. Psychological Warfare Division, overseas, 1943–4 ; Paris editor, Stars and Stripes. Columnist for International News and King Features Syndicate since 1945.

CELLER, Emanuel (1888–1981) : Brooklyn lawyer. Democratic Congressman from New York, 1923–73 ; Chairman of the House Judiciary Committee. One hundred per cent New Dealer. Author of You Never Leave Brooklyn.

CHANDLER, Albert Benjamin ('Happy') (b. 1898) : Lawyer. Democratic Governor of Kentucky, 1935–9, 1955–9; Senator, 1939–45. Resigned to become Commissioner of Baseball, 1945–51. Commissioner of the Continental Football League since 1965.

CHIANG KAI-SHEK, Chiang Ching-Cheng (1887–1975) : Commander-in-Chief, Chinese Armed Forces. President of Executive Yuan, 1935–8 ; Chairman, National Military Affairs Council, 1939–40 ; Director-General, Kuomintang Party, Republic of China, 1938–75 ; President of Nationalist China, 1938–75.

CHIANG KAI-SHEK, Madam Mayling Soong Chiang (b. 1899) : One of the famous Soong sisters. Strong-willed politician in her own right.

BIOGRAPHICAL NOTES

CHILDS, Marquis William (b. 1903) : Journalist with the *St Louis Post-Dispatch*, 1926–44 ; columnist with the United Features Syndicate, 1944–54 ; special correspondent with the *Post-Dispatch*, 1954–68.

CHURCHILL, Sir Winston Leonard Spencer- (1874–1965) : Prime Minister of the UK, 1940–5, 1951–5.

CICOGNANI, Amleto Giovanni (1883–1973) : Italian priest. Apostolic Delegate to the US, 1933–58 ; created Cardinal, 1958 ; Secretary of State to Pope John XXIII, 1961–3; Secretary of State to Pope Paul VI, 1963–73.

CIECHANOWSKI, Jan (1888–1973) : The Polish Government-in-Exile's (London) Ambassador to the USA, 1940–6.

CITRINE, Sir Walter McLennan, 1st Baron (b. 1887) : Rose through the Electrical Trades Union to be General Secretary of the British Trades Union Congress, 1926–46. President, International Federation of Trades Unions, 1928–45. Chairman, Central Electricity Authority, 1947–57.

CLAPPER, Raymond (1892–1944) : Newspaperman. Political commentator for Scripps-Howard newspapers, 1936–44. Faithful reflector of small-town America.

CLARK, Bennett Champ (1890–1954) : Son of Speaker of the House of Representatives (1911–19). Lawyer. Parliamentarian, House of Representatives, 1913–17. Democratic Senator from Missouri, 1933–45. Associate Justice, US Court of Appeals, District of Columbia, 1945–54. Past National Commander, American Legion ; ex-President, National Guard Associate of the US. Notable isolationist.

CLARK, David Worth (1902–55) : Lawyer. Assistant Attorney General of Idaho, 1933–5. Democratic Congressman from Idaho, 1935–9 ; Senator, 1939–45 ; defeated by the 'Singing Cowboy', Glen Taylor, and entered law partnership with Tom Corcoran (*q.v.*).

CLARK, Thomas Campbell (b. 1899) : Texas lawyer. Member of Department of Justice, 1937–45 ; Assistant Attorney General, 1943–5 ; Attorney General of the US, 1945–9. Associate Justice of the Supreme Court, 1949–67.

CLAY, General Lucius du Bignon (1897–1978) : West Point army officer. In charge of defence airport programme, Civil Aeronautics Administration, 1940–1 ; Assistant Chief of Staff for Materiél Service of Supply, 1942–4 ; Deputy-Director for war programmes, 1944 ; deputy to General Eisenhower, 1945 ; Deputy Military Governor of Germany (US), 1945 ; Commander-in-Chief of US Forces in Europe and Military Governor of US Zone, Germany, 1947–9. Chairman of the Board and Chief Executive Officer of Continental Can Corporation, 1949–62.

CLAYTON, William Lockhart (1880–1966) : Biggest cotton broker in the world. Vice-President, Export-Import Bank, 1940–2; Assistant Secretary of Commerce, 1942–4 ; Assistant Secretary of State, 1944–5 ; Under-Secretary of State for Economic Affairs, 1945–7 ; alternate Governor, World Bank, 1946–9.

COHEN, Benjamin Victor (b. 1894) : New York lawyer. Assistant General Counsel, Public Works Administration, 1933–4 ; Assistant General Counsel, National Power Policy Commission, 1934–41 ; Special Assistant to US Attorney General concerned with public utility holding company litigation, 1941–2 ; assistant to Director, Office of Economic Stabilization, 1942–3 ; General Counsel, Office of War Mobilization, 1943–5 ; counselor of Department of State, 1945–7. Noted as draftsman of much New Deal legislation.

COLE, William Sterling (b. 1904) : Lawyer. Republican Congressman from New York, 1935–57 ; member of the Joint Committee on Atomic Energy of US Congress, 1947–57, Chairman, 1953–4. Director-General, International Atomic Energy Agency, 1957–61.

COMMAGER, Henry Steele (b. 1902) : Leading American historian, biographer and champion of liberalism. Professor at New York University, 1931–8 ; Professor at Columbia, 1938–56 ; Professor at Amherst, 1956–72.

CONANT, James Bryant (1893–1978) : Chemistry Professor at Harvard University, 1916–33 ; President of Harvard, 1933–53. Chairman of the National Defense Research Committee and Deputy-Director, Office of Scientific Research and Development, 1941–6. US High Commissioner to Germany, 1953–5 ; US Ambassador to Germany, 1955–7.

CONNALLY, Thomas Terry (1877–1963) : Democratic Congressman from Texas, 1917–29 ; Senator, 1929–53 ; Chairman of the Senate Foreign Relations Committee, 1943–53. On domestic issues strongly critical of the New Deal ; on foreign policy initially somewhat more neutralist than the Administration, but subsequently a supporter of Hull and State Department.

CONNELLY, Matthew J. (1908–76) : President Truman's appointments secretary, 1945–53, and political operative ; one of Truman's poker companions. Found guilty in 1956 of conspiracy to defraud the Government, and of bribery and perjury. Jailed in 1960, pardoned after six months by President Kennedy.

COOLIDGE, Calvin (1872–1933) : Republican President of the USA, 1923–9.

COOPER, Kent (1880–1965) : General manager in charge of news service and personnel, Associated Press, 1925–48 ; Executive Director, Associated Press, 1943–65 ; Chairman, AP in Britain, 1938–51, and AP in Germany, 1939–51. President of the Press Association, Inc., 1940–51.

CORCORAN, Thomas Gardiner (b. 1900) : Lawyer. Associated with Benjamin Cohen in drafting New Deal legislation. Counsel of the Reconstruction Finance Corporation, 1932, 1934–41 ; Special Assistant to the Attorney General of the US, 1932–5.

COSTELLO, John Martin (b. 1903) : Lawyer. Democratic Congressman from Los Angeles, California, 1935–45. General Counsel and Manager of the Washington office of the Los Angeles Chamber of Commerce, 1945–7.

COUGHLIN, Father Charles Edward (1891–1979) : Detroit Catholic priest. Anti-Roosevelt and, by late 1930s, proto-fascist religious and political rabble-rouser.

COWLES, Gardner (b. 1903) : Executive editor of the Des Moines (Iowa) Register, 1931–9, President, 1943–71. President of Cowles Magazines, Inc. (publishers of Look) and Chairman of the Iowa (later Cowles) Broadcasting Company. Domestic Director, Office of War Information, 1942–3. He and his brother John were two of Willkie's staunchest adjutants.

COWLES, John (b. 1898) : Publisher of the Minneapolis Tribune, 1935–73 ; Chairman of the Des Moines Register and Tribune Company 1945–70. Special Assistant to the Lend-Lease Administrator, E.R. Stettinius Jr, 1943. Strong supporter of Willkie.

BIOGRAPHICAL NOTES

Cox, Edward Eugene (1880–1952) : Lawyer and judge. Democratic Congressman from Georgia, 1925–52 ; prominent member of the House Rules Committee. Intransigent conservative.

Cox, James Middleton (1870–1957) : Owner of newspapers in Ohio (The News League of Ohio) and Florida. Democratic Congressman from Ohio, 1909–13 ; Governor, 1913–15, 1917–21 ; Democratic presidential nominee, 1920.

Cox, Oscar Sydney (1905–66) : New York lawyer. Assistant to General Counsel, US Treasury, 1938–41 ; Counsel, Lend-Lease Administration, 1941–3 ; Counsel, Office of Emergency Management, 1941–3 ; Assistant US Solicitor General, 1942–3 ; Counsel, Lend-Lease Administration, 1943–5.

Coy, Wayne (1903–57) : Indiana State Administrator, Works Progress Administration, 1935–7 ; Administrative Assistant to US High Commissioner to the Philippine Islands, 1937–9 ; Assistant Administrator of the Federal Security Agency, 1939–41 ; Special Assistant to the President, and Liaison Officer, Office for Emergency Management, 1941–3 ; Assistant Director, Bureau of the Budget, 1942–4 ; Chairman of the Federal Communications Commission, 1947–52. President of the Twin State Broadcasting Co., 1957.

Crawford, Frederick Coolidge (1891–1978) : President since 1933 of Thompson Products, Inc. President of the National Association of Manufacturers, 1943.

Cripps, Sir Richard Stafford (1889–1952) : Lawyer. MP (Lab.), 1931–50. Solicitor General, 1930–1 ; British Ambassador to the USSR, 1940–2 ; Lord Privy Seal, 1942 ; Minister of Aircraft Production, 1942–5 ; President of the Board of Trade, 1945–7 ; Chancellor of the Exchequer, 1947–50.

Crossley, Archibald Maddock (b. 1896) : Marketing analyst. President of national research organization, Crossley, Inc., 1926–54.

Crowley, Leo Thomas (1890–1972) : President, Wisconsin General Paper & Supply Company, 1917–72. Chairman, Federal Deposit Insurance Corporation, 1934–45 ; Alien Property Custodian, 1942–3 ; Head of the Office of Economic Warfare, 1943, and the Foreign Economic Administration, 1943–5. Chairman, Chicago, Milwaukee, St Paul and Pacific Railroad, since 1945.

Curley, James Michael (1874–1958) : Democratic Congressman from Massachusetts, 1911–14, 1943–6 ; Mayor of Boston, 1914–18, 1922–6, 1930–4, 1946–50 ; Governor of Massachusetts, 1935–7. During his 1946–50 term as Mayor jailed for six months for mail fraud ; Truman gave him a full pardon, 1950. Inspired Edwin O'Connor's novel *The Last Hurrah* (1956).

Curran, Joseph Edwin (b. 1906) : Organized and became President of the (predominantly East Coast) Maritime Union, 1937–73 ; became President of the Greater New York Industrial Council, 1940 ; became Vice-President of the CIO, 1941. Member of the American Labor Party.

Curran, Thomas Jerome (1898–1958) : Lawyer. Alderman, New York County, 1934–7 ; President, New York County Republican Committee, 1940–58 ; Secretary of State for New York, 1943–58 ; Republican nominee (defeated) for Senator, 1944.

Currie, Lauchlin (b. 1902) : Economist ; President of Lauchlin Currie & Co., Inc. ; Assistant director of research and statistics, Board of Governors, Federal Reserve System, 1934–9 ; Administrative Assistant, White House Office, 1939–45 ; Deputy Administrator, Foreign Economic Administration, 1943–4.

BIOGRAPHICAL NOTES

DANAHER, John Anthony (b. 1899) : Lawyer ; Assistant US Attorney for Connecticut, 1922–34 ; Secretary of State for Connecticut, 1934–5 ; Republican Senator, 1939–45. Subsequently a US judge.

DANIELL, Francis Raymond (1901–69) : Journalist with the *New York Times,* 1929–67 : chief London correspondent, 1939–45 ; chief of the Berlin bureau, 1945–6 ; European correspondent for the *Times* Sunday Department, 1946–9 ; subsequently London correspondent.

DANIELS, Jonathan Worth (b. 1902) : Son of Josephus Daniels, who had been editor of the *Raleigh* (N.C.) *News* and Secretary of the Navy under Wilson. Correspondent for and later editor of the *Raleigh News and Observer,* 1933–42, 1948–70. Administrative Assistant, White House Office, 1943–5 ; Press Secretary to the President, 1945. Author of *Frontier on the Potomac* (1946) and other books.

DARLAN, Admiral Jean Louis Xavier Francois (1881–1942) : French Chief of Naval Staff, 1936–40 ; Minister of Marine, 1940–1 ; Vice-President of the Council and Minister of Foreign Affairs, Marine and Interior, 1941–2 ; Commander-in-Chief of the French Forces, 1941–2. Civil power was in the hands of Darlan in North Africa in late 1942 on the pretext that he represented 'the captive Marshall' Pétain. Assassinated.

DAVENPORT, Russell Wheeler (1899–1954) : Managing editor of *Fortune,* 1937–40 ; Chairman of the board of editors of *Fortune,* 1941 ; chief editorial writer, *Life,* 1942–4. On Willkie's personal staff in 1940.

DAVIES, Joseph Edward (1876–1958) : Lawyer and financier. Chairman, Federal Trade Commission, 1915–16. Vice-Chairman, Democratic National Committee, 1936–7. US Ambassador to the USSR, 1936–8 ; Ambassador to Belgium and Minister to Luxembourg, 1938–9 ; Chairman, President's War Relief Control Board, 1942–6. Married as his second wife the heiress Marjorie Post Hutton in 1935.

DAVIS, Chester Charles (1887–1975) : Native of Iowa, former editor and state commissioner of agriculture in Montana. One of the first farm leaders to support Roosevelt in 1932. Administrator of AAA, 1933–6 ; member of Board of Governors, Federal Reserve System, 1936–41 ; appointed to the National Defense Advisory Commission, May 1940, with special responsibility for farm production ; War Food Administrator, Department of Agriculture, March–June 1943. President of the Federal Reserve Bank of St Louis, 1941–51.

DAVIS, Elmer Holmes (1890–1958) : Rhodes Scholar. Journalist with the *New York Times,* 1904–24 ; freelance journalist, 1924–39. News analyst, CBS, 1939–42 ; Director of Office of War Information, 1942–5 ; news analyst, ABC, 1945–53.

DAVIS, Forrest (d. 1962) : New York journalist, first on the *Herald-Tribune,* then on the *World-Telegram,* 1922–35 ; general correspondent for Scripps-Howard, 1935–7 ; writer for the *Saturday Evening Post.* Adviser to Taft and McNary in presidential campaign, 1940. Author (with E.K.Lindley) of *How the War Came* (1942).

DAVIS, James John (1873–1947) : Born in Wales. Pittsburgh steel worker ; official of the Amalgamated Association of Iron, Steel and Tin Workers. Secretary of Labor, 1921–30 ; Republican Senator from Pennsylvania, 1930–45.

DAVIS, Norman (1878–1944) : Assistant Secretary of the Treasury, 1919–20 ; Under-Secretary of State, 1920–1. Chairman, US delegation to the Disarmament Conference, 1933, and to the London

629

BIOGRAPHICAL NOTES

Naval Conference, 1935. Chairman, American Red Cross, 1938, and thus in the Office of Civilian Defense. Head of the Security Advisory Committee of the State Department.

DAVIS, William Hammatt (1879–1964) : New York patent lawyer. Chairman, National Defense Mediation Board, 1941–2 ; Chairman of the National War Labor Board, January 1942–5 ; Director, Office of Economic Stabilization, March–September 1945.

DAWSON, William Levi (1886–1970) : Black lawyer from Chicago. Democratic Congressman from Illinois, 1943–70. Later Chairman of the House Government Operations Committee.

DAY, Stephen Albion (1882–1950) : Lawyer ; private secretary to Chief Justice of Supreme Court, Melville W. Fuller, 1905–7. Republican Congressman at large from Illinois, 1941–5. Devoted special attention to federal court matters and to corporate organization and reorganization.

DE GAULLE, Charles (1890–1970) : Army officer. French Under-Secretary of National Defence, May–June 1940 ; leader of the Free French Movement and Head of the National Liberation Committee, 1940–3 ; President, Committee of National Liberation, 1943–4 ; President of the French Provisional Government, 1944–6 ; Prime Minister, 1958–9 ; first President of the Fifth Republic, 1959–69.

DELANO, Frederick Adrian (1863–1953) : President of various railways, such as the Wheeling, Wabash & Monon, 1905–14. Chairman of the National Resources Planning Board, 1934–43. Roosevelt's uncle.

DENEEN, Charles Samuel (1863–1940) : Illinois lawyer ; State's Attorney for Cook County, 1896–1904. Mildly progressive Republican Governor of Illinois, 1905–13 ; Senator, 1925–31.

DE VALERA, Eamon (1882–1975) : American-born President of the Irish Republic, 1919–22 ; President of Fianna Fail Party, 1926–59 ; President of the Executive Council, Irish Free State, and Minister for External Affairs, 1932–7 ; Minister for External Affairs, 1937–48 ; Taoiseach (Head of Government), 1937–48, 1951–4, 1957–9.

DEWEY, Charles Schuveldt (1882–?1976) : Engaged in real estate business and a trust company in Chicago. Assistant Secretary of the Treasury, 1924–7. Banker in Chicago, 1931–40. Republican Congressman from Illinois, 1941–5.

DEWEY, Thomas Edmund (1902–71) : Lawyer. Special prosecutor in investigation of organized crime in New York City, 1935–7, and District Attorney, 1937–40. Unsuccessful candidate for the Republican nomination for President, 1940. Governor of New York, 1942–54. Republican presidential candidate, 1944 and 1948.

DIES, Martin, Jr (1901–72) : Democratic Congressman from Texas, 1931–45, 1953–9. First Chairman of the notorious witch-hunting House Committee to Investigate Un-American Activities, 1938–44.

DILL, Field-Marshal Sir John Greer (1881–1944) : Chief of the Imperial General Staff, 1940–1 ; Head of Joint Chiefs of Staff Mission to Washington, 1941–4.

DILLING, Mrs Elizabeth : Head of the anti-semitic and anti-Roosevelt organization 'We the Mothers' ; Director of the Patriotic Research Bureau ; author of *The Red Network*.

630

BIOGRAPHICAL NOTES

DINGELL, John David (1894–1955) : Newspaperman, pipeline construction worker, wholesale dealer in beef and pork. Democratic Congressman from Michigan, 1933–55. Author, with Senators Wagner and Murray, of an omnibus welfare bill to provide, *inter alia,* for compulsory health insurance.

DIRKSEN, Everett McKinley (1896–1969) : Lawyer and minor business executive. Republican Congressman from Illinois, 1933–49 ; Senator, 1950–69 ; Minority Whip, 1957–9 ; Minority Leader, 1959–69. Frequently reversed his attitudes on legislation.

DISNEY, Wesley Ernest (1883–1961) : Lawyer. Democratic Congressman from Oklahoma, 1931–45.

DITTER, John William (1888–1943) : Senior member of the law firm Ditter and Ditter. Republican Congressman from Pennsylvania, 1933–43. Chairman of the National Republican Congressional Committee. Vehement anti-Rooseveltite. Died in an air crash.

DIXON, Frank Murray (1892–1965) : Lawyer. Democratic Governor of Alabama, 1939–43. Dixiecrat leader in 1948.

DONDERO, George Anthony (1883–1968) : Small-town lawyer. Republican Congressman from Michigan, 1933–57. Author of the St Lawrence Seaway bill.

DONNELL, Forrest C. (b. 1884) : Lawyer ; sometime Chairman of the St Louis Advisory Board of the Salvation Army. Republican Governor of Missouri, 1941–5 ; US Senator, 1945–51.

DONOVAN, General William Joseph ('Wild Bill') (1883–1959) : New York lawyer and First World War hero. First Director of the Office of Strategic Services, 1942–5. Unorthodox and skilful bureaucratic infighter.

DOUGHTON, Robert Lee (1863–1954) : Farmer and stock raiser, 1894–1911 ; local banker, 1911–36. Democratic Congressman from North Carolina, 1911–53 ; Chairman of the House Ways and Means Committee, 1933–47, 1949–53. Conservative but generally loyal to Roosevelt.

DOUGLAS, Lewis Williams (1894–1974) : Democratic Congressman from Arizona, 1927–33 ; Director of the Budget, 1933–4. President of the Mutual Life Insurance Company, 1940–7, Chairman, 1947–59. Deputy Head of the War Shipping Administration, 1942–4. US Ambassador to Great Britain, 1947–50.

DOUGLAS, William Orville (1898–1980) : Member of the Law Faculty, Columbia University, 1925–8, Yale, 1928–34. Chairman of the Securities and Exchange Commission, 1937–9. Associate Justice of the Supreme Court, 1939–75. Mountaineer and civil libertarian.

DOWNEY, Sheridan (1884–1961) : Lawyer, who entered California politics as a supporter of Upton Sinclair's EPIC (End Poverty in California) movement, and national politics as an advocate of the 'Ham and Eggs' pension scheme. Democratic Senator from California, 1939–50. In the Senate he moved considerably to the right.

DRUMMOND, James Roscoe (b. 1902) : Journalist with the *Christian Science Monitor,* 1924–53 : executive editor, 1934–40 ; chief, Washington news bureau, 1940–53. Chief, Washington bureau, *New York Herald Tribune,* 1953–5 ; syndicated columnist for the *Los Angeles Times* Syndicate.

631

BIOGRAPHICAL NOTES

DUBINSKY, David (b. 1892) : President, International Ladies' Garment Workers Union, 1932–66. Force behind the American Labor Party and Americans for Democratic Action.

DULLES, John Foster (1888–1959) : Lawyer and diplomat, eminent Presbyterian layman. Secretary of State, 1953–9. Prominent in the formation of the United Nations.

DUNN, James Clement (1890–1979) : Career diplomat. Chief, Division of Western European Affairs, Department of State, 1935–7; adviser on political relations, 1937–4. Assistant Secretary of State, 1944–6 ; US Ambassador to Italy, 1946–52 ; Ambassador to France, 1952–3 ; Ambassador to Spain, 1953–5 ; Ambassador to Brazil, 1955–6.

DURR, Clifford Judkins (1899–1975) : Lawyer. Assistant General Counsel, Reconstruction Finance Corporation, 1936–41 ; member, Federal Communications Commission, 1941–8.

EARLY, Stephen (1889–1951) : Newspaperman. Member of the Washington staff of United Press, 1908–13, and of the Associated Press, 1913–17, 1920–7 ; Washington representative for Paramount News, 1927–33. Assistant Secretary to the President, 1933–7 ; Secretary to the President, 1937–45. Under-Secretary of Defense, 1949–50.

EASTMAN, Max Forrester (1883–1969) : Trotskyite writer ; a founder and editor of *The Masses*, 1911–17, and editor of *The Liberator*, 1917–22. He moved considerably to the right and became a roving editor for *Reader's Digest*, 1941–69. Author of *Enjoyment of Laughter* (1936), *Stalin's Russia* (1940).

EATON, Charles Aubrey (1868–1953) : Born in Canada. Baptist minister, 1893–1919, and part-time newspaperman. Republican Congressman from New Jersey, 1925–53. Signatory of the United Nations Charter.

EBERSTADT, Ferdinand (1890–1969) : New York investment banker ; assistant to Owen Young, Reparations Conference, 1929. Chairman of the Army and Navy Munitions Board, 1942 ; Vice-Chairman, War Production Board, 1942–3.

ECCLES, Marriner Stoddard (1890–1977) : President, Eccles Investment Co., 1929–51, and Chairman of various boards and companies. Chairman, Board of Governors, Federal Reserve System, 1936–48.

EDEN, Robert Anthony, 1st Earl of Avon (1897–1977) : MP (Cons.), 1923–57. Secretary of State for Foreign Affairs, 1935–8, 1940–5; Prime Minister, 1955–7.

EDISON, Charles (1890–1969) : Son of Thomas Alva Edison. Assistant Secretary of the Navy, 1937–9 ; Secretary of the Navy, 1939–40. Governor of New Jersey, 1941–4.

EISENHOWER, Dwight David (1890–1969) : West Pointer who saw no overseas service in First World War. Served in the Office of the US Chief of Staff under MacArthur and accompanied him as aide to the Philippines. Became Chief of Staff to the XXII Corps, 1940 ; Chief of Staff to the Third Army, 1941. His staff work led Marshall to bring him to Washington as head of the War Plans Division after Pearl Harbor. Went to London in April 1942 for consultation with the British. Appointed Commander of US forces in Europe, June 1942 ; Commander-in-Chief, December 1943 ; US Army Chief of Staff, 1945–8. President of the United States, 1953–61.

ELIOT, George Fielding (1894–1971) : Writer on military and international affairs, 1928–71. Military and naval correspondent, *New York Herald Tribune*, 1938–46 ; military analyst for CBS, 1939–47.

BIOGRAPHICAL NOTES

ELIOT, Thomas Hopkinson (b. 1907) : Democratic Congressman from Massachusetts, 1941–3 ; redistricted and defeated by Curley. Director, British Division, Office of War Information, London, and Special Assistant to the American Ambassador, January–November 1943. Chancellor of Washington University, St Louis, 1962–71.

ELLENDER, Allen Joseph (1891–1972) : Lawyer and cotton farmer. Member, Louisiana House of Representatives, 1924–36 ; Speaker, 1932–6, in the days of Huey Long, whom he succeeded in the Senate just after the assassination. Democratic Senator, 1937–72 ; Chairman of the Agriculture and Forestry Committee ; President *pro tem.* of the Senate (the oldest member), 1971–2. Noted for his travels at the public expense designed to expose extravagance of US overseas expenditure.

EVATT, Herbert V. (1894–1965) : Attorney General of Australia and Minister for External Affairs, 1941–9 ; member of the Commonwealth War Cabinet.

FARLEY, James Aloysius (1888–1976) : Archetypal unideological, ultimately conservative, Democratic politico. Origins in New York City politics. Chairman of New York State Athletic Commission, 1925–33. Secretary of the New York State Democratic Committee, 1928–44. US Postmaster-General, 1933–40. Chairman, Democratic National Committee, 1932–40. He broke with Roosevelt over the latter's bid for a third term, and openly opposed Roosevelt's renomination in 1944 ; thereafter devoted himself almost entirely to business, in particular the export of Coca-Cola.

FEIS, Herbert (1893–1972) : Economist. Economic Adviser to Department of State, 1931–43 ; special consultant to the Secretary of State, 1944–6 ; member of the Policy Planning Staff, Department of State, 1950–1. Author, *inter alia,* of *Three International Episodes* (1946), *The Road to Pearl Harbor* (1950), *Churchill-Roosevelt-Stalin* (1957) and *Between War and Peace* (1960).

FERGUSON, Homer (b. 1889) : Republican Senator from Michigan, 1943–55 ; US Ambassador to the Philippines, 1955–6 ; judge on the US Court of Military Appeals, 1956–71.

FIELD, Marshall, III (1893–1956) : Millionaire owner of Chicago department store; bank director. Founded the *Chicago Sun* in 1941 to provide morning competition to the *Chicago Tribune.* Owner of *PM,* a pro-New Deal New York daily.

FINLETTER, Thomas Knight (1893–1980) : Partner in the New York law firm of Coudert Bros. Special Assistant to the Secretary of State, 1941–4 ; Secretary of the Air Force, 1950–3 ; US Ambassador to NATO, 1961–5.

FISH, Hamilton, Jr (b. 1888) : Elected as a Progressive to the New York State Assembly, 1914–16. Major in First World War. Republican Congressman from New York, 1919–45 (his district included Roosevelt's Hyde Park) ; ranking minority member of the House Foreign Affairs Committee until 1942. Grandson of Grant's Secretary of State ; one of the organizers of the American Legion. Leading isolationist.

FLANDERS, Ralph Edward (1880–1970) : Began as machinist apprentice and draftsman, self-made and self-educated. President, Jones and Lamson Machine Company, 1933–46. Director, Social Science Research Council, 1932–6. Middle level bureaucrat in government (e.g., in the Office of Production Management), 1941–3 ; President, Federal Reserve Bank of Boston, 1944–6. Republican Senator from Vermont, 1946–59.

FLY, James Lawrence (1898–1966) : Lawyer. Chairman, Federal Communications Commission, 1939–44 ; Chairman, Board of War Communications, 1940–4.

BIOGRAPHICAL NOTES

FLYNN, Edward Joseph (1892–1953) : Boss of the Bronx and good personal friend of Roosevelt's. Polished and urbane lawyer who ran his organization like a smooth business operation. Secretary of State of New York, 1929–39. National Democratic Committeeman from New York State, 1930–53 ; National Chairman of the Democratic Party, 1940–2.

FOOTE, Wilder (1905–75) : Journalist, editor and publisher, *Brandon* (Vermont) *Union, Middlesbury Register, Bristol Herald,* 1931–41. Information officer, Office of Emergency Management and Office of War Information, in charge of Lend-Lease information, 1941–4 ; Special Assistant to the Foreign Economic Administrator, 1944–5 ; assistant to Secretary of State, 1945 ; officer of US Mission to the United Nations, 1945–7 ; Director, press and publications, UN, 1947–75.

FORD, Edsel Bryant (1893–1943) : With Ford Motor Co. from beginning of active career, later President, 1919–43. Since Henry Ford was alive, his authority as president was often nominal. In 1936 Henry and Edsel together established the Ford Foundation.

FORD, Henry, II (b. 1917) : With Ford Motor Co. since 1940 ; Vice-President, 1943–5 ; President, 1945–60 ; Chairman and Chief Executive since 1960.

FORRESTAL, James Vincent (1892–1949) : President of Dillon, Read & Co., New York investment bankers. Under-Secretary of the Navy, 1940–4 ; on Knox's death became Secretary of the Navy, May 1944–7 ; First Secretary of Defense, 1947–9.

FORTAS, Abe (b. 1910) : Assistant Professor of Law, Yale University, 1933–7 ; with SEC, 1937–9 ; General Counsel, Public Works Administration, 1939–40, bituminous coal division, 1939–41 ; with Department of the Interior, 1941–6 ; Under-Secretary, 1942–6 ; Associate Justice, US Supreme Court, 1965–9. Nominated by Johnson as Chief Justice, rejected by Senate, 1969.

FRANCO Y BAHAMONDE, Francisco (1892–1975) : Head of the Spanish State and Generalissimo of Land, Sea and Air Forces, September 1936–75.

FRANKENSTEEN, Richard T. (b. 1907) : Vice-President, United Automobile Workers' Union. Sometime Democratic candidate for Mayor of Detroit.

FRANKFURTER, Felix (1882–1965) : Born in Austria. Professor, Harvard Law School, 1914–39. In First World War Chairman of the War Labor Policies Board. In Roosevelt's presidencies he was a leading talent spotter and insatiable go-between for the White House. Associate Justice of the Supreme Court, 1939–62. Applied, for a liberal, a surprisingly restrictive interpretation of the Court's role.

FULBRIGHT, James William (b. 1905) : Rhodes Scholar, 1927–8. Lawyer with the Department of Justice, Anti-Trust Division, 1934–5 ; lecturer in Law, University of Arkansas, 1936–9 ; President of the University, 1939–41 ; also engaged in newspapers, business, banking and farming. Democratic Congressman from Arkansas, 1943–5 ; Senator, 1945–75 ; Chairman of the Senate Foreign Relations Committee, 1959–75. Sponsor of the Fulbright Act.

GALLUP, George Horace (b. 1901) : Public opinion statistician ; Director of Research, Young and Rubicam Advertising Agency, 1932–47. Established the American Institute of Public Opinion, 1935. In 1936 he correctly forecast Roosevelt's victory while the *Literary Digest* forecast Landon as victor.

GANDHI, Mohandas (Karamchand) Mahatma (1869–1948) : Indian nationalist and religious leader who exemplified the concept of non-violent protest.

BIOGRAPHICAL NOTES

GANNETT, Frank Ernest (1876–1957) : Owner of the Gannett chain of newspapers, centred on Rochester, New York. Father of the so-called Committee for Constitutional Government. Arguably the most reactionary newspaper publisher in the USA.

GARNER, John Nance (1868–1967) : Small-town Texas lawyer ; acquired extensive bank and real estate holdings, and became involved in local politics. Democratic Congressman from Texas, 1903–33 ; Speaker of the House of Representatives, 1930–2 ; Vice-President of the USA, 1933–41. Once in the House, he cultivated a reputation as 'Cactus Jack', archetypal poker-playing, congressional operator.

GATES, Artemus L. (1895–1976) : Banker, President of the New York Trust Company. Assistant Secretary of the Navy for Air, 1941–5 ; Under-Secretary of the Navy, July-December 1945.

GAUSS, Clarence Edward (1887–1960) : Career diplomat ; consul in China in various posts, 1907–40 ; US Minister to Australia, 1940–1 ; Ambassador to China, 1941–4. Member of the board of directors, Export-Import Bank, 1945–60.

GAVIN, Leon Harry (1893–1963) : Republican Congressman from Pennsylvania, 1943–63.

GEARHART, Bertrand Wesley (1890–1955) : California lawyer and District Attorney, Fresno County, 1917–23. Republican Congressman from California, 1935–49. Member of the Sons of the American Revolution and author of the Act establishing Armistice Day as a national holiday.

GEORGE, Walter Franklin (1878–1957) : Lawyer and judge. Democratic Senator from Georgia, 1922–57 ; Chairman of the Senate Finance Committee and member of the Foreign Relations Committee ; President *pro tem.* of the Senate, 1955–7.

GERRY, Peter Goelet (1879–1957) : Lawyer. Democratic Congressman from Rhode Island, 1913–15 ; Senator, 1917–29, 1935–47. Conservative. Came from a very old family and married a Vanderbilt.

GERVASI, Frank Henry (b. 1908) : Liberal journalist. A roving correspondent for *Collier's Weekly,* 1939–45.

GIBSON, Hugh (1883–1954) : Career diplomat. US Ambassador to Belgium, 1927–33, 1937–8 ; Ambassador to Brazil, 1933–7. Director-General for Europe of Commission for Polish Relief and Commission for Relief in Belgium, 1940–1.

GILLESPIE, Dean Milton (1884–1949) : Farmer and cattleraiser ; then moved into automobile and oil business. Republican Congressman from Colorado, 1944–7. Member of the Society for Research on Meteorites and owner of one of the largest private collections of meteorites in the world.

GILLETTE, Guy Mark (1879–1973) : Farmer and lawyer. Served in the Spanish-American War, 1898. Democratic Congressman from Iowa, 1933–6 ; Senator, 1936–45, 1949–55 ; isolationist member of the Senate Foreign Relations Committee. President of the American League for a Free Palestine, 1945–8.

GIRAUD, General Henri-Honoré (1879–1949) : Commander of French troops in North Africa and a rival of de Gaulle for leadership of liberated France. Resident in Vichy France but uninvolved in its politics, he replaced Darlan as Commander-in-Chief and High Commissioner in North Africa, December 1942. Under pressure, he co-operated with de Gaulle as Co-President, Committee of National Liberation, 1943 ; French Commander-in-Chief, 1943–4.

BIOGRAPHICAL NOTES

GOBITIS, Lillian and William : Children of Jehovah's Witnesses' parents whose refusal to salute the flag at their school, on grounds of conscience, precipitated the case of Minersville School District *v*. Gobitis, 310 US 586. The Court in 1940, Frankfurter delivering the majority opinion, found against the parents ; Justice Stone was the only dissenter.

GOEBBELS, Joseph (1897–1945) : Director of the Nazi propaganda machine from 1929 onwards.

GOLDEN, Clinton Strong (1888–1961) : Regional Director, United Steelworkers of America Organizing Committee, 1936–42 ; Vice-President, United Steelworkers, 1942–6. After his resignation, he lectured on labour problems at the Harvard Graduate School of Business Administration.

GOSS, Albert S. (1882–1950) : Involved in cereal and flour milling, general storekeeping, the telephone business and farming. Land Bank Commissioner, Farm Credit Administration, 1933–40 ; Master of the National Grange, 1940–50.

GRAFTON, Samuel (b. 1907) : Editorial writer, *Philadelphia Record*, 1929–34 ; associate editor, *New York Post*, 1934–49 ; writer of daily column, 'I'd Rather Be Right', widely syndicated, 1939–49.

GREEN, Theodore Francis (1867–1966) : Lawyer and company director. Democratic Governor of Rhode Island, 1933–6 ; Senator from Rhode Island, 1937–61 ; member of the Foreign Relations Committee and the Rules Committee. The oldest man in the Congress.

GREEN, William (1873–1952) : President of the American Federation of Labor, 1925–52. Initially a coal-miner, he rose through the United Mine Workers and, in 1913, was elected to the executive council of the AF of L. After the CIO was formed in 1935, he fought bitterly with John L. Lewis for leadership of labour. Sought to give an aura of respectability to the labour movement ; sworn foe of all traces of radicalism.

GREW, Joseph Clark (1880–1965) : Career diplomat. US Ambassador to Turkey, 1927–32 ; Ambassador to Japan, 1932–41 ; Special Assistant to the Secretary of State, 1942 ; Director, Office of Far Eastern Affairs, Department of State, 1944 ; Under-Secretary of State, 1944–5.

GROMYKO, Andrei Andreivich (b. 1909) : Counsellor, Soviet Embassy in Washington, 1939–43 ; Soviet Ambassador to the USA and Minister to Cuba, 1943–6 ; Soviet Foreign Minister since 1957.

GRUNDY, Joseph Ridgway (1863–1961) : Wealthy textile manufacturer. Head of the Pennsylvania Manufacturers' Association, 1909–30. Republican Governor of Pennsylvania, 1926–9 ; Senator, 1929–30.

GUFFEY, Joseph F. (1870–1959) : With the Philadelphia Co. (public utilities) from 1899, General Manager, 1901–18. An independent oil producer, he was President of the Guffey-Gillespie Oil Company, Atlantic Gulf Company. Democratic National Committeeman from Pennsylvania, 1920–32 ; Democratic Senator from Pennsylvania, 1935–47. After the First World War he worked in the office of the Alien Property Custodian and was indicted for fraud.

GURNEY, John Chancellor (Chan) (b. 1896) : Local businessman. Republican Senator from South Dakota, 1939–51. Member of the Civil Aeronautics Board, 1951–64.

HAGUE, Frank (1876–1956) : Worked his way up from ward heeler to police commissioner to Mayor of Jersey City, New Jersey, 1917, and state leader of the Democratic Party, 1919, both of which posts he held uninterruptedly until his death. He was uneducated, illiterate, teetotal, non-smoking, vindictive, ruthless and anti-liberal.

HALLECK, Charles Abraham (b. 1900) : Lawyer. Republican Congressman from Indiana, 1935–69 ; Majority Leader, 1949–50, 1955–6 ; Minority Leader, 1961–6. A Dewey man.

HALSEY, Admiral William Frederick (1882–1959) : An Annapolis man, he was a destroyer officer in the First World War. At sea when the Japanese struck at Pearl Harbor. In 1942 he provided a launching base for Doolittle's raid ; the same year he was appointed Commander of the US Fleet in the South Pacific. The symbol of aggressive action, he was appointed Commander of the 3rd Fleet, 1943. Supported MacArthur's Philippines landing at Leyte and later at Mindoro. Retired in 1947.

HAMILTON, John Daniel Miller (1892–1973) : Lawyer. Member of the Republican National Committee, 1932–40 ; Chairman, 1936–40. A Kansan, he was Landon's nominator in 1936.

HANNEGAN, Robert E. (1903–49) : Commissioner of Internal Revenue, 1943–5 ; Postmaster-General of the USA, 1945–7. Democratic National Committee Chairman, 1944–9.

HARDING, Warren Gamaliel (1865–1923) : Republican President of the USA, 1921–3.

HARNESS, Forest Arthur (1895–1974) : Lawyer. Lieutenant in First World War. Special Assistant to the Attorney General of the US, 1931–5. Republican Congressman from Kokomo, Indiana, 1939–49.

HARPER, Fowler Vincent (1897–1965) : Professor of law, University of Indiana, 1929–46 ; Yale, 1947–65. General counsel, Federal Security Agency, 1939–40 ; Deputy Chairman, War Manpower Commission, 1941–3 ; Solicitor to the Department of the Interior, 1943–5.

HARRIMAN, William Averell (b. 1891) : Chairman, Union Pacific Railroad, 1932–46. Lend-Lease Co-ordinator in London, 1941–3 ; US Ambassador to the USSR, 1943–6 ; Ambassador to Great Britain, 1946 ; Secretary of Commerce, 1946–8 ; Democratic Governor of New York, 1955–8 ; Ambassador-at-large, 1961, 1965–8 ; Assistant Secretary of State for Far Eastern Affairs, 1961–3 ; Under-Secretary of State for Political Affairs, 1963–5.

HARSCH, Joseph C. (b. 1905) : Journalist with the *Christian Science Monitor* since 1929. Washington correspondent, 1931–9 ; Rome, then Berlin correspondent, 1939–41 ; CBS news commentator, 1943–9 ; *Christian Science Monitor* foreign affairs columnist since 1952 ; NBC news commentator, 1953–67 ; ABC news commentator, 1967–71.

HART, Edward Joseph (1893–1961) : Lawyer. Democratic Congressman from New Jersey, 1935–55 ; Chairman of the House Committee on Merchant Marine and Fisheries ; Vice-Chairman of the Joint Committee on the Economic Report.

HASSETT, William D. (1880–1975) : Journalist with the *Washington Post,* 1909–11, with the Associated Press, 1911–15, the *Post,* 1915–21. National Recovery Administration, National Emergency Council, 1933–5 ; detailed to the White House, 1935 ; appointed Secretary (Correspondence) to Roosevelt, February 1944 ; Secretary to Truman, 1945–53. A solemn, scholarly Catholic ; part of Roosevelt's inner circle.

HATCH, Carl Atwood (1889–1963) : Lawyer. Assistant Attorney General of New Mexico, 1917–18 ; collector of internal revenue, 1919–22 ; district judge, 1922–9, 1949–62. Democratic Senator from

New Mexico, 1933–49 ; sponsor of the Hatch Act, designed to check abuses of political contributions from federal employees.

HAYEK, Friedrich August von (b. 1899) : Born in Vienna, emigrated to the UK in 1931. Tooke Professor of Economic Science and Statistics, University of London, 1931–50. His *Road to Serfdom* (1944) led to the invitation to become Professor of Social and Moral Science, University of Chicago, 1950–62. Returned to Europe in 1962 as Professor, first at Freiburg and later at Salzburg. Nobel prize-winner with Gunnar Myrdal in 1974.

HAYES, Carleton Joseph Huntley (1882–1964) : Professor of History, Columbia University, 1907–64 ; author of *A Generation of Materialism, 1871–1900* (1941). US Ambassador to Spain, 1942–March 1945 ; Catholic and conservative, and proportionately pro-Franco.

HEARST, William Randolph (1863–1951) : Newspaper publisher. Democratic Congressman from New York, 1903–7. By 1925 he owned a nationwide chain of newspapers, including the *San Francisco Examiner* ; he closed many of the papers when hit by the Depression. Fervently populist and jingoistic, he opposed the First World War and the League of Nations.

HEATTER, Gabriel (1890–1972) : With Mutual Broadcasting System, 1932–65. Master of Ceremonies for 'We, the People' from 1936 ; presented a television programme from Miami, 1951–65.

HÉBERT, Felix Edward (pronounced [sic] 'A-Bear) (1901–79) : Journalist on the *New Orleans Times-Picayune* and the *New Orleans States*. Democratic Congressman from Louisiana, 1941–77.

HENDERSON, Leon (b. 1895) : Economist. Director, Consumer Credit Research, Russell Sage Foundation, 1925–34 ; Director, research and planning division, National Recovery Administration, 1934–5 ; consultant economist, Works Progress Administration, 1936–8 ; commissioner, Securities and Exchange Commission, 1939–41 ; Administrator, Office of Price Administration, 1941–2 ; Director, Division of Civilian Supply, War Production Board, 1941–2.

HENDRICKSON, Roy F. (b. 1903) : Administrator of Agricultural Marketing, Department of Agriculture, 1941–4 ; Deputy Director-General of United Nations Relief and Rehabilitation Administration, 1944–5.

HERRING, Clyde LaVerne (1879–1945) : Farmer ; later active in the automobile business. Democratic Governor of Iowa, 1933–7 ; Senator, 1937–43. Active in 1937 against Roosevelt's Supreme Court bill.

HERSHEY, Major-General Lewis Blaine (1893–1977) : After serving since 1936 on the Joint Army and Navy Selective Service Commission, he was Director of the Bureau of Selective Service, 1941–6.

HESS, William Emil (b. 1898) : Lawyer. Republican Congressman from Cincinnati, Ohio, 1929–37, 1939–49, 1951–61.

HICKENLOOPER, Bourke Blakemore (1896–1971) : Lawyer. Republican Governor of Iowa, 1943–5 ; Senator, 1945–69. Bedrock conservative.

HILL, Lister (b. 1894) : Lawyer. Democratic Congressman from Alabama, 1923–38 ; Senator, 1938–69 ; Majority Whip, 1941–7. Liberal.

638

BIOGRAPHICAL NOTES

HILLMAN, Sidney (1887–1946) : President, Amalgamated Clothing Workers of America, 1915–46. Joined with John L. Lewis and others to form the CIO in 1935. Associate Director-General, Office of Production Management, 1941–3 ; in 1942, when the War Production Board replaced the OPM, Hillman became director of its labour division. In 1943 he became Chairman of the CIO's Political Action Committee.

HIROHITO (b. 1901) : Emperor of Japan since 1926.

HITLER, Adolf (1889–1945) : German Chancellor and Führer, 1933–45 ; German Supreme Commander, 1938–45.

HOARE, Sir Samuel John Gurney, 1st Viscount Templewood (1880–1959) : MP (Cons.), 1910–44. Secretary of State for Air, 1922–4, 1924–9, 1940 ; Secretary of State for India, 1931–5 ; Secretary of State for Foreign Affairs, 1935 ; First Lord of the Admiralty, 1936–7 ; Home Secretary, 1937–9 ; Lord Privy Seal, 1939–40 ; Ambassador to Spain, 1940–4.

HOBBS, Samuel Francis (1887–1952) : Lawyer ; judge, 4th Circuit Court of Alabama, 1921–6. Democratic Congressman from Alabama, 1935–51.

HOEY, Clyde Roark (1877–1954) : Democratic Congressman from North Carolina, 1919–20 ; Governor of North Carolina, 1937–41 ; Senator, 1945–54 ; represented the 'Shelby interest' – i.e., the textile nucleus in Cleveland County.

HOFFMAN, Clare Eugene (1875–1967) : Lawyer and prosecuting attorney for Allegan County, Michigan, 1904–10. Republican Congressman from Michigan, 1935–63 ; one of the most vituperative personal critics of Roosevelt.

HOLMAN, Rufus Cecil (1877–1959) : Local businessman. State Treasurer of Oregon, 1931–9. Republican Senator from Oregon, 1939–45. Isolationist.

HOLMES, Julius Cecil (1899–1968) : Career diplomat, 1925–37 ; President of General Mills, 1941–2. Brigadier-General, US Army, 1943. Assistant Secretary of State for Administration, 1944–5.

HOOVER, Herbert (1874–1964) : Engineer. Secretary of Commerce, 1921–8 ; Republican President of the USA, 1929–33.

HOOVER, John Edgar (1895–1972) : Lawyer ; Special Assistant to A.Mitchell Palmer, Attorney General of the US 1919–21 (during the period of the Red Scare) ; Director, Federal Bureau of Investigation, 1924–72.

HOPKINS, Harry L. (1890–1946) : Began as supervisor, Association for Improving Conditions of the Poor, New York City, and held a sequence of social work appointments, culminating in the office of federal administrator of emergency relief, 1933. Works Progress Administrator, 1935–8 ; Secretary of Commerce, 1938–40 ; from 1940 Special Assistant to President Roosevelt ; Head of Lend-Lease (1941), and confidential friend and agent of Roosevelt throughout the remainder of his time in office.

HOPPENOT, Henri Etienne (b. 1891) : Entered French diplomatic service, 1914. Minister to Uruguay, 1940–2 ; Director of Civil Services, French Military Purchasing Mission to the US, 1943 ; representative of the French Committee of National Liberation in Washington, 1943–4 ; Ambassador

639

to Switzerland, 1945–52 ; permanent delegate to the United Nations, 1952–5 ; High Commissioner in Vietnam, 1955–6.

HORNBECK, Stanley Kuhl (1883–1966) : Career diplomat. Chief, Division of Far Eastern Affairs, State Department, 1928–37 ; adviser on political relations, Department of State, 1937–44 ; Director, Office of Far Eastern Affairs, 1944 ; US Ambassador to the Netherlands, 1944–7.

HOWARD, Roy Wilson (1883–1964) : Initially assistant managing editor of the *Cincinnati Post,* he left in 1906 to join Scripps-McRae papers ; first general news manager of United Press, 1907 ; President of UP, 1912–21 ; Chairman of the Board and business director, Scripps-McRae papers (which became Scripps-Howard in 1925), 1921–36 ; President of Scripps-Howard, 1936–53. Anti-Roosevelt.

HOWE, Quincy (b. 1900) : Editor of *Living Age,* 1929–35 ; with Simon and Schuster, Inc., publishers, 1935–42 ; news analyst, CBS, 1942–9. Sometime President of National Board of Review of Motion Pictures. News analyst, ABC, 1954–63 ; Radio New York World Wide, 1966–70. Author of *England Expects Every American to Do His Duty* (1937).

HULL, Cordell (1871–1955) : Lawyer. Democratic Congressman from Tennessee, 1907–21, 1923–31 ; Senator, 1931–3. Secretary of State, 1933–44.

HURLEY, Patrick Jay (1883–1968) : Lawyer, mining company executive. Secretary of War, 1929–33. Negotiated between Mexico and five US expropriated oil corporations, 1940. Brigadier-General, 1941, on active duty 1941–2. Personal representative of President Roosevelt in various foreign countries, 1942–4. Republican.

HUTCHINS, Robert Maynard (1899–1977) : Lawyer. Professor of Law, Yale, 1927–9. President, University of Chicago, 1929–45 ; Chancellor of the University, 1945–51.

IBN-SAUD, Abdul-Aziz (1880–1953) : King of Saudi Arabia, 1932–53.

ICKES, Harold LeClair (1874–1952) : Lawyer. Initially a 'Bull Moose' (reform) Republican. Involved in municipal reform politics in Chicago ; Chairman of the Progressive Committee, Cook County, 1912–14 ; Chairman of the Illinois Progressive State Committee, 1914–16 ; member of the National Campaign Committee in charge of Charles Evans Hughes' campaign for President, 1916 ; Illinois manager of Hiram Johnson's presidential campaign, 1920 and 1924. But in 1928 he left the Republican Party and supported Al Smith in 1928 and Roosevelt in 1932. Secretary of the Interior, 1933–46.

JACKSON, Robert Houghwout (1892–1954) : New York lawyer ; joined the Department of Justice in 1936, and became the chief legal defender of New Deal legislation. Solicitor General of the US 1938–9 ; Attorney General of the US, 1940–1 ; Associate Justice of the Supreme Court, 1941–5, 1946–54 ; chief US prosecutor, Nuremberg trials, 1945–6.

JACKSON, Samuel Dillon (1895–1951) : Lawyer. Attorney General of Indiana, 1940–1. Democratic Senator from Indiana, January-November 1944.

JACOBSON, Leon Oris (b. 1911) : Physician and instructor in medicine, University of Chicago, 1942–5, becoming Professor in 1951. Associate Director of Health, Plutonium Project, Manhattan District, 1943–5 ; Director of Health, 1945–6. Director, Argonne Cancer Research Hospital, 1951–67.

JAECKLE, Edwin F. (b. 1894) : Buffalo lawyer and successful tax collector. Chairman of the New York State Republican Committee, 1940–4.

JAMES, Edwin Leland (1890–1951) : Journalist with the *New York Times,* 1915–51 ; managing editor, 1932–51.

JEFFERS, William Martin (1876–1953) : President, Union Pacific Railroad, 1937–46 ; Vice-Chairman, Board of Directors, 1946–53. Director of Office of Rubber, WPB, 1942–3.

JEFFRIES, Edward J. (1900–50) : Lawyer. Mayor of Detroit, 1940–50.

JOHNSON, Calvin Dean (b. 1898) : Building contractor. Republican Congressman from Illinois, 1943–5.

JOHNSON, Edd : Associate managing editor of *Colliers ;* foreign news editor of CBS. Chief of the Overseas Division, Office of War Information, 1942–4.

JOHNSON, Edwin Carl ('Big Ed') (1884–1970) : Wealthy rancher and operator of a farmers' milling co-operative. Served four terms in the Colorado House of Representatives. Democratic Governor of Colorado, 1933–7, 1955–7; Senator, 1937–55. Strong States' Righter ; anti-third term for Roosevelt.

JOHNSON, Hiram Warren (1866–1945) : Lawyer. Progresive reform Governor of California, 1911–17. Vice-presidential candidate with Theodore Roosevelt's Bull Moose Party, 1912. Republican Senator from California, 1917–45. In the Senate an implacable isolationist.

JOHNSON, Louis Arthur (1891–1966) : West Virginia politician and lawyer. National Chairman, Democratic Advisory Committee, 1936–40. Assistant Secretary of War, 1937–40 ; Secretary of Defense, March 1949–July 1950. Sent by Roosevelt on a vague military mission to New Delhi at the time of the Cripps Mission (March–December 1942).

JOHNSTON, Eric A. (1895–1963) : Organized the Columbia Electric and Manufacturing Co., Spokane, and was President, 1933–49, and Chairman, 1949–63. Director, Chamber of Commerce of the US, 1934–41, and President, 1942–6. President of the Motion Picture Association of America, Inc., 1945–63. Administrator, Economic Stabilization Agency, 1951 ; special representative of the President with the personal rank of Ambassador to the Middle East, 1953–63.

JOHNSTON, Olin DeWitt Talmadge (1896–1965) : Lawyer. Democratic Governor of South Carolina, 1935–9, 1943–4 ; Senator, 1945–65. He came from Spartanburg in the mill section of the state and so combined some labour sympathies with unblushing racism.

JONES, Jesse Holman (1874–1956) : Chairman of the Board of the Reconstruction Finance Corporation, 1933–9 ; Chairman of the executive committee, Export-Import Bank, 1936–43, Administrator, Federal Loan Agency, 1939–45 ; Secretary of Commerce, 1940–5.

JONES, John Marvin (1886–1976) : Democratic Congressman from Texas, 1917–41. Judge of the US Court of Claims, 1940–3 ; assistant to the Director of Economic Stabilization until 1943 ; Chairman of the American delegation to the Food and Agriculture Conference, 1943 ; Food Administrator, 1943–5. Judge, US Court of Claims, 1945–64 ; chief judge, 1947–54.

JUDD, Walter Henry (b. 1898) : Doctor. Medical missionary and hospital superintendent in China, 1925–31, 1934–8 ; he returned to speak throughout the USA to arouse Americans to the menace of

Japanese expansion and to secure an embargo on the sale and shipment of war matériel to Japan, 1939–40. Republican Congressman from Minnesota, 1943–63. Contributing editor, *Reader's Digest,* after 1963.

KAISER, Henry John (1882–1967) : Industrialist – builder of bridges, dams, docks and ships, maker of steel, aluminium and cement, all on a vast scale and mostly on the West Coast. Played key role in war production effort and subsequently went into car manufacturing in Detroit (Kaiser-Frazer).

KANZLER, Ernest Carlton (1892–1967) : President of Universal Credit Corporation, 1928–44 ; former Director of the Ford Motor Company. Deputy Chairman, Director-General for Operations, War Production Board, August 1942–February 1943.

KEENAN, Joseph Daniel (b. 1896) : Official in the International Brotherhood of Electrical Workers of America, and Secretary of the Chicago Federation of Labor from 1937. Associate Director, Labor Production Division, War Production Board, 1942 ; Vice-Chairman, Labor Production, War Production Board, 1943–5 ; Chief, Manpower Division, Allied Control Commission for Germany, 1945–7. Director, Labor's League for Political Education, from 1947.

KEFAUVER, Carey Estes (1903–63) : Yale lawyer. Democratic Congressman from Tennessee, 1939–49 ; Senator, 1949–63. Democratic nominee for Vice-President, 1956. Crusading supporter of New Deal and Fair Deal legislation. Ran for the Senate against Boss Crump's machine. Chairman of the Senate Judiciary subcommittee which investigated organized crime (televised), 1950–1. Glaswegian wife.

KELLAND, Clarence Budington (1881–1964) : Best-selling author of detective and humorous fiction and popular juvenile literature. Republican National Committeeman for Arizona, 1940 ; Executive Director (and publicity chief), Republican National Committee, 1941–3.

KELLY, Edward Joseph (1876–1950) : Machine politician ; Democratic Mayor of Chicago, 1933–47. In 1920 became chief engineer of the Chicago sanitary district – the foundation of a comfortable fortune and a successful political career. His machine was the strongest in Chicago's history, without being by any means the most corrupt.

KELLY, Frank V. (1880–1946) : Building contractor and insurance executive. Democratic boss of Brooklyn, 1934–46.

KENNEDY, Joseph Patrick (1888–1969) : Son-in-law of Irish-born Mayor of Boston. Banker and successful speculator in motion pictures and real estate. Supported Roosevelt in 1932. Chairman of the Securities and Exchange Commission, 1935–7 : US Ambassador to Great Britain, 1937–41 ; dismissed after a record of appeasement and defeatism. Father of President J.F.Kennedy.

KENNEDY, Martin Joseph (1897–1949) : Insurance broker. New York State Senator, 1924–30 ; Democratic Congressman from New York, 1930–44. Leader of Tammany Hall, 1942–9.

KENT, Frank Richardson (1877–1958) : Conservative newspaper columnist. With the *Baltimore Sun,* 1898–1923 ; managing editor, 1911–21 ; London correspondent, 1922–3. Writer of syndicated column carried by 100 papers.

KERR, Philip, Marquess of Lothian (1882–1940) : A member of the Milner 'Kindergarten', he was the first editor of the *Round Table* quarterly, 1909. Member of Lloyd George's private secretariat, 1916–23. Secretary of the Rhodes Trust, 1925–39. Chancellor of the Duchy of Lancaster, 1931. British Ambassador to Washington, 1939–40. Prominent member of the 'Cliveden Set'.

BIOGRAPHICAL NOTES

KEYNES, John Maynard, 1st Baron (1883–1946) : British economist. Fellow of Kings College, Cambridge, 1909–46. Wartime civil servant in the Treasury, 1915–19. Returned to the Treasury as an adviser, 1940–6 ; chief negotiator of the American loan to Britain, 1945.

KILDAY, Paul Joseph (1900–68) : Lawyer. Democratic Congressman from Texas, 1939–61. Judge, Court of Military Appeals, 1961–8.

KILGORE, Harley Martin (1893–1956) : Lawyer ; judge, State Criminal Court, 1932–40. Democratic Senator from West Virginia, 1941–56 ; member of the Special Senate Committee to investigate National Defense Program, 1941–6, Chairman, 1946 ; Chairman, Senate Judiciary Committee.

KIMMEL, Admiral Husband Edward (1882–1968) : Appointed Commander-in-Chief of the US Navy and Commander-in-Chief of the US Pacific Fleet, February 1941. Relieved of both commands after Pearl Harbor.

KING, Admiral Ernest Joseph (1878–1956) : Annapolis-trained Commander-in-Chief of the Atlantic Fleet, 1940–1 ; replaced Admiral Kimmel as Commander-in-Chief of the US Navy after Pearl Harbor, 1942–5 ; also replaced Stark as Chief of Naval Operations, March 1942. Member of the Combined Chiefs of Staff. The dominant American naval figure of the war.

KINGDON, Frank (1894–1972) : Methodist clergyman, of English birth, 1918. President, Dana College, Newark, NJ, 1934–40. Lecturer and radio news analyst.

KIRCHWEY, Frieda (?1894–1976) : Newspaperwoman on various New York papers, 1915–18 ; joined *The Nation* in 1918. Editor of *The Nation,* 1932–5, and editor and publisher, 1937–55.

KIRK, Alexander Comstock (1888–1979) : Career diplomat. US Minister to Egypt and to Saudi Arabia, and Ambassador to the Government of the King of the Hellenes, 4 June–25 November 1943 ; Ambassador to Italy, December 1944–March 1946.

KLEBERG, Richard Mifflin (1887–1955) : Grandson of the founder of the King Ranch in Texas (1,250,000 acres), and Chairman of the Board, 1934–55. Democratic Congressman from Texas, 1931–45. President of the Texas Agricultural Association, 1928–55.

KNIGHT, John Shiveley (1894–1979) : Editor of the Akron, Ohio *Beacon Journal,* the *Detroit Free Press* and other papers from 1933 to 1979 ; President of Knight Newspapers, Inc. Chairman of the Association of Newspaper Editors and Publishers. Censorship Liaison Officer in London, 1943–4.

KNOLLENBERG, Bernard (1892–1973) : Writer ; Librarian of Yale University, 1938–44. Senior Deputy Administrator, Office of Lend-Lease Administration, 1943–4 ; Division Deputy, Office of Strategic Services, 1944–5.

KNOWLAND, William Fife (1908–74) : Member of a California conservative dynasty ; owner of the *Oakland Tribune.* Republican Senator from California, 1945–59 ; Majority Leader, 1953–5, Minority Leader, 1955–9. Supported the Goldwater candidacy, 1964.

KNOX, William Franklin (Frank) (1874–1944) : A 'Rough Rider' ; served overseas in First World War. Associated with William Randolph Hearst in the 1920s, he became publisher of the *Chicago Daily News* in 1931. Republican nominee for Vice-President, 1936. Secretary of the Navy, 1940–4.

KNUDSEN, William S. (1879–1948) : Executive Vice-President, General Motors Corporation, 1933–7, President from 1937. Director of Production, War Department, 1941–5 ; Director-General, Office of Production Management, 1941–5.

BIOGRAPHICAL NOTES

KNUTSON, Harold (1880–1953) : Small-town newspaper editor. Republican Congressman from Minnesota, 1917–49 ; sometime Chairman of the House Ways and Means Committee ; Republican Whip ; Chairman, Joint Committee on Internal Revenue Taxation ; Chairman, Joint Committee on Reduction of Nonessential Federal Expenditures.

KROCK, Arthur (1886–1974) : Newspaperman. A Kentuckian, he edited the *Louisville Times,* 1919–23, and then worked for Will Hays, a motion pictures public relations man. Joined the *New York Times* Board of Editors in 1927, Washington correspondent for the *Times,* 1932–53, Washington commentator, 1953–67. Three times Pulitzer Prize winner. Broke with Roosevelt after the inception of the Second New Deal and became a pillar of right-wing opinion.

KRUG, Julius Albert (1907–70) : Chief power engineer, Tennessee Valley Authority, 1938–40, manager of power, 1940. Director, Office of War Utilities, 1943–4 ; Chairman, War Production Board, August 1944–5 ; Secretary of the Interior, 1946–9.

KRZYCKI, Leo (1881–1966) : Vice-President, CIO Clothing Workers' Union. National President, American Polish Labor Council ; President, American Slav Congress.

KUH, Frederick Robert (1895–1978) : Newspaperman. London correspondent of the *Chicago Sun-Times,* 1942–51, and Washington correspondent since 1951. Noted for hard leg work and successful scoops.

KUHN, Ferdinand, Jr (1905–78) : Newspaperman. With *New York Times,* 1925–40 ; chief London correspondent, 1937–9, editorial and special writer, 1939–40. Appointed assistant to Secretary of the Treasury, December 1940–2 ; Deputy Director, OWI (Overseas Branch), and chief (British Division), 1943–5 ; Head, International Information Service, Department of State, 1945–6. International affairs reporter, *Washington Post,* 1946–53.

LA FOLLETTE, Robert Marion, Jr (1895–1953) : Progressive Republican Senator from Wisconsin, 1925–47. Offspring of a dynasty which gave liberal rule to Wisconsin for the first half of the 20th century ; brother to Philip, who was Governor, 1921–33. Ardent New Dealer ; tenacious but not absolutely diehard isolationist. Driven out of politics by his electoral defeat by Joseph McCarthy, 1946.

LA GUARDIA, Fiorello Henry (1882–1947) : Elected to Congress as a Republican in 1916, but resigned to serve as a pilot in First World War ; returned to Congress in 1918. President of the New York City Board of Aldermen, 1920–1 ; Progressive Congressman from New York City, 1922–33. Mayor of New York City, 1933–45, on fusion ticket. Director of the Office of Civilian Defense, 1941, and Chairman of the Permanent Joint Board on Defense – US and Canada. Director-General of UNNRA, 1946.

LAMBERTSON, William Purnell (1880–1957) : Farmer. Speaker of the Kansas House of Representatives, and four years in the Kansas Senate. Republican Congressman from Kansas, 1929–45.

LAMONT, Thomas William (1870–1948) : Partner in J.P.Morgan & Company, 1911–40 ; Director, J.P.Morgan & Co., Inc., 1940–8, Chairman of the Board, 1943–8. Proprietor of the *New York Evening Post,* 1918–22 ; adviser to the American delegation to the Versailles Peace Conference, 1919 ; worked on Dawes Plan for German reparations, 1924 ; delegate to the World Economic Conference, 1933.

LANDIS, James McCauley (1899–1964) : Dean, Harvard Law School, 1937–46. Director, Office of Civilian Defense, and Chairman, Civilian Defense Board, 1942–3 ; Director of American Economic

Operations and US Minister to the Middle East, 1942–5 ; Chairman, Civil Aeronautics Board, 1946–7.

LANDON, Alfred Mossman (b. 1887) : A Bull Moose Progressive. Served in First World War. Republican Governor of Kansas, 1933–7 ; Republican candidate for President, 1936. Subsequently returned to oil business.

LANGE, Oskar (1904–65) : Polish-born economist who became Professor at the University of Chicago. Visited the USSR at Stalin's invitation in 1944 and endorsed the Polish Provisional Government in Moscow. Became its first Ambassador in the US, 1945 ; UN delegate, 1946–7.

LANGER, William (1886–1959) : Lawyer. Republican Governor of North Dakota, 1933–5, 1937–9 ; Senator, 1941–59. Central figure in the farmers' protest movement, the Non-Partisan League (within the Republican Party). Teetotaller, cheap money advocate, isolationist ; said to prefer to chew his cigars with their cellophane wrappers on.

LATTIMORE, Owen (b. 1900) : China specialist – engaged in business in China, 1920–6. Editor, *Pacific Affairs,* 1934–41. Professor, Johns Hopkins, 1938–63. Political adviser to Chiang Kai-shek, 1941–2. Deputy Director, Pacific Operations, Overseas Operations Branch, Office of War Information, 1942–4. Professor of Chinese, Leeds University, 1963–70.

LAVAL, Pierre (1883–1945) : French Foreign Minister, 1934–6 ; Foreign Minister of State and Vice-President of the Council in Vichy, June–December 1940 ; Head of Government, Minister for Foreign Affairs, the Interior and Propaganda, 1942–4.

LAW, Richard Kidston, 1st Baron Coleraine (1901–80) : Son of the British Prime Minister, Andrew Bonar Law. MP (Cons.), 1931–54. Junior Minister in the National Government, 1940–5.

LAWRENCE, David (1888–1973) : Washington correspondent originally with the Associated Press, 1910, and then with the *New York Post ;* an ardent Wilsonian. President and editor, *U.S. News,* 1933–48 ; founder and President, *World Report,* 1946–8 ; President and editor, *U.S. News and World Report,* 1948–59 ; Chairman of the Board and editor, 1959–73.

LEAHY, Admiral William Daniel (1875–1959) : Chief of Naval Operations, 1937–9 ; Governor of Puerto Rico, 1939 ; called out of retirement to be US Ambassador to France, 1940–2 ; Chief of Staff to Presidents Roosevelt and Truman, 1942–9.

LEE, Joshua Bryan (1892–1967) : Farmer. Democratic Congressman from Oklahoma, 1935–7 ; Senator, 1937–43. New Dealer. Member of the Civil Aernoautics Board, 1943–55 ; thereafter practised law.

LÉGER, Alexis (1887–1975) : Prominent figure with the Free French, in charge of publicity. Member of the French diplomatic service since 1914. Secretary-general, French Ministry of Foreign Affairs, 1933–40. Deprived of his citizenship, 1940–4 ; returned to France in 1957. Wrote poetry as St-John Perse and won the Nobel Prize for Literature, 1960.

LEHMAN, Herbert Henry (1878–1963) : Banker. Democratic Governor of New York, 1932–42. Director-General of OFRRA and then of UNRRA, 1943–6 ; Senator from New York, 1949–56. Called 'the conscience of the Senate' for his open opposition to McCarthy.

LEITH-ROSS, Sir Frederick William (1887–1968) : Entered the British Treasury in 1909. Deputy Controller of Finance, the Treasury, 1925–32 ; Chief Economic Adviser to the British Government,

1932–46 ; Director-General, Ministry of Economic Warfare, 1939–42 ; Chairman, Inter-Allied Post-War Requirements Committee, 1941–3 ; Deputy Director-General, UNRRA, 1944–5.

LEMKE, William (1878–1950) : Lawyer from Yale. Attorney General of North Dakota, 1921–2. Republican Congressman from North Dakota, 1933–41, 1943–50. Union Party candidate for President, 1936.

LERNER, Max (b. 1902) : Russian-born journalist and teacher. Taught at Harvard, 1935–6 ; editor of *The Nation*, 1936–8 ; taught at Williams College, 1938–43 ; editorial director, *PM*, 1943–8 ; Professor of American Civilization, Brandeis, 1949–73 ; columnist with the *New York Post* and *Los Angeles Times* Syndicate since 1949. Called a 'Neo-Marxist liberal'.

LESINSKI, John (1885–1950) : Engaged in the Building and real estate business in Detroit. President of the Polish Citizens' Committee of Detroit, 1919–32. Republican Congressman from Dearborn, Michigan, 1933–50.

LEWIS, John Llewellyn (1880–1969) : President of the United Mine Workers of America, 1920–60. Became a national figure in 1935 when he led a committee of the American Federation of Labor which organized mass production workers along industrial lines and became the Congress of Industrial Organizations in 1936, with Lewis as the first President. Resigned in 1940, and in 1942 withdrew the UMWA from the CIO. Lifelong Republican, but supported Roosevelt during his first two terms.

LILIENTHAL, David (1899–1981) : Lawyer. Worked with the Chicago labour lawyer, Donald Richberg, in the 1920s. Member of the Wisconsin Public Service Commission, 1931–3. Head of the Tennessee Valley Authority, 1933–46 ; Chairman of the Atomic Energy Commission, 1946–50.

LINDBERGH, Charles Augustus (1902–74) : Son of a Minnesota Congressman, he became an airmail pilot and, in 1927, made the first non-stop flight from New York City to Paris. Married Anne Morrow in 1929 ; in 1932 their son was kidnapped and murdered. In the 1930s he visited Germany and, in 1936, was decorated by the German Government. A leading member of the isolationist America First Committee, 1940–1.

LINDLEY, Ernest Kidder (1899–1979) : Rhodes Scholar. Correspondent for the *New York World*, 1924–31, and the *New York Herald Tribune*, 1931–7 ; Washington correspondent for *Newsweek*, 1937–61 ; syndicated political commentator for Tribune Syndicate, 1938–52 ; radio and television commentator, 1955–61. The archetypal New Deal newspaper columnist, he covered Roosevelt from the inception of his governmental career onwards.

LINDSAY, Sir Ronald Charles (1877–1945) : Career diplomat since 1899. British Ambassador to Germany, 1926–8 ; Permanent Under-Secretary of State at the Foreign Office, 1928–30 ; Ambassador to Washington, 1930–9. Married twice, each time to an American.

LIPPMANN, Walter (1889–1974) : Syndicated newspaper columnist, probably the most influential of his day, and author of books on American politics and foreign affairs. One of the founders of *The New Republic*. Assistant to the Secretary of War, 1917 ; aide to Colonel House at the Versailles Peace Conference, 1919. Editor, *New York World*, 1921–31 ; joined the *New York Herald Tribune* in 1931. Author of *A Preface to Politics* (1913), *A Preface to Morals* (1929), *The Good Society* (1937), etc.

LLEWELLIN, Colonel John Jestyn, 1st Lord (1893–1957) : MP (Cons.), 1929–45. Held minor ministerial offices until 1942, when he was successively President of the Board of Trade and Minister of

Aircraft Production ; Minister Resident in Washington for Supply, 1942–3 ; Minister of Food, 1943–5 ; First Governor-General of the Federation of Rhodesia and Nyasaland, 1953–7.

LLOYD GEORGE, David (1863–1945) : Liberal Prime Minister of Great Britain, 1916–22.

LODGE, Henry Cabot (1850–1924) : Republican Congressman from Massachusetts, 1887–93 ; Senator, 1893–1924 ; Senate Majority Leader, 1918–24. Chairman of the Senate Foreign Relations Committee, 1918 ; inserted 'reservations' to the Versailles Peace Treaty which President Wilson would not accept.

LODGE, Henry Cabot, Jr (b. 1902) : Republican Senator from Massachusetts, 1936–44, when he resigned to accept a commission in the US Army, and again 1946–53. Republican nominee for Vice-President, 1960. US Ambassador to Vietnam, 1963–7 ; Ambassador to Germany, 1967–9.

LONG, Breckinridge (1881–1958) : Lawyer. Assistant Secretary of State, 1917–20, 1940–December 1944. US Ambassador to Italy, 1933–6. Important in Democratic politics in Missouri.

LONG, Huey Pierce ('The Kingfish') (1893–1935) : Notorious demagogue and populist Democratic Governor of Louisiana, 1928–32 ; Senator, 1932–5. Assassinated.

LOTHIAN, *see* KERR.

LUCAS, Scott Wike (1892–1968) : Lawyer. Chairman, Illinois State Tax Commission, 1933–5. Democratic Congressman from Illinois, 1935–9 ; Senator, 1939–51 ; Senate Majority Leader, 1949–50.

LUCE, Clare Booth (b. 1903) : Author, playwright, journalist, wife of Henry Luce (publisher of *Time, Life, Fortune*, etc.). Republican Congresswoman from Connecticut, 1943–7.

LUCE, Henry Robinson (1898–1967) : Founder and editor-in-chief of *Time, Fortune, Life, Architectural Forum, Sports Illustrated, House and Home*. Founded *March of Time*, 1929.

LYTTLETON, Oliver, 1st Viscount Chandos (1893–1972) : MP (Cons.), 1940–54. President of the Board of Trade, 1940–1, 1945 ; Minister Resident, Cairo, 1941–2 ; Minister of Production, 1942–5 ; Secretary of State for the Colonies, 1951–4.

MAAS, Melvin Joseph (1898–1964) : Republican Congressman from Minnesota, 1927–33, 1935–45. On active duty (Marines), South Pacific, 1942–5. Stricken with total blindness in 1951. Chairman of the President's Committee on Employment of the Physically Handicapped, 1954–64.

MACARTHUR, General Douglas (1880–1964) : Commander, US Armed Forces in the Far East, 1941–5 ; appointed Supreme Commander, Allied Forces in the SW pacific, 1942. Commander, Occupation Forces in Japan, 1945–51. Supreme Commander, UN Forces in Korea, 1950–1. Dismissed by President Truman for insubordination, 1951.

MACKENZIE KING, William Lyon (1874–1950) : Liberal Prime Minister of Canada, 1935–48, and Secretary of State for External Affairs, 1935–46.

MACLEAN, Sir Fitzroy Hew (b. 1911) : Churchill's liaison officer with Tito and the Partisans. Member of the Foreign Office, 1933–9. Joined the Cameron Highlanders as a private, 1939 ; Brigadier commanding the British Military Mission to Yugoslav Partisans, 1943–5. MP (Cons.), 1941–74. Author of books on Russia and international affairs.

MacLeish, Archibald (b. 1892) : Poet. Served in First World War ; spent the years 1923–8 writing poetry in Paris. One of the original editors of *Fortune* until 1938 ; Librarian of Congress, 1939–44. Director of the US Office of Facts and Figures, 1941–2 ; Assistant Director, Office of War Information, 1942–4 ; Assistant Secretary of State for Public and Cultural Relations, 1944–5. Boyleston Professor of Rhetoric and Oratory, Harvard University, 1949–62.

Maloney, Francis Thomas (1894–1945) : Newspaper reporter, 1917–21 ; engaged in real estate and insurance business since 1921. Democratic Congressman from Connecticut, 1933–5 ; Senator, 1935–45. Independent-minded, moderate conservative.

Marcantonio, Vito (1902–54) : Lawyer ; a protégé of La Guardia's in the 1920s and 1930s. Republican Congressman from New York, 1935–7 ; American Labor Party Congressman, 1939–51. Established almost one hundred per cent Communist-line voting record.

Marshall, General George Catlett (1880–1959) : A graduate of the Virginia Military Academy, he served in the Philippines, 1902–3, 1913–16, and with the American Expeditionary Force in France, 1917–19 ; aide-de-camp to Pershing, 1919–24. Chief of Staff, US Army, 1939–45. Secretary of State, 1947–9, when he established the European Recovery Program (the Marshall Plan) ; Secretary of Defense, 1950–1.

Martin, Edward (1879–1967) : Lawyer. President of Dunn-Mar Oil & Gas Company. Commanding General, US Army, 1941–2. Republican Governor of Pennsylvania, 1943–7 ; Senator, 1947–58. Vice-President and Director, Pennsylvania State Sabbath School Association.

Martin, Joseph William, Jr (1884–1968) : Publisher of the North Attleboro *Evening Chronicle*, 1908–68. Republican Congressman from Massachusetts, 1925–67 ; Party Whip, 1933–9 ; Minority Leader, 1939–47, 1949–53, 1957–9 ; Speaker of the House of Representatives, 1947–9, 1953–5. National Chairman of the Republican Party, 1940–2. Taftite.

Matthews, H. Freeman (b. 1899) : Career diplomat. Counseler and then US minister in London, 1941–2 ; acting Chief Civil Affairs Officer, on Eisenhower's staff, London and Algiers, 1942–3 ; Deputy Director, Office of European Affairs, Department of State, 1944. US Ambassador to Sweden, 1947–50 ; Ambassador to the Netherlands, 1953–7 ; and Ambassador to Austria, 1957.

May, Andrew Jackson (1875–1959) : Lawyer and judge ; President of the Beaver Valley Coal Corporation. Democratic Congressman from Kentucky, 1931–47 ; Chairman of the House Military Affairs Committee, 1938–47.

Maybank, Burnet Rhett (1899–1954) : Engaged in cotton export business, 1920–38. Mayor of Charleston, 1931–8. Democratic Governor of South Carolina, 1939–41 ; Senator, 1941–54. Southern conservative.

McCarran, Patrick Anthony (1876–1954) : Farmer and stock raiser, lawyer and judge. Democratic Senator from Nevada, 1933–54 ; Chairman, Senate Judiciary Committee, 1943–6, 1949–53. Author of the McCarran Act, which obliged members of the Communist Party to register as foreign agents.

McCarthy, Frank (b. 1912) : Assistant Secretary, War Department General Staff, and Military Secretary to the Chief of Staff, 1941–3 ; Secretary, War Department General Staff, 1944–5 ; Assistant Secretary of State for Administration, 1945 (he had to retire almost immediately owing to ill-health after army service). Motion picture producer, 1949–77.

BIOGRAPHICAL NOTES

McCloy, John Jay (b. 1895) : New York Lawyer, 1920–40. Assistant Secretary of War, 1941–5 ; President of the International Bank, 1947–9 ; US High Commissioner for Germany, 1949–52.

McCormack, John William (1891–1980) : Democratic Congressman from Massachusetts, 1928–71 ; Majority Leader, 1940–7, 1949–52, 1955–61 ; Speaker of the House of Representatives, 1962–71. Consistent New Deal, Catholic and Irish voting record.

McCormick, Anne O'Hare (1882–1954) : Journalist with the *New York Times* ; originally a free-lance contributor, she was appointed to the staff in 1937. Pulitzer prize, 1937, for distinguished foreign reporting. Served on the State Department's post-war planning committee.

McCormick, Colonel Robert Rutherford (1880–1955) : Crusading proprietor of the isolationist and arch-Republican *Chicago Tribune,* whose influence extended throughout the Middle West. His cousin, Joseph M. Patterson, was proprietor of the *New York Daily News* and another cousin, Mrs Eleanor ('Cissy') Patterson, of the *Washington Times-Herald.* The similarities of their editorial stance stimulated employment of the phrase 'Patterson-McCormick Axis'.

McDermott, Michael James (1894–1955) : Career diplomat, concentrating largely on press relations and arrangements for conferences, e.g. he was chief press officer for Bretton Woods, 1944, and the San Francisco conference (to establish the United Nations), 1945.

McKellar, Kenneth Douglas (1869–1957): Lawyer. Democratic Congressman from Tennessee, 1911–17 ; Senator, 1917–53 ; Chairman of the Senate Appropriations Committee (and previously often acting Chairman). President *pro tem.* of the Senate, 1945–7, 1949–53. A thoroughgoing irreconcilable.

McKittrick, Roy (1888–1961) : Lawyer. Attorney General for Missouri from 1933.

McLean, Mrs Evalyn Walsh (d. 1946) : Celebrated Washington hostess who entertained at her home, 'Friendship'. Fifth wife of Robert Rice Reynolds, Senator from North Carolina, 1933–45. Author of *Father Struck it Rich* ; her mother owned the Hope Diamond.

McMahon, James O'Brien (Brien) (1903–52) : Lawyer and judge. Special Assistant to the US Attorney-General, 1933–5 ; Acting Assistant Attorney General, 1935–6 ; Assistant Attorney General, 1936–44. Democratic Senator from Connecticut, 1945–52 ; Chairman of special Senate Committee on Atomic Energy, 1945–7, and author of the McMahon Act for the control of atomic energy.

McNary, Charles Linza (1874–1944) : Lawyer and judge. Republican Senator from Oregon, 1917–44 ; Minority Leader, 1933–44. Republican vice-presidential candidate, 1940.

McNutt, Paul Vories (1891–1955) : Governor of Indiana, 1933–7 ; US High Commissioner to the Philippines, 1937–9, 1945–6. Administrator of the Federal Security Agency, 1939–45 ; Director of the Office of Defense Health and Welfare Services, 1941–3 ; Chairman of the War Manpower Commission, 1942–5. US Ambassador to the Philippines, 1946–7.

Mead, James Michael (1885–1964) : Democratic Congressman from New York, 1919–39 ; Senator, 1939–46 ; Chairman of the Senate War Investigating Committee. Chairman of the Federal Trade Commission, 1950–5.

Meany, George (1894–1980) : Plumber. Secretary-Treasurer, American Federation of Labor (AF of L), 1940–52 ; President, 1952–80 ; President, AF of L-CIO, 1955–80. Member, National War Labor Board, 1942–5.

BIOGRAPHICAL NOTES

MELLETT, Lowell A. (1884–1960) : Editor, *Washington Daily News*, 1921–7. Director, Office of Government Reports, 1939–42 ; Administrative Assistant to President Roosevelt, 1940–4.

MESSERSMITH, George S. (1883–1960) : Career diplomat. Minister to Uruguay, 1934 ; Minister to Austria, 1934 ; Assistant Secretary of State, 1937–40 ; US Ambassador to Cuba, 1940–1 ; Ambassador to Mexico, 1941–2 ; Ambassador to Argentina, 1946–7.

MEYER, Eugene (1875–1959) : Banker and publisher. Governor of the Federal Reserve System, 1930–3 ; 1st Chairman of the Board, Reconstruction Finance Corporation, February–July 1932. Editor and publisher, *Washington Post*, 1933–46 ; Chairman of the Board, 1947–59. First President, International Bank for Reconstruction and Development, June–December 1946.

MICHELSON, Charles (1869–1948) : Newspaperman on Hearst California papers, then chief Washington correspondent, *New York World*, 1917–29. Director of Publicity for the Democratic National Committee, 1929–40. Director of public relations, National Recovery Administration, 1933–4. Ghost writer credited with pinning the blame for the Depression on Hoover.

MIHAJLOVIC, General Draza (1893–1946) : Organizer of resistance movement in Yugoslavia after 1940 (the 'Chetniks') and appointed Minister of Defence by the Yugoslavia Government-in-Exile. At odds with Tito and his more aggressive Communist Partisans, whom the Allies at Tehran decided to support.

MIKOLAJCZYK, Stanislaw (1901–66) : Polish Minister of the Interior, 1941–3 ; Prime Minister, 1943–4 ; Minister of Agriculture and Deputy Prime Minister in the Polish Provisional Government, 1945–7. Subsequently in exile.

MILLER, Arthur Lewis (1892–1967) : Practised medicine, 1919–42. Republican Congressman from Nebraska, 1943–59. Director, Office of Saline Water, Department of the Interior, 1959–61.

MILLIKIN, Eugene Donald (1891–1958) : Lawyer ; President of the Kinney-Coastal Oil Co. Republican Senator from Colorado, 1941–57 ; ranking Republican on the Senate Finance Committee. One hundred per cent illiberal voting record.

MINTON, Sherman (1890–1965) : While at Yale Law School he organized the Yale University Legal Aid Society for the Poor (1916). Democratic Senator from Indiana, 1935–41 ; assistant Majority Whip and Chairman of the Senate's Lobby Investigating Committee. A strong supporter of Roosevelt's Supreme Court bill, and of the New Deal generally. Judge, US Court of Appeals, 1941–9 ; Associate Justice, US Supreme Court, 1949–56 ; his record on the Supreme Court was mildly conservative.

MOLEY, Raymond (1886–1975) : Professor of Public Law, 1923–8, and Professor of Government, 1928–54, both at Columbia. Effectively, the head of the first Roosevelt Brains Trust, and Assistant Secretary of State, 1933. Resigned September 1933, but continued in unofficial capacity as part-time adviser and speech-writer until 1936. An editor of *Newsweek* for much of 1937–68.

MOLOTOV, Vyacheslav Mikhailovich (b. 1890) : Soviet Minister for Foreign Affairs, 1939–49, 1953–6.

MONNET, Jean (1888–1979) : Chairman, Franco-British Co-Ordination Committee, 1939–40 ; on British Supply Council, Washington, 1940–3 ; on French Liberation Committee, Algiers, 1943–4.

MONTGOMERY, Field-Marshal Bernard Law, 1st Viscount Montgomery of Alamein (1887–1976) : Son of a bishop. Entered the army in 1908 ; served in France in First World War. Commander, 8th

Army, July 1942–4, in North Africa, Sicily and Italy ; Commander-in-Chief, British Group of Armies and Allied Armies, Northern France, 1944 ; Commander, 21st Army Group, 1944–5 ; Commander, British Army of the Rhine, 1945–6 ; Chief of the Imperial General Staff, 1946–8.

MOONEY, Edward, Cardinal (1882–1958) : Bishop of Rochester, New York, 1933–7 ; Archbishop of Detroit, 1937–46 ; Cardinal since 1946. Head of the National Catholic Welfare Conference.

MOORE, Edward Hall (1871–1950) : Lawyer, oil producer and cattle raiser, 1919–42. Originally a Democrat until 1940, Republican Senator from Oklahoma, 1943–9. Passionately reactionary.

MORGENTHAU, Henry, Jr (1891–1967) : Dairy and fruit farmer, fifteen miles from Roosevelt's Hyde Park ; personal friend of Roosevelt's until the latter's death. Publisher of the *American Agriculturist*, 1922–33. Chairman of the Federal Farm Board, 1933–4 ; Secretary of the Treasury, 1934–45. His conservative economic views, especially his desire to balance the budget, led to conflicts with Roosevelt. Resigned from the Treasury because of his disagreement with Truman over policy for the post-war reconstruction of Germany.

MORRIS, Newbold (1902–66) : Lawyer ; Republican, Episcopalian. President of the New York City Council, 1938–46.

MORRISON, Herbert Stanley (1888–1965) : Labour leader with roots in London, where he had been Secretary of the London Labour Party. MP (Lab.), 1923–4, 1929–31, 1935–59. Minister of Supply, 1940. Secretary of State for Home Affairs, 1940–5 ; Lord President of the Council and Leader of the House of Commons, 1945–51 ; Secretary of State for Foreign Affairs, 1951.

MORSE, Wayne Lyman (1900–74) : Dean and Professor of Law, University of Oregon, 1931–44. Progressive Republican Senator from Oregon, 1945–57 ; Democratic Senator, 1957–69.

MOSES, John (1885–1945) : Democratic Governor of North Dakota, 1938–45 ; Senator, January–March 1945.

MOUNTBATTEN, Albert Victor Nicholas Louis Francis, Earl Mountbatten of Burma (1900–79) : Commodore, Combined Operations, 1941–2 ; Chief of Combined Operations, 1942–3 ; Supreme Allied Commander, S.E. Asia, 1943–6 ; Viceroy of India, November 1947–June 1948 ; Chairman, Chiefs of Staffs Committee, 1959–65 ; Admiral of the Fleet since 1956. Assassinated in Ireland.

MOWRER, Edgar Ansel (1892–1977) : War correspondent for the *Chicago Daily News*, First and Second World Wars. Pulitzer Prize, 1932.

MOYNE, Walter Edward Guinness, 1st Baron (1880–1944) : Secretary of State for the Colonies, 1940–2 ; Deputy Minister of State, Cairo, 1942–4 ; Minister Resident in the Middle East, 1944. Assassinated by the Stern Gang.

MRUK, Joseph (b. 1903) : Retail jewellery business. Republican Congressman from New York, 1943–5 ; Mayor of Buffalo, NY, 1950–3.

MURPHY, Frank (1890–1949) : Democratic Mayor of Detroit, 1930–3 ; Governor of the Philippines, 1933 ; Governor of Michigan, 1936–8 ; notable for his refusal to use troops to break a sit-down strike. US Attorney General, 1939–40. Associate Justice of the Supreme Court, 1940–9. Notable defender of civil and minority rights.

MURPHY, Robert Daniel (b. 1894) : Career diplomat. Counsel-General in Paris, 1930–6 ; Counsellor in Embassy at Paris, 1940. Chief Civil Affairs Officer, American Forces Head Quarters, and

President's Special Representative in North Africa, 1942–3 ; political adviser, AFHQ, and American representative, Italian Advisory Council, 1943–4. US Ambassador to Belgium, 1949–52 ; Ambassador to Japan, 1952. Company Director.

MURRAY, James Edward (1876–1961) : Lawyer. Democratic Senator from Montana, 1934–60. Liberal. Campaigner for a Missouri Valley Authority on the lines of the TVA.

MURRAY, Philip (1886–1952) : Born in Scotland ; emigrated to the US in 1902. Organizer for the United Steel Workers of America from 1936 and President, 1937–52. President of the Congress of Industrial Organizations, 1940–52.

MURRAY, Wallace Smith (1887–1965) : Career diplomat. Saw active service in First World War. Chief, Division of Near Eastern Affairs, State Department, 1929–42 ; Director, Division of Near Eastern and African Affairs, 1944 ; Director, Office of Near Eastern and African Affairs, 1944–5. US Ambassador to Iran, 1945–6.

MURRAY, William Henry ('Alfalfa Bill') (1869–1956) : Rancher. Democratic Congressman from Oklahoma, 1913–17 ; Governor of Oklahoma, 1931–5. Champion of the interests of the Chickasaw (Indian) Nation.

MUSSOLINI, Benito (1883–1945) : Italian socialist who turned fascist after First World War. Head of the Italian Government, 1922–43. Declared war on France and the UK, 10 June 1940.

MYERS, Francis John (1901–56) : Philadelphia lawyer. Democratic Congressman from Pennsylvania, 1939–45 ; Senator, 1945–51.

NASH, Walter (1882–1968) : Deputy Prime Minister of New Zealand, 1940–9 ; Minister of New Zealand in Washington, 1942–4. Leader of the Opposition, 1950–7, 1960–3 ; Labour Prime Minister of New Zealand, 1957–60.

NATHAN, Robert Roy (b. 1908) : New Deal economist in the Commerce Department, 1933–40 ; Assistant Director, Bureau of Research and Statistics, Office of Production Management, 1940–2 ; Chairman, Planning Committee, War Production Board, and Acting Director of the Anglo-American Combined Production and Resources Board, 1942–3 ; Deputy Director, Reconversion, Office of War Management and Reconversion, 1945. Private consultant since 1946.

NEGRÍN, Dr Juan (1889–1956) : Physiologist. Last Republican Prime Minister of Spain, May 1937–9. Exile in Paris, Britain and the USA as head of the Government-in-Exile.

NIELSON, William Allan (1869–1946) : Born in Scotland. Scholar of English literature, especially of Shakespeare ; President of Smith College, 1917–39. Liberal.

NELSON, Donald Marr (1888–1959) : Vice-President of Sears, Roebuck. Executive Director of Supply Priorities and Allocations Board, 1941. Chairman of the War Production Board (set up to control the domestic economy in January 1942), 1942–4. Sent on special mission to China, 1944.

NICHOLS, John Conover (Jack) (1896–1945) : Democratic Congressman from Oklahoma, 1935–43.

NIEBUHR, Reinhold (1892–1971) : Pastor in Detroit, 1915–28 ; Professor, Union Theological Seminary, New York, 1928–60. Author of *Moral Man and Immoral Society* (1932) ; *Nature and Destiny of Man* (1941–3) ; *Irony of American History* (1952). Pioneer of the 'new theology' or Neo-orthodoxy, he combined Augustinian emphasis on the reality of sin with social radicalism. British wife.

BIOGRAPHICAL NOTES

NILES, David K. : Administrative Assistant, White House Office, and Hopkins' chief political adviser, 1943.

NIMITZ, Admiral Chester William (1885–1966) : Annapolis graduate. Replaced Admiral Kimmel as Commander-in-Chief of the Pacific Fleet after Pearl Harbor, 1941–5 ; commander at the battles of the Coral Sea, Midway, Guadalcanal, Marianas, Philippines Sea, Iwo Jima and Okinawa. Chief of Naval Operations, 1945–7.

NORRIS, George William (1861–1944) : Republican Congressman from Nebraska, 1903–13 ; Senator, 1913–43. Voted against US entry into First World War. Author of Twentieth Amendment abolishing lame duck sessions ; fought for government development of water power, especially in Tennessee ; co-author of Norris-La Guardia Act restricting use of injunctions in labour disputes. He endorsed Roosevelt in every election.

NYE, Gerald Prentice (1892–1971) : Republican Senator from North Dakota, 1925–45 ; defeated for re-election in 1944 and 1946. He was a leader of isolationism, and of Progressivism within the Republican Party ; Chairman of Senate committees investigating the Teapot Dome scandal, 1928, and the munitions industry, 1934–5.

O'CONNELL, William Henry (1859–1944) : Bishop of Portland, Maine, 1901–7 ; Archbishop of Boston from 1907, Cardinal from 1911. Powerful prelate who had his own registered lobbyist to handle liaison work with the state legislature, etc.

O'DANIEL, Wilbert Lee ('Pappy') (1890–1969) : Flour salesman and author of song, 'Beautiful Texas', with 'Pappy, Pass the Biscuits' as his motto. Democratic Governor of Texas, 1939–41, with the greatest majorities in the State's history ; Senator, 1941–8. Totally bogus reactionary.

O'DONNELL, John Parsons (1896–1961) : Reporter for the New York American, 1923–7, and for the New York Daily News, 1927–33 ; Washington correspondent, New York Daily News, 1933–61, war correspondent, 1939–40.

O'DWYER, William (1890–1964) : Born in Ireland. Began as a policeman, later a lawyer in New York City. County Court judge, 1938–9 ; highly successful District Attorney for Brooklyn, 1939–41 ; lost to La Guardia for mayoralty, 1941. Joined the army ; named Brigadier-General in 1944. Executive Director, War Refugee Board, 1944–5. Became Democratic Mayor of New York City, 1945–50.

O'LEARY, Thomas M. (1875–1949) : Bishop of Springfield, Massachusetts, 1921–49.

O'MAHONEY, Joseph Christopher (1884–1962) : Assistant Postmaster-General of the US, 1933. Democratic Senator from Wyoming, 1935–53, 1955–60. Independent-minded liberal. Dominant figure in anti-trust investigation by Temporary National Economic Committee (TNEC), 1939–42.

O'NEAL, Edward Asbury III (1875–1958) : President of the Alabama Farm Bureau Federation, 1923–47 ; President of the American Farm Bureau Federation, 1931–47.

O'TOOLE, Donald Lawrence (1902–64) : Democratic Congressman from New York, 1937–53.

OTTO de Bourbon Hapsburg, Archduke (1912–54) : Eldest son of Charles IV, upon whose death in 1922 he became the Austrian Pretender. In the USA March–April 1940, reputedly hoping to enlist the sympathy of American Catholics ; after the fall of France he and his family again came to the USA.

OUMANSKY, Constantine A. (1902–45) : Soviet Ambassador to the USA, 1939–41 ; he 'belonged to the new school of offensive Soviet diplomats' (Dean Acheson). Appointed Ambassador to Mexico, May 1943. Killed in air crash, January 1945.

PADILLA, Ezequiel (1890–1971) : Professor of Law and federal deputy. Foreign Minister of Mexico, 1940–6. Lost to Alemáin in the 1946 presidential election.

PASVOLSKY, Leo (1893–1953) : Born in Russia. Economist on the staff of Brookings Institute before the war. Special Assistant to the Secretary of State, 1936–8 and 1939–46 ; Chief of the Division of Special Research, State Department, 1941–2. Director, International Studies, Brookings Institute, 1946–53.

PATCH, General Alexander McCarrell, Jr (1889–1945) : Temporary rank of Brigadier-General, 1941 ; Major-General, May 1942. Commander, US forces on Guadalcanal ; as Lieutenant-General, Commander of the 7th Army, Allied invasion ground forces, S. France, August 1944. Eisenhower regarded him as the ablest army commander in the European theatre of operations.

PATMAN, Wright (1893–1976) : Democratic Congressman from Texas, 1929–76. Chairman of the House Select Committee on Small Business, and later of the House Committee on Banking and Currency. Liberal, cheap-money advocate. Author of 'bonus (i.e., gratuity) bill' for First World War veterans, which Roosevelt vetoed as inflationary in 1935 but which passed in 1936.

PATTERSON, Joseph Medill (1879–1946) : Newspaper editor and publisher. In 1914 became co-editor of the *Chicago Tribune* with his cousin, R.R.McCormick ; in 1919 founded the *New York Daily News,* the first tabloid.

PATTERSON, Robert Porter (1891–1952) : Republican ; New York lawyer and judge. Assistant Secretary of War, July–December 1940, and Under-Secretary of War, 1940–5, directing the army's procurement programme ; Secretary of War after Stimson, 1945–7.

PATTON, General George Smith, Jr (1885–1945) : West Pointer ; cavalry officer ; led 304th Brigade, Tank Corps, in First World War. Commanded Western Tank Force of 'Torch', N.W. Africa operation, 1942 ; commanded the 7th Army in Sicily, July 1943 ; under Bradley, led the 3rd Army and relieved Bastogne, December 1944.

PATTON, James George (b. 1902) : Director, National Farmer's Union, 1937–40 ; President, Colorado Farmer's Union, 1938–41 ; President, National Farmers' Co-Operative Union, 1940–66.

PATTON, Nat (1884–1957) : Judge, 1918–22 ; admitted to Texas bar to practise law, 1922. Democratic Congressman from Texas, 1935–45.

PAULEY, Edwin Wendell (b. 1903) : Chairman, Pauley Petroleum Inc. Treasurer, Democratic National Committee, 1944–5. US representative, Reparations Commission, 1945–7.

PEARSON, Drew Andrew Russell (1897–1969) : Syndicated newspaper columnist, notorious for his sensational investigative reporting. Reporter on the *US Daily,* 1926–33, and on the *Baltimore Sun,* 1929–32 ; author of column 'Daily Washington Merry-Go-Round' for the *Washington Times-Herald* since 1931. Author (with Robert S. Allen) of *Washington Merry-Go-Round* (1931). Son-in-law of Mrs Eleanor ('Cissy') Patterson, who owned the *Washington Times-Herald.*

PECORA, Ferdinand (1882–1971) : Born in Italy. Lawyer ; Counsel to US Senate Committee on Banking and Currency, 1933–4. Justice of the New York Supreme Court, 1935–50, from which he resigned to run (without success) for Mayor of New York City.

BIOGRAPHICAL NOTES

PEGLER, J. Westbrook (1894–1969) : Sports writer until he began his syndicated newspaper column in 1933 for United Features, in which he expounded the opinions of the 'average man'. In 1944 he switched to Hearst. Retired in 1962, but continued to write for the John Birch Society.

PELLEY, William Dudley (1890–1965) : Publisher. Founder of the Silver Legion of America (the 'Silver Shirts'), 1933, and of the Christian Party, 1935. Later jailed for sedition.

PENDERGAST, Thomas J. (1870–1945) : Democratic boss of Kansas City, Missouri. Active in politics from 1916 and dominant in the State from 1932 to 1938. Jailed in 1939 for tax evasion. Arguably the most powerful boss of his generation.

PEPPER, Claude Denson (b. 1900) : Lawyer. Member of the Florida State House of Representatives, 1929–30. Democratic Senator from Florida, 1936–51 ; defeated for renomination, 1950. Congressman since 1962. Totally loyal Rooseveltian.

PERKINS, Frances (1882–1965) : Industrial Commissioner of New York State, 1929–33. Secretary of Labor, 1933–45 ; longest serving member of Roosevelt's Cabinet.

PERKINS, Milo Randolph (1900–72) : Texas bag manufacturer. In the Agricultural Adjustment Administration, 1935–44, always as a close associate of Wallace. President, Federal Surplus Commodities Corporation, 1939–44 ; Executive Director of the Economic Defense Board, later the Board of Economic Warfare (BEW), 1941–4. Subsequently foreign trade consultant.

PERÓN, Juan Domingo (1895–1974) : Argentinian Army colonel who organized coup that overthrew President Castillo, June 1943. In ensuing provisional government he held increasing power. Ousted by liberals in 1945, returned as President, 1946. President, 1946–55, 1973–4.

PÉTAIN, Marshal Henri-Philippe (1856–1951) : Commander-in-Chief of the French Army in First World War. Head of the French Government (Vichy), June 1940–4.

PEW, John Howard (1882–1971) : President of Sun Oil Company, 1912–47 ; Director, 1947–71.

PEW, Joseph Newton, Jr (1886–1963) : Brother of John H. Pew. Vice-President, Chairman of Sun Shipbuilding and Dry Docks Company ; Chairman, Sun Oil Company, from 1947 ; publisher of agricultural journals. Estimated to have spent over $1 million by 1944 to oppose Roosevelt. Adopted John D. M. Hamilton, after 1936, as his chief campaign adviser.

PEYROUTON, Marcel (b. 1887) : Vichy Minister of the Interior, 1940–1 ; Governor-General of Algeria, 1943, dismissed by de Gaulle.

PHILLIPS, William (1878–1968) : Career diplomat. Assistant Secretary of State, 1917–20 ; US Minister to the Netherlands, 1920–2 ; Under-Secretary of State, 1922–4 ; Ambassador to Belgium, 1924–7 ; Minister to Canada, 1927–9 ; Under-Secretary of State, 1933–6 ; Ambassador to Italy, 1936–41 ; Director, Office of Strategic Services, London, July–December 1942 ; personal representative of the President to India, December 1942 ; Political Officer (US) on Eisenhower's staff, London, 1943–4.

PORTER, Paul Aldermandt (1904–75) : Newspaper reporter and lawyer. Special Counsel, Department of Agriculture, 1932–7 ; Washington Counsel to CBS and Vice-President, 1937–42 ; Deputy Administrator in charge of rent division, Office of Price Administration, 1942–3 ; Associate Administrator, War Food Administration ; Associate Director, Office of Energy Supplies, July 1943–February 1944 ; Campaign Publicity Director, Democratic National Committee,

February–November 1944 ; member of the Federal Communications Commission and Chairman, November 1944–6 ; Administrator, Office of Price Administration, 1946. Law practice, Arnold and Porter.

POWELL, Adam Clayton, Jr (1908–72) : Minister, Abyssinian Baptist Church, 1937–60. Democratic Congressman from New York, 1945–67, 1968–70. Expelled from Congress (where he was Chairman of the House Labor and Education Committee) in March 1967 (he had misused public funds for his own travel and living expenses). The Supreme Court reinstated him in 1969. Lost his seat in 1970.

POWERS, David Lane (1896–1968) : Republican Congressman from New Jersey, 1933–45.

PRICE, Byron (b. 1891) : With the Associated Press since 1912 ; executive news editor, 1937–41. US Director of Censorship, 1941–5. Assistant Secretary-General for administrative and financial services, United Nations, 1947–54.

PROCOPÉ, Hjalmar Johan Fredric (1889–1954) : Finnish Minister to the US, 1939–54.

PRYOR, Samuel Frazier, Jr (b. 1898) : With Pan American Airways, and Vice President since 1941. Republican National Committeeman from Connecticut, and Vice-Chairman of the National Committee, 1937–41 ; in charge of Willkie's Eastern headquarters during the 1940 campaign.

QUEZON Y MOLINA, Manuel (1878–1944) : President of the Philippines, 1935–44.

RANDOLPH, Asa Philip (1889–1979) : President of the Brotherhood of Sleeping-Car Porters, 1925–68 ; leader in Negro civil rights movement.

RANKIN, John Elliott (1882–1960) : Lawyer. Democratic Congressman from Mississippi, 1921–53 ; co-author of the Tennessee Valley Authority bill. Rabid racist.

RAYBURN, Samuel Taliaferro (1882–1961) : Democratic Congressman from Texas, 1913–61 ; elected Speaker of the House, 1940, and held that position, or that of Minority Leader, until his death. His forty-eight years in the House constitute a record. 'A Democrat without prefix, without suffix and without apologies.'

READING, Monsignor Michael Joseph (1893–1957) : Assistant General Secretary, National Catholic Welfare Conference, Washington, 1931–6 ; General Secretary, 1936–44. Bishop of Columbus, Ohio, 1944–57. Papal Chamberlain, 1934. Member of the President's Advisory Commission on Political Refugees.

REBER, Samuel (1903–71) : Career diplomat. Secretary, US Embassy, Rome, 1936–9 ; in the Department of State, 1939–42 ; member of the Allied Military Mission to Italy, 1943 ; assistant to the President's Special Representative to North Africa, 1943 ; political officer, Supreme Headquarters, Allied Expeditionary Force (SHAEF), 1944–5.

REED, Clyde Martin (1871–1949) : Post office official ; subsequently editor and publisher of small-town daily. Republican Governor of Kansas, 1929–31 ; Senator, 1939–49. Consistent and cantankerous anti-New Dealer.

REED, James Alexander (1861–1944) : Democratic Senator from Missouri, 1911–29. A leading anti-Prohibitionist of the period.

656

BIOGRAPHICAL NOTES

REED, Stanley Forman (1884–1980) : General Counsel, Reconstruction Finance Corporation, 1932–5 ; Solicitor General of the US, 1935–8 ; Associate Justice of the Supreme Court, 1938–57.

REID, Helen Rogers (Mrs Ogden Reid) (1882–1970) : Newspaperwoman. Wife of editor of the *New York Herald Tribune* ; proprietor, 1947–55.

RESTON, James Barrett ('Scotty') (b. 1909) : Born in Scotland. Reporter for the Associated Press, New York City, 1934–7 ; *New York Times* correspondent, London, 1939–41, and in Washington since 1941 ; chief Washington correspondent, *New York Times,* since 1953. Pulitzer Prize, 1945, 1957.

REUTHER, Walter Philip (1907–70) : Director of the General Motors Department, United Auto Workers Union, 1939–46 ; President, UAW, 1946–70. President, CIO, 1952–5. Helped forge unification of AF of L and CIO, 1955. Died in an air crash.

REVERCOMB, William Chapman (b. 1895) : Lawyer. Republican Senator from West Virginia, 1943–9, 1957–9.

REYNOLDS, Robert Rice (1884–1963) : Democratic Senator from North Carolina, 1932–45 ; Chairman of the Senate Military Affairs Committee. Red-neck fascist and founder of the American Nationalist Party.

RICKENBACKER, Edward Vernon (1890–1973) : Leading American air ace in First World War. President of Eastern Air Lines. Served as special observer for General Arnold of the US Army Air Force and for Secretary Stimson.

RIDDLEBERGER, James W. (b. 1904) : Career diplomat. In US Embassy, Berlin, 1936–41 ; Department of State, 1941–2 ; Board of Economic Warfare, 1942 ; in US Embassy, London, 1942–4 ; Chief, Division of Central European Affairs, Department of State, 1944–7 ; with the US Military Government in Germany, 1947–50.

ROBERT, Admiral H. : French (Vichy) High Commissioner, West Indies, 1940–3.

ROBERTS, Owen Josephus (1875–1955) : Associate Justice, Supreme Court, 1930–45 ; headed the commission which investigated Pearl Harbor. Dean of the University of Pennsylvania Law School, 1948–51.

ROBERTSON, A. Willis (1887–1971) : Democratic Congressman from Virginia, 1933–46 ; Senator, 1946–66 ; Chairman of the Senate Committee on Banking and Currency, and Chairman of the Joint Committee on Defense Production. Respectable and conservative.

ROCKEFELLER, Nelson Aldrich (1908–79) : Second son of John D. Rockefeller, Jr, the philanthropist. Co-ordinator of Inter-American Affairs, 1940–4 ; Assistant Secretary of State for American Republic Affairs, 1944–5. Sought Republican presidential nomination in 1968, but lost to Nixon. Appointed Vice-President by President Ford, 1974.

ROGERS, Will, Jr (b. 1911) : Democratic Congressman from California, 1943–4.

ROOSEVELT, Eleanor (1884–1962) : Wife of President Roosevelt. Visited the United Kingdom, 1942, and the South West Pacific, 1943. Syndicated news columnist. Held a position of great, if unofficial, influence, and actively promoted liberal causes.

BIOGRAPHICAL NOTES

ROOSEVELT, General Elliott (b. 1910) : Second son of President Roosevelt. Recalled to active duty from the Army Air Corps Reserve, 1940 ; became Brigadier-General, February, 1945. Served in N.W.Africa and on the staff of Supreme Air Command (SAC) in Europe.

ROOSEVELT, Franklin Delano (1882–1945) : President of the United States, 1933–45.

ROOT, Elihu (1845–1937) : Lawyer. Secretary of War under McKinley, 1899–1903, when he was mainly concerned with the disposition of former Spanish possessions, e.g. Cuba and the Philippines ; Secretary of State under Theodore Roosevelt, 1905–9 ; Republican Senator from New York, 1909–15. Reform Republican, close to Theodore Roosevelt, he supported US entry to the League of Nations.

ROPER, Elmo Burns, Jr (b. 1900) : Marketing consultant, 1933–67 ; Research Director, *Fortune* Survey of Public Opinion, 1935–50. Acted as a dollar-a-year man for Office of War Information ; Deputy Director, Office of Strategic Studies, 1942–5.

ROSENMAN, Samuel Irving (1896–1973) : Lawyer. Counsel to Roosevelt when he was Governor of New York, 1929–32 ; served on the New York Supreme Court, 1932–43 ; Special Counsel to Roosevelt and Truman, 1943–6.

RUSSELL, Richarl Brevard (1897–1971) : Lawyer. Member of the Georgia State House of Representatives, 1921–31 ; Democratic Governor of Georgia, 1931–3 ; Senator, 1933–71 ; Chairman of the Senate Immigration Committee, and subsequently of the Armed Services Committee. Powerful figure.

RUTLEDGE, Wiley Blount, Jr (1894–1949) : Dean of the University of Iowa Law School, 1931–9 ; judge on the Circuit Court of Appeal, District of Columbia ; Associate Justice of the Supreme Court, 1943–9. Liberal.

SABATH, Adolph Joachim (1866–1952) : Emigrated from Bohemia at fifteen. Practised law and real estate. Democratic Congressman from Illinois, 1907–52 ; Wilsonian, supporter of League of Nations, one hundred per cent New Dealer, on home and foreign affairs. Became Chairman of the House Rules Committee, 1939.

SALTONSTALL, Leverett (1892–1979) : Archetypal blue-blooded Yankee. Member of Massachusetts State House of Representatives, 1923–36. Became Republican Governor of Massachusetts, 1939, by defeating the notorious James Curley. His solid gubernatorial terms prepared way for his Senate victory in 1944, as successor to Henry Cabot Lodge, Jr. Retired from Senate, 1966.

SALVEMINI, Gaetano (1873–1957) : Italian anti-fascist historian who escaped from Mussolini in 1925 ; accepted the Lauro de Bosis Chair of History at Harvard, 1933. Returned to Italy in 1954.

SAVAGE, Carlton (b. 1897) : Career official in the State Department since 1927 ; general consultant to Secretary of State 1943–7. Assistant to the Assistant Secretary of State, 1941–3 ; Assistant to the Secretary of State, 1943–7 ; subsequently member of the Policy Planning Staff from 1947.

SCHROEDER, Werner William (1892–1960) : Chicago lawyer and insurance company director. Legislative adviser to the Governor of Illinois, 1923–8, 1941–7, 1953–9. Republican National Committeeman from Illinois, 1940–52 ; Vice-President, Republican National Committee, 1944–52.

SCHUBART, William H. (1893–1953) : Senior Vice-President, Bank of Manhattan, 1929–43. Director of the Bureau of Supplies, Federal Emergency Administration, 1943.

BIOGRAPHICAL NOTES

SCHWELLENBACH, Lewis B. (1894–1948) : Democratic Senator from State of Washington, 1935–41. Federal judge, 1940–5. Secretary of Labor, 1945–8.

SCOBIE, General Sir Ronald MacKenzie (1893–1969) : Official in the War Office, 1938–40. General Officer in Command (GOC) Tobruk, 1941 ; GOC Malta, 1942 ; Commander General Staff, Middle East, 1943 ; GOC British troops in Greece, 1944–6. Retired 1947.

SELVAGE James P. (b. 1902) : Washington reporter, Associated Press, 1929–33. Vice-President, National Association of Manufacturers, 1933–8, in charge of publicity ; member of public relations firm, Selvage & Lee, until 1958 ; assistant to the Chairman, Republican National Committee (as publicity expert), 1943–4.

SERVICE, John Stewart (b. 1909) : Career diplomat. Served in posts in China, 1935–43 ; attached to General Stilwell's forces in China, 1943–5 ; in the State Department, 1945 ; executive officer to US political adviser, Supreme Commander for Allied Powers, Tokyo, 1945–6. In 1945 charged (but exculpated) with turning documents over to fellow-travelling journal *Amerasia*.

SFORZA, Count Carlo (1872–1952) : Italian Foreign Minister, 1920–2 ; Ambassador to France, 1921–2, but resigned when Mussolini became President of the Council and Minister of Foreign Affairs. Head of the Mazzini Society, he spent most of the pre-war period in exile in Belgium and France, visiting the USA, to speak at anti-fascist rallies. After outbreak of war he took up residence in the USA, and became one of the chief spokesmen for the Italian political exiles, giving intellectual respectability (with Salvemini) to the anti-fascist resistance. Italian Minister Without Portfolio, June 1944 ; became Minister for Foreign Affairs, November 1944, and again in 1947.

SHAFER, Paul Werntz (1893–1957) : Lawyer and newspaper publisher. Municipal judge, 1929–36. Republican Congressman from Michigan, 1937–53.

SHAW, Gardiner Howland (1893–1965) : Career diplomat since 1917 ; specialist on Turkey. Assistant Secretary of State, 1941–December 1944.

SHEPPARD, Harry Richard (1885–1965) : Businessman who retired in 1934. Democratic Congressman from California, 1937–65.

SHERWOOD, Robert Emmet (1896–1955) : Playwright, Pulitzer Prize winner ; editor of comic magazine, *Life,* 1924–8. Special Assistant to Secretary of War, 1940 ; Director of Overseas Operations, Office of War Information, 1942–4 ; Special Assistant to Secretary of the Navy, 1945. Author of *Roosevelt and Hopkins : An Intimate History* (1949).

SHIEL, Bernard James (1886–1969) : Auxiliary Bishop of Chicago, 1928–69 ; titular Archbishop of Selge, 1959–69. Founder of Catholic Youth Organization. Critic of McCarthyism. His liberalism thought to have impeded his preferment.

SHIPLEY, Mrs Ruth Bielaski (b. 1885) : Joined US Civil Service, 1903. Spent 1909–14 in the Panama Canal Zone with her husband ; upon his death she returned and joined the State Department (her brother, Bruce Bielaski, was then head of the FBI). Chief, Passport Division, State Department, from 1928 to retirement.

SHIPSTEAD, Henrik (1881–1960) : Farmer-Labor Senator from Minnesota, 1923–47. Vigorous isolationist, domestic liberal.

SHORT, General Walter Campbell (1880–1946) : Commander, Hawaiian Department, February–December 1941. Charged with 'dereliction of duty' by the Roberts Committee's report,

BIOGRAPHICAL NOTES

February 1942, and retired on ¾ pay. Associated with Ford Motor Company as a traffic manager until 1946.

SIKORSKI, General Wladyslaw (1881–1943) : Polish nationalist leader in First World War ; Prime Minister, 1922–3, and then leader of the anti-Pilsudski group in Poland in the 1920s. Prime Minister of the Polish Government-in-Exile, 1939–43, as well as Commander-in-Chief. In 1940 moved his Government from Paris to London. In 1941 signed the Polish-Russian Agreement invalidating the Soviet-German partition of 1939. Killed in plane crash at Gibraltar, 4 July 1943.

SILVER, Abba Hillel (1893–1963) : Cleveland rabbi ; President of Zionist Organization of America ; Chairman of the Executive Committee, American Zionist Emergency Council.

SIMMS, William Philip (1881–1957) : Foreign editor of the Scripps-Howard Newspapers, 1922–50.

SINGH, J.J. : President of the India League of America ; former member of the All India Congress Committee.

SLICHTER, Sumner Huber (1892–1959) : Professor of Business Economics at Harvard University from 1930. Specialist in labour-management relations.

SMATHERS, William Howell (1891–1955) : Lawyer and judge. Attorney General of New Jersey, 1934–6. Democratic Senator from New Jersey, 1937–43.

SMITH, Ellison Durant ('Cotton Ed') (1866–1944) : Came of 18th-century family of plantation owners. Democratic Senator from South Carolina, 1909–44 ; last of the 'spittoon Senators'. Believed in states' rights, white supremacy and tariff for revenue only. New Deal unsuccessfully attempted to purge him in the 1938 primary.

SMITH, Howard Alexander (1880–1966) : Lawyer ; Executive Secretary of Princeton, 1919–27. Republican Senator from New Jersey, 1944–58. Consultant, Department of State, 1959–60.

SMITH, Howard Worth (1883–1978) : Lawyer and judge ; farmer. Democratic Congressman from Virginia, 1931–67 ; powerful Chairman of House Rules Committee, 1954–67. Extreme die-hard, co-author of the Smith-Connolly Act. Anti-labour reactionary.

SMITH, Joseph Luther (1880–1962) : Democratic Congressman from West Virginia, 1929–45.

SNYDER, John Wesley (b. 1895) : Banker. Office of the Comptroller of the Currency, Washington, DC, 1931–7 ; Manager, St Louis Loan Agency, Reconstruction Finance Corporation, 1937–43 ; assistant to the Director, RFC, 1940–4 ; Administrator, Federal Loan Agency, April–July, 1945 ; Director, Office of War Mobilization and Reconversion, July 1945–6 ; Secretary of the Treasury, 1946–53.

SOKOLSKY, George Ephraim (1893–1962) : Author, lecturer ; Shanghai correspondent for, *inter alia, New York Evening Post* and London *Daily Express,* 1920–30 ; editor, *Far Eastern Review,* 1927–30 ; contributor to *New York Herald Tribune,* 1935–40 ; syndicated columnist, *New York Sun* and other papers, 1940–50 ; syndicated columnist for King Features since 1944 ; commentator for ABC since 1948.

SOMERVELL, General Brehon Burke (1892–1955) : West Pointer and veteran of First World War. Works Progress Administrator for New York City, 1936–40. Appointed Assistant Chief of Staff

(Supply), War Department, 1941 ; Commanding General, Services of Supply and Army Service Forces, 1942.

SOONG, T. V. (1894–1971) : Educated at Harvard University. Brother of Madame Chiang Kai-shek. Minister of Finance, 1928–31 ; Vice-President, Chinese Executive Yuan, 1930–44 ; Chairman, Bank of China, 1935–41 ; Minister for Foreign Affairs, 1941–5 ; Premier of China, 1945–7 ; Governor of Kwangtung Province, 1947–9.

SOSNKOWSKI, General Casimir (1885–1969) : Won the only Polish victory over German invaders at Przemysl, 1939 ; on Polish collapse, fled to London. Polish Commander-in-Chief, 1943–4, when he left the Government.

SPANGLER, Harrison Earl (1879–1965) : Member of the Republican National Committee, 1932–52, and Chairman, 1942–4. Boss of Republican Party in Iowa.

SPELLMAN, Francis Joseph (1889–1967) : Ordained in 1916. Served in Roxbury and Boston until 1925 ; attaché at office of Secretary of State at the Vatican, 1929–32 ; consecrated Bishop, 1932 ; appointed Archbishop of New York City, 1939 ; Military Vicar of the Armed Forces of the USA (designated by Pope Pius XII), 1939–45 ; named Cardinal, 1946.

SPRAGUE, John Russel (b. 1886) : Lawyer ; New York Republican chief. Supervisor, Nassau County, 1930–7 ; County Executive, 1938–52. Republican National Committeeman for New York State. One of the main Dewey organizers in 1948.

SPRUANCE, Admiral Raymond Ames (1886–1969) : Annapolis graduate ; Rear Admiral, 1940. Led US forces at Midway, where he earned the DSM ; Chief of Staff to Nimitz ; directed Gilbert Islands operation ; Admiral, 1944 ; successes in Marshalls and Carolines ; commanded force attacking Iwo Jima and Okinawa ; named Commander of US 5th (Pacific) Fleet in succession to Nimitz, 1945.

STALIN, Josef Vissarionovich (1879–1953) : General Secretary, Central Committee of the Communist Party of the Soviet Union, 1922–53.

STANDLEY, Admiral William Harrison (1872–1963) : Veteran of Spanish-American War, 1898. Chief of Naval Operations, 1937–8 ; retired from active duty, but recalled during Second World War ; went to the USSR as a member of Allied aid mission, 1941 ; US Ambassador to the USSR, February 1942–3 ; member of Planning Group, Office of Strategic Services, 1944–6.

STARK, Admiral Harold Raynsford (1880–1972) : Annapolis graduate. Chief of Naval Operations, August 1939–March 1942 ; thought to have been less careful before Pearl Harbor than he should have been ; Commander, US Naval Forces, European Waters (i.e., chief liaison with British naval forces), 1942–5.

STARNES, Joe (1895–1962) : Lawyer ; First World War veteran. Democratic Congressman from Alabama, 1935–44 ; member, House Un-American Activities Committee, 1937–44.

STASSEN, Harold Edward (b. 1907) : 'Boy' Governor of Minnesota, 1938–43, and subsequently perennial candidate for Republican presidential nomination. Liberal who spent two hard years in the Navy as Assistant Chief of Staff to Halsey (1943–5).

STEAGALL, Henry Bascom (1873–1943) : Democratic Congressman from Alabama, 1915–43.

BIOGRAPHICAL NOTES

STEELMAN, John Roy (b. 1900) : Director of Conciliation, Department of Labor, 1937–44 ; public relations consultant, New York City, 1944–5 ; Director, Office of War Mobilization and Reconveision, June–December 1946 ; on Truman's White House staff, December 1946–53.

STEINBECK, John Ernst (1902–68) : Californian novelist. Author, *Of Mice and Men* (1937) ; *Grapes of Wrath* (1939) ; *Bombs Away : The Story of a Bomber Team* (1942) ; *Cannery Row* (1945). Served as war correspondent for the *New York Herald Tribune*. Pulitzer Prize, 1940 ; Nobel Prize, 1962.

STETTINIUS, Edward R., Jr (1900–49) : Chairman, US Steel, 1938–40. Chairman, War Resources Board, 1939–41 ; Administrator of Lend-Lease and Special Assistant to the President, 1941–3 ; Under-Secretary of State, 1943–4 ; Secretary of State, 1944–5 ; US representative to the UN, 1945–6.

STEWART, Arthur Thomas ('Tom') (1892–1972) : Lawyer ; prosecuting attorney at celebrated case in which the Tennessee schoolmaster Scopes was tried for teaching evolution (1925). Democratic Senator from Tennessee, 1939–49.

STILWELL, General Joseph W. ('Vinegar Joe') (1883–1946) : West Point graduate ; staff officer in First World War. Military attaché, Peking, 1935–9 ; learnt Chinese. Commander, 5th and 6th Chinese Armies in Burma, 1942 ; later Commander, US forces in China, Burma and India, and Deputy Commander, Allied S.E.Asia Command, 1943 ; recalled, 1944 ; appointed Commander, US 10th Army in Okinawa, 1945.

STIMSON, Henry Lewis (1867–1950) : Member of Elihu Root's law firm. Republican. Secretary of War, 1911–13 ; Governor of the Philippines, 1927–9 ; Secretary of State, 1929–33 (enunciated Stimson Doctrine, 1931) ; Secretary of War, 1940–5. Universally respected repository of Roman virtue.

STOKES, Thomas Lunsford, Jr (1898–1958) : Washington correspondent for Scripps-Howard Newspaper Alliance, 1936–44 ; Washington political columnist for United Features Syndicate, 1944–58. Pulitzer Prize, 1938.

STONE, Harlan Fiske (1872–1946) : Dean of Columbia Law School, 1910–23. US Attorney General, 1924–5 ; Associate Justice of the Supreme Court, 1925–41 ; Chief Justice, 1941–6. Great exponent of judicial restraint in area of economic regulation and of judicial defence of civil liberties.

STONE, Isidor Feinstein (b. 1907) : Liberal newspaper columnist for *PM* (Washington correspondent), 1941–52 ; Washington editor of *The Nation*, 1940–6. Editor and publisher, *I.F.Stone's Bi-Weekly*, 1953–71.

STRAUS, Roger Williams (1891–1957) : President of the American Smelting and Refining Company, 1941–7. Chairman or trustee of various Jewish organizations, and Co-Chairman (1944) of National Conference of Christians and Jews. Adviser to Dewey.

STRAUSS, Lewis Lichtenstein (1896–1974) : Banker. Secretary to Herbert Hoover, 1917–19. Partner in Kuhn Loeb, 1929–47 ; Lieutenant Commander, USNR, 1926 ; Admiral, 1945. Member (and hardliner) of the Atomic Energy Commission, 1946–50, and Chairman, 1953–8 ; Secretary of Commerce, 1958–9.

STREIT, Clarence Kirshman (b. 1896) : *New York Times* League of Nations correspondent, 1929–39. Launched the Federal Union Crusade in 1939 and became the first President.

STROUT, Richard Lee (b. 1898) : With the *Christian Science Monitor* since 1921, Washington correspondent since 1925 ; 'TRB' for *The New Republic*. War correspondent during Second World War.

SULLIVAN, John Lawrence (b. 1898) : Lawyer. Assistant Secretary of the Tresasury, 1940–4 ; Assistant Secretary of the Navy for Air, 1945–6 ; Under-Secretary of the Navy, 1946–7 ; Secretary of the Navy, 1947–9.

SULLIVAN, Mark (1874–1952) : Author and commentator ; initially a muckraker, later a conservative. Wrote *Our Times – The United States 1900–1925* (6 vols) and *The Education of an American*. With *McClure's Magazine*, 1904–05 ; *Collier's Weekly*, 1906–19, editor, 1913–17. Syndicated writer on national politics for *New York Evening Post*, 1919–23 ; columnist for *New York Herald Tribune*, 1923–52.

SULZBERGER, Arthur Hays (1891–1968) : Publisher of the *New York Times*, 1935–61, in succession to his father-in-law, Adolph S. Ochs, who had bought the *Times* in 1896.

SUMNER, Jessie (b. 1898) : Lawyer and county judge. Republican Congresswoman from Illinois, 1939–47.

SWEENEY, Martin L. (1885–1960) : Democratic Congressman from Ohio, 1931–43.

SWING, Raymond Gram (1887–1968) : Newspaperman and radio commentator. With London bureau of *Philadelphia Public Ledger* and *New York Evening Post*, 1924–34. Enjoyed large following as news commentator on American affairs for the BBC, 1935–45 ; commentator on foreign affairs for the Mutual Broadcasting System, 1936–45 ; commentator for ABC, 1942–8.

TAFT, Charles Phelps (b. 1897) : Liberal brother of Senator Taft. Lawyer. Director, US Community War Services, Federal Security Agency, 1941–3 ; Director, Wartime Economic Affairs, Department of State, 1944 ; Director, Transport and Communications Policy, Department of State, 1945. Mayor of Cincinnati, 1955–7.

TAFT, Robert Alphonso (1889–1953) : Son of President Taft. Lawyer. Member of the Ohio House of Representatives, 1921–6 ; member of the Ohio Senate, 1930–2. Republican Senator from Ohio, 1939–53 ; author of the Taft-Hartley Act, 1947 ; Senate Majority Leader, 1953. Defeated by Dewey for the presidential nomination, 1948 ; defeated by Eisenhower for the nomination, 1952. Known as 'Mr Republican'.

TALMADGE, Eugene (1884–1946) : Lawyer. Democratic Governor of Georgia, 1933–7, 1940–3. Demagogue whose power rested on an alliance between the 'forgotten man' and Georgia business interests.

TAYLOR, Glen Hearst (b. 1904) : Democratic Senator from Idaho, 1945–51 ; guitar-strumming 'cowboy Senator'. Progressive Party candidate for Vice-President, 1948.

TAYLOR, Wayne Chatfield (1893–1967) : Banker. Assistant Secretary of the Treasury, 1936–9 ; Under-Secretary of Commerce, 1940–5 ; President, Export-Import Bank of Washington, 1945–6 ; appointed assistant to Administrator of the Economic Co-operation Administration, 1948.

THACKREY, Mrs Dorothy Schiff (b. 1903) : President and publisher of the *New York Post* since 1942, owner since 1943.

BIOGRAPHICAL NOTES

THOMAS, Elbert Duncan (1883–1953) : Professor of Political Science, University of Utah ; author of *Chinese Political Thought* (1927) and other books. Democratic Senator from Utah, 1933–51. US High Commissioner with rank of Ambassador, Trust Territory of the Pacific Islands, 1951–3.

THOMAS, Norman Mattoon (1884–1968) : Presbyterian clergyman, 1911–31. Socialist Party candidate for Governor of New York, 1924 ; for Mayor of New York City, 1925 and 1929 ; and for President, six times 1928–48. A founder of the American Civil Liberties Union.

THOMPSON, Dorothy (1894–1961) : Foreign correspondent during the 1920s in Germany and Austria. Wife of Sinclair Lewis, 1928–42. Political commentator and columnist, *New York Herald Tribune* Syndicate, 1936–41, and for Bell Syndicate, 1941–58. Lecturer and radio commentator.

THYE, Edward John (1896–1969) : Farmer, 1922–69. Republican Governor of Minnesota, 1943–6 ; Senator, 1946–59. Moderate liberal ; protégé of Stassen.

THYSSEN, Fritz (1873–1951) : German steel magnate and financier of the National Socialist Party.

TINKHAM, George Holden (1870–1956) : Republican Congressman from Massachusetts, 1915–43.

TITO, Marshal Josef ('Broz') (1890–1980) : Yugoslav Partisan leader. President of the National Committee of Liberation, 1943–5 ; Prime Minister of Yugoslavia, 1945–80.

TOBEY, Charles William (1880–1953) : Businessman and banker. Speaker of the New Hampshire House of Representatives, 1919–20 ; President of the New Hampshire Senate, 1925–6 ; Governor of New Hampshire, 1929–30 ; Republican Congressman from New Hampshire, 1933–9 ; Senator, 1939–53.

TOBIN, Daniel J. (1875–1955) : General President, International Brotherhood of Teamsters, 1907–55 ; Vice-President, American Federation of Labor, 1933–55.

TOLAN, John Harvey (1877–1947) : Practising lawyer. Democratic Congressman from California, 1935–47.

TOWNSEND, Francis Everett (1867–1960) : Elderly California physician, who in 1934 launched the Townsend Plan, i.e. to retire everyone over sixty and pay each a $200 a month pension in scrip, to be spent within a month.

TRIPPE, Juan Terry (b. 1899) : Naval pilot during First World War and close friend of Lindbergh. Organizer and President of Pan American World Airways, Inc., since 1927.

TROTSKY, Lev Davidovich (1879–1940) : Russian revolutionary in US when the February Revolution broke out, but returned to become Chairman of the Petrograd Soviet, October 1917. First Commissioner for Foreign Affairs. Created the Red Army, and acted as the People's Commissioner for Army and Navy, 1919–23. With Lenin's illness and death, ousted by Stalin and deported in 1929 ; assassinated in Mexico by Stalinist agent, July 1940.

TRUMAN, Harry S. (1884–1972) : Haberdasher. Democratic Senator from Missouri, 1935–45 ; Chairman of the Truman Committee to investigate the war effort. Vice-President, January–April 1945 ; President, 1945–53.

TUNNELL, James Miller (1879–1957) : Schoolteacher ; later lawyer. Member of the Democratic National Committee since 1930. Democratic Senator from Delaware, 1941–7. Liberal New Dealer.

BIOGRAPHICAL NOTES

TYDINGS, Millard E. (1890–1961) : Engineer and lawyer. Served with distinction in First World War. Speaker of the Maryland House of Delegates. Democratic Congressman from Maryland, 1923–37 ; Senator, 1927–51 ; Chairman of the Senate Armed Services Committee. One of the most vehement Democratic critics of Roosevelt.

VANDENBERG, Arthur Hendrick (1884–1951) : Lawyer ; editor and publisher of the *Grand Rapids* (Michigan) *Herald*. Republican Senator from Michigan, 1928–51 ; a leading isolationist, he publicly reversed himself in 1945, supporting the founding of the UN and later of NATO.

VAN NUYS, Frederick (1874–1944) : Lawyer. Member of the Indiana State Senate, 1913–16. Democratic Senator from Indiana, 1933–44 ; Chairman of the Senate Judiciary Committee. Anti-Rooseveltian.

VIERECK, George Sylvester (1884–1962) : Born in Germany, settled in New York City in 1895. Novelist, essayist, playwright, editor of the *American Monthly*, 1914–27. Actively championed the German cause during First World War ; in Second World War, he was adviser to German Library of Information ; imprisoned, 1942–7.

VINCENT, Beverly Mills (b. 1890) : Lawyer. Democratic Congressman from Kentucky, 1937–45.

VINSON, Frederick Moore (1890–1953) : Democratic Congressman from Kentucky, 1923–9, 1931–8. Associate Justice, US Court of Appeals for the District of Columbia, 1938–43. Director of the Office of Economic Stabilization, 1943–45 ; Director of the Office of War Mobilization, 1945 ; Secretary of the Treasury, 1945–6 ; Chief Justice of the Supreme Court, 1946–53, where he was a liberal constructionist.

VOORHIS, Horace Jerry (b. 1901) : Democratic Congressman from California, 1937–47 ; protégé of Upton Sinclair ; keen advocate of co-operatives. Lost his seat to Nixon in 1946, after 'red' smear campaign. Liberal intellectual.

VORYS, John Martin (1896–1968) : Lawyer from Yale ; teacher in China, 1919–20. Republican Congressman from Columbus, Ohio, 1939–59 ; ranking Republican on House Foreign Affairs Committee. Internationalist.

WADSWORTH, James Wolcott (1877–1952) : Farmer and rancher. Speaker of the New York State Assembly, 1906–10. Republican Senator from New York, 1915–27 ; Congressman, 1933–51. Highly respected conservative internationalist.

WAGNER, Robert Ferdinand (1877–1953) : Born in Germany. Lawyer. Member of the New York State Senate, 1909–18. Justice of the New York State Supreme Court, 1919–26. Democratic Senator from New York, 1927–49 ; Chairman of the Senate Committee on Banking and Currency. Chairman of the National Labor Board, 1933–4. Liberal New Dealer and labor supporter ; author of the Wagner Labor Act.

WALKER, Frank Comerford (1886–1959) : Montana lawyer and businessman. Treasurer, Democratic National Committee, 1932. Executive Director, National Emergency Council, 1933–5, a sort of expanded Cabinet. Postmaster-General, 1940–5. Chairman, National Democratic Party, 1943–4.

WALLACE, Henry Agard (1888–1965) : Editor of farm magazines. Secretary of Agriculture, 1933–40 ; Vice-President, 1940–4 ; Secretary of Commerce, 1944–6. Presidential nominee of the Progressive Party, 1948.

BIOGRAPHICAL NOTES

WALSH, Arthur (1896–1947) : New Jersey Director of the Federal Housing Administration, 1934–5 ; with the FHA in Washington, 1935–8. Democratic Senator from New Jersey, 1943–4.

WALSH, David Ignatius (1872–1947) : Governor of Massachusetts, 1914–15 ; Democratic Senator from Massachusetts, 1919–47 ; Chairman of the Senate Naval Affairs Committee. Erratic, often isolationist, voting record. Big vote-getter ; in 1940 ran ahead of Roosevelt ; beaten in 1946 by Henry Cabot Lodge, Jr.

WARBURG, James Paul (1896–1969) : Banker and author. Special Assistant to Co-ordinator of Information, 1941–2 ; Deputy Director, Psychological Warfare Policy, Overseas Operations Branch (in London and Paris), Office of War Information, 1942–4.

WARING, Roane (1881–1958) : Lawyer. Served in First World War. National Commander, American Legion, 1942–58.

WARREN, Earl (1891–1974) : Attorney-General of California, 1939–43 ; Republican Governor of California, 1943–53 ; Chief Justice of the Supreme Court, 1953–69.

WATSON, Deneen A. (b. 1904) : Chicago lawyer. Chairman of Republican Post-war Policy Committee.

WEIR, Ernest Tener (1875–1957) : Pennsylvania millionaire. Founder and Chairman of National Steel Corporation, 1929–57 ; Chairman of other coal and steel firms. Very conservative and highly vocal opponent of New Deal.

WEIZMANN, Chaim (1874–1952) : Research chemist. President of the World Zionist Organization, 1920–31, 1935–46 ; President of the Jewish Agency for Palestine, 1935–46. First President of Israel.

WELLES, Sumner (1892–1961) : Career diplomat. Assistant Secretary of State, 1933–7 ; Under-Secretary of State, 1937–43.

WHEELER, Burton Kendall (1882–1975) : Lawyer. Democratic Senator from Montana, 1923–47 ; Chairman of the Interstate Commerce Committee. Initially an agrarian-progressive of the Norris-La Follette type ; in 1924 ran as candidate for Vice-President with La Follette on the Progressive label ; reverted to Democrat in 1928. A keen New Dealer during Roosevelt's first term, but after the Supreme Court fight became fiercely anti-Roosevelt as well as paranoiacally isolationist.

WHITE, Harry Dexter (d. 1948) : Economist. Director, monetary research, Department of the Treasury, 1940–2 ; Special Assistant to Secretary of the Treasury, 1942 ; assistant to Secretary of the Treasury, 1943–5 ; Assistant Secretary of the Treasury, 1945–6 ; US Executive Director, International Monetary Fund, 1946–7. Keynesian, contentious, disagreeable, but effective administrator. Accused after war of being a communist agent, which he denied under oath.

WHITE, Wallace Humphrey, Jr (1877–1952) : Republican Congressman from Maine, 1917–31 ; Senator, 1931–49 ; Senate Minority Leader, 1945. A mild middleman.

WHITE, William Allen (1868–1944) : Proprietor and editor, *Emporia* (Kansas) *Daily and Weekly Gazette,* 1895–1944 ; author. Founder and Chairman, Committee to Defend America by Aiding the Allies, 1940.

WICKARD, Claude Raymond (1893–1967) : Agricultural specialist from Indiana. Secretary of Agriculture, 1940–May 1945 ; Administrator, Rural Electrification Agency, May 1945–March 1953.

BIOGRAPHICAL NOTES

WILEY, Alexander (1884–1967) : Lawyer. Republican Senator from Wisconsin, 1939–63 ; ranking Republican member (relatively ineffective) of Senate Foreign Relations Committee in succession to Vandenberg.

WILLIAMS, Aubrey Willis (1890–1965) : Worked with the Federal Energy Relief Administration, 1933–5 ; with the Works Progress Administration, 1935 ; Administrator, National Youth Administration, 1938–43 ; Director of Organization, National Farmers' Union, 1943–5 ; nominated as Administrator, Rural Electrification Agency, but rejected by the Senate, 1945. Editor and publisher, *Southern Farm and Home*, 1945–62.

WILLIAMS, Clyde (1873–1954) : Lawyer. Democratic Congressman from Missouri, 1927–9, 1931–43 ; ranking member of Banking and Currency Committee ; member of the Temporary National Economic Committee, 1946–7.

WILLIS, Raymond Eugene (1875–1956) : Republican Senator from Anoolag, Indiana, 1941–7 ; deeply conservative but un-fire-raising.

WILLKIE, Wendell Lewis (1892–1944) : President of a utilities holding company, Commonwealth & Southern, who battled the TVA. Republican presidential nominee, 1940, and candidate for renomination, 1944. Anti-New Deal, but liberal, pro-civil rights, and internationalist ; author of *One World* (1943).

WILSON, Charles Edward (1886–1972) : Electrical engineer who became President of General Electrical Company, 1940–2, 1944–50. Executive Vice-Chairman, War Production Board, 1942–4 ; Director, Office of Defense Mobilization, 1950–2. Headed Truman's Committee on Civil Rights.

WILSON, General Sir Henry Maitland ('Jumbo') (1881–1964): British GOC Egypt, 1939–41 ; GOC Cyrenaica, 1941 ; Commander-in-Chief, Persia-Iraq, 1942 ; Commander-in-Chief, Middle East, 1943–4 ; Supreme Allied Commander, Mediterranean, 1944–5, and Field Marshal.

WILSON, Woodrow (1856–1924) : President of the USA, 1912–20.

WINANT, John Gilbert (1889–1947) : Liberal Republican Governor of New Hampshire, 1925–6, 1931–4 ; Chairman, Social Security Board, 1935–7 ; Director, International Labor Office, 1938–41 ; US Ambassador to Great Britain, 1941–6 ; US representative to the UN, 1946–7.

WINCHELL, Walter (1897–1972) : Child actor. Gossip columnist who began in 1922 on the *New York Graphic*. In 1929 he joined the *New York Mirror*. Very widely syndicated. Broadcaster.

WISE, Stephen Samuel (1874–1949) : New York City rabbi and Roosevelt's principal New York Jewish political manager. Founded the Federation of American Zionists in 1898, later known as the Zionist Organization of America ; President, 1936–8.

WOLCOTT, Jessie Paine (1893–1969) : Lawyer ; prosecuting attorney in Michigan, 1927–30. Republican Congressman from Michigan, 1931–55 ; ranking member of the Banking and Currency Committee ; delegate to (and supporter of) Bretton Woods.

WOOD, General Robert E. (1879–1969) : Veteran of the Spanish-American War and of First World War. President of Sears, Roebuck & Co. of Chicago, 1928–39 ; Chairman, 1939–54. Founder and President of America First.

WORLEY, Francis Eugene (1908–74) : Democratic Congressman from Texas, 1941–50.

667

BIOGRAPHICAL NOTES

ZEMURRAY, Samuel (1877–1961) : Born in Russia. Fruit importer ; President of the United Fruit Company. Assisted in framing Agricultural Adjustment Administration codes. Adviser, Board of Economic Warfare.

ZHUKOV, Marshal Georgi K. (1896–1974) : Soviet Chief of the General Staff, 1941 ; Deputy Supreme Commander, 1942–5.

List of Abbreviations

AAA   Agricultural Adjustment Administration
AF of L American Federation of Labor
ALP   American Labor Party
AP   Associated Press
BEW   Board of Economic Warfare
BIS   British Information Services
CCC   Commodity Credit Corporation *or* Civilian Conservation Corps
CIO   Congress of Industrial Organizations
FBI   Federal Bureau of Investigation
FCC   Federal Communications Commission
FDIC   Federal Deposit Insurance Corporation
FEA   *see* OFEA
FSA   Federal Security Administration *or* Farm Security Administration
FWA   Federal Works Agency
GOP   'Grand Old Party' – sobriquet of Republican Party
ILO   International Labour Organization
NAM   National Association of Manufacturers
NBC   National Broadcasting Corporation
NHA   National Housing Agency
NIRA   National Industrial Recovery Administration
NRPB   National Resources Planning Board
NWLB   National War Labor Board
NYA   National Youth Administration
OCD   Office of Civilian Defense
OES   Office of Economic Stabilization
OEW   Office of Economic Warfare
OFEA   Office of Foreign Economic Affairs
OFF   Office of Facts and Figures
OFRRO   Office of Foreign Relief and Rehabilitation Operations
OLLA   Office of Lend-Lease Administration
OPA   Office of Price Administration
OPM   Office of Production Management
OSS   Office of Strategic Services
OWI   Office of War Information
OWM   Office of War Mobilization
PAC   Political Action Committee

REA   Rural Electrification Administration
RFC   Reconstruction Finance Corporation
SD   State Department
SEC   Securities and Exchange Commission
TUC   Trades Union Congress (UK)
TVA   Tennessee Valley Authority
UMW   United Mine Workers' Union
UNRRA United Nations Relief and Rehabilitation Administration
UP   United Press
USCC   United States Commercial Company
WAC   Women's Army Corps
WFA   War Food Administration
WLB   War Labor Board
WMC   War Manpower Commission
WPA   Works Progress Administration
WPB   War Production Board

INDEX

A figure 2 in brackets immediately after a page reference indicates that the subject is mentioned in two separate despatches on that page. Words or phrases in brackets after a page reference are intended to locate the reference in cases where the subject is not mentioned by name. The Foreword and the Biographical Notes have not been indexed.

INDEX

Episcopalians, 413
Ethiopia Peace Society, 103
Europe, invasion of, European war (advocated, *see* Second Front), 32, 188, 189, 190, 212, 242, 298, 332, 348, 367–8, 370, 373–4, 376–7, 393–4, 402–3, 425–6, 481, 486–7, 488, 492–3, 497, 524, 531, 550, 553, 558, 615 ('Doenitz')
European Advisory Commission (EAC), 269 ('new commissions'), 327, 504
European federation, 172, 238, 284, 336, 429, 495
Evatt, Dr Herbert V., 160, 180

Facts and Figures, Office of, 18, 37, 61*n*.
Fair Employment Practices Committee/Bill, 141, 146, 204, 400–1, 576, 578, 586
Far East : Britain and, 31, 38 (*see also* Burma ; Hong Kong ; *and under* China ; Pacific War) ; Russia and, 603–4, 606–7, 611–12, 615–16 (*see also under* China ; Japan)
Farley, James A., 52, 56, 63–4, 68–9, 73–4, 75, 125, 153, 156, 162, 173, 232, 272, 312, 320, 354, 395, 453
Farm Bloc, 11, 12, 14, 16, 24, 35, 39, 40, 44, 55–6, 59, 60, 67, 72–3, 80–1, 82, 84–5, 87–8, 115, 117, 124, 127, 144, 155, 164, 175, 207, 214, 256–7, 271, 275–6, 278, 286, 291, 306, 318, 326
Farm Bureau Federation, 54, 80, 92, 164, 286, 428, 438
Farmer-Labor Party, 56
farmers, 76, 80–1, 85, 100, 112–13, 149, 208, 214, 221, 232, 271, 274, 276, 278, 380, 444, 457
Farmers' Union, National, 81, 92, 164, 250, 331

fascism and fascists, in US, 31, 37, 45, 61, 142, 208, 226, 232, 277, 307, 318, 407–8, 412, 430
Federal Bureau of Investigation (FBI), 53–4, 78
Federal Communications Commission, 195–6, 217–18, 256
Federal Council of Churches, 168, 222, 348, 472, 508, 530
Federal Deposit Insurance Corporation (FDIC), 255, 267
Federal Security Administration, 30
Federal Surplus Commodities Corporation, 38*n*.
Feis, Herbert, 183, 351
Fenton, Francis P., 305
Ferguson, Senator Homer, 525
Field, Marshall, 590
Field publications, 576
Fight for Freedom Committee, 147, 331*n*., 356*n*.
Fighting French movement (formerly Free French, *q.v.*), 109, 127, 154, 176*n*.
filibuster, 103, 118, 124, 256, 484, 586
Finland, Finns, *see* American–Finnish relations
Finletter, Thomas K., 249, 323
Fish, Hamilton, Jr, 42, 71, 107, 126, 145, 239, 352, 396, 399, 400, 440, 449, 454, 476
Flanders, Ralph E., 92, 557
Fly, James L., 218, 459
'Flying Fortresses', 34
Flynn, Edward J., 18–19, 36, 56, 125, 137, 140, 143–4, 146, 390, 463, 580
food, 221, 236, 238–9, 412 ; shortage, 101, 125, 137, 155, 172 ; 'muddle', 146, 149–50, 159, 210, 211, 339, 529, 530, 538 ; for Europe, 150, 294, 339, 352, 381, 530, 552, 557, 588, 592 ; conference,

175, 178–9, 182–3, 193–4, 198, 202, 204, 274, 323 ; *see also* rationing ; subsidies
Food Administration, *see* War Food Administration
Food Commission, International, 221
'Food for Freedom', 552
Food Requirements Committee, 76
Foote, Wilder, 475
Ford, Henry, 61
Ford Motor Company, 67
Foreign Affairs, 43
Foreign Agents Registration Act (1938), 226, 388
Foreign Correspondence, 480*n*.
Foreign Economic Administration, Office of (OFEA), 254, 266–7, 304, 609, 612*n*.
Foreign Economic Co-ordination, Office of, 254, 266
Foreign Policy Association, 542
Foreign Relief and Rehabilitation Operations, Office of (OFFRO), 144*n*., 206, 238, 239, 266
'forgotten man', 112, 113
Forrestal, James V., 186, 223, 329, 340, 354, 358, 397, 413 ('Sec. of Navy'), 464, 465, 579
Forte, Felix, 228
Fortune, 38*n*., 51, 70, 99*n*., 199, 231
Foster, William Z., 570
Fotich, Constantin, 288
France, French, Vichy government, 32*n*., 59, 284, 415, 516 ; Franco-Russian relations, 238*n*., 242, 479 ; *see also* American–French relations ; Anglo-French relations ; Committee of National Liberation ; Darlan ; de Gaulle ; Fighting French ; Free French ; Giraud ; Monnet ; *and under* North Africa

679

Pucheu, P., 346
Puerto Rico, statehood for, 380
Pulaski Day, 432–3

Quakers, 274, 462
Quebec conferences, 235, 240, 242, 248*n.*, 418, 419, 466*n.*, 486
Queeny, Edgar Monsanto, 265
Quezon, Manuel, 180
Quigley, James C., 312

race riots, 61, 203, 207–8, 212
radio, US, ix, 15, 149, 196, 218, 256, 363, 426, 458
Railroad Brotherhoods, unions, 92, 141, 235, 276, 287, 294, 305, 396
Ramsay, Captain, 374
Ramsey, Guy, 145
Randolph, Asa Philip, 141, 352*n.*
Rankin, John E., 156, 254, 496, 501
rationing, 10, 35, 42, 44, 72, 76, 101, 121, 134, 413, 496 ; petrol, 26, 28, 34, 36, 39–40, 67, 82, 90, 118, 125, 208, 225, 604 ; sugar, 28, 34, 36, 227 ; meat, 72, 76 ; coffee, 101, 227 ; food, 199, 210, 552, 557, 604
Rayburn, Samuel Taliaferro, 134, 140, 201, 213, 217, 284–5, 312, 360, 386, 440, 445, 546, 573
Rayner, Charles B., 329
Reader's Digest, 208, 534–5, 571
Ready, Mgr Michael J., 355
Reber, Samuel, 416
reciprocal trade, 132, 135, 181, 183, 185, 191, 198, 201, 382, 534–5, 545, 550, 576, 578, 601 ; *see also* free trade
'Reconstruction', 210*n.*, 381*n.*
Reconstruction, International Bank for, 460, 514
Reconstruction Finance Corporation (RFC), 124–5, 144, 506–7

reconversion, 276, 292, 322–3, 330–1, 367, 373, 397, 406–7, 408–9, 413, 420, 599, 601, 604, 604–5, 613
Red Cross, International, 183*n.*
Reed, Senator Clyde Martin, 69, 182, 400, 463
Reed, James A., 170
Reed, Philip D., 55
Reed, Justice Stanley Forman, 344
refugees, 172, 175–6, 178–9, 183, 275
Reid, Mrs Ogden, 282, 291, 379, 387
Reinsch, James L., 547
relief and rehabilitation, 123, 136, 137, 149, 165, 170, 199, 238–9, 266, 279–80, 294, 352, 543, 557 ; *see also* United Nations Relief and Rehabilitation Administration
Republican Party : platform (1942), 86, 125 ; and 1942 election results, 105–8, 113–16 ; St Louis meeting (1942), 118–19, 125, 126 ; National Chairman, 123–4, 125, 126, 275, 398 ; in Congress, 127–8, 155, 186, 208, 285, 326, 334, 463 ; National Committee, 145, 350 ; and B2H2 Resolution, 172–3 ; Mackinac Island meeting, *see* Mackinac ; Willkie and, 259, 265, 272, 275, 276–7, 285–6, 291–2, 343–4, 383, 401, 433–4 ; Convention (1944), 277–8, 281–2, 292, 350, 360, 375–6, 377–81, 396, 398, 407, 436, 457, 461–2 ; primaries (1944), 286, 312, 388–9, 396–7, 399–400, 451 (Illinois, 300, 347–8 ; California, 312 ; Wisconsin, 312, 323, 334, 338–9, 343–4, 347, 349 ; New Hampshire, 334 ; New York,

343, 400, 401 ; Nebraska, 347 ; Pennsylvania, 354 ; Indiana, 357 ; Ohio, 359 ; West Virginia, 359 ; Kansas, 400) ; pre-Convention politics, 308–9, 311, 313 ; Dewey and, 348–50 ; and labour, 395–6, 418 ; platform (1944), 378–81, 382–3, 384–5, 392, 393, 444 ; and Negroes, 539
Repulse, HMS, 4
Reston, James B., 410, 413, 445
Reuters, 283
Reuther, Walther P., 68
Reynolds, Quentin, 360
Reynolds, Senator Robert R., 148, 173, 252, 269, 277, 450
Ribbentrop, Joachim von, 310, 311
Richelieu, 154
Rickenbacker, Edward V., 145, 156
Riddleberger, James W., 589
Riley, Henry Ware, 267
Rinehart, Stanley Marshall, Jr, 52
Rio de Janeiro Conference, 14, 17
Robert, Admiral H., 52
Roberts, Justice Owen J., 589
Robertson, Senator Edward V., 463
Robeson, Paul, 352, 528
Robinson, Senator Joseph Taylor, 320
Rockefeller, Nelson A., 249, 318, 325, 478, 479, 485, 520–1, 554, 563, 587
Rogers, Will, Jr, 357
Roman Catholics, Catholicism : discrimination against, 31 ; anti-Roosevelt, 37, 66 ; anti-British, 37 ; hierarchy, 45, 123, 159, 189, 224, 283, 294, 307, 363, 387, 549, 570 ; Catholic vote, 63–4, 140, 162–3, 173, 201, 220–1, 255, 390, 440 ;